THE NOVELS OF CARMEN LAFORET
AN AESTHETICS OF RELIEF

LEGENDA

LEGENDA is the Modern Humanities Research Association's book imprint for new research in the Humanities. Founded in 1995 by Malcolm Bowie and others within the University of Oxford, Legenda has always been a collaborative publishing enterprise, directly governed by scholars. The Modern Humanities Research Association (MHRA) joined this collaboration in 1998, became half-owner in 2004, in partnership with Maney Publishing and then Routledge, and has since 2016 been sole owner. Titles range from medieval texts to contemporary cinema and form a widely comparative view of the modern humanities, including works on Arabic, Catalan, English, French, German, Greek, Italian, Portuguese, Russian, Spanish, and Yiddish literature. Editorial boards and committees of more than 60 leading academic specialists work in collaboration with bodies such as the Society for French Studies, the British Comparative Literature Association and the Association of Hispanists of Great Britain & Ireland.

The MHRA encourages and promotes advanced study and research in the field of the modern humanities, especially modern European languages and literature, including English, and also cinema. It aims to break down the barriers between scholars working in different disciplines and to maintain the unity of humanistic scholarship. The Association fulfils this purpose through the publication of journals, bibliographies, monographs, critical editions, and the MHRA Style Guide, and by making grants in support of research. Membership is open to all who work in the Humanities, whether independent or in a University post, and the participation of younger colleagues entering the field is especially welcomed.

ALSO PUBLISHED BY THE ASSOCIATION

Critical Texts
Tudor and Stuart Translations • New Translations • European Translations
MHRA Library of Medieval Welsh Literature

MHRA Bibliographies
Publications of the Modern Humanities Research Association

The Annual Bibliography of English Language & Literature
Austrian Studies
Modern Language Review
Portuguese Studies
The Slavonic and East European Review
Working Papers in the Humanities
The Yearbook of English Studies

www.mhra.org.uk
www.legendabooks.com

STUDIES IN HISPANIC AND LUSOPHONE CULTURES

Studies in Hispanic and Lusophone Cultures are selected and edited by the Association of Hispanists of Great Britain & Ireland. The series seeks to publish the best new research in all areas of the literature, thought, history, culture, film, and languages of Spain, Spanish America, and the Portuguese-speaking world.

The Association of Hispanists of Great Britain & Ireland is a professional association which represents a very diverse discipline, in terms of both geographical coverage and objects of study. Its website showcases new work by members, and publicises jobs, conferences and grants in the field.

STUDIES IN HISPANIC AND LUSOPHONE CULTURES

The Novels of Carmen Laforet

An Aesthetics of Relief

❖

CARAGH WELLS

LEGENDA

Studies in Hispanic and Lusophone Cultures 29
Modern Humanities Research Association
2019

Published by Legenda
an imprint of the Modern Humanities Research Association
Salisbury House, Station Road, Cambridge CB1 2LA

ISBN 978-1-78188-525-3

First published 2019

Copy-Editor: Dr Ellen Jones

CONTENTS

To my son Allód,
with love and respect

ACKNOWLEDGEMENTS

I would like to thank my sister Siobhan and brother-in-law Mark for supporting me during the early stages of researching and writing this book. Thanks also are due to my friends Emily, Joe, Miriam and Teresa, who were there for me at both a practical and emotional level. Norman Freeman's listening ear was also much appreciated. Support, insight and guidance was given by Clare Harris and Jim Sinkinson, whose professional knowledge of the human quest for relief was instrumental in aiding my understanding of Laforet's fiction. The work of Ann d'Arcy Hughes has been an important source of inspiration for my insights into the concept of relief. I am greatly indebted to Ann for giving me permission to use her print 'Thinking' for the cover of this book. My colleague Matthew Brown kindly read and commented upon the original book proposal for Legenda. At a crucial stage of writing this book, the simple, direct advice of Denis M. Donovan helped me to find my own perspective and interpretation of relief. I should like to record my thanks to the editors of the *Modern Language Review* for permission to re-use material from my previously published article: '"Su larga trenza de pelo negro": The Phenomenon of Disordered Mourning in Carmen Laforet's *Nada*', *Modern Language Review*, 107.4 (2012), 1123–1140.

This book could not have been written without the wonderful insights of my students, whose enthusiasm for Laforet's fiction over the years is evidence of how her novels still speak to us across epochs and generations. Finally, most thanks are due to my son Allód for his forbearance, humour and love. He has been a constant source of inspiration and endless joy.

c.w., Bristol, March 2019

INTRODUCTION

'Wherever sorrow is, relief would be'
Silvius, *As You Like It*, Act 3, Scene 5[1]

'Much of what we are doing is a question of changing the style of thinking.'
LUDWIG WITTGENSTEIN[2]

In his analysis of the human subject's desire for clarity, Henri Bergson discusses the 'clarity of the radically new and absolutely simple idea, which catches as if it were an intuition.'[3] The 'absolutely simple idea' of emotional relief, and its aesthetic representation in the novels of one of Spain's most important twentieth-century writers, forms the subject of this study. Although the idea of emotional relief may not be regarded as radically new, academic discussions of its centrality to human and animal life have been almost overlooked, perhaps due to its unconscious prominence within the texture of lived experience. Metaphorically speaking, relief exists in plain sight as one of the primary, motivating, emotional forces across the lifetime of the human subject, yet relief's simplicity and pervasiveness sustain its invisibility within conceptual discourses. To a large extent, relief remains beyond conceptual language, which may account for its as yet uncharted terrain within academic discourses.

This study does not seek to prove that Laforet's novels are autobiographical, nor does it wish to elucidate in depth her fiction as an example of life-writing. Nonetheless, given the evidence that has come to light in Caballé and Rolón's comprehensive biography, it now proves impossible to detach the circumstances of Laforet's personal experiences from her writing.[4] Thus, this study does not treat each novel as an autonomous textual artefact and series of linguistic signifiers in which the author's emotional and psychological imprint has left no trace.[5] Instead, Laforet's novels are read here as if they were a series of photographic negatives that bear the impression of aspects of Laforet's repressed unconscious emotions. In this respect, Laforet's novels are deeply autobiographical as they serve as vessels in which readers encounter the author's ongoing desire to find relief from a major, early life trauma, the death of her mother Teodora when she was thirteen years old. The psychological impact of Laforet's mother's death was further compounded by her father's swift re-marriage to Blasina, a woman who worked for Teodora, and whom Laforet suspected of having an affair with her father prior to the loss of her mother. Blasina ordered the removal of all reminders of Teodora from the house and refused Laforet and her siblings to speak about their mother. Laforet, who avoided interviews and discussions of her private life, spoke openly of her step-mother's actions on one occasion: 'Una persona que entró en nuestra familia se encargó de hacerlas desaparecer [las fotografías tomadas por don Eduardo], como casi todas los fotografías de nuestra infancia.'[6] The enforced eradication of her mother's memory led to Laforet's subsequent refusal to speak openly about her loss for the remainder of her life. Laforet's close friend elucidated her mutism surrounding the matter of her grief:

> No hablamos de la muerte de su madre, no sé cómo la vivió. Fue hasta el final una experiencia sellada en su vida, como tantas otras; un silencio o un modo de proceder que tal vez adoptara Laforet inconscientemente para sacudirse la angustia y seguir adelante.[7]

The enforced silence surrounding Teodora's life and death from both Blasina and Laforet herself led to the author's unconscious psychological pursuit of the figure of the substitute mother which manifests itself repeatedly throughout her novels through the figure of relief. As Caballé and Rolón note, 'la muerte de la madre significa la imposibilidad de romper simbólicamente con ella, proceso necesario a toda emancipación.'[8] The mother is therefore configured symbolically as both an absence and a presence throughout Laforet's novels and the trope of flight or *fuga* encapsulates the dual process of the pursuit of the mother (a longing for pleasure and a movement towards the lost love object) combined with a movement away from unpleasure (grief and a recognition of the absent mother).[9] Both movements are conjoined within the desire for relief, and one of the central questions to consider across this study is the extent to which Laforet's protagonists encounter relief through the various strategies that they adopt to contain and assuage their suffering. As Rita Frankiel avers in her discussion of the death of a primary beloved object, 'the loss of a loved figure in external reality has a profound effect on the sense of well-being because the loss puts the internal object world into disarray.'[10] As will be observed in subsequent chapters, Laforet's aesthetic response to 'the restoration of well-being' through her protagonists' actions, reveals the extent to which their internal worlds are in disarray. The repeated desire for dissolution of self-object distinctions signals a profoundly fragile self-concept and, potentially, evidence of Freud's Thanatos or death drive. Throughout Laforet's fiction, relief does not signal 'the restoration of the internal good object, which is the source of optimism and good feeling about self and the world'.[11] Instead, the search for the good object is re-sought in different guises across each of her five novels, suggesting a sustained depressive disposition as a result of a distortion in the mourning process, which is similarly accounted for within Laforet's personal history through her refusal to speak about her mother's death and her defensive sublimation of her grief. Freud made the early distinction between normal mourning and its more pathological form melancholia, whereby 'an object-loss [...] is withdrawn from consciousness'.[12] Non-pathological mourning remains within the individual's consciousness and defensive strategies are less present, but the melancholic mourner experiences 'an extraordinary diminution in his self-regard, an impoverishment of his ego on a grand scale'.[13] All Laforet's protagonists display fragile ego structures, and although they also disclose tendencies towards independence and resilience, the novels do not provide conclusive evidence that the protagonists have been able to construct self-regulating egos and stable identities.[14]

Their tendency to locate their sense of self within an Other, which can be translated as a form of psychic *cathexis*, suggests that their egos remain underdeveloped as they seek emotional stability through investment in something outside the self.[15] Thus, it is the impoverished egos of Laforet's protagonists that seek relief, sometimes through the aesthetic realm of art, music, architecture or nature or, on other occasions, through slavish admiration for another person or deity. Their weak ego structures are shored up temporarily, based on a mis-reading of the other's capacity to provide relief from their underlying sorrow yet, as Rasmussen avers 'there is quite a bit of "non" "sense" in many of our efforts to feel as good as possible'.[16] As the chapters of this study unfold, the extent to which each protagonist engages in non-sensical behaviour to feel relief will be considered. It is no coincidence that each of the protagonists of Laforet's novels have lost either one or both of their parents, a fact that cannot be overlooked in any discussion of her work. The voided space of maternal absence leads to her protagonists' desire for self-constancy which is symbolically displaced onto an Other. As this study will discuss, the pursuit of the stable and healthy self cannot emerge unless recognition of the original trauma occurs, as Bessel van der Kolk observes: 'Relief does not come until they are able to acknowledge what has happened and recognize the invisible demons they're struggling with.'[17] This suggests that psychological self-sustenance can only fail in the face of ongoing denial of the source of individual trauma. Although Laforet may have manifested a profound sense of psychological intuition in terms of her capacity to capture the complexities of the human psyche in her method of characterisation in her novels, she did not wish to gain a deeper understanding of the impact of the defensive patterns she herself established following her mother's death and her protagonists mirror this failure to confront the source of their instability.[18] In an intimate memoir of her mother's life, Cristina Cerezales Laforet reveals her mother's resistance to undergoing any form of therapy; she did not wish to 'emprender el dolorosísimo trabajo de hacer el recorrido inverso'.[19] The blockage that existed due to her refusal to talk about her mother's death, and the repression of her memory within the family as a result of her step-mother's domineering presence, is transformed into the unconscious creative drive behind Laforet's novels. Although creative writing can function to aid a traumatic wound to heal, what we witness in Laforet's fiction is the reverse. Writing keeps the wound hidden, occluded defensively within the aesthetic. As readers, what we receive through Laforet's writing and the actions of her protagonists is the imprint of defensive *cathexis*. Her novels contain the psychic processes through which she repressed her grief and thus the gaps, silences and lacunae that form the substructure of her novels reflect the defensive patterns that were laid down in Laforet's childhood as a response to her mother's early death. The autobiography of Laforet's life *is* then contained in her fiction both through what remains unsaid and through her protagonists' attempts to find relief from their ongoing suffering. Caballé and Rolón refer to the absent place of grief in Laforet's life as 'un no-lugar' which, once again, invokes the symbol of the photographic negative, an image that is there but not there, and can only be intuited from the reverse impression.

Laforet rebutted critics who sought to forge connections between her protagonists and her own life, but her responses were invariably defensive and suggestive of her own efforts to repress her emotional suffering over the loss of her mother. Despite Laforet's denial of the autobiographical traces in her fiction, it was impossible for her to distance herself from her protagonists; the objectivity she longed to instil in her novels ultimately failed to be put into practice.[20] Even though Laforet shifted to a male protagonist in *La insolación* and *Al volver la esquina*, the ideas expressed through Martín Soto reflect the author's personal dilemmas regarding the capacity of art to heal the psychological traumas of an individual's past. Notably, Martín is also lacking a mother figure in his life, as is the case for all Laforet's previous protagonists. Roberta Johnson, one of the few critics who has examined Laforet's *oeuvre* in detail, notes the absence of the mother figure across the novels, although she suggests that this allows for 'successful personal exploration and growth', whereby 'each novel may be seen as a progression of confrontations with and eventual rejection of role models'.[21] Although this perspective remains valid, the absence of the mother figure in Laforet's novels represents a veiled pursuit of, or repetitive flight towards, the missing mother, one that is manifested repeatedly through aesthetically charged tropes based on the need to find relief from psychological pain. Thus, each trope is structured around the same symbolic search for the lost mother based on the protagonists' subliminal desire to merge, either with an external phenomenon or another character.[22] While Lacan believed the unconscious was structured like a language, Maude Ellman takes his proposition further by suggesting the commonality of literary criticism and psychoanalysis in their attention to 'the boundless creativity of tropes'.[23] In their multifarious forms, the tropes discussed in the following chapters provide readers with a tentative language through which to read and interpret relief both in the novels of Laforet, but also, more broadly, as a type of experiential knowledge that individuals seek repeatedly across time, place and circumstance. We must therefore acknowledge Laforet as a deeply philosophical and humane writer who brings readers into contact with what might be argued is a common human goal, that of alleviating suffering and making sense of the human subject's need for relief at all stages of existence.

The *imago* of the dead mother then remains invariant across Laforet's fiction.[24] Here it is important to dwell on the concept of invariance and its significance as a methodological basis for reading Laforet's fiction. The literary understanding of invariance is best illustrated in Norman Holland's analysis of H.D.'s poetry and her memoir of her own experience of psychoanalysis.[25] Holland detects the invariant wish in her writing 'to fuse with, be devoured by, close the gap between herself and a mother perceived and felt as a timeless, uninterrupted, unbroken mystic level of experience'.[26] At the core of Laforet's writing we detect the same invariant drive towards symbolic merger with mother substitutes — Andrea's relationship with Ena in *Nada*, Marta's obsessive need to pursue Pablo in *La isla y los demonios*, Paulina's relationship with God in *La mujer nueva* and Martín's friendship with the Corsi siblings in both *La insolación* and *Al volver la esquina* — all of which are based on an ongoing psychological need to find relief. Although Holland's analysis arises out of close readings of H.D.'s formal approach to writing poetry, and the relationship between form and patterns of psychological defense, his ideas are applicable to a novelist's use of narrative techniques and the creative devices at play within novels, which similarly reflect repressed material in the form of desires, longings and unmet needs.[27] However, in Laforet's fiction it is not simply a matter of mapping the protagonists' psychologies onto those of their creator. It is, rather, as Frederick Hoffman observes in his analysis of literature's contribution to our understanding of psychoanalysis, more relevant to reflect upon the subtle arrangements within a novel 'which report and reflect on a high level of linguistic articulateness and subtlety the basic tensions, balances, imbalances, repressions, and compensations of psychic energies contained within a system such as Freud has described'.[28] The text thus provides clues or signs within the formal structure of language whereby we arrive at 'the aesthetic means of articulating psychic balance'.[29] Throughout this study, attention is focused on precisely how this psychic balance is sought and represented through the aesthetic means of language and, as subsequent chapters will reveal, how Laforet's treatment of language functions as both an acknowledgement of the need for relief, whilst at the same time employing aesthetic representation as a defensive shield against that need. By paying close attention to the tropes of relief across Laforet's novels, the reader comes into contact with the unconscious presence of the author's unacknowledged grief as well as the processes of denial and defense, which find themselves imprinted within Laforet's complicated and, at times, frustrating aesthetic style. Positive and negative aesthetic impulses punctuate her novels. On the one hand, the reader detects a desire to find relief through aesthetic means, whilst on the other, the actual source of psychological suffering is kept at bay through an aesthetic process of negation and refusing to name the source of personal trauma. It is as if Laforet's novels cancel themselves out, for although they purport to create an aesthetics of relief, the protagonists never find an endpoint to their search for inner stability. In this respect, her narratives represent an aesthetics of negation, yet it is through the imprint of such negation that grief speaks itself through silence, the muted nothingness or *nada* that cannot be expressed other than through the symbolic representation of relief, which Laforet articulates through the unconscious substructure of her novels.

It proves difficult to conceptualise relief within academic discourse, since by its nature it remains within the realm of the non-conceptual domain of emotions and of bodily sensations. As Silvius reminds us in the quote above, the underside of relief is grief or, more broadly, human suffering, which Buddhist thought contains within the concept of *dukkha*. Borrowing from the Buddhist tradition, psychoanalyst Barbara Low approximates an early conceptualisation of relief through her discussion of the *Nirvana Principle*, which Freud refers to directly in his study on masochism.[30] Freud envisages relief, although he does not name it as such, as a process aimed at 'keeping as low as possible, the sums of excitation which flow in upon' the subject's 'mental apparatus'.[31] The 'nirvana principle', according to Freud, contains the 'pleasure-unpleasure principle', an idea which encapsulates the concept of relief based on the Latin origins of the word, *solamen* and *allevatio*, connoting the acquisition of comfort and solace, and an elevation from one state, that of suffering or unpleasure to another, pleasure.[32] On closer examination of Freud's nascent discussion of relief, he recognises that there is a qualitative characteristic of the pleasure–unpleasure principle that he cannot name: 'Perhaps it is the rhythm, the temporal sequence of changes, rises and falls in the quantity of stimulus. We do not know.'[33] It is not about feeling pleasure as such, but feeling less bad; in other words, it is a process based on a different response to an existing negative reaction or feeling. Relief is then about the avoidance of feeling 'unpleasure' as much as it is about feeling good or happy. Rasmussen bases his discussion of relief on the work of Alfred Adler, who also approximated a conceptual formulation of relief within his idea of the 'felt plus' and the 'felt minus'. Rasmussen praises the Adlerian model for understanding 'that we humans do what works for us. While it may not be the most optimal response to life circumstance, if it works to resolve a felt minus, we are likely to use it again.'[34] Yet these strategies may also be maladaptive and do little to provide long-term relief; they may even serve to harm the development of a stable self-structure, which may aid regulation of the emotions. Laforet's fiction illustrates how just such negative strategies of short-term relief are pursued by her protagonists, who often encounter a 'felt plus' for a period of time, but do not find effective, long-term methods of healing their suffering or establishing stable psychological homeostasis. As the following chapters testify, what could be understood as evidence of lasting relief is often misconstrued or mis-read by Laforet's protagonists. Patterns of seeking relief then become 'maladaptive ways of protecting and enhancing the self', but have no long-term efficacy.[35] Tranquillity of being, in the sense that the Stoics conceived, remains elusive across Laforet's narratives. Stoic relief and the recovery of our true selves arose, according to Seneca, through the mind following a 'smooth and steady course, well disposed to itself, happily regarding its own condition and with no interruption to this pleasure'.[36] According to this view, Laforet's protagonists fail to find Stoic relief, although there are ample examples of them finding other forms of temporary relief from suffering, or Adler's 'felt-plus'. *Ataraxia*, a state of serene, lasting calmness, is never achieved. The deeper philosophical idea posited within her novels suggests that equanimous states may only be long-lasting for the deeply spiritual or devoutly religious, and that for those individuals who have suffered trauma in early life, relief arises like an enticing mirage, only to disappear again as the path of life proceeds.[37]

Nonetheless, the elusive quality of the emotional experience of relief need not deter us from discussing its aesthetic representations in literature. These are, arguably, ubiquitous within all forms of artistic representation, but they have, to date, not been framed within discussions of relief. Here my understanding of relief is aligned closely to Silvius's statement on relief as a counterweight to sorrow, something that is sought both consciously and unconsciously to make the individual feel better or worse in response to a given environment or set of stimuli. This understanding of relief emerges from Laforet's representation of her protagonists' varied responses to grief across her five major novels.[38] I have not sought to examine Laforet's short fiction here, as the novels illustrate more sustained meditations on the subject of relief, and they are bound together through the protagonists' common pursuit of the need for psychological relief. My analysis has deliberately focused on Laforet's protagonists, rather than providing a more diluted account that incorporates all of the secondary characters. Where they are discussed, they aid our understanding of how the protagonists use others, almost narcissistically, in their search for psychological stability due to deficits in their self-concepts. My argument will therefore remain concentrated on the idea that Laforet provides aesthetic representations of relief from which we gain insights into the pervasive nature of emotional relief within the traumatised individual, primarily as a response to the subject's need to mediate his or her life through an ongoing balance of Freud's unpleasure-pleasure principle.

Prior to any further exploration of the non-conceptual nature of relief and its resistance to aesthetic representation, it is important to explore Laforet's position as a writer in post-war Spain alongside a discussion of the methodological approach employed in this study. Within the field of post-war Spanish literary studies, Laforet is still considered to be pivotal to the regeneration of the novel in the aftermath of the Spanish civil war. To consider her work outside of this long-standing historical framework may appear boldly unconventional and dismissive of the oppressive conditions that existed in Spain under Franco's military dictatorship. However, it is only by re-positioning Laforet's narratives within the broader context of the psychology of the emotions and the concept of relief that the deeper, and profoundly radical nature of her fiction can be appreciated. My intention throughout this study is not based on a desire to detach Laforet's fiction from its historical context, but to move beyond overly contextualised readings in order to uncover how her writing speaks to the contemporary reader, thus adding to our existing knowledge of the subject's primary need for and pursuit of relief in the face of mental distress.[39] The subject of the historical contextualisation of literature has been debated widely in recent years, although less so within current scholarship on post-war Spanish narrative. The legacy of the Spanish civil war, and Franco's long dictatorship, still stands as the dominant framework through which to read fiction from the second half of the twentieth century. Yet one question to consider is what sort of interpretations get left out through our existing methods of reading texts from this epoch through a primarily historical context. There may be an argument for considering whether writers from the post-war period in Spain can *only* be read against the backdrop of Spanish history and, more particularly, Francoism. A further question to consider is whether some writers from this epoch deserve to be situated in a broader philosophical or psychoanalytical interpretative framework, so that their narratives can be understood more fully. The automatic move to historicise, or limit one's discussion to a clearly defined historical context, may result in readings that fail to honour the complexity of the text itself and its relationship to other epochs, thinkers and, indeed, different contexts. In her discussion of 'diachronic historicism' Wai Chi Dimmock suggests that when we only capture a literary text in its pastness, we 'cannot say why this text might still matter in the present, why, distanced from its original period, it nonetheless continues to signify, continues to invite other readings'.[40] Dimmock insists on texts being 'seen as objects that do a lot of traveling: across space and especially across time', which she sums up as the text's 'resonance'.[41] This study examines the extent to which Laforet's novels still have resonance today, and suggests that they continue to open up ideas that place them within and beyond their historical context. Michael Bristol builds on Dimmock's urge for literary critics to move beyond context in their interpretations. He conceives of texts 'inaugurating their own history, as advents that open up possible adventures in a future not yet determined'.[42] The text, through its existence as a cultural artifact will, at a future point in history, be read beyond the time and context of its production. It contains a series of potential temporalities that must then incorporate future readings and interpretations. Bristol elucidates: 'Rather than the present or the past, their temporality is that of a future still to be realized, a latency that may or may not become manifest, a meaning that is still deferred.'[43] It is interesting to note that Laforet expressed similar views on resonance and latency in her appraisal of Pío Baroja's fiction. She recognized that his novels were 'todavía un continente que no ha sido explorado del todo', and that he would be 'redescubierto' when his 'espíritu original poético, individualista' was fully comprehended by successive generations of readers.[44] The same can be said for Laforet, whose novels speak beyond their historical context to contemporary readers, and whose core thematic concerns provide nuanced perspectives on the methods employed by individuals to alleviate childhood trauma, grief and insecure self-concepts. As early as the 1950s, Laforet's fiction was recognised for its depth of meanings and expansive themes. Elena Fortún wrote to Laforet in 1951 telling her 'tu literatura es universal.'[45] However, due to ongoing disciplinary methodological rigidities, Laforet's novels remain trapped within critical interpretations that still tend towards historicisation; their latency has been curtailed and their resonance restricted within socio-historical readings.[46]

As the quote from Wittgenstein above suggests, one of the jobs of the philosopher and scholar is to change styles of thinking surrounding existing sets of ideas or concepts. Here, I do not seek to apply a theory or set of theories, psychoanalytical or otherwise, to Laforet's fiction. Rather, I am guided by the novels themselves and their capacity to unveil previously unknown areas of knowledge and ideas on the nature of relief as well as some of the various modes through which the human subject seeks relief. In this regard, my views align with those of Pierre Bayard and his poignant analysis of how literary texts may be put in 'the position of instructing psychoanalysis', rather than using literature to prove existing psychoanalytical theories or schools of thought.[47] A further aim of this book is to place equal emphasis on analysing each of Laforet's published novels. For too long, Laforet has been discussed as the author of *Nada*, the novel that signalled the beginning of a new era in Spanish writing following the civil war. *Nada* has generated more critical analysis than any of Laforet's subsequent novels, thus distorting its importance within her literary *oeuvre* and leading to the clichéd formulation: 'después de *Nada*, nada.'[48] This inaccurate view of Laforet's apparent failure to match the literary success of her first novel has arisen due to her later novels' resistance to socio-historical readings. *Nada*'s stark portrayal of the dissolution of family life in post-war Barcelona is repeatedly interpreted as a metaphor for the breakdown of Spanish society due to the fallout of the internecine struggles of the civil war.[49] However, her following four novels cannot be read using the same historicising approach and, as I will go on to argue in chapter one of this study, *Nada* also resists being framed exclusively within the context of post-war society due to its preoccupation with the psychological consequences of grief on Andrea and her efforts to alleviate her inner sadness. *La isla y los demonios* provides a sustained meditation on the pitfalls of obsessive love on women's psychology as well as exploring the philosophical concept of free will; the ancient Platonic debates on the importance of finding a balance between love and reason are revisited in Laforet's second novel. *La mujer nueva* focuses on the protagonist Paulina Goya's struggles with her Catholic faith, although the central question that arises from this novel is whether Paulina's search for spiritual freedom is another iteration of the invariant theme of the flight to find relief, a *fuga* Laforet herself undertook repeatedly. *La insolación*, arguably Laforet's most accomplished novel, examines Martín Soto's infatuation with Anita and Carlos Corsi, siblings with whom he repeatedly seeks to merge his identity during his summer vacations on the Alicante coast. Martín's neurotic attachment to Anita Corsi forms the core narrative theme of *Al volver la esquina*, the last of Laforet's novels to be published and, significantly, the only novel in which psychoanalysis is dealt with directly.

What is common, or, to invoke Holland's concept once more, remains invariant across all five novels, is each protagonist's desire to merge with an Other as a source of relief. This feature of her writing takes readers beyond the immediate historical circumstances of post-war Spain into the realm of the transcendental and locates her fiction within a much broader thematic framework than has previously been conceived. Indeed, it is here that Laforet's radical, yet still unnoticed, critique of Francoism can be found. Direct criticism of Francoist ideology is eschewed in favour of a stance based on the belief that, notwithstanding the censorship laws in place under the regime, one of the most effective ways to oppose oppression is to ignore its power over an individual's creative freedom, in other words, to adopt a form of radical disengagement, which is not the same as passivity or disinterest. As Manuel Vázquez Montalbán observed, as early as the 1940s in Spain, a counter cultural space began to be built within the edifice of Francoist ideology which he referred to metaphorically as 'la ciudad democrática'.[50] It is significant to note that he cites *Nada* as one of the early building blocks in the construction of this democratic space, 'aunque Carmen Laforet nunca tuviera la menor voluntad de convertirse en una escritora de resistencia'.[51] Through her rejection of any constraints upon her artistic freedom and her own desire for personal freedom, Laforet and other writers of the 1940s and 1950s began to create, 'una ciudad basada en la participación, abierta, plural, donde la libertad de la estética se interrelacionaría con la libertad del comportamiento, de la forma, de la innovación'.[52] The aesthetic freedom that Laforet chose meant that her novels stood above direct political critique and reached beyond their circumstances, marking a strong defiance towards censorship and, at the same time, a detachment from oppositional writers' attempts to align literature to political ends through, for example, the *novela objetivista*. If Laforet's fiction is to stand as a challenge and critique of Francoist ideology, then it does so through a defiant refusal to acknowledge any attempt to curtail artistic freedom. Similarly, it behoves the literary critic to respect Laforet's preoccupation with non-conceptual phenomena such as psychological relief, the emotions, and unconscious processes, and to honour the understated complexity of her novels.

Laforet was therefore less interested in constructing a strong, social critique of Francoism in her novels and more concerned with exploring the depths of the human emotions and the relationship between broad philosophical concepts and individual psychology. Although references to philosophers or established philosophical schools of thought remain absent throughout Laforet's *oeuvre*, her novels divulge an innate awareness of much wider and older discourses on what constitutes knowledge and experience. One philosopher, whose faint outline can be traced in Laforet's representations of non-conceptual experience, is Miguel de Unamuno. The tragic divergence between life as a lived and fecund substance and knowledge as its disembodied opposite is played out across her novels through their exaltation of intuition over intellection.[53] Laforet's own life was mediated through an ongoing struggle to reconcile her art to her more natural desire to experience life directly. If we are to return to the autobiographical features of her novels, it is through the protagonists' visceral interactions with their environments and other people that we encounter the author's non-intellectual mode of perceiving reality. As Johnson noted, Laforet worked 'primarily on intuition [...] with an avoidance of intellectualizing'.[54] As a writer then, Laforet seems to have had an awareness of the Schopenhauerian belief that 'intuitive cognition' [intuitive Erkenntniß], 'knowledge of perception' [anschauliche Erkenntniß] or 'feeling' [das Gefühl] exists as a form of non-conceptual knowledge.[55] We gain this knowledge, according to Schopenhauer, 'through aesthetic experiences of nature and art'.[56] There are numerous examples throughout Laforet's novels of such non-conceptual knowledge arising through either aesthetic or religious contemplation as well as through her protagonists' encounters with the natural world, all of which are simultaneously expressions of the search for relief. The epigraph to *Nada*, taken from a poem by Juan Ramón Jimenéz, demonstrates Laforet's appreciation of the centrality of the non-conceptual to human life, and how it functions as a conduit to a deeper truth beyond the realm of philosophical logic and conceptual reasoning.

> A veces un gusto amargo,
> Un olor malo, una rara
> Luz, un tono desacorde,
> Un contacto que desgana,
> Como realidades fijas,
> Nuestros sentidos alcanzan
> Y nos parecen que son
> La verdad no sospechada...[57]

This realm of the senses and the emotions, unmediated by thought or interpretation, resists conceptualization and remains complete unto itself. It is perhaps only the direct experience of our sensory relationship with the world, a pre-linguistic, haptic domain, through which relief is felt, a Freudian 'oceanic oneness' based on the subliminal desire to return to the undifferentiated state of merger with the mother. If we are to move closer to the basis of all efforts to find relief, perhaps we might find it here.

Laforet's novels therefore urge readers to step outside conventional representations of objective reality to enter the timeless space of what William James referred to as 'pure experience', where the mind has direct acquaintance with the object and true knowledge, 'la verdad no sospechada', arises from unmediated, direct experience.[58] At the core of James's radical empiricism lies the concept of merger, or what Taylor and Wozniak refer to as 'a radically pluralistic monism of pure experience', and it is this understanding of experience as an undivided whole that is reiterated across Laforet's novels and which also manifests itself as an integral feature of the author's pursuit of relief throughout her lifetime.[59] Laforet referred to the monism of pure experience as a realm or space of oneness: 'lo Único, indivisible, maravilloso', an incomparable physical and mental state for which no words exist, in which the author felt 'una armonía perfecta'.[60] At the level of aesthetic representation, states of oneness and the pursuit of pure experience appear as moments of transcendence throughout Laforet's novels, found either through music, art, nature, love and friendship or God. Traditional interpretations of transcendence assume that despite the temporary nature of the moment of pure experience, the subject emerges with greater self-knowledge and a firm resolution to live life within a different set of emotional or psychological co-ordinates; one's relationship to the self and the world has changed. Although Laforet's protagonists pursue and experience transcendence as a form of relief, it is important to note that their temporary state of merger and the suspension of subject-object distinctions does not produce the typical transformation associated with contact with pure experience. On the contrary, throughout Laforet's fiction we encounter both an attempt to articulate an aesthetics of relief intertwined with a broader aesthetics of failure, whereby each effort to find 'una armonía perfecta' or 'la verdad no sospechada' is undermined by an ineluctable pull backwards towards a state of grief and melancholia. Each novel marks a different *fuga* and the renewed pursuit of relief, but it is the same journey made over and over again, an aesthetic search for the absent mother whose *imago* is impressed across all of Laforet's longer narratives and suggests the impervious nature of grief, irrespective of psychoanalytical interventions. There is a clear case for arguing that Laforet's fiction is the embodiment of pessimism, although the temporary accounts of psychological relief do suggest that the mourning subject may encounter brief respite through contact with a deeper reality. Her novels recognise that the tragic sense of life is embodied in this conflict between human suffering and tranquillity of being.

Each chapter of this study undertakes an analysis of how, through different means, Laforet's protagonists attempt to encounter relief from emotional suffering. Chapter one establishes the relationship between Andrea's visceral reactions to her environment and her wider family with repressed grief due to the death of her mother. Chapter two assesses Marta Camino's wavering allegiance to either love or reason as methods of alleviating her anxiety and underlying distress due to losing both her parents by the end of the novel. Chapter three questions the extent to which Paulina Goya's conversion to Catholicism can be read as a spiritual awakening or whether it is a missed opportunity for Paulina to acquire deeper self-awareness. Chapter four considers Martín Soto's efforts to find relief through the Corsi siblings as a further example of mis-reading the potential solution to his sorrow, although he does come to a clear realisation towards the end of the novel. In the final chapter, Martín's account of a period of his life when he sought to merge emotionally with Anita Corsi suggests a level of self-reflection unseen in the previous novels. Relief is finally sought through therapeutic means, although the outcome of his encounter with analysis remains unknown as the manuscript of the last novel of the trilogy *Jaque mate* has never been found. The conclusion assesses whether true relief from sorrow arises through the course of Laforet's novels. The role of silence as a distillation of relief will be considered in the final pages of this study.

Any treatment of Laforet's novels as separate works of art proves problematic; collectively, they are one unified work of art, and it would make greater sense to work backwards from *Al volver* to *Nada* to understand more accurately the substance and treatment of relief across her narratives. Laforet used the symbol of the closed or open circle to describe the shape of *Nada*,[61] yet it is applicable as a metaphor for all her novels, as they each follow a pattern of return, undermining each protagonist's capacity to progress, a potent symbolic reminder of the shape of sorrow, whose underside, to return to Silvius once more, is relief.

Notes to the Introduction

1. *The Complete Works of William Shakespeare*, ed. by B. Hodek (London: Spring Books, 1958), p. 225.
2. Ludwig Wittgenstein, *Lectures and Conversations on Aesthetics, Psychology and Religious Belief* (Oxford: Blackwell, 2001), p. 28.
3. Henri Bergson, *The Creative Mind* (New York: The Philosophical Library, 1946), p. 40.
4. Anna Caballé and Israel Rolón, *Carmen Laforet. Una mujer en fuga* (Barcelona: RBA Libros, 2010).
5. Miguel Delibes's views on the autobiographical substance within a writer's work substantiate the idea that the writer's life seeps through into his or fiction at the level of ideas: 'Ya tenemos [...] una base autobiográfica en toda obra de ficción, base que no solamente se alimenta de la vida del fabulador, sino también de su propia filosofía. Miguel Delibes, *España 1936–1950: Muerte y resurrección de la novela* (Barcelona: Destino, 2006), p. 135. It is also evident that repressed material gets transferred into the unconscious of the text.
6. 'Carmen Laforet cuenta su vida' (II), *Pueblo*, 4 January 1961. Cited in Caballé and Rolón, p. 52.
7. Caballé and Rolón, p. 50.
8. Caballé and Rolón, p. 53.
9. Julia Kristeva suggests that the depressed subject 'wanders in pursuit of continuously disappointing adventures and loves' which reinforces the idea of the trope of flight or *fuga* that recurs across Laforet's novels. *Black Sun: Depression and Melancholia* (New York and Oxford: Columbia University Press, 1989), p. 13.

10. Rita Frankiel, Introductory Notes to Chapters 3, 4, 5, in Rita V. Frankiel, *Essential Papers on Object Loss* (New York and London: New York University Press, 1994), p. 37.

11. Rita Frankiel, Introductory Notes to Chapters 3, 4, 5, in Rita V. Frankiel, p. 37.

12. Sigmund Freud, 'Mourning and Melancholia', in Rita Frankiel, *Essential Papers*, pp. 38–51, p. 40. John Bowlby would develop Freud's analysis in his discussion of the concept of 'disordered mourning' which will be examined in greater detail in chapter one.

13. Ibid., p. 40.

14. Barry Jordan suggests that Andrea's ego remains stunted due to impediments to her psycho-sexual development but he does not trace the origins back to the protagonist's melancholic mourning. See Barry Jordan, *Laforet: Nada* (London: Grant & Cutler in association with Tamesis Books, 1993).

15. Here it proves useful to consider Julia Kristeva's views on depressive subjects and their tendency to 'cling to an other, perceived as supplement, artificial extension, protective wrapping,' Kristeva, p. 15.

16. Paul R. Rasmussen, *The Quest to Feel Good* (New York and London: Routledge, 2010), p. 6.

17. Bessel van der Kolk, *The Body Keeps the Score: Mind, Brain and Body in the Transformation of Trauma* (London: Penguin Random House, 2014), p. 211.

18. In one of the earliest studies of Laforet's fiction Graciela Illanes Adaro noted the author's deep 'intuición psicológica'. *La novelística de Carmen Laforet* (Madrid: Editorial Gredos, 1971), p. 132.

19. Cristina Cerezales Laforet, *Música blanca* (Barcelona: Destino, 2009), pp. 179–80. It proves difficult to ascribe a genre to this representation of Laforet's life. It is based on memoir and an imagined spoken dialogue between mother and daughter following Laforet's fall into silence, which may have been voluntary or linked to a debilitating, end of life illness. Cristina posits the idea of silent, extra-sensory communication with her mother based on intuition and non-verbal signals.

20. See Marie-Lise Gazarian Gautier, *Interviews with Spanish Writers* (Elmwood Park, Illinois: Dalkey Archive Press, 1991). Laforet contradicts herself in this interview and fails to provide a convincing defence when questioned about her writing as autofiction. Laforet mentions that her father wished her to be more objective in her future novels following the publication of *Nada*.

21. Roberta Johnson, *Carmen Laforet* (Boston: Twayne Publishers, 1981), p. 93.

22. Thus, I do not concur with Johnson's view that 'the basic theme of all her novels is the development of sexual identity at an archetypal level', although this may be a related psychological function within the grieving subject (Johnson, p. 98).

23. Maude Ellman, Introduction to *Psychoanalytical Literary Criticism* (London and New York: Longman, 1994), pp. 1–26, p. 5.

24. Kristeva describes the lost Object as 'the "Thing"' or 'the real that does not lend itself to signification', *Black Sun*, p. 13. Kristeva's views on depression and melancholia are only partially useful to our understanding of Laforet's fiction, since the depressive mood presented through Laforet's protagonists does not provide 'the self with integrity', Kristeva, p. 19. On the contrary, grief presents itself across Laforet's fiction as a process of hollowing out the establishment of a sense of self, which in turn triggers the repeated search for psychological relief.

25. H.D. also lost her mother at a young age.

26. Norman Holland, *Poems in Persons: An Introduction to the Psychoanalysis of Literature* (New York: W. W. Norton, 1973), p. 51.

27. Ibid., p. 56.

28. Frederick J. Hoffman, *Freudianism and the Literary Mind* (New York: Grove Press, 1957), p. 321.

29. Frederick J. Hoffman, p. 326.

30. Barbara Low, *Psycho-Analysis; A Brief Account of the Freudian Theory* (Harcourt Brace: London and New York, 1920), p. 76; Sigmund Freud, 'The Economic Problem of Masochism', in *Essential Papers on Masochism*, ed. by Margaret Ann Fitzpatrick Hanly (New York and London: New York University Press, 1995), pp. 274–85. Original essay in Freud, Sigmund, James Strachey, Anna Freud, Alan Tyson, and Alix Strachey. *The Standard Edition of the Complete Psychological Works of Sigmund Freud: Ego and the Id and Other Works. Volume IXX (1923–1925)* (London: Vintage, 2001), pp. 159–70.

31. Freud, in Hanly, p. 275.
32. Ibid., p. 275. Laforet frequently makes reference to the noun *desahogo* across her novels as a direct signifier for relief.
33. Ibid., p. 275.
34. Rasmussen, p. 79. Freud and Adler are referred to in *Al volver la esquina* (Barcelona: Destino, 2004), p. 185.
35. Rasmussen, p. 79.
36. Seneca, *On the Shortness of Life*, ed. and trans. by C. D. N. Costa (London: Penguin Books, 2004), p. 73.
37. For a more detailed discussion of the Stoic's belief in the restraint of emotion to bring about lasting relief see Richard Sorabji, *Emotion and Peace of Mind: From Stoic Agitation to Christian Temptation: The Gifford Lectures* (Oxford: Oxford University Press, 2002).
38. We must acknowledge, as Freud did in his study of masochism, that seeking unpleasure can be a source of relief. As I will go on to illustrate, this is borne out by the actions of several of Laforet's protagonists whose nascent masochism suggests the influence of traditional Catholic doctrine on the value of suffering and abnegation. The presence of Catholicism within Laforet's writing must be acknowledged as an important influence on her characters' behaviour and attitude towards suffering.
39. Laforet declared that the political situation in Spain did not interest her: 'Siempre he estado desinteresada, quizás por no tener simpatía por un lado o por otro', Geraldine C. Nichols, *Escribir, espacio propio: Laforet, Matute, Moix, Tusquets, Riera y Roig por si mismas* (Minneapolis: Institute for the Study of Ideologies and Literature, 1989), p. 136.
40. Wai Chi Dimmock, 'A Theory of Resonance', *PMLA* 112 (1997), 1060–1071, (p. 1061).
41. Dimmock, p. 1061.
42. Michael Bristol, 'Macbeth the Philosopher: Rethinking Context', *New Literary History*, 42, 4, (2011), 'Context?' Special Issue, pp. 641–62.
43. Bristol, p. 656.
44. Manuel Andujar et al, *Encuentros con Don Pío. Homenaje a Baroja* (Madrid: Al-Borak, N.D, 1972). 'Del diario de Carmen Laforet', pp. 205–06, p. 206.
45. *Carmen Laforet y Elena Fortún: De corazón y alma 1947–1952*, Cristina Cerezales Laforet, (Madrid: Fundación Banco Santander, 2017), p. 53. As Anthony Storr notes 'the function of the arts is not to depict particular instances of reality, but to represent the universals which lie behind the particular', *Music and the Mind* (London: Harper Collins, 1997), p. 134.
46. Barry Jordan however situates Laforet's first novel *Nada* within the framework of Freudian psychoanalysis. See 'Narrators, Readers and Writers in Laforet's Nada', *Revista Hispánica Moderna*, 46.1 (1993), 87–102; Jordan, Barry, 'Shifting Generic Boundaries: The Role of Confession and Desire in Laforet's Nada', *Neophilologus*, 77.3, (1993), 411–22; Jordan, Barry, 'Laforet's *Nada* as Female Bildung?' *Symposium: A Quarterly Journal in Modern Literatures*, 46.2 (1992), 105–18; Jordan, Barry, 'Looks that Kill: Power, Gender and Vision in Laforet's *Nada*', *Revista Canadiense de Estudios Hispanicos*, 17.1, (1992), 79–104. David William Foster was one of the first critics to situate *Nada* within a non-historical perspective and focus instead on the novel's generic features. 'Nada de Carmen Laforet (ejemplo de neo-romance en la novela contemporánea', *Revista Hispánica Moderna*, 32 (1966), 43–55.
47. Pierre Bayard, 'Is it Possible to Apply Literature to Psychoanalysis?' *American Imago*, 56.3, (1999), 207–19, (p. 214).
48. At the time of writing, the MLA bibliography listed more than one hundred items on *Nada*.
49. I will argue in chapter one that *Nada*'s central theme focuses on Andrea's attempts to find relief from melancholic or disordered mourning.
50. Manuel Vázquez Montalbán, *La literatura en la construcción de la ciudad democrática* (Barcelona: Crítica, 1998). Implicit in this argument is the view that censorship was, ultimately, less effective as a tool in Franco's arsenal of repressive measures against the Spanish population than was assumed.
51. Ibid., p. 61.
52. Ibid., p. 60.

53. Henri Bergson's ideas on non-conceptual knowledge also find a place in Laforet's fiction. For an excellent analysis of the relationship between Bergson and Unamuno see Benjamin Fraser, *Encounters with Bergson(ism) in Spain: Reconciling Philosophy, Literature, Film and Urban Space* (Chapel Hill: University of North Carolina Press, University of North Carolina at Chapel Hill for its Department of Romance Studies, 2010).

54. Johnson, p. 35.

55. Shapshay, Sandra, 'Schopenhauer's Aesthetics', *The Stanford Encyclopedia of Philosophy* (Summer 2018 Edition), ed. by Edward N. Zalta, <https://plato.stanford.edu/archives/sum2018/entries/schopenhauer-aesthetics/> [accessed 25 January 2019].

56. Ibid.

57. Carmen Laforet, *Nada* (Madrid: Aguilar, 1987), p. 7.

58. The Zen Buddhist concept of *satori*, which involves seeing deeply into the nature of existence as it is, approximates both James's 'pure experience' and Abraham Maslow's 'peak experience'. See A. Maslow, *The Farthest Reaches of Human Nature* (New York: Viking Press, 1971). For an excellent discussion of James's concept see *Pure Experience: The Response to William James*, ed. by E. I. Taylor & R. H. Wozniak (Bristol: Thoemmes Press, 1996). Bergson also believed that truth must be felt before it is conceived, rather than 'truth merely thought'. *The Creative Mind*, p. 259. It is worth noting that Laforet's trilogy, of which only the first two novels were published, was to carry the title *Tres pasos fuera del tiempo*.

59. Taylor and Wozniak, p. xiv.

60. Cerezales Laforet, *Música blanca*, p. 45.

61. Gazarian Gautier, p. 158.

CHAPTER 1

Grief and Relief
Nada (1945)

Carmen Laforet's first novel has generated a significant number of critical interpretations since its publication in 1945 and there has been little agreement amongst scholars on the meaning of both the defiantly negative title and the story of the protagonist's life during her year in Barcelona. *Nada* was initially read as a realistic account of post-war urban life in the Catalan capital; the internecine conflicts of Andrea's extended family were also read as a metaphor for the ongoing impact of the civil war on Spanish society. Both *Nada* and Camilo José Cela's *La familia de Pascual Duarte* (1942) were read as examples of *tremendismo* due to their explicit descriptions of violence.[1] During the mid to late 1950s, critical interpretations of *Nada* evolved; the novel began to be located within the broader, European tradition of existential literature. Andrea's quest for meaning and self-understanding amidst the hopelessness of her family environment was interpreted as evidence of a deeper, metaphysical crisis afflicting mid-twentieth-century Western society. The title suggests a loss of meaning, and the theme of alienation looms large throughout the novel as nearly all the members of Andrea's family suffer from a lack of psychological stability and alienation from their true selves. Juan and Román are clearly psychologically disturbed, Gloria is subjugated through domestic violence and the grandmother suffers from passivity and upholds dominant cultural gender norms.[2] In more recent years, *Nada* has been subjected to a variety of readings. Some of these have focused on Laforet's use of various symbols and imagery, while others have examined *Nada*'s structural complexity as well as the role of the narrator in the novel. One of the most penetrating interpretations of the novel is articulated in Barry Jordan's sophisticated critical guide in which he describes *Nada* as a work of 'psychological realism'.[3] Jordan was one of the first scholars to apply a broadly psycho-analytical approach to reading *Nada* and, through his analysis of Andrea's repression of her sexual desires, he refutes the idea, held by a number of critics, that the protagonist undergoes identity development during her year in Barcelona: 'Andrea, far from moving forward in emotional and psycho-sexual terms, is actually marking time, running on the spot and in the end, going nowhere.'[4] Although Jordan excels in his detailed psychoanalytical reading of the novel, he fails to engage fully with the root cause of the protagonist's failure to develop a more solid sense of self, and thus develop as a character. Jordan's analysis is grounded in Freudian thought and links Andrea's development, or lack thereof, to underdeveloped psychosexual maturity. Nonetheless, Jordan identifies that Andrea's failure to transition to mature adulthood 'is predicated on a return of the repressed', but he does not elucidate in depth upon what the repressed material consists of, although he intuits that it is connected to the figure of the dead mother and a return to 'a state of unity with the mother, of undifferentiation, of non-being, a paradise which is lost by the fall into socialization and growing up'.[5] This is the 'nada' into which Andrea, according to Jordan, seeks to dissolve her self.[6] It is important to extrapolate further on Jordan's analysis. The nothingness throughout the novel arises from the voided emotional space of traumatic grief, which remains beyond the realm of articulation and forms the 'oquedad' that exists within each of Laforet's novels. It is to this subject, and the need to relieve the psychological pain associated with this absence, that we must turn our attention.

Andrea's mother is only referred to once in the novel by name — Amalia — whose 'larga trenza de pelo negro estaba guardada en un viejo armario de pueblo muy lejos de allí'.[7] This image of her mother's mane of black hair, kept in a wardrobe far from Andrea, expresses the absence or 'nada' at the heart of Andrea's existence.[8] Like her mother's hair, Andrea's grief is locked away, hidden deep within her unconscious mind, inaccessible yet always pressing itself to emerge through her emotional responses to people, places, art, music, architecture, nature, and through her need to write, all of which manifest themselves within *Nada* through aesthetic representations of the pursuit of relief. *Nada* is a portrait of the consequences of the trauma caused to an individual's psychology through the process of what John Bowlby termed 'disordered mourning'.[9] In a strikingly similar manner to the mental processes involved in psychological trauma, the narrative is based on withholding information. *Nada* is punctuated by gaps and silences that are equivalent to a string of absences within the text, of that which cannot be articulated because it lies buried behind the barriers of Andrea's emotional defenses. Jordan recognises *Nada*'s 'elliptical quality' in which one finds 'gaps and ends untied and enigmas unresolved'.[10] The reader experiences a sense of frustration in relation to the facts of her life that remain unaccounted for, such as what happens to her following her departure from Barcelona as well as her wider life experiences prior to her arrival in the city. These lacunae within the narrative symbolise Andrea's underlying trauma. As Judith Lewis Herman has observed in her study of individuals who have experienced a major traumatic event and engage in the therapeutic process of re-telling it, 'Occasionally [...] major amnesiac gaps in the story remain even after careful and painstaking exploration.'[11] Irene Mizrahi has discussed *Nada* as a trauma narrative, suggesting that the retrospective narrative account of her life in Barcelona represents a form of entrapment for Andrea from which she cannot escape.[12] Mizrahi contends that *Nada* articulates the trauma of Andrea's repressed homosexuality, a view also held by Ana Figueroa.[13] This is the unsuspected truth — 'La verdad no sospechada' — according to Figueroa and Mizrahi, yet Andrea's sexual orientation does not account for the trauma that afflicts her, one which she carries with her, along with her overloaded suitcase full of books, to Barcelona. Indeed, her desire to attach herself to her friend Ena may be less a matter of sexual attraction and more a longing for merger with another human being, potentially a substitute mother figure.

This chapter will examine how Laforet's representations of Andrea's efforts to articulate her grief and find relief are fraught with difficulty due to an ingrained set of psychological defences stemming from the trauma of her mother's death. It appears to be the case that Andrea's outlet for her repressed emotions is her art: the novel she narrates from a position of greater maturity. However, as Gustavo Pérez Firmat indicates, 'Andrea is a narrator whose language insistently calls attention to itself but who is equally insistent in covering up or dissembling the act of narration.'[14] Yet for Andrea, the act of writing serves only in part as a tool for self-reflection; there are numerous examples of the older narrator examining the actions and motivations of her younger self. Nonetheless, writing also serves as a shield, as Pérez Firmat noted, behind which she hides her grief and through which she fails to find relief. Writing, her 'virtuoso scriptive performance' becomes the symbolic figuration of Andrea's psychological condition, a projection of her suffering and a defense behind which she hides her deeper emotional trauma associated with loss of the primary carer.[15] Relief appears to be experienced at certain moments in the novel, yet is presented in a highly aestheticised manner, as if to constrain its potency as a source of joy. These moments are attempts at a form of willed tranquillity on Andrea's part, yet they remain fleeting, as the epigraph to the novel suggests. As will be discussed below, Andrea demonstrates a complicated response to the realm of the aesthetic whereby she seeks to elicit an emotional response through contemplation of aesthetic forms, yet she still fails to articulate her suffering. Art, nature and other aesthetic forms do not therefore provide an effective outlet for Andrea's grief, although they may assuage it temporarily. Relief is also sought through Andrea's friendship with Ena, a disturbed and beautiful fellow student with whom Andrea seeks to merge her identity.[16] A psychoanalytical reading of Ena's role in the novel positions her as an idealised mother substitute in whom Andrea seeks to alleviate her suffering. Critical interpretations of Ena's relationship with Andrea have upheld the value of female friendship to the protagonist's self-development in the novel; however, as I discuss below, their friendship is fraught with difficulty and is based on Andrea's projected desire for merger with a substitute other, rather than a real, altruistic friendship. It is only towards the end of the novel that their friendship is cemented into something stronger. Their relationship prefigures all the later emotional bonds that each protagonist seeks to forge with substitute mother or father figures and reveals an attachment pattern that is based on unmet needs, dependence and rooted in phantasy.

Grief and Disordered Mourning

We should not look to the actual events described in the story of *Nada* to understand the 'nothing' that lies at the heart of this novel, but to what Andrea brings with her to Barcelona on the night she arrives at her maternal grandmother's apartment on Calle Aribau, namely, her grief and the impact of her disordered mourning on her psychology. Andrea may have placed physical distance between herself and her mother's 'larga trenza de pelo negro' but the legacy of her unresolved grief weighs down more heavily than the suitcase full of books that she carries with her. Throughout *Nada*, Andrea pursues relief as an antidote to 'disordered mourning', a now well-known term within the field of object-relations theory which was originally coined by John Bowlby. In his essay on 'Loss, Sadness and Depression' Bowlby discusses the impact of 'the disruption or threatened disruption of an affectional bond'.[17] Bowlby suggested that those who experience childhood mourning may go on to establish patterns of defence, resulting in 'the exclusion from further processing of information of certain specific types for relatively long periods or even permanently'.[18] Andrea fails to process the impact of her grief in any direct way throughout *Nada*; what results is a story that revolves around her defensive exclusion of her emotions associated with the loss of her mother and a description of the mechanisms she draws upon to defend against the expression of her feelings. The person who experiences disordered mourning, according to Bowlby, deactivates (to a greater or lesser degree) some behavioural systems, and 'when this occurs one or more other activities may come to monopolise the person's time and attention, acting apparently as diversions'.[19] This account of the creation of diversions as part of the defence mechanism that distorts 'healthy mourning' relates back to Freud's analysis of the pleasure-unpleasure principle and the human subject's pursuit of relief in the face of emotional suffering, sometimes even resulting in masochism towards the self.[20] The displacement of repressed emotional material functions as a form of relief yet also serves to avoid a confrontation with the source of suffering. In the case of Andrea, the 'diversions' she creates to clothe her grief manifest themselves within other activities, namely writing, and appreciating the aesthetic beauty of art and nature as well as her friendship with Ena. The fact that Andrea is involved in these activities undermines the view, held by Jordan, that Andrea is a passive character: 'The problem is that the main protagonist seems excessively passive as a character [who] does not act in the conventional sense of initiating things, of planning and executing ideas.'[21] The key word here is 'conventional' since Andrea is in fact permanently initiating things, planning and executing ideas through her creative imagination, an activity that Román recognises early in the novel: 'Ya sé que estás siempre soñando cuentos con nuestros caracteres' (p. 40). This metafictional moment signals Andrea's predilection for story-telling, one of her 'permanent diversions' through which she seeks, but does not appear to find, relief. *Nada* may even be described as an example of sustained metafiction since the overly dramatised characters of Román, Juan, Gloria and Angustias undermine verisimilitude and make us question whether the novel could ever be described as an example of post-war social realism. Laforet's characters may be too quixotic for the reader to take as approximations of real people, and Andrea herself is overly fictionalised as a character due to the extremity of her reactions and interactions with other characters. *Nada*'s peculiarity lies in its lack of familiarity and the exaggerated nature of its characters and situations. There are also moments in the novel when we find Laforet working effusively with language to create a startling image which conveys a deeper emotion, expressed with considerable force. For example, 'La locura sonreía en los grifos torcidos' (p. 18), 'el vientre de un cielo sofocantemente oscuro' (p. 280) or 'La tierra parecía hervir, jadear, desprendiéndose de todos sus venenos' (p. 284). The reader is forced to question whether Andrea is expressing unconscious projections of her emotions, through heightened aesthetic means, in order to cloak a deeper terror associated with her mother's death and its uncanny silencing throughout the novel. One striking illustration of the narrator's tendency to overlay her grief by turning towards an excess of aesthetic description occurs as she prepares for her first night in her grandmother's house. Having not found the love and security of her wider family in the flat in Barcelona, Andrea enters a state of shock which rapidly transforms her vision of the people and objects around her. As she looks up at the stars through a glass gallery, Andrea is struck by a wave of emotion and 'unas ganas súbitas de llorar, como si viera amigos antiguos, bruscamente recobrados' (p. 19). Alone in the world, with only the stars as her companions, her sense of isolation and disappointment is magnified, and she projects her emotions onto the bed with which she has been provided, comparing it to a tomb: 'aquella cama parecida a un ataúd' (p. 19). On the level of symbolic association, the bed may also trigger her to remember her mother's dead body, the primary trauma of which she cannot speak, the 'nada' that lies at the heart of her existence. Rather than escaping from her bereavement in Barcelona, Andrea is forced to confront it again and she draws upon her ingrained defense mechanisms to stave off her suffering, by using her imagination to deflect her (and the reader) from addressing the real reason for her suffering. The physical action of looking upwards and diverting the gaze away from an object forms a repetitive trope in *Nada* and symbolises the concept of relief, a turning away from a source of suffering towards an alleviating vista or object. It is a movement that hinges together flight from a phenomenon and the search for another object into which to project emotion; to invoke Adler again, this pattern signals an avoidance of a felt-minus and a searching for a felt-plus, and it is repeatedly used as an invariant trope of relief across Laforet's fiction.

There are clear signs throughout *Nada* that Andrea is suffering from a form of depressive illness. Combined with her state of semi-starvation, Andrea experiences nervous tension and shows frequent bouts of despondency; for example, she lies for hours on her bed with her eyes open with her gaze unfocused in a state of absorption reminiscent of a mystical trance. Her friend Ena describes how she first viewed her when she saw Andrea at university: 'Tenías los ojos brillantes y andabas torpe, abstraída, sin fijarse en nada...' (p. 174). The absent gaze of Andrea's eyes also suggests a state of dissociation, a traumatic defence mechanism which early practictioners of psychoanalysis such as Pierre Janet and Freud linked to symptoms of psychosis and trance-like states.[22] Throughout *Nada* there are repeated occasions when Andrea enters into an almost trance-like state in response to music, architectural form or nature. These states are almost always willed on her part and they provide further evidence of her seeking out methods of dissociation as a form of relief.

Although Andrea is vigilant to her fluctuating moods and psychological states, she seems unable to forge an association between her current responses to her environment and what appears to be a long-standing depression. The lugubrious, dirty and disorganised environment she steps into when she arrives in Barcelona only serves as a trigger for her existing feelings of isolation and desperate loneliness. The relief that she anticipates she will find in her grandmother's house in Barcelona remains unmet, and it is plausible that this will always remain for as long as she fails to confront her grief. It is as if Andrea encounters an emotional environment in Aribau that is not unfamiliar to her, and she suffers the subsequent disappointment of returning to a memory of rejection and an absence of love from which she had hoped to escape. Jordan draws our attention to the opening of *Nada*, 'a novel which begins on a note of severe disruption. Things, people, relationships, families and identities are out of place.'[23] This is not the environment in which, as an orphan, Andrea is going to find a way to alleviate her suffering. Jordan avers that Laforet's intention is to put things back in place by the end of the novel, but it is not clear that resolution occurs.[24] Andrea's apparent opportunity to move on with the help of Ena's family does not in fact signal any form of resolution but represents instead another attempt to find relief, a cyclical pattern that encircles Laforet's novels in an ongoing pursuit of tranquillity and inner peace which is only found through temporary *cathexis* into another phenomenon or person.

Andrea therefore arrives in Barcelona in search of something to assuage her emotional distress but, from the moment of her arrival, she is doomed to repeat the failure of her unmet desire for connection with a significant other or substitute for her dead mother. As Jordan states, *Nada* is 'a novel of stasis, circularity, repetition and entrapment, in which Andrea is fated to experience and repeat the same'.[25] Within the first line of the novel, the narrator informs the reader: 'no me esperaba nadie' (p. 12), alluding to the ongoing sense of absence that plagues Andrea and serves as a poignant symbol for her disordered mourning and subsequent psychological trauma. The verb 'esperar' appears as a leitmotif throughout *Nada*, as if hope of relief were always stymied by the void of nothingness that permeates Andrea's life. She herself describes her depressive state as 'aquella esperada tristeza' (p. 46). The use of the word 'esperada' here suggests the long-standing nature of Andrea's grief, providing some evidence that she is aware of her condition and that she is bringing her psychological difficulties with her to Barcelona. It is not the case that the family conflicts raging in the Aribau household function as the source of her suffering, although they may aggravate her fragile state of mind. Acts of self-punishment also indicate Andrea's unstable mental equilibrium; she refers to her 'instintos martirizados', which are possibly rooted in her Catholic upbringing, but also suggest a desire for self-denial due to unresolved issues over the loss of her mother associated with emotions of guilt and self-blame (p. 274).[26] As a result of not finding relief in her grandmother's home, a sense of hopelessness sets in to Andrea's life: 'Me acostumbraba a olvidarme de mi aspecto y de mis sueños. Iba dejando de tener importancia el olor de los meses, las visiones del porvenir' (p. 46). Throughout *Nada* the reader is forced to consider whether Andrea's depressed condition is caused by her experiences during her year-long residence with her family in Aribau or is in fact a continuation or re-activation of an earlier trauma that pre-dates this period of her life.

The question to consider is how the quest for relief is expressed throughout *Nada* and through which means Andrea tries to find temporary escape from her grief. At certain moments in the narrative, the conflict that exists between Andrea's defense mechanisms and her ongoing suffering is given representative form. Andrea is frequently engaged in aesthetic contemplation and it is during this act that her grief almost breaks through to expression yet is simultaneously withheld through a powerful, poetic style or aesthetic veneer. Bowlby noted that the process of defensive exclusion of significant information (in Andrea's case, information about her mother's death and her feelings about this event) 'may of course be less than complete'.[27] He goes on to state that 'there are times when fragments of the information defensively excluded seep through so that fragments of the behaviour defensively deactivated become visible'[28] (p. 66). The following examples illustrate moments when Andrea's grief almost seeps through her ingrained defences and readers gain an insight into her 'dynamic unconscious and the return of the repressed', in other words, her repressed grief.[29]

The first description of Andrea becoming absorbed in aesthetic contemplation occurs when she is listening to Román's music. It is important to register what immediately precedes this account. Román has been talking to Andrea about their wider family, which includes Román's sister, Andrea's mother Amalia: 'Tu madre evitó el peligro antes que nadie marchándose' (p. 42). Andrea does not press her uncle to find out more about the 'peligro' or gain information about her mother. She responds instead with a supplication to Román to play music for her as if to purge her of an emotion or sensation: '¿No quieres hacer música hoy, di?' (p. 42). There then follows a description of Andrea's psychological defence mechanisms partially receding due to aesthetic elevation. A sense of symbolic death, the ultimate relief, arises:

> En el momento en que, de pie junto a la chimenea, empezaba a pulsar el arco, yo cambiaba completamente. Desaparecían mis reservas, la ligera capa de hostilidad contra todos que se me había ido formando. Mi alma, extendida como mis propias manos juntas, recibía el sonido como una lluvia la tierra áspera. Román me parecía un artista maravilloso y único. Iba hilando en la música una alegría tan fina que traspasaba los límites de la tristeza. La música aquella sin nombre. La música de Román, que nunca más he vuelto a oír. (42–43)

Andrea's soul, her emotional core, appears to be momentarily bared and her self-willed hostility towards others, and part of her psychological defence mechanisms, are suspended. The protagonist continues to describe the impact of Román's music on her emotions:

> Y a mí llegaban en oleadas, primero, ingenuos recuerdos, sueños, luchas, mi
> propio presente vacilante, y luego, agudas alegrías, tristezas, desesperación, una
> crispación impotente de la vida y un anegarse en la nada. Mi propia muerte,
> el sentimiento de mi desesperación total hecha belleza, angustiosa armonía sin
> luz. (43)

This sequence endorses the view that Andrea's suffering pre-dates her arrival in
Barcelona. The account occurs too early in the novel for Andrea's description of
her 'tristezas' and 'desesperación' to be attributed solely to her difficult relationship
with Angustias and the unwelcoming atmosphere in the flat on Aribau. Román's
music stirs her to feel a variety of sensations linked to her past and present, yet
Andrea still refuses to inform the reader of what is at the core of her 'desesperación'.
What is made apparent is how her suffering is aestheticised through Román's music
and momentary relief through beauty arises: 'mi desesperación total hecha belleza'.
This statement is a condensed description of the entire novel as the aesthetic beauty
of the narrator's prose, and of Laforet the writer, is a sustained defence against
Andrea's grief and, arguably, that of the author herself. Writing, as such, does not
bring relief, yet beauty, in the form of Román's music, may provide temporary
respite for Andrea as she [seems to] merge with the sound of his violin. Anthony
Storr notes in his discussion of Schopenhauer's interpretation of music that it can
function as an 'aesthetic mode of knowing', enabling 'the individual to escape, for
the time being, from the never-ending misery of unsatisfied desire into a Nirvana
of spiritual peace'.[30] Relief arises momentarily for Andrea through Román's music,
only to dissipate once the sound of the violin stops.

Bowlby's ideas undergo slight modification with the examples drawn from *Nada*
as what is made visible is still partially defended against through Andrea's art.
Beauty and the aesthetic simultaneously function as a reflection of and a defence
against Andrea's grief and this seemingly contradictory dynamic is carried over into
Laforet's prose style, becoming ever more embellished as she approximates the state
of her true emotions: 'angustiosa armonía sin luz'. This poetic fragment articulates
the anguished, wan melody of Andrea's pain, yet it remains within the realm of
abstract metaphor. Relief is glimpsed but the reader is kept at a distance through
Laforet's aesthetic ingenuity. Art, music and aesthetic contemplation temporarily
ameliorate the 'nada' on which Andrea's story is based but the void over which her
emotions are permanently poised remains. When Román's music stops and he asks
her to express what she feels, Andrea replies 'nada', reiterating the cryptic word
towards which the entire novel gravitates, and which serves as a leitmotif for the fact
that the protagonist's knowledge that nothing will ultimately function as a source
of relief from her unconscious desire for a symbolic death and longed-for reunion
with her dead mother.

A further example of the role of aesthetic contemplation as one of Andrea's
methods of finding relief from grief is illustrated when she recounts her experience
while contemplating the façade of Barcelona's neo-gothic Cathedral. However,
we must look again to the events preceding this description to understand fully
the event narrated. Andrea has been enjoying an evening with Ena and her family
during which Ena's mother has been singing. The presence of a loving mother with

her wider family stands in contrast to Andrea's status as orphan and the absence of a caring extended family in the Aribau household; Andrea therefore finds herself in a state of heightened sensitivity to her own life circumstances. It is the power of music that touches Andrea again, awakening 'todos los pozos de sentimentalismo y de desbocado romanticism de mis dieciocho años' (p. 122). Her emotions are over-aroused and she feels 'ganas de escapar de todo lo demás que me rodeaba' (p. 122). The narrator informs us that she leaves Ena's flat in search of something that will satiate her desire for relief and is quenched by contemplating the architectural forms of the cathedral:

> apreté el paso hasta llegar a la fachada principal de la Catedral, y al levantar mis ojos hacia ella encontré al final el cumplimiento de lo que deseaba.
> Una fuerza más grande que la que el vino y la música habían puesto en mí, me vino al mirar el gran corro de sombras de piedra fervorosa. La Catedral se levantaba en una armonía severa, estilizada en formas casi vegetales, hasta la altura del limpio cielo mediterráneo. Una paz, una imponente claridad se derramaba de la arquitectura maravillosa. En derredor de sus trazos oscuros resaltaba la noche brillante, rondando lentamente al compás de las horas. Dejé que aquel profundo hechizo de las formas me penetrara durante unos minutos.
> (124)

Architectural beauty penetrates Andrea, yet this state of aesthetic absorption is purposely willed on her part, suggesting that she is invoking relief through beauty as a means of coping with, or perhaps more accurately, deflecting deeply felt emotions, a practice that appears to be familiar to her.[31] But the question that must be addressed is why Andrea feels compelled to seek a sensation of dissolution following her evening at Ena's. Jordan's reading of this moment is suggestive. He states that art and architecture 'act as a means of sublimation for Andrea's libidinal drives, which, like those of Román, include a desire for self-annihilation'.[32] The idea of Andrea repressing *something* is pertinent, and Jordan astutely notices that it is coming from the unconscious. However, it is Andrea's sense of grief, stimulated by the voice of Ena's mother singing, that has been aroused and which she attempts to repress through aesthetic contemplation. Art, or more specifically music and architecture, are co-opted as a way of both feeling and repressing emotions associated with the loss of her mother. A form of emotional displacement or *cathexis* occurs, and it is through this process that some alleviation arises, but it does not, again, address the source of her suffering. In both accounts of Andrea becoming absorbed in aesthetic contemplation, a distinct harmony is described: 'angustiosa armonía sin luz' and 'una armonía severa' both of which connect back to the musical harmonies that have stimulated her emotional reaction. Yet this harmony carries within it a disharmony, since it appears to be a thwarted form of relief, devoid of colour, anguished and severe. Relief as experienced by *Nada*'s protagonist is painful as it is an evocation of her traumatic loss which, through a not easily describable process of transmutation, is transposed through Román's music, and similarly projected onto the structural forms of the Cathedral. Transmutation and projection do not however lead to the written expression of the substance of Andrea's grief. This remains beyond the text, although it appears to find a proximate articulation through the harmonies and tones of music. As Jenefer Robinson suggests, 'Music arouses mood states from which we readily enter into emotional states.'[33] Although Andrea fails to express in any precise way what it is that Román and Margarita's music has stirred in her, this ambiguity towards her emotions may, according to Susanne K. Langer's discussion of the philosophy of music, convey how the 'real power of music lies in the fact that it can be 'true' to the life of feeling in a way that language cannot; for its significant forms have that ambivalence of content which words cannot have'.[34] We must return to Pérez Firmat's observation of how Andrea, the narrator, utilises language to dissemble; in other words, to not be true to her life of feeling. Art becomes a tool within her repertoire of defences against her grief. Andrea's response to music, and her sense of rapture through temporary dissolution of the self, suggests that she may be, according to Robinson's discussion of the effect of music on the emotions, 'under the influence of an unconscious emotional memory'; music may then have a similar effect upon the listener 'as if it were the forlorn cry of an unhappy child'.[35] According to this view, the 'angustiosa armonía sin luz' and 'una armonía severa' is the sound of her own unhappy child, from which there is no relief since the past cannot be altered. Readers sense the significance of these two moments on Andrea's emotions; deep feelings are being stirred within her due to the strength of her reaction and her need to turn towards beauty for relief. However, returning to Bowlby, 'the information defensively excluded' does not quite seep through but remains just below the surface of the narrative description. Writing may even be described as a form of defensive dissociation for Andrea: a 'distancing from the source of grief and painful mourning'.[36] Although, as Jordan suggests, it appears that writing or the aesthetic 'offers [a] realm of unity, harmony and stability, [a] fairy land behind the mirror', it remains an appearance and, 'ultimately is no more than a fantasy'.[37] What Jordan fails to recognise however is that Andrea the narrator appears to recognise this: hence the ironic title of the novel, a novel that expresses 'nada'. *Nada* is therefore a novel about art's failure to express Andrea's mourning as well as the fragile and temporary nature of relief arising from both aesthetic contemplation and the act of creation itself.

Another manifestation of Laforet's aesthetics of relief emerges through her representation of the city and Andrea's relationship with urban spaces. Barcelona is frequently naturalised as a space in which Andrea often finds temporary peace of mind, tranquillity and draws upon it as a source of beauty. The ravaged, bombed post-war city does not loom large throughout *Nada*. Instead, the city is transformed into a place of romantic mystery and, on occasions, melancholy beauty.[38] References to the sea, sky, stars, rain, sunsets, trees and other natural elements abound throughout the novel. As in the case of the Romantic poets, the contemplation of nature transforms itself into an aesthetic experience, but it is also linked to a desire for freedom, freedom from the flat on Calle Aribau and Andrea's ongoing state of disordered mourning. As in Thoreau's *Walden*, nature provides Andrea with 'an infinite and unaccountable friendliness', providing momentary relief to her acutely sensitive disposition.[39] When Andrea and Ena meet at the entrance to the University after Andrea has rescued her from Román towards the end of the novel, they stand in silence 'escuchando aquella lluvia que a mí me calmaba y me verdecía como a los árboles' (p. 283). Andrea also turns or deflects her gaze towards nature as a source of alleviation and silent contemplation. Prior to entering Ena's grandparent's garden she becomes absorbed in nature: 'Yo estaba apoyada contra los hierros de la gran verja del jardín. Olía intensamente a rosas y sobre mi cabeza voló un abejorro, produciendo un profundísimo eco de paz' (p. 227). Schopenhauer indicates the curative properties of contemplating nature which involve the suspension of the will, transporting the individual 'into a state of pure perception'.[40] Such states invoke James's concept of 'pure experience' in which subject-object distinctions dissolve and appear as aesthetic tropes of relief across Laforet's novels. But at times, even the aesthetic beauty of the city and the natural world do not provide her with the comfort she craves; her attempts to stem her grief through the contemplation of nature break down and her grief issues forth, revealing that the negative defense structures she has constructed to protect her are fallible:

> Una mañana de otoño en la ciudad, como yo había soñado durante años que sería en la ciudad el otoño: bello, con la naturaleza enredada en las azoteas de las casas y en los troles de los tranvías; y sin embargo, me envolvía la tristeza. Tenía ganas de apoyarme contra una pared con la cabeza entre los brazos, volver la espalda a todo y cerrar los ojos. (44)

Andrea's 'intimidades tristes', which remain 'espantosas', (p. 229) lie just below the surface of her consciousness and can only be assuaged temporarily through the natural world. However, perhaps the most important source of relief to which Andrea turns is her friendship with her fellow student Ena.

Relief and the Role of Friendship

If art and nature do not lead to lasting relief from grief, the matter of Andrea's relationship to a female Other as a source of comfort needs to be addressed. Bowlby's ideas prove instructive again in evaluating how Andrea's pathology is represented in the novel. He suggests that for the individual who has suffered a major disruption to the attachment bond, due to the death of a parent, 'a helpful companion may be of great assistance.'[41] Andrea seeks out friendship as another mode of ameliorating her distress.[42] However, we must be careful not to interpret Andrea's friendship with Ena as a resolution of the former's emotional suffering. According to Bowlby, through the presence of a friend in the bereaved person's life, her or his 'anxiety is reduced, his morale fortified, his evaluations made less hastily, and the actions necessary to meet a situation selected and planned more judiciously'.[43] This description of friendship as an aid to the grieving subject only serves in part to account for the representation of female friendship in *Nada*, which is in fact fraught with complications.

Although Ena eventually acts as an emotional support for Andrea, and recognises her distress, this only occurs towards the end of the novel. Andrea's friendship with Ena places her emotionally labile state and loneliness into high relief. From the very first line of the novel, readers are alerted to Andrea's sense of isolation, and the fact that she arrives alone in Barcelona with no one to meet positions her from the outset within a place of solitude. Andrea makes her way to her grandmother's house alone and when the door is finally opened, she is not recognised and is instead mistaken for Gloria, the grandmother's daughter-in-law. Andrea is therefore initially unmet and unseen by her closest family member, re-activating in her a sense of profound despair which then leads her to over-idealise the relationship with Ena at first. Their friendship is not based on mutual support, empathy, altruism and understanding. As Lawrence A. Blum has argued 'friendship involves a substantial concern for the good of the friend for his own sake, and a disposition to act to foster that good, simply because the other is one's friend. In this sense friendship is an altruistic phenomenon, and a locus of altruistic emotions'.[44] However, Ena's interest in Andrea is founded on ulterior motives based on her desire to get to know Andrea's uncle Román in order to avenge her mother's psychological degradation by him prior to her marriage to Ena's father. Andrea may be projecting her over-active desire for companionship onto a person who is not acting with the sufficient altruism that Blum argues is essential to friendship. In fact, Ena's initial attitude towards Andrea can at best be described as fickle: 'Yo estaba pensando que hacía solo unos minutos también me había sentido herida por burlas suyas de las que hasta entonces no tenían la menor idea [...] Pero ahora estaba ganada por su profunda simpatía' (p. 64). Similarly, the following sequence reveals the uneven nature of their relationship in terms of an equal exchange of personal information:

> Me gustaba pasear con ella por los claustros de piedra de la Universidad y escuchar su charla pensando en que algún día yo habría de contarle aquella vida oscura de mi casa, que en el momento en que pasaba a ser tema de discussion, empezaba a aparecer ante mis ojos cargados de romanticismo. Me parecía que a Ena le interesaría mucho y que entendería aún mejor que yo mis problemas. Hasta entonces, sin embargo, no le había dicho nada de mi vida. Me iba haciendo amiga suya gracias a este deseo de hablar que me había entrado (64–65)

Andrea's emotional defences prohibit her from speaking about her 'problemas' and she is confined to the role of listener. Her 'ojos cargados de romanticismo' cloud a more reasoned and accurate representation of Ena's true motivations for initiating their relationship, which is indicated in Ena's direct request to Andrea: 'Yo quiero que me presentes a tu tío' (p. 65). However, Andrea does not appear to notice that she is being subtly manipulated into doing Ena's bidding, providing an indication of Andrea's preparedness to tolerate a mediocre version of friendship based on her long-standing need for emotional connection.[45] Andrea's desire for emotional affiliation with an Other, based on her pathological need for love, therefore blinds her to a deeper understanding of friendship, although the older narrator may be relying on subtle irony to cover up her own earlier naive attitude towards her friend.[46] Andrea makes much of an act of beneficence towards Ena — she gives her a lace handkerchief, a present from her grandmother — as a sign of appreciation for Ena's financial generosity. But it is Andrea's account of her response to this action that requires close examination, as it reveals more about the protagonist's emotions than it does about Ena's attitude towards their relationship.

> Yo no me acordaba de que fuera tan bonito y la alegría de podérselo regalar a Ena me *compensaba* muchas tristezas. [...] Poder hacer a Ena un regalo tan delicadamente bello me *compensaba* de toda la mezquindad de mi vida.
>
> Ena se quedó conmovida y tan contenta cuando encontró en el paquete que le di la graciosa fruslería, que esta alegría suya me unió a ella más que todas sus anteriores muestras de afecto. Me hizo sentirme todo lo que no era: rica y feliz. Y no lo pude olvidar ya nunca. (73–75) [My italics]

According to Bowlby, friendship for the bereaved person has a compensatory function as it assuages the overwhelming sensation of grief associated with the loss of an important attachment figure. Relief is encountered through an emotional bond based on unconditional support from a friend. From the above quotation, it appears that Andrea's 'muchas tristezas', and the 'mezquindad de [su] vida', are ameliorated through her friendship with Ena. However, the gift of giving the handkerchief could also be interpreted as a self-focused, non-altruistic act, one that ensures the maintenance of a human source of comfort and protection. Andrea's action towards her friend therefore provides, for the time being, 'mood repair' until she is abandoned by Ena temporarily when she switches her attention to establishing a relationship with Román, returning Andrea to her depressed condition.[47] The relationship between these two female characters is subject to the competing forces of each woman's ego distortions and personal agendas, psychological and otherwise.

It is only after Andrea acts altruistically towards Ena that she receives emotional recognition from her. Following Andrea's attempt to rescue Ena from being harmed by Román, Andrea runs out of the flat on Aribau to the university garden where Ena finally finds her standing alone in the rain.

> ¿Comprendes, Andrea, comprendes, querida, que no te pudiese decir nada, que incluso llegara a maltratarte en la escalera? Aquellos momentos parecían borrados de mi existencia. Cuando me di cuenta de que era yo Ena, quien estaba viviendo, me encontré corriendo calle Aribau abajo, buscando tu rastro. Al volver la esquina te encontré al fin. Estabas apoyada contra el muro del jardín de la Universidad, muy pequeña y perdida debajo de aquel cielo tempestuoso. Así te vi. (291)

At this point, towards the end of the novel, Ena meets Andrea equally as a friend and sees her as an individual who has been diminished, 'muy pequeña y perdida', through grief and suffering. Finally, Andrea's grief finds a witness through the eyes of another and this act of recognition allows the protagonist's defended emotions to surface, whereupon relief is found. A concept of friendship based on reciprocity and moral responsibility emerges between the two women, as Ena goes on to support her friend through finding her employment in her father's company.[48] Both women have undergone a development by the end of the novel, a development in their moral responsibility towards each other. They have reoriented their emotions and being-towards-others. According to Blum, 'The moral motive must be a non-egoistic one. [...] The morally motivated action must be prompted by the actual moral considerations of the situation, not by particular and fortuitous aspects of the agent.'[49] Thus, it is only through her close female friendship that Andrea's defence against her suffering changes, as she herself recognises: 'Yo me sentía cambiada' (p. 292). Although Andrea does not directly attribute her changed state to the mutual trust that has grown between Ena and her, she does acknowledge a shift in her feelings which is also manifested at the level of bodily experience: 'Cada día mi cabeza se volvía más débil y me sentía reblandecida, con los ojos húmedos por cualquier cosa' (p. 292). Andrea also absorbs herself into a tripartite friendship involving Ena's fiancée Jaime. On a trip to the beach with Jaime and Ena, the narrator reveals once again her tendency to dissolve her sense of self in others and the surrounding environment:

> La dicha ésta, tan sencilla, de estar tumbada bajo un cielo sin nubes junto a mis amigos, que me parecía perfecta, se me escapa a veces en una vaguedad de imaginación parecida al sueño. Lejanías azules zumbaban en mi cráneo con ruido de moscardón, haciéndome cerrar los ojos. Entre las ramas de los algarrobos veía yo, al abrir los párpados, el firmamento cálido, cargado de chirridos de pájaros. Parecía que me hubiera muerto siglos atrás y que todo mi cuerpo deshecho en polvo minúsculo estuviera dispersado por mares y montañas amplísimas, tan desparramada, ligera y vaga sensación de mi carne y mis huesos sentía. (292)

Andrea's experience is one of transcendental bliss, akin to a state of religious mysticism or *henosis*, a return to the monad.[50] Freud's interpretation of relief within the concept of the 'nirvana principle' is evoked in Andrea's description. This type of transcendental, meditative state has been assisted by the proximity of friends and through concentrating her senses on elements from the natural world. This account differs to previous narrative descriptions of the dissolution of Andrea's sense of self through music, nature and architecture since it does not appear to be willed so actively, nor has it been stimulated by an aesthetic form. Andrea's condition of oneness is based on her desire for relief through communion with others and the natural world; neither art, nor aesthetic contemplation have produced the same emotional relief for her. For the first time in the novel a positive development in her psychological condition is attained; relief appears to have been found through the triangulated relationship of Andrea-Ena-Jaime, arguably a substitute for her missing family.[51]

However, the succession of narrative events throughout *Nada* is structured around a positive-negative dialectic of progression followed by regression. Thus, Andrea's opportunity for a sustained sense of relief and mental stability is undermined by Ena's imminent departure for Madrid and Román's suicide, with the latter throwing her into a state of extreme anxiety again. Andrea's response to Román's death is so profound that it suggests she may be experiencing a re-activation of the shock of losing her mother and, possibly also, her father. She is plagued by the image of his hands rotting in the earth: 'Aquellas manos hábiles [...] se me representaban torpemente hinchadas y blandas primero, tumefactas. Luego, convertidas en dos racimos de pelados huesos' (p. 310). She feels haunted and seeks solace by going for long walks around Barcelona to flee from 'los fantasmas' (p. 310). On one of these occasions, Andrea returns to the Cathedral, and enters a trance-like state:

> me vino una impresión de belleza casi mística. Como un deseo de morirme
> allí, a un lado, mirando hacia arriba, debajo de la gran dulzura de la noche que
> empezaba a llegar. [...] Era como si estuviese oliendo un aroma de muerte y me
> pareciera bueno por primera vez, después de haberme causado terror. (311)

Andrea describes herself as 'entontecida y medio estática' (p. 311), which is suggestive of Freud's discussion of hypnoid states induced by heavily defended
emotions. Freud suggested that 'the ideas which emerge in hypnoid states are cut
off from associative communication with the rest of the content of consciousness'.[52]
What emerges in Andrea's altered state is her unconscious desire to return to a state
of oneness with her dead mother, yet this information is withheld and deflected
through her reaction to Román's death.[53] Freud noted in his studies of neurotic
patients that such attempts to repress the upsetting idea 'did not succeed [...] but led
to various pathological reactions which produced either hysteria or an obsession or
a hallucinatory psychosis.'[54] Andrea's account of her psychological state following
Román's death suggests that she may in fact be hallucinating; she mistakes a sheet
hung out on a balcony for a shroud and admits: 'no tenía la cabeza buena aquel día'
and runs back to the flat on Aribau 'medio loca' (p. 311). Andrea's psychological
confrontation with Román's suicide therefore stirs the memory of what she seeks
to repress: her mother's death. But, as Freud observed, 'both the memory-trace
and the affect which is attached to the idea are there once and for all and cannot
be eradicated.' Despite Andrea's attempts to dissemble her grief through art and
aesthetic contemplation, *Nada* persistently reveals that the traces of her mourning
cannot be eradicated and that her defence against her suffering is also the hallmark
of her pain. We may then have to conceive of Andrea's friendship with Ena as only
a partial palliative to Andrea's suffering.

Although it appears that *Nada* ends on a note of optimism as Andrea leaves
to commence life in Madrid with the support of Ena and her family, there is no
evidence in the text to suggest that Andrea has left her grief behind. Rather, like
the suitcase of books she arrived with, Andrea's grief is carried with her to Madrid.
Particular weight has been placed on the final moment of self-reflection in the
novel when Andrea considers what she is taking with her following her year in
Barcelona:

> Me marchaba ahora sin haber conocido nada de lo que confusamente esperaba:
> la vida en su plenitud, la alegría, el interés profundo, el amor. De la casa de la
> calle de Aribau no me llevaba nada. Al menos, así creía yo entonces. (318–19)

Readers might assume that Andrea's insertion of the caveat signals the wise
reflections of the older narrator and that, with hindsight, she feels that she has taken
a plethora of experiences with her and turned them into fiction: the novel we are
reading. But this remains an assumption as readers are in fact left with no answer
to what Andrea believes she has taken from her year at her grandmother's house.
Readers are once again deflected away from further information as if the narrator
were stopping short of expressing something. It may be more appropriate to
consider Andrea's final action in the novel to assess what Andrea takes with her on
her departure from Barcelona. She turns her gaze upwards, a physical response that

she repeatedly performs throughout the course of the narrative, one that signals a move towards contemplation of an object or phenomenon, an action that symbolises her need to turn away from a deeply felt emotion: 'Antes de entrar en el auto alcé los ojos hacia la casa donde había vivido un año. Los primeros rayos del sol chocaban contra sus ventanas. Unos momentos después, la calle de Aribau y Barcelona entera quedaban detrás de mí' (p. 319). The image of light hitting the windows of the flat represents an obvious contrast to the darkness of the night of Andrea's arrival. On one level, this image provides a sense of a new beginning and hope for Andrea, yet it also indicates a final image of deflection, an apt metaphor for the entire novel and the protagonist's tendency to redirect her heavily defended emotions through the act of writing, aesthetic contemplation, nature or friendship. Thus, Andrea's hope of finding a loving family environment to heal her grief has been warded off, largely through her own self-willed defences. The narrative is constantly being deflected away from any real progression in terms of Andrea's self-development because the suppression of the memory of her mother's death, which she achieves through writing, is the narrator's primary activity. Writing then forms another core psychological defence pattern through which Andrea diverts her attention away from her loss. It therefore remains ambiguous whether the act of creation provides her with any sense of relief from her suffering and aids her maturation. Jordan suggests that Andrea can only find happiness through literature and art: 'only in artistic creativity [...] can [she] heal the wound of childhood separation from her mother and family and enter an imaginary world of stability and androgynous wholeness.'[55] Yet this does not appear to be the case at all. Following Bowlby's observations, Andrea's need to write, and the constant preparation of her materials through close observation of the world around her, acts as a permanent diversion from her suffering which she repeatedly fails to articulate directly. Writing is transformed into a manifestation of Andrea's disordered mourning, a way of concealing her suffering through aesthetic means, whilst at the same time expressing her inability to divulge what lies at the heart of her existence: melancholic grief and its unconscious pathological manifestations. The traumatic memory of Andrea's mother's death remains unarticulated and this may help readers better to understand *Nada*'s static quality. As Herman has observed, 'Traumatic memory [...] is wordless and static.'[56] Thus, Andrea cannot progress until she articulates her grief; hence Jordan's view of Andrea as a character who is 'going nowhere.'[57]

Although *Nada* closes with an image of movement away from the quarrels and violence of the Aribau household, Andrea does not leave her grief behind her. Relief may have been found on a few occasions but the novel we are reading indicates that her state of disordered mourning continues. Her departure signals a repetition of her arrival in Barcelona rather than evidence of progression. Andrea appears to move from a state of unhappiness to happiness through her promise of a new life in Madrid and relief from her past suffering seems certain. But, as Jordan notes, 'the narrator prefers to leave unexplained what happened after her departure for Madrid', creating 'a troubling gap in her record [and] 'an absence which could constitute *Nada*'s own dark double, the unwritten novel which, like a ghost, inhabits the interstices of the text presented to the reader'.[58] The dark double is the imprint of Andrea's grief, the photographic negative that cannot be eradicated from the story of her year in Barcelona and forms the unwritten, undeveloped novel within *Nada*. It is the text's unconscious story that prohibits Andrea's development and impedes lasting relief to her suffering. Andrea then leaves Barcelona seeking something else to assuage her pain, which she may or may not find in Madrid. As this chapter has illustrated, the creation of art and aesthetic contemplation form 'permanent diversions', according to Bowlby's theory of disordered mourning, from the grief that Andrea endures due to her mother's death, grief that is only temporarily assuaged through friendship. Permanent relief remains out of reach until the source of Andrea's trauma is articulated and recognised. *Nada* is a novel that is persistently warding off the real story of Andrea's trauma, a story of which she cannot speak and is repeatedly deflected through the aestheticisation of relief in different forms. In Laforet's second novel, *La isla y los demonios*, we witness a similar pursuit of relief from grief but, on this occasion, it is explored through a complicated dialectic of love and reason.

Notes to Chapter 1

1. *Nada* contains graphic accounts of domestic violence yet managed to avoid censorship, no doubt indicating the censors' lack of concern for this broader social ill.
2. She has overindulged her sons through favouritism because they are male.
3. Jordan, *Nada*, p. 29. He was not the first critic to observe Laforet's concern with psychoanalytical themes. Illanes Adaro's earlier study was the first critical appraisal of Laforet as a psychological writer.
4. Jordan, *Nada*, p. 16. Jordan's interpretation of the novel is compelling, but it has been refuted by the more recent work of Mark Del Mastro, who also adopts a psychoanalytical approach. Using the theories of Erik Erikson, Del Mastro links Erikson's ideas on adolescent identity development to the various characters in the novel who assist Andrea in forging a more stable adult identity. See 'Cheating Fate: Female Adolescent Development and the Social Web in Laforet's *Nada*', *Hispanic Journal*, 18.1 (1997), 55–66.
5. Jordan, *Nada*, p. 17, p. 90.
6. Ibid., p. 43.
7. Laforet, *Nada*, p. 107.
8. Caballé and Rolón note the impact of her mother's death on Laforet's psychological development: 'La pérdida exterior e innombrable impuso pues un vacío psíquico que se instaló en su lugar impidiendo el cumplimiento del duelo. La vida de la joven Carmen, casi una niña, se construye a partir de esa oquedad permanentemente contenida', p. 54.
9. John Bowlby, *Attachment and Loss, Volume Three: Sadness and Depression* (London: The Hogarth Press and the Institute of Psycho-Analysis, 1980).
10. Jordan, *Nada*, p. 15.
11. Judith Lewis Herman, *Trauma and Recovery: From Domestic Abuse to Political Terror* (London: Pandora, 2001), p. 185.
12. Irene Mizrahi, *El trauma del franquismo y su testimonio crítico en* Nada *de Carmen Laforet* (Newark, Delaware: Juan de la Cuesta, 2010).
13. Ana B. Figueroa, 'Nada de Carmen Laforet: la pulsión lésbica como verdad no sospechada', *Alpha*, 22 (2006), 169–81.
14. Gustavo Pérez Firmat, 'Carmen Laforet: The Dilemma of Artistic Vocation,' in Joan L. Brown, *Women Writers of Contemporary Spain. Exiles in the Homeland* (Newark: University of Delaware Press. London and Toronto: Associated University Presses, 1991), pp. 26–41 (p. 28).

15. Gustavo Pérez Firmat, p. 29.

16. We witness a pattern, or invariant trait, with Laforet's treatment of friendship in her novels. Marta in *La isla y los demonios* seeks to merge her identity into Pablo's. Similarly, Martín Soto undergoes a type of infatuation with both the Corsi siblings in *La insolación* and the with Anita Corsi in *Al volver la esquina*. These relationships provide ample evidence of object *cathexis*.

17. Bowlby, p. 441. More recent work has suggested that trauma in early childhood can lead to enhanced resilience to stressful life events in later life. See Sarah Becerra, *Death of a Parent in Childhood and Resilience in Adulthood* (Saarbrücken: Verlag, 2006). This may be the case for the older Andrea, but the young eighteen-year old student does not display signs of resilience during her year in Barcelona. She is often crying, emotionally overwhelmed or angry, suggesting her volatility and vulnerable state of mind.

18. Bowlby, p. 45.

19. Ibid., p. 64.

20. There are many examples of Andrea behaving masochistically towards her self. Her first cold shower in the Aribau flat is but one example.

21. Jordan, *Nada*, p. 63.

22. For further discussion see Herman, p. 12.

23. Jordan, *Nada*, p. 104.

24. Ibid., p. 104.

25. Jordan, *Nada*, p. 67. Freud's discussion of the repetition compulsion comes to mind since Andrea has not dealt with the traumatic legacy of her mother's death. Herman expands upon the concept of trauma haunting the individual: 'But traumatic events ultimately refuse to be put away. At some point the memory of the trauma is bound to return, demanding attention. Often the precipitant is a significant reminder of the trauma — an anniversary — or a change in the survivor's life circumstances that brings her back to the unfinished work of integrating the traumatic experience', p. 174.

26. Andrea needs to cleanse herself at various points in the novel, suggesting both a desire to rid the body of some malign phenomenon but also as another way of seeking relief. For a discussion of Laforet's treatment of water in Nada see: Currie K. Thompson, 'Perception and Art: Water Imagery in *Nada*', *Kentucky Romance Quarterly*, 32.3 (1985), 291–300.

27. Bowlby, p. 65.

28. Ibid., p. 66.

29. These moments border on epiphanies. However, a full epiphany would allow for profound self-insight following the experience but there is no evidence that this occurs. I would prefer to call such moments in *Nada* states of merger.

30. Storr, *Music and the Mind*, p. 136.

31. Schopenhauer suggested that aesthetic contemplation produced 'a mystical union of the subject with the object' which resulted in a dissolution of 'the subject-object distinction'. In the case of Andrea, such quasi-transcendental states appear to have the effect of numbing Andrea's emotions. *Schopenhauer, Philosophy, and the Arts*, ed. by Dale Jacquette (Cambridge: Cambridge University Press, 2007), p. 8.

32. Jordan, *Nada*, p. 81.

33. Jenefer Robinson, *Deeper than Reason: Emotion and its Role in Literature, Music, and Art* (Clarendon Press: Oxford, 2005), p. 294.

34. Susanne K. Langer, *Philosophy in a New Key* (Cambridge, Mass.: Harvard University Press, 1976), p. 43. Quoted in Robinson, p. 299. Storr makes a similar observation: 'What music expresses is the inner spirit', *Music and the Mind*, p. 140. He also suggests that music functions as 'a way of ordering human experience' which is pertinent to Andrea's need to find an outlet for her grief, p. 187.

35. Robinson, p. 410.

36. Bowlby, p. 138.

37. Jordan, *Nada*, pp. 81–82.

38. The opening paragraph of the novel provides a lyrical ode to the city's nighttime beauty.

39. Henri David Thoreau, *Walden* (Oxford and New York: Oxford World Classics, 2008), p. 120.

40. Cheryl Foster, 'Schopenhauer and aesthetic recognition', in Jacquette, pp. 133–49 (p. 138).
41. Bowlby, p. 232.
42. The importance of friendship in Laforet's first novel is made evident in the dedication to 'mis amigos Linka Babecka de Borrell y el pintor Pedro Borrell'. Laforet relied on a network of friends throughout her life to support her and provide her with the necessary strength to survive long-standing emotional traumas. Linka Babecka, on whom the character of Ena is based, remained her life-long friend.
43. Bowlby, p. 232.
44. Lawrence A. Blum, *Friendship, Altruism and Morality* (London, Boston and Henley: Routledge and Kegan Paul, 1980), p. 43.
45. This need is manifested directly when Andrea reflects upon her deepest need for close communion with a mother substitute: 'una necesidad física de tenura, ávida y polvorienta como la tierra quemada presintiendo la tempestad', p. 230. The suggestion here is that the desired kindness is long-standing, reinforcing the view that Andrea's emotional needs pre-date her arrival in Barcelona.
46. As the older narrator, Andrea provides no information on whether her friendship with Ena continues.
47. For an interesting discussion of the concept of mood repair and writing see Patrick Colm Hogan's discussion of grief in *What Literature Teaches us about Emotion* (Cambridge: Cambridge University Press, 2011), pp. 111–43. We witness a similar dynamic in Martín Soto's relationship with the Corsi siblings in *La insolación* and *Al volver la esquina*.
48. Although it could be argued that Ena's class and access to financial privilege undermines any possibility of equality in their relationship.
49. Blum, p. 3.
50. Jordan notes how Andrea 'finds her greatest satisfactions in experiencing a loss of identity, in merging into something else, in abandoning the contours of the self', *Nada*, p. 79.
51. The desire of the bereaved individual to merge within a surrogate family structure has been discussed by Edith Jacobson: 'They looked for superior, "worthy" — and frequently wealthy — people who might be willing to "adopt" them. Naturally, such attempts were bound to fail. The persons they selected could not live up either to the part they were supposed to play or to the patients' glorified imagery.' Edith Jacobson, 'The Return of the Lost Parent', in Rita V. Frankiel, *Essential Papers on Object Loss* (New York and London: New York University Press, 1994), pp. 233–50 (p. 233).
52. Sigmund Freud, 'The Neuro-Psychosis of Defence' in *The Complete Psychological Works of Sigmund Freud. Volume III, 1893–1899*, edited by James Strachey (London: The Hogarth Press, 1962), pp. 45–61 (p. 46).
53. Jordan intuits the relationship between aesthetic absorption, oneness and Andrea's unconscious desire for death following Andrea's response to standing in front of the Cathedral again: 'Andrea expresses a desire for an imaginary state of oneness, for a place which precedes the relativity and flux of ordinary existence and guarantees permanence, i.e. a symbolic death', *Nada*, p. 81.
54. Freud, 'The Neuro-Psychosis of Defence,' p. 48.
55. Jordan, *Nada*, p. 106.
56. Herman, p. 175.
57. Jordan, *Nada*, p. 16.
58. Jordan, *Nada*, p. 107.

CHAPTER 2

Reason as Relief:
La isla y los demonios (1952)

Before considering Laforet's deliberations on reason and its counterpart, love, as forms of relief from suffering in *La isla y los demonios*, I wish to reflect briefly on the view that her second novel is a thinly veiled re-working of her first. Rather than treating *La isla* as a re-writing of *Nada* or as a continuation or even prequel to Andrea's story, it proves useful to return to Holland's notion of 'invariancies' in a writer's work. What remains invariant across both novels is the protagonists' shared search for relief from anguish caused by personal loss and an unloving family environment. In this sense, Laforet's first and second novels bear significant similarities. Andrea arrives in Barcelona in the hope of finding a loving home as an antidote to her grief and leaves with the same desire, which is projected into Ena's family. Marta, 'anhelante y emocionada', stands at the opening of *La isla* on the quayside awaiting the arrival of her relatives from mainland Spain, who she believes will initiate change in her life and bring her emotional succour.[1] In both cases, relief is sought in the form of hope placed within the projected ideal of a loving family or person who, symbolically, serve as a substitute attachment figure for the mother. Andrea is an orphan; Marta's father is dead, and her mother exists in a catatonic state in an upstairs room in the family home. Grief and a frustrated mourning process pervade both protagonists' existences. However, although suffering and the search for psychological relief remain invariant features across both novels, what differs is the manner through which relief is sought in *La isla*. Whereas Andrea employs music, architecture, friendship, nature and writing as modes of exploring and experiencing relief, Marta replaces obsessive love with an increased awareness of the importance of reason as the primary mechanism through which to assuage her suffering and release her from an oppressive family environment.[2] However, prior to embracing reason as a route towards greater psychological freedom, Marta must engage with the 'demonios' of the title, irrational libidinal impulses which she ultimately rejects as she plans her escape from her family and the island. Laforet's treatment of love as a means through which to ameliorate human suffering is delineated with a significant dose of irony in her second novel. Contrary to the pervasive view that love has positive transformative properties, *La isla* presents love as a source of suffering and a misguided method of acquiring tranquillity. In this regard, *La isla* prefigures the views of several second-wave feminist thinkers on the dangers effected by romantic love on women's lives and capacity for self-agency. Other methods of pursuing relief represented in *La isla* will also be touched upon. For example, the role of art as an escape from suffering is explored through Marta's own creative impulses. The relevance of bodily relief through physical activity also emerges as a relevant sub-theme within *La isla* and will receive further critical attention in chapter four on *La insolación*.

At a stylistic level Laforet does not repeat the first person narrative style of *Nada*, switching instead to a third person narrative mode in her second novel, with additional interjections of free indirect discourse to convey Marta's interior thoughts. This technique permits readers access to the young protagonist's vacillating emotions which are made manifest through two competing voices that govern her thoughts and feelings and are referred to in the novel as 'dos Martas'. One of these voices represents her irrational, emotionally labile self; the other, more mature, self-reflecting voice issues from an older, wiser Marta, who is guided by reason and a nascent sense of self-agency. Although *Nada* displays a similar pattern through the presence of Andrea, the older narrator who is reflecting on her residence in Barcelona as a younger woman, the 'dos Martas' in *La isla* are presented simultaneously within the temporal framework of the novel. This technique of creating parallel voices within Marta establishes a greater sense of the struggle between love and reason that takes place within the protagonist's psyche. This stylistic feature allows for a greater sense of maturation within the protagonist, although it remains unclear whether Marta's pursuit of reason as a guiding force in her life will suffice to bring her long-standing relief from the emotional void that lies at the heart of her existence: the absence of loving parental figures.

Laforet indicated that writing *La isla* was an exercise in seeking relief but, in her typically guarded manner, she elides the matter of what the source of 'angustia' was at the time of her writing the novel:

> Escribir esta tontería me ha costado mucho. Escribiendo he tratado de librarme de muchos absurdos, de mucha angustia, y creo que eso tiene siempre un premio. Dominar lo peor de uno y convertirlo en arte... Creo que debe ser arte lo que salga, cuando se ha puesto en ello alma y vida, y no vaciedad.[3]

Here Laforet reveals important features of her approach to her craft: the difficulty she encountered in writing and her use of her art as a method of repression or defence, a mode through which emotions can be controlled — 'dominar lo peor de uno' — rather than as a source of relief from difficult emotions. Yet control is not the same as release, although it may result in a form of temporary psychological relief. Laforet also suggests in this quote that suffering can be transformed into art but this says nothing of what happens to the source of suffering if it does not get articulated. In one sense, Laforet is unconsciously describing how she herself established a method of not dealing with her grief and how writing became another defensive strategy within her psychic processes through which her emotions were contained. Through the character of Marta, readers are reminded of the autobiographical traces within Laforet's fiction and the author's personal deliberations on the concept of freedom for the individual as well as her own ongoing search for relief against the backdrop of her continuing grief over her mother's death and father's hasty remarriage. Laforet's daughter reflected on her mother's similarities to the character of Marta:

> Le [...] dices que sabes que Marta Camino es un personaje creado, y las circun-stancias de su vida son totalmente inventadas, pero el alma de Marta Camino, su espíritu sensible y salvaje, su vida de aventura y de inteligencia pertenecen a Carmen Laforet.[4]

However, *La isla* provides a projection of Laforet's psychology and not, as such, an attempt at explicit autobiography. All of Laforet's novels are meditations on questions that the author wished to pose and deliberate upon at the time of writing as well as revealing the impression of long-standing unconscious phenomena, rather than mimetic accounts of particular events of her life. However, the autobiographical features of Laforet's first two novels must not be entirely set aside, as Caballé and Rolón suggest:

> En ninguno de los libros (*Nada* and *La isla*) Laforet no puede dejar de escribir su verdad más profunda y arrojar sobre quienes rodearon su adolescencia y primera juventud la responsabilidad de su abandono y de su soledad afectiva. En sus dos novelas la orfandad de la protagonista es un rasgo determinante, una especie de mancha de aceite que va extendiendo sus límites y marcando a los personajes con ese hecho diferencial: la soledad familiar.[5]

In a similar manner, 'la soledad familiar' constitutes the source of Marta's suffering from which she seeks to flee towards the end of the novel. Marta longs for an external source — her extended family who are arriving from mainland Spain — to alleviate her ongoing unhappiness. The narrator informs us that Marta's emotional needs remain unmet within her family home: 'Allí dentro no había felicidad, ni comprensión, ni dulzura' (p. 24). Marta's suffering is made explicit: ' "He sufrido." Murmuró esto y sintió que se le llenaban de lágrimas los ojos' (p. 24). Her half-brother José rules over her with patriarchal authority, hits her and punishes her when she does not comply with his wishes and his wife Pino projects her anger and neurosis onto Marta.[6] Within our broader discussion of the pursuit of relief, Marta's psychological anguish is rooted in the absence of love that she experiences within her family home due to her mother's illness and her father's death.[7] From a psychological perspective, Laforet's representation of parent-child relationships and the consequences of the absence of parental love are incisive, and they concur with the observations of children's behaviour studied by both Bowlby and D. W. Winnicott in the 1950s and 1960s.[8] Laforet's novels provide evidence of her intuitive understanding of human psychology and her awareness of what we now commonly refer to as disturbed or disrupted attachment. *La isla* suggests that the attachment bonds between Marta and her mother have not only been interrupted by her mother's illness but are, in fact, long-standing. As is the case with *Nada*, *La isla* indicates how the temporal framework of the narrative extends much further into the past than the events of the actual story we are reading. Although she did not do so explicitly, Laforet connects her protagonists' present motivations within their early life histories, even though she withholds detailed information about their emotional response to parental loss.[9] Some insight is provided into the nature of Marta's relationship with her mother, although the cause of their compromised attachment bond is not divulged. When Marta enters her mother's room on one occasion, the narrative mode shifts to an intimate second-person voice:

> Es como si estuviera muerta. Nunca estuviste con ella. Nunca te necesitó... Ni la necesitaste desde que dejó de estar en tu vida. Desde que creciste pensaste, más que en ella, en tu padre, que te dejó un cajón lleno de libros en el desván. (193)

The meaning of the word 'nunca' remains ambiguous and its emphatic repetition indicates a historic absence of maternal love and thus a possible impediment to Marta's psychological development due to an emotional deficit or interruption to the mother-daughter relationship.[10] When Marta's mother dies, the protagonist's incapacity to feel emotion or empathy is disclosed:

> Estaba asustada porque le sucedía igual que cuando pensaba en la guerra y sus catástrofes y no podía sentir las mismas emociones que los demás sienten. Le parecía que una zona de su alma estaba seca y árida, y que solo infinitas desgracias, infinitas penas, podían redimirla de esta sequedad. (236)

The defensive process of denial of the emotions figures in Marta's reflections, indicating that her capacity to refrain from displays of feeling is historic and forms a well-established part of her psychic defences.[11] Given this engrained nature of Marta's psychological defence mechanisms, we must understand her desire for relief as being both magnified and curtailed by the impossibility of the task to overcome her suffering.

Much of *La isla* is structured around the pursuit of a stable parental figure who can act as a temporary surrogate, an external locus of regulation for Marta's psychological suffering, an Other who is less a bringer of pleasure than a source of stability in her life. Marta turns to Pablo the painter, who has travelled to the island with Marta's wider family to escape the final stages of the Spanish civil war on the mainland. It is through her obsessive relationship with him that Laforet constructs a biting critique of love as a source of relief for the human subject. It must be made clear from the outset that Laforet's depiction of Marta's love for Pablo is neither uniquely romantic, nor Platonic, but rather a form of hero worship which is intimately linked to the protagonist's damaged psyche and tendency to project her wishes onto others, albeit unconsciously. The only form of sexual love that she experiences is her physical attraction towards her fellow islander Sixto, yet she remains detached from any deeper emotional connection with him and rejects his offer of marriage. Marta's eagerness to pursue Pablo is evidence of an unconscious projected desire to re-incorporate herself within the body of a primary care giver. As Illanes Adaro notes: 'Marta está enamorada, pero puede decirse que no es al hombre al que ama, sino a una especie de ser abstracto que éste representa.'[12] From a psychoanalytical perspective, this form of idealised love and the construction of an imagined 'ser abstracto' is a common feature of love's complex tapestry, as Wendy Langford suggests in her critique of love's hold on the human subject: 'As we struggle to repress the painful knowledge of our own incoherence and the unsatisfactoriness of life, one apparent solution is the idealisation of someone who appears to be what we are not.'[13] Marta's love for Pablo is a classic case of psychological projection; her own nascent artistic desires as a writer are projected onto Pablo, whose artistic talents as well as his freedom to travel become sources of fascination for her. Laforet's protagonists repeatedly demonstrate a tendency to project their wishes or unconscious desires onto those around them, a common trait in human behaviour but one which is particularly exacerbated in people who have experienced dysfunctional attachments in early childhood.[14] Marta displaces her source of self onto others; initially her wider family and then, following their rejection of her, Pablo. When Marta's literary endeavours are ridiculed by her aunt Matilde she loses all hope of finding solace in her relatives' presence: 'Cuando pensaba en la manera como Matilde le había rechazado, hasta tenía ganas de llorar' (p. 67). The figure of Pablo is then transformed into the object of Marta's *cathexis*; she turns him into an idealised composite of the archetypal mother and father figure through which she hopes to find a source of meaning in her life and an end to her suffering. Her non-sexual, obsessive love for him impedes Marta's path towards individuation and self-understanding. What ensues across the novel is a competing dialectic between love and reason as sources of potential relief. Marta initially pursues love, or what she believes to be a higher form of non-sexual love, as a means of healing her psychic wounds and releasing herself within 'los brazos de alguien que fuese comprensivo y bueno' (p. 43), and this person is Pablo. On close reading, Laforet's representation of Pablo is subtle and ironic; he is a lonely artist, estranged from his wife, who seeks sexual alleviation through an affair with Marta's aunt Hones.[15] Laforet renders Pablo ordinary towards the end of the novel, ultimately demysti-fying him from Marta's fantastical projection of him as a tortured, artistic genius. Yet Pablo's function in the novel serves as a temporary buffer against Marta's psychic disintegration; he is a source of relief, albeit a false one, and also serves to propel her towards reason as an antidote to untrammelled grief and emotional instability.[16]

Marta identifies with a man whom she perceives to be suffering as much as her and who recognises her distress and lack of love from her wider family. Following a dance together and brief conversation at a gathering at her home, she transforms Pablo into an idealised emotional interlocutor: 'él la había mirado por dentro [...] Aún temblaba (p. 89). Marta's *cathexis*, or massive psychic investment in Pablo, centres around her discovery of his sketchpad which has been left on a sofa during the same evening. In it she encounters images of her aunt's legs, a 'demonio con patas de cabra' (p. 91) and a representation of José beating his naked wife on the back. Due to her naivety, Marta does not consider the obvious interpretation of the sketches — all symbolisations of sexual desire and fantasy, one of the primary forms through which the human subject seeks relief. Marta on the other hand believes that she has gained access to Pablo's creative genius and his emotional core. In fact, what she is seeking is for Pablo to recognise these aspects of her own character. Marta's response is so visceral and overwhelming that it constitutes an intimation of an awakening within her which goes beyond that of revealing Pablo's artistic genius: 'Casi temblando, escondió el bloc bajo el colchón de la cama turca y apagó de prisa la luz. Vibraba toda ella, como hacía rato le parecía haber visto vibrar a los instrumentos de cuerda, calientes aún' (p. 91). The reverberation of her own creative capacities is felt but, as will be discussed in the following chapter, an act of mis-reading occurs whereby Marta misses the opportunity provided by this experience to commune with her unconscious and access her true self. Marta's unconscious, her deeper self, calls to her, yet she lacks the reflective self-knowledge to recognise this: 'Una extraña llamada, como la trompeta alrededor de Jericó, derrumbaba muros, hacía desaparecer tabiques, habitaciones y gentes que la rodeaban. Allí, en la oscuridad, no escuchaba ni sentía más que un hondo y lejano rumor de su sangre' (p. 92).[17] Marta fails to recognise this moment of relief as a form of self-revelation and misattributes her emotions to Pablo's recognition of her as a subject. The feelings of love that surge up in her are misdirected and projected onto Pablo. As Langford observes, this process of falling in love is an unconscious, circuitous route back to the self which we mistake for love of another person: 'Love in itself does not so much take us higher, as round in circles; it takes us nowhere that we have not been before and does not allow us to develop into anyone substantially different from who we were in the first place.'[18] Marta's reaction to her discovery of the sketch pad indicates her tendency to over-embellish events with her own projected emotions as the content of the sketches represents an ironic and prophetic reflection on what will occur later in the novel: Marta awakening to the knowledge of Pablo's baser, but wholly natural, instincts and the 'demonios' of sexual desire. Prior to this revelation, however, Marta idealises Pablo beyond the bounds of reality:

> A veces se ruborizaba de orgullo, al recordar que era la mejor amiga y la confidente de un hombre extraordinario, que había llegado a la isla quizá solo para llegar a fortalecer e ilusionar su vida. (145)

Her transformation of him into a god-like figure who affords her salvation reveals the extent to which she is seeking a substitute parental figure as a source of consolation for her suffering: 'No sabía por qué Pablo le era tan necesario. Por qué tenía ganas de arrodillarse delante de él, suplicarle que le prestara un poco de atención. Decirle: "A usted yo puedo enseñarle mi alma"' (p. 156).

Laforet's representation of Marta's self-abnegation through love suggests a subtle, feminist critique of heterosexual relationships. La isla proposes that women who seek relief from a sense of worthlessness or inferiority through love ought not to displace their sense of self in an idealised male Other. According to Jessica Benjamin, self-abnegation leads to an avoidance of one's self in the pursuit of love.[19] Similarly, Langford writes: 'Psychoanalysts have argued that falling in love represents an attempt to escape from, and resolve, contradictions within the self.'[20] As outlined above, Marta's contradictory sense of who she is and what she desires have as their root cause attachment disturbance with the mother. Her obsessive love of Pablo is an attempt to repair an earlier damaged bond through a re-enactment of another bond in the present, which is doomed to fail as the first cannot be replaced by the second. Summarising Theodor Reik, Langford states that although we may think we love an actual person, 'the love object is [...] a phantom to a great extent, a peg on which we hang all the illusions of ourselves which we long to fulfil.'[21]

Yet Marta's failure to read the potency of her own self-awakening in response to the discovery of Pablo's sketch book is counteracted by the voice of the other Marta who implores her to use her reason and organise her life on her own terms. *Decathexis* or disinvestment in the desired object begins to occur following Pablo's rejection of their friendship due to gossip about them being seen walking and talking together being conveyed back to Marta's family.

> 'Acostumbrarte a la idea de que no tienes que perseguir a quien te rechaza
> [...] De ninguna manera.'
>   Se hizo esta reflexión, despacio, firmemente. Era como si hubiese dos Martas
> en la playa, una dispuesta a llorar a gritos, a patalear como una niña, a correr
> detrás del pintor para pedirle explicaciones de aquel brusco rechazo de su
> amistad, y otra muy implacable, hasta burlona, que le decía que no fuese pesada,
> que obrase por su cuenta, que no se dedicase a ser una histérica obsesa como
> Pino. (156)

Here Laforet's feminist voice rings clear and, through Marta's self-reflections, she articulates what Betty Friedan, over a decade after the publication of *La isla*, succinctly sums up as women's lot: 'they are in a trap, and to escape they must [...] finally exercise their human freedom, and recapture their sense of self. [...] They must begin to grow.'[22] In a similar vein, *La isla* deconstructs love as the cure to Marta's emotional and psychic pain. In order to grow, Marta must reject her idealised view of Pablo and this is what she does through the other, implacable Marta. Laforet recognised what many second wave feminist thinkers articulated in relation to women's perception of the role of love in their lives and its capacity to bring lasting relief to their existence. As Langford notes, love can 'hold us hostage to oppressive forces, lock us ever more securely within the confines of a stunted selfhood, and twist our desire for freedom into a neurotic and destructive craving'.[23] It is the emergence of another aspect of Marta's psyche, one which stands alongside the 'neurotic and destructive craving' of the emotionally underdeveloped girl that leads her towards a more balanced understanding of her capacity to set herself free. Although Laforet did not align herself with feminist ideas, her novels can be situated broadly within the discourses of second-wave feminism, especially those that sought to deconstruct romantic love. Once again, we find evidence of how Laforet's narratives speak to readers beyond a specific time and find an echo in more contemporary contexts.

In opposition to love stands reason and it is to this faculty that Marta turns in her search for relief.[24] Whereas Andrea does not find psychological relief in any full sense in *Nada*, *La isla* poses a more positive representation of the protagonist's search for relief such that the acquisition of reason develops through actions that enable Marta to assert her free will. More than any other protagonist in Laforet's novels, Marta experiences herself changing through the demystification of her child-like beliefs and her growing awareness of the dangers of love as an antidote to suffering and false form of relief. *La isla* therefore provides readers with an inquiry into the ancient philosophical concept of reason as a method of balancing unruly emotions, famously outlined in Plato's discussion of the charioteer in the *Phaedrus*. Marta's pursuit of love as a form of relief evolves into an inquiry into the importance of reason as a check on the *demonios* which Laforet referred to as 'la trama de pasiones humanas — siempre las mismas en todas las latitudes'.[25] Although Johnson posits the view that the central theme of Laforet's second novel is 'imagination and fantasy', this observation requires further consideration.[26] *La isla* is, in part, a warning against the pursuit of fantasy and the sway of the imagination over reason. On a general level, *La isla* exposes the restrictions placed on freedom of the will through an individual's life circumstances, society, gender and individual psychology but the novel also suggests that these conditions are not insurmountable, thus positing the possibility of an undetermined concept of free will. Laforet also renders problematic the gender-neutral accounts of free will that dominate philosophical discourse since the historically situated subject position of women cannot be divorced from accounts of free will. Laforet's inquiry into women's capacity to be free sits within the fact of their lack of control over their reproductive capacities due to an absence of access to contraception in post-war Spain.

However, Marta undergoes greater development than Andrea and transcends out of what Harry Frankfurt describes as a 'wanton' state.[27] It is within the enlightened condition of greater reason that Marta encounters relief. The more objective 'other' Marta within the narrative speaks to her through the discourse of reason and warns her against seeking out Pablo as a source of unpleasure for her anxious, traumatised psyche. *La isla* suggests that freedom of the will is not innate, but that it evolves within the individual over time through self-reflection and, according to Robert Kane's discussion of free will, 'self-forming actions' that assist in the construction of what he describes as personhood.[28] Laforet's representation of women's capacity to be free is complicated and, on occasions, contradictory. Her fiction sometimes posits a compatibilist notion of free will, a combination of biological determinism and a woman's capacity to exercise the choice to be free; while on other occasions, a more deterministic stance is represented, most notably in Paulina's decision to return to her husband in Laforet's next novel *La mujer nueva*. Overall, Laforet's novels tend to propose an evolutionary argument for free will, despite the regressive context in which the author was writing. If, as Daniel Dennett suggests in his evolutionary discussion of free will, 'culture [...] provides the fulcrum from which we can leverage ourselves into new territory' and therein 'provides the vantage point from which we can see how to change the trajectories into the future that have been laid down by the blind explorations of our genes',[29] then Laforet's novels pose an interesting case study.[30] If we conceive of Francoist culture negatively, then this same culture does not serve to lift the capacity for freedom beyond biological determinism. Yet Laforet's fiction functions to resist the cultural stagnation of the regime and suggests that women, to a greater or lesser extent, can rise above their historical circumstances and evolve beyond their biologically determined roles, although these may also be incorporated into the process. There is no doubt in *La isla* that Marta evolves and participates in a self-forming action that enables her to leave the island: she sells jewellery given to her by her mother and buys a ticket to take her on boat to mainland Spain. Through Laforet's creation of an internal dialogue between the 'dos Martas', a wiser and less wanton Marta begins to emerge who counsels the younger, less emotionally regulated aspect of her psyche: ' "Piensa en lo que te importa." Marta, de cuando en cuando, se interrumpía en aquella disparada facilidad de sus pensamientos... Hacía algún tiempo que había dos Martas dentro de ella. Una que ordenaba a la otra' (p. 177). Marta rejects Sixto's offer of marriage and refuses her biological destiny at this stage of her life. Reason and free will prevail as both methods of finding relief from her family circumstances and as a springboard towards the next stage of her life.

One of the most significant narrative sequences in the novel occurs during a dialogue between the opposing voices operating in Marta's psyche. Her culturally determined self, which carries within it inflections of patriarchal authority, engages with her deeper, wiser self — the emerging voice of reason that will guide her towards action and, eventually, enable her to leave the island. Each of Laforet's novels contains at least one narrative sequence or chapter to which all the other events of the text gravitate and acquire meaning. In the case of *Nada*, Andrea's account of her listening to Román's music and her experience in front of Barcelona's neo-gothic cathedral are representative examples. In the following chapter, detailed attention will be given to Paulina's experience in *La mujer nueva* on the train to Madrid, which forms an entire chapter of the novel and represents one the most significant aesthetic configurations of relief to be found across Laforet's novels. Collectively, these sequences form a connected chain of aesthetic questions on the nature of relief: how it is to be found, how it is to be experienced and how it is even possible to represent its non-conceptual properties within language.[31] In the case of *La isla,* these questions are posed during a sequence when Marta, disappointed at not finding Pablo on one of her walks, rests beside an ancient dragon tree in a park. She leans her head against its trunk, an action through which the desire for relief is expressed through bodily contact with a natural object. The tree functions on a variety of symbolic levels: it represents the tree of knowledge and experience as it appears to talk to Marta and encourages her not to act from her emotions. On a deeper symbolic level, the tree also serves as a projection of different parts of Marta's psyche — an admonishing superego, representing the voice of patriarchal culture and a more egocentric self, which encourages her to awaken to 'realidad' and employ reason within her life choices, although this voice has been emerging within Marta for some time.[32] Laforet also instils the dragon tree with the power of prophecy as it foretells the night when Marta discovers that Pablo and Hones are engaged in a sexual relationship. Laforet's prose shifts to an intense poetic register, as if to heighten the reader to the relevance of the content.

> Es un árbol de siglos, casi humano. Un árbol cuyo tronco retorcido finge cuerpos apasionadamente enlazados... No es bueno pensar en quién se quiere con la cabeza apoyada en este árbol de tierras cálidas. Su silencioso misterio no se envuelve en brumas, se recorta duramente en la luz deslumbrante y sin frío. Está pidiendo realidad. No quiere sombras; si el cuchillo le hiere, no disfraza sus zumos de frescura y de agua; suelta sangre como la carne de los hombres al herirse. [...] Marta sentía detrás de su cabeza la palpitación de aquella sangrienta sabiduría del drago. "Realidad, realidad, besos en la noche, besos... Realidad, Marta Camino." (128)

The image of the young Marta, with her head pressed back against the tree trunk delineates the protagonist's despair and her search for alleviation from her suffering and misguided emotional investment in Pablo. On the one hand, the tree appeals to Marta as a way of grounding herself in reality as opposed to fantasy. Reason is presented as an antidote to her fear of losing her friendship with Pablo when he leaves the island following the end of the civil war. There is a certain irony to Laforet's prose in this sequence as she enters fully into the realm of the symbolic imagination to represent Marta's struggle to free herself from her emotions towards Pablo. Laforet's over embellished style and exaggerated, surreal, symbolism belies another purpose, which is to explore the more unconscious and repressed thoughts of her protagonists. This technique entails a complex dynamic as readers experience a distancing effect through the intensity of the language or image, while simultaneously drawing them closer towards an understanding of the psychological struggles present within Laforet's protagonists. One aspect of this struggle is revealed through Marta's fictionalised dialogue with the dragon tree when it 'speaks' to her about the subject of gender and her reproductive capacity. Here, the punitive voice of a wider, culturally conditioned superego imposes itself, yet it also warns her against idealising Pablo.

> Te hace soñar en otros países, te hace soñar con la pureza de la vida y el del arte. Pero, qué es eso? La vida para una mujer es amor y realidad. Amor, realidad, palpitación de la sangre. [...] Tienes dentro de ti semillas de muchos hijos que han de nacer; eres como una tierra nueva y salvaje y debes esperar como la tierra, quieta, el momento de dar plantas. Yo tengo mil años de vida en tierras cálidas, y te digo: "No sabes nada, no busques nada. Eres una loca." (130)

Marta is reminded of her biological capacity for reproduction and her kinship with nature, which is posited alongside her fascination with Pablo's profession and, more importantly, his freedom to exist unencumbered by his gender. The voice that urges Marta to displace fantasy with 'realidad' suggests that this reality necessarily involves the realisation of the maternal archetype through sexual reproduction. The source of the voice can be interpreted as an extension of patriarchal ideology and traditional Catholic doctrine, all too familiar to Laforet and women of her generation. However, Laforet's purpose in introducing the theme of biological predetermination for women is to explore more deeply the relationship between gender and freedom of the will.[33] The representation of Marta's reproductive capacity is over-aestheticised as if to turn the female body into an exotic and mysterious natural object. The power of female reproduction appears to be upheld by the voice, yet it is juxtaposed alongside interjections that highlight the social limitations that exist for women in a patriarchal dictatorship. As is the case in *Nada*, Laforet suggests that her young female protagonists are aware of a tension between motherhood and freedom.[34] Perhaps what is most significant about the dragon tree sequence is the tree's role as a type of interlocutor, a substitute parental figure who offers guidance to the young Marta. However, the protagonist eventually rejects the role of motherhood; 'realidad', as Marta finally conceives it, can be elected through freedom of the will. Echoing the Stoic philosophers, reason is presented as the ultimate source of tranquillity, the place from which choices can be made, rather than the fluctuating domain of emotion and (returning to Frankfurt's concept of the wanton) irrational, disordered choices. Thus, the dragon tree sequence encapsulates the key thematic concerns present in *La isla*: it explores Marta's emerging sense of self-agency as she negotiates between her two selves, the wanton and the increasingly individuated, and it considers the wider issue of gender and whether free will is possible for women within a repressive society. There is also an ethical dimension to *La isla* intertwined within Marta's turn towards reason as a mode of relief and agent of change in her life. The emergence of a stronger self-concept that balances Marta's wanton tendencies provides a meditation on the ethics of the individual's responsibility to be free. It echoes the views outlined in existential philosophical debates, most notably de Beauvoir's understanding of women's moral responsibility to become agents so as not to remain trapped within a self-imposed inferior subject position. However, and perhaps ironically, it is only through Marta's abnegation of her sense of an authentic, independent self through her infatuation with Pablo that she awakens to reason.

I would like to dwell on other pursuits in which Marta engages to find relief, some of which are more successful than others in ameliorating her psychological pain. It is important to note that while Laforet's protagonists suffer from insecurity, anxiety and a deep sense of alienation from others, they simultaneously display high levels of psychological resilience. This is frequently aided by art, writing or fantasising, which serve as coping mechanisms in the face of the potential chaos of psychic despair. For example, Marta isolates herself from José and Pino's arguments 'en una especie de neblina detrás de sus propias imaginaciones' (p. 26). One of the means through which Marta has sustained a degree of psychic stability prior to the arrival of her relatives is through writing, which is described as a 'sarampión literario' (p. 18). The mythical stories of island gods fuel Marta's imagination and the figure of Alcorah, the ancient god of the Canary Islands is transformed into a symbolic, quasi-sexualised father figure who appears in her naïve tales. Marta's tendency to retreat into the realm of the imagination is mirrored by another interesting stance that she adopts which has much in common with psychological dissociation and may form part of the spectrum of her defence mechanisms. For Marta, self-willed defamiliarisation facilitates the process of deflecting her emotions away from the source of her anguish. Throughout Laforet's novels the trope of deflection, either through the protagonists' gaze being turned away towards another object or through a shift in perspective, signals a deeper, metaphorical figuration of a movement towards relief. The turning from one object or phenomenon towards another lies at the core of all her protagonists' quests for release from psychic pain and, more generally, is one of the key mechanisms in her subjects' search for relief. Early on in *La isla*, the narrator outlines Marta's capacity to imagine herself into a viewpoint other than her own. The metafictional properties of this narrative sequence are self-explanatory as we are given an insight into both the author's and Marta's capacity to project their imaginations into other selves: 'Trató de imaginarse que ella misma era una viajera recién llegada. Le pareció, solo de pensarlo, que el cielo se hacía más profundamente azul, las nubes blancas más inquietantes, los jardines más floridos' (p. 19). Marta deflects her accustomed response and adjusts her viewpoint to an unfamiliar perspective: 'Marta volvió a su abstracción: "Si yo no conociese esa alta palmera que en una vuelta da tanta gracia al paisaje, si yo no conociese estos jardines floridos de bugambillas [...] ¿qué pasaría? ¿Qué sentiría en este momento?" (p. 21). This abstract mode of thought poses the question of whether a human subject can relinquish her existing repository of knowledge and experience to observe reality from a different point of view other than her own. Marta's dissociative proclivities suggest that she is in pursuit of a different subject position both as an escape from her ordinary point of view and as a way of relieving her isolation and loneliness.

> Se fijo por primera vez en la casa donde había nacido. La miró críticamente como pudiera hacerlo una desconocida. [...] Trató de imaginarse que ella venía de un país muy frío, lleno de tinieblas, y llegaba a esta casa... Se sentó en el escalón de la entrada y puso la palma de su mano en el cálido picón que jamás había recibido la caricia de la nieve. (23)

By projecting her thoughts into the imagined subject position of another, and defamiliarising herself from familiar perceptive modes, Laforet posits at least the possibility of a form of knowledge or experience beyond one's immediate life experiences, which forms the basis of most novelistic production. Laforet's novels foster an important ethical discourse based on the individual's capacity to free themselves from restrictive modes of perception, an endeavour that was entirely relevant to the historical context of Franco's dictatorship, but can be applied more widely to the human condition across different epochs and geographical spaces. At a subtle yet no less significant level, Laforet encourages the reader to maintain an expansive vista in order to free the individual from patterns of behaviour and cultural practices that unconsciously saturate the psyche and impinge upon her freedom. Relief is then configured within the reading process through the expansive vistas opened up on occasions by each protagonists' distinct point of view.

However, as has already been outlined above, Marta appears to reject the realm of fantasy as a source of succour. By the end of the novel, and following her mother's death, Marta decides to burn her 'cuadernos' in which she has written her stories about the island. Critics have almost universally viewed the burning of Marta's manuscripts as evidence of Marta's development. Johnson believes that Marta discards art and experiences in 'an awakening to reality'.[35] The ritualistic rite of burning her stories signals Marta's passage from immaturity to adulthood: 'Aquello era, verdaderamente, convertir en cenizas su adolescencia' (p. 306). More generally, the pyre of manuscripts signals Laforet's scepticism regarding art's capacity to heal the wounded psyche. *La isla* posits the view that action in the world, reason and self-responsibility better aid the individual to cope with the slings and arrows of life, especially a life scarred by loss. Pablo's discourses on art as 'el único camino de salvación personal. El único consuelo de la vida' (p. 120) may be tinged with irony since art is finally rejected as an aid to Marta's salvation from suffering. Pablo also suggests that art in itself provokes its own 'demonios' due to the demands it places on the creative subjects' life and relationships, a subject to which Laforet returns in *La insolación*.[36] Throughout Laforet's fiction, participation in life, sociability and interaction with the natural world are set against the more secluded, inward domain of artistic creation. Her protagonists oscillate between art and life, never finding a home or happiness in one or the other, which begs the question as to where a sense of stability and calm arises in her protagonists' search for relief.

This leads me to some final considerations on the pursuit of relief in *La isla* and Laforet's insights into a non-aesthetic, non-intellectual domain through which pleasure or joy may be encountered and a return to the realm of the senses and the body enjoyed. Strangely, this does not include sexual intimacy, which Marta rejects, apart from her kisses with Sixto and her admiration of his youthful, healthy body. Both Marta and to a similar extent Andrea, feel a visceral disgust towards even the thought of the sexual act. When Marta catches sight of Pablo and Hones embracing in the garden of her house following her mother's death: 'Aquello la mareaba como puede marear la vista de la sangre saliendo de una herida [...] Empezó a sufrir de asco. Empezó a sentirse tan enferma, que tuvo ganas de vomitar' (p. 293). The realisation that Pablo is a sexual being like any other perhaps reflects Marta's sudden *decathexis* and comprehension of her own naivety, her tendency to project her desires onto others, and to structure her reality according to her fantasies. Although her love for Pablo has been 'demasiado espiritual, demasiado lleno de idealismo' (p. 293), her first hand evidence of his sexual desire for Hones serves the important purpose of re-directing Marta's attention towards reason and greater engagement with her less-wanton and rational side: 'Pablo no era, al fin y al cabo, un ser más extraordinario que Daniel o José, o ella misma' (p. 300).[37] It is only in Laforet's final novel, *Al volver la esquina* that sex is represented as a source of relief for the male protagonist Martín Soto.

Although the sexual act as a form of relief remains beyond the sphere of knowledge for both Andrea and Marta, the body is not fully rejected as a source of haptic pleasure. On the contrary, pleasure derived through physical movement, in Marta's case swimming and walking, induce what can only be described as joy acquired through bodily alleviation. A poetically infused description of Marta swimming naked in the sea during a full moon articulates a profound sense of happiness:

> El aire cálido y el mar lleno de luz plateada la llamaban. Se desnudó rápidamente en aquella profunda soledad de la arena con luna, y se metió en el agua.
> El mar guardaba el calor del día y Marta jamás había nadado así, con tal delectación, entre aguas cálidas llenas de luz. La vida le parecía irrealmente hermosa. Tendida sobre el mar, sintiendo flotar sus cabellos, empezó a reírse suavemente. [...] ésta era la felicidad. Profunda, plena, verdadera. Cada uno tiene una manera distinta de sentir la felicidad, y ella la sentía así. (214)

She then senses that the joy or 'dicha' that she experiences will be curtailed by her future destiny, intimating the limited nature of relief and the cycle of repetition, required to encounter similar states of being, which forms the invariant theme of Laforet's five novels: 'Y tuvo un temor grande y supersticioso de que el destino le guardara algo muy malo para vengar esta alegría que ella había alcanzado quizás indebidamente' (p. 214). The sea provides Marta with a sense of 'flojedad' and 'alivio' (p. 157) that permit a momentary feeling of dissolution of the self, an intimation of Freud's oceanic feeling again perhaps, or a cessation of suffering, as outlined in the nirvana principle. Although Marta goes on to embrace reason and rational motivation as a means of alleviating her emotional distress, *La isla* does not suggest that her more rational self is where she necessarily encounters joy and happiness. Reason is but one vehicle through which relief is sought for Laforet's protagonists but *dicha* — joy arising from transcendence of mind and body, embodied in Marta's fleeting experience of oneness, connoting death and a re-incorporation into the body of the lost parent — is the conduit to a higher realm of experience. Thus, although reason triumphs at the end of *La isla*, the novel simultaneously acknowledges that a tension exists between conceptual, rational knowledge and non-conceptual, pure, direct, physical experience with the environment.

Some of Marta's most intense moments of self-reflection and mental ease occur when she is walking alone around the city of Las Palmas.[38] In this regard, Marta and Andrea manifest a shared love of solitude and physical movement through urban space. Marta is referred to as a female 'vagabundo', a characteristic she has inherited from her father, as her grandfather informs her: 'Su propio padre había sido así, un bohemia, un vagabundo' (p. 27).[39] Yet when she asks her grandfather whether the figure of the female vagabond ever existed, he replies: 'No, una mujer no... Nunca oí eso. Iría contra la naturaleza' (p. 27).[40] This quotation arises early on in *La isla*, signalling Laforet's interest in the relationship between gender and freedom of movement, a theme that is repeated across her first three novels. As Marta acquires greater mobility in the capital as a result of her sister-in-law's jealousy of her travelling with José in his car, Marta's ability to find psychological freedom and relief from her family milieu is simultaneously enhanced. For Marta, walking facilitates a meditative state in which 'no hacía nada. Se dejaba vivir' (p. 125). The following narrative sequence illustrates the process through which Marta's outward contemplative gaze as she walks around the island's capital also leads to an inner state of augmented self-understanding that aids her reflections on her growing self-agency: 'La vida de la plaza había empezado. Campesinas acababan de llegar en los coches de hora, sirvientas madrugadoras movían por allí. Ella las miraba. A veces pensaba: "Soy yo, yo, Marta Camino, quien estoy libre en este día"' (p. 125). In Marta's case walking with no purpose other than the pleasure of looking, often associated with the lascivious gaze of the *flâneur*, leads her to reflect on her 'malos sentimientos' which have been fostered by her sense of oppression and lack of love within the family environment. In an interview with Geraldine C. Nichols, Laforet made the following observations on walking: 'tiene implicaciones trascendentes: puede hacer nacer en la mente imágenes, deseos, ideas y pensamientos que tal vez de otro modo nunca se gestarían. Ayuda a pensar. Facilita la sublimación del deseo.'[41] Not only does Laforet indicate contact with the realm of the transcendental, a central theme in her third novel *La mujer nueva*, but she also suggests that the peripatetic tradition aids the generation of ideas. For Marta, walking enables her to transcend her feeling of isolation within her family environment and measure her capacity to experience freedom of movement and thought.

In the final pages of the novel, Marta is better able to articulate her own wants and desires. She asserts her freedom to act unencumbered by love and the emotions: 'hay personas a las que el amor no quiere detener ni aprisionar. Ella estaba libre delante de su juventud. Para sus pies eran los caminos' (p. 303). *La isla* suggests that this path is best taken alone as Marta recalls how her greatest joys and sorrows have been experienced in solitude (p. 304). However, there is a moment of doubt as Marta reflects on how she might still give up her desire for flight and remain on the island as an act of abnegation which, she believes 'tenía una gran hermosura, que era necesario y hasta bello' (p. 290). Her newly found sense of agency is momentarily shaken by a culturally engrained feeling of self-sacrifice, indicating how Laforet's protagonists vacillate between acting for themselves and acting for the sake of others as they question which path will lead them towards a greater sense of ease and psychological freedom. In her next novel, Laforet turns to the theme of abnegation and denial of the self in the service of an Other as a method of encountering relief within the framework of religious belief. The subject of abnegation to God's will forms one of the primary themes in *La mujer nueva*.

Notes to Chapter 2

1. Carmen Laforet, *La isla y los demonios* (Barcelona: Destino, 1991), p. 11. First published 1952. Hereafter *La isla*.
2. It must be emphasised that the forms of relief sought across Laforet's novels are never presented as permanent solutions. Their interim function is a result of the protagonist's failure to address their deeper traumas.
3. Extract from a letter to Paquita Mesa quoted in Caballé and Rolón, p. 219.
4. Cerezales Laforet, *Música blanca*, pp. 116–17.
5. Caballé and Rolón, p. 235.
6. Pino represents the figure of the emotionally distant stepmother of Laforet's childhood.
7. It is interesting to note that in both *Nada* and *La isla* the mother's hair, or rather its absence, shares the same symbolic resonance of loss. During Teresa's illness she wears her hair, 'casi al rape' (p. 83) which echoes 'larga trenza de pelo negro' that is shaven off Amalia's head on her death and kept in a cupboard by one of Andrea's relatives.
8. I have not sought to engage in significant detail with the vast psychoanalytical literature on the absent mother figure since Bowlby's observations on object loss are foundational and pertain most closely to this study. This study is based primarily on close textual analysis, rather than a synthesis of psychoanalytical approaches to bereavement of the primary carer. My intention is to delve deeper into the strategies developed by individuals in response to object loss through my discussion of Laforet's fiction.
9. This temporal feature of the novels provides further justification for a primarily psychoanalytical reading of Laforet's fiction.
10. Johnson notes that 'what is largely absent in Carmen Laforet's familial structure is the good mother figure', p. 94. She also suggests, with reference to Marta, that she 'seems to have no feeling for her mother at all', p. 73.
11. Again, the parallels with Laforet's refusal to discuss her mother's death are obvious.
12. Illanes Adaro, p. 62.
13. Wendy Langford, *Revolutions of the Heart: Gender, Power and the Delusions of Love* (Routledge: London and New York, 1999), p. 56.
14. In *Nada* this is made explicit in Andrea's relationship with Ena, who is less of a friend than she initially perceives, as I have indicated in the previous chapter.
15. Hones is also held up for ridicule throughout the novel. Laforet's characterisation of certain

figures in her narratives demonstrates, on occasions, sarcastic cruelty. This mainly occurs with reference to secondary characters. Her protagonists are delineated as aloof and distant, and they frequently judge the attitudes and behaviour of others. In this respect, Laforet makes no effort to make her protagonists amenable to readers. On the contrary, it proves difficult to like her protagonists due to their selfish proclivities and obsessive natures.

16. Further evidence of Rasmussen's concept of ' "non" "sense" ' discussed in the introduction.

17. We witness a similar error of attribution during and following Paulina's conversion on the train to Madrid in *La mujer nueva*.

18. Langford, p. 150.

19. Jessica Benjamin, *The Bonds of Love: Psychoanalysis, Feminism, and the Problem of Domination* (London: Virago Press, 1990), p. 117.

20. Langford, p. 25.

21. Langford, p. 56.

22. Betty Friedan, *The Feminine Mystique* (London: Penguin, 2010), p. 249.

23. Langford, p. 150.

24. In a Jungian sense, Marta individuates and takes back her projections, although she does so at an earlier age than Jung suggests is normal for the process of maturation to occur. Marta is sixteen, yet Jung suggests that individuation arises around middle age. It is relevant to mention that on occasions Andrea and Marta display traits of maturity and undertake actions that are atypical of their respective ages. It has also been noted repeatedly by critics that Laforet's depths of insights into the human character in *Nada* were surprising for a woman of her age, yet her perceptive understanding of human psychology reveals the mature, intuitive knowledge of the world that the author possessed. For further discussion of the development of this psychological trait see Alice Miller, *The Drama of the Gifted Child: The Search for the True Self* (New York: Basic Books, 1997).

25. Carmen Laforet, *Mis páginas mejores* (Madrid: Editorial Gredos, 1956), p. 57.

26. Johnson, p. 73.

27. A similar trajectory is traced through the character of Paulina in Laforet's third novel, which will be discussed in the next chapter, although freedom is apparently achieved through a passion for God. Harry G. Frankfurt, 'Freedom of the Will and the Concept of a Person', *Journal of Philosophy*, 68,1 (1971), 5–20.

28. Robert Kane, *A Contemporary Introduction to Free Will* (New York and Oxford: Oxford University Press, 2005), p. 172.

29. Daniel C. Dennett, *Freedom Evolves* (London: Penguin, 2003), p. 165.

30. Dennett's view of culture is of course meant progressively, but he fails to consider the more nuanced nature of what culture means and the multifarious ways in which evolution and cultures converge and separate at different points in history.

31. These types of chronotypes recur across each novel. They are to be considered alongside Maslow's discussion of 'peak experiences' as they are also descriptions of merger with an object of contemplation or with nature itself.

32. I do not use the term egocentric to refer to a selfish, narcissistic sense of self but rather to the formation of a more stable self-concept within Marta's psyche. This is not possible without the basic structure of an ego.

33. The relationship between gender and free will is underexplored in philosophical discussions of free will. For a recent discussion of freedom of will and philosophy see Susanne Moser, *Freedom and Recognition in the Work of Simone de Beauvoir* (Frankfurt; New York: Peter Lang, 2008).

34. Laforet's views on motherhood and women's role in society cannot be easily categorised within any existing concept of feminism. Her discussion of how society might be organised to support mothers brings together elements of patriarchy and communism. See Caballé and Rolón, pp. 212–13. There is little evidence of motherhood being represented as a conduit towards relief, although Ena's mother does exalt motherhood to an extent in *Nada* during a private conversation with Andrea.

35. Johnson, p. 76.

36. Laforet struggled to reconcile her own problematic relationship with art and finally stopped

writing fiction. For the author, some relief appears to have arisen through giving up her artistic vocation.

37. Andrea is equally outraged by the encounter on the balcony between Gloria and Román. Paulina is similarly disgusted by her father's flirtations with the family maid. Paulina also struggles with her own sexual desire towards Antonio. Adult sexuality is rendered problematic in Laforet's fiction and suggests an uneasy relationship with natural bodily instincts and the power of libidinal drives. It is here that we witness the impingement of traditional Catholic doctrine on Laforet's writing.

38. For a more expansive analysis of Andrea's relationship to urban space see Caragh Wells, 'The City's Renovating Virtue: Urban Epiphanies in the Novels of Carmen Laforet, Carmen Martín Gaite, Montserrat Roig and Rosa Montero', *Journal of Romance Studies*, 7.1 (2007), 7–19.

39. Caballé and Rolón discuss how Knut Hamsun's *Un vagabundo toca con sordina* and Walter Starkie's *Aventuras de un irlandés en España* had an important influence on Laforet's desire to travel freely, p. 125.

40. Laforet's first three novels contribute to a wider critical discourse that was occurring in Spanish fiction of the 1940s and 50s on women's freedom of movement. See 'La chica rara' in Carmen Martín Gaite's *Desde la ventana: Enfoque femenino de la literatura española* (Madrid: Espasa Calpe, 1993).

41. Nichols, p. 132.

CHAPTER 3

Religion as Relief
La mujer nueva (1955)

On first appearance, Laforet's third novel bears few similarities to *Nada* and *La isla* due to the predominantly religious themes present within the narrative and the use of an older female protagonist. The novel closes with Paulina's return to her husband, which might be interpreted as an act of self-abnegation, based on the cultural expectations of female behaviour in Spain during the 1950s. Her action stands in stark contrast to the defiantly independent behaviour of both Andrea and Marta. However, on close analysis, we witness the same invariant features of Laforet's fiction arising within her third novel. Paulina is seeking relief from psychological despair which has its origins in the absence of both parents and the inability to find meaning within her current existence. Her family history has been troubled; she has had to witness her father's licentious behaviour towards household maids and her mother's supressed anger and passivity. Both parents are dead prior to the events of the novel, replicating the pattern of parental loss in *Nada*. The protagonist's efforts to ameliorate her emotional distress and pathological mourning process are diverted into religion, or more accurately, the experience of a living faith and a personal relationship with God. *La mujer nueva* is structured around Paulina's sudden conversion to Catholicism whilst travelling to Madrid by train and it is the experience of divine union as a method of seeking relief from grief that forms the subject of this chapter.[1] I challenge the view that *La mujer nueva* represents Laforet's attempt to write a Catholic novel and argue instead that the religious and mystical themes in the novel have more to do with the author's search for psychological repair due to her own incapacity to address the unresolved traumas of her past.[2] The spiritual relief and state of transcendence that can arise through mystical union with God may be better interpreted as the satisfaction of an unfulfilled longing for emotional safety and an effort to return to the primary love object. *La mujer nueva* therefore poses wider philosophical questions surrounding the extent to which mystical experiences can be attributed to religion or whether they are a manifestation of deeper, unconscious, psychological processes or neurological brain states. The complexity of representing these types of non-conceptual, unitive experiences in language also forms part of my discussion below.

The point at which *La mujer nueva* differs from Laforet's previous and subsequent novels lies in the text's more explicit autobiographical references, most notably the similarity between Paulina's conversion to Catholicism on the train to Madrid and Laforet's own experience of a sudden re-awakening to the Catholic faith.[3] In 1951 Laforet underwent a transcendental, spiritual experience whilst walking in the Retiro park in Madrid. This initiated a seven-year period of adherence to religious belief which, in its early stages, was nurtured by her friendship with the famous Spanish tennis player and sportswoman, Lilí Álvarez, who also wrote about religious matters and to whom *La mujer nueva* is dedicated.[4] Throughout her third novel, Laforet's own unconscious need for relief as a result of the early loss of her mother is projected through the character of Paulina, further problematising the author's desire to avoid the autobiographical features of her life leaching into her narratives. As is the case for all Laforet's novels, the psychological imprint of grief, or what I have referred to as a photographic negative, is etched into *La mujer nueva*, only on this occasion it is not art, music, nature or an idealised woman or man who receives the protagonists' *cathexis*, but God. Absorption is the invariant feature common to all the unitive experiences that populate Laforet's novels, a numinous state of oneness with another person or phenomenon. They signal an underlying desire for a suspension of grief and a merger with a deeply, longed for Other within whom reparation of suffering may be achieved. The mystical or unitive state may then be read as a desire for regression to an earlier period of one's life, a pattern already noted in the previous two chapters.[5] On an autobiographical level, Laforet's ongoing experiences of non-dual states are recounted by her daughter in *Música banca*. Having fallen into silence towards the end of her life, either through illness or voluntarily, Laforet wrote two words on a piece of paper and passed it to her daughter: '"UNA... ÚNICA".'[6] The author's desire for experiences of oneness is further articulated in Cristina's account; she recalls her mother's descriptions of moments of absorption, which, I would argue, are succinct accounts of psychological relief:

> A veces un estado de gracia desciende sobre mí y me envuelve en su pureza y formo parte de lo Único, indivisible, maravilloso. Cuando estoy en ese trance, no necesito ninguna clase de ayuda, incluso como sin dificultad, puedo tragar y podría hablar si no lo considerara absolutamente inútil porque no existen palabras para comunicar ese estado. No hay nada comparable con *eso*. [...] Todo mi ser tiende a mantenerse ahí, en esa armonía perfecta.[7]

It is Laforet's sustained aesthetic description of 'esa armonía perfecta' during Paulina's conversion in *La mujer nueva* that betrays the author's psychic search for relief and the experience of non-dual consciousness as a temporary negation of unpleasure.

According to contemporary accounts of non-dual experiences, the preconditions for transcendence often entail a sustained period of suffering or depression and thus Paulina's seemingly sudden conversion to Catholicism while travelling to Madrid on the train may not be as instantaneous as the narrator suggests. In other words, Paulina's historic psychic state predisposes her to spiritual awakening. The train journey to Madrid provides Paulina with the opportunity to reflect on her life and to assess the nature of her relationship with Antonio, her husband's cousin with whom she has been having an affair and who intercepts her when she changes trains. Paulina's recollections prior to her awakening reveal a life of suffering;

first, within her family of origin, and then, following the end of the civil war, her incarceration in a women's prison due to Eulogio's support for the second Spanish Republic. Paulina's relationship with both of her parents is unsatisfactory; and so, once again, Laforet represents an inadequate relationship with primary care givers, resulting in the absence of a stable psychic base from which to develop into adulthood. This absence is fulfilled, so Paulina believes, through her relationship with Eulogio, whom she also meets on a train, travelling to his family home in Villa de Robre from Madrid prior to the outbreak of the civil war. On Eulogio's return to Spain several years after the civil war, Paulina fails to re-encounter the union that she once felt with her husband, throwing her into deep emotional crisis. It is this loss of love, illness and subsequent depression that prompts her decision to travel to Madrid to evaluate the future direction of her life. Laforet's representation of Paulina's attitude towards relationships is complex and, on occasions, contradictory. On the one hand, Paulina admits 'no concibo la vida sin un amor grande' (p. 67), yet she has lived without the presence of a partner for six to seven years. Eulogio's return from America brings to an end Paulina's independent life as a single working-mother and she is forced to give up her teaching job and live off his small salary. Similarly, Paulina feels both sexually drawn to her lover Antonio but is also capable of dismissing their relationship as if it were of no consequence to her: '"¿quién es este hombre, qué hago aquí esta noche a su lado?"' (p. 88). Laforet is a remarkably astute observer of the vacillating nature of human emotions, actions and the motivating forces that lie deep in the psyche and unconsciously dictate human behaviour. Just as there are 'dos martas' in *La isla*, so too can 'dos Paulinas' be traced within *La mujer nueva*. A rational, wiser, less wanton Paulina frequently pulls her towards a more objective stance, as illustrated in her reflections upon her love for Antonio:

> De pronto, parecía que se le acabase a ella la vida y que el tiempo fuese un reloj sin manecillas y ella pudiese colocarlas en otro momento, en un momento en que el nombre de Antonio ni se sospechase en su existencia. En que todo en su vida respondía a su manera personal, libre y espontánea de manifestarse. (88)

Paulina's difficulty lies in maintaining her ability to respond 'a su manera personal' to the course of her life, as she finds herself drawn to merge with others rather than act as an independent agent. However, Paulina's fluctuating emotions towards Antonio suggest that she possesses a deeper knowledge of the source of relief — to live her life according to her own desires — yet her suffering stems from an impediment to her will to be free.[8] In other words, Paulina has a sense of what it is she is looking for, which is based upon a desire for inner freedom and self-possession, yet she is not able to embrace it fully through lack of self-awareness and an inability to engage with her deeper emotions.[9]

Paulina has been seeking relief from suffering for some time prior to her awakening on the train to Madrid. She relates her experience of a visit to a Carmelite convent with Blanca to her lover Antonio.[10] Although still sceptical about the nature of religious devotion, Paulina feels drawn to this group of women who have acquired the deep, inner peace which she lacks. It is the nuns' certainty about their purpose in life and clarity of conscience that impresses itself upon Paulina, rather than their religious vocation:

> están tan alegres porque están seguras de que al obedecer a su superior y cumplir la regla hace la voluntad de Dios... a mí, particularmente, me parece un absurdo... pero veo que esas mujeres tienen algo que a mí me falta esta temporada. Veo que obedecen a su conciencia. (118)

The nun's wills are undivided, unlike Paulina's. Her encounter with the Carmelite nuns enables her to see that the possibility of relief from suffering is not an illusion, as she witnesses their happiness as a living presence within their lives: 'algo muy sereno, profundo, verdadero, imposible de fingir' (p. 118). She admits to Antonio 'las he envidiado' (p. 118) and goes on to reflect privately, with greater objectivity and self-awareness, that her life seems to follow an ineluctable pattern of pleasure and disappointment: 'sólo la muerte podría desbaratar la carrera comenzada... Dejar a Antonio, quitarse esta pesadilla de amor de Antonio [...] y volver a empezar irremisiblemente, otra vez. Otra alegría, otra cadena, otra desesperación, otro amor' (p. 122). Paulina appears unable to insert herself as an active agent within this sequence of relationships with men, perhaps indicating Laforet's subtle feminist critique of some women's incapacity to forge independent identities outside of the parameters of love and relationships and thus find lasting relief from suffering and their ongoing state of immanence.[11] We must now turn to a detailed consideration of Laforet's most poignant and complex configurations of relief within her fiction, during which Paulina believes herself to have entered into divine grace and become unified with God's love.

The peace and harmony that the nuns display is revealed to Paulina during the most significant chapter in *La mujer nueva*, around which the rest of the narrative is structured. The 'segunda parte' of Laforet's third novel, running to only twenty-five pages and containing two chapters, differs from the familiar tripartite structure of her other novels.[12] The first chapter of the novel's central section is devoted to a lyrical description of Paulina's conversion to the Catholic faith. The second chapter recounts Paulina's arrival in Madrid at the apartment she once shared with Eulogio and her search for spiritual guidance through the figure of father González. The entire narrative is pulled towards the first chapter of the 'segunda parte'; Paulina's suffering, outlined in detail in the 'primera parte', and her ongoing suffering to commit her will to God, which is narrated in the 'tercera parte', is momentarily suspended during her spiritual awakening on the train.

Paulina wakes up to a sensation of profound peace and mental equanimity, yet only the previous evening she was feeling 'envuelta en una punzante alambrada [...] como estar en un infierno' (p. 72). Her journey up until this point has enabled her to reflect on a litany of events that have conjoined to turn her life into one of psychological despair: lack of love from her mother, her father's licentious character, Eulogio's patriarchal attitudes on his return from America, and the Church's condemnation of women as corrupting forces within society. Conversely, her experience of the civil war and early relationship with Eulogio during the conflict, as well as her subsequent imprisonment and the birth of her son Miguel in jail, are transformed into a romantic adventure, suggesting that the conditions of war have removed her from any thoughts about the reality of her future life once the war is over. The emotional impact of her encounter with Antonio the previous evening, combined with a full realisation of her suffering, has radically dissipated in the early morning light. The first thing to note about the conversion chapter is Laforet's treatment of language. In a letter to the author, Gerald Brenan praised her poetic style: 'dudo que haya en castellano unas páginas más maravillosamente poéticas que estas del primer capítulo [de la segunda parte].'[13] Laforet shifts her register towards poetic prose, signalling a different intention on the part of the author and a point of view suffused with greater emotional intensity which is, perhaps ironically, combined with a greater degree of objectivity towards the narrative description of the events occurring. Laforet challenges the Wittgensteinian proposition in the *Tractatus* that silence is the appropriate response to any attempt to express non-conceptual knowledge and mystical experience. She reveals in this chapter that she possessed the ability to put into words the experience associated with meditative states. Some philosophers from both Eastern and Western religious traditions have suggested that these states resist representation in language. William James observed that the inability to ascribe language to mystical experiences is a common phenomenon: '[the] incommunicableness of the transport is the keynote of all mysticism.'[14] According to this view, relief remains beyond the realm of linguistic expression and may only be experienced at the level of the senses or, as I shall discuss below, as a shift in cognitive focus. However, in Laforet's case, she draws her readers closely into a deeper form of knowledge and the non-conceptual experience of relief. Emotion, bodily sensation and language are folded into a monadic totality, a process of unification that promotes the dissolution of outer and inner, language and experience so that the language conveys, through its poetic register, part of the numinous experience. The Wittgensteinian gesture therefore does not replace language in Laforet's account of Paulina's mystical experience but rather language evolves into a linguistic gesture that incorporates sound, descriptive terms and the tenor and vehicle of metaphor.[15] In *La mujer nueva*, Laforet's aesthetics of relief are embedded within the language itself and although the source of suffering and unresolved grief that underpins her novels is never described directly, the emotional sensation of the experience of relief is conveyed at the linguistic level. Although Wittgenstein pursues his ideas in relation to the indescribability of an individual's response to a piece of music or poem, they pertain to the realm of the emotions and mystical experience as well. He states his proposition thus:

> ...it is true that again and again we do feel inclined to say: 'I can't describe my experience'. I have in mind a case that saying one is incapable of describing comes from being intrigued and *wanting* to describe, asking oneself: 'What is this? What's he doing, wanting to do here? — Gosh, if I could only say what he's doing here.'[16]

At the level of Laforet's description of Paulina's conversion, the 'wanting' to describe does not enact itself as a failure but is instead transmuted into the intimate gesture of her prose style in which the emotional experience of feeling the mystical state of transcendence and relief is made manifest. Wittgenstein's views on language undergo modification since, as has already been suggested, language, in this instance, becomes an expressive, poetic gesture in its own terms. Despite her capacity to bind emotion and language into a unified whole during certain narrative sequences in her fiction, Laforet's fiction also suggests that grief may also find its home in the gesture of silence, rendering Wittgenstein's proposition valid. It is commonly believed that sensory experience prefigures language; intuition, bodily contact with phenomena, and the immediacy of emotion all come prior to knowledge. We feel, we name, and we adhere a form of knowledge to the experience but by the third stage of the process we are normally at some remove from the first. As Thomas Dumm observes, language functions within a realm of contradiction when it comes to representations of the non-conceptual: 'The fact that we have words as instruments to describe what may be indescribable is paradoxical.'[17] However, Laforet's account of Paulina's awakening provides readers with an example of embodied experience within language, a literary feat that is more at work in poetry than prose. Laforet's poetic prose is perhaps an example of what Robert Louis Stevenson described as poetry's capacity to represent the ineffable: 'it was poetry's unique contribution to point us toward such moments of "true realism".'[18] Stevenson's account of poetry's power to access true realism, or 'la verdad no sospechada', points towards Laforet's success in drawing language as closely as possible to the felt experience of emotional relief provided by Paulina's mystical experience in La mujer nueva.

The physical location of Paulina's experience, the effect of movement on her body and the visual panorama outside the train are pivotal to understanding her numinous awakening. She is travelling alone and has woken up in her sleeping compartment. The narrator draws the reader's attention to the sensation of being rocked: 'era como una cuna. Tchak, tchak, tchak... un movimiento acompasado, monótono, profundamente monótono. Algo la abrazaba, la envolvía, la acunaba en el sueño' (p. 135). The evocation of Paulina's regression to an earlier phase of her life is clear as she finds herself 'mecida sobre las ruedas, con su cuerpo distendido, cómodo' (p. 135), as if she were being rocked in a cradle by her mother. The primary motif of the entire chapter is announced in the opening paragraph; Paulina awakens to a sensation of merger with nature which expands into the experience of direct communion with God's love. There is an element of psychological regression to Paulina's experience as her psyche detaches itself from present concerns over her relationship with Antonio and seeks to return to a pre-individuated state, one that may even be prior to maternal separation and recalls a watery oneness within the mother's womb.

Paulina awakens at dawn and, according to the American transcendentalist, Henry Thoreau, 'all memorable events transpire in morning time and in a morning atmosphere.'[19] She then looks out of the window and receives the beauty of the natural world as it passes in front of her: 'una pura y serena impresión de belleza que la dejó mucho rato quieto, sonriente. Absorta' (p. 135). The relationship between the beauty of music and architecture and moments of absorption was discussed in detail in chapter one. Nature acquires a similar role in La mujer nueva as Paulina feels herself merge with the landscape, prompting the reduction of her egocentric consciousness. The external vision of the Castilian countryside at dawn has a profound impact upon her emotions and a process of emptying out of her consciousness occurs: '...no pensaba en nada. Su cabeza, su cuerpo, sus sentidos todos, estaban serenos en este momento puro del despertar' (p. 135). The narrator's account of Paulina's equanimity bears the hallmarks of a state of consciousness known to practitioners of Zen Buddhist meditation as *kenshō* or *satori*, when the egocentric self dissolves and allocentric awareness arises. The combined movement of the train and the moving visual panorama have a physiological and psychological effect on Paulina, signalling the transition towards a state of joy or *gozo* which brings her relief. James H. Austin discusses how activity within the temporal lobes whilst on a train can induce the brain to evaluate a person's sense of themselves in relation to other moving objects.[20] In Paulina's case, her mind appears to project itself out into the Castilian landscape, as if her sense of self had dissolved and she had merged with her surroundings. Sensorial descriptions layer themselves into the narrative as Paulina traverses more deeply into her experience of peaceful merger and the dissolution of the anguish aroused through her encounter with Antonio the previous evening: 'toda aquella ardorosa, vulgar, pequeña intriga que era la vida. Lejos, el dolor del cuerpo y del alma... lejos todo, menos las inmensidades de la tierra y del cielo, alto y puro' (p. 136). Following Austin, Paulina is evaluating her sense of self with the assistance of the landscape as it moves in front of her field of vision. At this point in Paulina's conversion it is the comfort of the train, solitude and the natural environment that have induced her relief and her own capacity to imagine a life beyond the reach of others. This set of conditions does not at this stage appear to have anything to do with God revealing his presence to her. On the horizon, she notices a small cottage, above which hangs 'la última estrella, ennobleciéndola con una temblorosa poesía' and in which she fancies herself living, 'en un sitio así, rodeada de lo inmenso, para siempre olvidada y sola' (p. 136). Again, the theme of relief foregrounds itself in the narrative as well as the protagonist's search for a place of psychological freedom that transcends suffering and releases her from the will of others. The image of the house, far out on the horizon, plays a key role in aiding Paulina in shifting her perspective away from her suffering and towards a diminished egocentric consciousness, integral to the experience of relief. As Austin has observed, looking up and outwards onto a horizon can have an important impact upon the way that the brain processes previous traumatic events: '*out* means "out there," in the distance, toward distant events arising *farther away* from one's physical body.'[21] Interpreted thus, Paulina's method of projecting her consciousness into the distant object of the house provides temporary relief and reiterates the trope of deflection which enacts a cognitive shift and alters the emotions. It may then be the case that Paulina's state of transcendence is based on a physical change in her body and brain due to being on the train and looking out at the landscape and has little to do with divine intervention. This view would concur with Antonio Damasio's descriptions of changes in emotional states being defined by 'changes in the body's chemical profile' and 'changes in the collection of neural structures which cause those changes to occur in the first place and which also cause other significant changes in the state of several neural circuits within the brain itself'.[22] Relief may then be conceived as a cognitive or neurological shift from one set of neural circuits to another and, as such, the view of relief as a transitional state from one set of emotions to another reaffirms Adler's discussion of moving from a felt minus to a felt plus state and Freud's notion of the shift from unpleasure to pleasure, both of which are imprinted upon activity in the brain.

Paulina then indicates a conscious awareness of feeling her emotions. The transition from feeling to knowing has occurred, reinforcing Damasio's description of the process by which changes in neural patterns are accompanied by 'a sense of self in the act of knowing'; Paulina is therefore aware that she is feeling her feelings.[23] As the sensation of peace deepens within Paulina, which the narrator begins to describe as 'una sensación divina' (p. 136), she passively observes the sun rise on the horizon. What follows is a description of Paulina envisaging herself conjoined with the universe with the capacity to see the world *as if* from the perspective of a divine Other. It is an out of body experience akin to the Buddhist state of *nirvana* and Bucke's discussions of cosmic consciousness.[24] The beauty and strangeness of the description necessitates an extended quotation:

> ...tuvo la sensación de que veía todos los espacios del mundo a aquella hora: los anchos, solitarios espacios de las llanuras de toda la tierra y las soledades de las grandes montañas, altas, azules, espolvoreadas de nieve. Y los mares cálidos que, a aquella hora, se llenaban de sol hasta burbujear su belleza en manchas de color de plata, en mil espejeos de luz, en un suave, impalpable, tembloroso vapor... se imaginó también los mares fríos, con sus grandes sombras junto a las rocas, y los chorros de espuma de su oleaje, y los animales de los abismos, desplegando su color, su vida, a tanta lejanía de la mirada humana y, sin embargo, perfectos hasta el último detalle de su colorido y sus caprichos y sus instintos. (136–37)

Although we must acknowledge the presence of a narrating subject, Laforet attempts to diminish the egocentric concept of being as the self dissolves into a wider, cosmic or non-dual whole in which all phenomena are complete unto themselves. We are reminded of Heidegger's understanding of *Dasein*: 'projection into the Nothing. Projecting itself into the Nothing, Dasein indeed is beyond the world of beings. This being-beyond the world of beings we call Transcendence.'[25] Paulina's experience does not represent an existential alienation from the self, in the Sartrean sense of the *Néant* and *pour soi* of *Being and Nothingness*. She feels instead a deep sense of love and equanimity. At this stage in the narrative, the narrator refrains from discussing Paulina's feelings in terms of divine love, concentrating instead on describing the protagonist's gradual comprehension of what is happening to her. Paulina becomes aware of herself once more as a woman travelling on a train and asks herself what it is that she is experiencing. She describes the innate suchness of the world around her as she receives it through her senses: 'recibió en la cara el fresco aroma, el viento que la velocidad del tren producía, los chirridos de los pájaros, los fuertes colores de la tierra, que el sol caldeaba ya y que se confundían en el brillante amanecer' (p. 138).[26] Nature contains the harmony which Paulina seeks in order to unify her fragmented psyche and which she equates with love, sustaining all things within a unified whole:

> El amor se parece a la armonía del mundo, tan serena. A su inmensa belleza, que se nutre incluso de los muertes y las separaciones y la enfermedad y la pena... el amor es más que esta armonía; es lo que la sostiene... el amor recoge en sí todas las armonías, todas las bellezas, todas las aspiraciones, los sollozos, los gritos de júbilo... el amor dispone la inmensidad del universo, la ordenación de leyes que son matemáticamente las mismas para las estrellas que para los átomos, esas leyes que, en penosos balbuceos, a veces, descubre el hombre (138–39).

Paulina finally attributes her experience of feeling invaded by love to God: 'el amor es Dios' (p. 139). Here onwards, Laforet utilises capitals to refer to Paulina's attribution of her awakening to God's love: Gozo, Gloria de Dios, Universo, Hoguera de amor. The previous poetic descriptions of nature have given way to a similarly poetic language of mystical religious discourses, drawing on Santa Teresa's writings and Paulina's knowledge of St Paul's conversion on the road to Damascus. A state of *ekstasis* develops within her as she undergoes a ' "break-through", "ascent", or "flight" of the soul in attaining in its culmination the mystery, wonder, and awe of a theophanic Encounter, of a miraculous union between God and man.'[27] Time, space and her individual ego dissolve into this miraculous union through the experience of *gozo*: 'la dimensión de la vida que no se encierra en el tiempo ni en el espacio y que es la dorada, la arrebatada, la asombrosa, inmensa dimensión del Gozo. El porqué del Universo, la Gloria de Dios. El Gozo' (p. 139). Paulina's state of rapture is aligned with St. Paul's conversion and re-birth into a new man following his experience on the road to Damascus: 'Paulina a treinta y tres años. Recién nacida' (p. 143). Here the chapter draws to a close, and yet the matter of what really has happened to Paulina on the train persists in the novel's 'tercera parte'. She struggles to surmount her feelings for Antonio, before finally returning to Eulogio and agreeing to marry through the Catholic church.[28] Unlike St Paul's experience on the road to Damascus, Paulina has in no sense been re-born with absolute faith in God's love, even though her experience is attributed to mystical union with God. We must now consider further whether discussions of the attribution of mystical states and the extent to which they are Theophanic encounters or are rooted in the individual's unconscious desire for a state of embodied relief, as I believe to be the case in Paulina's conversion.

The first point to consider is the language used to describe the transcendental religious experience. Nieli points out how the ' "new" man [...] will often search for a new language — a search which for many ends in the acceptance of the theological idiom' since in 'ordinary language [...] the experience is inexpressible'.[29] Despite Laforet's Catholic upbringing and the pervasive influence of the Church prior to and during Franco's dictatorship, it is the psychological experience of transcendence and union that remained of interest to her as a writer. Based on what is now known about Laforet's relationship with her faith following her conversion, Paulina's interpretation of her mystical awakening may be considered, in part, an error of attribution. The language of religion is employed to describe the experience due to Laforet's knowledge of the Spanish mystics, most notably Santa Teresa, and she herself believed at the time of writing the novel that she had entered a state of grace based on her experience in the Retiro park. However, seven years after the event, Laforet realised that she too had made an error of attribution and accepted the theophanic idiom too easily. She described her seven-year period of strict adherence to the Catholic faith as an illness: 'Yo estuve enferma siete años [...] a consecuencia de ese mal enfoque de mi vida. De ese intento del peor de los suicidios que es intentar ser como no se es.'[30] Saint Augustine believed the theophanic experience to be a return to one's true self through God's guidance, yet Laforet suggests that the opposite effect occurred through her seven-year period of devotion to Catholicism.[31] Similarly, Paulina's rapturous union with God may be interpreted as a missed opportunity to encounter her true self as opposed to the ego-driven false self and the defensive psychological patterns developed to protect it from invasions of the unconscious. At one point later in the narrative when Paulina is considering entering a convent, she senses that there is something at odds with her religious faith, which suggests the imposition of false values upon her psyche: 'Había algo en sus propios razonamientos que le hacía daño, que no encajaba, que era como una dolorosa piedra incrustada en su carne. Había algo falso en todo aquello, pero no adivinaba qué era lo que pudiese ser esta falsedad' (p. 305). Paulina's, and arguably Laforet's awakening to faith, may therefore need to be reconsidered within a psychological rather than religious interpretations of noumenal states. If we are to understand Laforet's representation of non-dualism and states of absorption or merger, we must return to William James's subtle conclusions on the mystical experience and his attempts to understand the state of mystical transport. James situates the mystical experience within psychoanalysis without diminishing the validity of mystical revelation: 'we cannot, I think, avoid the conclusion that in religion we have a department of human nature with unusually close relations to the transmarginal or subliminal region.'[32] Here James is referring to the unconscious and he proceeds to note that this aspect of the human psyche is 'the fountain-head of much that feeds our religion'.[33] For those immersed in the religious life, access to the transmarginal 'region seems unusually wide open'.[34] In the case of *La mujer nueva* the inverse might be posed as a mode of interpreting Paulina's conversion and search for relief from the demands of her ego and its relation to the false self. What appears to be a religious experience is the gateway to the transmarginal or unconscious centre of Paulina's being. As a writer, Laforet was therefore addressing more than religious themes in her third novel. Paulina's experience of a state of nothingness and merger with the noumenal in fact represents her psyche's attempt to heal itself through the integration of a divided will, returning us again to the invariant theme of relief being sought as a counterbalance to the pain of repressed grief. As readers, we are given access to a manifestation of the psychotherapeutic process of *cathexis* as Paulina invests her self in God. This follows on from her dis-investment or *decathexis* from Antonio the previous evening, albeit temporarily. Paulina fails to invest her psychic resources inwards towards herself and, arguably, misses the opportunity to heal her suffering, as she searches for a divine Other in which to locate her sense of self.

What Laforet is describing through Paulina's conversion is not unique to Catholicism but is in fact integral to all mystical experiences. Absorption, the falling away of a sense of time and space, the appearance of a special type of bright light, joy, love, ecstasy — all of these have been conveyed by Eastern and Western religious practitioners and meditators. Austin provides a detailed account of the enlightenment that can occur during Zen Buddhist meditation:

> What happens when the lightning strike of *prajna* dissolves every *psychic* root of one's self into emptiness and — simultaneously — the brain awakens into that paradoxical fullness, the ineffable insight-wisdom of kensho-satori? In this state of 'suchness,' no self-identity remains. Such a moment of oneness is not owned by any imperial self. In this 'thusness,' no agency of an ego exists that must thrust its own personal top-down modes of discriminating discourse into complex, branching networks.[35]

Relief from Paulina's egocentric, suffering 'self-identity' dissolves into the ineffable 'thusness' of which Austin speaks. And, typical to these moments, or brain-states as Austin suggests, is a sense of *achronia*, as time appears to dissolve.[36] The 'pasos fuera del tiempo'[37] or sensation of transport above and beyond their suffering remain of more significance to Laforet's protagonists than the religious or mystical content of the experience. James observed that the mystical experience involved passing 'from a less into a more, as from a smallness into a vastness, and at the same time, from an unrest to a rest'.[38] The experience is therefore not one of stasis, certainly not psychological or emotional stasis, but movement, fluidity and flux from one mode of perception to another and, following Damasio, one brain state to another. The nature of this movement, according to James, involves removing 'an uneasiness' and glimpsing 'its solution'.[39] Yet in Paulina's case it is only glimpsed and then framed within the language of religious conversion. An 'allocentric frame of reference', based on an outward-looking, non-self-centred point of view, arises and offers her the opportunity to experience 'an astonishing, fresh perspective' but she fails to comprehend the relevance of her experience in terms of her need for psychic repair and discovery of her deeper, true self.[40]

In David Aberbach's discussion of mysticism and its origins in grief, he suggests that during the 'climactic stage in the mystical process, union with the divine presence, also has a parallel in the grieving process, in the form of identification with, or in some cases, an actual sense of union with the lost person'.[41] Aberbach suggests that 'mystical detachment' may be conceived as the unconscious search for attachment with the dead parent and could function as 'a practical and creative response to loss'.[42] Paulina's ecstatic experience on the train to Madrid may therefore be understood as an unconscious manifestation of her longing for parental love; God's love then becomes a balm for the pain of grief.[43] Aberbach also observes how the 'impulse to pantheism [...] is particularly strong among certain individuals bereaved in childhood who persist in searching for and finding the lost person, or some abstract substitute, in Nature'.[44] This may help to explain the relationship between Paulina and nature at the beginning of her conversion as she contemplates the Castilian landscape from her train compartment.[45] Her merger with the natural surroundings and then deepening cosmic vision symbolise the protagonist's unconscious desire for merger. As is the case for all Laforet's protagonists, they repeatedly betray a tendency to allow their selves to leak into the lives of others or other phenomena. Mystical union, art, music, friendship and nature function as emotional receptacles into which the protagonists project their search for relief and longed for merger with a parental substitute.[46] The movement within Laforet's novels is therefore predominantly backwards towards the gilded realm of infancy and proximity to parental safety. Following her conversion on the train, Paulina speaks to Antonio about her experience as a regression to her youth: 'Es como volver, remontando la corriente de los años, de todos los cinismos, de todas las suciedades de la mente, hasta llegar de nuevo a la fuerza limpia de la juventud...Sí, es como navegar contracorriente' (p. 278). As Maslow suggests, the mystical experience appears to replicate a deeper desire within the individual to produce the 'end of straining and striving, the achievement of the desire and the hope, the fulfillment of longing and yearning'.[47] Relief is therefore achieved through Paulina's conversion as she feels her yearning for what the Carmelite nuns possessed is now within her grasp. However, as I have argued above, *La mujer nueva* does not suggest that the relief that arises through Paulina's religious experience is lasting, primarily because it is based on a mis-reading of the source of the experience.

Failure to shore up the self through concentrated reflection on the causes of her suffering leads to Paulina's decision to return to her husband at the end of the novel. In what proves to be a problematic ending to *La mujer nueva*, self-abnegation is posed as a solution to Paulina's personal struggles. Drawing on the views of Gerald Brenan, Cristina Cerezales Laforet offers further information on the unsatisfactory ending of *La mujer nueva*:

> A Gerald Brenan le gusta mucho *La mujer nueva* pero no le convence el final, le parece una derrota, no un triunfo de la protagonista. Yo también lo pienso, pero no todos son triunfos en la vida... Pero claro, detrás de ella estaba yo, y yo lo presentaba como un triunfo cuando en realidad en lo más íntimo de mi ser no lo sentía, quería convencerme de ello haciéndoselo vivir a Paulina.[48]

This quotation suggests that the abnegation displayed by Paulina at the end of the novel is based on a form of false consciousness that presents itself through a deterministic version of free will. Kane notes however that for some ancient philosophers, true freedom was to be found only through self-restraint: 'Plato and many other ancient thinkers, such as the Stoics, thought that the freedom of reflective self-control was the "true" freedom, since it meant that the soul was in control of itself.'[49] According to this view, Paulina's decision to return to Eulogio is not an act of self-denial since she has subjugated her will to God, and not to her husband, an action that entails freedom from the ego's needs and demands.[50] However, as in the case of Andrea and Marta, readers are left unenlightened on the matter of the protagonist's future life and the outcome of her decision to live alongside her husband and son. We gain some insights into Laforet's reasons, however, for the way she depicted Paulina's final actions. The author disclosed a clear awareness of how individuals can falsely attribute a meaning and interpretation to events that have happened to them. Here, Laforet's words pertain directly to *La mujer nueva*:

> el miedo me ha ocultado la verdadera respuesta. En esos casos uno se aferra a una verdad acomodaticia e incluso cree en ella con toda la sinceridad de que es capaz en ese momento. Y se va construyendo la vida sobre esa base inestable y falsa, e incluso puede funcionar durante un tiempo. Pero la verdad acaba poniéndose, sobre todo después de haber vivido una experiencia como la que tú y yo vivimos, en la que la Gracia se hace presente y te hace partícipe de la Esencia Divina. Puedes tener entonces la seguridad de que Ella te proporcionará más de una ocasión en el resto de tu vida para que te liberes de los falsos límites y hagas la elección adecuada, la que te conduzca directamente a la cima, a la fusión con la Unidad.[51]

The 'verdad acomodaticia' of religion is drawn upon to interpret Paulina's experience of psychological relief, but as has already been suggested, it is not a matter of entering into the presence of God's love, but an encounter with her own divine essence in the form of a dialogue with her unconscious desires which, as Aberbach attests above, have more to do with union with the lost parent than mystical revelation. Although the mystical overtones are clearly stated, the roots of the experience reach back into Paulina's psychology and her unconscious longing to heal the traumas of the past.[52]

We may wish to return to the imprint of Laforet's life upon her fiction to assess the ending of *La mujer nueva*. As has already been outlined above, Laforet could not sustain her strict adherence to Catholic doctrine. What she perceived to be a source of emotional and spiritual freedom would become a constraint on her ongoing search for relief. Nonetheless, *La mujer nueva* suggests that Laforet believed at the time of writing the novel that emotional freedom was to be found through her commitment to Catholic beliefs, but her subsequent novels and re-examination of her own belief system indicate that her concept of religion changed as she pursued her inquiries into non-dualism and Eastern religious systems. As she grew older, Laforet read the work of Gary Snyder,[53] a Zen-Buddhist poet and ecologist, and began sketching out Chinese Hanzi on pieces of paper, even though she was not trained in the language.[54] The mystical or transcendental features of Catholicism remained of interest to Laforet, yet in a similar vein to Unamuno, she could not fully subscribe to the doctrinaire teachings of the Catholic Church.[55] *La mujer nueva* is, in part, a critique of traditional Catholicism and an acknowledgment of faith as a deeply personal relationship with God, rather than one based on prescriptive belief systems. Throughout her life, religion was but one of the means which Laforet drew upon as a form of relief. In her next novel, the author returns to the themes of art, nature and friendship as potential sources of solace.

Notes to Chapter 3

1. My analysis will concentrate almost entirely on this narrative sequence because it functions as the most important aspect of the novel and deserves detailed consideration.
2. Initial critical interpretations of the novel as a vindication of Catholic values may have fed into

the number of prizes awarded to *La mujer nueva*. It won the Premio Menorca 1955 and both the Premio Nacional and Premio Miguel de Cervantes in 1956. Rolón, in his introduction to the novel, refutes the idea that it is a Catholic novel: '*La mujer nueva* no fue y no es una novela de beatería ni el simple resultado de una crisis religiosa que tanto ha señalado la crítica.' His argument is framed within a feminist analysis: 'la autora se adentra, de forma sugestiva, en la vertiente feminista de su obra.' Prologue by Israel Rolón Barada, '*Carmen Laforet, La mujer nueva*' (Barcelona: Destino, 2003), pp. 7–16 (p. 15, p. 9).

3. The importance of travel and transport, implying movement and change, is relevant to Laforet's first three novels. Andrea arrives on a train and departs Barcelona in a car. Marta awaits the arrival of her relatives who are travelling by boat and she will leave the island using the same method of transportation. *La insolación* also opens with an arrival, on this occasion by car, and closes with a departure in a vehicle. The symbolic importance of movement from one place to another must be noted because it echoes each protagonist's pursuit of relief, as well as a movement away from unpleasure towards pleasure, or from states of grief to conditions that alleviate suffering.

4. It has been suggested by Caballé and Rolón that Laforet and Álvarez's relationship had a sexual component to it.

5. For an interesting discussion of the relationship between mysticism and unitive states see chapter two in Dan Merkur, *Explorations of the Psychoanalytical Mystics* (Amsterdam and New York: Rodopi, 2010).

6. Cerezales Laforet, *Música blanca*, p. 15.

7. Cerezales Laforet, *Música blanca*, pp. 45–46. [Italics in original] Laforet experienced difficulty swallowing on occasions due to an accident during her childhood when she ingested a toxic substance which burnt the lining of her throat.

8. The dialectic between immanence and transcendence as discussed by Simone de Beauvoir in *The Second Sex* is reiterated in part through Paulina's vacillating will.

9. Here one could make the feminist argument that it is the patriarchal conditions of Francoist culture that delimit Paulina's self-agency and journey towards de Beauvoir's concept of transcendence. However, this does not take account of Paulina's psychology and her unconscious motivations.

10. The Carmelite Order was founded by Santa Teresa de Jesús, who worked tirelessly to set up new convents within the Order.

11. While it is the case that this proved difficult for many women in 1950s Spain, Laforet was articulating a point of view that extended well beyond the borders of her own country and which became a central preoccupation of many second wave feminist thinkers.

12. I agree with Torrente Ballester's views on the structural weaknesses of *La mujer nueva*. He suggested that the final part of the novel appeared as if it were tacked on to the preceding narrative and that 'estorba a la economía y a la unidad de la novela'. Gonzalo Torrente Ballester, *Panorama de la literatura española contemporánea* (Madrid: Ediciones Gudarrama, 1956), p. 452.

13. Letter from Gerald Brenan to Laforet in Agustín Cerezales, *Carmen Laforet* (Madrid: Ministerio de Cultura, 1982), pp. 147–48.

14. William James, *The Varieties of Religious Experience: A Study in Human Nature* (London: Penguin, 1985), p. 405.

15. See Wittgenstein's essay 'From a Lecture Belonging to a Course of Lectures on Description' in Ludwig Wittgenstein, *Lectures and Conversations on Aesthetics, Psychology and Religious Belief* (Oxford: Blackwell, 2001), pp. 37–40.

16. Ibid., p. 37.

17. Thomas Dumm, *Loneliness as a Way of Life* (Cambridge, Mass. and London, England: Harvard University Press, 2008), p. 32.

18. James H. Austin, *Zen Brain Horizons* (Cambridge, Mass. and London, England: MIT Press, 2014), p. 61.

19. Austin, *Zen-Brain Horizons*, p. 78.

20. James H. Austin, *Zen-Brain Reflections* (Cambridge, Mass. and London: The MIT Press, 2006), p. 153.

21. Austin, *Zen-Brain Horizons*, p. 57.
22. *What is an emotion? Classic and Contemporary Readings*, Robert C. Solomon (ed.), (New York and Oxford: Oxford University Press, 2003), Antonio Damasio '*From* the feeling of what happens', pp. 152–57, p. 154. Damasio insists upon the neurological basis of the emotions: 'there is nothing vague, elusive, or nonspecific about emotional responses, and there is nothing vague, elusive, or nonspecific about the representations which can become feelings of emotions. The substrate for emotional feelings is a very concrete set of neural patterns in maps of selected structures,' p. 154. This view provides fruitful material for further investigation into states of bodily relief and their relationship to literature.
23. Damasio, p. 154.
24. Richard Maurice Bucke, *Cosmic Consciousness: A Study in the Evolution of the Human Mind* (New York: Dutton, 1954).
25. Introduction to the 5th edition of the Lecture (1949), cited in Nieli, p. 52.
26. Suchness or *tathātā* in Sanskrit.
27. Nieli, p. 71.
28. Paulina and Eulogio have had a civil marriage during the Second Republic, which would then not have been legally recognised under Franco's dictatorship.
29. Nieli, p. 76.
30. Cerezales Laforet, *Música blanca*, p. 223.
31. See Nieli for a more detailed discussion of this concept, p. 73.
32. James, *Varieties*, p. 483.
33. Ibid., p. 483.
34. Ibid., p. 484.
35. Austin, *Zen-Brain Horizons*, p. 59.
36. Ibid., p. 59.
37. *Tres pasos fuera del tiempo* is the title of the trilogy of Laforet's next three novels, only two of which were published.
38. James, *Varieties*, p. 416.
39. Ibid., p. 508.
40. Austin, *Zen-Brain Horizons*, p. 85.
41. David Aberbach, *Surviving Trauma: Loss, Literature and Psychoanalysis* (New Haven and London: Yale University Press, 1989), p. 91. See chapter five on grief and mysticism. He notes that Santa Teresa lost her mother when she was twelve years old and that a significant number of mystics suffered the loss of either one or both parents in childhood, p. 84, p. 104.
42. Ibid., p. 86.
43. Aberbach suggests that 'union with the lost person might become union with the divine being', p. 94.
44. Ibid., p. 100.
45. It is interesting to observe that Paulina's return to Eulogio will only be bearable due to the fact that she will be surrounded by nature in Las Duras: 'Imaginó su vida en Las Duras. En otoño, la lluvia de hojas de los viejos robles debería ser muy bella. Ahora estaba segura de que podría apreciar la belleza de aquellos grandes árboles y que la soledad le sería buena', p. 334.
46. Aberbach notes something similar: 'Unity, the 'lost parent', offers a haven of solace and hope which the actual lost parent can no longer supply [...] those who suffer childhood loss are more likely than others to feel abandoned and afraid and the need for emotional support, which mysticism, philosophy or art might provide', p. 106.
47. Abraham Maslow, 'Lessons from Peak-Experiences', *Journal of Humanistic Psychology* (1962), 9–18, (p. 10). Quoted in Nieli, p. 126.
48. Cerezales Laforet, *Música blanca*, p. 227.
49. Kane, p. 166.
50. Rolón Barada also suggests that despite Paulina's return to her husband, she does so from a position of psychological freedom: 'se encuentra en una posición de libertad para elegir su camino y su futuro,' Introduction to *La mujer nueva*, p. 13.
51. Cerezales Laforet, *Música blanca*, pp. 77–78.

52. Simone de Beauvoir's discussion of women's experience of mystical states in *The Second Sex* proves interesting. Although de Beauvoir admits that mystical fervour 'can be integrated into active and independent lives', such 'attempts at individual salvation can only result in failures', *The Second Sex* (London: Vintage Books, 2011), p. 734. She avers that the relationship the woman establishes with a divine other remains unreal and she then 'has no grasp on the world; she does not escape her subjectivity; her freedom remains mystified; there is only one way of accomplishing it authentically: it is to provide it by a positive action into human society', p. 734. Santa Teresa's achievements in establishing the Carmelite Order in Spain could be used to contradict de Beauvoir's assertions.

53. Towards the end of Laforet's life she became interested in Eastern thought and consulted works on sophrology. Cerezales Laforet, *Música blanca*, p. 30, p. 262.

54. Private conversation with Cristina Cerezales Laforet.

55. For an interesting comparative discussion of Unamuno's concept of religion and that of Bergson see Fraser, p. 89.

CHAPTER 4

Friendship as Relief
La insolación (1963)

In his introduction to *Al volver* Agustín Cerezales describes *La insolación* as his mother's 'obra cumbre'.[1] From a technical point of view, *La insolación* reveals Laforet at her most sophisticated, primarily through her capacity to represent the protagonist's relationship with his environment, the natural world and his friends Anita and Carlos Corsi through an intimate or watchful point of view.[2] In keeping with Laforet's previous novels, *La insolación* possesses a skeletal plot structure and focuses on Martín Soto's sense impressions which are conveyed through lyrical prose, often resembling ekphrasis. Martín is a talented young artist whose vision is transcribed as if he were painting the scenes depicted, even though he fails to paint consistently when he is on holiday. Through the narrative descriptions of Martín's three summers on the Alicante coast, where he visits his father and step-mother, Laforet reproduces a soporific effect; readers are transported into the hazy, timeless realm of adolescence, which is further enhanced by descriptions of summer heat and a sense of *achronia* associated with the more relaxed rhythms of time spent by the sea. The reading experience of *La insolación* is largely one of taking 'un paso fuera del tiempo' and stepping into Martín's sensation of *arrebato* which he experiences when he is with his bohemian teenage friends.[3]

As is the case for Andrea, Marta and Paulina, Martín is also seeking to alleviate his psychological suffering, the source of which lies in the loss of his mother to tuberculosis shortly after his birth. This has resulted in his acutely sensitive disposition and internal sense of shame.[4] He has inherited his artistic abilities and intelligence from his mother, who married a man of lesser intellect and cultural refinement. It is again clear from the start of Laforet's fourth novel that the representation of the psychological consequences of disruption to the relationship with the mother figure plays a major role in the protagonist's emotional responses to the people with whom he interacts and his distinct point of view, which shares similarities with the detached, observational stance adopted by both Andrea and Marta; one that it is watchful, rather than passive. In a similar manner to Laforet's previous protagonists, Martín searches for relief through a close bond of association with others, in this case the Corsi siblings, with whom he plays during the three summers that he spends in a fictional coastal village called Beniteca. His friendship with Anita and Carlos Corsi is based on the recurrent trope of merger as he seeks to absorb himself in their strange yet superficial bohemian world, one which also contains an absent mother.[5] The brother, sister and Martín seek relief from confronting their loss through distractions involving physical play, acting, childlike acts of revenge and bravado, which in fact mask their failure to articulate their feelings towards the emotional consequences of the loss of the mother. Anita and Carlos's personalities are excessively merged into one another; Carlos's level of psychic *cathexis* in his sister borders on the unnatural as she becomes a quasi-surrogate mother on whom he keeps a vigilant, oedipal-like eye throughout the novel. Martín is overly invested in his adoration for Carlos to whom he seems drawn ineluctably, despite the former's emotional investment in his sister. Martín is also prone to states of meditative absorption akin to the Zen concept of *satori* — a watchful state of contemplation — which may be linked to the psychological process of dissociation, a subject that receives significant attention in the following chapter. A third person omniscient narrator is utilised to articulate Martín's point of view and there are also narrative forays into free indirect discourse when the protagonist's interior thoughts and impressions dominate the narrative, both of which enhance the sense of watchfulness or meditative absorption that dominates the novel. This mode of narration, based on Martín's sustained epiphanic merger with the seaside environment and the Corsi siblings, is glimpsed in *Nada* during Andrea's description of her response to Román's music and her epiphany in front of Barcelona's neo-gothic cathedral; similarly, Paulina's religious conversion in *La mujer nueva* exhibits equivalent poetic properties as the author attempts to move readers closer to an understanding of 'la verdad no sospechada' or Jamesian 'pure experience' based on non-conceptual, intuitive knowledge. As discussed in the introduction, Laforet's treatment of language can provoke a fusion of the linguistic sign and its representational correlative within an experience of emotional totality, as if to create an effect of relief through the plastic properties of the creative act; imagery and word rhythms harmonise to emulate a pure, unmediated experience, wherein relief may come into being if we conceive of reading as a sensory and cognitive experience.

La insolación provides readers with the best example of the author's interest in intuitive understanding and non-conceptual knowledge, especially through direct experience with nature as a source of relief over intellectual interpretation. The invariant trope of oneness, associated with the temporary emotional feeling of relief from suffering, arises again through the narrative effect and one of the greatest achievements of *La insolación* is Laforet's ability to maintain such an effect across each of the three sections of the novel that recount Martín's three summers in Beniteca. Readers are drawn into the protagonist's seemingly passive observation of and absorption into the world around him. Two abrupt *intermedios* interrupt the state of *arrebato* experienced by Martín during his summers in Beniteca. The *intermedios* have a deliberate dislocative function, providing a sense of temporal reality to the atemporal, rapturous summers during which Martín exists beyond his routine commitments to education and family life with his grandparents. In the first edition, the typesetting of these sections is made larger as if to accentuate their separation from the accounts of the three summers on the Alicante coast. Laforet also switches to a more lucid, unembellished prose style to describe Martín's winters with his maternal grandparents in their home in the city, where he experiences acute hunger due to post-war shortages. His isolation from his friends and the beauty of the natural landscape also serve to fuel his deeper sense of alienation from a set of cultural expectations of male behavior which he witnesses as a young adolescent in Franco's Spain.

The theme of gender identity construction is addressed more overtly in Laforet's fourth novel, although on this occasion it is primarily male identity formation that concerns the author. As an adolescent male growing up within the patriarchal culture of Franco's Spain, Martín is expected to emulate the model of masculinity performed by his father, a high-ranking military officer, whose hyper-masculinity is verbalised frequently through his views on how his son is expected to behave. Anticipating Judith Butler's discussion of the performative nature of gender identity construction within a given culture, Laforet explores the manifold ways in which gendered cultural stereotypes act as constraints upon human freedom and stymie an individual's capacity to find tranquillity of being.[6] However, in keeping with Laforet's previous three protagonists, Martín's psychological issues stem from the absence of a loving mother and cannot be linked solely to his cultural experience of masculinity.

It is important to comment on Laforet's decision to switch to a male protagonist in her fourth novel. Martín's story was to be completed within the trilogy *Tres pasos fuera del tiempo*, of which only two novels were published with *Al volver la esquina* being the second part and *Jaque mate* the third.[7] One of the reasons for Laforet's decision to use a male protagonist appears to have been based on the autobiographical features of her first three novels, although it is fair to say that *La insolación* similarly bears the imprint of Laforet's psychological complexes and disordered mourning, impressed once again like a photographic negative within the narrative.[8] *La insolación* also contains the author's personal dilemmas on the relationship between the life of the artist and that of direct, lived experience based on sensorial immediacy. It is significant that Laforet made no mention of her decision to create a male protagonist in her introduction to *La insolación*; instead, she suggested that she was embarking on a new start in her writing career, almost certainly as an attempt to distance herself from the fame she had accrued due to the success of her first novel. Her trilogy, she stated, was to be: 'un comienzo de lo que puedo escribir', suggesting that her previous novels had been a prelude or series of narrative experiments prior to the creation of *La insolación*.[9] Roberta Johnson's views prove instructive on Laforet's decision to change to a male protagonist in the trilogy; she suggests that the male point of view enabled Laforet to 'efectuar sus propósitos feministas'.[10] Thus, Laforet utilises the male gaze and perspective to construct a critique of gender identity formation more generally. Laforet overturns the stereotypical, binary view of men and women possessing different subjectivities and types of emotions. *La insolación* tests the outmoded generalisation that men display traits that render them less emotionally sensitive to others, a role once thought to have stemmed from women's biological capacity to give birth and bond with their offspring. Martín's point of view overturns the idea that women are biologically pre-determined to be more emotionally attuned to their environment. The intimate stance articulated through Martín's point of view illustrates Laforet's understanding of how, at the primary level of experience and emotional response, men and women do not display significantly different modes of feeling and perceiving. *La insolación* also deconstructs the manifold ways in which gender identity is culturally constructed and can serve to distort men's sense of self-identity and delimit their freedom, just as it does for women. Here *La insolación* addresses the wider concept of the absence of psychological relief within society for those individuals who did not wish to conform to prescriptive cultural stereotypes of gender roles and behaviours associated with masculinity and feminity under Francoism. The contemporary relevance of her nascent critique of prescriptive gender roles once again indicates that Laforet was writing well ahead of her time.[11] Martín's decision to reject his father as a role model illustrates Laforet's desire to encourage different models of masculinity and to question all gender sterotypes. As Martín develops across the novel he realises that his father 'no era ahora para él más que una especie de maniquí de hombre fuerte y sano dominado por su mujer — otro maniquí — a los que Martín veía como a través de una niebla' (p. 196). Laforet's use of a male protagonist does, as Johnson suggests, allow her to pursue her feminist ideals, which broadly anticipate the feminist humanism of writers such as Montserrat Roig[12] and Rosa Montero whilst at the same time reiterating the views of earlier twentieth-century feminists such as Karen Horney.[13] There is a sense in which relief finds another iteration through Laforet's treatment of gender roles throughout *La insolación* as Martín seeks to define his identity and locate his sense of self through a critical stance towards men and women adopting false, gendered selves for the sake of social convention. For Martín, relief arises through looking at the world, to a large extent, through non-gendered eyes, although he occasionally falls foul of culturally constructed versions of masculinity. Yet Martín's point of view emanates primarily from a desire to see others as free individuals rather than simply as gendered subjects. When he reluctantly accompanies one of the local girls to a café one Sunday, the other women appear to him as 'maniquíes sin alma, con sus bocas pintadas, con sus ondas simétricas, sus uñas rojo sangre, sus monótonas conversaciones sobre el nacimiento de sus hijos' (p. 69). The perspective of the male narrator permits Laforet to convey her own views on women's entrapment within a narrowly defined femininity from a different and, arguably, more objective perspective than if she had chosen a female protagonist. Laforet is posing the following question: if men can see that women are trapped within limited gender roles then why can women not see this for themselves? The traps of false consciousness permeate Laforet's subtle but nonetheless critical analysis of women's gender roles in Franco's Spain. The women Martín observes remind him of flies who become trapped in spiders' webs who are then unable to release themselves. From that point onwards, he makes the decision to 'liberar a cuanta mosca viese en aquel trance' (p. 69), a direct appeal to the reader to awaken to the performative nature of gender roles and the unconscious processes that entrap individuals from finding their true selves.

However, a contradictory dynamic manifests itself when the actions of Laforet's protagonists' are analysed, as they themselves demonstrate unconscious tendencies to act like trapped flies by becoming enmeshed in relationships in their pursuit of psychological relief, only to end up compromising their freedom. As we have already witnessed with reference to Marta and Paulina, love and religion are explored respectively as forms of relief from personal suffering, yet it is questionable as to whether emotional alleviation is found through Marta's relationship with Pablo and Paulina's encounter with God's love. In Andrea's case, friendship with Ena is used as a means of attenuating the protagonist's suffering and disordered mourning and it is only towards the end of the novel that their relationship undergoes consolidation.[14] In the case of Martín, a similar contradictory dynamic can be traced through his desire for freedom from narrowly defined gender roles and his almost obsessional need to be with Anita and Carlos Corsi during their summer holidays. Whilst Laforet may be exploring the nature of adolescent relationships with their concomitant intensity of depth and fickleness, there is a more familiar pattern to Martín's pursuit of the Corsi siblings, arising from deeper psychological needs that have as their origin, once again, the absence of the mother. It is only through the framework of psychoanalytical thought that Martín's entrapment within his relationship with the Corsi siblings can be understood; his desire for their attention becomes a dramatisation or re-enactment in the present of a deeper longing for a past love, namely that of the mother, and a quest to encounter absolute safety and union with a caregiver.

The level of psychic *cathexis* that Martín invests in the Corsi siblings, especially Carlos, therefore discloses a deeper search for an end to the source of his suffering. The narrator informs us that his mother was also a painter, whose drawings still adorn his maternal grandparents' house (p. 20), and where her diplomas are kept in a box in a similar manner to the 'larga trenza de pelo negro' in *Nada* as a memento and symbolic figuration of the dead mother. The impact of her death on Martín's psychology is revealed indirectly through his reactions to others; he displays difficulty in regulating affect and has weak impulse control, features associated with deeply buried feelings of shame and early abandonment. When the Corsi siblings enter his father's cheaply furnished home, the narrator informs us of Martín's 'antigua vergüenza y timidez' (p. 43), yet we are not supplied with any detailed backstory to the source of his emotions, a typical feature of Laforet's treatment of her protagonists whereby the psychological reaction is described but the source of intimate emotional responses is withheld. We are later given an extraordinary insight into Martín's ingrained defence mechanisms and inability to control emotional hyperarousal which are manifested through anger, dissociation and rapid memory loss.[15] When his father threatens to beat him if the Corsis come into his house again, Martín's reaction is based on a deeper psychological fear than that of his father's violence and is linked to the same experience of disordered mourning felt by Andrea, outlined in chapter one with reference to the work of Bowlby.

> Seguía sintiendo como un resentimiento oscuro y triste que ya no era miedo a paliza alguna, sino algo así como si tuviese demasiado llena el alma y le desbordara anegando y diluyendo aquella alegría del tarde anterior. Horrorizado se dio cuenta de que ni siquiera recordaba cómo eran aquellos chicos, los Corsi. Quizá no los volvería a ver jamás. Sólo recordaba sus siluetas a caballo en lo alto del muro, pero aquellas figuras ahora no tenían cara. (59)

What Laforet shows readers is how the unconscious psychic structures that prevail from unhealed wounds from the past structure present emotional reactions.[16] In Martín's case, he engages in dissociation which, as I will go on to discuss in the next chapter, is characterised by memory loss of certain events. Martín also manifests an irrational fear of not being recognised by the Corsis following his return to Beniteca during the second summer at his father's house, signalling a weak sense of self and anxiety surrounding his relationship with others: 'Martín tuvo un impulso de timidez y de miedo a que los Corsi le desconociesen como le había desconocido Carmen la guardesa o que, como Adela, huyesen de él' (p. 99). Martín also manifests hyper-sensitivity to the pain of others, indicating a deeply held wound within his unconscious that can be re-opened when he witnesses suffering in another. When it is discovered that the Corsi's maid has been hiding her husband Damián in an unused part of the Corsis' rented house in Beniteca due to his alleged murder of a nationalist soldier during the civil war, Martín has a visceral, empathic response to her suffering: 'A Martín le pasó durante un instante algo muy curioso. Tuvo como una unión con el dolor de aquella mujer y casi sintió un desgarramiento físico' (p. 242). Martín's attunement to the suffering of others at such a profound bodily level signals a deeper trauma within the protagonist, yet, as is typical for Laforet's novels, the defensive pattern of non-disclosure of the primary wound or wounds is woven into the story as a narrative pattern of gaps, silences and undisclosed events within the text's unconscious psychic structures.

On occasions, Martín himself becomes the trapped fly in the web spun by the Corsi siblings. His emotional investment in the Corsis is based on an unwillingness to face the superficial nature of their personalities. Roberta Johnson affirms that Anita and Carlos are vacuous and treat Martín as 'their sidekick', someone who is 'generally available in a passive manner for the Corsi-planned activities. Martín does not initiate; he always follows'.[17] If, as Johnson suggests, Anita and Carlos are 'useless jesters' then readers are forced to question whether there are deeper motivations behind the sensitive and intelligent protagonist's reasons for spending significant amounts of time with them.[18] The narrator informs readers of Martín's irrational dependency on the brother and sister: 'No podía separarse de los Corsi. No podía pensar en un día sin ellos. Los Corsi, a veces, le desesperaban, pero no podía tomárselo en cuenta' (p. 77). Despite his awareness of the Corsis' superficiality, he remains drawn to them: 'Martín sabía todo. Sabía que para los Corsi lo importante eran ellos mismos, sus propias opiniones, su propio deseo de las cosas. Martín sólo contaba cuando era él la diversión, la compañía, el aplauso que necesitaban' (p. 85). If Martín knows this, then his relationship with the siblings constitutes a diversion from his deeper suffering and sense of isolation in the world due to the loss of his mother. Their narcissism and use of him as a disposable plaything is matched by

Martín's need to merge his identity temporarily. All parties to the relationship play out their unconscious need for emotional relief through different means; the Corsis sadistically manipulate Martín's need for them, while he subjugates his will to them, creating a collective *folie à trois* which is at some remove from friendship based on reciprocity and altruism. We are reminded once more of Andrea's early relationship with Ena and her search for a compassionate other in which to find solace.

If friendship as a source of relief is thrown into doubt in *La insolación*, there is one aspect of Martín's relationship with the Corsis that brings him pleasure. This has less to do with Anita and Carlos as individuals and is more deeply connected to the natural world in which the teenagers exist over the summer months. Laforet's fourth novel is a celebration of physical activity and play as a means of encountering relief from suffering as well as a positive representation of the form and energetic capacities of the human body.[19] Echoes of Laforet's appreciation of the physical and sensual aspects of the body can be found in Andrea's appraisal of Gloria's beauty while Juan paints her naked and in Marta's appreciation of Sixto's healthy, vital physique. More generally, Laforet pays attention to the quality of her characters' hair, skin tone and the shape of their hands, suggesting her attunement to the way in which early visual and haptic memories of the caregiver are imprinted upon the psyche and to which the human eye and hand return in adulthood as unconscious sources of comfort. Throughout *La insolación* there are frequent descriptions of the adolescents' bodies in action, either running towards the sea, chasing each other, swimming, dancing, climbing, sunbathing or engaged in playful wrestling. Non-sexual touching and kissing is represented as part of their activities, with Anita encouraging Martín and Carlos to kiss on occasions and Carlos taking Martín by the hand in an act of friendship. Throughout the novel, Laforet conveys the exquisite sensation of young people who are physically fit and enjoy the bodily sensation of play but who are also collectively in need of touch due to the absence of a mother. More recent studies of trauma posit the body and not just the psyche as the site of traumatic memory. Suffering is imprinted and retained within the body and the brain and Martín's obsessive need to be within the physical presence of the Corsis suggests that his suffering undergoes temporary relief at the level of the body rather than the intellect.[20] Thus, it is within their dynamic playful interactions that their relationship develops rather than through conversations about each others' emotions or inquiries into their past lives. When Martín attempts to talk to Anita and Carlos on one occasion about 'ciertas inquietudes de su espíritu y cómo había pintado aquel invierno a la acuarela y que empezaría con el oleo el próximo curso' they remain disinterested, shut off in their own 'mundo cerrado' (p. 123). His depth of feeling and intellectual curiosity sits oddly alongside their frivolous natures and disregard for anything that exists outside their domain of understanding. Martín's physical relationship with the Corsi siblings provides him with relief. Their corporal proximity forms the substance of the reality of their relationship: 'Lo más real era la sensación de sus tres cuerpos, sentados los tres sobre la pinocha' (p. 86). A bond based on physical association unites Martín with his friends and the tripartite unity of the three friends at play and at rest together symbolises the triad of mother-father-child which is replicated in the relationship between Andrea, Ena and Jaime in *Nada*.[21] At their core is a search for forgetting, a longing for relief from traumatic grief and a sense of living within a suspended moment outside of time, or taking, *un paso fuera del tiempo*:

> en general lo que hacían los tres era vivir juntos los días del sol — todos los días como un largo día con las interrupciones de la noche, de las horas de las comidas y de los domingos por la mañana —, y la felicidad de estar juntos los tres era algo casi intangible, a pesar de las pequeñas y grandes amarguras de Martín. (79–80)

The narrator suggests that Martín's 'amarguras' are still present despite the sensation of sunstroke or *achronia* that he feels when he is in the Corsis' company. Here we are provided with further evidence of how Martín seeks relief from a deeper anxiety and that his suffering persists within the present. When the Corsis' father returns temporarily to visit his children, who are being looked after by Frufru, a family friend, Martín's reaction unveils the deeper, subjective patterns of defence that structure his behaviour and his reactions to those around him. Anita and Carlos turn their attention to their father and Martín is left standing alone in front of their house:

> Se quedó solo otra vez. Tenía metido en los ojos el dibujo de aquella casa que veía enfrente, con sus viejos tejados, su torrecilla, sus ventanas enrejadas y la pintura roja y descascarillada en los lugares donde los muros no estaban cubiertos con reredaderas de jazmín o de flores azules. Aquella casa empezó a hacérsele extraña a Martín, extraña y enemiga. (249)

Laforet delineates the beginnings of the process of psychological dissociation through Martín's response as he transforms the house into an abstract representation that becomes unfamiliar and hostile, but it is his psyche that makes it so as he projects his anger onto the Corsis' house. He feels the Corsis' shift of attention towards their father as a sudden emotional disinvestment in him, but it in fact reveals an ingrained psychic response based on Martín's fear of abandonment, which has its origins in the early loss of his mother. He suddenly feels 'terriblemente solo cuando oyó las voces del señor Corsi y de sus amigos' (p. 249), signalling a rapid regression to a child-like state of fear and lack of protection. Friendship with the Corsis is a mask for a deeper longing for intimate association with the missing parent and Martín's sudden dissociation from the house where he has enjoyed a surrogate family life discloses Laforet's profound understanding of the psychological processes linked to traumatic loss, especially in relation to affect regulation. As Daniel Hill observes, underlying an individual's incapacity to regulate strong emotion is a feeling of shame which has its roots in attachment disorders: 'When shamed, we are rendered speechless and suffused with painful aloneness and exposure. It is an all-encompassing experience of hopelessness and helplessness in which the self, in its entirely, is felt to be devalued and shunned.'[22] Martín suddenly feels a loss of love due to the physical absence of the Corsi siblings; his primal fear of abandonment results in him running wildly back to his father's house, in flight from his emotions rather than from anything tangible: 'sin saber lo que hacía emprendió una retirada velocísima, corriendo pinos arriba, con desesperación' (p. 250).[23] Despite the 'insolación' that Martín feels during his summers in Beniteca with the Corsis, Laforet's representation of friendship is almost entirely negative in her fourth novel. Anita and Carlos fail to provide Martín with the inner security and emotional bond that he seeks and there is a case for arguing that the hollowness and instability of his relationship with the siblings on occasions represents a retraumatisation of his loss based on an unconscious and quasi-masochistic desire to repeat the past. It is significant that his friendship with the Corsis entails him forgetting his vocation and the development of his artistic skills every summer, even though the physical environment provides him with multiple opportunities for painting. This suggests that something is at stake through Martín's propensity to merge and lose his sense of identity within that of an Other, or others; as I have already outlined in chapter two, a similar process is at work in Marta's pursuit of Pablo's friendship. Laforet appears to be suggesting that feigned friendship based on need rather than altruism carries risks for the individual in pursuit of psychic relief. At the close of the novel, after he has fled his father's house due to a misunderstanding over Carlos sleeping in his bedroom one evening, Martín returns to his maternal grandparents' apartment and concludes that 'Ni siquiera los Corsi entendían la amistad. Nadie' (p. 363). As obsessive adoration of Pablo was for Marta, friendship serves as a *via negativa* for Martín, and a journey in search of relief is transformed into an awakening to the concept of true friendship: 'Don Narciso y los abuelos eran amigos' (p. 363).[24] Martín accepts his grandparents and a long-standing relationship with a family friend as sources of nuture at the end of the novel. Although Laforet continues the story of Martín's friendship with the Corsis in the second novel of the trilogy, a similar drama of intense association that finally leads to separation is played out again through the protagonist's relationship with Anita. The ending of *Al volver* delivers a further ambiguous conclusion to Martín's capacity to find relief and presents readers with a reiteration of Laforet's protagonists' cyclical quest for some body or phenomenon through which to end their despair.

Despite Martín's pursuit of intimate connection through friendship as a form of psychological relief, art is posited as a potential place where solace and the solitude he needs to develop his thoughts and individual perspective on his life might be found. *La insolación* contains a limited number of Martín's discourses on art, mainly arising when he tries to steer conversations with the Corsis towards a deeper intellectual level. Following a day spent on his own, when the Corsis are away from Beniteca with their father and one of his friends, Martín undergoes a sudden revelation about his future direction as an artist. In contrast to Paulina's spiritual merger with God, Martín's epiphanic experience is not described in detail, although the narrator provides an explanation of the outcome and his conclusions about his revelation. He relates his experience to Carlos: 'No te puedes imaginar lo que llegué a ver ayer. Un día sin importancia en que está uno solo sentado en las dunas: no sucede nada ni pasa nada alrededor y de pronto se ve claro' (p. 308). Solitude and absorption within the present moment leads Martín to a quasi-Nietzschian revelation, a form of radical nihilism which involves the severance of all intimate bonds, including that of friendship:

> No me podrá atar nada. Necesito una libertad absoluta. Ningún lazo familiar. [...] Ni ataduras de patria tampoco. Esa idea de la Patria es forzada, es utópica. Ni ataduras de religion, ni mucho menos sociales, incluso en las relaciones del sexo, incluso en eso he visto dos caminos de liberación; el de Freud, de no retener ningún impulso para que las inhibiciones no te aten, o el de los místicos, superándolo por el espíritu. Y desde luego, lazos familiares ninguno. Ya te lo he dicho. Ni ataduras de amistad. Nada absolutamente. [...] Creo que un artista tiene que ser eso, un hombre liberado en absoluto. Sólo así puede crear su mundo. (306–07)

Martín's rejection of all emotional ties in the name of his art smacks of hypocrisy, superiority and naivity since the Nietzschian superman existence he envisions runs counter to his deepest need — that of emotional intimacy. One is forced to consider whether Laforet is engaging in an ironic critique of the tortured artist as she did in *Nada*, through her depiction of Andrea's bohemian friends, and in *La isla*, through the representation of Pablo. Martín's sudden realisation of his need for emotional disinvestment and existential alienation from the world and others for the sake of his art rapidly dissolves as soon as he desires the company of the Corsis again and the sense of *arrebato* that he feels when he is in their presence. Throughout Laforet's novels there is little indication that artistic creation carries within it the healing properties necessary for psychic repair or even temporary relief. On the contrary, art appears to perturb Laforet's protagonists in both *La isla*, *La insolación* and *Al volver* through its failure to bring about sustained relief or facilitate a resolution of unresolved psychic trauma. In this regard, Laforet's fiction overturns the view within trauma theory that writing offers the possibility of facing and healing an individual's trauma. Laforet posits non-conceptual knowledge and direct experience as the conduit to experiencing states of relief; her narratives also suggest that joy or *gozo* is encountered in the non-representational, based on a negative movement away from artistic or linguistic expression towards Jamesian 'pure experience' or meditative states.[25]

La insolación provides important insights into states of relief as they are felt within the intimate realm of the emotions which, despite their resistance to linguistic representation, find aesthetic form through Martín's distinct mode of perceiving his environment, illustrated in detail on several occasions in the novel. In her introduction to *La insolación*, Laforet articulated her desire to represent a sensation of intimacy through Martín Soto. The novel, according to Laforet: 'narra un primer impacto adolescente y completamente íntimo, con referencias apenas esbozadas sobre los años cuarenta, cuarenta y uno y cuarenta y dos en España.'[26] It is not the historical milieu of post-war Spain that forms the subject of the narrative but 'el ambiente de arrebato y de interés que únicamente para un muchacho, Martín Soto, tienen los personajes y los sucesos que se narran.'[27] It is significant that Laforet re-employs the term *arrebato*, alerting readers to the invariant theme of a deeper, transcendent reality or state of oneness that her protagonists seek out at various stages in the three preceding novels, a state of pure being or the self being at one with itself. This inward state of relief is expressed through Martín's method of observing objective reality through which the object or phenomenon is perceived in its *suchness*, the condition of pure perception which transcends the ego of the perceiving subject. It was Laforet's desire in her fourth novel to construct a method of representing Martín's intimate perceptual world through a new aesthetic approach to narrative point of view. Laforet expressed an interest in Allen Ginsburg's efforts to encounter a 'new method for attempting to find the exact words to express pure sensation'.[28] This stance has left critics struggling to locate *La insolación* within a recognisable literary genre due to the author's distinct point of view, which works to defamiliarise readers from their more conventional perspectives on reality and open them up to a deeper level of transcendental experience and intuitive knowledge. Illanes Adaro suggests that Laforet shows evidence of being 'una escritora realista' but goes on to add 'pero su realismo es peculiar'.[29] Similarly, Elisabetta Noè struggles to articulate Laforet's version of reality and states that what the author creates is 'una realidad no fácilmente discifrable'.[30] We gain a sense of Laforet's efforts to describe 'pure sensation' in an article of 1951:

> El canto de un pájaro, una gota de agua que en un momento tuvo dentro de ella los colores del arco iris, sigue teniéndolos dentro de mi recuerdo, y quizá durante años estén dentro de ese organismo mortal que es mi cuerpo, y quizá siempre enriquezcan mi espíritu inmortal.[31]

Laforet gives us a description of what Russell T. Hurlburt describes as 'pristine inner experience' which has a longer history within Eastern Buddhist and Taoist traditions.[32] From simple, direct observation, dissociated from egocentric striving, arises a sense of anachronia or timelessness, a state of intimate experience which Laforet delineates through her treatment of point of view throughout *La insolación*. The term 'transcendental realism' is a fitting mode of describing Laforet's treatment of Martín's point of view, although even this term may prove inadequate to convey the mindful state of suchness projected through his inner experience and which stands as another trope of relief.[33] Hurlburt suggests that our pristine experience is our 'own ultimate intimacy', although he is sceptical about literature's ability to represent this state of being.[34] *La insolación* suggests otherwise as Laforet demonstrates her capacity to express Martín's intimate reality at the semantic level, challenging once again the Wittgensteinian view that gesture must replace language when it comes to representing non-conceptual knowledge. In Laforet's case, language is transmuted into the gesture of expressive intimate experience. As Johnson reminds us, for a writer such as Laforet 'observation and experience come first' and interpretation or conceptualisation of experience are of less importance.[35] This is reflected through Martín's method of observation whereby his sense of self drops away and he appears to fuse with the objects or scene under description. This sense of merger entails being fully immersed within the present moment as the narrator indicates: 'Lo importante era el minuto presente' (p. 318), with past and future falling away or collapsing into the oneness of the now. At an early stage in the narrative we are introduced to Martín's tendency towards full absorption in the present whilst he is watching his father cleaning his gun:

> Eugenio había sacado la pistol, la escobilla, trapos blancos y grasa para limpiar el arma. Todo esto estaba sobre el hule. Martín se sintió fascinado por

aquella pistol desde el primer momento. Le gustaba el olor de aquellos trapos
manchados de grasa, se los llevaba a la nariz. Se acumulaban alas transparentes
de hormigas voladoras sobre el hule. Estas hormigas daban vueltas alrededor de
la luz junto a las mariposas nocturnas y depués iban soltando sus alas.

   Un hermoso silencio entre el revolar de los insectos, un silencio cortado sólo
por las manipulaciones del padre con la pistol: pequeños golpes al dejarla en la
mesa, chasquidos del cargador vacío. (26–27)

Although this example indicates the presence of Martín's volitional self and thus
the presence of the ego, a pool of stillness is opened up both in terms of Martín's
absorption within the present moment and through the reading experience itself.[36]
Relief arises through both the narrative act of reading and Martín's mindful point
of view. The embellished, dark prose of *Nada* has evolved into the lyrical fluidity of
poetic prose in *La insolación*, which is enhanced by rhythmic assonance that sequences
into deeper musical resonance within the body: 'alas transparentes de hormigas
voladoras sobre el hule'. The aesthetics of relief are played out as a form of semantic
music that arises from the fusion of Martín's vision and the emotional reverberations
arising from Laforet's prose which impact the reader at the level of the senses. This is
an example of what Claudia Milstead has observed in the work of modernist poets,
most notably T. S. Eliot, whereby 'we release all barriers between the self and Other
and experience "music heard so deeply/That it is not heard at all, but you are the
music/while the music lasts" '.[37] Martín inhabits a Zen-like observational stance and
sees things in their pure simplicity: 'Las hormigas con alas y las mariposas volaban
alrededor de la lámpara. Llegó del jardín un olor a tierra reseca y, a ráfagas, el olor
del lejano jazminero. Martín miraba hacia el mantel mientras comía y sonreía a
la vez como un bendito' (p. 270). Laforet presents readers with an insight into the
intimate spaces of relief that exist within Martín's existence, spaces that lie outside
conventional understandings of time and are represented through an almost purely
objective point of view. Within these segments of Jamesian pure experience 'there
is no *inner dualism* of knower and known' and Martín becomes unified with the
moment and the phenomena under observation.[38] Self-transcendence brings inner
peace as he absorbs himself in the silent monadic experience of oneness during
which his pursuit of friendship with the Corsis is rendered insignificant.

   These silent moments of relief may provide readers with an insight into why
Martín refuses or is unable to paint while he is in Beniteca. Martín cannot represent
these experiences in his art either because he has not found an adequate form to
do so, or he refuses to attempt to shape the non-conceptual into artistic expression.
Relief is lived and sensually savoured, not removed from its source of experience
through representation, even though the irony of Laforet's writing is that she is
herself endeavouring to express the essence of relief through various means. *La
insolación* does not suggest that painting satiates Martín's desire for relief. It is
only during the first week of the first summer that he fills up a sketch pad with
drawings of his pregnant step-mother, soldiers, priests and young *falangistas* as he
records his new environment. He then stops and does not paint or draw apart from
his sojurns with his grandparents during the winter months. Yet Martín's painting
goes on by other means while he is in Beniteca as Laforet embeds descriptions of

the protagonist observing scenes as if he were painting them: 'El pueblo parecía blanco y dormido con sus calles estrechas. "Las sombras y la cal, eso es todo", pensó Martín sin darse cuenta de que lo pensaba. Sin darse cuenta de lo que recogía su cerebro como pintor' (p. 231). As a painter, his brain is receiving the scene as a series of shapes, tones and hues which are interlaced with his emotions; yet Martín does not seek to paint it, as he savours them in their state of purity as if to suggest that pristine experience negates artistic or possibly any form of representational expression. Another example arises later in the novel:

> En el sol de la mañana, el mundo era perfecto y simple tambíen. Adela reñía a gritos al asistente en el jardín, un pájaro se disolvía en la luz. Sombras y claridades vivas lo llenaban todo. Un mundo de claridad y de contornos para ser interpretado, dibujado, pintado. (338)

Laforet stops short of ekphrasis and instead gives semantic expression to Martín's mode of perception, the quiet, Zen-like observational stance of disengaged watchfulness: seeing phenomena in their purest state, ostensibly devoid of subjectivity. Milstead informs us that within the Zen tradition 'to name a concept or object forces it into a predetermined and intellectualised category', a process from which the follower of Zen philosophy refrains.[39] We detect a similar pattern of resistance to representation through Martín's refusal to paint subjects or experiences that strike him as beautiful or fascinating. For example, when Anita, Carlos and Martín gather at the burial of his family dog, poisoned by Damián, the protagonist knows that the event will be lost forever and that he will not be able to paint it:

> La escena que le rodeaba le pareció de pronto muy fantástica. Anita con su velo sobre la cabeza y sobre los hombres, Carlos con el brazo en cabestrillo y el cabello inflamado por el sol, las piedras, los cardos, el aire caliginoso, los golpes de azadón que daba Cirilio tan cerca de ellos. Era una escena que no se sentía capaz de dibujar. Que nunca dibujaría, ni pintaría. Una escena destinada a perderse para siempre. (186)

There is of course a certain rhetorical irony to this narrative sequence since although Martín cannot paint the scene, Laforet records it within the story of *La insolación*. Yet Martín's knowledge of its mutability expresses an essential feature of all artistic creation, namely the inadequacy of representational forms to express lived experience whether we consider that to be the abstract realm of our unconscious or the objects, people and rhythms of everday life. Laforet is suggesting that first order experience and emotion, Hurlburt's 'pristine' and James's 'pure' experience, remain detached from a secondary order of symbolic representation even though, as we have witnessed with reference to the conversion sequence in *La mujer nueva*, intimate states of pure experience are closely approximated by Laforet through language. Laforet's aesthetics of relief may then be construed as a problematic and contradictory encounter since the experience of solace and the temporary suspension of suffering defy representational expression yet as a writer she was striving to capture their impact upon subjectivity and the emotions. Martín's position towards his art whilst in Beniteca aligns itself with Laforet's attitude towards her art, illustrating the indirect correspondence that exists between the author's personal concerns and the actions and thoughts of her protagonists. As Johnson notes: 'when confronted with the choice between writing about life and experiencing it directly, Carmen Laforet prefers the latter', resulting in 'a serious obstacle to her publishing'.[40] Laforet's struggles between following her need to create and her longing to live life unmediated by art are directly encapsulated in Martín's attitude towards his vocation.

The idea of the unsayable and the inexpressibility of relief are pushed to their limits in *La insolación* when Laforet presents a narrative viewpoint that adopts a godlike or cosmic perspective on the events being narrated, as if to dimish the relevance of the human subject to an insignificant role. We have already glimpsed Laforet's treatment of allocentric awareness during Paulina's conversion on the train to Madrid when the narratorial point of view acquires a cosmic expansiveness and Paulina's dilemmas are reduced to nothing against the natural world. The *via negativa* of the self denying the self and subjugation to God, reminiscent of Juan de la Cruz's writing, is posited as the end to human suffering and, possibly, the quintessential expression of relief. *La mujer nueva* suggests that spiritual union with God as a source of emotional relief for Paulina, whereas *La insolación* promotes a non-individualistic, cosmic consciousness through which the human subject is diminished to a series of gestures against a unified universe.[41] In what is perhaps the most striking narrative sequence to be found in terms of narrative viewpoint across Laforet's novels, the centrality of human life within the wider cosmos is reduced to its true scale as the narrator's point of view vertiginously elevates itself above the events of the story to occupy a god-like perspective. In a moment of pure joy and enervation, Martín lets out a primeaval scream and runs into the sea with his friends:

> Corría detrás de Anita, y Carlos corría ahora detrás de él. No había complicaciones en el mundo. La tierra, ese planeta, giraba lentamente bañando de sol y de luna y de negrura, alternativamente, las distintas partes de su vientre. Desde los espacios nadie podría suponer la efervescencia de aquellos momentos, ni las muertes que estaban ocurriendo, no las vidas que llegaban nuevas, ni las floraciones periódicas, ni las nieves y hielos. Ni las injusticias ni los odios, ni los simples amores de las criaturas humanas. Ni la sencilla felicidad de sentirse vivos que tenían aquellos tres muchachos. Nadie más que el ojo de Dios podría traspasar todo ese vasto panorama aquella noche.
>
> Martín y sus amigos fueron sólo unas risas, un chapoteo en el agua templada. Tres sensaciones de vida, con el círculo brillante del verano — brillante de día, brillante de noche — envolviéndoles. (331–32)

Laforet's account of Martín's suffering, his painful sensitivity and regressive longing for merger with the Corsis, is rendered insignificant within the wider perspective of the cosmos and eye of God. Martín, Carlos and Anita are reduced to sounds and splashes within the water, gestures in nature rather than individuals with subjectivities. Their place in the world is diminished to a few chords within a wider, unified vibration of life, summer, days and nights. Laforet invokes the spirit of English Romanticism as the young people are 'rolled round in earth's diurnal course,' not conjoined through death but through the recurrent life force or spiritual presence of a being greater than themselves.[42] The invariant theme of oneness and non-dual merger is beautifully encapsulated in these lines which convey, better than any others in Laforet's novels, what she conceived as the source of relief: the loss of self within the wider world and the universe. Laforet establishes a point of view that 'views scenes *anonymously*' whereby the subject's 'perspective is emancipated', indicating the author's efforts to represent phenomena or experiences objectively, even though we must always recognise the presence of the narrating subject and creative presence of the author.[43] Embedded within the reading process is an appeal to readers to escape from 'an all-encompassing non-dual frame of reference' and for their perception to rise above 'so many Self-centred attachments'.[44] The spiritual overtones of Laforet's fiction arise again as she encapsulates, albeit inadvertently, the Buddhist concept of watchfulness:

> The wise man who by watchfulness conquers thoughtlessness is as one who free from sorrows ascends the palace of wisdom and there, from its high terrace, sees those in sorrow below; even as a wise strong man on the holy mountain might behold the many unwise far down below on the plain.[45]

Laforet's cosmic stance encourages readers to unimagine themselves as the centre of the world as one mode of finding relief. We must return to the author's intentions through her creation of such a watchful stance within her fiction, both at the level of the narrator and of the protagonist. There appears to be a desire on the part of the author to establish, as Gregory Currie has described it, 'a special mind-world transaction' within the narratorial point of view which 'challenge us to experience [...] events in unfamiliar ways'.[46] Taking on the watchful perspective of Martín, or even God, acquires a moral dimension 'either because it reveals merit in a point of view to which we were previously insensitive, or because it helps us understand, from the inside, the attractions of a distorted way of seeing things'.[47] The moral and didactic properties of Laforet's fiction issue from her efforts to distort readers' ordinary way of seeing things and to conjoin their experience with that of the protagonist and, at times, the narrator in a bid to enlargen readers' own point of view. Thus, the god-like stance, which looks down on Martín and his friends in the sequence previously quoted temporarily becomes that of the reader. The self transcends the self through the aesthetic representation and, I would argue, experience of relief is evinced through language. Laforet, following Currie's arguments, elicits 'an experience of sharing that depends on psychologically important mechanisms of joint attention and imitation'.[48] I would go further and suggest that the author and reader meet within the space of linguistic merger, creating the possibility of a new transactional, atemporal space; readers temporarily take 'un paso fuera del tiempo' and relinquish their point of view into a psychologically liberating domain. The performance of relief within the aesthetics of language has occurred.

And yet, Laforet illustrates the short-lived nature of relief. *La insolación* demonstrates how the human subject must always return to the self with its complex needs, deficits and unresolved anguish. At the level of abstract intellect Martín states that he has the capacity to 'prescindir de todo' (p. 310) for the sake of his art but his behaviour towards the Corsis and the ending of the novel suggest that his emotional needs require contact with loving others. Self-transcendence, or even art for that matter, cannot substitute the relief provided by physical and emotional intimacy. When his father mistakenly suspects Martín of a homosexual encounter with Carlos following his discovery of them asleep in the same bed, Martín is forced to flee and return to his grandparents' apartment, a place that provides him with the familiar, mundane and steadfast presence of stable, loving relationships. Refuge and relief lie not in the tantalising bohemian Corsi household but in the simple space of Martín's room as he reimagines it:

> La idea de su cuarto con el escritorio, con el ventanillo junto al techo donde entraba por las noches la luz del patio que se reflejaba en la pared de enfrente en cuadrados superpuestos como en una pintura, le dio la sensación de un refugio deseado. (364)

Martín feels a final, primal desire to flee as he stands below the windows of his grandparents' home. The figure of Martín standing alone in the street with his suitcase, recalls Andrea's arrival at her maternal grandparent's house on *calle* Aribau in Barcelona; both protagonists embody a posture of departure and arrival which is conjoined in a trope of stasis and uncertainty about the future direction of their lives and finding a means through which to end their internal psychological despair. The final physical gesture of *La insolación* is that of Martín being welcomed by his grandmother's hands as she extends them towards him in a familiar fashion. The dual features of flight and the pursuit of safety are encapsulated in the closing pages of the novel. Friendship, abstract reasoning about his art and dissolution of his self through moments of absorption have not borne Martín towards the feeling of absolute safety and relief from suffering that he desires and which have their origins in the premature death of his mother. The simplicity of his grandmother's gesture, the haptic encounter of hand to hand and body to body brings Martín a sense of peace but, as the second novel in the trilogy suggests, it is shortlived as the protagonist continues to pursue his search for psychological repair.

Throughout *La insolación* it is not the historical circumstances of Franco's Spain that Laforet seeks to foreground but the deeper inner reality of the protagonist and his 'reacciones psicológicas'. Yet Laforet does not abdicate her concern with the nefarious features of Franco's dictatorship and its culture of repression. On the contrary, she recognised how the individual's natural quest for self-exploration and freedom from psychological despair remained uncurtailed in Spain during the post-war years, despite the regime's efforts to enforce a form of homogeneity on the country's collective psyche. At a more general level, Laforet's novels pose important questions about the treatment (or lack of it) of mental health conditions arising from attachment disorder, domestic violence and other psychological illnesses associated with parental loss and trauma.[49] For example, Román and Juan both have pervasive mental health issues, while Angustias and Pino exhibit chronic anxiety problems. It remains too simplistic to attribute their pathologies to the legacy of the Spanish Civil war and post-war deprivation since each novel reveals that the cause of their pathologies runs deeper and, more often than not, it is disordered attachment, family trauma, sexual repression and the effects of a patriarchal, religious society that lie at the heart of her characters' distorted psychologies, all of which existed within Spanish society prior to Franco's victory in 1939. While other writers of her generation such as Juan Goytisolo and Josep Maria Castellet focused their attention on the role of the writer under dictatorship conditions and, in the 1950s, set about formulating narrative strategies to avoid censorship through the techniques of *objetivismo*, Laforet was exploring the ongoing subject of psychological suffering at the level of the individual. The underlying intention of Laforet's writing was not to depict 'una psicología de masa', but to focus on the intimate reactions and sensations of each of her protagonists.[50] Although we may encounter some correspondences, one cannot rely on simple, causal connections between the representation of the personal suffering of Laforet's protagonists and the wider social context. The intricacies of an individual's psychology and the shaping of human consciousness across a life time remained the foundation upon which her novels were built rather than her concerns with immediate historical reality. It may come as no surprise then that Laforet's final novel takes as its central theme the subject of psychiatry and an exploration of the relationship between patient and doctor as a means of finding relief through the therapeutic encounter.

Notes to Chapter 4

1. Introduction to *Al volver la esquina*, (Barcelona: Destino, 2003), p. 10.
2. Here I am again drawing on the Zen concept of *satori*: a watchful state of contemplation.
3. During the late 1950s Laforet spent time with her husband in Tangiers. There she enjoyed the company of an ecletic range of people who may have served as her inspiration for the bohemian approach to life of the Corsi family in *La insolación*.
4. The relationship between grief and shame remains an important feature of Laforet's fiction and will be discussed in greater detail in the following chapter.
5. Throughout *La insolación* it is never made clear how the Corsi family's mother died.
6. Judith Butler, *Gender Trouble* (London: Routledge, 1990).
7. The manuscript of *Jaque mate* has not been found to date. It may have been lost in a suitcase that Laforet used during her period of residence in Rome and subsequent travels.
8. Prior to the publication of *La insolación*, Laforet's husband and closest critic had been encouraging her to adopt a more objective stance in her novels and to concentrate less on her own personal struggles as material for her narratives. They separated in 1970 but never formally divorced.
9. Carmen Laforet, Introduction to *La insolación*, p. 7.
10. Roberta Johnson, 'La novelística de Carmen Laforet y el género negro', *Arbor*, 720 (2006), 517–25, (p. 521).
11. Although Laforet never aligned herself with feminist thought or feminism as a political movement or philosophy, her representation of gender roles in *La insolación* locate her alongside other contemporary Western feminists who were discussing women's sense of entrapment within patriarchal social structures. Betty Friedan's *The Feminine Mystique* was published in the same year as *La insolación*. Laforet's close friend Lilí Álvarez wrote the introduction to the first Spanish translation, indicating that she may have had a deeper knowledge of second wave feminism than might have been originally thought.
12. See, for example, Roig's *Mujeres en busca de un nuevo humanismo* (Barcelona: Salvat, 1981).
13. Here again we witness the difficulty of locating Laforet within strict historical and national parameters.
14. It is significant that the older Andrea makes no mention of Ena, suggesting that Andrea is more self-sufficient and less in need of their relationship than her younger, defended self.
15. There is an early indication of Martín's tendency to experience dissociative amnesia, a subject that will receive greater attention in the following chapter.

16. Here we discern the extent to which Laforet's novels facilitate greater understanding of psychoanalytical concepts, rather than the other way around. For further discussion of this point see Pierre Bayard, *Peut-on appliquer la littérature à la psychoanalyse?* (Paris: Minuit, 2004).

17. Johnson, *Carmen Laforet*, p. 86.

18. Ibid, p. 92.

19. Swimming forms an important physical diversion for Marta Camino as it did for Carmen Laforet.

20. For a comprehensive discussion of the imprint of trauma within the body see: Bessel van der Kolk, *The Body Keeps the Score: Mind, Brain and the Body in the Transformation of Trauma* (London: Penguin Random House, 2015).

21. Laforet also utilises the figure of three within the relationships between Eulogio, Antonio and Paulina in *La mujer nueva* and Anita, Zoila and Martín in *Al volver*.

22. Daniel Hill, *Affect Regulation Theory: A Clinical Model* (New York and London: W. W. Norton and Company, 2015), p. 123.

23. There are several moments in *Nada* when Andrea is described as taking sudden flight through the act of running. The connection with anxiety and the stress response are clear.

24. For an interesting discussion of Martín's psychological process of maturation see Mark P. Del Mastro, 'Identity Achievement and Lost Innocence in Carmen Laforet's *La insolación*', *Ojáncano: Revista de Literatura Española*, 25 (2004), 43–60.

25. This may go some way towards explaining why Laforet stopped writing novels after *Jaque mate*, although she did publish a limited number of articles and two travelogues. Correspondence with friends and fellow writers also continued.

26. Carmen Laforet, 'Por qué de esta trilogía' in *La insolación*, pp. 5–10, p. 8.

27. Ibid, p. 8.

28. Johnson, *Carmen Laforet*, p. 40. Ginsburg had tried using a variety of methods to do this, one of which required attaching an electrical device to his head to activate brain cells that are used less frequently (Johnson, p. 40). Here we note the similarities between contemporary neuroscientific research into left and right brain hemisphere activity under certain conditions. Laforet was primarily interested in representing alternative cognitive states, and her fiction suggests direct knowledge of such experiences. Overall, it was her writerly intention to create as style that emanated from a position of pure seeing, although whether this is ever possible for the perceiving subject is a matter of debate.

29. Illanes Adaro, p. 194.

30. Elisabetta Noè, 'Otro paso "fuera del tiempo": *Al volver la esquina* de Carmen Laforet', *Revista de Literatura*, 69 (2007), 559–76, (p. 562).

31. Carmen Laforet, 'El reloj interno' *Destino*, August 4, 1951.

32. Russell T. Hurlburt, *Investigating Pristine Inner Experience* (Cambridge: Cambridge University Press, 2011).

33. Here I am not referring to Kant's discussion of transcendental realism but to Laforet's unique representation of a numionous realm of experience.

34. Hurlburt, p. 411, p. 412.

35. Johnson, *Carmen Laforet*, p. 41.

36. As Illanes Adaro notes, 'Carmen Laforet le da mucha significación al momento en sí', p. 58.

37. C. Milstead, *The Zen of Modern Poetry: Reading Eliot, Stevens, and Williams in a Zen Context* (unpublished doctoral thesis, Knoxville, University of Tennessee, 1998), p. 93.

38. Taylor and Wozniak, p. xvi.

39. Milstead, p. 180.

40. Johnson, *Carmen Laforet*, p. 34.

41. Wittgenstein's views on gesture replacing language are pertinent here, although Laforet attempts to provide the gesture with a linguistic correlative.

42. William Wordsworth, 'A Slumber Did My Spirit Steal' 1799.

43. Austin, *Zen-Brain Horizons*, p. 146.

44. Ibid.

45. *The Dhammapada* (Harmonsworth, Middlesex: Penguin Classics, 1975), p. 28.

46. Gregory Currie, *Narratives and Narrators: A Philosophy of Stories* (Oxford: Oxford University Press, 2010), p. 219, pp. 86–87.

47. Ibid, pp. 86–87.

48. Currie, p. 87.

49. This is a subject that deserves more detailed inquiry within the study of post-war Spanish and Catalan culture. The quality of mental health provision is touched upon Laforet's short story *El regreso* (1954).

50. 'El por qué de esa trilogia'?, *La insolación*, p. 9.

CHAPTER 5

Psychoanalysis as Relief
Al volver la esquina (2004)

'Todo es un círculo que se cierra, todo.'[1]

The symbol of the closed or open circle which Laforet used to describe the form of her first novel serves as a more encompassing figure for all her novels. The last novel to be discussed here, *Al volver la esquina*, is situated on an arc that curves back towards *Nada* and it provides a broader explanatory framework for the invariant theme of relief that dominates Laforet's narratives. Reading Laforet's novels along a reverse trajectory enables us to link her protagonists together on a path that always leads backwards toward the figurative absence of the dead mother and the vacant, yet emotionally replete, space of silent grief. This method of reading the novels serves as a metaphor for the process of psychoanalysis, which forms the central narrative theme of *Al volver* and has informed the methodological basis of this study. Laforet's final novel functions as a container for each preceding novel; like a series of Russian dolls, each protagonist's psyche is merged within Martín Soto's. Indeed, her protagonists may be read as one collective psyche, even as each one embarks on a different journey to seek objects, others or experiences through which to find relief from their suffering.[2] Laforet's novels collectively suggest that an endpoint to the protagonists' quest is out of reach, and that the cycle of repetition and a renewed search for relief remains imminent within the return to the starting point. This circular pattern reiterates the psychoanalytical view of the human subject's unconscious search throughout her lifetime for a return to her beginnings in spite of the seemingly temporal progression of life.[3] Within Laforet's novels readers hear the faint echo of the Homeric odyssey, only it is a journey transposed onto the psyche of each protagonist, each one in pursuit of an elusive feeling of safety, combined with a sense of encountering a home. Once more, it is through Martín Soto's 'reacciones psicológicas' in Laforet's last published novel that we witness the pattern of searching and not finding an endpoint to suffering. Relief is sought, found temporarily and lost again, reiterating the pattern of circularity that shapes Laforet's novels and the various *fugas* that she herself embarked upon to ease her psychological pain as a result of her mother's death.

    Al volver was finished in 1973 when Laforet was in her early fifties, but the manuscript remained unpublished until a few months after the author's death in 2004.[4] It was to form the second novel in the trilogy *Tres pasos fuera del tiempo*. *Al volver* is primarily a first person account of an older, forty-seven-year-old, Martín Soto who is trying to recuperate memories of a period of his life between April and December 1950, when he was twenty-four years old. As in the case of Laforet's narratives, the historical reality does not form the substance of the story but is instead back staged, deliberately, as Laforet herself corroborated:

> No me propongo en esta novela, ni en ninguna, dar una secuencia histórica y documentada de los hechos del mundo y de mi país, sino captar, con la veracidad que me sea posible y dentro de las limitaciones argumentales del libro, un momento circunstancial al mismo tiempo que el momento íntimo del personaje que sirve de base a todo lo demás.[5]

While the context of Francoist repression seeps through as a mode of further aggravating the protagonists' sense of alienation from his environment, Laforet takes the intimate, interior world of Martín Soto as the subject of her inquiry, reaffirming the claims of both Illanes Adaro and Jordan that Laforet was primarily a psychological writer. For the first time in Laforet's fiction, readers are introduced directly to the process of psychoanalysis. The older Martín, whose narrative we are reading, has submitted himself to the professional care of a female psychoanalyst called Doctor Leutari, who is overseeing the process of Martín's retrieval of his lost memories. The doctor is first introduced to readers in chapter six of the novel and Martín informs readers that he has made her a promise to 'proyectar las imágenes perdidas en el recuerdo, tal como se vayan presentando a la memoria' (p. 71). The doctor has asked Martín to write his memories down as a basis for their therapeutic work. *Al volver* could be mistaken for a novel about the inadequacy of human memory to recall the events of a human life yet, as Santos Sanz Villanueva has noted, what readers are presented with is a description of a 'reconstrucción psicoanalítica'.[6] Readers are placed into the role of the analyst throughout *Al volver* as they sift through the material recounted by Martín as analysand. Johnson, who has argued the case for the influence of detective fiction upon the novel, suggests that the mystery underlying *Al volver* is 'la personalidad de Martín'.[7] Johnson intuits the difficulties faced by the reader in attempting to formulate a detailed sense of Martín's personality and psychological traits. Similarly, Sotelo Vázquez argues that as readers 'adivinemos más que veamos [...] como si tratara de fotografías sepias que el tiempo ha envejecido'.[8] The reader's role is rendered more active throughout *Al volver* as she tries to assemble Martín's fragmented narrative through which he persistently withholds information about his past and present.[9]

Al volver is divided into two sections: 'La noche toledana' and 'Y lo demás', differing from the tripartite narrative structure of previous novels. Critics of the novel have pointed to its structural flaws, with Janet Pérez stating: 'No le faltan aristas'.[10] Sotelo Vázquez describes *Al volver* as 'una novela rara' in which some of the situations represented 'rayan lo grotesco o lo absurdo'.[11] There is a sense from chapter seventeen onwards that the novel weakens in terms of its structure and purpose as many details appear irrelevant. However, we must bear in mind that the narrative represents an effort to record the process of recall within the framework of the therapeutic transaction between Martín and Doctor Leutari. The loose, unreliable and irrelevant or absurd events that Martín includes in his story are consistent with the flotsam and jetsam thrown up from an individual's unconscious whilst undergoing psychoanalysis; order, consistency and relevance are not the primary goals of analysis. Martín's account also indicates that the experience of psychoanalysis may in fact reiterate the embedded defence patterns laid down within an individual's psyche that have arisen due to an earlier traumatic event. As was the case for *Nada*, direct references to the dead mother are excluded from Martín's narrative, yet it is through his recollections of his intimate encounters with other characters in the novel that the traces of his loss are delineated. The permissive use of lacunae on the part of Laforet's narrators and the author herself function as silent pools replete with meaning, akin to the unconscious material that lies dormant within the human psyche. The silences in Laforet's novels are no less relevant to her fiction than the events and experiences narrated. In keeping with Sotelo Vázquez's photographic analogy, Laforet's narratives encourage readers to engage in a form of interpretation that intuits what remains undeveloped within the stories of the novels yet is imprinted within her protagonists' 'reacciones psicológicas', the unsaid or *nada* within each text which contains repressed unconscious material and is rooted in the traumatic loss of the mother.

Martín's orphanhood is well established prior to the events narrated in *Al volver*. The death of Martín's mother during his early childhood forms the backdrop to his experiences in *La insolación*, and the death of his father sometime after his three summers in Beniteca is mentioned by the narrator in this novel.[12] *Al volver* suggests that both of Martín's maternal grandparents are dead by the time of his early twenties and that he has inherited a sum of money. Martín has entered psychoanalysis with Doctor Leutari due to an inability to recall a period of several months in his early twenties during which time he re-encounters the Corsi family. Through Martín's attempt to formulate a narrative of these months, he discloses the fragile nature of his mental health as a young man. Laforet permits her protagonist to engage in a greater level of self-scrutiny than in any of her previous novels, although self-disclosure is controlled by Martín's defensive strategies that prohibit detailed discussions of the source of his emotional suffering. On one occasion, he discusses the state of his feelings following a trip to Alicante, which occurs just before his chance meeting with Anita Corsi in Toledo in April 1950. Martín refers to this as 'la temporada más gris de mi vida [...] andaba como embotado, sin fuerzas para salirme de aquella situación' (p. 80). The 'noche toledana', which will be discussed in further detail below, suggests a hiatus in Martín's otherwise depressive state, although the birth of his child, mentioned towards the end of the novel, signals the potential for more permanent change in his otherwise self-oriented inner world. On occasions, Martín ponders on the matter of his personal sanity, his tendency towards introversion and his incapacity to empathise with others, although there is no indication of him endeavouring to connect his early life experiences with his later 'reacciones psicológicas'. When Anita compares Martín to Don Quijote, he reflects on his mode of viewing reality and considers whether he may in fact be mad: 'En realidad yo era loco, si ser loco quiere decir tener un mundo distinto al de los demás, pero mi locura terminaba en los límites de mi frente' (p. 51). He recognises that he often feels the world to be 'lejano y fantasmal' (p. 51) and that he cannot adapt himself to collective social norms, suggesting an ongoing dissociation from others and his environment. In this regard, he replicates the alienated subject position of Andrea, Marta and Paulina who feel similarly detached from their families and their society due to their distinct point of view and emotional needs. When viewed collectively, Laforet's protagonists display depressive traits in one form or another. Andrea, Marta and Martín's early life experiences have produced unintegrated ego structures that do not serve them well as young adults within their society. Martín is therefore not mad in the sense that Don Quijote may be, even though they are both engaged in a form of psychological projection. The knight errant's vision has become saturated through reading too many chivalric novels, whereas Martín's relationship to reality arises from his unconscious search for the figure of the lost mother, which is illustrated through his interactions with both Anita Corsi and Zoila, Carlos's wife. Martín's detachment or dissociation from his society stands in stark contrast to Don Quijote's over-engagement with all that is occurring on his quest, albeit mediated through the lens of his imagination. Laforet's protagonists share Quijote's stubborn will to see the world through their own eyes with little regard for others' realities.

In the case of Martín, his narrative of the lost months of his early twenties provides an insight into his self-centredness and latent narcissism, both of which are associated with distortions in the formation of a healthy ego structure during childhood development. As a young man, Martín accompanies a friend who is visiting *chabolas* in Madrid. His lack of engagement with the plight of others illustrates his incapacity for empathy: 'no me interesaba más que lo que me parecía que iba a servirme en lo mío. [...] Sólo me interesaba mi propio negocio, no podía pensar siquiera en la injusticia o bondad de aquello. Yo me escapaba' (pp. 200–01). This is not evidence of madness; rather, Martín's attitude indicates an incapacity to understand the emotional needs of others. All Laforet's protagonists reveal similar traits and are concerned with pursuing their own ends. The exception is Paulina in *La mujer nueva* who returns to her husband towards the end of the novel, although there is a case for arguing that she is still seeking her own desires through her actions and that her apparent subjugation to Eulogio is illusory since she is returning of her own volition. Martín's tendency towards extreme self-centredness is revealed in a morally dubious act, an account of which Martín includes in his diary of recollections which he is writing to aid his analysis with Doctor Leutari. Whilst visiting Beatriz Din, the daughter of his colleague Jiménez Din, in a mental institution, he has sex with her in a secluded part of the asylum. Martín 'forgets' this event and when he recalls it several months later, he ponders again on the state of his mental health: 'Era yo quien necesitaba el psiconanálisis y no Anita' (p. 187). The police report kept by Luis López also reveals Martín's use of prostitutes as a young man, despite him giving others the impression that he lives only for his art. Laforet makes no effort as a writer to make her protagonists likeable or represent their actions as morally exemplary. The source from which Laforet's fiction springs is her close observation of human psychology; the protagonists of her novels reveal how individuals act from contradictory impulses that are based on reason as well as unconscious processes and unmet needs rooted in childhood trauma. Martín's account suggests that, during his early twenties, he remains childlike and is moved too easily to act upon impulse without consideration for others. Without divulging the relationship between the dead mother and Martín's psychological state, *Al volver* makes it clear that he bears the traces of an earlier life trauma. Nonetheless, the question of Martín's sanity remains pertinent throughout *Al volver*, and the matter of whether he finds psychological relief through psychoanalysis remains open to question.

Martín's sexual encounters with Carlos Corsi's wife Zoila are indicative of how the figure of the dead mother is alluded to but, in a similar manner to Andrea, never stated explicitly. Zoila's function as a sexual partner assists Martín in stemming the flow of grief associated with his loss which is referred to as a wound: 'Sólo esa herida por donde mi sangre quería escapar en busca de ella como única cura. Sólo esa obsesión de fundirnos uno con otro todos los días luminosos' (p. 250). Sex becomes a substitute for another type of merger, a form of relief which is suggestive of the primal bond with the mother, prior to birth or the infant's early consciousness of separation from the maternal object. Similarly, Martín's friendship with Anita, with whom he forms a deeper attachment in *Al volver* than he did with Carlos in *La insolación*, is transformed into a source of both pleasure and pain as it is associated with feelings of oneness and intimacy with a close Other which simultaneously carry the potential for rupture and permanent loss. Anita becomes the object of Martín's projections, just as Pablo did for Marta in *La isla* and Ena for Andrea in *Nada*. *Cathexis*, or psychic investment in another human being, re-opens the original wound associated with the loss of the mother. Martín's account of his relationship with Anita transforms her into an idolised female Other, whom Martín wishes to marry yet also seeks to maintain a sisterly, non-sexual friendship. In the following quotation Martín's projection of his desire for a more innocent union with a surrogate mother figure is made manifest as he walks around Madrid holding Anita's hand:

> El color de la primera hora de la noche en primavera. [...] Era un azul fresco y profundo de una suavidad que hacía pensar en algo florido. Nos sentíamos dentro de una corola en forma de copa invertida; en el interior de una inmensa campánula azulada, ancha como el universo, donde, según íbamos andando, con las manos enlazadas, veíamos encenderse las estrellas poco a poco. Dentro de aquel azul de la noche olvidé el cansancio y la pesadumbre de la vida y hasta empecé a pensar si aquella gran mentira del amor completo por un ser humano, no sería una gran verdad algunas veces. (91–92)

Laforet posits the apparent innocence of the parent-child relationship as the crucible of true love as opposed to sexual or romantic love. Although Anita and Martín kiss at one stage in *Al volver*, their relationship is not based on sexual desire; rather, Martín behaves like a possessive child towards her across the narrative.[13] When she leaves Madrid to embark upon a relationship with Dr Tarro at the end of *Al volver*, Martín recognises that he must return to a more adult state of being. Anita's departure serves as 'Un pozo de agua helada al que me arrojé de cabeza y que apagó las llamas; un hierro candente para curar una llaga que se había enconado' (p. 250).

The reference to a wound is repeated, yet, once again, Martín fails to elucidate on its source. People, sex and, as the following example illustrates, nature, function as modes of alleviating the permanent psychic wound that Martín carries which bears the imprint of maternal loss. Having escorted Zoila home, he turns to nature for its curative properties: 'andando bajo las estrellas del cielo, andando hacia el oleaje de luces, del centro de la ciudad, curándome el alma con el aire fresco, el olor a pinos que llegaba de la Sierra, a ozono, a tormenta primaveral. Sin psicoanálisis' (p. 188). The ironic quip at the end of the quotation suggests that psychoanalysis serves little function in alleviating Martín's suffering and the reader is drawn to question to whom the comment is directed.[14] Martín is perhaps reflecting on the process to which he has submitted himself and wishes his therapist to be aware of his scepticism towards the task she has set him in and its effectiveness in healing his emotional trauma. The possibility of psychological cure for Martín's memory lapses and underlying depression are thrown into doubt throughout *Al volver*, as is the process of writing as a mode of reducing the impact of traumatic memory. By the end of the novel, it remains unclear whether Martín benefits psychologically through his transcription of past events from his life and although writing facilitates a degree of recuperation of his lost months during his early twenties, the veracity of his account is consistently undermined. There are multiple examples of Martín reflecting upon the process of writing, mainly in the form of reminders to himself to keep to the instructions laid down by Doctor Leutari. She insists that he includes only his recollections in his account and not those of others linked to his past. However, intertexts from a pseudo-police report, written by Luis López following his disappearance over a number of months, appear in the novel alongside narrative sequences which Martín refers to as 'el cuento de Soli'. The incursion of other people's accounts into Martín's story signals Laforet's attempt at inter-textual experimentation, yet these seemingly digressive micro-narratives also suggest a subtle critique of the psychoanalytic process, as the authority of a personal life narrative divulged to a therapist has the potential to be undermined through another person's point of view. The incompleteness and fallibility of Martín's life story is further challenged throughout the narrative through Martín's reticence to disclose information about important events in his life such as the birth of his son. However, this technique of enforced silence preserves the space of traumatic grief as a pristine, nameless experience, one that is situated beyond language and remains within the realm of the emotions and the unconscious. The scant references to Andrea's dead mother that appear in *Nada* have been transformed into the silent figuration of grief in *Al volver*, only seeping through Martín's narrative through his muted references to the 'herida' or 'llaga' for which he has sought therapeutic treatment in later life. A form of 'música blanca' or white noise muffles out the expression of grief throughout Laforet's writing and functions as a muted corollary of her own silence surrounding her mother's death.

The deliberate exclusion of information from Martín's narrative is compounded by his self-willed forgetting of the lost months of 1950, when he sought to merge his life with that of Anita Corsi and her wider circle of friends. Martín steps out of his normal and familiar frame of reference and takes 'un paso fuera del tiempo', arguably into the space of his unconscious, unmet childhood needs and a separate emotional reality to that of his life as a professional painter.[15] In this regard, Laforet presents an interesting case of the power of unconscious drives to find their way into daily existence, despite the ego's efforts to maintain control over intrusions from the subconscious. Laforet's representation of Martín's rememoration of this period of his life is both an account of the search for relief in the present through psychoanalysis and an exploration of his attempt to alleviate his suffering as a young man through a renewed friendship with the Corsi family. What remains significant throughout Martín's account is that he has deliberately pushed his recollection of his chance meeting with Anita in Toledo in 1950 out of conscious recall. The reasons behind him doing so are excluded from his narrative, although readers become aware that this period permitted him to experience intense human association, renewed acceptance within a surrogate family, as well as sexual pleasure through his relationship with Zoila. Martín's 'lost' months are not simply a *lapsus memoriae* due to the passing of time and the process of ageing. An ingrained defensive reaction of forgetting forms part of a recognisable pattern across his lifetime, as he admits himself: 'después de haber estado encerrado y perdido en ese rincón secreto que la doctora Leutari me ha hecho descubrir, es para explicarme a mí mismo otros olvidos' (p. 272). The pattern of forgetting events rapidly is present in *La insolación*. When he returns to his grandparents' house after the third and last summer in Beniteca, Martín forgets everything: 'No recordaba nada ya. Beniteca, el verano larguísimo y ardiente y los Corsi, se habían esfumado de su cabeza.'[16] Martín's propensity to forget indicates an ingrained defence mechanism which, atypically, involves dissociation from positive experiences with a close Other or Others, a psychological response that has its origins in an earlier stage of his life but which he fails to associate with his later emotional response systems. As van der Hart, Nijenhuis and Steele observe, when an individual fails to comprehend the roots of their suffering as a result of an early life trauma, they 'may find the past too painful to integrate, so that they continue to respond to potent reminders of traumatic experiences with alarm or other defensive reactions'.[17] In Martín's case, memories associated with love and human association are defensively sequestered away within his psyche, forming gaps in the narrative of his life and problematising the process of recollection. Relief arises through the negation of a seemingly positive memory. However, this defensive pattern further reinforces Rasmussen's understanding of how the individual's attempts to feel good are often based on 'quite a bit of "non" "sense"'.[18] *Al volver* appears to suggest that the older Martín may have begun to acknowledge that what once served him as a protective defence pattern against psychological pain, a type of enforced amnesia, has been transformed into a debilitating pathology requiring treatment with Doctor Leutari.[19]

Al volver reveals the complexity of Martín's psychic structure through his account of his psychological reactions to others and his emotional dependence on Anita Corsi and her wider family. As Hill reminds us, 'Affect tells us what matters,'[20] and it is through an examination of Martín's affective bonds, primarily with Anita, that the deeper material that lies buried within his psyche comes to light, thus enabling readers to see the fuller image that is imprinted within the photographic negative etched into the novel. We must recall Laforet's intentions in *Al volver* to capture 'el momento íntimo' as Martín experiences it. On occasions, his emotional responses to others are often extreme and disproportionate to the situation in which he finds himself. For example, when Anita makes a throwaway comment in relation to Doctor Tarro, with whom she starts an affair, Martín feels himself wounded and recalls how the encounter unleashed 'mi ansiedad de corazón, mi angustia infantil y absurda' (p. 104). Buried beneath Martín's reactions is a deeper sense of shame which is associated with longing for a relationship based on an exclusive bond and bears the traces of his unmet longing for his lost mother. As Hill notes with reference to the pathology of shame, it represents 'an overwhelmingly frightening, unexpected severance of the attachment relationship and disorganisation of the self. In a flash, one is exposed, and alone: in pain, paralyzed, and helpless'.[21] It is precisely because Martín's shame and longing remains unspeakable that it is not made explicit in the narrative. The structural gaps and silences are symbolic manifestations of the protagonist's dissociation of painful psychic material from his past. Martín's non-sexual relationship with Anita triggers the deeper painful emotions from which he has defensively disassociated in relation to his mother and which, as a young adult, he continues to exclude: 'Todos esos momentos de emociones desagradables o turbadoras han estado arrinconados hasta hoy en el cajón del olvido junto a las escenas mañaneras en el comedor de los Corsi' (p. 194). What Martín seeks to exclude are memories of certain emotions associated with people and events, not the events themselves. The emotions bear traces of previous traumatic events which he cannot articulate, and they then become part of his repressed psychic material. Nonetheless, the traumatic past intrudes into the present of current affective relations. Hill notes with reference to Pierre Janet's discussions of the sequalae of trauma and affect regulation, that dissociation is rooted in 'a fear of the affective component of the memory'.[22] The source of the intense emotion associated with trauma is normally linked to a negative experience that the subject annexes, according to Janet, 'in the form of continuous and retrograde amnesia'.[23] Yet Martín's dissociation of past events is, on one level, linked to positive memories, although underlying his relationship with Anita Corsi exists a more primal longing for the mother figure, as has been illustrated above. His need for intimacy and friendship has been pushed out of conscious recall, primarily memories associated with the renewed bond of friendship with Anita Corsi: 'sólo olvidé esos momentos en que me veo junto a Anita en intimidad y amistad, que sí había olvidado por completo al pensar en esa época' (p. 205). Bessel A. van der Kolk and Rita Fisler provide a rare insight into the relationship between trauma and the concept of longing, of which Martín's case provides an important literary example and supports Bayard's views on the manifest ways in which literature has much to teach psychoanalysis. They write: 'any affect related to a particular traumatic experience may serve as a cue for the retrieval of trauma-related sensations, including longing, intimacy and sexual arousal.'[24] Martín's amnesia is connected to the emotion of longing for a feeling of psychological safety within a collective of other human beings, one in which he feels recognised, loved and needed by the Corsi family, but which is in fact a projection of an idealised surrogate family, sense of self and home. As a response to his ongoing desire for relief, Martín dissociates himself from memories associated with the temporary satiation of this need, resulting in him pushing these memories out of conscious recall. Within this process lies a hidden sense of shame over the realisation that the relief he encountered with Anita and family and friends was based on unmet emotional needs and, to all extents and purposes, did not constitute an authentic experience of alleviation to his suffering but was instead an illusory and temporary palliative.[25]

One of the most salient features of the pursuit of relief arises through the experience of *arrebato*, a state of transcendence that suggests a partial dissolution of Laforet's protagonists' defensive psychic structures during which deeper psychological processes reveal themselves. If we return to the structural form of the circle in Laforet's narratives, the representation of *arrebato* can be traced back through each novel to Andrea's moments of rapture while listening to Román's music and standing in front of Barcelona's cathedral. Similarly, Martín's 'sensación de arrebato fuera del mundo conocido y cercano' (p. 268), which he experiences around the Corsi siblings throughout much of Laforet's fourth novel is, arguably, a reiteration of Paulina's state of rapture during her sudden conversion to Catholicism on the train to Madrid in *La mujer nueva*. There is a case for arguing that Laforet's descriptions of *arrebato* are also accounts of dissociative states based on a defensive response to a deeper psychological trauma arising from unbearable emotions linked to the lost bond with the primary caregiver. The common root to Laforet's aesthetic representations of merger lie in the experience of the self as undifferentiated and unified with either the object of contemplation or sensory environment such that a sensation of no self or *Samadhi* arises. In this state, temporary emotional and physical relief arises. Hill has argued that during these types of altered states of consciousness, the subject's attention can become 'hyperfocused and narrowed [...] resulting in depersonalization and derealisation, total absorption and/or a sense of time slowed down'.[26] This description concurs with the accounts of *arrebato* that occur across Laforet's novels and outlines the intimate state of being that Martín recounts early on in *Al volver* during his first attempt at conveying his lost memories to Doctor Leutari. In this instance, the state of *arrebato* is stripped of its religious associations and is transposed onto the therapeutic encounter between analyst and analysand. It is not clear initially whether Martín is describing a dream or day-dreaming about a memory of the Corsi's flat near the Retiro park in Madrid. The oneiric quality of his narrative mixes up memories, thoughts, emotions and, as the narrative proceeds, the unreliability of Martín's account emerges, yet this remains unimportant within the therapeutic encounter as a desire for a memory to be real is as valid as a concrete factual experience. Martín mixes unconscious desires of longing with what appear to be real memories of the Corsi's apartment:

> El sueño se me está escapando como el humo de una hoguera. (Humo de hogueras. San Juan, las vacaciones de la infancia. Saltos sobre el fuego.) En el sueño

estoy en mi casa: puertas blancas, cortinas blancas del techo al suelo, pasillos empapelados con papeles de rosas rojas o rosas azules sobre fondo gris. Y sobre todo esa insoportable ternura que amenaza hacer estallar el corazón a la vista de los muebles sólidos, ni feos ni hermosos, pero vividos usados, nuestros. (19)

Martín's account seems to be a recollection of his childhood but as the narrative develops we learn that this is not the case; he is in fact creating what he wants to remember — an imagined sense of home wherein the state of relief, 'esa insoportable ternura' is projected as if it were a reality that once existed. Longing is symbolically configured within Martín's account of his suspended state, a liminal space where fantasy, desire and reality coexist. It must be noted that the corollary of longing is the absence of the person or thing that is missed which, in Martín's case, is an intimate feeling of oneness with a place and others even though it remains a fantasy. However, although Martín invents this memory, his sense of longing for an unbearable tenderness is, within the realm of his emotions, a reality: 'Si he soñado ha sido sobre algo que existe, que permanece, que podré encontrar aquí o donde sea cuando despierte' (p. 19). Laforet's poetic prose conveys the complex, intimate space of unconscious processes where time and space are displaced, and emotion and present experience dominate and constitute the real for the analysand. With acute attention to the semantic capacities of the Spanish language, Laforet provides the clearest articulation of longing for relief to be found within her novels, although the defensive dyadic pattern of dissolution of the self and resistance to articulation of deeper emotions is manifested through the over embellished prose style: 'pasillos empapelados con papeles de rosas rojas o rosas azules sobre fondo gris' (p. 19). Laforet's purple prose functions as both an intimation of emotion as readers are lulled into the rhythms of the words, inducing a temporary soporific state of aural and cognitive unity, yet their aesthetic beauty defensively overlays the deeper emotions being expressed by Martín: his longing for this to be a real memory. In the case of Laforet's narrative style, representations of relief remain indirect and obtuse; there is always a more complex set of emotions and desires at work beneath the surface of her, at times, florid and exuberant prose.

Martín is at pains to capture the memory through the childlike use of possession and familiarity: 'La vida empieza lentamente en mi calle, en mi casa, en este piso grande y un poco destartalado del que conozco todos los ruidos y donde he visto con emoción hasta los deterioros del tiempo' (p. 21).[27] He recalls an emotion of 'algo muy real' (p. 21) which, at the level of his psychology and intimate emotions, is real.[28] Martín's recollections under therapy develop into an almost Proustian recollection of a being a child in a familiar room: 'Recuerdos de toda una vida, de toda una infancia, de un calor, de una dicha perdida permanece en este cuarto' (p. 21). Something has been lost, something charmed and pristine, yet, as is common in Laforet's fiction, further information is suddenly excluded, as if to contain the emotional content of the experience the protagonist is undergoing. A series of sensations falls under description but the deeper emotional trauma from which longing or suffering arises is left for readers to intuit as if they were to play the role of the analyst who is required to sift through Martín's account. It becomes clear that Martín is projecting his desires within his recollection of living in the Corsis' flat: 'he vivido una vida entera en esta casa de Madrid, en este piso, y he regresado a esta dicha perdida después de un largo abandono y eso ha ocurrido en sueños' (p. 21). Readers know that Martín has not lived in Madrid as a child, but with his maternal grandparents in Alicante following his mother's early death. However, psychoanalysis permits him to relive a different childhood temporarily and to evoke the 'dicha perdida' of an early life experience he has always longed to have, which has been triggered by his relationship with the Corsis.[29] Martín informs Doctor Leutari, that he has invented this dream: 'me repito que he soñado toda una vida en esta casa. Yo nunca viví una infancia en Madrid frente al Retiro en este piso' (p. 22). Laforet seeks to identify with the deeper structures of the unconscious where desires, memories, concepts of self and impulses remain intertwined; as readers, she encourages us to take 'un paso fuera del tiempo' to explore a different mode of experience akin to the state of *arrebato*. Laforet's representation of Martín's recollection serves as an invitation to enter into a different level of reality wherein the possibility of relief is posited. Yet the state of suspension from the more familiar coordinates of existence must, in all cases of transcendence, come to an end, which Martín finally accepts: 'Al fin lo acepto: el sueño ha cambiado las medidas del tiempo; quizá en otra vida he estado aquí entre estas cortinas blancas, este viejo tresillo, estos espacios vacíos que me emocionan como algo tan mío' (p. 22).[30] The dream reflects Martín's quixotic propensity to project his desires onto the world around him as if they were real. His expectations are that others should function as players within a narrative based on his need for them to fulfil his childlike, unconscious desires. When they do not, as is made evident through Anita leaving to pursue a relationship with Doctor Tarro later in the novel, Martín's sense of self collapses, as if the actors within his fantasy were responsible for his sense of self.[31]

Martín's dreamlike account of living in the Corsi's flat extends into a description of 'La noche Toledana' in chapter two, although the entire first section of the novel bears the same name.[32] As was the case in *La insolación*, Martín stops painting when he is in the company of the Corsi family, suggesting that he sets his creative drives aside to accommodate his deeper emotional needs. As Martín recalls his re-encounter with Anita, the narrative creates a sense of temporal confusion and unreality which is compounded by torrential rain, stimulating Martín to recall a line from Valle-Inclán: 'dijo que si lloviese con fuerza sobre Toledo, se desharía en barro' (p. 29). However, it is not the city that is dissolving, but Martín's already fragile self-concept. There is a precise moment at which this happens, according to Soli, the young daughter of one of Martín's acquaintances in Madrid who accompanies him on his trip to Toledo. Soli states that the 'noche toledana' occurs 'cuando Zoila se acercó a nuestra mesa en el café grande de Zocodover' (p. 28). Zoila is intimately connected to the Corsis through her marriage to Carlos and it is this connection that leads him to find Anita; meeting her again instigates a change in Martín's mental state, 'ese cambio mío, ese desenfoque de la realidad... La noche toledana (p. 38).[33] Although Johnson suggests that '"La noche toledana" es una metáfora para el régimen franquista y los valores tradicionales bajo los cuales los españoles habían vivido desde 1940', it in fact serves as an important clue to Laforet's primary concerns within *Al volver*, namely, to explore Martín's psychological reality, rather than the historical circumstances of Franco's Spain.[34] 'La noche toledana' indicates Martín's defensive exclusion or dissociation of material from conscious recall: 'Yo mismo cerré la memoria a todas las nimiedades de mis primeros pasos en la noche toledana y lo demás que siguió, o al menos una gran parte de todo aquello' (p. 55). The events that occur during the 'noche toledano' possess an 'incomprensible encanto' (p. 55) and Martín becomes 'hipnotizado' (p. 65) by his renewed association with Anita. Yet the hypnotic state induced by Anita Corsi evokes anger in Martín when he manifests a deeper awareness of her superficial character and that of her family: 'La rabia de sentirme atraído otra vez por un hechizo hacia esa raza de seres vacíos, egoístas, inconsecuentes (había pensado así de Carlos muchas veces), me heló' (p. 115). Anita's presence enables Martín to numb himself from his depressive tendencies, allowing him to 'vivir el tiempo en un presente continuo' (p. 116). Here Martín manifests a latent awareness of how he uses others to satisfy his need for relief. Through his reliance on others to fulfil his unmet needs, Martín's methods draw him away from his true self and from the development of a secure, internal object, a process necessary for individuation and maturational growth. There is also the matter of the excessive nature of his investment in the Corsis that deserves further consideration. The intensity of emotional communion sought by Martín reveals his emotional and psychological deficits. He offers too much of himself to the Corsis, as if he were in expectation of a similar investment on their part, which is never the case, neither in *La insolación* nor in *Al volver*. On one occasion, when he enters the sea to swim whilst on holiday with Anita, Carlos, Zoila and their friends, Martín reveals his capacity to invest excessively in people whom he himself believes to be shallow and incapable of a reciprocal level of friendship.

> Mi espíritu se expandía, sin atadura alguna; me sentía tan capaz de entregar mi amistad y con ella lo más puro, lo más generoso, lo mejor de mí a los dos hermanos, cuando volvíamos juntos hacia la casa, como si aún no la hubiese empañado ni el tiempo, ni el olvido ni otros sentimientos espinosos como zarzas. (249)

Martín reveals much of himself here, although he also refuses to expand on the deeper trauma associated with 'otros sentimientos espinosos como zarzas'. Rather than Martín's defensive, aloof and detached charateristics, the voice of the child and its unconditional love for the parent seep through his narrative. The trope of merger, symbolised by the sea and the three friends submerged together, is framed within a description of excessive emotion towards the siblings. The type of love he describes, and which is offered up to the Corsis, does not match their emotions towards him. His feelings of an excess of love are rooted in the real object which he seeks, the figure of the lost mother. Once again, projection of a desired but unreal relationship is manifested within Martín's 'reacciones psicológicas.'[35]

The figure of absence is symbolised in the final image of Martín at the close of *Al volver* which starkly situates him in a space, now voided of emotional connection: the vacant Corsi flat. He returns one day to find it empty, without the presence of

Anita and her family:

> encendí todas las luces, todas las habitaciones de la casa, los pasillos, todo. Y
> la iba buscando en cada cuarto que dejaba iluminado. Las lámparas encendidas
> parecía que me quitaban algo de la negrura que sentía en mi alma. Por un
> instante, entre tanta luz, soñe que oía a los perros acudiendo a mi llegada, los
> pasos de la niña, la voz de don Carolo, la risa de Anita. (284)

As has already been discussed, Martín constantly projects his unconscious desires
onto his environment, only this time it is a space and not a human subject that
functions as a receptacle for his emotions. The final image of Martín frames him
within a lonely, empty space, 'entre el vacío y las cortinas blancas...' (p. 284). The
ellipsis points towards the unfinished nature of Martín's quest for relief as well as
his refusal to divulge the source of his psychological suffering, the ever present
'negrura' that stalks his unconscious. The ending of the novel undercuts the positive
hope of a cessation of Martín's despair and depressive tendencies due to the birth
of his son. Relief through parenthood is at least suggested through the emphatic
nature of Martín's reaction to the knowledge that Jiménez Din's daughter Beatriz
has given birth to his son:

> Fue el principio de una recuperación. [...] Era como si hubiese caído en un
> abismo y de pronto encontrasen mis manos unas raíces fuertes para agarrarse.
> Volví a saber en qué día vivía, qué hora era, para qué vivir, para qué quería y
> luchar. (283)

At one level, Laforet may have elected the more inconclusive ending of Martín
positioned in the void of loneliness in the Corsi apartment as an ironic reflection on
the illusion of finding happiness through another person, in his case, his newly born
child. He sits alone, waiting for the presence of someone in whom he can invest his
emotional needs just he as did when he met Anita again in Toledo. The arc of the
circle returns to its beginnings, reinforcing the motif of circularity and repetition
that occurs across Laforet's novels. Whether Martín acquires psychological peace
through fatherhood remains unknown; the answer may lie in the lost manuscript
of *Jaque mate*.

   The act of writing as an aid to lasting release from earlier, traumatic life events is
once again drawn into question in *Al volver*. Readers have Martín's account of his
efforts to recover his past through writing under Doctor Leutari's instructions, but
his narrative remains inconclusive and tells us nothing of the relationship between
writing and recovery from early childhood trauma. Standard interpretations of
the relationship between trauma and writing suggest a dual process of abreaction
and integration, a mixture of expulsion of repressed emotional material within
the psyche followed by assimilation of its content through conscious processes
enacted through writing. This provides too simplistic an explanation for Laforet's
treatment of the process of writing with reference to Martín or, for that matter, the
author herself. In Antony Storr's discussion of the relationship between creativity
and psychological defence mechanisms, he draws on the work of Anna Freud
to elucidate creativity as a form of defence in itself, whereby the act of creation
becomes a 'means by which the ego wards off unpleasure and anxiety.'[36] Storr

notes that creative activity 'is particularly apt for defensive purposes'.[37] The writer may therefore remain in control of his or her art and elect 'how much of himself to reveal and how much to keep secret'.[38] In the case of Laforet's protagonists who write, the creative act evolves into an aesthetic veneer, behind which little is revealed directly, although much is said through the protagonists' psychological reactions or, as Currie suggested with reference to novels more generally, the 'mind-world transactions' that arise from fictional characters' emotional responses to phenomena. Laforet does not suggest that Martín's task of writing as an aid to recall some of the 'olvidos' of his past serves any positive, integrative function. The value of writing and psychoanalysis in *Al volver* remains ambiguous. Readers gain a sense of ongoing sublimation within Martín's narrative which reiterates Winnicott's views on an inherent dilemma which the artist faces through the process of creation: 'the co-existence of two trends, the urgent need to communicate and the still more urgent need not to be found.'[39] The latter urge predominates Laforet's fiction and disclosure of each protagonists' 'llaga' is elided repeatedly. A psychic place of safety remains elusive for Laforet's protagonists.[40] Although Storr suggests that through the creative act the artist may find that 'some part of his inner life is being accepted which has never been accorded recognition before',[41] Laforet's novels suggest otherwise since the thing that requires recognition, in other words, the longing for the absent mother figure, is not directly acknowledged. This absence remains a part of her protagonists' inner lives that cannot be articulated explicitly yet finds itself expressed through symbolic aesthetic figurations of relief.

If writing fails to bring relief for the protagonist of *Al volver*, the effectiveness of the therapeutic relationship also remains unresolved as readers are not privy to the effectiveness of Martín's psychoanalytical treatment with Doctor Leutari. As Noè notes, Martín's search for 'una deseada serenidad' does not occur.[42] Del Mastro also casts doubt on the extent to which Martín's search for stability has come to an end at the close of the novel, through parenthood or otherwise: 'the reader wonders if a now 47-year-old Martín has made any progress in reconciling his identity during his lifetime, or if perhaps 23 years later he is still searching.'[43] *Al volver* does not resolve this matter and the narrator fails to provide evidence of relief arising through the process of writing his narrative as an aid to combat his dissociative amnesia. The fact that he has been able to recuperate his memories of his lost months during 1950 does not equate to psychological repair. Indeed, Laforet's final novel suggests the author's underlying scepticism towards the possibility of long term psychological repair. Her aesthetics of relief retain a pessimistic undercurrent, linked no doubt to the author's own personal life circumstances.

Although it has not been my intention throughout this study to situate Laforet's novels within the genre of life writing, the autobiographical features of her work emerge repeatedly. According to Del Mastro, Laforet's final novel represents her 'most complex portrayal of the lifelong quest for identity that she attempted to reconcile for herself via her literature, beginning with *Nada*'.[44] Yet it is not an identity as such that is being sought but, as this study has argued, the quest for relief, for only a secure identity can arise once psychological suffering has been recognised and given expression. Laforet's ongoing battle with depression and anxiety indicates that the source of her suffering persisted. Her biographers state that 'en los años sesenta ya había aparecido el fantasma de la depresión que acaba de engullirla'.[45] It has already been noted in the introduction how Laforet suffered from an ongoing tendency to block out anything that caused her to experience emotional pain, a repetition of the affective response mechanism that she used following her mother's death: the silencing and defensive repression of her grief. Her art is perhaps best described as a sustained example of literary *alexithymia*, of having no words for feelings. Laforet often transcribes substitutes for words that describe her protagonists' loss and longing, metonymic figures of relief created through representations of transcendence or merger with another being or phenomenon.

Laforet's strengths as an artist arise, as Storr notes more generally for creators of works of significant quality, from her ability to relate her 'personal deprivations to the discontents implicit in being human'.[46] Each novel is a renewed attempt to articulate the subject of psychological suffering with each also serving as a defensive restraint on expressing the source of trauma. Expression may be desired, yet it remains impossible, even within the therapeutic encounter, as Martín's case attests in *La insolación*. More broadly, within Laforet's novels the desire to express something manifests itself as a repressed confession. Here the words of Ted Hughes prove instructive to our analysis and are pertinent to both the poet and the novelist. Hughes takes poetry to be 'a revealing of something the writer doesn't want to say, but desperately needs to communicate, to be delivered of'.[47] He continues:

> The writer daren't actually put it into words, so it leaks out obliquely, smuggled through analogies. We think we're writing something to amuse, but we're actually saying something we desperately need to share. The real mystery is this strange need. Why can't we just hide and shut up? Why do we have to blab? Why do human beings need to confess? Maybe, if you don't have that secret confession you don't have a poem — don't even have a story. Don't have a writer. If most poetry doesn't seem to be in any sense confessional, it's because the strategy of concealment, of obliquity, can be so compulsive that it's almost entirely successful.[48]

Laforet's novels are structured around such strategies of concealment. As a writer, Laforet was almost successful in concealing her grief across her novels yet, inscribed within her writing, one hears the echoes of her suffering imprinted through a confession communicated through silence, perhaps the most appropriate articulation of relief.

Notes to Chapter 5

1. Cerezales Laforet, *Música blanca*, p. 78.
2. If we are to take the view that Laforet's fiction is primarily autobiographical, then we are essentially dealing with only one psyche, that of the author herself.
3. The metaphorical allusions to Freud's death drive and his discussion of repetition compulsion are obvious.
4. Laforet experienced difficulties with her editor at Destino, which led to the author withholding publication until 2004. See Caballé and Rolón, especially chapter 17.

5. Carmen Laforet, 'Por qué de esta trilogía', *La insolación*, p. 8.
6. Review of *Al volver la esquina* in *El Cultural* de *El Mundo* (13 May 2004). Quoted in Marisa Sotelo Vázquez, '"*Al volver la esquina*" de Carmen Laforet: Las fotografías de la memoria', *Revista Hispánica Moderna*, Año 58, 1–2, (2005), 107–17, (p. 109).
7. Roberta Johnson, 'La novelística de Carmen Laforet', p. 521.
8. Sotelo Vázquez, p. 115.
9. This may account for the use of intertexts, such as Luis López's pseudo-police reports and 'el cuento de Soli', as they provide information that Martín leaves out.
10. Janet Pérez, '*Al volver la esquina*', *Hispania*, 87.4 (2004), 744–46, (p. 746).
11. Sotelo Vázquez, p. 114.
12. Laforet's narrators will, on occasions, provide some information concerning the protagonists' future lives.
13. Martín's obsessive need to be around Anita and monitor her movements borders on the pathological.
14. *Al volver* suggests that Laforet was well acquainted with the experience of psychoanalysis although there is no evidence that she underwent treatment herself. She was interested in its major figures; for example, Freud and Adler are mentioned in passing in her novels. Her close friend Fernanda Monasterio was a well known psychiatrist in Spain and Latin America.
15. Comparisons arise again with Don Quijote who leaves reason behind to embark on his imaginary chivalric quest.
16. Laforet, *La insolación*, p. 365.
17. Onno van der Hart, Ellert Nijenhuis and Kathy Steele, *The Haunted Self: Structural Dissociation and the Treatment of Chronic Traumatization* (New York and London: W.W. Norton and Company, 2006), p. 53.
18. Rasmussen, p. 6.
19. All we know as readers is that Martín has sought therapy to deal with the gaps that exist in his memory. Since he is able to recall them through the assistance of Dr Leutari it is not the case that these memories have been permanently wiped from conscious recall, although Martín has been an active agent in the process of forgetting.
20. Hill, p. 135.
21. Shame is illustrated in Martín's reactions to the Corsis in *La insolación*. Although he is anxious to see them again after a winter at his grandparents', he feels ashamed of his feelings: 'Cuando oyó voces y risas se incorporó de un salto conteniendo el extraño deseo de echar a correr. Retrocedió unos pasos cuando les vio aparecer entre las dunas, pero se quedó quieto al fin arrodillándose en la arena como si quisiera disminuir de estatura y desaparecer disuelto en la luz', *La insolación*, p. 100.
22. Hill, p. 42.
23. Pierre Janet, *Les nervoses* (Paris: Flammarion, 1909), p. 1607, cited in Bessel A. van der Kolk and Rita Fisler, 'Dissociation and the Fragmentary Nature of Traumatic Memories: Overview and Exploratory Study', *Journal of Traumatic Stress*, 8.4 (1995), 505–25, (p. 511).
24. van der Kolk and Fisler, p. 510.
25. Ena's family provide an interesting point of comparison with reference to Andrea's longing for an alternative to her family in the flat on calle Aribau.
26. Hill, p. 159.
27. The theme of an absence of home recurs in Laforet's fiction. Andrea lacks a home, Marta leaves her home and Paulina lives uneasily in both her husband's home and their flat in Madrid. Martín lives with his grandparents and then on his own when he becomes a successful artist. Each protagonist is seeking the stability of home yet cannot seem to find it. The trope of Laforet's ongoing psychological *fuga* and itinerant existence in later life is echoed in her protagonists' lack of a stable physical space which they can call their home.
28. Laforet repeatedly deconstructs traditional conceptions of family relationships and substitutes these with sometimes odd formations that are both a substitute for and challenge to the nuclear family. For example, following Martín's meeting with Anita in Toledo, the tripartite relationship of Anita-Martín-Soli is formed, based on non-familial connections. There is no

positive representation of the family in Laforet's novels. Andrea's initial idealisation of Ena's family is undermined through the revelation of Ena's mother's infatuation with Román.

29. *Al volver* suggests that within the psyche, our deepest longings form memories in themselves, even if they remain within the realm of desire.

30. For an interesting discussion of the relationship between trauma and the tendency towards absorption see Auke Tellegen and Gilbert Atkinson, 'Openness to Absorbing and Self-altering Experiences ("Absorption"), a Trait Related to Hypnotic Susceptibility', *Journal of Abnormal Psychology*, 83.3 (1974), 268–77.

31. His reaction once again suggests an impingement to the normal processes of maturation and individuation.

32. The term 'una noche Toledana' refers to a night of disturbed sleep. Soli's father don Amando states that it is: 'dos noches con un día en medio' (p. 46).

33. The story of Zoila, Obdulia and Anita Corsi's reasons for being in Toledo is convoluted and lacks veracity, although it introduces a degree of farce or melodrama into the novel.

34. Johnson, 'La novelística de Carmen Laforet', p. 519.

35. This idea of excessive love is mirrored in both Andrea's love for Ena and Marta's for Pablo. It is also reiterated in Paulina's love of God. In Laforet's letters to her fellow Spanish writer Elena Fortún, we witness a similar outpouring of affection. Although Fortún remained an important literary influence on Laforet, in their correspondence Laforet raises her to the status of a substitute mother: 'Tú sin saberlo has sido un poco mi madre, o un mucho, y yo te quiero así, sin reservas', Cerezales Laforet, *Carmen Laforet y Elena Fortún*, p. 93.

36. Anna Freud, *The Ego and the Mechanisms of Defence* (London: The Hogarth Press and the Institute of Psycho-Analysis, 1968), p. v. Quoted in Storr, *The Dynamics of Creation*, p. 45.

37. Storr, *The Dynamics of Creation*, p. 45.

38. Ibid., p. 57.

39. D. W. Winnicott, 'Communicating and Not Communicating Leading to the Study of Certain Opposites', in *The Maturational Processes and the Facilitating Environment* (London: The Hogarth Press and the Institute of Psycho-Analysis, 1965), p. 185, quoted in Storr, p. 58. Laforet stated that writing functioned as a 'huida de mis malos fondos revueltos[...] aunque me angustie escribir también', Cerezales Laforet, *Carmen Laforet y Elena Fortún*, p. 39.

40. Del Mastro touches upon this point with reference to Martín: 'the protagonist's identity search continues', 'Reflections of Oneself: Reconciling Identity in Carmen Laforet's *Al volver la esquina*', *Hispania*, 97.4 (2014), 555–65, (p. 563).

41. Storr, p. 58.

42. Noè, p. 567.

43. Del Mastro, 'Reflections of Oneself', p. 558.

44. Mark P. Del Mastro, 'Carmen Laforet: A Tenth Anniversery and Something after *Nada*', *Hispania*, 97.4 (2014), 552–54, (p. 553).

45. Caballé and Rolón, p. 19.

46. Storr, p. 237.

47. Interview with Ted Hughes, *Paris Review*, Spring 1995. <https://www.theparisreview.org/interviews/1669/ted-hughes-the-art-of-poetry-no-71-ted-hughes> [accessed 9 July 2017].

48. Ibid.

CONCLUSION

Silence and Relief

'...to speak is to say less'
GEORGE STEINER[1]

The source of Laforet's novels flows from the well-spring of tragedy; their pessimistic undercurrent connects her writing back to a previous generation of writers in Spain, notably Unamuno and Baroja, yet her style remains *sui generis* and is intimately linked to Laforet's personal life experiences, rather than a set of defined literary or philosophical influences.[2] Critics have compared her first novel to Emily Bronte's *Wuthering Heights* and Proust's *À la recherche du temps perdu*. J. D. Salinger's prose style has been suggested as a possible influence, yet it proves enduringly difficult to compare Laforet's novels to any author or to fit them into a clearly defined genre. Each novel is an oblique reflection of her own unique mode of experiencing reality based on the imprint of the events of her personal life on her psyche. Although this may be said of any writer, Laforet was at pains to hide the confessional features of her fiction within the silent discourse of relief which, as the previous chapters have illustrated, arises under different guises. The narrative representations of moments of merger and transcendence symbolise the author's efforts to express and withhold deeply felt emotions simultaneously.

The intention of this study has been to draw out the significance of relief as an invariant theme across Laforet's novels without endeavouring to align closely the events of Laforet's life to the fictional events that occur in her texts. The much broader matter of how the human subject encounters relief, or attempts to do so, in the face of grief and early life trauma remains the more important subject of investigation. Laforet changes our style of thinking about grief so that it may be viewed as a series of exercises or efforts to assail suffering across a lifetime rather than focusing on the process of resolution or healing. Here her approach to writing overturns the widely held view that creativity can lead to integration of the subject's disordered mourning. Aberbach suggests that:

> Creativity may also serve to confront and attempt to resolve emotional conflicts and heal wounds caused by the loss itself, or by unhappy elements in the relationship which the loss revives. The satisfaction of creating a thing of beauty may palliate the artist's grief, and the distancing of the self from grief through art may be similarly therapeutic.[3]

However, in Laforet's case grief's resistance to integration within the psyche emerges as an important aspect of her fiction; rather than conceiving of suffering as something that reaches an end point or assimilation within the psyche due to a successful grieving process, Laforet's novels suggest that relief arises in discrete moments linked to feelings of merger or an encounter with the transcendental realm, that it is transitory and sometimes sought in the wrong places. As Rasmussen observes, 'it is wise to look for forms of relief from distress that are more optimal (e.g., long term or permanent) rather than simply immediate.'[4] Laforet's protagonists appear to fall foul of such immediate forms of relief rather than finding 'optimal reliefs [which] are often harder to come by and slower in their effectiveness'.[5] There is no evidence of her protagonists finding optimal reliefs, that is, long term or permanent alleviation of their suffering. They remain instead lonely, searching for, but not finding psychological peace. Within the matrix of loneliness, as Dumm notes more generally, 'remains the matrix of the missing mother', whose presence cannot be re-encountered.[6]

For Laforet herself, the act of creation did not provide her with the relief that she sought for her emotional wounds. Laforet felt compelled to write due to her vocation, yet she simultaneously found writing to be a form of suffering. In a letter written to Elena Fortún in 1951, she discussed her desire for her daughters not to become artists or writers: 'que no tengan esa terrible carga de crear, aunque sepan que no vale nada lo que hacen. Esa manía espantosa que a mí me amarga la vida.'[7] Her daughter also recalled her mother's relief at the prospect of not writing: 'Ya no tengo que escribir. ¡Qué liberación!'[8] Laforet experienced writing both as a compulsion and as a source of suffering, perhaps because it did not permit her to express her grief. It is perhaps no surprise then that the author fell into silence towards the end of her life. The missing manuscript of *Jaque mate*, the final novel in the Martín Soto trilogy *Tres pasos fuera del tiempo* may one day be found and add to our knowledge of Laforet's treatment of relief. We have only the title of this last novel to reflect upon, which evokes curtailment and the sense of an ending. The king is hemmed in with no possible exit and the game is over, a fitting prophetic symbol for Laforet's silence in later years.[9]

A haunting silence pervades Laforet's novels and the unsayability of grief becomes the unacknowledged substance of her writing. We are reminded of Wittgenstein's famous words at the end of the *Tractatus* which pertain to the philosopher's silence in the face of describing the non-conceptual or mystical in language. Wittgenstein's proposition brings together sorrow and relief, echoing Silvius's words quoted in the introduction to this study. A sense of sorrow surrounds the inexpressibility of the unsayable; that human suffering cannot be honed into language, yet this condition of silence remains the purest distillation of relief, a source of comfort when words are effaced by the phenomena or emotion under description.[10] Nieli proposes the sacred nature of silence that is alluded to in Wittgenstein's discussion of language: 'Silence may [...] be held as the only manner of symbolization which does not profane, either by suggesting that the experience is an act of human will, or that the Reality revealed through it is like an everyday "thing" in the mundane world.'[11] Similarly, Steiner's reading of the end of the *Tractatus* reiterates the positive nature of silence whereby 'we look out of language not into darkness but light' which emanates from the 'mute radiance' of Wittgenstein's writing'.[12] In the case of Laforet's silent confession, it is less a mute radiance that emanates from her fiction and more of the 'angustiosa armonía sin luz' referred to in *Nada*. Direct expression of the grieving subject's emotions cannot be made into a mundane thing in the world and blanks language out of its expressive capabilities.[13] Thus, semiotic failure occurs and stands in contrast to Kristeva's views on the melancholy person triumphing 'over the sadness at being separated from the loved object through an unbelievable effort to master signs in order to have them correspond to primal, unnameable, traumatic experiences'.[14] In Laforet's case, there is no sense of triumph or mastery over the traumatic experience; failure is acknowledged in the face of melancholic grief and the signifier is subsumed within the negative poetics of her writing. The inability to grieve and represent the loss of the mother figure enclosed Laforet within 'un círculo de angustia' from which she could not find a way out: 'Nada puedo hacer, nada puedo... Cerrar la luz.'[15] The light shuts off and the interminable darkness of grief or 'círculo de angustia' engulfs the word, leaving only silence or *nada* as the appropriate method of articulating relief. We return to the analogy of the photographic negative, which presents itself in Laforet's fiction as a silent imprint, always there and not there as an anguished 'música blanca'. As readers, we sense the shadow of anguish casting itself across Laforet's novels, despite the protagonists' endeavours to find relief through various means. Laforet's fiction suggests that the absence of the loved and lost parent occupies a space of muted loss, forming the *nada* or nothingness which receives syntactical equivalence through the frequent use of ellipsis within or at the end of sentences. Something is running on or within these gaps, as if the author were intimating that she wished to express more but could not do so, or was, perhaps consciously or unconsciously, withholding some piece of information. Laforet's use of ellipsis contains a prophetic symbol for the end of her novelistic production and refusal to speak towards the end of her life.[16]

If we are to make any conclusions about Laforet's ongoing relevance as a writer, then it is important to assess her contribution to our understanding of human psychology and the emotional impact of grief on the individual. Her novels enrich our knowledge beyond that of her personal life history; they contain 'an Idea which can only be manifested in a particular, but which itself transcends particulars'.[17] As Storr suggests of Eliot, Tolstoy, Freud and Proust, Laforet used her imagination and creative talent 'to penetrate below surface appearances to reach a deeper and richer truth'.[18] Her fiction is a sustained aesthetic meditation on one of the most common of all human pursuits, relief, and its place within human experience. To evoke Bayard's propositions on the relationship between literature and psychoanalysis again, we must recognise Laforet's capacity to 'teach us today about the psychic life' and ask why her novels 'remain for us, even coming from another era, sources of knowledge and reflection'.[19] Beyond death and beyond the historical epoch in which Laforet wrote her novels, her work still speaks to us and unfolds new perspectives on the aesthetic revelation of relief in literature and, more generally, within the human condition.

Notes to the Conclusion

1. George Steiner, *Language and Silence: Essays 1958–1966* (London: Faber and Faber, 1967), p. 68.
2. Nietzschean pessimism forms an undercurrent in Laforet's writing.
3. Aberbach, p. 23. Storr reiterates this view: 'In so far as [...] literary efforts serve a 'therapeutic' or healing function, they may be compared to abreaction: the provision of an opportunity to 'blow off steam'; to rid the psyche of impulses which cannot find expression in ordinary life, as well as compensating for the disappointments of reality.' *The Dynamics of Creation*, p. 27. More recently, van der Kolk has suggested otherwise, illustrating Laforet's relationship to writing out her trauma in her novels: 'telling a story about the event does not guarantee that the traumatic memories will be laid to rest', *The Body Keeps the Score*, p. 219.
4. Rasmussen, p. 165.
5. Ibid., pp. 165–66.
6. Dumm, p. 24.
7. Cerezales Laforet, *Carmen Laforet y Elena Fortún*, p. 61. In another letter to Fortún she writes of her creative work as an 'huida de mis malos fondos revueltos' (p. 39) which causes her anguish, once again indicating that writing did not provide psychological relief.
8. Cerezales Laforet, *Música blanca*, p. 185.
9. Although Laforet's novelistic production stopped after *Jaque mate*, she continued to publish articles for *Destino* during the 1970s and wrote letters to friends. She also wrote two works of travel writing: *Paralelo 35* (1967) and *Mi primer viaje a USA* (1981). On a personal level, Laforet continued to seek relief; in her later years she explored sophrology and showed an interest in Eastern thought and religion. See Cerezales Laforet, *Música blanca*, p. 85, p. 262.
10. Consider how loss is commemorated through silence.
11. Nieli, p. 89.
12. Steiner, p. 40.
13. van der Kolk notes that 'Traumatic events are almost impossible to put into words', *The Body Keeps the Score*, p. 231.
14. Kristeva, p. 67.
15. Cerezales Laforet, *Música blanca*, p. 262.
16. *Música blanca* is an extraordinary account of how Laforet's daughter communicated non-verbally with her mother during Laforet's period of silence. There is much to be discovered within this memoir on the subject of non-verbal relationships and the augmentation of other forms of communication including visual cues and extrasensory perception.
17. Storr, *Music and the Mind*, p. 134.
18. Storr, *The Dynamics of Creation*, p. 27.
19. Bayard, 'Is it possible', p. 218.

BIBLIOGRAPHY

ABERBACH, DAVID, *Surviving Trauma. Loss, Literature and Psychoanalysis* (New Haven and London: Yale University Press, 1989)

ANDUJAR, MANUEL, et al., *Encuentros con Don Pío: Homenaje a Baroja* (Madrid: Al-Borak, 1972)

AUSTIN, JAMES H., *Zen-Brain Reflections* (Cambridge, Mass. and London, England: The MIT Press, 2006)

——*Zen-Brain Horizons* (Cambridge, Mass. and London, England: MIT Press, 2014)

BAYARD, PIERRE, 'Is it Possible to Apply Literature to Psychoanalysis?', *American Imago*, 56 (1999), 207–19

——*Peut-on appliquer la littérature à la psychoanalyse?* (Paris: Minuit, 2004).

BECERRA, SARAH, *Death of a Parent in Childhood and Resilience in Adulthood* (Saarbrücken: Verlag, 2006)

BENJAMIN, JESSICA, *The Bonds of Love: Psychoanalysis, Feminism, and the Problem of Domination* (London: Virago Press,1990)

BERGSON, HENRI, *The Creative Mind* (New York: The Philosophical Library, 1946)

BLUM, LAWRENCE A., *Friendship, Altruism and Morality* (London, Boston and Henley: Routledge and Kegan Paul, 1980)

BOWLBY, JOHN, *Attachment and Loss, Volume Three: Sadness and Depression* (London: The Hogarth Press and the Institute of Psycho-Analysis, 1980)

BOYLE, RICHARD P., *Realizing Awakened Consciousness: Interview with Buddhist Teachers and a New Perspective on the Mind* (New York: Columbia University Press, 2015)

BRISTOL, MICHAEL, 'Macbeth the Philosopher: Rethinking Context', *New Literary History*, 'Context?' Special Issue 42.4 (2011), 641–62

BROWN, JOAN L., *Women Writers of Contemporary Spain: Exiles in the Homeland* (Newark: University of Delaware Press; London and Toronto: Associated University Presses, 1991)

BUCKE, RICHARD MAURICE, *Cosmic Consciousness: A Study in the Evolution of the Human Mind* (New York: Dutton, 1954)

BUTLER, JUDITH, *Gender Trouble* (London: Routledge, 1990).

CABALLÉ, ANNA, and ISRAEL ROLÓN, *Carmen Laforet: una mujer en fuga* (Barcelona: RBA Libros, 2010)

CEREZALES, AGUSTÍN, *Carmen Laforet* (Madrid: Ministerio de Cultura, 1982)

CEREZALES LAFORET, CRISTINA, ed., *Carmen Laforet y Elena Fortún: de corazón y alma 1947–1952* (Madrid: Fundación Banco Santander, 2017)

——*Música blanca* (Barcelona: Destino, 2009)

CURRIE, GREGORY, *Narratives and Narrators: A Philosophy of Stories* (Oxford: Oxford University Press, 2011)

BEAUVOIR, SIMONE DE, *The Second Sex* (London: Vintage Books, 2011)

DEL MASTRO, MARK P., 'Identity Achievement and Lost Innocence in Carmen Laforet's *La insolación*', *Ojáncano: Revista de Literatura Española*, 25 (2004), 43–60

DEL MASTRO, MARK P., 'Reflections of Oneself: Reconciling Identity in Carmen Laforet's *Al volver la esquina*', *Hispania*, 97.4 (2014), 555–65

DEL MASTRO, MARK P., 'Carmen Laforet: A Tenth Anniversary and Something after *Nada*', *Hispania*, 97.4 (2014), 552–54

DELIBES, MIGUEL, *España 1936–1950: Muerte y resurrección de la novela* (Barcelona: Destino, 2006)

DENNETT, DANIEL C., *Freedom Evolves* (London: Penguin, 2003)

The Dhammapada (Harmondsworth, Middlesex: Penguin Classics, 1975)

DIMMOCK, WAI CHI, 'A Theory of Resonance', *PMLA*, 112 (1997), 1060–1071

DUMM, THOMAS, *Loneliness as a Way of Life* (Cambridge, Mass. and London, England: Harvard University Press, 2008)

ELLMAN, MAUDE, *Psychoanalytical Literary Criticism* (London and New York: Longman, 1994)

FIGUEROA, ANA B., '*Nada* de Carmen Laforet: la pulsión lésbica como verdad no sospechada', *Alpha*, 22 (2006), 169–81

FELSKI, RITA, *The Limits of Critique* (Chicago and London: Chicago University Press, 2015)

FRANKFURT, HARRY G., 'Freedom of the Will and the Concept of a Person', *Journal of Philosophy*, 68.1 (1971), 5–20

FRANKIEL, RITA V., *Essential Papers on Object Loss* (New York and London: New York University Press, 1994)

FRASER, BENJAMIN, *Encounters with Bergson(ism) in Spain: Reconciling Philosophy, Literature, Film and Urban Space* (Chapel Hill: University of North Carolina Press, University of North Carolina at Chapel Hill for its Department of Romance Studies, 2010)

FREUD, SIGMUND, JAMES STRACHEY, ANNA FREUD, ALAN TYSON, and ALIX STRACHEY. *The Standard Edition of the Complete Psychological Works of Sigmund Freud: Ego and the Id and Other Works. Volume IXX (1923–1925)*: (London: Vintage, 2001)

FRIEDAN, BETTY, *The Feminine Mystique* (London: Penguin, 2010)

GAZARIAN GAUTIER, MARIE-LISE, *Interviews with Spanish Writers* (Elmwood Park, Illinois: Dalkey Archive Press, 1991)

HANLY, MARGARET ANN FITZPATRICK, ed., *Essential Papers on Masochism* (New York and London: New York University Press, 1995)

HERMAN, JUDITH LEWIS, *Trauma and Recovery: From Domestic Abuse to Political Terror* (London: Pandora, 2001)

HILL, DANIEL, *Affect Regulation Theory: A Clinical Model* (New York and London: W. W. Norton and Company, 2015)

HODEK, B., ed. and intro., *The Complete Works of William Shakespeare* (London: Spring Books, 1958)

HOFFMAN, FREDERICK J., *Freudianism and the Literary Mind* (New York: Grove Press, 1957)

HOGAN, PATRICK COLM, *What Literature Teaches us about Emotion* (Cambridge: Cambridge University Press, 2011)

HOLLAND, NORMAN N., *Poems in Persons: An Introduction to the Psychoanalysis of Literature* (New York: W. W. Norton, 1973)

HURLBURT, RUSSELL T., *Investigating Pristine Inner Experience* (Cambridge: Cambridge University Press, 2011)

ILLANES ADARO, GRACIELA, *La novelística de Carmen Laforet* (Madrid: Editorial Gredos, 1971)

'Interview with Ted Hughes', *Paris Review*, Spring 1995. <https://www.theparisreview.org/interviews/1669/ted-hughes-the-art-of-poetry-no-71-ted-hughes> [accessed 9 July 2017]

JACQUETTE, DALE, ed., *Schopenhauer, Philosophy, and the Arts* (Cambridge: Cambridge University Press, 2007)

JAMES, WILLIAM, *The Varieties of Religious Experience: A Study in Human Nature* (London: Penguin, 1985)

JOHNSON, ROBERTA, *Carmen Laforet* (Boston: Twayne Publishers, 1981)

——'La novelística de Carmen Laforet y el género negro', *Arbor*, 720 (2006), 517–25

JORDAN, BARRY, 'Laforet's *Nada* as Female Bildung?', *Symposium: A Quarterly Journal in Modern Literatures*, 46.2 (1992), 105–18

——'Looks that Kill: Power, Gender and Vision in Laforet's *Nada*', *Revista Canadiense de Estudios Hispanicos*, 17.1 (1992), 79–104

——'Narrators, Readers and Writers in Laforet's *Nada*', *Revista Hispánica Moderna*, 46.1 (1993), 87–102

——'Shifting Generic Boundaries: The Role of Confession and Desire in Laforet's *Nada*', *Neophilologus*, 77.3 (1993), 411–22

——*Laforet: Nada* (London: Grant & Cutler in association with Tamesis Books, 1993)

KANE, ROBERT, *A Contemporary Introduction to Free Will* (New York and Oxford: Oxford University Press, 2005)

KRISTEVA, JULIA, *Black Sun: Depression and Melancholia* (New York and Oxford: Columbia University Press, 1989)

LAFORET, CARMEN, 'El reloj interno', *Destino*, August 4, (1951)

——*Mis páginas mejores* (Madrid: Editorial Gredos, 1956)

——*Tres pasos fuera del tiempo: La insolación* (Barcelona: Planeta, 1963)

——*Nada* (Madrid: Aguilar, 1987)

——*La isla y los demonios* (Barcelona: Destino, 1991)

——*La mujer nueva* (Barcelona: Destino, 2003)

——*Al volver la esquina* (Barcelona: Destino, 2004)

LANGER, SUSANNE K., *Philosophy in a New Key* (Cambridge, Mass.: Harvard University Press, 1976)

LANGFORD, WENDY, *Revolutions of the Heart: Gender, Power and the Delusions of Love* (London and New York: Routledge, 1999)

The Literary Freud: Mechanisms of Defense and the Poetic Will, ed. by Joseph H. Smith, (New Haven and London: Yale University Press, 1980)

BARBARA LOW, *Psycho-Analysis; A Brief Account of the Freudian Theory* (Harcourt Brace: London and New York, 1920)

MARTÍN GAITE, CARMEN, *Desde la ventana: enfoque femenino de la literatura española* (Madrid: Espasa Calpe, 1993)

MASLOW, ABRAHAM H., *The Farthest Reaches of Human Nature* (New York: Viking Press, 1971)

MERKUR, DAN, *Explorations of the Psychoanalytical Mystics* (Amsterdam and New York: Rodopi, 2010)

MILSTEAD, CLAUDIA, *The Zen of Modern Poetry: Reading Eliot, Stevens, and Williams in a Zen Context* (unpublished doctoral thesis, Knoxville: University of Tennessee, 1998)

MILLER, ALICE, *The Drama of the Gifted Child: The Search for the True Self* (New York: Basic Books, 1997)

MIZRAHI, IRENE, *El trauma del franquismo y su testimonio crítico en Nada de Carmen Laforet* (Newark, Delaware: Juan de la Cuesta, 2010)

MOSER, SUSANNE, *Freedom and recognition in the work of Simone de Beauvoir* (Frankfurt; New York: Peter Lang, 2008)

MURRAY PARKES, COLIN, *Bereavement: Studies of Grief in Adult Life* (London: Penguin, 1991)

NICHOLS, GERALDINE C., *Escribir, espacio propio: Laforet, Matute, Moix, Tusquets, Riera y Roig por sí mismas* (Minneapolis: Institute for the Study of Ideologies and Literature, 1989)

NIELI, RUSSELL, *Wittgenstein: From Mysticism to Ordinary Language: A Study of Viennese Positivism and the Thought of Ludwig Wittgenstein* (Albany, New York: State University of New York Press, 1987)

NOÈ, ELISABETTA, 'Otro paso "fuera del tiempo": *Al volver la esquina* de Carmen Laforet', *Revista de Literatura*, 69 (2007), 559–76

PÉREZ FIRMAT, GUSTAVO, 'Carmen Laforet: The Dilemma of Artistic Vocation', in *Women Writers of Contemporary Spain: Exiles in the Homeland*, ed. by Joan L. Brown (Newark: University of Delaware Press. London and Toronto: Associated University Presses, 1991), pp. 26–41

PÉREZ, JANET, '*Al volver la esquina*', *Hispania*, 87.4 (2004), 744–46

RASMUSSEN, PAUL R., *The Quest to Feel Good* (New York and London: Routledge, 2010)

ROBINSON, JENEFER, *Deeper than Reason: Emotion and its Role in Literature, Music, and Art* (Clarendon Press: Oxford, 2005)

ROIG, MONTSERRAT, *Mujeres en busca de un nuevo humanismo* (Barcelona: Salvat, 1981)

SENECA, and C. D. N COSTA, ed. and trans., *On the Shortness of Life* (London: Penguin Books, 2004)

SHAPSHAY, SANDRA, 'Schopenhauer's Aesthetics', *The Stanford Encyclopedia of Philosophy* (Summer 2018 Edition), ed. by Edward N. Zalta <https://plato.stanford.edu/archives/sum2018/entries/schopenhauer-aesthetics/> [accessed 25 January 2019]

SOLOMON, ROBERT C., ed., *What is an emotion? Classic and Contemporary Readings* (New York and Oxford: Oxford University Press, 2003)

SORABJI, RICHARD, *Emotion and Peace of Mind: From Stoic Agitation to Christian Temptation: The Gifford Lectures* (Oxford: Oxford University Press, 2002)

SOTELO VÁZQUEZ, MARISA, '"*Al volver la esquina*" de Carmen Laforet: Las fotografías de la memoria', *Revista Hispánica Moderna*, 58.1–2 (2005), 107–17

STRACHEY, JAMES, ed., *The Complete Psychological Works of Sigmund Freud. Volume III, 1893–1899* (London: The Hogarth Press, 1962)

STEINER, GEORGE, *Language and Silence: Essays 1958–1966* (London: Faber and Faber, 1967)

STORR, ANTHONY, *The Dynamics of Creation* (London: Secker and Warburg, 1972)

——*Music and the Mind* (London: Harper Collins, 1997)

TAYLOR, E. I., and R. H. WOZNIAK, eds., *Pure Experience: The Response to William James* (Bristol: Thoemmes Press, 1996)

TELLEGEN, AUKE, and GILBERT ATKINSON, 'Openness to absorbing and self-altering experiences ("absorption"), a trait related to hypnotic susceptibility', *Journal of Abnormal Psychology*, 83.3 (1974), 268–77

THOMPSON, CURRIE K., 'Perception and Art: Water Imagery in *Nada*', *Kentucky Romance Quarterly*, 32.3 (1985), 291–300

THOREAU, HENRI DAVID, *Walden* (Oxford and New York: Oxford World Classics, 2008)

TORRENTE BALLESTER, GONZALO, *Panorama de la literatura española contemporánea* (Madrid: Ediciones Gudarrama, 1956)

VAN DER HART, ONNO, ELLERT NIJENHUIS and KATHY STEELE, *The Haunted Self: Structural Dissociation and the Treatment of Chronic Traumatization* (New York and London: W.W. Norton and Company, 2006)

VAN DER KOLK, BESSEL A., and RITA FISLER, 'Dissociation and the Fragmentary Nature of Traumatic Memories: Overview and Exploratory Study', *Journal of Traumatic Stress*, 8.4 (1995), 505–25

VAN DER KOLK, BESSEL A., *The Body Keeps the Score: Mind, Brain and Body in the Transformation of Trauma* (London: Penguin Random House, 2014)

VÁZQUEZ MONTALBÁN, MANUEL, *La literatura en la construcción de la ciudad democrática* (Barcelona: Crítica, 1998)

WELLS, CARAGH, 'The City's Renovating Virtue: Urban Epiphanies in the Novels of Carmen Laforet, Carmen Martín Gaite, Montserrat Roig and Rosa Montero', *Journal of Romance Studies*, 7.1 (2007), 7–19

WITTGENSTEIN, LUDWIG, *Lectures and Conversations on Aesthetics, Psychology and Religious Belief* (Oxford: Blackwell, 2011)

WOLLHEIM, RICHARD, *On the Emotions* (New Haven and London: Yale University Press, 1999)

ZUBIRÍ, CARMEN CASTRO DE, 'Los ojos del Alcorah ven el mar', *Clavileño*, 14 (1952), 47–49

INDEX

CW00688342

RAF
AND THE
SOE

Special Duty Operations
in Europe During WW2

RAF
AND THE
SOE

Special Duty Operations
in Europe During WW2

An Official Account

Frontline Books

RAF AND THE SOE
Special Duty Operations in Europe During WW2

This edition published in 2016
and reprinted in this format in 2022 by Frontline Books,
an imprint of Pen & Sword Books Ltd,
47 Church Street, Barnsley, S. Yorkshire, S70 2AS,

This book is based on file reference AIR 20/8459, Second Draft, at The National
Archives, Kew and licensed under the Open Government Licence v3.0. Appendix
XII based on file reference AIR 20/8450 at The National Archives, Kew and
licensed under the Open Government Licence v3.0.

ISBN: 9-781-39901-978-1

CIP data records for this title are available from the British Library
For more information on our books, please visit
www.frontline-books.com
email info@frontline-books.com
or write to us at the above address.
Printed and bound by CPI Group (UK) Ltd, Croydon, CR0 4YY
Typeset in 10.5/13 Palatino

Contents

Preface

Few people in the summer of 1940 could possibly have envisaged just how extensive and effective an organisation the Special Operations Executive would become by the time of the Normandy landings just four years later. Even today, despite the many studies and memoirs that have been published, the scale of the destruction and disruption achieved by the SOE, and the Resistance movements it co-ordinated, supported and supplied, is rarely understood or appreciated.

This vast network, operating in every region of France, as well as in countries and regions such as Belgium, Holland, Denmark, Norway, Poland, Italy and the Balkans, required enormous logistical support, and possibly the most remarkable aspect of the whole SOE story was how this organisation was maintained in the field. In preparation for the widespread campaign of sabotage planned to inhibit the Germans response to Operation *Overlord*, 10,000 tons of supplies were dropped secretly into France or transported across the coast, which included weapons for more than 350,000 men, 600 tons of explosives and 800,000 hand grenades.

When the Resistance leaders received word that *Overlord* had begun in June 1944, they started their campaign of sabotage and disruption all across France. For months prior to D-Day, SOE headquarters at Baker Street in London had studied the French infrastructure and planned an enormous programme that effectively shut down German communications throughout the country. This involved, for example, sabotage against the rail system and electrical facilities (mainly power lines), attacks on German command and control centres, or the destruction of enemy ammunition depots and fuel dumps. The Resistance also obstructed the movement of the German forces that could potentially reinforce the troops defending Normandy by blocking roads and demolishing bridges, while telephone and teleprinter cables, whether above or below ground, were cut.

At the most crucial time of all – when the Allies began landing on the flat beaches of Normandy – the Germans suddenly found much of their communications cut, their railways and roads blocked and saw their fuel and ammunition storage facilities blown sky high. Had it not been for the activities of the SOE and the Resistance, the Allied troops in Normandy would have had a far more difficult task establishing a foothold in France and even more difficulty breaking out from the beach-heads. Much of this was only made possible by the secret and highly dangerous operations of the RAF.

Any present-day historian endeavouring to relate these activities, or other operations conducted by the SOE, is hindered by the dearth of original material. There are a number of reasons for this. The first is that it was initially a new department under the Minister of Economic Warfare with no existing structure, central registry or departmental filing system, and the very nature of its 'cloak and dagger' operations attracted individuals more interested in action than administration. This lack of, or disregard for, thorough record keeping was further compounded by the rapid growth of the organization. At its peak, the SOE employed some 13,000 agents and staff (10,000 men and 3,000 women), with around a million sub-agents across all theatres and regions around the world.

The second reason, as the historian of the SOE in France, M.R.D. Foot discovered, was because of 'the dense fog of secrecy in which it lived'. Foot found that 'wisps of [that] fog still keep getting in the way of the seeker of past truth'. There were a number of known instances where betrayals by individuals led to mass arrests, torture and murder. Mistakes were also made, even by senior staff, which had similar consequences, and in the dark world in which the agents worked it was not always clear who was the enemy. It was no doubt thought that such things were best forgotten and efforts by historians to dig up the past were not encouraged.

The third, and principal reason, for the existing lack of original documentation is more related to smoke than fog. In 1946 the SOE was closed down. It wound up its operation, as Nigel West put it, 'with inordinate haste, destroying documents wholesale'. As the organisation was being dismantled its files were 'roughly weeded' by staff members who had helped to compile them.

Many of these papers were taken onto the roof of the Baker Street building where they were burnt; on one occasion this was witnessed by personnel at the nearby headquarters of Marks and Spencer. Unfortunately, the fire got out of hand and the fire brigade had to be called. Just how much material was intentionally destroyed and how much accidentally lost is not known, but Norman Mott, the head of the SOE Liquidation Section in Baker Street, claimed: 'The entire contents of my office where I was holding a considerable number of operational files … In addition, all the handing-over briefs from the SOE Country Sections were destroyed as well as a good deal of material relating to investigations into blown *réseaux* [circuits].' What remains of the SOE material is estimated to amount to no more than fifteen per cent of the original total.

We are extremely fortunate then in possessing the Air Ministry's report on their contribution to the activities of the SOE which was compiled before the loss of the papers in the Baker Street fire. Because of the fundamental link between the RAF and SOE, this account includes much information on the establishment of the SOE and its subsequent activities across Europe. As a result, this Air Ministry report is as much a history of the SOE as it is an account of the air operations which made such activities possible.

Behind the details of the air support provided by the RAF are the untold stories of the pilots and crews who flew unescorted and often unarmed deep into enemy territory. Small dark-camouflaged Lysanders landed in rough fields with just a number of tiny lights to guide them. They would remain on the ground for only a few dangerous moments, barely stopping as agents leapt down from or clambered into the confined cockpit, before accelerating across the bumpy ground desperately seeking the speed that would lift the small high-winged 'planes into the night sky for the perilous journey back to the UK. Or the lumbering Whitley and Halifax bombers that had to fly low and slow to parachute equipment and personnel into the dark and possibly into the unknown.

Those are the personal sides of the story. This book is, in effect, the background to those highly secret and hazardous missions. It is a 'history' that is reproduced here in the form that it was originally written. Aside from correcting obvious spelling mistakes or typographical errors, we have strived to keep our edits and alterations to the absolute minimum. A direct consequence of this policy is that there are inconsistencies in the text. For example, 'guerilla' is spelt throughout with a single 'r', whilst words such as partisan and meeting are used with and without a capital P or M. It is also important to point out that a small number of short appendices containing personal information on those involved have been omitted in order to comply with the terms of the Open Government Licence. This detail can of course be viewed by a researcher in an original copy of the report held at The National Archives, Kew. The last major difference in our publication is the addition of Appendix 11: 'SOE/SIS – A History of Bomber Command Support'. This was a shorter, separate report written after the war, and has been added here to provide additional detail to this account.

Such alterations aside, what follows is, in effect, one of, if not the most comprehensive study of the RAF and its support for the Special Operations Executive ever compiled.

John Grehan
Storrington
August 2016

Air Ministry Note

This History is intended to cover the work carried out by the R.A.F. on behalf of S.O.E. in Europe.

Part I, divided into three Sections, covering respectively the periods 1940-42, 1942-June 1944 and June 1944-May 1945, will describe the setting up of S.O.E., the Directives given to the Organisation by the Chiefs of Staff and the efforts of S.O.E. to obtain more aircraft in order to fulfil these Directives. Views expressed by the Combined Chiefs of Staff, the Prime Minister, the Foreign Office, the A.O.C.-in-C, Bomber Command and the various Theatre Commanders on the policy to be followed with regard to resistance movements will also be included. The story of the development of resistance will be told chronologically, and several main threads in the pattern will appear more than once: the particular problems of the four most important countries for which extra S.D. aircraft were required (France, Poland, Yugoslavia and Italy), the Gestapo penetrations and the parachute problems. Although a chronological treatment of the subject will involve a certain amount of repetition, it is felt that this is the only way in which the interlocking of all the various factors can be clearly shown.

Part II details the actual squadrons engaged on S.D. operations and describes the administrative and technical problems involved together with the staff work and procedure employed in the mounting of operations. It will include a short account of the landing operations undertaken by the R.A.F., and a general survey of successes, failures and losses. Assistance given by the R.A.F. to S.O.E. other than by S.D. aircraft, will be briefly described.

Part III consists of a very short account, country by country, of the growth and work of the Resistance Movements, showing how the material delivered by S.D. aircraft was used in the field.

Chronology

	Military Operations	UK Based SD Operations	Mediterranean Based SD Operations
1940			
June	Capitulation of France Dunkirk		
July	Battle of Britain Establishment of SOE		
Aug	Battle of Britain	419 Flight set up at North Weald	
Sep	Battle of Britain		
Oct		419 Flight moves to Stradishall	
Nov		SOE's First Directive	
Winter		First SD Operations into W. Europe from UK.	
1941			
Feb		419 Flight moves to Newmarket.	

	Military Operations	UK Based SD Operations	Mediterranean Based SD Operations
July	Germany invades Russia		
Aug		419 Flight becomes 138 (SD) Squadron	
Sep		First SOE Lysander pick-up in France	
Oct			SD Flight to be formed in Middle East
Dec	Japan attacks Pearl Harbor		
1942			
Feb		161(SD) Squadron formed at Newmarket	
Mar		138 and 161 Squadrons move to Tempsford	
May		SOE's Second Directive	
Oct	El Alamein		X Flight of 148 Squadron operating from Delta
Nov	Operation *Torch*		
1943			
Jan	Relief of Stalingrad		

	Military Operations	UK Based SD Operations	Mediterranean Based SD Operations
Mar		SOE's Third Directive	X Flight reconstituted as 148 Squadron
Apr		SD Ops placed under Bomber Command	624 (SD) Squadron established at Blida
May	*Trident*		
Jul	Invasion of Sicily	Parachute crisis First JIC report on penetration of SOE circuits	
Aug	*Quadrant* Italy surrenders		149 Squadron at Toccra
Sep	Invasion of Italy	Decision to allocate two USA squadrons for SD work	
Oct		Appointment of the Air Adviser to SOE	
Nov	*Sextant*		Base for Polish Ops moved to Mediterranean
Dec		Second JIC report on penetration of SOE circuits Suspension of air ops to Poland, Denmark and Holland	

	Military Operations	UK Based SD Operations	Mediterranean Based SD Operations
1944			
Jan			SO(M) set up.
			SD bases move to Italy
			334 Wing formed at Bari
Feb		Large supplementary air lift from 3 group allocated to France, February, March and April	DC recommend trebling deliveries to Poland Steady increase in Special Duties aircraft (including Italian and US aircraft)
Jun	*Overlord*	EMFFI set up	Formation of BAF
Aug	*Dragoon*, Warsaw Rising		
Sep			2641 Special Group (USA) formed at Rosignano
Nov		SOE's Fourth Directive	
1945			
May	Germany surrenders		

Abbreviations

AA	Anti-Aircraft
ACAS	Assistant Chief of the Air Staff
ACIU	Allied Central Interpretation Unit
AEAF	Allied Expeditionary Air Force
AFHQ	Allied Force Headquarters
AI	Air Intelligence
AL	Air Liaison
AMSO	Air Member for Supply and Organisation
AOC	Air Officer Commanding
AOC-in-C	Air Officer Commanding-in-Chief
ATC	Air Transport Command
ATF	Air Transport Form
BAC	Balkan Affairs Committee
BAF	Balkan Air Force
BAS	British Army Staff
BBC	British Broadcasting Corporation
BLO	British Liaison Officer
BOAC	British Overseas Airways Corporation
CAS	Chief of the Air Staff
CCS	Combined Chiefs of Staff
CIGS	Chief of the Imperial General Staff
C-in-C	Commander-in-Chief
CIU	Central Interpretation Unit
CLE	Container Light Equipment
COS	Chief of Staff
COSSAC	Chief of Staff, Supreme Allied Command
DCAS	Deputy Chief of the Air Staff
DDI	Deputy Director of Intelligence

DMO	Director of Military Operations
D of I	Director of Intelligence
DR	Dead Reckoning
EAM	Ethniko Apeleftherotiko Metopo (National Liberation Front (Greece))
EDES	Ethnikos Dimokratikos Ellinikos Syndesmos (National Republican Greek League)
ELAS	Ellinikós Laïkós Apeleftherotikós Stratós (Greek People's Liberation Army)
EMFFI	Etat Major, Forces Francaises de l'lnterieur (an administrative headquarters)
EPF	Equipment of Patriot Forces (Committee)
ETOUSA	European Theater of Operations, United States Army
FFHQ	Free French Headquarters
FFI	French Forces of the Interior
F/Lt	Flight Lieutenant
GHQ	General Headquarters
GI	Government Issue/General Issue (American soldier)
GOC	General Officer Commanding
HB	Heavy Bomber
HMG	His Majesty's Government
HQ	Headquarters
ISSU.6	Inter-Service Signal Unit 6
JIC	Joint Intelligence Committee
JPS	Joint Planning Staff
KLM	Koninklijke Luchtvaart Maatschappij (Royal Dutch Airlines)
LG	Landing Ground
LNC	Lëvizja Nacional Çlirimtare (National Liberation Movement (Albania))
MAAF	Mediterranean Allied Air Forces
MATAF	Mediterranean Allied Tactical Air Force
ME	Middle East
MEW	Ministry/Minister of Economic Warfare
MI.9	Directorate of Military Intelligence Section 9
MU	Maintenance Unit
OR	Other Ranks
OSS	Office of Strategic Services
PIAT	Projector, Infantry, Anti-Tank (anti-tank weapon)
PWB	Psychological Warfare Branch

QMG	Quartermaster General
RAF	Royal Air Force
RAAF	Royal Australian Air Force
RCAF	Royal Canadian Air Force
RNZAF	Royal New Zealand Air Force
RVV	Raad Van Verzet (Dutch Council of Resistance)
SAAF	South African Air Force
SACMED	Supreme Allied Commander, Mediterranean Theatre
SACSEA	Supreme Allied Commander South East Asia
SAS	Special Air Service
SCAEF	Supreme Commander Allied Expeditionary Force
SD	Special Duties
SEAC	South East Asia Command
SHAEF	Supreme Headquarters Allied Expeditionary Force
SIO	Senior/Station Intelligence Officer
SIS	Secret Intelligence Service
S/L	Squadron Leader
SNCF	Société Nationale des Chemins de fer Français (National Society of French Railways)
SO	Supply Officer
SOE	Special Operations Executive
SO(M)	Special Operations (Mediterranean)
STS	Specialized Training School
TC	Troop Carrier
USAAF	United States Army Air Force
VCAS	Vice-Chief of the Air Staff
WAAF	Women's Auxiliary Air Force
W/T	Wireless Telephony

Introduction

On September 1st, 1939 the German armies invaded Poland; and on September 3rd, in accordance with her pledges, Great Britain with her ally France declared war on Germany. The rest of the world at this stage of the second Great War, with the exception of Russia, which invaded Poland, was neutral. The campaign in the east was soon over and in the first few weeks of the war Poland was overrun to join Czechoslovakia in the ranks of the occupied countries. After a pause of nearly six months 'phoney' war the German forces once more took the offensive and on the 9th April 1940, Norway and Denmark were invaded. On 11th May the Low Countries were attacked and by the last week in June the struggle in Western Europe was temporarily at an end.

By this time Denmark, Norway, Holland and Belgium had also fallen under German occupation. The northern part of France was completely in German hands, the southern part under the rule of the Petain Government which had no power to oppose German wishes. There was clearly nothing to prevent the Germans from extending their occupation to whatever other countries on the Continent they chose, occupying them according to their convenience either as their enemies or their allies; and in the course of a year they thus added to their dominions Hungary, Rumania, Bulgaria, Yugoslavia and Greece. Italy lost most of the reality of her independence after the fiasco of her Greek campaign in the winter of 1940-41 and fell to a status but little less humiliating than that of the more definitely occupied countries.

In the summer of 1940 Great Britain alone stood undefeated, the rock on which Hitler's dreams of World domination were doomed eventually to founder. But though at that time the British Government was determined not to surrender, it was impossible not to recognise the fact that there was no prospect for many years to come of our army being able to conduct any successful campaign on foreign soil against the German army. It was indeed far from easy to see how we should ever be able to invade the Continent unless other great countries – Russia and the United States – which up to that time had shown little sign of any wish to come into the war against Germany, should somehow become involved in it as our Allies.

At the same time, if we were not going to surrender it was useless to await the German assault on these Islands in a state of mere inaction, and we must make the most we could, limited as our power might be, of all available means of hampering the German war effort. Accordingly we attempted to blockade the Reich by sea, even though it was evident that, with the Russian trade still open, with the Italian Alliance, and with our naval position in the Mediterranean wholly insecure, no very spectacular success could be expected from such a policy. We set to work slowly and patiently to make up our deficiencies in arms and in particular to build a bomber force which could carry the attack into the very heart of Germany itself; and to the Blockade and the Bomber we added a third policy of planned and co-ordinated sabotage which should hamper Germany's war effort in all the occupied countries and compel her to disperse her armed forces.

Already in the autumn of 1940 there were contacts with rebellious patriots in Poland and Czechoslovakia and small quantities of arms and explosives were being smuggled into these countries. In the other occupied countries also the spirit of resistance was spontaneous. Although defeat seemed to have temporarily stunned the peoples of some of the occupied countries, the will to resist was not lost and everywhere was fanned into flame by the violence, cruelties and mass murders which were the routine Nazi methods of occupation. The Germans could hardly have expected to be made welcome in any event, but had they had the political wisdom to pursue a conciliatory policy they might well have been accepted in the end by large numbers of people on the argument that their strength was overwhelming and their victory inevitable. Instead of this, however, they displayed the usual Teutonic lack of understanding of other nationalities, and prepared to use every traditional and modern weapon in the ruthless enforcement of a policy of rigorous suppression. Fortunately for the future of Europe they behaved in such a way that to masses of people in the occupied countries any suffering, however desperate the hope of deliverance, was thought better than submission.

Here was a situation which, great as were the difficulties, it was possible for British policy to exploit. Had it been left to little knots of desperate men in this country and that country to carry out their acts of resistance without extraneous assistance then, under modern conditions of war, the German task would have been an easy one, and there could have been no results save the useless sacrifice of gallant lives. If anything was to be effected, action must be co-ordinated and timed. This could only be done from the one free base in England. The small scale smuggling of arms into Poland and Czechoslovakia must be expanded and intensified until channels of communication were established between England and the occupied countries by which men, material and messages could be delivered. It was important that England should give such help not only for its material but also for its moral and political value. By our policy we showed the oppressed people of Europe that they were not forgotten, and gave proof that even in our darkest hour we remembered that we were fighting not only for our own freedom but for that of all the world.

In order to implement this policy the Special Operations Executive was set up in the summer of 1940 with orders to "co-ordinate all action by way of subversion and sabotage against the enemy overseas."

The business of supporting organised Underground Resistance Movements in enemy-occupied or enemy territory was not an entirely new one. At various periods in the history of the world it had been attempted by different Governments within the framework of the particular conditions of their time. The Trojan Horse is perhaps the earliest example of S.O.E. work, although here the 'resistants' were not indigenous but were infiltrated from outside. In general the effort of an enemy, sometimes military, but more especially political, is to overcome his opponent from the <u>inside</u> (which is also in a military sense his rear) and so to save the risk of loss of battle. At this art the Mongols were especially expert and much of the rapidity of their success in their Western advances across Asia was due to their skill in subversion, as also to corruption and intimidation, the other main branches of 5th Column Activity. National states as they developed were comparatively invulnerable on this head; but states still had an Achilles heel in the shape of minority or oppressed populations; Spain for example, had a permanent weakness in Catalonia, England in Ireland. English sixteenth-century history provides several examples of the support of rebel elements by an enemy power. In England itself, the use by Spain of the Catholic minority, culminating in an extraordinarily widespread, yet close-knit, network of Underground Organisations is in the best S.O.E. tradition. Ireland and Scotland, the two vulnerable points through which England might be attacked, were both encouraged in rebellion, financed and, to some extent, armed by the enemies of England: the one by Spain and the other by France, through Mary Queen of Scots. In the Napoleonic wars the Alliance between the leaders of the French Revolution and Wolfe Tone who aimed at (and very nearly achieved) a French invasion of Ireland which would have been supported by Irish patriots is another example of the use of an "occupied" country by an enemy, while on the other hand the English, playing the same game, encouraged and supplied the patriots of Portugal and Spain in their resistance to the Grand Army. In the First Great War, the famous Casement affair, in which an Irish rebel movement was encouraged and financed by Germany, is a very fair parallel to S.O.E.'s work. Other German activities in that war which bear a striking resemblance to S.O.E.'s work between 1940 and 1945 were the sabotage carried out by von Rintelen in the United States and the well-timed smuggling of Lenin back to Russia in a closed train.

It was part of the traditional policy of Great Britain to oppose the exclusive domination of an aggressive power on the Continent of Europe by encouraging and supporting European allies – if possible, even after they had been defeated or overrun. Money, equipment and even troops were distributed widely by the British Government during the Napoleonic wars in an effort to keep some Continental armies in the field and so disperse the enemy's forces. The weakness of England as a military power made such a policy essential, while her tremendous strength at sea made it practicable. In the Second Great War Hitler's successful occupation of most of the continent, like Napoleon's, left England isolated and without active Allies. Until her inferior military strength had been built up she could not hope to obtain a foothold in Europe. Meanwhile the enemy's forces must be dispersed and worn down as far as possible, and since there was no regular army in the field against him he must be attacked by subversive methods. The German occupation of all her continental allies provided England, armed with the appropriate modern weapons (notably aircraft and W/T), with an opportunity to strike at the enemy from inside his fortress. The Prime Minister, with his imagination and historical insight, was the first to seize on this and his personal influence on the policy of encouraging resistance forces was felt again and again.

It fell to S.O.E., staffed by amateurs (since England had no history and tradition of this type of warfare) to exploit with the aid of these modern weapons the possibilities of underground resistance. Clearly its first task must be that of establishing channels of communication between the occupied countries of Europe and the United Kingdom so that agents, instructions and supplies could be infiltrated to the resistants while they, on their side, were enabled to send out intelligence, requests for help, reports on results, and military and political representatives. Above all W/T links must first be forged, and for this wireless sets and wireless operators must be sent into Europe. There were two possible methods by which men and material might be conveyed: by sea or by air. It is with the story of the R.A.F.'s part in the supply of Resistance throughout Europe that this narrative is concerned.

Part I

The Charter and Directives Given to the SOE
by the Chiefs of Staff and Allocations of Aircraft
on Special Duties

Chapter 1

The Pioneer Phase

1940 to November 1942

Special Operations Executive was established, and its first Directive given, in a War Cabinet Meeting Memorandum of July 1940, in which it was recorded that the Prime Minister had decided, after a consultation with the Ministers concerned that a new organisation should be established forthwith to co-ordinate all action by way of subversion and sabotage against the enemy overseas.

WP(40)271, 19 July 1940
S.O.E. was to be under the Chairmanship of Mr. Dalton, Minister of Economic Warfare, who would have the co-operation of the Directors of Intelligence of the three Service Departments, and of the Secret Intelligence Service (M.I.6), for the purpose of the work entrusted to him. The Memorandum emphasised that the general plan for irregular offensive operations should be kept in step with the general strategical conduct of war, and that Mr. Dalton should therefore consult the Chiefs of Staff as necessary keeping them informed in general terms of his plans, and in turn receiving from them the broad strategic picture.

COS(40)27(0), 25 November 1940
In November 1940 the Chiefs of Staff issued their first Directive to S.O.E. In this paper the importance of planning subversive activities within the framework of military strategy was underlined again, and S.O.E., the Joint Planning Staff, the Director of Combined Operations, and the Air Staff were told to keep in close touch with each other. The Directive stated that the process of undermining the strength and spirit of the

1

enemy armed forces, especially those in the occupied territories, should be the constant aim of S.O.E. On a long view, it should be S.O.E.'s particular aim to prepare the way for the final stage of the war, when by co-ordinated and organised revolts in the occupied countries and by a popular rising against the Nazi Party inside Germany, direct and decisive military operations against Germany herself might be possible.

After explaining the impossibility of laying down with any precision the areas in which military operations would eventually take place, the Chiefs of Staff said:

> "We are, however, very conscious of the important and even decisive part which subversive activities may play in our strategy … we feel that if we are to exploit the use of subversive activities to the full, these activities must be planned on a very big and comprehensive scale. Our aim, in fact, should be to get subversive activities laid on and ready for execution in all areas where there is any chance that they may be needed, so that, wherever the fortune of war may require action, the ground will be prepared in advance."

In the enemy countries S.O.E.'s aim was to be the creation of political disunity, discontent, economic disorganisation and dislocation of communications.

Offensive operations by the Allies in Western Europe and the Mediterranean were envisaged, and S.O.E. was directed to encourage subversive activities in the enemy-occupied countries of these areas. The importance of guarding against any premature revolt was emphasised and S.O.E. was warned that abortive attempts could only lead to the elimination of individuals and organisations which might later be needed.

Necessity for Use of Aircraft by S.O.E.

3039/PDDO, 20 August 1940
Deep penetration of the enemy's Fortress of Europe, as envisaged by the Chiefs of Staff, necessitated the use of aircraft as a means of transport. The difficulties of transporting supplies inland from the coast, and the increasing German surveillance of the coastal areas, particularly in Western Europe, served to put the emphasis more and more upon air transport. As early as the summer of 1940, therefore, the first aircraft

were set aside for S.D. work, when the Director of Plans, Air Ministry announced the formation of No.419 Flight at North Weald. These aircraft were not allotted for S.O.E.'s exclusive use but were to be shared between S.O.E. and S.I.S.

First S.D. Operations and S.O.E. Reports on Results

During the winter of 1940-41 the first operation to Western Europe was carried out by this Flight, and although the weather was consistently unfavourable and the number of successful operations correspondingly small, organisers, W/T operators and coup-de-main teams were dropped in the countries of Western Europe.

Assistance had been given to the Services in a number of operations by S.O.E. The first raid on the Lofoten Islands and operations "Shamrock," and "Hemisphere" and particularly "Rubble" owed something of their success to intelligence and special equipment supplied by S.O.E. or to personnel trained by S.O.E. R.A.F. raids on the Bergen/Oslo railway and on Hoyanger were given assistance by S.O.E. agents who arranged for light signals to be shown on the ground, and in the former case the raid was planned on photographs printed by S.O.E. Apart from these semi-military operations, small scale sabotage had been carried on continuously against enemy communications by organisations financed and supplied with material by S.O.E. Attacks on railways and locomotives and a number of acts of industrial sabotage had met with a wide measure of success.

S.O.E. Plans: General Necessity for Aircraft, April 1941

On 21st April 1941, a paper entitled "The Prospects of Subversion," was submitted to Lieut. General Sir Hastings Ismay by S.O.E. After recording that considerable progress in the organisation of Resistance had been achieved, S.O.E. pointed out that there was still immense scope for development in this branch of warfare. The possibilities in all parts of the world were now being studied while existing fields were being further exploited, and support given. Like the other Services, i.e. the Navy, Army and Air Force, S.O.E. were handicapped by the existing shortages of arms, of aircraft and of transport facilities; when these were made up, progress was expected to be quicker. If S.O.E. were to be responsible for the organisation of the "Fifth Column of the Free" they declared that provision must be made for their needs, and urged that long-term planning should take place at once, unless S.O.E. were to lose their whole raison d'etre they would have to train and infiltrate large numbers of agents during the coming year. Four to five hundred men were actually already in training. Suitable aeroplanes in sufficient numbers must be made available, and above all communications ensured.

A letter to H.M.G. Jobb, Esq., 24 April 1941
General Ismay replied that it would be asking for the impossible to expect the Chiefs of Staff to give a definite undertaking that they would make available, from their respective Services, the men and material necessary for carrying out all the S.O.E. plans. This would commit them to an almost unlimited liability. Unfortunately the Chiefs of Staff were at present faced with the problem of having to feed many hungry mouths with bread, on which the butter had to be spread very sparingly, and he felt sure that though they would agree, in principle, with S.O.E.'s paper, they would not be prepared to give S.O.E. the carte blanche for which they asked.

S.O.E. Plans: Sabotage and Secret Armies

COS(41)147(0), 21 July 1941
In July 1941, a paper submitted by S.O.E. to the Chiefs of Staff set forth an outline plan of S.O.E. operations from September 1941 to October 1942. S.O.E. working to a target date of the autumn of 1942, had evolved plans for the organisation both of subversive sabotage groups and of Secret Armies for guerilla warfare, had strongly urged that the formation and equipment of Secret Armies should be undertaken. The total number of aircraft sorties, which, it was estimated, would be necessary to fulfil the plans, was, 2,334, of which 584 were needed to equip the sabotage and subversive groups, and 1,750 for the Secret Army.

JP(41)649, 9 August 1941
This paper was considered by the Joint Planning Staff, and later by the Chiefs of Staff Committee, and both emphasised the distinction between the two types of organisation which S.O.E. proposed to encourage. The Joint Planning Staff suggested that sabotage might be a most valuable

complement to the bombing effort of the R.A.F. and should therefore be directed chiefly in accordance with the bombing policy aim. The organisation of Secret Armies on the other hand, should be limited to those areas where it was anticipated that an Allied Offensive would later be possible, and since they could not operate until bombing had first created suitable conditions, it would be unsound to sacrifice the effectiveness of our bombing effort to these activities. The Joint Planning Staff therefore recommended that subversive activities should be given preference over Secret Armies.

COS(41)287th Meeting, Item 10, 14 August 1941
The report of the Joint Planning Staff was considered by the Chiefs of Staff Committee who agreed that subversive activities should be given every encouragement but the prospects of raising Secret Armies, which depended on our ability to provide arms and ammunition, were to be reconsidered at a Chiefs of Staff Committee meeting the next day.

Increase of Aircraft for S.D. Work, October 1941

If subversive activities were to be given every encouragement the first essential was an increase in the number of aircraft allotted to S.D. work, so that men and supplies could be sent in to the occupied countries to intensify Resistance activities. From the R.A.F.'s point of view the allocation of more aircraft for S.D. work inevitably meant a loss to the bombing effort. The D.C.A.S., in a minute to the Director of Plans on 10th August 1941, pointed out the difficulty of deciding whether the sacrifice to the Bomber effort was compensated by an equal or greater success in sabotage, and also remarked that the fact that S.D. operations could be carried out only during the moon periods meant that aircraft engaged on this work were used much less intensively than normal Bomber Squadrons.

DDP/598, 5 October 1941
The Director of Plans, however, writing to the V.C.A.S. argued that although the diversion of two or three Heavy Bombers from Bomber Command would entail a proportionate drop in the bomber effort, it was possible that the results obtained by sabotage might outweigh the loss. Germany was now intensifying her efforts to crush the Underground organisations in the occupied countries and this might

well be the most appropriate moment to show by practical help that these subversive activities were valued. It could be argued that the ultimate aim of the bombing policy and the purpose of S.O.E. activity were identical. Without the lifeline of air transport, resistance could not continue on an effective scale.

COS(41)287th Meeting, Item 10, 14 August 1941
The Chiefs of Staff Committee, therefore, in directing that subversive activities were to be encouraged took note that the Air Ministry would try to expand as soon as possible the Special Flight. By the end of 1941, 138 Squadron had been formed, and was engaged on S.D. operations. In the spring of 1942, a second Squadron (161) was also allotted to S.D. work, and for the greater part of the next two years it was left to these two Squadrons to carry out the operations from the U.K. necessary to implement the Chiefs of Staff Directives to S.O.E.

Secret Armies

COS(41) 288th Meeting, Item 14, 15 August 1941
As had been arranged, the problem of the Secret Armies was further discussed by the Chiefs of Staff when the Committee agreed to reconsider the raising of Secret Armies after the War Office report on the availability of the necessary arms and equipment had been circulated.

JP(42)465, 1 May 1942
A Joint Planning Staff paper of May 1942 reports, however, that at the above Chiefs of Staff Meeting, it had been decided that secret armies and sabotage organisations in the nearer countries (Northern France, Belgium, Holland and Norway, in that order of priority) should be supported by the delivery of personnel and materials, while action in Poland and Czechoslovakia must be limited to the support of sabotage groups alone, as sufficient supplies for a secret army could not be transported without an unwarrantable diversion of bomber effort.

S.O.E.'s Second Directive, May 1942

COS(42)133(0), 12 May 1942
In May 1942, S.O.E. received its second directive from the Chiefs of Staff. Future military operations were expected to comprise a series of raids

to be carried out on the coast from the north of Norway to the Bay of Biscay; an active air offensive over North Western Europe; a large scale raid to bring about an air battle and/or the capture of a bridgehead in France; and a large descent on Western Europe in the spring of 1943. S.O.E. were required to ensure that plans for the use of Resistance conformed with this general military strategy, and was instructed to work in continuous collaboration with the Planning Staffs. In particular S.O.E. should endeavour to build up and equip para-military organisations in the area of the projected operations. The action of such organisations would be directed particularly against the enemy's road, rail and signal communications.

The emphasis was already beginning to shift from the exclusive support given to clandestine sabotage: in future S.O.E. were requested to plan for more military organisations which were, in effect, the Secret Armies of which they had long dreamed.

First Operations in the Mediterranean: Yugoslavia

As early as the autumn of 1941 reports from Yugoslavia had shown that guerilla activity was growing up under a more or less unified command, and in October the A.O.C.-in-C. Mediterranean and the C-in-C Mediterranean agreed to allocate two Wellesley Bombers based on Malta and three bomber sorties from Cairo for dropping supplies to Montenegro.

COS(41)339th Meeting, Item 2, 1 October 1941
At a Chiefs of Staff Meeting, a statement was given of S.O.E.'s transport requirements in Malta and the Middle East. A telegram dated 29th September which had been received from the Middle East reported that the M.E.W.S.C. had agreed, with the approval of A.O.C. Middle East, to proceed with the immediate formation of a small flight to be supplied, operated and maintained by the R.A.F. and capable of expansion as demands increased. S.O.E.'s representative agreed that this arrangement went a long way towards meeting their requirements.

British Liaison Officers despatched by sea succeeded in contacting General Mihailovic, at that time the most promising leader in Yugoslavia. Two Whitleys were sent to the Mediterranean, but they proved to be too slow for daylight sorties, and owing to their general limitations only one sortie was successfully completed. Ill luck continued to hamper Yugoslav plans: of the four Whitleys allotted to Malta, one burnt out in England and two were destroyed or badly damaged on the ground in Malta by enemy action.

COS(42)139, 26 February 1942
A memorandum by the Secretary of State for Foreign Affairs reported that Great Britain's policy towards the revolt in Yugoslavia had hitherto been that although we were not in a position to give any substantial military assistance we would do our utmost to provide the rebels with the supplies necessary to maintain the movement in the hills. Circumstances, had, however, rendered even this moderate degree of help unattainable.

COS(42)215, 10 April 1942
In April a memorandum was received from the Yugoslav Legation which, after stressing that General Mihailovic had by this time been leading a fight in Yugoslavia against enormous odds for nine months, stated that it was essential that the material help, already prepared in Malta should be transmitted to General Mihailovic as soon as possible, and urged that a Bomber Squadron or Flight of long range aircraft should be formed as soon as possible for liaison with General Mihailovic.

COS(42)117th Meeting, 13 April 1942
The Chiefs of Staff considered the problem and agreed that it was very desirable to give such support as could be afforded to General Mihailovic, whose activities in Yugoslavia had become "an extremely valuable contribution" to the Allied cause. On the subject of the provision of long range aircraft, the V.C.A.S. said that Liberators were the only aircraft suitable for the task of dropping supplies to Yugoslavia. Two were already available in the Middle East and the Commander-in-Chief had been asked to modify the remaining two. The Committee agreed that when additional Liberators became available in the Middle East (probably in the following month) it would be for the Commanders-in-Chief to decide where they should be employed.

Review of 1941 and 1942

1941 and 1942 were the lean years for Resistance. The speed of the lightning German advances and the apparently irresistible strength of their forces had combined to stun the peoples of Occupied Europe, and apathy and confusion were widespread during the early months.

The spirit of Resistance, however, had not been long in showing itself, and although the process of contacting indigenous Resistance Movements and organising subversive groups was, in the first two years, painfully slow, S.O.E. by the end of 1942, had established a network of clandestine organisations in most of the occupied countries of Europe. The work had not been carried out however without some setbacks and many losses. The principle difficulty inherent in the task allotted to S.O.E. was that sabotage had to be carried out continuously, whilst the organisation was being developed and nursed, to enable it to play a fuller part when the immediate support of regular forces was required. The more active resistance organisations became, the greater was the risk of penetration by the enemy; and in attempting to fulfil the dual task of inflicting day-to-day damage to the enemy, and yet preserving its striking power for D-Day, the Resistance Groups in the field had inevitably suffered certain losses in men and material. Similarly, coups-de-main carried out directly from England by specially trained parties had led to reprisals which had caused temporary setbacks.

The results on the whole however had been satisfactory. By the end of 1942, sabotage was on the increase throughout Europe, although if S.O.E.'s tasks were to be fulfilled it must be stimulated much further. There were many reports daily of bomb outrages, arson, destruction of property and of power supplies and interference with communications in occupied territories. Even in the enemy countries themselves, sabotage had increased during 1942. The tempo and success of sabotage activity varied considerably, but although in some areas the sabotage organisations in the various countries had been penetrated and broken up, yet on balance the strength of these organisations was increasing. Side by side with violent sabotage, methods of "insaisissable" sabotage had been developed to hamper the German machine in every way possible.

The equipment of Secret Armies had as yet hardly begun, although their organisation was beginning to take shape. The main reason was the shortage of transport facilities for arms and materials. Deliveries had increased from 20 or 50 containers a month in 1941, to over a hundred in the months of September, October and November 1942. Even this number, however, had proved wholly insufficient to meet demands from the field.

Chapter 2

The Beginning Of The Offensive

November 1942 to June 1944

By the end of 1942 the Allies had succeeded in building up their strength and were ready to take the offensive on a limited scale. The landing in North Africa inaugurated a new phase of the war in which for the first time the Allied Commanders, not the enemy, held the initiative. In occupied Europe the Resistance Movements also felt the new impulse. The capture of bases in North Africa facilitated S.O.E. work in Southern France and Italy. There was greatly increased activity in the Balkans and an increased volume of supplies poured into Western Europe. Resistance was everywhere intensified. Despite the vigilance of the Gestapo and a number of losses new groups were established and sabotage increased. By D-Day the patriots of Western Europe were ready to take the game into their own hands and the summer of 1944 saw a great flaring up of resistance activity in that area while in Eastern Europe the guerillas maintained their steady pressure on the enemy.

S.D. Aircraft Situation at the Beginning of 1943; Diversion of S.D. effort; A/c for Poles and New S.D. Base in North Africa

Plans/350/764, 8 February 1943
In February 1943 the Director of Plans of S.O.E. reviewed the case for S.O.E.'s aircraft requirements, and recapitulated the situation up to that date. The Air Staff, and more particularly the C-in-C Bomber Command, were bound to see in the provision of aircraft for S.O.E. a diversion for a job which to them must be of less importance than the Bomber Offensive. In spite of this they had provided first of all a Special Flight,

which was later expanded into a Squadron. In September/October of 1942 when S.O.E's demands for air transport operations increased considerably, he, The Director of Plans, had pointed out to the Air Ministry that S.O.E. would require more and more aircraft, and the increase in the establishment of No. 138 Squadron and the use of No. 161 Squadron were to some extent the result of his verbal representations. These representations had fallen under four main headings: efforts to increase the number of aircraft allotted to S.O.E. both in the U.K. and in the Middle East; efforts to retain the aircraft allotted to S.O.E. by trying to prevent their diversion to other work; and efforts to obtain extra aircraft specifically for the Poles.

MO/B2/337, 11 September 1942
The Director of Plans reported that during the last months of 1942 S.O.E. had several times put on record their conviction that an increased number of S.D. aircraft based in England would shortly be required. Efforts had also been made to obtain aircraft from American sources.

MOA/1174, 1 October 1942 (to S.O.E. representatives in Washington)
CMcVG/1408, 10 October 1942 (to Col. Guenther of O.S.S.)
As far as the Middle East was concerned Air Ministry had promised to provide six Halifaxes for S.O.E. work by the end of February. These were on their way but for various reasons it was feared that they might not prove suitable for work in that Theatre. The Western Mediterranean had also by now become a sphere of S.O.E. operations. An S.O.E. base had been established at Algiers at the end of 1942 to work into Italy, Corsica, Sardinia and Southern France, and S.D. aircraft were required in North Africa.

Plans/350/118, 22 March 1943 (to DDI(2))
The use of S.D. aircraft for other duties had become a serious problem. At the end of 1942 there were 18 + 2 aircraft available in the U.K. for S.O.E. and S.I.S. work, and 10 in the Middle East.

Plans/350/798, July 1943
Unfortunately it had not even been possible for S.O.E. to retain the whole-time services of the aircraft that had been allotted to them. It was true that during these early years there were months when S.O.E.'s operational programme was not sufficiently large to keep the aircraft

11

of two Squadrons fully employed. In order to make full use of the squadrons, therefore, Bomber Command occasionally withdrew aircraft for bombing operations. Even when this practice was confined to the non-moon periods, it was liable to have serious results for S.O.E. Aircraft might become unserviceable or due for major inspections when they were required for S.O.E. work; there was the possibility that aircraft and their specialised crews might be lost while engaged on bombing operations; less time would be available during the non-moon period for training, practice and development in S.O.E. work; and even at best the operational flying life of the highly trained crews employed in the S.D. squadrons was reduced so far as S.O.E. operations were concerned. Aircraft from S.D. squadrons were also used for the transport of essential stores to the Middle East and North Africa. Here again there was a serious risk that the modified aircraft and trained crews essential for S.O.E.'s work would not be available in England when they were required. Even if all went well, and the aircraft were able to return on schedule, this diversion meant a serious loss to S.O.E., but on more than one occasion, S.D. aircraft engaged on this type of work suffered casualties. In November 1942, eight Halifaxes from 138 Squadron were sent to the Middle East to transport a quantity of urgent stores. Of these aircraft only four returned to England: two crashed, although the crews were saved, and two more, including a Polish crew and the only Czech crew, were lost.

CMcVG/964, 12 June 1942 (to DDI.2)
CMcVG/54, 18 November 1942 (to A.C.A.S.I.)
CMcVG/131, 7 December 1942 (to Brig. Hollis of C.O.S.)
CMcVG/226, 22 December 1942 (to A.C.A.S. (I).)
CMcVG/115, 2 December 1942 (to A.V.M. Medhurst)
CH/4314

A series of letters from S.O.E. to the Air Ministry during 1942 requested that diversions of S.D. aircraft to other work should not be made unless absolutely essential. On 24th January 1943, Major-General Gubbins wrote a personal letter to Air Chief Marshal Sir Charles Portant asking him to use his influence to ensure that aircraft and crews should not be removed from S.D. work. The C.A.S. replied [...] that, while he appreciated S.O.E.'s anxieties, there were occasions when the diversion of S.D. aircraft was absolutely essential to the success of other operations. He pointed out that every suggestion for the use of S.D.

aircraft on other work was put to the Chiefs of Staff for final decision.

So far as the Poles were concerned they had made their own approaches both to the Air Ministry and to the Americans, and although S.O.E. had represented their case to the Air Ministry from time to time it was largely due to their own efforts that Polish crews were introduced into the Squadron and the extra long-range Halifax was provided.

JSM/544, 9 December 1942
The U.S. Chiefs of Staff, who had received a request for aircraft from the Polish Military Attaché in Washington, and replied that they could not take action on this request without jeopardising basic agreements between the United States and Great Britain in accordance with which Poland was within a British theatre of operations and responsibility. The Polish request had therefore been referred to the British Chiefs of Staff. On January 8th, 1943, the President wrote to the Prime Minister: "I feel however that his (General Sikorski's) proposal had a great deal of merit and I told him therefore that I would refer the matter to you with the request that you would give it all possible consideration."

Plans/350/764, 8 February 1943
The Director of Plans concluded his review by pointing out that the Air Ministry could not be blamed for not giving S.O.E. a larger share of what was after all their own principal weapon. It was up to S.O.E. to represent their case to the Chiefs of Staff who must decide whether bombing, convoy protection or S.O.E. work was the most important, and who must lay down what proportion of the Bomber Force was to be allotted to each.

DCDO/553, 12 February 1943
At the request of the War Secretariat, however, S.O.E. were requested to postpone the submission of a paper on aircraft requirements until the Chiefs of Staff had issued their now comprehensive Directive to S.O.E.

S.O.E.'s Third Directive, March 1943

COS(43)142(0), 20 March 1943
The Chiefs of Staff directive to S.O.E. for 1943 laid down that S.O.E. activities should be concentrated to the maximum extent in support of military strategy, and in general emphasis should be laid on current

activities rather than on long-term preparations. Sabotage must be pursued with the utmost vigour and should as far as possible be co-ordinated with the aims of the Bombing Policy, and full advantage should be taken of bombing cover for the execution of sabotage operations. In general the organisation of active guerilla formations should not be permitted to interfere with current activities. An order of priority was given: first, the Italian Islands, Corsica and Greece, where S.O.E. was to encourage revolt against the Fascist Government and the Germans as a part of the overall plan of eliminating Italy during 1943; the Balkans, where an intensified campaign of sabotage and guerilla activities during spring and summer was considered to be of the first strategic importance in order to impede the concentration and consolidation of German forces on the Eastern front; France, where industrial sabotage and attacks on communications were to be continued in conjunction with the supply, when practicable, of Resistance Groups, which might later play an active part in support of Allied strategy; Poland and Czechoslovakia, where the sabotage of German communications to the Russian front was of primary importance, but the organisation of Secret Armies should be continued as far as possible; and Norway and the Low Countries, where sabotage and coup-de-main attacks were to be increased. The Chiefs of Staff then invited S.O.E. to prepare an appreciation stating what could be done with the available resources for the support of United Nations strategy in 1943 in accordance with this directive.

COS(43)175(0)

On 3rd April the Committee for the Equipment of Patriot Forces reported to the Chiefs of Staff recommending that equipment should be provided for Resistance Groups of a total strength of 300,000 and that this should be taken as the target at which S.O.E. should aim.

COS(43)267(0), 22 May 1943

In a supplementary report in May, the E.P.F. Committee pointed out that one of the factors contributing to the selection of the figure of 300,000 as the target (as against the total of a million given by S.O.E. as the potential strength of Resistance Groups) was the fact that 300,000 seemed the highest figure which it was possible to justify in relation to probable future facilities for delivery.

CC(43)43, 6 April 1943
S.O.E.'s directive for 1943 was examined by the Joint Operational Staff who reported that they were satisfied that S.O.E.'s present activities were in accordance with the new directive and were being carried out effectively in so far as limitations imposed by shortages of aircraft would allow.

S.O.E.'s Appreciation of this Directive

COS(43)212(0)
The Appreciation called for by the C.O.S. Directive was submitted by S.O.E. on 24th April. It emphasised the importance of the production of adequate transport facilities and pointed out that the demands for transport exceeded the means of delivery by about 200%. Since one of the essential characteristics of Resistance Groups was that unless they were served sufficiently to enable them to retain their dynamic quality they tended to disintegrate, the demand for supplies was progressive and the lack of adequate transport facilities not only retarded their expansion, but threatened their very existence.

JP(43)170, Final, 10 June 1943
The Joint Planning Staff considered S.O.E.'s appreciation of their directive and suggested that the order of priority in some areas already given to S.O.E. should be slightly amended to read: Corsica, the Balkans, France and Poland. The Joint Planning Staff further suggested that the equipment of at least three hundred thousand personnel of Resistance Groups, by 30th September 1943 in the case of the Balkans, and by 1st April 1944 for all other areas, was desirable for the implementation of future strategy.

The air transport requirements and the implication of its fulfilment must be balanced against the major claims of the bomber offensive, and the transport requirement for airborne forces. The Joint Planning Staff therefore invited the Air Ministry, in conjunction with S.O.E., to examine immediately and report to the Chiefs of Staff ways and means of increasing deliveries by aircraft: by improving the facilities for aircraft at present allotted to S.O.E.; by meeting S.O.E.'s present request for an initial increase of 18 first-line aircraft and the necessary training flight, and by assessing the aircraft required to meet S.O.E.'s full requirements.

COS(43)128th Meeting (0), Item 4, 17 June 1943
In June the Chiefs of Staff Committee approved the amended order of priority given by the Joint Planning Staff, and invited the Air Ministry in conjunction with S.O.E. to examine and report on the possibility of increasing aircraft deliveries.

Yugoslavia: Shortage of Aircraft.

By this time the position with regard to Yugoslavia had become acute. During the winter of 1942/43 several requests by S.O.E. for additional aircraft had been made with special reference to the Mediterranean Theatre.

CO5/3594, 30 January 1943
A telegram from S.O.E.'s Cairo H.Q. reported that it was becoming increasingly difficult to convince people in the Middle East that British interest in Serb resistance was serious, especially in the face of intensive Allied propaganda regarding air supremacy and current production. The Prime Minister himself during his visit to Cairo in February 1943 took a particular interest in the support of guerilla activities in Yugoslavia.

COS(43)44, 11 February 1943
At his own request he was given a memorandum on this subject prepared by S.O.E. and G.H.Q. Middle East which stressed the necessity of increasing the volume of supplies to the guerilla fighters if resistance was to be maintained and raised to a level where it would be of real military value to the war effort. The Prime Minister himself showed this note to General Eisenhower in Algiers with a view to enlisting his interest and possibly his support.

Srl. No. DM/2/3, 12 February 1943
On his return to England the Prime Minister minuted to Major Morton:

> "Please show Lord Selborne the report I had from the S.O.E. section dealing with Yugoslavia (COS(43)44 of 11th February 1943). I agree with this report in general terms. I consider it is a matter of the greatest importance to establish the desired closer contacts with Yugoslav leaders. The number of enemy divisions being contained in these regions is most remarkable.

"I appealed strongly to General Arnold as he passed through Cairo to give us eight more Liberators fitted for discharging paracargoes or agents. He was going off the next morning, but gave instructions to General Spaatz. I believe a meeting was held with S.O.E. people on the subject. I also spoke to General Eisenhower in favour of the eight additional aircraft.

"Pray let me know how the matter stands and whether there is anything more we can do. If you show me where it is being held up, I can probably get the block removed."

This minute was sent to the Minister of Economic Warfare by Major Morton on 15th February 1943, who replied (unreferenced):

"The Prime Minister kindly refers in his minute to the possibility of further action on his part. I think there are two ways in which he can help. The first is to intervene again with the Americans about the eight Liberators for the Middle East if his previous intervention does not do the trick. The second to be so good as to inform the Chiefs of Staff of his interest in the question of aircraft for S.O.E. at the time when they receive from the J.P.S. for consideration the new directive now being prepared. If the Prime Minister would be willing to do this I would, of course, let you know immediately the J.P.S. have this new directive ready to submit to the Chiefs of Staff."

On 23rd February, Major Morton wrote to the Acting Secretary of the Chiefs of Staff Committee (unreferenced):

"When in Cairo and since his return, the Prime Minister has taken a special interest in the provision of aircraft for S.O.E.'s operations, both from the Middle East to serve Yugoslavia and from England, especially in co-operation with the Poles.

"At the Prime Minister's direction I have had correspondence with Lord Selborne on this subject, while the Prime Minister himself has addressed minutes to Ministers and Chiefs of Staff."

COS(43)94(0), 2 March 1943
Support was also given by the Secretary of State for Foreign Affairs to S.O.E.'s request for additional S.D. aircraft in the Middle East.

CC/195, 22 February 1943
A minute from the Secretary of State for Foreign Affairs and the Minister of Economic Warfare on a M.E. telegram of 22nd February in which the M.E.D.C. reported that S.O.E. had asked for an increased allocation of aircraft which could not be supplied from the present Middle East resources, stated that they felt that an extension of the activities of the Secret Organisation in the Balkans was highly desirable in view of the approach to the Eastern Mediterranean of war developments.

COS(43)76, 23 February 1943
The view had been expressed in a note on a Chiefs of Staff meeting to consider the telegram that the allocation of aircraft which had already been made for the support of operations in Yugoslavia was about correct, and that it would not be right to send further aircraft from the United Kingdom for this purpose. Mr. Eden and Lord Selborne felt that the present scale of support to Mihailovic in Servia must be maintained, and that operations to gain contact with and give support to resisting elements in Croatia and Slovenia should be started as soon as possible; they therefore urged that eight more Liberators with trained crews should be allotted for this purpose, in addition to the six Halifax bombers already promised to S.O.E. Cairo.

COS(43) 38(0)
On 25th February 1943, the Chief of the Air Staff reported that he had now seen the Foreign Office's paper stating that our ability to embark on a new policy towards the Anti-Axis parties in Yugoslavia depended entirely on whether we could or not increase the aircraft available in the Middle East, and considered that he could increase the establishment of special aircraft in the Middle East by an additional 4 Halifaxes with only very slight set-back to Bomber Command expansion.

COS(43)34th Meeting.(0), Item 7
At a later meeting the Chiefs of Staff approved the proposal of the Chief of the Air Staff to increase the establishment of special aircraft in the Middle East by four Halifaxes, but it was generally agreed that further aircraft could not at present be provided for these special operations.

This brought S.O.E.'s aircraft allocation in the Middle East up to fourteen. Further efforts on the part of S.O.E. in the Middle East to obtain more aircraft were unsuccessful.

No.83 ARFAR

On 3rd April, the Minister of Economic Warfare, replying to the Minister of State, Cairo, who had reported S.O.E.'s requests, declared that he sympathised with the requests but it had to be remembered that S.O.E. Middle East already had a large proportion of the total aircraft available to S.O.E. – in fact, a larger proportion than the number of their operations compared with those mounted from the U.K. would strictly justify. Moreover, it had not yet been established by actual trial to what extent the fourteen aircraft allocated to S.O.E. Middle East would be able to fulfil S.O.E.'s needs in the Balkans when their crews were fully trained and full experience of their handling had been gained. He felt, therefore, that until the existing facilities had been fully tried out he could not justify a further approach to the Chiefs of Staff for more aircraft for S.O.E. Middle East.

COS(43) 336(0), 23 June 1943

The Minister of Economic Warfare sent to the Prime Minister a report by S.O.E. on the position in Yugoslavia showing that the inadequacy of the support to the guerillas was seriously hampering their activities.

   The Prime Minister minuted to the Chiefs of Staff:

> "All this is of the highest importance, and should be brought before the Chiefs of Staff Committee and C.A.S.
>
>   "I understood when I was last in Cairo that an additional number of aircraft were to be made available. I consider that at least a dozen should be placed at the disposal of the S.O.E. authorities for this, and that this demand had priority even over the bombing of Germany.
>
>   "We might discuss this after the Staff Meeting at 5.30 p.m. on Wednesday (tomorrow). The Minister of Economic Warfare should be invited with anyone he wishes to bring."

COS(43)135th Meeting (0), Item 2

The Staff Conference was held at No. 10 Downing Street on Wednesday 23rd June 1943, when the Prime Minister emphasised the very great importance, particularly at the present time of giving all possible support to the Yugoslav Anti-Axis movement which was containing some 33 Axis divisions in that area. This matter was of such importance that he considered that the small number of additional aircraft required to increase our aid must be provided, if necessary at the expense of the bombing of Germany and of the anti-U-boat war.

Air Chief Marshall Sir Charles Portal said that he proposed to place the 22 Halifax aircraft which would be shortly available for S.O.E. and S.I.S. operations in the Mediterranean Air Command. With these aircraft, and using aerodromes in Tunisia and Libya approximately 150 tons of supplies could be delivered each month in Yugoslavia. The Prime Minister said that the delivery of the increased amount of supplies was a small price to pay for the diversion of Axis forces caused by Resistance in Yugoslavia, and every effort must be made to increase the rate of delivering supplies, working up to 500 tons or so each month by September. It was essential to keep this movement going. The Conference therefore approved the Air Ministry's arrangements to increase delivery to the Resistance Movements in Yugoslavia and for Greece up to 150 tons each month.

General Shortage of S.D. Aircraft

The serious effects of the shortage of S.D. aircraft were not limited to Yugoslavia however. On 21st July 1943, the Minister of Economic Warfare wrote to the Prime Minister setting out the difficulties with which S.O.E. had found themselves faced as a result of the small number of aircraft available for S.D. operations. He reported that for some weeks past he had been in communication with the Air Ministry on the question of increased supply of aircraft for S.O.E. As far as the Balkans were concerned, it had been decided at the Staff Conference held on 24th June that S.O.E. must increase the rate of deliveries to 500 tons per month by 30th September. This would require 35 additional Halifaxes. Increased supplies were also needed urgently for the rest of Europe. After two-and-a-half years intensive preparation, S.O.E. were servicing movements in Poland, France, Norway, Czechoslovakia, Holland, Belgium and Denmark, most of which were now expanding rapidly. The contribution that they were making in sabotage and subversion was a powerful auxiliary in the softening of German resistance, and the contribution that they could make to the operations of the Allies' regular forces on D-Day was very considerable.

After analysing various figures and calculations, the Minister assessed the increase required at a total of 63 aircraft, 28 for the U.K. and Algiers bases, and 35 for the Eastern Mediterranean; and he concluded by saying that unless aircraft could be soon provided on the scale he had suggested, S.O.E. would be unable to fulfil the directives it had received.

S.O.E./Air Ministry Report on S.O.E.'s Aircraft Requirements

COS(43) 404(0)
The joint S.O.E./Air Ministry Report for which the Chiefs of Staff Committee had asked in June was submitted, with a covering note by the Chief of the Air Staff, on 25th July 1943. The report showed that in order to achieve the target figures of men armed and tons of stores infiltrated, S.O.E. had at present in all theatres only 47 aircraft, or about the equivalent of three Heavy Bomber Squadrons, and would need over the period an average of 117 aircraft or 4½ additional Heavy Bomber Squadrons. The report pointed out that one Halifax Squadron would on average drop 240 tons of bombs a month on the enemy, and since the present operational strength of Bomber Command in Heavy Bombers was 40 Squadrons, the full S.O.E. requirements of 7½ squadrons would represent a substantial diversion from the Bomber Offensive.

C.A.S.'s Views

The C.A.S.'s note is worth quoting at length, since it sets out the problem, to the Air Staff, of diverting aircraft from Bomber Command to S.D. work.

> "This proposed diversion is so great that it leads me to call in question the whole basis of our S.O.E. plans in relation to our general strategy. Desirable as it may be to maintain and foster S.O.E. activities, we must bring the problem into focus with the whole strategic picture.
>
> "The issue is a plain one. As we cannot provide aircraft for the transport of arms and materials to Resistance Groups except at the direct cost of the Bomber Offensive, what is the exact price which we are prepared to pay? I suggest that the answer should turn, not on a C.O.S. directive issued in general terms in March last, but on an impartial consideration of the present strategical situation.
>
> "We are unquestionably obtaining great and immediate value from the bomber offensive. For all that, the weight of our attack falls

far short of what it should be. At the end of June we were still 3 Heavy Bomber Squadrons below the target figure of 58, and in spite of every effort it has only been possible to increase the number of effective Medium and Heavy Bomber Squadrons in Bomber Command by 2½ in the last three months.

"I have no doubt about the value of what is being done by S.O.E. in the Balkans, or about the need to do as much more there as is possible. These activities accord with our general strategic plan, they exploit our present successes and should give us good and immediate results.

"The same, however, cannot be said about the rest of Europe, where the efforts of Resistance Groups cannot be really profitable until next year. The real value which we shall obtain from these Groups will be an up-rising. If such an up-rising is to be successful – and it can only succeed once – it will demand conditions in which German resistance in the West is reaching the point of disintegration. We are not in a position to begin to apply the necessary pressure for another nine or twelve months, unless the German war machine cracks seriously in the meantime. The most likely cause of this accelerated collapse is the bomber offensive which must not be handicapped by diversions to an operation whose value is obviously secondary.

"Thus on strategic grounds, while I feel that there is a very good case for providing aircraft to back S.O.E. activities in the Balkans, even at the cost, as it must be, of some small detraction from the direct attack on Germany, I feel that it would be a serious mistake to divert any more aircraft to supply Resistance Groups in Western Europe, which will only be of <u>potential</u> value next year, when these aircraft could be of <u>immediate and actual</u> value in accelerating the defeat of Germany by direct attack."

The C.A.S. went on to suggest that the total number of aircraft allotted to S.O.E. before January 1944, should be limited to 58. 36 of these should be based in the Mediterranean Theatre, of which 4 would be in North West Africa for the use of Resistance Groups in Corsica, Southern France and North Italy, while the remaining 32 would be available for the Balkans. This represented an increase of 14 aircraft over the present establishment in the Mediterranean area.

In the U.K. the present establishment of 22 aircraft for operations to Western Europe should be maintained, and should be capable of sustaining Resistance Groups in lively and vigorous condition until we could concentrate in turn on their ultimate exploitation. The C.A.S. added that he was investigating what contribution towards S.O.E. requirements in France could be made by Squadrons in Bomber Command without prejudice to their offensive against Germany and Italy.

COS(43)173rd Meeting, 27 July 1943
This proposed allocation of aircraft for S.O.E. purposes to cover the period up to 1st January 1944, was approved by the Chiefs of Staff in July.

Defence Committee Consider Aircraft for S.O.E

COS(43)176th Meeting (0), Item 7, 30 July 1943
The problem, however, was not yet settled. Three days later the Chiefs of Staff were informed that the question of aircraft for S.O.E. purposes was to be raised at a Defence Committee to be held on August 2nd.

DO(43)17, 30 July 1943
This meeting was called by the Prime Minister himself, who sent a minute to General Ismay for the C.A.S. and C.O.S. Committees pointing out that a political and not only a military appraisal of the profit and loss must be sought.

DO(43) 7th Meeting
The Defence Committee met on Monday 2nd August and had before them minutes by the Prime Minister, the Minister of Economic Warfare and the Chiefs of the Air Staff regarding the allocation of aircraft to the Special Operations Executive. Lord Selborne reported that Resistance movements throughout territories that had been overrun by the Germans had, during the last eight months, been booming. The problem of keeping these movements alive by the provision of supplies was becoming increasingly difficult. These movements could not be left unassisted until D-Day: if they were not continuously stimulated by the supply of arms and ammunition they would die; and it would be deplorable to allow all the work that had been put in during the last three years to go for nothing.

The proposals made by the Chief of Air Staff for the provision of aircraft for the Balkans met the essential requirements of S.O.E. but they were made at the expense of the requirements of Western Europe and Poland. During the summer months it was only possible to carry out special operations in France and the Low Countries, but when the nights lengthened there would be an increasing demand for operations in Norway and Poland. The Prime Minister stated that he had no doubt of the value of resistance operations. The question the Committee had to decide, however, was the relative priority to be accorded to particular areas, and the most economical use that could be made of the resources at our disposal. At present the Balkans took first place.

The C.A.S. explained the difficulty of allocating a large number of S.D. aircraft for the permanent use of S.O.E. in Western Europe, but suggested that if the control of all aircraft used for this purpose were transferred to Bomber Command from Air Ministry, Bomber Command would then undertake the responsibility for the provision when needed of supplementary aircraft for carrying out S.O.E. operations, provided that the priority of these operations was settled by the Chiefs of Staff.

The Secretary of State for Foreign Affairs recorded his conviction that there was no doubt that the first call on our resources at the moment must be the Balkans since it was there that the largest dividends could be earned. The Prime Minister again emphasised the immense value to the war effort of stimulating resistance amongst the people of Europe. He recognised that acts of rebellion against the Germans frequently resulted in bloody reprisals, but the "blood of the Martyrs was the seed of the church," and the result of these incidents had been to make the Germans hated as no other race had ever been hated. Nothing should be done which result in the falling off of this most valuable means of harassing the enemy. The Committee finally agreed:

(i) That S.O.E. should retain, as a minimum, their existing lien on 22 special aircraft based on the United Kingdom.
(ii) That Bomber Command should undertake the responsibility for carrying out such additional work for S.O.E. as S.O.E. required to be undertaken, subject to the direction on priorities as decided by the Chiefs of Staff.
(iii) It is open to the Minister of Economic Warfare to appeal to the Defence Committee, if at any time he considers that S.O.E. requirements are not being given a sufficiently high priority.

S.O.E. and the Chiefs of Staff

COS(43)180th Meeting (0), Item 5, 4 August 1943
COS(43)505(0)
The meeting also discussed S.O.E.'s position vis-a-vis the Chiefs Of Staff. It was decided that the Chiefs of Staff were to be kept continually informed of S.O.E. activities and intentions, and that S.O.E. should be given opportunities to express their views in person to the Chiefs of Staff Committee when S.O.E. matters were under discussion.

COS(43) 240th Meeting, 7 October 1943
A Committee was later appointed to study the question of closer liaison between the Chiefs of Staff and S.O.E., and its recommendations, including the submission of a weekly report by S.O.E., were accepted by the Chiefs of Staff Committee in October.

Bomber Command's Responsibility for S.D. Operations from U.K.

180th Meeting (0), 4 April 1943
Further clarification of Bomber Command's responsibilities towards S.O.E. was given at subsequent meetings of the Chiefs of Staff. In April the C.A.S. reported that the Air Ministry were preparing a draft directive to Bomber Command regarding their responsibilities in connection with S.O.E. activities. In future the operational as well as the administrative responsibility for S.D. aircraft based in the U.K. was to be undertaken by Bomber Command, with the object of bringing the Special Operations more closely into line with the normal operations of Bomber Command, and of facilitating the employment when necessary of supplementary aircraft for S.D. work.

Parachute Crisis

At the end of June 1943, a shortage in another supply vital to S.O.E., this time parachutes and containers, threatened to curtail the number of S.D. operations that could be undertaken, and was sufficiently acute to have a direct bearing on the number of aircraft which S.O.E. could employ.

During 1941 and 1942, parachutes and containers were obtained by A.I.10 for S.O.E. on the requisitions placed by the Operational Sections for Western Europe and the Middle East. Six monthly estimates were given to the R.A.F., but these were always on a small scale as the number of aircraft available for S.D. operations was very limited, and for this reason Air Ministry would never undertake a big production programme for S.O.E. At the beginning of 1943, with the volume of S.D. operations increasing, S.O.E. began to build up a reserve of parachutes and containers in anticipation of increased air resources in the early summer. A reserve of five thousand parachutes and containers, as well as a number of packages was aimed at in April. The Middle East Sections, who had hitherto been operating on a very small scale, had now asserted that their claims would require considerably large quantities of these stores than had been anticipated, and at the beginning of May some immediate shipments to Cairo were authorised. Meanwhile S.O.E. instructed A.I.10 to request increased production.

236/43/DDI2, 13 May
On 13th May, D.D.I.(2) informed S.O.E. of the position with regard to parachutes and containers. The Director-General of Equipment had visited A.C.A.S.(I) to explain that unless provisioning was done on the largest scale, there would be a serious shortage of all parachute equipment in the future. The growth of demands for containers, parachutes and other stores from the Middle East had been considerable, and it is likely that existing stocks would have to be shared by all 'customers'.

In June the situation became critical. Two main problems now faced S.O.E.: the immediate supply of containers and parachutes for Cairo and the U.K., and the long-term requirements up to the end of 1944. During June the stocks in the U.K., including the London reserve, were depleted as far as possible so as to increase the supplies sent to Cairo to tide over their immediate difficulties in that area. As production became available it was allocated and the Cairo portion shipped or flown on the highest priority. In addition a number of parachutes and containers were allocated from Airborne forces for use in the Mediterranean.

On 28th June, Major-General Gubbins wrote to the V.C.A.S. asking him to give warning to A.M.S.O. of S.O.E.'s increased requirements of containers and parachutes. It seemed that the limiting factor in any expansion of aircraft resources would be the provision of these items. Sudden increases in the delivery of material from the Middle East into the Balkans had led to a much heavier consumption than S.O.E. had anticipated, and if a further increase were to be decided upon by the Chiefs of Staff, S.O.E. requirements would be still greater. It appeared that it was going to be extremely difficult to meet S.O.E.'s requirements. Present production was round about 2,000 per month while S.O.E.'s requirements now were 3,300 and would rise to 7,144 if they were called upon to meet the full commitment in Europe.

During August the problem of production was continually under examination on Air Staff level at Air Ministry, and two main questions of priority began to arise: on the one hand between the availability of the fabrics for parachutes and other uses such as balloons, and on the other hand between the various users of parachutes, principally the Airborne forces and S.O.E.

Plans/358/907, 11 August 1943
In a letter to D.D.I.(2) S.O.E. emphasised that although no immediate increase had been made in the number of aircraft available for S.D. operations it was perfectly possible that circumstances might arise during the next year when an increased allotment would be made. Unless planning was carried out now, S.O.E. could not guarantee to have the necessary number of parachutes and containers available, and it was essential that both in the U.K. and in Overseas Theatres some reserve should be built up against future contingencies. Even in present circumstances there was a variable and possibly very large factor in the air lift available to S.O.E. since Bomber Command had been directed to provide what additional assistance they could, and there was always the possibility that this might be on a very considerable scale.

Plans/358/1024, 1 September 1943
By September, the position had become slightly easier. A minute from D/Plans of S.O.E. to senior S.O.E. officers reported that the allocation of Supply Dropping parachutes to D. of Ops (Tac), i.e. Airborne forces, and A.I.10 was to be 65% of the total requirements of each.

COS(43)336(0)
Moreover, in view of the fact that A.I.10 were engaged in continuous ops, they were to be given first priority for 1943.

Production was increased as far as possible, but the problem of distribution to the Mediterranean Theatre still remained.

IM/1117/43 (D.D.I.2. to D.W.O.)
That Air Ministry were aware of the urgency of the requirements is shown in a letter from D.D.I.(2) which stated that unless the maximum speed and priority was given to the shipment of containers and parachutes to the Mediterranean area, there was every likelihood, within the next few months, that operations scheduled to be undertaken from Mediterranean bases would be held up, even though the parachutes and containers are in existence and allocated to A.I.10. Addressees of this letter were therefore requested to take concerted action to ensure a high priority in the movement of this equipment.

"Big Three" – Washington (Trident)

The activities and support of Resistance Groups in occupied Europe were by this time sufficiently important to be included in the agenda at the "Big Three" meetings. At the Washington Conference in May 1943, the problem of providing support in some form to the Partisans in the Balkans was introduced into the discussions by the British representatives, but there were no policy decisions made, and the subject was not specifically included in the "Agreed Summary of Conclusions," presented by the Combined Chiefs of Staff to the President and the Prime Minister.

"Big Three" – Quebec (Quadrant), Resistance in Europe

At the Quebec Conference in August 1943, the active problem of providing some support for Resistance Movements in Europe was given consideration, and at the conclusion of the conference it was recorded as part of the agreed policy that help should be afforded to them.

COS 303/3, 17 August 1943
In a paper on the "Agreed Strategic Concept of the Defeat of the Axis in Europe," which was considered by the C.C.S., there was included among recommended operations "Air Supply of Balkan Guerillas."

COS 110th Mtg, Minute 1, of 17 August 1943
After discussion the C.C.S. approved the recommendations contained in the paper.

1st Plenary Mtg., 19 August 1943
The Prime Minister at the first plenary meeting remarked on the possibility of supporting by air French partisans in the south-east of France as an alternative to a beach landing. He described the operation he had in mind as "air-nourished guerilla warfare."

2nd Plenary Mtg., 23 August 1943
The meeting agreed that the possibilities of the Prime Minister's suggestions should be explored. The President, at the second plenary meeting, expressed the view that guerilla operations might be initiated in south central France as well as in the Maritime Alps.

Possible activities in Sardinia and Corsica were also discussed, and the C.C.S. agreed to send a telegram to General Eisenhower calling attention to the excellent conditions then existing, with Italy in a state of confusion, for establishing such conditions in Corsica and Sardinia as would lead to unopposed occupation.

CCS 113th Mtg., Minute 4, of 20 August 1943
It was suggested that S.O.E. and O.S.S. (their American counter-part) might collaborate in these operations. It would be an excellent opportunity for both organisations to gain experience.

2nd Plenary Mtg., 23 August 1943
The Prime Minister expressed his approval of this action.

CCS 319/5, paras: 15,16,17,65, of 24 August 1943
The action finally recommended with regard to the support of the Partisans in Europe is given in the summary of the C.C.S. decisions presented at the conclusion to the President and Prime Minister. It is as follows:

> i) Under "Air Operations" – "Air Supply of Balkan and French Guerillas."; ii) Under "Operations in Southern France" – "Air-nourished guerilla operations in Southern France, will, if possible, be initiated."; iii) Under "Special Operations in Sardinia and Corsica." General Eisenhower has been asked to examine the possibilities of intensifying subversive activities in Sardinia and Corsica, with a view to facilitating entry into these islands."

The problem of support of the Polish Resistance Movement did not, it may be noted, enter into the discussion or recommendations at any point.

CCS 329/2, Para: 9, 29 August 1943
The Combined Staff Planners were then instructed to estimate the availability of actual resources necessary to implement the operations agreed upon at the Conference. Regarding support to the Partisans movements, they remarked that the extent of air operations would be limited by the supply of heavy bomber aircraft, and must in any case be related to the advantages likely to accrue. They also made the following definite recommendations.

CCS 329/2, Annex IV, Appendix E, 29 August 1943
i) British aircraft were allocated to the support of Resistance Groups in Europe and the Balkans as follows:

	Heavy Bombers.	Miscellaneous Aircraft.
U.K. Bases	22	14
Mediterranean Bases	36	Nil

ii) No further allocation of heavy bomber aircraft could be made for this purpose without affecting the build-up of heavy bomber squadrons in the British Bomber Command.
iii) Aircraft for the support of Resistance Groups in Greece and in the Balkans had recently been given priority.
iv) Further assistance to Resistance Groups in Europe could only be given at the expense either of the Combined Bomber Offensive or of the support of the partisans in Greece and the Balkans.
v) The heavily-armed, high-altitude day bombers as used by the U.S.A.A.F. were not suitable or available for night operations in support of the guerilla forces.

British C.O.S. on Balkan Resistance

CC/266 of 30 July 1943, (Answer to F.O. tel, DEDIP, 2365 quoted in COS(Q)17 of 11 August 1943)
A purely British comment on the support to the Balkan Partisans is recorded in an exchange of telegrams between the Commanders-in-

Chief, Middle East and the British Chiefs of Staff. The Commanders-in-Chief stated that agents were being used in, and supplies sent to, the Balkans to the limit of aircraft availability, and that an increase in the number of aircraft would be welcome.

COS(ME) 4025, August 1943
General Eisenhower had agreed verbally with General Wilson that facilities for an advanced base for S.O.E. and raiding parties would be granted in captured areas west of the Adriatic.

COS(ME) 4025, August 1943
The British Chiefs of Staff replied with the approval of the Foreign Office that the question of increasing still further the number of aircraft available for the Commanders-in-Chief, Middle East for the above purpose was being actively considered.

U.S. Point of View on Resistance

COS/317, 18 August 1943
The U.S. point of view on the support of Resistance Groups in Europe is indicated in a paper which was prepared by the U.S. Staff Planners at the time of the Quebec Conference, but upon which action was deferred by the C.C.S. They postulated their problem: "To consider requirements for material for equipping allies, liberated forces, and friendly neutrals, and determination of basic policies which will govern the meeting of such requirements."

So far as support by air was concerned, they made the following observations:

a) Balkans. In the past, the supply of these guerilla forces had been carried out by Middle East Command in some 100 scattered sorties, dropping only bare necessities, e.g. medical supplies etc. Their principal needs were machine guns, light (horse) artillery, and medical supplies. After stating the decision of the conference that equipment to be supplied to the Balkans would be limited to support of guerillas by air and sea transport, the U.S. Planners said that for planning purposes the forces to be equipped must be limited to 175,000 men (six divisions) and supporting troops.

b) Poland. According to U.S. Intelligence sources, the Polish "Secret Army" was estimated at some 65,000 men. Equipment for this organisation would require 500 sorties initially. In the past the British had occasionally dropped small quantities of explosives and of communications equipment. The Polish plan (see para 26) envisaged transporting the Polish forces then in U.K. and M.E. by air after the "break-through contact with the Secret Army had been established." The U.S. Planners estimated that support of this operation would need some 2,000 sorties by heavy transport planes, and that such an air lift was not possible without a serious effect on other air operations. The U.S. Planners therefore recommended that no equipment should be provided for Polish Forces in Poland except that which could be flown in to guerilla and underground forces extant within the limits of Poland. (The limitations imposed by the fact that all material must be flown in by air would restrict the forces that could be supplied to an optimum figure of 50 modified infantry battalions). This would be a British commitment.

c) France. The U.S. Planners' comment was brief. Certain Resistance Groups in France were being equipped by air delivery with small arms. This was a British commitment. Any demands on U.S. for weapons or equipment for this purpose would be negligible.

Special Problem of Poland – Polish Plan and C.C.S. View

CCS 267 Series
Further information on the views of the Combined Chiefs of Staff with regard to the support of the Polish Secret Army is given in a series of C.C.S. papers prepared for the consideration of the Standing C.C.S. Committees in Washington. Towards the end of June 1943, the Polish Liaison Officer within the C.C.S. had produced a lengthy paper on "The Armed Forces and Secret Military Organisation of Poland as a Factor in General Allied European Planning."

CCS 267, 30 June 1943
This paper outlined the plan of the Polish Commander-in-Chief to prepare the Polish armed forces abroad and the "Secret Armies" in Poland, for the primary purpose of obtaining control of central Poland. His plan regarding the Secret Army was divided into two phases: – Phase 1; starting in September 1943, there would be intensified sabotage together with the continuation of the Polish Intelligence system: phase 2; an insurrection of the Secret Army would take place in co-ordination

with, and in support of, contemporary Allied operations. It was believed that the Secret Army could exist in isolation for only 20 days. The timing of the insurrection would therefore have to be carefully considered.

Attached to Plans/401902, 6 August 1943
S.O.E.'s views on this plan were given in a paper of August 1943, and the necessity was emphasised of obtaining a greatly increased number of aircraft, if the plan, especially the part of it which envisaged the use of the Polish Parachute Brigade, were to be implemented.

CCS 100th Mtg.
The plan was the subject of discussion at a C.C.S. Meeting of 2nd July 1943, but no comments were made.

CCS 267/1, 3 September 1943
Early in September 1943, the Combined Staff Planners submitted their observations regarding the plan and, after some minor amendments had been incorporated, their recommendations were approved by the C.C.S. These recommendations were: i) that no approval would be given at that time for the furnishing of supplies necessary to equip the Secret Army, but that supplies necessary to maintain the sabotage and intelligence activities would be furnished to the Polish Government in London from both U.S. and British sources.

CCS 267/3 of 17 September 1943
ii) that no U.S. Heavy Bomber aircraft would be assigned at that time to the Polish Government for the delivery of supplies to Poland. As soon as possible, without interference to the Combined Bomber Offensive, one Squadron initially, and eventually two Squadrons of U.S. Heavy Bombers would be organised to operate from the U.K. for this purpose. These Bombers should be such as were not operational for full daylight combat, and should operate under the command of the Commanding General, 8th U.S. Army Air Force.

CCS 267/4
The Polish Liaison Officer was informed that the C.C.S. had approved the above recommendations in a letter dated 23rd September 1943. Owing to the heavy operational requirements of active theatres; the

inability of the Secret Army to take part against the Axis until direct land or sea communications were immediately in prospect, and the lack of suitable aircraft for the delivery of large quantities of supplies to Poland, the Combined Chiefs of Staff were unable to see their way to the allocation of the equipment required for the Polish Secret Army. Supplies for sabotage and intelligence activities had been approved, but there was still a shortage of heavy bomber aircraft and it was not possible to allocate such aircraft to the Polish Government.

The Combined Chiefs of Staff, however, were anxious to give what help they could, and with this in view, one squadron and eventually two squadrons of U.S. Heavy Bombers, which were not operational for full daylight combat, would be organised to operate from the U.K. under the commanding General of the 8th Air Force for the support of sabotage and intelligence activities by Polish and other underground groups in Europe.

Allocation of American Aircraft for S.D. Work

CCS. 119th Mtg., 17 September 194
During the discussion on the C.S.P. recommendations the Head of the British Joint Staff Mission in Washington, Field Marshal Sir John Dill, expressed his pleasure at the decision to allocate some U.S. Heavy Bombers to these activities, and pointed out that S.O.E. co-ordinated all such activities in the European Theatre and that the R.A.F. Bomber Command worked closely with them and were responsible for these operations.

R-3223, 17 September 1943
A telegram from Combined Chiefs of Staff to ETOUSA confirmed the allocation of one squadron initially and eventually two squadrons of U.S. Heavy Bombers for S.D. work.

Difficulties of Polish Operations

The Polish Government, however, were not content with the arrangements made for their operations, and their dissatisfaction was aggravated during the next months of 1943. In September, the first month of operations to Poland, only 16 flights were successful; and before the October moon period began Polish H.Q. transmitted orders to Poland for the preparation of no fewer than sixty reception committees

– a figure considerably in excess of that advised by S.O.E. Experience during September, however, had shown that enemy opposition on the route previously used for flights to Poland was considerably heavier than had been the case in previous months. Out of a total of twenty-two aircraft despatched to Poland during September six did not return.

It was therefore necessary to consider a new routeing for these flights, but the decision of the Station Commander was not made known to S.O.E. until the first day of the October moon period. The new route was longer than that used hitherto and resulted in all but six of the sixty reception committees becoming out of range, a fact which naturally upset the Polish Government. They further complained that aircraft allotted for their work were being diverted to other tasks, but this complaint, in the opinion of S.O.E. revealed a fundamental misconception on the part of the Polish H.Q. Six of the Tempsford aircraft were manned by Polish crews, but it had already been made clear to the Poles, that, although primarily intended for the work in Poland, these aircraft must be regarded as an integral part of the Squadron, subject only to the overriding Polish priority; and in addition to this, R.A.F. Station Tempsford, had in fact given assistance whenever possible from their own aircraft for Polish operations. On one occasion in the September moon period no fewer than eleven aircraft were despatched on Polish operations.

Plans/410/1459, 16 October 1943
An S.O.E. paper of October 1943 suggested that certain deeper causes of discontent lay at the root of the Polish dissatisfaction. The desire of the Polish Government to be responsible for the organisation of resistance in their own country without the necessity of working through the medium of S.O.E., their growing suspicion of Russian influence, and the Polish desire that their own aircraft should be employed on supply dropping to Poland, were among the causes of discontent of the Polish Government. This analysis of the psychology of the Polish Government was true not only at this moment but throughout the period of S.D. operations to Poland.

Proposed Move of Polish Base to Mediterranean

It was hoped that the establishment of a base in the Mediterranean from which operations to Poland could be conducted would provide a shorter and safer route to the target area, and discussions were held between S.O.E. and the Air Ministry to obtain Air Ministry's approval of this project.

0601

A telegram from M.A.C. to the Air Ministry of 20th October reported that: "We can accept Polish S.O.E. Flight consisting of 3 Liberators and 3 Halifaxes in December."

The Poles Complain of Shortage of Aircraft

On 21st October 1943, the Minister of Economic Warfare reported to the Prime Minister that the Polish Commander-in-Chief, General Sosnkowski, had lodged a serious complaint concerning the degree of help that S.O.E. were able to give to the Polish Resistance Movement. After the R.A.F.'s decision on re-routeing aircraft to Poland, Polish G.H.Q. had boiled over with indignation, and had intimated that unless facilities could be materially increased they would be forced to give orders for the cessation of resistance in Poland and of transmission of intelligence.

The Minister considered that there were only two possible methods by which the programme for Poland might be fulfilled: firstly by basing the bulk of the Polish operations on S. Italy instead of England. By this means it should be possible to obtain a shorter route into S. Poland and to avoid the German night fighter belt. It was important, however, that the aircraft which were sent from England for this purpose should be ear-marked for Polish work and should not be regarded as part of a pool which M.A.C. could order into France or Yugoslavia in priority to Poland. The Poles had been told by both the Secretary of State for Air and the C.I.G.S. that these aircraft were "primarily at their disposal."

The second method by which deliveries to Poland might be stepped up was an all-round increase of S.D. aircraft. The supplementary assistance which Bomber Command, at the Defence Committee of August 2nd, had been instructed to give, had not so far amounted to very much, primarily because the crews were not trained in S.D. work. On the other hand, S.O.E. now had a promise of two U.S. Squadrons and there was a fair prospect that the first of these would be operating by December. The Chiefs of Staff had recently decided that 25% of the total S.O.E. air effort available for Europe, less the Balkans, should be allotted to Poland, Czechoslovakia and Hungary, which meant that the Poles would have a prior claim upon six aircraft out of the present 26, and an additional 3 as each U.S. Squadron came into service. They should, therefore, reach a total of 12 by January. In the circumstances, the Minister did not propose to ask for an increased allotment of aircraft for S.O.E. work at that moment, but he said that he would feel bound to ask shortly for more aircraft for 1944 and the claims of Poland would occupy a prominent place in his case.

He went on to say that he sympathised with the Polish standpoint and added "For the Poles to be told that Britain cannot afford them more than 6 aircraft is a bit hard." The case for increased assistance to Poland rested less on strategy than on Polish morale, to which the Minister attached great importance.

The Air Ministry Replies

A copy of the Minister of Economic Warfare's Minute was also sent to the Secretary of State for Air who replied on 30th October 1943 that Bomber Command had in fact done its best to help. In the previous month they had suffered between 25% – 30% casualties on S.D. work – six times the normal rate of casualties in Bomber Command. Arrangements had been made for the Polish Flight to operate from a base in the Mediterranean area in the near future.

This would have distinct advantages over a flight operating from the U.K. and should do much to relieve the Polish difficulties. Meanwhile, Sir Archibald Sinclair assured Lord Selborne that the Air Ministry would do all it could, in the present air situation, to help the Poles.

Polish Base Transferred to Mediterranean

LI/43/D of I(R), 3 November 1943
In November 1943 a letter from D. of I(R) to the Polish General Staff recorded that preparations were in hand for the move of the Polish Flight from Tempsford to the Mediterranean. The problem of continuing operations to Poland from the U.K. was a difficult one, since the removal of 6 aircraft of the Polish Squadron meant that there would be only 10 plus 2 Halifaxes in No. 138 Squadron and 6 in No. 161 Squadron to undertake work to all countries with the exception of Poland and the Balkans. S.O.E. were prepared to continue to observe the principle that

Polish operations should be undertaken from England. In view of the limitation of the number of aircraft available, however, S.O.E. did not feel able to undertake more than nine sorties to Poland in any one month. Moreover, in making such attempts, not more than three aircraft would be made available on any one night.

Ops. 1(s) 217/43, 13 November 1943
The R.A.F. authorities, however, were very anxious that in order to overcome the difficulties of routeing aircraft from England to Poland all S.D. operations to that country should be carried out from the Mediterranean, and a letter from the Commander-in-Chief, Bomber Command urgently requested that all flights to Poland on behalf of S.O.E. should be carried out from an advanced base in the Mediterranean.

Organisation and Control of S.O.E. in Middle East

Meanwhile the whole problem of S.O.E.'s work in the Middle East had come to a head. As guerilla activities in the Balkans grew in 1942 and 1943 their closer integration with military plans became essential. The task of equipping and controlling guerilla armies in the Balkans inevitably raised disputes on the extent of S.O.E.'s Charter and led to a large expansion and modification of its structure.

CRME/78674/G(0), 9 September 1942
In September the Commander-in-Chief, Middle East had described the long-term object of S.O.E. in the Middle East as the organisation of a concerted rising amongst the peoples of territories occupied by the Axis, while the short-term policy of S.O.E. was to create as much administrative difficulty as possible for the Axis. At this date the short-term policy was clearly of more immediate interest to the Army, and numerous suggestions for operations of a sabotage nature were received from the Services for execution by S.O.E. if possible. In fact the activities of S.O.E. at this date impinged only in a minor degree upon the sphere of military action.

During the next months, however, and throughout the summer of 1943, the activities of S.O.E. in the Balkans necessarily assumed an increasingly military character. Sabotage and guerilla activities in Yugoslavia, Greece and Albania were containing substantial Axis forces, and the Middle East Defence Committee considered that Resistance activities were likely in the future to be an increasingly important factor in the planning and execution of operations in the Mediterranean.

COS(43)519(0), 8 September 1943

In these circumstances, the M.E.D.C. in September 1943, suggested a re-organisation of S.O.E. in the Middle East since the S.O.E. organisations in the Balkans had become a predominantly operational instrument of war, and were of such importance that it was essential that their activities should be co-ordinated and controlled by the responsible Commanders in the Theatre.

They recommended, therefore, that S.O.E. Cairo, in so far as activities in and on the Balkans were concerned, should now be brought directly under the control of M.E.D.C. and become in effect a branch of G.H.Q. Middle East.

COS(43)531(0)

A Memorandum on this subject by the Minister of Economic Warfare was circulated to the Chiefs of Staff Committee in which he agreed that, although S.O.E. Cairo, should be entirely subject to the military direction of the Commander-in-Chief Middle East, and the political direction of M.E.D.C., but explained why it must be an integral part of the S.O.E. organisation able to deal direct with S.O.E. London, on technical questions, supplies, personnel, and on matters both operational and administrative, which had a bearing upon S.O.E. activities outside the Middle East Theatre.

COS(43)594(0), 30 September 1943

In September the Chiefs of Staff Committee considered the proposed re-organisation of S.O.E. and recorded that the S.O.E. organisation had been built up over a period of years into an effective machine. They considered that any drastic change of the organisation itself at this eleventh hour would militate against its efficiency at the very time when it was required to play a prominent part. On the other hand, there were military advantages to be gained by transferring the higher control and direction of the organisation to the Chiefs of Staff, acting in consultation with the Foreign Office. The Chiefs of Staff therefore considered that arrangements in the Middle East should be on the broad lines proposed by the Minister of Economic Warfare.

COS(43)618(0).

A Meeting of Ministers, at which the Prime Minister was in the Chair was held on 30th September 1943, to consider the whole problem. The Conference agreed that S.O.E. organisation should preserve its integrity under the Minister of Economic Warfare. The main policy for S.O.E. would be settled in London between the Foreign Secretary and the Minister of Economic Warfare, while the execution of S.O.E. policy in operational theatres would be under the sole control and direction of the appropriate Commander-in-Chief.

S.D. Operations in the Mediterranean

The transfer of the Polish Flight of 138 Squadron to the Mediterranean, together with the establishment in the autumn of a base at Blida from which S.D. aircraft could operate to southern France and Italy, raised once more the problem of the S.D. aircraft available in that Theatre. A meeting was held in the Air Council room on 15th October 1943 to consider the conduct of S.O.E. air operations in the Mediterranean Theatre. The V.C.A.S. and the A.O.C.-in-C., Middle East, were present, together with a number of senior R.A.F. officers and representatives from S.O.E. and S.I.S. (There are no referenced minutes of this meeting). The A.O.C.-in-C., Middle East said that the Balkans had now developed into a military theatre and the Commanders-in-Chief Middle East looked upon S.O.E. as their agent for the conduct of operations there.

The V.C.A.S. referred to proposals to establish a base in Italy from which aircraft of the Special Units would be able to operate more economically into the various territories, and the Meeting agreed that H.Q. No.334 Wing should eventually be moved to this base and that all units permanently employed on these special tasks should be controlled by it. It was also agreed that it would greatly simplify the control of operations if an S.O.E. co-ordinating section under a senior S.O.E. Officer could be set up close to the Wing H.Q. to control S.O.E. administrative arrangements in connection with air operations, and to indicate priorities to the C.O. of No.334 Wing.

Both S.I.S. and S.O.E. requested that aircraft for landing operations should be established in the Middle East and the V.C.A.S. said that if there really was a role for the Lysander there should be no difficulty in transferring some from this country.

S.O.E. Report, April to October 1943

In spite of the shortage of aircraft and other difficulties a large measure of success had been attained by S.O.E. in their work in occupied countries during the year.

SOE(43)R23

In October 1943, S.O.E. submitted a report to the Chiefs of Staff Committee on the extent of fulfilment of their 1943 directive during the period 1st April – 1st October. This report recorded a notable increase in subversive activities all over Europe. In Italy groups controlled by, or in touch with, S.O.E. had played a substantial part in the stimulation of Anti-Fascist feeling and the riots which had followed the fall of Mussolini. In Greece an intensive campaign of sabotage and guerilla activities was achieved during the spring and summer, and planned attacks on communications immediately prior to "Husky" caused up to two German Divisions to be diverted to Greece in anticipation of an Allied landing.

Over 20,000 men had been armed and organised in Greece by this time, but progress was threatened by political crises, and internal feuds. In the Balkans guerilla activities had contained over 30 Axis divisions, Yugoslavia being the main centre of activity, and Partisan forces now numbered 180,000. Though the Chetniks under Mihailovic and the Partisans under Tito were continuing to fight each other they were also, especially the latter, harassing the enemy.

In Albania guerilla activities had been organised on a substantial scale, though training and equipment was still inadequate. In France sabotage against communications and military and industrial objectives had risen to a high level during the summer of 1943. Plans for assisting military operations were being co-ordinated with COSSAC, and were making good progress.

In the Low Countries Resistance had increased, and a high level of sabotage activity had been maintained. Activities in Poland had been curtailed by the extremely small quantities of supplies which it had been found possible to deliver during the summer months, but minor sabotage of communications was continuing.

In Denmark a major sabotage campaign had been planned and carried out with complete success, leading to riots and disorders, and forcing the Germans to take control of the administration of the country. Norway, like Poland, had suffered from the limitations on air transport during the summer months, and no sabotage of importance had been achieved except attacks on shipping.

Earlier in the year, the attack by a coup-de-main team on the Norsk Hydro "Heavy Water" plant had met with complete success, and had resulted in the putting out of action of the enemy's principal source of Heavy Water production. Air operations during the six months up to 1st October had succeeded in delivering to Europe 587 men, and over 1,500 tons of stores for the loss of 16 aircraft.

Penetration by Gestapo, Summer 1943

Within the normal cycle of resistance activities in the field such a volume of sabotage activity was bound to bring in its train an intensification of Gestapo activity. The Gestapo method of concentrating in force upon a limited area and waging an intensified battle against resistance movements within a certain town or district inevitably attained a certain measure of success. The special task with which S.O.E. circuits in the field were called upon to perform inevitably left them vulnerable to Gestapo penetration. Their very raison d'etre lay in the volume of activity in terms of sabotage which they could maintain, therefore their membership must increase and the security of any clandestine organisation is bound to be diminished if the organisation contains a large number of persons. Throughout the whole period of occupation individual resistance organisations were penetrated in this manner by the enemy: and although this was usually discovered by S.O.E. at an early date by means of a complicated system of checks on signals and by personal questions to agents, there were occasions when the Gestapo were successful in maintaining the deception over a comparatively long period.

In the summer of 1943 with the tempo of resistance activity rising there were a number of arrests by the enemy. In France particularly both the Independent British-controlled French and the Fighting French de-Gaullist organisations suffered from the loss of several of their most valuable leaders. In the case of the Independent circuits, where the principle was always maintained that each organisation was independent from its neighbour, the arrests, while extremely serious locally, were limited in their effect. Arrangements were made by S.O.E. to send out new organisers and W/T operators and, while old organisations were written off, the work went on again under the leadership of new officers. The Fighting French organisation in the field, since it was highly centralised, was more affected by the enemy's successes. The arrest of several senior members of the organisation together with the "blowing" of a number of codes had the effect of temporarily decapitating the Fighting French organisations in the country. The occasion was seized by S.O.E. to urge once more upon General de Gaulle and F.F.H.Q. the necessity for observing the principles of independence and separation in the organisation of clandestine activities.

COS(43), 173rd Meeting(0), Item 11, 27 July 1943
In July 1943 the C.A.S. reported at a Chiefs of Staff Meeting that he had received a note based on reports from "Most Secret" sources on the situation of certain of the resistance groups in France.

COS(43), 178th Meeting(0), Item 12
He suggested, and the Chiefs of Staff agreed, that the Joint Intelligence Sub-Committee should be instructed to examine these reports.

JIC(43)325(0)
The minutes of a later Chiefs of Staff Meeting recorded that the Chiefs of Staff took note that the J.I.C. report was to be considered at the Defence Committee Meeting on August 2nd.

DO(43), 7th Mtg.
At this meeting the C.I.G.S. referred to the receipt of information on resistance groups by the Chiefs of Staff from S.I.S. and drew the moral that a closer relationship was required between S.O.E. and S.I.S. He considered it was wrong that important information had reached the Chiefs of Staff in this way and they should have received it from S.O.E. themselves. This is the only mention at this meeting of the S.I.S. report on penetration of S.O.E. circuits. Arrangements were made however for closer co-ordination between S.O.E. and the Chiefs of Staff. (see para 19).

Control by Theatre Commanders of S.O.E.

By the end of 1943, S.O.E. was organised into an H.Q. and three main groups corresponding to the principal theatres.

COS(43), 237th Meeting(0), Minute 11, 15 May 1943
The North West Europe or London Group was placed under the operational control of COSSAC as soon as COSSAC became an operational H.Q. The functions of COSSAC were later taken over by SHAEF.

COS(43)618(0)
Similarly, it was agreed that S.O.E. activities under the then Middle East Theatre should be under the operational control of the Commander-in-Chief, Middle East. The same principal had always been in operation in the Western Mediterranean Theatre controlled by A.F.H.Q. It was confirmed by the Allied Commander-in-Chief that this principle was to continue throughout the new unified Mediterranean Theatre.

Operational control of S.O.E. activities in all parts of Europe had therefore been divided between the two Allied Commanders in London and the Middle East. The only exceptions to this rule were Poland and Czechoslovakia; activities in these two countries, and for a time in Austria, remained directly under the operational control of the Chiefs of Staff.

S.D. Aircraft Available at the End of 1943, U.K. and Mediterranean Bases

The total number of aircraft now engaged on S.O.E. operations was approximately four Squadrons: two of these (161 and 138) based on Tempsford in the U.K. while the remaining two were in North Africa, 148 at Toccra, and 624 at Blida. Temporary increases to the number of S.D. aircraft available were made by Bomber Command in the last months of 1943 by the addition of some Stirlings, and later of some Lancasters, to the aircraft strength at Tempsford. Two American Squadrons of Liberators had been allotted (see para 27), for this work, but were not yet operational.

CCS.267/3, 17 September 1943
The increase was comparatively small, and the airlift available was still entirely inadequate for S.O.E.'s work.

"Big Three", Cairo (Sextant): Support of Balkan Partisans

The problem of supplies for the Balkan partisans was considered at the "Big Three" conference in November/December 1943, and the Prime

Minister showed himself markedly interested in the problem. The question of support to the French and the Polish underground movements, however, was not brought up in any of the recorded discussions.

COS(Sex) Prelim, 18 November 1943
At a preliminary C.O.S. Meeting in Malta with General Alexander, Admiral Sir John Cunningham, and Air Chief Marshal Tedder attending, the Prime Minister referred to the deterioration of the situation on the Dalmatian coast, where the Germans were pushing back the Partisans. The C.I.G.S. commenting upon the Prime Minister's remarks observed that a General Officer had now taken over there, working in close collaboration with S.O.E. and the other two services.

COS(Sex)1(Revise), 20 November 1943
Two days later, en route to Cairo, the Prime Minister submitted to the British Chiefs of Staff a minute in which he indicated the general line he proposed to take at the Plenary Conference in his review of the current situation in Europe. He expressed his view in unequivocal terms on the generally unfavourable situation in the Mediterranean.

Regarding the Balkans, he remarked that we had failed to give any real support to the Partisans in Yugoslavia, and Albania – they had, he said, been nourished up to that time only be droppings from the air; and from his subsequent remarks it was clear that such efforts as had been made to assist the Partisans were viewed by him with unconcealed dissatisfaction.

The cause of this failure to provide effective support, he attributed to the artificial and unsatisfactory lines of demarcation between the areas over which the Commander-in-Chief, A.F.H.Q., and the Commander-in-Chief, Middle East, respectively, had responsibility. So far as the Balkans were concerned, General Wilson had the responsibility without the forces necessary to provide adequate support: General Eisenhower had the forces, but not the responsibility.

This unsatisfactory state of affairs was used by the Prime Minister as a cogent argument for unification of command in the Mediterranean area as a whole – a policy which was strongly championed by the British representatives at this Conference, and which was unanimously approved.

COS(Sex), 1st Mtg., Minute 3., 22 November 1943
COS(Sex), 2nd Mtg., Minute 1, 23 November 1943
The British Chiefs of Staff considered the Prime Minister's minute, and offered their comments. On the Balkan issue, they remarked that they shared the Prime Minister's views and considered that the reasons for the unsatisfactory state of affairs were: i) the divided command in the Mediterranean; ii) the fact that the operation had grown beyond the capacity of S.O.E. to organise and control.

The fault given in ii) above was in process of being remedied.

2nd Plenary Mtg., 24 November 1943
The Prime Minister at the second Plenary Meeting reviewed the general European situation on the lines he had indicated in the minute which he had submitted to the British Chiefs of Staff, and conveyed to the meeting his thoughts on the Balkan support question, advocating as a definite item of our combined policy in Europe the provision of supplies to Yugoslavia. There was no specific comment on this item by the U.S. Representatives.

COS(Sex), 4th Mtg., Minute 3, 25 November 1943
That the British Chiefs of Staff themselves had misgivings regarding the handling of the Balkan support by Middle East authorities is indicated by a discussion at one of their earlier meetings at Cairo.

CC/351
The C.A.S., referring to a telegram from the Commander's-in-Chief Middle East, observed that it would appear that such steps as had been taken regarding the provision of support to the Balkan guerillas did not altogether meet the wishes of the Chiefs of Staff Committee as expressed in a telegram which had been sent by the Committee to the Commander's-in-Chief, Middle East.

COS/ME/439
The C.I.G.S. said that in his view what was required was the appointment of one man, assisted by an inter-service Staff, responsible for organising the delivery of supplies by land, sea and air, and for co-ordinating the employment of any aircraft operating in support of the Partisans. He suggested, however, that the matter be held in abeyance pending the decision of the conference regarding the proposal to unify

command in the Mediterranean. A telegram was sent to the Commander's-in-Chief, Middle East, conveying the sense of the C.I.G.S. remarks.

COS(Sex), 2nd Mtg., Annex I, Para 15, 23 November 1943
It may be noted from a comment by the British Chiefs of Staff on a proposal by the Prime Minister that a bridgehead should be established on the Dalmatian coast, that they were not in favour of such an operation (although they had been at the Quebec Conference), and that their disfavour was shared by General Alexander, who had confirmed the opinion expressed by General Marshall at Washington in May, that the operation would be required too great a proportion of the Allied resources. They further stated that in their view as much support could be given by smuggling operations along the coast and by air, and that successful prosecution of the operations depended much more on good organisation. They re-iterated that the business had got too big for S.O.E., and should be taken over by a proper Staff.

CCS, 131st Mtg., 25 November 1943
General Eisenhower and Air Chief Marshal Tedder were invited to give their views on the Mediterranean operations at one of the C.C.S. Meetings. As far as the Balkans were concerned, General Eisenhower reported that one officer had been placed in charge of all operations regarding the supply of equipment to Yugoslav guerillas, and the arms captured in North Africa and Sicily were being sent in. He believed all possible equipment should be sent to Tito as Mihailovic's forces were of little value. Air Chief Marshal Tedder said that he felt that the present system of air operations into the Balkans worked reasonably well. The tactical commander in Italy was given targets by the Middle East organisation. He agreed with the C.A.S. that a Joint Staff under the officer responsible for Balkan operations would lead to a better co-ordination of effort.

CCS, 132nd Mtg., 20 November 1943
At the meeting of the C.C.S. prior to their final meeting with Marshal Stalin at Teheran, when the specific items of future policy on which they felt it desirable to reach agreement with Marshal Stalin were under discussion, it was decided that one item should be: "All possible help to the Partisans in Yugoslavia."

This item of proposed policy was agreed at Teheran and was incorporated in the list of agreed decisions.

CCS,426/1, Para 9(a), 6 December 1943
CCS,133rd Mtg., Minute 2, 3 December 1943
The Combined Staff Planners were then instructed to prepare the necessary directive to implement this decision.

CCS, 425, December 1943
Their recommendations appeared as a C.C.S. paper which was approved by the C.C.S., who gave instructions for its inclusion in the comprehensive directive, then in course of preparation, which was to covey to the Commander-in-Chief Allied Forces, North Africa, the C.C.S. decision to unify command in the Mediterranean.

CCS, 135th Mtg, Minute 6, 5 December 1943
CCS/387/3, Appendix B, 5 December 1943
The instruction regarding Balkan support appeared as an appendix to the main directive, and informed the Commander-in-Chief that it had been agreed at the Conference at Teheran that the support of the Balkan Partisans for which he would now be responsible should be intensified: support should be provided to the greatest extent practicable by increasing the supply of arms and equipment, clothing, medical stores, food and such other supplies as might be necessary. The Commander-in-Chief should furnish whatever air support he considered advisable, taking into account the overall situation. The possibility should be examined of continuing to supply the Partisans with Italian equipment, with which they were already familiar, making good any deficiencies so far as necessary with available British or American equipment. This Mission was regarded of such importance that it was best controlled on a regular basis by a Special Commander, and a Joint Staff.

The Combined Administrative Committee were then instructed to consider the availability of resources necessary to give effect to the Conference decisions.

CCS/428, Encl. Annex IV, Appendix F, 15 December 1943
They reported that aircraft based as follows were allocated to the support of Resistance Groups in Europe and the Balkans:

	Heavy Bombers
U.K. Bases	16
Mediterranean Bases	42
TOTAL	58

The formation within the 8th U.S. Army Air Force in the U.K. of two squadrons of Liberators had been agreed. No Liberators suitable for day combat duty should be allocated for this purpose. Support given to the Resistance Groups in Europe would not cause any interference with the intensification of the Combined Bomber Offensive.

Penetration by Gestapo, Investigations December 1943 to January 1944

During the autumn of 1943 further reports were received from the field showing the extent of the enemy's success in penetrating certain of the S.O.E. organisations, and in particular those in Holland. On December 1st, while the Cairo Conference was still sitting, the Secretary of the Chiefs of Staff Committee informed the Deputy Prime Minister that information had just come into the hands of the Vice-Chiefs of Staff which seemed to show that the whole S.O.E. organisation in Holland was penetrated by the Germans, and had been run by the Germans for the last year.

This information came from two agents who were dropped in Holland – one in December 1942, and one in March 1943 – who were received by the Germans and placed in a prison camp, from which they had now escaped. If this information was accurate, it meant that for over a year every man and container of material sent to Holland had fallen directly into the hands of the Germans, and that the Germans had been operating wireless sets in Holland which communicated with S.O.E. in England. The Vice-Chiefs of Staff regarded the position with great disquiet. Action had been taken to suspend all S.O.E. operations to Holland, where for some time past R.A.F. losses on S.O.E. sorties had been abnormally high (18%).

The A.O.C.-in-C., Bomber Command, had gone further and temporarily suspended all S.O.E. operations over Europe, but the Secretary of State for Air was looking into this, as so drastic a step might not be necessary. The Vice Chiefs of Staff proposed that an enquiry should be conducted by the Joint Intelligence Committee who should be instructed to investigate the truth of the allegations concerning S.O.E. operations in Holland and, if these allegations proved to be well founded, to examine the position elsewhere, so as to find out the extent of the German penetration of the S.O.E. organisation in Europe.

F1145/127
The next day the Minister of Economic Warfare wrote to the Deputy Prime Minister about the manner in which S.O.E. affairs were apt to be handled. It had been known in London for some ten days that there were very grave doubts about the integrity of the S.O.E. organisation in Holland. Information had accordingly been given to the Air Ministry by S.O.E. that they did not intend to ask for any sorties to Holland other than to drop 'blind' (that is without Reception Committees) two Organisers intended to lay the foundations of a new D-Day organisation in that country.

On 30th November, the A.O.C.-in-C., Bomber Command, without any prior consultation with S.O.E. had cancelled all S.O.E. air sorties from the U.K. and on 1st December the whole question, again without any reference to S.O.E., had been considered by the Vice Chiefs of Staff. In fact, the first official notification which the Minister himself or S.O.E. received of the whole question had been a copy of Brigadier Jacob's Minute to the Deputy Prime Minister informing him of the Vice Chiefs of Staff discussions. The Minister protested strongly against the tendency for other Government Departments to consider themselves entitled to discuss and sometimes even to take decisions upon matters connected with S.O.E. without prior reference to or consultation with that Organisation. In such circumstances it was extremely difficult for S.O.E. to do the work with which they had been charged by H.M.G.

Suspension of Operations, Poland

A meeting was held at Air Ministry on December 2nd to discuss the question of the suspension of Polish operations at which the Minister of Economic Warfare, the Secretary of State for Air, D.C.A.S., A.C.A.S.(I) and the Vice Chief of S.O.E. were present. Although it had been arranged that Polish operations were to be flown from a base within the Mediterranean Theatre the Polish Government had certain important agents whom they wished to infiltrate immediately from England. This would involve nine sorties. Since the re-routeing of the aircraft on the

Polish run the casualty rate had dropped most satisfactorily, and since it appeared that C-in-C, Bomber Command's worries over Poland were not concerned with the security of the Polish organisations but with the operational hazards of the flight itself, the S.O.E. representatives suggested that these nine sorties should be authorised without any Polish enquiry by the J.I.C.

The D.C.A.S. said that in his view the operational hazards, which he agreed the J.I.C. were not competent to judge, were so great that the C.-in-C. was anxious to discontinue all sorties to Poland from the U.K. at the earliest possible moment. It was therefore agreed that the Polish agents should be ferried to North Africa immediately in order to enable them to be dropped into Poland by the Polish Flight operating from North African territory.

The next day, however, the Minister of Economic Warfare reported in a minute to the Secretary of State for Air that the arrangements which had been agreed at the meeting to ferry Polish agents to North Africa in order to enable them to be infiltrated into Poland from there was for various reasons unsatisfactory. After strongly pressing the Polish case and underlining the difficulties of the Reception Committee in the field, he suggested that his argument should be put to the C-in-C. Bomber Command with the request that he should most urgently reconsider his present refusal to allow Polish operations to be flown from the U.K. and also that the J.I.C.'s enquiry into the security of the operations in Poland should be called off.

The Minister sent a copy of this minute to the Deputy Prime Minister on December 5th and reported that the C-in-C. Bomber Command had now agreed to permit the sorties to take place, by a new route which was unfortunately not only safer but also longer. None of the Reception Committees which had been arranged and were already standing by in the field could be reached if this route were followed. The previous difficulty over ranges and routes was recapitulated and the Minister added that if the C-in-C. Bomber Command refused to allow the use of the shorter route (which his officers had previously approved), then in fact none of the sorties from the United Kingdom, upon which the Poles had been relying, could take place, and it would be impossible to send any money for the maintenance of their organisations in Northern Poland. This would be a disaster of first-class magnitude.

A Staff Conference was held on 6th December at which were present the Deputy Prime Minister, the Secretary of State for Air, the C-in-C.

Bomber Command, the Minister of Economic Warfare and the R.A.F. and S.O.E. representatives. The Minister of Economic Warfare said that at the previous Staff Conference held on December 1st he had been surprised to learn that the C-in-C. Bomber Command, required that S.O.E. operations from the U.K. over Poland and Denmark as well as over Holland should be suspended. He, the Minister of Economic Warfare, had been very willing that the suspension of S.O.E. operations over Holland should be continued pending the result of the enquiry by the Joint Intelligence Sub-Committee. He had also agreed at the meeting to the suspension covering Denmark and Poland. The Joint Intelligence Sub-Committee had produced their report regarding Denmark with considerable speed and as a result it had been possible to lift the ban on operations over that country. He had realised after the meeting that he should not have agreed to the ban on operations over Poland. He recounted the difficulties in which S.O.E. and the Polish Government found themselves as a result of the cancellation of the Polish operations from U.K.

The C-in-C. Bomber Command said that since the middle of November, it had been increasingly borne in upon him that flights over the northern route to Poland involved an unjustifiable risk. The heavy Allied attacks on Berlin were resulting in considerably increased air defences in Northern Europe.

The Deputy Prime Minister pointed out that S.O.E. had a valid cause for complaint since they had believed that a firm commitment had been entered into by the Air Ministry. There appeared to be a lack of proper liaison between the Air Minister and S.O.E. This whole matter had risen out of a meeting on 1st December called to consider the alleged penetration of the S.O.E. organisation in Holland. It was now clear that the Air Ministry's objection to operations over Poland from the U.K. was not based on any suspicion of penetration by the enemy of the organisation in that country.

The Secretary of State for Air suggested that a solution to the problem might be found by the Air Ministry agreeing to send out the necessary aircraft to the Mediterranean so that the sorties could be flown from an advanced base in Italy, and this was agreed by the meeting. It was further agreed that the C-in-C. Bomber Command would make up the effort on S.D. operations from the U.K. which would otherwise be lost by the despatch of four Tempsford Halifaxes to North Africa. The meeting further invited the Secretary of State for Air and the Minister of

Economic Warfare to arrange for closer association of the R.A.F. liaison staff with S.O.E. planning at all stages.

J.I.C. Report on S.O.E. Penetration

JIC(43)517, 22 December 1943
The J.I.C. report on the degree of penetration by the enemy of S.O.E. organisations in Europe was considered at a Meeting of the Defence Committee on January 14th.

DO(44), 2nd Meeting
The principal conclusions of the J.I.C. were that the organisations established by S.O.E. in Holland had for a long time been penetrated, that there was doubt as regards the situation in Poland owing to the lack of information on this subject, and that in France there was a tendency to centralisation in those resistance organisations which were directly under the control of Fighting French Headquarters.

The Minister of Economic Warfare stated that while it was easy to be wise after the event, S.O.E. themselves now thought that they might have been more suspicious regarding the situation in Holland. He reminded the Committee, however, that S.O.E.'s principal function was to fight. It was not until June 1943 that his organisation seriously suspected that penetration in Holland had taken place. They had hoped that two parts of the Dutch organisation had even then escaped penetration. In agreement with the Air Ministry they had therefore decided to test out these two parts. The event showed that the entire organisation had been penetrated.

The Secretary of State for Air said that S.I.S. had been consulted and in the summer of 1943 had been unable to produce any evidence of penetration of the S.O.E. groups in Holland. The air evidence on the whole question had been important: those who were concerned with the air operations carrying agents into Holland did have their suspicions aroused and had remarked on the apparently unnaturally good reception arrangements. He stressed his opinion that Air Ministry representatives in S.O.E. should be much more than advisers but should be brought into consultation on every stage of planning special operations of this nature. The Minister of Economic Warfare asked that decisions should be taken as soon as possible on the question of renewing operations to Holland and on the allocation of aircraft for

S.O.E. purposes. The Secretary of State for Foreign Affairs strongly supported the Minister of Economic Warfare.

The Committee in conclusion recorded their opinion that R.A.F. officers attached to S.O.E. should be associated at all stages with the planning of S.O.E. Air Operations. They also agreed that S.D. operations over Holland should be resumed and developed if feasible, invited the Chiefs of Staff to give urgent consideration to the question of S.O.E.'s aircraft requirements, and recorded their opinion that high importance should be attached to the development of special operations during the coming months.

R.A.F./S.O.E. Co-ordination, Appointment of Air Adviser to S.O.E.

The problem of R.A.F./S.O.E. co-ordination, thrown into relief by the news of the penetration of S.O.E. organisations, had been under discussion for some time. Verbal arrangements between the Air Ministry and S.O.E. had led in the autumn of 1943 to the appointment of a senior Air Adviser within S.O.E.

Circ. within SOE as VCD/588 of 22 October 1943 (Under Heading "Status and Responsibilities of the Air Adviser to SOE."
After this officer had been working in S.O.E. for some weeks it was found necessary to clarify his duties and responsibilities, and a Directive was therefore agreed between S.O.E. and the Air Ministry. This document laid down that the Air Adviser would be responsible to the Air Staff for all liaison between S.O.E. and the Air Ministry on matters concerning the air policy and air operations undertaken on behalf of S.O.E. He would represent S.O.E. at discussions involving demands for increased aircraft and would act as the senior R.A.F. Liaison Officer between S.O.E. and H.Q. Bomber Command. He would also keep both Air Ministry and S.O.E. fully informed as to the general purpose and aim of projected S.O.E. operations on the one hand and the capabilities and limitations of air operations on the other.

As the volume of S.D. operations increased, the importance of good liaison between the R.A.F. and S.O.E. and of machinery that would work both efficiently and rapidly for the mounting of S.D. operations became of greater importance. Various suggestions were put up as to ways in which the existing liaison and machinery could be improved. For instance, the Air Adviser to S.O.E. in November raised the question of A.I.2(c)'s responsibility for passing the pinpoints for S.D. operations and suggested that this function might be transferred either to Bomber Command or to R.A.F. Station Tempsford. The necessity for S.O.E. air operations officers to make frequent visits to the Air Ministry authorities responsible for passing pinpoints was a serious objection to this suggestion, since both Bomber Command and Tempsford were situated at some distance from S.O.E. H.Q. The question of strengthening the liaison between R.A.F. and S.O.E. by the provision of additional R.A.F. officers to the staff of S.O.E. H.Q. was also put forward.

A meeting was held at the Air Ministry on December 2nd at which were present the Minister of Economic Warfare, the Vice Chief of S.O.E., the Secretary of State for Air, D.C.A.S., and A.C.A.S.(I). This meeting was convened primarily to discuss the question of the suspension of S.D. operations as a result of the allegations that had been made as to the penetration of S.O.E. circuits, but it went on to consider the question of organisation and procedure as between S.O.E. and the R.A.F.

V/CD/751, 2 December 1943
The D.C.A.S. said that Air Marshal Harris was not satisfied that the operations carried out from S.O.E. were properly considered from an air operational point of view. The Air Adviser to S.O.E. had suggested to him that the right solution would be for Bomber Command to put an R.A.F. officer with operational experience into every country section of S.O.E. The C-in-C. was also anxious that the Station Commander should have a veto of sorties not only on grounds of weather but also if he considered that the operational hazards of a proposed flight were too great.

The Minister of Economic Warfare said that S.O.E. welcomed any suggestion for strengthening liaison with the R.A.F. and good operational officers would be most welcome. He could not agree, however, to the expansion of functions proposed for the Station Commander. At this point A.C.A.S.(I) remarked that the C-in-C. seemed to be under a misapprehension if he was worrying about the D. of I(R) and A.I.2(c) went most carefully into the air operational considerations of every single projected sortie, and none were accepted on behalf of the Air Ministry or passed to Tempsford until experts in the Air Ministry were fully satisfied with the pinpoint and route to be taken, the defences in the neighbourhood, the meteorological aspect and all the other technical considerations involved. Both the Secretary of State and

D.C.A.S. said that they had on the previous day received the impression that the C-in-C. Bomber Command had not known anything about these arrangements and did not realise that the operations received this consideration from Air Ministry experts. It was undoubtedly largely for this reason that he had asked for reassurance and it was clear that some misunderstanding had occurred.

The Meeting therefore agreed to set up a Committee immediately to consider the whole question of the aims and conduct of air operations carried out on behalf of S.O.E. The constitution of this Committee and its terms of reference were to be agreed between D.C.A.S. and the Vice Chief of S.O.E. and then submitted to the Secretary of State and the Minister of Economic Warfare for approval. The general conclusion of the Meeting was that it was most desirable to improve the relationship between the Air Ministry and S.O.E. to tighten up the whole system and to do everything to promote easy and harmonious working.

Ad Hoc Committee on R.A.F./S.O.E. Liaison

A Committee, consisting of representatives of S.O.E. and of the R.A.F., was accordingly set up and meetings were held during December and January. It was clear throughout that the views of the C-in-C. Bomber Command were fundamentally opposed to the continued maintenance of special squadrons engaged on S.D. work.

At a meeting held on January 4th the C-in-C. Bomber Command said that in his view all heavy bombers should logically come under the operational control of Bomber Command. He believed that it should be perfectly possible for Bomber Command to play a full part in meeting S.O.E. requirements, more particularly since under present conditions Bomber Command tended not to operate under the moonlight conditions which were particularly suited to S.O.E. operations. He was aware that co-operation between Bomber Command and S.O.E. had not been very satisfactory, and this was largely because Bomber Command had not felt satisfied that S.O.E. operations were planned with full knowledge of the air aspect involved. If, in the past, experienced R.A.F. officers had been available in S.O.E. he was of the opinion that many losses and abortive efforts could have been avoided, and a much greater effort put out.

It was in his view essential that competent R.A.F. officers should be associated with S.O.E. activities from the initial planning stages. If full support were to be forthcoming from Bomber Command, he would wish to be assured:

  a) that for any given operation the risk in aircraft and crews was justified.

  b) that the operation was tactically practicable.

Under present arrangements and in the absence of experienced air advice he could not feel satisfied that the risks taken by Bomber Command in carrying out S.O.E. operations were justifiable.

The S.O.E. representative pointed out that a suggestion had been made that the S.D. aircraft might be placed under the control of COSSAC, in which case the removal of 138 and 161 Squadrons from the control of Bomber Command would be involved. It was true that S.O.E. would then have to sacrifice the supplementary effort which they had received from Bomber Command but there was hope that A.E.A.F. might possibly be able to contribute towards S.D. work in the same way as Bomber Command were contributing. With regard to the question of wasted effort he was in entire agreement that competent air advice should be available at all stages in the carrying out of operations, but he was doubtful if the advice of Air Officers situated in the country sections of S.O.E. could be of assistance in the initial planning of operations. The broad directive for S.O.E. was laid down by the Chiefs of Staff and faulty operations arose usually as a result of some contretemps on the ground side. It was questionable whether it would be either practicable or useful to train airmen to work in S.O.E.'s country sections.

In the opinion of the S.O.E. representative the solution was that the special Air Section of the London Group should be so qualified as to have the confidence of the R.A.F. authorities concerned, in this case Bomber Command, that its views on the feasibility and worth of a projected operation would be accepted by them.

In discussion it appeared that there were two levels on which the Air Ministry required strong representation within S.O.E.: both on the S.O.E. Council, where officers of Air Rank would be concerned with the high policy of S.O.E. as a whole, and on the executive level of the Air Transport Section. The C-in-C. Bomber Command added that in his view it was essential that the Command concerned in the air operations should be fully represented throughout the planning departments of S.O.E. by Air Force officers of operational experience, organised as an Air Staff and directly responsible to the Air Officer on the S.O.E. Council. The Air Officer on the S.O.E. Council would thus be enabled to keep his finger on the pulse of the entire organisation from top to bottom.

The meeting also considered the arrangements which should be made for improved liaison between the Air Ministry and S.O.E. H.Q. and it was generally considered that it would be very desirable to have one officer in the Air Ministry as the channel through which all S.O.E. operations should flow. Both D. of I(R) and A.C.A.S.(I) were at present concerned with S.O.E. air operational affairs and it was suggested that a new directorate might be formed to cover all Air Ministry functions with regard to S.O.E. It was further suggested that this post should be amalgamated with that of the Air Adviser to S.O.E.

The Meeting recommended that there should be appointed within the Air Ministry a new Director under A.C.A.S.(Ops) charged with the responsibility for all questions affecting air operations on behalf of S.O.E. and S.I.S. This officer, would also hold the appointment of Air Adviser to S.O.E. Council. The operational control of the S.D. Squadrons should be transferred to No.38 Group, A.E.A.F., under COSSAC. In the event of such a transfer taking place, Tempsford should be retained as the S.D. airfield. The Head of the Air Transport Command Organisation in S.O.E. and certain of the staff should be provided by the Command responsible for S.O.E. air operations, and should be responsible to the C-in-C. of the Command concerned and also to the Controller of the London Group.

The C-in-C. Bomber Command, however, dissociated himself from the conclusions.

On 14th January the Minister of Economic Warfare wrote to the Secretary of State for Air asking that the necessary new R.A.F. officers should be appointed to S.O.E. as soon as possible. Further discussions and correspondence ensued on the question of the transfer of S.D. Squadrons to A.E.A.F., the responsibilities of the Air Adviser on the S.O.E. Council, and the amalgamation of the various departments within Air Ministry concerned with S.O.E. affairs. A letter from the Secretary of State for Air to the Minister of Economic Warfare, dated 23rd January (no reference) proposed that there should be no doubling of the roles of Air Ministry Air Staff Director and Air Adviser within S.O.E., that the S.D. Squadrons should be transferred to A.E.A.F., that one R.A.F. officer should be appointed to the staff of the country sections concerned with Western Europe and that the Head of the Air Transport

Section in S.O.E. and certain of his staff should be provided by the R.A.F. Command responsible for S.D. operations.

VCAS, DO/8/44/CMS.407

The proposal to transfer the Tempsford units from Bomber Command to A.E.A.F. was held in abeyance in view of the special effort required from Bomber Command during the early months of 1944. However, arrangements for the co-ordination of functions within Air Ministry proceeded and Air Marshal Evill writing to S.O.E. on 1st February 1944 stated that the Air Ministry recognised that a single authority was needed within the Air Staff who would be responsible for S.O.E. requirements and operations and for general co-ordination of the Staff action on these and cognate matters for S.I.S. He proposed therefore that D of I(R) should become the responsible Air Staff Director for S.O.E. and S.I.S. operations.

The question of the R.A.F. representation in S.O.E. was also settled during February and further R.A.F. officers were appointed to the Staff of S.O.E. H.Q. R.A.F. officers were appointed to the Western European Country Sections of S.O.E. and the duties of the Air Liaison Section were laid down. (see Appendix "C" for details). At the same time the status and responsibility of the Air Member of S.O.E. was defined again.

S.O.E.'s Aircraft Requirements, January to March 1944

The paper on which the Minister of Economic Warfare had asked at the Defence Committee on January 14th for an urgent Chiefs of Staff decision was S.O.E.'s "Air Transport Requirements for January to March 1944."

In Western Europe all roads now led to Overlord. For some months, S.O.E. had been making plans in conjunction with COSSAC for the use of the Resistance Forces in the countries of Western Europe, and it was evident that if Resistance organisations were to fulfil the role that had been allotted to them enormously increased quantities of stores must be despatched to the field.

France had by now become a special problem: the imposition by the Germans of the Réleve [*sic*] had resulted in the establishment of large groups of "Maquisards" all over the country and particularly in the mountainous areas in the South East. These Groups urgently required both food and clothing with which to maintain themselves in the mountains, and arms and ammunition with which to fight off the Germans who were making every effort to liquidate a threat so vital to themselves.

SHAEF/2142/25/SD, 14 January
A Meeting was held at S.H.A.E.F. on January 14th at which senior R.A.F. and S.O.E. representatives were present. The tonnages of stores required for the implementation of the D-Day plans, for arming guerillas and for maintaining current sabotage were estimated, and it was clear that with only the present number of aircraft available for S.D. work there would be a serious deficiency. The importance of weighing carefully any demands which required a diversion of bomber effort from Overlord was stressed and various means were considered to fulfil essential requirements without further demands. The Meeting however came to no definite conclusion.

COS(44), 15th Mtg.(0), Item 14; SOE(43)Plans/350 circ. as COS(43)781(0), 22 December 1943
On January 19th, the Chiefs of Staff considered the problem of S.O.E.'s aircraft requirements as set forth in the Memorandum which they had submitted in December 1943. The anticipated monthly lift of the aircraft at present available to S.O.E., together with the target figures for the various areas was shown as follows:

	Present A/c	Present Monthly Tonnage	Target Monthly Tonnage
Balkans:	32	278	680
Italy & S. France:	4	20	168
Western Europe:	16	86	560
Central Europe:	6	20	60
	58	404	1468

If all the Directives issued to S.O.E. were to be implemented then theoretically the effort of 300 aircraft would have to be employed if the full target commitment, amounting to over 1400 tons per month, was to be met. In the Mediterranean, the unification of command under S.A.C. MED, and M.A.A.F. would permit the pooling of all aircraft in accordance with strategic requirements for the supply of the Balkans, North Italy, South France, and Central Europe. In Western Europe, it had to be remembered that the first three months of 1944 were the vital period, after which little could be done to influence D-Day plans. With the present resources there was a very considerable gap of over 1,000 tons per month between the operational requirements and the estimated lift, and S.O.E. suggested that all squadrons engaged on S.D. work should be brought up to full strength; this, together with the addition of American Squadrons, would result in a total of 54 aircraft in the Mediterranean and 44 based on the U.K. Even this would not be adequate, and S.O.E. suggested that a supplementary effort should be made available to enable the Organisation to fulfil its plans.

The Chiefs of Staff Committee at the same meeting considered a Memorandum by S.O.E. on their plans for the intensification of sabotage and guerilla activity in Poland, and a request from the French Committee of National Liberation for increased supplies of material for Resistance Groups inside France. The Committee agreed that the French requests for increased supplies was now a matter which should be considered by the Supreme Allied Commander who had been made responsible for all S.O.E. operations in France. With regard to Poland, the C.A.S. said that any substantial increase in the air effort available for Polish operations must come out of the general allocation of aircraft for S.O.E. purposes.

In considering S.O.E.'s paper on their aircraft requirements, the C.A.S. remarked that there appeared to be no record of a target commitment of 1,400 tons per month having been accepted by the Chiefs of Staff and the S.O.E. representative explained that this figure had been calculated from the general directive which had been approved by the Chiefs of Staff.

The C.A.S. then emphasised that Bomber Command were between 70 and 80 Halifaxes short of their expansion programme. The provision of any additional aircraft for S.O.E. would cause a corresponding increase in this deficiency. He considered, therefore, that apart from expanding some of the present S.D. Squadrons, the maximum contribution to subversive operations that we could possibly afford to make at present was a supplementary effort of some 60 sorties per month by the Stirlings of No.38 Group. This would mean an additional delivery of approximately 60 tons per month. The Committee agreed that these proposals represented the maximum justifiable allocation of aircraft to S.O.E. operations for the current quarter, and further agreed that an approach should be made to the U.S. Chiefs of Staff for additional aircraft for O.S.S./S.O.E. work in the Mediterranean as well as the Western European Theatre.

COS(44), 23rd Meeting(0), Item 13, 25 January 1944
COS(W)1095, 25 January 1944
A telegram, approved by the Chiefs of Staff was therefore sent to Washington, requesting that the Americans should increase their contribution of aircraft for S.D. operations.

JSM/1509, 12 February 1944
The reply from Washington reported that the American Chiefs of Staff were considering every possibility for increasing their activities of this type, but owing to their commitments of personnel and equipment to various theatres the prospects were not hopeful. General Arnold had stated that no additional aircraft could be allocated from the United States Army Air Force specifically for S.D. purposes, but local United States Commanders had been directed to employ for this purpose any aircraft that could be spared.

After learning the decision of the Chiefs of Staff on S.O.E.'s aircraft requirements, the Minister of Economic Warfare wrote to the Prime Minister on 26th January 1944 that he was afraid their conclusions would mean that the Resistance Movements in Europe would be greatly disappointed. He pointed out that the increased allocations just made by the Chiefs of Staff still left a very large gap between the quantity of material which could be delivered to the field and the quantity necessary to enable S.O.E. organisations to fulfil their directive. He emphasised the importance of the time factor, recalling that the consideration of his paper of 18th December on S.O.E.'s aircraft requirements had been held up pending the result of the J.I.C. enquiry. So much time had been lost through this cause that the additional assistance could not now be ready in time to affect S.O.E.'s Overlord plans. The responsibilities of the British Government towards Resistance Groups in occupied territories was a solemn one. These groups were already extremely dissatisfied with the amount of support they had received, and the effect of further disappointment on their morale would be serious.

Prime Minister Calls a Meeting on France

During January, General de Gaulle and M. Emanuel d'Astier de la Vigerie, (Commissioner for the Interior, French National Committee, and prior to that one of the three heads of Resistance inside France), had seen the Prime Minister at Marrakesh on the subject of supplies to the guerillas in France, particularly in the south east, and had succeeded in interesting him in the problem.

COS(44)92(0), 29 January

A Meeting of Ministers was held on Thursday, 27th January, at which were present the Secretary of State for Air, the C.A.S., the Minister of Economic Warfare, M. d'Astier, and representatives from the Foreign Office and S.O.E. The Prime Minister stated that he had called the meeting to consider what could be done to assist the Resistance Movements in France during the coming critical months: a matter to which he attached high importance. The Minister of Economic Warfare said that S.O.E. were giving every assistance that lay within their power, but their help was limited by the number of aircraft that the Air Staff could make available for S.D. work. M. d'Astier pointed out that the situation of the bands of patriots in the Maquis, particularly in south-eastern France, was now acute and their needs were urgent. The Prime Minister said that he wished and believed it possible to bring about a situation in S.E. France comparable to that existing in Yugoslavia. Brave and desperate men could cause the most acute embarrassment to the enemy, and it was right that we should do all in our power to foster and stimulate so valuable an aid to Allied strategy.

The C.A.S. said that, while the Air Staff fully recognised the urgent need to assist the Resistance Movement in France, he must ask that no decision be taken which would result in the diversion of any part of the major bombing effort over Germany. The Secretary of State for Air asked that the Air Staff should not be asked to allocate at this stage particular squadrons for full time duty on this task, and requested that the Prime Minister should give the Air Ministry instructions that the effort of Bomber Command during the month of February should be directed primarily to the Bomber Offensive, but that the Maquis should be given priority over other activities of Bomber Command.

The Meeting agreed that during the month of February 1944, the primary effort of Bomber Command should be directed to the bomber offensive against Germany and that, subject to the needs of S.I.S., and the first two priorities of other operations of Bomber Command during that month should be the Maquis, and other S.O.E. operations. The Minister of Economic Warfare, in consultation with M. d'Astier and the Air Staff was invited to enquire into the air facilities that could be made available for S.O.E. operations in support of the Resistance Movement in the Maquis during February, and to prepare an outline plan of assistance and to submit a report to the Prime Minister by 31st January.

Annex V to COS(44)125, 3 February 1944
On the scheduled date the Minister of Economic Warfare reported to the Prime Minister on the conclusions of his Committee, submitting for the Prime Minister's decision a plan for arming Resistance Groups in the French Maquis during the February moon period which embodied the unanimous view of the Committee.

The scale of air effort which the Air Staff proposed to use in order to implement the plan included the reinforcement of the Tempsford Squadrons in order to bring their total strength to twenty Halifaxes, the use of one American Liberator Squadron which was by now converted and trained for special duties, a supplementary effort by No.38 Group sufficient to provide a total of 60 attempted sorties, and two squadrons of Stirlings. Arrangements were also under consideration by C-in-C. M.A.A.F., to provide a total of 120 attempted sorties from North Africa into Southern France.

The Minister pointed out that this plan had been made at short notice (in fact S.O.E. were only able to begin work on it four days before the February moon period began), and that about half of the air crews engaged would be undertaking S.D. work for the first time, and concluded by requesting that his committee should be instructed to prepare less hurriedly another special effort for the March moon, when prospects of achievement were likely to be considerably improved.

Annex I to COS(44)125(0), 3 February 1944
On February 2nd, The Prime Minister wrote to the Minister of Economic Warfare and the Chiefs of Staff:

> "I approve the proposals in your minute of 31st January for arming the Maquis, but if through bad weather or any other reason the number of sorties in February looks like dropping below your

estimate, I want extra effort made to improvise additional sorties to the Maquis on nights when conditions are favourable. Even if fully successful the February programme is not enough. Pray start at once on a programme for the March moon. Let me see it in plenty of time. I want March deliveries to double those planned for February. I am told that the stocks of ammunition in the Maquis are far below what is reasonable, even for the few weapons they possess. M. d'Astier has also asked me to send in some concentrated foods and vitamins. You should consult with the French about all this and arrange to pack accordingly your containers to be dropped in March."

ACASP/5974, 28 January
At the end of January a letter from the Air Ministry to Bomber Command recorded the steps taken by the R.A.F. to increase the aircraft available for S.O.E. purposes. Large scale operations were to be undertaken to the Haute Savoie, without prejudice to the Bomber effort. Proposals to transfer 138 and 161 Squadrons to 38 Group were in abeyance, and the re-equipment of Bomber Squadrons with Lancasters was to be carried out in such a way as not to affect the crews experienced on S.D. work until as late a date as possible.

COS(44), 37th Meeting (c), Item 12, 7 February 1944
The Chiefs of Staff considered the correspondence between the Prime Minister and the Minister of Economic Warfare, and took note, with approval, of the arrangements proposed for February for delivering supplies to the Maquis.

Annex VIII to above ref.
The Secretary was instructed to submit a reply to the Prime Minister's Minute of 2nd February reporting that a plan for considerably increased deliveries during March was being worked out by the Air Staff and S.O.E.

CCS.492, 17 February 1944
A French suggestion that representatives of the American, British and French services should meet to discuss plans for assisting Resistance did not meet with the approval of the Combined Chiefs of Staff who considered it unnecessary since General Eisenhower had the machinery within his staff to handle the matter of procurement and distribution of

material and he was responsible for the co-ordination of the activities of these groups with his military forces.

The Defence Committee Consider Aircraft for Poland

DO(44), 4th Meeting, Item 2
Meanwhile the problem of increased supplies to the Polish resistance groups had once more been raised and was considered at a Defence Committee held on 3rd February. The Minister of Economic Warfare asked the Committee to give directions for an increase in the assistance to be given to the resistance movements in Poland, since at present only six aircraft had been allocated for this work. He urged the Committee to authorise the allocation of seventeen aircraft for Polish operations. The Chief of the Air Staff said he felt confident that an increase of supplies to Poland could be achieved were the pool of aircraft for S.O.E. operations in the Mediterranean not restricted as to the operations they were permitted to carry out, instead of being limited to Balkan operations.

The Foreign Secretary stated that the number of aircraft allotted for S.O.E. work over Yugoslavia, Greece and Poland seemed a very small allocation in view of the importance at this stage of the war of encouraging the patriot forces in those countries. The Chief of the Air Staff said that our supreme task in the air was to sustain the battle which was being waged by Bomber Command, and which might prove decisive if we did not allow ourselves to be drawn away by less essential calls on our resources. The Prime Minister said that he considered it a matter of high public importance that greater assistance should be given by the Air Staff to Resistance Movements in occupied Europe, even at some small expense of the other responsibilities of the R.A.F. Treble the present allocation of aircraft to Poland should be accorded. A diversion of 12 aircraft from the bomber effort over Germany was a small price to pay.

After discussing the question of the control of special operations in Poland and Czechoslovakia and deciding that it should remain, as at present, with S.O.E. London, subject to the direction of the Chiefs of Staff, the Committee invited the Air Ministry to submit proposals for tripling the load dropped in Poland during February, March and April without reducing the support given to the Resistance Movements in Yugoslavia, Greece and France.

F.1676/125
On February 8th, the Minister of Economic Warfare wrote to the Polish Prime Minister to confirm that it had been decided to increase three-fold the aircraft allocated to S.O.E. for Polish operations. The services of other aircraft in the general pool would be added to these whenever the opportunity arose.

F.1914/125
Further information on the increase of aircraft for Polish operations was given by the Minister of Economic Warfare to Polish G.H.Q. on February 24th. Six special Halifax aircraft were to be flown to Italy by Polish crews, bringing the first-line strength of the Polish Flight up to 12 aircraft. The balance of effort required to raise the figure of 18 was to be provided by Air Marshal Slessor, from his Halifax squadrons at Brindisi. The Air Ministry was also providing a reserve of two aircraft for the Polish Flight.

The Minister explained that the Deputy Air Commander-in-Chief in the Mediterranean was anxious that all resources at his disposal should be pooled, thus enabling him to devote the maximum effort, on any one night, to an area to which weather might permit operations. He had undertaken to support the effort to Poland with extra aircraft on nights when weather conditions were favourable for flights to Poland, and the Minister felt that Air Marshal Slessor's plan should be accepted. General Sosnkowski, replying to the Minister, agreed that the principle of pooling aircraft resources was reasonable.

J.C.S./334, 10 March
In March a telegram from H.Q. M.A.A.F. assured the Poles that whenever weather permitted all available aircraft would be put on to their targets up to the limit of capacity for reception at any one time.

M.A.A.F.'s Contribution

COS(44), 43rd Meeting(0), Item 7, COSMED. 27, 10 February 1944
At their meeting on 10th February 1944, the C.A.S. reminded the Chiefs of Staff that General Wilson had not yet been informed of recent decisions to increase the scale of air effort to be devoted to S.O.E. operations for sustaining resistance groups in Axis-occupied Europe. A telegram to General Wilson was therefore approved by the Chiefs of Staff reporting that the Defence Committee who were much impressed

with the results which might be expected from a larger scale of operations in the French Maquis and to Poland, had directed that operations to these two areas should be considerably extended.

In order to supplement the greatly increased scale of effort to be exerted from the U.K., M.A.A.F. were to carry out if possible a total of 60 successful sorties during the February moon period rising to 120 successful sorties during March. The load to be delivered to Poland was to be trebled, and the effort available for Yugoslavia, Greece and other areas was not to be diminished. With the exception of the Polish Flight in the Mediterranean all R.A.F. S.D. Squadrons in M.A.A.F. were to be regarded as a single pool for employment wherever suitable.

General Wilson was further informed that the Chiefs of Staff recognised that the numbers of S.D. aircraft available in M.A.A.F. must be increased if full success was to be achieved. An appeal had already been made to the U.S. Chiefs of Staff, and the C.A.S. was in contact with Air Marshal Slessor about the despatch of further aircraft and crews for S.D. Squadrons and for the Polish Flight. The telegram reported that the C.A.S. had also suggested to Air Marshal Slessor that the greatest possible use should be made of any other aircraft of M.A.A.F. which could be spared from urgent operations. In particular, he hoped that considerable help could be provided by transports and possibly by night bombers.

Supplies to the French Maquis

The delivery of supplies to the Maquis in the mountainous country of south-eastern France in the month of February was never considered very practical by the air authorities. Events confirmed the difficulty of the operation.

On 9th February 1944, the Minister of Economic Warfare reported to the Prime Minister that the results achieved during the first half of the February moon in increasing the volume of supplies to France had so far been extremely disappointing. The sole cause had been the fact that nearly every night clouds had lain over the Maquis area which rendered operations in mountainous country impossible. The great majority of sorties had therefore been directed to normal S.O.E. work in other parts of France, and although the Maquis had every priority it seemed unlikely that it would receive anything like the supplies projected during the February moon period. In the meantime the Germans and the Vichy authorities had organised a concentrated drive of 10,000 troops on the Maquis who had appealed to S.O.E. for help. The Minister suggested that the only other method of delivering stores might be by mass daylight operations: but he added that it was probably true to say that the time for an operation of this character had not yet come. The Minister's opinion on the feasibility of daylight operations was confirmed by the Air Ministry, when D. of I(R) reported that the Air Staff after careful consideration had decided not to approve the proposal since for various reasons it would involve a very high casualty rate of aircraft.

66/44D. of I(R), 12 February, to S.O.E.'s Air Adviser
The success to be anticipated would be of a very low order and certainly not sufficient to justify the high risks involved.

The Prime Minister's views on the Minister's report were contained in a letter by Major Morton to the Minister of Economic Warfare dated 14th February. The Prime Minister felt that the French should be urged to organise themselves better for the acceptance of sorties in the Maquis. He was afraid that M. d'Astier and his people were too complacent about this and were inclined to regard it as our fault if the sorties failed. If we were to help them, they must help themselves and make really strenuous efforts to mark dropping places with bonfires, or by other signals easily recognisable by the less skilled pilots. In general the Prime Minister felt that the French must show much greater zeal in trying to remedy their own considerable defects.

After a run of bad weather during the first half of the February moon period it was decided to mount a special operation ("Fumiste") in which the pilots, after a dead reckoning run of not longer than 30 miles from a definitely identified pinpoint dropped their load from a considerable height and through cloud. This operation was attempted on three nights and a total of 220 containers were dropped. An agent reported "Haute Savoie delighted parachute operation," but it was inevitable that a proportion of material dropped from so great a height should fall into the wrong hands. A Vichy broadcast claimed that a large quantity of stores parachuted into France had been seized by the Germans of the Vichy authorities.

M.123/4
On February 16th, the Prime Minister wrote to the Minister of Economic Warfare asking for a report on the alleged loss of stores: "What

proportion does this represent of the arms which were actually dropped? Were they dropped in the wrong place, or how is it that the right kind of Frenchman was not in the right place to receive them?"

F.1905/38

The Minister of Economic Warfare reported on February 17th that during the February moon 2,237 containers had been dropped in the whole of France of which 495 had been delivered to the Maquis area. Full reports had not yet been received from the field but it was known that 2% of the containers sent to the Independent French circuits and 4.5% of those delivered to the de Gaullist French had been lost. It was probable that the remaining 98% in the case of the Independent French had reached their proper destination. Acknowledgements of the remainder of the de Gaullist French were still far from complete. Even if the Vichy broadcast were entirely correct – and the quantity of arms and explosives cited did not correspond with the makeup of container loads – the estimated maximum number of containers involved would represent only 4.6% of the total delivered to France during February. In view of the large number of untrained crews employed and the unfavourable weather conditions, the Minister submitted that this wastage was rather less than might have been expected.

On February 23rd the Minister wrote to the Prime Minister outlining S.O.E.'s plans for the March moon period. A further air effort from Bomber Command and the 2nd American Liberator Squadron was expected to be more than sufficient to double the February effort to the Maquis. The weather was the principal limiting factor, however, and instructions had therefore been given that on nights when it was possible to fly to France, but not to the Maquis areas, aircraft were not to be allowed to stand idle but were to be used for S.O.E. operations required to fulfil S.H.A.E.F. Directives. Arrears in the Maquis programme were to be reduced as far as possible by using all the available aircraft, including those set aside for normal S.O.E. operations, on any night when the weather was favourable in the Maquis area; and by still greater air efforts from 38 Group and Bomber Command.

F.1965/38, Annex I to COS(44)212(0), 3 March 1944

By the end of February sufficient reports had been received from the field to give a fairly clear picture of the results achieved during the

February moon period. On February 28th, the Minister reported to the Prime Minister that out of the target figures of 126 sorties from England, 102 had actually been flown, and form North Africa 28 out of 60. The total number of successful sorties were 47; 37 from England and 10 flown from North Africa. The causes of the comparative failure were bad weather, insufficiently expert aircrews and Reception Committees, and lack of time in which to perfect arrangements. The Minister stressed the difficulty of rapid extensions and improvisation in clandestine warfare, and pointed out that S.O.E. work needed much preparation and training.

Annex II to COS(44)212(0), 3 March 1944
The C.A.S. also submitted a report to the Prime Minister in which he admitted that the results achieved in Poland and to the Maquis had been very disappointing, owing primarily to the weather though a contributory cause in the Maquis area had been the inadequacy of some of the reception arrangements.

At the beginning of March it was suggested that the Committee set up under the Chairmanship of the Minister of Economic Warfare to consider the arming of French Resistance should include a representative from S.H.A.E.F. The Prime Minister agreed to this suggestion while making it clear that he did not wish the plans for the March moon period to be altered. Difficulties between the French and the Americans, however, led to instructions to General Eisenhower from the President that he was to have nothing whatever to do with the French, and in these circumstances General Eisenhower gave orders that no member of his Staff, British or American, was to attend any meeting at which Frenchmen were present. The proposed inclusion of a S.H.A.E.F. representative therefore fell through and it was left to the S.O.E. representatives, an American and a British officer, to keep S.H.A.E.F. fully informed.

On March 21st, Major Morton wrote to the Vice Chief of S.O.E. to explain the Prime Minister's wishes with regard to the respective claims of the Maquis and of the Overlord plans to deliveries in the March moon. Major Morton reported that whereas the Prime Minister wished no alteration to be made in the plans for the March moon as submitted by Lord Selborne to him, he agreed that General Eisenhower's wishes in respect of Overlord should be given prior consideration in regard to any plans for the April or other future moons.

F.1359/38

The report on the March moon operations submitted by the Minister to the Prime Minister on 27th March, showed a very great increase in the number of successful sorties compared with the February moon. 358 sorties had actually been flown from the U.K. although the target figure was only 261 and of these 192 were successful. From North Africa 83 sorties had been flown out of a target of 120 and 23 had been successful. A sufficient quantity of stores had been delivered to the Maquis to provide arms for 18,000 men. As a result of the greatly increased number of sorties a certain quantity of material had inevitably fallen into enemy hands: as far as was then known this proportion was in the region of 6%, and it was not expected that subsequent reports would greatly increase this figure.

In view of the comparatively satisfactory results of the March moon and of the substantial quantities of equipment delivered to the Maquis areas, S.O.E. agreed with S.H.A.E.F. that priority of effort for the April moon should be directed into northern France to complete the deliveries required for the D-Day railway and road plans, and for arming Resistance for guerilla warfare. On March 23rd, the Minister reported this change in priority to the Prime Minister for his approval and also asked for instructions that the deliveries to be effected during the April and subsequent moons were to be made in accordance with the instructions of the Supreme Allied Commander. The Prime Minister agreed to this.

During the April moon period the supplementary effort allotted for air operations was reduced, and the weather was less favourable than in March; 3,325 containers were delivered to France, as against 3,895 in the March moon period. In accordance with directions from the Supreme Commander the first priority was given to the north of France and the remainder of France including the Maquis was accorded second priority.

ADE/29, 29 April

It was estimated by S.O.E. that the deliveries during the March moon period would provide arms for twenty-three thousand men, and taking into account February and April as well it could be said that arms had been provided for approximately 65,000 men.

On 18th April, Major Morton wrote to the Vice Chief of S.O.E. that the Prime Minister was not satisfied with the proportion of failures, apparently due to no reception in the field. In view of the urgency with which M. Emanuel d'Astier pressed him to increase British efforts to arm the Resistance Movement in France, the Prime Minister did not feel that the French had done their fair share in making the resultant British effort a success. It was wrong to risk the lives of British air crews on hazardous operations doomed to failure from the outset through lack of efficiency in reception arrangements at the other end.

F.1525/38, 25 April
In forwarding S.O.E.'s report on the April moon to the Prime Minister, the Minister stated that neither the R.A.F. nor S.O.E. considered the proportion of unsuccessful sorties to be unduly high. Out of the total sorties attempted in January 56% had been unsuccessful and in February 60%. This figure had been reduced in the last two months: in March 53% and in April 47% of the sorties had failed. Apart from the ordinary difficulties of enemy opposition, engine trouble and navigation, which accounted for a small proportion of the failures, the main reasons of failure of S.O.E. operations were always weather and "No Reception." The Minister pointed out that the evidence of non-reception was based largely on Pilot's reports and in many cases no evidence confirmatory or otherwise was received from the field. Since the pilots could be interrogated and the committee could not, the percentage of failures due to the absence of reception committees was probably less than appeared and accounted for to some extent by faulty navigation. The percentage of failures was in fact pretty constant and much the same as in the northern countries of Europe.

Operations to France in May were to some extent handicapped by the necessity, for deception reasons, of directing a large proportion of the operations into northern France, which had first priority, into the area north of the Seine, including Holland and Belgium. This meant that aircraft had to operate over the most heavily defended area in France. The supplementary effort from U.K. was reduced although the long expected increase in aircraft began to materialise in North Africa. In spite of the difficulties, operations in the May moon period were the most successful so far carried out, and a total of over six thousand containers were delivered to France and three hundred and sixty four to Belgium. The proportion of heavier arms delivered was higher than in the past and P.I.A.T.S., Bazookas and Brens were to some extent substituted for Sten guns. The deliveries to the whole of France would, it was estimated, arm 37,500 men and this added to the February, March and April deliveries would result in 102,500 men being armed.

The Prime Minister received Lord Selborne's Minute concurrently with a Minute from the C.A.S. reporting air operations in support of S.O.E. and S.I.S. during the moon period, and minuted on the latter: "Good. Press on."

Difficulty of Expanding Reception Committee Machinery to Meet Increased Aircraft Resources

The sudden and enormous increase during the early months of 1944 of the number of aircraft available for S.O.E. operations raised an acute problem in Western Europe, where, apart from a few areas such as the south-east of France, the countries were still rigidly policed and controlled by the enemy.

The Resistance organisation was necessarily less flexible and less capable of sudden expansion than in the Balkans, where partisan control of large regions made the receipt of bulk supplies and the arming of large numbers of men an altogether easier task. For well over a year many S.O.E. groups in France, Belgium, Holland and Scandinavia had been begging and bullying, cajoling and cursing for increased supplies: the shortage of aircraft in 1943 had inevitably discouraged some groups who now found themselves, with very little warning, called upon to receive vastly increased quantities of stores. Reception Committee machinery had to be expanded at a moment's notice in order to provide the R.A.F. with a reasonable choice of operations through a moon period, spread over as wide an area as possible. All organisers were asked to lay on as many operations as they could take; and by repeating deliveries to the same ground and mounting multiple operations (especially in the Maquis) enough work was provided to keep the R.A.F. busy on those nights during the February moon period when the weather permitted operations.

In March, with the further increase of aircraft and good weather throughout the moon period, S.O.E.'s operational programme proved to be too small to allow the U.K. based aircraft a reasonable choice of grounds and even, on one or two nights, did not provide enough operations for the aircraft available. The organisers had again been asked to send in their maximum programmes, but a certain time lag was inevitable before the extent of the increase was realised: particularly in view of their long months of disappointment. This was the only month when S.O.E. were unable to make full use of the aircraft at their disposal. By April the field had realised how much greater were the facilities for supplying them and the operational programmes in the May and June moons proved larger than the aircraft could complete.

American Contribution to French Resistance

AGWAR to ETOUSA, W 24345, 17 April 1944
The great bulk of the increased supplies delivered to France in the early months of 1944 had been carried by aircraft of the R.A.F. For political reasons the State Department, Washington, became interested in destroying an impression that the British were doing all that was being done in the field, but General Eisenhower, replying to the American Chiefs of Staff, pointed out that in the past the effort had been preponderantly British since no American aircraft had been made available for the delivery of supplies until January. The permanent allotment of aircraft for S.D. work in the U.K. was 32 American and 22 British, but a very large supplementary British air lift had now been made available.

S/51066; S/51396, 6 May 1944
In answer to a request from the Combined Chiefs of Staff for detailed facts and figures, S.H.A.E.F. sent a report showing that in the months of February, March and April, American planes, flying 209 sorties had delivered 190 tons; British aircraft flying 1,292 sorties had delivered 1,113⅜ tons.

COS/429/4, 29 May 1944
The French apparently continued to believe that the increase in the delivery of stores was mainly due to the British; and the United States Chiefs of Staff submitted a memorandum to the Combined Chiefs of Staff recommending that the French Committee of National Liberation should be informed that the supply of Resistance Groups was a matter of combined United States/British responsibility.

Chapter 3

Climax In Europe

June 1944 to May 1945

The tide which had turned for the British Armies at El Alamein was now about to flood into Western Europe and the invading regular Armies of the Allies were to receive substantial assistance from the Resistance forces now reaching their climax of guerilla activity. The patriots of France, the Low Countries and Scandinavia organised, trained and armed, were ready to rise against the hated oppressor and revenge themselves for four years of slavery. For this moment they had waited long and anxiously, sometimes in doubt and disappointment, and now that their call to action had been sounded their response was immediate and overwhelming. Throughout Western Europe the patriots sprang to arms during the summer of 1944: in Eastern Europe the climax was to come a few months later with even greater intensity.

Overlord

So great a weight of supplies had been delivered to Western Europe during the first months of 1944 that on the eve of the invasion French Resistance movements everywhere found themselves sufficiently well equipped to fulfil, even beyond S.O.E.'s expectations, the role which they had been allotted. The D-Day plans were implemented on the receipt of the B.B.C. messages; railways and roads were attacked and the enemy found his lines of communication continually cut, while isolated German units were harassed by guerilla bands. The action of the Resistance Groups south of the Loire resulted, according to

S.H.A.E.F. in an average delay of 48 hours in the movement of enemy reinforcements to the bridgehead area, and in some cases this period was much longer.

"The Value of SOE Operations in the Supreme Commander's Sphere", 13 July 1944
From the mountainous areas the men of the Maquis were able to take the offensive and in southern and central France the enemy found himself faced with a battlefield behind his own lines.

M.733/4, Annex I to COS(44)556(0), 22 June 1944
On 20th June 1944, the Prime Minister sent a minute to the Minister of Economic Warfare:

> "The Maquis has started open guerilla warfare and is in temporary control of certain areas of southern France. The Germans are reacting strongly with fully armed troops. Every effort must be made to supply the Maquis at once with rifles, Bren guns, Piat guns, mortars and Bazookas with ammunition, and whatever else is needful to prevent the collapse of the Movement and to extend it. What is being done about this? Have you any difficulty in getting men to repack containers with the right sort of weapons? Could General Wilson help from North Africa? Pray tell me if I can help you to accelerate action."

Annex II to COS(44)556(0), 22 June 1944
The Minister replied on the same day pointing out that with proper support it would be possible for the guerilla fighting to be so developed as to become a most important factor in deciding the Battle of France. He envisaged an increased supply of stores by mass daylight operations by the 8th U.S.A.A.F. and possibly employment of bodies of regular troops to stiffen resistance and enable it to take over control of large areas; he also suggested that at a later stage a mass up-rising in France might be called for.

COS(44), 208th Meeting, Item 7, 24 June 1944
This exchange of correspondence was considered by the Chiefs of Staff two days later when the C.I.G.S. said that in so far as the Resistance

movements in the centre and south of France were concerned, Generals Eisenhower and Wilson were in close touch and were co-ordinating their plans.

The Minister also reported the integration of S.O.E.'s Anglo-American staff with French Officers provided by General Koenig. He advised the Prime Minister that S.O.E.'s requirements were for continuous sorties on a big scale to maintain the forces in the field, for certain types of heavier arms and for parachutes. In a separate minute of the same date he reported the successes achieved by Resistance action, and added that chaotic conditions had been created in large parts of France, generally hampering the German military machine. In limited areas, Resistance was in complete control. The continuation of aggressive offensive action depended largely on supplies by air and measures were being taken to increase these. S.H.A.E.F. were well satisfied with the results [that had] so far been achieved.

S.O.E., O.S.S., E.M.F.F.I.

As early as 1942 it was agreed between S.O.E. and O.S.S. (S.O.) (their American counterpart) that the field force should be treated as a single Fifth Column organisation to assist an invasion force, whether British or American. Co-ordination was to be effected in London.

COS(W)810, 15 September 1943
JSM.1174, 31 August 1943
This principle was the main condition made by the British Chiefs of Staff in September 1943 when giving the formal consent requested by the United States Chiefs of Staff for the operations of O.S.S. (S.O.) in North Western Europe, which at that date was a British Theatre. American Liaison Officers were attached to S.O.E. in the summer of 1943 and an integrated Anglo-American Staff was established to cover the countries within the sphere of S.H.A.E.F.

Immediately after D-Day, the Resistance forces in France were placed under the command of General Koenig and an Anglo-American-French staff known as E.M.F.F.I., which separated from the main S.O.E. organisation and worked operationally directly under S.H.A.E.F. The difficulty of this arrangement, as far as air transport was concerned, was set out in a letter of October from S.O.E.'s Air Adviser to D. of I(R).

AIR/506/725, 17 October 1944

S.H.A.E.F.'s instructions that General Koenig, with a tripartite staff, mainly French, should plan all operations behind the enemy lines in France meant that S.O.E. had virtually no control over these operations and had become in effect merely agents to carry out General Koenig's plans. The Air Adviser had explained this to V.C.A.S. at the beginning of August and V.C.A.S. had accepted the position. All S.O.E. operations to France had therefore been conducted in accordance with General Koenig's plans which were, of course, approved by S.H.A.E.F.

Air Lift in the Mediterranean for S.D. Operations: Organisation of SO(M), Liaison with Russians

The liberation of the heel of Italy enabled the R.A.F. to establish bases on the mainland of Europe. The S.D. Squadrons, moved from North Africa into southern Italy in January, were now based considerably nearer their target areas and deliveries were consequently facilitated.

JSM.1506
CCS.387/3, Appendix B
On 11th February the United States Chiefs of Staff asked for details to be obtained from the Allied C-in-C. Mediterranean as to the steps taken to implement the directive regarding the supply of arms and equipment to Resistance groups in the Balkans.

COS(44)163
A Memorandum by S.O.E. dated 14th February 1944 described the organisation of Special Operations in the Mediterranean. In the early autumn of 1943, Force 133 (i.e. S.O.E. Middle East) was centred at Cairo under the control of C-in-C. Middle East, and entrusted with all operations to the Balkans. An advanced base of Force 133 was set up in the Bari area.

In January 1944, when the command of the Eastern and Western Mediterranean was unified under A.F.H.Q., it was agreed that it would be necessary to have a corresponding central H.Q. to co-ordinate all special operations in the Mediterranean Theatre. It was then decided to establish H.Q. Special Operations (Mediterranean), known as S.O.M. which after an interim period came into existence officially on 12th April 1944, responsible for the co-ordination and technical efficiency of all

S.O.E. units in the Theatre; the co-ordination of S.O.E. and O.S.S.(S.O.) activities and the co-ordination of S.D. operations for all special agencies, S.O.E., S.I.S., O.S.S., M.I.9. and P.W.B. The S.O.E. Units working into different countries under the operational control of various military commanders were as follows:

	Unit	Military Command	Target Area
1.	I.S.S.U.6	7th Army (Force 163)	S. France
2.	Special Force	15th Army Group	Italy
3.	Adv. Force 133	SOM (till June 1944)	Yugoslavia
	(later Force 266	BAF (from June 1944)	Albania
	and Force 399)		Hungary
4.	Force 133	G.H.Q. Middle East	Greece
			Rumania
			Bulgaria
5.	Force 139	C.O.S. London	Poland
		(thro' SOE London)	Czechoslovakia
6.	Mil.Est.43	A.F.H.Q.	Austria

H.Q. S.O.M. was established near Bari, having liaison staffs with A.F.H.Q. (first at Algiers and then from July 1944 at Caserta) and M.A.A.F.

COS(44)163(0)
S.O.E.'s Memorandum also set out the position with regard to S.D. air operations. The high priority accorded to operations in support of the Maquis in southern France had necessitated the transfer of aircraft from Brindisi to Algiers. Demands for operations to Northern Italy had also to be met and the consequent loss to Balkan operations was made good by the movement to Brindisi for work into the Balkans of two Squadrons of D.C.3s. In February the S.D. aircraft consisted of a Squadron at Algiers working into southern France (624), three Squadrons in the Brindisi area working into northern Italy and the Balkans (148), and two Squadrons of D.C.3s. A packing station and air supply base had been set up near Brindisi airfield. In addition to these a certain number of Italian aircraft of the Italian Air Force were operating from southern Italy primarily to maintain Italian forces co-operating with the Balkan partisans.

COS(W)1149

The British Chiefs of Staff informed the Americans of the position in a telegram of 15th February.

MEDCOS.44

During the next months the problem of liaison with the Soviet authorities concerning action in the Balkans became increasingly important. On 26th February General Wilson reported that he was concerned with the lack of any operational liaison between his command and the Russian Service Authorities.

MEDCOS.93

In this telegram the C-in-C referred only to liaison on normal military operations such as air bombing, but in a later telegram dated 14th April, he again raised the question of the establishment of some form of liaison between his Headquarters and the Russians and added that some co-operation on the subject of air supply to Tito's Partisans was now becoming necessary since Russian aircraft were understood to be already operating into Tito's country from the East.

COS(W)1288

A telegram from the Air Ministry to the Joint Staff Mission, Washington, repeated to General Wilson, reported that the Air Ministry did not see much hope of successful co-ordination of bombing operations in the Balkans between the Russian Air Force and M.A.A.F., and were also doubtful about the wisdom of attempting to co-ordinate air supply to Tito. It was considered that the co-ordination of supplies to the Partisans would be much better done in Yugoslavia and in Italy.

COS(44)342(0), 15 April 1944

A Chiefs of Staff paper of 15th April set out a report recently submitted by A.F.H.Q. to the Combined Chiefs of Staff describing the organisation of control of Special Operations in the Mediterranean Theatre.

The increase of aircraft establishments for Special Operations had recently been authorised and the strength of 624 and 148 Squadrons and of the Polish Flight was to be increased. C.47 aircraft were temporarily undertaking S.D. operations under 334 Wing when their normal work permitted, and an American contribution was being made by 68 American Reconnaissance Group. The Italian Bomber Transport Force of approximately 40 aircraft was also engaged on S.D. operations.

S.D. Operations to Poland

C.5451/451G
An increase in the number of S.D. operations to Poland had been effected in the months of March and April. On 23rd April the Polish Prime Minister saw Mr. Churchill and expressed his warm gratitude for the notable increase which had taken place in supply droppings during recent weeks. Mr. Churchill said that he was very glad to hear this and he wished the proper British authorities to be instructed to make every effort to see that supplies to Poland were kept at the highest possible level during the next weeks.

As the Russian Armies approached Poland, it became evident that the time was approaching when action by the Polish Secret Army would be most likely materially to assist the operations on the Eastern front and Allied operations in general. Moreover if the Secret Army did not act soon it was likely to be overrun by the Russian advance without ever having acted at all.

JIC(44)204(0), Final
In May the Joint Intelligence Sub-Committee, in consultation with S.O.E., reported how the activities of the Polish Underground Movement could be related to allied strategy and forthcoming operations.

COS(44), 165th Meeting, Item 8, 20 May 1944
This report was considered by the Chiefs of Staff Committee who agreed that the timing of the rising in Poland must be left to the Polish Commander on the spot. The C.A.S. pointed out that the possibility of increasing supplies to Poland would depend largely on the time of year at which the rising took place. It was in any case doubtful if the supplies which could be introduced by air would be sufficient to make any material difference in the event of a general rising.

The Committee therefore agreed that the responsibility and the timing for a general rising in Poland must be left to the Polish authorities and the Polish Commanders on the spot respectively, that planning should continue on the basis that the scale of assistance to Poland would not be greater than it was at present, and that we should concentrate on urging the Poles to intensify partisan sabotage and diversionary operations. S.O.E. should meanwhile continue their efforts to arrange for better co-ordination between the Russians and the Polish Underground Movement.

COS, Special Meeting 241

On 12th June, General Tabor of the Polish Secret Army had the opportunity of speaking to the Combined Chiefs of Staff on the subject of assistance to the Polish Underground Army, but no decisions were taken.

In the next few weeks the Polish Government made further efforts to increase the flow of supplies to Poland. It was suggested that air operations should once more be undertaken from the U.K. or, if this were impracticable, Liberator aircraft might be substituted for Halifaxes and the proposed Stirlings for operations from Italian bases.

CCS.612/2, 1 August 1944

The Combined Chiefs of Staff, however, agreed that the decision of types of aircraft to be used must be made by the Air Ministry in conjunction with the Polish authorities concerned.

At the end of July the aircraft available for flights to Poland consisted of 1586 Flight (14 aircraft: 11 Halifaxes, 3 Liberators) and aircraft from 334 Wing which could be used for Polish operations if they were not operating to other countries. During the four months from April to July over 150 successful sorties had been flown and 231 tons had been delivered to the country. All but a few tons of this material had been delivered to the Governor Generalship of Warsaw.

The Warsaw Rising

4155

On 1st August the Polish Commander in the field, encouraged by the Soviet broadcasts, ordered a general rising of the Secret Army. On 3rd August, the Chiefs of Staff informed A.F.H.Q. and M.A.A.F. that telegrams had been received by the Polish Government in London from the Commander of the Polish Secret Army, reporting the outbreak of hostilities in Warsaw and urgently requesting stores. An immediate

Russian attack from outside the city was also called for. A.F.H.Q. were instructed to communicate this information to the Soviet Military authorities and to inform them that the request for supplies had been passed to our authorities in Italy for immediate action.

4154

Another telegram from the Chiefs of Staff reported that the Polish Government had made a most earnest appeal to the Prime Minister for supplies to be delivered to Warsaw if possible that very night and added that His Majesty's Government attached the greatest importance to complying with this appeal if operational factors permitted.

The weather fought against the Poles, however, and it proved impossible to make any deliveries in the next two nights.

F.79096

On 4th August General Wilson and Air Marshal Slessor reported to the Chiefs of Staff that the delivering of supplies to Warsaw seemed to them to be an impractical proposition, even if weather permitted – which seemed unlikely. The losses in aircraft would probably be considerable and this would in turn reduce activities in other areas which were equally important. If deliveries were made by daylight, the height from which they would have to be dropped made it almost certain that a very large proportion of the supplies would fall into German hands. They were therefore forced to the conclusion that this was just not an operation of war. Pressure should be exerted on the Russians, who were in a much better position to know exactly what was going on in Warsaw.

COS(44), 261st Meeting, Item 8, 5 August 1944

The Chiefs of Staff agreed with the view put forward by General Wilson and Air Marshal Slessor and it was therefore suggested to the Soviet authorities that they should examine the possibilities of dropping supplies to the Polish Secret Army. An appeal was also made by the Polish Government to the American Air Force to carry out a daylight drop.

COS(44)704(0), 7 August 1944

The Polish authorities then asked that at least the Polish Flight in the Mediterranean might be allowed to carry out operations to Poland.

COS(44), 262nd Meeting, Item 4
The position was considered at a Chiefs of Staff Committee Meeting on 7th August. The C.A.S. said that from the many approaches made by the Poles in the course of the last few days it appeared that they were trying to pass on to us the responsibility for failure of the operations of the Polish Secret Army which might result from this force having undertaken open warfare prematurely.

Operations to Poland had been attempted from the Mediterranean on the night of August 4/5 and had resulted in the loss of 5 out of 13 aircraft despatched. These aircraft had been despatched to selected areas in open country which were likely to be undefended. If they had been sent to Warsaw the losses would almost certainly have been greater. He agreed with General Wilson and Air Marshal Slessor that the delivery of supplies to Warsaw by aircraft of M.A.A.F. was not a practicable operation.

T.1571/4
The Committee also took note of a telegram from Marshal Stalin to the Prime Minister suggesting that the information communicated to the latter by the Poles was greatly exaggerated.

COS(44), 263rd Meeting, Item 4, 9 August 1944
At a Meeting the next day the Chiefs of Staff considered the Polish request to allow the Polish Flight to carry out supply dropping operations to Warsaw. The C.A.S. reported that, in anticipation of the approval of the Committee, he had already obtained the concurrence of the Secretary of State for Air in the despatch of a telegram to Air Marshal Slessor instructing him to permit the Polish Flight to carry out these operations.

COS(44)711(0), 8 August 1944
A letter from General Sosnowski to the C.I.G.S. recapitulated the development of the situation from the initial rising in Warsaw. Operations of the Russian Army on the Warsaw sector had virtually ceased, while on the other hand the Germans had brought heavy armour into action against the insurgents within the city: "The people are either being massacred or used as mass shields for German tanks trying to break into Polish barracks."

In spite of this, the G.O.C. in Warsaw has stated that he could hold the major part of the city if he received immediate assistance in supplies and air cover.

The first supply dropping operations to Warsaw had been flown on 4th August. On the 8th, 9th, 12th and 13th, operations were again carried out, but the Germans had by then moved in very strong anti-aircraft defences and the aircraft losses were very heavy.

4347

On 11th August, the Chiefs of Staff informed the Joint Staff Mission in Washington that the seriousness of the situation in Warsaw was fully realised. The responsibility for helping the Poles in Warsaw must rest primarily with the Russians and Marshal Stalin had accepted this responsibility. The short nights and the full moon had prevented large scale dropping operations but Air Marshal Slessor was now hoping to start operations immediately on a large scale with British crews.

By 12th August reports from Warsaw indicated that the Poles were losing ground and stated that without immediate support the fight would collapse in a few days.

4375

A telegram from the Chiefs of Staff to General Wilson and Air Marshal Slessor reported that Marshal Stalin had agreed to send help, but there was no indication as to the form this would take or its extent.

COS(44), 273rd Meeting, Item 7, 12 August 1944
At a Chiefs of Staff Meeting on 12th August, Sir Douglas Evill said that the C.A.S. had received a further letter from General Sosnowski and that he, the V.C.A.S. had answered it, explaining that even before the Chiefs of Staff Meeting a personal telegram had been sent to Air Marshal Slessor from the C.A.S. emphasising the importance of delivering supplies to Warsaw and expressing the hope that he would be able from henceforth to make a substantial British contribution. It was also agreed at the Meeting that an approach should be made to the United States Chiefs of Staff for American assistance.

JSM/199, 15 August 1944
A telegram from Washington confirmed that General Eaker still held his former opinion that it was definitely an impracticable operation to

deliver stores by daylight to Warsaw area. The United States Chiefs of Staff had therefore asked General Eisenhower if the Air Forces under his command could give any assistance to the Poles.

COS(44), 277th Meeting, Item 10
At a Chiefs of Staff Meeting on 16th August the C.A.S. reported that, on the night of the 14/15th August, out of 26 aircraft despatched to Warsaw 8 were missing. As a result of this Air Marshal Slessor intended to direct further operations to the areas immediately outside the city. General Spaatz had hoped to carry out a supply dropping operation with American heavy bombers the previous day, but had been unable to clear the matter with the Russians. The operation would be launched as soon as the necessary arrangements could be made. The Committee were informed that the British Ambassador in Moscow had reported that he had discussed this question with the Russians whose attitude to affording assistance to the Poles fighting in Warsaw had been unhelpful.

Annex to COS(44)755(0), 21 August 1944
A telegram from Air Marshal Slessor to the C.A.S. five days later reported that the Russians were still being unhelpful. It was difficult to resist the conviction that the Russian failure to supply Warsaw was a deliberate policy. Air Marshal Slessor added that the assistance being given by M.A.A.F. to the Russian activities in Yugoslavia might be used as a bargaining counter for obtaining Russian help for Warsaw.

COS(44), 285th Meeting, Item 2
The Foreign Office agreed to this suggestion, but at a Chiefs of Staff Committee Meeting two days later the V.C.A.S. pointed out that the aircraft concerned on the Russian-Yugoslav operations actually belonged to Russia and that the Russians intended to employ them on a shuttle service between Russian or Russian-occupied territory and Italy, carrying out dropping operations to Yugoslavia en route.

A letter to the Foreign Office was therefore approved by the Chiefs of Staff stating that everything practicable had already been done to persuade the Russians to take measures for the assistance of the Poles in Warsaw; it would be quite impracticable to suggest that their shuttle service to Italy for the supply of Yugoslavia should be made contingent in any way upon their so doing.

COSMED.174

On 23rd August a Polish appreciation of the situation was forwarded to A.F.H.Q. and Washington. The Polish authorities requested that the Polish crews should be allowed, regardless of losses sustained, to fly to Warsaw and Poland and to be used exclusively on operations to Poland, and that the British crews and aircraft of 148 Squadron should continue their assistance by carrying out operations to southern Poland. These night operations to relieve Warsaw should be attempted independently from American daylight operations from the U.K.

COS(44), 297th Meeting, Item 3

The problem of daylight deliveries hinged on the Russian willingness to permit the use of their bases for shuttle operations. At a Chiefs of Staff Meeting on 4th September, the C.A.S., discussing the possibility of a large scale operation to Warsaw by Bomber Command, stated that in view of the distance involved, the heavy losses which would probably be incurred, and the small proportion of the supplies dropped likely to fall into the right hands, the Polish authorities should be informed that the project was not practicable. As the Russians had refused to allow American aircraft to land on airfields in Russia the only practicable method of delivering supplies to Warsaw was by operations from the Mediterranean. The A.O.C. in that theatre had been instructed to consider how the scale of air assistance to Warsaw could be increased.

5157

On 10th September, a telegram to General Eisenhower from the Combined Chiefs of Staff informed him that the British Ambassador to Moscow reported that the Soviet Government were now prepared to co-operate with the British and Americans in organising assistance to Warsaw.

Agreement with the Russians for the attempt of a daylight shuttle operation and for their own despatch of supplies had at last been reached, and on 10th September, and after several abortive attempts, the Americans staged a mass daylight flight to Warsaw of 110 Fortresses escorted by fighters. Of the three dropping areas, two were missed completely and the central area of Warsaw alone received 380 containers. The material result of the operation was therefore inconsiderable however great was its moral encouragement. One bomber and one fighter were lost.

A certain quantity of stores was delivered by Russian aircraft, but the Russian support was on too small a scale and offered at too late a date to affect the final issue. A further American operation was laid on, but owing to bad weather it was never carried out. The food situation within the city was now desperate, and although the small Russian deliveries included food as well as ammunition the supplies were dropped without parachutes and were of poor quality. On October 2nd, Warsaw finally capitulated and the long drawn out tragedy came to an end. During the whole of the siege only 1,719 containers and 254 packages had been received within the city.

Emphasis on Yugoslavia: B.A.F

After the refusal of Mihailovic to accept the directive issued to him by H.M.G. in the summer of 1943, increasing support had been given in supply dropping operations to Marshal Tito and his Partisans at the expense of the Chetniks. The establishment of air bases in the heel of Italy in January 1944 greatly facilitated S.D. operations to Yugoslavia and it was, moreover, possible to infiltrate considerable quantities of stores by sea.

The conflict between Partisans and Chetniks continued, however, and it became increasingly obvious that the value of the forces commanded by General Mihailovic to the cause of the United Nations was practically nil since, as he himself admitted, he regarded not the Germans but Tito as his real enemy. Marshal Tito's Partisans, on the other hand, were carrying out constant attacks on communications and upon enemy units, and guerilla activity in the Balkans was containing a number of German divisions.

In May 1944, the Secretary of State for Foreign Affairs suggested that the best possibility of resolving the conflict within Yugoslavia would be to increase the size of the Partisan groups in Serbia owing allegiance to Tito, by making it plain that they could fight as separate units within his forces: if this were done, then the King might appeal to the Serbs to join up with Tito on these conditions.

COS(44)412(0), 11 May 1944
The military issues of this suggestion, were, on the Prime Minister's instructions, referred to the Chiefs of Staff, who instructed the Joint Planning Staff to prepare a paper on the subject.

JP(44)133 (Final), 24 May 1944
The Joint Planning Staff considered that the limiting factor in the implementation of the plan was the means of transporting supplies. There were considerable strategical advantages in increasing the size and power of Partisan Resistance Groups in Serbia, but it would be impossible to deliver sufficient supplies to enable the Foreign Secretary's proposal to be implemented at present. No increase in transport facilities was likely to be possible until further transport aircraft could be allotted or until the reduction of the German garrison in Yugoslavia permitted an extension of air and sea operations. The Chiefs of Staff agreed with these conclusions.

COS(44), 174th Meeting, Item 13, 27 May 1944
The increasingly military character of Partisan operations in Yugoslavia, and the consequent quantity of stores which they required, meant that support of the guerillas was by now less of a "Special Operation" than a military commitment. In May 1944, General Wilson submitted to the British and United States Chiefs of Staff a suggestion for the introduction of a measure of unified control of Trans-Adriatic operations at a lower level then A.F.H.Q.

MEDCOS.121, 20 May 1944
This involved the formation of a co-ordinating authority which, in this case, General Wilson considered should be the Airmen.

JP(44)144(?), Final.
This proposal was considered by the Joint Planning Staff and by the Chiefs of Staff, who agreed and issued the Directive to the Commander, Balkan Air Force, in June.

COS(44)552(0), 21 June 1944
The Commander was informed that he would be responsible for ensuring the co-ordination both on the planning and of the conduct of combined amphibious operations and raids on the islands and shores of the Adriatic and Ionian Seas. The system of joint command would be followed in Trans-Adriatic operations: directives and special instructions would be issued to the Commander as appropriate by the Supreme Allied Commander, defining the policy to be followed in the conduct of regular and special operations in the area of joint

responsibility. B.A.F. were to exercise operational control of Special Operations in Hungary, Yugoslavia and Albania. Liaison with Marshal Tito was effected through a British Mission led by Brigadier Maclean whose rear headquarters would be located at B.A.F. H.Q.

For air operations the Commander, B.A.F., was to be responsible under the air C-in-C. Mediterranean. While B.A.F. were not responsible for the control of Special Operations in Italy, Bulgaria, Rumania, Greece, Czechoslovakia or Poland, it was to be responsible for the operation of Special Duty aircraft employed in these areas through the various S.O.E. H.Q.'s concerned. The allocation of the available air lift to various territories would continue to be laid down by A.F.H.Q. and the Commander, B.A.F. was to act as Chairman of a Special Operations Committee which would ensure day-to-day co-ordination of the air aspect of Special Air Operations over the various territories and advise A.F.H.Q. on the allocation of effort.

This arrangement, by which the Commander was wholly responsible for certain areas and in addition responsible for providing air effort to areas outside his theatre, was not entirely consistent. Apart from operations into Yugoslavia, Albania and Hungary, B.A.F. acted more as a transport agency making deliveries to meet the requirements of SO(M) on behalf of A.F.H.Q.

JP(44)291 (Final), 24 November 1944
In November 1944, the Joint Planning Staff, after examining a telegram from General Wilson asking for guidance on the policy regarding supplies to Yugoslav Partisans concluded that the present policy of equipping 300,000 Partisans with guerilla-type equipment only should be continued. Further heavy equipment should not be provided.

Mediterranean Air Lift – Autumn 1944

By now, rather later than in Western Europe, Resistance activities in Eastern Europe were reaching their climax. During the summer of 1944 the demands on S.D. aircraft for supply operations into Poland, Yugoslavia and Italy continued to increase. On 6th October, S.O.E. submitted a paper to the Chiefs of Staff on "Special Operations Mediterranean Theatre: Air Lift Requirements." It was pointed out that since the allocation early in 1944 of additional Special Duty aircraft for operations from the Mediterranean Theatre the military situation had changed completely.

Whereas at that time the Balkan countries had been the primary target, the progress of the war during the past four months had given considerable impetus to the growth of resistance in more distant areas such as Poland, Czechoslovakia, Northern Italy, Austria and Hungary. The resulting air lift requirements were becoming greater than could be met by the heavy aircraft at present available. Two of the countries concerned, Poland and Czechoslovakia, were outside SACMED's theatre, but support to them must be provided from the Mediterranean. Apart from the battle for Warsaw, active resistance to the enemy was being carried out by the Polish Secret Army in those areas still under German domination, and supplies were urgently needed. The Foreign Office were keenly interested for political reasons in the maintenance of supplies to Poland and the War Cabinet had recently agreed that S.O.E. observers (British personnel) should be sent to join the movement behind the enemy lines. In Slovakia revolts had broken out, and although S.O.E. were not at present delivering supplies to the insurgents, the Foreign Office had agreed that an S.O.E. party should be sent to that province. This would involve a minor supply commitment. Bohemia and Moravia were, it had been decided by the Chiefs of Staff, a Russian commitment, but there were already some parties in position who had been sponsored by S.O.E. and a small commitment for their maintenance already existed.

Of the countries within the theatre of SACMED, Northern Italy had proved very fruitful ground for the organisation of partisan warfare, and the enemy had been compelled to maintain considerable forces in the area in an attempt to preserve order and maintain the security of his communications. Action had already been taken by A.F.H.Q. on the representations of H.Q. SO(M) to increase supplies to meet the requirements of the partisan groups and B.L.O.s in Italy, and the delivery of 600 tons during October had been fixed as the target. In Austria, although there was no effective organised resistance, S.O.E. had established a series of despatch posts manned by British officers situated along the Austro-Italian and Austro-Yugoslav frontiers. Resistance activity was also being carried out by the Slovene minority in South Carinthia. As far as Hungary was concerned the air lift requirements concerned only the introduction and maintenance of British Missions into the country, involving an estimated average of eighteen sorties per month.

Although the nearby Balkan areas could be served from Italy by unarmed transport aircraft, the penetration of more distant countries necessitated the use of heavy armed aircraft. The only S.D. heavy aircraft in the Mediterranean were those of 148 Squadron and 1586 Polish Flight. With these it had not proved possible, even in the best month of the summer, to meet the requirements of the Resistance forces, and the position had recently been worsened by the losses sustained over Warsaw. In the winter months weather conditions would probably militate against the success of S.D. operations, and it was clear that the existing resources were insufficient to provide the air lift requirements to meet the needs of Poland, Austria, Hungary and the small commitment to Czechoslovakia. S.O.E. therefore requested that the Chiefs of Staff should consider the importance which they attached to Special Operations in these countries and should give guidance to SACMED accordingly.

Supplies to the Italian Maquis

MEDCOS/205
On 24th October, General Wilson reported to the British and American Chiefs of Staff on his plans in the Mediterranean. After outlining his proposed Italian campaign, he added that the situation in the Balkans called for some immediate preparatory action. If we were to take advantage of the opportunity offered by the enemy's present critical position east of the Adriatic to destroy as large as possible a proportion of his forces now in Greece and Yugoslavia, we must accept some immediate reduction in the weight of our air offensive in North Italy. Only the partisans and the Air Force could act in Yugoslavia before the winter set in, and the winter itself might set the seal on their efforts. The air resources which were essential to early and decisive results in the Balkans could be found only at the immediate expense of the offensive in Italy.

General Wilson had therefore requested the Air Commander-in-Chief to give priority for air supply to the Partisans in northern Yugoslavia over those of northern Italy, and to be prepared to divert heavy and light bombers for operations in Yugoslavia, either bombing or supply dropping, as might be required by the Commander, Balkan Air Force.

Annex I to COS(44)933(0), 29 October 1944
On the same date the Minister of Economic Warfare wrote to the Prime Minister to emphasise the importance of delivering supplies to the

Italian Maquis. He pointed out that General Alexander himself had testified to the excellent work which these Partisans were doing and there was no doubt that their action had considerably assisted regular military operations. General Alexander had planned an important role for them during the coming months. But the winter would be a hard time for the Partisans, and if we could not send them the reinforcements and supplies they needed we should be depriving ourselves of a valuable weapon, crippling the existing Missions in the field and laying numbers of Italian communities open to fearful German reprisals.

The target of 600 tons which Air Marshal Slessor had agreed should be delivered to Italy in October had been beyond reach: meanwhile, as a result of bad weather the total had been very disappointing, and only 45 tons had so far been delivered. The Minister referred to a proposal to move to Italy the two American Liberator Squadrons which had been assisting in the support of French Resistance and said that he felt it was important, for political reasons, to maintain the British effort as well. He felt strongly that at this stage priority should be given to the Italian Partisans in view of their direct contribution to our main military operations in Italy.

MEDCOS/205
On 26th November, the Minister again wrote to the Prime Minister, after having seen General Wilson's telegram, to protest against the decision to give Yugoslavia priority over northern Italy.

Annex 2 to COS(44)933(0), 29 October 1944
"Acting on instructions I called the Italian Maquis out and they have done a magnificent job, far better than I ever expected; in fact, just as good as the French did.

"The decision now is that supplies to Northern Italy be restricted to minimum tonnage necessary for the maintenance of existing commitments. I plead that this be liberally interpreted.

"When you have called a Maquis out into open warfare it is not fair to let it drop like a hot potato. These men have burned their boats and have no retreat. If we fail them with ammunition, death by torture awaits them.

"General Alexander will tell you that Italian resistance has paid a rich dividend. I plead that if more support is to be given to Marshal Tito it should not be at the expense of the Italian partisans."

The Prime Minister then wrote to General Ismay for the Chiefs of Staff on 28th October:

D.258/4
"While I am well aware of the views of Air Marshal Slessor, I still think that it is of the utmost importance to keep the Italian Maquis in the field, and anyhow General Alexander's opinion must be sought upon this. The demand is not a large one and it ought to be possible to move these small quantities without abandoning our other plans."

COS(44), 352nd Meeting, Item 4
The matter was considered by the Chiefs of Staff on 30th October. The C.A.S. reported that the two American Squadrons which had been employed on supplying French Resistance had now returned to their normal bombing role. It was generally agreed that the Yugoslav Partisans could, under present circumstances, make a greater contribution to operations against Germany than could those in Northern Italy, and that the decision as regards the priority for air supply would be allotted to the two areas was one which must be taken by General Wilson.

Parachutes Again

Encl. l. to Air 2/0.0/81(C), 8 December 1943
With the growth of the Airborne forces the War Office became seriously concerned with the availability of parachutes, and in November 1943, the Q.M.G. had formed an inter-departmental Committee on Maintenance by Air upon which S.O.E. were represented, which was to plan, inter alia, production and requirements of parachutes. The question of priorities as between Airborne Forces and S.O.E. was agreed not to be the responsibility of the Air Ministry, but that of the Chiefs of Staff who delegated this to the Director of Air, War Office, subject to the right of appeal by S.O.E. to the Chiefs of Staff.

At S.O.E.'s suggestion it was agreed that a reserve of five thousand parachutes should be prepared in the U.K. for use in operations either by Airborne forces or by S.O.E.

During November and December the Maintenance by Air Committee endeavoured to ascertain the total requirements and supply position of parachutes. With the greatly increased aircraft resources supply at S.O.E.'s disposal during the early months of 1944 the demand on parachutes and containers became correspondingly heavier. S.O.E.'s demands for those supplies were supported by S.H.A.E.F. who after March themselves made the allocation between the users in their Theatre.

Minutes of 4th Mtg. of Army Requirements Supply Committee, Maintenance by Air, 8 April 1944
BN.359/43Q (Ops D&T)
A reserve of some twenty thousand packed containers was built up in the U.K. In April A.F.H.Q. supported S.O.E. in the Mediterranean for further increased demands of parachutes. In May S.O.E. drew four thousand parachutes from the S.H.A.E.F. reserve in preparation for Overlord, and a further five thousand in mid-June. American G.I. type parachutes were converted for use with British containers, and the position for S.O.E. was thus eased.

AIR 3/00/476
At the beginning of November 1944, the greatly increased air lift in the Mediterranean caused a fresh crisis in parachute supply in that area. This was reviewed at a War Office Meeting on 1st December at which S.O.E.'s revised requirements were accepted. With the increased use of Dakotas and the rapid liberation of France and Belgium, demands for parachutes diminished considerably in January 1945.

Post D-Day Resistance in Western Europe

After the invasion of France, S.D. Squadrons based in the U.K. continued to supply Resistance in the areas behind the enemy lines. A number of mass daylight deliveries were made by American Fortresses of the 8th U.S.A.A.F. to Maquis Groups in Southern and Central France, and open warfare was carried out in these areas on a scale more nearly approximating to the Balkan guerilla activities than anything else in Western Europe.

On the invasion of Southern France from North Africa the Allied Armies found that large areas had already been taken over by the Resistance Forces and their advance was very materially assisted by the Forces Françaises de l'Intérieur.

Meanwhile, deliveries to the Low Countries and to Scandinavia continued. As the Allied Armies advanced and larger areas were freed from German domination the demand for supplies to Resistance contracted. In August the two American Squadrons were withdrawn from S.D. work and returned to a normal bombing role, and S.D. operations were flown by the two Tempsford Squadrons and aircraft of 38 Group.

S.O.E.'s 4th Directive, November 1944

COS(44)957(0), 9 November 1944
In November 1944, the Chiefs of Staff issued to S.O.E. their fourth Directive. (It is worth noting that no Directive was given to S.O.E. between March 1943 and November 1944.) S.O.E. were once more instructed to ensure that subversive activity was planned in close co-ordination with strategical policy and operational plans. Where S.O.E. activities came within the operational theatres of S.C.A.E.F., S.A.C.M.E.D., or S.A.C.S.E.A., operations would be directed by the responsible Supreme Commander within general provisions of the Directive.

The general object of sabotage was to promote economic, industrial and military disorganisation and the dislocation of communications in German-occupied Europe. Sabotage should be pursued with the utmost vigour; attacks on communications and other targets must be carefully regulated and integrated with our operational plans. Sabotage against oil targets, enemy U-boats, air operations and shipping was of special importance. In organising guerilla activities S.O.E. was reminded that they should be aimed at hindering as far as possible the concentration and consolidation of German forces on the respective fronts. They should also aim at intensifying Germany's already severe shortage of man-power by increasing her internal security commitments in occupied territories. Resistance Groups should be prepared to act in support of any United Nations Forces which may operate in their countries but any premature uprising is to be discouraged.

In Western Europe all S.O.E. military operations were to be carried out in accordance with directives from S.C.A.E.F.; in Southern and Central Europe in accordance with directives from S.A.C.M.E.D. In Poland and Czechoslovakia, the two countries in which S.O.E. were under the operational direction of the Chiefs of Staff, every possible support should be given to the Resistance Movements. However, S.O.E. must not encourage either the Polish or Czech authorities to believe that sufficient arms and supplies would be forthcoming from the Western Allies for a general rising.

Poland: Russian Attitude

After the fall of Warsaw the Polish Secret Army continued to attack the Germans in the areas still under German domination, but the difficulties of distance and weather and the shortage of heavy aircraft on S.D. operations from the Mediterranean limited the quantity of supplies which it was found possible to deliver to Poland.

F.3279/125

On 30th October 1944, the Minister of Economic Warfare wrote to the Secretary of State for Air to ask for an increased allocation of S.D. aircraft for Poland. General Tabor of the Polish General Staff had been to see him to ask if it was possible to reopen S.D. flights to Poland from the U.K. in order to supplement the effort from Italy, a suggestion which the Minister strongly supported. It was clear that the Poles felt that the Prime Minister's ruling, given at the Defence Committee held on 3rd February 1944, for an increase in the airlift to Poland from Italy had never been fully implemented in practice. Since his return from Moscow the Prime Minister had urged Lord Selborne to put as many people into Western Poland as possible and to do everything possible to support the Polish Home Army there. This could not be done without some augmentation of the effort which the available Italian-based aircraft were likely to be able to achieve.

The Secretary of State for Air replied on 14th November to say that authority had just been given for the issue of an extra twelve new Liberators to the Polish Squadron in M.A.A.F. This should go a long way towards giving the Polish Army the extra support which General Tabor desired. He reported that the Air Ministry felt unable to adopt the suggestion of renewing operations to Poland from the U.K.: the difficulties of routeing aircraft on this trip were, if anything, even greater than they had been, and if Bomber Command were to attempt deep penetration as far as Poland they would have to expect prohibitive casualties. He concluded by quoting figures to show that the Air Ministry had done all within its power to implement the Defence Committee's ruling, concerning the trebling of deliveries to Poland.

F.3355/125

On 22nd November the Minister again wrote to Sir Archibald Sinclair thanking him for the reinforcements of Liberators, but reiterating his request that operations should be undertaken to Poland from U.K. He pointed out that the figures quoted by the Secretary of State for Air were not exactly the same as those compiled by S.O.E. and by the Poles. He concluded by urging very strongly that, on the few nights when Polish operations from U.K. were possible, these should be undertaken within the limits of existing resources.

Meanwhile, operations continued from the Mediterranean; but the weather was bad and the refusal of the Soviet authorities to allow S.D. aircraft to fly over their lines, thereby forcing them to make the more dangerous trip over the enemy lines, did not help matters.

On 24th November the Minister of Economic Warfare wrote to the Prime Minister, sending a copy of his minute to the Secretary of State for Air. He reported that the number of Polish operations successfully completed in the last eight weeks had been extremely disappointing. He recommended that most vigorous representations should be made to Moscow over the Russian refusal to allow flights from Italy across Hungary, that the importance of flights to Poland at that moment should be confirmed to Air Marshal Slessor, and that S.O.E. should be permitted to use S.D. aircraft based in the U.K. for flights to Poland whenever weather conditions permitted.

The Secretary of State for Air replied on 28th November that the A.O.C.-in-C. Bomber Command was emphatically of the opinion that the northern route to Poland was one which would undoubtedly involve heavy casualties without helping the Poles to the extent which they expected. He did not consider it a reasonable operation of war. The Air Ministry remained convinced that the casualty rate over the northern route would be so great as to make the operation impracticable. The position regarding the Minister's other two recommendations in his Minute to the Prime Minister was that the C.A.S. had given the Prime Minister a draft telegram to Marshal Stalin urging that flights to Italy across Hungary should be allowed, and that Air Marshal Slessor certainly appreciated the importance of the flights to Poland.

COS(44), 382nd Meeting, Item 6, 28 November 1944

Changes in the Polish Government and political friction between Poland and Russia aggravated an already difficult situation. The problem was considered by the Chiefs of Staff on November 28th when the C.A.S. reported that the Foreign Office had asked the Air Ministry to suspend, for the time being, the delivery of supplies to Poland. The necessary instructions were therefore being issued by the Air Ministry to the Mediterranean Air Force.

PM/44/742, 4 December 1944
Six days later, however, the Foreign Secretary suggested to the Prime Minister that, irrespective of any approach to the Russians, the Polish crews should be allowed to continue their flight to Poland. The Minister of Economic Warfare also wrote on 8th December to the Prime Minister to support the Foreign Secretary's suggestion and pointed out that whatever Polish Government was in office, it was the people inside Poland who had proved themselves so loyal to the Allies, and who still turned to us for assistance in their need.

PM/44/763, 12 December 1944
The Secretary of State for Foreign Affairs again wrote to the Prime Minister on 12th December. Recent developments had shown clearly that the Russians desired to prevent us from sending further assistance to the Polish Underground Movement.

The only way to ensure the maintenance of reasonably effective support to the Poles was for the Prime Minister to approach Marshal Stalin and try to persuade him to change his attitude, but Mr. Eden was not hopeful of such an approach proving successful. It might even prove prejudicial to our hopes of Soviet co-operation and it was doubtful whether we should run this risk, when the military advantages of sending supplies into Poland were so small. On the other hand, Mr. Eden was reluctant to abandon the Polish Underground Army, and he suggested that a possible compromise might be to authorise the resumption of flights to Poland by the longer route over German-held territory, or even to resume direct flights to Poland from the U.K.

F.3533/125, 9 January 1945
On 9th January, the Minister of Economic Warfare wrote to the Foreign Secretary to say that he personally felt most strongly that both our honour and our interest demanded a continuance of the supply flights. Political and military considerations alike demanded that we should

continue to make deliveries to Poland even although they could only be in insignificant quantity.

By this time however, the largest part of Poland had been freed by the Russian Armies from German domination and the Chief of the Polish General Staff informed the Combined Chiefs of Staff of the disbandment of all units of the Polish Secret Army within the Soviet occupied part of Poland.

CCS.645/8
A few air operations were flown to Poland during the months of January and February, but by 15th February, the Polish President felt compelled to order the dissolution of the Polish Secret Army.

The Last Winter of Occupation

During the winter, S.D. operations to Yugoslavia and Northern Italy continued. The Partisans in Italy were warned by General Alexander that it would prove impossible during the winter to give them the supplies they desired; they should therefore conserve their energies and lie low until deliveries could be made to them.

In the early spring large scale dropping operations were carried out by day and by night chiefly into the Apennine regions, and thus armed the Partisans were able to take the offensive, engaging the enemy in pitched battles and gaining control over large areas including a number of important towns in Northern Italy. When the Germans began seriously to withdraw their forces from the Balkans action by Yugoslav guerilla bands was directed towards harassing them. The advance of the Russian Armies removed Bulgaria, Rumania, and later Austria and Hungary from the sphere of Special Operations.

In Western Europe S.D. operations were flown throughout the winter of 1944/45 to the Low Countries and to Scandinavia. One of the Squadrons that had been engaged for so long on S.D. work returned to normal bombing duties on the understanding that a corresponding effort should be made available to S.O.E. when necessary from 38 Group.

SHDCS/TS.1122
In March 1945, Tempsford Station passed under the control of 38 Group and it was agreed that on the termination of hostilities it should become

a Transport Command Station. Its period of service under 38 Group lasted therefore only two months.

CMcVG/6093, 15 June 1945
On 15th June 1945, the Head of S.O.E. wrote to Air Vice Marshal Williams to record the end of S.D. operations in Europe:

> "I confirm that S.O.E. no longer requires S.D. facilities either in the U.K. or in the Mediterranean and I note that Transport Command could probably undertake any further work which we might have …
>
> "I should like to take this opportunity of expressing the most sincere thanks, not only of myself, but also of the whole of S.O.E. for the magnificent work which the S.D. Squadrons in Europe have accomplished; these have contributed in no small degree to the discomfiture of the enemy."

Part II

Assistance Given by the RAF to the SOE: Problems
and Procedure of Special Duty Operations

Chapter 4

The Scope of the Problem

From 1942 to 1945 the total of all operations in Europe by British Airborne Forces involved the parachuting or landing of thousands of troops and thousands of tons of stores. These operations were regular military operations carried out in force at considerable intervals of time. During the same period the organisation and supply of resistance movements in enemy-occupied Europe, carried out continuously under exacting conditions of secrecy and security, involved the parachuting or landing of 6,700 personnel of 18 different nationalities and 42,800 tons of stores.

The continuous clandestine air transport of this tonnage and the large number of highly trained organisers and specialists required no fewer than 33,000 sorties by aircraft of the R.A.F. and ultimately the U.S.A.A.F. These 33,000 sorties (except for a small percentage of formation flights under specially favourable conditions and a number of sorties in which two or more operations were combined in the same aircraft) represented an equivalent number of separate individual operations, each one separately planned, involving navigation by night to an exact pinpoint in enemy-occupied territory and (with an almost negligible number of exceptions, namely "blind" drops) requiring the presence of a Reception Committee at that same pinpoint at the right hour to receive, hide and distribute the stores and personnel to be dropped.

Of these 33,000 sorties over 22,000 were successful and nearly 11,000 were failures. With the exception of the few "mass" drops and "blind" drops every single sortie, whether a success or failure, involved an average of 3 or 4 signals between base and the men in the field, the special briefing of the aircrew and the packing and loading of the particular supplies required. In the early days of 1941 and 1942 sorties were few and far between; the supply requirements were small and the base organisation was in the workshop stage of development; the mounting of every individual operation and the packing of its supplies could be and normally was supervised by an officer personally familiar with every detail of the requirements of the man in the field. But from 1943 to 1945 the underground movements in Europe had been built up to operate on an increasing scale; the base organisations (both in the U.K. and the Mediterranean) passed into the factory or mass production stage, each one being eventually capable of handling up to 100 or more sorties a day, which according to the type of aircraft employed might involve anything from 1,000 to 2,000 containers or packages a day, and corresponding amounts of parachutes and supply dropping equipment. During the climax of the summer of 1944, operations, both in the U.K. and the Mediterranean were being mounted from 6 or 7 different airfields to scores of different pinpoints in several different countries.

The total figures, details of which are given in the Appendices, were as follows:

Bases	Total sorties	Successful sorties	Gross tonnage	Personnel delivered	Personnel evacuated	Aircraft lost
U.K.	11,894	7,602	11,141	2,028	559	154
M.T.O.	21,501	15,304	31,685	4,683	20,173	115
Totals	*33,395*	*22,906*	*42,826*	*6,711*	*20,732*	*269*

S.D. operations were undertaken at different times by different types of aircraft: the Wellington, Whitley, Wellesley, Halifax, Hudson, Dakota, Lancaster, Liberator, Stirling, Albemarle, Mosquito and Fortress all played their parts. Each of these carried a different quantity of stores and most had to be specially modified in order to take containers and packages. To the Bomber pilot dropping supplies was perhaps less exciting than dropping bombs, but to the people in the occupied countries the supply bomber represented their hope, not only of deliverance, but of participation in victory.

Not only were supplies delivered by parachute to occupied Europe, but in many countries landing operations also were carried out. This was perhaps the most spectacular activity of the R.A.F. in helping Resistance Movements. In some countries it was never possible throughout the whole war to arrange for such an operation, owing to the difficult nature of the terrain or the particularly vigilant control of the enemy. Norway, Denmark, Holland, and Austria never received any landing operations; but conditions in other countries were less difficult, and in Yugoslavia, Greece and France these operations, carried out by Lysander, Dakota and Hudson, became an important source of supply, and an invaluable method of transporting reports and personnel back to S.O.E. Headquarters. The evacuation of personnel by 'pick-up' operations was an important and remarkable feature. It made possible the quick return to base of officers and agents, whose missions had been accomplished, to report and give the first-hand and up-to-date intelligence which was vital for the clear appreciation of the progress and problems of the resistance movement. It enabled leading personalities to be brought out for consultation or rescued from immediate danger: a few prominent examples being General de Lattre de Tassigny (France), M. Arciszewski and General Tabor (Poland), Marshal Tito and his G.H.Q. Staff (Yugoslavia), General Zervas and General Sarafis (Greece): (see Appendix L). Finally under favourable conditions it enabled wounded officers or Partisans to be rescued; from Yugoslavia nearly 18,000 wounded or sick Partisans were evacuated to Italy.

The organisation of air supply to resistance movements in Europe was thus a major task; it had to combine flexibility, speed and accuracy and to deliver big loads of stores covering a wide range of items without neglecting the individual needs of every customer. When the first tests and experiments were carried out in England in 1941, it appeared doubtful in the extreme whether it would ever be possible to overcome the many obstacles; the air problems of navigation by night to a pinpoint in enemy-occupied territory, locating the feeble torches of friends on the ground, and distinguishing them from casual lights or from deliberate enemy deception; the ground problems of patriots assembling secretly, waiting perhaps night after night for their aircraft to appear, retrieving and hiding in the dusk twelve or twenty heavy containers or packages dropped at night; and the communications problem of maintaining speed and cypher security. It can at least be said with certainty that none of those who took part in the pioneer work in 1941 could have anticipated or even hoped for results on the scale achieved in 1944.

Chapter 5

Squadrons Engaged on Special Duties Work (UK and Mediterranean Bases)

The setting up of 419 Flight at North Weald in August 1940 was the first contribution made by the R.A.F. to S.O.E.'s work.

3039/PDDO, 20 August 1940
This flight was to consist of 2 plus 2 Lysanders of which two were to be fitted with long range tanks. It was to be shared between S.O.E. and S.I.S. By October 1940 the establishment of the S.D. Flight was increased by 2 plus 1 Whitley V modified for dropping and fitted with long range tanks.

S.5998/01, 2 October 1940
In October the Air Ministry suggested to Bomber Command that since the Special Duty operations of 419 Flight were more closely akin to the operations of Bomber Command, than those of Fighter Command, and since the Flight used Bomber Command lanes 419 Flight should move to one of their Stations.

DC/S.24455/ORG, 6 October 1940
Bomber Command suggested that the most suitable aerodrome would be Stradishall of 3 Group and in October 419 Flight was transferred from Stapleford Abbots of Fighter Command where it had latterly been stationed. At Stradishall better maintenance and other facilities were available for the Whitleys, but the station was not very convenient for the Lysanders. Facilities were therefore arranged at Tangmere which was used as an advanced base for pick-up operations.

The first S.D. operations were carried out by 419 Flight to Western Europe during the winter of 1940/41. In these early days many of the difficulties were still unsolved: shortage of staff, lack of accommodation and a general uncertainty as to the exact position of S.D. operations in the R.A.F.'s scheme of things increased the difficulties that had to be faced by 419 Flight. In addition, the weather during the first winter was consistently bad and very few sorties could be attempted. During 1941, however, a number of successful dropping operations were carried out, including the first S.D. operation to Poland (Adolphus, February 1941), and the first Lysander pick-up operation carried out for S.O.E. (Levee/Facade, September 1941). Events had already shown that S.D. operations in Western Europe would mainly take the form of supply dropping: there would be comparatively few landing operations since only small quantities of stores could be infiltrated by this means into countries where German control was comprehensive and always alert.

In February 1941, the S.D. Flight was moved from Stradishall to Newmarket still in No.3. Group, and was renumbered 1419 (S.D.) Flight. The aircraft establishment had now become:

> 3 + 1 Whitleys.
>
> 1 + 1 Lysander.
>
> 1 Glen Martin 167 for possible pick-up development.

During the summer action was taken to raise the aircraft establishment to 6 plus 1 Whitleys and a Polish and a Czechoslovak crew were added to the air crew strength.

In August 1941, 1419 Flight was raised to Squadron status as No.138 (S.D.) Squadron, and steps were taken to raise the aircraft establishment to 8 plus 2 Whitley V and 2 plus 1 Halifax I, the Halifax being intended for the Polish sorties which were beyond Whitley range. At the same time it was recommended that the Squadron be moved to a station nearer London, to render the despatch of agents easier. In October a Wellington was added to the establishment for experimental purposes, and the Glen Martin, which was never used, was removed.

A second squadron was made available in February 1942, when No.161 (S.D.) Squadron was formed at Newmarket, the basis of the Squadron being the aircraft and personnel of the King's Flight, under the command of its Captain. The consent of His Majesty was obtained for this action. The aircraft establishment of this Squadron was 4 plus 1 Whitley V, 6 plus 1 Lysanders (transferred from 138 Squadron), 2 Wellingtons (for experimental purposes), and 1 Hudson I (ex-King's

Flight). At the same time the establishment of 138 Squadron was altered to 8 plus 2 Whitley V and 5 Halifax I or II. All pick-up operations were henceforward undertaken by 161 Squadron whose establishment included the Lysanders and Hudsons, while 138 Squadron was concerned only with dropping operations.

On 11th March 1942 both Squadrons were moved to R.A.F. Station Tempsford still in No.3 Group, Bomber Command, from which Station they operated until the end of the War in Europe. In the early stages Graveley was used as a satellite airfield.

In June 1942, the aircraft establishment of 138 Squadron was changed to 10 plus 2 Halifax II and 5 Whitley V, to allow for a continued increase in the demands for long range sorties. By November, however, it had been decided that the continued employment of Whitley aircraft was no longer sound or economical, and they were replaced in both Squadrons, the respective establishments then becoming:

138 Squadron: 13 plus 2 Halifax II.
161 Squadron: 5 Halifax II, 6 plus 1 Lysander, 1 Hudson I and 2 Wellingtons (for development).

In the early days these Squadrons were not engaged full time on Special Duty work, since time was needed after the dropping of the original organisers for their circuits to grow and for their demands for air supply to increase. In June, July and September 1942, 161 Squadron was mainly used for bombing work and only a certain number of "Nickel" raids were carried out on behalf of S.O.E. The pioneer stages of the work largely took the form of transporting to enemy-occupied countries, notably France, those agents whose mission was to organise resistance groups in selected areas. Meanwhile the pick-up Flight was engaged on extremely valuable work in withdrawing from enemy-occupied France S.O.E. officers and senior French military and political resistance leaders.

In 1942, a second base for Special Duty operations was established in the Mediterranean when 'X' Flight of 148 Squadron (Liberators) began operations into the Balkans from the Delta. In March 1943 the Flight was reconstituted as 148 Squadron with the reinforcement of fourteen Halifaxes. From the Delta the supply dropping aircraft had already moved their base westwards more than once, to Gambut and then to Shandur. During the first part of 1943 they again moved behind the advancing Desert Armies first to Derna and in August to Tocra. In the summer of 1943 the dropping of supplies to Marshal Tito's forces required the use of an advanced base at Protville but even then the fitting of three overload tanks to Halifaxes was necessary to give them sufficient range. If the Special Duty aircraft were unable to meet their operational commitments the A.O.C.-in-C. M.E. sometimes permitted the occasional use of a Wellington for a Special Duty operation.

During the summer of 1943 a second Mediterranean base was established for S.D. operations when 624 Squadron, based on Blida, was made available for supply dropping work in Southern France, Corsica and Italy.

During 1943 the work of supplying resistance from England was continued by 138 and 161 Squadrons. 161 Squadron's first responsibility was to S.I.S. and only in default of S.I.S. operations could these aircraft be used by S.O.E. The S.O.E. operations were therefore flown mainly by 138 Squadron, although S.I.S., by the very nature of their work, needed far less supply dropping to do and 161 was thus able to aid S.O.E. to a considerable extent. Until the autumn of 1943 all Special Duty operations flown to Europe were the work of these two Squadrons.

Towards the end of 1943, however, it became obvious that these two Squadrons alone could not hope to meet the growing demands from the field. All over Western Europe the number of resistance groups was increasing and their appetite for supplies becoming correspondingly larger. Squadrons of Stirling aircraft were therefore allocated by Bomber Command during the autumn of the year for Special Duty operations, normally remaining at Tempsford for a period of about a month. For a short time the co-operation of some Lancasters was also given. The two American Liberator Squadrons allocated for S.D. work in Western Europe arrived at Tempsford towards the end of 1943 and it became the task of 138 and 161 Squadrons to train these enthusiastic helpers to that pitch of efficiency already attained by their tutors. In the early days of 1944 these Squadrons moved to Alconbury and were later transferred to Harrington where they continued Special Duty operations until the eve of D-Day. This cumulative and sustained effort on the part of Tempsford over a period of over three years (April 1942 until May 1945) resulted in the delivery to the field of a total of nearly 29,000 containers, over 1,000 personnel and nearly 10,000 packages.

The Prime Minister's decision at the beginning of 1944 that the volume of supply operations was to be increased resulted in the allotment of more aircraft, both in the Mediterranean and in England for

S.D. work. In England 161 and 138 Squadrons continued to operate from Tempsford and the two American Liberator Squadrons became fully operational during the first months of the year. In February, only four days before the moon period began, a supplementary effort of thirty-two Stirlings from 3 Group and sixty aircraft sorties from 38 Group was added to the S.D. aircraft allocation in England. Two new aerodromes were involved in this increase, (Hurn and Lakenheath) and only standard load operations were attempted by them.

An even greater variety of aircraft had now been reached: in addition to the Halifaxes and Liberators at Tempsford and Alconbury, Stirlings and Albemarles were also used. In spite of the fact that they had never before embarked on Special Duty operations both Hurn and Lakenheath achieved a considerable measure of success during their first moon period. In March the effort was further stepped up and seventy-two Stirlings from 3 Group together with ninety aircraft sorties from 38 Group were allocated for S.D. work. S.D. operations were now flown from Lakenheath, Tuddenham, Mepal (3 Group), and at different times from Harwell, Keevil, Fairford, Brize Norton, Earls Colne, Tarrant Rushton, Wethersfield, Great Dunmow, Shepherds Grove, Rivenhall (38 Group). This was the largest number of aircraft ever made available from England: by April the supplementary effort was reduced and during the succeeding months, as the occupied countries were liberated by the advancing Allied Armies, the demands for S.D. work and therefore the number of aircraft engaged on it were steadily diminished. During the summer of 1944, American Liberators of Air transport Command, operating from Leuchars, carried out a number of S.D. operations to Scandinavia.

Meanwhile, in the Mediterranean 624 Squadron had received an increased number of aircraft, and some American fortresses were also based on Blida for S.D. work. The liberation of the heel of Italy opened up bases for S.D. aircraft much nearer to their targets; and in January 1944, 624 and 148 Squadrons were combined to form 334 Wing and transferred from North Africa to Brindisi. The Polish Flight 1586 was also assigned to Special Operations in Italy. In February, however, 624 Squadron moved back to Blida in order to serve the duties of supplying organisations in Southern France, and in March three American heavy bombers were added to the aircraft available at this base.

In January 1944 a transport group of D.C.3s was moved to Brindisi to join 334 Wing and in the summer of 1944 the Polish Squadron 301 came into operation with Poland as its first priority target, Czechoslovakia as its second. For political reasons these aircraft were not used over Yugoslavia.

267 Squadron (D.C.3s) based on Bari also delivered supplies during the early part of 1944 to Yugoslavia and Italy, but as Italy became too dangerous for this type of aircraft in view of the concentration of flak, the Squadron was used mainly for Yugoslavia, and in the summer of 1944 did a number of landing operations in that country. 267 Squadron left for Burma in July 1944 and was replaced by 44 S.A.A.F. under 236 Wing. A Russian Squadron of Dakotas also based on Bari flew to targets given by the Russian Liaison Officers in Yugoslavia and worked in fairly close liaison with 267 Squadron. From Lecce the Italian Air Force carried supplies to Yugoslavia and at Foggia 205 Group consisting of normal bomber aircraft were used extensively on Italy and Yugoslavia for mass dropping operations. Their work to Yugoslavia often under fighter escort was especially successful.

In the Mediterranean, as in England, assistance in this work was also given by American Squadrons, 885 Squadron U.S.A.A.F., based at Blida operated to Southern France until October 1944 and then operated from Brindisi to Northern Italy and the Balkans. It was reinforced late in 1944 by 859 Squadron to form 2641 Special Group, (subsequently known as 15 Bomber Group Special). At the end of March 1945 this Group moved its base north to Rosignano and until VE-Day was solely responsible for all sorties to Italy, Austria and Czechoslovakia, while 334 Wing and 205 Group remained at Brindisi and Foggia and were exclusively responsible for S.D. sorties to Yugoslavia.

A further American S.D. contribution in Italy was made by 64 Troop Carrier Group U.S.A.A.F. operating first from Malignano in December 1944/January 1945 and subsequently Rosignano, into N.W. Italy. This contribution arose from the representations made in October/November 1944 regarding the need for maintaining Italian Resistance through the winter, notwithstanding the higher priority accorded to Yugoslavia. To meet the North Italian requirements M.A.A.F. in November 1944 invited M.A.T.A.F. (operating in support of 15th Army Group) to provide a supplementary S.D. effort for Italian partisans. From December 1944 M.A.T.A.F. made available up to 20 C47 (Dakota) aircraft out of 64 Troop Carrier Group. The maintenance of Partisans in N.W. Italy during the winter was largely due to the effort of this U.S. Unit.

After the invasion of France the volume of supplies delivered to resistance groups was substantially increased by a number of mass daylight dropping operations carried out by 8th U.S.A.A.F. to various parts of France where the Maquis were in open conflict with the enemy. An operation of a similar type was later carried out in Belgium and also in Holland. As the Allied Armies advanced the delivery of supplies to the still unliberated areas of Western Europe continued, while in the Mediterranean, where the crisis was to reach its height several months later than in Western Europe, supplies continued to pour into the Balkans and North Italy.

In the Autumn of 1944 Bomber Command requested that 138 Squadron should be released for normal bombing duties and S.O.E. agreed to this, provided that a corresponding air effort was made available if necessary from 38 Group. At a meeting held at Air Ministry on Thursday, 4 January 1945 the S.O.E. representative declared that his organisation "wished to record how extremely sorry S.O.E. were to lose 138 Squadron with whom they had worked in the closest co-operation for so long. They had done a marvellous and efficient job."

D of I (R/154/45), 27 February 1945
D of I (R/181/45)
In February it was decided that 161 Squadron at Tempsford should be transferred to 38 Group at an early date and this was effected on 10th March 1945. It had already been agreed by S.O.E. that at the conclusion of hostilities in Europe R.A.F. Station Tempsford should be transferred to Bomber Command and since victory in Europe was declared on 8th May, Tempsford's sojourn under 38 Group lasted for only two months.

Similarly, as the enemy's retreat in southern and south eastern Europe culminated in surrender, the M.A.A.F. squadrons employed on S.D. work were transferred to other duties.

Chapter 6

Types of Aircraft

The first aircraft to be used on S.D. dropping operations were Whitleys. In the spring of 1941 the first supply delivery to Poland was made by an aircraft of this type – a round distance of 1,700 miles. Targets at this range, however, were clearly beyond the normal capabilities of Whitley aircraft and the Poles very soon began to ask for the use of Halifaxes on their operations. Owing to the demands of Bomber Command these aircraft could not be spared for S.D. work until the autumn of 1942, when both 161 and 138 Squadrons began to change over from Whitleys to Halifaxes. By the spring of 1943 Whitleys were no longer used for S.D. operations flown from England and throughout that year the great bulk of deliveries were made by Halifaxes.

The increased allocation of aircraft for S.D. work by Bomber Command in the autumn of 1943 brought both Stirlings and Lancasters on to this type of operation, and with the allotment of sorties from 38 Group during the spring of 1944 Albemarles were also included. Certain types of dropping operations, including only personnel and packages, were also conveyed by Hudson during 1944.

The American effort from the U.K. consisted of Liberators which came into operation in the spring of 1944.

When an S.D. base was set up at Blida in the summer of 1943 the first aircraft used were Halifaxes which operated into Southern France and Italy. At a later date the Americans contributed both Fortresses and Liberators to this force.

Each of these different types of aircraft carried a different quantity of containers and packages at various ranges. A table is attached at

Appendix K showing the various aircraft used on S.D. work from England in the Mediterranean, and Appendix D shows the capacity of the aircraft from Albemarles to Stirlings. Aircraft which were allocated permanently for S.D. work were modified in order to facilitate the storage and release of containers and packages.

The first aircraft to operate from Egypt into the Balkans were Liberators: by the time it was possible to establish air bases in Italy the value of transport aircraft for delivering supplies to the Balkan areas had been recognised. Enemy opposition here was comparatively slight and it was therefore possible to use unarmed Dakotas and Italian aircraft which could not have faced the more formidable defences of Western or Central Europe, It was at first proposed that Stirlings should be sent out as the supplementary effort with which to equip the increased forces available for S.D. work in Italy, but after they had been actually ordered they were cancelled on Air Marshal Slessor's intervention and Dakotas were sent out instead. The Italian Air Force, flying S.M. 82s and Cant. Z.1007s with no instruments, were also engaged on supply dropping in Yugoslavia. The normal bomber aircraft of 205 Group (Liberators and Wellingtons) were used extensively in both Italy and Yugoslavia.

Landing Operations

In Western Europe the first aircraft to attempt to land in enemy-occupied territory were Lysanders. The first Hudson landing operation was carried out in February 1943. Lysanders were frequently used in pairs and even in threes: even Hudsons were occasionally used in this manner. American crews flying Dakotas carried out a number of landing operations in France in the months after D-Day.

In Western Europe, where small groups of resistants controlled only limited areas of country, it was essential that a small, light and easily manoeuvrable aircraft should be used for these operations. The length of runway for a Lysander was substantially shorter than that needed for either a Hudson or a Dakota, and it was therefore considerably easier to discover fields suitable for pick-up operations by Lysander. In the early days it had been suggested that a Glen Martin aircraft could be used for pick-up operations, but the high landing speed of this aircraft necessitated a long runway and made its use less practicable from the point of view of the men in the field.

Conditions in the Balkans were very different from those in Western Europe. In Yugoslavia and Greece powerful Partisan Forces were able to control large areas of country, and could even, if necessary, build their own landing strips. A small number of operations was carried out by Lysander to Northern Italy and Yugoslavia; but the most successful aircraft for work in the Balkans, on landing as on dropping operations, was the Dakota, since it is easily handled, has a comparatively low landing speed and a large capacity for passengers and stores.

Fast Dropping Operations

In certain circumstances, when organisations were in urgent need of money or W/T equipment but unable to receive large quantities of stores, the most efficient way of delivering material was by fast aircraft. From North Africa this was successfully attempted once by Spitfire on a daylight operation when the pilot threw a package to the waiting Reception Committee.

In 1943 and 1944 operations of this type were occasionally flown from the U.K. by Mosquito aircraft.

117

Chapter 7

Foreign Air Crews

It was natural that the Allied Governments co-operating closely with S.O.E. in the organisation of Resistance within their countries, should regard the employment of their own nationals on supply dropping operations as an ideal arrangement. There was in fact no other way in which an exiled Pole or Czech could give direct assistance to his oppressed countrymen; and many of the Allied Governments were anxious that their Air Forces should be used for S.D. work.

The problem was first raised during 1941, when the Polish, Czech and French Governments each separately requested that air-crews of their own nationalities should be used on S.D. operations. The practical disadvantages of this policy, however, were considerable. It was argued by the Air Ministry that the local knowledge a Pole or a Czech might have of his own country could not be at once sufficiently comprehensive and sufficiently detailed to help materially in carrying out S.D. operations. Moreover the standard of R.A.F. crews was on the whole higher than that of foreign crews, with the possible exception of the Polish Air Force, and the general standard of S.D. operations would undoubtedly decline if a large percentage of other nationals were employed on this work. In addition to this, the use of foreign crews only on operations to their own countries would inevitably involve a lack of economy; and if they were to be allowed to fly to countries other than their own, there would seem to be little point in the plan. The administration of a mixed squadron composed of nationals from various countries was bound to be difficult, and later experience showed that it did in fact involve a degree of disunity under the Squadron Commander, and sometimes even of disloyalty towards him.

S.5998/DCAS

The D.C.A.S., however, agreed in August 1941, that one Czech and one Polish crew should be posted to 1419 Flight in order "to make use of their special knowledge and experience." In September 1943 the Polish crews in 138 Squadron were formed into a Polish Flight and the Squadron establishment was increased by 3 plus 0 Liberator III. During most of the period a Czech crew was attached to the S.D. Squadrons. Apart from this, however, S.D. operations were undertaken from the U.K. entirely by the R.A.F., later assisted by the U.S.A.A.F. and the R.C.A.F. (Mosquito operations).

In October 1943 when the base for S.D. operations to Poland was transferred to the Mediterranean, the Polish Flight were moved to this theatre as 1586 (S.D.) Flight, and by the summer of 1944 the Polish Squadron 301 was carrying out S.D. work from Italy.

A Czech S.D. crew was also transferred to the Mediterranean and for a short time Italian crews belonging to the Italian Air Force were also employed on supply dropping in Yugoslavia. In this theatre, also, however, the great bulk of the work was undertaken by British, Dominions and American crews.

Chapter 8

Containers and Packages

Stores were dropped from aircraft both by container and package, the containers fitting into the bomb-bays and the packages being stowed in the fuselage of the aircraft and then either dropped out of a hole or pushed out of the door. The limiting factor to the amount of stores that could be carried by an aircraft generally proved to be volume rather than weight.

The containers took up about the same space as bombs but were considerably less heavy. Packages were used in order to increase the pay load on each sortie: here again the limit to the number of packages that could be carried was fixed by the storage capacity of the fuselage of the aircraft rather than by their individual weights. It should be remembered also that for security reasons the aircraft could not remain for too long a time over its dropping point.

The Reception Committees themselves sometimes specified that only one or two runs over the target were to be made; even if this was not definitely laid down by the field, pilots were always instructed to make as few runs as possible and thus draw as little attention to the area as they could. The number of containers and packages was therefore further limited by the speed of release: only a certain number of containers, and particularly of packages which were rather slower in release, could be despatched over the target area on any one run.

Containers

Different types of containers were used by S.O.E. at different times. The first to be used was the "C" type container, consisting of an outer shell or casing with three inner cells, the outer shell hinged to allow the cells to be lifted out with ease. The containers were cylindrical, of 5ft. 8ins. overall length and 15ins. diameter; their gross weight was 330lbs. and the pay load (i.e. the weight of the stores that could be carried exclusive of the container) 220lbs.

The "H" type container was invented in 1943 by Polish officers in conjunction with the Polish Country Section of S.O.E. The hard nature of the Polish soil did not lend itself to the disposal of the "C" type outer shell and the Poles required a container that after dismantling would leave very little extra material for disposal. The "H" type container was produced with the assistance of the staff of the South Metropolitan Gas Company and the prototype came off the assembly line within three weeks. After much trial and error and many drop tests, which were carried out by 138 Squadron, a satisfactory container was evolved. It consisted of five cells interlocked together and joined into one unit by metal rods. No outer casing was employed and five webbing carrying straps were sent with each container to enable the cells to be transported separately on the backs of the members of the Reception Committee. Its overall length was 5ft. 6ins. and its diameter 15ins; its gross weight was 330lbs. and the pay load 235lbs. The "H" type container had two main advantages over the "C" type: it could deliver a higher pay load to the field, and the absence of an outer casing meant that stores could be carried more quickly easily from the reception ground, while there was no extra covering to be buried or otherwise hidden.

The "H" type came into general use during 1943, but the "C" type container was still used for certain stores such as the larger types of Small Arms. Rifles, Brens, Bazookas and Piats were packed in the "C" type container with its inner cells removed; petrol and oil was also delivered by the cell-less "C" type container with Jerrycans, divided by plywood and hairlok as a shock absorbent, packed inside its outer shell.

During 1944 the rate of delivery to the field exceeded the supply of containers delivered from the manufacturers, and the C.L.E. container normally used by the Airborne Division was therefore employed by S.O.E. It was similar to the S.O.E. "C" type container but had an additional bracket for attachment to the aircraft. As soon as delivery of the "H" and "C" type containers was stepped up the use of the C.L.E. was discontinued.

The rate of descent of a container was 28ft. per second and its striking force was therefore roughly equivalent to a drop from a twelve foot wall. Each container was fitted with a buffer head which absorbed ten percent of the shock of impact. Containers were identified by stencilled numbers on the container head and also on the parachute bucket.

Until 1944 packing material such as fibre, corrugated cardboard and paper waste was used to fill spaces within containers, but in the delivery of bulk stores to the Maquis of France, clothing was used as packing material so that no inch of space should be wasted. In the Mediterranean, where food and clothing had for long been essential stores for the partisans, blankets, battle-dress, shirts, pants and vests, socks and scarves were despatched in this way.

Containers were packed at Special Packing stations both in England and the Mediterranean which were situated as close as possible to the airfields used by S.D. aircraft. In the early years each container was individually ordered by the Country Sections concerned, but as the volume of deliveries increased it became necessary to institute a system of standard packing. The separate cells were standardised first, but in a short time the complete container had become the standard unit. There still continued to be a large proportion of "Special" containers, but the standardisation of the bulk of the container deliveries considerably reduced the amount of work and time involved in packing.

Packages

Packages, designed primarily for the packing of stores too delicate or too bulky for packing in containers, were used more and more in order to employ aircraft capacity to the full, were packed in England at R.A.F. Station Henlow and in the Mediterranean at the S.O.E. packing stations.

The resilient material used in the making of the first packages, in 1941, was sorbo rubber sheeting. This material was cut according to the size of the stores to be parachuted and the whole was enclosed in a tailor-made canvas outer-cover. In 1942, hairlok – 2ins. thick sheeting of horse-hair impregnated with latex – superseded the sorbo rubber which was in short supply. Moulded boxes of hairlok were also available in different sizes, but for the most part packages of hairlok were made up from hairlok sheets. Until December 1943 all packages were packed in hairlok, and as the vast majority were tailor-made this was a long process, especially as each harness also had to be made individually as it depended upon the size of the package.

Mainly because of a hairlok shortage, but also because a speedier method of packing was necessary in order to keep pace with increasing package commitments, a pannier was introduced. The package pannier resembled a laundry basket in design in that it was in two parts which fitted one part into the other. It comprised a springy wire frame with a canvas cover: it was hinged with fittings at each corner to allow of its being opened out flat – an advantage to concealment in the field. These panniers were available in three sizes and were used, as far as size permitted for the packing of all items of a robust nature. Thus agents' suitcases of effects, food, clothing, and medical stores were packed in panniers, whilst W/T equipment and other fragile stores were still packed in hairlok.

Early in 1944 the 15in. "C" type container cell was put into use for package dropping. Ammunition and small arms were packed in this way. These cells required only a resilient base and top, for which hairlok discs were normally used. As the size of the cell was constant the web harness could be made up in advance in quantity.

In 1944 curled koran fibre was introduced as a supplementary packing material. Koran was a fibrous material of little resilience, but as it was available either loose or needled on canvas it could be used either for wrapping or for internal packing. Special packages of unusual size, such as skis, rifles, Bren guns, etc. were wrapped in needled koran with hairlok sheeting as a base.

The size of packages was limited by two factors, the size of the aircraft's despatching hole; and the ability of the despatcher to handle the packages. In the Halifax, the despatch hole was 40ins. in diameter. Packages were therefore restricted in size to a base of approximately 20ins. square with a height of say 30ins. The taller the package the narrower it had to be. Thus, skis, rifles, Brens, etc., being long but narrow, could comfortably be tipped out through the hole. Although Stirlings Mk V had large rectangular holes for despatching, package sizes were not increased because of the despatchers' difficulty in handling them.

The internal dimensions of the wire panniers were:

Type 'A'	22" x 16" x 16"
Type 'B'	24" x 18" x 20"
Type 'C'	29" x 18" x 13"

The 'C' type container cell had a height of 19ins. and a 15in. diameter.

The weight of packages was limited by the despatcher's ability to handle them, as each package had to be stored forward for take-off and brought to the rear for despatching. A limit of 120lbs. was therefore imposed for all packages. In exceptional circumstances – e.g. packages for special parties, when it was essential to keep the number to a minimum – weights up to 140lbs. were allowed, but the airfield had to be warned in advance so that arrangements could be made to provide an additional despatcher if need be.

Except for a few parachutes which had a single point, all parachutes had a two point suspension. The snaphooks on the parachute engaged the triangular rings sewn into the web harness of the package. The diameter of the canopy employed varied with the packed weight of the package thus:

> Weight up to 40lbs.   12'
> Weight 41 to 80lbs.   16'
> Weight 81 to 120lbs.   20'
> Weight 121 to 160lbs.   24'
> Weight 161 to 200lbs.   28'*
> * used only for "double" packages hooked together in the aircraft

Bulk delivery of clothing was carried out by dropping the bales as received from Ordnance on a 62in. parachute which acted as a drogue.

Packages, like containers, were identified by a stencilled number and were also in the later stages standardised. The number of packages carried in an aircraft was determined by the stowage space in the fuselage, Halifaxes could carry only six packages normally, although on some occasions the Halifaxes operating from Blida took as many as fifteen. A Stirling Mk V carried up to ten and a Liberator twelve packages.

Free Drops

Tests were carried out for the free dropping of packages (i.e. without parachutes) but the danger to the Reception Committees and the difficulty of dropping both parachuted and non-parachuted material at the same time were objections to this method. It was hardly ever used from England, but in emergencies when parachutes were in short supply it was a necessary expedient, and in operations to the Balkans was employed more extensively. It was possible to overcome the objections mentioned above in areas where large scale guerilla activities prevailed.

Where large areas were held by guerillas large bonfires could be lit at the dropping grounds and the Reception Committee could take post (if necessary) well back from the dropping ground. The suggestion was received from an Italian Partisan area in 1945 that in order to give warning of a free drop the aircraft should switch on its landing lights for some seconds on its run in. This suggestion was, after some discussion on security grounds, tried out and proved satisfactory, but it was only possible under two conditions: a strongly held Partisan area and the absence of any reasonable risk from enemy night fighters.

Types of Stores

The variety of stores delivered to the field both by container and package was tremendous. Every type of small arms from pistols to bazookas, together with the necessary ammunition; quantities of high explosive and made up charges; food, clothing and W/T equipment were the most important of the stores delivered.

In the later stages when groups of resistants had become more organised and more powerful, large quantities of petrol and oil were despatched in order to enable them to run their own transport. Instructions and explanations in various languages were sent with the arms and devices to enable resistance organisations to recognise and use them even if they had no trained operator in their midst. On one occasion, when dried egg powder had been sent to the Balkans for the first time, a message was received at Headquarters: "Thanks for new explosive. Please send instructions for use."

Officers in the field frequently asked for the delivery of special stores and these were often of a peculiar nature. As far as possible their requests were met. One woman officer in France who had a wooden leg was supplied with special socks over a period of several months. Special demands for sleeping pills or, more melodramatically, for poison pills were also received. On one occasion a layette for twins was delivered to the field in response to an urgent demand, and articles of minor sabotage value such as itching powder were often included. Perhaps one of the greatest packing achievements was the delivery to France of two hundred glass bottles of Printers' Ink – not one bottle was cracked.

Chapter 9

Technical Problems Confronting the RAF

The nature of the work undertaken by the S.D. Squadrons produced problems which often differed from those faced by aircraft engaged on normal bombing operations.

Navigation

In particular, the difficulties of navigation were especially acute for the S.D. crew, the success of whose work necessitated pin-point accuracy on a small, often ill-defined target after hours of flying across enemy country. The navigation, both on the journey and on the approach to the target, must obviously be of a very high order. Reception Committees were instructed to choose sites for their dropping grounds which could easily be seen from the air: but for many reasons this was often not possible for them, and the aircraft, after having found its target area, might have to search for some time before discovering lights half hidden by a wood, or obscured in a valley.

As far as possible the ordinary navigational aids such as Gee were used: but to Mediterranean based aircraft these advantages were denied, and in any case Gee assistance could not be accurately obtained at low altitudes. Ultimately the navigator nearly always had to rely on map-reading and D.R. and in order to enable him to do this, the pilot would take his aircraft across enemy-occupied Europe at a low altitude. Lysander pilots, with no wireless operator to help them, were especially dependent on accurate reading.

Terrain and Enemy Opposition

The necessity for low-level flying in turn raised its own problems. In some countries the absence of distinguishing land-marks made navigation difficult even from this height. The Belgian Ardennes, and the forested hills of Czechoslovakia were always particularly difficult areas for the S.D. crew to tackle. On the other hand, the presence of mountains made low-level flying particularly dangerous. In Yugoslavia, Austria and S.E. France, Reception Committees were often found in the steep valleys between the mountains.

If the release of supplies was made form a considerable height containers and parachutes might drift for miles and their discovery by the Germans would alert the whole district. Experiments were made from time to time with a device for delaying the opening of the parachute, but on the whole these did not meet with much success. If the load was not to be scattered over a wide area the pilot would have to take his aircraft down to a height of less than a thousand feet above the floor of the valley: a height which was often very much below the surrounding mountain tops. Handling a heavy bomber at this height in enclosed country, and at night, was a task requiring steady nerves and the highest possible degree of skill. A British Liaison Officer with a party on the Austrian border commented particularly in his report on the bravery of the R.A.F. crews in flying below the level of the mountain tops in order to make accurate drops in the valleys.

Whereas the high flying Main Force bombers were more susceptible to heavy flak and fighters, the low flying S.D. aircraft were extremely vulnerable to light flak of all types but to a lesser degree to fighters. Should, however, a fighter attack develop when S.D. aircraft was flying at 600-700 feet above ground level, with flaps down and at a reduced speed preparatory to dropping supplies, it would fall a certain victim owing to its complete inability to manoeuvre under such conditions.

Weather

One of the chief considerations for any aircraft flying by day or by night must be weather conditions. In the execution of a job in which accurate navigation was essential weather was even more important, and could spell the whole difference between success and failure. Bad visibility on the journey would mean that map-reading was impossible, and would to low flying aircraft inevitably increase the dangers of crashing into hills. If, when the target area had been successfully located, it was found to be covered in cloud, the pilot would be prevented from seeing the Reception Committee lights and be unable to make his drop. Moreover, when the lights were only ordinary hand torches it did not need thick cloud to obscure them, and they were often hidden by light ground haze or the local river mist that is frequently found in valleys.

Navigational Aids

In order to reduce the number of operations that failed because the aircraft could not find the Reception Committee (due either to navigation or to weather conditions), two instruments were employed which, it was hoped, would help to guide the aircraft to its target. The supply of these instruments was never large enough to meet the demand, and in most countries this proved the limiting factor to their use. Moreover, the delivery of highly complicated and fragile machinery to the field involved an inevitable percentage of loss by damage. Agents had to be specially trained to use them accurately, and often time could not be spared for a recruit to undertake this extra course.

Even if a serviceable instrument belonged to a Resistance Group which boasted a trained operator, it was not always possible for him to be present at every dropping operation – Reception Committees might be scattered over a large area. To the man on the ground the employment of these instruments meant the transport of additional and compromising material: to the aircrew, their use involved yet another set of buttons and gadgets which needed attention. The problems of fitting and maintenance of a highly technical instrument in the aircraft were also considerable.

Rebecca/Eureka

This was a type of "beam" navigational aid which enabled an aircraft fitted with Rebecca to home on to a Eureka sometimes from a distance of 70 miles. In Western Europe, and above all France, Eurekas were dropped throughout 1943, and the field was urged to use them whenever possible. Yet results were on the whole unsatisfactory: a large proportion of the Eurekas despatched were never heard of again, and the R.A.F. were not always able to attempt the few operations which were mounted with the aid of Rebecca/Eureka, to the discouragement of the field. Of these operations which were attempted with Rebecca/Eureka assistance a very high proportion of success was achieved. Towards the end of 1943, a system of "Depot" grounds was employed in France on which permanent Reception Committees, usually with a Eureka, watched for aircraft who were unable to locate their primary target. The system was very successful, and over a period must have saved the R.A.F. many abortive sorties, and provided Resistance with many container loads which would otherwise have been returned to base. Eurekas were also used to a lesser extent in the Low Countries and in Scandinavia, and achieved perhaps their greatest success in Norway.

A fixed "Beacon Grid" was planned for France during 1943, involving the use of larger and more powerful Eurekas than were normally sent to the field. These were to be under the control of a specially trained operator who would come on the air in answer to a special B.B.C. message. The locations of these Beacons were fixed by the R.A.F. at sites which would most help the aircraft operating into France, and the fixed Beacon operator was usually independent of any Reception Committee, and did not himself receive any stores direct. This grid proved extremely difficult to put into practice at a time when conditions in the field were becoming more and more dangerous; but several beacons were eventually set up, and proved of inestimable value.

In the Mediterranean, the supply position proved the chief limiting factor to the use of Rebecca/Eureka, but during 1944 a number were despatched to the field. Eureka was used with great enthusiasm on the part of the Air Force for daylight operations. Whenever possible the R.A.F. squadrons engaged on S.D. work in the Mediterranean theatre were equipped with Rebecca. No Beacon Grid system was adopted here, since it was impossible to obtain the more powerful Eureka sets. As in England, the Eurekas were packed and held by S.O.E., but the R.A.F. authorities were responsible for their maintenance, and of course for the fitting and maintenance of Rebeccas.

S-Phones

A method by which direct telephonic communication is established between ground and air would, it was hoped, fulfil a navigational function, since the agent on the ground could direct the aircraft towards him. Owing to language difficulties, however, and to the fact that in practice it proved more complicated than at first sight it seemed to direct one out of probably several aircraft flying in the neighbourhood, this particular function was not developed very far in Western Europe.

In the Mediterranean the difference of language did not present the same difficulty since there were nearly always British Liaison Officers at the dropping grounds. One of the most interesting uses of an S-phone was by Pilot Officer McGregor who landed in Yugoslavia with an S-phone and a collapsible bicycle, found a landing-ground the same night, and as a one man Reception Committee received a Dakota a few hours later. On several occasions when French or Belgian Reception Committees had had to move their grounds at the last minute, as a result of German measures, the S-phone was used to instruct the pilot on the location of the new ground. There was the time when an aircraft operating to an area near Bordeaux searched in vain for some time for the lights of the Reception Committee. At last the rear gunner saw them over his shoulder, and shouted over the inter-com "There they are! What bloody awful lights!" The voice of the officer on the ground came immediately back to him by S-phone and inter-com: "So would yours be, if the Gestapo were only a mile away from you!"

But the principal value of S-phones in Western Europe turned out in the end to be their use as a method of passing information. It was unlikely in most cases that a Reception Committee could provide an English speaker (and only too often a crew would be forced to switch off the S-phone as soon as contact had been established since a flood of Gallic eloquence was preventing the use of the inter-com). S.O.E. Country Section Officers were therefore allowed in the aircraft by special permission. On these occasions, while the aircraft was making its circuit and dropping the containers a long conversation could be held between the agent on the ground and his Country Section Officer in the aircraft. In the case of organisers who had lost their W/T operator or his set, an S-phone conversation might be the only means of re-establishing contact with H.Q. By this means much valuable and up-to-date information was transmitted.

Chapter 10

Reception Committees

Throughout the whole period the development of Resistance depended to a very considerable extent on the efficiency of Air Supply as a channel of communication. In Western Europe the difficulty of delivering stores by Sea in the face of the increasing German surveillance of the Coastal areas served to put the emphasis still further on supply by Air. This in itself involved a developed organisation in the field, at S.O.E. Headquarters, and in the R.A.F.

In general, the ideal organisation of Resistance as S.O.E. saw it involved the setting up of small independent clandestine groups, each one separated from its neighbour so that security should not be endangered, and with the emphasis all the time on the establishment of small bands of entirely reliable men rather than the collection of large conglomerations of amateurs and enthusiasts.

The conditions in different countries, however, had obviously to be taken into consideration by S.O.E.; and these varied considerably. In Poland, for example, where a long history of underground warfare had already given the people intensive experience of the methods of conducting such a campaign, the English had little to teach and a great deal to learn, and S.O.E. confined itself mainly to supplying the already existing and well organised underground armies in Poland. In France, two separate types of Resistance Organisation grew up: the one inspired by, and owing its military allegiance to, General de Gaulle, the other a British-controlled network of small S.O.E.-type circuits headed by British officers. In the Balkans and Italy where considerable national movements were already in operation, S.O.E.'s task was to send political and military liaison Missions to make contact with the various leaders. In Scandinavia, Holland and Denmark, various types of indigenous Resistance movements grew up, and to these S.O.E. sent technical instructions on such subjects as weapons, explosives, and sabotage, and liaison officers to co-ordinate their activities and also brought leaders to England for instruction.

Whatever type of underground armies developed in a country, the organisation of an efficient system for ordering and receiving supplies by air was clearly a task of the very first importance, since only by this means could the resistants hope to collect sufficient equipment and reinforcements. The training of both agents and aircrews in Reception Committee procedure was obviously essential if air supply was to be carried out efficiently, and in 1943 a special "Reception Committee" School was established by S.O.E. in which Organisers learnt the principles of reception procedure including selection of grounds, lights, disposal of stores and S-phone and Rebecca/Eureka drill. It was perhaps unfortunate that such a school was not established earlier both in England and in the Mediterranean since there is little doubt that its effect on the ratio of success of air operations was considerable. Training for pick-up operations was particularly intensive: for these agents who it might be expected, would later need to lay on such operations, a special week's course was organised. During this period agents were taught the particular problems faced by the Lysander or Hudson pilot, the varying lengths of fields necessary for the different types of aircraft and above all the importance of transferring the incoming and the outward loads as quickly as possible. It was obviously essential for both pilot and Reception Committee that the aircraft should remain on the ground for as short a time as possible: and agents were therefore taught how to transfer baggage and passengers with the minimum delay.

Since it was the Air Force upon whom fell the burden of transporting stores for long distances over enemy country, it was essential that whatever system was used should be acceptable to and fully trusted by the Air authorities. The R.A.F. themselves decided what system of lights on the ground should be used in order to help their aircraft to find the dropping point. This lighting system might vary from country to country, but basically it consisted of torches or bonfires arranged in a certain pattern, with a flashing light which gave an agreed Morse recognition signal.

Owing to the difficulties of navigating to a small pinpoint at night the bulk of the work undertaken by the R.A.F. from the U.K. was done on moonlight nights. The later development of navigational aids such as Rebecca/Eureka and S-phone, and also the relaxation of German control, which permitted the use of bonfires, enabled the R.A.F. to increase the quantity of material delivered during the non-moon periods; but even then it was during the two weeks immediately before and after full moon that the weight of these supplies were delivered.

The Mediterranean-based S.D. aircraft, owing to the very different conditions within the countries to which they operated, were able to carry out their work in moon and non-moon periods alike. Apart from the moon, the working time of Reception Committees was determined by the "stand-by" times, which were fixed by the R.A.F. in order to allow for variation in the weather. For U.K.-based aircraft, for instance, the Reception Committees normally stood by for four hours. A week or ten days before the beginning of each moon period, the Reception Committee were given reception instructions and the times of stand-by. In some cases, particularly in the early days, an agent might report that owing to security difficulties he could not arrange to stand-by at the regulation times; if possible the R.A.F. would then accept curtailed or alternative stand-by times for his particular operation.

The selection of grounds suitable for "parachutages" was one of the most important functions in laying on an air delivery, since a badly placed Reception Committee in a valley or near a wood could only be spotted from an aircraft with the greatest difficulty. Wide open spaces, if possible near some landmark, such as a river, lake, or railway line were the best grounds for Reception Committees; but these, of course, while perfect from the R.A.F. point of view, were often unsafe for the men in the field. Reception Committees, emulating the Butcher, often "Fixed the spot unfrequented by man: A dismal and desolate valley", which, though comparatively safe for them, was practically undiscoverable from the air.

A balance had always to be struck between security on the ground and the necessity for easy recognition from above. The co-ordinates of chosen grounds were sent in by W/T to the appropriate Country Section of S.O.E. by map reference, and the grounds, if agreed by the Air Ministry, were confirmed back to the field. In this way a register of grounds was gradually built up until at D-Day there were over 5,500 dropping grounds in France and in Yugoslavia.

The initiative in arranging for an actual dropping of material was nearly always taken by the field, although Country Sections might sometimes make suggestions to their Organisers. As a rule, however, the agent concerned, having decided that he needed a delivery of stores, would select a suitable ground, and arrange for a Reception Committee to man it. This Reception Committee worked under a Chief, and was of varying size, depending on the strength of the circuit, and the number of containers that it would have to receive. The Reception Committee was sometimes as small as three men: in the later years, and in some countries such as Poland, sometimes as large as five hundred. In the Balkan countries the same dropping zones were used over and over again for air deliveries with an almost permanent establishment of Partisans to act as Reception Committee. The co-ordinates of the ground (if they had not previously been submitted), details of the stores required, the signal letter to be flashed by the Reception Committee, and the B.B.C. message to be used as their signal for the alert, were all sent by W/T to S.O.E. H.Q. In addition, if the Organiser possessed a Eureka or S-phone, the intended use of this instrument would be given. If for any reason the Reception Committee was unable to stand-by for the whole of the moon period, the alternative dates would be sent.

The operation, after having been agreed by the R.A.F. and the Air Liaison Section of S.O.E., would be mounted by the Country Section, and the agent in the field would be notified to that effect.

It was now only a question of waiting for the weather – often and especially in winter, a long, dreary, and disappointing period. Sometimes the squadrons would think during the day that an operation could be attempted that night, and the appropriate B.B.C. message would therefore be transmitted; but later the weather might close down and the aircraft would be unable to fly. By then it would be too late to warn the Reception Committee, who were doomed to spending four hours in vain out on a field in the middle of the night.

Balkan Reception Committees were given warning of an operation directly by signal while the B.B.C. messages which were used to alert the Reception Committees of Western Europe including Italy, were usually transmitted in news bulletins.

In the case of France, for instance, they went out after the French News at 1.30, 2.30, 6.30, and 9.15. They consisted of a short, and usually meaningless phrase, and were introduced by the announcer as "messages personelles." To anybody not concerned, ten minutes worth

Above: Westland Lysander R9125 in the markings of a Special Duties squadron. This aircraft is known to have been taken on charge by 161 (Special Duties) Squadron at RAF Tempsford (which also had a forward operating base at RAF Tangmere, Sussex, from where Lysander sorties were usually flown) in October 1944.

Below: Pilots of 'A' Flight of 161 (Special Duties) Squadron with their CO. Pictured lined up beside a Lysander, they are, from left to right: Pilot Officer J.A. McCairns, Squadron Leader H.B. Verity, Wing Commander P.C. Pickard (CO), Pilot Officer Vaughan-Fowler, and Flying Officer F.E. Rymills.

Above: The Special Duties
squadron Westland
Lysander flown by
Squadron Leader J. Nesbitt-
Dufort after an accident
whilst landing in France.

Right: A cargo of SOE mail.
Seen here is the volume of
courier mail brought back in
a single Special Duties
squadron pick-up mission
on the night of 2-3 June 1944,
pictured after having been
unloaded from the aircraft
involved.

Above: A Lockheed Hudson of an RAF Special Duties squadron.

Below: A rare photograph of a 138 (Special Duties) Squadron Short Stirling at RAF Tempsford during 1944. The individual in the foreground is believed to be the bomb aimer of this aircraft. (Courtesy of Mark Hillier)

Above: An airman in the cockpit of a 138 (Special Duties) Squadron Stirling Mk.IV at RAF Tempsford, 1944. (Courtesy of Mark Hillier)

Below: Ground crew loading supply canisters into a 148 Squadron Handley Page Halifax, BB335 coded 'FS-M', at Foggia in the summer of 1944. (The Andy Thomas Collection)

Above: A 148 Squadron aircraft drops supplies to Tito's partisans during 1944. (The Andy Thomas Collection)

Above: The RAF's support of SOE and the various Resistance units came at a cost. This is the wreckage of the 218 (Gold Coast) Squadron Short Stirling, BK712, coded 'HA-D' and flown by Pilot Officer W.G. Shillinglaw and his crew, which was shot down during a supply drop on the night of 21/22 June 1943. A victim of the Messerschmitt Bf 110 flown *Leutnant* Schnaufer, BK712 crashed near the village of Langdorp, just east of the town of Aarschot. (The Andy Saunders Collection)

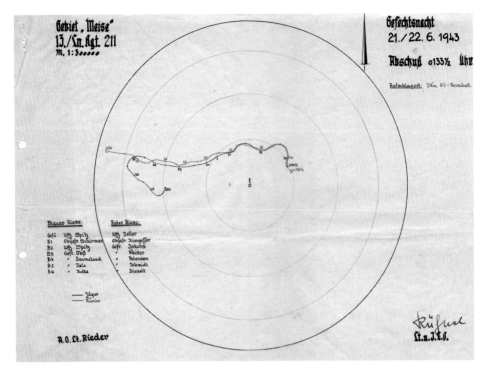

Above: A plot which shows the course taken by Pilot Officer Shillinglaw's Stirling during the pursuit by *Leutnant* Schnaufer's and *Leutnant* Baro's Messerschmitt Bf 110 in the early hours of 22 June 1943. The path of the British bomber is indicated by the lower, curving line, which charts its flight path between 01.26 hours to 01.33 hours, whilst the top line is that of the *Luftwaffe* night fighter. (The Andy Saunders Collection)

Right: Dated 9 November 1942, this briefing photograph shows a landing site codenamed *Eclipse*. It maybe that this was the very airfield to which Squadron Leader Hugh Verity, at the controls of a 161 (Special Duties) Squadron Lysander, was tasked to fly, from RAF Tangmere, on the night of 24 February 1943. If so, it is a field near Issoudon, south of the Loire near Bourges. Verity's passenger was Jean Moulin. The flight was unsuccessful, fog forcing a return to the UK.

Left: The unveiling of the SOE and Resistance memorial in the village of Beleymas in the Dordogne in the years after the Second World War. Part of the memorial's inscription states that, 'At this place was made the first parachute drop of personnel and equipment for the resistance in France by the British War Office'. This was Operation *Corsican*, the first simultaneous drop of men and weapons (which were in two containers) in France. (Courtesy of Mark Hillier)

Above: A view of the ante-room at SOE's cottage at Tangmere in West Sussex, which was used by agents en route to or from their missions to the Continent. The original caption points out the 'remains of presents [champagne bottles] brought by agents to the pilots may be seen on the mantelpiece'.

Above: Described as 'one of the most secret airfields of the war', RAF Tempsford in Bedfordshire was the home of a number of Special Duties squadrons. Located near to the end of one of the runways on the airfield, this structure, the Gibraltar Farm Barn, was adapted to continue looking like a normal farm barn but in fact served as the holding point for SOE agents immediately before they were taken to the aircraft that were to transport them into Europe. Here agents were also supplied with their equipment. (Courtesy of Peter Skynner; www.geograph.org.uk)

Below: An original memorial plaque that used to hang on the wall inside the Gibraltar Farm Barn at Tempsford. It can be seen at on display in The Fenland and West Norfolk Aviation Museum, whilst a replacement is at Tempsford. Some of the names associated with Tempsford and the Gibraltar Farm Barn are Odette and Peter Churchill, Violette Szarbo, Wing Commander Yeo-Thomas, and personnel involved in Operation *Gunnerside*, the destruction of the heavy water plant in Norway. (Courtesy of Evelyn Simak; www.geograph.org.uk)

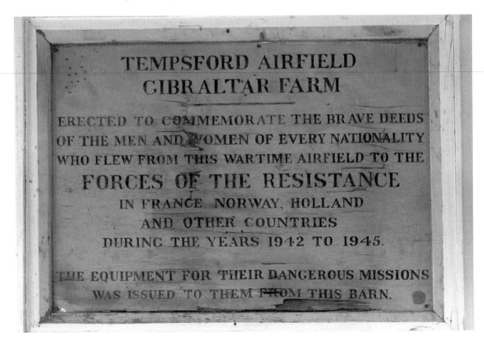

TEMPSFORD AIRFIELD
GIBRALTAR FARM

ERECTED TO COMMEMORATE THE BRAVE DEEDS
OF THE MEN AND WOMEN OF EVERY NATIONALITY
WHO FLEW FROM THIS WARTIME AIRFIELD TO THE

FORCES OF THE RESISTANCE
IN FRANCE NORWAY, HOLLAND
AND OTHER COUNTRIES
DURING THE YEARS 1942 TO 1945.

THE EQUIPMENT FOR THEIR DANGEROUS MISSIONS
WAS ISSUED TO THEM FROM THIS BARN.

of "messages personelles" must have been boring in the extreme: but to the men of the Reception Committees waiting all over France it was the call to action. When they heard their particular message – "Les lions sont terribles," or "Adolf a deux sous" – they would leave their homes and families, and go out into the night to the pre-arranged ground, carrying with them such material as was necessary to their task. The most important equipment they needed was their torches. These were ordinary, unmarked hand-torches, pathetically small from the pilot's point of view, but as large as a man dared carry about in France.

After a time the Gestapo learned to know these torches, and any man caught with one in the country after dark was immediately under suspicion. An S-phone could be strapped round a man's waist and hidden fairly effectively under a raincoat. A Eureka involved carrying two heavy suitcases. Every pound of such equipment made the task of the Reception Committee, not only more arduous, but also more dangerous. They would collect on their grounds in ones and twos, on foot or by bicycle, sometimes even by car or lorry. It was essential to have a good excuse for being out so late at night, in view of the curfew which the Germans imposed on the country. Sometimes the ground chosen was a field belonging to a nearby farmhouse, and the farmer and his labourers would form the Reception Committee. Sometimes a Reception Committee was less lucky, and might have quite considerable distances to cover to reach the appointed place.

When they had reached the field, there was nothing to do but wait, alert all the time for the sound of aircraft engines, or the noise of a German patrol. There was no way of telling which was their particular aircraft of all the aircraft flying in the region, and often Reception Committees would take up their positions and flash their torches, only to hear the aircraft disappearing into the distance, possibly to deliver stores to another point, possibly on a bombing operation. Sometimes the aircraft was not English at all, and Reception Committees would flash hopefully at a passing Junkers or Dornier. At last, if the weather had been kind to them, the aircraft destined for their particular ground would arrive, circle once or twice and drop its containers and packages.

A great deal depended on the accuracy of the drop. If the stores fell on the ground, or close to it, the work of collecting them was comparatively simple and rapid; but if, as often happened (particularly if the aircraft made the drop from a greater height than usual or if there was a strong wind), the containers and packages were dispersed over a large area, the Reception Committee might well spend the rest of the night looking for them. To leave containers with their parachutes in a spot where they might be discovered by the Germans was to invite Gestapo examination of the whole district, and could not be risked.

When the material had all been collected, it was either buried near the ground or taken away at once and stored elsewhere; then in the early hours of the morning – and sometimes, if there had been difficulties, even after daylight – the Reception Committee would return to their homes, knowing that they had to face a normal day's work since it was impossible for them to admit that they had not been sleeping soundly all night. Even this was not necessarily the end of the story. The cover which was usually given for S.D. operations in Western Europe was the dropping of leaflets usually on a town at some distance from the target area, though care had to be taken in choosing a district which would not compromise other dropping grounds. At least one indignant agent reported that after spending the night on Reception Committee work, he had been forced by the Germans to spend the whole of the next day picking up the leaflets which had been dropped by S.D. aircraft.

The work of Reception Committees in partisan-held areas was less dangerous than that of their colleagues elsewhere, but certainly not less arduous. The disposal of hundreds of containers delivered by large scale operations involving scores of aircraft, and the management of a landing field, where Dakotas came in one after another throughout the night, demanded a high degree of organisation.

After the operation, the results were immediately sent to the Organiser or the local Air Operations Officer, who transmitted them by W/T to S.O.E. Headquarters. In the Mediterranean, particularly full and detailed reports based on a standard questionnaire were despatched after every air delivery. By the time they arrived the Country Section would also hold the pilot's report on the operation. Discrepancies might arise between the two reports, and the Country Section would then do its best to clear them up. If some containers had hung-up in the aircraft a telegram would be sent at once to the field to set the minds of the Reception Committee at rest and to prevent their searching uselessly for containers that had not in fact been dropped.

Sometimes a Reception Committee would receive by mistake the loads of two aircraft, and this would then be explained to them; sometimes, on the other hand they might receive nothing, and the operation would then be remounted. If the pilot of the aircraft reported that although he had found the exact pinpoint there had been no Reception Committee, enquiries were made from the field. The ground might be badly placed, torches might have been too dim; a German patrol might have scattered them at the last minute, or the B.B.C. message might not have been heard – there were any number of reasons why a Reception Committee could not be completely reliable. On the other hand, since the navigation of an aircraft to a small pinpoint in enemy territory is not an easy matter it was also possible that the pilot was mistaken in thinking he had found the right spot. An analysis and comparison of the reports received from the field and from the Squadrons not only gave details of how much material had been dropped and received, but also constituted a valuable survey of the efficiency of [the] Reception Committee system.

In different countries the reception of supplies varied both in method and in the conditions in which the work was carried out. In Poland, for instance, the organisation of Reception Committees, like the rest of the Resistance movement, was on a more military basis than in any other country. Committees were usually large, enabling the men to deal with large numbers of containers very quickly, especially as the "H" type container was normally used in Poland with each of the five cells packed as a complete unit so that each member of the Reception Committee could take one and carry it home himself immediately. The difficulties with which the Reception Committees had to contend were much the same as in other countries: curfew, problems of transport, and weather. Farm carts were often used to carry containers from the dropping grounds and sometimes a civilian Pole employed on transport work by the Germans would bring along his lorry. The weather in winter was bitter and one Polish Officer who came out of the country reported that members of Reception Committees had been known to freeze to death in the snow while waiting for their aircraft. Torches were usually used for signalling, and in the later stages it was possible in some areas to light bonfires.

Throughout the period the Poles themselves showed the greatest determination not to lose an aircraft load and waste a sortie. Reception Committee exercises in England, which were later used for all Country Sections, were first instituted by the Poles. Nearly all the operations laid on were given alternative points and often in addition a "safe area" in which the pilot might drop his load if both the first Reception Committees were absent.

The strongest measures were taken against defaulting members of Polish Reception Committees, on more than one occasion the death sentence was carried out. The organisation on the ground, the collection of containers, and the checking of stores was astonishingly detailed and efficient, and several times the Polish Quartermaster in the field was able to report minor variations of load even before the Packing Station had noticed them.

Since Reception Committees were the only means by which the Resistance Organisations could be fed with arms and supplies it was naturally to their interest to ensure that they were as efficient as possible. No amount of enthusiasm in the field, however, could compensate for a mistake made in England. The procedure for arranging a supply dropping or landing operation was necessarily extremely complex and involved, and while the chain from the Resistance Groups' demand for supplies to their receipt was very long, a weakness in any of the links would render it useless. A very high degree of efficiency in the staff work entailed in mounting S.D. operations was therefore required both at S.O.E. H.Q. and on the part of the R.A.F. authorities concerned, all of whom were conscious that their work directly affected the safety and lives of men in the field.

Chapter 11

SOE and RAF Procedures, UK and Mediterranean

In the first two years the only aircraft available for S.O.E. operations (and these were shared by S.I.S.) were those of 1419 Flight. These resources were increased, until in 1944 Special Duty operations were being flown by Tempsford, 3 Group, 38 Group and 46 Group. It was therefore was necessary to develop a very complex system of control and liaison.

The normal method of control of its squadrons by the R.A.F. – from Command through Group to Station – had, in the case of S.D. operations, serious disadvantages. The main consideration, of course, was that of security: in order to safeguard the lives both of the men in the field and of the aircrews it was essential that as few people as possible should know that operations of this type were being carried out. The details of the actual pinpoints must be transmitted only to those persons whose work necessitated a full knowledge. Moreover, each S.D. operation was an individual mission – each aircraft had to be specially loaded and each aircrew separately briefed.

On a good night operations from Tempsford might be flown to five or more countries of Western Europe. Above all, the staff procedure employed must be both flexible and speedy: decisions must be taken quickly and passed immediately to the authorities concerned. There must be the least possible delay in notifying all the various departments of the operational programme. The troops served by the S.O.E. and R.A.F. authorities by means of S.D. operations, were, unlike normal troops, not in easy communication with their commanders. Apart from the known dangers faced by a W/T operator every time he came up on the air, his periods of contact with H.Q. were necessarily limited and defined. S.O.E., and to a less extent the R.A.F., were bound to work within the framework created by this fixed timetable of W/T schedules.

The normal R.A.F. machinery which was built for the requirements of large scale, multiple-aircraft operations, whether bomber or fighter, was clearly not the ideal means of controlling an aerodrome from which operations so diverse and so individual were undertaken. It was therefore considered by the R.A.F. that some procedure other than that usually adopted must be used to control the S.D. squadrons, and from the beginning the Air Ministry itself took a special and direct responsibility in this connection.

3039/PDDO, 20 August 1940

On the formation of 419 Flight it was ruled that while 11 Group of Fighter Command should be responsible for its administration the Flight should, for operational control, come directly under the Air Ministry. In October of 1940, when 419 Flight was transferred to the Bomber Command Station of Stradishall, Bomber Command took up the problem of the operational control of the Flight and suggested that unless its work was very specialised it should be controlled in the normal way.

M/XX/382, 24 February 1942 (in S.O.E.'s files)

A meeting was held at Air Ministry on 24th February 1942 at the instance of D.C.A.S. to discuss the question of the control of 138 and 161 Squadrons and to consider whether control could not be exercised by Bomber Command through the Director of Bombing operations at the Air Ministry.

It was decided that some deviation from the normal machinery of operational control of Bomber Command was essential; that the higher authority must on many matters deal directly with the unit (and not through the normal channels of the group); and that an R.A.F. officer should be posted or attached to S.O.E. to organise the air transport side of S.O.E.'s work.

BC/s.24455/Ops.1(B) and S.5998/01

After correspondence between Bomber Command and the Air Ministry, it was agreed that while the details of the task to be undertaken by 419 Flight would be communicated direct to the Station Commander, the normal machinery of operational control within the Command would otherwise operate, and the Station Commander, in conjunction with his meteorological advisers, was responsible for deciding whether operational conditions were practicable. This method of R.A.F. operational control was maintained until the autumn of 1943.

The Air Ministry department responsible for the detailed operational control of the S.D. squadron, under A.C.A.S.(I) was A.I.2.(c), working directly under D.D.I.2., later D. of I.(R). The duties of this department included the "vetting" of pinpoints submitted by the field and, in the early years, the day-to-day operational control of S.D. operations on behalf of the R.A.F. A.I.2.(c)'s opposite number in S.O.E. was the Air Liaison Section(AL), commanded at first by a Lieutenant Colonel and later by a Group Captain. In the autumn of 1943, in order to strengthen the liaison between S.O.E. and the R.A.F. on a higher level, a senior R.A.F. officer was appointed as Air Adviser to S.O.E. (see Part I. Section 43).

Within S.O.E. the work of laying on air operations was shared between the Country Sections and AL. It was the Country Sections who were responsible for the Resistance Organisations within their particular country, for the despatch of all W/T messages to and the receipt of all W/T messages from the field, and who therefore were the first to deal with requests for air deliveries and details of dropping or landing.

It was AL who had to arrange with the R.A.F. authorities for the despatch of aircraft in answer to these requests and who acted as the channel between S.O.E. and the Air authorities concerned with S.D. operations. Direct communication between AL and the R.A.F. authorities at Tempsford was not permitted, however. AL worked with A.I.2(c) only, but an S.O.E. Liaison Officer was attached to every airfield from which S.D. sorties were flown. (See Appendix G for Directive to Liaison Officer). This Officer's duties included receiving agents, checking their equipment and preparing them in their striptease suits for their drop, the correct selection of packages and containers for each operation and each aircraft, and the briefing of the despatchers. Being of course in direct communication with the Air Liaison Section, he was often able to inform S.O.E. of decisions made at the airfield before the news would otherwise have reached them through the normal A.I.2(c) channel.

Telegrams from the field requesting air deliveries which were received by S.O.E. were sent simultaneously to the Country Section concerned and to the Air Liaison Section. After a preliminary check the Country Section Air Operations Officer would request AL to proceed with the operation. The pinpointing section within AL would then work out the ground in detail, plotting the proposed dropping or landing ground on a large scale map, and pass it to A.I.2(c) for their approval (see Appendix E for details). A.I.2(c)'s primary responsibility was in the selection of suitable pinpoints for S.D. operations: if the ground appeared to be too near a danger spot such as a night fighter aerodrome or flak emplacement, A.I.2(c) refused to accept it and the field was told to select a point further away.

If the ground was approved, AL informed the Country Section who in their turn signalled the field. The Country Section then ordered from the stores department of AL the necessary containers and packages for the operation, and if personnel were concerned arrangements were made for their kitting up. The B.B.C. messages were laid on by the Country Sections, stores were packed and full details of the operations were then sent out by AL to the aerodromes whose squadrons would carry them. Even after A.I.2(c)'s approval the Station Commander might refuse to accept certain pinpoints, but this happened rarely; normally when suggested grounds had been agreed by A.I.2.(c) they were accepted by the squadrons concerned.

It should be noted that this procedure for the meticulous checking of dropping points was evolved only after some experience of S.D. operations: in the early days rather more amateur methods were used. Country Sections would tell AL that they wished to drop a man within a certain area and AL would obtain Air Ministry approval not for a pinpoint but for a whole area. An S.O.E. officer would go down to the aerodrome with the agent and the two of them would go into conference with the pilot of the aircraft to decide upon the exact pinpoint. This might not be fixed until as late as 1600 hours – when take-off might be at 1900 hours.

Once details of the operations had been passed to the aerodromes the Operations Room within AL Section took over S.O.E.'s share of control, working in the closest liaison with both the R.A.F. and the Country Sections. Once an operation was ready – operational orders having been sent to the airfields and the necessary stores having been packed – there was nothing to do but wait for good weather: a very variable period. In some cases operations were held up for as long as five months, in others they might be despatched the very next night. Even when all arrangements had been made between the field and H.Q. and between S.O.E. and the R.A.F., there were circumstances which necessitated the cancellation or temporary withdrawal of an operation. The Organiser in the field or his W/T operator might be arrested; the Germans might unexpectedly intensify their controls in the area – sometimes even camping their troops on the prospective dropping ground by unlucky accident; messages or codes might be captured. Daily alterations in the list of "Operations Ready" were inevitable and could only be met by daily confirmation and reconfirmation by the Operations Room to the R.A.F. authorities.

Since the number of aircraft allotted to S.O.E. was, from 1942 onwards, unable to meet the increasing demands from the field, the list of "Operations Ready" was almost always far larger than the squadrons could possibly hope to complete. It was therefore necessary for S.O.E. to indicate the priority of the various operations, so that at least the most important deliveries could be attempted. Priority was shown by means of "stars" which were allotted by S.O.E. A Country Section Head could accord an operation one "star", a Regional Head (covering more than one Country Section) two "stars". Three "stars" were allotted by the Brigadier commanding the London Group of all S.O.E.'s Western European Country Sections, and were only given for vital and urgent operations such as coups-de-main. The "star" value of operations was included in the list of "Operations Ready" given to A.I.2(c).

During the early years the Operations Room's opposite number in the R.A.F. was A.I.2(c), who carried out in the same way a day-to-day control of operations on behalf of the R.A.F. A list of the operations ready for the next night together with their "star" priority was checked by the Operations Room with the Country Sections and passed to A.I.2(c) each afternoon. It was then transmitted by them to Tempsford (see Appendix F for details of Tempsford procedure). Conversely, the Station Commander's decision on which operations were to be attempted each night was sent along the same channels in reverse – to A.I.2(c) and so on to S.O.E.'s Operations Room. The Operations Room, acting as link between the R.A.F. and the Country Sections, then passed the list on to the Country Sections concerned who arranged with the B.B.C. for the transmission of the appropriate messages. At the airfields, the R.A.F. authorities, in conjunction with the S.O.E. Liaison Officer, was responsible for loading and briefing the aircraft and aircrews for the separate operations; A.I.2(c) had satisfied themselves that the grounds to which sorties would be flown were operationally practicable; and from S.O.E. H.Q. the B.B.C. messages or signals advising the field of the intended despatch of an aircraft were being transmitted. The chain was now complete, and everything possible had been done to ensure that the Reception Committee and the aircraft met at the same point in time and space.

Last minute changes in the programme were notified by A.I.2(c) to the Operations Room and passed on to the Country Section in the normal way; but after the final B.B.C. message transmissions of the day it was impossible to cancel the Reception Committee's attendance on the field. A Duty Officer was present in the Operations Room throughout the night to deal with emergencies, and to receive the reports telephoned through by the S.O.E. Liaison Officers at the aerodromes from the returning aircrews. In the morning these results were passed on to the Country Sections who were thus in a position to assess the situation. As the list of "Operations Ready" was telephoned by the Operations Room to A.I.2.(c) on the afternoon of the day before they were to be attempted it was not normally possible to make changes based on the results of the previous night, but in special cases – for instance if the men in the field were actually engaged with the enemy – the R.A.F. were prepared to accept last minute amendments to the list that had been given.

Pick-up operations, which were flown by "A" Flight of 161 Squadron, were arranged in much the same way as dropping operations. As an additional check on the description of the ground submitted by an agent, air photographs of the grounds considered were always obtained in the case of landing operations. Requests for such photographs were submitted to R.A.F. Station at Medmenham (A.C.I.U.) Z Section (G.I.L.D.) by Air Ministry.

MIM/MS/16 opened 1 September 1942, which was changed to MIM/TS/212/1/Ops
In the early days of 1942 requests came through A.D.I.(Ph) and were dealt with by R Section (Combined Operations). With the increase in demands for this type of work, and the preoccupation of R Section with preparations for the African landing, the requests were passed through R Section to Z Section, where they were dealt with by one or two senior or experienced interpreters. A.I.2(c) now became known as the originators and it began to appear more clearly what was required. A

more detailed and specialised form of report was evolved. In order to save time requests were often submitted by telephone as well as by correspondence, and the volume steadily increased throughout 1943 and 1944. A very large number of Topographical Reports were produced at A.I.2(c)'s request at short notice, and the technique evolved and the extremely speedy manner with which all demands were dealt with deserved the highest praise. A very high proportion of successful landing operations in Western Europe can be directly attributed to the work done at Medmenham.

During the first years "A" Flight moved to an advanced base at Tangmere for the moon period, and although no permanent S.O.E. Liaison Officer was attached to them there an AL Section Officer and a Country Section Officer went down to the aerodrome on operational nights to give the pilot last minute information on the security of the ground and to welcome any agents that he brought back. In the winter of 1943/44 it was decided that "A" Flight should remain at Tempsford in spite of the extra flying distance this often involved.

In the autumn of 1943, when Bomber Command took over operational control of S.D. aircraft in England, the day-to-day operational control hitherto vested in A.I.2(c) was transferred to Bomber Command to which S.O.E. and S.I.S. Liaison Officers were posted. A.I.2(c) continued to receive the details of all proposed pinpoints and in the first instance to accept or refuse them; and especially on landing operations the department maintained its interest and influence. The daily list of "Operations Ready" however, was no longer the concern of A.I.2(c) and was now transmitted direct from S.O.E.'s Operations Room to Bomber Command. The use of 3 Group aircraft in the early months of 1944 involved no problem, since this Group came under Bomber Command; but further complications were introduced when 38 Group, under A.E.A.F., also joined the S.D. effort. S.O.E.'s Operations Room was then responsible for dividing the list of "Operations Ready" between A.E.A.F. and Bomber Command and for ensuring that each authority was informed when necessary of the operations being undertaken by the other.

As a rule 38 Group undertook only "standard load" operations for S.O.E. owing to the difficulties of transporting special containers. For the same reason, aircraft operating from the more distant 3 Group airfields carried only standard loads. All "special load" operations were carried by Tempsford or by the American Squadrons at Alconbury (later

Harrington) since these airfields were in close proximity to the packing stations.

Occasionally, Mosquito operations were carried out by 46 Group for S.O.E. These involved only a small quantity of stores and were used only when organisations in the field had urgently requested some small but vital store, such as money or W/T crystals, and were unable to receive the normal Halifax container load. There were few of these operations and each was arranged individually with 46 Group. S.O.E. Liaison Officers normally went down to the aerodromes concerned in order to assist at the briefing and to hear the reports of the returning aircrews.

The American contribution to the S.D. effort consisted of two Liberator Squadrons of the 8th U.S.A.A.F. based first at Alconbury and later at Harrington which became operational in the first months of 1944. Pinpoints for operations to be carried out by these squadrons were submitted by S.O.E. to A.I.2(c) in the normal way, but the Americans, while accepting the facilities afforded by the R.A.F., did not consider themselves bound in the same way by A.I.2(c)'s decisions. S.O.E.'s Operations Room was responsible for allotting, from the complete list of "Operations Ready", a suitable selection for the American Squadrons, and this list was telephoned through to the airfields concerned.

The system of direct communication between S.O.E. and the American aerodromes proved more flexible and satisfactory than the procedure enforced by the R.A.F., by which all contact between S.O.E. and the squadrons at Tempsford had to go through Air Ministry. Since the American squadrons were working under a different operational command and with different meteorological advisers it not infrequently happened that there was a considerable difference between the conditions under which they would operate as compared with the R.A.F. squadrons. On certain nights and to certain areas the Americans might agree to attempt operations though the R.A.F. refused, while the opposite might be true on other occasions. These anomalies were sometimes difficult for S.O.E.'s Country Sections to understand.

The advantages of the establishment of all S.D. aircraft under a single command were stressed by S.O.E. in the autumn of 1944 when, on reduction of demands for supply dropping from Western Europe, 138 Squadron was withdrawn from Tempsford for normal bombing duties. S.O.E. then suggested that 161 Squadron and R.A.F. Station Tempsford should be transferred to 38 Group (which was then responsible for allocating an air effort corresponding to 138 Squadron if necessary) in order to have all S.D. aircraft under the same operational command. This was agreed by the R.A.F. and in March 1945 Tempsford and 161 Squadron were transferred to 38 Group, and operated under this command for the remaining two months of the European war.

Although throughout the four years the character of S.D. operations to Western Europe remained basically the same, their scope and scale expanded enormously as the Resistance forces in the occupied countries gained strength. In the early years Reception Committees were usually small in size and could handle only a limited number of containers. In order, therefore, to use the full pay-load of the aircraft two or even three Reception Committees were served in one sortie. The selection of containers and the briefing of navigator and despatcher were more complicated when two separate pinpoints had to be located and the correct load dropped on each one. If three operations were combined in the same aircraft the third Reception Committee was not infrequently disappointed: The aircraft, after searching for its first two pinpoints, often arrived at the third after the stand-by times were over and the Reception Committee had gone home. As the patriot organisations developed it became normal for a Reception Committee to receive not the half but the full load of a Halifax, and fifteen containers were the standard delivery.

The use of many different types of aircraft each carrying a different quantity of containers and packages made the work of the Reception Committee more confusing and more difficult, since they could not always be warned in advance whether to expect a Halifax (fifteen containers) a Stirling (twenty-four containers on short range), a Liberator (twelve containers) or one or more Albemarles (six containers each). In the areas in Western Europe in which the sparks of partisan activity developed in the later stages to the forest fires of guerilla warfare, large-scale multiple-aircraft deliveries added the necessary fuel to the flames, and operations involving anything from two to twenty aircraft were carried out to the same pinpoint or to Reception Committees in close proximity serving the same guerilla bands.

After, D-day, deliveries to the field were further supplemented by mass daylight operations carried out by bomber aircraft of the 8th U.S.A.A.F. These operations, under fighter cover, resulted in the delivery of very large quantities of arms and ammunition. As many as thirty-six and sometimes even seventy-two aircraft dropped their containers to the same pinpoint. The tremendous development of S.D. operations from the early days of 1941, when personnel together with only one or two containers or packages were despatched, to the mass operations of 1944, had placed a heavy strain on the machine. Both the procedure and the personnel involved had been tested. Fortunately for the men in the field, they were not found wanting.

Procedures in the Mediterranean

From the summer of 1940 S.O.E.'s H.Q. at Cairo dealing with the Balkan countries and the Middle East maintained communications with the Continent of Europe by courier and there was no requirement for S.D. aircraft. By the middle of 1942, with the growth of patriot Resistance Movements in the Balkans, it became evident that deliveries by air would have to be undertaken. As in England the beginnings were small. The first to be placed at S.O.E.'s disposal in the Mediterranean were two Wellesley bombers, based on Malta, supplemented by Whitley aircraft sent from England. In 1942, at about the same time as the Allied landings in North Africa four Liberators of X Flight of 148 Squadron based in Egypt, were allocated to S.D. work. These resources were gradually expanded, until by the middle of 1943, the whole of 148 Squadron was engaged on S.D. work.

The organisation in the field of Reception Committees and the machinery at base for receiving air deliveries were set up in much the same way as in Western Europe. At Cairo (and from 1944 at Bari) S.O.E. had its own Signals Station, Country Sections, and Air Liaison Section, and requests for air deliveries from the field were dealt with very much as in Western Europe, with H.Q. R.A.F. Middle East filling the place of Air Ministry and Bomber Command. Operations were mounted from Cairo, and the distance to the airfields which were moved westwards behind the advancing Desert Army together with the inadequate telephone communications were a fertile source of difficulties.

In the winter of 1942/43 an S.O.E. Mission was established at Algiers to work into the countries of the Western Mediterranean. A second S.D. base was later set up at Blida from which aircraft of 624 Squadron carried out deliveries into Southern France, Italy and Corsica, on operations arranged by S.O.E. Algiers. During the early months, only a limited number of aircraft were available and the weather was consistently unfavourable. The main bulk of stores delivered by the

Blida-based aircraft during 1943 was to Corsica. At the beginning of 1944 624 Squadron was brought up to strength and American aircraft were also added. The weather improved and operations to southern France were conducted on a considerable scale.

While it was obvious that deliveries to the South of France could more economically be made from Blida than from England this was not easy to arrange. In the first place Southern France, although not within the theatre of S.C.A.E.F., was an area with which he was necessarily concerned, since Special Operations conducted there might affect his plans in the more northern areas. S.O.E. Algiers had therefore to ensure that the organisations built up in the South of France conformed with the overall strategy planned for the whole of France. Moreover, the actual day-to-day running of air operations from two bases as far apart as Tempsford and Algiers into the same country, and sometimes even to the same Resistance Groups, necessitated an extremely complicated procedure. The agents despatched by London were in W/T communication with England; those sent in by Algiers with Algiers. Certain of the London agents were in the extreme South of France, and on the other hand, certain of the Algiers agents were located further north. Four types of French S.D. operations now existed: by U.K.-based aircraft to organisations in W/T communication with England; and by U.K.-based aircraft to organisations in W/T communication with Algiers. On the other hand, the S.D. aircraft based at Blida served all organisations in the South of France, including both those in touch with Algiers, and those in touch with England. Telegrams from the field concerning air operations, dropping points, stores required and so forth, were therefore not necessarily received at the S.O.E. H.Q. which would be responsible for mounting the air operation. By means of correspondence, and above all of telegrams, between S.O.E.'s London and Algiers H.Q.s, the Air Operations Sections of both were kept fully informed. In order to cover the innumerable daily variations, a system of crack signals between the two Headquarters was instituted by which four-figure groups of numbers were translated into phrases such as:

"Intend to attempt Operation Monkeypuzzle tonight."

"Our programme remains unchanged."

"All operations cancelled owing to weather."

These crack signals operated at fixed times during the day and were scheduled to fit in with the B.B.C.'s transmissions, so that if necessary the B.B.C. Reception Committee messages could be cancelled. The system, though extremely complex, worked very well, and certainly resulted in a valuable economy of effort. With the exception of operations carrying special stores, Reception Committees in both Southern and Northern France were served by aircraft flying from the nearest base and able to carry the maximum load.

A small number of "shuttle" operations were flown between England and Algiers, in which the aircraft, after leaving the U.K., carried out its dropping or landing operation and then went straight on to North Africa. A second operation might be attempted on the return journey. Where special personnel or stores had to be delivered to areas which, because of the short nights, could not be served by aircraft returning to the U.K. this type of operation was extremely valuable, but so many problems of organisation were involved that the R.A.F. would agree to attempt only a limited number of high-priority deliveries by "shuttle" service.

Meanwhile, S.O.E. Cairo continued to arrange for the despatch of increasing quantities of stores to the Balkan countries where partisan activity had now become a real menace to the enemy. In the summer of 1943, as a result of the Prime Minister's intervention, the number of aircraft available for S.D. operations into the Balkans was increased. Deliveries were facilitated towards the end of the year by the liberation of the heel of Italy which enabled Packing Stations and air bases to be established much nearer the target areas served by the aircraft.

The S.D. base at Blida was maintained for operations into Southern France; but from January 1944 aircraft carrying supplies to Central and Eastern Europe were now based in the heel of Italy. S.D. operations to Poland, Czechoslovakia, Austria and Germany were now also flown from Mediterranean bases instead of from the U.K. in order to shorten the length of the flight involved, and to avoid the formidable defences of N.W. Europe. In the winter of 1943/44 the amalgamation of the Eastern and Western Mediterranean theatres under A.F.H.Q. and M.A.A.F. radically altered the situation in the Mediterranean.

The S.O.E. Units at this time consisted of Force 133 at Cairo, Advanced Force 133 at Bari, No. 1 Special Force at Monopoli, and I.S.S.U.6 at Algiers. I.S.S.U.6 at Algiers now worked directly with A.F.H.Q., though in close conjunction with S.O.E. London. In April Special Operations (Mediterranean) (SO)M)), was created with Headquarters near Bari. Its tasks were to centralise the administration and control of all S.O.E. Units and to provide central air operations and technical services and to a large extent the provision and packing of stores, not only for S.O.E. but for all Special Services such as S.I.S., O.S.S., M.I.9., and P.W.B. Thus SO(M) had a dual responsibility to S.O.E. London and A.F.H.Q. for the administration and efficiency of S.O.E. Units, and to A.F.H.Q. for servicing and co-ordinating air sorties for several agencies.

Both operational and administrative control of the pool of S.D. aircraft in the Mediterranean was vested in M.A.A.F., who established a special section to handle the problems of S.D. operations. The allocation of tonnages of stores to be dropped month by month in each country was fixed by Special Operations Committee at A.F.H.Q., (including representatives of M.A.A.F., S.O.(M), O.S.S. and the Political Advisers), who decided the competing priorities on the basis of the requests submitted not only from S.O.E. and O.S.S., but also from S.I.S., P.W.B., and M.I.9.

In June 1944 the Balkan Air Force was created as Theatre Commander under A.F.H.Q., for Yugoslavia, Albania and Hungary, and was also made responsible for the air aspect of S.D. sorties not only in those countries, but in all countries served from Mediterranean bases, with the exception of France. The division of functions was as follows:

> A.F.H.Q. Special Operations Section
>> Policy and strategy.
>> Monthly allocation of air lift to the various countries.
>> Overall co-ordination.
> M.A.A.F. Special Operations Section
>> Air policy
>> Allocation of aircraft to meet A.F.H.Q. requirements.
>> Provision of air bases.
>> Provision of air statistics.
>> Technical efficiency and training of S.D. squadrons.
> S.O.(M)
>> Adviser to A.F.H.Q. on special operations, including monthly allocation of airlift.
>> Day-to-day control of S.D. sorties (from June 1944 jointly with Balkan Air Force) for all countries and agencies within the framework of the monthly A.F.H.Q. allocations.
>> Provision and packing of supplies.

B.A.F.

> Theatre Commander, responsible to A.F.H.Q. for Yugoslavia, Albania and Hungary.
>
> Responsible to M.A.A.F. for day-to-day control of S.D. sorties on the air aspect for all agencies, and countries (less France).
>
> Responsible to M.A.A.F. for technical efficiency.
>
> Responsible to M.A.A.F. on air aspect of S.D. sorties and training of S.D. squadrons.

(Note: In March 1945 M.A.T.A.F. took over from B.A.F. all responsibility for S.D. sorties to Italy, Austria, and Czechoslovakia, and from that date to VE day B.A.F. was responsible only for Yugoslavia.)

It will thus be seen that S.O.(M) and B.A.F. had each a dual role and a dual responsibility. In the case of B.A.F. the appointment of A.O.C. B.A.F. as Theatre Commander was due to the special circumstances of Trans-Adriatic operations. In 1944 in spite of various projects for raids or the establishment of bridgeheads on the Dalmatian or Albanian coasts, resources were not sufficient for any substantial measure of ground support to the Yugoslav or Albanian partisans. Air supply and air support, bomber and fighter, were the only available means, apart from the delivery of supplies by sea on a more or less clandestine footing. The creation of B.A.F. was therefore a logical step. But B.A.F. was often placed in a difficult position by reason of its two roles of Theatre Commander for three countries and S.D. air transport agency for seven other countries.

In July 1944 the Yugoslav Country Section and Field Missions of S.O.E. were converted into a regular military mission, known as 37 Military Missions, under B.A.F., as liaison with Marshal Tito, now recognised as an Allied Commander. It was found at the time quite impossible for technical reasons for Army or Air Force Signals to take over communications with mobile stations operating at long range in enemy-occupied countries. S.O.E. therefore continued to handle both the signals and the packing of stores for enemy occupied Yugoslavia, but the operational control of activities in that country passed to 37 Military Mission under the command of B.A.F.

Meanwhile, the advance of the Allied Armies up Italy enabled both S.O.E. and R.A.F. bases to be established further north. In September, operation Dragoon effected the liberation of Southern France which therefore ceased to be a sphere of Special Operations. In October operation Manna similarly liberated Greece. By the end of the year Albania, Rumania, and Bulgaria had also been evacuated by the enemy and were of no further concern for S.D. operations. Poland, Czechoslovakia, Austria and Northern Italy remained (apart from Yugoslavia) the only countries in which Resistance movements still required support.

Complex as the situation was in England in the summer of 1944, it was even more involved in the Mediterranean. Under A.F.H.Q. no fewer than four Theatre Commanders (Seventh Army, 15th Army Group, B.A.F. and G.H.Q. Mid. East) were involved; and in addition S.D. operations were flown to countries under the direct control of the Chiefs of Staff. S.O.E. in the Mediterranean was split into several sub-Headquarters at Cairo, Algiers and several bases in Italy, all co-ordinated under S.O.(M) but under the operational control of the various military commanders. There were aircraft engaged on Special Duty work based at half a dozen different aerodromes in Italy and North Africa.

The problems of packing and transporting containers to these separate bases in countries where communications by telephone, road and rail were always bad and where all stores had to be imported in the first place from overseas, were enormous. The co-ordination and control of S.D. work was made possible by a relation at once closer and more elastic between S.O.E. on the one hand and the R.A.F. and military authorities on the other than was attained in England. In the semi-"active service" conditions of N. Africa and liberated Italy it was easier to establish close personal liaison between S.O.E. and R.A.F. officers than in the office-bound atmosphere of London. Moreover, since S.O.E. in the Balkans had a more definitely military role to fulfil, the considerations of secrecy and security which in England often confused the R.A.F. were in the Mediterranean not permitted to hamper to the same extent.

Chapter 12

Landing Operations

The problem of secretly withdrawing agents from enemy-occupied territory is even more difficult to solve than that of introducing them. On the establishment of the enemy's "Fortress of Europe", all normal channels were closed, and new and clandestine transport arrangements had to be made. In some cases the traditional method of crossing the frontier into a neutral country could still be used: in other cases agents might be brought out at night from lonely parts of the coast by submarine or motorboat. A third method was by air transport, and involved night landing by aircraft in enemy-occupied territory.

The pick-up operation is not new. During the First World War, aircraft were used fairly extensively for carrying agents across the lines and back: but the problem then was in some ways easier. The aircraft were only required to fly short distances. They were slow, with low wing loading, and low landing speeds, and could alight easily in small fields almost without noise. As they were so light the risk of their becoming bogged in an ordinary meadow was small. Enemy opposition, in the form of night fighters or A.A., was not then a serious risk. Moreover, because the distances involved were short, the aircraft could cross the lines by twilight and land in enemy territory at dusk, so that navigational difficulties were slight and no Reception Committee was needed on the landing ground to lay a flare-path.

In 1941, however, the requirements were different. The distances involved were very much greater. From Tangmere for instance, landing aircraft were frequently required to carry out operations to points as far distant as Lyons, and even the shortest mission necessitated a long sea crossing or a journey across enemy defended territory which could only be penetrated during the hours of darkness. The navigational difficulties were therefore considerably greater. The aircraft used required a good range and a reasonably high cruising speed. This in its turn meant that the aircraft would be heavier, and have a higher landing speed, than those of 1914-18, and would therefore need a larger field to land in and a smooth firm surface. The necessity for night landings moreover, meant that trained agents must be on the ground to lay a flare-path. The amount of light which could be shown on the field was not enough for landings to be made safely except in moonlight, and this factor combined with the navigational difficulties restricted operations to the moon period.

Landing operations were carried out by the R.A.F. for S.O.E. into France and Belgium from the U.K., and on a much larger scale, from the Mediterranean into the Balkan countries. A small number of Lysander and Dakota operations were also carried out into Northern Italy, and three Dakota landings were made in Poland. The methods used in each country were very similar, but the conditions varied enormously. In the Balkans, the landings of aircraft on prepared landing strips became almost a Transport Command function: in France, on the other hand, the Germans were in complete control of all districts and landing operations, if they were to be successful at all, must be conducted clandestinely.

The most suitable aircraft available for operations from the U.K. was the Westland Lysander. Designed for Army co-operation it could cruise at 165 m.p.h. and land in restricted spaces. Its normal range was short, but fortunately it was found possible to place a large extra tank between the legs of the under-carriage which gave the aircraft an operational range of 900 miles. To compensate for this extra weight, all armament and armour had to be removed together with all wireless equipment, except for an R/T set worked by the pilot. Thus modified, the Lysander could carry three passengers in the rear cockpit and weighed about four and a half tons fully loaded. It required a landing strip 600 metres long, with clear approaches and a firm level surface. Specially trained and experienced pilots were needed for Lysander operations: not only had the pilot to land by night in a small unknown field on a flare-path, composed of three dim lights, but he had to find his way there, navigating single-handed by map-reading, across enemy country.

The second aircraft to be used for landing operations was the Lockheed Hudson twin-engined bomber. This aircraft was armed and carried a crew of four; its range allowed it to operate anywhere in France from England, and it could carry ten passengers. The all-up weight was about ten tons, and the Hudson needed a landing strip 1,000 metres long with clear approaches. The presence of a navigator in the Hudson crew removed most of the navigational difficulties inherent in Lysander operations, but on the other hand the aircraft was a good deal more difficult to land under clandestine conditions than the Lysander, and a more elaborate flare-path was needed.

The third and last type of aircraft to be employed on this work was the Douglas Dakota or D.C.3. which carried a crew of four. This aircraft was extensively used in Yugoslavia, from February 1944, and during 1944 was also employed on French operations. It had much the same range as the Hudson, and needed a landing strip of the same length with the same type of flare-path, but it could carry twenty passengers or two tons of freight. Like the Lysander it was unarmed.

The Lysanders and Hudsons employed on landing operations from England belonged to "A" Flight of 161 Squadron, and were stationed at Tempsford with an advanced operational base at Tangmere. The Dakotas belonged to the U.S. 8th Air Force, and operated from Harrington.

In the Mediterranean a Lysander flight carried out the small number of Lysander operations into Southern France and Northern Italy. The Dakota operations were carried out by a number of Dakota Squadrons: 267 R.A.F. and 44 S.A.A.F., and also by the U.S.A.A.F. Dakotas of 51 T.C. wing and 60 T.C. Group.

If training was necessary for both agents and aircrews in the conduct of dropping operations, this was doubly true for landing operations. Since so much depended on the establishment of mutual confidence between pilot and Organiser, special training was always undertaken in order to qualify agents to mount landing operations, and in this course the landing pilots were themselves the instructors. The course aimed at teaching the agent the requirements for an acceptable landing ground as regards dimensions, approaches, slopes and surface; how to survey it and describe it to London; how to lay a flare-path and flash a Morse signal letter with pocket torches; and how to organise the rapid exchange of passengers and luggage so that the aircraft spent as short a time as possible on the ground.

The difficulties of selecting a suitable ground for landing operations were obviously even greater than in the case of parachutages." In the early days disused airfields were sometimes used, but the enemy soon realised what was happening and ordered all disused landing grounds to be obstructed so that the agent had to fall back on large meadows. More than that the enemy tried to put these too out of action. Farmers were ordered to plough up large fields or even obstruct them, but there were usually methods of getting round this difficulty. The farmers might not have enough petrol to carry out their orders, or fences and posts planted as obstructions might be removed at the last minute to leave a clear field. In countries such as Greece and Yugoslavia the geography itself was such that fields of sufficient size were practically non-existent.

Where nature had failed to provide, man must improvise; and the partisans themselves, under the guidance of Army and R.A.F. Liaison Officers, constructed landing strips out of the unpromising terrain. This of course was a major activity which could hardly be conducted in secrecy. A B.L.O. organising a landing ground at Trikkila in Greece reported that he had had to employ for the purpose a steam roller which belonged to the local village. In such circumstances, probably even the Germans themselves realised what was happening, but fortunately the partisans were strong enough to be able to hold the districts concerned against the enemy. In Western Europe it was usually impracticable for security reasons to do much work on fields to make them fit for landings, but it was sometimes possible to persuade the owner to plant lucerne or clover on a suitable large field in order to give a good surface for aircraft to land.

Apart from the difficulties of choosing the ground, the agent had to arrange for a nearby safe-house to receive the incoming passengers and to shelter the outgoing ones during the period of waiting for the aircraft. When the ground had been accepted by the R.A.F. authorities and the operation had been confirmed back to the agent by signal, he assembled his passengers there and waited for the pre-arranged B.B.C. message. Owing to bad weather the waiting period was sometimes long, and the presence of the prospective passengers, always liable to be an embarrassment, might become an acute danger to the Organiser.

In the Balkans the use of improvised landing strips within partisan-controlled areas made large scale landing operations possible, and the main problem became purely one of traffic control.

In Western Europe, however, the position was very different. On receipt of the arranged B.B.C. message the Organiser conducted his passengers to the landing point, posted his guards and waited. When an aircraft came near he challenged it with an ordinary pocket torch in Morse, and on receiving the correct reply lit his flare-path. The aircraft approached, touched down by the first lamp where the agent was standing with his passengers, and at the end of its landing run turned round and taxied back to a point alongside the agent. It then turned round again and stood facing into the wind, with the engine ticking over ready to take off. Even a Lysander makes a considerable amount of noise in the silence of the night.

A twin-engine aircraft such as a Hudson or Dakota was inevitably even more disturbing; and yet there were occasions on which landing operations were carried out within three or four miles of German troop detachments. Clearly the most important thing was to keep the aircraft on the ground for as short a time as possible. The passengers and luggage were quickly exchanged and the aircraft opened up its engine and took off. All lights were then extinguished and removed, leaving no trace of the operation except perhaps wheel marks in the grass. The time spent on the ground was usually about three minutes. Sometimes two aircraft were used; in this case the second landed immediately after the first had taken off and the total time on the ground for the two aircraft was about eight minutes. Both Lysanders and, at a later date, Hudsons operated in this way, and occasionally even treble Lysander landing operations were carried out. Sometimes when this was done, one of the aircraft would beat up an area some distance away as cover for the others' landing.

The actual procedure by telegram and telephone for mounting a landing operation was similar to that used for dropping operations. Since the operations were known to be especially difficult and hazardous, even greater care was taken in the selection and acceptance of grounds and the other necessary details. The over-riding priority accorded to S.I.S. for landing operations meant that S.O.E., who shared the same aircraft, sometimes suffered delay. S.O.E. landing operations had to wait until the weather was good and the aircraft available – two conditions for which they might sometimes wait a long time.

Practically every one of the landing operations carried out from the U.K. is worth a whole story to itself. The first (*Levée/Façade*, 4/5th September 1941, S/L. Dufort), attempted in September 1941, was rather an inauspicious start to S.O.E. pick-ups. The agent laying the flare-path was disturbed by the police and could not use his original field which had been accepted for the landing. He managed, however, to lay the flare-path in an adjacent field which of course had not been passed. The aircraft landed safely, but struck some wires on taking off and was damaged, although not sufficiently to prevent it getting home.

The next operation, delayed owing to priority difficulties, was not attempted until December 1941 (*Stoat*, 8/9th December 1941, F/Lt. Murphy). The pilot found his landing point without difficulty shortly after midnight, but was not entirely satisfied with the signal he received, and the lights were not correctly laid. He circled around for some time, and eventually decided to land, using his landing light. As he touched down he saw a trench running between the lights of the flare-path. He immediately opened up his engine, and then landed on the other side of the landing ground about 400 yards away, where he waited for the agent to come over to him.

Although suspicious, he was not seriously alarmed until he saw in the moonlight a line of figures advancing towards the aircraft. He was then fired on and wounded, but managed to take off; and in spite of considerable loss of blood he landed at Tangmere 3½ hours later. It subsequently transpired that the Organiser of the operations had been surprised and captured by a chance patrol, which then improvised an ambush for the aircraft. In the confusion caused by the shooting and the aircraft taking off the agents had managed to make their get-away. Although the Gestapo often tried to organise a false reception this was the only time an aircraft was ever ambushed, and it was the only S.O.E. pick-up operation ever attempted in Belgium. The density of population increased ground security difficulties, and together with good strong A.A. defences ruled the area out altogether for landing operations.

By 1942 the drill for pick-ups had been developed from early experiences and the procedure was fully organised. Nine Lysander operations were completed during the year, including a double. The only serious incident occurred in December (*Chubb Minor/Merhaden/Starfish*, 17/18th December 1942, S/L Lockhart), when a Lysander, in making a landing along a bumpy field, damaged the tail wheel and partly jammed the elevator. This caused the aircraft to climb steadily during the homeward flight, and the pilot was only able to maintain the required low altitude by throttling back and stalling the aircraft every few minutes in order to lose height.

Operations completed in 1943 showed a big increase over the 1942 figures. Requirements had increased to such an extent that nearly all

Lysander operations were doubles and one treble operation was successfully completed. For the first time Hudsons were used on this work and one double Hudson operation was carried out. A total of thirty-nine operations were successfully completed, involving thirty-eight Lysander, and sixteen Hudson landings. One Lysander was lost (*Sten*, 10/11th December 1942, F/O Bathgate), the pilot and his passengers being the only losses sustained on S.O.E. landing operations.

1943 was perhaps the best and most important year for this type of work. The missions were flown by a hand-full of pilots, all of whom were experienced in pick-up operations. The success of these operations during this critical period was an important factor in maintaining a close liaison between S.O.E. H.Q. and the Resistance Groups in the field, and the information and personnel brought back to England were of the greatest value to S.O.E. in formulating its future plans.

1944 was a more difficult year for many reasons. The heavy bomber attacks had led to an intensification of the German anti-aircraft defences, and the enemy's determined efforts to eliminate Resistance Groups before the anticipated invasion took place increased the ground risks. Towards the end of 1943 the Lysander Flight had suffered several casualties, and most of the remaining pilots had completed their operational tour: this meant that very few of the original pilots were left.

A Hudson operation early in the year (*Bludgeon*, 8/9th February 1944, F/O Affleck), which nearly ended in disaster, did much to damage the good relationship between the pilots and the agents. The aircraft got bogged on the landing ground and was extricated only after three hours of concentrated work on the part of the Reception Committee, the entire local village, three horses and two oxen. Eventually the aircraft managed to take off and returned safely. It was argued that in this case the agent should not have allowed the aircraft to land, and the confidence of the Squadron and Air Ministry in the reliability of agents' judgment was badly shaken. The agent concerned, however, had been waiting for a landing operation for some months and was anxious to send both personnel and reports to England at the first possible moment. He knew the ground was soft and realised the danger to the aircraft. When he heard his B.B.C. message he had a difficult decision to make. From the R.A.F.'s point of view he chose the wrong course, and for some time afterwards was forbidden to arrange further landing operations.

In this year the Lysander pick-up Flight was formed in the Mediterranean to operate from Corsica to the South of France. The difficulties of communication by signal and crack signal were very great and had serious results on one occasion (Thicket 2, 11/12th July 1944). The signal from Bari was not received in London in time for the Reception Committee to be warned and when the aircraft arrived at the landing point there was no reception. Had the pilots of the two Lysanders carried out the correct drill and returned to Corsica without landing all would have been well, but they knew the ground from previous visits and decided to land in the moonlight using their landing lights. One of the aircraft overshot badly on landing and ran into some rough ground. This caused the engine to stop and the pilot was unable to re-start it.

A farmer from a nearby farm, which had been used as a safe house for previous operations had heard the aircraft circling and now arrived on the scene. The pilot of the disabled aircraft got into the other aircraft which took off and returned to Corsica without further incident. The farmer looked after the incoming passengers, and as the Reception Committee had not been warned there were no outward passengers waiting. The farmer then set the disabled Lysander on fire. When it was completely destroyed he telephoned to police and told them that an unidentified aircraft had crashed into his field and burst into flames. The police were unable to prove anything against the farmer and finally decided that it was an ordinary flying accident. The Gestapo might have been more difficult to convince, but the situation in France was developing rapidly and they were presumably occupied with other matters. This was fortunate, since if the Gestapo had made a serious enquiry the farmer would almost certainly have been arrested and probably shot. Once again the moral was underlined: stick rigidly to the agreed drill.

The most interesting development during the year was the entry of the U.S.A.A.F. Dakotas into the field of pick-up operations. These aircraft needed the same length of landing strip as the Hudson but could carry twenty passengers or about two tons of freight which made them extremely valuable. The first Dakota operation (*Mixer* 1, 7/8th July 1944, Col. Heflin) was to a ground near Nantua not far from the Swiss border. The ground was in a small controlled area, and as the nights were too short to allow the return journey to be made in darkness it was arranged that the aircraft should land in the dark, remain hidden during the following day, and return to the U.K. at nightfall. The Dakota was hidden with branches and camouflage netting and weather reports were passed by pre-arranged B.B.C. phrases. The aircraft took off from Harrington on 7th July and owing to bad weather at base had to remain hidden at the landing point for two days. The pilot, who was the Station Commander, spent the time in inspecting the local guerillas and accepting French hospitality. The aircraft took off again on 9th July and returned to U.K. after a completely successful trip.

There were several subsequent Dakota operations to this ground. The Dakotas were also used extensively after D-Day for taking heavy weapons to controlled areas – a much more economical method of delivering material than by parachute. Large numbers of Allied airmen were brought out by Dakota and Hudson. On one operation (*Gunner*, 2/3rd September 1944, Lt. Col. Brekerson and Major Saunders), two Dakotas brought out forty evacuees: a record exfiltration for French landing operations.

By now the character of landing operations in France had changed, and from being fully clandestine they were developing into something comparable to the Yugoslav pattern. Night landings were carried out into controlled areas and finally by the middle of September it was possible to operate by daylight.

The extraordinarily high ratio of success of landing operations and the even more surprisingly low percentage of losses in aircraft were perhaps due in part to the very audacity of the scheme. Even when the enemy had realised that such operations were taking place it is unlikely that he grasped the scale on which they were being used. In the Balkans the areas surrounding the landing grounds were in any case protected by strong partisan forces. In Western Europe, where landing operations had to be conducted clandestinely, the Germans were always slow in reacting and ordering their counter-measures. Another factor, and one of the most important, was the high degree of training imposed on both agents and pilots, which engendered complete confidence between the two.

In many cases they knew each other personally, having taken part as trainees or instructors on the same courses. Moreover, because the operations were prima facie so difficult and dangerous, special care was always taken in arranging them. The agents' reports on the ground were very detailed and were always supplemented by photographic reconnaissance of the grounds by the R.A.F. But after everything else has been taken into consideration, the skill and daring of the pilots concerned in navigating an aircraft – in the case of Lysanders singlehanded – to a point sometimes hundreds of miles within enemy-occupied country, and in landing at night on a strange field known to them only by description and photograph, remains the principal reason for the success of this type of operation.

Chapter 13

Failures and Losses

The difficulties and hazards of S.D. operations inevitably resulted in a proportion of wasted effort. Success here did not depend entirely on the R.A.F.: unlike their other operations, supply dropping required the help of trained assistants on the ground. In bombing the pilot could be certain that his target was there – even though he could not see it; but a Reception Committee did not, and could not, attain such reliability.

The pilot had his own special problems, arising principally from the need for absolutely accurate navigation and low level night flying; the Reception Committee faced all the dangers of clandestine life. Arrests, curfew times, German patrols, jamming of the B.B.C., the difficulties of obtaining torch batteries, the problem of transport; all these, and many other circumstances might prevent the Reception Committee from being present on the ground, or, if there, from being seen. The position in the field altered not only from day to day but from hour to hour, and there might not be time to warn the R.A.F. of the changed conditions. In spite of all that skill and staff work could do there remained a wide margin of luck. Every separate S.D. operation was, to some extent, a chancy affair and its success required good fortune as well as good management.

The success/sortie ratio was therefore often disappointing. For the U.K.-based aircraft, operating into countries where Resistance could only exist clandestinely, the average proportion of successful flights on dropping operations varied between 45% and 65%. In the later stages, improved methods and the relaxation of German control increased the chances of success. For landing operations the proportion was considerably higher: between 75% and 85%.

In the countries served from the Mediterranean bases the situation on the ground was easier and the proportion of successful sorties was higher than that achieved from England: on Yugoslav operations, an average of nearly 80% of the total sorties were successful, on Greek 80%. Of flights to Poland, 49% were successful: a very high figure in view of the special difficulties of operations to Poland, and achieved partly by the determination of the Polish Underground Army not to waste a sortie and partly by the skill of pilots operating at extreme range over difficult country.

Of the sorties which were unsuccessful, by far the largest number failed for one of two reasons: bad weather, or "No Reception Committee". The need for absolutely accurate navigation enhanced the importance of good weather conditions. An average of 25% of the unsuccessful sorties was due to bad weather conditions. In the winter months this proportion might rise to as high as 35%. The exact number of operations which failed because the Reception Committee were not present on the agreed spot at the agreed time is difficult to determine. In a number of cases when the pilot reported that, after locating the pinpoint he had been unable to find the Reception Committee, the organisers in the field insisted that the Reception Committee had in fact been present. There is no doubt, however, that a very large proportion of the failures was due to the Reception Committee's inability – no doubt through circumstances beyond its control – to keep its appointment. The reason for over a third of the failures, on an average, was recorded as "No Reception".

The remaining unsuccessful sorties were due to a variety of causes. A proportion varying between 5% and 15% was due to navigation, the pilot himself reporting that he had got lost. A smaller number failed owing to engine trouble or other mechanical failure in the aircraft. In a number of cases – a proportion varying considerably – the aircraft failed to return, although sometimes information was received from the field that the operation had been completed, and the aircraft had presumably crashed on its return.

On the whole, the proportion of aircraft lost on S.D. work was extraordinarily small, (see Appendix J for details). In Western Europe it never exceeded the Main Force ratio, and was usually substantially lower. On French operations the number of aircraft lost varied between 1.5% and 3% of the total sorties: in Holland and Belgium it was a good deal higher. The Scandinavian losses averaged roughly 2.5%. The situation was even better for the Mediterranean-based aircraft operating into Central Europe and the Balkans: over the whole period only approximately .1% of the aircraft flying on S.D. work failed to return. For Polish operations the normal loss ratio was 2%: but in the attempt to fly supplies to Warsaw the losses suffered were as high as 25%.

The low incidence of loss among the pick-up aircraft was even more surprising. In France, only two Lysanders were lost in the four years during which 112 landing operations (including twenty Dakotas) were successfully completed, and of these one pilot was successfully brought out later. In Yugoslavia, up to June 1944, five aircraft were lost for 186 successful operations; and in Greece nine landing operations were carried out up to the end of 1943 but no aircraft were lost.

Chapter 14

SOE Assisting Air Force Escapees

On many occasions the crews of aircraft that crashed in enemy-occupied country were looked after by S.O.E.'s Resistance Groups in the field and were guided over the frontier into neutral countries. Sometimes landing operations were laid on by S.O.E. to evacuate such personnel. Several of the S.D. crews were assisted in this way by the men in the field for whose sake they had undertaken the operations.

The crew of an S.D. aircraft that crashed in Denmark, for instance, was sent over to Sweden within a matter of days. A number of aircrews baling out over France were escorted to Switzerland or Spain. Perhaps the most interesting case was that of S/L Griffiths who, after his aircraft had crashed on Operation *Pimento 12*, leaving him the sole survivor, joined the Maquis and after many adventures eventually reached Switzerland.

The total figure for the number of airmen who escaped from Western Europe through S.O.E. channels, including R.A.F., U.S.A.A.F., R.C.A.F., and R.A.A.F. is as follows (there is no record before September 1943):

September – December 1943	40
1944	245
1945	45
Total	*330*

Chapter 15

Assistance Given by the RAF to SOE Other Than Special Duties Operations

The help which the R.A.F. gave to S.O.E. was not confined to S.D. operations, although these were by far its largest contribution. Normal bombing operations were sometimes mounted by the R.A.F. at the request of Resistance Groups in the field, and moreover the Air Force were able to supply S.O.E. with air transport, with stores and equipment, and with personnel, both Staff officers and agents.

Bombing

There were a number of occasions on which Resistance Groups in the field found themselves in urgent need of assistance by Allied bombers, since some of the opposition with which they were faced was too strong for them to deal with by the ordinary methods of sabotage and guerilla attack.

Targets for which bombing was requested by the field included Gestapo and Quisling Headquarters, local enemy troop headquarters and enemy units who were attacking the Resistance strongholds. There were also occasions on which S.O.E. Officers in the field were able to give information on military targets. In 1941-1942 two members of the Air Ministry Bomb Target Section were transferred to S.O.E., and S.O.E. were represented at every weekly meeting of the Bomb Targets Committee at Air Ministry. Industrial records and often plans of every factory of importance were thus available to S.O.E. through this arrangement, while Bomber Command received a corresponding benefit.

Requests for bombing received from Western Europe by S.O.E. were forwarded to the Air Ministry for such action as they considered practicable.

SHAEF/17240/10/Ops, 15 May 1944
A procedure for handling such requests for air assistance to Resistance Groups was laid down. This procedure worked smoothly as regards the actual passing of the requests, but in view of the many other calls on air effort it was not possible to give sufficient priority to Resistance targets. It was decided, however, that the procedure was adequate and should be maintained.

SHAEF/17240/10/Ops, 30 July 1944
A letter from S.H.A.E.F. to S.F.H.Q., S.O.E. reported that the Army Liaison Section at Air Headquarters of S.H.A.E.F. were fully apprised of the urgency of meeting requests for air assistance from Resistance Groups. Requests of this nature should be transmitted by S.O.E. to the Ops. 'C' Sub-Section at S.H.A.E.F. (Main) who would notify S.O.E. on the acceptance of the proposed targets, and forward requests without delay to the Liaison Section at Air Headquarters.

SHAEF/R/A/HEPW/DO, 17 November 1944
In November 1944 this procedure was slightly elaborated S.O.E. was to signal bombing requirements to their representative at S.H.A.E.F. Air Main, repeating the signal from S.H.A.E.F. Air Rear. If urgent action was required S.H.A.E.F. Air Rear would clear the operation with S.H.A.E.F. Air Main in the shortest possible time, but would only take action on S.O.E.'s requests if speed was essential, as it was important that the two Staffs should not concern themselves with the same operational problems.

Difficulties were sometimes experienced in obtaining the agreement of the Allied Governments concerned to the bombing of targets within their countries and this necessity for political clearance sometimes involved delay. Operations were flown either by the Tactical Air Force or, if it was considered more suitable, by Bomber Command. In Western Europe there were only a limited number of bombing attacks carries out at the request of Resistance Groups, two of the most spectacular and successful being the attacks on the Gestapo Headquarters in Copenhagen and Oslo.

In the Mediterranean requests for such special air assistance were forwarded by S.O.E. to M.A.A.F. (or B.A.F. or M.A.T.A.F.) who dealt with them as and when conditions permitted. When the front was moving it was difficult for S.O.E. to get facilities for bombing operations since all bomber aircraft were engaged on tactical work in support of the current military operations.

During the static periods, however, bombing operations in support of, or on information supplied by, Resistance Groups in the field was provided by the Air Forces very generously. Information on troop movements, for instance, was signalled by agents in the field to S.O.(M) and passed to the appropriate military authorities who arranged for bombardment. A particularly flexible W/T system was established whereby information was passed to the Air Forces until the last possible moment. Diversionary bombing to cover sabotage attacks was also undertaken by the Air Forces based in the Mediterranean Theatre, and sabotage and bombing were used as complementary methods of attack to an unusual degree.

Air Transport

By the nature of its work, S.O.E. required to use air transport facilities to a considerable extent, and in the transportation of S.O.E. personnel overseas by air, the Air Ministry gave generously of its own limited resources.

In 1941 the air transport situation was very bad indeed. The most crowded route was England to Cairo. The B.O.A.C., operating a service to Cairo via West Africa, ran one aircraft every ten days which carried five passengers, and these seats were sought after by all Government departments. Bombers going out to reinforce the Air Forces in the Middle East occasionally carried passengers, but the priority had to be very high indeed to displace the urgently required operational spares normally carried by these aircraft.

As a result of the congestion and uncertainty of this route – often a selected passenger was turned off at the last moment to make room for someone with an even higher priority – it was quicker to send passengers for Cairo to West Africa by sea and from there by air to Cairo and, when this route too became congested, by sea to Durban and then on by air.

In March 1941 a priorities board was formed to collate and grade the various applications for air passengers to the Middle East and onwards and to allocate seats on the aircraft available, both British and American. Since the formation of the Board S.O.E. was always given fair treatment whenever adequate reasons were quoted for the passages requested.

Another congested route was the one operated by B.O.A.C. with K.L.M. crews from England to Lisbon. Although this was a daily service it was the only air link with the American trans-Atlantic Clipper and with enemy-occupied Europe, and bookings had normally to be made about three weeks in advance. However the Air Ministry were very helpful in unloading passengers, and sometimes freight, so as to carry S.O.E. passengers at short notice.

In addition to these regular services, B.O.A.C. operated an irregular service to Stockholm from which S.O.E. derived the most benefit. At first the only aircraft available for use on this flight was an old Lockheed, but this was later augmented by three Hudsons, and by two Lodestars purchased from America by the Norwegian Government. Some Whitleys were added and later some Dakotas operated by American A.T.C. crews. Mosquitos were also used on this route, the passengers travelling in the bomb bay. In spite of the number of aircraft available it was never possible to operate a regular service to Stockholm as it was so dependent on the weather, and the aircraft were liable to be attacked when passing over the tip of German-occupied Norway.

As air transport facilities increased, B.O.A.C. and Transport Command carried an increasing number of S.O.E. passengers, and the following approximate figures will give some idea of the extent to which S.O.E. is indebted to them and particularly to the kindness and patience of the staff of Transport Command and A.C. Admin. Air Ministry:

1941

To and from Shetlands	81
U.K. to Lisbon	78
Takoradi to Cairo	43
Durban to Cairo	10
Belfast	5
Far East via Takoradi	5
Toronto	5
Far East (direct)	3
Far East via Durban	3
Cairo (direct)	2

New York	2
West Africa	2
Russia	1

1st June 1944 to 31st May 1945

India and Ceylon	354
Italy	218
To and from Shetlands	210
North Africa	81
Cairo	37
Australia	33
France	20
New York	14
Lisbon	13
Gibraltar	11
Madrid	9
Australia sea/air	3
Moscow	3
Switzerland	3
China	2
Tangier	2
Athens	1
Iceland	1
Leopoldville	1
Teheran	1

Since June 1942 no air passages have been paid for by S.O.E., all costs being charged by Air Ministry to normal public funds.

Equipment

Early in 1941 S.O.E. began to find that the R.A.F. possessed certain articles of equipment which would be very useful both for operations and for use in the United Kingdom. Earliest among these were rubber dinghies and sorbo rubber pads for packing containers.

A.I.10, as an Intelligence branch, had no power to indent for R.A.F. equipment, and as the requests from S.O.E. became more frequent and varied it became obvious that special arrangements would have to be made to deal with them. Eventually, after some discussion, A.M.S.O.'s department at the Air Ministry agreed that all requests for R.A.F. equipment should be initialled by A.C.A.S.(I) or his representative and passed to a central equipment branch who would authorise the issue of the equipment which would then be struck off charge and no further accounting action taken.

At first this arrangement only covered normal Air Force stores, but in September 1941 it was decided to include containers and parachutes, which had formerly been made by Air Ministry contractors but had been paid for in cash by S.O.E.

The following are the approximate figures of containers and parachutes received from the R.A.F. (N.B. Containers and parachutes made locally in India and the Middle East are not included.)

Issue of Supply Dropping Equipment to All Theatres (Approximate Numbers)

MIDDLE EAST
Parachutes, Container, 28'	20,000
Containers, Type "C"	10,000
Containers, Type "H"	200

N. AFRICA
Parachutes, Container, 28'	25,000
Containers, Type "C"	14,000
Containers, Type "H"	8,000

ITALY
Parachutes, Container, 28'	100,000
Containers, Type "C" & C.L.E.	26,000
Containers, Type "H"	20,000
Parachutes, Type "X"	500

INDIA
Parachutes, Container, 28' 30,000	
Container, Type "C"	20,000
Container, Type "H"	16,000
Parachutes, Type "X"	2,000

AUSTRALIA

Parachutes, Container 28′	500
Containers, Type "C"	510
Containers, Type "H"	120

U.K.

Parachutes, Container 28′	150,000
Containers, Type "C" & "H"	116,250
Parachutes, Type "X"	3,150

Since this arrangement came into operation early in 1941, S.O.E. received from the R.A.F. what was virtually a gift of many millions of pounds worth of equipment including such things as machine guns, air-sea rescue boats, wireless transmitters and receivers, generators, mobile wireless workshops, motor vans, flying clothing and countless valves, plugs and sockets and other wireless parts.

Some of S.O.E.'s wireless stations were largely equipped with material supplied from R.A.F. sources. In addition, the Air Ministry photographic staff carried out much work in connection with the reproduction of codes for use in the field.

Personnel

As far as personnel were concerned S.O.E. obtained from the Air Force the services of a number of senior and junior R.A.F. and W.A.A.F. officers and a small number of other ranks. Some of these were used on work concerned with Air Operations, in Sections such as the Air Liaison Section while others took their place in S.O.E.'s Country Sections and in other S.O.E. Departments.

Sixteen R.A.F. officers and 10 W.A.A.F. officers volunteered for duty as agents in the field, the Air Ministry agreeing to give special commissions in the W.A.A.F. to a number of the brave women who were under S.O.E. training. One of the most outstanding of these was W/Cdr. Yeo Thomas, who carried out three separate missions to France, acting as a senior British Liaison Officer to the Fighting French organisations. On his last mission he was captured by the Gestapo, and after fifteen months in various prisons and camps, including Buchenwald, succeeded in making his escape.

Part III

Resistance in Europe

Chapter 16

The Outline Story

The outline story of Resistance in the occupied countries necessarily follows in general the same pattern, although the details and the timing may vary considerably. The organisation of sabotage groups and Secret Armies can be divided into three main stages:- the pioneer phase, in which organisers and W/T operators are dropped in order to contact indigenous Resistance movements and report on their potentialities; the second period, which may last some years, of building up the groups which have been initiated and contacted, of encouraging clandestine sabotage activity and preparing the ground for offensive action later; and the final stage, not necessarily attained in every country, in which large and well-equipped partisan formations are in a position to take the offensive against the occupying forces.

Within this broad framework, however, the tempo and efficiency of Resistance activities might vary considerably. In Germany and its satellite countries it might never be possible to get beyond the first phase: in the more bitterly resistant of the occupied countries the third stage might be reached long before the Allied Forces were able to land and take part in military operations with them. In other areas, such as Scandinavia, where there was less necessity and less scope for guerilla activities, the organisation of Resistance activity might reach its fullest development in the second stage.

In analysing the work carried out by S.O.E. with the help of the R.A.F. it is convenient to divide the countries of occupied Europe into three categories: those in the West (France, Holland, Belgium, Norway and Denmark) which were served throughout the whole period mainly by aircraft based on the U.K.; Central Europe, (Poland, Czechoslovakia and Austria) which were served during the early years from the U.K. and later from Mediterranean bases; and the countries of Southern Europe and the Balkans (Italy, Yugoslavia, Greece, Rumania, Bulgaria, Hungary, Albania, Crete and Corsica), to which stores were delivered by aircraft based first in North Africa and later in Italy itself.

It is worth emphasising, in fairness to the people of the occupied countries themselves, that this brief record is concerned only with their operational activities. The work which they carried out for the Intelligence Services is not considered here.

Chapter 17

Western Europe, Supplied by UK-based Aircraft

By the winter of 1940-41, S.O.E.'s first recruits were ready to go to the field, and the earliest operations carried out included the dropping of coup-de-main teams in France.

France

The reports of the members of these teams (who had been sent in by the "Independent" French Section of S.O.E.), convinced General de Gaulle that Resistance was a force to be reckoned with, and after some persuasion the Fighting French proceeded to make their own contacts with the Resistance movements in France through S.O.E. A Fighting French Section was accordingly set up in S.O.E. to work in liaison with General de Gaulle's staff, but the Independent circuits already established were maintained and expanded, since it was recognised in this country that many Frenchmen, although definitely anti-German, were not pro-de Gaulle.

From the beginning, H.M.G. reserved its right to contact any Resistance element in France of whatever political faction, while at the same time giving General de Gaulle such facilities as he needed for his own work. In a letter from the Secretary of State for Foreign Affairs of November 1941, it was laid down that: "H.M.G. must be free to co-operate meanwhile with any Frenchmen who are willing to aid the common cause."

The continued existence of the British controlled circuits in France was a perennial bone of contention between de Gaulle and H.M.G. But the soundness of our policy was proved both by the extent of the support given by Frenchmen in France to the Independent organisations, and the consequent success of their work, and by the higher standard of security which was attained. Security is an indispensable condition of existence for clandestine organisations but was also, apparently, an idea foreign to the officers of Fighting French Headquarters. If all the subversive organisations in France had been under the control of Fighting French H.Q., it is unlikely a network of efficient and active circuits could have been maintained in the face of the repeated Gestapo drives. As it was, the existence of the two organisations allowed for complementary activities and for planning in duplication and in depth. Moreover, they were on occasions able to be of assistance to each other: for example the Leader of the Resistance Movement "Liberation", a de Gaulle contact and a later member of the Provisional Government, was brought to this country by the Independent French Section at the General's request.

The methods used by the two sections were very different. The nucleus of the Independent French circuit was the organiser with his W/T operator: British officers were generally employed, and round these centres small watertight circuits were gradually built up all over France. If the Gestapo succeeded in breaking up a circuit a new organiser would be sent to the area and the work would begin again. In general the size of these circuits was limited; in some cases it became considerable, but a large organisation nearly always proved insecure in the long run, and the organisers were instructed to confine themselves to establishing small bodies of well trained and entirely reliable men. Fighting French Headquarters, on the other hand, for political reasons, aimed at reaching the masses of the French people. General de Gaulle, having failed to create his own Resistance Movement responsible directly to him, began in 1942 to try to make contact with those indigenous Resistance Movements already in existence. To this end French Liaison Officers and W/T operators were despatched, together with a co-ordinator to control their activities, and Resistance Leaders and politicians representing every shade of French political opinion were brought back to this country. By the end of the year most of the great Resistance Movements had agreed to recognise de Gaulle's military, though not his political, leadership.

By the autumn of 1941 information showed that sabotage in France was on the increase. In September, nineteen separate sabotage "incidents" on communications were reported together with a number of fires which had damaged petrol stocks and lorries. The coup-de-main operation "Josephine" had succeeded in affecting the electrical supply for a wide area around Bordeaux, and the Germans were offering a one million franc reward for information leading to the arrest of saboteurs. The turn-tables at Le Mans were put out of action, and the first Lysander pick-up operation was successfully carried out in this month.

This operation is perhaps worth recording in greater detail. The officer who was to be picked up had engaged rooms in a hotel about 15 kilometres from the landing ground, for himself and a French assistant. On the evening of the day on which he heard the warning B.B.C. message the hotel was visited by the Police who examined the papers of every person staying there, and prevented his leaving the hotel until sometime after he had planned. When they were at last free, he and his assistant took to their bicycles and throughout a hot summer evening cycled furiously along the hilly roads of France, in an effort to make up for lost time. As they neared the landing ground they could hear the Lysander circling above them in the darkness, and since they were already very late, they were afraid that the pilot might soon decide to abandon the attempt if they did not show their flare-path quickly. They, therefore, chose the nearest field which, as far as they could see, would be suitable for the operation, climbed over the hedge, and laid out the flare-path. The Lysander landed without mishap. It had brought over another officer who now quickly climbed out while the returning organiser took his place after a brief hand-shake. The 'plane took off but on its way hit the telegraph wires alongside the road and several yards of wire became attached to the 'plane. On reaching England the pilot found thick ground mist and at the same time his wireless failed. Listeners at the aerodrome heard him circling around and he was given his direction by search-light signals. Meanwhile, the officer who had landed was quietly setting off along the road when he heard a voice hailing him. This was the Frenchman who had assisted in laying the flare-path. However, he was not to know this, and immediately assuming it was the Police he set off at a great speed, hotly pursued by the eager Frenchman who was encumbered with two bicycles.

In spite of this series of misfortunes, the operation had succeeded, and the Lysander brought back important reports from the field.

During the winter of 1941-42, more organisers and W/T operators were dropped both to the Occupied and the Unoccupied zones. The weather was poor, however, and the number of successful sorties was small. In April and May it was discovered that some of the subversive groups had been penetrated by the Gestapo, but new plans were ready, new men were sent to the field, and the work went on. A coup-de-main attack by Fighting French agents on Radio Paris wireless station, the main channel for Axis and collaborationist propaganda, was extremely successful.

In the autumn more stores were dropped and five Lysander operations were completed bringing out from France, among others, some senior Staff officers of the Fighting French Organisations. The first water-drop was carried out in the December/January moon period when an organiser with his W/T operator were successfully dropped into a lake.

The effect of the Allied invasion of North Africa was to enhance the French sense of alliance and participation, and the consequent German occupation of Southern France, while immediately unfortunate since it resulted in many arrests, caused a powerful resurgence of patriot feeling of which S.O.E. was not slow to take advantage.

At the beginning of 1943 the Independent French Section sent into France an officer specially trained for pick-up operations. The number of landing operations increased. In March, the first reports were received of the existence of Maquis groups in the Haute Savoie. The Germans, in an effort to relieve their man-power shortage were now making serious efforts to conscript labour from the occupied countries, and many young men preferred outlawry in the mountains to deportation to Germany. The existence of these Patriot Groups was a considerable problem to S.O.E., who had not sufficient aircraft resources to maintain them in hiding against the inevitable German counter-measures, and who, moreover, were afraid that large deliveries of stores to them might encourage premature revolt in France. It was decided that a limited quantity of stores, sufficient to keep the Maquis alive, should be despatched, and in the March/April moon period a quantity of food, 270 Stens, and 1,350 Grenades were sent to the Haute Savoie. A British Staff Officer was despatched to France with a senior Staff officer from Fighting French Headquarters to review and report on the position generally.

The weather throughout the summer of 1943 was fortunately good, and the R.A.F. made an outstanding effort. In the April/May moon period 331 containers were sent to the field, in the July/August moon,

660, August/September, 1,446, which included 10,000 Stens, 2,600 pistols, 20,000 Grenades and nearly 18 tons of high explosive in addition to essential wireless equipment. Over the September moon period, an average of 7½ flights per crew was made – or an operation more often than every other night.

The response to the increased quantity of stores delivered was terrific. In April one organiser reported that his group alone wrecked several railway engines a month. In June, 14,000,000 litres of alcohol in a distillery at Saint L'Aumond, and 1,000 tons of rubber at the Michelin factory at Clermont Ferrand were destroyed. By the summer rail cuts, attacks on rolling stocks, and train derailments, had reached a daily average of 100, and so intense was the sabotage activity that the Germans were led to believe that the Allied invasion was impending. The Hispano Suiza works and Tarbes were virtually put out of action. A transformer station at Le Creusot was damaged by a coup-de-main team, and the attack on the Gigny Dam, scheduled to coincide with the invasion of Sicily, succeeded in preventing for five weeks the transport southward along the Saone [Saône] of German naval craft. In September 1943, the total strength of the Independent Groups was estimated at 100/200,000 men, and in addition powerful Fighting French groups were directed and equipped by S.O.E. in collaboration with Fighting French H.Q. Attacks on German personnel had succeeded in killing 800 and wounding 8,500 during the previous six months. Damage to railways had been very great and over 200 locomotives and 2,000 waggons had been affected.

During the autumn the volume of supplies fell off, as a result of poorer weather, but sabotages continued on a high level. An aviation fuel dump for the aerodrome at Istres (1 million litres) and 12 million litres of oil at Varennes-le-Grand were destroyed. Attacks on waterways were extremely successful: in one "incident" the Rhine/Marne Canal was emptied for a stretch of 17 miles.

A second attack on the Gigny barrage once more closed the Saone to shipping. In November, a British officer recently returned from a two months tour of inspection in France reported that the rank and file of Resistance was sound and pro-British: the officers on higher levels were less reliable, being preoccupied with the question of "prise de pouvoir."

The establishment of an S.O.E. Mission at Algiers (Massingham) and an S.D. base at Blida enabled operations to be carried out into Southern France – an area difficult to reach from England. S.D. operations were first attempted from here during the second half of 1943, but it was not until the beginning of 1944 that, with increased aircraft resources and better weather, they reached a significant level.

Two new developments in the technique of relating sabotage to bombing were made during the autumn of this year. An S.O.E. officer in France reported that the workmen and management of one of the Peugeot factories were prepared themselves to sabotage the works provided that the R.A.F. should refrain from bombing them. After consultation with the Air Ministry, S.O.E. replied that the factory must be put out of action for at least six months, and photographs must be produced in order to substantiate the claims of the saboteurs. The sabotage was successfully executed. In the months that followed this "Blackmail" technique was developed further, and several factories were put out of action by either the workmen or the management, who preferred this method to bombing raids by the R.A.F.

Among the stoutest Resistance supporters were the "Cheminots" who themselves suffered considerable loss of life as a result of the R.A.F. train-busting activities.

Annex to COS(43), 287th Meeting
On November 15th, the Minister of Economic Warfare wrote to the Prime Minister, on the subject of fighter attacks on French locomotives:

> "S.O.E. agents returning from France have for some time past called attention to the disproportionate loss of life among drivers and firemen of locomotives attacked by Fighter Command aircraft in comparison with the damage done to the locomotives themselves. The French assert that the average period for which the locomotives are out of action after attack is between 36 and 48 hours whereas many drivers and firemen have been killed.
>
> "Our agents emphasised the adverse effect of these attacks on the morale of the S.N.C.F., the Trade Union of railwaymen, who are among S.O.E.'s best contacts and wholeheartedly working for the Allies."

The message went on to cite the example of the Peugeot factory, and reported that S.O.E. had now received information that effective sabotage had resulted in putting the plant completely out of action for one month and to the extent of 70% of its capacity for a further five months: "If S.O.E. can make bargains on behalf of the R.A.F. we may be able to get the necessary damage done better and without sacrificing French lives."

He therefore asked that the Chiefs of Staff Directive to Fighter Command on the subject of locomotive attacks should be rescinded.

COS(43), 287th Meeting, Item 7

The Chiefs of Staff considered the problem at their 287th Meeting. Sir Douglas Evill said that the Air Ministry had gone into the question and were prepared to agree with the views expressed by Lord Selborne. Operations against locomotives in enemy-occupied N.W. Europe had now been cancelled: "S.O.E. had been informed of the action taken and had been invited to do everything possible to interfere with transportation by stepping-up sabotage operations on the French railway system."

The railway workers played their part, and in the event more locomotives were put out of action through sabotage than had been possible by air attack. This policy was to the material advantage of the French people, and of Fighter Command.

D-Day plans for France were by this time fairly well-developed, and the tremendous increase in the number of S.D. aircraft in the early months of 1944 led to an increase in the quantity of stores sent to the field. In many areas the Maquis had now for some time been in open revolt. In the Haute Savoie, regular German Army divisions had finally had to be employed in the effort to overrun the Maquis strongholds. Allied Missions, consisting of British, American and French officers, were despatched to the chief Maquis areas to strengthen and direct Resistance activity, and a large proportion of the supplementary air lift was used to send stores and supplies to these areas. The arming of groups in strategic areas such as Normandy was clearly desirable: but the cover plan laid down by S.H.A.E.F. decreed that at least twice – sometimes three times – as much material should go into the area north of the Seine as into Normandy. The first fast dropping operation was carried out in January 1944, when a Mosquito delivered a small package of money, and W/T equipment to the field. This type of operation was never widely employed, but on some occasions was invaluable.

In April, the Timken ball-bearing factory was put out of action by "Blackmail" sabotage. The volume of sabotage activity was now rising steeply. As a result of the increased air deliveries of the last few months, Resistance was now well-equipped to play its part within the general military strategy. On June 1st the "warning" signal for the D-Day plans were transmitted, and these were followed on the evening before D-Day by the "action" messages. The subversive groups all over France went into action; and a very high proportion of the allotted targets was attacked. News of the Invasion of France stimulated Resistance activity to the highest possible pitch, and thousands of Frenchmen joined the Maquis Groups. The Germans found themselves faced with a continual disruption of their lines of communication: attacks on railways and roads delayed the employment of reinforcements to the Bridgehead area, telephone communications were constantly put out of action, so that the Germans were unable to issue orders to their subordinate formations, and in many areas the Maquis, at last taking the offensive, was able to attack individual German units. The mass daylight operations by the 8th U.S.A.A.F. supplied the guerilla groups with quantities of arms and ammunition, and the execution of both Overlord and Anvil was materially assisted by the action of the Resistance forces behind the enemy lines. Deliveries were continued to the still unliberated areas of France until the winter.

Holland

Holland was among the most difficult of the Occupied countries in which to organise Resistance. The tough, stubborn nature of its people and its important geographical position made it one of the areas most severely controlled and suppressed by the Germans. Moreover it is a small country, very flat, and well-populated; there are practically no districts in which the nature of the terrain lends itself to Maquis work. In Holland Resistance organisations had to remain clandestine or be liquidated: there was no possibility of retreat to the hills.

The first officers to be despatched to Holland were dropped on 7th September 1941, and consisted of two couriers whose mission was to establish contact with local Resistance movements. In November an organiser and W/T operator were dropped, and in December the first W/T message was received. During 1942, a small number of operations were completed, delivering a quantity of stores and more agents to the field. The building up of clandestine organisations went on slowly throughout the winter and spring of 1943. In the last three days of the

June moon period 25 containers and 4 packages were despatched to the field, but the high percentage of aircraft losses on Missions to Holland caused the Air Ministry to cancel all operations to Holland for three months.

DD12/441/43, 4th September 1943
In September it was agreed that two sorties should be attempted, but neither aircraft returned from its Mission. In November it was confirmed that the para-military organisation in Holland had been penetrated by the Gestapo some months previously and must be considered as a total loss. Air operations to Holland were once more cancelled.

It is unlikely that the high percentage of loss on supply dropping operations to Holland was a result of the enemy's knowledge of the Resistance movements. From the Gestapo point of view, the shooting down of a few English bombers could not be as valuable as the knowledge of Resistance plans which they could continue to acquire so long as the British were in ignorance of the fact that the organisations were penetrated. The less attention that was drawn to them, the longer they might continue to play a double game. It is more likely that the aircraft lost were due to the normal enemy anti-aircraft defence measures. At this time, when Bomber Command was making a series of major attacks on the Ruhr and the Rhineland, both the ack-ack and the night fighter defences in Holland were formidable. Moreover, supply dropping bombers, flying singly and usually low, were easily tracked in by the enemy and were an easy prey to his fighter aircraft.

In spite of the loss of so much of the Resistance organisation, information from Holland showed clearly that the Resistance spirit itself was still very much alive. At the beginning of 1944, the Air Ministry agreed to undertake operations to Holland once more, although these were to be limited at first to the "blind" dropping of agents. More officers and W/T operators were sent in, and the work of contacting and establishing Resistance Groups was begun again from the beginning. A tremendous leeway had to be made up, however, since the quantity of stores delivered to the field was already well behind schedule.

Sabotage in Holland was encouraged by the news of the Allied landing in June, and in August S.O.E. was able to report that the principal Resistance Movement (R.V.V.) was sound. Aircraft losses were still high, however: out of a total of nine sorties three had been lost between May and August. In September, a vastly increased quantity of stores was delivered. Two operations had been successfully completed in August: in September, 42 out of 86 sorties were successful, delivering 111 tons of stores to the field. In November there was another wave of arrests in the country, but the impetus of Resistance was by now too powerful to be checked. Operations continued on a small scale in the winter of 1944 and the spring of 1945, and in March, 25 out of 40 sorties were successful.

Despite the limitations imposed on it by the severity of the German control and by the difficulty of delivering supplies by air, Dutch Resistance had played a not unworthy part. The sabotage of communications and waterways throughout the country, which had been continued over most of the period, with increased enthusiasm after the invasion of France, provided the enemy with a considerable problem. The flooding of large areas of the country was the only answer the Germans could find to the tough and resilient spirit of the Dutch.

Belgium

By the summer of 1941 reports from Belgium of fires and industrial sabotage showed that the spirit of Resistance was active here too, and organisers and W/T operators were despatched to the field in the autumn.

The first agent, who had been dropped on the night of 12/13th May, sent his first message on 14th September, reporting that he had been landed about forty miles N.E. of his intended pinpoint; that he had found himself on the German side of the border in a prohibited area, and had had great difficulty in escaping to Belgium. Not until four months afterwards was he able to contact one of the S.O.E. wireless operators whom he had known in this country, and report on the progress he had made. He stated that he had been busy organising sabotage groups, and that the Belgians were waiting impatiently for help to be sent to them from England. When the necessary materials could be delivered there was a great deal of good work to be done.

Bad weather during the winter of 1941-42 limited the number of successful operations, but in the spring the quantity of stores delivered began to increase to about 2½ tons per month. Industrial sabotage, and attacks on communications began to increase. In September, a big power station was attacked, and in November an attack on railways and locomotives carried out by saboteurs under cover of an R.A.F. raid was partially successful. Bad weather prevented the R.A.F. from taking part on the scale originally planned, and only a few Intruder aircraft were used. The careful timing of this operation necessitated the establishment of daily communications with the field who were not, however, warned that the R.A.F. would be helping them in their work.

COS(42)386(0), 7th November 1942
S.O.E.'s work in organising Resistance work in Belgium was severely handicapped by the lack of co-operation by the Belgian Government. In spite of the C.I.G.S.'s Memorandum outlining S.O.E.'s responsibility as the co-ordinating authority dealing with the General Staffs of the Allied Governments of the occupied territories, and in contrast to the loyal and cordial co-operation received from the Belgian General Staff, the Belgian Government broke off relations with S.O.E. in August 1942. By November, S.O.E. had again established relations with the Belgian Government, but the task of obtaining help and support from them was always difficult.

It was discovered in the autumn of 1942 that the Gestapo had succeeded in penetrating many of the subversive organisations in Belgium and only two of the S.O.E. groups could be regarded as reliable (the same two that had carried out the locomotive attack). Once more the work had to begin again; but Belgian Resistance was luckier than Dutch in that there was more time for reorganisation, and for the despatch of new officers and stores. Aircraft losses in Belgium, although higher than those in France, never reached the Dutch level, and during 1943 operations continued to this country.

In September 1943 S.O.E. reported that contact with Belgian Resistance movements had been maintained and a total of some 350 containers had been sent into the country. Sabotage was continuing although it was less successful than in some other countries. In the winter bad weather once more curtailed the number of successful operations, but by the spring the number was increasing. In May, 32 out of 62 sorties was successful, and although on the Allied invasion, Belgian Resistance was still sadly under-equipped, the execution of their D-day plans was carried out with proportionately even greater success than in France.

Between 10th and 20th June, 153 sabotage operations were carried out including a high percentage of road and railway destruction. Sabotage of telecommunications was widespread and effective. During July, clandestine attacks on all types of communications increased – 800 rail cuts were reported together with 42 derailments, and the destruction or damage of 65 road and railway bridges. A daylight operation carried out by the 8th U.S.A.A.F. to the Belgian Ardennes, where a large number of insurgents had found refuge, delivered a considerable quantity of stores to the Belgian Maquis, who were able to take the offensive and carry out minor harassing attacks on German formations.

The liberation of large areas of France increased the number of aircraft available for supply dropping operations to Belgium, and stores continued to pour into the country. At the request of the Army authorities, Belgian Resistance carried out a large number of mopping up operations, and in this way dealt with many isolated German units. Highly successful anti-scorch action of vital importance to the Allied Armies operating against Germany was completely successful, especially in Antwerp. By October 1944, the work was done, and Belgium, thanks in part to the efforts of her own patriots, had been liberated.

Norway

By the autumn of 1941 direct W/T contact had been established with the military organisation of Resistance in Oslo. The R.A.F. raid on the capital was reported to have had a tonic effect and its success facilitated S.O.E.'s work in the direction of Resistance. An example of the type of minor sabotage carried out in all the occupied countries was given by a Norwegian nurse who escaped to England and reported that Norwegian hospital staffs, ordered to hand over blankets to the German authorities, had caused them to be infected with scabies before complying with the order. Bad weather in the winter limited the number of successful operations: this was particularly unfortunate since operations to Norway could not be flown during the summer months owing to the distance involved and the short hours of darkness. One of the last operations carried out in the spring of 1942 was the successful landing of a Catalina, which delivered two couriers and special stores to the Norwegian Resistance Groups.

Operations were resumed in September, but the weather was still unfavourable, and the number of successes was small. The R.A.F. raid on the Knaben mines on 3rd March 1943, was based to a considerable extent on intelligence provided by S.O.E. who were also able afterwards to report that the main objective had been demolished. In February the coup-de-main party "Gunnerside", that had been standing-by for some months was at last sent to the field, and carried out its attack on the Norsk Hydro Heavy Water plant with amazing success. Now that the story of the research on the atomic bomb is told, the importance of this attack, which destroyed the German's main source of heavy water, and was carried out on instructions from the War Cabinet, can be seen in its true perspective.

COS(43), 89th Meeting, Item 2, 12th April 1943
"Instructed the Secretary to convey their warmest congratulations to S.O.E. in the outstanding success achieved in certain recent operations in Norway."

By May 1943 S.O.E., in reviewing its activities, was able to report that the Norwegian Secret Military Organisation had been maintained, and was continuing Resistance in accordance with a planned programme. A large number of coup-de-main attacks on various targets had met with considerable success. In the autumn air operations were once more resumed to Norway, and although a number of arrests were made during the winter the organisation of Resistance remained fundamentally sound and substantially intact.

News of the Allied landing in France stimulated the morale of the Norwegian Resistants, but instructions were issued that no premature risings should be made. Sabotage continued in spite of the inadequate supplies which were delivered to the country as a result of bad weather and partly because of the comparatively low priority of Norwegian S.D. operations. By the spring of 1945 the volume of supplies had risen sharply; only 7 deliveries were made in January, but in February, 187, and in April, 156 operations were successful.

Resistance organisations were by now in a sufficiently strong position themselves to take over the country, and even before the formal surrender of the German Command in Chief of the area, all real authority had been wrested from him, and was in the hands of the men who had opposed him for so long.

Denmark

S.D. operations to Denmark began in the autumn of 1941. One of the earliest of these resulted in tragedy.

Two agents were dropped, but the parachute of one failed to open and the officer who was to have been the chief organiser of Resistance in Denmark was killed. His W/T operator however, landed safely – in spite of the fact that with his equipment he weighed eighteen stone and on his practice jumps had first broken his leg and then injured his pelvis. The body of the officer who was killed was discovered by the Germans, and for security reasons it was decided that no more air operations should be attempted for three months.

Throughout 1942 deliveries to Denmark continued on a small scale. In May, and again in December, Gestapo activity and arrests in the field caused the postponement of operations. In the autumn the first water-drop into the open sea was successfully completed when an important Danish representative was dropped into the sea 150 yards off the north coast of Zealand. This drop, which required the highest degree of accuracy from the pilot lest the man should be dropped to far out and caught in the tides, was extremely well done.

In January 1943, the R.A.F. carried out a raid on the Burmeister and Wain factory – a raid for which S.O.E. had pressed since January 1941, and for which they were able to provide detailed intelligence. After the raid a Danish officer was instructed by the Germans to deal with the delayed action bombs, and instead of removing them he insisted that they would have to be exploded on the spot. The Germans believed this. He was able to carry out his programme, and the amount of damage done on this raid was considerably increased by his efforts.

In the summer of 1943, a considerable increase in the number of sabotage incidents was reported. Among many other objects, the Scandia railway carriage shops at Randers were put out of action, and the factory of stores (valued at 400,000 pounds) of A.T. Hansen, which were working for the German army, were destroyed by fire. By September, a well-knit organisation had been created in Denmark, and had been responsible for a wave of sabotage throughout the country. The Germans were compelled to take over the control of a country which, until now, they had considered a model of the "New Order."

The delivery of stores continued on a small scale. By November the nightly average of sabotage attacks had risen to twenty, in spite of the enemy's precautions. In December an aircraft failed to return from a Danish S.D. operation, but its crew of eight landed safely and were passed through to Sweden by the S.O.E. Underground Groups.

On D-Day Resistance in Denmark, as in Norway, was not called into the open, but clandestine sabotage was continued. During the first week of July the tension prevailing as a result of the Allied invasion and the consequent increase of sabotage culminated in a spontaneous strike in Copenhagen which spread to other towns under the Danish Freedom Council. This strike was so successful that the German authorities were forced to give way to the demands of the Freedom Council.

In September, Danish resentment at German oppression once more found expression in a strike, but by November a series of arrests carried out by the Germans had caused the partial eclipse of the Freedom Council as the central authority of Resistance in the country, and general lawlessness prevailed throughout Denmark. The number of deliveries had by this time considerably increased; in September, 26 sorties were successful, and in February, 49. In March, the R.A.F.'s attack on the Gestapo H.Q. in Copenhagen was extremely successful, and Resistance was still further encouraged. 96 stores deliveries were made in March, and in April the figure had risen to as high as 155.

Owing to the German capitulation, Danish Resistance had no time to come into the open. Sabotage operations, however, continued on a large scale until the 5th May, when orders were sent for all activities to cease. In its way Danish Resistance had been as successful as any other in Europe, and had certainly learnt how to obtain the maximum results for the minimum losses.

Chapter 18

Central Europe, Supplied by Aircraft Based in the UK and Mediterranean

Throughout the whole war, the main difficulty inherent in operations to Central Europe was the distances involved, and aircraft, whether based in England or the Mediterranean found themselves operating at the extreme limit of their range. This often entailed special modifications to the aircraft, so that they could carry extra petrol tanks.

Poland

The shortness of the summer nights made it impossible for flights to be undertaken to Poland or Czechoslovakia during the hours of darkness, and therefore there was a period during the summer when no air operations could be flown to these countries.

In Poland, a country where the technique of Underground Warfare is part of the national tradition, the Secret Army was organised on a more military basis than in any other country of Europe. Resistance activity began almost as soon as the Germans had occupied the country, and requests for help and supplies were soon being received by the Allies. The first operation to Poland was flown by a Whitley in February 1941, and involved a flight of 1,700 miles. In the autumn, the first two Halifaxes were made available for operations and were modified for long range work. By the spring of 1942 a number of men and a small quantity of stores had been despatched to Poland. Operations were then suspended for the summer months, and although they were resumed in the autumn the weather severely limited the number of successful flights.

Sabotage in Poland had continued steadily throughout 1941 and 1942. In the four months between April and August 1941, a report from the field showed that 876 locomotives had been damaged, and 2,699 acts of industrial sabotage carried out. By the third quarter of 1941, the total number of sabotage acts had risen to 7,446 and included the damaging of 543 locomotives and 22 aircraft. By the end of 1942, the strength of the Secret Armies was estimated at 300,000. Wireless communications were good, and it was reported that 50 Reception Committees could be set up at once if necessary. In the autumn of that year the execution of simultaneous attacks on railway lines, which was carried out by personnel trained in the U.K. included great damage, and caused the Germans to carry out heavy reprisals.

Operations during the winter of 1942/43 were curtailed by a run of bad weather, but during the spring a number of successful flights were made, including deliveries during the non-moon period. At the end of April, operations were once more suspended until the autumn.

During the first part of 1943 operations to Poland were continued from the U.K., but in the autumn it was decided that in order to shorten the length of the flights involved and to avoid some of the most dangerous German anti-aircraft defences in the West, S.D. operations to Poland should be undertaken from the Mediterranean. A Polish flight was set up near Tunis, but at first results were disappointing owing chiefly to the bad weather throughout the winter of 1943/44. In April, however, when the air base had been established at Brindisi, conditions began to improve, and 66 out of 130 sorties were successfully completed during the moon period, resulting in the delivery of 70 tons of stores to the Polish Secret Army.

The first landing operation to Poland was carried out in the same month, when three senior Polish Officers, including the second in command of the Secret Army, were brought out of the country. Two more landing operations, one of which brought out valuable information on the enemy's V.2 weapon, were also carried out this year. At the end of July, the Resistance forces in Warsaw rose to attack the enemy and supplies were then urgently demanded.

An increased allocation of aircraft was made and a large number of sorties were flown from Italy, including normal bomber aircraft, to the relief of the Secret Armies. In order to obtain pinpoint accuracy on the squares and streets of Warsaw the aircraft had to fly low over the city and were attacked by every type of German anti-aircraft gun posted on the roofs of the houses. The aircraft losses were considerable: in August, 30 aircraft failed to return from Polish operations and at one time the proportion of losses on Warsaw deliveries was as high as 25%. In spite of the efforts of both the R.A.F. and the U.S.A.A.F., however, the Secret Armies, after a protracted and gallant fight were forced to capitulate, and on October 2nd, resistance in Warsaw came to an end.

Operations continued to Poland after this, but were not made easier by the Russian refusal to allow S.D. aircraft to fly over their lines. In November after the failure of negotiations between M.A.A.F. and the Soviet authorities, flights to Poland were resumed, but aircraft were forced to fly to the west of the Russian-occupied territory.

During the winter supplies were delivered to the German-occupied areas of Poland, but by February 1945, the Russian forces had liberated the whole country. Resistance in Poland, although well organised and heroically led, had been severely handicapped. The difficulty of sending supplies to so distant a country resulted in the Secret Army being permanently under-nourished with arms and ammunition. After years of stubborn resistance, the Russian attitude towards them caused bitterness and resentment. The Polish Secret Army was perhaps the first weapon of Underground Warfare in Europe, but for reasons beyond its control – and beyond the control of S.O.E. or the R.A.F. – it was never used to its full extent.

Czechoslovakia

Resistance in Czechoslovakia, although rigorously suppressed by the Germans, began to show itself soon after the enemy occupation of the country. The entry of Russia into the war in 1941 had a strong moral effect on the patriots, and during September 14 major acts of sabotage and a large total of minor activities were carried out. In the autumn agents and W/T sets were dropped, and although weather was bad in January and February operations were later resumed. In an attack by Bomber Command on the Skoda Works at Pilsen, Czech resistants helped to guide the aircraft by lighting fires near the target.

In May 1942 the execution of Heydrich by Czech patriots despatched from this country by S.O.E. resulted in a German reign of terror. Organised cruelty and brutality on such a scale could not fail to be effective, and many Resistance organisations were broken up while others were forced to go to ground. In March, 1943, the leader and W/T operator of the last remaining S.O.E. party were arrested and committed suicide, but their reserve operator was still able to send messages, and reported that he was in contact with another Resistance group.

In the autumn of 1943, it was decided that air operations to Czechoslovakia should in future be flown from the Mediterranean, and attempts were once more made to rebuild Resistance organisation in the country. The success achieved, however, was small. The distance involved, the almost continuous bad weather, and the difficulties of navigation in Czechoslovakia combined to make S.D. flights to that country particularly difficult. Moreover, the German grip on Czechoslovakia throughout 1943 was still too tight to permit the establishing of subversive groups. A small number of operations were despatched during 1943 and 1944, carrying organisers, W/T operators and a limited quantity of stores to the field.

COS(44)902(0), 14 October 1944
In October 1944 the Foreign Secretary wrote to the Chiefs of Staff, agreeing with the view taken by the C.I.G.S. that large scale air operations to assist a general rising should now be more properly conducted by the Soviet Air Force, and a letter embodying this argument and suggesting that sabotage activity should be continued was sent to General Ingr.

Annex to COS(44), 339th Meeting, Item 9, 16th October 1944
The Slovak rising which later took place was regarded as primarily a Russian responsibility. In January 1945, the Chiefs of Staff authorised A.F.H.Q. to undertake 10 successful operations per month to Czechoslovakia, but bad weather once more prevented the implementation of these plans, and in the January moon period only one daylight stores drop by fighter aircraft was successful. The weather continued poor throughout the spring; in February, 4 out of 15 sorties were successful; in March, 5 out of 14 and in April 13 out of 61.

SOE/45/R.42
A message from the Council of Three of April 1945 sums up the Air force assistance to their country: "We thank you and Allied pilots for the operations. Few weapons were supplied, but nevertheless you have saved many lives, national property, and you have increased Anglo/American prestige. Every weapon will be multiplied many times."

Austria and Germany

Germany naturally presented the most unfavourable ground for the organisation of Resistance, and the people of Austria, whether because they favoured the Nazis or because they were too cowed to show their resentment, were almost as unpromising material as the Germans themselves.

A small number of operations were flown to both countries from the U.K., until in the autumn of 1943, the aircraft base for operations to Central Europe was transferred to the Mediterranean. A number of agents were despatched to Germany to organise sabotage and go-slow methods, but comparatively little material was sent. Efforts to penetrate Austria were made during 1943, from bases in Yugoslavia, and in North Italy, and by February 1945, a small number of S.O.E. officers had been dropped or infiltrated by land-line, into Austria. The achievements of the Anti-Fascist Groups in this country, however, were throughout the period comparatively insignificant.

Chapter 19

Southern Europe, Supplied by Mediterranean-based Aircraft

From the very beginning, conditions in the occupied countries of the Balkans were very different from those in Western Europe. Powerful indigenous Resistance movements sprang up in countries such as Yugoslavia and Greece, where their historical traditions enabled the people to take to a guerilla life with ease and enthusiasm. As early as 1941, reports from these countries showed that Resistance was already beginning to crystallize around its own leaders, and to undertake sabotage and sometimes even military action against the occupying forces. In order to continue their work, however, it was obvious that the patriots needed supplies of military equipment, of food and of clothing.

Yugoslavia

Ante-occupational work carried out by S.O.E. in Yugoslavia had to some extent prepared the ground for resistance to the enemy. In the autumn of 1941, after widespread activity, reports showed that some guerillas were operating under more or less unified command, and in October, the A.O.C.-in-C., Mediterranean, and the C.-in-C. Mediterranean, agreed to allocate two Wellesley Bombers, based on Malta, and three Bomber sorties from Cairo for dropping supplies to Montenegro. British Liaison Officers were despatched by sea, and by October were able to report that they had made contact with Mihailovic.

By November, however, the first signs of internal disunity were seen, and in Montenegro Mihailovic and his Chetniks were reported to be fighting the Communists. An appeal, suggested by S.O.E., was made to both Moscow and King Peter to do their best to bring about a united front within Yugoslavia, but the Russians proved unwilling, and the King unable, to assist in dissolving the conflict.

Meanwhile, the lack of aircraft was seriously handicapping operations. Two Whitleys were sent to the Mediterranean, but they proved to be too slow for daylight sorties, and owing to their lack of de-icing and oxygen apparatus, only one sortie was successfully completed. Difficulties of maintaining communications with Mihailovic made air deliveries almost impossible. Ill-luck continued to hamper Yugoslav plans: of the four Whitleys allotted to Malta, one burnt out in England, and two were destroyed or badly damaged on the ground in Malta by enemy action. During 1942, a limited quantity of stores was delivered to Yugoslavia by the aircraft of 148 Squadron. Sabotage directed by the British Liaison Officers on the spot had achieved some success and in the spring of 1943, with the news that Mihailovic had apparently accepted H.M.G.'s directive on his future action, prospects for Yugoslavia were brighter. In May 1943 the first British missions to the Partisans were dropped in Croatia and the first British mission under Major Deakin was dropped to Tito's Headquarters, then in Montenegro. In May the Chiefs of Staff, reviewing the operational policy in Yugoslavia, ruled that in the immediate future S.O.E.'s capacity to supply stores to the guerilla forces should be at the rate of 150 tons per month, rising as soon as operations elsewhere permitted, to 500 tons. The Prime Minister himself, after his visit to the Mediterranean emphasised the over-riding importance of giving help to the Yugoslav resistants immediately, and at a Staff Conference held on 23rd June, it was decided that the scale of support both to Mihailovic and to the partisans should be considerably increased.

The number of S.D. sorties to Yugoslavia was accordingly stepped-up. Further British Liaison officers were sent in to both the Chetniks and the Partisans, and by September 1943 the senior British missions at the respective H.Q. of Tito and Mihailovic had been reinforced and each was headed by a Brigadier. In the July/August moon period, 27½ tons were despatched to Mihailovic's forces, 17¼ to Tito's. In the August/September moon these figures had practically doubled: 33¾ tons were sent to the Chetniks, and 34 tons to the Partisans, by a total of 51 successful operations. By this time there were 26 Allied missions in the field, including 33 British officers, 37 British O.R.'s and 2 American Liaison officers. The total equipment delivered up to

September 1943 included 118 tons of stores to Mihailovic and 71 tons to the Partisans; the strength of the guerilla forces was then estimated at 20,000 Chetniks and 75,000 Partisans.

Mihailovic had always shown a tendency to refrain from action against the Italians, but after the Italian armistice in September 1943 it was becoming increasingly clear that Mihailovic was becoming reluctant to use his forces even against the German occupying forces; on one occasion he went so far as to declare that he regarded Tito, and not the Germans, as his chief enemy. An Army which practically refused to fight the Germans was obviously of little value to the cause of the United Nations, and in January 1944, the Chiefs of Staff directed that the Partisans under Tito should receive 80% of all air sorties to the Balkans. Shortly afterwards it was decided to withdraw all British missions from the Chetniks and the evacuation of over 100 personnel was completed by air at the end of May 1944.

The establishment of air bases on the heel of Italy, which placed the S.D. aircraft at a comparatively short range from their targets, and the increased aircraft allotment for S.D. work in the Mediterranean, permitted a terrific expansion in the quantity of stores despatched to the field. Landing operations, which had been carried out on a small scale during the autumn of 1943, were now used to deliver equipment by the ton and to exfiltrate Liaison Officers, military and political delegates, and wounded guerillas by the hundred.

In April, 303 tons of stores were sent to the Partisans. In May, 418 out of 714 sorties were successful, and 582 tons of stores were delivered; 42 landing operations were completed, and 627 persons were brought out of Yugoslavia. June beat all previous records when 970 sorties were successful. In addition, on the night 3/4th June Tito himself, his H.Q. Staff and British, American and Russian missions totalling over 150 personnel were evacuated by air from an untried landing ground by American and Russian Dakotas at less than twelve hours notice, in response to an S.O.S. message resulting from a German concentrated drive.

These figures steadily increased. In July, under the pressure of a temporary parachute shortage, 386 landing operations were completed, delivering supplies and bringing out 4,880 people; in August 4,032 persons were evacuated. The record monthly tonnage was reached in November, when mass drops by 205 Group brought the number of successful sorties up to 1032.

Throughout the whole period, guerilla activities in the Balkans, centering mainly on Yugoslavia, had succeeded in containing a number of German divisions which could ill be spared. Large areas of country had been cleared of German and Italian occupying forces, and were entirely controlled by the Partisans. It was of course this circumstance which made possible the unparalleled use of transport aircraft on landing operations.

Towards the end of 1944, the Yugoslav guerillas took advantage of the enemy's increasing weakness to increase their pressure, and by the spring of 1945 the Germans were withdrawing in large numbers from Yugoslavia. The long and bitter fight carried out from the inhospitable hills was over, and the Partisans had re-occupied their own country. In two years from June 1943 to May 1945 (see Appendix I.3) over 13,000 tons of stores were delivered by air and over 17,000 personnel, mostly wounded or sick Partisans were evacuated by air. In addition even larger quantities of stores had been delivered by sea.

Italy

From Italy, reports were received during 1941 and 1942 that strong Anti-Fascist underground groups existed in the north. One operation, delivering two men was successfully completed by U.K.-based aircraft in 1941, but Italy was not really a practical proposition for S.D. operations from England. In the summer of 1943, the establishment of an S.D. Squadron at Algiers made it possible to supply the Italian groups by air, and one Liaison officer and some W/T operators and stores were dropped into the country before the end of the year. When Marshal Badoglio sued for peace, it was S.O.E. who provided a wireless operator and set to establish contact between his H.Q. in Rome, and A.F.H.Q. at Algiers.

The 1943 Armistice caused large numbers of deserters from the Italian Army and other resisters to take to the hills. This was the first beginning of the Italian Partisan movement, and although many bands had a good deal of arms and equipment at the outset, the demand for stores in N. Italy was far in excess of Allied capacity until the beginning of 1945.

Italian organisers and W/T operators continued to be dropped to the biggest groups in north Italy to report on their potentialities. In the winter, however, bad weather limited the number of operations, but by the spring of 1944 the increased airlift made available and the use of

Italian bases increased the number of sorties attempted and the volume of supply went up by leaps and bounds. In May, 48 out of 106 sorties were successful, in June, 107 out of 197. British Liaison officers in uniform began to be dropped in June. The Partisan movement grew so rapidly in the summer of 1944 that the bands in the hills reached a figure of well over 100,000.

By October 1944, when it was clear that the war would last to 1945, the position of the Partisans, faced by winter conditions and enemy reprisals, was extremely grave unless the airlift could be substantially increased. In November, mass daylight and night deliveries were made as an emergency measure to Partisan Groups in the mountains, but were not on the whole very successful. 205 Group, which carried out these Missions, were inexperienced in this type of work, and the delay action devices on the parachutes were not properly operated by the aircrews. The high drops, therefore, caused a great deal of scatter, and so much German activity was roused and it was decided that this method of supply should be discontinued.

From January 1945, however, mass drops were attempted with greater success by Dakotas with fighter escort, based on Rosignano and between 1st February and 30th April over 2,700 tons of stores were poured into Northern Italy, largely by this means. Several pick-up operations by Lysander were also successfully carried out, and British Liaison Officers were withdrawn from the country to report on their work.

By April, 1945, S.O.E. missions in Northern Italy numbered over 100 British officers and O.R.s and Resistance was sufficiently organised and well-equipped to make a tremendous response to the Allied appeal for guerilla activity in support of 15th Army Group's offensive and anti-scorch. The Partisans, under Allied officers, mainly British, were able to establish their authority over large areas of Northern Italy seizing Milan, Genoa, Turin and many other important towns, and capturing over 50,000 German prisoners. Italian Resistance, though late in the field, had proved itself to be one of the most successful of the patriot movements in Europe.

Albania

Albania had of course been occupied by the Italians in 1939, and therefore when the Italians launched their attack on Greece from

Albanian bases in 1940, there was a certain chance of organising Albanian risings against the Italian rear. S.O.E. officers, including Abas Kupi a well-known supporter of King Zog, entered Albania from Yugoslavia in 1941 but were unable to achieve a substantial rising.

It was not until the summer of 1943, when British missions to the Greek guerillas had been established in Epirus, that it was possible for a British mission to be dropped in Epirus and move overland northwards into Albania. They found plenty of potential resistance elements, the right wing Balli Kombëtar [literally National Front], the Zogist movement under Abas Kupi and the left wing L.N.C. or Partisans under Enver Hoxha. But organisation, training, equipment and co-ordination were non-existent. Consequently in the autumn of 1943 further missions were dropped, including a Senior Mission under a Brigadier, and the work of training and organisation proceeded throughout the winter, in spite of casualties including the Brigadier himself who was wounded and captured.

The supplies which began to go into Albania in 1943 were dropped from Halifaxes of 148 Squadron. With the Italian collapse the Italian troops either took to the hills or were murdered and the Germans moved in to occupy Albania. At the same time the policy of the support and unification of two rival bands proved in Albania, as in other countries, to be full of difficulties. Both bands were mainly concerned with the prosecution of their private ends and it was difficult to decide which was the genuine Resistance movement.

However, the Balli Kombëtar tended more and more to a policy of collaboration with the enemy, M. Hoxha had the support of Marshal Tito, and therefore when we supported Tito in Yugoslavia we had to support M. Hoxha in Albania. Wherever his writ ran, he instituted a reign of terror and denounced as collaborators all those who would not obey him. He raised complaints against the British because they gave refuge in Italy to those "war criminals" (his rivals) who were fleeing from his vengeance.

The Germans were in possession of the country's few landing grounds, of which that of Tirana was the best. There is no level space in Albania. Improvised landing grounds were therefore not possible, no landing operations were carried out until the German withdrawal in November, over 900 tons of stores were dropped during 1944, (in addition to considerable tonnages delivered by sea), and the Partisan resistance to the Germans, which kept 2 or 3 divisions tied down, was of definite value to the war effort, since, apart from the casualties inflicted on the Germans, these divisions were diverted from reinforcing German troops in Greece, Yugoslavia or elsewhere.

The Germans eventually withdrew of their own accord from Albania in the autumn of 1944 immediately after their withdrawal from Greece. M. Hoxha claims the credit of having driven them out, but the claim is absurd. The German tactics were to announce beforehand the date of their withdrawal from a place, and to declare that if they were attacked the place would be burnt down. In obedience to this arrangement and timetable, the Partisans would enter the town some half-hour after the Germans had freely left and announce that they had captured it.

The German departure left the country in a desperate need of food, particularly in the south, some food was supplied by the British, but it was mostly delivered by sea, and in any event was in no way a Special Operation. With the beginning of 1945 the Albanian Section was closed down and Albania removed from the theatre of Special Operations.

Greece

Preparations for the organisation of Resistance in Greece had been made in the early months of 1941 before the country was overrun by the Germans, and the organisation of clandestine resistance among the Greeks themselves began from the first moment of German occupation. Resistance began clandestinely in the towns, and strikes and sabotage developed throughout 1942, S.O.E. maintained communications and sent in funds and small scale supplies by overland routes from Istanbul and by caique through the Aegean from Smyrna.

The prime mover in organising Resistance was the left wing group known as E.A.M. and it was clear even in 1942 that British support to this group would produce political complications, unless the Royal Greek Government was prepared to broaden its composition to include representatives of the Resistance movement. The other chief leader was Colonel Zervas, who after prolonged pressure by S.O.E. in 1942 took to the hills.

In September 1942, a party of British officers was dropped in Central Greece to destroy the Gorgopotamos Bridge on the Salonica-Athens railway, so as to cut one of Rommel's main supply lines in preparation for the El Alamein offensive. They contacted Zervas and local E.A.M. supporters, and persuaded these rival bands to unite for the attack on the bridge which was carried out with complete success. The party was originally briefed to withdraw after the operation but were now instructed to remain in Greece and organise guerilla activity.

The party was therefore supplemented by other British missions throughout Epirus and Central Greece and began the task of organising and reconciling the main rival bands, E.L.A.S. which was the paramilitary wing of E.A.M. and E.D.E.S., the guerilla organisation of Zervas.

Throughout the spring and summer of 1943 Halifaxes of 148 Squadron were operating almost continuously in dropping missions and supplies every night during the moon period and every other night during the non-moon period – twenty nights a month from April to August. A large part of the supplies to Greece however went in not by air, but by caique through Smyrna.

August 1943 saw the first landing operations in Greece. On 7th August Squadron Leader Harris dropped a Flight Lieutenant with equipment to lay out a flare-path, and on 9th himself landed there in a Dakota and after eleven minutes on the ground took off the Senior B.L.O., Brigadier Myers and six guerrilla leaders for consultations in Cairo with G.H.Q. Middle East and the Greek Government.

Unfortunately these talks proved abortive and thereafter there were such bitter divisions among the rival Greek Partisans that it was doubtful wisdom to supply them with further arms. The problem of reconciling conflicting political views with the necessity for military actions became acute. After the failure of out attempt to hold Cos and Leros the Greek situation deteriorated very rapidly. With the exception of Colonel Zervas, there was little guarantee that the Greek Partisan leaders would use arms to fight against the Germans. They were far more likely to use them, as they did in the case of Captain Hubbard on 14th October 1943, to murder British officers.

With the growing strength of Marshal Tito in Yugoslavia, it was thought that our major effort could be more usefully transferred to that country. In November 1943, the Prime Minister specifically forbade the supply of any further arms to E.L.A.S. in Greece, though this ban was later modified in favour of E.L.A.S. bands known by B.L.O.'s to be actively fighting the Germans. At the end of the month Lysanders of C Flight of 148 Squadron brought out the Resistance leaders to attend the Lebanon Conference, returning them later to Greece.

In August 1944, Zervas and Sarafis, the leader of E.L.A.S. were brought out by air to attend the Caserta Conference at which the areas to be held by E.D.E.S. and E.L.A.S. were laid down in anticipation of the German evacuation and British occupation. The network of British missions supplied to General Scobie and A.O.C. B.A.F. a volume of tactical intelligence throughout operation Manna, including intelligence on fighter and bomber targets during the German withdrawal. They also assisted in preparing advanced L.G.'s for R.A.F. fighters before the Germans withdrew. The Greek Resistance movement did not of course compel the German withdrawal but made valuable contributions by harassing and delaying the withdrawal and by anti-scorch activity which saved a number of important installations especially in Athens and the Piraeus.

Resistance in Greece, more than anywhere else had been embittered and dissipated by internal feuds and the tide of patriot feeling had been lost in the sands of political rivalries. Although much useful work had been done, the Greeks themselves had reduced the value of their Resistance forces by disunity and, when the enemy withdrew, were to poison the liberation which had been achieved partly through their own efforts, by civil war.

Chapter 20

The Satellite Nations

Rumania, Bulgaria and Hungary provided, like Austria, unfruitful ground for S.O.E. activities. In December 1943, a party of three British Liaison Officers were dropped in Rumania but were caught and immediately placed in a villa surrounded with barbed wire by the local Rumanians.

The Germans, hearing of this, asked that the British officers should be handed over to them, but the Rumanians refused to do this, and for seven months, until the coup d'etat, the British Liaison officers remained safe in Rumanian hands. A small number of S.D. operations completed in 1944, but results were negligible.

In September 1943, S.O.E. had established W/T communication with elements in the Kallay Government who offered unconditional surrender; S.O.E. then began to prepare a mission to be despatched to Hungary, but political difficulties, however, delayed this departure until after the German occupation of March 1944. It was not dropped until May 1944, and all the members of the party were captured. The aircraft which carried out the operation did not return, and the Senior British Liaison Officer, who later escaped through Poland, and made his way back to this country, reported that while he himself was still actually in the air, he saw a German night fighter take up its position behind the bomber and begin its attack. A small quantity of stores was sent into the country during 1944, and one pick-up operation which evacuated four persons was successful. By November the Russian forces had overrun the country.

A much larger quantity of stores was sent to Bulgaria than to the other two countries. The Russians were asked to assist Bulgarian partisans but their attitude was unhelpful. As many as four British Missions were at one time established within the country, but two of these were captured by rival Bulgarian organisations, and the officers, after hideous tortures, were executed and their heads stuck on spikes over Sofia station.

Although a fair quantity of stores was sent to Bulgaria, small dividends in the way of sabotage were paid, and most of the equipment was apparently used for the prosecution of civil war within the country.

Crete

Although most of the supplies sent to Crete went by sea, a small number of dropping operations were carried out during the autumn of 1943, and during 1944.

Corsica

Corsica provided a good example of the success that can be achieved by Resistance organisations under a unified command, well-equipped with arms, and directed in accordance with military strategy. Colonna D'Istria, the man who achieved and maintained the unity of the patriot forces on the island was personally responsible in large measure for the success of the Resistance campaign.

During the first seven months of 1943 organisers were sent in to the Island, and the R.A.F. operating from N. Africa succeeded in dropping large quantities of stores. The Partisans of the Maquis were soon able to take over control of whole mountain areas, and the work of supply dropping was made easier by the use of bonfires. Stores were delivered sufficient to equip 12,000 men, and the Partisans then found themselves sufficiently well-armed and equipped to take the offensive against the Italian and German occupying forces, and to harass their withdrawal.

Though the withdrawal was due mainly to the Allied landing at Salerno, the island was in fact liberated without the employment of any regular Allied troops, except one French Bataillon de Choc, who had received special training from S.O.E. officers with a view to collaboration with the Maquis. Although of minor significance, the liberation of Corsica provided a classic of successful resistance activity.

Part IV

Chapter 21

The Conclusion

It is impossible to estimate the value to the war effort of the work done by the R.A.F. on S.D. operations without assessing the effectiveness of Resistance activities. The Squadrons of Bomber, Coastal and Fighter Command in reviewing their work were able to report material and direct results; so many towns had been bombed, so many submarines destroyed, so many aircraft shot down. The S.D. Squadrons could report on the quantity of stores they had delivered and the number of men they had taken in and out of occupied Europe, but so far as direct damage to the enemy was concerned they had nothing to show. They were in the position of a Transport Unit, responsible for feeding an Army which was constantly engaged with the enemy. In the last resort the value of their work could be judged only by the use which was made by that Army of the stores they delivered.

That it would have been impossible to organise and sustain Resistance Movements without the help of the R.A.F. is patent. An Army – even a Secret Army – must have supplies. Even communications, the other vital necessity, depend on supplies: of W/T operators, of W/T equipment, of codes and cyphers. Without the food, clothes, arms and ammunition sent in from outside, the patriots of occupied Europe must have battered themselves uselessly against the Nazi armour. The Germans, who know as much about methods of oppression as any other nation has ever learnt, would not have found it difficult to deal with unarmed and unorganised rebels. The leaders of the Resistance Movements would probably have been captured and killed and the rank and file might have found it difficult to sustain their enthusiasm without direction and guidance. It may be said therefore that the very existence of organised and efficient Resistance groups depended on the work of the R.A.F.

The S.D. Squadrons themselves, trained to a pitch of technical efficiency hardly surpassed in the R.A.F., carried out their work in extremely difficult conditions with amazing skill and fortitude. Much depended on the efficiency with which the task of delivering stores and personnel to the field was carried out. A drop made from too great an altitude might mean a wide scatter of containers and packages on the ground and a consequent focussing of German interest on the neighbourhood; a drop made from too low might result in injury to personnel and damage to stores. The security on the ground of the Resistance group was inevitably endangered every time it received a stores delivery; only the R.A.F. could reduce this necessary risk to a minimum.

There were, of course, occasions on which mistakes in dropping were made. On the whole, however, the standard of efficiency of the S.D. crews was extremely high. The R.A.F. personnel themselves realised how much depended on their efforts, and the skill with which they faced the innumerable problems of Special Duty work was equalled only by their courage and determination.

Types of Resistance Activity

However efficiently the S.D. operations were conducted, the results to which they contributed depended primarily on the men in the field. Broadly speaking the activities of resistance groups in Europe may be divided into two types: clandestine sabotage and guerilla warfare. In nearly every case, Resistance activities began with sabotage, and only later developed into semi-military offensive action against the enemy. This second stage was not necessarily attained in every country.

Value of Sabotage Compared with Bombing

It was early realised that the maximum value of sabotage attacks could only be obtained if they were based on strategic requirements and fitted into the plans for the bomber offensive. Sabotage and air bombardment must be regarded as complementary methods of attack.

In their first Directive to S.O.E. the Chiefs of Staff emphasised this point and it was reiterated in every later Directive. Sabotage by itself cannot possibly obtain the results which may be reaped from large scale and continuous bombing, which include not only material damage, but also the moral effect on the enemy. Moreover, sabotage can only be carried out effectively within the conditions created by bombing. In Germany itself sabotage was as might be expected, on a small scale and it fell to Bomber Command to carry out the necessary attacks here. In the enemy-occupied countries the sabotage undertaken by Resistance would have been much less effective without the heavy bombardment to which German cities and industries were subjected.

On the other hand although sabotage action cannot operate on so wide a scale as air bombing it is in some circumstances the most economical and effective method of attack. An onslaught directed against the enemy's industrial machine can only reach its maximum efficiency when either an important plant, preferably in the nature of a bottle-neck, is put out of action for a long time, or when all the factories of a certain type are simultaneously damaged. The industrial machine is normally sufficiently flexible to withstand the destruction of one or two cogs without causing more than a minor delay in production.

It must always be remembered that sabotage and bombing were complementary methods of attack. The material damage and moral effect of a heavy bombing raid can hardly be overestimated.

Within its own limitations, however, sabotage might be more accurate and more deadly. It could not effect such general destruction, but it might reach the heart of its objective more surely. Air bombardment is not always a certain method of destroying the essential parts of a factory. Sabotage was able, at least to some extent, to fill these gaps.

Where Bomber Command might hesitate to undertake heavy bombing raids on factories in enemy-occupied countries because of the inevitable loss of life to our Allies, sabotage attacks could be carried out in such a way that the casualties were reduced to a minimum. Other targets unsuitable for bombing might be tackled by sabotage action. In some specific cases Resistance forces were able to attack targets which had been unsuccessfully bombed by the Allied air forces.

When the top priority on the target list was ball-bearing factories, S.O.E. was able to organise attacks on such factories in France and Norway and thus to complement the bomber raids staged by Bomber Command in Germany itself. On the other hand, sabotage attacks, in certain instances, were able to affect the vital parts of their objective more than bombing attacks. S.O.E.'s saboteurs, trained in England by industrial experts on the best methods of sabotaging every sort of machine and plant, could place their charges on the most vulnerable point, and with a couple of pounds of explosive do more damage than tons of bombs.

Sabotage by Resistance

Throughout the five years of occupation both major and minor acts of sabotage were carried out by the Resistance forces of Europe, under the direction of trained agents and in conformity with a plan prepared at S.O.E. H.Q. under the instructions of the Chiefs of Staff and the Theatre Commanders and in co-ordination with the Air Forces. Coup-de-main teams were also sent in by S.O.E. to attack specific targets of high importance. Among the most effective of the major sabotage attacks were the destruction of Radio Paris, the damage inflicted in two separate attacks on the Gigny Dam and the destruction of the Gorgopotamos Bridge.

The most important coup-de-main operation planned by S.O.E. – by now famous, since the story has been reported in the press and by the B.B.C. – was the attack on the Norsk Hydro factory in Norway from which the Germans obtained the "Heavy Water" necessary for their research on the Atom Bomb. If S.O.E. had done nothing but the organising of this one operation, and the S.D. Squadrons had delivered only this one party of men with their stores, it might well be true that they had sufficiently justified their existence.

Apart from the major operations there were literally thousands of sabotage attacks on every sort of objective. Factories, rail and road transport, telecommunications, waterways, individual enemy soldiers and collaborators were all targets for this type of attack. Each individual act might be in itself unimportant, but the cumulative effect, on the morale both of the Germans and of the people of the occupied countries, was enormous. Moreover a dividend of more direct military value was paid, in that the Germans were forced to extend and increase their occupation forces in order to maintain control over the countries which they had incorporated into the "New Order." Large numbers of troops must be used on police duties; and as Resistance feeling grew stronger and sabotage intensified the number must be increased. The relentless pin-pricking of sabotage activities caused a steady drain on the enemy's resources.

Guerilla activities by Resistance

The second type – and the second stage – of Resistance activities was guerilla warfare. Harassing action by bands of under-equipped patriots is unlikely to achieve startling results against well-armed regular troops. On the other hand, guerilla activities, well planned and well led, conducted from safe bases in the hills and carried out with the advantages of surprise and mobility, could do much to throw the enemy's troops into confusion. Guerilla bands, even more than saboteurs, need regular supplies, and it was the S.D. Squadrons who provided them with the food, clothes and arms without which they could not have maintained themselves. The very existence of armed bands in the hills compelled the enemy to maintain strong garrisons and large occupation forces and to mount punitive expeditions. In the Balkans the Partisans succeeded in containing a remarkably large number of German divisions throughout the whole period of so-called occupation. In south eastern France, Panzer divisions had to be employed against the Maquis.

In guerilla activities, as in sabotage, the work of the Resistance Movements must be co-ordinated with general military requirements – in this case: tactical rather than strategic. It was undoubtedly always a good thing to attack German troops on the move: it was even better if an attack could be made on a particular division which was known to be moving up to the front. S.O.E. H.Q. was informed by the military commanders of suitable targets of this sort, and instructed their officers in the field accordingly. The military authorities were by this means able to command the services of an Army behind the enemy lines.

Tributes to the work of Resistance

In the various theatres of Europe the efficiency and value of Resistance activities was vouched for by military and political officers.

CinC/695
On January 20th 1945, the C.-in-C. Middle East Forces wrote to Lord Selborne on the occasion of the disbandment of Force 133: "I would like to take this opportunity of expressing my appreciation of the excellent work done by this organisation whilst under my command."

The C.-in-C. reviewed S.O.E.'s activities in the various countries of the Middle East and concluded: "I have been able to follow in detail the achievements of many of the personnel and have been glad to be able to confer a relatively large number of immediate awards. Their record in this respect bears witness to their courage and devotion to duty. I am satisfied that this Force has played a worthy part in the defeat of the enemy in this theatre of operations."

A copy of this letter was sent to the Minister Resident in the Middle East who wrote on the 26th January:

> "I was deeply thrilled by the account of the Force's activities which I heard last week, and I should like to associate myself unreservedly with the praise bestowed upon it by Sir Bernard Paget. Its achievements by sea, land and air were evidently due to its excellence in two ways – the imagination, resourcefulness and high courage of the officers composing it, and the really marvellous feat of organisation by which they were so successfully launched and so consistently supported. I must add the splendid esprit de corps which animated and inspired them.
>
> "I frankly never dreamt, when you invited me to your headquarters, that I should hear and see in a small room in the course of one short hour so much that made me proud of my country and of the younger generation of my fellow-countrymen. I trust the epic for which they were responsible will be written and published as soon as possible. They have worked and dared with such amazing secrecy that very few at home have the remotest inkling of their existence, far less of their achievements. That secrecy was no doubt essential to our success while they were operating and may be desirable for other reasons a little longer. But the whole Empire should hear their story worthily told at the earliest possible moment.
>
> "When it does, the Force will have the honour it deserves and will assuredly go down to history as proof that the spirit of Elizabethan times is still alive in all its brilliant daring. In the meantime I rejoice to have had the chance of hearing a little of that story betimes and of paying my small tribute to a most Gallant Company of Gentlemen Adventurers."

To the Italian patriots many messages were sent from military commanders and political leaders, including the Prime Minister himself.

On 7th May Field Marshal Alexander sent a message to the President of the National Liberation Committee for North Italy: "Now that the operations in Northern Italy have been victoriously concluded I should be grateful if you would make known to General Cadorna" (the military commander of all the Partisans in Northern Italy) "and all delegates of the Partisan Command my admiration and gratitude for the part they have played both in the destruction of the enemy and in the preservation of the plant and factories essential to the life of Italy."

Sir Noel Charles, reporting to the Foreign Office from Rome on 11th May said:

> "I should like to pay high tribute to the S.O.E. British Liaison Officers in Northern Italy who for the past month have been our main source of contact with the local committees of National Liberation and patriot local authorities. You will no doubt receive reports from Field Marshal Alexander on the military aspects but on the political side their work has been no less valuable … I think it can safely be said that maintenance of law and order up till arrival of Allied troops and Allied Military Government and avoidance of arbitrary or independent action on the part of northern committees has largely been due to the tact and ability with which these officers have carried out their duties."

A tribute to S.O.E.'s work in Western Europe was paid by General Eisenhower himself, who on May 31st 1945 wrote to General Gubbins:

> "Before the combined staff of Special Force Headquarters disperses I wish to express my appreciation of its high achievements.
>
> "Since I assumed the Supreme Command in January, 1944, until the present day its work has been marked by patient and farsighted planning, flexible adaption to the operational requirements of Supreme Headquarters, and efficient executive action during operations. In no previous war, and in no other theatre during this war, have resistance forces been so closely harnessed to the main military effort.
>
> "While no final assessment of the operational value of resistance action has yet been completed, I consider that the disruption of enemy rail communications, the harassing of German road moves and the continual and increasing strain placed on the German war

economy and internal security services throughout occupied Europe by the organised forces of resistance, played a considerable part in our complete and final victory. In Denmark and Norway the commanders concerned have already reported on the great help which they have received from resistance forces in maintaining law and order during the early stages of liberation.

The combination of certain sections of your two organisations, first established as Special Force Headquarters under the joint command of Brigadier Mockler-Ferryman and Colonel Haskell, was the means by which these resistance forces were so ably organised, supplied and directed. Particular credit must be due to those responsible for communications with occupied territory. I am also aware of the care with which each individual country was studied and organised, and of the excellent work carried out in training, documenting, briefing and despatching agents. The supply to agents and resistance groups in the field, moreover, could only have reached such proportions during the summer of 1944 through outstanding efficiency on the part of the supply and air liaison staffs. Finally, I must express my great admiration for the brave and often spectacular exploits of the agents and special groups under control of Special Force Headquarters.

"I would be grateful if you would convey, as a personal message, my thanks to everyone at Special Force Headquarters for their work. And through you I would like to express my gratitude to the two parent organisations, without whose co-operation and help the great success of Special Force Headquarters could not have been achieved."

The Naval Authorities also bore witness to the value of Resistance activities. On June 14th Rear Admiral Mansfield wrote:

"On completion of hostilities in Europe and with the end of the German U-boat war, I would like to take the opportunity of thanking you for the valuable and gallant assistance which your organisation has rendered to the Anti-U-boat war effort, particularly in Norway.

"I well know the losses which have been suffered and the dangerous and arduous work which has been undertaken to interfere with U-boats and their facilities in harbour. Apart from the tangible results (such as the destruction of large quantities of diesel oil, of the torpedo store and workshops at Horton, of the accumulator factories in Denmark, and of U-boat battery acid factories in the Oslo area) the intangible results on U-boat morale and the feeling of insecurity which you engendered have been of the greatest value. The other multitudinous activities not specifically aimed against U-boats, such as destruction of communications, continually pin-pricked the enemy and made his operating conditions more difficult.

"Although I realise that this has been only a small part of their duties as a whole, nevertheless I would be grateful if you would convey to all concerned … the war appreciation of the Navy on their fine efforts."

A special Order of the Day of November 2nd 1944 records that:

"His Majesty the King has been graciously pleased to convey to Lord Selborne his great interest in the account, which was circulated to the Cabinet, of S.O.E.'s role in the preparation and execution of the invasion of France, and his admiration for the resource and courage shown by all concerned. He further directed that his hearty congratulations be sent to all who contributed to the success of the operations."

S.H.A.E.F. Study of Resistance Work

The most detailed study from a military point of view of the work of Resistance Forces in the field was made in a S.H.A.E.F. Memorandum of 13th July 1945. This paper stated that: "Resistance assisted the Supreme Commander's operations in the two broad fields: Political and military."

The existence of organised resistance had fulfilled an important role in setting the oppressed peoples at loggerheads with the occupying power and thus keeping the enemy continually on the "qui vive". Militarily, organised resistance helped the main operations of the Allied Expeditionary Force by sapping the enemy's confidence in his won security and flexibility of internal movement; by diverting and dispersing enemy troops; by causing delay to the movement of enemy troops; by disrupting telecommunications in France and Belgium; and by enabling Allied formations to advance with greater speed through being able to dispense with many normal military precautions, such as flak protection and mopping up.

In discussing the delay inflicted on enemy movements by rail to the Normandy beach head the paper stated that:

> "Any consideration of this subject must be prefaced by an emphatic statement that the major cause of delay to enemy troop movements was action by the Allied strategic and tactical air forces. Resistance action was only a secondary element in causing delay. The widespread and continuous sabotage (3,000 confirmed rail cuts between 6th and 27th June) in this field, however, caused an effect outside the capabilities of Allied air effort unless it had been concentrated on railways to the exclusion of other priority tasks."

The programme of railway sabotage in France and Belgium resulted in delays to all troop movements; a reduction in the stock of serviceable locomotives to a point where there was an actual deficiency in the number required by the enemy at the time of and following the Normandy landing; an increase in the number of repairs required and a consequent swamping of the repair facilities; the increased use of steam locomotives and coal at a time when valuable stocks of both were depleted; and the deployment of railway troops and guards of all kinds to rebuild and protect the vital lines.

Apart from direct sabotage S.O.E. had encouraged slow-downs, absenteeism and strikes. S.H.A.E.F.'s paper reports that:

> "In this connection Rundstedt's Director of Military Transport has cited the slow-down of French railway as one of the significant contributory factors which led to the German failure to maintain transport facilities adequately to contain the Allied bridgehead in Normandy."

As far as sabotage of telecommunications was concerned the interrogation of German Commanders had shown that the effect was greater than had been anticipated, largely owing to the extreme stress under which the staffs were already working.

A somewhat unexpected role was fulfilled by the Resistance Groups in their execution of minor military roles such as flank protection, the containing of isolated enemy garrisons, mopping up and the custody of prisoners. In Denmark and Norway, the Allied Forces on arrival found that Resistance had actually taken over control of essential services already. The effectiveness of anti-scorch action carried out by Resistance was considered, and S.H.A.E.F. concluded that whenever the enemy had sufficient time adequately to prepare his demolitions, Resistance could not stop him effecting them. A striking success was, however, attained in the case of Antwerp, which was preserved intact very largely through the action of Belgium Resistance Groups which had been organised for that purpose.

The value of the guerilla activities carried out in France was also considered. In June 1944 the Germans had been forced to employ 5,000 troops to disperse the guerillas in the Correze [Corrèze], and approximately 11,000 with artillery, were engaged against Resistance in the Vercors in July. On one occasion 18,000 men out of a column of 20,000 which was unable to escape eastwards because of the control exercised by Resistance on all lines of escape, were taken prisoner:

> "There can be no doubt that at a time when the Germans were exerting every effort to obtain more manpower, the dispersion of troops in protective and internal security duties had an effect on the land battle."

In conclusion the S.H.A.E.F. Memorandum stated that:

> "S.O.E. operations made a substantial contribution to the victory of the Allied Expeditionary Force. Widespread and continuous sabotage action against railways and telecommunications supplemented the air effort and completed the confusion of the enemy."

Allied Governments

The foreign Governments for whom S.O.E. had worked so long recorded their appreciation of the work which had been done. The Belgian Minister of Justice writing on September 2nd 1944 to General Gubbins speaks of, "la collaboration qui, grace à vous, a pu aller en s'amplifiant entre l'effort allie et mes camarades de la Résistance."

M. Gerbrandy of the Dutch Government wrote to the Minister of Economic Warfare on October 4th:

"I shall always be grateful for the assistance we have received in this country, and in this you have played a major part. Your work has been of the greatest importance to us.

"I shall never forget the readiness with which you have always been willing not only to discuss the problems I have laid before you, but to tackle them. I have much admired the way in which you, and the men of your organisation, have solved our difficulties. Your wholehearted co-operation has so immensely lightened my own task."

ADE/5349, 11 May 1945
Prince Bernhardt also sent a message to S.O.E.:

"Splendid results achieved by our interior forces are due to very large extent to the Organisation and guidance from your H.Q., for which these Forces and I are extremely grateful; also on their behalf I should like to express our appreciation to all your personnel for the great work they have done. The co-operation with you was always ideal, for which I want to thank you personally."

The S.D. Squadrons

The number of aircraft engaged on the work of supplying Resistance Groups was, for three of the five years of occupation, extraordinarily small. Three principal squadrons were responsible for S.D. operations throughout the war: Nos. 138, 161 and 148. No. 624 Squadron also carried out these duties from the summer of 1943. In the last two years additional squadrons were allocated to Special Duties and played a distinguished part in the delivery of supplies to the field, but it is the four squadrons who initiated the work in the early difficult days and who carried it through to the end whose names will be chiefly remembered in connection with Resistance.

Many telegrams received from the men in the field gave high praise to the work of the R.A.F. on S.D. operations. A large number of foreign decorations were awarded to the aircrews of the S.D. squadrons, who also received an unusually large number of British decorations. H.M. the King was graciously pleased to award as many as 142 decorations to the aircrews of No. 161 Squadron, one of the Tempsford squadrons engaged on S.D. work for five years.

Although the work of the S.D. Squadrons did not, and could not, itself result in direct military damage to the enemy, it was more than justified by the achievements of Resistance, to whose success it had made a major contribution. Without supplies, the Resistance forces must have languished: with them, they were able to cause severe punishment to an enemy many times their weight. The value of the work carried out by Resistance in all theatres of Europe has been declared by senior military, naval and political officers, and the R.A.F.'s part in this work was of incalculable value.

Of the three services, it was the R.A.F. from whom S.O.E. required the most and to whom they could give the least. Apart from the sabotage of a number of aircraft factories and of occasional aircraft there was little that Resistance could do to help the R.A.F. The chief benefits of Resistance activities were reaped by the Navy, and, above all, by the Army. In carrying out S.D. work, therefore, the R.A.F. themselves gained little; but the S.D. Squadrons had the satisfaction of knowing that they had made the major contribution to Resistance activities – one of the most outstanding success stories of the war.

List Of Appendices

Appendix I

Control of Operational Units engaged on SOE and SIS (Operations from the UK)

Sir,

I am directed to refer to the recent discussions which have taken place between representatives of the Air Staff and your Headquarters to inform you that it has been decided that you shall undertake full operational and administrative responsibility for the operational units engaged in S.O.E., and S.I.S. activities conducted from the United Kingdom.

2. The objects underlying this revision of the existing system of control are:

(i) To bring these special operations more closely into line with the normal operations of Bomber Command in order to ensure the maintenance of the highest possible standard of operational efficiency.

(ii) To facilitate the employment when necessary of some portion of the normal Bomber Command effort on S.O.E. and S.I.S. activities, so as to supplement that of the squadrons specifically allotted for this purpose: and

(iii) To ensure that no worthwhile opportunity is lost of providing this supplementary effort, whenever it can be made available.

3. The operational control of the S.O.E./S.I.S. units has hitherto been exercised by A.C.A.S.(I) whose staff has been responsible, in conjunction with S.O.E. and S.I.S., for the detailed planning entailed. It has now been

decided that while full operational control of these units is to be transferred from A.C.A.S.(I)'s Branch to Bomber Command, the former will continue to be responsible for the initial planning of parachute dropping operations and for the selection and approval of landing grounds for pick-up operations.

4. Once planned, all S.O.E. and S.I.S. requirements will be communicated in a standard form to Bomber Command for executive action. Copies of the relevant instructions will be forwarded for information direct from the Air Ministry to the Base or Station Commander immediately responsible for the execution of the operations. This action has been agreed in order to obviate delay in the eventual execution of any urgent operation. These instructions will in any event be subject to your approval.

5. Any operations required by S.O.E. and S.I.S. (excluding those which are undertaken by Coastal or other Commands) which involve a departure from the normal form of these operations, will be submitted to you for consideration in the initial stages of planning. This procedure will cover for example:

(i) Ad hoc requests for the temporary use of other types of aircraft not allotted for these special operations;
(ii) The extension of operations to ranges or countries notpreviously involved;
(iii)Operations demanding air cover as a diversion.

6. In order that the requirements of S.O.E. and S.I.S. may be fully represented to you it has been agreed that you shall have authority to consult directly with the R.A.F. representatives of S.O.E. and S.I.S. These representatives can speak with full authority for their respective organisations. They will also advise their organisations on the practical limitations which govern your operations generally.

7. In order to assist you in implementing these instructions, a further communication will be addressed to you by A.C.A.S.(I), outlining broadly the responsibilities allocated to S.O.E. and S.I.S. respectively. In addition A.C.A.S.(I) will be responsible for forwarding to you each month a Directive outlining in broad terms the air effort required in

various geographical areas for the ensuing month. Specific day to day requirements will be communicated to you in accordance with the procedure outlined in paragraph 4 above.

8. In regard to the supplementary effort which can be provided by your normal squadrons, it is accepted that this must be limited to operations not involving the dropping of personnel, for which major modifications to aircraft would be essential. For your information the operations which your normal squadrons will be called upon to perform and which will involve the dropping of equipment only, are limited for the time being to France.

9. The extent of the supplementary effort which you can provide must naturally depend on operational and other circumstances prevailing at the time. It is clear that you will not normally be in a position to forecast the precise extent of the help which you can provide. These S.O.E. and S.I.S. operations, however, play a very important role in the general strategical plans approved by the Government and are largely complementary in their effort to that of the Bomber offensive itself. Consistent with the needs of your main current directive you should, therefore, make every effort to ensure that your contribution to these special operations is sufficient.

10. The revised procedure is to be introduced with effect from the 1st September, 1943. This will enable the operations already planned for August to be carried out without undue disturbance and will at the same time permit your staff to function under the new organisation in the arranging of operations to be undertaken in September and subsequently.

11. I am to request that you will submit your recommendations for any changes in establishments which you consider necessary under this revised organisation.

I am, Sir,
Your obedient Servant,
Air Marshal,
Deputy Chief of the Air Staff.

The Air Officer Commanding-in-Chief,
Headquarters, Bomber Command.

Appendix II

Status and Responsibilities of the Air Adviser to SOE

The Air Staff have had under consideration the question of the status and responsibilities of the officer holding the appointment of Air Adviser to S.O.E. and as Senior R.A.F. Liaison Officer between that organisation, Air Ministry and Bomber Command. In agreement with C.D., the following lists of duties and responsibilities have been approved:

(i)   The Air Adviser to S.O.E. will be a Member of the Council of S.O.E.

(ii)   He will be responsible to the Air Staff for all liaison between S.O.E. and the Air Ministry on matters concerning air policy and air operations undertaken on behalf of S.O.E.

(iii)   He will when necessary inform the Air Ministry of the general purpose and aim of any projected S.O.E. operations and satisfy them that the air effort required is justified. For this purpose he will have access to the Air Ministry branch or department appropriate to the subject concerned. He will, however, normally deal with the Assistant Chief of the Air Staff (Intelligence) who is responsible for the co-ordination of the detailed planning of S.O.E. air operations.

(iv)   He will exercise general control over S.O.E. air transport operations conducted from the U.K. If at any time he considers that any projected air operation is of doubtful value in relation to the operational risks entailed he will represent to the appropriate S.O.E. authority the need for modifying or abandoning any planned operation.

(v)   He will represent S.O.E. initially in any discussions which involve demands for increased aircraft establishment and will be required to speak with full authority and knowledge of the reasons and circumstances from which such demands arise.

(vi)   In relation to S.O.E. operations conducted from the U.K. he will act as the Senior R.A.F. Liaison Officer between S.O.E. and H.Q. Bomber Command. In this capacity he will speak with full authority on behalf of C.D. in so far as air matters are concerned.

(vii)   He will be responsible for keeping the A.O.C.-in-C., Bomber Command informed of the extent of supplementary air effort which may be required from time to time.

(viii)   He will advise C.D. of the views of the Air Ministry and A.O.C.-in-C. Bomber Command as to the capabilities and limitations of air operations in aid of S.O.E. work.

(ix)   He will be responsible for ensuring that operational experience obtained in special air operations is disseminated to S.O.E. organisations in all theatres.

(x)   He will advise S.O.E. of any special methods or types of aircraft suitable to particular conditions of operations in theatres overseas.

(xi)   He will be responsible for representing to the Air Ministry circumstances which may render necessary a re-distribution as between the various theatres of operations of the aircraft allotted for S.O.E. work and for keeping S.O.E. informed of the general distribution and employment of such aircraft in theatres abroad.

(xii)   He will be responsible for keeping S.O.E. informed of such technical developments in R.A.F. aircraft and equipment as may be of value for special operations.

(xiii)   He will be responsible for keeping the Air Staff generally informed of the progress of S.O.E. activities.

Appendix III

Duties of the Head of the Air Transport Organisation of SOE London Group

Appointments

The Head of the Air Transport Organisation of the London Group of S.O.E. should be a Group Captain and he and the R.A.F. officers on the staff of this section will all be selected by the Air Ministry after consultation with the R.A.F. Commands concerned.

Responsibilities

2. The Head of the Organisation will be responsible to (the Commands concerned) and to the Controller, S.O.E. London Group in respect of the matters set out below:

R.A.F. Commands

(i)   Consideration of the practicability and feasibility of all projected S.O.E. operations involving air operations, having regard to their importance and the risks involved.

(ii)   The preparation of operation orders for individual operations.

(iii) In conjunction with the Air Ministry (D. of I(R)), checking of dropping areas and landing grounds.

(iv) The transmission of operation orders to the Group and R.A.F. Station concerned.

(v)   The delivery of agents and S.O.E. stores to the R.A.F. Station for despatch overseas.

(vi) The preparation and submission of operational reports and returns to R.A.F. Commands concerned.

(vii)   Advice on the employment of such supplementary effort as No. 38 Group can make available from time to time.

(viii) Liaison between S.O.E. R.A.F. Commands and the R.A.F. Stations concerned, in connection with the use of special S.O.E. equipment such as radio-navigation aids, pick-up devices, etc.

The Controller S.O.E., London Group

(i)   Advice on the air aspect of projected S.O.E. operations.

(ii)   The preparation of particulars of landing grounds and dropping points and their submission to the Air Ministry (D. of I(R)) for approval.

(iii)   Recording of dropping points and landing grounds.

(iv)   Liaison with S.O.E. Country Sections on the air aspect of their operations.

(v)   The training of agents in air dropping and air landing and pick-up operations, and their final preparation in these matters, but not including training in parachute jumping.

(vi)   The training of S.O.E. personnel in the air aspect of reception committee work.

(vii)   Control of the S.O.E. packing station and despatch centre.

(viii) The transport of agents and stores to the airfield.

(xi)   Demanding of stores and special equipment required at the packing station for transport by air.

(x)   Drop-testing equipment and devices to be delivered by air.

(xi)   Preparation of special packages for despatch, and liaison with No.13 M.U., R.A.F. Henlow, on the provision of special type of parachutes and packages.

(xii)   Liaison with the "special pigeon service."

3. He will be guided in the planning of air operations by principles laid down by the Air Member of the S.O.E. Council.

Status within S.O.E.

4. The Head of the Air Transport Organisation will have direct access to the Controller of the London Group and will be responsible for

representing to him any objections he may have to planned operations, which, in his opinion involve undue risks to R.A.F. aircraft or unjustifiable effort. He will obtain from the Country Section concerned full explanations as necessary, including their exact significance and importance. In the event of his objections not being accepted by the Controller of the London Group he has the right to represent the case to the Air Member of the S.O.E. Council. He will also have the right to discuss problems affecting the R.A.F. with the Air Member.

Staff

5. The staff of the Air Transport Organisation will consist of:
    (i) R.A.F. staff appointed by the Air Ministry.
    (ii) U.S.A. and U.S.A.A.F. staff appointed by O.S.S. and Headquarters, VIIIth U.S. Air Force.
    (iii)S.O.E. staff.

Appendix IV

Air Liaison – SOE Pinpointing Section

1. SUBMISSION OR DROPPING POINTS FROM THE FIELD

a) <u>France: First Method</u>

The agent in the field pinpoints his dropping ground onto a Michelin map, which has a scale of 1/200,000 and is divided by longitudinal and latitudinal grade lines which are sub-divided into fifths of a grade. These grade lines form large squares on the Michelin map.

To submit his dropping ground to London, the agent employs a celluloid grid which is divided by vertical and horizontal lines, the intersection of which form squares equal in area to 1 Kilometre on the ground. The squares running from West to East are lettered commencing from 'L' and those from North to South are numbered commencing from 11. Thus the top left hand square is called 'L.11'.

The agent fits his celluloid grid into the appropriate square formed by the grade lines on the Michelin map. He then transmits to London the number of the Michelin map, the name of the largest town lying within the square, and the letter and number of the small square on his grid in which his dropping ground is situated. Latterly the agent was required to give the distance and direction of his ground from the large town indicated. Each fold of the Michelin map is numbered round the edge; as an additional check the agent indicates the number of the appropriate fold.

Each dropping ground is allotted a code name by the agent.

Example of message:

"New dropping ground VIOLET stop Michelin 59 Fold 15 bearing 14 Kms. South South East CERCY Yorker 28….."

In the London office the pinpoint is interpreted by placing an identical celluloid grid over the appropriate grade square on the Michelin map and the point is ascertained by reading off the correct letter and number quoted and checking the distance and direction of the point from the town.

b) France: Second Method

The agent in the field pinpoints his dropping ground onto a Michelin map (as previously described).

To submit his dropping ground to London, the agent measures the number of millimetres East and North of the appropriate grade lines. He must always give the distance and direction of the point from the nearest town and state the number of the Michelin map.

The information he transmits would be as follows:

Name: OLIVE

Michelin: 60

48 mm. East of 03 grade 00

49 mm. North of 54 grade 40

101 mm. E.S.E. of St. GENT

In order to cut down the number of words involved in sending these co-ordinates, a special system was evolved. The message is divided into five distinct parts as follows:

PRIMO: OLIVE (Code name of the ground)

SECUNDO: 60 (Number of Michelin map)

TERTIO: 48 (Number of mm. East of grade line)

30 (Two central figures of the number of the grade line)

QUARTO: 49 (Number of mm. North of grade line)

44 (Two central figures of the number of the grade line)

QUINTO: 101 East South East St. GENT

c) Other Methods employed

Agents submitting dropping grounds from countries other than France employ various methods. In Norway, for example, the agent submits co-ordinates based on the meridian of Oslo, in Holland a six-figure grid reference is employed, and in Denmark he uses a map book in general use in the country, describing the position of his ground by means of page numbers and numbered squares on the page. The principle of always identifying the position of the ground in relation to nearby towns or landmarks is followed throughout.

2. ACTION TAKEN BY COUNTRY SECTION AS AFFECTING PINPOINTING SECTION

On receipt of the signal giving the new dropping point, the Country Section copies the details onto a form and submits them to the Pinpointing Section. The details must be copied exactly, even in cases where the agent has made an error, or the signal is mutilated.

3. ACTION TAKEN BY PINPOINTING SECTION

a). The pinpoint is not always used for an operation immediately. It is important, therefore, to record all details of the point carefully until such time as it is required.

The signal is filed in a box file under the name of the agent. An index card is made and filed under the code name of the ground. This card shows the reference number and date of the signal and the name of the agent. Any signal referring to the ground passing between the Country Section and the field are noted.

It is advisable to place the point on the Michelin map immediately it is received in order that any error in the co-ordinates may be noted and the error pointed out to the agent before any valuable time is wasted. The field are always asked to reconfirm co-ordinates which arrive mutilated in the signal.

b). When the pinpoint is required for an operation it is placed on the Michelin map by the method already indicated. Every detail of the agent's co-ordinates must be correct. It is very easy for the pinpointing section to guess what the agent really means if he has made a slight mistake, but equally easy to make the wrong guess. In case of doubt the agent is always asked to reconfirm his co-ordinates.

Having found the point on the Michelin map, the pinpointing section transfer it onto a large scale map and work out the co-ordinates in degrees of latitude and longitude based on the meridian of Greenwich. The same set of maps is used for every dropping point and every point is marked on the map and labelled. In this way it is impossible for two agents to submit the same dropping-point without the pinpointing section being aware of the fact. Similarly the pinpointing section can make a note of any two points lying within three kilometres of each other and be certain that operations are not laid on to both grounds on the same night. If a new point lies very close to a point belonging to a different Country Section, the original 'owner' of the area is consulted before an operation can take place on the newer point.

The co-ordinates of the new point are then telephoned to the Air Ministry who are responsible for checking that the pinpoint lies in suitable flying country, that the aircraft will not fly into a flak belt of night fighter area, and that it is within range of aircraft based in Great Britain.

When the pinpoint has been accepted it is allotted its own permanent reference number. France, for instance, was split up into twenty areas and numbers allotted to each pinpoint in these areas consecutively. Thus the first point in area 11 in France would be called 11F/1, the second 11F/2 and so on.

4. PERMANENT RECORDING OF PINPOINTS
a) Code Number Card

This card gives the Air Ministry co-ordinates of the point and the number of the large scale map. It is filed according to the reference number of the ground, e.g. 11F/1. The code name of the ground, the code name of the agent who submitted it and the date on which it was accepted by the Air Ministry are shown on the back.

If a successful operation takes place on the ground, the date and name of the operation are added.

b) Code Name Cards

This card gives the reference number of the point, the name of the agent who submitted it and the references of any correspondence referring to the point passing between the pinpointing section and the Country Section. It is filed alphabetically according to code names. The life history of the ground is shown in this card. All notes of other points in the area, dates on which the area has been loaned to another country section, adverse security reports from the field, etc. etc., are kept up-to-date. The signal letter allotted to the ground is usually noted, but this is really the responsibility of the Country Section. Once a successful operation has taken place on the ground, this card is "starred" so that in case of a future unsuccessful operation to the same ground the pinpointing section can be sure that the faults lie with the navigator or the reception committee and do not require to re-check their co-ordinates.

c) For system 1(a) as described [previously] a further index card is necessary to cross reference 'CERCY Yorker twenty-eight' with the Code Name Card and the Code Number Card.

5. LAYING ON OF OPERATIONAL PROGRAMME
The agent submits his programme for each moon or non-moon period about ten days before the period starts. The Country Section is responsible for assembling the programme, but the pinpointing section check all signals to and from the field and are able to examine the dropping grounds before the Country Section send in their operational order.

As soon as the Country Section have checked the programme they telephone to the pinpointing section a list of the grounds required and the pinpointing section, having previously assembled their own list from the signals are usually able to pass or refuse the grounds immediately.

At the same time the Country Section are informed if any of their grounds fall within three Kms. of a ground belonging to a different Country Section and they are required to come to an agreement with the other Country Section as to which operation may take place first and inform the pinpointing section of the arrangements made. (This applied only to France).

The Country Section then submit an Air Transport Form No.1. to the pinpointing section, giving the code name and code number of the ground, the code name of the operation, the signal letter, load to be carried and any further particulars, such as S-Phone, Rebecca/Eureka, alternative pinpoints, interval between operations etc. The pinpointing section check all details from the signals, although the responsibility for the accuracy of the programme rests with the Country Section.

The pinpointing section issue the operational order, called Air Transport Form No.6.This gives all the details included in the A.T.F.1. and in addition the flying co-ordinates and map reference of the pinpoint.

Each ground, having been allotted an <u>operational</u> code name (not to be confused with the code name of the ground itself) is given a separate A.T.F.6. The same A.T.F.6. and operational code name are used for one ground from one moon period to another, so that if ground OLIVE is given operational code name CHARLEY 1, CHARLEY 1 will always be the name of any future operation laid onto the ground, except that the second successful operation to the ground would be known as CHARLEY 1A, the third CHARLEY 1B, and so on.

The A.T.F.6. is issued at least two days before the moon period begins to all who are concerned in any way with operation: i.e.

> COUNTRY SECTION
> CONFERENCE ROOM
> AIR MINISTRY
> BOMBER COMMAND
> ALL AIRFIELDS WORKING FOR S.O.E.

From this moment the responsibility for the operation passes to the Conference Room and the Country Section, although the pinpointing section continue, in fact, to watch all signals from the field and to keep a check on all operations mounted each day. Alterations and additions to the programme and new dropping points arrive daily from the field. The pinpointing section issue these orders and amendments to the old orders to all who received copies of the A.T.F.6.

North Africa/London procedure:_S.O.E.'s H.Q. in North Africa (Massingham) was allotted a definite area in the South of France in which to operate. All grounds lying within that area were automatically passed to Massingham and the operations carried out from there. There were occasions, however, when the agent required special stores held in London to be delivered into the Massingham area. In this case the ground was loaned to London pinpointing section until the operation had been completed and a careful note of the arrangement held by the pinpointing section and the section dealing with Massingham operations in London. For obvious reasons it was important that one ground should not be served from both London and Massingham on the same night.

6. OPERATIONAL RESULTS

The pinpointing section record the result of each operation on their card index and keep a card index of all successful operations showing the date on which it was carried out and the code number of the pinpoint.

If a pilot had reported that he found no reception at the pinpoint, the point is rechecked before the operation is attempted again. The pilot's operational report is studied carefully for any adverse criticism of the pinpoint, and in the case of a very bad report the pinpoint is cancelled for further use.

The signals from the field giving their operational results are likewise studied and the pilot's report and the agent's report compared. If the agent has by any chance confused the code names of the two grounds it is often very easy to see by this comparison where he is confused and to ask the Country Section to clarify the matter with the field.

7. MASSINGHAM

Procedure in Massingham was in all respects similar to that outlined above with the exception of a few minor differences.

Appendix V

Tempsford Procedure

The list of operations was phoned from the Conference Room to the Intelligence Section on the scrambler. It was given in priorities, one, two or three stars indicating the degree of importance of the operation. The points on the A.T.F.'s were plotted on maps in a room set aside for the purpose. When the daily list was received from the Operation Room, the priorities were shown by marking the target with a coloured ticket. Blue was used for the starred points, and the priority was marked in black. Green was used for non-starred targets. The American list was plotted in brown and the Three Group allocation in red. Any changes subsequently phoned through were also altered on the maps.

At 0930 hrs the following morning a Met Conference was held by the Station Cmdr., Sqdn. Cmdrs., Nav. Officer, Int. Officer and the Met. Officer. Suitable areas for operations that night were discussed and then in the planning room targets were chosen in order of priority, the more difficult ones being given to the more experienced crews.

Once the allocations had been settled the chosen points were plotted on 1/1,000,000 maps, and routes were decided upon. Petrol loads were given by Sqdn. Cmdrs. and loads were worked out by the Liaison Officers. Timing was then done by the Navigation Officers, the necessary information being given to Ops for the Form J. All target points were then checked with the A.T.F. information and plotted on a 1/500,000 map, so that when the crews were briefed they could see their exact dropping point and the navigator could work out his best D.R. run.

Briefing was held as soon after lunch as possible and each crew was told the route, the load, height of drop, difficulties of terrain and such information as was available to intelligence about local Gestapo activities etc. Met. then gave the weather picture and the crews made final preparations for their operations.

As each aircraft became airborne Control informed Group and the W/T Section stood by to give assistance if required. Group were again informed as each aircraft landed, and the specialist officers congregated in Intelligence to interrogate crews. When targets were widespread interrogation lasted for several hours and often the night duty people were still working on the Form Y when the day shift arrived.

After the nights work, diaries and Captains records had to be brought up to date, the daily summary completed and (if the weather allowed) the days operations commenced.

When Bomber Command in Feb' 44 installed a section to effect liaison between Air Ministry and Tempsford the procedure was very similar but necessarily slowed up as everything had to go through an extra channel.

Appendix VI

Instructions to SOE Liaison Officer at RAF Station Tempsford

1. You are appointed as S.O.E. Liaison Officer at R.A.F. Station, Tempsford.

2. Your duties are:

(i) To ensure that personnel to be carried by No. 138 Squadron aircraft arrive at the aerodrome in time to prepare themselves for emplanement at the time required by the Squadron Commander, that they are properly dressed and equipped, and that they are fully informed on the drill for leaving the aircraft over the Dropping Point; you are also to ensure that the Dropping Point given to Aircrews corresponds to that given to the personnel to be dropped, by their appropriate Country Section Officers

(ii) To inform the Officer Commanding S.T.S. 61, after consultation with the Squadron Commander, which particular operations are scheduled for each night, and to ensure that the material required for each operation is delivered to the aerodrome in adequate time to be loaded on to the aircraft.

(iii) To see that, in the event of an aircraft having to return without dropping its load, the equipment and containers are marked with the code name of the operation concerned before they are returned to S.T.S. 61.

(iv) To attend at the briefing of the crews at the time laid down by the Squadron Commander, and to check that the briefs given to crews conform to the instruction in A.T.F. 4 or A.T.F.

2b. Should there be any discrepancy between the requirements stated in the A.T.F.'s and the instructions given by the Officer in charge of Briefing, you should point this out to the S.I.O. or his Staff.

(v) In consultation with the Station Parachute Officer, to ensure that all Parachuting equipment in aircraft scheduled for operations is complete, correctly fitted, and in good condition, and that no indication of the name of the operation is marked on containers or equipment after they have been loaded on to aircraft.

(vi) To ensure that Transport of S.T.S. 61, while at R.A.F. Station, Tempsford, is controlled in conformity with the Orders laid down by the Station Commander.

(vii) To see that adequate arrangements are made for the reception of personnel returning from uncompleted or unsuccessful sorties, and for their immediate return to S.T.S. 61.

(viii) To attend at the interrogation of crews from sorties and to obtain detailed information on the delivery of personnel and containers, including the efficiency of Reception Committee arrangements, so far as this Headquarters is directly affected. Any questions you may wish to put to crews for this purpose are to be asked at the conclusion of the interrogation by the S.I.O. or his staff.

3. In order to carry out these duties, you should normally report to the Squadron Commander by 1200 hours daily during the operational period.

4. You are not to discuss details of Dropping Points, or the method of conducting particular operations, with Aircrews before the official briefing takes place, nor are you in any way to alter instructions given by the Intelligence Staff at any time. Should late information necessitate any alteration in briefing, you will inform S.I.O. immediately.

Signed C.M. Grierson.
22.7.42

Appendix VII

STATISTICAL APPENDICES:
Totals for Special Duties Operations From the UK, 1941–1945

NOTES:

1. The figures for aircraft missing years 1941 and 1942 are not available in this office.

2. The figures for sorties attempted years 1941 and 1942 are also not available in this office.

3. The figures given are compiled from monthly totals as far as possible, but in some cases there may be an overlap of the moon or non-moon period into the next quarter.

4. Tonnage delivered is worked out on the basis of 10 containers, and 20 packages, to the ton – to the nearest ton.

5. Figures include both landing and dropping operations.

VII A
Totals For Special Delivery Operations From the UK, 1941-1945

COUNTRY	SORTIES		MEN			TONNAGE
	Attempted	Successful	Dropped	Out	Home	DELIVERED
France	8,651[+]	5,634	868[∅]	293	559	8,455½
Belgium	529[+]	342	198	-	-	484
Holland	630[+]	372	120	-	-	554
Germany	43	26	42	-	-	1
Poland	102[+]	77	197	-	-	37
Czechoslovakia	19[+]	14	33	-	-	1
Italy	2[+]	2	2	-	-	-
Norway	1,241	717	200	-	-	933
Denmark	677[+]	418	55	-	-	676

[+] *No record of sorties attempted for 1941 and/or 1942*
[∅] *No record of men dropped for 1941 and/or 1942*

VII B

Special Duty Operations to France Undertaken by RAF Aircraft Based in the United Kingdom (Including Pick-ups)

DATE	SORTIES		MEN			TONNAGE DELIVERED	AIRCRAFT MISSING	REMARKS	
	Attempted	Successful	Dropped	Out	Home			Containers	Packages
1941	22+	22	-	1	1	1½	-	9	11
1942	93+	93	140	15	19	23		201	64
1943									
January-March	79	22	18	13	18	20	2	170	57
April-June	342	165	18	23	43	148	5	1,361	236
July-September	630	327	52	40	76	277	6	2,566	399
October-Dec.	298	101	20	30	56	133	6	1,202	263
Total	1,349	615	108	106	193	578	19	5,299	955
1944								Including pick-ups	
January-March	1,046	557	77	11	15	693	13	6,096	1,676
April-June	1,163	748	70	18	19	1,162	20	12,188	2,828
July-September	2,358	1,644	189	69	113	3,223	21	29,832	4,591
October-Dec.	65	46	-	12	23	44	-	374	125
Total	4,632	2,995	336	110	170	5,122	54	48,590	9,220
Total 1941-1945	6,096+	3,725	584°	232	383	5724½	73#	54,099	10,250

+ *1941 and 1942 figures for attempted sorties – no records obtainable*

° *No record for 1941 – men dropped*

No record for 1941 and 1942 – aircraft missing

VII C

Special Duty Operations to France Undertaken by USAAF Aircraft Based in the United Kingdom (Including Pick-ups)

DATE	SORTIES		MEN			TONNAGE	AIRCRAFT	REMARKS	
	Attempted	Successful	Dropped	Out	Home	DELIVERED	MISSING	Containers	Packages
1944									
January–March	119	52	6	–	–	73	2	619	228
April–June	545	344	76	–	–	524	4	2,063	2,359
Daylight Op.[+]	180	177	–	–	–	209	2	2,088	–
July–September	1,445	1,076	195	61	176	1,615	7	12,328	7,642
Daylight Op.[∅]	195	192	7	–	–	229	–	2,286	–
Daylight Op.[#]	71	68	–	–	–	81	–	814	–
October–Dec.	–	–	–	–	–	–	–	–	–
Totals	2,555	1,909	284	61	176	2,731	15	20,198	10,229

[+] *Operation Zebra, 25 June 1944*

[∅] *Operation Brick, 1 August 1944*

[#] *September 1944*

249

VII D
Special Duty Operations to Belgium Undertaken by RAF Aircraft Based in the United Kingdom

DATE	SORTIES		MEN	TONNAGE DELIVERED	AIRCRAFT MISSING	REMARKS	
	Attempted	Successful				Containers	Packages
1941	11+	11	12	1	-	8	7
1942	56+	56	70	22	-	214	10
1943							
January-March	25	6	7	3	-	23	7
April-June	19	11	16	7	1	50	24
July-September	14	10	10	6	-	51	18
October-Dec.	24	6	3	5	2	53	1
Totals	82	33	36	21	3	177	50
1944							
January-March	23	13	18	11	-	81	29
April-June	50	24	22	37	5	347	49
July-September	159	119	2	267	2	2,247	840#
October-Dec.	19	19	-	45	-	452	
Totals	251	175	42	360	7	3,127	918#
Total 1941-1944	400+	275	160	404	10⊘	3,526	985#

+ *No record of sorties attempted for 1941 and 1942*
⊘ *No record of aircraft missing for 1941 and 1942*
Twenty-six men out/1 home

250

VII E

Special Duty Operations to Belgium Undertaken by USAAF Aircraft Based in the United Kingdom

DATE	SORTIES Attempted	Successful	MEN	TONNAGE DELIVERED	AIRCRAFT MISSING	REMARKS Containers	Packages
1944							
January–March	9	5	–	3	1	24	5
April–June	84	40	10	53	3	467	97
July–September	36	22	28	24	–	248	105[#]
Totals	129	67	38	80	4	739	207[#]

[#] 5 men out/5 home

VII F
Special Duty Operations to Holland Undertaken by RAF Aircraft Based in the United Kingdom

DATE	SORTIES Attempted	Successful	MEN	TONNAGE DELIVERED	AIRCRAFT MISSING	REMARKS Containers	Packages
1941	2+	2	4	-	-	-	3
1942	49+	49	43	27	-	255	24
1943							
January-March	26	13	11	12	-	114	15
April-June	20	14	6	15	5	135	28
July-September	2	1	-	1	2	13	1
October-Dec.	1	1	2	1	-	-	2
Totals	49	29	19	28	7	262	46
1944							
January-March	-	-	-	-	-	-	-
April-June	3	2	6	-	1	-	4
July-September	64	37	13	33	4	315	38
October-Dec.	288	152	4	244	4	2,302	274
Totals	355	191	23	277	9	2,617	316
1945							
January-March	52	25	8	51	-	458	96
April-May	123	76	23	171	4	1,576	264
Totals	175	101	31	222	4	2,034	360
Total 1941-1945	630+	372	120	554	20⊘	5,168	749

+ No record of sorties attempted for 1941 and 1942
⊘ No record of aircraft missing for 1941 and 1942

VII G
Special Duty Operations to Germany Undertaken by RAF Aircraft Based in the United Kingdom

DATE	SORTIES Attempted	Successful	MEN	TONNAGE DELIVERED	AIRCRAFT MISSING	REMARKS Containers	Packages
1943							
January-March	1	1	1	-	-	-	1
April-June	-	-	-	-	-	-	-
July-September	1	1	1	-	-	-	1
October-Dec.	1	-	-	-	-	-	-
Totals	3	2	2	-	-	-	2
1944							
January-March	1	1	1	-	-	-	1
April-June	3	1	2	-	-	-	-
July-September	1	1	1	-	-	-	-
October-Dec.	3	2	3	-	1	-	1
Totals	8	5	7	-	1	-	1
1945							
January-March	21	11	17	1	-	12	4[+]
April-May	11	8	16	-	2	-	4
Totals	32	19	33	1	2	12	8[+]
Total 1943-1945	43	26	42	1	3	12	11[+]

[+] Includes six men out

VII H

Special Duty Operations to Poland Undertaken by RAF Aircraft Based in the United Kingdom

DATE	SORTIES		MEN	TONNAGE DELIVERED	AIRCRAFT MISSING	REMARKS	
	Attempted	Successful				Containers	Packages
1941	3+	3	12	1	-	8	3
1942	14+	14	76	5	-	42	24
1943							
January-March	51	34	76	14	1	179	116
April-June	1	1	1	-	-	-	1
July-September	24	17	29	13	6	103	57
October-Dec.	9	8	3	4	1	34	19
Totals	60	85	109	31	8	316	193
Total 1941-1943	102+	77	197	37	8⊘	682	220

+ *No record of sorties attempted for 1941 and 1942*
⊘ *No record of aircraft missing for 1941 and 1942*

254

VIII I

Special Duty Operations to Czechoslovakia Undertaken by RAF Aircraft Based in the United Kingdom

DATE	SORTIES Attempted	SORTIES Successful	MEN	TONNAGE DELIVERED	AIRCRAFT MISSING	REMARKS Containers	REMARKS Packages
1941	4[+]	4	8	-	-	-	6
1942	10[+]	10	25	1	-	4	10
1943							
January-March	5	-	-	-	-	-	-
April-June	-	-	-	-	-	-	-
July-September	-	-	-	-	-	-	-
October-Dec.	-	-	-	-	-	-	-
Totals	5	-	-	-	-	-	-
Total 1941-1943[#]	19[+]	14	33	1	-[ø]	4	16

[+] No record of sorties attempted for 1941 and 1942
[ø] No record of aircraft missing for 1941 and 1942
[#] No operations from the UK in 1944 and 1945

255

VII J

Special Duty Operations to Italy Undertaken by RAF Aircraft Based in the United Kingdom

DATE	SORTIES Attempted	Successful	MEN	TONNAGE DELIVERED	AIRCRAFT MISSING	REMARKS Containers	Packages
1941	1+	1	2	–	–	–	–
1942	–	–	–	–	–	–	–
1943							
January-March	–	–	–	–	–	–	–
April-June	1	1	–	–	–	–	6
July-September	–	–	–	–	–	–	–
October-Dec.	–	–	–	–	–	–	–
Totals	1	1	–	–	–	–	–
Total 1941-1943#	2+	2	2	–	–	–	6

+ *No record of sorties attempted for 1941 and 1942*
# *No operations from the UK in 1944 and 1945*

256

VII K
Special Duty Operations to Norway Undertaken by RAF Aircraft Based in the United Kingdom

DATE	SORTIES		MEN	TONNAGE DELIVERED	AIRCRAFT MISSING	REMARKS	
	Attempted	Successful				Containers	Packages
1941	–	–	–	–	–	–	–
1942	22	11	21	6	–	53	14
1943							
January-March	16	6	14	5	–	39	26
April-June	4	3	2	3	–	23	7
July-September	4	3	4	3	–	25	10
October-Dec.	26	12	25	13	–	104	52
Totals	50	24	45	24	–	191	95
1944							
January-March	17	13	3	17	–	151	42
April-June	30	23	6	31	–	271	63
July-September	2	2	2	3	–	23	22
October-Dec.	144	50	33	90	4	762	276
Totals	193	88	44	141	4	1,207	403
1945							
January-March	497	326	40	533	9	4,800	1,065
April-May	280	170	25	255	10	2,304	494
Totals	777	496	65	788	19	7,104	1,559
Total 1942-1945	1,042	619	175	959	23	8,555	2,071

VII L

Special Duty Operations to Norway Undertaken by USAAF Aircraft Based in the United Kingdom

DATE	SORTIES Attempted	Successful	MEN	TONNAGE DELIVERED	AIRCRAFT MISSING	REMARKS Containers	Packages
1944							
January-March	6	4	-	5	-	48	6
April-June	2	2	-	3	-	24	9
July-September	61	33	-	47	1	396	138
October-Dec.	2	2	-	3	-	24	6
Totals	71	41	-	58	1	492	159
1945							
January-March	24	11	3	16	-	132	53
April-May	104	46	22	71	4	551	309
Totals	128	57	25	87	4	683	362
Total 1944-1945	199	98	25	145	5	1,175	521

VII M
Special Duty Operations to Denmark Undertaken by RAF Aircraft Based in the United Kingdom

DATE	SORTIES Attempted	Successful	MEN	TONNAGE DELIVERED	AIRCRAFT MISSING	REMARKS Containers	Packages
1941	–	–	–	–	–	–	–
1942	4+	4	12	–	–	–	3
1943							
January-March	4	2	8	1	–	4	5
April-June	4	4	7	2	–	14	3
July-September	9	8	3	7	–	61	8
October-Dec.	8	5	3	2	1	21	2
Totals	25	19	21	12	1	100	18
1944							
January-March	3	3	2	3	–	24	3
April-June	8	7	3	8	1	72	10
July-September	12	12	2	15	–	144	6
October-Dec.	104	71	10	143	3	1,402	54
Totals	127	93	17	169	4	1,642	73
1945							
January-March	83	54	5	109	4	1,059	59
April-May	174	114	–	218	8	2,061	231
Totals	257	168	5	327	12	3,120	290
Total 1942-1945	413+	284	55	508	17⊘	4,862	290

+ *No record of sorties attempted for 1942*
⊘ *No record of aircraft missing for 1942*

VII N

Special Duty Operations to Denmark Undertaken by USAAF Aircraft Based in the United Kingdom

DATE	SORTIES		MEN	TONNAGE DELIVERED	AIRCRAFT MISSING	REMARKS	
	Attempted	Successful				Containers	Packages
1944							
January-March	-	-	-	-	-	-	-
April-June	1	-	-	-	1	-	-
July-September	23	9	-	10	-	104	-
October-Dec.	-	-	-	-	-	-	-
Totals	24	9	-	10	1	104	-
1945							
January-March	86	36	-	45	-	426	54
April-May	154	89	-	113	-	1,037	178
Totals	240	125	-	158	-	1,463	232
Total 1944-1945	264	134	-	168	1	1,567	232

Appendix VIII

STATISTICAL APPENDICES:
Totals for Special Duties Operations From
the Mediterranean

NOTES:

1. From April 1944, operations carried out on behalf of other agencies are incorporated in these figures, as it is not possible to extract them from the totals. However the proportion of these operations is very low:

Date	Total Successful Sorties	Total Successful Sorties for Other Agencies
1944		
April to June	2,729	71
July to Sept.	3,829	117
Oct. to Dec.	3,217	73
1945		
Jan. to March	3,216	81
April to May	1,196	29
	14,187	*371*

2. Personnel infiltrated on both landing and dropping operations are given as a combined figure.

3. These figures are for operations carried out by <u>all</u> aircraft working from the Middle East of S.D. operations – landing and dropping operations.

4. Figures prior to June 1943 are not obtainable.

VIII A

Totals For Special Delivery Operations From the Mediterranean

COUNTRY	TOTAL SORTIES	SUCCESSFUL SORTIES	GROSS TON DELIVERED	PERSONNEL DROPPED	PERSONNEL LANDED	PERSONNEL EXFILTRATED	PWB LEAFLETS IN TONS
Yugoslavia	11,632	8,640	16,469	-	2,500[2]	19,000	536
Greece	2,064	1,714	4,205	85	300	600	106
Albania	673	572	1,205	134	201	502	74
Corsica	89	79	140	2	-	-	4
S. France	1,713	1,129	2,878	578	31	34	98
Poland	619	289	501	132	12	13	200
Italy	4,280	2,652	5,907	538	-	24	169
Hungary	28	14	16	14	-	-	11
Romania	9	4	2	6	-	-	10
Bulgaria	183	107	218	22	-	-	-
Czechoslovakia	114	39	58	42	-	-	11
Austria	72	45	47	76	-	-	10
Crete	31	20	39	10	-	-	-

[2] *Records not available to distinguish between personnel dropped and landed in Yugoslavia. However, it is known that comparatively few were parachuted because of the large number of available landing strips.*

VIII B

Special Delivery Operations To Europe Undertaken by Aircraft Based in the Mediterranean Area

DATE	FRANCE SORTIES		ITALY SORTIES		POLAND SORTIES		CZECH SORTIES		BALKANS© SORTIES		GERMANY & AUSTRIA SORTIES		HUNGARY SORTIES		REMARKS
	Att.	Suc.	Att.	Suc.	Att.	Suc.	Att.	Suc.	Att.	Suc.	Att.	Suc.	Att.	Suc.	
1944															
January-March	246	91	207	78	19	1	-	-	555	327	-	-	-	-	4 a/c missing; 2 crashed on take-off
April-June#	651	396	477	269	253	140	4	3	3,286	2,344	4	4	12	9	22 a/c missing; 9 a/c crashed
July-September	743	593	642	369	280	135	5	4	2,496	1,856	3	2	5	4	49 a/c missing; 16 a/c lost in crashes
Oct-December	-	-	959	554	67	18	7	2	3,156	2,594	4	4	-	-	26 a/c missing; 6 a/c lost in crashes
Totals	1,640	1,080	2,285	1,270	619	294	16	9	9,493	7,121	11	10	17	13	101 a/c missing; 33 a/c crashed

VIII B (continued)

Special Delivery Operations To Europe Undertaken by Aircraft Based in the Mediterranean Area

DATE	FRANCE SORTIES		ITALY SORTIES		POLAND SORTIES		CZECH SORTIES		BALKANS[∅] SORTIES		GERMANY & AUSTRIA SORTIES		HUNGARY SORTIES		REMARKS
	Att.	Suc.	Att.	Suc.	Att.	Suc.	Att.	Suc.	Att.	Suc.	Att.	Suc.	Att.	Suc.	
1945															
January-March	-	-	1,533	976	-	-	32	9	2,707	2,160	25	11	-	-	11 a/c missing; 4 a/c lost in crashes
April-May	-	-	697	504	-	-	60	16	695	639	43	25	-	-	3 a/c missing; 1 crashed
Totals	-	-	2,230	1,480	-	-	92	25	3,402	2,799	68	36	-	-	14 a/c missing; 5 a/c crashed

[∅] Balkans: Greece, Yugoslavia, Albania, Romania, Bulgaria and Aegean.

[#] From May, figures for other agencies included.

264

VIII C
Special Delivery Operations To France Undertaken by Aircraft Based in the Mediterranean Area

DATE	TONNAGE	MEN Out	Home	REMARKS
1943				
June	1	2	-	-
July to September	1	3	-	-
October to December	6	4	-	-
Totals	8	9	-	-
1944				
January to March	172	20	-	February and March figures for bodies not available
April to June	794	96	30	-
July to September	1,100	474	30	-
October to December	-	-	-	-
Totals	2,066	590	30	-
1945				
January to March	-	-	-	-
April to May	-	-	-	-
Totals	-	-	-	-
Total 1943 to 1945	2,074	599	30	-

VIII D

Special Delivery Operations To Yugoslavia Undertaken by Aircraft Based in the Mediterranean Area

DATE	TONNAGE	MEN Out	Home	REMARKS
1943				
June	37	18	-	-
July to September	144	81	-	-
October to December	125	17	-	-
Totals	306	116	-	-
1944				
January to March	251	14	89	No figures for men out February to March
April to June	2,602	235	3,674	-
July to September	3,014	919	9,247	-
October to December	2,398	1,812	1,184	-
Totals	8,265	2,980	14,194	-
1945				
January to March	3,347	882	2,135	-
April to May	1,158	31	1,353	-
Totals	4,505	913	3,488	-
Total 1943 to 1945	13,076	4,009	17,682	-

VIII E
Special Delivery Operations To Italy Undertaken by Aircraft Based in the Mediterranean Area

DATE	TONNAGE	MEN Out	MEN Home	REMARKS
1943				
June	1	–	–	–
July to September	4	8	–	–
October to December	1	5	–	–
Totals	6	13	–	–
1944				
January to March	92	34	–	No figures for February to March
April to June	398	143	–	–
July to September	650	171	–	–
October to December	780	109	7	–
Totals	1,920	457	7	–
1945				
January to March	1,669	225	5	–
April to May	875	244	20	–
Totals	2,544	469	25	–
Total 1943 to 1945	4,470	939	32	–

VIII F

Special Delivery Operations To Greece Undertaken by Aircraft Based in the Mediterranean Area

DATE	TONNAGE	MEN		REMARKS
		Out	Home	
1943				
June	146	22	–	–
July to September	395	84	–	–
October to December	234	51	23	–
Totals	775	157	23	–
1944				
January to March	290	12	–	–
April to June	201	42	15	–
July to September	219	57	336	–
October to December	428	594	347	–
Totals	1,138	705	698	–
Total 1943 to 1944	1,913	862	721	–

VIII G
Special Delivery Operations To Crete Undertaken by Aircraft Based in the Mediterranean Area

DATE	TONNAGE	MEN Out	Home	REMARKS
1943				
June	-	-	-	-
July to September	2	-	-	-
October to December	10	-	-	-
Totals	12	-	-	-
1944				
January to March	-	-	-	-
April to June	3	-	-	-
July to September	6	-	-	-
October to December	15	6	4	-
Totals	24	6	4	-
Total 1943 to 1944	36	6	4	-

VIII H

Special Delivery Operations To Germany and Austria Undertaken by Aircraft Based in the Mediterranean Area

DATE	TONNAGE	MEN Out	Home	REMARKS
1944				
April to June	4	3	–	–
July to September	.3	6	–	–
October to December	2.4	11	–	–
Totals		6.7	20	–
1945				
January to March	4	16	–	–
April to May	25	39	–	–
Totals	29	55	–	–
Total 1944 to 1945	35.7	75	–	–

VIII I

Special Delivery Operations To Sardinia Undertaken by Aircraft Based in the Mediterranean Area

DATE	TONNAGE	MEN		REMARKS
		Out	Home	
1943				
June	3	6	-	-
July to September	.1	4	-	-
October to December	-	-	-	-
Total 1943	3.1	10	-	-

VIII J

Special Delivery Operations To Corsica Undertaken by Aircraft Based in the Mediterranean Area

DATE	TONNAGE	MEN Out	Home	REMARKS
1943				
June	-	-	-	-
July to September	93	2	-	-
October to December	-	-	-	-
Total 1943	93	2	-	-

VIII K

Special Delivery Operations To Albania Undertaken by Aircraft Based in the Mediterranean Area

DATE	TONNAGE	MEN Out	Home	REMARKS
1943				
June	4	-	-	-
July to September	57	28	-	-
October to December	76	34	-	-
Totals	137	62	-	-
1944				
January to March	121	-	-	No figures for February to March – Men out and home
April to June	81	30	-	-
July to September	259	99	-	-
October to December	463	108	245	-
Totals	924	237	245	-
1945				
January to March	34	102	187	-
April to May	5	4	70	-
Totals	39	106	257	-
Total 1943 to 1945	1,100	405	502	-

VIII L

Special Delivery Operations To Czechoslovakia Undertaken by Aircraft Based in the Mediterranean Area

DATE	TONNAGE	MEN Out	Home	REMARKS
1944				
April to June	1	11	-	No Ops first quarter
July to September	2	14	-	-
October to December	2	5	-	-
Totals	5	30	-	-
1945				
January to March	9	5	-	-
April to May	28	-	-	-
Totals	37	5	-	-
Total 1944 to 1945	42	35	-	-

VIII M

Special Delivery Operations To Hungary Undertaken by Aircraft Based in the Mediterranean Area

DATE	TONNAGE	MEN		REMARKS
		Out	Home	
1944				
April to June	10	4	–	–
July to September	2	5	–	–
October to December	–	–	–	–
Totals	12	9	–	–
1945				
January to March	–	–	–	–
April to May	–	–	–	–
Totals	–	–	–	–
Total 1944 to 1945	12	9	–	–

VIII N

Special Delivery Operations To Bulgaria Undertaken by Aircraft Based in the Mediterranean Area

DATE	TONNAGE	MEN Out	Home	REMARKS
1943				
October to December	-	-	-	-
Totals	-	-	-	-
1944				
January to March	58	3	-	-
April to June	76	2	-	-
October to December	-	-	-	-
Totals	134	5	-	-
Total 1943 to 1944	134	5	-	-

VIII O

Special Delivery Operations To Romania Undertaken by Aircraft Based in the Mediterranean Area

DATE	TONNAGE	MEN Out	Home	REMARKS
1943				
October to December	.08	3	-	No ops. before this date
Totals	.08	3	-	-
1944				
January to March	-	-	-	-
April to June	.04	2	-	-
July to September	2	27	36	-
October to December	-	-	-	-
Totals	2.04	29	36	-
Total 1943 to 1944	2.12	32	36	-

VIII P

Special Delivery Operations To Poland Undertaken by Aircraft Based in the Mediterranean Area

DATE	TONNAGE	MEN Out	Home	REMARKS
1944				
January to March	3	–	–	–
April to June	153	38	8	–
July to September	163	10	5	–
October to December	24	33	–	–
Total 1944	343	81	13	–

Appendix IX

Aircraft Missing, Yearly Totals

YEAR	UK BASED	MED. BASED	REMARKS	TOTALS
1941	-	-	-	-
1942	-	-	-	-
1943	38	-	-	-
1944	79	101	33 aircraft crashed in Middle East	180
1945	37	14	5 aircraft crashed in Middle East	51

N.B. These figures are incomplete – there are no figures available for aircraft missing for 1941-1942 for UK-based aircraft, and 1941-1943 for Middle East-based aircraft

Appendix X

Aircraft Available, UK and Mediterranean

United Kingdom

<u>TEMPSFORD</u>

Squadron:	138	
	161	
10.3.45	138 Squadron to Bomber Command	
	161 Squadron to 38 Group (Fighter Command). Last operation for this Squadron was to Norway 2.5.45.	

<u>38 GROUP</u>

Squadrons:	161	From 10.3.45
	190	Stirlings
	196	Stirlings
	295	Albemarles
	296	Albemarles
	297	Albemarles
	298	Halifaxes
	299	Stirlings
	570	Albemarles
	620	Stirlings
	644	Halifaxes
Aerodromes:	(Headquarters: Netherhaven)	
	Harwell	
	Keevil	

Brize Norton
Fairford
Tarrant Rushton
Tain
October 44.   (Headquarters: Markshall, Earls Colne)
Gt. Dunmow
Rivenhall
Wethersfield
Earls Colne
Shepherds Grove
Period of operation on S.O.E. operations: 3.2.44 to 26.4.45.

3 GROUP

Squadrons: 75   Stirlings
90   Stirlings
149   Stirlings
199   Stirlings
218   Stirlings
(Majority of operations carried out by 90 and 149 Squadrons)
Aerodromes: Lakenheath
Mepal
Tuddenham
Methwold
Period of operation of S.O.E. operations: 4.2.44. to 10.7.44.
(214 and 617 Squadrons based on Tempsford supplementary effort from 10.12.43 to formation of Bomber Command supplementary effort in Feb. 44)

MOSQUITO OPERATORS

Squadron: 418 Mosquito Intruder Squadron
Aerodromes: Holmesley South
Ford
The first operation was flown on 21.1.44.

U.S.A.A.F.

Operated from Harrington and Leuchars
Period of operation: 16.12.43. to 26.4.45.

Middle East

Squadrons:

	148 Squadron	Halifaxes
	1575 Flight	Polish operations (Disbanded July 1943)
	624 Squadron	Halifaxes (Formed August 1943)
	Italian Flight	S.M. 62s and CANT. Z.1007s (January 1944)
	1586 Flight	Halifaxes and Liberators (January 1944)
	62 T.C.	February 1944
	267 Squadron	Dakotas (March 1944)
	68 Recce Group	Mitchells (March 1944)
	122 Squadron	(March 1944)
	51 T.C. Wing	Dakotas, Fortresses, Liberators (March 1944)
	Lysander Flight (May 1944)	
	60 T.C. Group	Dakotas (May 1944)
	885 Squadron	Fortresses, Liberators (June 1944)
	205 Group	Liberators and Wellingtons (October 1944)
	859 Squadron	Liberators and Fortresses (December 1944)
	38 Squadron	Wellingtons (December 1944)
	44 Sqn SAAF	Dakotas (February 1945 in place of 267 Sqn; Moved to SEAC)
	301 Polish Sqn	Halifaxes and Liberators (November 1944 – March 1945)

Appendix XI

Summary Of Landing Operations

The importance of evacuation of personnel by air can be seen from the following summary of landing operations:

France	R.A.F.	383
	U.S.A.A.F.	176
	Total	*559*
	(Including Gen. de Lattre de Tassigny)	
Belgium	R.A.F.	1
	U.S.A.A.F.	5
	Total	*6*
Poland	R.A.F.	4
	Total	*4*
	(Including M. Arciszewski, last Premier of London Govt., and Gen. Tabor, D.M.O. Polish Secret Army)	
Yugoslavia	R.A.F.	
	U.S.A.A.F.	
	U.S.S.R.A.F.	19,000 combined
	(Including Marshal Tito and his G.H.Q. Staff and Allied Missions – over 100 personnel at 12 hours' notice)	
Greece	R.A.F.	721
	(Including 6 representatives of ELAS, EDES and other guerillas in August 1943 and Gen. Zervas and Gen. Sarafis and staffs for the Caserta Conference in Aug. 1944)	

Appendix XII

SOE/SIS – History of Bomber Command Support

INTRODUCTION

1. This is an historical record of the part played by Bomber Command, its aircraft and its crews, in support of special duty operations for S.I.S. and S.O.E.

2. After the fall of France arrangements were made by S.I.S. for the dropping by parachute of intelligence agents in enemy and occupied territory, and for supplying them by air with stores and equipment when necessary, and also for picking agents up in France and flying them back to this country.

3. Later, another organisation known as S.O.E. (Special Operations Executive), more directly concerned with military plans, was formed, whose function it was to organise and supply the underground resistance movement in France, now known as the F.F.I. They were also charged with arranging and co-ordinating various acts of sabotage on the Continent from Trondheim to the Pyrenees.

EARLY ORGANISATION

4. On the 9th October 1940, the C. in C. of Bomber Command agreed to the transfer of No.419 Flight, which consisted of 3 Lysanders and 2 Whitleys from Fighter Command to his command: it being considered that the type of operations envisaged would be more akin to Bomber Command operations than those of any other. The Flight was put in No.3

Group and located at Stradishall. The question of its operational control was the subject of much discussion and it was eventually agreed that details of the tasks required to be undertaken would be communicated by Air Ministry A.I.2(c) direct to the Station Commander Stradishall, and that in all other respects normal operational control within the Command would be applicable in exactly the same way as with Squadron aircraft; thereby permitting the Station Commander to decide upon the feasibility or otherwise of particular operations on any particular night.

5. The channels for laying on an operation were for S.O.E. and other organisations to make an operational request to Air Ministry A.I.2(c) who would then examine the operation from the flying aspect. For example, range, proximity of the pinpoint to flak areas or mountains etc. had to be considered. If it were found acceptable, the pinpoint and details of the load were passed on to the Station Commander for the flight to be carried out when the right conditions, such as weather and moonlight, made it possible.

EQUIPMENT AND AIRCRAFT USED.
6. Three types of loads were delivered by the Whitleys: containers, packages and personnel. The containers were long cylindrical metal holders with a parachute stored in one end. Two types of loads were known to Bomber Command, the standard load and the special load. In the standard load, usually dropped to the F.F.I. elements, were small arms, ammunition, hand grenades and other useful accoutrements whilst the special loads were made up of particular types of explosives and perhaps tools specifically collected for a particular set of sabotage against a known target. These containers were stored in the bomb bays of the aircraft in the same manner as a bomb. The packages were steel framed boxes more or less 2½' square and weighing an average of 100-140 lbs. A small number of these could be placed inside the fuselage and manhandled out of the despatching hole in the fuselage floor by one of the aircrew known as the despatcher. Their contents were similar to those in the containers and they had parachutes and static lines which operated in just the same manner as for parachutists.

7. The passengers who were dropped varied in their functions. Some were dropped to set up the organisation of French and Belgian

Resistance, others were dropped with their own special containers to carry out pre-arranged sabotage of industrial plant or communication lines, others for purposes we were not told about, and towards 'D' Day S.A.S. (Special Air Service) troops were put into France.

8. The method of dropping was for the aircraft to navigate to its pin-point where the reception committee would have three lights set out in an equilateral triangle with an additional signalling light at its apex. On the receipt and reply of the correct code letters, a run-up would be made and the load dropped.

9. The Lysanders, who have made by far one of the most romantic chapters of the war, landed on the Continent and took off again. The method of operation was for an aircraft to fly to a field or landing ground, the topography of which, after photographic cover, had to be approved, by the Air Ministry A.I.2(c). On the ground were partisans and in some cases British Officers too. The agent in charge of the landing field had previously been trained in his duties in this country; carrying out practical exercises with the Lysanders. The flare path consisted of 4 white lights and another at the downwind end forming an L. The lights were no more than hand torches tied to stakes and at No.1 flare stood the operator with white hand torches who flashed the challenge and reply code letter to the aircraft. On a day when it was known the weather would be favourable for an operation, a wireless signal was sent during the day warning the party to proceed to the ground at a pre-arranged time. The various methods of getting to the ground, often far from the partisans homes, were on occasions extremely ingenious.

1941

CHANGES OF STATION AND COMMAND
10. In March 1941, the Flight, under S/Ldr. E.V. Knowles D.F.C., was renumbered 1419 Flight and with 4 Whitleys and 3 Lysanders moved to Newmarket on the 22nd May.

11. On August 26th 1941 the Flight was expanded and 138 Squadron was formed under W/Cdr. W.J. Farley D.F.C. with 7 Whitleys, 2 long

range Lysanders and a Maryland. On the 18th December the Squadron moved from Newmarket to Stradishall and the growing incidences of their tasks has brought about an increase in their establishment giving them 12 Whitleys, 3 Halifaxes, 3 Lysanders.

LYSANDERS

12. With the close of 1941 no less than 7 clandestine landings had been made in France by the Lysanders. The Prime Minister had promised France we would go back; in fact W/Cdr. Farley was the first, he beat 'D' Day by nearly 4 years, landing his aircraft near Montigny on the night of 20th October, 1940. These flights called for a high degree of skill, courage and initiative. There were the difficulties of navigation to overcome. The smallness of the aircraft precluded a navigator with the many navigational aids available in a night bomber. The pilot had to map-read his way by the aid of the moon; he had then to make a night landing on a field he had never seen before, being guided in for a landing by hand torches manipulated by partisans. The work went on.

1942

No. 161 SQUADRON

13. The organisation over the channel was taking root. Increasing loads of arms, ammunition, and explosives were needed and on 14th February 1942, No.161 Squadron commenced to form at Newmarket under the command of W/Cdr. E.H. Fielden, M.V.C., A.F.C., to an establishment of 7 Lysanders, 5 Whitley V's, 2 Wellingtons and 1 Hudson from the King's Flight.

FURTHER MOVES

14. The Squadron moved to Graveley on March 1st and were followed by 138 Squadron on the 14th March. 138 Squadron had handed over its pick-up aircraft to 161 Squadron and were now equipped with 5 Halifaxes and 12 Whitleys. In April both Squadrons moved to R.A.F. Station Tempsford, under the command of G/Cpt. A.H. MacDonald, where they have remained ever since.

OPERATIONAL CONTROL

15. On February 24th 1942, a meeting was held at the Air Ministry to

discuss the re-organisation of 138 and 161 Squadrons and it was agreed that the present policy of control exercised by A.C.A.S.(I) through A.I.2(c) should continue, subject to the principles that the normal channels within the Command, both for operations and administration, should be used to the greatest possible extent. The decision was arrived at when it became evident that if the special requirements of the S.O.E. commitments and of other organisations were to be made and special arrangements for their security were to be adequately covered, it would be impossible to bring them within the normal operational machinery of the other squadrons within Bomber Command.

16. To implement this decision it was proposed that A.I.2(c) be established permanently to fulfil the functions of control; that consideration be given to the establishment of an R.A.F. Officer of the rank of Group Captain or Wing Commander in the operational planning branch of S.O.E.: that Bomber Command considers in conjunction with D.D.I.2 (standing between A.C.A.S.(I) and A.I.2(c)) the establishment of the Station Headquarters organisation at Tempsford having regard to the special day to day direction and control of the squadron operations, and finally that Bomber Command give sympathetic consideration to any particular proposals submitted by the Station Commander for ensuring that adequate facilities in terms of buildings, security measures etc., be provided on the Station.

POLISH CREWS

17. Two days before 138 Squadron moved from Stradishall a visit was paid to them by D.C.A.S., D.B. Ops., D.D.I.2 and S.A.S.O. Bomber Command to discuss the possibility of forming a Polish Flight in the Squadron. S.O.E. were now envisaging operations to all enemy occupied countries in Europe. It was the view of the Squadron Commander however, that it was unnecessary for operations over various countries to be carried out only by crews of the nationality concerned. Nevertheless it was decided to establish 3 complete Polish crews to carry out operations to Poland with the proviso that they would be available for other flights when no polish operations were called for. They were to come under the direct control of the Station Commander for all operational and technical matters.

TRAINING AND SUPPLEMENTARY BOMBING

18. In April 1941 the Air Officer Commanding No.3 Group suggested that No.1419 Flight should be expanded up to at least Flight strength or preferably Squadron strength and then undertake normal bombing missions when special duties could not be attempted. He felt that as at present constituted, the Flight was uneconomical since the peculiar conditions which must obtain for special operations meant that only about 8 nights per lunar month could be used. It was however decided that no change would be made since the specialised type of flying necessitated considerable extra and individual training which could only be undertaken at the unit and then in the non-moon, i.e. non-operational, period. It was realised that, at this stage, to introduce a different type of operations would only confuse the issue to the detriment of both the special duties and the bombing.

19. Nearly a year later in February 1942, another request was made by the A.O.C. of No.3 Group that No.138 Squadron be permitted to carry out bombing attacks on selected targets. He considered that this would give additional training to crews in map reading to targets in occupied territory without giving rise to suspicion as to the purpose for which they were training; it would give security cover in this country to the true role of the Squadron and when not required for special operations would be able to inflict bombing attacks upon the enemy. It was also pointed out that the most useful targets for training the pilots in map reading would be those remote from towns and other well defined landmarks. This type of target also had the advantage that they were not likely to be heavily defended and in consequence would not impose an undue strain on crews operating at the relatively low altitude necessary for effective close-work map reading.

20. A list of bomber aerodromes in Franc3e and a list of targets submitted by H.R.H. Prince Bernhard of the Netherlands was forwarded to Air Ministry with a request for authority to attack them. Approval was given on the 1st June.

SUPPLY DROPPING

21. With the arrival of the two Squadrons at Tempsford, work was started in earnest and the summary of the work carried out until the

end of the year tells its own story of ever increasing effort. What has to be borne in mind in reading these figures is that as the nights decrease in the summer so the range of operations decrease, and as their targets were usually well into Europe they were affected to a greater extent than would be the case with a normal bomber squadron.

22. The versatility of the Squadrons is worthy of note. Not only were passengers and packages parachuted through the floor of the fuselage, and containers dropped from the bomb-bays, but pigeons, nickels, incendiaries and bombs were also sent down.

23. In the period 16th March – 14th April, despite bad weather, a record number of passengers were dropped and the newly formed 161 Squadron carried out its first operation which was successful. In the following moon period the amount of cargo delivered to the Continent was doubled, and the first bombing attacks were carried out. On 15/16th April, 3 Whitleys successfully attacked the Burmeister and Wain Works on Amager Island, near Copenhagen, and a Polish crew, flying a Halifax bombed Konigsberg. The attacks were intended primarily to act as 'cover' for dropping operations. The shorter nights in the May/June period cut out all Polish and Czechoslovakian operations. The same number of containers were dropped as in the previous period, and the number of successful sorties was higher than ever. An increased weight of bombs were dropped on targets, all of which were attacked from low level, and the record number of over 7½ million pamphlets were distributed.

24. In June and July the shorter range for special operations permitted an increase in bombing, even the Lysanders taking a hand in this form of sport. One attack was particularly successful, P.R.U. cover confirming that the explosives factory at Oissel was very badly damaged.

25. During the period 14th July/11th August, special operations were carried out exclusively by 138 Squadron, 161 Squadron confining themselves to low level bombing. The best effort was an attack on the Tank Farm at Gien. 3 Whitleys attacked on 28/29th July, followed by 4 Whitleys and 2 Halifaxes of 138 Squadron the following night. P.R.U. confirmed that out of 100 bombs, 91 fell on the target. Other attacks

were made on Folligny Marshalling Yard, Cholet Power Station and Serqueux Marshalling Yard. Pigeons were dropped in such widely scattered areas as the Loire, Ardennes, in Holland and as far North as Jutland. In the period 12th August/9th September, a record number of passengers was carried due chiefly to the seasonal resumption of operations to Poland. Five flights were undertaken to Poland in spite of indifferent weather, and four were successful. The Halifaxes taking part were manned by Polish crews and each round trip represented a distance of about 2,100 miles, involving an operational flying time of 12 hours or more. 23 passengers were successfully delivered in Poland, besides containers and packages. Fresh country was broken during the period by the successful delivery of a passenger and containers in the difficult area east of Antwerp, the approaches to which are heavily defended by flak and searchlights and strongly patrolled by night fighters. 8 Whitleys and 6 Lysanders of 161 Squadron carried out bombing sorties against railway communications in France with some picturesque results. One Whitley met the Paris/Bordeaux express, to the detriment of the express and the annoyance of Vichy. On Queen Wilhelmina's birthday 3 Whitleys of 161 Squadron distributed over one ton of cigarettes over wide areas of Holland, a task performed the previous year by 138 Squadron. A new record in pigeons, containers, and hours flown was set up.

26. During the next moon phase the weather was the worst experienced since the previous February. A large programme had been arranged, against which little headway could be made until the moon was already on the wane, when conditions improved. Determined flying by both squadrons reaped a last-minute harvest of success, the number of passengers, including an increase in the traffic to Gibraltar, exceeding any previous period. Other passengers were successfully dropped in various parts of France, Belgium, Holland, Norway and Poland. The Norwegian flights were carried out with practically no moon, and all four Polish flights performed at maximum range succeeded at the first attempt. A record of 67 sorties was flown.

27. The operational period from 10th October to 14th November is significant in that flights were carried out to nearly all parts of occupied Europe, France, Belgium, Holland, Norway, Denmark, Poland,

Czechoslovakia and Estonia, which was a remarkable achievement in view of appalling weather, which made possible only two nights upon which full-scale operations could be attempted.

28. A new method of delivering passengers was successfully attempted on two occasions. One person was dropped in the sea near the coast of Denmark, and another in a lake near the Mediterranean shore. They were dressed in rubber suits with dinghies attached. Seven Lysander landings were made in France, two in adventurous circumstances, resulting in 3 passengers being delivered and 3 being flown back. As cover bombing, Okecie A/F near Warsaw was successfully bombed, as was Pardubice A/F, 60 miles east of Prague, by Czech crew. On the lighter side several hundred small bags of coffee were dropped in Belgium.

28. A feature of the last period was the despatch to Cairo of 8 Halifaxes with a heavy load of cargo, and 7 Halifaxes to Algiers with a load of A.A. guns. These special flights overlapped the moon period for special operations, and continued into the dark period, placing a considerable strain on the resources of the Squadrons. Despite this a large number of sorties was made to France, Belgium and Holland, and 6 successful Lysander landings were made in France.

PICK-UP OPERATIONS
29. As an instance of the hazards involved and the initiative demanded on Lysander operations, the operation attempted by S/Ldr. J. Nesbitt-Dufort D.S.O. on 28/1/42 is worthy of record. He had crossed the French coast in cloud, experiencing slight icing, and after pin-pointing himself on the Seine map-read to the landing-ground south of the Loire where he handed over his passenger and took off again with two other passengers. He set course for Fecamp, but before Fecamp was reached his intercom had failed and the weather had deteriorated. The clouds were down to 700□ and he was hedge-hopping in heavy rain. Glazed frost was starting to form on the windscreen and leading edge and the pilot took these as symptoms of a cold-front so he decided to fly back on the reciprocal and then turn again and climb up over the bad weather. From a D.R. position due south of the Seine below the first loop, course was set for Beachy Head. He started to climb up through

continuous thick and bumpy cloud. Slight misting of the windscreen at first gave way to rain at 7,000′ and at 8,000′ severe icing began; the engine gave indications of icing in the air intake and three or four inches of clear ice started to form on the leading edge. He pulled the over-ride in the hope of climbing out of the ice layer but at 8,500′ his aircraft was gaining no height at all and was almost unmanageable. (It must be remembered he had two passengers and luggage in the back.) He estimated his position between the Seine and the French coast so he throttled back and shouted to his passengers to bale out. They did not hear him. His aircraft would not now maintain height even at full throttle so he let the nose drop and tried to edge her round on a reciprocal course. In achieving this his aircraft had dived up to 240 mph and at 2,500′ he started to ease her out and broke cloud at 1,000′. He then found he could just keep her flying straight and level at a speed over 150 mph. He then flew west for 40 miles and then back east for 70 miles hoping to find a break in the front. There wasn't one. He was now running short of petrol so decided that in view of the type of passengers he was carrying he would fly back and try to force land in the vicinity of Chateauroux. He re-crossed the Loire at Orleans and set for Issoudun. He selected a field and came into land. There was a ditch at the far end which he could not see and this smashed the undercarriage and turned the aircraft on its nose. The axe was jammed so a pen-knife had to be used to get at the petrol tank with the object of setting the aircraft alight. When it was well alight they all ran for it. He had been in the air for 7 hours. For the next 30 days he was obliged to remain indoors as he was without identity card or food ticket.

30. On the night of their departure S/Ldr. Nesbitt-Dufort was joined by four other passengers and after a square meal set off to walk to the landing field. They rested for 15 minutes and then laid out the flare-path at 9.45. By 10.00 hours all were in position lying on the ground. Only a barking dog gave cause for anxiety. There were two false starts and on each occasion the flare-path was lit and frantic signals made to the aircraft. They turned out to be friendly Whitleys going about their unlawful occasions. At midnight the E.T.A. was up and S/Ldr. Dupont was approached on the subject of abandoning operations. They decided to wait until one o'clock. At 12.15 the noise of an Anson was heard approaching from the north. The flare-path was lit and the challenge

letter flashed to the aircraft which landed without mishap. It was quickly signalled to the edge of the field where embarkation was carried out at high speed. The increased load and the surface and length of the take-off run proved something of an embarrassment to the Anson as it is reported that by the time Nos.2 and 3 flares were passed she had reached a ground speed approximating to a steady trot. It says much for the pilot's skill and coolness that he got his aircraft airborne and so brought his precious cargo home. The Anson was flown by S/Ldr. A.M. Murphy D.F.C. and the date was 1st March.

31. Although quite a number of landings were carried out without any untoward excitement this story is typical of the resourcefulness and daring which always had to be available.

32. Other landmarks in the history of the pick-up flight were the attempt on the 18th November to carry out a double pick-up operation and the first attempt to land a Hudson in France, which was made by G/Cpt. Fielden. Both, unfortunately were unsuccessful. In the case of the Lysanders the aircraft were unable to locate the target and on the return S/Ldr. Lockhart was engaged by flak and searchlights over St. Malo and later over Jersey was attacked by 7 F.W.190's. Two attacked head-on and another from the rear starboard quarter. The pilot spun down to cloud cover and was again fired upon so he dived to sea level. He climbed back into cloud and finally got away.

33. In the case of the Hudson the Loire was followed to Avignon from where course was set to the landing ground which was easily found but no lights were seen. The pilot circled the area for half an hour and still nothing was seen. They had no alternative but to return.

CHANGE OF COMMAND

34. On 1st October, 1942 W/Cdr. Fielden M.V.O., A.F.C., Captain of the King's Flight, was promoted to the rank of Group Captain and took over the command of the station from G/Cpt. A.H. MacDonald.

35. His place as Commanding Officer of No.161 Squadron was taken by W/Cdr. P.C. Pickard D.S.O., D.F.C., who will always be remembered as the pilot in "Target for Tonight".

36. W/Cdr. W.I. Farley D.F.C. went missing on 20.4.42 and command of No.138 Squadron was taken over by W/Cdr. R.C. Hockey, D.S.O., D.F.C. who was later to receive the Czechoslovakian Military Cross, the Polish Military Cross of Valour and the Croix de Guerre.

1943

SUPPLY DROPPING

37. 1943 was to see great increases in the number of containers and packages dropped and in the number of operational hours flown.

38. At Appendix 'B' [missing] is a summary of the Squadrons' work for the year. This is more comprehensive than the previous summary and a point to be noted is that it shows operations attempted and those of them which were completed as well as the number of sorties flown. This arises and is best set out in this manner because in this special work one sortie does not necessarily imply only one operation, and vice-versa. For example, the London organisation may require 5 containers of special equipment to be dropped on each of three different reception points which may be 10 or 40 miles apart. The total number of containers is 15 which is the full load of a Halifax. Therefore one aircraft is employed. This is then recorded as one sortie carrying out 3 operations. And again, it may arise that one operation is mounted by S.O.E. which calls for 45 containers in which 3 aircraft would be employed on one operation. In fact, operations with varying loads were mounted in every Department of France and it was the responsibility of the Station Commander so to combine and allocate his aircraft available against operations offered on a particular night in the most economical manner.

39. Other new points are that Hudsons were employed on dropping as well as pick-up operations.

40. It will be seen that bombing ceased altogether owing to the organisations being able fully to employ both Squadrons on dropping and pick-up work.

41. In January and February the weather restricted operations somewhat but all possible effort was made since to complete 10

operations successfully by the moon phase ending 14th January no less than 56 operations were attempted. Of the six aircraft that were returning from Egypt unfortunately only three got back safely with passengers and mail. The others crashed on their way back and two experienced crews were lost. By the end of January all the Whitleys had left the Station. Up to 3rd February 4 long distance flights had been made to Norway, 2 to Poland and 2 to Czechoslovakia.

42. In February great strides were made: the number of passengers and containers jumped to the record figure of 64 and 177 respectively on operations which covered Germany, Austria, Poland and Norway. The next month still greater progress was made; 70 passengers and 292 containers being dropped. The operational flying hours reached the record of 749 hours. No less than 34 visits were made to Poland and flights were also carried out to Czechoslovakia, Norway and Corsica. One Halifax successfully carried out a "shuttle service" operation which meant that it flew out to Tunisia, carried out an operation from there, and then returned. In April the shorter nights precluded visits to Poland, Czechoslovakia and Austria, yet the number of containers dropped rose again to 423. The number of containers dropped in the ensuing months were to rise progressively to 594, 742, 716 reaching in August the giant figure of 1,523. In April Italy was successfully visited for the first time. In the May period, 5 Halifaxes were sent out again to North Africa to carry out clandestine operations from there to places in the Mediterranean Theatre.

43. On 8.5.43 the establishment of 138 Squadron was amended and increased to stand at 20 Halifax Mk. Vs two of which were dual conversion aircraft.

44. The June period had the shortest nights of the year yet the top score of 742 containers were dropped.

45. The following month was marred by bad weather and bad receptions, out of 215 operations attempted only 99 were completed. The pilot often pin-pointed himself over the target but either no one was there or if they were the presence of German patrols may have kept them down. In all these cases the load had to be brought back. Despite this, the operational flying hours rose to 947.50.

46. August was the record month of the year 1,288 operational hours were flown and 1,523 containers were dropped. There was a mixed flying bag; apart from special operations there was a flight from North Africa, Havocs flew Ascension sorties (of which more will be said later) and Air Sea Rescue sweeps were carried out. Some other factors contributing to these fine results were the great improvement in receptions and a supreme effort by the Engineering Staff. The policy of not re-attempting a "non-reception" operation until a satisfactory explanation has been received from "The Field" produced quick and salutary results and had a heartening effect upon the crews.

47. The September period was marred by bad weather and the loss of 8 valuable crews. Two aircraft were missing on Dutch operations where the enemy defences had been stiffening for some time and the other six aircraft were lost on Polish flights. 3 Liberators joined 138 Squadron and 3 Stirlings from Chedburgh were attached to 161 Squadron. They arrived too late in the period to make their weight felt; they did however carry out 7 Stirling and 2 Liberator sorties before the moon went down.

48. The next moon period was from 29th September to 20th October and many long flights under bad weather conditions occasioned a number of diversions which in turn weakened the battle order. Aircraft took off from advanced bases and tried a new and successful route to Poland, other aircraft went out to North Africa, others took off from Kinloss to carry out operations in the Narvik area. To carry out these distant operations showed ambition on the part of the station; with aircraft diverted, landing in other theatres of war and working advanced bases the increased strain on maintenance, organisation and administration was severe – and, alas, often forgotten.

49. Six Stirlings from 214 Squadron were again attached to 161 Squadron for the next moon period and the Polish flight in 138 Squadron was re-formed into 1586 Flight and sent overseas. Also personnel of the 22nd Anti-Submarine Squadron of the U.S.A.A.F. were attached to the station for instruction in the organisation and execution of dropping personnel and materials in enemy territory.

50. The year went out with extremely bad weather. Between the 28th November and 26th December, the Squadrons were able to operate on

only 6 nights. The night of 16th December was particularly disastrous. Owing to an inaccurate Meteorological forecast for base conditions a total of 6 Halifaxes and 2 Lysanders crashed, causing a high number of casualties among the crews. The station was again supported by 6 Stirlings of 214 Squadron plus 4 Lancasters from 617 Squadron. Four Halifaxes and one Hudson were detailed to carry out operations to Poland taking off from Italy, but having arrived at the latter country bad weather prevented them achieving any success: only two operations could be attempted.

51. It brought to a close a year of outstanding achievement. 465 people had been parachuted to earth in occupied territories and 6,720 containers with them. Hitler was to regret this.

TACTICS

52. In the tactical sphere enemy opposition was mounting and Holland in particular was to be treated as a proposition.

53. It is as well, at this juncture, to appreciate some of the tactical difficulties involved. The best dropping height for passengers and containers is about 500□ which unfortunately is the "suicide" height for flying over light flak. At night, at that height, light flak positions cannot be seen until they have already opened fire, when avoiding action is often too late. Operating singly, these aircraft did not enjoy some of the safety measures available to the main bomber force, such as radio jamming, intruder support against enemy night fighter aerodromes, protection afforded by density of attack. If they were intercepted by fighters they could look for little help elsewhere but to fight it out at low level. There was little chance of baling out in such encounters. However, on more than one occasion, Tempsford aircraft gave as much as they took.

ASCENSION OPERATIONS

54. A most important, although unspectacular part of the clandestine flying carried out by Tempsford were the Ascension flights. Havocs of 161 Squadron were employed. Early flights were made as far back as 1941. They consisted of patrolling along a predetermined route just off the enemy occupied coast and speaking over the R/T to agents at some

pre-arranged place and time. By this means most important information was brought back to this country. These operations were often extremely hazardous for the individual operating the land-based set and in consequence many flights proved to be fruitless; there not being sufficient time, when the agent was surprised by the Germans shortly before time of commencement, to organise the W/T signal telling the aircraft not to take off. As an example, in July 1943, 18 Havoc sorties were made of which only 8 were successful, yet the information brought back was vital to the Allied Supreme Command formulating their plans for the invasion of N.W. Europe.

PICK-UP OPERATIONS

55. Among the outstanding pick-up flights of 1943 were two early in the year carried out by W/Cdr. Pickard; who also carried out the first pick-up operation in a Hudson on 13th February. On the 26th January, flying a Lysander, he arrived over the pin-point at 0130 hours. He had great difficulty in finding the field, owing to bad visibility and little moon. No lights were seen on arrival, yet he continued to circle the area until 0315 hours when a light was flashed to which he replied. He landed, remained on the ground 3 minutes, and took off with his new passengers. He had been in the air so long that when he landed at Predannack his petrol tanks were empty.

56. On 24th February he took off in a Hudson to make a landing somewhere between Dijon and Lyon. When he arrived over the field fog was already forming and this, plus the awkward position of the field made the approach very difficult. No less than 20 attempts were made to get in, and even then they landed heavily and to the side of the flare path; to make matters worse they got bogged at the end of their run. With the aid of some onlookers the aircraft was dug out after ½ hour of toil, but they had only taxied about ¼ mile when the aircraft became bogged again. The situation had now become serious, but with superb coolness and energy the crew set about organising half the people of the village who had by now gathered round, and just before 0530 hours the Hudson was dug out for the second time. They then experienced great difficulty in finding out from the French the distance available to them for a take-off run. Finally they taxied back as far as possible, turned and opened the throttles. Just as they were

airborne the aircraft struck a tree with its wing tip, but it kept on flying and as W/Cdr. Pickard crossed the French coast, dawn was already breaking.

57. On January 26th, the first double Lysander operation was carried out. It was the practise for the Lysander Flight to be attached to Tangmere for the moon period, and on this occasion it was under the command of S/Ldr. Verity. Three aircraft took off between 2200 and 2215 hours flown by S/Ldr. Verity, F/O. Rymills and P/O McCairns, the intention being for the third aircraft to cover any eventualities. After crossing the French coast a recall signal was sent out but only P/O McCairns received it. He was unable to contact the other two who, in the meantime, had reached the target. F/O Rymills landed and changed passengers, taking off at 0140 hours. In the air he made contact with S/Ldr. Verity and told him it was alright to land, which he did at 0141 hours. He was met by the Mayor of the village among others. Both aircraft returned safely.

58. There was plenty of excitement for others in the detachment. Sharing a double Lysander operation on the 17th March, F/O Fowlers' engine caught fire as he made contact with foreign soil. He switched off and stuffed his Mae West up the exhaust to extinguish the flames. Taxying back for take off after this interlude, his aircraft hit a bump and the engine cut, this time of its own volition. He reached base at 0320 hours.

59. In the case of F/Lt. Brider, he was attempting a landing in the Clermont-Ferrand area on the 16th April. Coming in over an escarpment he fell victim to a down current which caused him to land with too much speed. He opened up again but in doing so he crashed through some H.T. wires which gave a vivid flash, yet he managed to stagger into the air, complete a circuit and land. On examining the damage he found that he had hit the wires with his wheel and had burst the tyre, so he had no more ado than to puncture the other, after which he brought his aircraft and passengers back to England.

60. On 15th May a Hudson pick-up in the South of France was unsuccessfully attempted by the Station Commander, G/Capt. Fielden; fog was over the target when they got there. He set out again four nights

later for the same place, and this time landed successfully, taking six passengers on board. By this time there was not enough of the night left to reach the Channel before dawn, so he flew South and landed in North Africa at 0555 hours. They left the same day and were in England by 0600 hours on 21st May. His example was to be followed in the ensuing summer months, and so the shortening nights did not stop their work continuing.

61. In September the record number of 25 sorties were made, out of which 19 were successful. During this month a brilliantly executed triple landing was made. The three Lysanders made rendezvous near the landing ground. S/Ldr. Verity went down, landed, changed his passengers and taxied off the flare path. He the signalled F/O McCairns to come in and land. He came in, changed his load and took off. F/Lt. Fowler did the same, after which S/Ldr. Verity turned about and did likewise. The whole change went off without a hitch in the remarkably short space of 9 minutes.

62. In November their run of good luck was to break. On the 16th November, F/Lt. Hooper failed to return. Later it was learned that his aircraft had become hopelessly bogged and he had had to burn it. He was safe and was "lying up", so he was put on the passenger list for the next moon period, and so on the 16th December W/Cdr. Hodges the O.C. the Squadron, took off early in the evening in a Lysander and brought him back. Unhappily there was little rejoicing as the other two Lysanders operating that night both crashed on return with fatal results, as their pilots were attempting to land; the weather had closed right down. And so came to an end a year of outstanding achievement and brilliant airmanship.

CHANGES OF COMMAND AND AWARDS
63. On 5th May, W/Cdr. D.M. Hodges D.F.C., took over command of No.161 Squadron from W/Cdr. P.C. Pickard D.S.O., D.F.C.

64. On 28th February W/Cdr. K.F. Batchelor, D.F.C., took over command of No.138 Squadron from W/Cdr. R.C. Hockey, D.S.O., D.F.C., who commanded until 3rd June when we handed over to W/Cdr. R.D. Spear, D.F.C.

65. S/Ldr. H. Verity D.F.C., received the D.S.O., and later a bar to it. Other D.S.O.'s were awarded to W/Cdr. Hodges, D.F.C., S/Ldr. Hooper, D.F.C., and F/Lt. Broadley D.F.C., D.F.M.

1944

PICK-UP OPERATIONS UP TO 'D' DAY

66. The pick-up unit started the year with 10 Lysanders and 5 Hudsons: the latter were of course used for the triple purpose of landing, dropping and Ascension flights. They flew on every occasion when the weather was fit.

67. A particularly stout effort was made by F/O Affleck on the 8th February. He landed successfully in a Hudson but owing to the water-logged state of the ground the aircraft became bogged and the engines had to be stopped. The aircraft was eventually manhandled into wind at the take off point where the engines were re-started. It was then found that the tail wheel had sunk deep into the mud and the engines had to be switched off again. Undaunted, horses and oxen were recruited in the Allied cause, but even these attempts to drag it out were of no avail. The pilot then decided to dig two sloping trenches in front of the wheels and try to taxi out and it was calculated that they had until 0300 hours in which to do it. After that hour they would not have sufficient time to get out of France before dawn and would therefore have to set fire to their aircraft. The digging was finished in time and he taxied out and attempted to take straight off. This he found impossible as the field was so soggy that he could not get enough speed to become airborne. He had to throttle back and whilst taxying round for another attempt bogged again. They managed to get out of this again and made another attempt to take off. This time when nearing the boundary of the field the aircraft hit a bump and bounced into the air at a speed of no more than 50 knots per hour. With superb skill F/O Affleck kept her airborne and so flew back to base.

68. On the 8th February, the first mail pick-up flight was successfully carried out by F/O Bell in a Lysander. To carry out this Flight – of which there were to be more, known as M.P.U.'s – the pilot had to fly at a

height of about 12☐ between two poles over the tops of which was stretched a cord with a mail-bag attached. The aircraft lowered from its undercarriage a pick-up hook which caught the wire and so lifted away the mail-bag. In darkness such flying called for great skill and precision.

69. The number of passengers flown to and from France was remarkable. In the February/March period 38 were ferried and in March/April 48 people were taken and brought back. In May, a very successful triple Lysander operation was carried out by S/Ldr. Ratcliff, F/Lt. Large and Lt. Hysing-Dahl of the Royal Norwegian Air Force. They were on the ground no longer than 10 minutes, taking a total of 6 people out and bringing 8 others back. The last landing operations before 'D' Day were on the night of the 2nd June when three very successful operations were carried out by F/Lts. Taylor and Turner, and F/O Alexander.

SUPPLY DROPPING UNTIL 'D' DAY
70. With the approach of 'D' Day the dropping of supplies was stepped up still more. Everything that they got into France now would mean so much more to our force when they stormed the beaches of Normandy.

71. An examination of Appendix 'C' [missing] shows the rising number of containers and fighting men dropped. In February, March and April, the outstanding figures of 77, 78 and 94 men were put secretly into Europe, and in the same months 1375, 1691 and 1190 containers were dropped: in May the record figure of 2276.

72. At the start of the year bad weather made flying possible on only 4 nights in the moon period and on 2 nights in the moonless period. These moonless operations were made possible by the use of wireless homing sets which were operated by agents in the field. The operator in the field transmitted from his set in the field and the aircraft picked it up on its own special instruments and homed to the field. Whilst this new innovation called for increased skill on the part of the aircrews, the darkness tended to give better protection against night fighters. A special operation was carried out by 3 aircraft which dropped 573 pigeons in France.

73. Besides the operation for the first time of U.S.A.A.F. crews carried out in their Liberator aircraft, the following also operated in support: 6 Stirlings from 214 Squadron, 2 from 199 Squadron and one from 149 Squadron.

74. The following month a Hudson was successfully used for the first time for the dropping of passengers by parachute, the aircraft having been modified for this purpose. The weather improved for the period 23rd February to 22nd March, and the new record of 1666 operational hours were flown from Tempsford. Between 23rd March and 20th April, the record number of 94 people were set down in occupied territory; sorties being made to France, Belgium, Holland, Denmark, Norway and Germany. The following month the same countries were visited again.

SUPPLEMENTARY EFFORT

75. At the end of January, Bomber Command received instructions from the Air Ministry to the effect that the Prime Minister had ordered special arrangements to be made for supplying arms and equipment to French Resistance in the Haute-Savoie area. It was decided that all Stirling Squadrons would be employed in the moon period primarily upon this task, and the Director of Intelligence (R), Air Ministry, ruled that the Stirlings be available for operations to other parts of France when the weather precluded visits to the Haute-Savoie.

76. It was decided at a meeting held at Bomber Command at the beginning of February that, owing to the shortage of containers held by S.O.E., No.3 Group would supply 32 Stirlings and not the entire force. 12 of these were to be attached to Tempsford during the moon period, and the remainder would operate from Lakenheath. Between the 4th-15th February, No.149 and 199 Squadrons carried out 117 sorties. In the middle of February the Prime Minister directed that the supplementary effort for the March period must be double that of January/February and to this end it was agreed at Bomber Command on 22nd February that 12 Stirlings of 218 Squadron would be attached to Tempsford and the remaining Squadrons would operate from Lakenheath, Tuddenham and Mepal. It was agreed that Ops.1(s) at H.Q. Bomber Command would co-ordinate the selection of operations by Tempsford and 3

Group from the lists submitted by S.O.E. Ops.1(s) had been established at Bomber Command in October 1943 and was, in effect, a miniature operations room for all special duties aircraft. The branch was formed under W/Cdr. Kynoch, whose function it was to co-ordinate and filter all operations between S.O.E., other London organisations and the Squadrons. During the period 29th February to 16th March, Nos. 75, 90, 149 and 199 Squadrons attempted 263 sorties, apart from their aircraft attached to Tempsford. In the March/April period, 32 Stirlings were called upon and they attempted 106 sorties. None were attached to Tempsford. In the last period in which they were called upon, 27th April to 11th May, only 24 were used. However, the bulk of their work had been done and their contribution was greatly appreciated. General Koenig, Commander of the F.F.I., sent a personal message of thanks to the C. in C. expressing his gratitude for the invaluable work of the crews.

JUNE 1944

77. 'D' Day came, not surprisingly, in the moon period. Sorties were confined to France, Belgium and Holland, and the large number of 1240 pigeons as well as a large number of leaflets were put down in France. Many of these were later to bring back vital information from behind the German lines. (It is feasible that a few may have served in a less dignified manner: finding their way into the pie)

78. As 'D' Day approached, an increasing number of the "passengers" were S.A.S. (Special Air Service) Troops. They were usually parachuted in batches of 6, and remained together as a military unit upon landing. They were to take action on 'D' Day in direct support of the landing forces and of the Airborne Division. Officers with the Supreme Commanders plans' for the F.F.I. were dropped. The Maquis were ready. The stage was now set. The people were armed, the bridges were mined, the crossroads were covered; and so it was that when our troops first set foot on French soil, the bottom fell out of Hitler's tub.

AFTER 'D' DAY

79. The invasion itself meant no relaxation for Tempsford. As shown in the Appendix [missing], 251 Halifax sorties were flown between 21st June and 20th July. The beach-head did however, have a secondary

effect in their effort. Large areas of the English Channel were prohibited to our aircraft. There were large concentrations of Allied shipping standing off the coast of Normandy which quite naturally would engage anything above them either seen or heard. Behind the beach-head the Germans were re-distributing their defences, night fighters were coming into the area and light flak was moving up. It so happened that Cabourg had for years been the place on the French coast where both Halifaxes and Lysanders had crossed into France. This was now denied to them, and seriously cut down the operation of the Lysanders. The nights were the shortest of the year and to go round the restricted areas by way of Devon and across to St. Malo meant they would be unable to get inland more than a few miles in the time available. However, 1 Hudson and 3 Lysanders managed to get through and brought back military information of vital importance to Allied arms. In this same period important operations were carried out to the South of France in support of the coming landing on the Riviera. These flights had perforce to be shuttle operations. Nine Halifaxes, dropped containers, packages and agents and then proceeded on to Blida in North Africa. Some came back by the same route completing another operation on the way. Advantage was taken of the fact that the enemy had few fighters in Southern France and as such our aircraft were able almost to reach the French coast before nightfall.

80. An interesting point in this period is that moonless operations were undertaken on 9 nights; the same number as on moon nights. This was particularly gratifying to S.O.E. since it meant that there was now no interruption in the flow of supplies. In the following period, operations were undertaken on 10 nights in the dark period and 9 in the moon period, sorties being undertaken to France, Belgium, Holland and Denmark.

81. At the end of August, the Squadrons started to re-equip with Stirling aircraft and in the period 20th August to 18th September both types were in operation. With the swift Allied advance across France, it now became possible for daylight operations to be carried out to certain areas, night operations being confined to the Dijon-Lyons area. The Hudsons were successful on 21 out of 23 operations and ferried over 135 people to Belgium and France.

82. In the September/October period owing to bad weather it was possible to operate on 5 nights in the moon period and two nights in the dark period, but daylight operations, both parachute and landings, were carried out on most days. A very successful landing operation was carried out by 4 Stirlings and 6 Hudsons transporting a special duty Army Unit and their equipment to Belgium. A continuous shuttle service to Belgium was also kept up taking supplies of arms and ammunition to the Belgian Resistance Forces, whilst on the afternoon of the 10th September, 15 Stirlings flew over a reception ground near Brussels and dropped urgently needed supplies.

83. The weather continued to affect operations considerably during the next period and permitted operations to be undertaken on only four nights during the moon period and one night in the dark period, although sorties were made to Denmark, Norway, France and Holland.

PICK-UP OPERATIONS
84. The Lysanders were out again in the first moon period after 'D' Day successfully completing two out of three sorties. One Hudson also landed in enemy territory and in all 27 passengers were ferried between England and France. On the night of 7th July, Lt. Hysing-Dahl had a narrow escape. A change in the winds upset his navigational calculations and in consequence he found himself over the beach-head. He was engaged by flak and his Lysander was hit in several places, he also got a shrapnel wound in the hand. He decided he would have to land in the sea, and when about 20 miles out to sea his engine cut and he had to glide in at about 70 mph. The Lysander went over on its nose on making contact with the sea and he found himself sitting in the cockpit under water. His Mae West wouldn't inflate, but he managed to get out and inflate the dinghy: he finally got his 3 passengers on it. After 2½ hours they were seen and rescued by an American M.T.B. and picked up at 0710 hours. Unfortunately one passenger died on the vessel and one was drowned.

85. With an improvement in the routeing, our Lysanders were able between 21st July and 19th August to carry out 11 sorties, and the Hudsons had an outstandingly successful run attempting and completing 8 operations, one of which was a double. Of the 9 sorties

this entailed, W/Cdr. Boxer brought off three of them. The Lysanders were detached to R.A.F. Station, Winkleigh in Devon as it was considered that it would be better to use it as an advance base for routes crossing in over the Brittany coast. They moved there under the command of S/Ldr. Radcliffe, and it was from there that two successful mail pick-ups were carried out. W/Cdr. Boxer and F/O Ibbot successfully carried the first double Hudson operation on 6th August, bringing back over 20 passengers between them.

86. By September the war had brought about a number of changes, and as such the Lysanders could not be fully employed. An arrangement was made, however, to fly a shuttle service each day to Belgium carrying photographs between the P.R.U. at Benson and the 21st Army Group Headquarters in Belgium. The Hudsons were employed in a similar role taking a total of 135 passengers from this country to France and Belgium. It was in this month that W/Cdr. Boxer made further pick-up history by successfully carrying out the first non-moon pick-up, which he did in a Hudson to the South of France.

87. In the period between 19th October and 17th November, the weather again continued to be unfavourable: operations were, however, carried out to France, Norway, Denmark and Holland.

88. In the last period of the year Stirling operations were confined solely to Norway and Denmark, over 69 sorties being made. On the 26th November, 6 Hudsons made a strong bid to get into Germany, 3 were successful, 2 were defeated by the weather and one, although it was subsequently learnt that he completed his task, fatally crashed behind our own lines on the way home. Many Ascensions were attempted but bad luck was with them and it seemed that when there was contact at the other end some slight technical hitch necessitated the aircrafts' early return.

CHANGES OF COMMAND
89. On May 9th, W/Cdr. W.J. Burnett, D.F.C., took over command of No.138 Squadron from W/Cdr. R.D. Spear, D.S.O., D.F.C. and bar, Croix de Guerre, and he handed over again to W/Cdr. T.C. Murray, D.F.C. and bar on 8th November.

90. In No.161 Squadron, command was handed over from W/Cdr. D.M. Hodges, D.S.O., D.F.C. and bar, Croix de Guerre to W/Cdr. A.H. Boxer, D.F.C., Polish Virtuti Militari, on 9th March.

ROPLEY'S LEGACY

THE RIDGE ENCLOSURES, 1709 TO 1850:

Chawton, Farringdon, Medstead, Newton Valence
and Ropley and the birth of Four Marks

CHRIS HEAL

Published by Chattaway and Spottiswood
Four Marks, Hampshire
www.candspublishing.org.uk
chrisheal@candspublishing.org.uk

A catalogue record for this book is available from
the British Library.

5 4 3 2 1

ISBN 978-1-9161944-3-4

Designed and typeset: Mary Woolley, www.battlefield-design.co.uk
Cover and maps: Paul Hewitt, www.battlefield-design.co.uk
Cartoons: Stella, Radical Cartoons, www.spanglefish.com/stellaillustrator
Translations: Brooke Westcott
Index: Holly Fletcher
Print on Demand: IngramSpark

DEDICATION AND ACKNOWLEDGEMENT

In 2020, in the *Castle of Comfort* in Medstead, I fell into conversation with two young people. They complained of how little there was to do locally. 'Nothing ever happens here.'

This book is dedicated to my two casual acquaintances and to the poor people of the founding parishes of Four Marks.

Supported by
Financial assistance from the Hampshire Archives Trust
Ropley History Network and Archive
David Rymill, archivist, and staff at the Hampshire Archives

Using additional original research material from
Alresford Historical & Literary Society
The British Newspaper Archive
Find My Past
Parliamentary Archives
Surrey Archives
The National Archives
Winchester Cathedral Archive
Winchester College Archives

I stand on solid ground, on solid ground

It's the land - it is our wisdom
It's the land - it shines us through
It's the land - it feeds our children
It's the land - you cannot own the land
The land owns you
Solid Ground: **vocals Dolores Keane; lyrics Dougie MacLean**

Even if the small farmer received strict justice in the division of the common fields, his share in the legal costs and the additional expense of fencing his own allotments often overwhelmed him and he was obliged to sell his property. The expenses were always heavy … The Lords of the Manor could afford to bear their share because they were enriched by enclosure: the classes that were impoverished by enclosure were ruined when they had to pay for the very proceeding that had made them the poorer.
J. L. and Barbara Hammond, *The Village Labourer*

It was all 'a plain enough case of class robbery'.
E. P. Thompson, *The Making of the English Working Class*

What the history of land ownership in Britain proves, and modern political economics demonstrate, is the inseparable bond between land and power … that the fortunes of 5,000 landowning families have been revived by a surge in demand for development land, something which has not been investigated by the media and is a hugely significant development.
Kevin Cahill, *Who Owns Britain*

CONTENTS

PREFACE

I first met England's enclosures when I studied the background of a handful of villages in nineteenth century South Gloucestershire. What I uncovered surprised me for I had no idea such careless brutality had been inflicted openly by greedy landed aristocracy on the peasantry. Reading the great standard bearers like E. P. Thompson and the Hammonds, I found a call for recognition of the wrongs done.[1]

Elements of the historical establishment suggested that my preferred sources were a touch *passé* and their Marxist undertones more than dated. Worse, the academic world seemed to believe that their own reasoned review of enclosure was largely done. Other subjects beckoned. For my part, I felt, in my naïve sixties, that the enclosures, as few other episodes in England's history, should never be allowed to slip away: they remained important and new breath should be applied with every generation so that the young could hear the stories for the first time. There was no room in my thesis for more than half a chapter on these disturbing events.[2] If opportunity arose, I decided to return to the subject.

In early Covid days, I met two young men in the *Castle of Comfort* in Medstead and fell into casual conversation. Their complaint was normal: there was nothing to do locally, nothing ever happened. I argued, but lost. 'The routine of daily life leaves fewest documents. The daily and yearly round of [agricultural] work was so ordinary and so completely taken for granted that little was ever written down.'[3]

Perhaps, with this book, I can now persuade them otherwise.

The very first private parliamentary enclosure was in 1709 in Ropley. Driven by the bishop of Winchester, it was a highly contested affair with angry petitions and lies told on the floor of the House. The enclosure's consequences, its legacies, were remarkable and remain largely unknown: venison raids by armed, black-faced men against church, gentry and the crown, troops stationed in Farnham, the Hampshire smugglers to the fore and local men called to form regiments to back the invasion of the Stuart pretenders. England's most vicious piece of suppressive legislation, the *Black Act*, was a direct result of what happened in Ropley. There was much more: fraud, nepotism, the 'South Sea Bubble', evictions, impoverishment, the established church against Catholics, near revolution, hangings, transportation and a long list of, shall I say, misdemeanours committed by some of the county's richest and most powerful men, many of them absentee landlords.

---

1   J. L. and Barbara Hammond, *The Village Labourer*. E. P. Thompson, *The Making of the English Working Class; Whigs and Hunters.*
2   Heal, 'The Rise' and 'The Fall'.
3   Orwins, *Open Fields*, p. v.

The lessons of Ropley's enclosure were learned quickly by landowners in surrounding parishes, especially along the ridge that runs through modern Four Marks, and which contributed quietly to its twentieth century formation.

Ropley's legacy is a tale of small battles, all won by unscrupulous and determined people and lost by labouring families without a voice. 'The poor, the losers in the struggle for control of the land, did not often have the wherewithal to write their story.'[4]

You will readily realise that in my research journey, I have taken sides. I am angry. As an 'impartial' historian by training, I know some will disapprove. However, I believe, as Francis Pryor of *Time Team* wrote, that 'history (and archaeology) is a personal discipline and [I] consider it misleading to suggest that there are such things as impersonal, dispassionate or objective history books'. If historians care about their subject they will have 'axes to grind and I prefer to sharpen mine in public'.[5]

I also prefer my history to be like an acquaintance or friend: human, fallible and sometimes hard to explain. I don't mind mysteries. I prefer a mystery rather than seeking *any* explanation. I also believe a sense of community is important, especially with adopted places, in a world which becomes increasingly selfish and self-centred.

Ropley's Legacy is in two parts.

The first consists of twelve conventional chapters that take you from the beginning of the eighteenth century to the present day. Some chapters provide important background to help place local enclosures in their hungry and demeaning context. I have sought to bring these to life with twelve new or redrawn maps (many of the originals are too damaged for useful reproduction), a dozen more illustrations and a series of new, *Punch*-like cartoons that I hope bring 'attitude' and emotion to the story. I have also quoted extensively from the works of John Clare whose biographer, Jonathan Bate, called 'the greatest labouring-class poet that England has ever produced'. Clare wrote of the 'breaking up of customary relationships'.[6] He is the best respected of the enclosure poets including Oliver Goldsmith.

The second part comprises twenty-five appendices, longer than the tale itself, some of them translations and many complete transcriptions, reprinted for the first time from original documents. In their various ways, they tell the story of the enclosures, their background and their reality. Hopefully, they will prove interesting to those who like to read for themselves what was said at the time. I also hope that they will provide a springboard for those who wish to continue their investigation. There is a great deal of material here on local fields and landmarks and the genealogy of owners and tenants which I leave to others.

---

4 Munsche, *Gentlemen and Poachers*, p. ix.
5 Francis Pryor, *Britain AD*, pp. xvii–xxi.
6 Neeson, *Commoners*, pp. 10-11.

There is a glossary of the more unusual terms on pages 430-434.

Research and publication has become an expensive business so many thanks are due to the Hampshire Archives Trust for their grant and to the Ropley History Network and Archive for their support. Thank you also to Diane, my wife, and to Jacqui Squire for their 'background' readings and comments, to Mike Overy and Keith Brown for their willing sharing of material, to Manni Kirchner for map preparation, and to Holly Fletcher for help with transcriptions, the population study and the index.

One purpose of this book is to put the area around Ropley, Four Marks, Chawton, Farringdon, Medstead, Newton Valence and East Tisted into a new perspective, to give these places more of their long-term history.

Another intent, after your examination of the facts and arguments, is to nudge you to take sides. Perhaps the resulting tussle with your conscience will make you look anew at the actions of the church, the gentry and the middling landowners in this part of the world.

When you turn the last page, I hope you will be angry, too; not just for yesterday, but for today as the process of land closure, your land, continues.

Chris Heal
Four Marks
October 2021
chrisheal@candspublishing.org.uk

MAPS

CARTOONS

ILLUSTRATIONS

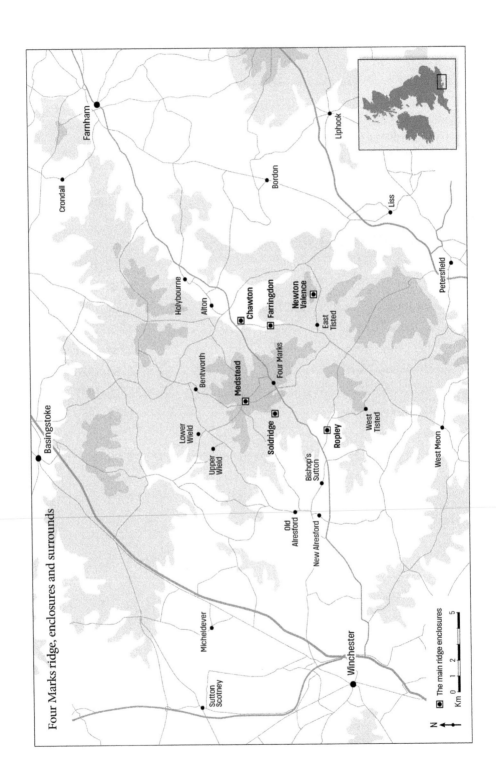

Four Marks ridge, enclosures and surrounds

1 CHURCH DEBT AND PERSONAL GREED

Squeezing the bishop of Winchester's assets, 1707-1709

The privileged classes have set up a code under which no labourer could take a single step for the improvement of the lot of his class without putting his life and liberties in a noose.[1]

Perhaps, sometimes, we are lazy or uninformed and find ourselves caught in silent traps. We assume that the way it is now is the way it has always been or, at least, little has changed. Telling the story of what used to be, writing history, either by ignoring the truth, or by suppressing it, is usually the prerogative of the victors. In the main sources of this book, that prerogative belongs to the landowners, the gentry and the established church or the professional men who took their silver and did their bidding. Truth, however, is not eradicated so easily. Eventually, a later generation asks the pertinent questions and searches the records for answers.[2]

Sir Jonathan Trelawny, baronet, was not a man to admire for his charity, religion or rectitude. Beneath the *bonhomie*, he was an obsequious schemer devoted to the worship of money. Had he held a lesser rank, certainly if he had lived in a later time, he would likely have found himself standing before a court. His lawyer might have whispered to plead guilty and accept a lesser sentence.

But Trelawny had no such temporal worries unless he upset, for instance, his occasional patron and High Church Protestant, Queen Anne, because Trelawny was the Bishop of Winchester. From the day he was translated to the city in 1707, Trelawny saw an opportunity to repair his finances for his new diocese was one of the richest in the land.

With few exceptions, ecclesiastical landowners in the eighteenth century rarely retained properties in their own lands save for the houses in which they actually lived and, for the more important like Trelawny, that included adjacent parkland stocked with deer.[3] Wolvesey, the bishop's castle in Winchester, had been in long-term decline and was abandoned as an episcopal house in the 1680s.[4] Despite building a new palace next to the medieval site, successive bishops often preferred Farnham Castle in Surrey with its large park as their main

---

1 Hammonds, *Village Labourer*, p. 272.
2 Smith, *Fighting Joshua*, p. 1.
3 Clay, 'Greed of Whig Bishops?', pp. 129-30.
4 Wolvesey was neglected and the baroque palace was largely demolished in 1786. The west wing survives and remains the current bishop's residence.

residence. When in London, there was a palace in Chelsea, once Winchester House, dismantled in the nineteenth century.[5] Trelawny's Winchester estates comprised at least fifty manors with another twenty attached to the cathedral.[6] These properties stretched over seven counties from Surrey to Somerset. Income was generated from land rents, sales of produce and fees imposed at the manor courts. Each year, estates sent their profit in cash directly to the bishop's treasury. Four hundred years before, in 1301-2, this profit totalled £5,188, over £3½ million at today's values.[7]

Trelawny was born in 1650 in the family manor of Trelawne at Pelynt in Cornwall. His grandfather, Sir John, the first baronet, and his father, Sir Jonathan, both fought for the king in the Civil War. At his own expense, Sir John raised a regiment of Cornish infantry which worsted the parliamentary forces in 1643 at the battles of Stratton, Cornwall, and Lansdown Hill, near Bath. Sir Jonathan was a member of the garrison of Pendennis Castle when that royalist stronghold was the last in England to surrender. After the war, both men were charged with delinquency to Parliament and to the Commonwealth. Their estates in danger, they paid fines of over £600. To these was added another £700 which had been taken by the Prince of Wales's Council from the rival Buller family in the early days of the war. The Trelawnys, father and son, were sued and locked up until they agreed to repay this 'debt'.[8] The son corresponded regularly with King Charles in exile and was imprisoned several times.

In 1681, bishop Trelawny inherited his family's estates and launched on a scramble for unearned income amid a continuing battle against bankruptcy. Over his career, there were particular costs to add to the long-standing family debts – the cost of his arrival at his bishoprics, particularly Winchester, his installation as Prelate of the Order of the Garter and, when living at Farnham Castle, which was always greedy, money for rebuilding.

Trelawny was never entirely a victim of circumstance as was evidenced by his discretionary expenditures. He erected a new chapel at Trelawne, laid new gardens at his palace in Winchester and installed a 'vast' episcopal Grecian throne there for his own use.[9] At his death in 1721, he was pulling down part of Trelawne House as a preliminary to extensive new work. Cash for builders was a higher priority than wages for his staff. He was spending money so quickly that some of his servants' wages were perpetually in arrears. One litigant, awarded costs by the Court of Exchequer in 1719, had to wait until 1736 before payment

---

5   Nicholas Riall, 'A 'lost' palace of the bishops of Winchester', *Society for Medieval Archaeology*, 2021.
6   Thomson, 'Estate Management'.
7   Winchester Pipe Rolls, J. T. Beaumont, *English Heritage Book of Winchester* (London, 1997). TNA, currency converter.
8   Hearne, *Remarks and Collections*, i, 165.
9   The throne was acquired much later by Trelawny's descendants.

because he had refused to accept in the bishop's lifetime an 'insultingly low offer' of twelve pence in the pound.[10]

Importantly for the story to come, Trelawny, from 1685, by virtue of his Cornish landholdings, was also a freeman of Liskeard, an alderman of Lostwithiel, a justice for Truro and a justice and free burgess of Fowey. These positions made him a powerful broker of parliamentary seats.[11] Nine politicians owed their places in London to Trelawny in the General Election of 1710.[12] He was convinced that the safety of his Church was 'best lodged in the hands of the gentry who should occupy the bulk of the seats in the House of Commons and support any ministry that was anti-Jacobite and an enemy to the pretensions of France'.[13] Trelawny was one of twenty-two noblemen and gentry favoured with a personal letter from the Privy Council urging them to employ all their efforts to see that only approved persons became members. This appropriation of the electoral process, now illegal but not entirely eradicated, was then the norm. Nepotism and relationships based on favours was second nature to the bishop and his circle; however, implementation was a further drain on his strained finances.

Throughout his life, Jonathan Trelawny was moved by three great loves: Cornwall, the honour of his ancient family and the Protestant religion. He was swayed by other loyalties like the Royal House of Stuart and Christ Church, Oxford, but they had ultimately to reconcile with the first three if they were to receive his support.

It was, thought historian E. P. Thompson, 'difficult to know how he became a priest'.[14]

Trelawny received his first bishopric not because of his piety but because of his powers of military organisation. He was sent by King James to Cornwall to prepare forces in 1685 in anticipation of the Duke of Monmouth's invasion through which he planned to install himself as a Protestant king. Three days later, the duke arrived at Lyme Regis. It was no part of Monmouth's plan to march west so the mobilisation and defensive arrangements of the Cornish militia which Trelawny carried out with great enthusiasm were not tested.[15] The Government, however, was pleased and sent Trelawny a congratulatory letter just before the Battle of Sedgemoor when Monmouth's ragtag 'pitchfork' army was routed. For his pains, Trelawny was made bishop of Bristol, a post he received with abject dismay because it would 'break his estate'. 'Peterborough, Chichester – anywhere but Bristol,' he begged.[16] The one saving grace was that the king by royal diploma appointed Trelawny a Doctor of Divinity, without study, to go

10 Devon Record Office, C.R. 636.
11 Smith, *Fighting Joshua*, p. 19.
12 Smith, *Fighting Joshua*, p. 169.
13 Smith, *Fighting Joshua*, p. 178.
14 Thompson, *Whigs and Hunters*, p. 123.
15 Smith, *Fighting Joshua*, pp. 17-20.
16 Letter to the Earl of Exeter 10/7/1685, Strickland, *Seven Bishops*.

with his MA, earned by attendance. Finances were hardly improved when, later, Trelawny was given Exeter.

Trelawny, 'the fighting Joshua', was singled out for vicious abuse over his 'doings' against Monmouth's supporters in a, no doubt, scurrilous pamphlet of the time:

> ... *though he cannot preach, or pray, or write,*
> *He 'gainst his country and his king can fight.*
> *What wonders in the field were lately done*
> *By fighting Joshua, the son of Nun;*
> *He bravely Monmouth and his force withstood.*
> *And made the Western land a sea of blood;*
> *There Joshua his reeking heat assuage,*
> *On every sign-post gibbet up his rage;*
> *Glutted with blood, a really Christian Turk*
> *Scarcely outdone by Jeffreys or by Kirke* ...[17]

This unlikely bishop did little to commend himself for advancement on grounds of pastoral care or academic distinction. He was a 'hearty Christian' enjoying good wine and tobacco and to be found in boisterous company. He was a frequent and dedicated user of bad language and later used to explain that he swore not as a bishop but as Sir Jonathan Trelawny. He was academically lazy, never mastering any subject, but widely read judging only by his bookshelves. He was renowned for using language of 'nauseating obsequiousness' when seeking preferment.

One other aspect of Trelawny's life sets him apart, even, perhaps, sets him beyond the civilised pale. It is a characteristic of modern liberal culture to excuse behaviours that seem wrong today but can, at least, be sidestepped because they were reasonable when set in their historical context. Others, like the British slave trade and all its practices, are harshly unforgiven. Where does one stand then on Trelawny's choice of wife in 1684: Rebecca, daughter of Thomas Hele of Babcombe in Devon, and an heiress?

Rebecca was barely fourteen; Trelawny was an experienced man-about-town of thirty-four.[18] Is there not something in that sexual juxtaposition between a bishop, or any man, and any child that will always remain deeply disturbing?

Rebecca began producing babies immediately. Eleven of her thirteen children survived. Some claim the relationship grew into a 'loving' marriage. The eldest child, Charlotte, was born with a humped back which she concealed by sitting alone in the dark corners of rooms, her deformation so pronounced that she was

---

17 'The Tribe of Levi', quoted in Strickland, *Seven Bishops*. George Jeffreys was the hanging judge after the rebellion. He sentenced 251 men to death, although only seventy-one were hanged, drawn and quartered with their heads then displayed on spikes in Dorchester and other towns around Dorset. Percy Kirke led a regiment at the Battle of Sedgemoor who ruthlessly hunted down fugitives.

18 Smith, *Fighting Joshua*, pp. 4-5.

buried in a square coffin. A son, Charles, was ordained at eighteen and provided with the Rectory of West Meon and, then, the Rectory of Cheriton. Charles also leased part of the bishop's estates, South Farm, East Meon, in 1709, and was given the office of Keeper of the Wild Beasts in 1711 at £20 a year. Daughter Rebecca, who was known as a 'beauty', was forced by her father to marry the disfigured John Francis Buller to heal the financially damaging rift from the Civil War.

With both Rebeccas, mother and daughter, Trelawny's actions can best be understood by his desperation for money.

Church estates tended to be dispersed more widely than was normal with lay concerns. The only way an amateur bishop landlord could make himself knowledgeable about his land was to pay for professional surveys and dedicated managers. However, 'surveys were expensive and likely to soak up a large part of the fine resulting from any rent increase. Bishops also knew that they might be dead by the time the next opportunity for an increase came around and so were reluctant to incur costs only for the benefit of their successor. Therefore, they were often in the dark as to the true value of their holdings'.[19]

Trelawny, though, was not a novice having much experience through his family estates in Cornwall. The problem became finding sufficient good information to enable a bargain on something like a equal footing. The last thing a tenant would normally admit was what the land they leased was really worth. The opposite was considered remarkable. One of the bishop's bailiffs sent in some figures which he considered to be unusually reliable. 'I wish I had as good information concerning several estates to our church which lie as near and which I have labour'd after a long time with Art and Assiduity. But I told you, people hereabouts are close mouth'd, and for what Reasons, and you must take advantage of their Resentments to one another to squeeze any Intelligence from them.'[20]

There was a further problem with the 'quality' of the tenants. Accounts from not long after Trelawny's death show that many senior church estates had a handful of titled peers among their lessees, often leading gentry families of the areas where the estates lay, leavened here and there by prominent local merchants and successful London-based money-men.[21] The bishop of Winchester's lessees included the Earl of Kingston, the Earl of Clarendon, the Countess of Ross, the powerful Wiltshire landowner Sir James Ashe, Richard Aldworth and Hungerford Dunch (both major proprietors in Berkshire and elsewhere), the politician Anthony Henley, the former banker and cashier of the excise, Charles Duncombe, and the financier-official of the Ashburnham Toll. Of these, Aldworth, Dunch, Henley and Duncombe were MPs. Thirty years or so later, most of these individuals or their immediate heirs were still in possession and

---

19 Clay, 'Greed of Whig Bishops?', pp. 139–45.
20 Clay, 'Greed of Whig Bishops?', p. 147.
21 Clay, 'Greed of Whig Bishops?', p. 136.

the survivors had been reinforced by the dukes of Norfolk, Argyll and Chandos, gentleman MP Bulstrode Peachey and the Knight family of Chawton. These lessees could not be easily browbeaten by any bishop if a dispute arose over tenancy.

This was not the case with the small tenants. If money was to be squeezed from the bishop's assets, then it was best if it involved the lesser landowners – the low hanging fruit. As a country gentleman, Trelawny was in a position to known what changes were taking place both in the freehold price of land and in the bargains being struck between landlords and their tenants. In practice, Charles Heron, Trelawny's steward, observed, that episcopal tenants 'have an interest in their estates almost as good as inheritance because your Lordships the Bishops will always renew'.[22]

Nor did the bishops of Winchester tend to let out important parts of their estates at a 'rack rent', that is rents which represented the full economic value of the land to a tenant. People like Trelawny invariably let their land on beneficial leases. The tenant purchased his lease by the payment of a lump sum known as a 'fine' at the beginning of the term so as to give early, desperately needed cash and thereafter paid only a 'reserved rent' which was normally a small fraction of worth, often less that 10 per cent.[23] A high proportion of beneficial leaseholders and copyholders, particularly but not only those with large holdings, sublet them to others who then paid a full rack rent. Laymen often bought and sold church leasehold in the same way as they did their own freehold.

Both leasehold and copyhold tenancies were commonly let for a number of lives rather than a term of years. Both types involved the tenant in financial obligations of an archaic hue, notably the rendering of a heriot, in effect a death duty payable in kind. The important difference was that copyhold depended on the customs of the manor and, however favourable or unfavourable this might be, it always placed some limit to the extent to which the landowner could force his will.

In June 1707, Trelawny arrived in Winchester giving 'great disgust to many (including leading bishops), he being considerable for nothing but his birth and his election interest in Cornwall'. After impassioned debate, it was promised that future preferments should be 'bestowed on men well principled ... and on men of merit'.[24]

Trelawny soon brought the 'vigorous' Charles Heron to join him. He was a man who had been in and out of Trelawny's employ for more than twenty years. Heron, sometimes 'Herne', quit the service of the Duke of Somerset in order to work as the bishop's business manager, overseeing lesser stewards and manorial

---

22 Clay, 'Greed of Whig Bishops?', p. 153. Thompson, *Whigs and Hunters*, p. 128.
23 Clay, 'Greed of Whig Bishops?', pp. 129-30.
24 Historian Gilbert Burnet, Bishop of Salisbury, quoted in Strickland, *Seven Bishops*.

officers, negotiating fines on renewals of leases and on proposals for enclosures.[25] Trelawny held Heron in such esteem that he secured him a senior degree at the University of Oxford.

The duties of a 'good' steward were laid out in a tract by Edward Laurence in 1727.[26] Stewards should be 'zealous for his lord's sake in purchasing all the freeholders out as soon as possible'. Laurence also suggested that all small farms let to poor indigent tenants should be moved to larger farmers who were better able to stock, equip and seed the land bringing higher profit. However, Laurence cautioned, that 'it was a work of Difficulty and Time' and should be accomplished 'without oppression' for 'it would raise too great an Odium to turn poor Families into the wide World by uniting all farms at once in order to make an Advance on Rents'. Pragmatically, Laurence suggested waiting until a tenant's death until applying the pressure so that the family may 'betake themselves to other employments'.[27]

There can be no doubt that Trelawny knew exactly the nest of wasps he would excite. He needed money and Heron was set loose with orders to tighten the administration of the manors which had grown particularly slack after twenty-two years under his predecessor, bishop Peter Mews.[28] Mews was 'entirely careless of discharging the duty of his function' and had shown a 'total neglect of discipline in the diocese'. To be slightly fair, Trelawny inherited a moribund financial estate system. The records still included 'sales of works', that is payments for labour services obsolete for some 350 years.[29] During Mews' declining years, the cottagers, farmers and foresters had 'discovered they could live very well without a bishop'.[30] The officers, mainly country attorneys and clerks, but also small gentry and clergy, had found ways of making themselves comfortable, taking fees for themselves, 'allowing customary perquisites to enlarge' and 'winking at certain offences'.

In pursuit of his policy of squeezing his assets, in fact the livelihoods of others, Trelawny, with the enthusiastic support of Heron, was 'prepared to use fair means and foul'.[31] This is quite an admission for Trelawny's modern-day biographer and careful cheerleader, the Reverend Michael Smith.

In short order, Heron was a hated man in Hampshire. His methods as a business agent 'aroused deep fear and resentment', particularly but by no means exclusively among tenants in Ropley and Farnham.[32] One of the main duties of a steward, Laurence advised all noblemen, 'and others', was not to sit in an office

---

25 HRO, Bishopric of Winchester: Estate Administration, Eccles 415809, E/B9-E/B13.
26 Wrightson, *Earthly Necessities*, pp. 282-3.
27 Laurence, *Duty of a Steward*, p. 3.
28 Capes, *Rural Life in Hampshire*, p. 271.
29 Clay, 'Greed of Whig Bishops?'.
30 Thompson, *Whigs and Hunters*, p. 125.
31 Smith, *Fighting Joshua*, p. 169.
32 Smith, *Fighting Joshua*, p. 169.

like a country attorney and collect money, but rather to be a 'living instructor amongst ignorant farmers' to teach them how to improve their farms and thereby 'happily increase their rents'.[33] Heron was not the teaching sort, but would rather spend hours watching in the rain to sniff out a petty financial misdemeanour. At a whiff of success, he raced to scour manorial records for proof in Farnham, Bishop's Sutton or Winchester. On a fresh horse, he sped back to levy a fine or issue a summons on an unsuspecting cottager or small farmer.[34]

Tactics varied. Trelawny disputed with neighbouring owners over rights in the common fields. The manorial courts were used to break old tenures and to press contractual fines when leases were renewed. When tenants died, worthwhile heriots were extracted from their belongings, usually a live animal, and often at the time of the bereaved families' greatest need. Whenever trees were cut, the threatened people of the forest villages – Frensham, Binsted, Bentley and Kingsley – 'avowed they had the right' to the 'offal' or stack wood.[35] Poor plot holders were prosecuted for the custom of taking timber for which they forfeited their copyhold tenancies. Trelawny and Heron then fraudulently concealed their own tree felling from Robert Kerby, the bishop's woodward, the guardian of the church's forests, and quietly sold the timber. Kerby was 'perhaps the most powerful among the bishopric's bureaucracy, holding his office for life, by patent, with perquisites enforceable by law'. He could not be dismissed by Trelawny and was, perhaps, disappointed at not getting Heron's job.[36]

Kerby lost income as he had the right to licence all wood cutting and to take up to a third of the value of the timber as his fee. After fifteen months of provocation, he made himself the spokesman for the newly hard-done-by, and drew up a series of accusations against Heron which survive in the Hampshire archives together with the steward's replies.[37]

Historian E. P. Thompson studied the charge sheet and ripped into Heron. It is worth quoting from his study at some length.[38] It should also be noted that Trelawny's sympathetic biographer, the Reverend Smith, said of Thompson's interpretation that 'it is written from a Marxist standpoint and includes a caricature of Trelawny worthy of the pages of the Soviet satirical magazine, *Krokodil*'.[39] Having read, transcribed (and slightly modernised) the originals, I side with Thompson (*Appendix 6*).

It is an extraordinary miscellany of complaint. Heron had clearly offended the entire bureaucracy as well as the clergy and gentry with whom they

33 Laurence, *Duty of a Steward*, p. 4.
34 Thompson, *Whigs and Hunters*, p. 125.
35 Thompson, *Whigs and Hunters*, p. 244.
36 Thompson, *Whigs and Hunters*, p. 125.
37 HRO, 'Articles against Heron' and 'Heron's replies', 11M59/F/GBP/E/B12.
38 Thompson, *Whigs and Hunters*, pp. 126-7.
39 Smith, *Fighting Joshua*, p. 173

associated. Some of the accusations are highly personal. He chose scandalous and ill-famed servants, making them his informers; he spread false stories about the bishop's established officers; he was a 'very haughty imperious man and of a rigid temper', used 'base and unmannerly expressions' to the tenants, 'is a person that swears and dams your Lordship's servants, officers and tenants', is a frequent sabbath breaker' who spent his Sundays in searching records, 'is by same a necessitous man and lives separate from his wife, and is very vicious', and (when invited to stay at Kerby's house) 'he behaved himself so to his maid servant, by using such violent temptations to her by way of debauchery, that she would not go into his chamber ...'

To the last accusation Heron replied, 'I am so very innocent, that I cannot recollect what manner of person she is; 'tis possible I might offer to kiss her, it is an innocent liberty I have often taken, carelessly and without design ...'

A related group of accusations concerned his slighting of the existing officials: 'By his pride he's above advice of the ancient officers of your lordship's bishopric who know the customs thereof.' He had threatened Wither, the Steward of the Land, with the forfeit of this office; he had refused to Wither's groom a customary allowance, and told Wither in public court that, 'if he did not like it, he could carry his portmanteau himself' ... He told Kerby much the same. The affront was the worse, since these officers are 'gentlemen ... and better men than Mr 'Herne' were he out of your lordship's service'. He had defrauded the officers of their allowances for entertainment at manorial courts, and had usurped their functions and their fees.

Mr 'Herne's' intent is to break them all, that he may be sole officer to your lordship, and then he might be at liberty to make such accounts as he pleased, and not be detected.

Heron replied uniformly: he was following Trelawny's instructions, he acted only when officers or tenants were negligent or 'incroaching' and he was restoring lost rights to the bishopric.

The archives at Farnham and Winchester are studded with examples of disquiet among the tenantry. At Farnham in 1707, they claimed as socagers the absolute security of heritable tenure.[40] As Thompson explained, 'if the bishop wished to increase his rental, his steward had to have recourse either to raising fines upon death and renewals or to breaking the old tenures' through courts actions proving, for example, forfeit, waste or debt and then releasing the land at a higher rate.[41] Actions started for a waste of timber led to forfeits of copyhold. Proceedings became bitter. Nineteen jurors were required by Heron to give up seven other tenants as having forfeited their estates by cutting oak and elm

---

40 Farnham Custom Roll, 1707, Winchester Cathedral Library.
41 Thompson, *Whigs and Hunters*, p. 128.

without licence. 'They severally refused' and were fined twenty shillings each. At the next court, a juror was fined 'for giving sawcy language to the Court'. There were disputes about cattle rescued from the pound where they had been sent for trespassing in the lanes and several more jurors were fined for 'refusing to present the offenders'.

The records for 1707 to 1709 show more than thirty other cases when Heron battled the tenants who placed their complaint on record damning both Heron and, by blunt inference, Trelawny,

> *Every new Lord brings in a new procurator, who for private gain racketh the custome and oftentime breaketh it, soe shifting that sometimes they have put the Steward out of his place, and sate themselves (which ought not to be) it being all one as if the Lord sat himselfe ... for his owne profit. Whereas a Steward who knoweth the customes ought to be judge, and not such procurators, seeing the Custome of the Manor hath always been that there was at all times a Man of Worship, faithful, honest, and true chosen (of the country) to doe justice and equity between the Lord and tenants ...*[42]

---

42 Farnham Custom Roll, 1707, Winchester Cathedral Library.

2 CHURCH LAND AND PARLIAMENTARY POWER

The Ropley enclosures, 1709-1710

The fault is great in man or woman
Who steals a goose from off the common;
But what can plead that man's excuse
Who steals a common from a goose?[1]

Charles Heron was now under a cloud, his employment threatened by a rising tide of hatred from the bishop's officials, the tenantry and the common people. He spent increasing time in manorial courts either fighting for Trelawny's 'rights' as he interpreted them or defending his methods with Trelawny's employees. Despite the discontent, or perhaps because of it, Heron urged Trelawny to press 'the business of the copyholders to a conclusion and particularly to order executions [collections] against those who have forfeited since the fines'.[2]

It was Heron, evidence suggests, who, probably in 1708, came up with a corrupt plan to solve the problem of troublesome tenants. Enclosure of the common lands was a contested practice from the fifteenth century; often in the early days by force, but increasingly by agreement.[3] For now, suffice to say, that the wider debate swayed between, on the one hand, a perceived need to enclose common fields to increase holdings and rents and, perhaps, to allow more efficient agriculture to feed the country and, on the other, the long-held rights of commoners to continue to crop in the old way with its important element of independence.

By 1700, 70 per cent of England's cultivatable land was enclosed. The spreads of leasehold tenures and the process of enclosure 'entailed a hardening of property rights over land. The ambiguities of custom were gradually washed out by the powerful certainties of ownership and contract.'[4] Almost inevitably, as the larger landowners made their move, small farmers and cottagers who had encroached on the commons to build their shacks lost their rights without any compensation. The loss of a subsistence living reduced poor families to a search for work – a result welcomed by the new landowners who sought, often engineered, an available, compliant and dependent workforce.

---

1 *The Tickler Magazine*, 1/2/1821, cited in *The Oxford University Press Dictionary of Quotations*, 1985.
2 Farnham Court Presentments, 30/3/1708, 14/9/1708, 15/3/1709; HRO, 11M/59/B14B/3/2.
3 The process is examined in Chapter 5.
4 Wrightson, *Earthly Necessities*, pp. 273-6.

Seeking justice: 'What stand could the small proprietor make against such forces? He would be warned that the success of the enclosure was certain and that those who obstructed it would suffer. His only prospect ... lay in his ability to move a dim and distant parliament of great landlords.'¥

¥ Hammonds, *Village Labourer*, p. 45

The idea from Heron, thoroughly endorsed by Trelawny and by the wardens of Winchester College, was for the largest tenants in Ropley, which was at that time part of the parish of Bishop's Sutton, to enforce enclosure while bypassing the need for the commoners' agreement. The largest landowner was the bishop himself with other common land held by the college's Ropley Manor. An act of parliament would grant authority for enclosure to a trio of 'independent' commissioners who would then allocate the common land based, supposedly, on previous ownership. The commissioners would hold complete authority to make this allocation, instruct the building of hedges and new roads and, crucially, decide who would pay and how much. Those who did not want enclosure would have no choice but to accept their allotment, fair or not, and would then have to pay for the privilege.

Recent history supported the idea. A survey by scholars of surviving Hampshire enclosure agreements shows that Ropley's Act was not completely new, but had been 'tried and tested in agreements'.[5] In 1685, as the lax Bishop Mews took over at Winchester, 300 acres of Windley Common at Bishop's Sutton, firmly under episcopal control, were enclosed and cultivated by informal agreement.[6] The commissioners were William Godwin and Henry Budd. Godwin was to play a major role in the contested Ropley enclosure. The extended Budd family were prominent, on one side or the other, in almost every local enclosure, for the next 150 years. An agreement of 1706 for Ibthorpe near Hurstbourne Tarrant allowed three commissioners to lay out highways and private ways ... and to 'appoint each commoner to inclose land with quickset (living) hedges'.[7] Two years after Ropley in 1711, when commons and wastes were to be enclosed by agreement at Faccombe, north of Andover, three commissioners were appointed to allot and divide the land in just proportion.[8] The term waste is potentially misleading. The land was not necessarily 'waste' or 'wasted', but was any common land not in pasture or used for cultivation. It was often 'used in many socially and economically productive ways' which will also be discussed later.[9]

The genius of Heron's plan, of course, was that Trelawny's bill would be taken for approval before a parliament of senior clergy and large landowners some of whom had been placed there by Trelawny himself. Many others would be interested in the bill's progress in London to gauge how the procedure could be used again to their own pecuniary advantage. One calculation, taken much later, identified more then 600 landowners, almost the entire capacity of the House of Commons, who sat as MPs at one time or another; of the 580 members of the

---

5   Chapman and Seeliger, 'Formal and Informal Enclosures', p. 7.
6   HRO, 11M59/E1/152/4/42.
7   Corpus Christi College, Oxford, CL 6/5.
8   HRO, 2M37/18.
9   Christophers, *New Enclosure*, p. 80.

Part of the first page of the Ropley Enclosure Act, 1709.

Lords, 500 were significant landowners and 'were either father, brother or cousin of the landowners sitting as MPs'.[10]

Trelawny piloted a bill to enclose Ropley Commons and to 'improve' Farnham Old ('disparked') Park through the Lords and Commons in 1709. The act was passed on 27 March, after a counter-petition was brushed aside, and received royal assent on 5 April. It was the first ever private enclosure bill in England, a foregone conclusion and a trailblazer (*Appendix 7*).[11]

---

10 Cahill, *Who Owns Britain*, p. 25, and quoting statistics from John Bateman, *The Great Landowners of Britain and Ireland* (4th edition, Harrisons & Sons 1883), which further argues that not much changed until the Second World War.

11 Parliamentary Archives, HL_PO_PB_1_1709_8&9An41, 8 Anne c. 16. The second private paliamentary act in 1713 took another five years (13 Anne, c. 7) and concerned two 'great open common fields and a large open greensward common down' in the manor and parish of Thormarton, alias Farmington, in Gloucestershire. The next two were in 1717: Baltonsbury Common, Somerset (5 Geo. 1, c. 5) and Gratwood Heath in Eccleshall, Staffordshire (5 Geo. 1, c. 7). These were followed by Lighthorne, Warwickshire, 1720 (7 Geo. 1, c. 3); Stokesby Common, Norfolk, 1720 (7 Geo. 1, c. 4); Ellenhall, Seighford and Ronton, Staffordshire, 1720 (7 Geo. 1, c. 26); and Glastonbury Common, Somerset, 1721 (8 Geo. 1, c. 16). The Commons Journals reported no dissent or petitions.

Tenants on Ropley Common, said the bill, had sole rights to pasture their cattle 'levant and couchant', rising and lying over night. The central argument for enclosure was that the land was of 'little annual value' but capable of improvement if the tenants could only fence it for ploughing and sowing. 'Complete' ownership would be allotted according to the owners' 'due share and proportion according to their respective interest and right of common'.

This, in turn, meant that those people who were not owners, the subsistence farmers and small encroachers who were entitled to common rights, by long practice if not always by law, would lose their day-to-day entitlements.

Here the bill made a duplicitous acknowledgement of that loss: 'many poor people would be employed in making such improvements which will tend to the public good'. In other words, the poor would no longer have access to the commons to support themselves, but would have to work to boost the profits of those whose access and ownership was enshrined.

Decisions on the allotment of the land were to be placed in the hands of three yeomen commissioners: William Godwin, late of Ovington and a commissioner at the Bishop's Sutton 'voluntary' enclosure twenty years or so before;[12] Richard Seward, late of Bishop's Sutton; and Henry Whitear, of Lanham in Old Alresford. These three would decide on the allotments and then order the fencing and hedging of the new fields and ensure their 'good repair'.

Godwin, Seward and Whitear were, of course, the bishop's placemen chosen, most probably, by Charles Heron, and willing to act as instructed. Godwin and Seward were reeves of Cheriton, both directly in Trelawny's employment and in which they continued until the 1720s.[13] Seward, a conscientious recorder judging by his list of successful fines in the Court Rolls, had recently taken a lease on two coppices from St Cross Hospital in Winchester: Westercott and Great Priestwood, adjoining Ashton common in Bishop's Sutton.[14] It is likely that a third lease for Moor Court in Romsey was also held by him.[15]

Whitear was even more deeply implicated as he leased Abbotstone Farm from Charles Paulet, the Duke of Bolton, part of the 'very handsome' Abbotstone House, visited by Daniel Defoe in 1719.[16] Paulet played a leading role in the first parliamentary committee to review the Ropley enclosure act, as evidenced shortly. Paulet's father, John, was the defender of Basing House near Basingstoke during the Civil War. The family's favoured property was Hackwood House just south of the town. Whitear also worked extensively as an administrator for the

12 Chapman and Seeliger, *Guide to Enclosure*, p. 72, says there is reference to unauthorised enclosures in the common fields of Bishop's Sutton in 1742 (HRO, 10M54/108) and to Kytes Piece Common Filed in 1776. The last piece of Sutton Farm in the common field was enclosed between 1776 and 1781 (HRO, 8M49/E2). See main text for perambulation in 1744 and commons enclosure in 1685.
13 HRO, 11M59/B2/13/72, 74 and 88. HRO, 11M59/B2/13/67 and 83.
14 HRO, 11M59/B2/13/67, 1707; 111M94W/Q2/2/7, /Q1/1 p. 177.
15 English Heritage, 101093649. HRO, 111M94W/Q2/2/8.
16 HRO, 11M49/418. Defoe, *Tour*, Vol. 1, p. 181. Hampshire Gardens Trust, HCC 1538.

bishop's estate regularly posting bonds as he dealt with the probates of deceased tenants.[17]

With the choice of these men and their new-given parliamentary and, therefore, absolute authority lies two great untruths: Trelawny's bill claimed that the tenants had agreed, first, to the process of enclosure and, second, that 'each and every one of them' would accept the commissioners' impartial decisions to be made in writing and 'enrolled' in the manor courts.

The Lords approved the bill on 17 March and passed it on to the House of Commons where, the next day, it was read for the first time and, two days later, read again. The bill then passed to twenty-five members for discussion in committee that afternoon at five o'clock.[18] The wheels of government were moving remarkably quickly.

> *The eighteenth-century parliament ... took no precautions at all to obtain a disinterested court. Indeed, the committee that considered an enclosure was chosen on the very contrary principle ... Each bill is committed to the member who is charged with its management and such other members as he may chose to name and the members serving for a particular county and the adjoining counties and consequently ... the members to whom bills have been committed have been generally those who have the most interest in the result.*[19]

To understand the extent of the loaded dice in the Commons chamber, it is worth listing most of the professional politicians, military men and landowners called to the committee. The roll included all the members of the counties of Southampton (Hampshire), Surrey and Wiltshire and, by name, Anthony Henley of The Grange, near Alresford, MP for Weymouth and a tenant of Trelawny; Thomas Jervoise, of Herriard Manor, Hampshire, MP for Hampshire; Lord William Powlett, MP for Winchester and Deputy Lieutenant and JP for Hampshire; John Smith, of Tedworth House, Tidworth, then Hampshire, Chancellor of the Exchequer and MP for Andover; Charles Paulet, 2nd Duke of Bolton, Lord Marquess of Winchester, Lord Lieutenant of Ireland, Member of Parliament for Hampshire, leaseholder of commissioner Henry Whitear, and a 'great booby' according to Jonathan Swift.[20] Involvement in the dispute was important enough for Thomas Jervoise to keep a copy of the Ropley Commons bill in his papers and it is, today, in the Hampshire Archives.[21]

---

17 HRO, 21M65/D4: 1709/59 Mary Swan of Bishops Waltham, 11/2/1710; 1715B/48 Tenement at Bishops Waltham 1715; 1740/78 Estate Abigail Maddin, Itchen Stoke 22/1/1741; 1749/4 Estate John Aslett Bishop's Sutton 15/3/1749. The will of Henry Whitear of Abbotstone, Itchen Stoke, 1759, is at HRO, 1759A/147.
18 HoC Journals, XVI, 1709, pp. 374, 376
19 Hammonds, *Village Labourer*, pp. 45-46.
20 Swift, 'Remarks on the Characters of the Court of Queen Anne'.
21 HRO, 44M69/G2/190.

'My friends and I can assure My Lords and Members of the House, that the rights holders of ROPLEY COMMONS are COMPLETELY behind us on the matter of this Act of Inclosure'.

Behind the lies: *'It would requite a considerable act of imagination to suppose that the parliamentary committee spent very much time or energy on the attempt to give body and form to this hazy and remote society and to treat these shadows as living men and women about to be tossed by this revolution from their ancestral homes.'¥*

¥ Hammonds, *Village Labourer*, p. 53.

Denzil Onslow, MP for Guildford, was an out-ranger for Windsor Forest, a sinecure responsible for deer which escaped the forest bounds, which has significance shortly. Sir Francis Masham was a 'rather stupid' MP in Essex where he held large estates and was a close friend of Trelawny's set of Whig bishops.[22] There were three members from Trelawny's 'personal' seats in Cornwall: Joseph Addison, MP for Lostwithiel and founder of the *Spectator* magazine; and William Bridges and John Dolben, MPs for Liskeard.

Others who can be identified were Joseph Austin, MP for Perth; Thomas White, MP for East Retford and a major landowner; Lieutenant General Charles Rosse, MP for Ross-shire; Sir Rushout Cullen, a landowner of Upton House and MP for Cambridgeshire; Waller Bacon, landowner and MP for Norwich; Sir Robert Eden, 1st Baronet, of West Auckland; one of the two Neville's, father and son, of Billingbear House in Berkshire and MPs for the county; Sir Richard Farington of Farington House, Chichester, MP for his town where his grandfather had been mayor three times; Major Robert Yate; Sir Walter Yonge of Escot House, a grand mansion in Talaton, Devon, MP for Honiton; George Evelyn, MP for Bletchingley, Surrey; and Theophilus Oglethorp, MP for Haslemere, whose sister was a reputed mistress of James II, and who joined the Old Pretender as a Jacobite baron in the court-in-exile in St Germain.[23]

Three days later, the first lie was exposed when a petition arrived from the tenants of the manors of Ropley and Bishop's Sutton with nine signatories — John Soper esquire, headed the complainants, followed by three Budds, James junior, Robert senior and Thomas; John Gilbert; John and Nicholas Mayhew and Richard and Robert Yalden. The group claimed to represent 'several others' (*Appendix 8*).[24] The petitioners were 'possessed of divers freehold, copyhold and leasehold estates' worth over £500 with right of common on Ropley Commons. These were no small objectors. They asked that their counsel be allowed to speak against the bill. The august parliamentary committee was recalled for the next day.

The role of the Yalden clan may be complex. Petitioner Robert could well be associated with William Yalden who was involved in the Itchen Stoke Commons Fields enclosure by agreement in 1787. Here, no punches were pulled. William threatened an unnamed recipient with an Act and a forced expense equal to one year's rent if there was no agreement on enclosure.[25] The agreement was signed in the following year.

---

22 The History of Parliament online.

23 There seems to be no complete and authoritative list of members with their affiliations for this period. There are regular comings and goings and variations in name spelling. Some gentlemen appear as members of committees for whom there was no formal record of their being a member. Please excuse any inconsistencies.

24 HoC Journal, XVI, 1709, p. 381.

25 HRO, 27M92/51. 'I take this opportunity ... of writing to acquaint you that Mr. Earle and myself with the approbation of the Duke of Bolton and the Duke of Chandos and also of Mr. Smith the vicar (making four fifths of the property) have agreed to apply to parliament the next sessions for a Bill to

It is likely William ran two farms called Newhouse, in Alresford, and Kitwood, in today's Four Marks, in 1795.[26]

The objection to enclosure of Ropley Commons was also all for naught. Lord William Powlett, well known to Bishop Trelawny, reported back to the House on 25 March that the 'allegations of the bill and the petitioners' had been heard. The bill, without amendment, was 'laid on the Clerk's table', a euphemism for 'no action'.[27]

The House moved on quickly to order the burning by the Public Hangman in the Palace Yard at Westminster of a book called 'A Defence of the Rights of the Christian Church' as scandalous, seditious and blasphemous and which contained 'libels, highly reflecting upon the Christian religion, and the Church of England, and tend to promote immorality and atheism and to create divisions, schisms and factions among Her Majesty's subjects'.

This was a time of general concern about the harvest and fear of price rises: a cold winter was followed by a rainy summer; a quarter of wheat rose from 27s 3d to 81s 9p in eighteen months.[28] On 3 February 1710, almost a year later, the second lie in Trelawny's act was laid bare by two more fruitless petitions.[29] The same eight previous petitioners had added another six to their number: Margaret Battel, James Blanchard, Robert Budd junior, John and Richard Oliver, and Jason Smith who claimed that,

> *Several of the Petitioners opposed the passing* [of] *that Act, well knowing they should have no Benefit by the Inclosure; and the Three Persons have acted so partially in the Premises, that several of the Petitioners, who always had right of Common, have no Part allotted to their Estates, and to others they have not allotted half their Proportion, to their very great Oppression: And praying, that the Clause in the said Act for inclosing the said Common, may be early repealed, or that the Petitioners be otherwise relieved in the Premises, as the House shall think fit.*

This was now something more than another country squabble. Principles of power were at stake. The church and the great landowners, the very essence of control and wealth, were under direct challenge. Should the House deign to react when a bill, already on the statute book, was questioned? There was a split along mainly party lines with some Whigs standing by Trelawny and alongside the

---

enable us to inclose Stoke Common Fields. Your brother Farmer Thorn does not seem to approve of it – if he and you consented to the enclosure we should be able to complete our wishes without the expense of a Bill, which will be about a year's rent to each individual – if you do not consent we must then proceed as I have stated to you and whether you consent or not you must pay your share in the expense.'

26 *Hampshire Chronicle*, 16/3/1795. The farms were for rent but 'in the occupation of' Yalden.
27 HoC Journal, XVI, 1709, p. 385.
28 Rudé, *Crowd in History*, p. 36.
29 HoC Journal, XVI, 1710, p. 476.

landowning Tories. A new committee of thirty-eight members was suggested consisting of only four of the old hands. This was a manoeuvre often used when serious opposition was feared and became a regular procedure after the Ropley bill was passed. No enclosure bill ever failed to get through when this tactic of a delaying committee of landed interests was called following a second reading.[30]

For Ropley, a vote was forced and Trelawny lost the skirmish. The tellers against further consideration were William Bridges, one of Trelawny's Cornish placemen, and Anthony Henley, Trelawny's tenant at the Grange, near Alresford, who counted seventy-six votes. The 'Yeas' won the day with 129 votes with tellers Sir Simeon Stuart and Charles Cholmondley.

In quick order, the new committee was handed a third petition from gentlemen and freeholders living near Ropley Commons who described how the enclosure would 'incommode' them so that they were unable to travel by horse, carts and other carriages. This was, presumably, because of new fences that landlocked their tenancies.

Then, three weeks later, on 21 February, before a reaction had been assessed, a counter petition from Ropley arrived at parliament. The forces for enclosure had felt it necessary, or perhaps been encouraged, to restate their case.[31] The eight tenants, no doubt the primary beneficiaries, disputed that the commissioners had made 'partial and unjust allotments'. They had incurred great expense in fencing their new allotments. They would be ruined if the Act was overturned and their money wasted. The group was led by the Reverend John London, the vicar of Ropley, incumbent since 1672, and who, one has to believe, was doing his master's bidding. Its other members were John Bull (one wonders), Robert Cranston, John Gilbert, James Godwin (the same surname as one of the three commissioners), Robert Harwood and Thomas Warrenton.

And there, at least in a parliamentary sense, it all died. The establishment of a committee had been a pyrrhic victory. The bill was not brought back to the House because the Committee did not 'think fit'. The bill had already been given the Royal Assent and the Committee thought it unnecessary to reconsider the bill or the new petitions before the House. Trelawny had prevailed.

John Soper, who led the petitioners, was no small landowner. There will be space later to examine the pedigree of a few of the families whose interests in the several village enclosures around the Four Marks ridge spread over the next 150 years. However, the Soper family is worth noting now. They reach back at least to Winchester in the thirteenth century and probably extend with the Gilberts and the Gascoines to Norman times.

---

30 This stalling and diversionary procedure was recognised by such unlikely academic bedfellows as the Hammonds, *Village Labourer*, p. 40, and Tate, *English Village Community*, p. 84, and later confirmed by Neeson, *Commoners*, pp. 191-97.

31 HoC Journal, XVI, 1710, p. 509.

Soper properties were extensive and, while concentrating on Titchfield and Dummer, extended throughout Hampshire. Another John Soper, died 1688, married Elizabeth Venables of Ropley in 1677 in Bighton. Possibly our John Soper was a reeve and farmer in 1706-7, mentioned in the Church Commissioners' manorial accounts for Bishop's Sutton.[32] From the early eighteenth and into the nineteenth centuries, there were numerous Soper records in and around Ropley, mostly of agricultural and domestic occupations as their star fell. One Henry was landlord of the *Shant Inn* at Ropley Soke and another a servant to Abraham Crowley, the Alton brewer.[33]

The feud between the disagreeing parties in Ropley must, on any determination, have torn the village apart. Trelawny's party, backed by his own officers and those tenants who had gained from the enclosure, and led in the final rebuff by Ropley's long-term vicar, John London, were triumphant. If the claims in the petitions were even part true then many families were dispossessed of their commons rights or given a lesser proportion of land than they deserved.

Petitions only tell us of families that had a voice and had the determination and the knowledge to write to parliament and to employ counsel. Many others, without the skills to debate in a lawyer's world, would have been cast out of their cottages as strong hedges were planted, locked gates inserted and fields made private. Lands that used to provide communal pasture and strip farming, forest foods, building materials, and fuel for warmth and cooking were closed forever. Cottagers who once worked when they chose were now driven to accept paid labour at rates and times specified by the now dominant landlords: Bull, Cranston, Godwin, Harwood and Warrenton. Left glowering over the fences were Batel, Budd, Mayhew, Oliver and Yalden. Many of these names on both sides were long-term residents and can be found over a hundred years before in local tax lists.[34]

The rifts extended into local families, the Gilberts, Godwins and Smiths had men on both sides of the divide. One suspects that feelings ran deep for many years and helped to explain a local antipathy by some to the church. Enclosures, once decided, were usually quickly enforced, but there is evidence that those at Ropley were still incomplete in 1712 despite a parliamentary target of 1710.[35]

In the 1990s, historian Jeanette Neeson wrote one of the most influential books on enclosure and studied in depth the results across many occurrences.

Broadly, opposition came from the landowning tradesmen and artisans who may have augmented their land by renting, the victuallers, butchers and weavers, and the elderly cottagers of modest means, and cottagers in general.

---

32 HRO, 83M76/PI4/64.
33 Soper family, rootsweb.com.
34 Davey, *Hampshire Law Subsidy Rolls, 1586.*
35 The target was 20/12/1710. HRO, Letter from Thomas Cranley, steward, to Trelawny, 18/5/1712, Trelawny MSS I misc. 12, cited in Thompson, *Whigs and Hunters*, p. 133.

Support for enclosure came from the farmers, husbandmen and graziers, the
landlords and the biggest landowners. Those who remained anonymous were
of the poorer sort, less likely to generate records; those fired with a dislike of
enclosure, cottagers, land-poor commoners and friends of commoners.[36]

Neeson made a particular study of enclosure in two villages in Northamptonshire.
They give useful leads about the likely effect in Ropley. Cottage commoners
fared badly: first in losing their common right which destroyed an economy
based on the use of land belonging to others; second, enclosure took land from
those cottagers who were landowners of whom a third lost everything. None of
those who petitioned for enclosure lost land; all but two of those who petitioned
against it either lost land or had to sell out altogether.[37]

Some of the unintended consequences were nasty. Enlarged estates not only
meant an absolute decline in the numbers of small owners following enclosure,
but chid mortality rates rose as families moved from subsisting off the land to
working as paid labourers.

Im swordy well a piece of land
That's fell upon the town
Who worked me till I couldn't stand
& crush me now I'm down

There was a time my bit of ground
Made freeman of the slave
The ass no pindard dare to pound[38]
When I his supper gave

The gipseys camp was not afraid
I made his dwelling free
Till vile enclosure came & made
A parish slave of me

Alas dependence thou'rt a brute
Want only understands
His feelings wither branch & root
That falls in parish hands[39]

The last element for immediate consideration is the whereabouts of Ropley
Commons, estimated in the act at 500 acres made from a 'tract of ground' from

---

36 Neeson, *Commoners*, pp. 191-97, 205.
37 Martin, 'Small Landowner … Warwickshire'.
38 'Pindar': an impounder of strayed cattle.
39 Clare, 'The Lament of Swordy Well', c. 1822

both Bishop's Sutton and Ropley manors. This suggests a continuous if not homogenous assembly. Five hundred acres, at 640 acres to a square mile, provide an area equivalent to a circle of one mile diameter. There is no found map or convenient list, but there are mentions which give persuasive clues and lead to a general picture.

Shore, one of Hampshire's many historians, said that the 'long parallel at the east [of Ropley] denoted their situation while the old tenements, lanes and gardens at the west show where the ancient village existed'.[40]

The old boundary between Ropley and Farringdon, before Ropley became an independent parish in 1882 and the 1932 formation of the new parish of Four Marks, shows the line running from Telegraph Lane-to-be and cutting through Alton Lane at about third its distance down the hill from the ridge. This line was the point below which land was auctioned for bungalows and smallholdings around 1900.[41] The boundary with Farringdon was marked by the 'Ropley Hedge' and is a reference point in the Farringdon enclosure act of 1748. Farringdon Common came up to the hedge and met on the Ropley side an 'inclosure of a certain heath'. Heaths are not generally small so one can assume it stretched from the old boundary hedge south through Four Marks at least to Lymington Bottom. William Dunce, who received an allotment on Farringdon Common, was ordered to fence his land on each side except the south because there the 'Hedge' bordered its enclosed common.

Pre-enclosure field hedges had a character of their own, always crooked due to the difficulty of ploughing a straight furrow with slow-plodding oxen. They were also composed of a variety of trees and shrubs, maple, elder, holly, sloe, whitethorn, hazel and, surprisingly dominant in some districts, crab-apple.[42]

Ropley Manor, some of whose lands were part of the enclosure, is an odd beast, an artificial construct 'thrown together between 1390 and 1476' by William of Wykeham, bishop of Winchester and Chancellor of England, and his successors, in order to provide income for his new college.[43] Much of the Manor was the bishop's land taken from his Manor of Bishop's Sutton.

Wykeham's career brought him great personal wealth some of which he applied to a university college, New College, Oxford, and to a feeder school in Winchester, St. Mary's Winchester College. The College provided education for ten fee-paying scholars ('commoners') and seventy poor scholars intended to replace clergy and administrators lost during the Black Death. In the early fifteenth century, the requirement was that scholars come from families where the annual income was less than five marks sterling (£3 6s 8d). By comparison, the contemporary reasonable annual living need by a yeoman was £5.[44]

---

40 Shore, *Hampshire*, p. 267.
41 Heal, *Four Marks Murders*, 'Conclusion'.
42 Bovill, *English Country Life*, p. 4.
43 Kirby, 'Charters of Manor of Ropley', p. 1.
44 Harwood, 'Winchester College', pp. 166, 171, 173.

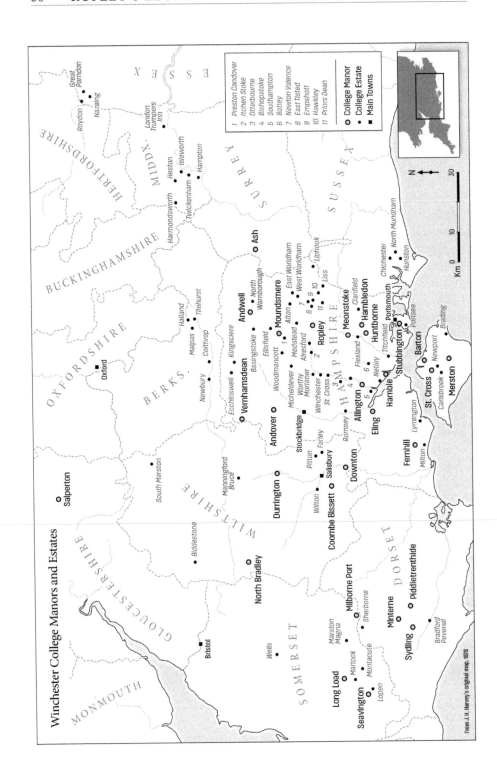

Winchester College Manors and Estates

1 Preston Candover
2 Itchen Stoke
3 Otterbourne
4 Bishopstoke
5 Southampton
6 Botley
7 Newton Valence
8 East Tisted
9 Empshott
10 Hawkley
11 Priors Dean

○ College Manor
● College Estate
■ Main Towns

From J.H. Harvey's original map, 1978

Consequently, Ropley Manor is not a cohesive property, nor is it by any means the entirety of the College lands, nor does it hold ownership of much more than ten per cent of Ropley. The bishops of Winchester still held much of the remainder and unexpected owners spring up like Queen Elizabeth and Newark Priory which stands on the banks of the River Wey near Ripley in Surrey, one of the monasteries dissolved by Henry.[45]

The majority of the manor's early land bought by Wykeham came from a family named Gerveys, by escheat or forfeiture for a term of one hundred years. These freeholds and leaseholds were joined with lands at Ropley North Street and at Hattingley and Medstead and the Minchins in Wield.[46] The ancient rents were reserved 'so that the see should be no loser'.[47] In the fifteenth century, the College employed two stewards, one of whom looked after the estates in Hampshire and Wiltshire, the other dealt with those in Berkshire and Middlesex. These men were from families of the lesser gentry who had legal training and were 'closely connected with the bishopric'.

In the 1780s, Ropley Manor consisted of plots in Ropley parish, 42 per cent providing 41 per cent by value of the annual rent, Medstead (28 per cent, 24 per cent), and other pieces scattered in Bighton, Bishop's Sutton, Itchen Stoke, Wield and Winnall in Winchester. In a Winchester College terrier of Ropley Manor in 1786-8, compiled by New Alresford surveyor Morley Copeland, thirteen pieces of land in Ropley parish, about sixty acres, were recognised as being 'inclosed commons' and these would have most likely come from Trelawny's 1709 enclosure of Ropley, with the College having part rights to the common land, being swept along by his administrative coat tails (*Appendix 19*). Named pieces include Bogmere, Little Broom Field, Two Acre Close by Old Down, The Hanger Piece near Collin's Wood, land abutting the north side of the Turnpike Road near Ropley Soke, and two pieces off the King's Highway leading from Medstead to East Tisted, one adjoining Kitwood Road.

In addition, truculent local farmer William Budd held a four-acre piece of Ropley Common inclosed 'adjoining to the north side of the road by Farringdon Common'.[48] In 1797, a minute entered into the terrier noted a dispute over the value of land between Budd and the College. The surveyor, Tredgold, wrote that 'the lands of Ropley differ greatly in value: those of the north side (part of the waste and commons) are by no means as good as those of the south'. Tredgold will be met again during the second Medstead enclosure.

Among the documents left in 1900 by the speculator of Lymington Park Farm, to the south east of the junction of Brislands Lane and Lymington Bottom, is acknowledgement that this was once known as Common Farm, confirmed by

---

45 Shore, *Hampshire*, p. 131.
46 35 Henry VI; 12 & 15 Edward IV.
47 Kirby, 'Charters of Manor of Ropley', p. 2.
48 Winchester College Archives, 21412, no. 40.

the The Ordnance Survey map of 1893. Marianna Hagen in the *Annals of Old Ropley* claimed that 'one of the earliest of the modern enclosures was that of the common land near Kitfield, Ropley'. Kitfield Farm is that site of many changing uses on the corner of Gradwell Lane and the road by the primary school up to Kitwood.

3 ARMED RAIDS AND THE SUPPRESSION OF THE BLACKS

Farnham Castle and the bishop's deer parks, 1710-1730

When the gentry lost their monopoly on game, Sir John Shelley told the Commons, it would not be long before the nation would dwindle into that which it had been contemptuously asserted by Buonaparte to be, 'a nation of shopkeepers'. On the other side, Lord Suffield said that the law was founded on exclusive rights, supported on selfish principles and its chief enjoyment consisted in the possession of what your neighbour has not and perhaps cannot have. It was hardly surprising that such a system inspired resentment against society's 'natural leaders' among men who should have been their principal supporters: the farmers, small freeholders and reputable tradesmen of rural England.[1]

Bishop Trelawny finally lost patience with his steward Charles Heron not because of underhand or illegal ways of doing business, nor for his blasphemy, nor disrespect, nor the sexual misconduct outlined in Woodward Kerby's articles of complaint. Heron committed two greater sins in the bishop's eyes. First, for all Heron's busy work against the episcopal tenants, he had not raised sufficient rent to meet Trelawny's financial target. Second, Heron had failed, negligently thought Trelawny, to knock down the bills of the tradesmen working on the bishop's palace in Chelsea. Even worse, one tradesman won a successful suit against the bishop for debt.[2]

Heron wrote to Trelawny in 1708 that he had persuaded the painter and glazier at Chelsea to settle at a 20 per cent discount, a saving of £50, but that others were 'holding out'.[3] Heron suggested calling on Sir Christopher Wren, through his work for the clergy and their buildings, because Wren had 'absolute command' over one of the tradesmen, Mr Jackson, 'the great incendiary'. Alternatively, Trelawny could write to friends in the lawcourts to arrange a delay in any court appearance for debt.

As Thompson put it, 'Heron had, of course, the necessary money to meet the bills in his hands. The difficulty lay in the bishop's scruples: he did not like to pay his bills in full.'

---

1 Parliamentary debates, 1819 and 1823: xvii, col. 269, 737; xl, col. 364; xvii, col. 737; xxxix, col. 1090.
2 Thompson, *Whigs and Hunters*, pp. 132-3.
3 HRO, Heron to Trelawny, 11M59/F/GBP/E/B, 6/11/1708.

Heron disappears from the records in 1712 when he was arrested by a tenant for the wrongful seizure of heriots. When the bailiffs arrived, they 'found him delirious'.[4]

While Heron's disgrace and departure is not a main theme in this story, it does, if any more proof is needed, show Trelawny's absolute commitment to making money. There was no pause as he chose Edward Forbes as Heron's replacement. Forbes was the steward of the Farnham Court and 'had been the officer most responsible for pressing the case against the Farnham copyholders'.[5]

One must look to Forbes for the curious attachment of Farnham Old Park to the Ropley Commons bill, a combination that was to have national consequences and to ruin many lives. Thompson described the park as 'being quietly tacked on'. I suspect that its inclusion was more deliberate. Bishop George Morley, one of Trelawny's predecessors, had turned over half the park's 1,000 acres to small farmers to raise revenue. In the remaining half, Trelawny and Forbes encountered the same old problems, commoners evading payments and claiming their 'rights', especially with regard to timber. Trelawny told parliament that Lawday House in the north of the park had accidentally burnt down and he wanted to rebuild it and also to make improvements by enclosing the land for 'the encouragement of the said tenants therein'.[6] Farnham Castle, the bishop's residence, separated by its defensive bank and ditch, lay in the south and provided the park entrance.[7]

Whatever improvement was implemented, the common rights in the park were extinguished after a couple of years and it is inevitable, as at Ropley, that tenants were cheated. Regularly contested claims included grazing and access to clay, marl, chalk, earth, stones, peat, turf and heath.[8] The principal beneficiary was Edward Forbes, Trelawny's new steward, who rented the entire park at the low sum of £70 a year.[9] Forbes's widow, Sarah, renewed the tenure at the same rental from 1734 to 1768.

Towards the end of 1720, just months before his death, Trelawny suffered a great shock to his finances which may have hastened his final days. He was one of the many aristocrats and landowners who following their personal greed and credulousness, lost serious amounts of money in the business scandal known as the South Sea Bubble. As the Bubble collapsed, Trelawny's wider family was deeply involved to many thousands of pounds. His last visit to the Lords six weeks before his end was to attend a debate on the company.[10] A manuscript copy of

---

4   HRO, Cranley to Trelawny, MSS I/12, 6/5/1712.

5   Thompson, *Whigs and Hunters*, p. 133.

6   Lawday House, or its replacement, still stands at the north of the park at the junction of Folly Hill and Upper Hale Road (English Heritage, 443034).

7   The bishopric sold the park to the town of Farnham in 1930. Roe deer and cattle continue to graze. There is a golf course centred on the Ranger's House and the surrounding pleasure grounds are now in private ownership. A medieval field system has been uncovered.

8   This list was presented in the Farnham Customs Roll of 1707 and contested by the steward.

9   HRO, 11M59/F/BP/E/B19.

10 R. J. E. Boggis, *History of the Diocese of Exeter*, p. 440 (Exeter, 1922).

Farnham Castle and park, 1830
Engraving, W. J. Cooke

the report of the government's secret committee on the South Sea Company was kept in the family papers.[11] All this added to the failure of the Cornish Wheal Vorr tin mine in 1718 in which Trelawny had invested. Trelawny's son John was bought an expensive army colonelcy; he also owned £1,000 of South Sea stock.

The South Sea Company, founded in 1711 with the Chancellor of the Exchequer Robert Harley as its governor, was a public-private partnership to consolidate the national debt (over £50 million by 1719) which had run out of control and was threatening to bankrupt the country. It was, from the beginning, a criminal enterprise seeking to defraud its investors who included the royal family, parliamentarians and much of the landowning class. Many of these 'senior' investors were bribed to the tune of over £1 million to encourage the company's promotion. One share's starting price was £100 in a time when to earn £500 in a year was to be wealthy.[12]

The company behind the Bubble began by making sword blades and then ran a national lottery. To help fund the master plan of turning government debt into shares, it became a trading company with a monopoly to supply African slaves (the *Asiento de Negroes*) to the mainland of South America and its 'South Sea islands'. The government's propaganda machine was ably spearheaded' by Daniel Defoe, the novelist, and by Jonathan Swift, the poet, political pamphleteer and

---

11 Smith, *Fighting Joshua*, p. 171.
12 Most of what follows is taken from Malcolm Balen's book on the scandal, *A Very English Deceit*.

South Sea House in its pomp in Bishopgate Street, 1754
Engraving, Stowe's Survey of London

satirist. The Prince of Wales took over from Harley as governor in 1715 followed, in 1717, by King George.

Share dealers were 'raucous, seedy, unscrupulous and rough'. Their aim, in the saying of the day, was 'to sell the bear's skin before they have caught the bear': they were selling stock before they had paid for it in the hope that they would meet the cost from the profit – or 'bubble' – on the deal. If the shares were in demand, the directors could continue to issue more at higher prices and, to do this, their trick was to offer cut price opportunities to corrupt royalty and politicians. As long as confidence held, there would be no limits to growth. Few who took part in the headlong rush to invest saw fit to question the profitability of the company that was driving such paper wealth. There was a vacuum at its heart: no business plan, no market for its goods and no financial prospects whatsoever. However, it attracted investors because it attracted investors. The company's share price had to keep climbing; within 1719, it increased tenfold.

When the bubble burst in September 1720, 'England's investors resembled the half-drowned survivors of a ship wreck, washed up on dry land. The country's sudden transformation from a seaworthy vessel, capable of defying the elements, to a mass of flotsam tossed about by the waves was deeply felt.' One loser, Jonathan Swift, was inspired to write *Gulliver's Travels* that same year, sending his hero to the 'South-Seas' where he was overcome by a violent storm. 'Like

Gulliver, England's shareholders lay exhausted, gasping for breath and numb with shock, not knowing whether they would live or die.'[13]

In the aftermath, some parliamentarians who were involved through just buying shares now saw the absurdity of what had been done. However, they were ranged against many others who had been bribed and who needed to disguise the depth of their corruption. In all, more than 450 MPs held stock during the year and 122 out of 200 peers had been shareholders. Their complicity was hidden when record books were forged and rushed abroad. Months were wasted because the prime minister-to-be, Robert Walpole, was determined to limit and steer any enquiry in order to protect those in power, deflect his own involvement and, in doing so, seize control of government for himself.[14] Trelawny declared himself in word and action a strong supporter.[15]

In the countryside, too, the impact of the Bubble's collapse was felt deeply, especially among the families who had borrowed against their new riches and acquired large, mortgaged estates. With the South Sea Company's decline came an inevitable slump in land prices which hurt those who had not even bought stock. England suffered a economic downturn that led to heightened social tensions.

However, the South Sea Bubble had made the 'present juncture … so favourable' for those looking for a way out.[16] Ropley's recent revolutionary enclosure bill showed commons landowners a route to help repair their fortunes.

Trelawny died intestate which 'shipwrecked' his charitable intentions – some £2,000.[17] However, in each of the previous eight years, he received a full income, at least £25,000. Near the end, he declared he had 'smarted too much by mortgages to bring any person I have a kindness for under that plague which seldom is cured and leaves many great scars behind.'

---

13 As an example, the Duke of Chandos was £300,000 down and would never quite recover. When he died a quarter of a century later, his great house at Cannons in north London, where Handel was composer-in-residence, was pulled down and its contents sold piecemeal by his son to pay the debts he had inherited. Today, its grand colonnade stands outside the National Gallery in Trafalgar Square; its gates at Trinity College, Oxford; the font and altar from the chapel in the parish church of Fawley in Buckinghamshire; while its stained-glass windows, ceilings and the organ used by Handel are installed at Great Whitley in Worcestershire. Avington Park, near Alresford, received the reredos from the Cannons altar, which is now in St. Mary's Church, Avington, and was recently restored. The church also holds a 'Vinegar Bible', named after a prominent misprint, 'vinegar' instead of 'vineyard', and two large prayer books which also came from Cannons (private email, Jacqui Squire, 27/5/2021).

14 Black, *Walpole in Power*, Chapter 1. Balen, *English Deceit*, throughout. There is no date for when the office of prime minister first appeared as the role was not created, but rather evolved through a merger of duties. The term was regularly if informally used of Robert Walpole by the 1730s. Modern historians generally consider Walpole as the first and longest-serving prime minister, but the title is applied to early prime ministers only retrospectively. The first prime minister of the United Kingdom of Great Britain and Ireland was William Pitt the Younger. The first to use the title in an official act was Benjamin Disraeli in 1878.

15 Smith, *Fighting Joshua*, p. 149.

16 G. V. Bennett, *The Tory Crisis in Church and State 1688-1730: The Career of Francis Atterbury, Bishop of Rochester* (Oxford University 1975), p. 228.

17 ODNB, Trelawny, Andrew Coleby.

With his actions, Trelawny had blazed a trail across church exchequers.[18] Ecclesiastical landlords, bishops and bodies relating to the great cathedrals, were happy to follow his aggressive style of land management and enclosure after it was seen to increase income when there might be difficulties with the users of the common land.

Trelawny was replaced by Charles Trimnell, raised from Norwich, a political churchman, but with his roots more firmly based in Christianity. However, the land policies instigated by Trelawny were continued by Trimnell and pursued with vigour by Heron's successor, Forbes.

There can be no doubt that the church's tenants, in Hampshire in particular, hated episcopal interference and despised the bishop's officers for the passion with which they went about their work. There had always been deer stealing from the bishop's various parks. Venison was a profitable booty, selling in London in 1722 for between £3-5 a haunch.[19] However, there was a marked increase in thefts from the time of the 'improvement' and enclosure of Farnham Park and Ropley Commons.

The choice, from many options, of Farnham Park to become the specific target of organised poaching in 1721 suggests that the general unhappiness had become personal: the bishop against his tenants. Historian Rogers felt the first big attack on the Park 'rose out of private spite' and agreed with Defoe that Trelawny 'had not been so indulgent' as his predecessor, Peter Mews, 'in letting his neighbours make bold with some of his Venison'. One might think that, when it came to rights of commons, 'indulgent' was not a word that should be placed in the same sentence as 'Trelawny'.

According to an anonymous pamphleteer, 'scandalous' events began 'in about the Times of the general Confusion when the late pernicious schemes of the South-Sea company bore all things down before them, and laid Waste what the Industry and good Husbandry of Families had gather'd together'. The pamphlet, *The History of the Blacks of Waltham in Hampshire; and those under the like Denomination in Berkshire*, was printed in London in 1723 by A. Moore and sold for sixpence. Reasonable conjecture is that 'A. Moore' is akin to 'A. N. Other' and that the work was written by Daniel Defoe.[20] The best interpretation comes from Thompson in his acclaimed history, *Whigs and Hunters*.

There were three small royal forests in south-eastern and north-eastern Hampshire. From Portsmouth, it was possible to ride across forest territory, through Bere, Woolmer and Alice Holt, and a stretch of private property, to Farnham in Surrey; and from there to Bagshot Heath and the Forest of Windsor. Woolmer was an unwooded expanse of peatbog, fern and sandy heathland on

---

18 Clay, 'Greed of Whig Bishops?'.
19 Thompson, *Whigs and Hunters*, p. 159.
20 *The History of the Blacks of Waltham in Hampshire* is a 32-page pamphlet written chronologically from 1721-23. Rogers, 'Waltham Blacks', p. 466. Thompson, Chapter 5.

which some red deer ran. Alice Holt lay south-east of Farnham, contiguous to the lands of the Bishop of Winchester. It was heavily wooded with plenty of good oak and stocked with fallow deer.

The first mounted raid at Farnham took place in October, just three months after Trelawny's death. Perhaps there was a pause in plans to see whether Trimnell would be more lenient? Perhaps the poachers waited for darker nights; the 'hours between sunset and sunrise were the poacher's day when he made his rounds, setting his snares and taking away the squire's expensively reared game'?[21] Perhaps, the poachers needed a few weeks to make contacts and to gather equipment? Thompson claimed that in Hampshire 'all the components' of the raiders were 'fully assembled by 1718'; however, it was only in 1721 that the attacks 'assumed a new and even more highly organised form'.[22]

The following story is taken from press reports many of which were combined in 'Defoe's' anonymous pamphlet.

In 1671, the Game Act gave hunting privileges to every sporting country gentleman. Where previously, the king was the only 'mighty hunter' across the land, the game laws 'raised a Nimrod in every manor'.[23] All the members of parliament, particularly for the hunting counties like Hampshire, were invited to attend a Commons committee to consider the bill. Forest laws were a valuable source of crown patronage, especially in the rights of park, chase and free warren claimed by landowners in every part of the country. These franchises allowed the hunting of deer and game within certain areas. Parks and chases were, respectively, enclosed and unenclosed sanctuaries for deer while free warrens protected game. No one was permitted to hunt in these areas without the permission of the holder of the franchise. These franchises could be inherited, as by bishops, but holders could not punish poachers summarily, as could the king, and had to seek redress through common law courts – which often amounted to the same thing. At root, was the monarch's claim that all game across the whole of England was the king's game and that, in effect, royal hunts could go wherever they pleased.[24] The gentlemen of England took to guarding their special amusements by methods of which a member of parliament declared that the nobles of France 'had not ventured on their like in the days of their most splendid arrogance'.[25]

Sixteen deer poachers broke into Farnham park and took three deer, leaving two more dead. A keeper was 'shot thro' the Body, tho' he afterwards recovered'. Bishop Trimnell instigated a search and four arrests were made: two poachers were sent sent to prison in Guildford and two to Winchester, the latter by Sir Simeon Stuart, one of the tellers in the passing of the Ropley Commons act. The four were tried at the next Lent assizes where two were acquitted for lack of

21 Munsche, *Gentlemen and Poachers*, p. 115.
22 Thompson, *Whigs and Hunters*, pp. 140-42.
23 Blackstone, *Commentaries on the Laws of England*, p. 416.
24 Munsche, *Gentlemen and Poachers*, pp. 9-15.
25 Hammonds, *Village Labourer*, p. 187.

evidence. The two convicted men were pilloried for an hour and then imprisoned for a year and a day and fined £20.

> *Their Comrades were no sooner apprehended and imprison'd, but this Gang of Banditti meditated nothing but Revenge; and having formed themselves into a numerous Band, and taken an Oath to stand by one another to the last Extremity, under these Anarchical and confus'd Principles they chose to be under a mock Kingly Government, and therefore elected a very robust, enterprising and substantial Gentleman, yet unknown, for their King.*

A much larger gang returned to Farnham Park and took eleven deer with as many left dead. They then rode through the town at seven o'clock on a market day morning in 'open triumph' wearing masks and black gloves which gave rise to their popular name – the Blacks. When, later, faces were blackened in disguise the nickname was assured. For the next two years, the park was attacked repeatedly, the herd of deer substantially reduced, lodges burned, young timber destroyed and cattle shot. Defoe, in his country-wide tour, noted that 'some of the country folks' at Farnham 'notwithstanding the liberality and bounty of the several bishops' have 'of late been very unkind to the bishop in pulling down the pale of his park and plundering it'.[26]

To most country gentlemen, the primary characteristic of a poacher was simply that he was not a sportsman. Where the former revelled in the excitement of the chase, the poacher did not, but instead snared game when it was most vulnerable. Sportsmen never sold their kills. Poachers, however, violated this cardinal rule.

The gentry professed to hold 'the mean rascal who kills game and sells it' in great contempt, but there was more to their attitude than simple indignation. Fear was also involved. The fact that the vulgar sort, and men of small worth, were making a trade and a living by killing game was seen as a threat to social order.

'Most country gentlemen believed that the only thing which stood between the poor and immorality was the necessity of having to work for a living. Without the discipline of constant labour, they agreed, the lower classes would soon sink into lives of crime and debauchery and they would inevitably lead to their own, and society's, ruin.'[27]

A royal proclamation offered £100 for information on the deer thefts and that led to arrests. More raids followed and the Government was finally aroused.[28] A detachment of soldiers was sent to Farnham warned to look out for men with

---

26 Defoe, *Tour*, p. 142. Court records of the time are sparse, but see Surrey Record Office quarter session rolls, 1721, bundles 239 and 240, concerning Richard Morris, deer stealing, and Robert Sturt, cow shooting.
27 Munsche, *Gentlemen and Poachers*, p. 53.
28 Rogers, 'Waltham Blacks', pp. 468-70.

masks or blackened faces and Sir Francis Page, a notorious hanging judge, went to Winchester Assizes to preside over any prosecutions.

The rioters conferred and judged it advisable to 'go further afield for fresh plunder'. They chose another of the bishop's game chases near the village of Waltham, nestled against Bishop's Waltham, about ten miles from Winchester. The band's name changed in the newspapers and government reports to the 'Blacks of Waltham'.

> *What they committed in the Park were but Trifles to what they acted in the Chase where, tho' large Heads of Deer were to be seen in Droves before, scarce were to be seen in two Months Time two of the creatures grazing together: Insomuch that they render'd themselves terrible to all the adjacent Country, who were not only fearful of the Loss of Game, but their very lives, from the circular Letters which were sent from this tumultuous and terrible Assembly, who threaten'd with burning down their very houses in case of Opposition to their search after further supplies of Venison.*

These attacks were clearly of a different calibre to what had gone before; not only well organised, but also exhibiting social resentment highlighting a 'fairly direct class hatred'. This was about the bishops of Winchester. Farnham and Waltham deer parks were chosen with a determination for all to see.[29] The good income from their venison sales was a bonus.

There were many references to a pseudonymous leader, who styled himself King John, a device common later in the nineteenth century popular protests.[30] King John, whether one person or many, exhibited political sophistication and literacy. At one incident, when challenged as to his station, he pulled off a glove and showed the white hand of a gentleman. He was named in one official document as 'Captain Clavered, Hampshire, head of the Blacks, a person yet unfound in today's records. Perhaps, it is better to recognise in the root of his surname, the old verb 'to claver' or to 'to talk idly'.

At first the brigand king was 'treated flippantly and dismissively', but he was soon taken seriously.[31] The Hampshire Blacks not only stole deer but openly provoked the foresters and gamekeepers with exchanges of shot and occasional woundings and used arson, animal maiming and beatings to intimidate. Threats were sometimes made to the local population when it showed sympathy with the forest guardians.[32]

---

29 Rogers, 'Waltham Blacks', p. 468.
30 Rudé, *Crowd in History*, throughout.
31 Rogers, 'Waltham Blacks', p. 469.
32 Broad, *Whigs and Deer-Stealers*, p. 57.

Unless one leaps to sympathy for the park rangers and keepers, it was commonly alleged that they 'milked the spoils of office'.[33] Defoe, in 1724, singled out these men as worse offenders than any Black, despite their many perquisites. One keeper sent over twenty hares at a time into a small Hampshire inn for a half-a-crown a piece which were sold on at 3s 6d to a London poulterer.[34]

In 1725, Robert Walpole's eldest son was appointed a ranger of Richmond Park.[35] Walpole himself, married to Catherine, was a deputy ranger. His affairs became the 'talk of the town', and he regularly retreated to the ranger's lodge at weekends to spend time with his mistress, Maria Skerrett, who gave him two daughters.[36]

The authorities saw acts of terror and extortion, but in the eyes of peasant farmers and poor tenants, the deeds spoke more of vigorous chastisement. A farmer who informed had fences broken and cattle driven into standing corn; the widow of a ranger was forced to return £10 received for a game offence; a landowner near Farnham who had bark stripped from his trees was relieved of money he had received in recompense; a widow at Wickham fighting for parish pews had her garden despoiled; a parson's beehives were thrown into the highway; a carpenter from Farnham was sent to gaol in Winchester following a dispute over a bill with a gentlemen, but the magistrate was ordered to bail him (which he did) or the King of the Blacks would 'take very severe revenge upon him'. Despite rewards and threats, local inhabitants were reluctant to give up names.

The rituals of the raids strongly suggests the defiance of anonymous, mostly agricultural, people against exclusive parks and their protected and nurtured game. Such impudence was a shock to those in power unused to having their authority challenged in an organised way. The royal forests were no longer the impressive preserves of timber and deer that the Normans had created. For centuries they had run wild. In 1660, the forest laws were restored along with the other institutions of monarchy, but after the long neglect and decades of encroachment and virtually uninterrupted plundering, reinforcement was patchy and often disregarded.[37]

According to the justice, Sir William Blackstone, the Waltham gang modelled themselves on the followers of Robin Hood.[38] King John issued printed manifestos and called a meeting at Waltham Chase to answer published criticism. He took his 'Posse out near a Publicke House on the Chase' and 'fifteen of his smutty tribe appeared; some in Coats made of Skins, others with their fur Caps. They

33 Thompson, *Whigs and Hunters*, p. 160.
34 Bovill, *English Country Life*, p. 178.
35 TNA, E 403/2473, p. 44.
36 ODNB, Stephen Taylor, 'Walpole', 28601. Lord John Hervey, *Some materials ... King George II*, Vol. 3, p. 832.
37 Munsche, *Gentlemen and Poachers*, pp. 9-10.
38 Blackstone, *Commentaries on the Laws of England*, p. 255.

were all well armed and mounted, and at least 300 People assembled to see the Black Chief and his Sham Negroes'. There could be no clearer indication of the popularity of the band, or, at least, its capability of exciting interest. Large numbers of the local population attended without fear or sign of aggression and without an appearance from the authorities. Watchers thought that the band's members were not local men.

King John told the crowd that the Blacks had,

> No other Design than to do Justice, and to see that the Rich did not insult or oppress the Poor: that they were determined not to leave a Deer on the Chase, being well assured it was originally designed to feed Cattle, and not fatten Deer for the Clergy.

At the close of the speech, the King, Prince and Princesses drank Loyal Healths and rode off.[39] One can almost hear the laughter over the years.

At about this time, an offshoot of the Hampshire Blacks set up near Windsor Great Park and a copycat gang operated in Berkshire. The Blacks 'made a dreadful havoc in Windsor Forest; a Crime more audacious than hitherto committed, because it was the property of the Crown'. Other attacks at Bagshot and Caversham Park, owned by the Earl of Cadogan, followed with a series of increasingly audacious raids in 1722 and 1723 including one in which a gamekeeper's son was killed and the father escaped only because a gun misfired.

At the leading instigation of Bishop Trimnell, smarting from the attacks to his estates at Farnham Park and Waltham Chase, the Black Act was passed in 1723 'for the more effectual punishing wicked evil and disposed Persons going armed in Disguise and doing injuries and Violence to the Persons and Properties of His Majesty's Subjects, and for the more speedy bringing the Offenders to Justice' (*Appendix 9*).[40] Trimnell died at Farnham Castle in 1723.

No other single statute passed during the eighteenth century equalled the Black Act in severity and none appointed the punishment of death in so many cases.[41] To hunt deer at night or in disguise, or in a forest, and armed with swords, firearms, or other offensive weapons, in any enclosed ground, brought the death penalty without benefit of clergy.[42]

The death penalty was introduced for over fifty criminal offences which were all already well covered by the law. Over the previous thirty years, the penalties for a number of these offences, especially the unlawful hunting of deer, had increased first to a £30 fine, then in 1719 to seven years' transportation and, finally, to the gallows. The Black Act was the only eighteenth-century piece of hunting

---

39 *Stamford Mercury*, 17/1/1723.
40 'The Waltham Black Act'. Thompson, *Whigs and Hunters*, p. 119.
41 Radzinowicz, 'Waltham Black Act', p. 56.
42 'Benefit of clergy' was a provision by which clergymen could claim that they were outside the jurisdiction of the secular courts and should be tried instead in an ecclesiastical (and more lenient) court under canon law.

and game legislation which invoked the death penalty 'so lavishly applied to other areas of criminal law'.[43] The Act was expanded over the years and greatly strengthened the criminal code by specifying over 200 capital crimes.[44]

Any offender who with a blacked face, armed or otherwise, disguised, merely blacked, merely disguised, accessories after the fact or 'any other person or persons' involved, anyone in one of the above categories found in a forest, chase, down or Royal Park could be sentenced to death. It was an offence to hunt, kill, wound or steal deer in those locations with the first offence punishable by fine and the second by penal transportation.

Other criminalised activities included fishing, the hunting of hares, the destruction of fish-ponds, the destruction of trees and the killing of cattle, the last of which was also punishable by death. Within its brief time before parliament, extra offences were added daily. An offender could also be executed for setting fire to corn, hay, straw, wood, houses or barns or shooting another person. The same penalties applied to attempting to rescue anyone imprisoned under the act or attempting to solicit other people to participate in crime that violated it.[45]

Three of the Blacks' leaders were captured during the passage of the bill although one escaped. A series of raids captured thirty-two Blacks who were tried in Reading. Four were sentenced to death for the killing of the gamekeeper's son and were executed two weeks later in June 1723 and 'made an exemplary end'.[46] Six others were ordered to be transported for deer stealing.[47]

In 1723, a major expedition was mounted to defeat the Windsor Blacks; the government used paid informers to arrest over forty suspects.[48] Trials continued while seven more poachers were captured, transported or hanged, marking the end of the Blacks of Berkshire and Windsor.

In retaliation, at least ten Blacks raided Southwick Park near Fareham and took several deer after feeble resistance. Three 'fat bucks and several hogsheads of the richest French wines' were intercepted at Alresford on their way from Southampton to Frederick, Prince of Wales.[49] The Hampshire Blacks looted Stratfield Saye, the park of George Pitt, sometime MP for Hampshire, part of the Ropley Commons committee, and committed other 'outrages' on the Wiltshire border.

King John then announced the retirement of the Hampshire Blacks, but 'as they had begun their riotous Assemblies with Ravages and Insults on the Bishop of Winchester's Premises so they likewise would end them there'.

---

43 Broad, 'Whigs and Deer-Stealers', p. 57.
44 9 Geo. 1 c. 22, 27/5/1723. The Act was largely repealed in 1823 after a reform campaign.
45 Radzinowicz, 'Waltham Black Act', pp. 57-72.
46 Leonard Thorn, the shooter; John Hawthorn; John Gilbert and Thomas Hatch.
47 Edward Collier, Joseph Mercer, Joseph Magnar, John Chapman, Andrew Hughes and Charles Grant.
48 Broad, *Whigs and Deer-Stealers*, p. 57.
49 The record says 'Aylesford' not 'Alresford', but is most probably a mistake. Aylesford in Kent is an odd route from Southampton to London.

Seven blacked men were sent to Farnham in September 1723 and raided the forest at Alice Holt, adjoining Farnham Park, killing three deer.[50] One poacher, James Ansell, was captured by the keeper and his men as he ran to give the alarm. Six more men of 'the same sooty Complexion' were spotted and 'very civilly desired to quit the Ground and retire'. Arguing face to face, 'one of the Villains (Henry Marshall) cock'd his piece and shot the Keeper (John Ellicker) unexpectedly in at the Breast and out at the Back, that he died immediately on the Spot'. A severe fight ensued. One servant, John Barber, was wounded in the thigh by one of his companions who, in turn, in falling, fired and wounded a gang member who was taken. Barber was carried to a private house in Binsted. Marshall, Ansell, Edward Elliott and Robert Kincot were soon caught. Three more of the gang, John and Edward Pink, labourers ('remarkable for their Ignorance and Brutality'), and Richard Parvin, a publican, got away but were taken in Portsmouth, their home town, a dangerous place at the time with the assize records full of street murders, assaults and robberies. The men were taken to Winchester Jail.

In November, a detachment of the Duke of Bolton's Blue Guards escorted the seven to Westminster for trial. The duke, Charles Paulet, of Abbotstone House near Alresford, it may be remembered, was a prominent member of the first Ropley committee in the House of Commons. The men pleaded 'Not Guilty', but three were convicted of wilful murder and the other four, under the Black Act, of being armed and in disguise in a deer park. They hoped for transportation. All were hanged at Tyburn. Several of the bodies were immediately bought and taken away for dissection and experiment.

The paradox, in London, Winchester and Oxford, for example, was that game was bought and sold openly with little interference from the authorities. The large quantities could not have come from professional fowlers and country folk. 'Poaching was a learned trade providing an income of £100 a year and more.'[51]

It is important to appreciate the fanaticism with which the English nobility and gentry sought and guarded their ownership of land and the pivotal role deer and game played in their relentless deprivation of the poor. Permission from the owner to hunt was all important.

'Except in a few forests and chases where the ancient privileges conferred by the forest laws and royal franchises still applied, no deer or rabbit could be legally hunted except with the permission of the landowner. This legal status was not proclaimed in Parliament, but rather came about as a natural consequence of the enclosure of deer in parks and rabbits in warrens. By their enclosure, they had ceased to be wild animals. When game became property, poaching became an offence against property and that in the eighteenth century was a very serious matter.' Additionally, as long as the gentry retained their legal monopoly

50 The anonymous pamphlet says 'Colt' not 'Alice Holt'.
51 Munsche, *Gentlemen and Poachers*, pp. 55, 65.

over game, lesser landowners were denied the right to hunt on their own land whatever damage the game was doing to their crops or how hungry was their family.[52]

The game laws imposed a property qualification on sportsmen and effectively gave the gentry the exclusive right to hunt game in England. This monopoly was enforced by the gentry themselves in their capacity of justices of the peace by means of summary trials and severe punishments. As a consequence, the game laws were bitterly resented and, in many cases, violently resisted.[53]

To the Webbs, the game code was 'an instrument of terrible severity, leading, not infrequently, to cruel oppression of individuals of the lower orders'.[54] The Hammonds said the code 'spilt the blood of men and boys ... for the pleasures of the rich'. Even historians sympathetic to the gentry, like J. D. Chambers, thought enforcement 'tyrannical'.[55]

Munsche explained some of the seeming contradictions,

> *Game refers only to hares, partridges, pheasants and moor fowl (like grouse). Animals which were not protected by any statute, wild ducks, foxes, otters or badgers, were classed as vermin rather than game. There was no operative property qualification for deer or rabbits, they were not seen as game, but in some situations it was a crime. There was also one set of laws for rabbits and another for hares. The explanation for the apparent confusion was 'enclosure', not the enclosure of fields, but the process by which wild animals were confined, fed and protected in a specific area where they were bred and nourished until the landowner decided they were to be hunted and killed. After enclosure, an animal ceased to be wholly wild and became part-domesticated property. By definition, a wholly wild animal had no owner and, therefore, at its death no one suffered a loss. An intruder who took a wild animal off someone's land could, of course, be sued for trespass, especially if that property was specifically protected.*[56]

The large landowners feared that if game became a saleable item, it would lose its significance and assume a 'mercenary sordid character'.[57] Worse still, reform would undermine the difference in outlook which distinguished the landed from the moneyed classes. Gentlemen did not need to work. It would degrade the country gentlemen into hucksters, men who were not mindful of 'gentlemanlike and liberal feelings', but interested only in 'paltry profit'. The game which they preserved would no longer be a symbol – 'a sort of feather in their cap' – of their

52 Munsche, *Gentlemen and Poachers*, p. 114.
53 J. D. Chambers, *Nottinghamshire in the Eighteenth Century, a study of life and labour under the squirearchy*, pp. 74-5. Also, Mingay, *Gentry*, pp. 131-33; Munsche, *Gentlemen and Poachers*, p. 1.
54 Webbs, *Parish and the County*, p. 598.
55 Hammonds, *Village Labourer*, p. 187.
56 Munsche, *Gentlemen and Poachers*, pp. 3-4.
57 Munsche, *Gentlemen and Poachers*, p. 166.

special position in society. Instead it would become a commodity, available to anyone with money enough to purchase it.

Gilbert White of Selborne was just a boy when the last of the deer raids occurred, but he wrote of hearing the tales of the Blacks in their old age.[58] 'Our old race of deer-stealers are hardly extinct yet. It was but a little while ago that, over their ale, they use to recount their exploits and trot out various ways of catching deer.

'Such forests and wastes are of considerable service to neighbourhoods that verge upon them, by furnishing them with peat and turf for their firing; with fuel for the burning their lime; and with ashes for their grasses; and by maintaining their geese and their stock of young cattle at little or no expense.'[59]

Spasmodic deer thefts at Farnham Park continued through 1745, a date whose significance will become apparent in the next chapter.[60] At about the same time, Benjamin Hoadly, bishop of Winchester for almost thirty years from 1734, of whom more follows, was asked to re-stock Waltham Chase with deer. Hopefully at embarrassment at the actions of his predecessors, he refused, claimed Gilbert White, saying that the Black Act 'had done mischief enough already.'[61] In 1783, a warrant was issued to all constables in Surrey for the arrest of several named men and for the search of their houses and outhouses for the skins or carcasses of fallow deer stolen from the Farnham Park.[62] Poachers returned there in 1795, killing one servant, but one of their own was shot dead. As a result of this and other gangs, parliament passed the Ellenborough Act in 1803 by which anyone who offered armed resistance to lawful arrest was to be hanged as a felon.[63] Waltham Chase was enclosed in 1870, since when the timber has been entirely cut down, though the name forest still clings to the locality.

And, as for the fate of King John? Well, who knows?

58 White, *Natural History*, Letter VII, 'The Waltham Blacks'.
59 White, *Natural History*, p. 24.
60 *Derby Mercury*, 7/3/1745.
61 Gibson, *Enlightenment Prelate*, p. 257. British-history.ac.uk/vch/hants/vol3/pp276-282.
62 HRO, 44M69/G3/1050.
63 Bovill, *English Country Life*, p. 179.

4 SMUGGLERS AND JACOBITES

Thickening the Ropley enclosure plot, 1719-1745

'One thing which most of Sir Robert Walpole's admirers did not lack was money. Most were rich and many immensely rich landowners, though some of them become immensely poor suddenly on the wrong turn of a card or throw of a dice. Rich noblemen bet wildly on anything, and and drank prodigiously and spent fortunes keeping whores ... They behaved arrogantly and abominably because they were aristocrats and reckoned themselves above having to behave like gentlemen.'[1]

How much does all this claim and counter-claim, anger, deer-stealing, shooting and cocking a snook at authority have its genesis in Ropley? The story began with the never-ending search by that unpriestly bishop, Jonathan Trelawny, for cash to pay his debts and for his excesses. No corner of the episcopal estates was safe from the zeal and unkindness of Trelawny's stewards and their officers who chose Ropley and Farnham Park to use parliamentary coercion to enforce enclosure. The result was most keenly felt by the commoners and, afterwards, the Blacks at Farnham. When the park was almost stripped of venison, the Blacks reinvented themselves at Waltham Chase, another space where deer, said King John, was 'fattened' for the Winchester clergy.

The trail leads from Winchester to Ropley and to Farnham Park, and then thirty miles back to Waltham Chase and to Winchester. Ropley lies half way between the two deer-stealing centres, fifteen miles, an easy evening's ride.

Did the small landowners and poorer citizens of Ropley, stung by their unfair enclosure and ignored by the great landowners gathered in London, figure in the popular, public and violent reaction. What other evidence exists?

Historian E. P. Thompson conducted a small survey using state papers into the occupations of the Hampshire Blacks and concluded that 'it was quite possible' that none of King John's men was detected by the authorities. Local tradition, fragmentary evidence and the logistics of travel to their targets, suggested that gentlemen, or at least yeomen of substance, were involved. It was the best explanation of why so many of the affrays were led by well-mounted, well-spoken men with firearms. Good horses and reliable guns, both normally out of reach of labourers, hint at a wealthy captain. In Hampshire, 'there were gentlemen sufficiently at odds with the forest and episcopal authorities to have given the Blacks at least passive support'.[2]

---

1   Frank Muir, *The Walpole Orange* (Corgi 1993), p. 29.
2   Thompson, *Whigs and Hunters*, pp. 156-7.

How did the Blacks' organisation come about? There was the normal great and continual movement across the country, but it was largely undertaken by those with money, landowners with estates to manage and enjoy, and merchants with goods to sell. This was still a time when the majority of the population seldom left their home and then only to travel to a close village or the nearest small town. Until the nineteenth century, the concept of the county was familiar among the gentry, but 'not to the masses'.[3]

Secret communications were dangerous. Post was routinely opened by government spies, fearful of French and Spanish invasions and with the exiled Stuarts, the Jacobite Pretenders, plotting at home and overseas. Lists of captured Blacks are remarkable for the diversity of homes; their villages and small towns are seldom repeated.[4]

How did these Blacks, drawn piecemeal from across the South of England, learn of each other's existence? Observers talk of the ability to call on over a thousand men. How did they agree to act in concert? To their rules of operation? To their travel without discovery to their targets? These practicalities suggest the Blacks were leaning heavily on some pre-existing community with particular skills which might be predisposed to criminality.

Only one community fits the bill and which, not by chance, has a proven and lengthy association with Ropley. The government's loud encouragement of enclosure and crop specialisation benefitted the larger landowners, but created little opportunity for the small farmers and the labouring poor. Smuggling was well established, a means of supplementing low rural wages.[5]

The first smuggling gangs were formed around 1714, but there is evidence of co-ordinated smuggling networks from the 1690s.[6] In Hampshire in 1734, a gang of Sussex smugglers attacked and robbed the home of George Wakefield at night, dragging the man from his bed. Wakefield turned to his neighbour the Duke of Richmond for help. 'He is afraid to move towards justice lest a greater evil should fall upon him and dares not complain of it even to his neighbours.'[7] In 1748, another Hampshire landowner, Henry Foxcroft, also wrote to Richmond. 'I have had abundance of mischief done me in the night time, my gardens have four times been cut to pieces, near 700 trees of nine years growth, utterly destroyed ... water poisoned ... summer house burnt down.'

In a number of accounts, the Hampshire Blacks were described as smugglers or, at least, as gathering around them 'owlers' (wool smugglers), poachers, and 'other malcontents' who had formed gangs and 'by open force run their goods'.[8] Knowledge of smugglers remains minimal although tens of thousands of people

3   David Hey, 'Countries and Pays' in Jones, *Farmers*, p. 13.
4   TNA, 35/33/192; 35/43/18, 23, 30, 43-46; 44/81/236.
5   Monod, 'Dangerous Merchandise', p. 158.
6   Monod, 'Dangerous Merchandise', p. 152.
7   East Sussex Record Office, Sayer MSS, 269, 1/10/1734.
8   *Weekly Journal*, 4/5/1723. Thompson, *Whigs and Hunters*, p. 158.

were thought to be involved. Their stories are often ignored in social histories, but an investigation of parliamentary records, local newspapers and court lists corrects any misconception that serious crimes against the Revenue in the countryside were infrequent.[9]

Smugglers on a beach, undated
George Morland, National Trust, Mottistone Estate, Isle of Wight, NT 1412311

Smuggling of wool was the custom of 'men of substance, the landowners and farmers'. Britain had to pay for its constant wars of the eighteenth century until the final defeat of Napoleon at Waterloo. Amidst the fighting and the conquest of new lands, expanding trade brought exotic commodities. The difficulty of levying productive taxes on income and wealth to offset the national debt meant that import duties took a large part of the burden.[10] As more revenue was required, more items were taxed. By 1760, 800 items had levies at import and a further

9   Cal Winslow, 'Smugglers' in Hay, *Fatal Tree*, p. 121. Rudé, *Crowd*, p. 35.
10   Peter Hogarth, 'Ropley in the Age of Smuggling', No. 84, p. 2.

1,300 were added in the next fifty years.[11] At its height, smuggling was believed to account for up to a third of all trade in England.

With the development of the illicit, high-profit trade in tea, a lower class of smuggler joined in and brought with them additional brutality. Before the 1740s, it was a guerrilla war. Daniel Defoe, toured the coast and 'perceived several dragoons, riding officers, and others armed and on horseback, riding always about as if they were huntsmen beating up their game'.[12]

> *The insolence and outrageous behaviour of the smugglers in your parts has been, in my judgement, a public concern for some time, and calls loudly for a parliamentary redress. They are a standing army of desperadoes, who must pay themselves, and can subsist by no other means but public rapine and plunder, and if they cannot be broke, shut up Westminster Hall, and disband all your officers of justice as an expensive but useless incumbrance on the nation.*[13]

France provided most of the smuggled items and the French Government encouraged the illicit trade to England. While Kent was closer to London, the biggest market, its seaboard was exposed and watched. Cornish and Devon coasts were more treacherous. Hampshire, Sussex and Dorset were the greatest smuggling counties. Their coastal areas were also favoured for their indentations which were less well guarded. Once landed at, say, one of the many creeks of the harbours at Langstone, Emsworth (supposedly then by a tunnel under Tower Street and into the cellars of Trentham House or to the Smugglers' Rest and on to a notorious pub near Nore Farm Avenue)[14] and at Chichester (to be hidden in old gravel workings off Brandy Hole Lane),[15] there were rough cart tracks heading north up river valleys and across open country.[16]

Widely differing profits are quoted depending on circumstance and time, the amount of tax sought, the distance travelled and the number of men involved. Goods might be unloaded defiantly in broad daylight, or in a secluded cove or be attached to a raft and floated deep into a harbour. After unloading, local purchasers took their share. The bulk, still unsold, was loaded onto carts and taken inland to a distribution point. At each stage, until trust was established, it was cash on the nail. Up to five times the purchase price might be available for expenses. At the inland centre, everything needed to be rehidden until

---

11 In 1842, Prime Minister Robert Peel reintroduced income tax which foreshadowed less reliance on import duties. Britain adopted a free-trade policy and in three acts from 1842 to 1846, 1,200 items were freed of duty, Trevor May, *Smugglers and Smuggling* (Shire, Oxford 2014).

12 Defoe, *Tour*, p. 139.

13 Letter, Henry Simon, solicitor to the Commissioner of Customs, 11/12/1744, East Sussex Record Office, Sayers MSS 3871.

14 A. J. C. Reger, *Short History of Emsworth* (Havant Borough History, No. 6).

15 *Chichester Post*, 11/8/2018.

16 Chris Hare, *Secret Shore: Tales of Smuggling from Sussex and Hampshire* (South Downs Society 2016).

firm contracts were made for onward distribution to a customer, or another intermediary, probably in a major town.

The route taken to Ropley was from the harbours at Langstone, or adjacent coves, then to Titchfield and up the Meon Valley through Soberton, where a vault close to the chancel door at St Peter and St Paul was sometimes used for concealment, before cutting over to Cheriton and East Down Farm, near Sutton Scrubs in fox-hunting territory, a staging post used to keep an eye on the activities of the authorities.[17] Cheriton was also part of a gin smuggling route; many bottles from Holland have been found in contemporary cottages.[18]

Contraband did not arrive in Ropley unexpectedly. Hiding places were ready; and 'fences' alerted in Alton, Guildford, Reading and Winchester and, it is reported, as far as Bristol, Gloucester and Worcester. Transportation and concealment around Ropley was so extensive that almost every able-bodied man was used to some degree and to some purpose.

There can be little doubt that all knew. Women were an essential part of this 'land smuggling'. They sold, transported or hid contraband in their homes or about their person; they provided protection, alibis and assistance.[19] Those few villagers outside the group were encouraged, as Rudyard Kipling put it, to '*Watch the wall, my darling, while the Gentlemen go by!*'.[20]

As the smuggling trade grew, so did the rewards and the risks. 'An exasperated government applied increasingly severe penalties and, for their part, the smugglers responded with escalating violence.'

Sir John Cope's parliamentary enquiry of 1736 highlighted the audaciousness of the gangs:

> *The smugglers being grown to such a degree of insolence, as to carry on their wicked practices by force and violence, not only in the country and remote parts of the kingdom, but even in the city itself, going in gangs, armed with swords, pistols and other weapons, even to the number of forty or fifty, by which means they have been too strong, not only for the officers of the revenue, but for the civil magistrates themselves who have not been able to put a stop to these pernicious practices, even by the assistance of regular forces as have been sent to their aid. The sloops and boats appointed for preventing the running of goods have likewise been beaten off by a greater number of armed men on board smuggling vessels ... The number of custom-house officers who*

---

17 Richard Platt, *OS Guide to Smuggler's Britain* (Cassel, London 1991). 'East-down farm' mentioned in Duthy, Sketches of Hampshire, 1829, as being near a wood called Sutton Scrubs from which Waller's forces were forced to retire before the Battle of Cheriton.

18 Geoffrey Morley, *Smuggling in Hampshire and Devon 1700-1850* (Countryside Books, Newbury 1994), p. 42.

19 Richard Platt, *Smuggling in British Isles* (History Press, Stroud 2011).

20 Rudyard Kipling, 'A Smuggler's Song', *Puck of Pook's Hill*.

have been beaten, abused and wounded since Christmas 1723, being no less
than 250, beside six officers who have been actually murdered.

Numerous anti-smuggling acts were passed which equalled in savagery any eighteenth-century legislation.[21] A witness at a government enquiry proposed that 'future smugglers should be deemed to be within the Black Act'.[22] Under the provisions of the new act, numerous activities, such as being assembled 'in the running, landing or carrying away of prohibited or uncustomed goods', having a blackened face or wearing 'any wizard mask or other disguise', or wounding an officer of the Revenue, were made felonies, with the convicted to suffer death. However, when offenders were brought before the courts, the local magistrates, were often lenient as local law officers were sometimes beneficiaries. Even if the proof 'was ever so clear against the [prisoner], no magistrate in the county durst commit him to gaol; if he did he was sure to have his house or barns set on fire, or some other mischief done him, if he was so happy to escape with his life'.[23]

One can track the complicity of the judiciary by the low levels of punishment meted out. In Ropley, no case ever made it to court.

Why did Ropley become a centre for inland smuggling operations?

There are a number of logistical and geographical reasons. The area was more than twenty miles inland. Cart journeys could finish after dusk without having to climb the Four Marks ridge. It was a remote dispersed community, off the turnpike, and could be reached by little-travelled paths well away from regular Revenue searches. It was beech wood country with a large number of country houses and farms with cellars and out-of-the way fields, reaching to isolated places in current day Four Marks at Brislands, Cobb, Headmore, Hawthorn and Kitwood.

No other village away from the coast has such a concentration of verbal and written record backed by open rumour and known locations for hiding contraband.[24] The village also enjoyed the active connivance of the clergy, like William Evans, in position for seven years, who allowed free use of the church and its tithe barn, as did his partner-in-Christ at Medstead where goods were stored in the belfry. A favourite place for brandy in that village was in tubs used for pig food.[25] Ropley and Alton were also convenient, neutral and discreet meeting places for the men from the cities who financed the smuggling operations.

It was Ropley for all of these things, but also one more which was the greatest.

The local gentry were the organisers who carried on the trade 'with a high hand for many years'. Local support was shown by open fairs of smuggled goods

21 Hay, *Fatal Tree*, p. 134.
22 Commons Journal, Vol. xxv, 1745-50, p. 109.
23 Anon, 'Gentleman of Chichester', c. 1749, West Sussex Record Office, MSS 155/H 128.
24 Heal, 'Smugglers and the Vicar', *Four Marks Murders*, pp. 60-5.
25 Moody, *Short History of Medstead*, p. 25.

at nearby Monkwood on Sunday afternoons.[26] A small clearing in the woods was laden with deliveries: wine, gin and brandy; silk, lace and fine handkerchiefs; perfumes; items for gambling like ivory dice and back-woven playing cards; sugar, chocolate and the increasingly sought after oilskin bags of tea.[27]

The gentry also ran the local courts. They were the stalwarts of the community who the authorities turned to in time of trouble. One needs first to look in the records for men who got rich quickly and lived comfortably in big houses. The not-too-distant ancestors of many of those who now live a quiet and honest life, prominent in the Ropley community, were criminals.

Among them, Major John Lavender, of Ropley Grove, a much-respected Justice of the Peace, a churchwarden and a subscriber to the Hunt, stands tall. Lavender was everything that a respectable country squire ought to be except that he was also a smuggler.

One noon, Revenue Officers arrived requesting Squire Lavender to sign a search warrant for what is now Smugglers' Cottage in Monkwood where contraband was thought concealed.[28] Lavender offered them dinner. Meanwhile, his groom was sent to warn the cottage where the goods were lowered into a 200-foot well.[29] In 1928, the then owner of Ropley Grove, Vice-Admiral Wilfred Henderson, found under the stone floor of his dining room a brick-lined, seven-foot cubic chamber, empty apart from earth and rubble, a storage place for contraband.[30]

What is less well known is that Lavender's cousin, also John, a blacksmith, lived on Portsea Island, a smugglers' haunt, and a short distance from Langstone Harbour. He was rich for a blacksmith and owned several houses in Hanover Street. 'The generality of the people on the coasts are better friends to the smugglers than they are to the Custom House officers.'[31]

Here is the underlying reason why Ropley was the northern centre of the trade. The Lavender cousins managed the opposite ends of the land corridor. The Lavenders' Portsea address, and their inn, the Blacksmith's Arms, has increased significance shortly.

There are many traditions of local smuggling adventures with 'hairbreadth escapes and tales of caves, secret cellars beneath cottages, and stores of spirits, tobacco and other smuggled goods'.[32] Neighbourhood caves, with locations

---

26 Hagen, *Annals of Old Ropley*.
27 Mason, *Ropley*.
28 Morley, *Smuggling*, p. 42. Hagen, *Annals of Old Ropley*.
29 This story is covered at length in Hagen's *Annals of Ropley* and was confirmed by local resident, George Hale.
30 Letter from Henderson, 7/10/1928. Henderson was appointed to command the 1,500-strong First Royal Naval Brigade to help defend Antwerp at the beginning of WWI. The Brigade was cut off. Rather than surrender to the Germans and become prisoners of war, Henderson led his men across the border into Holland where they were interned for the duration. He was ordered not to escape.
31 Commons Journals, Vol. xxv, 1745-50, p. 104.
32 Shore, *Hampshire*, p. 269.

since lost, may be a stretch of the imagination but they signified holes dug in embankments and old quarries. The list of hiding places is too long to ignore.

In and around Ropley, the church tower and the tithe barn at the Old Parsonage were regular storage spaces. The younger Mr Duthy of Ropley House covertly encouraged the smugglers and lent his father's horses at night. Ropley House was built upon the foundation of a much older house. During renovations, a flight of steps was discovered 'leading down no one knew where'; a villager described a 'Mediterranean' passage leading to the old school.

One man from Monkwood, Henry Prior, obtained a cart-load of whisky kegs at Portsmouth. Revenue men gave chase. Prior galloped the twenty-five miles and arrived safely with his kegs which were then hidden in the big beech wood on Monkwood Hill.[33]

Just beyond Lyewood House, a narrow lane drops down right into a gorge while the Petersfield Road continues up the hill. This is Smugglers' Lane and on the right near its bottom is the white-walled house called 'Smugglers' with its deep well and whose occupants were alerted by Lavender.

In Medstead, contraband was stored in the church tower.[34] The *Castle of Comfort* was hazarded as a smuggler's pub.[35] There is a large, hollow buttress in the sizable cellar of the old *Lymington Arms* on Lymington Bottom Road, now with a blocked entrance under the floor of Clementines fruit and vegetable shop. Goatacre Farm had a smuggling cave, a sister to another between the village and Wivelrod. A secret room was found in the chimney of an old South Town house.[36] Two wells were used as dumps in Preston Candover with a cave near one reputed big enough to accommodate a coach and horses.[37] The tower of Alresford church was used for storage while, remembered a late rector, 'the vestry was considered a particularly safe place as it was certain that no one would enter it from Monday morning till Saturday night'.[38] There is a Brandy Mount off East Street in Alresford; a Brandy Mount Cottage in Cheriton; a dung heap, long gone, and used for storage where the Bighton road joined Winchester Road; at West Tisted, a 'nest with forty eggs in it', a dell with forty tubs at the bottom; hiding places at Herriard Park and the little church of Nateley Scures, near Hook.[39]

Bishop's Waltham, the second deer park target, was also involved in smuggling. In 1748, a number of men from the Customs House in Southampton travelled to the home of Captain Gwyn in search of contraband goods. On the way, they sought the support of soldiers quartered nearby. When the party arrived, they

33 Or Henry Price of Monkwood, story from James Smith, Ropley.
34 Platt, *Guide to Smuggler's Britain*.
35 Terry Townsend, *Hampshire Smugglers' Pubs* (PiXZ Books, Wellington 2016).
36 Moody, *History of Medstead* (1932).
37 Platt, *Guide to Smuggler's Britain*.
38 Curtis, *Alton and Villages*.
39 Mason, *Ropley*.

found the house surrounded by a posse of Gwyn's neighbours. The local constable and a passing Marines officer joined the 'gentlemen' and the Customs officers retreated in face of an increasingly hostile crowd.[40]

When a parish priest, Samuel Maddock, arrived in Ropley and stood against smuggling, he took on more than his own village flock some of whom tried to kill him. His predecessors were deeply embedded in the trade. Maddock was unable to turn to his fellow priests for support for, in almost every direction, they were mired in the business of concealment and freely lent their own churches for the purpose.

The smugglers had a more sinister purpose. Many were in league with Jacobites. Jacobitism is a term derived from the Latin *Jacobus* which means James. Jacobites were opposed to the Glorious Revolution of 1688 which thrust James II of England (and James VII of Scotland) from the throne.

> *They showed their loyalty to the exiled senior line of the royal house of Stuart by a series of plots and risings which have left imperishable memories of self-sacrificing heroism on the battlefield and the scaffold. Failure has not dimmed its glamour.*[41]

From the day of the Stuarts' exile to the Battle of Culloden in 1746, successive protestant British monarchs: William III[42] and Mary II, Queen Anne, and Hanoverians George I and George II were threatened with invasion by the Catholic Stuarts: the deposed King James II; his son James, the Old Pretender; and his grandson Charles, the Young Pretender.[43] The Stuarts were forced to leave France under the Treaty of Utrecht in 1713 and went to Bar-le-Duc in the hospitable and independent Duchy of Lorraine. They made many efforts, some stillborn, to recover their throne with the rebellions of 1715 and 1745 popularly best remembered. All the time, Jacobite supporters 'working secretly within England on their behalf'; a 'hidden stream of political subversion, a mysterious shadowy presence, too vague to grasp, too volatile to define, influencing both the adoption of religious toleration and the enactment of repressive legislation': The Riot Act, 1714, allowed local landowners to read a proclamation ordering illegal gatherings of more than twelve people to disperse on pain of death; the Septennial Act, 1716, increased the maximum length of a parliament to seven years; and the Black Act.[44]

The Church of England, through the pulpits, was 'the most effective means of communications with a large population'. The church also dominated the

---

40 Hay, *Fatal Tree*, p. 143.
41 Lenman, *Jacobite Risings*, p. 11.
42 William of Orange was also a Stuart by family and marriage. The Stuarts were a cadet branch of the English Fitzalan family.
43 William III and Mary II (1689-1702), Queen Anne (1702-1714), and Hanoverians George I (1714-27) and George II (1727-60).
44 Monod, *Jacobitism*, p. 1, 11. Biddell, 'Jacobitism in Bishop's Waltham', p. 229.

universities, especially Oxford, a great centre of Royalism and seminary of the Church of England, which 'excelled in extravagant support for the concepts of divine right and passive obedience to authority'.[45] Led by Trelawny and his fellow bishops, loyal messages were hammered home.

The disdain of the public was first centred on a small circle of discontented Jacobite gentlemen, displaced functionaries and cashiered army officers. 'The most reckless and audacious of these men were the ex-officers, who delighted in outrageous displays of their treasonable allegiances.' John Childs estimated that one third of James II's army officers followed him to France and Ireland (from an army of 35,000 men) and another third retired or were dismissed from the new king's service.[46] The government press represented them as wild, desperate individuals. However, this 'ramshackle structure was able to plan two rebellions and countless conspiracies without complete discovery by the government'. The presence of over 10,000 uprooted, impoverished and disaffected former soldiers soon became a serious social and political problem.[47] Many Jacobites joined gangs involved in highway robbery, smuggling and poaching.

Robert Walpole and his government were acutely aware of widespread collusion between Jacobites and large-scale smuggling in Essex, Kent, Sussex and Hampshire.[48] A blow against one group, they realised, would injure the other. The Smuggling Acts of 1698, 1717, 1721 and 1745 were passed amid great anxiety over Jacobite activity.[49]

The South Coast smugglers had sound financial reasons for liking the Stuarts because their trade was dependent on the connivance of the French authorities, the allies of King James.[50] The monthly crossings of Jacobite agents and messages across the channel was a profitable if dangerous business. In 1690, an innkeeper from Rye was hanged, drawn and quartered for conveying letters to the French fleet. Three years later, the notorious 'Farmer' Hunt, smuggler of French brandy and English Jacobites, made over £3,000.[51] Ordinary smugglers gradually absorbed a measure of Jacobite political culture.

Of course, Ropley, as a cornerstone of one of the main inland contraband routes, would also have provided safe passage for Jacobite spies.

Here, we have a moment of possible enlightenment. Historian Sir Geoffrey Elton claimed the Black Act was 'passed not in order to suppress legitimate protest but because organised gangs were destroying deer and planning a Jacobite uprising.[52] The central part 'played by nebulous fears of Jacobite plots

---

45 Lenman, *Jacobite Risings*, p. 15.

46 John Childs, *The Army, James II, and the Revolution* (Manchester 1980), p. 206.

47 Monod, *Jacobitism*, pp. 96, 102, 111-2. Narcissus Luttrell, *Brief Historical Relation*, Vol. 1, pp. 494-5, 505.

48 Monod, 'Dangerous Merchandise', pp. 153-5.

49 Lenman, *Jacobite Risings*, p. 16.

50 Monod, *Jacobitism*, pp. 113-15.

51 Luttrell, Vol. ii, pp. 124, 135.

52 Elton, *The English* (Blackwell, London 1992), p. 186.

... has perhaps been underplayed in its effect on the government's parallel attack on the Blacks'. The severity of the Black Act has much to do with the hysteria whipped up by Walpole who was juggling several problems simultaneously. Like any politician, he was only too happy to find a joint solution.[53] Walpole was also known to enjoy bottles of untaxed wine.

Paul Monod noted that the underworld of Jacobitism handled the everyday business of the cause – hatching conspiracies, transporting agents and recruiting. They also engaged in 'special acts of publicity, defiance and sedition'. They were not 'ordinary' people. They were generally members of strictly defined occupational groups, like ex-officers or smugglers. Their commitment to the Stuart cause was unusually strong. They made little attempt to conceal their sentiments and often indulged in bold displays of loyalty. In their taverns and clubs, they cultivated a Jacobite sociability. 'To outsiders and ordinary countrymen, they displayed a dream of unity and peace that had wide appeal.'

In the reconstructed maps of uprisings and discontent, Hampshire's emptiness suggests at least an acquiescence if not an agreement with King William and his policies, but this was not so.[54] The royal presence was weak in Hampshire where there was no strong local leader. A great deal of Jacobite support derived from regional hostility to central government.[55]

Open hostility was all about and punished. A man from Alton got into trouble for drinking a toast to 'King James the Third and Eighth'.[56]

Winchester was one of the favourite national Jacobite schools.[57] Disaffection thrived under the headmastership of Robert Friend, brother of a Jacobite MP. The son of the rebel Scot, the Earl of Mar, was enrolled at the school in 1716 and Dr. Friend was said to be 'as careful of him as if he were his own son', encouraging the boy to head the Jacobite party among his schoolmates.[58] Winchester was even more notoriously hostile to the Hanoverians. In 1717, the wardens, fellows, masters, usher and children of the school were taken to the grand jury of Hampshire Assizes 'for their known disaffection and corruption of manners'.[59] The tactic did not work for in August, 1718, the boys 'came into Church in the middle of the service with Rue and Time in theire breasts, and others with Crape hatt bands in their hatts'.[60] A government minister ordered that 'these poor children' be whipped.

On both the Sussex and the Hampshire sides of the county border, there were long-standing smuggling routes. East Hampshire was full of Jacobite gentry,

53 J. H. Plumb, *Walpole, Statesman*, pp. 120-2. Broad, 'Whigs and Deer-Stealers', p. 71.
54 Monod, *Jacobitism*, pp. 125, 135, 137, 274, 314.
55 Lenman, *Jacobite Risings*, p. 51.
56 HRO, QS B/xvib/2/5. Thompson, *Whigs and Hunters*, p. 164.
57 Alongside Westminster.
58 HMC, Stuart, Vol. iii, p. 143.
59 *VCH Hampshire and the Isle of Wight*, Vol. ii, p. 344.
60 *VCH* and TNA SP, 35/12/97, SP 44/79A, pp. 212-13.

particularly around Petersfield, and all were subject to humiliating discrimination: double land tax and exclusion from the civil service and the armed forces.[61] Catholic nobles and gentry, previously dependent on the rents from their estates, had to look for other sources of income. 'Jacobitism against the Hanoverians thrived near the estates of sympathetic owners.'[62]

The Caryll family was connected with Catholics in exile in France who provided them with smuggling opportunities. Alexander Pope, the poet, was a protégé of the cultivated John Caryll II. In 1717, Pope wrote to him asking for bottles from a hogshead of good French wine at the estate in Ladyholt Park near Harting. It was in the well on the estate that the notorious murder of Daniel Chater by the Hawksworth gang of smugglers took place.[63]

The Mayfield gang, ardent rivals of the Hawksworth men, struck up an arrangement with the Jacobite Sir Henry Goring who came from Highden near Steyning in Sussex. Goring was a member of parliament for Horsham for 1707-8. His family was notable for its loyalty to the Stuarts and its early involvement in the smuggling trade.[64]

In July 1720, revenue officers fought a pitched battle near Billingshurst with about 200 Mayfield gang members. One of these smugglers told the beleaguered officers, perhaps accurately, that 'they were the Farnham Blacks'.[65] Goring was there and confirmed the connection. He was so impressed that he set about employing the Blacks for the coming rebellion.

Goring wrote to James Stuart, the 'Old Pretender' in Bar-le-Duc, in May 1723, about Mr Philip Caryll, nephew to the late Lord Caryll and who lived at North House, Catherington, near Petersfield. The letter was recently found in the Queen's Archives at Windsor Castle and turns previous perceptions on their head.

> *Caryll, knowing him to be a man of good sense, few words and well acquainted with most of the Gentlemen of Hampshire that were well inclin'd* [to the Jacobite cause] *and it being impossible for me to carry on my project alone ... he knew the Countrey very well was us'd to travel alone, knew all by Roads ...* [but] *as I was unfortunate in my choice of a friend, so I was fortunate in not trusting him with a great deal more than I did, for I had*

---

61 Erskine-Hill, *Social Milieu*, p. 63.
62 Monod, *Jacobitism*, p. 161.
63 In 1748, members of the notorious Hawkhurst Gang kidnapped a witness, Daniel Chater, and William Galley, the minor customs official taking him to court,. The victims were tied to ponies, carried across the countryside and beaten until nearly dead. After a terrifying night at the *Red Lion Inn* at Rake, Galley was buried alive and Chater was taken to a Harris's Well in Ladyholt Park. Here the gang tried to hang him, but the rope was too short, so they threw him into the well and tossed stones down until his cries were silenced. Seven members of the gang were convicted of the crime at Chichester Assizes, six were hanged, while the gang leader died in gaol before the sentence could be carried out.
64 Calendar of Treasury Books, 10:23; 13:69,70, 172, 259.
65 East Sussex Record Office, Sayer MS 266, 334. Monod, 'Dangerous Merchandise', pp. 164-5.

settled an affair with five gentlemen of that county who were each of them to raise a regiment of dragoons well mounted and well armed which I knew they could easily do for the men had horses and homes of their own, and were, to say the truth of most of them, the persons who some time since robbed the late Bishop of Winchester's Parke, and have increas'd in their number ever since they now go by the name of the Waltham Blacks tho' few of them live there which is a most loyal little town ...

I once saw two hundred and upwards of these Blacks in a body within half a mile of my house. They had been running brandy. There was 24 customs officers following them who they abused heartily and carried off their cargo. I am told there is no less than a thousand of them and indeed I believe they now have taken loyalty in to their heads, and will I hope prove very useful.

This Mr Caryll was the Person who I intended to send to give these Gentlemen before mention'd, their orders when to rise and to tell them the place of Rande-vous, but I thought it was not necessary to acquaint him with it till nearer the time ... I yet cannot but thinke that have used torture to the man to get from him what they have ....[66]

Goring's letter confirmed Abel Boyer's statement that the Waltham Blacks were smugglers and involved in a Jacobite plot centred on the Tory bishop of Rochester, Francis Atterbury.[67]

René de Saunière de L'Hermitage, was an English Huguenot envoy with the Dutch and an experienced diplomat.[68] He reported in May 1723 that the Waltham Blacks were a gang running contraband on the south coast and that Sir Henry Goring, heavily in debt, had helped them organise diversionary tactics against customs officers. In return, Goring had received money from these Blacks.[69] This smuggling involved running wool from the English coasts, destined for Lille and other French textile towns, and bringing back mostly brandy, but also wine and tea. The trade accounted for the bulk of Calais's export and a substantial part of that of Dunkirk.

After 1720, the volume of contraband declined sharply because the government began to employ fast sloops against the smugglers with devastating effect.[70] It was this, L'Hermitage said, that drove the Waltham Blacks to turn to deer stealing.

Caryll made frequent visits to several inns in Hampshire and Sussex. His favourite inn, the *Blacksmith's Arms*, was kept by a Mrs Howard in Portsea at Portsmouth and there was a presumed direct link through the inn with the

---

66 Windsor Castle, Royal Archives, Stuart MS 67/16, letter from Sir Henry Goring to James [III], 6/5/1723, quoted in full in Cruickshanks and Erskine-Hill, 'Waltham Black Act', pp. 359-60.

67 Abel Boyer, *The Political State of Great Britain*, (London, 1711-40), Vol. 25, p. 667.

68 L'Hermitage is a much respected primary source for this period, especially noted by Thomas Babington Macaulay, the English historian.

69 British Library, Additional MS 17677 KKK5, folios 548-9.

70 Cruickshanks and Erskine-Hill, 'Waltham Black Act', pp. 361-2.

smuggling Lavender family of Ropley.[71] In March 1723, Caryll was arrested for drinking to the Old Pretender's health in the inn, home of the latter's former nurse in Portsea and drinking toasts to 'Mrs Howard's nurse child'. An innkeeper in Horndean testified that Caryll held meetings with Goring who fled to France after the Jacobite Atterbury Plot had been discovered in August 1722.

Goring played a central part in the organisation of the Atterbury Plot and was sent by Atterbury to Rome to settle the final arrangements for invasion with the Pretender who promised him a peerage in the event of restoration.[72] Goring wrote in 1721 to the Duke of Ormonde who commanded the Irish troops in Spain: 'The whole kingdom begs a reprieve ... and if you would come with 1,000 soldiers and 10,000 arms, it is safe again.'

The plot was to erupt during the general election of 1722 linking domestic uprising with an invasion up the Thames by Ormonde. It did not develop well and by late March 1722 Atterbury had washed his hands of it as wild and impracticable.[73] Trelawny had been a good friend to Atterbury, but in the later years the relationship became increasingly distant as Atterbury took no pains to hide his Jacobitism.[74]

Walpole's own attitude to Jacobitism had been opportunistic. However, he did not hold the king's steadfast confidence so 'nothing was better calculated to fix him in the heart of that stupid but complicated and demanding sovereign than the "discovery" of a good-going Jacobite plot and the salutary, indeed preferably sanguinary, punishment of the plotters'.[75]

State papers throng with accusations of Jacobite plots, pamphleteers and secret agents. 'Soldiers were arrested, troops massed and big parades held in Hyde Park to raise the political temperature during and after the 1722 general election.' The judiciary was constantly interfered with especially in counties like Hampshire where juries might be suspect. Every agency of government from post office to the munitions works was thoroughly purged in order to weed out malcontents. Government supporting landlords in the counties were rewarded with encouragement to consolidate adjoining lands and to enclosure.[76]

In August, Atterbury was arrested and committed to the Tower where he remained for almost a year before being sent into exile. During this time, came the Black Act, the suspension of *Habeas Corpus* and the imposition of a £10,000 fine on Roman Catholics. 'Atterbury's full state trial for treason would have been an even more attractive propaganda coup, but Walpole found it very difficult to find evidence of sufficient weight to commit him.'[77]

71 TNA, State Papers, SP 35/42/309, 367, 369.
72 R. Sedgwick, *The House of Commons, 1715-54*, two vols. (London 1970), 2:72.
73 ODNB, Stephen Taylor, 'Walpole', 28601.
74 Smith, *Fighting Joshua*, pp. 147-8.
75 Lenman, *Jacobite Risings*. Fritz, *English Ministers*.
76 Monod, *Jacobitism*, p. 346.
77 Lenman, *Jacobite Risings*. Fritz, *English Ministers*. Broad, *Whigs and Deer-Stealers*, p. 68.

Walpole turned his investigation to the activities of Goring and Caryll at the inns in Horndean and Portsea, frequented by people disaffected to His Majesty and His Government. The Horndean innkeeper, William Basing, was arrested and turned king's evidence. A week later, Caryll was taken at his house near Petersfield.[78] Caryll confessed that Goring had told him the main outlines of the projected invasion.[79] Three witnesses testified that recruits were enlisted by a well-dressed man who gave the Blacks five guineas each, the promise of a horse, and a further fifteen shillings a week for the horse's feed. It was this discovery of the Jacobite allegiance of the Blacks, said L'Hermitage, that was the primary reason for the passing of the Black Act.[80]

Faced with charges that the Blacks were not only poachers but revolutionaries, 'judged by some who were in the Secret of Affairs to be in the Pretender's Interest and went about thus Arm'd to be prepar'd for a general Insurrection', his 'mock Majesty' gave out a message in a printed manifesto. King John claimed that he and his followers were 'faithful and true Subjects to their Liege Lord and Sovereign King George and would stand by the Succession in the illustrious House of Hanover to their last drop of blood'.[81] At their well-publicised parade on Waltham Chase, dressed in furs and mad hats, King John and his lesser royalty reinforced the loyal message.[82] Many historians took this disavowal at face value and dismissed any Jacobite connection.[83] In retrospect, the pantomime seems a barely-disguised piece of jovial insolence designed to deflect speculation and reprisal.[84]

The Blacks began and ended their activities in Farnham Park and Waltham Chase in personal conflict with bishops Trelawny and Trimnell. Half way between the two deer parks lay the smugglers' inland distribution centre of Ropley, inextricably linked through Trelawny's enclosure act with Farnham Park and through smuggling with the *Blacksmith's Arms* in Portsea where the Old Pretender's nurse lived. It is a real possibility that part of the Jacobite army comprising up to three regiments of dragoons of Hampshire Blacks, were to meet somewhere between Ropley, Bishop's Waltham and Petersfield while waiting for news of Ormonde's invasion, but melted away when the plot was uncovered. 'Sympathisers to the Jacobite cause would much prefer to rise in arms after the arrival in the British Isles of a substantial foreign professional army.'[85]

---

78 TNA, SP 35/42/302. Cruickshanks and Erskine-Hill, 'Waltham Black Act', pp. 363-5.
79 Boyer, *Political State of Great Britain*, 25:432-36.
80 British Library, Additional MS 17677 KKK5, folios 548-9. Monod, *Jacobitism and the English People*, p. 116.
81 Anon, *History of the Blacks*.
82 *Stamford Mercury*, 7/12/1723.
83 Broad, *Whigs and Deer-Stealers*, p. 71. Thompson, *Whigs and Hunters*. Richard Vann, 'Reviews', *American Journal of Legal History*, 21, 2.
84 Monod, *Jacobitism and the English People*, pp. 116-117. Cruickshanks and Erskine-Hill, 'Waltham Black Act', pp. 358-365.
85 Lenman, *Jacobite Risings*, p. 109.

Barbara Biddell speculates that there was a secret Jacobite society in Bishop's Waltham some twenty years later from 1740-6.[86] She also identifies other prominent Catholic Hampshire families: Matthew of Heath End, Petersfield and Sir Henry Tichborne of Tichborne, Alresford with their private chapels; Matthew Friend of Curdridge and John Friend of Ashton; Augustine Fisher of Bellmore farmhouse; William Fisher, Chawton; Francis Fisher, Durleigh; Edward Molton, Soberton; John Wybarne, South Stoneham; Mary and John Collins, Catherington; and Mary Cole, Catherine Glasspool and Henry Wells, in Twyford.[87]

Wells, a recusant, was arrested after he raised a glass in 1745 as the Jacobite rebels advanced into England.[88] At the height of the Jacobite alarm, constables were ordered by the Privy Council to bring all Catholics in Hampshire to the Guildhall in Winchester to swear the oaths of allegiance and their homes were searched for arms.[89]

At the same time, newspapers reported that the Blacks had reappeared in Hampshire, stolen deer and sheep and robbed parks.[90]

86 HRO, 30M77/PO4. Biddell, 'Jacobitism', pp. 235-9.
87 TNA, FEC (Forfeited Estates Commission).
88 TNA, SP 36/73, folios. 52-4; SP 37/83, folios. 9, 11, 200.
89 HRO, W/K5/7, *W. H. Jacob's Scrapbook*, No. 6, f. 1. Gibson, *Enlightenment Prelate*, p. 253.
90 *St James's Evening Post*, 5638, 8-11/3/1745.

5 STEALING FROM THE POOR

Understanding enclosure

In the Dark and Middle Ages,
If we trust to History's pages,
You might search the landscape round,
Not a hedge was to be found.
Instead of little tidy squares,
Mine, and his, and yours, and theirs,
My field, his field, your field, their field,
All formed one enormous bare field.[1]

Hampshire's countryside with its hedged and very private fields is seen by many today as quintessentially English. However, for those alive at the beginning of the eighteenth century when much of the county's arable land still lay in medieval open fields, it might seem a foreign landscape.[2]

All local land in 1709 at Ropley's enclosure had a legal owner. If land was held 'in severalty', the owner was free to use it as they wished. It seems likely that many did and gradually elbowed the poor from places where their cottages and gardens were inconvenient.

Some land, however, was subject to a form of communal right which restricted an owner's freedom of action. Joan Thirsk distinguished what she called 'common fields' from other kinds of land systems, identifying their four key elements: strips of arable for crops and meadows; pasturing on both immediately after harvest and during fallow seasons; joint rights over the 'wastes' or commons beyond the arable for foraging and grazing; and the administration of the whole complex system of usage and rotation by a manorial court or village assembly.[3]

Peasants' plots were scattered in a multitude of unfenced furlong strips; the most convenient length for a lumbering, cumbersome team of oxen that 'no ploughman would wish to turn more often than necessary'. The animals and men required made excessive demands on limited resources and so individual families had to work together. Having jointly equipped the plough, they naturally apportioned each day's finished land equally and in this way 'each man received a share of good and bad'. When allowed, commoners' stock often 'wandered unconstrained'.

---

1 R. H. Charles, *Punch* magazine
2 Chapman and Seeliger, *Formal and Informal Enclosures*, p. 1.
3 Thirsk, 'Common fields', pp. 3-4. Williamson, 'Jane Thirsk' in *Farmers*, p. 37.

Large landowners claimed that these common rights became so firmly entrenched in law that they came to constitute an 'insuperable obstacle to any change of use'.[4] 'Enclosure' was the process by which these communal rights were abolished and the land divided among the more powerful. Enclosure could be by agreement, by practice over time or by force. The latter could be easily employed in isolated villages with a dominant and determined lord of the manor who reduced the terms of access for cattle, the stint, or imposed a brute introduction. Writing in 1738, Thomas Andrews claimed that lords and richer freeholders had deprived many of the 'Meaner Sort of People whereby their Ancient Privileges are taken away and given to the rich'.[5]

> *The true interest of the nation was served by a society in which most people could live without wages. But here is a sharper criticism: enclosure impoverished twenty small farmers to enrich one. It reduced the size of holdings that were once nine or ten acres to only six or seven. Rents rose and prices followed. Commoners became labourers, mere 'tools'. Landlords grew lazy, some little better than tyrants who when they had less wealth were more sensible of their dependence and connections, and could feel for both the poor and the public upon every emergency.*
>
> *Their claim to the exclusive enjoyment of their land was nothing more than an excuse for shutting out the poor from their rights on the common fields, from gleaning, from getting turf and furze.*
>
> *And the fear: in destroying village relations, enclosure also endangered relations in the nation as a whole. It brought about an open dissatisfaction that risked mob rule and encouraged sedition, even Jacobitism. In essence, either farmers should have authority over those forced into labour or you believed in an independent peasantry able to set their own definition of happiness* [which might] *include gathering fuel, seen as wasted time when a wage would allow them to buy coal.*[6]

During the eighteenth and nineteenth centuries, most estimates suggest that just under 60 per cent of English agricultural land was enclosed, eight million acres by private agreement and six million by private parliamentary act. A further five million acres of English and Welsh waste land were enclosed.[7]

> *In short, the enclosure movement scythed through the British landscape, utterly transforming half or more of British land and the social relations that it sustained. By the time it was complete, precious little common land*

---

4   Chapman and Seeliger, *Formal and Informal Enclosures*, p. 1.
5   Andrews, *Enquiry ... Miseries of the Poor*, pp. 38-40.
6   Coventry, *Observations*, pp. 5-6, 8, 10-14.
7   McCloskey, 'Enclosure of Open Fields', pp. 15-16.

"I remember, before you children were born, we had rights of common in that field, and the one beyond. They were full of coppices where we collected kindling for cooking and the fire. We had two pigs rooting the land, and some chickens..."

remained, just 1½ million acres, or less than 3 per cent of all British land, when the Commons Act brought effective closure to the process.[8]

Ropley's act was the start of the 'final and most contentious wave' when parliamentary authority was added to the methods for the gentry and clergy to get their way. Private acts were sought when avenues to slip enclosure through without a fight seemed closed. They cut short difficult protests from the lower orders.[9] There was almost no appeal and those few complaints, as with Ropley, that made it to the ears of a landowning government always failed. Few could afford to fund opposition: the small man felt the burden of costs much more than the large proprietors. In a great injustice, he would naturally be shy of adding to enforced heavy expenses unless he stood a good chance to defeat the scheme.[10]

During the fourteen years from 1786 to 1799, 707 bills came before the House. None were defeated. Their fees amounted to £59,867 6s 4d, an average of £85. The money covered bill fees, small fees, committee fees, housekeepers' and messengers' fees and engrossing fees. The separate costs in the Lords amounted to near the same for bill fees, for the yeoman, usher, door-keeper, and order of committee and committee fees.[11] To these must be added all the local costs of lawyers, commissioners, surveyors, copyists and ground works. All in all, it could amount to £10 an acre, a 'crippling figure to all but the rich'.[12]

When the all-powerful commissioners had made their decisions, change on the ground was usually rapid. Where there were once large, communal open fields, new boundaries appeared. Land was now hedged, fenced off and gated. Private roads were built and footpaths opened to give access to landlocked estate. 'Keep Out' signs took root.

Faced with a debilitating and demeaning transformation, the small tenant farmer and the poor either gave in or were driven to violence. The enclosure riot was well established as an act of protest: hedge-levelling was seen as a 'national pastime'.[13] Any disorder could be deplored and put down by the gentry because they managed the clergy, the law enforcers, the local courts and administered the punishments.

There were originally far more commons in Hampshire than open fields. The parishes that would come to contribute to the formation of Four Marks–Chawton, Farringdon, Medstead, Newton Valence, Ropley and, slightly, East Tisted–each had upland commons with poor chalk and clay soils suited more for sheep pasture. They were sited alongside bracken-filled wastes, appreciated by pigs and geese, and stretched almost unbroken for six miles from Soldridge to

---

8 Cahill, *Who Owns Britain*, p. 37.
9 Fairlie, *Land*, p. 24.
10 Hammonds, *Village Labourer*, p. 52.
11 Hammonds, *Village Labourer*, p. 76, fn.
12 Bovill, *English Country Life*, p. 5.
13 Healey, 'Political Culture', p. 267.

the western edge of Newton Valence along what is now the Four Marks ridge. This ridge, an early drovers' way, was used for the seasonal passage of animal herds.

Primitive clearings were hacked for agriculture by the end of the Bronze Age.[14] When the Anglo-Saxons came the names they introduced 'were actually given to places that had been in existence very much earlier'. In Andreaswald, the great forest which covered much of Kent, Sussex and Hampshire, men settled in the denes or dens, which were hollows and valleys in the woods. They were attracted by the water and the shelter and by the ease of communication along the rivers. Some took to the high ground for protection and to gain easy access to the old roads. The surrounding unclaimed forest gave pannage and rough grazing. The whole of the local arable land was claimed at an 'infinite expenditure of manual labour from natural woodland'.[15]

The first farmers cleared the country of wood and scrub, providing grazing for their animals, and made land fit to grow corn. The farmer was not a politician, but first and foremost 'a hungry animal combining with his neighbours to wring a living from the land' and 'never certain until the harvest was gathered whether he would survive or starve in the ensuing year'.[16]

> *From these centres began the attack by man upon Nature, with inadequate weapons and at great personal cost and, little by little, the woodland gave way to pasture and to cultivated land, the process continuing until none of it was left except in places associated with the wetter or more intractable soils … The struggle must be continuous for land in a state suitable for agriculture is something entirely artificial and Nature, never finally subjugated, is ever waiting the opportunity to shake herself free from the costume of civilisation and to resume her first covering of woodland, water and wild grass. These 'deans', 'hursts' and 'steads' are indicative of these settlements in woods which have long since been cleared.[17]*

Among the Saxons, the pig was the most important source of meat with two fat animals killed and salted, one at the beginning of the winter, the other just before the coming of the spring.[18] Cattle came next in importance supplying milk for drinking, for butter making, and particularly for cheese. As late as Cobbett's day, cheese was still made by families for their own consumption. 'On the farm, if not the road, oxen were used for draught until the last 200 years. Their heavy shoulders and light quarters depicted in eighteenth-century illustrations, before the work of the early livestock improvers, show how work rather than beef was

---

14 Prior, *Britain AD*, pp. 192-4.
15 Orwins, *Open Fields*, p. 15.
16 Thirsk, preface, Orwins, *Open Fields*, p. vi.
17 Orwins, *Open Fields*, pp. 16-20.
18 Orwins, *Open Fields*, p. 56.

their first function. Chickens ran free. Sheep were kept more for their wool than for their mutton and might be milked. Medstead in the eighteenth century was a centre of the local wool industry.[19]

The problem of maintaining livestock along the Four Marks ridge has always been how to provide enough water and winter food. In hard times, effort centred on breeding and the young stock needed to replenish flocks and herds. There was a general killing of other animals as autumn drew on and fodder dwindled; carcases being salted for winter meat.

I have no penny for pullets for to buy,
Nor neither geese nor pigs, but two green cheeses,
A few curds and cream and an oaten cake,
And two loaves of beans and bran baked for my youngsters.
And yet I say, by my soul I have no salt bacon;
Nor no hen's eggs, by Christ collops for to make.
But I have parsley and leeks with many cabbages,
And a cow and a calf, a cart-mare also
To draw dung afield while the drought lasts,
With this for our living we must live until Lammas time come.[20]

The commons ran down the chalk slopes almost to the hearts of the circling villages and their more fertile valley land. The last great spread of woodland, Chawton Park, linked Medstead to Alton and held both the old Roman Road from London to Winchester and the rutted, busy and dangerous King's Highway leading to Bighton, Bishop's Sutton and Alresford.[21]

The ridge was a significant watershed. Rains to the north drained to one source of the Wey at Flood Meadows in Alton and from thence to the Thames. Move a few inches south on the ridge and the seepage fed the springs of the Arle at Bishop's Sutton and then the Itchen to reach the Solent. The southern slopes were dotted with old farms like Kitwood, Grove, Goatacre, Soldridge, Stankham and Pullinger which claimed the higher ground, or like Lymington, Brislands, Common, Budget, Kitfield, Cobb and Hawthorn, which lined the course of the ancient waterway along today's Lymington Bottom. This countryside held the patchwork remains of Andreaswald, like the woods of Weathermore, Old Down, Dogford and Plash. Sir John Gate in the sixteenth century surveyed Medstead and noted that it was 'very well wooded with great beeches and some oaks on every side of the great woods.'[22] William Cobbett in his *Rural Rides* described riding in 1825 from Alton to Alresford via Medstead 'in order to have fine turf

19 Moody, *Short History of Medstead*, p. 21.
20 Langland, *Vision of Piers the Plowman*. Collop: a slice of bacon.
21 Richard Whaley, edited, Vol. 3, Parts 1-3, 'Collected Reports on the Roman Road' (NEHHAS, 2018). M. T. Clanchy, edited, 'Highway Robbery and trial by battle in the Hampshire Eyre of 1249', in R. F. Hunnisett and J. B. Post, *Medieval Legal Records* (HMSO, London 1978).
22 *Victoria County History*, Vol. 3, pp. 327-9.

to ride on and to see, on this lofty land that is, perhaps, the finest beech-wood in all England'.

There were always avaricious landowners. Agricultural common land was enclosed from as early as the twelfth century as holdings were consolidated into individually-owned or rented fields. They were aided by the law amid the squabble for power. The *Statute of Merton* of 1235 is acknowledged as the first parliamentary statute. Its terms were agreed by Henry III in another example, along with *Magna Carta* twenty years previously, of the struggle by the barons to limit the king's rights. The statute allowed a lord of the manor to enclose common land provided that sufficient pasture remained for his tenants and also set out when and how lords could assert rights over waste land, woods and pastures.[23]

A number of early authorities identified that Hampshire in the north west and centre had early three-field open systems, for instance, in Lasham in 1336-7 and at East Tisted in 1334-5.[24]

During the Tudor period, owners saw enclosure as a more economical way of farming. The medieval large estate owners sought to convert arable open fields and communal pastures and 'cleared the small tenants from great tracts of land in order to create sheep pastures to profit from the thriving wool trade'.[25] After a period of disuse, the *Statute of Merton* was revived in 1550 by lords wishing to enclose their land at their own discretion. Villages were depopulated across England and several hundred all but disappeared, including, latterly, Hartley Mauditt, an old deer pasture, near Alton, and Colemore.[26] With the Stuarts, the intent of enclosure was the reclamation of old forest areas. Crown lawyers for the first Charles raised extra income by the enforcement of forest rights which had 'fallen into desuetude'.[27] Towards the end of the sixteenth and throughout the seventeenth centuries, Hampshire was one of the counties where extensive enclosure took place by Chancery decree.

Fields multiplied whenever new land was taken into cultivation from waste. As the parcels of each cultivator became more scattered, regulations had to be introduced to ensure that all had access to their own land and to water, and that meadows and ploughland were protected from damage by stock.[28] The community was drawn together by sheer necessity to co-operate in the control of farming practices. All the fields were brought into two or three large units. Regular

---

23 See also the *Statute of Westminster*, 1285.
24 Tate, 'Field Systems', p. 257; H. L. Gray, *English Field Systems*, frontispiece; Orwins, *Open Fields*, pp. 64-6.
25 Chapman and Seeliger, *Formal and Informal Enclosures*, p. 2. Dyer and Jones, *Deserted Villages Revisited*, p. 6.
26 Hartley Mauditt was first documented as *Herlege* ('hartland', a pasture for deer). The manor was granted to William de Maldoit (corrupted to 'Mauditt') by William the Conqueror and, later, owned by John of Gaunt, the Duchy of Lancaster, the Crown, and then, in 1603, Nicholas Steward, a politician and lawyer.
27 T. E. Scruton, *Commons and Common Fields* (1887), p. 112.
28 Tom Williamson, 'Jane Thirsk' in *Farmers*, p. 39.

crop rotation was agreed and it became possible to organise more efficiently the grazing of stubble and aftermath. Thereafter, the scattering of strips, which had at one time been a handicap, became a highly desirable arrangement since it gave each individual a proportion of land under each crop in the rotation.[29]

Leland discovered that a 'very considerable portion of Hampshire was in open field especially to the north of the county.[30] Defoe in 1724 noted that a good deal of the Hampshire down country had been converted from sheep walk to wheat land.[31] In 1756, Hale regarded Hampshire as a county whose agriculture cried out for further improvement, at any rate in its 'starving parts' which like similar areas of Wiltshire could be made as fertile as Buckinghamshire and Hertfordshire by enclosure.[32] Young, in his second tour of 1771, noted the land south of Winchester as poorly cultivated with unenclosed chalk hills, though, throughout the county, he saw turnips, clover and sainfoin, 'infallible indications of improved husbandry'.[33] The county agricultural survey in 1792 reported 'immense tracts' of open heath and uncultivated land which 'tend to remind travellers of voyages among barbarians'.[34]

Disputes over these common rights were frequent, believed by the poor and illiterate to be about 'time hallowed custom', but rejected by the landowners in 'time hallowed ways'.[35]

The peasantry responded with a series of ill fated revolts.[36] Enclosure was a secondary issue in the Peasants' Revolt of 1381, but in Jack Cade's rebellion of 1450, land rights were a prominent demand especially against the clergy. The first recorded written complaint against enclosure was made by a Warwickshire priest, John Rous, in his *History of the Kings of England*, published around the second half of the fifteenth century. The complaint was taken up sardonically in 1516 by Thomas More in *Utopia*, a vision of what should be rather than what was. Criticism of the selfish role of churchmen was a consistent theme in all complaints.

> *Your sheep that were wont to be so meek and tame and so small eaters, now, as I hear say, be become so great devourers and so wild, that they eat up and swallow down the very men themselves. They consume, destroy, and devour whole fields, houses and cities. For look in what parts of the realm doth grow the finest and therefore dearest wool, there noblemen and gentlemen,*

---

29 Thirsk, 'Common fields', p. 14.
30 John Leland, *John Leland's Itinerary: Travels in Tudor England*, edited, John Chandler (Sutton, Gloucester 1993; revised 1998).
31 Defoe, *Tour*, pp. 180, 187.
32 Thomas Hale, *Compleat Body of Gardening*, p. 100.
33 Young, *Eastern Tour*, Vol. III, pp. 204-41.
34 *General view ...*, pp. 13-15.
35 Thompson, *Customs in Common*, p. 104.
36 Tate, *English Village Community*, pp. 122-5. Andy Wood, *Riot, rebellion and popular politics in early modern England* (Palgrave, Basingstoke 2002).

yea and certain abbots, holy men no doubt, not contenting themselves with the yearly revenues and profits that were want to grow to their forefathers and predecessors of their lands, nor being content that they live in rest and pleasure, nothing profiting, yea, much annoying the weal-public, leave no ground for tillage: they inclose all into pastures; they throw down houses; they pluck down towns, and leave nothing standing but only the churche to be made a sheep-house. And as though you lost no small quantity of ground for by forests, chases, lands, and parks, those good holy men turn all dwelling places and all glebeland into desolation and wilderness.[37]

Robert Kett's rebellion began in Norfolk in 1549 and spread to Hampshire although little is recorded locally. Enclosure was a main issue; landowners' hedges destroyed.[38] Enclosure reared again in the 'Captain Pouch' revolts of 1604-1607 around Warwickshire, led by John Reynolds, when the terms *levellers* and *diggers* appeared, referring to those who levelled the ditches and fences erected by enclosers. 'Tudor and Stuart monarchs took note and introduced a number of laws and commissions which managed to keep a check on the process of enclosure.' Charles I was deemed 'the one English monarch of outstanding importance as an agrarian reformer'.[39] Prominent figures like Thomas Wolsey, Hugh Latimer, William Tyndale, Lord Somerset and Francis Bacon spoke out against the practice.[40]

In 1649, Gerrard Winstanley and fellow diggers started cultivating land on St George's Hill, Surrey, and proclaimed a free Commonwealth with a manifesto.

The earth (which was made to be a Common Treasury of relief for all, both Beasts and Men) was hedged into Inclosures by the teachers and rulers, and the others were made Servants and Slaves ... Take note that England is not a Free people, till the Poor that have no Land, have a free allowance to dig and labour the Commons, and so live as Comfortably as the Landlords that live in their Inclosures ... If the wasteland of England were manured by her children it would become in a few years the richest, the strongest and the most flourishing land in the world.[41]

'In some ways, the Diggers foreshadowed the smallholding and allotment movements of the late nineteenth and twentieth centuries and the *partageux* of

---

37 Moore, *Utopia*, p. 22, 1516, in *Three Early Modern Utopias* which includes Francis Bacon, *New Atlantis*, 1627, and Henry Neville, *The Isle of Pines*, 1668.

38 Wood, *Riot, Rebellion*, p. 61. Also E. Lamond, edited, *Calendar of the state papers domestic series of the reign of Edward VI* (1992), p. 58.

39 Tate, *English Village Community*, pp. 124-7.

40 Fairlie, *Land*, p. 20.

41 William Everard, *The True Leveller's Standard Advanced* (1649). Gerrard Winstanley, 'A Letter to the Lord Halifax and his Council of War' (Giles Calvert, 1649).

the French revolution – poor peasants who favoured the enclosure of commons if it resulted in their distribution amongst the landless.'[42]

Conflict over 'botes' or 'estover', small wood for fencing, building repair, fuel, or 'turbary', turves and peat for fuel, was never-ending, but only occasionally reached the courts or became a fight between villages. Thompson thought there 'cannot be a forest or a chase in the country which did not have some dramatic episode or conflict over common right in the eighteenth century'.

The soil itself, the land, was not the commoner's, but the use of it was. That use, what the law called a *profit à prendre*, was common right. It was a custom long held by those peasants who occupied the lowest rung on the property ladder. These peasants were the distinguishing mark of the old village; able to get a living, but who could never accumulate capital. They worked the land themselves, rarely employed others and shared a common culture: customary behaviour, joint agricultural practice, mutual aid and sometimes political solidarity.[43] They were relatively independent of wages, markets and poor relief.

Neeson and Thompson captured the commons way of life. 'The shifting components of their family incomes, the histories of their trades and manufactures, the balance of power in their villages, their very sense of who they were and how well they lived were all in part dependent' on the survival or decline of the commons.[44]

> *Custom passes into areas altogether indistinct – into unwritten beliefs, sociological norms, and usages asserted in practice but never enrolled in any by-law. This area is the most difficult to recover because it belongs only to practice and to oral tradition. It may be the area most significant for the livelihood of the poor and the marginal people in the village community. Customs and by-laws should not be taken to be an exhaustive accounting of the actual practice of common right usages, especially where these bear upon the fringe benefits of common, waste, the herbage of lanesides, to the landless inhabitants or the cottager. For these documentary sources are often partisan briefs drawn up by the lord's steward, or by the substantial landowners on the in-coming of a new lord; or they are the outcome of bargaining and compromise between several propertied parties in the manorial court, in which the cottager or the landless had no voice.[45] ... They are always made by parties having a positive interest in gaining the greatest extent of property possible.[46]*

---

42 Fairlie, *Land*, p. 21.
43 Neeson, *Commoners*, pp. 299-300, 313.
44 Neeson, *Commoners*, p. 1.
45 Thompson, *Customs in Common*, pp. 100-1.
46 Stacey Grimaldi, 'Report upon the Rights of the Crown in the Forest of Whichwood' (1838, section on 'timber and saplings within manors').

Commoners were poor, but they were not paupers; their cottages and commons were miniature farms. Most had some pasture, a slice of an arable field or fruit trees. 'The interest which a commoner had in a common was, in the legal phrase, to 'eat the grass with the mouths of his cattle'.[47] On the ground, the range of common produce was as broad as were the uses to which it was put. No defender of Commons assessed the retail value of commons until the late 1760s when it was put at a quarter to a third of the rent; the calculation varied considerably from place to place.[48]

The livestock of the open-field farmers was fed on the natural greenery of those parts of the parish which were not under the plough, the woodlands and waste of the parish that were over and above what was needed or were unfit by reason of soil or situation. All those who occupied lands in the common fields had the right to graze stock on the common wastes. 'As the needs of a growing community caused the fields to encroach more and more upon the wastes, the grazing rights were stinted with the number of animals and grazing time limited.'[49]

The wastes or commons were a source of fuel. The right to cut gorse or turf was valuable, but was often limited by how it was carried away, for instance, 'on their backs, but not otherwise'. Gorse, reeds and weeds were taken for fodder and litter and for firing ovens, bakehouses, lime and brick kilns and woolcombers' pots as well as cottage hearths and last-ditch winter fodder when bruised.[50] Commoners gathered furze from where they could.[51] It was particularly abundant and in the twentieth century showed old common land that had failed to be turned into valued pasture.[52]

Hazel brushwood was unfit for deer to browse on so forest keepers lost nothing when it was taken. Quick growing hazel made hurdles for folding sheep, to mend hedges and make fences. Thin tributary branches made good beanstakes; a long hazel rod tied around with holly sprigs made a chimney brush. On heathland, fern and bracken made ash balls to be used as lye for soap and its high potassium made it valuable as potash in glass-making and bleaching. It also made better litter than straw in the winter because it held less moisture and when stalls were cleared it could be composted and ploughed in. Its resistance to moisture made it a good base for a haystack, when set over stones, helping it dry quickly. Rodents had no appetite for it.

Shepherds left old ewes unshorn in order to keep them warm. The result was that by August these ewes trailed around pastures with 'disreputable clots of wool dropping off them'. This was the kind of wool commoners gleaned from common

---

47 Hailsham, ed., *Halsbury's Laws of England*, 1932.
48 Homer, *Essay*, p. 76
49 Orwins, *Open Fields*, p. 57.
50 Neeson, *Commoners*, pp. 166-69.
51 Vancouver, *General View*, p. 390.
52 Neeson, *Commoners*, p. 160.

pastures for spinning. As well as being free, it was tapered at both ends making a fine, even thread.

An acre of coppice when the hazel bushes were uncut could yield 30 cwt of nuts. Mushrooms were free for soups and stews, or dried, threaded and hung on the mantle pieces. Truffles sold at 2s 6d a pound. Herbs were used for cooking and healing: wild chervil, fennel, mint, wild thyme, marjoram, borage, wild basil, tansy, and young leaves for salads, hawthorn, sorrel, chicory, dandelion, burnet, nettles, catsear, goatsbeard, sow-thistle, fat-hen, chickweed, yarrow, charlock and goosegrass; and fruit plentiful: elder, blackberry, barberry, raspberry and strawberry, rosehip, haw and sloe.[53]

Most commoning economies were extinguished by enclosure at some point between the fifteenth and nineteenth centuries. The pace of the change was uneven. Much of England was still open at Ropley's turn in 1709, but most of it was enclosed by 1840.

Each case of enclosure was different, depending on the size and nature of the land affected, the motives and personalities of the participants and their ability to talk to each other with respect and understanding. Argument swayed back and forth over the years as enclosers sought the approval of government and educated opinion. It was one long public relations battle where the money, skills and access lay with the ruling landowners until the commons had all but disappeared.

The debate was straightforward, but all views leant heavily to one side or the other.[54] If you favoured enclosure, you believed that the open field system prevented improvement, for example the introduction of new breeds, new crops like clover and turnips and new practices like four course rotations. Commoners could never agree to innovate. You saw the waste lands and common pastures as worn out places, or full of scrub, and overstocked with half-starved beasts. Commoners were lazy and not inclined to work for wages: enclosure would force them into employment.

> For the most part the common fields were in a deplorable condition. An immutable system of cultivation had exhausted the fertility of most of them; no winter crops could be grown because from harvest till spring they were subject to common rights of pasture; a slovenly cultivator could poison his neighbour's land with weeds; the balks that divided strip from strip harboured twitch, thistles and other noxious weeds. The wastes were in no better shape. Often unstinted, there was no limit to the number of beasts that might be grazed on many of them. Where there were restrictions they were often ignored by large holders at the expense of the poor.[55]

53 Mabey, *Plants with a Purpose.*
54 Fairlie, *Land*, p. 24.
55 Bovill, *English Country Life*, p. 2.

Neeson noticed that the eighteenth century enclosers' excuse was always argued as the national interest, but never for the landlord's profit despite damning evidence.

In many cases, little improvement occurred. Money gained went for private pleasure, to deal with the heavy cost of Walpole's government, or to write off gambling debts.[56] Andrews said he was 'willing to excuse these Rich Men, as far as can be, from the Circumstances of the Times – The Publick Taxes, the Luxury of the Age, and Expensive Elections, do force, even, the Great to Shifts which their Forefathers knew nothing of; and almost every one is willing, where he can, to turn off the Burthen upon another, rather than bear it himself'.[57]

In the name of the national interest, improvers deplored the insubordination of commoners, the unimprovability of their pastures, and the brake on production represented by shared property.'[58] In many a village, it was claimed, an intransigent minority of one blocked the road to progress.[59] The national interest demanded harsh decisions. Timothy Nourse, an Oxford man and a Catholic priest, wrote nine years before the Ropley Act:

> *Commoners were very rough and savage in their dispositions, being of levelling Principles, and refractory to Government, insolent and tumultuous … more dangerous than mastiffs and stallions, they needed the same harsh treatment, civility was futile, it will be much more easy to teach a hog to play upon the bagpipes than to soften such brutes by Courtesy … Such men are to be looked upon as trashy Weeds or Nettles, growing usually upon dunghills, which if touch'd gently will sting, but being squeez'd hard will never hurt us … The commons gave only a lean and hungry soil to lean and hungry stock. The men, as the cattle, are unfit for the dairy or the yoke … Common field agriculture provided soldiers and sailors excellent good Food for Powder.*[60]

Or, to put it another way:

> *And you, good yeomen,*
> *Whose limbs were made in England, show us here*
> *The mettle of your pasture; let us swear*
> *That you were worth your breeding: which I doubt not;*
> *For there is none of you so mean and base,*
> *That hath not noble lustre in your eyes.*[61]

56 Hammonds, *Village Labourer*, p. 69.
57 Andrews, *Enquiry … Miseries of the Poor*, pp. 38-9.
58 Neeson, *Commoners*, p. 7.
59 Bovill, *English Country Life*, p. 3.
60 Nourse, *Campania Foelix*, pp. 15-19.
61 William Shakespeare, *King Henry V*, Act III, Scene 1

If you stood against enclosure, you knew that the common pastures and waste lands were the mainstay of the independent poor; overgrazing was often the fault of the wealthiest commoners, the very people agitating for enclosure. Experience showed that enclosure would enrich already wealthy landowners, increase rents, force commoners into low wage dependency on an uncaring gentry, depopulate the village, or drive the poor off the land and into urban slums. The Earl of Fitzwilliam spent over £10,000 in connection with his enclosure for which, thanks to increased rents, he gained a 30 per cent return.[62]

The difference in position was often irreconcilable. What was the advantage to a landowner in building an estate if there was no ready-made subservient workforce at hand to work it? The best a poor commoner could hope for was some form of recompense for their loss; 'even supporters of enclosure for conversion of arable land to pasture sought full and proper compensation'.[63] If a rural labourer's wages could not support his family, he must turn to the poor rates and these rates were gathered from all landowners whether involved in enclosure or not. The great landowner's profit was supported by low wages compensated for by his neighbours who had had little interest in enclosure.

Neeson contrasted the romance against the hard-headedness:

> *Sauntering after a grazing cow, snaring rabbits and birds, fishing, looking for wood, watercress, nuts or spring flowers, gathering teazles, rushes, mushrooms or berries, cutting peat or turf. When critics of commons weighed the value of a common they did so in their own terms, the terms of the market. They talked about wage labour or the efficiency of the market. But commoners lived off shared use of the land. To some extent they lived outside the market. They lived on invisible earnings.*[64]

There were good arguments on all sides for providing the dispossessed with sufficient land to keep a cow and tend a garden.[65] The land was available. It would have made very little impression upon the final settlement of most enclosure acts if areas of wasteland had been sectioned off and distributed as secure, decent-sized allotments to those who had lost their common rights. In a number of cases where this happened (for example in Farringdon in 1748, the village of Dilhorn or on Lord Winchelsea's estates), it was found that cottagers hardly ever needed to apply for poor relief. Moreover, it was shown by research conducted by the *Society for Bettering the Condition of the Poor* and the *Labourer's Friends Society* that smallholdings cultivated by spade could be more productive than large farms cultivated by the plough.[66]

---

62 Bate, *Clare*, p. 52.
63 Neeson, *Commoners*, p. 19.
64 Neeson, *Commoners*, p. 40.
65 Andrews, *Enquiry … Miseries of the Poor*, pp. 38-40.
66 Fairlie, *Land*, p, 26.

Often, compensation was egregiously withheld. Low-paid employment was the only option. This disagreement was about 'the worth of each class'; neither side doubted that enclosure turned commoners into labourers, but it left 'a bitter sense of betrayal amongst commoners'.[67] Andrews told a story foretelling the truck system applied to the navvies who built the nation's canal and railways.

> *... Going into the house of a poor neighbour, a woollen manufacturer, I saw several Loaves and some pieces of linen and taking them for Signs of Plenty began to congratulate the poor man. 'Ah! Sir,' said he, ''tis my Misfortune to have these. I am forced to take them of my Master instead of Money, for my Work. I told him there was a penalty imposed on a Master who pays in that Way ... He told of a Weaver who got a Warrant for his Master and forced him to pay in Money ... and the Master would let him have no more Work. He went to all the Masters round the Country, who refused him; nor had he been able to get any ever since, and must have starved or come to the Parish if he had not learned to work at Husbandry.*[68]

The argument whirled back and forth and became a controversial pamphlet war. An important, and successful, function of critics of the commons, and later on the reporters to Prime Minister William Pitt's new *Board of Agriculture*, was to change public opinion on the issue of enclosure, to turn it from hostility to approval. The Board 'was not a Government department, like its modern namesake, but an association of gentlemen, chiefly landowners, for the advancement of agriculture, who received a grant from the government'. Their writers were making a case rather than conducting an enquiry; 'exaggeration and licence played their part,' and they benefited considerably from state support.

The loudest voice for improvement was former failed farmer Arthur Young, the first Secretary of the Board of Agriculture, who set about publishing, in 1793, a series of *General Views on the Agriculture of all the Shires of England*. Tate observed, 'The ninety odd volumes are almost monotonous in their reiteration of the point that agricultural improvement has come through enclosure and that more enclosure must take place.' The public nature of the debate also raised a warning flag, and still does, that any anecdotal story about enclosure needs to recognise the partiality of its author. Little of enclosure debate was backed by hard evidence.

What became clear from both sides was that commoners were well-dispersed throughout the country; common right gave commoners an income and independence they found valuable; and the extinction of common right marked the decline of small farms and a transition from some degree of independence to complete dependence on a wage.[69]

---

67 Neeson, *Commoners*, p. 18.
68 Andrews, *Enquiry ... Miseries of the Poor*, p. 41.
69 Neeson, *Commoners*, p. 9.

The modernisers eventually won the argument by continuously identifying private parliamentary enclosure with the national interest and to such an effect that it became public policy in the middle of the eighteenth century. Private Acts began to flow and, from the 1750s, became the norm. The final and most contentious wave of land enclosures in England occurred between in the hundred years to 1850 and included the last local private act at Newton Valence in 1848.

It was all, said E. P. Thompson, 'a plain enough case of class robbery'. William Cobbett thought the 'poor were sacrificed and needlessly sacrificed'.[70] Arthur Young, who suffered a dramatic change of heart, declared,

> By nineteen enclosure bills in twenty [the poor] are injured, in some grossly injured. It may be said that commissioners are sworn to do justice. What is that to the people who suffer? ... It must be generally known that they suffer in their own opinions, and yet enclosures go on by commissioners, who dissipate the poor people's cows wherever they come, as well as those kept legally as those which are not ...
>
> The poor in these parishes may say, and with truth, Parliament may be tender of property, but all I know is, I had a cow, and an act of Parliament has taken it from me. And thousands may make this speech with truth.[71]

Commoners did not always object loudly to enclosure, but often they did. Of the smaller commoners many lost land as well as grazing. They lost a way of life, too.[72]

> These paths are stopt – the rude philistine's thrall
> Is laid upon them and destroyed them all
> Each little tyrant with his little sign
> Shows where man claims earth glows no more divine
> But paths to freedom and to childhood dear
> A board sticks up a notice 'no road here'
> And on the tree with ivy overhung
> The hated sign by vulgar taste is hung
> As tho the very birds should learn to know
> When they go there they must no further go
> This with the poor sacred freedom bade goodbye
> And much they feel it in the smothered sigh
> And birds and trees and flowers without a name
> All signed when lawless laws enclosure came.[73]

70 Thompson, *Working Class*, p. 237. Cobbett, *Rural Rides*. Also, well worthwhile for acerbity and poetry, Curtler, *Enclosure and Redistribution*; Neeson, *Commoners*; and Johnson, *Disappearance of the Small Landowner*.

71 Arthur Young, *An Inquiry Into the Propriety of Applying Wastes to the Better Maintenance and Support of the Poor* ... (1801), pp. 538-9.

72 Neeson, *Commoners*, p. 5.

73 John Clare, 'The Motes'.

John Clare, the enclosure poet, 1820
William Hilton, National Portrait Gallery, NPG 1469

6 THE FIRST OFFICIAL BITE OF MEDSTEAD COMMONS

The Soldridge private parliamentary enclosure, 1735-36

Phsaw! Thou wert vulgar – we are splendid now.
Yet, poor man's pudding – rich with spicy crumbs,
And tiers of currants, thick as both my thumbs, –
Where are thou, festal pudding of our sires? –
Gone, to feed fat the heirs of thieves and liars[1]

Medstead, a border parish with Ropley, underwent at least three, four, or continuous, eighteenth century enclosures. It is likely more than 1,000 acres were involved. On two occasions, in 1735 and 1798, private parliamentary acts were organised as mainly external gentry were concerned that village opponents would hinder their plans. Damage to village life and landscape was extensive as landowners, backed by peers in London, had their way. Ropley's legacy, the bill of 1709, which told lies and ignored the majority wishes of its commoners, provided the pattern for most that followed in this quiet and probably unsuspecting corner of Hampshire. This chapter discusses the enclosure act and its award of 1736. They are fully transcribed in *Appendices 10-11*.[2]

Following the Ropley enclosure with its very public challenge in the House of Commons, a divided village and slow implementation, few landlords nationally were quick to move to all out attack. Whisps of evidence of much quieter local enclosure, enforced by the clergy and gentry, came from the villages of Bishop's Sutton, Bighton and Wield.

In Bishop's Sutton, Thomas Hawsted surrendered to his lord at a relaxed Winchester court in 1615 a close of purpresture land gained by encroachment from the commons at *Ramscombes*, Ranscombe. Hawsted had just built a cottage for Robert Mason who was to pay £40.[3] In 1685, the bishop of Winchester, Peter Mews, informally enclosed about 300 acres in Bishop's Sutton.[4] The commissioners were William Godwin and Henry Budd. By 1725, half the parish was lost by the commoners.[5] Soon after 1733, the gentry shut off the main North and South open fields; a glebe terrier contains their last clear reference.[6]

---

1 Ebenezer Elliott, 'Feast of the Happy Village! Where are thou?'.
2 Award: HRO, 21M65/I/2/A/157.
3 HRO, 11M59/C2/54.
4 Montgomery, HGS, *Bishops Sutton*, 68, pp. 10-11.
5 HRO, 58M71/E/B37.
6 HRO, 35M48/16/29. Montgomery, HGS, *Bighton*, p. 4.

Labourer Richard Cranston walked the boundaries to support his claim to two purrocks which had been enclosed for three years and which abutted Medstead Common and Stancombe.[7]

A memorandum of 1742 records a disagreement about 'lately made' enclosures in the common fields, a double fence and a quickset hedge having been built by a mason from Old Alresford.[8] Litigation was threatened in order to secure a 'speedy stop', but the fields were nevertheless ultimately shut.[9]

Two small unofficial enclosures took place in 1745 and 1776 in Bighton under one of two lords of the manor, father and son, the Dukes of Buckingham.

A map of the estates of George Bridges Rodney and others in Upper Wield of 1779 'provides a tantalising hint at some kind of more formal enclosure': open fields called Coppice Field, Middle Field and White Lain Field with part of the latter marked as 'an allotment to Lord Portsmouth in respect of estate held by lease of Lord Rodney'.[10] Elizabeth Gibson gives a detailed account of other piecemeal enclosures and confirms completion by 1799 when 'produce was almost double than when the lands were in common and more labourers are employed'.[11] A surrender dated 1821 refers to lands 'formerly in diverse common fields but now enclosed'.[12] Bingley's *History*, compiled between 1807 and 1813 confirms that the parish was enclosed by that time.[13]

One suspects enclosure was often a careless presumption in these agricultural backwaters. The Buckinghams in Bighton were absentee landlords. They were prime examples of all that was distasteful in the English aristocracy, cloaking themselves in arrogance, debt, illegitimacy and dangerous seduction, including among royalty and their neighbours.[14] One Buckingham, with three local clergy, became notorious in a renowned case of poaching injustice which his victim, Richard Deller, an Easton farmer, took to parliament to seek redress.[15] Appropriately for this short-lived third creation of the dukedom, the family descended from Sir Edmund Sheffield, a second cousin of Henry VIII, who was killed in the streets of Norwich during Kett's Rebellion against land theft by the gentry.[16] John, the father, a solider, sailor, poet, one-time Jacobite and Tory politician, was so unpopular that rumour described how, when ordered to relieve Tangiers, he was given a rotten ship in the hope he would not return. He died in 1721 in his home in St James's Park on the site of the current royal palace. Edmund, the son, died of tuberculosis in Rome in 1735.

---

7 HRO, 13M53/1.
8 HRO, 10M54/108.
9 Chapman and Seeliger, *Formal and Informal Enclosures*, p. 4.
10 HRO 105M88/3. Chapman and Seeliger, *Formal and Informal Enclosures*, p. 4.
11 Gibson, 'Rodney Family'.
12 HRO 38M48/159.
13 HRO 16M79/25.
14 Wikipedia.
15 'Petition of Richard Deller', Hansard, 25/4/1823.
16 Wikipedia, Dukes of Buckingham.

Admiral Rodney of Avington Park, Hampshire, was lord of the manor of Wield, inherited from his wife, Jane Compton. Her sister, Elizabeth, married Henry Drummond, who played a leading part in the second parliamentary enclosure of Medstead in 1798. Rodney was a brilliant and flawed seaman, renowned for his successful naval battles, much criticised by his subordinates for his arrogance and for his devotion, above all, to gaining prize money. Addicted to gambling like his father, he was much in debt through buying his parliamentary seats and a 'foolish agreement' with a loan shark ruined him. Rodney's soldier father was a politician and a Jacobite, entertaining the second Charles at Avington, and who lost heavily in the South Sea Bubble. Rodney's mother was the notorious mistress of the Duke of Buckingham of Bighton.[17]

The first Medstead parliamentary act, passed in 1735 with the award made the following March, was a rapid piece of work.[18] The wording and arrangements showed that careful attention had been paid to its parent in Ropley. It was planned to cover a similarly sized area: an estimated 500 acres of 'certain Commons or Tracts of Waste Grounds called Stankham and Soldridge Common', although the exercise eventually scooped just over 650 acres, an increase of about a third.

Old Alresford Manor comprised almost all the modern parishes of Old Alresford and Medstead and part of the parish of Wield, except that in Medstead the land was dotted by pieces belonging to Winchester College under the Manor of Ropley. Medstead Manor was large, 3,671 acres, gravel at its lowest levels around its streams giving way to loam on chalk on the drier uplands where wheat and oats were grown.

The primary protagonists in the 1735 Medstead enclosure act were the lord of the manor of Old Alresford, Benjamin Hoadly, also bishop of Winchester and patron of the rectory of Old Alresford, which included Medstead; and John Shackleforth, lord of its subsidiary or 'inferior' manor of Medstead. This pair were closely supported by the Warden and Fellows of Winchester College, the President and Fellows of Magdalen College in Oxford and Joseph Soley, Rector of Old Alresford. Of course, the wardenship and the rectory were both in the gift of the bishop.[19]

Perhaps Shackleforth doesn't bear tracking too closely. For whatever reason, death or cashing in, the lordship was in the hands of Edward Rookes by 1744 when he led a village 'perambulations and treadings' of his new manor (*Appendix 15*).[20] Rookes was accompanied by his steward Thomas Peace and several parishioners, who on Rookes's instruction made over twenty 'ancient bound crosses cutt a fresh' to restate the boundary points. Among the parishioners were

---

17 Wikipedia, the Rodney family.
18 Private Act, 9 George II, c. 19, HL/PO/PB/1/1735/9G2n47; HRO, 109A05/PX/10.
19 Gibson, *Enlightenment Prelate*.
20 HRO, 107M89/22, 9/10/1744.

several of the participants, like Richard Wake, aged sixty, and John Budd of Trinity, aged seventy, named in the enclosure act.

Hoadly is an interesting character, a more important and nuanced man than Trelawny, his rapacious predecessor. Hoadly is a dichotomy: a man of intellect and evident charity, yet one who signed approval for the first Medstead act of enclosure surely knowing the consequences. The national public debate on the unfairness, even wickedness, of enclosure, was in full flurry around him. Perhaps he was distracted.

Hoadly hated that the sacrament of communion was being used as part of a legal examination for gaining political power. In 1735, the year of the Medstead act, he published *A Plain Account of the Nature and End of the Sacrifice of the Lord's Supper*, against the warnings of friends. Next year, he repeated his arguments for the repeal of the *Test Acts*, which provided onerous religious examinations for people seeking any public office, and was designed to keep Roman Catholics and dissenters out of power. Three years later, Hoadly published his full position.[21] Although Hoadly seemed 'unabashed at the storm he had unleashed', opprobrium was heaped upon him.[22]

Those who disparaged Hoadly at the time or later were unforgiving.[23] He was condemned as 'the worst bishop of Winchester'.[24] Sir Leslie Stephen, the Victorian editor of the *Dictionary of National Biography* described him as probably 'the best-hated clergyman of the century amongst his own order' and as popular as a 'trades unionist who should defend his masters'. 'Had Hoadly been honest and honourable he would have withdrawn from the Church.'[25] G. R. Cragg, reviewing Hogarth's portrait of Hoadly, claimed the bishop's advancement was 'perhaps the most savage indictment of the eighteenth century Church' ... and that his face betrayed 'lust of the flesh, the lust of his eyes and the pride of life ... depicted with merciless candour'.[26] Herbert Vaughan in a biographical chapter written in 1931 accused Hoadly of pluralism, nepotism and absenteeism.[27]

On all three of Vaughan's charges, Hoadly stands convicted. By pluralism, Vaughan likely meant appointing favoured clergy to multiple livings of which more shortly. But another pluralism was at the heart of his philosophy and many today would see this as being to his great credit. The idea that individuals, with different beliefs could worship independently without fear of state or church repression infuriated his high church colleagues. They wished to draw up the

---

21 Hoadly, *Objections Against the Repeal of the Corporation and Test Acts Considered* ... . Rutherford, 'Sacramental Tests'. Gibson, *Enlightenment Prelate*, pp. 236-7. Only those people taking communion in the established Church of England were eligible for public employment. Severe penalties met those who refused to comply.

22 Gibson, *Enlightenment Prelate*, pp. 247-8.

23 Pugh, 'Hoadly', p. 243.

24 John Hervey, *Lord Hervey's Memoirs* (1952), pp. 160-1.

25 Vaughan, *From Anne to Victoria* (Methuen 1931).

26 Earl of Ilchester, *Lord Hervey and his friends, 1726-1738* (John Murray, London 1950), p. 149.

27 See also Pugh, 'Hoadly', p. 243.

pastoral drawbridge against, not only all papists, but against all dissenters, too, no matter how small the doctrinal differences. Hoadly was for a more inclusive church and was firmly in favour of liturgical reform, laxity some would say, to achieve it.[28] However, welcoming Catholics into the fold of God would always be a step too far.

On nepotism, at Winchester, several senior family appointments were made. Hoadly's son John, aged twenty-five, the 'apple of his father's eye', was appointed chancellor of the Diocese of Salisbury in 1735 and ordained a deacon in the next month.[29] John was appointed chaplain to the Prince of Wales on Boxing Day and then, in swift succession in 1737, livings at Michelmersh, Wroughton, Alresford (which included Medstead) at £400, a prebend at Winchester and, in 1743, St. Mary's, Southampton, at £600, in 1746 Overton, and in 1760 the Mastership of St Cross Hospital in Winchester, a lucrative sinecure.

The sum of all these gifts made bishop Hoadly complicit in another sort of blind pluralism as he showered livings on his son. John Hoadly, to be fair, was reported to maintain high standards of clerical duty, carefully tending his cures, and ensuring that curates took the services. He was meticulous in repairing his parsonages and churches, in two cases entirely rebuilding them and in one case endowing it against future repair.[30] However, Duthy said Medstead's St. Andrew's church in 1839 was a rude old structure, gnarled and plastered and patched all over with modern repairs amidst which a few features peep out hinting at its remote origin.[31] Moody in 1932 described the curate's cottage as 'quaint in the extreme with dormer windows and an interior which reflects its suitability as an old-time parsonage. Visitors are struck with its peaceful atmosphere.'[32]

John Hoadly was appointed just in time to help oversee the implementation of his father's enclosure of Medstead, an implementation named in the act to conclude by 25 March 1737. John also inherited Medstead's long serving curate, Stephen Stephens, in post since 1702.

On absenteeism, Benjamin Hoadly's visits to Hampshire were occasional, even rare. He spent most of his time in his fashionable town residence, Winchester House, in Cheyne Walk, Chelsea, overlooking the Thames. Here, Hoadly was close to the political centre and able to represent himself in his many controversies. Much of his lack of mobility may be attributed to his lifelong lameness which meant that he was unable to ride a horse.[33] He did visit Farnham Castle, indeed he married there, but perhaps only because of the vicious reaction in the capital to a bishop being so shameless as to marry a second time.[34]

---

28 Gibson, *Enlightenment Prelate*, pp. 254-5.
29 Gibson, *Enlightenment Prelate*, pp. 250-1.
30 Southampton Record Office, PR5/1/1, 2, 18 and 6/1.
31 Duthy, *Sketches of Hampshire*, pp. 100-1.
32 Moody, *Short History of Medstead*, p. 17.
33 Pugh, 'Hoadly', p. 246.
34 Gibson, *Enlightenment Prelate*, p. 249

Crocodile tears: Was it a good thing that the parson should be put in the position of a farmer, that he should be under the temptation ... that he should be relieved from a system which often caused bad blood between him and his parishioners? Would it make him neglect the sacred forms of his ministry? ¥

¥ Hammonds, *Village Labourer*, p. 56.

By contrast, Hoadly's reputation in the United States was such that he is today seen as 'one of the intellectual fathers of the American Revolution', linked to Abraham Lincoln's pronouncements and someone who directly influenced the form of the *Declaration of Independence*.[35]

Bishops waxed fat on their lands, as did rectors on their tithes. Hoadly derived a large income from his estates.[36] 'His chief source of wealth apart from rents being the woods and coppices, the great pond at Alresford, fisheries and mills.'[37] He may not have been so distanced from the countryside for he advised a protégée not to give up a church living in the autumn because it would be far better to move 'at a time of year when the main harvest will be his'.[38]

The church had to play an active role in the enclosure following Hoadly's lead role in the published act. The church door of the chapelry at Medstead was the board to which all notice of meetings over the assessment period had to be fixed.

> *The said Commissioners ... are hereby required to give Notice at the Door of the Parish Churches of Old Alresford and Medstead upon some Sunday Morning immediately after Divine Service, of the Time and Place of the first Meeting of the said Commissioners for the executing of the Powers herby vested in them at least Ten Days before such Meeting.*

The rector and curate, as future landowning beneficiaries, and knowing the bishop and commissioners personally, would be the obvious sounding ground for village concerns. If there were questions or discontent about the enclosure, or the role of the church in the process, or indeed the very authority of the established church, here was a potential flashpoint. Not all people submitted willingly to Church discipline, but the Church's response was stern. Between 1700 and 1755, the diocese issued 101 writs of excommunication, the vast majority either for refusal to submit to punishment for defamation or for failure to undertake administrative functions such as the exhibition of inventories for tithes and the disbursement of legacies following probate.[39]

Hoadly's diocese was accounted 'an opportunity lost' for Methodism. Even the hotbeds of Wesleyanism in London did not influence Hoadly's northern domain across the river in Surrey.[40] There is no found evidence of trouble in Medstead despite John Wesley's stand against enclosure, but then murmurings may not have been recorded. Wesley had a low view of his Hampshire audiences and referred to them as like 'the wild beasts of Ephesus', 'slow of heart and dull of

35 Gibson, *Enlightenment Prelate*, pp. 34-5.
36 Rathbone, *Chronicles*, p. 50.
37 VCH (London 1908), Vol. 3, pp. 304-6. This version of the county history also declares that there was no enclosure in Medstead.
38 Gibson, *Enlightenment Prelate*, p. 259.
39 HRO, 21M65, C13/2/1-101.
40 Ward, *Parson and Parish in Eighteenth Century Surrey*, pp. xi-xiii.

understanding' and 'dead stones'.[41] In 1753, he exclaimed in Portsmouth, 'I was surprised to find so little fruit here after so much preaching.'[42]

Hoadly's strategy of the 'better' pluralism bore fruit. Ten former dissenters received ordination to the Anglican priesthood in the diocese of Winchester during the eighteenth century. Four of these confirmed during Hoadly's episcopate and had previously been dissenting ministers.[43] With them, they brought the laity in scores.[44] By the end of the eighteenth century, Hampshire's Christianity was still overwhelmingly that of the Church of England.[45]

Medstead's first parliamentary enclosure made fifty awards in ninety-six pieces to thirty-four individuals and to one group. The land stretched from the border with Bighton, through Stankham and Soldridge, along the London Road and Ropley border to almost the centre of Medstead village, where the main commons were left untouched for now. Within the lands to be enclosed there were both commons for pasture and open fields with shared furlong strips of long usage. A rental of Nicholas Wyard of lands he held in Medstead in 1391 shows these fields and furlongs for the first time with the farmers and owners. Strip farming was practised over seventy acres, divided into forty plots:

> ½ an acre in furlong called Ton furlong opposite Sowycom ... 7½ acres + ½ acre near Rycroft ... Another acre between the land of Robert Bud and Joye [?] in a field called Pays Feld ... 1 acre in furlong versus Stancumbe between the land of Walter Day and Golfridi Horesbarne.[46]

Those few open fields which survived 1736 were taken by the second parliamentary enclosure in 1799.[47] Finding physical traces of land lost is relatively difficult in Hampshire. 'Ridge and furrow' undulations in pasture ground are extensive in the Midlands, but the 'survival of these marks is dependent on formal arable being left unploughed as pasture and in Hampshire most of the old open fields have continued in arable use'.[48] The ploughing-up campaigns of the First and Second World Wars were responsible for the destruction of much remaining evidence. Most difficult of all to trace on the ground are the lost commons. Often the plots were simply absorbed into adjoining fields. Where much of the land

41 F. Baigent & J. Millard, *A History of Basingstoke* (Basingstoke 1899), Vol. 2, p. 547.

42 For details of the High Church attacks on dissenters in Hampshire in the eighteenth century, see W. Gibson, 'A Happy Fertile Soil which bringeth forth Abundantly: The Diocese of Winchester, 1689-1800' in J. Gregory & J Chamberlain, editors, *The National Church in Local Perspective: The Church of England and the Regions, 1660-1800* (Woodbridge 2002).

43 A.J. Willis, editor, *Winchester Ordinations, 1660-1829* (Folkestone 1964), Vol. 1.

44 Gibson, *Enlightenment Prelate*, p. 266.

45 Ward, *Parson and Parish*, p. xxxviii.

46 Rathbone, *Chronicle*, p. 24.

47 Rathbone, *Chronicle*, p. 29; a terrier of Medstead tything made by the newly-installed rector, William Buller, in 1776.

48 Neeson, *Commoners*, p. 171.

was unsuitable for arable farming, encroachment into the wastes provided the characteristic pattern of cottages and small plots.[49]

As at Ropley, there is no enclosure map at Medstead although there would have been one at least showing all the surveyor's calculations. However, in the way of the time, it was the written word which counted and much effort was taken to list the various allotments and instructions. Prior to 1845, there was no general system in place for the recording of parliamentary awards.[50] Private Acts allowed for the parties to make their own arrangements for keeping the award and, from the middle of the eighteenth century, a copy was normally deposited with the Clerk of the Peace of the county, or in the local church, or both. There were often many copies in circulation for each participant was entitled to his own. The Clerk's copy is now usually to be found in the county archive, in this case the Hampshire Record Office. It is written in at least three hands. While writing style was standard, these different clerks with their degrees of haste and care cause some confusion on the spelling of names of people and places. Capitalisation is random and often ornate. The transcription in the appendices will no doubt have some errors. Additionally, there is a rework of the award, taking each recipient in turn called the Commissioners' Allotment.[51]

Unusually, six commissioners are named (three is more the norm), all landowning stalwarts: The Honourable Edward Stawell, Norton Pawlett, Norton Pawlett junior, Thomas Bonham, Robert Cropp and William Yalden, who had experience as a failed petitioner at Ropley.

If the commissioners' work was to be equitable then each allottee had to have 'land of proportional monetary value, regardless of extent and area'. Medstead's open fields varied in quality. The scattered strips would have gone a long way to ensuring quality differences were shared among holders. As consolidation was a principal aim of enclosure, there was a 'danger that a holder would receive a new block solely within a good or bad area'. Compensation was calculated by varying the quantity allotted to each individual.

Commissioners also needed to establish the status of the land since illegal encroachments, normally those made within the previous twenty-one years, were held to remain part of the common land.[52] The problems of landless labourers deprived of access to the commons were sometimes ameliorated by allocating land for the 'labouring poor'. Other benefits of commons, such as the collection of fuel, were only formally written into enclosure legislation from 1845.

It seems that the proprietors in 1735 had experienced some opposition to their plan and reached for an act to close the door on the troublemaker(s). They claimed that they had the 'sole right of commoning and de-pasturing their cattle

---

49 Chapman and Seeliger, *Formal and Informal Enclosures*, p. 17.
50 Chapman and Seeliger, *Formal and Informal Enclosures*, p. 8.
51 HRO, 87M87/98.
52 Chapman and Seeliger, *Formal and Informal Enclosure*, p. 11.

therein, exclusive of all other persons whatsoever' and that they had agreed to enclosure because it would 'tend to the publick good and be a great advantage to the several parties' concerned. There was a significant 'but' as they admitted that the matter 'cannot be effectually settled to answer the Intention of the Parties interested in the said Commons or Wastes without the Aid and Authority of Parliament'. This was an expensive step and indicated worrying dissention. The owners authorised the commissioners to inspect the 'yearly Value of each Person's Estate', the land tax and Poor Rates and to 'inform themselves by every other way they shall think proper and necessary'.

There was also an air of determination and threat.

> *When the said Commissioners shall have fully completed ... the said Partitions ...* [they] *shall at all Times hereafter be admitted and read as Evidence in all Courts whatsoever ... and that every Person ... shall accept the Part allotted to him within six months ...* [if refused they] *shall absolutely forfeit the Part ... allotted ... and shall be entirely excluded from all Benefit, Right of Common, Estate, or Interest in any of the Lands ... and then and in such Case, the Part ... shall be divided amongst the rest of the Persons ... proportionably.*

Likewise any husband, trustee, guardians, attornies or committee of any person under coverture, under-age, idiot, lunatic, or beyond the seas, or otherwise incapable by law had the same six months to get their act together or forfeit. It really was a case of 'Do or Die'.

In the 1736 Medstead award, each allotment, its recipient and its size, is baldly stated with a list of abutting lands, few of which are given names. Here is a simple example:

> *To John Doary for his freehold* [is given] *fifty perches:*
> * *The land of the widow Stooll on the North,*
> * *The land of William Sawkins on the East,*
> * *The land of Joseph Smith on the South, and*
> * *The Road leading from the London Road towards Medstead on the west*

It follows that each award is like a piece of a jigsaw with the allotment in the middle and, at least, one property given for identification on each of the four compass points. These surrounding lands could be other allotments or could be land with no connection other than proximity to the enclosure. With a large table and patience, something useful might be achieved. The task of developing a reconstructed map is a complex one and probably needs the commitment of someone who knows the area well.

One of the many useful clues occurs with roads. In the example, for instance, London Road is named, and together with His Majesty's Highway, features twenty five times. Land under the estates of Winchester College and Magdalen

College, Oxford, are painstakingly given as are boundaries to land in Bighton and Ropley parishes. Several allotments concerned straight copyholds, copyholds of inheritance, of lives, and leaseholds of a thousand and two thousand years.

Four landowners were to be immediately enriched by the enclosure taking together 53 per cent of the commons and open fields: Shackleford, lord of the manor, 107 acres, 16 per cent; John Barnard of New Alresford, 86, 13 per cent; John Budd of Tenantry, 76, and John Budd of Lower House, 73, both 12 per cent, and both of Medstead. Some twenty-six dells, other stony ground and land taken by roads, almost six acres, were identified as lost to waste or spoiled. Other land was given in compensation. Dells, mostly old chalk workings, were seen as valueless.

Eight other farmers received substantial portions of the commons: Richard Wake, 47 acres; John Burnell, 38; John Hicks, 36; John Price, 33; John Budd of Shalden, 20; John Bulbeck, 28; John Camois, 24; and William Budd of Soldridge, 12.[53] Armiger Baily was given five acres instead of his 'twenty Sheep Commons and two Hog Commons in the Bishop of Winchester's late Wood call'd Stankham'. All these beneficiaries were taking land based on their previous ownership of the commons; the amount bore no relation to their holdings elsewhere in Medstead and in other places which may have been substantial in their own right.[54]

The Budd family, if a cohesive unit, amassed over 30 per cent of these newly enclosed commons. Their lands are identified over fifty times within the document.

The two clergymen, Joseph Soley, John Hoadly's immediate predecessor as rector, and his curate and employee, Stephen Stephens, swapped their glebe and other lands for almost four acres. Stephens's home and landholdings can be found in a glebe terrier of November 1695, forty years earlier, and may have been unchanged.[55] The terrier was signed by John Carter, Stephens's predecessor as curate and in post from 1613 to 1702.

One cottage containing three little rooms on the floor below and two little rooms above stairs with one little garden and the feed of the Churchyard. And one barn containing six bays of building and the yard wherein it standeth bounded on the east with a Meadow belonging to Henry Budd of Maydsted and on the west, north and south with the street of highway. From one acre and a half of arable ground in the Upper Church Field. And one little acre in

---

53 Camois is a surname variously spelled during these awards and, particularly, in later enclosures: Camice, Camiss and Camish.
54 This category of nine people probably includes James Budd, 8 acres; his brother John, 5; widow Elizabeth Pryor, 6; John Finden, 5; John Spencer, 4; William Pryor, 4; Richard Bone, 4; William Skinner, 3; and Mary Budd of Ropley, 3.
55 HRO, 21M65 E15/94/2.

the Lower Church Field. And one quarter of an acre in the same field [and other small pieces of field adding to] *five and a quarter acres.*

Richard Wake of High-Holmes, John Budd of Tenantry, Elizabeth Prior, widow, John Spencer and John Prior were all named in a separate document as Winchester College tenants who benefitted from the enclosure.[56]

There the dispensations might end except for some unusual and interesting items, not hidden, but mentioned matter-of-factly within the text.

First, there had been at least two undated enclosures previous to 1736, no doubt informal, and acquired by a, perhaps, mild application of force. Part of John Shackleford's allotment of over one hundred acres bordered his already 'enclosed lands'. John Budd of Shalden's newly enclosed twenty acres abutted 'an enclosure of his own'.

Second, the interests of the poor received a lot more care than at Ropley. There is evidence to suggest that lessons from the 1709 enclosure had been, at least, heard. Perhaps bishop Hoadly's beneficial influence, or the experience of William Yalden, played a part. The care surfaced in several ways.

The first allotment listed in 1736 was forty perches in Soldridge Bottom, a quarter of an acre, 'little more or less', 'left waste to the poor of Alton' so that it could be foraged and used as wild pasture. It provides a small mystery. William Curtis in his *History of Alton* of 1896 describes a charitable donation to the town's poor as,

Half an acre of land behind a barn called Spital Barn. An acre of land in Medstead lying in a field called Middle Field, and near a stile called Bar Stile.[57]

In a side note, Curtis says the half acre was sold in 1873; the acre commuted in 1824 into a tithe payment of five shillings a year by Mr. Budd, 'but this has not been paid for many years'. Rathbone then quotes from the Medstead's rector's terrier of 1776 that a quarter of an acre in Bath Stile furlong was given by two maiden ladies at a time when the Plague [1665-6?] was so bad in Alton that the streets were green with grass. The occupier of the land was William Budd of Tenantry (*Appendix 25*).'[58]

The remaining ten of the thirty-five allotments in the 1736 awards were all of small amounts: John Harrison, 2.59 acres; Thomas Hockley, 2.32; Edward Woolls, 1.91; William Sawkins, 1.89 acres in two lots; John White, 1.27; John Beagley, half an acre; and Nicholas Wilks, John Doary and Joseph Smith, 50 perches each. Notwithstanding that any of these men, certainly like Edward Woolls, could have rich holdings elsewhere, what we see is a recognition of the

---

56 Winchester College, I/2/A1/157.
57 Curtis, *History of Alton*, p. 111.
58 Rathbone, *Chronicle*, p. 30. HRO, 32M94/1/71.

small encroachers who had nudged their cottages onto the Commons and were tolerated and, perhaps, valued.

During the eighteenth century, the produce of a cow over the course of a year could be worth almost half as much as the wages of a fully employed male agricultural labourer.[59] Most common right cottages came with rights to two cows and could therefore have given significant independence. Arthur Young in the course of his travels came to realise that in those parishes where the cottagers had been able to keep a patch of property, they had 'shown a Spartan determination to refuse the refuge of the Poor Law'. Young found that enclosure, when it took away the property of the poor, destroyed one of the great incentives to industry and self respect. His previous view that the benefit of the commons to the poor was 'perfectly contemptible' and 'when it tempts them to become owners of cattle or sheep was usually ruinous' was fundamentally wrong.[60]

The Hammonds declared that, in these cases, 'The anchorage of the poor was gone.'[61]

It seems we have, in 1736 in Medstead, evidence of a partly enlightened policy. The agricultural poor had lost their valuable commons rights, but at least kept a house and garden. We also have a near complete list of the village poor, especially when names mentioned in the award for positioning allotments are added: widow Martha Stool, next door to Doary, Sawkins, Smith and Wilks; Thomas Cane with his garden by The King's Highway; a cottage and garden of William Crockford near the 'poor' allotment and, grouped together, land of Thomas Mould, garden and paddock of William Mould and the gardens and cottages of William Lover and the widow Olive Hall.

These extra eight families when added to the previous possible ten cottagers provide equivalent people to fill Medstead's poor roster. When compared to the 1744 village perambulation, there is great similarity to those identified as owners of cottages 'on the waste of the manor'.[62]

William Mould's property, mentioned above, is important for it bordered a footpath to be built, specified as four feet wide, which was a 'Water Way for the poor people to drive a wheel barrow to fetch water' from Hacket Pond, by-passing now enclosed fields, and to be repaired by the parish. Another water lane from widow Hall's to the pond was to be built for the same purpose. Further, Hacket Pond on Stankham Common and the pond on Soldridge Common called Five Ash Pond 'shall remain as they were before the enclosure, for the use of the Publick, and that no one shall enclose any part of them nor dig within their Land adjoining so as to drain the water from them'. The importance of water supply in this river-less parish is discussed in the penultimate chapter.

---

59 Humphries, 'Enclosures, Common Rights ...', pp. 23-32.
60 Hammonds, *Village Labourer*, p. 82. Young, *Annals*, i/52.
61 Hammonds, *Village Labourer*, p. 97.
62 HRO, *Bounds of the Manor of Medsted Taken 9/10/1744*, 107M89/22.

In view of what is to come in Medstead's second enclosure in 1799, the 1736 award gives little specific instruction on fencing, probably a lesson still to be learned. One exception called for a 'good quantity of fencing to fence off from roads the said piece called Towzer's bank, it is thought necessary and convenient that the said Elizabeth Prior … may erect and set up a gate at the north end of the said road to keep back the cattle which are feeding in the lanes, from feeding in the said road [and] Towzer's Bank'.

However, the general instructions were clear enough. Proprietors were banned from planting trees so near neighbours' hedges or fences that they might 'hinder or hurt'. They were also individually responsible to 'sufficiently ditch, fence, hedge, and enclose' their land as the commissioners, with full power and authority, directed and without appeal. It was understood that 'Great Hurt and Damage may happen unto the planting and setting Quick Wood [live plants], or any other Wood [used in fencing] by Sheep or Cattle going in any of the Lanes or Roads'. Proprietors had 'full Liberty' for twelve years to erect gates across any roads against their lands to keep out sheep or cattle so as to prevent them destroying quick wood. Private roads were to have a gate at either end. In effect, this was open season for gate construction.

Amusingly, towards the end of the award, all the parties sought to protect themselves against the others. First came the gentry:

The Right Reverend Father in God, Benjamin Lord Bishop of Winchester, the present Lord of the said Manor of Old Alresford, and his successors, the future Lords of the same Manor for the Time being, and also the said John Shackleford and his Heirs or Assigns, Lords of the said Manor of Medstead, shall, notwithstanding such Inclosure and Division of the said Common or Waste Grounds, be intitled to and have, receive, and enjoy, all Rents, Fines, Services, Suits of Court, and all Royalties belonging to the said Manors, as fully and effectually as if this Act had never been made.

Rector Soley insured himself and his successors against any loss of annual tithes from the newly enclosed lands. The proprietors then sought protection from the lord of the manor raising his fines and rents because of any perceived increase in land value. Finally, the commissioners made it clear that all the charges for passing this act and for surveying, allotting, dividing, and enrolling, and all their charges and expenses were to be paid proportionably by the proprietors and, on that subject, the commissioners would be their own judge and jury.

The 1736 enclosure changed the landscape of Medstead forever, first by the gates, hedges and fences set up to guard its privatised commons against public access, and then by the plethora of roads and footways which were needed to provide new access to enclosed land. No other new roads or ways, public or private, on foot or with horses, cattle or carriages, were allowed. The London Road, mentioned in two parts, was specified to be sixty feet wide; six other public

Why should I pay? 'Even if the small farmer received strict justice in the division of the common fields, his share in the legal costs and the additional expense of fencing his allotments often overwhelmed him and he was obliged to sell his property.' ¥

¥ Marshall, *Appropriation and Enclosure of Commonable ... Lands*, p. 52.

causeways on Soldridge Common, each thirty feet wide, were detailed. A further six private roads were for the use of one or more of John Shackleford, John Barnard, Richard Wake, William Prior, John Budd of Shalden, James Budd, widow Mary Budd of Ropley, and John Camois. Camois's road branching from the London Road was to be used by horses, carts, waggons and ploughs 'to his land called Hides keeping the same in good repair and not drive any cattle loose'.

Lastly, there were to be ten new footways, many probably in use today and, with their hedging and fencing, keeping the public from the fields that were once common land in Stankham and Soldridge.

George Morley
1662-1684

Peter Mews
1684-1706

Sir Jonathan Trelawny, 3rd Baronet
1707-1721

Charles Trimnell
1721-1723

Benjamin Hoadly 1734-1761

Brownlow North 1781-1820

Sir George Pretyman Tomline,
5th Baronet
1820-1827

Charles Sumner
1827-1869

7 USING THE ROPLEY MODEL

The Chawton and Farringdon enclosures, 1740 and 1748

Ah cruel foes with plenty blest
So ankering after more
To lay the greens and pasture waste
Which profited before[1]

The decade following Medstead's first private parliamentary enclosure, the 1740s, saw two further agreements that shut the commons and common fields of Chawton and Farringdon completely and forever. On the ground, there was little to differentiate the adjoining areas with their several small farms which reached down the valley to their respective villages.[2] These community lands were essentially sheep country that filled the whole of the north side of Four Marks ridge from the Winchester turnpike across to Newton Valence where they met the two Newton Commons. In practice, the two enclosures could not have been more different. Chawton was a near fiefdom where the commoners and their cottages were quietly swept away. In Farringdon, limited provision was made for the voiceless poor.

Chawton was originally occupied by a Saxon called Odo. It was given by the Conqueror to Hugh de Port, a large Hampshire landowner. The village held nineteen free residents, eight smallholders, six slaves (part of the sixty-seven slaves in the area from Alresford to the ridge parishes) and woodland with fifty pigs.[3] Several farms were well watered by the springs of the Lavant Stream, one of the sources of the River Wey. The parish's old boundaries ran from the Four Marks quadripoint to include the Alton Butts, the northern half filled by Chawton Park Woods. Chawton never developed into a settlement of substance, 'possibly because the lords of the manor wished to keep the area for themselves'.[4] The result was that a large part of the parish was developed into parkland and forests for hunting. The manor was sold in 1578 to Nicholas Knight whose family had been its lessees for fifty years. Although the manor remained under the Knight

---

1 Clare, 'The Lamentations of Round-Oak Waters'.
2 Wrightson, *Earthly Necessities*, p. 273.
3 Munby, *Domesday Book*, 23-25. Slave count: Alresford (including Medstead) 19; Bishop's Sutton (including Ropley) 32; Chawton 6; East Tisted 2; Farringdon 2; Newton Valence 6 (*Appendix 2*). For the complex nature of slavery in Anglo-Saxon and Norman history, see Pelteret, *Slavery in Early Medieval England*.
4 Montgomery, *Chawton*, p. 4.

name until the last century, this was sometimes achieved by cousins inheriting it and then changing their name to Knight.

In the seventeenth century, many landed families were struggling to keep their bitterly won estates in one piece. At the end of the Civil War, Royalists, including large numbers of families in Hampshire, like the Pinchin family of Shalden, forfeited their all for treason.[5] From 1646, many of these 'traitors' were allowed to buy back their lands, especially after the restoration of the monarchy in 1660.[6] This did not apply to the Pinchin family who scattered away from Hampshire. Their land eventually fell into the hands of Edward Knight.

However, there was still a 'legacy of debt and straightened circumstances'. Two legal developments, the 'strict settlement' and the 'equity of redemption', eased the way for the continuation of the great estates and also provided access to borrowed money. These changes were welcomed amongst the landed class, including crucially the lesser gentry, and made funds available for, among other matters, enclosures. 'Strict settlement' was a device for effecting the orderly transmission of property through primogeniture, preserving its integrity while providing for the well-being of dependents like widows and siblings. 'Equity of redemption' extended greater security to those who sought to raise capital by mortgaging property, previously an extreme risk with a high prospect of forfeiture.

Chawton's private parliamentary enclosure took place in 1740-1 when a bad harvest followed a severe winter and eighteen food riots were recorded over large parts of the country.[7] However, the Chawton act was mostly about sheep and its private act was merely the confirmation of an agreement already made (*Appendix 12*).[8]

There is a considerable history of early management of the commons thanks to the chronicler of Chawton Manor, William Austen Leigh, in a book published in 1911. Leigh inspected and transcribed many of 2,000 aged documents now held in the Hampshire Record Office, but which are rarely available because they were badly, some irreparably, damaged by damp prior to deposit.[9] Of particular interest are the records of the Courts Leets and Baron held in the sixteenth and seventeenth centuries (*Appendix 4*).

The account of the court of 1558, for instance, shows careful decisions about the control of sheep and hogs, engaging new sub-tenants, repair of houses, payment of heriots, and cutting of undergrowth. A common complaint was that a tenant failed to fence his land's ends, the strips that abutted on a road or

---

5   Heal, *Four Marks Murders*, p. 152. C. H. Firth and R. S. Rait, edited, 'An Additional Act for Sale of several Lands and Estates forfeited to the Commonwealth for Treason', 1652, *Acts and Ordinances of the Interregnum, 1642-1660* (HMSO, London 1911), pp. 623-52.
6   Wrightson, *Earthly Necessities*, pp. 275-7.
7   Rudé, *Crowd in History*, p. 36.
8   Private Act, 14 George II, c. 12 (HL/PO/PB/1/1740/14G2n44). Also HRO, 155M89/1.
9   HRO, 18M61.

common way.[10] These concerns would have varied little, one suspects, from similar courts in Farringdon, Medstead and Ropley.

Enclosure was nothing new in Chawton. In 1605, a court held by John Knight recognised that for the last thirty or forty years a 'great part' of the commons had been enclosed by tenants with the consent of the lord. However, these tenants still kept the same number of sheep on the reduced common land to everyone's detriment.

Records of the final and full enclosure in 1740 led Leigh to question the morality of what had happened,

> *It seems not improbable that … the lord of the manor, or possibly some of the larger commoners, had been buying up the rights of smaller inhabitants for, when the Enclosure Bill was passed, there were only seven commoners besides the lord and the rector to receive allotments of land, and of these seven, two were non-resident corporations. The number appears insignificant when compared with those who attended the earlier Courts, and who displayed so much activity and interest in the life of the parish … The enclosure appears to have been carried out most carefully and systematically.[11]*

Village regulation is often drawn by middle and small farmers whose reputation for hardheadedness or even meanness is notorious. Yet, even in hardheaded terms, there are sound reasons for affording latitude in minor common rights. It is better that a labour force should remain resident and available for the heavy calls of hay and harvest.[12]

The slow, negotiated process of piecemeal enclosure in which closes or woods were taken out of the system and common rights were abated by general agreement were disappearing. 'In its place came a process that dispensed with the need for much agreement and enclosed an entire parish in five to ten years and when it was done all common right had gone.'[13]

The enclosed lands at Chawton came from the 312 acres of Common and from 309 acres made up of seven common fields: Ridgefield, Southfield, Northfield, Upper and Lower Eastfield, Whitedown and Winstreetfield (*Appendix 13*).

The lord, Thomas Knight, newly in position and a lucky man, did very well. His existing local estate already comprised fifteen houses and 1,569 acres: 734 of arable land, 108 of pasture, 56 meadow, 615 woodland and 55 rough heath. Now, through enclosure, he added 156 acres from the common and 143 acres from the common fields, 48 per cent of the available total, and almost 2,000 acres altogether in Hampshire.[14] Knight's allotment was increased by the herbage of

---

10 Orwins, *Open Fields*, p. 55.
11 Leigh, *Chawton Manor*, pp. 41, 47.
12 Thompson, *Customs in Common*, pp. 130-1.
13 Neeson, *Commoners*, p. 187.
14 Leigh, *Chawton Manor*, p. 46.

North Field, Chawton, in common, before 1740

There were seven fields worked in strips by the commoners in Chawton. As an example, the strips of
North Field (38 acres 2 roods 28 perches) are shown before their allotment to the feoffees of Eggar's
School (a), Alton; Winchester Corporation (in two parts) as trustees for Peter Symonds School (b);
and Robert Eames (c) (William Austen Leigh, *Chawton Manor and Its Owners*, pp. 178-9, 209).

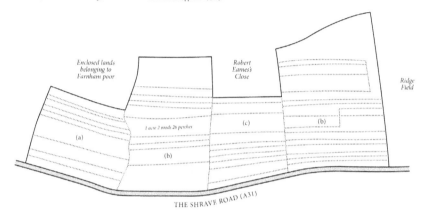

Chawton Commons enclosure, 1740

Not all allotments are named; some are unreadable
(William Austen Leigh, *Chawton Manor and Its Owners*, p. 207)

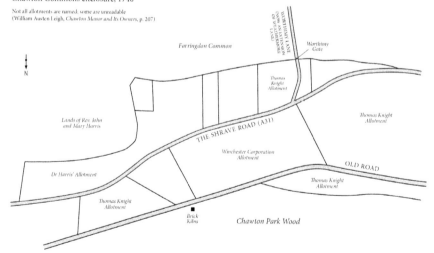

"MORE kindling? You want MORE ?"

More kindling? 'The property of the proprietors, and especially of the poor ones [is] entirely at [the commissioners'] mercy: every passion of resentment and prejudice may be gratified without control for they are vested with a despotic power known in no other branch of business in this free country.' ¥

¥ Young, *Six Months' Tour*, Vol. I, p. 122.

all the highways on the Common, and, because he was the lord, 'free liberty' by June 1742 to 'sell, cut down, grub up, take, cart, and carry away' all the timber trees, pollard trees, bushes and wood, anywhere on the Common for which his workmen could enter any allotment at any time.

Herbage was no small benefit. It meant the tended animals of the poor could no longer graze at the lane verges. Stripping the land of bushes and snapwood further encouraged the poor to move away. Throughout much of England 'no small part of the sufferings of the poor was due to the high cost of firing, to the problem of how to get enough fuel for cooking, let alone keep themselves warm.[15] Cobbett once wrote of the grasslands of Hampshire that 'these countries have one great draw-back: the poor day labourers suffer from their want of fuel and they have nothing but their bare pay. For these reasons they are greatly worse off than those of the woodland countries.'

All the Chawton common land was to be fenced and roads made with responsibilities for maintenance allotted to each of the recipients. Knight also had the right to set unlocked gates where he controlled the way. Leigh thought these roads, ways and droves were 'very much as now exist': the 'Shrave Road' (before the Turnpike Act of 1753), the highway, 'Pace-way Road', the brick kilns, and other place names. Several gates are mentioned and probably link to controlled Saxon entry points and stiles: a 'first' mention of 'Four Mark Gate' (singular), Worthimy Gate, Summergate and Crockland Gate.

Medstead land was scattered with dells, pits, copses and stony ground while the Chawton land had few of these: only trees (one wood) which was measured in sheep use (a stint of three to an acre) and one acre was specified for a new pond to be made near Worthimy Gate (where the track leaves Weathermore Wood onto the A31) and for a chalk pit to be dug for shared use for marling, the neutralising of acid soil.[16]

The look of the country went through a quick and fundamental change: hedged and fenced fields which were once open or farmed in strips were now crossed by gated roads, and were denuded of most of their trees, including those grown for pollarding, and their bushes and undergrowth.

> *I always admire the kindling freshness that the bark of the different sorts of tree and underwood assume in the forest – the 'foul royce' twigs kindling into a vivid colour at their tops as red as woodpigeon's claws, the ash with its grey bark and black swelling buds, the birch with its 'paper rind' and the darker mottled sort of hazel, black alder with the greener hues of swallow willows and the bramble that still wears its leaves with the privet of a purple hue while the straggling wood briar shines in a bright and more beautiful green, odd forward branches in the new laid hedges of white thorn begin to freshen*

---

15 Bovill, *English Country Life*, p. 21.
16 Mathew, 'Marling', pp. 97-8.

> *into green before the arum dare peer out of its hood or the primrose and*
> *violet shoot up a new leaf thro' the warm moss and ivy that shelter their*
> *spring dwellings, the furze too on the common wear a fairer green and here*
> *and there an off branch is covered with golden flowers and the ling or heath*
> *nestling among the long grass below (covered with the wither'd flowers of*
> *last year) is sprouting up into fresh hopes of spring, the fairey rings on the*
> *pasture are getting deeper dyes and the water weeds with long silver green*
> *blades of grass are mantling the stagnant ponds in their summer liveries.*[17]

There is no mention at Chawton of encroachments, peasants' cottages, or peasants' rights of common forage and the rest. This was entirely an arrangement between the owners of the land for their individual benefit. From lists in Leigh's book, one might have expected over thirty families to have held an interest, but all but one were already gone, not just from the Commons, but, soon, from the village entirely (*Appendix 4*). 'A thick cultural and social wedge was inserted between the *improving* husbandmen, the better sort of the parish, and the poor.'[18]

The Hammonds said it was of 'capital importance' to remember that the listing of consents,

> *... took account only of proprietors. It ignored entirely two large classes to*
> *whom enclosure meant, not a greater or lesser degree of wealth, but actual*
> *ruin. These were such cottagers as enjoyed their rights of common in virtue of*
> *renting cottages to which such rights were attached, and those cottagers and*
> *squatters who either had no strict legal right, or whose rights were difficult*
> *of proof. Neither of these classes was treated even outwardly and formally as*
> *having any claim to be consulted before an enclosure was sanctioned.*[19]

Thomas Knight, lord of the manor and chief protagonist, was a gentleman and hunter with a chequered heritage, not uncommon amongst a Knight family that regularly had a lack of children to inherit. He was born Thomas Brodnax and educated at Balliol College, Oxford, and studied law. When his parents died, he received the Godmersham estate, near Canterbury. Through his mother, Anne May, Thomas added another estate, Rawmere, near Chichester. In 1726, Thomas Brodnax became Thomas May and acted as High Sheriff of Kent in 1729. 'He was now a rich man and could afford in 1732 to commence the great work of building the present mansion of Godmersham Park.'[20] In 1734, he became MP for Canterbury. By a further confusion of cousins, Mrs Elizabeth Knight, the last of her tribe at Chawton was without heir.

---

17 Neeson, *Commoners*, p. 158. Clare, *Selected Poems and Prose*. 'Foul-rush' is either dogwood or the spindle tree (Mabey, *Plants with a purpose*).
18 Hindle, 'Sense of Place', in *Communities*, pp. 19-49.
19 Hammonds, *Village Labourer*, p. 52.
20 Leigh, *Chawton Manor*, pp. 137-45.

She fixed upon [Thomas] *as her successor. She was of a disposition to value both his sterling qualities and also his more adventitious advantages of wealth and position. He would represent the family creditably and she could provide in her will for the continuance of the family name. But she perhaps overlooked the fact that he already possessed a home to which he was warmly attached, and the probability that even the expression of her strong desire for regular residence during half the year at Chawton would be insufficient to overcome his prepossession for Godmersham. This proved to be the case and occasional business visits (especially when the line taken by the Squire was so unpopular as the attempted sale of the church bells) were hardly likely to endear him to the tenants.[21]*

Thomas Brodnax who had become Thomas May now became Thomas Knight. This misfortune or carelessness over children had other consequences. Late in the eighteenth century, Thomas Knight's son, also Thomas, having no heirs, 'adopted' Edward Austen, the son of a distant cousin, the Reverend George Austen, parson at Steventon. Edward changed his name to Edward Austen Knight and eventually inherited Chawton Manor and estate. In 1809, he provided a house in the village for his widowed mother Cassandra and sisters Cassandra and Jane, who wrote popular novels.[22] Edward lost £20,000 as a guarantor for his brother Henry when a bank in Alton collapsed. Matters worsened when he paid £15,000 to distant family to rid himself of an embarrassing claim. He had fallen foul of a deed, written in 1755, that, in the event of Thomas Brodnax having no issue, the estate would revert to the heirs-at-law of his benefactor, Elizabeth Knight.[23] 'This it was, I believe,' wrote a niece some fifty years later, 'that occasioned the great gap in Chawton Park Wood, visible for thirty years afterwards and probably not filled up again even now.'

The enclosure of Brodnax's Chawton estates was built on confidence in his place in a landed society where deference was the keynote. He stood at the head of the landed interest with substantial estates.

Much of institutional transformation of the rural economy had been accomplished at their behest, or with their compliance, and its character reflected their priorities and their values. Tawney wrote of the 'calm, proud faces' of their portraits which hang still on the walls of the country houses from which they ruled Britain, staring down on us with 'the unshakable

---

21 Leigh, *Chawton Manor*, p. 143; the story of the bells, Chapter III.
22 The house in Chawton is now open as a museum commemorating Jane Austen. Godmersham Park House was inherited by Edward Austen, Jane Austen's brother, in 1794. The house is closed to the public, but there is a footpath through the grounds. *Pride and Prejudice* depicts characters and scenes from Godmersham and, because of this, the house is shown on the £10 note issued in 2017. *Mansfield Park* is said to be based on Godmersham Park. In 2001, Godmersham Park became the home of the *Association of British Dispensing Opticians* and is used as a training college.
23 Leigh, *Chawton Manor*, pp. 170-1.

assurance of men who are untroubled by regrets or perplexities, men who have deserved well of their order and their descendants' … They stood for tradition and hierarchy, but they were thoroughly imbued with the values of the market. They revered lineage and ancestry. Yet they measured one another first and foremost in terms of the round figures of estimated annual income … They appreciated to the full the benefits of capital enterprise.[24]

Any suggestion of a right of resistance horrified the bulk of the articulate ruling class. The importance of landowners, the county elite, in protecting their power over the land through enclosure, and the holding of all rights to hunting, cannot be underestimated. It was reinforced at justices' meetings and assize dinners as well as at sporting events such as race days and the general social round. A master who wanted his servants to defer to him; a husband who expected his wife and children to defer to him; a gentleman who demanded of his tenants the deference he himself showed towards the nobility – all must ultimately, through the great chain of human ranks, defer to the king, the supreme guarantor of deference and social order.[25] That said, new fences built for enclosure, were always criticised by foxhunters. Byng wrote in 1781 of his neighbourhood, and of Gloucestershire, 'formerly so noted for hunting and now spoilt by enclosures'.[26]

E. P. Thompson wrote of the paradox whereby the popular culture of the eighteenth century was simultaneously rebellious and traditional.[27] 'The conservative culture of the plebs as often as not resists, in the name of custom, those economic rationalisations and innovations (such as enclosure, work-discipline, unregulated 'free' markets in grain) which rulers, dealers or employers seek to impose. That is why, said Jonathon Bate, biographer, that the poet John Clare conformed to this model. He was 'deferential to the local grandees – with their sense of *noblesse oblige* – but bitterly satirical towards the newly prosperous, socially aspirant farmers who benefitted from enclosure at the expense of the rights and customs of his own class.'[28]

The Church of England preached with sustained and fanatical enthusiasm the doctrine that 'deference was only safe when universally respected'. The Reverend Master John Baker, rector at Chawton for over twenty years and whose patron was the lord of the manor Thomas Knight, was one of the preachers. For his glebe land, he received the Parsonage Common and part of the common fields, totalling nearly twenty-three acres.

Even with all the influence at his disposal and with an agreement in his pocket, Brodnax needed to look to parliament to secure his coalition: 'mutual benefit

---

24 Wrightson, *Earthly Necessities*, pp. 274-5, quoting Tawney, *Agrarian Problem in the Sixteenth Century*, p. 314.
25 Broad, *Whigs and Deer-Stealers*, p. 71.
26 Bovill, *English Country Life*, p. 200.
27 Thomson, *Customs in Common*, p. 9.
28 Bate, *Clare*, p. 58.

[on the Commons] should be divided and inclosed and to avoid difficulties that might arise touching such division and inclosure the said Commoners did submit themselves respectively to the award …'.

'Determined enclosure by landholders almost always won the day' … Large landowners began to resort to parliamentary enclosure which 'automatically extinguished common right and gave commissioners a free hand to offer as little compensation as they wished with little redress.'[29] While the lesson of Ropley was learned and improved private acts were embraced, it was still clear that enclosure might not take place unless by due parliamentary process 'even if one humoursome landholder dissented'. Just one wayward voice could cause trouble and delay.

A young gentleman wrote on behalf of his mother to a noble patron in 1741 about her predicament in the village of Oakley, near Basingstoke.

> *My Mama has the largest farm there upon her hands and she finds it a very difficult thing to get a tenant for it, no person caring to take it unless the parish was enclosed, there being so great a disagreement among the farmers that in mere spite to each other they will not manage the Common Fields so as to make the best advantage of them …*[30]

The Chawton provisions came into effect in September 1741. There were seven arbitrators, rather than commissioners, for this was a parliamentary endorsement of a private deal. The list includes many familiar names. One can easily see how the round of local enclosures involved a coterie of social landholders from the immediate district. Three of the chosen men, John Barnard from New Alresford, John Budd of Trinity, yeoman, and John Camish (Camies), both from Medstead, were prominent recipients from the 1735 Medstead enclosure. This was surely no chance selection. One can all but hear the chink of glasses while the details of the deal were discussed around the brass fire-dogged chimney piece in the Great Hall at Chawton Manor. The other arbitrators, all yeomen, were taken from different villages at least a parish away from Ropley and one wonders at the logic. Were they there to ensure fair play as independent players or, more likely, as business friends looking to assess the process and value for their own lands and pockets: Benjamin Reynolds, Fleet; Bernard Burningham, Binsted; Thomas Stevens, Wield; and Thomas Earwaker, Neatham. Budd of Trinity did not sign the final adjudication; he was certainly alive at the time. His motive is considered later.

Once again there is no formal map of the enclosures, although a drawing of Knight's estate is held at Hampshire Record Office (*Appendix 17*).[31]

---

29 Neeson, *Commoners*, p. 108.
30 Thompson, *Customs in Common*, pp. 109-10.
31 HRO, 18M61/Map 3.

Edward Knight's Chawton Manor estate, 1768-1852

For field codes, see Appendix 17

12
Greenwood
Coppice

13
Jays Bottom

Alresford

9
Great
Common

FARRINGDON PARISH

11
Lower
Greenwood

10
Upper
Greenwood

4 Row

14
Old Gardens

3
Upper
Barn Field

8
Green
Common

Pits

15 Row

19
Long
Close

6 Row

16
The Six Acres

20 Row

Farmhouse

Pond

17 Row

7 Row

5
Lower
Barn Field

Glebe

18
The Seven
Acres

23 Row

*Crocklands
Coppice*

22
Little
Crocklands

*Inbook
Coppice*

26
Hatch
Gates

25 Row

*Edward Knight's
land*

24
Crooked
Crocklands

30 Row

27
Upper
South Field

29
Yew Tree
Piece

28
Lower
South Field

31
Great
Bean Field

Alton

N

32
Little
Bean Field

Metres   0   50   100   200

However, Leigh helpfully detailed Chawton Commons and included hand-drawn, often difficult, maps in his book:

> ... *beginning at the Lower Road or 'Shrave' where there was a gate, called the Hatch Gate. It followed the hedge of Hatch Gate and Imbook to the top of the hill; then turned west to the north-west corner of Greenwood Copse, where it turned south again; outside the copse across Jays Bottom to the Farringdon boundary. Here it turned west, and continued along the parish boundary hedge to the Four Marks, where was another gate. Still keeping to the parish boundary – here against Medstead – it continued in a northly direction as far as the bank and ditch of Red Hill Cut in Chawton Park, where it turned east, following the boundary bank of Chawton Park as far as the King Tree Gate. Here it turned south across Great Reads by the west side of Read's Copse to the Shrave, thence along the south side of Read's Copse to the Hatch Gate.*[32]

The allotments were made at the behest of only nine owners of the commons. Knight and Baker, his rector, have been discussed. Unusually, there were two corporations among the commoners. The largest was Winchester City, which received over 100 acres, almost 20 per cent, and acted as the trustees of Peter Symonds School in the town. The other was of the trustees of the free Grammar School in Alton of John Eggar of 'Moungomeryes'. In 1638, Eggar, a local farmer, set up a trust deed to initiate his idea of a school and, in the next year, the freehold to Mounter's Farm, thirty-nine acres, was acquired by the feoffees of Eggars. In 1641 by act of parliament, the school was set up with the farm to provide the endowment.[33] At some time, the school became a holder of rights of common and was awarded some twenty-three acres, about 8 per cent, of the Chawton enclosure.

Two of Chawton's oldest families, Morey / Fisher and Prowting were owners of common's rights .[34] Fisher was represented through a complicated route by Mary Forbes and her second husband, the Reverend Doctor John Harris of Ashe, and the couple received over seventy acres, 11 per cent. Another Harris, Michael, a copyholder, received twelve acres. Two copyholders, widow Joan and Rowland Prowting, received twenty-seven acres, less than 5 per cent. The Prowtings had held land in Chawton since the reign of the later Charles. Their family included a justice of the peace and a deputy lieutenant for the county.

Within a few years, the Prowtings were in an open fight against Thomas Knight for his 'miserable scheme', backed by the bishop of Winchester, Benjamin Hoadly, to reduce the three bells in the church to one to save money on repairs. Hoadly, claimed Leigh, was a 'prelate more conspicuous for friendly good nature

---

32 Leigh, *Chawton Manor*, p. 47.
33 HCC Regulatory Committee, Item 10, 27/6/2007.
34 Leigh, *Chawton Manor*, pp. 42-4.

than for love of church order or dignity of worship'. Prowting made 'such a clamour amongst the mob that there [was] hardly any passing through the street. I [Randall, Knight's steward] am told they called after you as you passed through Alton to know if you had a bell in your coach. [Prowting] has said you wanted to sell the bells to put money in your pocket'.[35]

The final commoner was Robert Eames, who sided with Knight over the bells. He received almost twenty-five acres through enclosure. With the Eames family, one finds a number of connections. Ann Eames married into the Budd clan in Medstead, probably about 1650. The family was one of the feoffees of Eggar's school. Their lands included a malthouse at Chawton, commons in Alton where there was also property in the High Street and in Mount Pleasant Lane and connections in Winchester which included Hyde Brewery. They were prominent in the last ridge enclosure at Newton Valence over a hundred years later.

Perhaps there was another moment of village tension here. Within a few years of the enclosure, a new rector, John Hinton, signed a petition with his churchwardens, overseers and two parishioners 'that no Public House may be licenced hereafter for the selling of Beer, Ale, Wine, Brandy, Punch or other Liquors within the said Parish of Chawton'.[36] This may have been particularly short sighted as Chawton village lay one mile from Alton and on a junction where plans were already under way to turn its rough roads into turnpikes from London to Gosport and to Winchester bringing coaching business to hostelries, blacksmiths and ostlers.[37]

It is worth recognition that three families connected with the enclosure, Barnard, Knight and Morey / Moorey / Moor were already in positions of local power 135 years before and during the Courts Leet and Baron.

The commoners' costs were £223 16s 11½p, paid by a levy of 7s 1½p an acre on all the commoners in proportion to the number of acres allotted.[38] The principal expenses were paid to their surveyor, Edward Randall, who was also the main contact with the committees of both Houses in London. He travelled twice to town with John Barnard and charged £6 9s 10½d. Randall claimed separately for surveying the common fields at 12p an acre, £15 9s, and for the commons at 8p an acre, £10 14s. The whole team met four times at the *George* in Alton at a cost of £11 1s 9d.

Randall was clearly a well-trusted man, but that was because he was also Thomas Knight's steward who looked after the estates at Godmersham and Rawmere as well as at Chawton: not only trusted, but with great influence.[39] For Knight, having his own steward manage the enclosure promised welcome security.

---

35 Leigh, *Chawton Manor*, pp. 57-60.
36 1748, Leigh, *Chawton Manor*, p. 45.
37 By 1903, Chawton parish also accommodated three railways passing from Alton to Basingstoke, Fareham and Winchester.
38 Leigh, *Chawton Manor*, pp. 49-50, Appendix IX (rough maps).
39 Leigh, *Chawton Manor*, pp. 143-5.

Mention has been made that one of the arbitrators, John Budd of Trinity in Medstead, did not sign the award. Those who have already sensed sufficient evidence of a landowners' conspiracy in the arrangements at Chawton may have further grist. Among the associated papers at the Hampshire Record Office is a draft memorandum, unsigned, but from the commoners and dated April 1741, some months before the Act was to be put into effect (*Appendix 14*).[40] The document gives to Thomas Knight the right over almost 120 acres of enclosed land to make ditches, but 'so as not to to hinder any sheep from passing and repassing and feeding' and also 'free Liberty to Denshire' after sheep had been removed. Denshire is the practice of improving land by burning heaps of turf and stubble and then spreading the ashes over the ground as a compost. This would be the death knell for the old commoners' free fuel.

The right to 'Denshire, Chalk, Break up, Plow', was passed by Knight to John Budd of Shalden who had 'hired all those allotments on the said Common ... assigned to Thomas Knight'. One assumes a relationship between Budd of Trinity and Budd of Shalden. Perhaps the lack of signature was a sign of discretion.

Budds feature throughout this book. Rathbone thought the name's root came from 'to swell' as in a bud and the nickname might also donate a fat individual. There was an Israel Budd farming in about 1290 and many of the early Budds had been 'of Hattingly'. Rathbone speculated that the first Budd of Medstead may have been a corpulent son of one of the 'de Hattingeles'.[41]

The local enclosing gentry moved their caravan to Farringdon in 1748.[42] The evidence that survives is in two parts: the first found formal map of a ridge enclosure, worn around the edges with damp marks, but listing all the recipients and placing their allotments; and five handwritten early drafts with multiple gaps, insertions, crossings out, corrections and spelling inconsistences in proper nouns that have been badly treated with tears and staining.[43] Few Hampshire maps have decorative cartouches: the Farringdon map is a notable example where the 'explanation' is elaborated with 'what seems to be mermaids with wings'.[44]

There were five arbitrators appointed to 'avoid difficulties and disputes that might arise touching divisions and allotments'. This standard phrasing does suggest that disagreement was a feared possibility. First among the arbitrators was Edward Randall, gentleman of Chawton, Thomas Knight's steward, and who, as the surveyor, worked in 1741 on Chawton's enclosure under Thomas Knight's close direction. Then came two Budds, the ever present and one might suggest reliable, John of Trinity in Medstead, the arbitrator who had failed to sign the Chawton agreement, and the second, John of Shalden, who had taken the tenancy of much of Knight's allotments in Chawton, land which adjoined the

40 HRO, 39M89/E/B562.
41 Rathbone, *Chronicle*, p. 56.
42 There seems to be an error in date here in Chapman's *Guide to Enclosure*, cf., pp. 35, 141.
43 HRO, 18M61/MP19. HRO, 39M89/E/B562.
44 Kain et al, *Enclosure maps*, p. 73.

Farringdon common lands now under review. The last two assessors were John Richardson, a carpenter of Ropley, an unknown, and John Baigen, a member of one of Chawton's oldest landowning families. Baigen can be connected to Symond's Farm and through marriage with the equally ancient Moorey family.[45] In the affair of the bells, Baigen also sided with the rudely treated Thomas Knight and Robert Eames.

The occupied lands of Farringdon stretch back to the iron age and later accommodated the incoming Saxons. Faringdon Episcopi, superior to a second manor, Faringdon Popham, was mentioned at the time of Edward the Confessor as held by Godwin the priest.[46] The place was linked to the church of Bosham on the south coast, which in turn belonged to bishop Osbern of Exeter, the first of the ridge commons to escape the baleful influence of the bishops of Winchester. Apart from a brief period in the thirteenth century, Exeter retained control until 1546 when it was exchanged for manors elsewhere. A year later, the much married Henry granted it to the Wriothesley family who, in 1596, conveyed it to Robert Cage.[47]

It was Lewis Cage, as lord of the manor, who led the enclosure request followed by familiar names: William Knight and Thomas Eames, yeoman, all Chawton, 1740; and Richard Wake, senior and junior, and John and William Finden, all Soldridge, 1735. There was one named newcomer to the enclosure lists, John Tribe, and a group called 'others'.

The Farringdon enclosure, apart from its descriptive contents, is remarkable for two elements (*Appendix 16*).

First, it is the only enclosure agreement along the Four Marks ridge not to have the approval of a parliamentary act. Considering the desperation in the previous fifty years to secure acts for Ropley, Soldridge and Chawton, this needs explaining. Thoughts go back to the ragtag collection of scruffy copies at the Hampshire Record Office that hold the written form of the agreement, without 'hands', signatures, marks or seals. Perhaps there is no final legal document? Could it be the basis for the ownership of the old commons is built on shaky ground? Might the common people of Farringdon today be encouraged to round up their sheep and hogs and reclaim their birth right?

A clue that something different was happening lies in the agreement's salutation. To date, the enclosures had all called at their start on the good offices of the monarch of the day. In Farringdon, one reads, 'To All Christian People [torn and stained] shall come, Greeting'. Clearly, this was not going to be presented to the king.

Then, there is evidence of the enclosure map carefully drawn to Randall's instruction, detailed and complete in every way. There could be no doubt about what was agreed.

---

45 Hurst, 'Baigens, Chawton'.
46 Domesday Book.
47 Montgomery, *Farringdon*, p. 4.

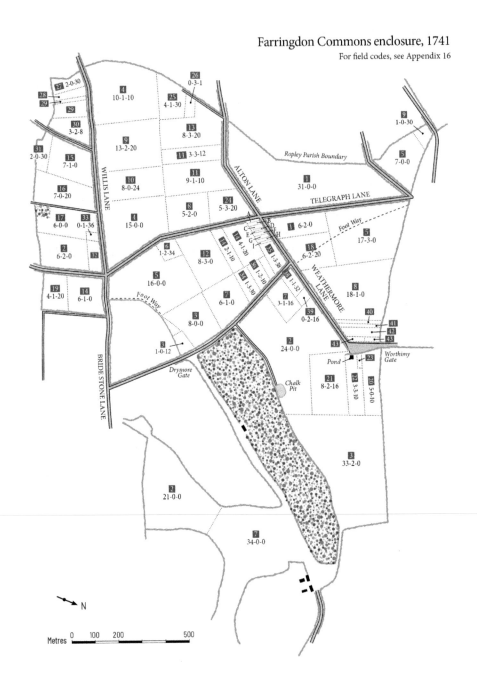

Farringdon Commons enclosure, 1741

For field codes, see Appendix 16

One of the Chawton Manor documents reviewed by Leigh suggests another pragmatic possibility for incompleteness. In June 1749, Thomas Knight consoled Randall on the death of his son by drowning on the coast of China.

By going out of the ship in the boat, as they lay in the River Canton, his foot slipped and he fell into the water and though there was help enough at hand, he never rose again for them to save him; and it is a remarkable quality of the water that a person falling does not rise. I know this must be grief to you and Mrs Randall but you must inform her of it in the gentlest manner you can; and it must be comfort to you that you did your part in bringing him up, and have provided for him in the best manner you could, and that he received his fate by the hand of providence to which we must all submit.[48]

Could it be the fast-moving landowners, with all their experience of previous enclosures quickly made the assessors' decisions a reality and negated a signed document? Supporting this view is the second remarkable aspect of the Farringdon enclosure: the 427 acres were divided between fifty-three entities, almost all individuals. Five families took almost 60 per cent of the land: John and William Finden, 17 per cent; William Knight, 12; John Tribe, 10; two Richard Wakes, father and son, 10; and Lewis Cage, under 9. The only other significant holdings were by Mary Windybank, nearly 6 per cent; Elizabeth with Thomas Fielder, just over 5 per cent; and John Langrish, Robert Rogers, and John with Jane and James Fry, each above 3 per cent. A paltry 0.1 per cent, less than half an acre, was set aside for the poor of Farnham (not Alton).

The remaining thirty-seven parties all received less than 2 per cent of the land; twenty of them less, or much less, than two acres.

Here are the independent commoners so significantly missing from the Chawton enclosure. It was the reason that the Farringdon agreement was relatively secure. No cottager, it seems, was thrown from their encroachment or rented plot. The lord, Lewis Cage, did not have the power, or perhaps wish, of his neighbour, Thomas Knight. He was a lesser amongst equals who accepted his smaller share. The poor finally had a voice: not a voice which built a future, but one which at least maintained their past and a modicum of independence from deferential labour.[49]

Nor did the Cage family's hold on their unencumbered land last for long. In 1758, they sold to Thomas Brodnax Knight, joining their estates with those in Chawton. The Knights remained lords of the two manors, and their several other estates, into the twentieth century.[50]

---

48 Leigh, *Chawton Manor*, p. 145.
49 Newby, 'Deferential Dialectic'.
50 Chawton House was sold on a 125-year lease in 1993 to a charity that became Chawton House Library.

8 HUNGER ACROSS HAMPSHIRE
Dearth and landowners' justice, 16th-18th centuries

Yet, it was thought, the sword she [Justice] bore
Check'd but the Desp'rate and the Poor;
That, urged by mere Necessity,
Were tied up to the wretched Tree
For Crimes, which not deserv'd that Fate
But to secure the Rich, and Great.[1]

Casual readers faced with the many stories of greed and disregard that emanate from the enclosures along the Four Marks ridge may wonder why there is not more record of widespread, even violent, dissent. Well, all is not yet told. There are still two private parliamentary acts to come, the second Medstead act and the final flourish in Newton Valance in 1854. The affair at Medstead in 1799, following a hiatus of fifty years after Chawton and Farringdon, is the most underlyingly vicious enclosure of all. And yet, for all that, the number of local people with ruined lives is small and none of their complaints are written down.

The ridge and other enclosure villages were often less than 400 people. The grumblings and threats of the poor met with implacable reactions from gentry and small farmers who controlled their reins and who saw a way to increase wealth with little effort or risk. On the one hand, discontent across the country was frequent, sharp-edged and people died. On the other, once departed, and quickly, the dispossessed commoners would be silent. The village would settle to a new, quieter, less happy way of life with more fences and more low-paid agricultural labouring. The powers would still expect unquestioning respect; the tugged forelock remained steadfastly in place. Of course, the winners, the rich or their friends, got to write the history or, as is more likely the case, chose to forget what had actually happened and to write about something else or not at all.

One could accept the view that Hampshire, especially around Medstead, Ropley and the rest, was a backwater where little untoward occurred and deference was a way of life. Violence does not suit a modern view of this part of the county. However, there are many examples of unpleasantness which make it difficult for sleeping dogs to lie. My last book, *The Four Marks Murders*, which told of some sixty deaths in twenty stories, brought a handful of unspecific denials from

---

1 Mandeville, 'The Grumbling Hive', *Fable of the Bees*, p. 67. The *Fable*, written in 1705, was vilified in the press, the pulpit and the courts with the Grand Jury of Middlesex condemning it as a 'public nuisance'.

readers who felt it was wrong to disturb the calm, even if its tales were accurate or, as admitted, near accurate.[2]

This chapter places the story of public food and land riots in Hampshire in a wider context up to the end of the eighteenth century. The story of agricultural improvement, corn prices and suppression by the gentry is a large subject. There is no pretence here to write that whole story, but more a need to give some chronology and to show the variety of local disorder. Those interested will find several suggestions for further reading in the footnotes.[3]

Perhaps the county, and particularly the area around Four Marks, was not as quiescent as it might at first seem?

Local early history was particularly lawless. In the thirteenth century, the Pass of Alton, that stretch of the King's Highway through today's Chawton Park Wood and broke cover near Red Hill in Medstead, was a feared and dangerous place. This was the main road from Alton to Winchester. Foot travellers, horses and carts that crawled to the high point were vulnerable to daily attack by bands of people led by the area's gentry. In 1248, two merchants from Brabant were robbed of 200 marks and complained to King Henry. The dramatic consequences, told in contemporary reports, shook Hampshire as the king sought to impose order.[4] Two of the principal accused, John de Bendinges and John Barkham, were men of knightly status. At least twenty of the sixty-four persons indicted were freemen of the Alton region. Richard Kitcombe from Kitwood in today's Four Marks was hanged. Gilbert, and his son William, from Hattingley, the Medstead hamlet, were charged with harbouring robbers. Other bandits came from Odiham, Petersfield, Priors Dean, Selborne, Upton Grey and West Tisted.

Their relevance here is not just that twenty-five men were found guilty of being principals in the thefts, or of being corrupt jurors, with, perhaps, nine hanged nor that many others were convicted of lesser offences and fled the country, nor that there was likely a trial by battle near today's car park in Boyneswood Road with the loser, Hamo Stare, left to rot as an example in the gibbet in the copse of that name. The point of this chapter is that the excuse offered by the men as they awaited the noose was that they were hungry.

Tell the king that he is our death and the chief cause of it by having so long withheld the pay which was due to us when we were in need. We were

---

2   I would like to take this opportunity to apologise to the people of Ropley for the one great error in the book. The old house of William Howley, later archbishop of Canterbury, remains in Ropley across the road from the village pond. It was not sited opposite the Four Marks pond as I claimed.

3   A good start is recommended in Outhwaite's *Dearth, public policy and social disturbance in England, 1550-1800*.

4   The story can be read in Heal, *Four Marks Murders*, Chapter 13. Also, M. T. Clanchy, edited, 'Highway Robbery and trial by battle in the Hampshire eyre of 1249', in R. F. Hunnisett and J. B. Post, *Medieval Legal Records*, edited in the memory of C. F. Meekings (HMSO, London 1978). Reverend J. A. Giles, translated, *Matthew Paris's English History*, 1235-1273, Vol. 2 (c. 1250) (1853; Scholar Select reprint 2020).

obliged to turn thieves and freebooters, or to sell our horses, arms, or clothes, which we could not possibly do without ... [When the king heard this he] *was touched with shame and grief and gave vent to his sorrows in protracted sighs.*

In more recent law, if just three or more people made menacing gestures or speeches, or destroyed an enclosure, the trespass was considered a riot; if more than forty it was treason.[5] Records of enclosure disturbances vary from study to study, but one can look back to, for instance, over twenty across England between 1530 and 1550 when the riotous levelling of hedges became the pre-eminent form of social protest.[6] Discontent in Hertfordshire in 1548 encouraged the government to announce a commission head by John Hales.[7] Large scale rioting followed in Somerset, and flowed into Gloucestershire, Wiltshire and Hampshire. Hales was criticised by Protector Somerset for his enthusiastic removal of enclosures. His diligence stirred the population into such a 'marvellous trade of boldness' that the rioters thought they were enforcing official policies.

Next year, 1549, saw the rebellion, mentioned earlier, of Robert Kett in Norfolk against the fencing of common lands by landlords for their own use. Labourers were forced off the fields and cottagers deprived of grazing. With a force of 16,000 distressed peasants, Kett captured Norwich. Of course, it all ended badly with Kett, after trial, swinging from gallows on the city walls.[8] Hampshire commoners joined Kett to voice their discontent and set up a rebel camp in the county which was in correspondence with the government. Accompanying riots took place in the wood-pasture parts of the county.[9]

Early in May 1586, Zachery Mansell, a weaver, and William Mitchell, a tailor, both from Hartley Mauditt, set out to deliver a load of kerseys to Guildford. Between Holybourne and Froyle, they met a 'Western man' and fell to talking about the lack of work and the price of corn.[10] 'Hampshire must have been buzzing' with the news that a group had tried forcibly to stop a landowner in Romsey from sowing woad, an intrusive dye crop still found in today's hedgerows, which everyone blamed for pushing up grain prices. Planting woad in Hampshire was illegal by a proclamation of the previous year.

As the party reached the signal beacons at Crondall, the 'conversation took on a seditious tone'. The effects of the accidental firing of beacons, readied to warn

5   Blomley, 'Private Property'.
6   Sharp, *Contempt of All Authority*, p. 184.
7   Wood, *Riot, Rebellion*, p. 61.
8   Frederic William Russell, *Kett's Rebellion in Norfolk: being a history of the great civil commotion that occurred at the time of the Restoration* (London 1859), digitised by the British Library.
9   Wood, *Riot, Rebellion*, p. 65.
10 The stories are taken from a set of papers which describe the interrogation of prisoners in what became known as 'The Hampshire Beacon Plot'. The full story is told in White, 'Hampshire Plot', 1934, improved by Jones, 'Beacon Plot', 1968, and in Sharp, *Contempt of All Authority*, 2010, pp. 9-26. TNA, Acts of the Privy Council, Elizabeth, Vol. 6, 2/14, 12/191/15 and others.

of a Spanish invasion, on the Isle of Wight and at Portsdown were well known. A plan was hatched at a Farnham inn for the deliberate firing of eight beacons, most in Hampshire, on a night early in June in order that people would gather. They would be issued with weapons and then loot grain barns and warehouses.

A rendezvous was agreed in Alton. Mansell set about recruiting William Stevens, a Farringdon tailor. 'If thou willt do what I and others will doe then ryse and have Corne.' Others followed: Selborne tailor Richard Passenger; Richard Noyse, a Hartley farm worker; Geoffrey Carey, a weaver from Alton; Richard Deacon, a tanner from Worldham; and Robert Hassall, a butcher from Farringdon.

There was talk of firing the houses of woad-growing landowners, of 'hearing mass said again', of a French fleet standing off Portsmouth, and of pulling Thomas Cooper, the bishop of Winchester, 'owt of Wolsey' and cutting off his head. The plot spread too far and the authorities were warned and strengthened the beacon guards. Altogether twenty-two men were arrested, 'all simple folk', including three more from Farringdon: Robert Wolfe, mason, William Faythful, smith and William Stevens, tailor; and two from Alton: William Arthur, weaver, and William Newman, tailor. Their punishment is unknown, but it is possible they were all released on promises of good behaviour after some time in Marshalsea prison in Southwark.

In December 1630, the kersey-making areas of Hampshire were in straits after another harvest failure. Merchants refused to buy cloth from the clothiers because the market had dried.[11] A justice reported that 'the daily complaints of the poore about me so fill my eares with their miserable wants who at this present are like to perishe with their families for want of worke to maintaine their charge'. The situation had been desperate since the beginning of the year. 'We are streightly required to see that clothiers keepe their workmen and people in imploiment which in this case we cannot tell how to helpe.'[12]

Corn was being brought to market, as provided by the *Book of Orders for the Relief of Dearth*, a 'sprawling sets of good intentions' that empowered justices to organise searches, watch over transactions and punish hoarders.[13] First issued in 1586, the *Book* was regularly updated in years of serious shortages. It appeared in 1630 for the last time, but 'the poore wanting worke had no money to buy and so lack bread.'[14] In Basingstoke, sixty households who depended on the clothier trade, 300 people, were forced onto the alms of the parish and a petition was sent to London.[15] In July 1631, in Winchester, 500 unemployed were reported

---

11 TNA, State Papers 16/176/36, Thomas Jenoise, J.P., to Viscount Conway, Lord President of the Council, 6/12/1630.
12 TNA, State Papers 16/182/45, JPs of Hampshire, 12/1/1630.
13 Outhwaite, *Dearth, Public Policy*, pp. 32-3.
14 Sharp, *Contempt of All Authority*, pp. 41-2.
15 TNA, State Papers 16/182/45, petition of clothiers.

in serious need. The judges of assize ordered an increase in the poor rates to set them to work, but by next February 'no effective relief had been provided'.[16]

The commons were policed in the manor or courts baron as was shown at Chawton. Suits over common land devoted most time to establishing 'long usage'. This was the crucial plank of legal 'custom'. For practice to be customary it must have occurred from 'time immemorial', technically this meant uninterrupted since 1189, as well as being 'reasonable' and 'compatible with natural and divine law'. Physical access was crucial: if a group of putative commoners could be excluded from the land, any claim of long-usage was meaningless. Enclosure, in the physical sense, was the best-known way to seize possession of a common.

The 'Clubmen' of the Civil War seem to be little known. These bands of local defence vigilantes tried to protect their localities against the excesses of both armies. Clubmen joined to prevent their wives and daughters being raped, themselves being forcibly conscripted, their crops and property being damaged or seized by the armies and their lives threatened or intimidated by soldiers, battle followers, looters, deserters or refugees. As their name suggests, they were mostly armed with cudgels, flails, scythes and sickles. They distinguished themselves by white ribbands.[17]

In 1645, Clubmen were active in Hampshire and therefore qualify for this chapter by the defence of their land.[18] Their activity at this time would hardy be a surprise after Cromwell's major muster, probably on Chawton Common, two bloody skirmishes in Alton and the turning point of the Battle of Cheriton in the preceding years.[19] During the whole of this war, a great deal of military traffic passed between Alton and Winchester: scouts, baggage, message takers, retreating soldiers one way, reinforcements the other. Necessarily, any movement had to cross the ridge at or near Medstead. Troops of both sides caused widespread damage including firing Alresford, looting during a retreat to Basingstoke and some incidental murders.

Initially, Clubmen gathered spontaneously in response to the actions of soldiers in their localities and were of a third party, neither Royalist nor Parliamentarian. In some areas, Clubmen were organised by the local gentry and churchmen and were a force which both sides in the war repressed severely, particularly in the south and west. Oliver Cromwell attacked a group of over 1,000 in the ancient fort on Hambledon Hill in Dorset. After an hour's fighting, sixty Clubmen were killed and 400 captured, half of whom were wounded.

From 1680 to 1692, there were twelve successive years of favourable seasons and low prices. The exception was the winter of 1688-9 which was particularly bleak with great storms and much hardship amongst the poor because of soaring

---

16 TNA, State Papers 16/185/2345, 188/55, 189/43, Assizes 24/20, ff. 31, 44.
17 Wikipedia.
18 Wood, *Riot, Rebellion*, p. 145.
19 Godwin, *Civil War in Hampshire*, p. 314. Adair, *Cheriton 1644*.

grain prices. The grain shortage was partly the result of the freezing rivers and streams which prevented mills from grinding corn.[20] A wet autumn in 1692, however, ushered in six lean years, heralded by the catastrophic harvest of 1693, said to have been the worst recorded since the reign of Elizabeth, and harvests were not really good again for almost a quarter of a century.[21]

Breaking the ice, 1792
George Morland, Museums Sheffield
George Morland was probably the most popular painter in the late eighteenth century. He felt strongly about the world lost to the enclosures. He is often criticised today for his sentimentality manifesting a 'flight from realism'. In his time, his critics thought him 'too accurate, too unsentimental and reluctant to argue a case'.

Moral judgements were often passed on those claiming or defending common rights. To an extent, this was a legal tactic to taint an opponent, but it also suggested the use of gossip in which the 'common fame' of individuals could be related to their claim as litigants.[22] 'Thievish places' gave liberty and opportunity

20 Lenman, *Jacobite Risings*, p. 11.
21 Rose, 'Price Riots', p. 281.
22 Healey, 'Political Culture', pp. 269-279.

to villainous minds which sought to shake down trees, maim animals, place cattle on a disputed enclosure or break down hedges.

Until about 1700, manorial courts were relatively active in the direction of communal agriculture where it still existed. Particular attention was paid to the stinting of communal pastures and the control of animals. Encroachments onto common land of any kind were, on the whole, vigilantly policed, the encroachers having to throw down their fences and remove buildings. After 1700, there was a great deal of variation in the completeness of the functioning of manorial courts. By the end of the eighteenth century, most court books merely record the various and inevitable changes of tenant and there is little discussion of husbandry. Most telling of all is the attendance record. The freeholders, leaseholders and copyholders were expected to present themselves at the manorial court on a regular basis. However, it is clear that in some manors regular attendance became the exception quite early in the eighteenth century.[23]

> *Most deponents were old men who were overwhelmingly representative of the rural middling sorts. There were some labour deponents, but the majority were yeomen and husbandmen. It was the politics of the elite, not the politics of the weak.*[24]

The medieval village had been gradually transformed by the impact of trade, civil war, sales of land, enclosure and the invasion of domestic crafts. There were seldom lords and peasants. In place of the old feudal lord of the manor, the squire ruled in the village, sat on the county bench, appointed the church of England parson, leased land to the tenant farmer and, like him, employed rural workers. The merchant who owned land sat beside the squire in Parliament and proved their common interests by jointly voting enclosure acts, subsidies and Corn Laws; upholding the Poor Law and Acts of Settlement for the better regulation of the poor; and promoting tolls and turnpikes, measures against smuggling and bringing in Militia Acts. In 1705, a mob of over twenty attacked soldiers escorting a 'disorderly fellow' from Romsey who had been impressed for the army by justices.[25]

> *All these measures were of considerable concern to the cottagers, small freeholders and the labouring poor. Having no political rights and no other means of redress of grievance, the lower orders resorted to the traditional riot. On such occasions, frequent in the eighteenth century, market towns and country lanes echoed to the sound of marching feet, burning stacks and*

---

23 Chapman and Seeliger, *Formal and Informal Enclosures*, p. 4.
24 Healey, 'Political Culture', p. 284.
25 TNA, State Papers, Anne, MS, p. 244. Beloff, *Public Order*, p. 121.

of uprooting fences as working men and women settled accounts with corn factors, religious dissenters, mill owners, farmers or enclosing landlords.[26]

In the eighteenth century, there were riots, at some time, almost across the country and for many reasons. There were sporadic disturbances over England in 1714 and 1715: Bedford, Birmingham, Chippenham, Norwich and Reading on the King's coronation day. Oxford, the citadel of High-Anglican clerical Toryism was in perpetual uproar. During parliamentary elections, non-voters rioted at the polls in Brentford, Bristol, Cambridge, Hereford, Leicester and Taunton.

Roman Catholic chapels were pulled down in Sunderland and Liverpool in 1746, in London and Bath in 1780, and Methodist meeting houses everywhere and regularly. The Irish were attacked in London in 1736 and 1763, and extensively in 1780. There were protests against turnpikes around Hereford and Worcester in 1735-6 with a mass destruction of toll gates in 1753 in Bristol, Leeds, Wakefield and Beeston, and lesser affairs when the Alton to Winchester turnpike act was passed. Attempts to impose excise duties and to stop smuggling met with staunch resistance.

The Militia Acts stirred massive protests in 1757 in East Anglia, Lincoln, Nottingham, Yorkshire, and in 1761, in Northumberland ninety miners were killed and wounded. Frequent non-compliance continued to the turn of the century. Village militias were formed to shape haphazard local groups into a third line of defence behind the army and the regular militia. But, of course, once formed, they could be used by the government for any purpose thought fit. Every village, Medstead and Ropley included, had to provide a certain number of men, either as volunteers or through compulsory ballot. Those who volunteered received a bounty of two guineas while those enrolled through the luck of the draw received nothing. The commitment was for four years with four weeks' annual training.[27] Failing to attend was called desertion with a fine of £20.

Hostility to enclosure, mainly after 1760, can be instanced by riots in Northampton, Wiltshire, Norwich, Oxfordshire, Boston, Worcester, Sheffield and Nottingham. The poor were of course bitterly hostile. 'This appears not only from the petitions presented to parliament, but from the echoes that have reached us of actual violence.'[28] There was more opposition to enclosure than used to be supposed.[29]

For every serious incident, there were many more occasions of sullen resistance where a gate was thrown off its hinges, a hedge uprooted, or the notice of enclosure pulled down from the church porch. Enclosure protests were rarely reported in the newspapers. Before 1760, references are most often found in the exchange of letters between an estate steward and his master. Thus, in 1710,

---

26 Rudé, *Crowd in History*, pp. 33-4.
27 Bate, *Clare*, pp. 77-9.
28 Hammonds, *Village Labourer*, p. 63.
29 Andrew Charlesworth, *An Atlas of Rural Protest*, 1983.

Walpole heard of a mob, some in disguise with masks and women's cloaks, with axes, spades and pickaxes saying they would persist in the claim to a right of common and next year hoped to see the hedges demolished'.[30] Thompson gives numerous examples in Atherstone, Coventry, Newbury, Nottingham, Sheffield, Streatham and Sutton Coldfield.[31]

Perhaps the most famous case was at West Haddon in the 1760s. Fourteen months after enclosure, the fence posts and rails were burnt as they lay in the fields ready for construction with estimated damage at £1,500. Invitation for the riot came in an advertisement for a football match printed in the *Northampton Mercury*.[32] 'After the match they turned themselves into a tumultuous mob.' The landowners offered financial rewards to catch the perpetrators. Sir Thomas Ward of Guilsborough, was the third to do so, offering £20 on conviction of 'any persons of property'. He also threatened prosecution under the *Black Act*. Legal punch and counter punch eventually led to five men receiving sentences at the Assize of two to twelve years' transportation.[33]

But by far the most numerous riots in the eighteenth century, the 'most persistent, widespread and stubbornly promoted, were those occasioned by a shortage of, or a sudden rise in, the price of food. 'Rebellions of the belly' were the most common type of outbreak. Of some 275 disturbances noted between 1735 and 1800, two in every three were for this purpose.[34] Riots were triggered by soaring prices, by malpractices among dealers and by hunger.[35] Mob pressure tried to impose fixed prices on the market or to attempt to force local magistrates to decree maximum prices.[36]

> *These grievances operated within a popular consensus as to what were legitimate and what were illegitimate practices in marketing, milling, and baking. In turn this was grounded upon a consistent traditional view of social norms and obligations, of the proper economic functions of several parties within the community, which, taken together, can be said to constitute the moral economy of the poor.*[37]

When prices were high, more than one-half of the weekly budget of a labourer's family might be spent on bread. Dealers were hedged around with many restrictions codified in the reign of Edward VI. No-one could buy or sell by sample, parcels of corn in a bag or handkerchief, nor buy standing crops, nor buy to resell in three months within the same market at a profit. No sale could

---

30 Cambridge University Library, C(H) MSS 608, John Wrott to Walpole, 31/5/1710.
31 Thompson, *Customs in Common*, pp. 123-54.
32 *Northampton Mercury*, 29 July, 5, 26 August, 2 September 1765.
33 Neeson, *Commoners*, pp. 191-97.
34 Rudé, *Crowd in History*, pp. 35-6.
35 Thompson, 'Moral Economy', pp. 78-9.
36 Rose, 'Price Riots', p. 279.
37 Thompson, 'Moral Economy', p. 188.

be made at market before stated times when a bell would ring; the poor would have the first opportunity to buy grain, flour or meal in small parcels. When their needs were satisfied, a second bell would ring and licensed larger dealers might buy. In fact, many millers and merchants bought secretly at the farm door by samples.

Outhwaite warns that the counting of food riots is a 'perilous activity'.[38] Riots were not often reported to London for the fear that local officials might be castigated for their deficiencies in allowing them to occur. Troops might be sent in order to restore order burdening the locality with extra mouths to feed. Today's knowledge is constrained by the availability of newspaper resources. 'No region has been subjected to lengthy, intensive historical scrutiny.' However, the eighteenth century appears to have witnessed 'the most extraordinary rise in the extent and frequency of grain riots': 1708-12, 1727-9, 1739-40, 1756-7, 1766-8, 1772-3, 1783, 1795-6, 1799-1801, 1810-13 and 1816-18.

'A decided drop in prices' was not sufficient to ensure safety for dealers in 1712 when Sir John Lambert asked for protection for corn bought in Hampshire and stored in warehouses near Redbridge, Southampton, ready for export. The life of his factor had been threatened in a letter in a large, illiterate hand and the warehouses besieged by a mob for several days apparently with the full approval of the more substantial inhabitants in Romsey and the unwillingness to help of the local justices.[39]

Hampshire was heavily involved in the two most serious periods of widespread rioting: in 1740 when the deficient harvest of the previous year was followed by dearth and over 140 incidents took place in at least thirty counties; and, again, in 1756-57, with over twenty-four counties involved. These last 'were the most extensive rural disorders in a century when food riots became chronic'.

In 1766, the south and west of England, from Cornwall to Hampshire, exploded over twelve weeks with numerous riots over food prices. More than sixty violent incidents were reported in the press in a dozen weeks, including in Hampshire. Average wheat prices per quarter measure in the next thirty-six years were four times higher than before and reached a peak in 1800 of 128 shillings.

Consumers panicked and poured into the markets or raided flour mills. In October, civic leaders in Alton were so alarmed by a threatening letter that 'in great consternation', they consented to lower the prices of provisions to the poor.[40] Across the country there were hundreds of reports of markets sacked, grain stolen, merchant property looted and burned. The King ordered that no more grain was to be exported. Several rioters were shot dead. Special Commissions were set up in Wiltshire and other counties. Aggrieved landowners responded through the courts: three looters were sentenced to death in Reading, eight at

---

38 Outhwaite, *Dearth, Public Policy*, pp. 38-41.
39 TNA, State Papers, Anne, bundle 37. Beloff, *Public Order*, p. 70.
40 Rudé, *Crowd in History*, p. 42.

Norwich and four at Salisbury. At Gloucester, nine were sentenced to be hanged and seven to transportation.[41]

Harvests became regularly and considerably worse. Fifty years of relatively cheap food were followed by a second-half century of 'high and generally rising prices'.

The landlords closed their ears and pushed through more and more enclosures. Protests and petitions were ignored and the opposition charged that the customary rights and needs of commoners, once acknowledged, were now denied.[42] There was a fear that enclosure threatened internal peace. It was thought a decline in small farmers would weaken England's military strength; that tillage was more beneficial to the public than pasture; and it was gradually realised that enclosure was inimical to the very being of some communities.

The Marquis of Anglesey was asked in a letter where now was the 'degree of interest that could resist virtue?'

> Should a poor man take one of Your sheep from the common, his life would be forfeited by law. But should you take the common from a hundred poor mens sheep, the law gives no redress. The poor man is liable to be hung for taking from You what would not supply You with a meal & You would do nothing illegal by depriving him of his sustenance; nor is Your family supplied for a day by the subtraction which distress his for life! ... Yet the causers of cries are more guilty than the perpetrators. What must be the inference of the poor? When they see those who should by their patterns defy morality for gain, especially when, if wealth could give contentment, they had enough wherewith to be satisfied. And when the laws are not accessible to the injured poor and Government gives them no redress?

The Duke replied, 'Excepting as to the mere fact of the Inclosure, the forming of which no one has the right to comment, All your statements are without foundation & as your language is studiously offensive I musty decline any further communication with you.'[43]

At Atherstone, commoners asked,

> *What must we think of those who can Cloak themselves with Indifference and Neutrality while an affair of such importance to the said Town is depending that must we look upon those to be who byass'd by some sinister and selfish ends and views will give their vote for such an Inclosure?*[44]

---

41 *Annual Register*, IX, 9/1751; *Gentlemen's Magazine*, XXXVI, 30/12/1766; *Gloucester Journal*, 12/1766; TNA, TS 11/795/3707, 11/1116/5728. Neeson, *Commoners*, p. 22.
42 Neeson, *Commoners*, pp. 326-27.
43 Staffordshire Record Office, D603/K/16/104, Reverend C. Landor to the Marquis of Anglesey, 26/4 and 3/5/1824.
44 Warwickshire Record Office, HR 35/14.

In some towns, like Alton, small riots became endemic. A concerned citizen wrote in 1786 that 'scarce a Sabbath ever returns, but disturbance prevails in different parts of the town with impunity'.[45]

The year 1795 brought the revolt of the housewives. A Hampshire contributor to the *Annals of Agriculture* explained that the poor 'have erroneously conceived that the price of grain is increased by the late alteration from a nine-gallon bushel to the 'Winchester' eight-gallon at the moment of a rising market.[46] In the 1760s, Charles Smith estimated that of a supposed population of about six millions in England and Wales, 3,750,000 were wheat-eaters, 888,000 ate rye, 739,000 ate barley and 623,00 oats. By 1790, two-thirds of the population were eating wheat.[47] It was a time when one popular mill could provoke the people to fury by a sudden rise in the price of flour or an evident deterioration in its quality.

Exceptional scarcity sharpened the edge of the misery in 1795 and was marked by a series of food riots all over England.

> *These disturbances are particularly interesting from the discipline and good order which characterise the conduct of the rioting women. When they found themselves mistress of the situation, they did not use their strength to plunder the shops: they organised distribution, selling the food they seized at what they considered fair rates and handing over the proceeds to the owners.*

Among many, Sarah Rogers in company with other women started a cheap butter campaign. She took some butter from Hannah Dawson 'with a determination of keeping it at a reduced price' an escapade for which she was afterwards sentenced to three months' hard labour at the Winchester Assizes. 'Nothing but the age of the prisoner (being very young) prevented the Court from passing a more severe sentence.'[48]

The class conflict over land enclosure, corn prices and much else carried over into that other great preoccupation of the landed gentry, the gentlemen's game laws, discussed briefly in Chapter 3.

In 1389, in the wake of the Peasants' Revolt, Parliament was disturbed to learn that on days 'when good Christian people be at church hearing divine service', servants and labourers were often out hunting and 'sometimes under such colour they make their assemblies, conferences, and conspiracies for to rise and disobey their allegiance'.

To prevent such seditious gatherings, persons with lands worth less than 40s a year were forbidden, under pain of a year's imprisonment, to keep hunting dogs or to use ferrets, nets, hare-pipes of any other 'engine' to take deer, rabbits, hares or other 'gentlemen's game'. After 1610, there were different qualifications

---

45 *Hampshire Chronicle*, 20/11/1786.
46 Thompson, 'Moral Economy', pp. 102-5.
47 Charles Smith, *Three Tracts on the Corn-Trade and Corn-Laws* (London 1766), pp. 140, 182-5.
48 *Ipswich Journal*, 8/8/1795.

for hunting deer and rabbits and the rest. To hunt partridges, and pheasant, for instance, a person had to possess freeholds worth at least £40 a year, leaseholds worth at least twice that amount, or good or chattels at £400 or more. The property qualification for hunting deer was higher.[49]

The instruments to deal with 'stubborn, cross-grain'd rogues' like poachers were at hand,

> *Beadles, Catchpoles, Gaolers, Hangman, with such like Engines of Humanity are the fittest Tools in the World for a Magistrate to work with in the Reformation of an obdurate Rogue, all which, I say, may be so used and managed by him as not to endanger his own Fingers or discompose his thoughts.*[50]

The enforcement of the game laws, like the pursuit of all game, was the prerogative of unpaid country gentlemen. 'Here were the real rulers of most of England and the essential mechanism whereby the will of central government was made effective in the provinces.'[51] As prosecutors, as justices nominated by the sovereign, as grand jurors and as employers of the gamekeepers who appeared as witnesses, the gentry dominated the legal system which determined the poacher's fate and most other petty criminals. It was, in fact, possible for a gentleman to perform several of these roles at the same time and in private.[52] However much individuals might be victimised, the class-interests of the landed aristocracy were ultimately safe.

In one celebrated case in the 1820s, a Hampshire farmer named Richard Deller was convicted by the Duke of Buckingham on the information of the latter's gamekeeper and the testimony of another of his servants – all in the Duke's own drawing room in his house at Avington. If he uttered 'one impertinent word', Buckingham warned Deller, 'there was a constable in the room to take him to 'gaol or the stocks'.[53] Deller tried for several days to gain a fair hearing, but was given the run around by three clergymen including Edmund Poulter, one of the bishop's placemen to whom in 1791 was given the Rectory of Crawley, then that of Barton Stacey, then that of Meonstoke and a prebend in Winchester Cathedral and, finally, exchanging Barton Stacey for Alton. Poulter's dignity was somewhat impaired by his unfortunate tendency to fall into fits on the bench. After several attacks, he sank into a long decline and died in 1830.[54]

---

49 Munsche, *Gentlemen and Poachers*, p. 11. Pheasants were sometimes scarce in Hampshire. Between 1802 and 1853, Peter Hawker killed to his own gun 7,053 partridges, but only 575 pheasants (Hawker, *Diary*, throughout).
50 Nourse, *Campania Foelix*, pp. 273-4.
51 Lenman, *Jacobite Risings*, p. 94.
52 Munsche, *Gentlemen and Poachers*, p. 76.
53 Commons debate, viii, cols, 1292-8, 25/4/1823. Also Cobbett, *Rural Rides*, Vol. 1, pp. 191-3.
54 Martin, 'Better than Ambition', *Enter Rumour*, pp. 148-149.

Historians have very little to say about the summary trials of poachers before justices. The surviving evidence makes it very difficult to be sure what actually occurred. Before 1770, justices were not even required to record cases held out of sessions. Even in Wiltshire, where over a thousand conviction certificates survive, only 30 per cent between 1750 and 1800 can be found. How many summary trials of a poacher by a country gentlemen under unjust laws were a mockery of justice? Deller's plight was not unique. In 1769, for instance, Robert Barfoot, another Hampshire farmer, was charged with possessing a brace of hares and tried 'before some gentlemen ... assembled at the house of Mr. H − (where there is a monthly meeting held for the preservation of game)'. Not surprisingly, he was convicted and fined £10.[55]

Country gentlemen were hostile towards alehouses as the traditional social centre for the lower classes and there was no safer place where smugglers and poachers could meet, particularly if the place was run by someone involved in the trade.[56] The justices of Hampshire complained in 1778 that it was the practice of some public houses to sponsor shooting matches, 'whereby the servants in husbandry, and the other lower sorts of people, learn and are taught to shoot and destroy the game, and are seduced from the respective labours and employments'.[57]

To judge from the press notices, man traps and spring guns were not used by game preservers in parts of Hampshire before the 1790s. Robert Thistlethwayte, for example, announced in 1793 that traps and guns would be set in all the covers on his estate because he had been plagued by poachers for more than a decade.[58] In 1785, a Hampshire gentleman gave this description of what happened when 'thigh-crackers, body-squeezers, spring guns, and man traps' were set:

> *This hardened banditti disregarding the notice that was given of what was prepared for their destruction, ventured in the night, as had been their usual custom, into the wood, where no less than four of them were found in the morning caught in these terrible engines, three had their thighs broken by the crackers and traps, and the fourth was found dead in a body-squeezer.*[59]

The rulers of eighteenth century England cherished the death sentence. In place of police, propertied Englishmen had a fat and swelling sheaf of laws which threatened thieves with death.[60] The number of capital statutes grew from about fifty to over 200 between 1688 and 1820.[61] 'This flood of legislation is one of the great facts of the eighteenth century and it occurred when peers and gentry

55 Munsche, *Gentlemen and Poachers*, pp. 93-4.
56 Munsche, *Gentlemen and Poachers*, pp. 67, 73.
57 *Salisbury Journal*, 23/3/1778.
58 *Salisbury Journal*, 16/9/1793.
59 *Salisbury Journal*, 28/11/1775.
60 Hay, 'Property' in *Albion's Fatal Tree*, pp. 17-18.
61 Radzinowicz, *English Criminal Law*, Vol. 1, p.4.

held power with the least hindrance from crown or people.' According to Gilbert White, even bishop Hoadly opposed the harsh game laws in Hampshire.[62]

> *Property became officially deified. It became the measure of all things. Even human life was weighed in the scales of wealth and status. 'The execution of a needy decrepit assassin,' wrote Blackstone, 'is a poor satisfaction for the murder of a nobleman in the bloom of his youth and full enjoyment of his friends, his honours and his fortune.'[63]*

Parliament was not prepared to allow property to suffer when some mills were torn down in the national-wide riots of 1766-1767. An act plugged a gap in the law by making such destruction a capital offence.[64] If death for food rioters was an excellent idea so was transportation for enclosure rioters. Within three days, the bill was enlarged so that gentlemen busy on the expropriation of common lands by Act of Parliament were as well protected as the millers. By the time the bill became law two weeks later, it had also become a transportable offence to meddle with the bridges and steam engines used in the mines which were bringing ever-increasing revenue to the gentry and aristocracy. Within decades the death penalty extended to forgeries and frauds of all kinds.[65]

The landowners based their defence of judicial terror on comparisons with French tyranny or the occasional punishment of a great man. 'All men of property knew that judges, justices and juries had to be chosen from their own ranks.' The jury, the supposed guarantee that an Englishman would be tried by his equals, had a 'sharp property qualification'. The reason, simply put, was that the 'common Englishman could not be trusted to share in the operation of the law. A panel of the poor would not convict a labourer who stole deer or wood from a lord's park, a sheep from a farmer's fold, or corn from a merchant's yard'.[66]

'The effects were made the more disastrous after 1793 by England's entry into the European war.'[67] Under the shadow of the French Revolution, as farm gate prices rose dramatically, the English governing classes regarded all associations of the common people with the utmost alarm. In this general terror, lest insubordination and riot should develop into rebellion, 'the capitalist's objection to high wages and the politician's dislike of democratic institutions' were merged into repressive legislation.[68] The *Combination Acts* of 1799, developed to halt putative trade unionism, were joined by a stream of restrictive legislation: *Treasonable and Sedition Practices and the Seditious Meetings and Assemblies Bills* (1795); in the wake of naval mutinies, the *Seduction from Duty and Allegiance Act*

---

62 Hoadly, *Enlightenment Prelate*, p. 257.
63 Backstone, *Commentaries*, Vol. II, p. 7, in Hay, 'Property' in *Albion's Fatal Tree*, p. 19.
64 9 Geo III, c. 39, 12/4-1/5/1769.
65 Hay, 'Property' in *Albion's Fatal Tree*, p. 21.
66 Hay, 'Property' in *Albion's Fatal Tree*, p. 38.
67 Rudé, *Crowd in History*, pp. 37-39.
68 Webbs, *Trade Unionism*, p. 73.

(1797); two *Newspaper Publications Acts* (1798-1799); *Administering Unlawful Oaths* (1797); and an *Act for the more Effective Suppressions of Societies established for Seditious and Treasonable Purposes* (1799). Almost every town in the country rushed to support this government attack on freedom of association. New Alresford held solidarity meetings and placed newspaper advertisements, listing their prominent citizens, who declared that they would 'support and defend the constitution of our country consisting of king, lords and commons as established at the Glorious Revolution'.[69] In fact, they were doing the opposite.

The rising panic, especially but not only among the propertied classes, was magnified by Government manipulation. Three junior ministers masterminded Press propaganda. One of them, Francis Freeling, ran the Post Office from 1797-1836 and through it a large national spy network. Letters to suspect citizens in Hampshire were opened and reports made from Winchester Post Office to Government figures in London.[70] Surviving secret service accounts reveal that in the early 1790s, the Government spent about £5,000 a year on press subsidies and that the two alarmist newspapers, the *Sun* and *True Briton*, were both started with ministerial help in 1792-1793.

All in all, it was no time for a lowly labourer to join with his fellow victims to kick up a fuss about a nasty parliamentary enclosure bill in, say, Medstead in 1798.

---

69 *Hampshire Chronicle*, 7/1/1793.
70 Hilton, *Mad, Bad, and Dangerous People?*, p. 65. Chase, *Early Trade Unionism*, pp. 72, 83. Orth, *Combination*, p. 197.

9 THE RECTOR, THE WARDEN AND THE OLD BOYS' CLUB

The Medstead private parliamentary enclosure, 1798-99

Wee are confused, and infused,
and our hedges broken.
I faith, quoth Bars, I tell you sirs,
my fields they lye all open,
Faith, quoth old Neale, the poor will steale,
before they'll fall to working.
I and whoore for all they're poore,
they care not for a lerking.
These hedgebreakers I thinke it fit,
that at next léete wee paine them[1]

Agricultural workers lived in villages in which they were 'organisationally outflanked': separated from other parishes; dependent on the goodwill of a particular employer if they were regularly hired, in daily competition with their fellows for a day's work if they were not; embedded in local power structures controlled by the gentry and their friends; and vulnerable to the petty vindictiveness which was the other face of village paternalism. In such a situation, it would be a brave man or woman who tried to bargain too determinedly with an employer.[2]

Yet, if an onlooker viewed our species from a distance, what would probably most surprise would be the almost universal subjection of strength to weakness. The physical strength lies with the governed. At least, this was the view of William Paley in 1785. How is it, he asked, that the opinion [of the landlords] prevails over the strength [of the poor]. The motives by which the 'many are induced to submit to the few becomes an enquiry which lies at the root of almost every political speculation'.[3]

Writers at the end of the eighteenth century suggest little strength left for fight among poor cottagers.[4] Cobbett thought 'of all God's creation what is so miserable to behold or to think of as a wretched, half-starved family creeping to their nest of straw, there to lie shivering till sent forth by the fear of absolutely

---

1   Extract from an English ballad, *The Countrey Man's Chat*, c. 1632.
2   Wrightson, *Earthly Necessities*, p. 326.
3   William Paley, *Principles of Moral and Political Philosophy*, 1785, Book VI, Ch. 2.
4   Bovill, *English Country Life*, pp. 24-5.

*"Gentleman, welcome. To be thoroughly impartial after the Act
is passed, I will need to know your precise requirements quite soon."*

A thoroughly impartial business: 'The whole plan is generally settled between the
solicitor and two or three principal proprietors without ever letting the rest of them into
the secret.' ¥

¥   Stephen Addington, *Inquiry into the Reasons for and against Inclosing* (1772), p. 21.

expiring from want?'[5] Benjamin Disraeli, in *Sybil*, described the peasant's return after cultivating the broad fields of merry England to 'the squalid hovel which profaned the name of home ... over which malaria hovered and round whose shivering hearth were clustered other guests – fever in every form, pale consumption, exhausting Synochus and trembling ague'.[6] In 1788, John Byng described the lives of Sussex labourers, 'How wretched do the miseries of a cottage appear; want of food, want of fuel, want of clothing! Children perishing of an ague and an unhappy mother unable to attend to, or relieve their wants, or assuage their pains.'[7]

The general harvest failure in 1799-1800 was accompanied by a dozen or more food riots against price fixing of wheat, flour and bread. Farmers and grain merchants sold to merchants for the best price and left local workers short of food. Rioters forced the sale of wheat at the normal, or 'fair', price of 5s or 5s 6d a quarter. Millers were made to sell flour at less than 3d a pound and bakers their bread at 6d for a quatern loaf. Other forced sales included butter, cheese, meat, potatoes, bacon, malt, candles and soap. The *Hampshire Chronicle* reported that committees were instituted to prosecute forestallers and regraters and 'to defeat the many artifices too successfully practised to plunder the poor'.[8]

New powers to speed the enclosure process and granted to landowners under an act of 1773 were often abused: the preliminary meetings where enclosure was discussed were intended to be held in public but, by the time public meetings were advertised, the deals had already been cut.[9] Landowners then chose their own commissioners, lawyers and surveyors.

As a result, parliamentary acts for enclosure became a soulless production line. In 1778, a total of eighty-eight private acts on all matters were approved by parliament of which fifty, including that for Medstead and Bentworth, were for enclosures. The remainder concerned nineteen naturalizations and a collection of divorces and estate reconstructions for the aristocracy. Next year, 1799, there were sixty-one enclosures among 120 bills. This was the year that Napoleon seized power in France in the *Coup de 18 Brumaire*. The government's attention was firmly centred on this growing threat and on its own flood of repressive legislation. What scrutiny might Medstead's application receive? The answer was none as England's larger landlords poured through the legislative gap. The broader battle was lost: in 1786, there were still 250,000 independent landowners; within thirty years the number was reduced to 32,000.

5   Cobbett, *Rides*, Vol. 1, pp. 18, 35, 73, 321, 380, 382; Vol. 2, pp. 26, 298, 348, 387; *Cottage Economy*, pp. 11-2, 29, 32, 77.
6   Consumption: pulmonary tuberculosis; synochus, possibly typhus. Benjamin Disraeli, *Sybil*, Chapter III.
7   John Byng, *Rides Round Britain*, Vol. 1, p. 369; Vol. 2, p. 108.
8   *Hampshire Chronicle*, 15/9/1800.
9   The Inclosure Act 1773, 13 Geo. 3 c. 81.

"Gentlemen - and Ladies! The Medstead inclosures of 1736 were a good start, but our grandfathers lacked a little ambition! There are almost 300 Acres of common not yet fully in our hands. Why don't we finish the job?"

The Medstead and Bentworth enclosure act of 1798, held in the parliamentary archives, sets out to 'allot all the open and common fields' (*Appendix 20*).[10] After the last forty years of experience and lawyers' attention, acts were now much more complex and lengthy documents. There is also a sense of unfinished business from the first Medstead, or Soldridge, act of 1735. The aftermath of this second foray gutted Medstead of its commercial life and blighted the village.

The charge was led by the gentleman trustees of a deceased Henry Drummond, esquire and lord of the manor, his nephew Charles Drummond and George Wheatley.[11] For the first time, there is no prominent part for the bishop of Winchester, now Brownlow North, but his son stood in his place: Francis, the rector of Old Alresford, worth £560 a year, whose remit included the chapelries of New Alresford, £250, and Medstead, £600 (*Appendix 5*). Six months later, his father presented him with the largest parish in Southampton, St. Mary's, administered by a pair of curates to be each paid, perhaps, £50 a year out of an income of £2,000.[12] Much more will be said of Francis later.

Then follows a list of five well-known surnames and 'divers others', among them Budd, Wake, Camies, Bone and Hicks. Here is the unfinished element – all of these families were central to the previous parliamentary enclosure sixty years before and their descendants were returning to complete the job.

The three commissioners were Thomas Fleet, Thomas Hasker and John Tredgold. They charged £500 for their work. Their surveyor was Thomas Richardson, their clerk Edward Hopkins and their clerk's clerk, David Weddell.

Tredgold, of Chilbolton in 1798 and 1809 and Winchester from 1802-5, was by far the most experienced. Government sponsored reports mentioned him as prominent among the local improvers, a 'very understanding farmer much employed as a commissioner in enclosures and in valuing land'.[13] Chapman notes him as the most active commissioner in Hampshire with fifteen county awards and two others as an umpire and a quality man and one more in orchestrating an agreement. Within his enclosure briefs were Basing (1796), Old Alresford (1803), Romsey (1804) and Fareham (1805). He was also involved in two other counties. One must take him to be a professional, available for hire by the landowners to help drive their enclosure acts through the Lords and Commons and evidently trusted to achieve the right result when it came to the awards. It is likely that Tredgold was also a bondsman in Winchester, lending money as a surety for bail for the appearance of a defendant in court.

Hasker had experience in Basing, and in Basingstoke (1786) and Monk Sherborne (1792). It seems likely that he knew Tredgold well. At this time, Hasker owned Chineham Estate having bought the land from the family of the

---

10 Private Act, 38 George III, c. 35. Parliamentary Archives, HL/PO/PB/1/1798/38G3n99.
11 TNA, PROB 11/1263/76, will of Henry Drummond, proved 7/1775.
12 Martin, 'Better than Ambition', in *Enter Rumour*, p. 154.
13 *General View ...*, 1792, p.13.

Earl of Dartford and which was sold later to Lord Bolton. Hasker served as a guardian of the Basingstoke Union workhouse.

Fleet had been an overseer at Preston Candover Hall, an adjunct to the Basingstoke Union, and later found the money to become a yeoman in Hatch Warren. He had no previous positions as a commissioner, but was to take part in the later Old Alresford enclosure with Tredgold.[14] This juxtaposition of enclosure officers having a vested interest in managing the county's poor is disquieting.

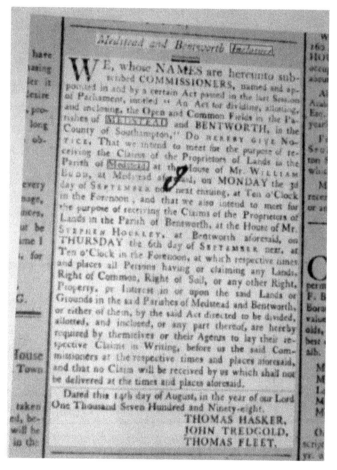

The Hampshire Chronicle's advert for the Medstead and Bentworth enclosure, 1798.

"Oh, you are Commoners. How delightful! Claims are being heard today. Let me have your letters drawn up by your attornies, and I will see that they get full attention".

Claims are being heard today! *'If there was no lawyer there to put his case, what prospect was there that the obscure cottager who was to be turned adrift ... would ever trouble the conscience of a committee of landowners?'* ¥

¥ Hammonds, *Village Labourer*, p. 52.

The commissioners placed three front-page advertisements in the *Hampshire Chronicle* announcing they would hear the claims of the proprietors of the common lands.[15] Notice of the commission was nailed to Francis North's church door in Medstead on 14 August. One can imagine the cluster of commoners straining to interpret the official language and trying to assess the change that would shortly come to their lives. The old among them would remember Chawton and Farringdon, and there would also be tales of land lost to the large farmers in 1736. The first meeting was at the home of William Budd in Medstead at ten in the forenoon on Monday, 3 September. Only those who could prove they were a proprietor would be heard. Budd, of course, was a prominent petitioner, making it tougher for unrepresented and, possibly, illiterate complainants to visit, for the first time, a house always beyond their means and then to stand, cap in hand, and state their case.

> Claims must be sent 'in Writing under their Hands, or the Hands of their Agents, distinguishing in such Claims the Tenure of the Estates in respect of which such Claims are made and stating therein such further Particulars as shall be necessary to describe such Claims with precision.' This was a difficult enough fence for the small proprietor so what must have been the 'plight of the cottager'? Unable to read or write, he knows only that he has enjoyed some customary rights of common without any idea of their origin or history or legal basis : knowing only that as long as he can remember he has kept a cow, driven geese across the waste, pulled his fuel out of the neighbouring brushwood and cut turf from the common and that his father did all these things before him. He was to present his evidence on a certain day to the landlord's bailiff, or to the parson, or to one of the magistrates into whose hands he has fallen before now over a little matter of a hare or partridge, or to some solicitor from a country town, a clear and correct statement of his rights. These commissioners can reject his claim on any technical irregularity.[16]

Such nailings were ill received elsewhere. In 1814, in Oxfordshire, 'it was found impracticable to affix the notices on the church doors of two parishes owing to large mobs armed with every description of offensive weapon having assembled for the purpose of obstructing the persons who went to affix the notices and who were prevented by violence and threats of immediate death'.[17]

The Medstead and Bentworth enclosure award in the Hampshire Record Office is not the master document signed on 21 May 1799 at the *Swan Inn*, New Alresford, but it is close.[18] Deputy clerk of the peace, Peter Kerby, who signed approval on 5 September 1800, called it a 'copy examined against the original'.

---

15 *Hampshire Chronicle*, 20, 26/8 and 3/9/1798.
16 Hammonds, *Village Labourer*, p. 63.
17 Hammonds, *Village Labourer*, p. 90.
18 HRO, Q23/2/82. Also Winchester College Archives, 3538.

Again, there is no map for Medstead or Bentworth. There were surveyor's maps of all the enclosure work and, in reverse of what we expect, these maps were painstakingly turned into words as the preferred way of presenting legal matters. If the maps still exist they will probably lie in a solicitor's records.

The Medstead copy award contains more than 24,000 words and weighs over two-thirds of a kilogram (*Appendix 21*). The Bentworth content is kept apart, but it is from the same 1820 copy.[19] The act states, pages 12 and 14, that the Medstead and Bentworth awards were to be treated and charged separately within the same Award; Bentworth proprietors held separate meetings. The original award says, page 16, that it contains twenty-two parchment skins; the Medstead part of the copy contains eight, double sided, making sixteen, the Bentworth copy is on six sheets, five double-sided.

The act estimates 400 acres to be enclosed in Medstead and Bentworth. The Medstead allotments, including new roads, come to just over 231 acres in spreadsheets constructed from the award document. The 'missing' 169-ish acres are in the Bentworth award which has not been transcribed, not being a 'ridge' parish. A reported final 'skin' containing all the signatures and seals of the participants is missing.

In 1776, twenty-three years before the enclosure award, Medstead parish contained 2,257 acres of arable and pasture land according to a terrier, a private inventory, made to record the tithings 'as far as the plough and scythe go' (*Appendix 18*).[20] When all the boundary information is stripped away from the 1799 enclosure, the Medstead Commons constitute the whole of the forty-one awards of 229.69 acres made to fourteen or fifteen people:[21]

- Lower Church field   14 awards   41.38 acres
- Upper Church field   1 award   2.09 acres
- Upper Pace field   6 awards   39.99 acres
- Lower Pace field   6 awards   38.61 acres
  (including Broom Corner)
- Middle field   11 awards   103.90 acres
- North field   3 awards   3.71 acres

The five main recipients were Charles Drummond (for the dead Henry), 29.4 per cent, Ann Woolls of New Alresford, 27.5 per cent (but with Edward Woolls

---

19 HRO, Q23/2/10.

20 HRO, 43M74/PB1, terrier of the rectory of Old Alresford, 1776. Rathbone, *Chronicle of Medstead*.

21 The document says that the whole of the Medstead awards amounted to 229.43 acres, a discrepancy of a quarter acre to my total. Within that, there exist seven small discrepancies adding to 0.37 acres where fields known to be the same have small 'perch' transcription errors, one to another. Not a bad result. A further 2.24 acres were used for all new roads and footways (making 231.66 acres). The complication over recipient numbers is that William Budd of Soldridge died during the process; there are awards to 'Richard Wake (trustee for William Budd)' and separately to 'the late William Budd'. Another William Budd is a main beneficiary. These Budds were variously described as gentleman, 'of Tenantry', 'copyhold tenant of Ropley, of Old Alresford and of Selborne', and 'late of Soldridge'.

of Farringdon, 31.1 per cent), William Budd, 12.2 percent (but with other Budd allotments, 15.1 percent), Richard Wake, 10 per cent and Robert, William and John Andrews, of Farringdon, 6.8 per cent. Five families received 92.4 per cent of the total with eight of the individuals living outside the parish.[22]

There is good reason to add Francis North into this leading group. He took only 1.6 per cent for which, as the local rector, he was exempt from fees. North, already identified as the son of bishop Brownlow North, educated at Eton and Christ Church, Oxford University, was twenty-seven-years-old at enclosure, just married to his first wife, Esther Harrison. His family was illustrious and extremely well connected. Many close relations were strongly Jacobite. His father's half-brother was Frederick, Lord North, prime minister from 1770-1782.[23]

Brownlow, the elder son of the first Earl of Guilford (now 'Guildford'), received most of his degrees at All Souls and Trinity, Oxford, by virtue of being kin of the founder, Sir Thomas Pope. Ironically in view of his name and offsprings' careers, Pope was active in the sixteenth century dissolution of the monasteries. He oversaw acquisition of the properties of smaller religious organisations and, through this, developed a personal portfolio of almost thirty manors, the foundation of the Norths' wealth. Brownlow's first religious position was as a rector in Warwickshire when he was appointed by his brother-in-law, John, 6th Lord Willoughby de Broke. He received the see of Worcester even before his predecessor had died after falling from a horse – 'incontinently given' as Walpole archly reported. He was to be bishop of Winchester for almost forty years.

Bishop North and his first wife, Henrietta Bannister, suffered poor health which required them to make a four-year expedition to Italy and Southern Germany returning to England just before the Medstead enclosure. Henrietta's reputation was of extravagance and gambling – 'the devil on earth'.

Mrs. North kept up the rounds of a woman of fashion, hobnobbing with the royalty of miniscule German courts, quarrelling with her countrywomen abroad, flirting with their husbands, and by her constant display of bad taste embarrassing her children and her indulgent husband. For their travels, which were complicated by children and an attendant retinue of servants, the Norths had three enormous coaches, numbered so that the servants would know into which of them to put the proper baggage. Like the greatest of milords, the Norths whirled around western Europe.[24]

---

22 The Bentworth allotments, calculated from the shared costs of £390, were made primarily to Thomas Coulthard, Esquire, £263 13s 3d, 67.6 per cent rounded. The others were Thomas Hickery, 13 per cent; Thomas Hall, Esquire, 7.7; John Andrews, 4.9; Joseph Page, 3.5; William Winter, 1.9; John Paddick, 0.5; and the unnamed proprietor of Hall Place Farm, 0.4.

23 Nigel Aston, 'Frederick, Lord North', ODNB, 3/1/2008.

24 Martin, 'Better than Ambition', in *Enter Rumour*, pp. 145-6. Mrs. North made a 'solitary and uncomfortable' trip to the Holy Land where she gathered cones from the Cedars of Lebanon and brought them back to plant at Farnham Castle where the trees still grow.

Brownlow extracted maximum familial advantage through his acknowledged generosity and connections. Twenty-six close and distant relations received about seventy appointments to fifty churches through his influence between 1785 and 1820.

A good example is the bishop's third son, Charles Augustus, ordained deacon by his father in 1809 as he left his studies at Oxford. Ten weeks later, young North was ordained a priest so that, as a wedding present, he could become rector of Havant with an income of £500.[25] Later the same year, the bishop presented him with Alverstoke, worth £1,500 with a rectory house which was said to be the finest in England. 'As a *bonne bouche*', Charles was made perpetual curate of Gosport at £300. In 1812, he became a prebendary at Winchester, worth £1,000, and then registrar of the diocese which paid about £200. In short order, Charles was receiving £3,500 annually, exclusive of fees, glebes and various houses.

Francis North quickly followed his success at Medstead with further enclosures to two other parishes in his immediate benefice, Old and New Alresford.

At Old Alresford, his main parish, 104 acres of Nythen (also Nythe) Commons were enclosed by parliamentary act in 1805.[26] Brownlow, his father, was lord of the manor, and received over four acres of arable land in lieu of commons rights. John Tredgold and John Fleet, trusted business partners from Medstead, again acted as commissioners. With the consent of his father, Francis exchanged three pieces of glebe orchard, close and meadow for three acres of arable land called Voxe's which bordered the vestry. Francis then exchanged a further three acres of glebe called Collyers for three acres of arable called Priors belonging to Henry Lord Viscount Gage and Margaret, widow and trustee of General William Sheriff. Gage, another absentee landlord, and his wife, Susannah Skinner, had their main estate at Firle near Glyndebourne. Gage was accounted the 'most opulent peer in the kingdom', partly on account of the great parcels of land in the state of New York brought to the marriage by Skinner.

Encouraged by his two enclosures successes, Francis moved on to his glebe land at New Alresford.[27] The award of 326 acres of common fields and Commons Marsh, eighty-four acres, was around the centre of the town and made in 1807.[28] Here, there is a clear map.[29] There were a number of abutting older enclosures. The two largest allottees with over 10 per cent, with twenty-one others, were William Harris and Sir Henry Tichborne, whose family is briefly discussed elsewhere. Francis received twenty-one acres behind the church. Among other allotees were several parcels given to Winchester College, six acres to the trustees of Perins free school, and a small piece to Francis's churchwardens: one wonders why this should be so.

---

25 Martin, 'Better than Ambition', in *Enter Rumour*, pp. 151-2.
26 43 Geo. III, c. 67, 1803.
27 45 Geo. III, c. 61, 1805.
28 HRO, Q23/2/93/2.
29 HRO, Q23/2/93/1.

Following the deaths of a series of childless relatives, Francis became 8th Baron of Guilford and 6th Earl of Guilford in 1827. He inherited Waldershare Park, near Dover, and Glenham Hall in Suffolk, worth £18,000 a year.[30] After his extreme good fortune, he resigned only the prebend at Winchester.

Francis North was connected to Henry Drummond, the chief beneficiary of the Medstead enclosure. Drummond purchased a seat in parliament at Wendover, Buckinghamshire, in 1774, and consistently supported prime minister North in government before becoming disillusioned by North's policy in North America.[31] Brownlow North also provided automatic support to his brother when he managed to get to London.

Drummond was another absentee landlord: John Wyeth was his tenant farmer and his rent was increased as a result of the benefit of the Medstead enclosure.[32]

Henry Drummond came from solid Jacobite stock. His father, William, 4th Viscount of Strathallan, took part in the 1715 Jacobite rising, supported Prince Charles Edward Stuart in 1745 joining his privy council, and commanded the Jacobite forces in Scotland as Charles advanced into England. He was killed the next year at Culloden.[33]

As a young man, Henry lived at his uncle's bank in London. His fortune was made by acting as agent for eighteen army regiments. With Richard Cox, an existing land agent, the two men were paymasters to the Royal Artillery.[34] In a later iteration, the business was taken over by Lloyds Bank. In 1787, Henry bought The Grange, near Alresford, where he died in 1795. Neither the property at Medstead, nor The Grange, is mentioned in Drummond's will, only his 'real estate in the County of Southampton' (which, until 1959, was the formal name of Hampshire). However, neither might be a major matter when seen among his London mansion at St James's Square and 'all those my manors or lordships' in Northamptonshire.

Henry's son, also Henry, inherited, age nine, and leased The Grange as a hunting lodge with over 400 deer to George, Prince of Wales. This second Henry was 'one of England's great eccentrics' and a long-standing parliamentarian. He transformed The Grange into an enormous Greek temple to upstage his neighbour, Sir Francis Baring, head of the banking family and owner of nearby Stratton Park. By 1817, Henry got 'bored' and sold the estate to Alexander Baring, son of Sir Francis.[35] He became intimately involved in the Catholic Apostolic Church of which he was considered an apostle.

30 *Gentleman's Magazine*, 11/1827.
31 Philip Winterbottom, 'Henry Drummond', ODNB, 23/9/2004.
32 The Wyeth family had extensive farming connections with the land in Medstead and along Four Marks ridge, including working the farm at the Telegraph Lane semaphore station. Gerald Wyeth published an undated *Four Marks School Boy's Memories*.
33 Murray G. H. Pittock, 'William Drummond', ODNB, 3/10/2013.
34 John Booker, 'Richard Cox', ODNB, 3/1/2008.
35 https://thegrangefestival.co.uk.

"My dear fellow, what do you say to a small piece of apple orchard for your delicious arable field?"

The five remaining small awards at Medstead, together less than 6 per cent, went to commons users with good lands elsewhere. Richard Bone, John Camies, John Hicks of West Meon, John and Ann Hoare of Froxfield, and Robert Pullinger of Itchinswell [now Ecchinswell], were mostly from outside the immediate area.[36] There were no allotments among the village's encroachers and poor commoners.

One aspect of the Medstead enclosure award which sets it apart from others is that the actual allotments take up only a small part of the document.

The commissioners made their decisions based on ownership of the commons, but also adjusted allotment sizes based on quality of land: a good acre near your home might be worth more than two poor acres in four pieces at a distance. In practice, what suited one farmer, land for an orchard, for instance, would not suit another seeking only to graze cattle or to grow cereals. Values were adjusted by previous use, slopes, water access, drainage, fertility and by an ability to be reached easily without having to cross another's land.

The remainder of the award, therefore, was a giant exchange of land between all the participants, agreed privately but formalised in the award document so that there could be no subsequent argument 'by and with the consent and approbation of the said Commissioners and are hereby ratified and confirmed by them'. The stated purpose of these exchanges was land consolidation and greater profit. Everyone participated.

There were 107 exchanges involving 114 parcels of land amounting to 376.12 acres. Several were sequential where, for example, A gave to B who gave to C, or even A gave to B who gave back to A, presumably as they haggled. The accounting in the copy document of who exchanged with whom is not wholly accurate. At one stage, the scribe seems to lose a little concentration, at another forgetting to record the recipient. However, the discrepancies are too small to much affect the whole. The 1799 award acreage constituted just 27 per cent of the 114 exchanges. The remaining pieces of land came from the 1736 award, 55 per cent, and other lands, inherited or bought, 17 per cent. Most exchanges were more a case of sorting out both small, long inefficient, disparate 1736 enclosures and also existing 'family' pockets to make them 'contiguous', as they said, with their new 1799 allotments. The exchanges allowed landowners, like William Budd, to 'ascertain the Situation of the Lands held by him [in, for instance] the Manor of Ropley, to lay the same as [contigious] and convenient to each other as possible and to render them of greater value'.

One imagines some tension in these arrangements. In 1810, sections of the exchanges were recopied and, later, found their way to the Winchester College

---

36 For instance, HRO, 43M74/PB1, terrier of the rectory of Old Alresford, 1776: Richard Bone, 12 acres (William Bone, 126); John Camies, 86; HRO, Q22/1/1/246, Medstead Land Tax Assessment, 1799: Pullinger (Pullinger Farm), £6 2s 10d; John Hicks (Hick's Farm), £6 3s 4d; Mr. Hoar, renting land to William Andrews, 3s.

archive.[37] The extract covers eighteen pages. Each piece of exchanged land was named with its acreage, its provenance and its bordering lands and roads to all points of the compass. This provides the ability for an enthusiast to construct a mini-map for each piece of exchanged land. For example, a part of *Middle Field* at almost fourteen acres was awarded to William Budd who exchanged it with Charles Drummond. The award had nine surrounding properties, including tilled land, meadows, a highway and two cottages. These mini-maps become important pieces of a jigsaw (as discussed with the first Medstead enclosure); bordering properties often touching other exchanged lands which have their own mini-map.

Here lies another value of the extract. When the exchanged properties are added to their individual surrounding lands, there is a list of 121 pieces of Medstead. This is a rich vein for a patient historic field reconstructor.

To continue with the example of William Budd: in 1799, he began the day of the awards with forty-two identified pieces of land amounting to 108 acres to which by the end of the day he had added in thirteen exchanges another forty-two acres. However, he also agreed to give away ninety acres in thirty exchanges. He was left with sixty acres, compared to his original 108, but the equation either must have been satisfactory to him or, unlikely, he was a weak negotiator.

Two men signed the extract, both seemingly acting for a third party. Why were they engaged? Perhaps, one of the original exchangers needed proof of ownership in a dispute, in a further sale, for a marriage contract? John Dunn was a prosperous New Alresford attorney with a house and office at 7 East Street.[38] Alresford was one of eleven Hampshire towns given the responsibility for French officers, captured and given parole. Each town had an agent, in Alresford it was Dunn, who saw to billeting prisoners with suitable families and dealing with complaints.[39] He joined a High Street, Winchester, bank, Bulpett, Mulcock & Dunn, which many years later through serial amalgamations became the National Westminster. Dunn also gave regularly to the poor. Nothing is known of William Rous, although an Edward Rous was landlord of *The Swan* at Alresford and befriended the Tichborne Claimant when he came to the town to regain his supposed fortune.[40]

Seven new roads and footways were instructed for the new owners to gain access to their enclosed awards (private, fenced and gated) that would otherwise be marooned as allotments within what had been large open commons and fields.

The final part of the 1799 document concerns a further twenty-nine roads and footways that needed to to be diverted to take account of the post-exchanged

37 Winchester College Archives, Miscellaneous items in tin box, 16800.
38 *TNA*, ADM 98/201, 207.
39 Deacon, 'French Prisoners of War', Hampshire Field Club.
40 Douglas Woodruff, *The Tichborne Claimant* (Hollis & Carter, London 1957).

land, either to stop people having access to now consolidated land or to provide a better access from the new estates to the public roads and access to markets.

Once a decision was made, everyone was certainly in a hurry. On the 19 December, Francis North's church door was put to further devastating use: all rights of common were 'extinguished': 'No rights of Common shall hereinafter be claimed or enjoyed over all or any part of the said Lands or Grounds or any part thereof'.

Of the poor in Medstead, the cottage dwellers on the commons, there is only the briefest, passing information: a few curt surnames as points of reference. Certainly, there was no home for them now, nor was there any indication of compensation in terms of land, access or money.

Landlords and farmers are found generally to own about 80 per cent of common-right cottages. Traders and artisans owned most of the rest.[41] The cottages in agricultural villages mostly belonged to the principal landowners, if not part of the manorial estate. The carpenter, the smith or the mason may posses a cottage or tenement to which may be annexed a right of common; but as to 'the poor husbandman, who is alone an object of charitable purpose, it is rare indeed that he has an house of his own'.[42]

There are to hand two unexpected methods of counting the human cost of 1799 to Medstead.

First, at the end of the description of a perambulation of Medstead in 1744 (*Appendix 15*), there is a list of the seventeen owners of all the cottages built on the manor's waste. Many of the names are familiar from the 1736 Medstead award: Allen, Budd, Cane, Camies, Crockford, Dorey, Loveyer, Mould and Silvester. Where had the majority of these homes and families gone?

Second, censuses from 1801-1831 are little used, even known, because they do not contain people's names. Families and visitors in individual houses can be identified by surname every ten years but only from 1841. In 1801, and through to 1831, the authorities sought mainly to count the population and number of houses, occupied or not, by parish, and to assess local prosperity. This included full numbers of those working in agriculture. Awkwardly, the measure for those specifically in agricultural employment changed from 'persons' in 1801 to 'families' in later surveys to 1831. The 1801 census was conducted by the victors of enclosure: 'substantial landowners', their stewards, the local clergy and the overseers of the poor. The statistics were sworn before justices and sent to the Home Office to be laid before parliament. Incidentally, Laurence, in his *Duties of a Steward*, advised 'persons of quality', necessarily away from their land for much of the time, 'to have always one of the farmer's sons in their eye' to take on the role of emergency steward.[43]

41 Shaw-Taylor, 'Labourers, Cows ...', p. 104.
42 Young, *General Report on Enclosure*, pp. 167-8.
43 Laurence, *Duty of a Steward*, p. 16.

In Alton, in the immediate aftermath of the 1799 enclosure, there were minor skirmishes against turnpike roads, not as bad as the destruction of gates and tollhouses elsewhere. In 1800, local field workers marched, as in many places in the county, in protest against their 'distressed condition'.[44] 'Labour was abundant, work was scarce in winter, and wages were low.'

The population of Medstead dropped from 393 in 1801 to 350 in 1811, a fall of 11 per cent. Within the 1801 population, 330 people were in agriculture, 84 per cent of both sexes and all ages, and fifty-six people, 14 per cent, in 'trade, manufacturing and handicrafts'. By 1811, the 330 people in agriculture were reduced to fifty-five families. Using the 1801 ratios, the fifty-five families in agriculture equates to 271 people in 1811, implying some fifty-nine people left parish agriculture, just under 18 per cent of the 1801 total. More shocking, perhaps, is that the fifty-six people in trade, etc, reduced to just three families. There was no squire, no retired officer or business man and no commuter. With the loss of the cottagers, small farmers and traders, the lifeblood had been sucked from Medstead. It had declined into an economy based on wage labour. By 1831, the proof is evident: eight 'occupiers' (employers) employed seventy-three agricultural labourers with only four independent 'occupiers' who worked alone.

Most, if not all, the Medstead commoners who were evicted in the enclosure also lost their homes. Occupied houses fell from sixty-one in 1801 to forty-five in 1811 – a significant drop of 26 per cent in the village stock. These censuses also give the number of uninhabited houses for these two survey years. It was zero in each case.

These missing houses were not left empty; they were pulled down. They would have been sited either on the newly-enclosed commons or on the land that was exchanged to consolidate the winners' holdings. The houses were in the way. Labourers were either no longer needed to manage the much bigger plots, with perhaps changed methods or, most likely, crops turned to pasture. The families were unable to sustain themselves in the village without access to the benefits of the lost commons.

These 1801 figures are extracted from a census which took place on 10 March. It is possible, even probable, that the damage to community life was even higher for there is no record of what happened in the fifteen months from enclosure to this first census. Chawton, similarly populated in 1801 with 372 people and the only other parish to clear its commons completely, was the only other ridge village to track Medstead. Generally, all local villages picked up inhabitants from 1821-1841.

Among the unsung sufferers from the enclosure acts were the gypsies who always made the commons and wastes their principal home. 'They already called themselves *Travellers*, but they lived wholly in tents and held the caravan-

---

44 Shore, *Hampshire*.

dwelling *Gorgio* in great contempt.'[45] There is no known evidence for gypsies in Medstead, but the route of the drovers' way suggests it is likely. A map from around 1900 still showed 'Gypsy's Copse' nearby, just south of the later Telegraph Lane in Ropley. It was probably the loss of their traditional camping grounds that compelled the true gypsies, at the end of the nineteenth century, to take to the caravan. John Clare, the enclosure poet, loved to spend time in his childhood with the gypsies who camped on the commons and margins.[46] 'Where were they to go?' he asked.

Medstead was no piecemeal enclosure with land gradually brought into the new estates over many years. It happened almost over night, with 'old boy' owners, after the extensive exchanges, given a year till 1 December 1800, on threat of fine and other heavy penalties, to finish all the roads, hedges and fences and, of course, to pay the bills both for these works and for the commissioners' efforts.[47] Fencers and hedge planters listened out in the alehouses for news of where they could find the work that came with enclosure.[48]

Reducing small famers to labourers was thought worth the price, 'disagreeable and painful as it may be to the tender and feeling heart', because it would encourage population growth.[49] Labourers married early and had more children. The poorer they were the earlier they married. They felt their 'growing poverty less keenly' than those with more money having already 'trod the rugged path and felt its thorns and briars'.[50]

Landlords were told that 'once commoners were dependent, care should be taken to prevent labourers becoming in any way independent of the wage again'.[51] Even planting new hedgerows required careful thought. Medlars, for example, should never be used among the poor because 'it is bad policy to increase temptations to theft; the idle among the poor are already too prone to depredation and would be still less inclined to work' if every hedge furnished the means of support.

When evicted from commons by enclosure, said Vancouver and Rudge, labourers must live in cottages belonging to farms and at a distance from the corrupt solidarity of the village or they might live in large houses of industry.[52] Worse, Hampshire foresters were an 'idle, useless and disorderly set of people' whose first act of plunder was to steal the materials for the very roofs they lived under. Additional useful hands for agricultural employment would come from 'gradually cutting up and annihilating that nest and conservatory of sloth, idleness

45 Bovill, *English Country Life*, p. 26.
46 Bate, *John Clare*, p. 49.
47 Neeson, *Commoners*, p. 193.
48 Bate, *Clare*, p. 75.
49 Neeson, *Commoners*, pp. 27-9.
50 Howlett, 1781, *Examination of Dr. Price's Essay*, pp. 26-29.
51 Rudge, *General View ... Gloucester*, pp. 97, 50. Also cited in Neeson, *Commoners*, p. 29.
52 Vancouver, *General View*, p. 495 ff.

and misery, which is uniformly to be witnessed in the vicinity of all commons, waste lands and forests'. Vancouver also feared teaching commoners to read and write: 'Independence had become a threat, however beautiful it may be in theory, to raise the lower orders to a situation of comparative independence.'

By 1810, Vancouver thought there were opportunities for work if men were prepared to travel. In North West Hampshire, where labouring families 'readily earned a guinea a week in the summer season by travelling a few miles to the Berkshire peat meadows'. There was work in the forests, wastes and woodlands cutting wood and raising fuel. There was also summer work in the saltings and fisheries on the coast and there was constant employment in the transport of timber from the woods to the canals and rivers. Portsmouth and other shipyards drew the best labourers 'leaving behind feebleness and debility to carry forward the common labours of the county'.[53]

The loudest complaints about the unavailability of commoners for work came from the Hampshire downs. Even Gilbert White regretted the idleness and sporting nature of the local commoners. Though otherwise steady, they succumbed too easily to the 'allurements and irregularities' that took the shape of rabbits and deer.[54]

The line between proprietor and labourer must be drawn firmly. Labourers must be labourers, not more. The lesson of the commons had been learned.

Hedges had always been the first fighting ground in any battle over enclosure. Conrad Heresbach in 1586 saw them as protection, 'well enclosed both from unruly folks and thieves and likewise from beasts'; Estienne, 1600, said fences provided 'so that no man can come except he enter in at the gate'; Leonard Mascall in 1640 saw hedges as 'a sure defence against rude persons'; and, in 1669, John Worlidge, saw them as 'protection against the lusts of vile persons'.[55]

In 1600, hedgebreakers in Essex were to be whipped until they 'bled well' while receivers of stolen wood were confined to the stocks all Sunday. A 1601 statute placed the 'breaking of hedges, pales or other fences' by 'lewd and idle' persons under the summary jurisdiction of magistrates. In 1607, the gentry of Northamptonshire suppressed a crowd in Newton which had 'cast down the hedges of Thomas Tresham', a particularly aggressive encloser. Up to fifty of the protesters were killed which, perhaps, should be remembered alongside modern-day films and books on Peterloo.[56]

Whitethorn, or hedging hawthorn, was the 'paragon of hedging plants', adaptable, hardy and tolerant of both dryness and excessive moisture. It got its

---

53 Vancouver, *General View*, p. 505.

54 White, *Natural History*, p. 24.

55 C. Heresbach, *Four Bookes of Husbandrie* (London 1586); L. Mascall, *The Country-Mans Recreation, of the Art of Planting, Graffing, and Gardening, in Three Bookes* (London 1640); T. Tusser, *Five hundred Pointes of Good Husbandrie* (London 1580); J. Worlidge, *Systema Agriculturae, being the Mystery of Husbandry Discovered and Layd Open* (London 1669).

56 Blomley, 'Private Property'.

name from the Old English *haga* meaning hedge or enclosure, a wall of closely knit shield bearing warriors affording an impenetrable barrier to man and beast. Planting a hedge may be laborious but, once established, it would last almost indefinitely with maintenance. A living quickset hedge was a statement of permanence distinct from a dead, temporary fence of interwoven branches.[57] Laurence even suggested investing in a 'nursery of quicks upon new inclosures'.[58] Fields in Medstead with stretches of hawthorn can likely date their planting to 1800.

> *Hedges wrought a profound remaking of the rural landscape. A new visual order signalled a new social order. Enclosure was not simply economic in its effects, but helped sustain a revolutionary shift in self-esteem. There was a shift from communal culture with a vigorous co-operative spirit in which country people worked, lived and governed together from field to village to one of privatisation. After enclosure, where every man could fence his own piece of territory and warn his neighbours off, the discipline of sharing things fairly with one's neighbours was relaxed and every household became an island unto itself.*[59]

The hedge came to be the principal symbol of private ownership of land and a sign of law. One need only look at the private gardens of housing in the ridge parishes today.

Clearly 1799 was a time when the wise counsel and intimate local knowledge of a good rector and his curate would provide welcome spiritual if not pecuniary help. Alas, not so. Francis North perhaps cannot be blamed for so freely lending his church door as a noticeboard, but he was a leading member of the enclosing fraternity and had such a close interest in acquiring money that he was guilty of a particularly bad fraud.

> *Love and meekness, lord,*
> *Become a churchman better than ambition.*[60]

In 1808, the bishop of Winchester, Brownlow North, gifted the Mastership of the Hospital of St. Cross in Winchester, with its gothic tower and alms square, to his son, Francis. The Hospital was founded in the twelfth century by another bishop, Henry de Blois, to give aid and shelter to 'thirteen poor impotent men and so reduced in strength as rarely or never able to support themselves without the assistance of another'. One hundred 'other poor men of good conduct and of the more indigent' were to be given free dinners. The income was derived from the tithes of a number of churches, mostly in Hampshire.

---

57 Blomley, 'Private Property'.
58 Laurence, *Duty of a Steward*, p. 46.
59 Thirsk, *Agrarian History*, Vol. IV, pp. 200-55.
60 Shakespeare, *Henry VII*, v, iii, pp. 62-3.

After quarrels in 1696 between the master and the brethren, a *Customary* was agreed which stated the master was to receive all profits and revenues out of which he was to bear the whole charges of the establishment and that, if there was any surplus, he had the right to retain it himself.[61]

It was not the money made by Francis North from the endowments and rents that caused the stir. That amount over nearly a half a century was never clearly established; estimates ranged from £45,000 to more than £300,000. What North pocketed immorally were windfall fines levied on Trust properties for the official commutation of tithes.[62] The affair broke with the revelation that from a fine of nearly £13,000 from the great tithes of Crondall, near Alton, North had taken £10,706. All the money received was for doing nothing more than signing leases; management was left to the steward and spiritual welfare to the chaplain.

The Globe reprinted an article from the *Hampshire Independent* in 1843.[63] The great tithes of Fareham and Twyford were called into question. Other newspapers began noticing Lord Guilford's income including the *Daily News*, *The Times*, the *Morning Post* and the *Morning Chronicle*. However, the religious press neglected the situation almost completely.[64]

A reformer, the Reverend Henry Holloway, took up the case. 'No one ever nosed out malfeasance with more pleasure than did Mr. Holloway.' By 1849, the management of the affairs of the Hospital had reached such notoriety that Joseph Hume, one of the leaders of the radical party in parliament, was granted a resolution calling for an investigation by the attorney general.

The next year, North advertised the sale of the contents of his expensively refurbished rectory at Alresford: more than fifteen four-poster beds, sixty-two dozen bottles of choice old port, claret, madeira, sherry, champagne and hock. In October, from his lavish Dover estate, he wrote his resignation of Old Alresford, including Medstead, which was accepted by the bishop three days later. In December, he resigned St. Mary's, Southampton.

The case was finally heard in 1853 when the Master of the Rolls found against North. 'A more shamefaced and shameful document than the *Customary* could not be imagined, nor could a more manifest and wilful breach of trust have been committed.' North was made responsible for fines taken in the last five years. The Hospital was put into receivership. The bishop, now Charles Sumner, refused North's resignation as master until building repairs were instituted and fines repaid. North retired to Waldershare Park, an old and supposedly broken man.

In 1855, Anthony Trollope wrote his fourth novel, the first of his Barchester series, *The Warden*, about the Reverend Septimus Harding and largely based on North's humiliation.

---

61 'Consuetudinarium', a Customary.
62 HRO, 111M94W.
63 *Hampshire Independent*, 21/10/1843.
64 Martin, 'Better than Ambition', in *Enter Rumour*, pp. 167-173.

Eager, pushing politicians have asserted in the House of Commons, with very telling indignation, that the grasping priests of the Church of England are gorged with the wealth which the charity of former times has left for the solace of the aged, or the education of the young. The well-known case of the Hospital of St. Cross has even come to the law courts of the country and the struggles of [the reformer] *have met with sympathy and support. Men are beginning to say that these things must be looked into.*[65]

By contrast, at the turn of the century, the average family of agricultural labourers earned seven to nine shillings a week. This was less than was required to keep them all sufficiently fed, clothed and housed. The paradox here was that the three-fifths of English families whose productive labour sustained the national economy were considered to be 'decreasing the wealth of the kingdom'.[66] These families were not allowed to leave the parish where they legally resided unless they could support themselves in their new parish.

Figures were collected for a family of six in Longparish, Hampshire, in 1789.[67]

Expenses per week:	£	s	d
Bread and flour	0	5	0
Yeasts and salt	0	0	3
Bacon or other meat	0	1	0
Tea, sugar, butter	0	0	6
Cheese	0	0	5
Soap, starch and blue	0	0	2
Candles	0	0	2
Thread, thrum and worsted	0	0	3
Total	0	7	9
Total per annum	20	3	0
Rent, fuel, clothes etc	7	0	0
Total expenses per annum	27	3	0
Earnings per week:			
The man	0	8	0
The woman	0	1	0
Total	0	9	0
Total earnings per annum	23	8	0

In 1820, after years of patiently endured infirmities, bishop North died at Winchester House in Chelsea, having served his diocese from afar as shepherd for thirty-nine profitable years. As befitted the son of an earl, the

---

65 Trollope, *Warden*, p. 8.
66 Wrightson, *Earthly Necessities*, p. 307, based on Gregory King.
67 Davies, *Case of Labourers in Husbandry* (1795), p. 166, from Hammonds, *Village Labourer*, p. 398.

brother of a prime minister, and a great prince of the church, he was buried with solemn honours beneath the ancient arches of Winchester cathedral ... His body was carried to its tomb by six dignitaries of the mourning diocese, all prebendaries and all relatives.[68]

---

68 Martin, 'Better than Ambition', in *Enter Rumour*, p. 154.

10 THE DUKE OF WELLINGTON'S WRATH

Napoleon, the Swing Riots and the Newton Valence enclosure, 1800-1850

Unbounded freedom ruled the wandering scene
Nor fence of ownership crept in between
To hide the prospect of the following eye
Its only bondage was the circling sky ...[1]

While England was at war with Napoleon and his republic food prices rose rapidly to offset harvest shortages and the pressure of high taxation. This was good for indebted landowners because the extra cash largely took care of the cost of their enclosures. Most were keen to sell their crops to the highest bidder, even to the French and even if it meant shortages in their own parish. It was, of course, a disaster for agricultural labourers like the discarded Medstead families who, without the comfort blanket of the commons, could no longer make ends meet. Worse, the gentry steadfastly refused to increase wages despite the speculative boom. Year by year, the poverty deficit widened. In Hampshire, it was a powder keg waiting for a careless spark.

By 1810, business was in depression. Investment in American markets failed. Credit tightened amidst a wave of bankruptcies which 'produced inevitable consequences: unemployment, diminished earnings, and bitter trade disputes which, in turn, degenerated into riots'.[2]

When peace came in 1815, there was an inevitable national slump. Disturbances were the most widespread, persistent and dangerous short of actual revolution or civil war known in modern times. A greater force, provided by the returning armies, and more exceptional measures, were employed to restore order than had ever been used before.[3] Political and industrial leaders, like William Cobbett, were 'getting the ear of the country'. Those who were opposed to the existing order of nobility and landowners were no longer inarticulate and desperate. They found ready outlets for their energies and hopes.

The consequences reached into the heart of local communities on the ridge and across the county, in fear of new agricultural machinery, in government legislation to control corn prices, in attempts to overturn the centuries-old tithe system, in poaching and food riots and even in the sorts of trees grown locally.

---

1 John Clare, 'The Mores'.
2 Darvall, *Popular Disturbances*, pp. 201-2.
3 Darvall, *Popular Disturbances*, pp. 306-7.

The slump may have helped old enclosure obligations, but new enclosures of the commons which could bring in increased rents to maintain old dissolute lifestyles were under threat for lack of seed money. Among the plentiful prospects noticed by Sir Francis Eden when he visited Hampshire to investigate local poverty in 1795 were 'commons in three parishes including two of 150 acres at Newton Valence'.[4] At Hawkley, he recorded 'no commons or alehouses'.

There was much campaigning in parliament to find ways to reduce the cost to landowners of seizing commons. No thinking gentry could allow enclosure to cease so ways had to be found to recover the heavy initial outlay. 'To many landowners, the planting of timber which, during the Napoleonic wars commanded high prices, seemed to offer the easiest way of doing this ... by sticking trees in every yard of a hedge or fence.'[5]

Some landowners planted the two most valuable trees, oak and ash, but there was a marked preference for elm. Oak was too slow growing and, in many soils, too uncertain. Ash, as Cobbett said, 'will grow anywhere and is fit for the wheelwright at the age of twenty years more or less'. However, from the farming point of view, it is the worst possible tree for a hedgerow. 'It is the grossest feeder of all our trees, no farm crops will grow within reach of its hungry roots; no cattle will graze where its leaves lie.'

Elm was free of all these faults and produce saleable timber quickly. Elm wood had a remarkable durability under water and high prices were won for planks in naval ships. The drawback was irregular supply because the elm is usually a lone rather than a woodland tree. It was ideal for hedge infill. It was because of this need for cash for more enclosure that the English countryside 'acquired the hedge row timber to which it once owed so much of its beauty'. This also explains why, today, there are so many gaps where majestic, defining elms have fallen to disease.[6]

At the same time, many of the local woods disappeared. Much of the timber in the great forests, like the beechwoods on the chalk at Chawton and Medstead, was unattractive to the husbandman. The beeches on the Boynes at Medstead, best suited for furniture making, were sold for felling in 1811. One resident believes that the name *Boynes* is a reference to beech woods. The last of the Boynes beeches was felled only a few years ago by the builders of a new house on the corner of Stoney Lane. 'It was a gnarled old thing.' A retired Forestry Commission arboriculturist thought that it had been left behind as being of no commercial value.[7]

Landlords also attached great importance to hedgerows as cover for all kinds of game. Tenants might be forbidden to trim them more than once in seven

4   Eden, *State of the Poor* (1797), pp. 194-9.
5   Bovill, *English Country Life*, pp. 5-6.
6   Orwins, *Open Fields*, p. 17.
7   Private email, 2021, Dr. Keith Brown.

years. Sometimes they were not allowed to touch them at all. It is no surprise to read of tenant farmers complaining of having to pay rent for land which not only could not be used, but which harboured hares and rabbits which attacked their crops and drains.[8]

Winter crops were first introduced into Britain in the 1790s. Within a few years, once secure rabbit warrens, which abounded locally especially around Ropley, proved porous as the animals dashed for the freely available new food. There was also protection at the field edge from a decreasing number of predators, like the stoat, reduced as more land was taken for the new crops.

Hunger rioting became a less important method for the working class to express popular discontent, particularly in the northern industrial areas. Here, they turned to Luddism, machine-breaking, rick-burning, industrial combination and political agitation.

Luddism was reputed to have its origins near Leicester in 1779 when Ned Ludd, a weaver, broke two stocking frames in a fit of rage.[9] When the Luddites emerged in Nottingham in 1811, his identity was appropriated to become the folkloric character of Captain Ludd, also known as King Ludd or General Ludd. The parallel with the deer-stealing King John and, later, with Captain Swing, Hampshire and the wider south's own agricultural revolution, is evident. Luddism spread rapidly throughout England over the following two years. The middle and upper classes strongly supported the government which used the army to suppress unrest. At one time, more British soldiers battled the Luddites than there were with Wellington fighting Napoleon on the Iberian Peninsula.[10] Dozens of machine wreckers were shot out of hand and dozens more were hanged and transported. Parliament made machine breaking a capital crime.[11]

The Peterloo Massacre took place at St Peter›s Field, Manchester in 1819. Eighteen people died when cavalry charged into a crowd of around 60,000 who had gathered to demand the reform of parliamentary representation.[12] This movement for votes was, in a few years, to contribute to the development of Four Marks and is discussed in the next chapter.

The decline in the incidence of price-fixing riots may have been hastened by the spread of the much disputed 'Speenhamland' system of poor relief. Pauper families received an individual subsidy adjusted to the price of bread supplemented by parish funds up to a minimum figure. One of the system's purposes was to discourage the movement of paupers from parish to parish. 'This

---

8 Bovill, *English Country Life*, p. 8.
9 Hobsbawm, 'Machine Breakers'. Rudé, *Crowd in History*, Ch. 5. Thomson, *Making of the English Working Class*. Bailey, *Luddite Rebellion*.
10 Darvall, *Popular Disturbances*, p. 260.
11 Frame Breaking Act, 1812.
12 Poole, *Politics of Regicide*. See also, 'Forty Years of Rural History from Below: Captain Swing and the Historians', *Southern History*, Vol. 32, 2010, pp. 1-20.

was a mixed blessing as it allowed farmers to keep wages low.'[13] As a result, the taxes of the small landowner who worked his own land went to subsidize the labour costs of the large farmers who employed the landless. This, in turn, added to the pressure to sell up to aggrandizing landowners.

Poaching and the gallows were so familiar to Englishmen of every class that they were rarely of more than local interest. However, at the Lent Assizes at Winchester in 1821, something happened which deeply shocked usually insensitive public opinion. Two young poachers were among the prisoners. One, James Turner, aged twenty-eight, was accused of assisting in the killing of one of Thomas Assheton Smith's gamekeepers at Tidworth; the other, Charles Smith, aged twenty-seven, was accused of shooting at a keeper employed by Lord Palmerston of Broadlands.[14] Both men were sentenced to death and were hanged together on the same gallows.

> The eminence of the two squires involved, the one a great landowner and the other the Secretary of War, was enough to excite more than the usual interest in a double execution which otherwise would have escaped notice. Certain unpleasant facts about the two trials quickly became widely known. These were, first, that of the sixteen prisoners condemned to death at those assizes these two poachers were the only ones to be hanged; second, the jurors had recommended both young men to mercy; third, in passing sentence, Mr. Justice Burrough observed, to quote Cobbett, that 'it became necessary in these cases, that the extreme sentence of the law should be inflicted, to deter others, as resistance to gamekeepers had now arrived at an alarming height, and many lives had been lost'. [15]

The lives of keepers, employed to protect the game of the rich, were evidently thought more sacred than those of men less valuably employed. Cobbett, among others, denounced the hangings as for 'the preservation of the game ... for the preservation of the sports of the aristocracy'. In the period, there were several stories of men from Wield being transported under the harsh game laws.[16]

In truth, there was little difference when it came to defending the gentry's property. Twice a year in Hampshire, the scarlet-robed judge of assize put the black cap of death on top of his full-bottomed wig to expound the law of the propertied and to execute their will. This was the climactic moment in a system of criminal law based on terror. 'If we diminish the terror of house-breakers,' wrote a justice in 1819, 'the terror of the innocent inhabitants must be increased and the comforts of domestic life must be greatly destroyed.'

---

13 Bate, *Clare*, p. 52.
14 Mingay, *Gentry*, p. 181.
15 Bovill, *English Country Life*, pp. 184-5.
16 Gibson, 'Rodney Family'.

The Bench, 1758, William Hogarth, The Fitzwilliam Museum, Cambridge, 727, engraved from an original painting.
Four judges listen to a case in the Court of Common Pleas. Though intended purely as piece of comical caricature, much of the imagery reflects common perceptions of senior judges at the time: pompous and indifferent men, inattentive to most of their case, and half asleep or even drunk when cases were being heard.

In 1822, Sir Thomas Baring, brother of Alexander of the bankers at Stratton Park, connected through Henry Drummond to the 1799 Medstead enclosure, decided to set a county limit to poor law handouts. He headed a self-elected meeting of eight magistrates, of whom five were parsons, to introduce a Hampshire scale of relief. This allowed one gallon loaf a head, with 4d per head in addition to a poor family of four persons. The extra allowance was reduced by a penny when there were six in the family and by twopence when there were more than six. Cobbett wrote one of his liveliest articles on these suggestions. He lambasted Baring for exceeding his authority and being so out of touch with the real state of poverty in the county. He set out the number of incomes held by the five parsons including an archdeaconry, two prebends, one canonship, four rectories, two vicarages and three other livings 'besides what things are in the possession of their relations'. The list included the clerical magistrate Robert

Wright of Itchen Abbas and Ovington in Baring's bailiwick.[17] Cobbett suggested that farmers look to pay tithes in a parish only to the amount that local rectors paid their curates.

> *Gentlemen, Farmers of Hampshire, it appears to me that it is impracticable ... for you to carry on your affairs without giving to the labourers a sufficiency to enable them to work and to keep them in health. I am aware that you cannot do this, and pay rent and yield tithe, and pay, besides, all the taxes that are levied directly and indirectly upon you ... The labourer, the suffering, the half-famished, the ragged, the cold, the desperate labourer ... will look to the farmer only.*

Cobbett described elsewhere a group of women labourers whom he met by the roadside in Hampshire as 'such an assemblage of rags as I never saw before even amongst the hop-pickers in Farnham'. Of some labourers he wrote, 'Their dwellings are little better than pig-beds and their looks indicate that their food is not nearly equal to that of a pig. These wretched hovels ... seem as if they had been swept off the fields by a hurricane and had dropped and found shelter under the banks of the roadside.'

Writing from Ropley to Hampshire's Lord Lieutenant, John Duthy added his voice, 'The year will long be remembered by the excessive dearness of every article of life. The grievous pressure induced ... make it the duty of every man to endeavour to trace out the productive causes of the overwhelming evil.'[18] After diagnosing the problem, Duthy was clear that he had 'no hesitation in saying that this master-mischief is the War'.

Munsche declared there was a 'great deal of evidence to suggest that the increase in poaching was directly related to the depression which hit the countryside at the end of the Napoleonic wars'.[19] Ropley, the smuggling centre, shows a big population dip from 1801 to 1811, 642 to 533, 17 per cent, but its inhabited houses remain stable.[20] Was this the young leaving to find work elsewhere?

Poachers excused their activities by pointing out their 'distress'.

'Tell me, then fellow, why do you go out poaching?' asked one justice in 1828. 'Because I am poor your worship,' he answered. 'I can get no work; and unless I take a gun now and then, I must starve.'[21] These statements were corroborated by the observations of the gentry. Sir Thomas Baring, for example, concluded that most of the men who were committed for offences against the game laws in Hampshire had poached 'in consequence of not being able to obtain employment or such employment as was equal to their support'. One year later, a committee of

---

17 *Cobbett's Weekly Political Register*, 21/9/1822, Columns 705-48.
18 Duthy, *Observation*, pp. 3-4.
19 Munsche, *Gentlemen and Poachers*, p. 148.
20 1801-11 censuses.
21 *The Times*, 10/11/1828. Hammonds, *Village Labour*, pp. 188-9.

Hampshire justices echoed their agreement.[22] They pointed out the comparative youth of offenders who were of a 'different description from those committed formerly … They were young, industrious, healthy men who were in distress and want of employment.'

Men without large families were discriminated against in the distribution of both work and relief in favour of those who had many mouths to feed. Was it any wonder, asked Lord Malmesbury, that men who 'had been reduced to work on the roads for half a crown a week … should have recourse to unlawful measures to obtain the means of subsistence'?[23]

The tinder had been lit. Throughout the south and west of England late into 1830 agricultural workers undertook acts of violent, local protest. Hampshire was, with Wiltshire, the most troubled county in Britain. It is now evident that 'many events went unreported and the full extent of rural protest was greater' than official records.[24] Anger was widely directed: against new machinery, rapacious landlords, the local church and far-away tithe holders supported by a hated tax, the lack of employment, the declining price paid for labour and the rising cost of bread and beer. The air was full of recrimination with crops destroyed and machinery and buildings that symbolised repression burned. One justice ascribed it with little accuracy to a 'wild dissolute population of poachers, smugglers and deer stealers'.[25]

The county's landowners had gone too far and were in fear of loss of their historic authority, particularly in the setting of wages. Their natural allies, the local clergy, reeled from personal attacks and, in some cases, took up arms to fight their flock. The garrison at Winchester was emptied as mounted troops raced to Hampshire's small towns to suppress discontent. Within months, ten local men, most from Headley and Selborne, were sentenced to death although all were transported.

The discontent became known as the *Swing Riots* although a single name could never encapsulate the complexity of hunger, hatred and disparate targets. 'Swing' was derived from Captain Swing, a fictitious name often signed to the threatening letters delivered to farmers, magistrates and parsons in the dead of night. The Captain became the shady figurehead of the rising, like King Ludd and King John before. With its sinister implications, Swing 'became a bogey which held half England in terror'.[26]

In the early days of the rising in Hampshire, Wiltshire and Berkshire there was great sympathy with the labourers. A meeting was convened in Winchester by the mayor to 'preserve the peace not to appoint special constables'.[27] Dr.

22 *The Times*, 29/1/1829.
23 Parliamentary debate, Hansard, viii, col. 735.
24 Kent, *Popular Radicalism.*
25 Hobsbawm and Rudé, *Captain Swing*, p. 128.
26 Bovill, *English Country Life*, p. 36.
27 *Hampshire Chronicle*, 22/11/1831.

Newbolt, a clergyman and a magistrate, described his own dealings with one of the mobs who said they wanted a wage of 12s a week. Newbolt and the mayor thought this a reasonable demand; Newbolt acted as a mediator.[28] The farmers agreed and the labourers returned to work, 'abandoning their project of a descent on Winchester'.

> *No one that had the misfortune to reside during the last winter in the disturbed districts of the south of England will ever forget the awful impression of that terrible time. The gathering of misguided peasantry amongst the wild hills, partly heath and partly woodland of which so much of the northern part of Hampshire is composed, dropping in one by one, and two by two, in the gloom of evening, or the dim twilight of a November morning; of the open and noisy meetings of determined men at noontide in the streets and greens, and even sometimes in the very churchyards, sallying forth in small but resolute numbers to collect money or destroy machinery and compelling or persuading their fellow labourers to join them at every farm they visited ...*[29]

The story of events around the ridge parishes is well documented. Dr. William Curtis, who founded the Curtis Museum in Alton, rode across the hill at East Worldham on his way to Kingsley when he was stopped by some 300 excited rioters. 'Oh, Mr. Curtis,' they said. 'It is a pity you were not at Headley when we broke into the workhouse. You would have laughed if you had seen the tiles fly. Tell the people in Alton to look out as we are intending to attack the workhouse and breweries after we have been to Selborne.'[30]

The threat contained farce. Abraham Crowley, owner of one of the town's two breweries, was Curtis's brother-in-law. When Curtis got to Alton, he went straight to Crowley and raised the alarm. A messenger was sent to Winchester to ask for protection. Alton citizens, perhaps 140, town gentry rather than men of the soil, were sworn in as special constables. Crowley's old hop store on the corner of Turk Street became a guard room. A troop of thirty Life Guards, the senior British regiment, arrived and were quartered at the *Crown Inn.*

Up to 1,500 men gathered from all the villages about Alton, but 'became disorganised' at the news of armed resistance. Gestures were made instead. The labourers and their local leaders acted openly and fearlessly because they 'expected that their protest would be tolerated'. Rioting and protest had a 'certain historical legitimacy' because both rulers and ruled understood that disorder and even violence were part of a popular culture.[31]

The Heighes brothers broke a threshing machine at Wyck in Binsted, an 'established way to put pressure on an employer using new technology'; there

28 Hammonds, *Village Labourer*, p. 265.
29 M. R. Mitford, *Our Village*, 2 vols. (London 1839), pp. 287-91, 324.
30 Curtis, *Alton*, pp. 125-6.
31 Palmer, *Police and Protest.*

were assaults and robbery at Farringdon and Greatham; and disturbances at Liphook.[32] William Hibberd and Isaac Butcher were charged with riotous assembly in Bighton, but both were 'discharged for want of prosecution'.[33] Rioters set fire to a public house, perhaps the *Horse and Groom*, and a barn at Newton Common.

At Selborne, as promised, the occupants were turned out of the Union workhouse, the fittings and furniture burned or broken and the roof pulled down.[34] The unloved Reverend William Cobbold was forced to sign away part of his tithe rights. In repayment, he later fought tirelessly to halt any thoughts of pardons or leniency. It was a similar story at Headley where the Reverend Robert Dickinson was made to agree a reduction in his tithes to £350 a year. At his village workhouse, the mob 'rushed like a torrent into every room'. For ninety minutes, windows were torn out, the stairways broken, ceilings pulled down. Up to 50,000 tiles were stripped from the roof.

A farmer told Cobbett that there could not be a 'more unhappy place in England' than Selborne. A shot was fired through the window at the vicar, possibly because of his lawsuits against the people.

Although, in 1830, the mob cried off, the local hop workers assembled near William Complin's brewery at Holybourne to try to get higher wages because the 'present allowance was really insignificant' to support their families.[35] Complin, who ran several public houses, was under direct threat from the wider rioters angry at an employers' conspiracy to reduce wages. He met with other farmers who reversed their decision and agreed to 'give a reasonable price for their labour'. The *Hampshire Chronicle* reported that the 'men appeared perfectly satisfied, and return to their work'. The newspaper couldn't resist betraying its own sympathies as it observed that 'the conduct of the men towards their employers was orderly and respectful. They declared they did not intend to join with any persons not belonging to the parish, and only requested as much as would enable them to live.' Perhaps the men's public position was not surprising with the Life Guards waiting nearby. Two days later, the Life Guards faced off a large mob, partly from the hop fields, that gathered outside the *Swan Inn* in Alton's High Street.

A recent analysis identified 3,283 incidents during the unrest in the countryside.[36] Open dissent began in Kent, another 'hop' county, in November 1830, spread into Sussex and parts of Surrey in the same month, then moved outwards by way of Berkshire, Hampshire and Wiltshire before heading westward and northwards. The highest concentration of lawlessness fell south of a line drawn between Hampshire and the Wash.[37]

---

32 Hobsbawm and Rudé, *Captain Swing*, Chapter 6.
33 HGS, *Bighton*, p. 5.
34 Smith, *Workhouse riots*.
35 *Hampshire Chronicle*, 29/11/1830.
36 Family and Community History Research Society, 2005.
37 Hammonds, 'The Last Labourers' Revolt', *Village Labourer*, Chaps. XI and XII.

Events reported in Winchester through November and December included 'evil-minded and dishonest men wandering about in predatory hordes exacting money and provisions from several gentlemen and farmers' and the moving of the 47th Regiment from Portsmouth and the 3rd Dragoon Guards from Southampton to guard the centre of the city. Special constables led by two reverend gentlemen attacked with bludgeons a mob of 300 at Avington and took fifty prisoners ('this instance of prompt and successful resistance, being opposed to a lawless mob, cannot be sufficiently applauded,' said the Duke of Wellington). A large group rioted at Itchen Abbas; at Martyr Worthy the mob set about the rector, Sir Henry Rivers. Five hundred men extorted money from the inhabitants of Swaythling and Stoneham where fifty-three were taken; prisoners were brought into the city from Basingstoke; money and provisions were taken from Littleton; threshing machines were destroyed at Wickham, Botley, New Alresford and Durley; men rioted in Upham; at Swanmore and Soberton 'many who have hitherto borne excellent characters have been carried away by the madness of the moment'; at Stockbridge, men with clubs and staves demanded a reduction in tithes and two sovereigns; at Nether Wallop, a wage rise of 25 per cent was agreed with local farmers; there were large gatherings of land occupiers and owners at Titchfield and Hambledon and, at a meeting at the *Swan Inn*, Alresford, 'the whole of the male population' voluntarily came forward to form horse and foot patrols. The county gaol held over 200 prisoners charged with having riotously assembled and destroyed machinery at Rockbourne, Basingstoke, Andover, Weyhill, Upper Clatford, Fordingbridge, Romsey, Buriton and Wickham.[38]

The historian George Rudé was at pains to point out that the wider business involved threatening letters, assaults, robberies to tithe, enclosure and food riots and that in 'every one of the twenty-five counties affected, there was rickburning, and the firing of farms, barns and country mansions'.[39] The Hampshire newspaper letter columns were full of the worthy lamenting the state of affairs and declaring the reasonableness of working men wishing to earn enough to feed their families. The establishment and the legislature were somewhat tougher:

> *Every friend to good order and the well being of society must deeply lament the existence of an insurrectionary spirit among a portion of the agricultural labourers, which is fast spreading, and if not timely checked, will be productive of the most serious results to the country at large ... A Royal proclamation offers a reward of £50 on the conviction of every person guilty of acts of outrage and violence, with His Majesty's pardon if the offence shall be made by an accomplice. £500 are offered, to be paid on conviction of any person for secretly setting on fire ricks of corn, hay, buildings, or other property in the countries of Hants, Kent, Wilts, Berks, Sussex and Surrey ... Let then the*

---

38 *Hampshire Chronicle*, 29/11/1830.
39 Rudé, *Crowd in History*, p. 151.

misguided men who, in an evil hour, have listened to the pernicious counsels of designing individuals, and gone astray, quickly reduce their steps and return to their peaceful avocations, lest they be destroyed by their faithless associates ...'[40]

The government of the Duke of Wellington had been well warned of the likelihood of trouble. In his *Political Register*, radical politician and writer, William Cobbett, commented:

The time is at hand when it will become a choice of labourers, certain death from starvation, or the chance of death by rope or gun, and, be assured, my Lord Duke, that Englishmen will prefer the latter. Think, then, betimes, of the consequence of parish after parish combined till there be half a country in commotion.[41]

The Duke of Wellington responded by inducing the magistrates to 'put themselves on horseback, each at the head of his own servants and retainers, grooms, huntsmen and game-keepers, armed with horsewhips, pistols, fowling pieces and what they could get, and to attack in concert, if necessarily or singly, these mobs, disperse them, and take and put in confinement those who could not escape'. This was done in a spirited manner. 'It was astonishing how soon the county was tranquilised.'[42]

The gentry substituted action for diplomacy. Little resistance was offered. Lord Melbourne, the Home Secretary, urged the lord-lieutenants and the magistrates to firmness and to vigour in quelling disturbances and virtually promised them immunity from illegal acts done in discharge of their duty. A village here and there continued to give Hampshire magistrates unease, for example, Broughton 'an open village in an open country where there is no gentleman to overawe them', but these were exceptions. By early December, *The Times* correspondent in Hampshire could report that quiet was restored, that the peasantry were cowed and that the men who had been prominent in the mobs were being picked out and arrested every day. The gaols were full to overcrowding, the movement crushed and the time for retribution come.

By year end, 1,000 men awaited trial in Hampshire, 2,000 across the country. Melbourne accused local magistrates of being lenient. In Hampshire, and four other counties, he appointed Special Commissions to try offenders outside the usual court schedule. These commissions were used when exemplary hangings or, at least, exemplary trials were deemed necessary for the public peace. Gentlemen often petitioned for them when riot in their counties was becoming too serious

---

40 Hampshire Chronicle, 'Summary', 29/11/1830.
41 Political Register, 23/10/1830.
42 Cited by D. Williams, *John Frost* (Cardiff 1939), pp. 59-60.

or when the violence associated with popular crimes, such as smuggling, verged on insurrection against their authority.[43]

The first commission started in The Castle in Winchester on 20 December. Sir John Vaughan, Baron of the Exchequer, was the chief judge, assisted by Sir James Parke and Sir Edward Alderson. The Duke of Wellington, in his capacity as Lord Lieutenant of Hampshire, also travelled from London to sit on the bench. Juries were selected from a list of twenty-three gentlemen, thirteen of whom were baronets or knights, and lasted, with a break of two days for Christmas, through until the end of the month. Badly scared and indignant, the landowning class would have its reckoning.

Judge Alderson said, '[We] do not come here … to inquire into grievances. We come here to decide law.'[44] The severity of the Winchester court, egged on by Wellington, can be seen in its unprecedented use of transportation in comparison with other counties. Two-thirds of those tried at Winchester were convicted, 101 prisoners capitally and 152 were transported, mostly for seven years. Those who were sentenced to death had their sentences commuted to transportation, often for life. However, six were hanged while public indignation saved another four.[45]

The public were aghast and the people of Winchester were harrowed by the appalling emotions which surrounded them. 'The scenes of distress about the jail are most terrible,' wrote *The Times* correspondent. 'The number of men who are to be torn from their homes and connexions is so great that there is scarcely a hamlet in the county into which anguish and tribulation have not entered. Wives, sisters, mothers, children, beset the gates daily, and the governor of the jail informs me that the scenes he is obliged to witness at the time of locking up the prison are truly heart breaking.'[46]

The antics surrounding the twice-yearly visits of the high-court judges, let alone a special commission with the prime minister, had considerable psychic force. The assizes and special commissions were a formidable spectacle in any county town, the most visible and elaborate manifestation of state power to be seen in the countryside apart from the presence of a regiment. The town was crowded with barristers and jurors. County meetings were often held in the same week. The cream of county society attended the assize ball, the event of the year. Tradesmen and labourers travelled to enjoy the spectacles, meet friends, attend the court and watch the executions.

The court arrived in town with traditional and calculated panoply. 'The judges,' wrote a French observer, 'upon their arrival are received by the sheriff and often by a great part of the wealthiest inhabitants of the country. The latter come in person or send their carriages with their richest liveries to serve as escort and

43 Hay, 'Property' in *Albion's Fatal Tree*, p. 31.
44 Hobsbawm and Rudé, *Captain Swing*, p. 259.
45 Wallis, 'We do not come…'. Bovill, *English Country Life*, p. 44.
46 *The Times*, 7/1/1831.

increase the splendour of the occasion. They enter the town with bells ringing and trumpets playing, preceded by the sheriff's men, twelve or twenty, in full dress armed with javelins.'[47]

In the court room, the judges' every action was governed by the gravity of the spectacle. In recognition of their importance, their annual pay had doubled in thirty years to £3,000, a sum beyond the dreams of most of their supplicants. The chief judge sometimes permitted his bench to be invaded by a throng of spectators and thus found himself surrounded by the prettiest women of the county – the sisters, wives or daughters of grand jurors. 'They are attired in the most elegant *négligé* and it is a spectacle not a little curious to see the judge's venerable head loaded with a large wig peering among the youthful female heads.'[48]

The charge to the grand jury was ostensibly directed to the county gentry and was a statement of central policy. At the appropriate time, judges castigated Jacobitism and smuggling, denounced attacks on game and seditious libels over government policy, attacked Catholicism and upstart non-conformists, or gave the official line on the South Sea Bubble.[49]

These secular sermons of the criminal law became more important than those of the church. 'Too many Englishmen had forgotten the smell of brimstone and the clergy, lazy, absentee and dominated by material ambition, were not the men to remind them.'[50] 'The diminished effectiveness of damnation to compel obedience was accentuated by the decline in ecclesiastical courts to mere arbiters of wills and marriages and occasional cases of slander.'

At one time or another, almost all the worthy bishops discussed in this book, and their jostling potential successors, gave the assize sermon in the cathedral before joining the ball.

It was William Cobbett of all people, scourge of the indolent and avaricious clergy, who wrote in 1831 that he had 'at last found a bishop of Winchester to praise'.[51]

> [Charles Sumner, who ascended in 1827] *in coming from Winchester to his palace at Farnham was met ... by a band of sturdy beggars, who some call robbers. They stopped his carriage and asked for some money which he gave them. But he did not prosecute them; he had not a man of them called to account ... the next day* [he] *set twenty-four labourers to constant work; opened his castle to the distressed of all ages, and supplied all with food and other necessaries who stood in need of them.*

---

47 Charles Cottu, *The Administration of Criminal Justice in England*, 1822, p. 43.
48 Cottu, *Administration*, pp. 103-4.
49 Hay, 'Property' in *Albion's Fatal Tree*, pp. 27-9.
50 Hay, 'Property' in *Albion's Fatal Tree*, pp. 29-30.
51 *Cobbett's Weekly Register*, Columns 158-9, 13/1/1831.

One execution stays in the local public consciousness to the current day. There had been a riot near the Barings' mansion in Stratton Park. The Baring family and their men, including those at The Grange at Alresford, were on high alert. Several hundred Hampshire farm labourers went on the rampage in the Dever valley smashing threshing machines. They reached Northington Down Farm where they destroyed machinery and demanded two sovereigns from the owner, Thomas Dowden. William Baring arrived from The Grange to confront the angry mob. Their spokesman John Silcock stepped forward and Baring grabbed his collar 'prompting the labourers to pour forward' to the rescue.[52] Accounts then vary as Henry Cook, aged twenty-one, some say nineteen, a ploughboy, stepped forward. He was carrying a pole or a sledgehammer, raised it and struck the brim of Baring's hat and then his shoulder causing Baring to fall to the ground. Seemingly, little serious damage was done.

'His pride more than anything was hurt,' claims local historian David Findley. 'You just could not have a farm worker hit a member of the aristocracy.'

For knocking off the hat of a landowner and Justice of the Peace, Cook was hanged and 'all those under sentence were gathered in the prison yard to watch'.[53] A newspaper reporter said, 'I cast my eyes down into the felon's yard and saw many of the convicts weeping bitterly, some burying their faces in their frocks, others wringing their hands convulsively, and the others leaning for support against the walls of the yard and unable to cast their eyes upwards.'

> *The gentlemen, the clergy and the newspapermen of England invented stories to show that Cook was brutal and callous. 'Justice', declared The Times, 'has seldom met with more appropriate sacrifice.' His age was said to be thirty, his wages were raised from 5s to 30s, his character and alleged crimes were painted in the blackest colours.'*[54]

In 1831, three convict ships sailed with 457 men and boys, the *Eliza* and the *Proteus* for Van Diemen's Land, and the *Eleanor* for New South Wales.

> *These were not pickpockets, thieves and murderers ... but were mostly farm workers, torn from families and friends ... all because, starved and oppressed, they had gathered in crowds, had escorted a few brutal Poor Law Overseers out of the villages, had asked for more wages or had broken a few of the newly introduced threshing machines ... they were jailed, loaded with chains and carried far across the seas to the grim penal settlements where shame and servitude and life–long separation would be their lot ... Few came back.*[55]

---

52 *Daily Echo*, 'Plaque commemorates Henry Cook', 12/6/2009, an interview with David Findley, Dever Valley Local History Society.
53 Groves, *Sharpen the Sickle!*, pp. 14-15.
54 Groves, *Sharpen the Sickle!*, p. 14.
55 Groves, *Sharpen the Sickle!*, p. 13.

Winchester citizens met at the Guildhall in May 1832 and decided to form an 'efficient police establishment' for the suppression of vagrancy.

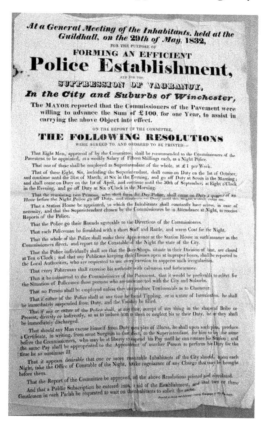

Formation of the Winchester police
establishment, 1832. *HRO, 92M95/F2/13/2*

The commissioners of the pavement advanced £100 and agreed seventeen resolutions. Seven night police were to be appointed at a weekly salary of fifteen shillings, with a superintendent paid £1, to start at six in the evening on the first of October. Each policeman was to receive a short staff and rattle and a warm coat for the night. One duty was to ensure beer shops closed at ten in the evening. Officers were encouraged to exercise their authority with 'calmness and forbearance'. Tippling, intoxication and acceptance of bribes or presents would meet with instant dismissal.[56]

In 1834, Thomas Ellery, a constable at Micheldever, brought before justice Sir Thomas Baring a case of creating a disturbance. Two men, Edward Bishop and

---

56 HRO, 92M95/F2/13/2. Poster illustration.

John Ride, had inflamed a crowd of a hundred people. Despite orders to stop, they continued, the crowd swelling to 200. The subject of the harangue is not mentioned, nor the consequences. [57]

The infamous events at Tolpuddle in Dorset in the same year, where the government conspired to ruin a legal trade union, may not at first sight seem closely linked to Hampshire, but they were and led later to strong unionism in the county. Wellington and the gentry's vengeance left bitter memories in the south and the spark of revolt was far from diminished. In Kent, Hampshire and Suffolk, labourers acted with some organisation and discipline. In Hampshire, wage rises from 7s 8d to 10s a week were agreed. In Tolpuddle, there were similar meetings with the same outcome. The farmers were met in a conference presided over by the vicar, Dr. Warren, who pledged,

> *I am a witness between you men and your masters that if you will go quietly to your work you shall receive for your labour as much as any man in the district, and if your masters should attempt to run from their word, I will undertake to see you righted, so help me God.*[58]

The farmers broke their agreement, paying only 9s, then cutting the wages to 8s. The vicar 'flatly denied having given any pledge' and the magistrates, all landowners or clergymen, instructed that the men must work for whatever the farmers decided. The farmers dropped wages to 7s and threatened 6s. The men formed a Friendly Society as did numbers of other workers towards the end of 1833, inspired by Robert Owen's plans for a new society.

It was no longer illegal for workmen to combine for trade purposes. The government, local magistrates, clergymen and landowners, however, thought it was best to break the resistance by suggesting the men had broken an act of 1797 which forbade secret oaths, an act passed specifically to deal with a naval mutiny.[59] Spies were planted, a warning posted, but on the next day at dawn, six leading trade unionists were arrested, five of whom were Wesleyan preachers. A trial was hurried forward before a picked jury and a hostile judge. After the evidence, the men's leader George Loveless handed the judge a note,

> *My Lord, if we have violated any law, it was not done intentionally; we have injured no man's reputation, character, person or property; we are uniting together to preserve ourselves, our wives and children from utter*

---

57 HRO, 92M95/F2/13/2.

58 Groves, *Sharpen the Sickle!*, pp. 16-23.

59 W. H. Oliver, 'Tolpuddle Martyrs and Trade Union Oaths', *Labour History*, No. 10, May 1966, p. 10. Also Edward Carleton Tufnell, *Character, Object and Effects of Trades' Unions; with some remarks on the law concerning them*, British Labour Struggles: Contemporary Pamphlets 1727-1850 (London, Ridgway 1834, reprint New York, Arno Press, 1972), pp. 66-73. *The Story of the Tolpuddle Martyrs Centenary Commemorations* (London, Trades Union Congress General Council 1934). Joyce Marlow, *The Tolpuddle Martyrs* (London, Grafton 1985).

degradation and starvation. We challenge any man, or number of men, to prove that we have acted or intended to act, different from the above statement.

The six men were sentenced to seven years' transportation. Eight days later, five of them were sent chained and manacled to Portsmouth to ship for New South Wales. The sixth, Lovelace, taken ill, followed a few weeks later to Tasmania. 'Step by step the government was forced to relent. After two years, a free pardon and passage back to England had been secured but all manner of delay and subterfuge was used to prevent the men returning for a further two years.'

Cobbett did not let up on the clergy's clinging to tithe rights. In one village, mounted, he laid his whip on the door of the curate, calling on the incumbent to come out and to debate. His open letters 'To The Hampshire Parsons' in his *Weekly Register* were avidly read, but sometimes in private behind closed doors.

> *Parsons, 'How long, how long, O Lord! Wilt thou stay thy hand?' ... Now I remind you of it once more, and give you my opinion, that it is not long now before all my prophesies ... will be fulfilled ... For many years, you have accused me of disaffection, disloyalty, infidelity, and all sorts of crimes, for no other cause that I have proposed to take away the tithes from the clergy ... It has always been seen, when any long-established body or corporation or fraternity, is placed in dangerous circumstances; when there is no possible means of saving a part of it, but that of timely conciliation; it has always been seen that such a body never conciliates; that in whatever degree it had become the object of hatred and hostility, it became resentful, and stuck to its obsolete rights, clung to the things that tended most to render it odious, still closer and closer, as its powers of retention grew weaker and weaker.*[60]

Tithes were still collected, mostly in kind, by the parson; no harvest could be carted until each tenth stook had been marked before being put into one of the ridge villages' tithe barns. In 1842, a meeting was held in the *Windmill Inn* at which the rector, the Reverend The Right Honourable the Earl of Guilford, soon to be accounted a fraudster, claimed the tithes for Medstead. It was the last collection before the tribute was forced by law into monetary form only.

Later that year, the apportionment of Medstead charges in lieu of tithes was made by Thomas James Tatham, assistant tithe commissioner. With the tithe commuted, Rector North wished to dispose of his unnecessary tithe barn and to use the money from the sale for the enlargement of the Old Rectory cottage for the 'permanent use of himself' and his successors. There was no possibility of North with his large estates and substantial income living in the cottage; it was sold a few years later for £104.

---

60 *Cobbett's Weekly Register*, 15/1/1831, Col. 162; 7/9/1833, Col. 607 ff.

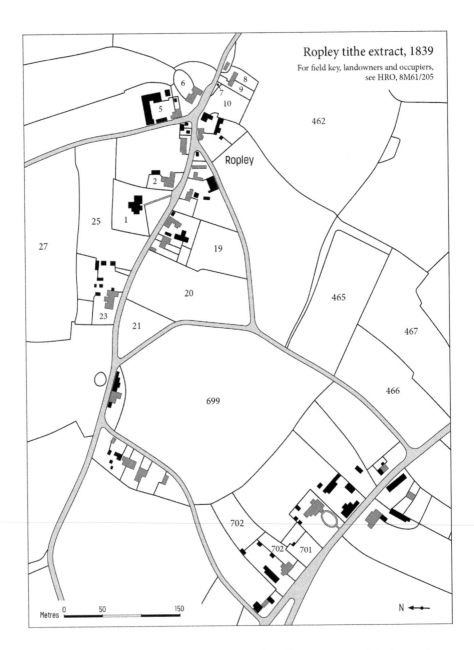

Extracts from two of the title maps showing the village centres of Ropley and Medstead.

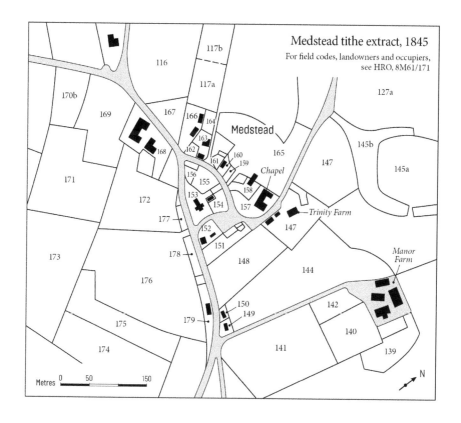

The parish consisted of 2,113 acres of arable land, 130 acres of meadow, 447 acres of woodland and eight acres of glebe land. Its tithes were worth £580, but North had been paying the curate just £60 a year. When criticised, he replied, 'I keep good curates and give largely to the poor.'[61] In 1846, Medstead's crops were counted: wheat 552 bushels at 7s ¼d; barley 979 bushels, 2s 11½d; and oats 1,410 bushels, 2s 9d.[62] North resigned in 1850 while under investigation for fraud by the attorney general. Three years later, his reputation was ruined by the Master of the Rolls.

The 1840s were the last decade in which the English version of *taxation populaire* was significant. In this decade, the general strengthening of the machinery of public order resulted in the decline of the riot as an endemic symptom of social discontent.[63] The General Enclosure Acts of 1836 and 1840 made it possible for landowners to enclose land without first making reference to parliament as long as a two-thirds majority of proprietors by value and number

61 Rathbone, *Chronicle*, p. 50. Moody, *Short History of Medstead*, p. 18.
62 Moody, *Short History of Medstead*, p. 26.
63 Rose, 'Price Riot', p. 282.

agreed to do so.[64] The acts' effect was that of a cheaper individual parliamentary process. The General Enclosure Act of 1845, and later amendments, attempted to provide better protection for the interests of small proprietors and the public.[65]

Newton Valence was authorised to be enclosed in 1848 in the Second Enclosure Act of that year along with fifteen other disparate places, with only Greatham also in Hampshire. It was further evidence of a government and landowners' conveyor belt (*Appendix 22*).[66] The parish had a long tradition of hunting with evidence of medieval deer parks linking with Chawton and Farringdon. The vicar in 1696 completed a comprehensive glebe terrier listing tithes of wool, hops, lambs, calves, pigs and apples.[67] The glebe consisted of a house, cottage, orchard, fifty-five acres of fifteen named fields and parts of several woods.

The enclosure business was now such that a local professional land surveyor and valuer was employed. Richard Wakefield Attree of Bishearne in the parish of Liss produced a rapid, but competent, report allotting almost 150 acres among nine groups consisting of eleven people with a further six acres specified for roads and a pond (*Appendix 23*).[68] In these more enlightened times, the pond was to be a 'public watering place' at Upper Common on the Ropley and East Tisted border and marking a continuum of old commons all the way to Soldridge.

The pond can be seen today at Headmore Farm on Headmore Lane in what was the furthest point in Newton Valence from the village centre. 'Cleansing and repairs' were allocated to Henry Chawner, the largest land recipient and lord of the manor by purchase. A further two fenced acres were allotted to the churchwardens and overseers of the poor in trust 'as a place of exercise and recreation for the inhabitants ... of the neighbourhood'. Attree's two detailed maps survive.[69]

The connected Upper and Lower Commons were the centre of interest running half-way down what is now Mary Lane, including Common Barn Farm, and was then called Common Road. Three public carriage roads, twenty-six feet wide, were directed and laid out on the maps. The usual responsibilities for fencing newly-enclosed land were specified.

Richard Attree was born at Blackmore House, Selborne, but he had roots in Corwen in North Wales where he died. His memorial is in Selborne churchyard.

---

64 6&7 William IV, c. 115, 1836. 3&4 Victoria, c. 31, 1840.

65 8&9 Victoria, c. 118, 1845. This General Act created the Inclosure Commission in London where a copy of anything carried out under the legislation had to be deposited. This body was later absorbed into the Ministry of Agriculture and its awards ultimately passed to The National Archives (Chapman and Seeliger, *Formal and Informal Enclosures*), p. 8.

66 Parliamentary Archive, HL/PO/PU/1/1848/11&12V1n303, The Second Annual Inclosure Act, 4/9/1848, 11&12 Victoria, c. 109. Greatham, HRO, Q23/2/56, 1851, but also HRO, Q23/2/57, Southern Common and Ridges Green, Greatham, 1868.

67 HRO, 21M65/E15/12 (under Ropley).

68 HRO, Q23/2/94 (with map). Chapman and Seeliger, *Guide to Enclosure*, p. 115, say the actual acreage was 166.43 which I am unable to reconcile. They also state four recipients exceeding 10 per cent of the allotments, whereas I count five.

69 TNA, MAF 1/543.

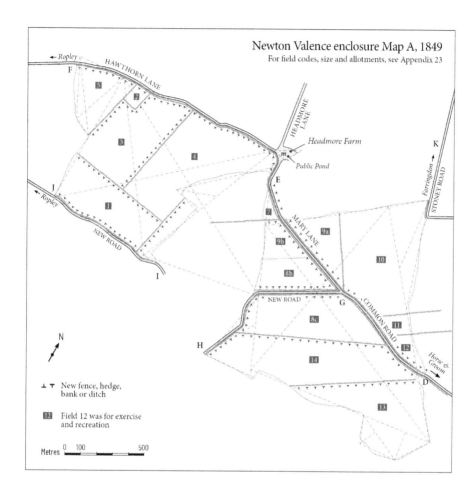

Newton Valence enclosure Map A, 1849
For field codes, size and allotments, see Appendix 23

From his London business address at 8 Cannon Row, he worked on sixteen enclosures, six of them later in Hampshire, all near Petersfield and all serving significant knights and esquires: Ramsdean and Langrish in East Meon in 1859, 123 acres; Petersfield Heath, 1859, seven acres; Sheet, 1859, 269 acres; Buriton, part of Petersfield Heath, 1861, forty acres; Liss, 1864, 662 acres; and East Meon Manor, 1866, 146 acres.[70]

Henry Chawner, a freeman of the Goldsmiths' Company of London, married an heiress named Hore of Esher in Surrey. His company, inherited from his father, Thomas, produced some of the city's finest silver, specialising in tableware, like candlesticks, coffee pots, sugar bowls and sauce ewers. In 1810, he bought the

70 Ramsdean and Langrish, HRO, Q23/2/41, TNA, MAF 1/562 (map); Petersfield Heath, HRO, Q23/2/109; Sheet, HRO, 8M61/16 (map), TNA MAF 1/557 (full text and map); Buriton, HRO, Q23/2/109, TNA, MAF 1/1063 (map); Liss, HRO, Q23/2/76/1-2, TNA, MAF 1/768 and 1/1008 (maps); East Meon Manor, HRO, Q23/2/123, TNA MAF 1/909 (map).

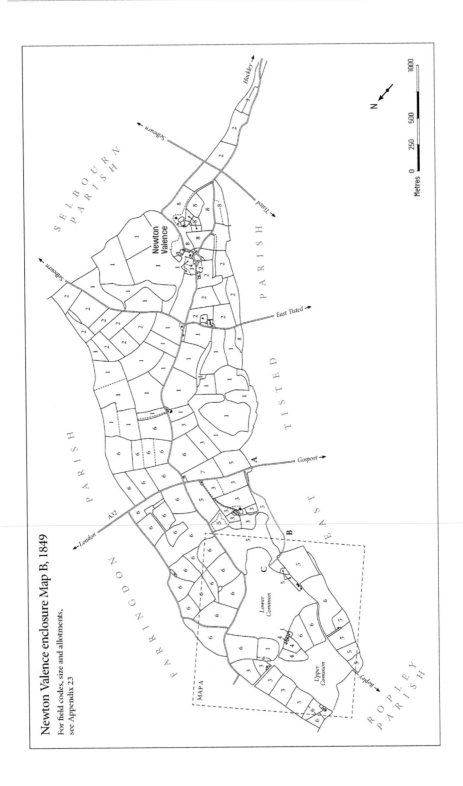

Newton Valence enclosure Map B, 1849

For field codes, size and allotments,
see Appendix 23

manor house in Newton Valence, noted for its designed landscape, and converted the old building into domestic offices and added a Grecian villa. They were filled with a large collection of paintings and other works of art including a hard paste *Duc d'Angoulême* Porcelain China vase from Paris, mounted in ormolu, after it was rejected by George IV because of a small fire flaw.[71]

Chawner was one of five who received over 10 per cent of the Newton Valence commons, 53 acres, 27.7 per cent, in three lots, to add to his existing 517 acres. The others were Robert and Henry Knight, 21.6 per cent in three lots; Eli Turvill, 13.9 per cent; James Winter Scott, 11.4 per cent and Captain George Ouvry Sampriere, 10.3 per cent.

Robert and Henry Knight were related to the widespread Knights and Eames of Chawton and Farringdon and other places; they added thirty-two acres to their existing 397. Turvill may only have received 21 acres, but he held almost 200 elsewhere in the parish. He was born in the parish, one of sixteen children, but his vigorous father, also Eli, was from Hartley Mauditt. Three other recipients, William Carter, John and Edward Hunt, and William Warner, were small farmers who had previously taken sizable bites of the land.

The last landowner to receive a share of the commons was the Reverend Thomas Snow. His glebe brought him just over thirteen acres. Snow's bishop at Winchester was George Pretyman.

Pretyman was a 5th Baronet, confidant of William Pitt the Younger, at one time his private secretary after the 1784 general election victory, and a staunch opponent of Catholic emancipation. Already wealthy through his father, a prominent Suffolk landowner, Pretyman, in 1803, inherited extensive property from an unrelated Marmaduke Tomline and took his surname. George Pretyman Tomline succeeded Brownlow North as bishop of Winchester in 1820 having declined the bishopric of London as 'too onerous'. When he died, Tomline was worth £200,000, close to £20 million today. Snow was one of his inherited headaches.

Thomas Snow was the fourth son of the banker, George Snow. After graduating from Cambridge, he rapidly became the vicar of Winterbourne Stoke, near Salisbury, and, just as quickly, was appointed the vicar of Micheldever and East Stratton by an old acquaintance of these pages, the banker and opinionated magistrate, Sir Thomas Baring.

'Gradually, Snow was drawn into the small group of Anglican discontents known collectively as the *Western Schism*' led by Baring. The Schism was the creation of a network of mostly well-connected Evangelicals, with strong direction provided by Harriet Wall, Baring's sister. The 'Baring party' were characterised by their strict Calvinistic principles and their rejection of infant baptism.[72] In

71 Bonham's website and HCC, *Integrated Character Assessment*, Newton Valence, Farringdon and East Tisted Downs, 5/2012. *Victoria History of Hampshire*, 'Newton Valence', 1908.

72 G. Carter, *Anglican Evangelicals. Protestant Secessions from the Via Media c. 1800-1850* (Oxford 2001),

1815, Snow married a widow, Maynard Eliza D'Oyly, daughter of a baronet, at Baring's home in Stratton Park. The next year, he was baptised by full immersion and Wall opened for him 'Snow's Chapel' in Cheltenham.[73] He officially left the Anglican priesthood for a number of years amid much episcopal distress.

Between 1822-26, Snow became again a compliant member of the Church of England. He wrote to Pretyman, just before the bishop's death, and to the bishop of Bristol, and submitted to the latter a confession of error.[74] Snow said that he now saw that it was wrong for clergy to separate from the Church of England and then to set themselves up as teachers and to gather around them congregations. Snow then served two curacies in the Bristol diocese and returned to Cheltenham. In 1842, under the benign influence of bishop Charles Sumner, he was invited to Newton Valence and bought the patronage, living there for many years until resigning in 1860.

East Tisted is the one remaining parish, which includes Rotherfield Park, of the six from which pieces were taken to form Four Marks in 1932. There is no found record of its enclosures except two brief notes to say that all the fields were shut by informal means.[75] A terrier of 1635 refers to land in the common field.[76] The names Great, Upper and Lower Common Fields, Brambly and Dun Furlongs survived until 1841.[77] Travelling south on the A32 towards Gosport, there is a long stretch of woodland on the right between Rotherfield Park estate and Lawns Hotel at Privett. Ordnance Survey maps of 1810-17 identify these woods today as much reduced contiguous commons, the first East Tisted, then Colemore, and finally West Tisted.

By 1850, at the last enclosure of the ridge parishes, Hampshire labourers were paid 10-11s a week, the wage of the Swing Riots, and their womenfolk 8d a day, mostly for weeding, spreading manure or stone picking. The Poor Law had been radically reformed in 1835. The largest parishes were grouped together to provide an efficient workhouse which was designed to be as unpleasant as possible so that only direct need would drive men and women to seek relief. 'The separation of husband, wife and children, coarse diet, severe discipline and hard tasks meant that workhouses were long hated and dreaded by the rural poor.'

Two Unions, workhouses, served the ridge parishes: Alresford dealt with Ropley among seventeen other parishes; eighteen villages, including Chawton, Farringdon, Medstead, East Tisted and Newton Valence, joined with Alton. Alresford's workhouse was built the year after the act for £5,350 at Tichborne Down, two doors along from the Cricketers Arms, with a capacity of 280

---

pp. 105-151.

73 Munden, 'Thomas Snow and the Western Schism', pp. 331-41

74 The correspondence was published as *Two Letters from the Right Reverend the Lord Bishop of Bristol to the Reverend Thomas Snow and his reply to each.*

75 Montgomery, *East Tisted*, p. 10. Chapman and Seeliger, *Enclosure in Hampshire*, p. 75.

76 HRO, 35M48/16/113.

77 HRO, 4M51/272.

paupers. Children were not allowed to mix with the adults. The site later became Tichborne Down House Hospital and, today, private residences.[78] The Guardians of the Poor in Alton gradually extended their existing workhouse. It was built for £4,000 in 1793 on Anstey Road on three acres known as Merriott's Purrock.[79] By the 1840s, it cost each taxpayer between £1-2 a year. Men were provided with a coat and waistcoat of woollen cloth and trousers of corded fustian with a round frock and stockings. The women wore linsey gowns. Able men pounded stones and gypsum, the old men worked in the garden. The women were divided into 'well-behaved' and 'bad character'. Today, the workhouse has been converted into residential housing called Adams House.

In 1851, Alresford Union had 103 inmates, Alton 86, the majority either lumped as paupers or from the agricultural trades, with several from outside the county.[80] Across the two workhouses were, somewhat surprisingly perhaps, a Henry Knight born in Chawton; young female house servants from Newton Valence and Chawton and another, Eliza Budd, from Medstead; William Pullinger from Ropley, with nine others born in the village; and five from Medstead, including Caroline Budd; and four men from Farringdon.

All but one of the Tolpuddle Martyrs emigrated to Canada. James Hammett remained working as a labourer. Old and blind, he refused to be a burden to his children and went into a workhouse to die. When Hammett was buried in Tolpuddle churchyard, the squire stood by the grave to make sure that no one spoke for or on behalf of trade unionism.[81]

78 HRO, 12A20/1, 4894/B6, 12A20/1.
79 HRO, 21M71/PO, 29M84/PK, 145A06/PL5/2, including the punishment book.
80 1851 census.
81 Groves, *Sharpen the Sickle!*, p. 23.

11 END OF THE CIRCLE: THE MAKING OF FOUR MARKS

Votes for all, freehold land, good profits and fresh air

And you that will come to this feast,
Come let's go chase the Deer,
For Hunting it is a pleasant sport
Fit for a Lord or Peer.[1]

The modern village of Four Marks was founded almost by accident at the end of the nineteenth century on little developed old commons and wastes mostly left from the 1709 Ropley enclosure. These largely empty lands on sloping ground in the north-west corner of the parish were bordered by road and rail routes from London to the south. The great agricultural depression from 1873-1896, driven by two faraway wars and then by the advent of cheap grain from the American prairies, undermined local landowners, forced bankruptcies and made the poor clay and chalk soil on the ridge so cheap that it could hardly be given away.[2] Much of the local countryside was neglected. Hedges were left untrimmed, pastures weed-ridden and buildings unrepaired. While the 40 per cent fall in farm prices benefitted the factory worker, it ruined a number of local smallholders.[3] Ropley and district saw a reported spate of suicides.

Coincidentally, two great British political movements sought, first, to extend the voting franchise through low-level property ownership and, second, to entice ordinary city dwellers to affordable plots in the 'idyllic' countryside. The waste suddenly had an unexpected value.

Land speculators and idealists in the 1890s, and through to the First World War, grasped the opportunity, sold or bought up land and then cleverly marketed regimented plots and down-market bungalows to Londoners. However, the new homes on the ridge's southern incline came with a heavy and often little understood burden: they were without power, water or sewerage or any civic or commercial facilities. This was community building from scratch. Families without agricultural skills or deep pockets met serious difficulties.

This chapter explains the background to Four Marks, named after a boundary stone, and enlarges on the world and national forces that fed a cycle of boom

---

1 Fritz, *English Ministers*, p. 107. '*The Hunting of the Newfound Dear with its Last* Legacy' portrays King George as a stag to be hunted, killed and cut up.
2 Mills, *Four Marks*, p. 1.
3 Collins, *Agrarian History*. Hunt and Pam, 'Responding to Agricultural Depression'. Perry, *British Agriculture*.

and bust. In under forty years a new Hampshire parish was formed that was very different from its neighbouring, traditional villages.

Alresford once included most of the lands of Bishop's Sutton, Ropley and Four Marks. The area was given by King Cenwalh of the West Saxons to the bishopric at Winchester starting a chain of ecclesiastical management through to the current day (*Appendix 1*). The commitment was confirmed in writing by a successor, King Ine, in A.D. 701.[4] It is an early English story of plot and counterplot as Walkelin, the first Norman bishop of Winchester, reputedly forged the record to confirm church ownership after the land had been granted to Saxon nobles. Fraud or not, the grant contains a detailed description of points on Alresford's early boundaries. One of them, *Lammeres Gate*, 'Claypond Gate', with eight other gates, show that ancient Four Marks was at the centre of important Saxon husbandry. In each case, the gate names are compounded with *mere* suggesting the 'internal division of wood pasture and the controlling of access to watering holes'.[5]

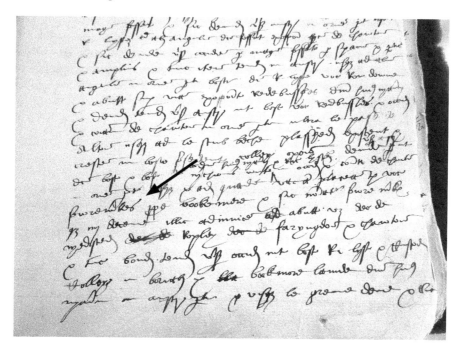

The first known mention of 'Four Marks' (at the beginning of a line), c. 1550
HRO, 11M59/A1/2/4.

---

4   British Library, London, *Codex Wintoniensis*, Additional Manuscript 15350, folios 20v-21r, Numbers 56 and 57 (s. xii).
5   Grundy, 'Saxon Land Charters', pp. 69-77, transcribed in Appendix 1.

The first document found to date to actually name 'Four Marks', written *Fowremarkes*, is recorded in Latin about 1550. It is deep in a record of a perambulation of Alresford manor and is not easy to spot. A perambulation is a walk to check and re-establish boundary markers and follows any 'ancient watercourse, the hedges of closes, and at each boundary point a cross or mark was made in the ground.'[6]

> ... *a certain empty place of land called Four Marks near Bookemere, and named thus, Four Marks, because four tithings abut there mutually, that is to say, the tithings of Medstead, Ropley, Farringdon and Chawton ...* (*Appendix 3*)[7]

'Bookemere' is interesting, important enough to be mentioned as a direction to the meeting point of the four tithings. It is repeated a line further on: 'the lord of this manor's Bookmore Launde'; so, perhaps, not a 'mere', or old pond, but a 'moor', or waste. It also occurs, 'Bokmeres stile', in the A.D. 701 Saxon boundary list and is further suggested by classical historian George Grundy to be the Old English *maere*, a balk of ploughland. The 1845 Ropley tithe map names 'Bogmore' as being in plots 68-9 (with a pit), today approximately at number 37 Thorn Lane in Four Marks. Probably, in the sixteenth century and before, the moor covered much more than a modern residential plot.[8] The immediate area has history. A denarius, the standard Roman silver coin, of emperor Marcus Aurelius, A.D. 161-180, was picked up in a Thorn Lane garden.[9] A lynchet, an ancient ploughing bank, was excavated at number 89 and contained large amounts of postmedieval and modern building debris.[10]

Apart from the accident of boundaries, 'Four Marks' for almost all of its prehistory and most of its modern times was an empty, but busy, place. People passed through without great notice. It was a chalk ridge, capped with clay and flints, that separated Alton from Alresford.

The ridge reaches its high point of about 215 metres on a line between Telegraph Lane and the centre of Medstead. It is no mountain, but it was a simple, tiring climb. The ridge was an inconvenience, a barrier to travel, to commerce and to community. People who gained the foothill on either side wanted to get to the bottom on the other side. For the walkers and riders of years ago, it made little sense to seek a long route around.

The ridge had two principal geographic and historic effects: to provide a home for those who sought a benefit from high ground and, a much larger affair, the founding of routes across or through the barrier.

---

6   Thompson, *Customs in Common*, p. 98.
7   HRO, 11M59/A1/2/4, p. 117. In my last book, *The Four Marks Murders*, I wrongly stated that this reference had been lost. My apologies to the archivist at the Hampshire Record Office.
8   With thanks to Manni Kirchner, 2/7/2021.
9   Historic Environment Record, HER 19130.
10 Historic Environment Record, HER 50278.

The high homes and work places span the centuries. North-west of Medstead Manor, there is a strong, rectangular defensive enclosure, or ringfort, now part of a copse near the convent.[11] It is possibly Iron Age, about 500 B.C., but could be medieval. Nearby, to the north, there are two tumuli, burial mounds, overlooking the countryside which are believed to date from 500 years earlier. A pre-Roman ridgeway from the Old Sarum area, the Lunway, crosses through Four Marks from the north following the drier southern side of the hill and is itself crossed near the *Windmill* by a summerway from today's Alresford following the quickest, driest, 'up-and-over' route to the Wey.[12] Medstead village is a hill settlement noted tangentially in 1086 in the Domesday Book (*Appendix 2*).

> As the early people spread and explored, established their camps and traded, so the first Celtic network of 'roads' evolved. The earliest of these are known, generally, as Ridgeways. This is because the first settlements were on the higher ground and the 'ways' which joined them ran along or just below the ridges; as far as was possible they avoided rivers and low ground. The main highways ran west and east across the southern downs from Cornwall to Kent; the most southerly of these came from the west, crossing the river Candover at Totford, and then going along the south side of Wield Wood and on to Burkham. At Barton's Copse, a branch ridgeway broke off and went south past Heathgreen to Hattingley and then to the present centre of Medstead, where it continued south past Roe Downs to leave the parish somewhere near the Windmill Inn. These were foot-paths made only by man and beast walking along the same track for countless generations.[13]

After these early herders had driven their sheep or cattle along the ridgeway, the Romans forged their main and, partly lost, route from Neatham up a carefully worked zigzag in Chawton Park Wood towards Winchester, possibly a three-lane highway with military traffic at its centre.[14] This way is under intense scrutiny at the moment, but there is good evidence of centuriation, the Roman method of surveying land for development. If events in Rome had taken a different path in the early 400s, this ridge down to Ropley might have been a large estate.[15]

There is a long-term debate about the path that pilgrims travelled after 1170 from Winchester via Alresford across the ridge to Canterbury. This pilgrimage was the great adventure of the Middle Ages. Five suggested routes are probably equally correct as travellers adapted to the weather, threats from robbers and varied advices given. Fearon advocated a northern route via Medstead and Wield before dropping down to Chawton.[16] A second road went through Bighton and

---

11 Williams-Freeman, *Field Archaeology*.
12 These routes are discussed in Hawkes, 'Old Roads'.
13 Rathbone, *Chronicle*.
14 NEHHS.
15 Heal, *Four Marks Murders*, Chapter 5.
16 Fearon, *Pilgrimage*.

missed Medstead. The third line followed close by the valley floor to Ropley where it briefly parted company with a fourth way up Blackberry Lane, once called Furse Bush Lane.[17] The final option was to cut across country from Ropley to West Tisted and Pelham Place, once Pilgrim Place, *pèlerin* being French for pilgrim.[18]

The King's Highway travelled from Bighton past Medstead and down through Chawton Park Wood from at least the thirteenth century.[19] There is a later branch to Odiham.[20] A system of quite passable bridleways existed across the kingdom. There was comparatively little wheeled traffic and only of the most primitive kind. Everyone travelled on foot or on horseback and nearly all goods were carried on the back of animals. Heavy materials were taken by water, 'going by small boats far up the most insignificant streams'. Roads made long circuits to reach fords where they could cross streams; they chose the high ground to escape the bogs, and they deviated from the straight course at all obstructions.[21]

As wheeled transport became more common, the road through the Chawton wood deteriorated although it was in heavy use well into the early twentieth century. A turnpike was deemed the answer to the muddy, potholed mayhem with its travellers forced to contribute at tollhouses to the upkeep of a safe and fast path. There were, however, several cherished local ways over the ridge: up Swelling Hill from Ropley Soke; tracks from Farringdon past the Woodside Farms (which extended to Alton) and by the current St Swithun's Way; along Brightstone, Kitcombe and Mary Lanes; and other routes from Colemore, Monkwood and West Tisted.

The Webbs, renowned husband and wife early historians, saw from *Piers Plowman* and Chaucer, from municipal and manorial records, and from the drawings of the period, a vision of a 'really enormous amount of wayfaring life' in the fourteen and fifteenth centuries.[22]

> The more important landowners usually held estates in different parts of England so that there was a perpetual coming and going between them. The practice of appeals to Rome involved an astonishing amount of journeying of ecclesiastic and legal agents of one kind or another. The common people seem always to have been on the road, on pilgrimages, seeking employment, or visiting the towns. The innumerable local markets, and still more, the periodical great fairs, must have required huge concourses of travellers from longer or shorter distances.

17 Cartwright, *Pilgrim's Way*. Belloc, *Old Road*.
18 Curtis, *Alton*.
19 Heal, *Four Marks Murders*, Chapter 13.
20 Rathbone, *Chronicle*.
21 Jackman, *Transportation*.
22 Webbs, *Kings Highway*.

All the kings and queens, indeed everyone of importance travelling from London to Winchester, passed over the ridge: every army, from marauding pre-historic bands to the Romans and Saxons, possibly the Vikings, certainly the civil war soldiers of Stephen and Matilda and the Roundheads and Cavaliers to the Tommies and Canadians on their way to Flanders trenches and the Yanks with their tanks in World War II.

Where any four boundaries meet is called a quadripoint. This coming together is near the current Boundaries surgery, marked by a 'large white stone' in 1759, and which was reported destroyed by workmen during road construction in the 1960s.[23] An old photograph notes its site tucked into a roadside hedge.[24]

Edward Rookes led a perambulation of his newly-acquired manor of Medstead in 1744 (*Appendix 15*).[25] He was accompanied by Thomas Peace, his steward, and twelve 'parishioners and inhabitants', including the usual sprinkling of Andrews, Budds and Wakes. On his journey, Rookes ordered over twenty-five 'Ancient Bound Crosses' in the ground to be immediately 'cutt afresh'. This sounds like a long-term lack of maintenance of some wood structures. More likely, they were boundary stones which could equally be 'cut afresh' when their letters were worn.

With a quadripoint, as at Four Marks, that marker should be evident in all the perambulations and enclosures of adjoining parishes. It was the site of a gate of unknown size or importance close by the junction with today's Boyneswood Road (*Appendix 13*). The Chawton enclosure map of pre-1740 shows another nearby parish gate, called Worthimy, at the boundary with Farringdon near where the old extension of Weathermore Lane meets the Shrave. On an 1839 map, the lane was called 'Four Marks Lane'.[26]

It is worth comparing the practice of bounds in Chawton which were holes dug and filled with stones and approved by village elders (*Appendix 4*). In 1744, particular attention was called, first, to a 'very remarkable Ancient Bound mark this day cutt afresh being an Old Bound Mark for Four Parishes that is Medsted Rapley [sic] Chawton & Farringdon & is about Six Yards from the hedge belonging to [erased] on Medsted Side', [note the toponym 'Four Marks' is nowhere used]; and, second, to a 'Very Ancient Bound Cross', [note the 'very'], by 'Ramscomb Gate'. Does this suggest that these two points have direct Saxon connections?[27]

There are two helpful perambulations made around Bishop's Sutton, the first also in 1744, by a local labourer Richard Cranston seeking to prove his right to

---

23 Mills, *Four Marks*. Cornick, *Early Memories*, p. 37.

24 Heal, *Four Marks Murders*, p. 293. Shore, *History*, p. 63: Primitive marks of some kind are denoted by many local names: Lee Marks, Alverstoke; Marks Lane, east of Stubbington; Markwell Wood, north of Finchdean; Worting Mark; Mark Lane, Mottiston; West Mark, Petersfield; Markfield, Bishop's Sutton; and, even, Ropley Mark.

25 HRO, 107M89/22. See also Alton Papers, No. 13, 2009, Margaret Prior, 'A Perambulation of Medstead in 1744', pp. 23-32, which includes the clockwise route laid on an Ordnance Survey map.

26 Four Marks Village Design Statement, 2001.

27 There is a group of mile and boundary stone enthusiasts in Hampshire: www.milestonesociety.co.uk.

two purrocks; the second a more formal affair in the following year with fifty-seven named people.[28] Cranston explained:

> *At the most remarkable Places where Crosses were made thirty-six* [thirty-five noted elsewhere] *Bound Mark Stones are now erected the first inscribed 'Bp's Sutton' on the East Side and 'New Alresford' on the West Side of it and the Rest have the letters 'B. S. P.' on them.*

It seems like crosses were attached to or engraved on stones. Cranston also made a small list of damaged and fallen stones: 'broke off', 'out of the ground' and 'loose'.

The c. 1550 survey called the area around the Four Marks boundary stone a *certain empty place of land*. It remained that way until deep into the nineteenth century except for two inns, two windmills, a turnpike and the odd cottage. The early route of the present A31, chosen to be widened and repaired for the turnpike in 1753, was an existing path through largely open terrain. There was no habitation in the way and no easy chance for long-distance travellers to dodge sideways and miss the tolls. This road from Alton passed through Chawton, parted with the Gosport turnpike, and climbed the ridge along the Shrave. The likely most disturbing consequence was the free use made of the local pits to provide road-building materials. Those responsible for maintenance had a legal *carte blanche* to raid properties for what they needed.

This was the time of the stagecoaches from the capital to Winchester, mostly leaving London in the morning, but carrying the Royal Mail in the evening. The route was competitive: Collyer's coach took ten hours, but the 'Independent', the 'Eclipse' and 'The Age' claimed eight hours. *Paterson's Itinerary* of 1785 ignored the turnpike and passed through Chawton Wood to near a marked South Town, by Medstead, again without mention of Four Marks.

A 1759 map of Hampshire shows two windmills: one behind the site of the *Windmill Inn*, a converted farmhouse, and a second, all traces gone, where the once important thoroughfare, Barn Lane, joins the A31. The inn, and the *Lymington Arms* on the site of Clementine's greengrocery store, have limited claims to be coaching halts, concentrating on attracting lesser traffic. *The Anchor* at Ropley Dene is the stop most mentioned in contemporary timetables, eight miles being sufficient for tiring horses facing or just finishing a major climb.

Canal mania in the 1790s stirred the newspapers, but nothing happened on the ground. There were three projected routes: two proposed long tunnels under Four Marks, the other a barge-carrying railway crossing from Ropley to near Rotherfield Park.[29]

---

28 HRO, 13M53/1. The 1745 Bishop's Sutton perambulation has been transcribed and placed with maps at www.bishopssutton.org.uk.
29 Heal, *Four Marks Murders*, Chapter 15.

The numbers of inhabitants are wrapped in the parishes which oversaw local government before 1932. Holly Fletcher conducted a population study of Four Marks in 2018 based on the decennial censuses. She traced the paths walked by enumerators as they travelled from house to house to compile their lists. It is not always possible to know whether a house, pulled down over a hundred years ago, was one side or the other of a later parish line. Some street and house names have changed. However, none of this is a serious concern when looking at the total count and long-term trends.[30]

In the years 1841–1861, comfortably under a hundred people lived in twenty dwellings in the parish-to-be. The great majority of them were far from the ridge, the boundary stone and the turnpike and were instead clustered around the long-established farms, mainly at Hawthorn and Kitwood. Today's housing centres were rough pasture or bracken, furze and brambles.

The years between 1853 and 1862 were described as the golden age of British agriculture, benefitting from decades of experimentation and investment. War in the Crimea and in America prevented cereal imports and protected the country. Lord Ernle said 'that crops reached limits which production has never since exceeded, and probably … never will.'[31]

In 1862, the United States passed the Homestead Act which led to the settlement of a large part of the Midwest. The United States also witnessed a great increase in railways, mainly across the prairies. Refrigerated steam ships drove down the cost of transatlantic food. In 1860, a quarter of wheat from Chicago to Liverpool cost 15s 11d, in 1890 3s 11d. The advent of the reaper-binder in 1873 allowed one man to do the cropping work of two on the American corn lands. The bad harvests in England of 1875 and 1877-79 disguised the real cause of the depression. 'Many thought that it was a temporary state of affairs and would correct itself.'

With attention centred on the explosion in manufacturing industry, and little protection from government, farming ceased to be Britain's major industry, 'in terms of employment, labour and capital and of social and political influence, or the source of the greater part of the nation's food supply'. Its contribution to the gross national product fell from 20 per cent in the late 1850s to 6 per cent in the late 1890s. It was a time of agricultural depression: falling prices, numerous bankruptcies, lower rents and untenanted farms.[32] Land used for cereals fell by 22 per cent and, by 1900, by 50 per cent. Almost 100,000 labourers left the industry. Between 1809 and 1879, 88 per cent of British millionaires had been landowners; between 1880 and 1914, the figure dropped to 33 per cent.

---

30 Data added to the population study from 1931 onwards came from a number of official sources and is specific to the newly-formed Four Marks, including the 1939 Register.
31 Ernle, 'The Great Depression and Recovery, 1874-1914' in Perry, *British Agriculture*.
32 Perry, 'Editor's Introduction', *British Agriculture*, pp. xi-xvi.

For landed business, it was a matter of commercial survival; 'improvement' was no longer the priority, enclosure no longer attractive. For the remaining field labourers, it was a question of keeping families alive. Memories of Swing and Tolpuddle were ingrained and led many Hampshire workers to look to trade unionism to increase their weekly wage.

One man, Joseph Arch, exemplified the nascent Farm Workers' Union.[33] Arch, from Warwickshire, started work at nine years, scaring crows for twelve hours a day. He became a plough boy and gradually learned the agricultural skills enabling him to travel for work. Arch saw the terrible conditions in which the majority of agricultural workers lived. He educated himself from newspapers and supported Liberalism. Destitute fellow workers turned to him to help fight for a living wage. At his first public meeting, Arch expected an attendance of fewer than thirty, but over 2,000 turned out. As president of his Union, Arch organised a strike which initially broke landowners' reprisals and saw a temporary rise in in wages.[34]

No records remain of Arch's trade union which collapsed in 1896 following farm owners' lock-outs. However, from newspapers reports and biographies, it is clear that Arch visited Hampshire, as well as Wiltshire and Dorset, several times looking to organise local labour and founding clubs and co-operatives. He was also at Tolpuddle in 1875 to make a presentation to James Hammett, the last martyr.

> *The labourer breakfasts on tea-kettle broth, hot water poured on bread and flavoured with onions, dines on bread and hard cheese with cider very washy and sour and sups on potatoes or cabbages greased with tiny bits of fat bacon. He seldom more than sees or smells butcher's meat.*[35]

Alton opened its station in 1852 connecting the town to London. An extension joining this new terminus to Winchester had been a gleam in the eye since the 1840s. Two tunnels were considered, but rejected as too expensive. A great gouge was instead cut at the highest point at the bridge in Boyneswood Road. The line was finally built in 1865, but was of little immediate benefit to the villages centres of Medstead and Ropley which it avoided. It followed closely the route of the turnpike, but always sought the best gradient for the steep climb over the ridge to aid early steam locomotives. The crews called it 'going over the Alps'. Alresford was the only town of note along its seventeen-mile route; Medstead got its station in 1868, although almost two miles away from the village. If one of the railway tunnels had been built, there would have been no station at Medstead.[36]

---

33 Horn, *Joseph Arch*.
34 Groves, *Sharpen the Sickle!*.
35 Canon Girdlestone, Groves, *Sharpen the Sickle!*, p. 33.
36 Heal, *Four Marks Murders*, Chapter 1.

In the ten years to 1871, the population in Four Marks increased to 139, the dwellings to thirty-two. At first thought, this would suit the claim in Wikipedia and elsewhere that the area was initially settled by returning soldiers of the Crimean War, 1853–56. The idea that a grateful government would give out land it did not own for a tiny selection of ordinary veterans is dubious, especially given practice to the current day. If the increase had been the result of the war, one might expect it to have happened before 1861 and not ten years later. A close examination of the occupants in 1861 suggests no war-weary from Sevastopol, but a less exciting handful of fertile local families who worked the land: agricultural labourers, farmers, carters and a shepherd. The influence of Hawthorn and Kitwood remained strong. The attractive Crimean story is a myth.[37]

The 1870 Ordnance Survey map notes only a couple of dwellings near the *Windmill Inn*. The inn, for some ten years from 1875 called the *Four Marks Inn* as it was near the boundary stone, was well established, set back at an angle from the road with a large paddock in front for resting horses or over-nighting drovers' charges.[38] One census night, the building might be almost empty, but ten years later holding thirteen people: the publican and family, servants and travellers.

The period from 1871–1891 was static: under 140 people lived in less than forty dwellings. *Black's Guide* of 1879 had no place for Four Marks in its map of Hampshire, but it did recognise North Street in Ropley. Opposite the *Four Marks Inn* in 1875, there was a 'Four Marks Cottage', later 'Four Marks House' which became the post office. A money order date stamp exists for 'Four Marks, Ropley' for March 1897; by 1907, it was 'Four Marks, Alton'.[39] Along Semaphore Lane, in 1891, the Farnham Brewery Company leased a copyhold plantation from Edward Knight of Chawton.[40] For the first time, in 1897, there are identifiable concentrated dwellings, perhaps nine spaced houses in an area called 'Four Marks'.

Why was there no significant development in or near 'Four Marks' before the end of the nineteenth century? The land around the *Windmill* is dotted with clay and chalk pits and kilns to provide road and building materials. From Saxon times, the great impediment to growth was the lack of water. There are no ridge rivers, only memories of an ancient stream along Lymington Bottom where some ten gravel pits indicative of a watercourse have been found. Local gravels include Early Stone Age implements and contemporary shells and fossils of red deer and of a famous elephant, *elephas primigenius*, the woolly mammoth.[41] The old river likely connected the ponds at Medstead and Five Ash to the road lake

---

37 See also Jane Hurst, letter Four Marks News, 10/2020.
38 *The Windmill* was replaced by a new building in 1935 and is now a Co-op shop and Post Office.
39 Mackay, *Sub Office Date Stamps*, p. 156.
40 HRO, 18M61/Box/B/13/1, 12/11/1891. *Village Design Statement*, p. 8.
41 To be seen in the Curtis Museum. Curtis, *Alton*. Shore, 'Hampshire Valleys'.

at the primary school crossroads and to the run of marling pits leading to Plain Farm pond.[42]

Chalk downland has few surface streams.[43] Under the skin of loam, there are two layers of chalk, the first coarse and impregnated with yellow stones, the second altogether finer and stone free.[44] The lower layer rests on a bed of impervious clay. Rain falling on the downs percolates through the chalk to the bed and then builds upwards saturating as it goes. When the chalk can take no more, the water flows over the clay until the chalk above is thin enough for it to push through the surface as springs. In the 1930s, these springs could be seen rising on the grass verges opposite the *Anchor Inn*.[45] Water is now extracted across the road from the *Shant*.

Consequently, on the ridge and dependent on agriculture, locals looked to rainwater, to wells and to dew ponds.

The main farms had always dug deep wells. A will of Roger Gerveys in 1392 lists a well rope and an iron hooped bucket. Four wells were noted by Moody in Medstead: Stancombe Farm had a well 'of great depth'; Goatacre Farm had a remarkable artesian well in its cellar, 225 feet deep; another remained opposite Trinity Farm until it was filled in during the latter part of the twentieth century; one more at Southdown was of 260 feet, dug by hand through the chalk without lining of any sort except for a short length at the top, and needed two men to walk inside the treadwheel.[46] In 1920, water pumping was still done by a donkey in a large oak wheel at the Manor House, now the Convent of St Lucy. The well was 308 feet deep; it took a quarter of an hour for each bucket to reach the top. Another donkey worked a wheel in Bighton in the outbuildings of the new manor house of the Reverend John Thomas Maine.[47]

Dew or mist ponds or meres, 'natural' to the clay, chalk and flint-laden land would have provided a sufficient, if meagre, supply of drinking water for animals and men.[48] The side and bottom of a dew pond, shallow and saucer-shaped, was lined with insulating straw and then impermeable clay, often puddled by cattle, to retain the water which generally came from rainfall rather than dew.[49] A layer of soot or lime deterred earthworms which burrow upwards. The trick was to keep the pond at a lower temperature than the surrounding earth. Ponds dotted the high ground as at the top of Blackberry Lane and the current Four Marks fishing haunt. It is why Jack and Jill went up the hill to fetch a pail of water.[50]

---

42 HRO, 38M48/5. Also, Box, 'Hampshire in Early Maps'.

43 Shore, 'Springs and Streams'.

44 Cobbett, *Rural Rides*: 'deep loam bordering on clay, rich in colour and full of yellow-looking stones, which still rise up on ploughing'.

45 Mason, *Ropley*.

46 Rathbone, *Chronicle*, pp. 23-4, 46. HGS, *Medstead*, p. 5. Moody, *Short History of Medstead*, pp. 19, 21.

47 HGS, *Bighton*, p. 10.

48 Rathbone, *Chronicle*, p. 8.

49 Mayhew, *Geography*, p. 129.

50 Martin, *Dew-Ponds*. Hubbard, *Neolithic Dew-Ponds*. Pugsley, *Dewponds in Fable and Fact*.

The enclosures of the ridge caused several new upland ponds to be made as the hedges and gates cut off access to previous water supplies. A pond a few feet away from Medstead church was used as drinking water for cattle; it was filled in over a century ago.[51] In 1736, the commissioners decided that Five Ash pond on Soldridge Common, and Hacket Pond on Stankham Common, should 'remain as they were before enclosure for public use' and that 'no one shall enclose any part of them nor dig within their land adjoining so as to drain the water from them'.[52] A lane a rod and a half wide from the 'Widow Hall's to William Lovers, William Moulds and John Smith' to Hacket Pond was designated 'for the use of the poor people' as well as a four foot wide way for the 'poor people to drive a wheel Barrow to fetch water on the West'. The pond at Worthimy Gate in Weathermore Wood was constructed during the Farringdon enclosure; the one at Headmore Farm during that at Newton Valence in 1850.

At least five major developers, one unidentified, descended on waterless Four Marks in the years between 1894 and World War I intent on social improvement or plain commercial gain. Winchester College Estate conducted at least two major sales: 350 acres in Medstead and Soldridge offered in April 1894 and, in May 1912, around the main road in Four Marks.[53] The Land Company of London held two auctions at Lymington Park Estate in 1896 offering over 140 plots with a hotel and shops on a farm bought from Charles Frederick Hemming, landowner and farmer.[54] Lymington Park Estate surrounded Lymington Farm, a substantial set of buildings on the corner of Brislands Lane, grandly renamed Lymington Park Road for the auction, and Lymington Bottom, called Medstead Main Road. At almost the same time, William Carter, owner of Herbert Park, offered large opportunities in Alton and Kitwood Lanes. A local man, Frank Gotelee, who in 1901 acquired much of the land in Medstead which had been accumulated in the 1850s and 60s by William Ivey, tried to sell freehold plots for development although with less success.[55]

Here was the true birth of a new village. In the ten years to 1901, the settlement around Four Marks doubled: inhabitants to 279 and dwellings to sixty-seven, and by 1911, a further increase to 334 people and to eighty-seven homes.

---

51 Moody, *Short History of Medstead*, p. 22.
52 1737 Soldridge award. 'Hacket' in Medstead is variously transcribed as Hac(r)ket(t) in this book and in the tithe, often in the same sentence. It may be two names or one. Grundy, *Appendix 1*, suggests that Hacket was originally a corrupted place name for the Saxon 'Eacges Geate', the name of three fields which lie on the east boundary of Bighton, just north of the road from Bighton to Soldridge. Hacket has been preferred.
53 Winchester College Archives, L14/49/9, 'Copy and draft deeds and other papers relating to property in Medstead, 1864-1912.
54 Kelly's Directory, 1889.
55 Dr. Keith Brown: The estate contained 'valuable brick earth, gravel and chalk'. The site was offered for let, including a pug mill for clay mixing, in 1865. Ivey claimed 'considerable loss' in a legal claim the following year, and offered the whole for auction in 1871 (*Hampshire Telegraph*, 12/5/1865; *Hampshire Chronicle*, 8/7/1865; William Ivey v. Mid-Hants Railway Co, 26/11/1866; *Hampshire Chronicle*, 26/8/1871), private email, 2020.

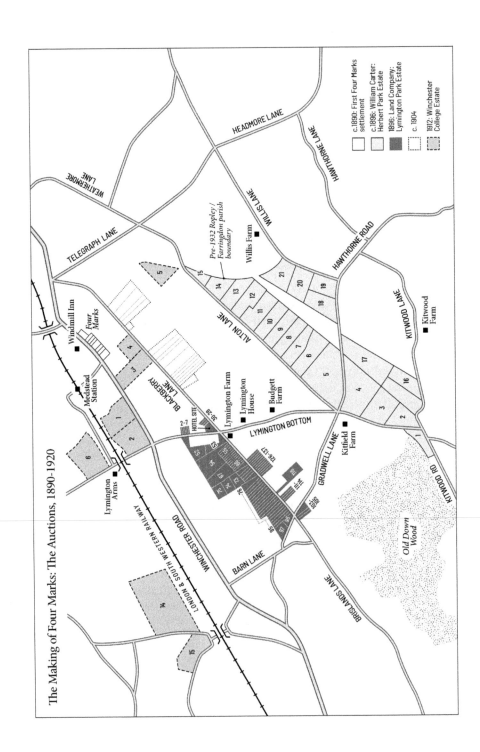

The Making of Four Marks: The Auctions, 1890-1920

c.1890: First Four Marks settlement
c.1896: William Carter: Herbert Park Estate
1896: Land Company: Lymington Park Estate
c. 1904
1912: Winchester College Estate

Three maps of the sales survive for Winchester College, The Land Company and for Carter's Herbert Park.[56] Together, they contain 242 plots comprising an estimated 251 acres, about half the total acreage enclosed in the 1709 Ropley enclosure and on approximately the same land. The maps also cover almost every nook and cranny of the early Four Marks developments with the exception, a big one, of the early bungalows on the southern side of Blackberry Lane; about twenty-three according to the 1912 map of Winchester College. It follows that, in order to complete the picture, at least one major sale or new developer is missing from the years before World War I. It also follows that, while some bungalow constructions may have been haphazard and built upon sub-divided plots, there were no significant independent land grabs. All these first buildings originated from land provided by a handful of speculative developers.

The College's brochure promised 'Valuable Freehold Small Holdings, Accommodation Fields, Splendid Building Sites and Bungalow Plots'. One catalogue for a sale in the *Swan Hotel* in Alton has pencil notations of the sale prices from a disappointed bidder. Lots 1 and 2 (both at £140) offered over fourteen acres in land east from Lymington Bottom between the railway and the Winchester Road. One half was seen as a splendid building site with 'Southern Slope and Grand Views' and the second an 'important corner building plot' for use as a 'fine site for a residence' or 'exceptionally adapted for profitable development by sub-division'. Lots 3 and 4 (together £190) promoted almost ten acres for building, with a combined 730 feet of frontage, to the north of the middle of Blackberry Lane. Both were occupied by A & C Wyeth. Lot 5 was an isolated four acres in country south of Telegraph Lane ideal for an 'Accommodation Plot'. Lot 6 was two 'valuable fields' (£190) of a combined twelve acres north of the railway between Lymington Bottom and Stoney Lane, also suitable for sub-division. There were further lots in Soldridge.

There may be a tendency to dismiss Four Marks' initial growth spurt at the turn into the twentieth century as nothing more than speculators on the make with a ready market of dreamy, hopeful smallholders with more money than sense. To do so would be a big mistake.

The move to Four Marks was given impetus by an important radical movement that is little remembered today. The Four Marks phenomenon was founded in the aspirations of the skilled working and trading lower middle classes and the wresting of the parliamentary vote away from the aristocracy and the landowners. In doing so, it provided a watershed to the development of friendly and mutual building societies.

'A key part of the explanation is to be found in the freehold land movement, a loose confederation which emerged in the late 1840s, causing a short-lived but illuminating flurry in political circles ... It came close to dominating popular

---

56 HRO, 38M48/5, Herbert Park.

politics.'[57] The fight, over many decades, is not a subject to condense or digest easily, but it is one on which the modern-day universal franchise was dependent.[58] It helped the Liberal Party rise to power on a broad programme based on the supremacy of parliament, expansion of the franchise, free trade, the abolition of slavery and, eventually, the completion of equal rights for Catholics.

Land societies, of which there were many hundreds across England and Wales from London northwards, signed tens of thousands of members within five years. They were offered freehold properties at cost together with the associated advantage of a vote in parliamentary elections.[59] Democrats and Liberal activists thought there was an imperative need to extend the franchise to develop 'working-class self respect and improvement'.

'The wish to improve their condition is taking root in the universal heart of the working classes,' observed Thomas Cooper in 1850.[60] That same year, one of the five newspapers founded exclusively to serve the freehold movement asserted, 'A new era has commenced.'[61] The 'discovery' … in practical politics was the facility to create forty-shilling votes in the counties:

> *Why should an Englishman henceforward supplicate parliament, in vain, to grant him a vote, when he may owe to his virtuous prudence and economy his own enfranchisement. The cost of a single pint of beer a day [over several years] amounts to more money than would buy a country qualification.*[62]
>
> *The Freeholders' Union are engaged in the two-fold labour of extending the franchise and multiplying the number of landed proprietors. We hardly know which of these two is the more important and needful. The monopoly of political power and the monopoly of the land are the two parent evils in this country, from which a multitude of lesser ones grow; and it is not possible to attack the one but through the other, or to effect any great or beneficial change in the condition of the mass of the people, until both these monopolies are abolished.*[63]

The purchase of the county forty-shilling franchise was a relatively simple exercise made possible by a miscalculation by the landowners when they moved to thwart attempts to extend the vote and to retain their own influence. The retention of an old clause in the 1832 Reform Act meant all owners of freehold property worth forty shillings or more, £2 (at a notional annual rental of 5 per

---

57 Chase, 'Out of radicalism'.
58 Gillespie, *Labor and Politics*. Hamer, *Politics of Electoral Pressure*. Prest, *Politics in the Age of Cobden*, Chapter 4.
59 Ritchie, 'Freehold Land Societies'.
60 *Cooper's Journal*, 17/1/1850.
61 *Freeholder*, 1/1/1850.
62 *Reformer's Almanac*, 'The Freehold Franchise', 1849.
63 *Freeholder*, 1/6/1850.

cent), or who owned a £10 house, were eligible to vote.[64] The legality of the clause was fought through the courts by the landowners when they realised their mistake, but they lost handsomely. It was observed that 'it did not take much more than a paddock and a pigsty to qualify'.[65]

Freehold land societies offered plots of land grouped on estates to be used as allotments and, in some cases, developed houses on them. The cost of conveyancing had always been a major disincentive to working-class purchases so building and legal costs were shared and, thereby, kept to a minimum.

Those workers and artisans who joined the movement, or took advantage of the friendly and mutual building societies which resulted, were generally examples of probity, self-help and thrift. A source in Birmingham reckoned that 'out of £50,000 paid into one freehold-land society, one-third was rescued from the public-house'.[66] It was not surprising, therefore, that the societies' ranks contained considerable numbers of radical thinkers, non-conformists and teetotallers. One might expect that the migrants' arrival in bulk in, say, Four Marks brought with them 'respect, order and sobriety.'[67]

> *Such a man will infuse fresh blood into the constituency. He will not give a vote like a browbeaten tradesman or a dependent tenant-farmer. His landlord will not be able to drive him to the polling-booth like a sheep. On the contrary, he will go there erect and free – a man not a slave.*[68]

These incomers were roundly supported by Liberal parliamentarians, a few of whom had their seats saved, or returned, by an influx of new voters targeted at their constituencies.[69] Chief among them were Richard Cobden and John Bright, leading free traders, famous for battling the scourge of the Corn Laws.[70] Cobden saw the freehold land movement as 'the only stepping stone to material change' and meant it to clothe an attack on the landed interest. In a speech in London, Cobden took the example of Hampshire in 1841 where there were 93,909 male adults over twenty years, but only 9,223, less than 10 per cent, registered electors (no female having the vote).[71]

Over time, the political and altruistic elements of the movement dwindled. Building Societies became more hard-headed. The National Freehold Land Society, set up in 1849 to extend the franchise through property ownership,

---

64 Prest, *Politics in the Age of Cobden*, p. 121.
65 Nossiter, *Influence*.
66 Beggs, 'Freehold Land Societies', p. 346.
67 Chase, 'Out of radicalism'.
68 Ritchie, 'Freehold Land Societies'.
69 Beggs, 'Freehold Land Societies'. Ritchie, 'Freehold Land Societies'. Chase, 'Out of Radicalism'.
70 Beggs, 'Freehold Land Societies', pp. 338-9.
71 Cobden public meeting, the *London Tavern*, 26/11/1849, in *The Times*, 27/11/1849.

transformed in 1856 into The British Land Company which, in one of its early iterations, may have been called the Land Company.[72]

British Land today has about £15 billion of assets under management with past developments including London's iconic 'Cheesegrater' (the Leadenhall Building), the Corn Exchange, Broadgate, Plantation House and Regent's Place, Meadowhall and, in Dublin, St Stephen's Green.

For at least twenty years, the marketing tactics of the Land Company changed very little: extensive newspaper advertising; empty country sites near railway stations; large, 'choice' community developments, mostly in Essex and Hampshire, for like-minded people from close-knit urban areas, often the East End of London, always suitable for allotments, bungalows and poultry farms; the offer of cheap home construction; the suggestion of hotels and shops; a surface affinity with the Freehold Land Movement; a free, or cheap, train ride to view the site and, later, to enjoy 'family' visits; a free lunch followed by an auction in a marquee; and easy terms made palatable by centralised, legal services and costs.[73]

In one auction on Wednesday, 10 June 1896, a steam locomotive from Waterloo eased to a halt at Medstead Station. All the 2s 6d single seats were taken. A large tent was pitched ready near the junction of Lymington Bottom and Blackberry Lane. The travellers inspected plans for 145 'small villa farm sites' ranging from 50 x 500 feet to two, three and five acres, part of the 'Lymington Park Estate near Medstead'.[74] There was no mention of 'Four Marks'. The intending buyers gazed at models of cottages they could order, £100 for brick and £80 for wood, supplied by Messrs Allen & Co of Charing Cross. The more adventurous might have showed interest in a 'bold hotel corner plot'. There were also twenty-five 'shop and cottage' opportunities. Adverts for the sale had been placed exclusively for the last month in *The East London Advertiser*, the *Westminster Gazette*, the *Essex Guardian* and *The Tower Hamlets Independent and East End Local Advertiser*.[75]

More than half of the 'very choice' freehold sites, the 'cheapest and highest on the market', had been bought at the first auction in April.[76] This day was to be the last chance to own a piece of this 'lovely rural rustic part of sunny Hampshire, within easy drive of Winchester City and Cathedral, and near the celebrated Sir Roger Tichborne's Rich Estates'. The mention of Tichborne was

---

72 Smith, *No Stone Unturned*. Marsh, *Centenary of British Land*. The British Land Company has no record of 'The Land Company' believing the full company name was always used. Records of this time were almost all destroyed following bombing in the Blitz. As a result, there are no records of sales in Hampshire or of a company office in Cheapside, only in Moorgate Street, London (private email 2020).

73 For example: *Southend Standard and Essex Weekly Advertiser*, 22/2/1894; *Barking, East Ham & Ilford Advertiser, Upton Park and Dagenham Gazette*, 10/8/1895; *Daily Telegraph and Courier*, 2/6/1896; *London Evening Standard*, 2/6/1896; *Westminster Gazette*, 10/7/1901; *London Daily News*, 13/7/1901; *Daily Mirror*, 17/5/1907, 4/11/1907; *East London Observer*, 3/8/1907; *Tower Hamlets Independent and East End Local Advertiser*, 17/8/1907; *West London Observer*, 18/10/1907.

74 Sale map, 10/6/1896, courtesy of Norman Read.

75 16, 23, 30/5 and 6, 8, 13/6/1896.

76 23/4/1896 at 1 pm, *St James's Gazette*, 18/4/1896.

to impress. The reason lay in the 'Tichborne Claimant', a legal cause célèbre and long-running court case avidly followed by newspaper readers. An imposter presented as Sir Roger, heir to the family fortune, thought dead in a shipwreck off Brazil in 1853. Arthur Orton, the claimant, after conviction and many years' hard labour, finally confessed to the crime in 1895, the year before the auction. The Tichborne name and the 'richness' of its estates would have been well known to many of the railway passengers.

With favoured plots selected, the substantial luncheon free to buyers began at noon: cold beef, ham, pies, cheese, salad and beer with juices for the ladies. At 1.30, directly the plates were cleared, the auctioneer mounted a platform and began his work.[77] Those whose bids were successful received free return train tickets, free deeds, abstracts and plans, and suffered no tithe or land taxes. There was a choice between outright purchase or a 10 per cent deposit followed by sixteen quarterly payments.[78]

Within five years, the population of this small area to the south and east of the London to Winchester road had almost trebled to close to 250 people with over thirty new homes.[79] These people who visited this unknown and unremarkable empty quarter of Hampshire came from all parts of London. Policemen were reported good purchasers at a similar contemporary sale in Essex along with 'licensed victuallers, pawnbrokers, housekeepers, caretakers, chemists, small tradesmen, engravers, fish porters, ivory turners, tennis-bat makers and others'.[80] Many new inhabitants, noted in later censuses, had some unusual birthplaces for north Hampshire: some just 'London', but also Battersea, Bloomsbury, Bow, Bowes Park, Camberwell, Chiswick, Ealing, Holborn, Hornsey, Islington, Kilburn, Kingston-upon-Thames, Leyton, Old Bailey, Paddington, St Pancras, Stamford Hill, Tooting, Tottenham, Tower Hamlets, Walworth, Westminster and Windsor.[81]

At the sale in Essex, buyers gave their reasons: 'Healthy place to live', 'A fine place for a Sunday outing', 'The cheapest railway in the kingdom', 'A place to retire and keep poultry', 'It's for my wife and children', 'An investment', 'To build on', 'For resale'.

From today's house distribution, many plots were bought together to provide large gardens or smallholdings. Few of the shops materialised. The hotel, a standard suggestion in all Land Company's estate offerings, was never built, but then, its presence had already given authority to the plan.

---

77 *The Pall Mall Gazette*, 9/7/1891, reporting a similar sale in Benfleet, near Southend-on Sea.
78 *The Tower Hamlets Independent and East End Local Advertiser*, 13/6/1896.
79 Discounting the inhabitants of the much older farms at Kitwood and Hawthorn which later became part of Four Marks parish (Fletcher, Population study).
80 *The Pall Mall Gazette*, 9/7/1891.
81 Fletcher, Population study.

What the Land Company's exciting auctions established was the legitimacy of local development. Speculators were hard at work seeking to buy, to wait and to resell.

William Carter was an early entrant to the list of developers interested in Four Marks. Carter was born in Dorset in 1852, the son of a master builder.[82] In America, he made a fortune in property. In the 1880s, he returned to Poole and acquired Kinson Pottery from which, much later, would come the decorative Poole Pottery. At the end of the nineteenth century, Carter bought vacant sites in the south of England with the idea of encouraging people back to the land by offering one-acre smallholdings at a reasonable price. His company, initially William Carter Estates, later became Homesteads Limited. Some of his purchases were local: Ropley Common Farm; Beech Place Estate and Goatacre Estate, both in Medstead; Down House Estate, Andover; and at East Oakley and Kempshott Village Estate, near Basingstoke.[83]

At least part of Carter's land in Four Marks, originally part of Bailey's Farm, was renamed Herbert Park. This area included the whole of the south of Alton Lane to the Farringdon parish boundary, including the current Jocks Lodge (1916) and Pooks Hill (1917) and all the land on the south of the road from Hawthorn Road past the school-to-be to Kitwood and, there, at the crossroads, the land on the north by a then much larger Old Down Wood.

The Homestead Movement had defining characteristics: cheap, rural or semi-rural land suitable for market gardening or self-sufficiency, and the option of a basic house, usually single-storey 'colonial' style bungalows in a 'do-it-yourself' community. 'Colonial' was a trade name with the several standard designs, mostly one, two or three bedrooms with a living room and kitchen costing from £100 upwards.[84] The higher prices also brought tile roofs instead of corrugated iron.

Homestead's influence extended to the United States, Australia and New Zealand. Initial pride-of-place in England went to Carter's development at Kempshott, advertised widely as a 'well located freehold property on high ground above Winchester'. The land was 'very good, having grown as much as forty-two bushels of wheat to one acre and specially adapted for cutting into poultry'. Several standard 'colonial bungalow' designs were available for submitting to Basingstoke Borough Council. Homestead's developments were sold without utilities: no clean water (use of a water tank or a well to be dug), no electricity (generator, solid fuel stoves and fireplaces, kerosene or gas lamps) and no sewerage (outside earth closet toilet).

In West Oxfordshire, in the town of Carterton, is a Four Marks twin and William Carter development. Homesteads bought local land in 1894 which was divided into plots of six acres. Each sold for £20 with bungalows costing

---

82 Jane Hurst, kempshotthistorygroup.org.uk.
83 HRO, 79M78/P4, Beech Place Estate.
84 Examples of the designs are held at the HRO, 38M48/5 with early pictures of the serried developments.

£120. It was a colony of smallholders and became renowned for black grapes and tomatoes, sold at Covent Garden. Many of the settlers were 'retired soldiers and people moving from the towns'.

However, to put all these developments by Winchester College, the Land Company and William Carter, in perspective, as late as 1920, Kelly's Directory felt able to say that Ropley parish contained several small scattered hamlets of which Lyeway, The Soke, Charlwood, Kitwood and Monkwood were the principals, with no mention of Four Marks.

The effect of the auctions and direct sales on the landscape of Four Marks was dramatic. Within a few years, Hilaire Belloc, seeking the Pilgrim's Way, described a recent and 'extraordinary little town of bungalows and wooden cottages' in Blackberry Lane as he walked the area in 1909.[85] Isolated bungalows sprang up along other side lanes like Alton and Willis. As the working man's wage grew, the demand for wheat fell and was replaced by calls for a 'good chop'. Husbandry was more profitable than tilling the fields. Pigeon and rabbit became staples.

The years before World War I were not a good time for a move to a rural idyll, especially for that part of the incomers who depended on working the land for a living. The weather was harsher in Four Marks than in the surrounding countryside and this was an exceptionally cold period. Today, one result of the village's elevation remains a particular micro-climate. In winter, the approach roads can be snow-blocked while Alton enjoys rain. In summer, Four Marks may be covered in cloud, especially in the morning, while Alton is in sunshine. It was a hard life with no telephones to call for help. In those early years, a few people were reported found frozen in their homes.

The lack of water was a never ending theme.[86] In time of drought, like in 1911, when the omnipresent rainwater butts and underground tanks that fed from the roofs of the house and buildings were empty, residents rose at four in the morning to get their water for the day from the springs at Beech, Bighton or Bishop's Sutton. There were three cottages at Heath Green whose inhabitants used to walk a mile each way with buckets to get their water.[87] A queue was not unknown. Often, the poor had to content themselves with polluted water from the ponds. It was part purified with alum or wood ash before drinking.

There is the tale of a man who, because the village ponds were dry, had gone to the Bighton spring to fetch water. On his way back, a storm broke. When he reached the bottom of Common Hill he found water pouring down it. He emptied his two large buckets and walked up the hill only to find that no rain had fallen on Medstead.[88]

---

85 Belloc, *The Road*.
86 Moody, *Short History of Medstead*, pp. 24-25.
87 Rathbone, *Chronicle*, p. 40.
88 Rathbone, *Chronicle*, p. 47.

Two underground water tanks supplied Medstead Station. A hand pump allowed water to be pumped into a slate tank to flush the gentlemen's toilets.[89]

In 1925, the area of Alton Rural District Council was supplied chiefly by wells, fourteen of which were repaired and four condemned that year. Medstead was the exception relying on underground rainwater tanks 'owing to its high situation and depth of water-bearing strata'.[90] By 1937, Four Marks, Ropley and West Tisted had joined Medstead. Rainwater tanks for new buildings were legislated to be of a minimum capacity of 5,000 gallons.

During the First World War, Mrs Beatrice Jervoise, manager of Church Farm at Lasham, brought in a dowser with great success. The resulting Herriard and Lasham Water Company, with reservoirs in Lasham Wood, had, by 1938, the statutory power to pipe water to a dozen villages around, but had not yet exercised their rights to Four Marks and Medstead. Wey Valley Water Company provided water to Chawton and Farringdon with plans to reach Newton Valence. In 1948, Medstead had seventy-six houses directly supplied with a further thirty-four using standpipes; Chawton 75 direct, 0 standpipes; Farringdon 87, 30; Newton Valence 13, 0; Ropley 39, 0 and none at all in East Tisted and Four Marks although work was at last underway. The following year, 63 of 420 houses were connected in Four Marks; 123 of 401 in Medstead and 100 of 398 in Ropley. Work progressed gradually into the early 1960s.

Four Marks was circled at some distance by long standing, traditional villages, Medstead, Chawton, Farringdon, Newton Valence, West Tisted and Ropley, with their medieval churches, village greens or halls where fairs or markets were once held, schools, alehouses, general and food shops, a heritage of agriculture with busy forges, road and path connections to neighbouring places, carriers for transport, and functioning social infrastructure.

Four Marks had no beating heart. The most needed infrastructure was built by its new inhabitants before the war. The school was largely a gift of two benefactors. Marianna Hagen of Ropley was the driving force. She bought the plot of land, part of Homestead Farm on Hawthorn Road, in 1902 from J Tomlinson, a farmer. Tomlinson, in turn, gave the purchase price towards the cost of construction. At first, church services were held in the school. In 1908, Miss Hagen moved the 'Iron Room', a corrugated iron and timber hut from Ropley Soke to opposite Belford House where it became the mission; now, sadly, a derelict eyesore.[91] Around 1910, a social and multi-purpose Institute was formed which met in borrowed premises. A permanent building arrived in 1913 and this has since been incorporated into today's Village Hall in Lymington Bottom.

---

89 Dr. Keith Brown, archivist, Mid-Hants Railway Preservation Society, email 5/4/2021.

90 Annual Reports: Medical Officer of Health, Alton Rural District Council: 1926; 1937, p. 2; 1944, pp. 1-2; 1945, p. 2; 1948, p. 4; 1949, pp. 11-12; 1951, pp. 10-11; 1963, p. 12.

91 The mission was reported to have been first built to save the souls of the Irish navvies working on the railway. The mission's replacement, the Church of the Good Shepherd, opposite the village hall, was built in 1953 and later enlarged.

Four Marks' next phase followed the end of World War I and meshed with a Government promoting the development of smallholdings in the hope of reducing unemployment. Land was cheap as the 'rural elite had suffered many casualties and could no longer manage their estates'.[92] Some claim that between 1918 and 1922, 25 per cent of the area of England was bought and sold although this claim, much repeated, relies on a single suspect magazine article.[93] Parcels of land were acquired from hard-pressed landowners by those looking for the romanticised life of the countryside. Buyers were encouraged by an unlikely consortium of politicians, like Stanley Baldwin, by the Board of Agriculture looking to dispose of surplus army huts, by the Arts and Crafts movement,[94] and by books from the travel writer H. V. Morton and the romantic novelist Mary Webb.[95] Companies were formed, many unscrupulous, to facilitate the sales of 'plots of heaven'. There were ready buyers and, with minimal building guidelines for the country and little enforcement, temporary buildings were constructed on plots of one to two acres, selling in 1932 for £200.[96]

The shacks that went up alongside Carter's 'colonial bungalows', a few ordered by near-penniless owners, were sometimes worse than those from the last invasion. These new homes were often sorry affairs of wood, sheets of uninsulated asbestos pasted with wallpaper and corrugated iron roofs.[97] Even chicken houses were given a new lease of life. There were similar developments, especially in the Monkwood area. Newcomers turned their hands to pig breeding or to chicken farming on the poor chalk and clay soil.

During the Great Depression of the late 1920s, economic output fell by over 25 per cent and did not recover until late in the 1930s. Smallholders again felt the pinch with falling gate prices. People rushed to sell and land prices plummeted. Another wave of migrants followed as even poorer aspirants found they could now afford to move from town to country.

Until 1911, those in paid employment in Four Marks numbered less than one hundred, four times that in 1841. Between 1911 and 1939, the number leapt to over 400. The traditional occupations in agriculture saw steady growth as more land came into cultivation. To be expected, the number of transport and construction workers grew to support the building boom.

Population growth continued to 754 in 1931, an increase over 1911 of 470 per cent, and to 1,574 in 1939, living in just under 400 dwellings, an increase over 1931 of 455 per cent.[98] Two new employment categories entered the list by

92 Mills, *Four Marks*.
93 *Estates Gazette*, 12/1921. Shrubsole, *Who Owns England?*, pp. 84-5.
94 A descendant of the movement can be found at the Edward Barnsley Workshop in Froxfield.
95 Morton, *In Search of England*: 'I have gone round England like a magpie picking up the bright things that please me' (1927).
96 Cornick, *Early Memories*.
97 Cornick, *Early Memories*.
98 ONS. The 1939 Register.

1939. The first, a professional and clerical class of about seventy people, catered for the needs of the new population of over 1,500. The second was a Four Marks peculiarity: the growth of poultry farming, the dominant occupation for all those looking for low-skill, low-labour, 'get rich quick' schemes on smallholdings. Just before the war, there were thirty-four owner-occupied egg farms with nineteen employed poultry hands, a workforce of over seventy. The local countryside at the outbreak of war still provided over half of all employment.[99]

Of the much-discussed invasion by the retired military there are only occasional signs. What one does see, forcefully from 1891, is the arrival of people 'living on own means'. After World War I, Four Marks provided, for an increasing number, an attractive, and perhaps cheap, retirement home.

Civic Four Marks is less than ninety years old. It was deemed worthy of its own identity in 1932.[100] The following year, Joseph's Arch's union's successor, the Farm Workers' Union, noted that wages in Hampshire were cut by a shilling to 27s for a fifty-four hour week. In 1938, the county received its first professional union organiser, Harry Pearson.[101]

When the boundary of the new civil parish of Four Marks was drawn, lands from six parishes were included. Parts of Chawton (1 per cent of the new parish), Farringdon (17 per cent, 252 acres) and Newton Valence (13 per cent, 189 acres) were acquired so that a straight line above of the whole of Telegraph Lane – effectively the ridge line – could mark the new northern boundary. Medstead (4 per cent) lost a sliver to make the railway the new divider to the west. A small parcel of land just the other side of the railway bridge (including Norman Read's, butchers) was placed in Four Marks until 1981 when it reverted to Medstead. The rest of the new parish, other than a small piece from East Tisted (2 per cent), came from Ropley (64 per cent, 958 acres) with an ugly dogleg divider to make sure the village pond and Kitwood were part of Four Marks while Old Down Wood was not. The new civil parish lines were almost everywhere well within the ecclesiastical boundary. To recognise Four Marks' new status, the railway station's name was changed to 'Medstead and Four Marks' in 1937.

A separate development, which began slowly shortly after the turn of the century, was an entirely different example of social change. The invention of two new popular forms of transport, bicycles and motor vehicles, transformed Winchester Road along its length.[102] This single-carriageway was eventually dotted with flowering cherry and ornamental apple trees. In a steady growth

---

99 Fletcher, *Population study*.
100 The Local Government Act 1929 dealt with, first, management of the country's poor and, second, redrawing local government footprints to provide greater efficiency. All boards of guardians for poor law unions were abolished and their responsibilities transferred to county authorities. Separately, some urban and rural areas had diminished populations unable to provide the resources needed to deliver modern local government services. As a part of this review, Four Marks was seen as a new parish capable of standing on its own two feet as a part of Alton Rural District.
101 Groves, *Sharpen the Sickle!*, pp. 224, 238.
102 Mills, *Four Marks*. Cornick, *Early Memories*.

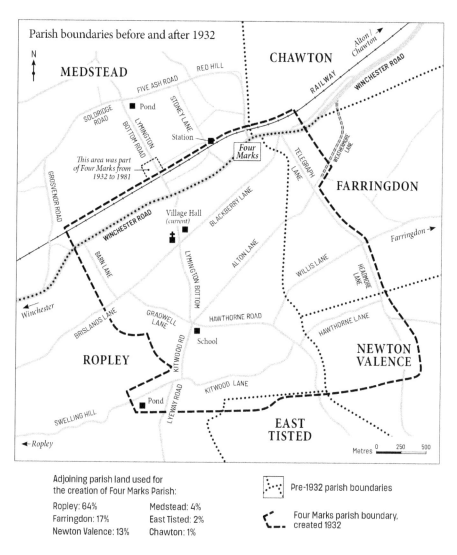

Parish boundaries before and after 1932

Adjoining parish land used for the creation of Four Marks Parish:

Ropley: 64%   Medstead: 4%
Farringdon: 17%   East Tisted: 2%
Newton Valence: 13%   Chawton: 1%

Pre-1932 parish boundaries

Four Marks parish boundary, created 1932

from between the wars and into the 1950s, businesses catered for a 'mobile, fine evening and weekend pleasure pursuing population' heading for the country. Premises 'sprouted like mushrooms' providing fuel and mechanical assistance for motorists and cyclists and, with the townies who came by railway, for sustenance with general stores, road houses, wholesome refreshment rooms, small shops, cafés, the *Windmill Inn* and, even, *The Blinking Owl*, a good class restaurant with a dance floor. Those smaller shops, which might otherwise have spread around the side streets with the bungalows, instead congregated prominently on Winchester Road taking best advantage of the needs of both visitors and locals. Many of the shops were made of rickety ex-Canadian Army huts, bought as a job lots and patched up by John Merlin Hutchings, son-in-law of the Tomlinson who had provided the land for the school.[103]

The railway station and a good road helped provide a destination for the energetic or a family trip from either side of the hill. There is a seedy side to this good life along the A31. Two contrasting aspects of Four Marks operated side-by-side and happily enough. Some of the buildings, dangerous to health and limb, were erected by local characters who might politely be called 'wide boys'. Loans were always available, but slipped repayments were vigorously pursued. Scrap businesses, stolen property and, later, war surplus, some of dubious origin, abounded. Village drinking houses were places of assignation for those who preferred not to be seen together in their home towns. There were at least two brothels, repeatedly named in verbal reminiscences, and a night club where 'loose' women attracted visitors.

By 1951, dwellings had stabilised at just under 400 while the population had declined by 300 to 1,233 whether lost in the war, not yet returned or moved away. It is noteworthy that throughout the period from 1841–2011, the male to female ratio in the village area remained steady, 48:52, reflecting no more variation than a national average which contained more longer-living women. This is the period of happy childhood recalled by today's oldest living village generation.

The village population study is able to provide an insight into the rate at which people from outside Four Marks came to live there. Initially, from about 1861, incomers were mainly from nearby parishes or wider Hampshire. The rush of people from outside the county began in 1896 so that, by 1911, more than half of all inhabitants were 'foreigners' without Hampshire birth links.

In its current and ongoing phase from 1961, Four Marks began to change forever: the population more than tripling in the next fifty years, the number of dwellings quadrupling. There were 3,893 inhabitants in 2011. There has been an explosion in piecemeal and large estate development in the last ten years.

In 1841, there were twenty-three men working in agriculture, farmers and labourers, in the Four Marks area. Almost a century later, in 1939, there were 281 in agriculture and poultry farming, an over twelve times increase. However, statistics can mislead. In 1841, those twenty-three men represented 96 per cent of the male working population; in 1939, 50 per cent were in agriculture; by 2011, less than 1 per cent (not counting horse stables).[104] Despite its many enclosed green fields, Four Marks is no longer an agricultural community.

103Hutchings gave his middle name to Merlin Road, off Blackberry Lane.
104Fletcher, Population study. Nomis, Four Marks Parish, Local Area Report, 2011, p. 28.

12 DISAPPEARING LAND
Theft, trespass and the problem of measurement, 1066-2021

> *By Langley Bush, I roam, but the bush hath left the hill;*
> *On Cowper Hill I stray, 'tis a desert strange and chill;*
> *And spreading Lea Close Oak, ere decay had penned its will,*
> *To the axe of the spoiler and self-interest fell a prey;*
> *And Crossberry Way and old Round Oak's narrow lane*
> *With its hollow trees like pulpits, I shall never see again:*
> *Inclosure like a Bonaparte let not a thing remain,*
> *It levelled every bush and tree and levelled every hill*
> *And hung the moles for traitors – though the brook is running still,*
> *It runs a naked brook, cold and chill.[1]*
> *Any friend of mine walks where he likes in this country,*
> *or I'll want to know the reason why.[2]*

The word *acre* once meant 'open country, untenanted land', but by the time of the parliamentary enclosure in Ropley, an acre had hardened to an exact measurement, standardised across the country to facilitate sales and acquisitions. *Forest* was first a legal construct, a term given to an appropriated piece of land, wooded or not, where hunting privileges were limited to the king. By the 1200s, there were almost 2,000 deer parks across England. Two years after *Magna Carta*, when the barons sought to protect their land from a king's whimsy, there was an almost forgotten second 'poor man's' agreement, the *Charter of the Forest*, which pressed the Crown to respect rights customarily held by commoners.[3] 'All woods made forest ... shall be immediately disafforested', a removal from the jurisdiction of the Norman kings. The most telling word change was in the use of *property*. In feudal times, *property* spoke of what could be done on a piece of land and what reciprocal duties were attached. Medieval lawyers did not write of owning land, but rather of holding it, echoed today in terms of *freehold* and *leasehold*: yours to use, you hold it but do not own it.[4]

If you stroll along the ridge, that piece of land that includes the high points of the villages that were reduced to form Four Marks, there are some good views: the hedged fields to Bentworth, the remains of the beech forest down to Alton,

---

1 Clare, 'Remembrances'.
2 Grahame, Mr. Badger, *Wind in the Willows*.
3 British Library, Add. Ch. 24712.
4 Hayes, *Book of Trespass*, p. 52.

the old commons that reach to Farringdon and Chawton, and the undulating acres towards Ropley. The sad truth is that you have almost no right to enter any of the property that you can see across this wide open landscape.

There are woods and plantations, like Chawton Park, Weathermore and Old Down, remnants of old deer parks with tracks where you are allowed to walk with the permission of the owner. Sometimes this access is not so courteous and can be easily withdrawn. You probably have no interest in entering the gardens of strangers. You do have a right to follow the public highways, the high-hedged communal footpaths and enclosure ways when not blocked by bramble, nettles and muddied puddles. You can also go to any recreation ground, hall, church or graveyard if unlocked.

In reality, there are few places as far as the eye can see where you are allowed by law to be. If you religiously do as you are told, keep to the codes of conduct, follow the signposts and notices, hug the hedges, fence lines, walls and tracks, you may be content and never question the restraint. Alternatively, you might wonder how this restrictive state came to be. You might be tempted to cross a line.

The enclosure movement was brought to an end when it upset the middle classes.[5] It wasn't the harm done to the agricultural poor or the arrogant posturing of the gentry that caused the distress, but decreasing facilities for recreation and allotments in the cities. In 1869, out of 6,916 acres scheduled for enclosure, just three were allocated for recreation and six for allotments.

Four years before, a group headed by Lord Eversley, a Liberal MP, and John Stuart Mill, the political thinker and philosopher, formed the *Commons Preservation Society*, today Britain's oldest national conservation body.[6] This became *The Open Spaces Society* when, in 1876, the *Commons Act* stipulated that enclosure could only occur where there would be a public benefit.[7] 'The Society was not afraid to support direct action, such as the levelling of fences, and did so successfully in Epping Forest and Berkhamsted Common to initiate court cases which drew attention to their cause.' In the last quarter of the nineteenth century, only a handful of parliamentary enclosures took place; the final enclosure bill, for Elmstone Hardwick in Gloucestershire, was enacted in 1914.

Two other founders of the Society, Sir Robert Hunter and Octavia Hill, along with Canon Hardwicke Rawnsley, founded the *National Trust* in 1895. In an indirect and unintentional way, the *Trust* is another of Ropley's legacies.

Today, the use of commons is primarily recreational, like London's Hampstead Heath and Clapham Common, and local societies have sprung up to preserve the public's access.[8]

---

5   Fairlie, 'Enclosure', p. 28.
6   Christophers, *New Enclosure*, p. 81.
7   Commons Act, Vic. 39 & 40, c. 56, 1876.
8   Manning, *Village Revolts*.

Writer and activist Nick Hayes tells a story about walking home with his mother after lunch in a pub. They entered a pig farm so that he could show her a kingfisher. A quad bike chugged across the paddock. The driver said that they had no right to be there: they were trespassing. Without a moment's thought, Hayes and his mother apologised and left.

Later, Hayes marvelled at the power of the man's words which had reversed the direction of two free-willed adults, imposing his will on theirs.

'It was as if he had cast a spell that had tied our feet and dragged us away ... There were many ways to cut the cake of what my mum and I were doing. To a literalist, we were walking, putting one foot in front of another; to a romantic, bonding; to a nutritionist, digesting a meal; to the metaphysical we were seeking a glimpse of the world through a kingfisher. But this man had managed to reframe all these subjective assessments into one objective assertion: we were trespassing. None of these other perspectives counted quite so much as his.'[9]

The famous sign *Trespassers will be Prosecuted* is an 'out-and-out lie', claims Hayes. Since, 1964, the misdemeanour of trespass has been one of civil, not criminal, law, and can only be brought to court if damages have occurred. However, if you resist the landowner's command to go, or if you are impolite, the police can be called (it would be interesting to see if they would come locally, given their record for attending other crimes). If you then resist the police, you can be arrested for a breach of the peace, or for obstructing a police officer. 'A landowner is allowed to use reasonable force to encourage you to quit, though no one can agree what that means.' The landowner cannot detain you, nor are you compelled to give your name and address. It is your right to use the nearest exit. If you go back, the landowner is allowed to apply for an injunction, but he doesn't have your address. If you do receive the injunction and return, you will be in contempt of court and face a fine or imprisonment.

However, through two recent pieces of legislation, trespassing can be seen as criminal.

In 1994, the *Criminal Justice and Private Order Act* introduced a new crime of 'aggravated trespass'.[10] 'Aggravated' can be anything thought to increase guilt or enormity, for instance, carrying a knife. It could include two people meeting for a common purpose, like rambling; twenty or more people dancing to amplified music, like ravers; or protesters on private land whose actions obstruct or disrupt. This last was intended, primarily, for hunt saboteurs, but is now used for protests on any matter from fracking to animal rights to disagreement with a war.

The right to protest is secured by the 1950 *European Convention of Human Rights*, but for the last twenty years if you do protest anywhere but in your back garden or on a highway, you can be arrested and sent to jail. 'In short, if you are doing something that is not illegal, like dancing, while doing something that

---

9 Hayes, *Book of Trespass*, pp. 14-5.
10 Shrubsole, *Who Owns England?*, p 25.

is not criminal, like trespassing, you can be arrested and liable to six months in prison.'[11]

The *Serious Organised Crime and Police Act* (SOCPA) of 2005 extended the arrest powers of the police and allowed them to keep DNA evidence of suspects even after they had been cleared. An extra section that received no debate in parliament created a deterrent to intrusions at high profile secure sites and enabled the arrest of trespassers where no other existing offence had been committed. One of its aims was to end long-standing unauthorised demonstrations in Parliament Square. On this and fifteen other specified sites, walking is now a criminal act. The list includes Buckingham Palace, GCHQ, Westminster and land owned privately by the Queen and her offspring.

Criminalisation of trespass is probably coming. In 2018, a delegation of thirty Tory backbenchers, mostly with landowning connections, signed a letter calling for it, a pledge that had already been mooted in their manifesto of 2010.

Brett Christophers, author and geography professor at Uppsala University in Sweden, argues that everyone in Britain should care who owns its lands.

> It is the literal foundation of people's lives; we need it for shelter, work, mobility, play and protest. And because land matters, so too does land ownership. Whoever owns the land has the ability to determine how it is accessed and used, and by whom ... The public, at least in a democracy, in principle has the power ... to shape how the land is used. If the government disposes of public land, it disposes of the public power associated with it. There surely cannot be many government decisions that matter more in a democratic society.'[12]

So, where and when did this 'ownership' of land begin and reach today to the heart of England on this small Hampshire ridge? Was it always the case that one individual, presumably as a result of force, claimed exclusive right to vast acreage? Christophers argues that 'we need to think much more closely about what it means to *own* land. The idea that land can and should be owned is not a natural or timeless one, characteristic of all human societies and cultures. How and why did land ownership become normalised?'[13]

When the Romans invaded, they brought with them, courtesy of Emperor Justinian, four different rules about what should not, could not, be privatised: *res communes*, the air and the sea; *res publicae*, the rivers, parks and public roads; *res universitas*, public baths and theatres and council amenities; and *res nullius*, wasteland, cattle pasture, woodland and wild animals.[14]

---

11 Hayes, *Book of Trespass*, pp. 15-7.
12 Christophers, *New Enclosure*, pp. 4-5.
13 Christophers, *New Enclosure*, p. 23.
14 Hayes, *Book of Trespass*, p. 29.

The laws of King Ine, who ruled Wessex and controlled Hampshire from A.D. 688, survive.[15] Ine, a devout Christian, abdicated in 726 to go to Rome leaving his kingdom to 'younger men'.[16] This is the same Ine who posthumously suffered a fraudulent charter which later set out to prove the bishop of Winchester's claim to the lands of Bishop's Sutton as far as the Four Marks boundary. Ine's codes read like basic modern law, standardising redress and compensation for various acts of harm and damage inflicted by one on another. They contain rules over fighting in church, blood feuds, regulating the actions of traders, forfeiture of land due to lack of military service. Fences and hedges existed, but for the purpose of containing livestock, not for the restriction of free movement. Nowhere is trespass mentioned.[17]

When William, first set foot on the English south coast, he proclaimed to his men, 'I have seized England with both my hands.' In truth, it was a more awkward moment for so propitious an event. William stumbled on landing, but a quick-witted soldier pointed to the clod of earth that a kneeling William clutched and called, 'You hold England, my lord, its future king'.[18]

After Saxon Winchester surrendered the next month without a fight, indeed the citizens went out of the city to meet the Norman army with gifts, the way was opened for a flank march on London.[19] On Christmas Day, William placed the English crown on his own head at Westminster after opposition in the south melted away. He took control of all the royal lands, those of the counter-claimant Godwine family and of all those who had fought against him.[20] Initially, he left other Anglo-Saxon aristocrats in control of their estates, but after three more years of campaigning and further uprisings, principally at Exeter and in the North where the Anglo-Danish supporters were most savagely suppressed, he changed policy. By Domesday, only a handful of Saxon aristocrats were left on their estates. William distributed his new lands among about 180 of his barons. The land was only given by his consent and could be taken back. These 'lords', literally the original land-lords, in turn parcelled out 'their' land to various tenants further down the food chain of feudal tenure. This was always at a price, sometimes in money, sometimes in service. Feudal service was not done away, in theory at least, until the *Tenures Abolition Act* of 1660.

William kept a fifth of England for himself. He established his chases, long cuts through the woods, where deer found large tracts to live undisturbed until the hunt, his consuming passion. 'Arms and horses and the exercise of hunting and hawking are the delight of the Normans.'[21] Commoners lost their rights to

---

15 British Library, *Laws of King Ine in a Legal Compilation*, Cotton MS Claudius D II, 1321.
16 Bede, *Chronicle*.
17 Hayes, *Book of Trespass*, p. 29.
18 Gabriel Ronay, *The Lost King of England* (Boydell Press, Woodbridge 2000), pp. 154-6.
19 Biddle, *Winchester in the Early Middle Ages*, p. 470.
20 Chibnall, *Normans*, pp. 42-44.
21 Gaufridi Malaterra, 'De rebus …', I, iii, p. 8, in Marjorie Chibnall, *The Normans* (2000), p. 24.

graze cattle and pigs, to take wood (estover), to dig peat and gravel (turbary) and to fish the ponds (piscary). These were the areas that became known as the forests, from the Latin *foris*, meaning 'outside' because they operated outside of common law. At the time of Hastings, a quarter of England was tree-covered including most of Hampshire. Villages were burned, roads re-routed and farmed fields left to grow wild to make the forests. It is here that we start to find references in the archives to trespass in its most primitive form.

Subsequent to declaring himself head of the Church of England in 1531, Henry disbanded the monasteries and disposed of their assets. In a second windfall for the new aristocracy, the bulk of these Catholic lands were acquired by the landed gentry, many claiming descent from Norman barons. One estimate puts the land grab, and the accompanying settling of Henry's debts, at two million acres, almost 20 per cent of the country's cultivated land. One of the underlying reasons why Bonnie Prince Charlie, the Catholic pretender in the eighteenth century, failed in his bid for the throne was because of the English aristocracy's fear that if he took power, he would reclaim for his faith the monasteries, abbeys and lands acquired in the dissolution.[22]

There was a third windfall for the followers of Cromwell a hundred years later. In 1651-2, two acts authorised the confiscation and then sale of all the royalist manors, lands, estates, tenements and hereditaments, except rectories and tithes, which had been forfeited for treason.[23] Parliament needed a 'considerable sum of money for carrying out the services of the Commonwealth', mainly for the navy, and intended to borrow £600,000 against the security of the lands 'of the said Traytors'. The list for the county of Southampton of 18 November 1652 had thirteen names including John Pinchin of Shalden.[24] Pinchin was a captain of musketeers whose son was murdered in Blackberry Lane, Four Marks, in flight after the Battle of Cheriton. The leading perpetrator, Richard Kiddle, was hanged in Farnham.[25] Pinchin's old manor was ceded at the beginning of the nineteenth century to the Knight family of Chawton. In 1840, it was sold on by Edward Knight. While some of these Catholic lands were restored with the restoration of Charles, many others were not and so further engrossed the estates of major Protestant landowners.

The ongoing pursuit of enclosure, the primary subject of preceding chapters, constituted the last windfall for Hampshire landowners until the great

---

22 Shrubsole, *Who Owns England?*, p. 65.

23 Heal, *Four Marks Murders*, p. 152.

24 *An Additional Act for Sale...*, 1652: Henry Fowel, Abbots-Ann; Anthony Gosling, Morestead; Dr. Laney, Petersfield; James Mallett, Portsmouth; John Pinchin, Shalden; John Unwyn, Ennington; William Budding, Clinton; William Chamberlain, Nash; Thomas Chamberlain, Lyndhurst; Anthony Hide, Woodhouse; James Linkhorn, Bowyet; Miles Philipson, Throp; Swithin Wells, Eastleigh. To these were added the estates of Sir Charles and Sir John Somerset, Sir Richard Tichborne and the manors of Blendworth, Catherington, Chalton and Clanfield.

25 Heal, *Four Marks Murders*, Chapter 11. Adair, *The Court Martial Papers of Sir William Waller's Army, 1644*.

privatisation of public land, largely unrecognised, during the time of Margaret Thatcher (and which will be discussed shortly). Enclosure turned a collective interest into an individual one.[26] It compromised the 'very survival' of land uses that didn't suit individual interests and thus the survival, too, of associated ways of living.[27] Hedges, ditches and fences came to signify a different type of country. What had been an open field with balks between ploughed patches, a communally shared resource, became a 'private, owned and managed boundary with threatening notices and locked gates, a large step on the road to a modern conception of private and guarded land bordering all footpaths and roadways'.[28]

Public discussion of land ownership has been hampered for centuries by the near-impossibility of obtaining proper information. Accurate facts, figures and maps detailing the ownership of English land are very hard to come by. The Ordnance Survey's hold over mapping licences makes it difficult to properly map land ownership in England. The OS has been called 'the great vampire-squid wrapped around the face of UK public-interest technology' by one frustrated researcher. The Land Registry has not released details of one-third of land in England and Wales owned by companies, public sector bodies and landed interests. It remains resistant to overcoming the final taboo, the long-term concealment of who owns England.

In the past 200 years as England has become an industrial democracy, its governments have chosen to survey land ownership on multiple occasions only to swiftly suppress knowledge of the results. The past two centuries have seen four 'modern Domesdays': the tithe maps of the 1830s-40s; the 1873 *Return of Owners of Land*; the 1910-15 Valuation Maps; and the 1941 *National Farm Survey*. In each cased these investigations faced huge opposition, and most have been all but forgotten.[29]

The tithe maps of much of England are readily accessible to everyone and are usually accompanied by a list of occupants that match their numbered fields.[30] They claim to show who ultimately owns the land: a tenant is one thing, but an owner is often someone completely different.

The *Return of Owners of Land* was commissioned in 1872 as a result of a disagreement in parliament on land monopoly.[31] Until 1867, only about one-eighth of the adult male population had the right to vote, but the *Second Reform Bill* extended the franchise to about one third. For the first time in British history, most of the electorate were not landowners and soon appointed the Liberal

---

26 Bromley, 'Enclosure, Common Right', pp. 311-31.
27 Christophers, *New Enclosure*, p. 14.
28 Blomley, 'Making private property'.
29 Peter Meyer, Alan Pemberton, HM Land Registry, *A Short History of Land Registration in England and Wales* (London 2020). Shrubsole, *Who Owns England?*, pp. 25-6.
30 Maps 7, 8, and 10 for tithe extracts centred on Ropley and Medstead villages and on an extended view of Newton Valence tithe showing that parish's enclosures.
31 Cahill, *Who Owns Britain*, Chapter 3.

government of William Ewart Gladstone, belligerent to landowners and the Conservatives. Radical politicians like Richard Cobden, John Bright and John Stuart Mill revived the arguments that land value enhancement was unearned wealth that ought to be taxed.[32] Bright used the 1861 census to charge that there were only 30,000 landowners.

A small number of gentry stood accused of owning much of the country. The aristocracy, led by the Earl of Derby, thought the opposite and had a vision of widespread ownership, but they needed facts to counter the clamour whipped up by the press. Charles Woods, a former Chancellor of the Exchequer, condemned in the Lords, 'the absurd statements made in certain newspapers and at some public meetings respecting the wonderfully small number of landed proprietors in this country' and that documenting actual land ownership patterns would quell public disquiet.[33]

'Is a Domesday Book more difficult now than in the days of the Conqueror?', asked the 1870s legislators. It was a task that would be impossible today despite the expensive presence of the Land Registry, still slaving away after years of non-achievement.

The facts to compile the *Return* were to hand in the ratings records held by the Local Government Board which were used to assess the parish poor rate. All of England, except London, nearly 15,000 parishes, was surveyed within two years. The *Return* was published in 1875 at 10s 6d for each of two volumes.[34] It contained, of course, many errors.

It fell to an author and country squire, John Bateman, to interpret and popularise the *Return*. In 1876, he published *The Acre-Ocracy of England* in which he summarised the owners of 3,000 acres and above. It became a best-seller, going through four editions and updates and culminated in 1883 with *The Great Land-Owners of Great Britain and Ireland*.

Bateman's analysis confirmed the radicals' worst fear. Everyone had guessed wrong, but the results were still shocking: just 4,000 families owned over half of all land. Meanwhile 95 per cent owned nothing at all and had no right of access to almost the whole of the country. Landowners hated it. It was set upon by *The Times*. The official *Return* was swiftly buried because of its embarrassing findings. [35]

Interpreting the results today for Hampshire and the ridge parishes has severe limitations.[36] The holdings for each landowner, down to a single acre, are grouped by county. One cannot tell if the land is in one piece or split many ways. If the

---

32 Peter H. Lindert, 'Who Owned Victorian England?, The Debate over Landed Wealth and Inequality', *Agricultural History*, 61, 4, pp. 25-51. Cahill, *Who Owns Britain*, pp. 29-30.

33 House of Lords, debate, 19/2/1872, c. 642.

34 John Lambert, edited, *England & Wales (Exclusive of the Metropolis); Return of Owners of Land, 1873; Presented to both Houses of Parliament* (HMSO, London 1875).

35 Shrubsole, *Who Owns England?*, p. 30.

36 Cahill, *Who Owns Britain*, pp. 38-48.

landowner owns lands in another county, it must be found separately. The only clue lies in the owner's address which, in the case of Hampshire, could be in a parish or a house anywhere in the country. One large guestimate has been made in the following figures: if a small landowner lives in a local parish, then that is where most of his land is likely to be.

Hampshire in 1871 covered 963,492 acres with a population of 544,684 living in 98,283 habitations in 345 parishes. The remains of the county's commons and wastes occupied 78,843 acres (8.2 per cent), mostly in the New Forest.

Just 27,472 people owned any land in Hampshire (5.04 per cent; 4.5 per cent nationally) which meant that 95 per cent (95.5 per cent nationally) owned no land, not even a blade of grass.[37] The majority of the county was owned by 6,236 people (1.1 per cent of population) with one acre or more totalling 878,900 acres (91.2 per cent). A further 21,236 people (3.9 per cent of population) owned less than one acre totalling 5,749 acres (0.6 per cent).[38]

In terms of concentrations of ownership in Hampshire, 164 people (0.03 per cent of population) held more than 1,000 acres (a total of 565,710 acres; 58.7 per cent of all acres). The first item in *Appendix 24* is a list of the forty-six aristocrats, gentry and organisations holding over 4,000 acres. Many of these names will be familiar and are unlikely to be much different today. It is headed by Lord Bolton of Hackwood Park with 18,808 acres, followed by the Earl of Portsmouth at Micheldever with 16,401 acres. The Duke of Wellington, scourge of the Swing food protestors, at Stratfield Saye, given by a grateful parliament, is third with 15,847 acres. Edward Knight of Chawton is there at number thirty-five, plus the Tichborne family, Jervoise of Herriard park, Shelley of Avington, the Marquis of Winchester at Amport, and Ashburton and Dutton at Alresford. The College of Winchester (including Ropley Manor), the Dean and Chapter of Winchester and the War Department are prominent.[39] While individually not making the top list, eleven other colleges, mainly from Oxford, but topped by King's, Cambridge, Queen's, Oxford, and Magdalen, Oxford, hold together almost 9,000 acres including land known to be in the ridge parishes.

The ownership of land on the ridge is revealing. When a parish includes a single significant owner, as with Knight of Chawton or Henry Mulcock, a banker and farmer of Ropley House (2,572 acres), the land claimed by that person can exceed the size of their home parish, showing a widespread estate.[40] The records for the London & South-Western Railway (with 1,450 acres in the whole county) have been added and are split within appropriate ridge parishes.[41]

---

37 Cahill, 'The Great Property Swindle: Why Do So Few People in Britain Own So Much of Our Land?', *New Statesman*, 11/3/2011.
38 Cahill, *Who Owns Britain*, pp. 12-15. For holdings of the Church of England, Chapter 12.
39 In Hampshire, the Aldershot Complex, with 21,000 acres, is the home of the British Army.
40 For H. J. Mulcock, see Hagen, *Annals*; Mason, *Ropley Past*; and Richard Mills, '200 Years of Banking in Alresford'.
41 With thanks to Dr. Roger Burt and Dr. Keith Brown.

Of the 'ordinary' small landowners, the percentages of parish land held by people whose home is within the parish are: Chawton, four people, 3.4 percent; East Tisted, two people, 1 per cent; Farringdon, 20 people, 9.8 per cent; Medstead, eighteen people, 33.2 per cent; Newton Valence, 10 people, 75.4 per cent; and Ropley, 17 people, 26.4 per cent. In the known cases of parliamentary enclosure, individual comparisons between the *Return* and enclosure allotments have a distinct correlation. These percentages show that a significant amount of land was held in each village by unknown, or only guessed at, outsiders. Again, presumably, little has changed.

The land situation in Scotland is far worse, but at least the records are open. In 2015, 432 people, 0.025 per cent of the population, owned 67 per cent of Scotland's rural land; 10 per cent of Scotland is owned by just sixteen individuals or groups. In terms of land ownership, Scotland is one of the most unequal countries in the world.[42]

The 15th Earl of Derby with 30,000 hectares in 1881, the driver behind the *Return of Owners*, let slip exactly how much land ownership mattered to him and why.[43]

> *The object which men aim at when they become possessed of land in the British Isles may, I think, be enumerated as follows. One, political influence; two social importance (deference) founded on territorial possession, the most visible and unmistakable form of wealth; three, power exercised over tenantry; the pleasure of managing, directing and improving the estate itself; four, residential enjoyment, including what is called sport; five, the money return – the rent.*[44]

Derby's political influence was secure. Land and power are intimately entwined; arguably this has been nowhere more true than in Britain. The nation has always been governed by the landed proprietor, said John Stuart Mill in 1871. Influence was yoked to land ownership whereby the right to vote in elections was dependent on it. In Britain, the extension of suffrage through the first, second, third and fourth Reform Acts of 1832, 1867, 1884 and 1918 respectively was achieved in significant part by lowering the land and property thresholds at which voting rights were allowed.[45] The *Return of Owners* showed not only the extreme concentration of ownership in the hands of the aristocracy but that almost every one of the top hundred landowners was also a member of the House of Lords.[46]

The hypnotic effect of social deference, of being heard first and getting one's way, is socially entrenched among many even today. Some see deference

---

42 Christophers, *New Enclosure*, p. 52.
43 Christophers, *New Enclosure*, p. 25.
44 Cahill, *Who Owns Britain*, p. 8.
45 Christophers, *New Enclosure*, pp. 26-7.
46 Christophers, *New Enclosure*, pp. 74-85..

as a set of attitudes, most centrally a set of beliefs about the nature of society. Specifically, these beliefs involve a group 'endorsing a moral order, which legitimises its own political, material and social subordination'.[47] Why do individuals continue to defer after the coercive constraints have been removed? The degree of dissemblance involved in overtly deferential behaviour, however, is often considerable – 'deference becomes the necessary pose of the powerless'.[48]

Owning land is a secure investment for the long term conferring power over resources found on and underneath. One has the right within reason to do with one's land and its resources as one sees fit and to decide who does and who does not get to enjoy it and under what conditions.[49] Farming rarely achieves great wealth with its considerable outlays and the effects of poor harvests, but losses can be more than recouped by unsympathetic rents.

At the extremes, activists demand the complete elimination of large landed proprietors or call, at least, for all their rents to go to the state. They claim this would do away with the need for all other taxes, such as income or capital gains tax, and provide a single, but adequate source for all government expenditure.[50]

To the surprise of many, all land in Canberra and in the Australian Capital Territory is publicly owned. In the 1890s, 'the political leaders planning federation were anxious to avoid in the new capital the land speculation which had occurred in the established cities. Edmund Barton, Australia's first prime minister, pointed out that the value of urban land results from the actions of the community as a whole rather than those of an individual landowner and the increase in value should therefore accrue to the community rather than to private owners'.[51] A tax on the 'unimproved' value of the land is another way to channel land-value gains to a wider society that generates them.

This idea of landowners benefitting unfairly from unearned income caught fire again in England in the 1900s. Try to guess the origin of this quote:

> *Roads are made, streets are made, services are improved, electric light turns night into day, water is brought from reservoirs a hundred miles off in the mountains and all the while the landlord sits still. Every one of those improvements is effected by the labour and cost of other people and the taxpayers. To not one of those improvements does the land monopolist, as a land monopolist, contribute, and yet by every one of them the value of his land is enhanced. He renders no service to the community, nothing to the process from which his own enrichment is derived.*[52]

---

47 F. Parkin, 'Working Class Conservatism', *British Journal of Sociology*, Vol. XVIII, 1967, pp. 280-90.
48 Newby, 'Deferential Dialectic', pp. 142-50.
49 Christophers, *New Enclosure*, pp. 28-9, 35.
50 Christophers, *New Enclosure*, p. 47.
51 M. Neutze, 'A Tale of Two Cities: Public Land Ownership in Canberra and Stockholm in the Early 1980s', Scandinavian Housing and Planning Research, 6:4, 1989, pp. 189-99.
52 Churchill, House of Commons, 4/5/1909.

It was Winston Churchill, who together with Lloyd George, spoke out. They saw land as a community good; people ought to contribute to their communities if they chose to use land exclusively. The politicians sought to introduce a land value tax of 20 per cent on future unearned increases in land value. To do so, however, would require a full survey of the ownership and value of land across the country and this was dubbed 'Lloyd George's Domesday'. Lloyd George's tax measures, which included a super tax on the very richest, triggered a constitutional crisis. The *Land Valuation Act*, mentioned earlier, took five years from 1911 and produced an astonishing amount of data with 95,000 ledgers and some 50,000 maps. It all came to a sorry end with the coming of the Great War and was repealed in 1920. The unfinished survey was forgotten and lies today, undigitised, in The National Archives (TNA).

In similar fashion, the *National Farm Survey* of 1941 covered all farms over five acres – around 320,000 in total. The government needed to find how much land could be brought under the plough to meet wartime demand and how farms could be improved.[53] The results were not made available for general use until 1992 and still remain on paper only in TNA, with no funder found for digitisation.[54]

The idea of unfair capital gain, taken tax free, was also seen to have dire consequences. Where none of the capital gain accrues to the state it is 'necessary for the state to fund itself by taxing effort, ingenuity and foresight'. One reporter wrote:

> In 1984, I bought my London house. I estimate that the land on which it sits was worth £100,000. Today, the value is perhaps ten times as great. All that vast improvement is the fruit of no effort of mine. It is the reward of owning a location that the efforts of others made valuable.[55]

By many estimates, land today represents on average about 70 per cent of the sale price of a residential property in England. When people buy houses, they are principally buying land.[56] The story told is that this is because of a land shortage, but this seems incorrect. Only 5 per cent of land in England has been urbanised; the remainder is just not released for sale for building. If ever this matter is discussed, land hoarders like building companies and supermarkets are quickly blamed. Of course, that is partly true, but the real hoarding lies on the landed estates. A release of this land at lower prices would solve the housing crisis at once, but so would the accumulated unearned price of residential homes fall alongside the value of every landed estate in the country.

---

53 TNA, 'Guide to National Farm Survey of England and Wales 1941-1943'
54 Shrubsole, *Who Owns England?*, pp. 32-3.
55 Martin Wolf, *Financial Times*, 2010.
56 Christophers, *New Enclosure*, p. 32.

Here is the greatest irony of all. The government pays billions of pounds in the way of farming and windfarm grants to the great landowners enabling them to keep land from sale. What is more, all governments refuse to say who receives this public money.[57]

> *Who owns England has also been literally hidden from plain sight. Large landowners have inherited or built high walls around their estates to keep out prying eyes. The English countryside still bristles with a profusion of 'Keep Out' and 'Private Property' signs. Rich businesspeople and celebrities live in gated communities protected by private security. For many decades through the Cold War, some Ministry of Defence sites were literally erased from maps.*[58]

The Crown owns half a million acres plus the same again of half of all foreshores, the coastal land between high and low waters, and river beds. Virtually all the sea bottom around England, Wales and Northern Ireland from twelve nautical miles out to the edge of UK territorial waters is crown property and thus the royals have a great interest in promoting off-shore windfarms by leasing anchorage. The Queen is the largest landowner in the world with 6.6 billion acres across the globe. She owns 12,000 times more than the runner up, the king of Saudi Arabia.[59] The land the Queen and her family profit from directly amounts to about half a million acres in three distinct holdings. Two of them are secretive duchies that pay no corporation tax: Lancaster, 172,000 acres with a portfolio valued at £534 million, including the Savoy precinct in London, and Cornwall, 255,000 acres across 22 English counties, owned by Prince Charles until he becomes king, with an income of £21.7 million. The third asset, the Crown Estate at 336,000 acres, including almost all of Regent Street, London, is the most significant holding.[60]

Despite losing the monasteries, the Anglican church in 1873 still owned a vast estate of 2.13 million acres, making it the single largest landowner in England. Under the threat of centralisation, individual rectors began selling off the glebe lands. In 2011, one MP accused the Church Commissioners of 'putting profit before people'. The journalist Harry Mount argued that a ruthless commercialism belied its otherwise affable reputation. 'The sleepy old Church of England is a greedy, money-grubbing property tycoon.' Professor Chris Hamnett castigated the Church's outlook as being one of 'philanthropy at 5 per cent'. Their limited 'social investment' was 'marginal to their major objective of income growth'.[61]

---

57 Shrubsole, *Who Owns England?*, p. 270. Cahill, *Who Owns Britain*, p. 5, and fn. 6, p. 402, states that the Ministry of Agriculture Fisheries and Food noted payments of £2.3 billion in 1999. EU figures, however, suggest that total UK figure is closer to £4 billion.
58 Shrubsole, *Who Owns England?*, p. 24.
59 Hayes, *Book of Trespass*, pp. 348-9.
60 Cahill, *Who Owns Britain*, Chapter 6, Duchy of Cornwall; Chapter 7, Duchy of Lancaster.
61 Shrubsole, *Who Owns England?*, p. 71.

Guy Shrubsole, researcher, writer and campaigner, in 2020 gave his best estimate in percentages of who owned England.[62]

Crown	1.4
Church	0.5
Public sector	8.5
Conservation charities	2.0
Companies & LLPs[63]	18.0
Aristocracy & gentry	30.0
New money	17.0
Homeowners	5.0
Total	**82.4**
Unaccounted	17.0 approximately.

Shrubsole felt that much of the missing 17 per cent was actually aristocratic land which had remained in the family for centuries, but had never been sold and therefore never registered. Land was passed on by the 'feudal practice of male primogeniture', added to over the years by monastery land bought from Henry, Catholic land bought from the Commonwealth, the profits from West Indian sugar estates, and from enclosure. If so, the proportion today was in the region of ten to one: 50 per cent for the aristocracy to 5 per cent for all English home owners, very much in line with the *Return of Owners*.

Kevin Cahill disclosed that there is a single family whose descendants, direct and indirect, have 'owned about 10 per cent of the landed wealth of England for most of the last 840 years'.[64] As a family group, they are still worth over £4 billion and own over 700,000 acres, about the size of an average county. 'They clung to power so tenaciously that when Tony Blair evicted the hereditaries from the House of Lords, he threw out forty-nine of them ... no less than twenty-three have appeared in the *Sunday Times* Rich List over the past thirteen years.' None bears the actual family name: the Norman French *Plantagenet*, 'henchmen of William the Bastard's robber gang', a family unmatched for 'bloodiness, violent warfare and internecine murder'.

Brett Christophers asked in 2015 what had been Britain's biggest privatisation to date. Someone suggested the Royal Bank of Scotland which had been rescued with a £45 billion bailout in 2008. Another thought it was the sale of council houses worth 'some £40 billion in its first twenty-five years'. Both were wrong, he said, and 'not just slightly, but spectacularly'.[65] Since Margaret Thatcher entered Downing Street in 1979 to 2018, the state had sold some two million hectares,

---

62 Shrubsole, *Who Owns England?*, pp. 267-3.
63 LLP: Limited Liability Partnership.
64 Cahill, *Who Owns Britain*, p. 27; Chapter Nine, 'The Plantagenet Inheritance'.
65 Christophers, *New Enclosure*, pp. 1-2.

about 10 per cent of the British land mass, of public land to the private sector. This was likely worth about £400 billion, the equivalent of more than twelve RBSs.

'We have, then, a puzzle', said Christophers. 'On the one hand a massive decades-long British privatisation, dwarfing all others in value. On the other, a lack of recognition of this most significant of all transfers of public assets to the private sector.'

He claimed that the logic of land privatisation has been 'deeply flawed, its process deeply problematic and its consequences deeply deleterious'. Land privatisation in Britain has generally not delivered the benefits that successive UK governments promised: value for public money; new jobs and homes; more efficient land allocation. It has also contributed substantially to three decidedly negative broader trends: a rise in private-sector land hoarding; Britain's growing transformation to one increasingly dominated by rents paid by the many to the affluent, landowning few; and widespread social dislocation.[66]

Public land is simply land owned by hundreds of public bodies and some are vast landowners: the Forestry Commission owns over one million hectares, much of it in Scotland. Many of the major public enterprises sold to the private sector during the past four decades, the electricity suppliers, the coal industry and, most significantly, the water authorities, were themselves major landowners. The land that they owned was generally privatised along with them, indeed was one of the key assets. Royal Mail, 60 per cent privatised in 2013 at £3.3 billion, is a good example. Its freehold estate was about 24 per cent of the cost, but was probably significantly higher in value judging by post-privatisation sales.[67] The NHS has also significantly disinvested.

The land transferred from the time of Margaret Thatcher in 1979 from public to private ownership is about half the land that was publicly owned at the end of the 1970s.[68] The two corporate sectors that have arguably benefited most from land privatisation in Britain are the property sector (developers, housebuilders and investors) and financial institutions. At the same time, these same two sectors have long been significant Conservative Party donors, the two very biggest since 2015.[69]

Privatisation of public land heralds the end of public space. When public space is genuinely open it contributes materially to social well-being and the pleasure people take in living nearby. In addition, the crisis of homelessness is made worse when there is no public space and people are driven away from villages towards places, like towns, where ironically there is more public space.[70]

---

66 Christophers, *New Enclosure*, p. 4.
67 Christophers, *New Enclosure*, pp. 6-7.
68 Christophers, *New Enclosure*, pp. 322-3.
69 Christophers, *New Enclosure*, p. 125.
70 Christophers, *New Enclosure*, p. 43.

One of the most historic land rights changes in the British context occurred in 1925 when, with the abolishment of customary copyhold tenure, the freehold to land still under copyhold passed to tenants, but with the former landowner often retaining mineral rights. This splitting of rights recently became news when it emerged that various present-day owners of such mineral rights, prominently the Church of England, had been stung into action by a change in the law meaning the rights could be lost if not registered. Since 2010, claims to mineral rights in around 10,000 separate locations have been recorded. The Church has accounted for over half of these claims, registering its ownership of around 235,000 hectares of resources under land owned by others with deposits of stone, metals and minerals and particularly where fracking may be anticipated – a far greater area than the Church's current estimated total surface land holdings of approximately 40,000 hectares.[71]

The Church has explained that it is simply re-registering ancient rights as part of an updating process mandated by the Land Registry and that it has few active plans to exploit these rights with new mines or quarries. But, there are ongoing efforts by shale gas companies to frack across large swathes in the north. In 2016, the Church Commissioners gave permission for a fracking firm to carry out underground seismic surveys on its Ormskirk estate in Lancashire. They argued that fracking could be 'morally acceptable' if properly regulated.[72]

A recent investigation found that the petrochemical giant Ineos had approached local authorities in the East Midlands with cash incentives to allow it to search for shale gas 'under council play parks, allotments, football pitches and, even, a council war memorial'. Most of the councils resisted the approach.[73]

Much further down the scale, but still part of the same chain of events, the lead set by Heron and Trelawny in Ropley transformed the landscape of local villages like Medstead, Chawton, Farringdon and Newton Valence into private, hedged fiefdoms and deliberately turned several generations of poor but independent smallholders into subservient and desperate wage earners.

As has been seen, however, residential owners in these parishes today do not own their land, but *hold* it beneath the Crown. The Crown, benefitting from the invasion of 1066, remains the only true owner of land in Britain.[74] If you die without a will, and if no heirs come forward who can claim under intestacy laws, any land you own will revert to the Crown through the law on *bona vacantia*.

Ropley's legacy with its first private parliamentary enclosure reaches in many unintended ways. Properties sold today, for instance and, at least, in Alton Lane,

---

71 Christophers, *New Enclosure*, pp. 8-9, fn. 3. K Burgess and L. Goddard, 'Church of England tells landowners it owns their mineral rights', *The Times*, 9/1/2018.

72 Shrubsole, *Who Owns England?*, pp. 71-2.

73 A. Roswell and M. Jones, 'East Midlands parish councils Reject Ineos' Assault on Community Spaces', 16/2/2017, at spinwatch.org.

74 *Land Registration Act*, 2002, c. 9. Christophers, *New Enclosure*, pp. 76-8. Cahill, *Who Owns Britain*, p. 397.

Four Marks, have covenants in favour of the Ecclesiastical Commissioners for England, Lords of the Manor of Bishop's Sutton, claiming all mines and minerals below 200 feet. These indentures also forbid the sale of intoxicating liquor and the building of schools, institutions, lunatic asylums, homes for inebriates, consumptives or persons of unsound mind, or of any shop, trade or factory.

Perhaps local businesses had better keep quiet.

APPENDICES

Appendix 1: Grant of King Ine to Winchester Cathedral of land at Alresford, A.D. 701

The *Codex Wintoniensis* is a handsome twelfth century manuscript, 400 x 280 mm, in brown leather and wooden covers which contains the Winchester Cartulary, a collection of 185 historical records pertaining to the cathedral priory of Winchester (Old Minster). The records were written in Latin and Greek by sixteen scribes over three centuries. Parts of included leaves are, possibly, eighth century and written in Italy. The book contains numerous large initials in red, green and yellow, many with penwork and foliate decoration in the same colour with rubrics, document headings, in red. Winchester Cathedral sold the manuscript in 1844 to the British Museum. It is now held by the British Library.[1]

The importance of the *Codex* in the context of *Ropley's Legacy* is the inclusion of a supposed charter of Ine, king of Wessex, 688-726, dated 701. This is a grant of an estate of forty hides, perhaps 120 acres to the hide, at Alresford to the Church of Saints Peter and Paul, now the Cathedral, confirming a previous grant by King Cenwalh [or Coenwealh], 643-72.[2] Within the charter are the boundaries of Alresford with named Saxon stiles and gates, a number of which are known by other names in current day Four Marks, Medstead and Ropley.[3]

The charter is thought by most modern academics to be a fake.[4] King Ine is correctly dated to 701, but his name is an alteration written over an erasure. The 'text is recognisably tenth-century in its vocabulary, inflated style and content'. The wording also resembles clauses in charters in the reign of Eadgar, 959-75, and is 'duplicated almost word for word in other Winchester charters which also appear spurious'. While authentic in its purported time (and therefore knowledgeable), it has a dubious witness list which has been altered and derives from a charter more of the 730-40s. The grant was supposedly confirmed by Egbert, 826; Edward the Elder, 956; and by Eadgar.[5]

There is a suggested explanation. In the late ninth or early tenth century, bishop Denewulf leased the Alresford estate to a layman named Ælfred for his lifetime. In 956, king Eadwig granted the land to another layman, Ælfric, said to be Ælfred's son, in a 'permanent alienation'. Ælfric 'of Hampshire' was from royal company. From the beginning of the reign of Æthelred, the boy-king was advised by a 'small cabal of close kinsmen'.[6] These ealdormen were related though blood or marriage one to another.

---

1   British Library, London, Additional Manuscript 15350, folios 20v-21r, Numbers 56 and 57 (s. xii). Birch 398. Kemble 1039. Sawyer 242

2   David Rymill, Winchester Cathedral archivist, HRO.

3   Grundy, 'Saxon Land Charters', pp. 69-78. Langlands, *Ancient Ways of Wessex*, p. 82. Rathbone, *Chronicle of Medstead*.

4   The following opinions have been adapted from two unpublished Ph.D. theses: Alexander Richard Rumble, 'The Structure and Reliability of the *Codex Wintoniensis*', University of London, 1979, and Heather Edwards, 'The Charters of the Early West Saxon Kingdom', University of Glasgow, 1985.

5   William Dugdale, *Monasticon Anglicanum*, 2 vols., 1655, 1661, reworked from the original by Roger Dodsworth.

6   Fleming, *Kings and Lords in Conquest England*, pp. 36-7.

Three died or retired and Ælfric was one of the replacements in the years 982/3.[7] His inconstancy was remarkable: fighting with the Danes, advising the king to sue for peace, evading leading a Hampshire army against the Danes leaving Wilton open to pillage, and dying fighting for Edmund Ironside in 1016.[8]

One can speculate there was a struggle over ownership of the estate before it was recovered by the church. By 1086, it was held by the Norman bishop of Winchester, Walkelin, and assessed in the Domesday Book at fifty-one hides. It seems likely that the church, after 956, in an effort to regain Alresford, drew up various false charters that confirmed the restoration of the estate. It must have ben a concerted effort because of the twenty-three places granted to laymen in Hampshire between 871 and 1066, 70 per cent were in the hands of either Winchester Old or New Minster by the conquest.[9]

Notwithstanding the evident doubt, the 'forgery' may have been no more than a clumsy restitution of a lost document. It is most likely that the Alresford boundary names, the main interest here, are necessarily accurate for the content to be respected. The landbounds of Alresford, translated into English, are:

> *First from Candover on this side, along this side in the White Ditch, along the ditch in the Barrow Meadow, along the boundary ways in the small valley, thence to the Buck's Horn, thence to the ford between the valley, along the valley to the wood, so by the bounds to Greenmeres stile, thence to Lameres gate, from that gate to Bokmeres stile, thence to Bealmeres gate, from that gate to Hamerdene gate, thence to Hremmescumbe gate, thence to Elges (?) gate, thence to Dunnes stile, thence into White Meadow, thence to the Broad Oak, thence along the bounds to Drayton in the ford, from that ford to Woodford, thence south along the bounds to the south end of the gorse (furze), thence along the bounds into Ewillas, along Ewillas into Tichborne (Ticceburnam), along Tichborne in Itchen, along Itchen where Candover and Itchen come together, along Candover, where it went up.*[10]

The bounds were investigated and translated by George Grundy who said he used a later and slightly variant copy of the boundary survey in which the grant is, reputedly, reconfirmed by Egbert:

Ecgbert confirms to Winchester cathedral 40 hides at Alresford.[11] Reputed date, A.D. 802-839. A duplicate and slightly variant copy of the survey is attached to B.938. Only the variants are here quoted in brackets.

---

7 Charter attestation lists among S 843-944.
8 S 876; *Anglo-Saxon Chronicle*.
9 Fleming, *Conquest England*, p. 17.
10 Duthy, *Sketches of Hampshire*, Appendix 5, pp. 466-8 (with the original Latin) and p. 83.
11 Grundy: Alresford [*Alresford* or *Alresforda* in the various AS. Charters]. AS. *Alres-ford[a]* 'Ford of the Alder-tree', the genitive form of the first element of the name implying that it was named after a particular tree, and not from the presence of alders generally in the neighbourhood. Inasmuch as the river on which the town stands is called Alre at the present day, it might seem as if the name meant

1. *Erest of Cendefer on tha Andheafd:* 'First from Candover (ie, the brook) to the Headland of the ploughland.'[12] This is where the boundary leaves Candover Brook, ¼m west of Fob Down Farm, and a little more than 1m west of Old Alresford.

2. *Andlang Andheafda on tha Witan Die:* 'Along the Headland on the White Dyke.' This must have been on the north west boundary somewhere about where the road from Old Alresford to Abbotstone crosses it, ie ¼m north of Fob Down Farm.

3. *Andlang Die on Burclea:* (probably *Beorcleah)*[13] 'along the Dyke on the Lea where Birch-trees grow.' The further points show that this lea was probably at the bend which the boundary makes ¼m south of the earthwork known as Oliver's Battery.

4. *Of Burchlea andlang Mearc Weges: (mereweges.* B.938) 'from Birch (or Camp) Lea along the Boundary Way.' All traces of this track have, as far as I can see, vanished; but it must have run north east along the south edge of Lower Abbotstone Wood.

4a. (B.938 only). *Be tham Wege on Hae Dene: (? Haga Dene)* 'By the track on the Dean or Valley of the Game Enclosure.'[14] This is almost certainly the dean through which the road from Andover to Preston Candover runs.

5. *On Smalandene:* 'To the Narrow Dean.' This is the dean which runs up into Armsworth Park from the south.

5a. (B.938 only). *Andlang Hlinces:* 'Along the Lynch (shelf of ploughland).'

6. *Thanan to Bucgan Oran:* 'Then to Bucga's Hillside or Slope.' This is mentioned in the Brown Candover charter. The name is preserved in part in that of Bugmore Hill at the south east corner of Brown Candover parish. That hill is part of a long ridge which runs along the boundaries of Brown Candover, Chilton Candover, Godsfield and Wield. The 'Bucgan Ora' was evidently the whole slope of this ridge. The present boundary comes to it on the north west boundary of Wield parish where, in Chilton Candover and Preston Candover, are several fields called Bangor or Bangar, a corruption of the old name 'Bucgan Ora.' (See notes on Chilton Candover). This actual point in the survey was probably about ¾m north west of Wield village, where the road to Preston Candover crosses the boundary of Wield.[15]

'Ford over the Alre'. But the last few points of the charter imply that the river now called Alre was looked on in Saxon times as the upper waters of the Itchen; and what is now the upper Itchen was then called *Ticce-burna* [Tichborne]. I fancy that this is one of those rather numerous cases of back-formation, where the river-name has been deduced from the name of the town.

12 Grundy: 'Heafod' means the headland of a ploughland. I strongly suspect but cannot prove that *Andheafda* was, as it were, the headland of a headland, ie, the place where the plough was turned when the headland came to be ploughed. It would thus be always at the corner of a ploughland.

13 Grundy: I am very doubtful about this reconstruction of the term. It may be *burbleah*, 'lea of the camp'. Is Oliver's Battery an old camp? If so, this is very probable. Also there is a Burley mentioned in Alresford, temp. Edw. III.

14 Grundy: 'Haga' is a curious word about which, though it is very common, we have only the general knowledge that it means 'hedge'. But so does 'hege', and the Saxons did not indulge in synonyms. I find 'Haga' is always used, as far as my experience goes, of a hedge surrounding a wood, intended evidently to prevent the larger game from getting onto the cultivation. 'Haga' has produced 'haw' in hawthorn and 'hege' has produced 'hay', an enclosure. But I am inclined to think that the two words got confused in post-Saxon times through the influence of the O.F. 'haie' which = hedge, for I have come across instances in which 'haga' is represented by a modern 'hay', a phenomena which cannot be due to linguistic evolution.

15 Grundy: In the *Victoria County History of Hampshire*, under Gods Field, it is stated that constant reference is made in medieval charters of Gods Field and Swarraton to the wood of Buggenore, and to

a.   From this point the survey cuts across the present parish of Wield in a general direction south south east. The old boundary between the two parts of Wield is described in a sixteenth century perambulation of the bounds of Alresford Liberty as going from Bugner Corner 'then to the park of Welde, and round the park east to the common of Welde'. [16]

b.   Great Park and Lower Park are two fields on the south boundary of Wield towards its west end. But the passage of the boundary through the parish is clearly marked in the charter.

7. *Thonan ford* (forth) *be Wyrtwalan to Wiglumes Putte:* 'Then forth by the Hillfoot to (?) Wighelm's Pit.' B.938 inserts a point before the above pit, viz., 'on the Rode', 'on the rood of land.'[17] One MS. reads 'Wyrt Dene' for 'Wyrtwala'. This need not trouble us, for the 'wyrtwala' was evidently the foot of the slope of one side of the dean, and the dean referred to is that ½m west of wield village, called stony dean in the TA. The pit is perhaps the old chalk-pit three furlongs west south west of the village.

8. *Thonon to Spreot Mere:* 'Then to Pole Pond.' Not identifiable.

9. *Thonan tha Twigbutme Del:* 'Then to the Double-bottomed Quarry.'[18] This quarry is clearly the old chalk-pit Pugdells, ¼m south west. of Wield village. It is marked in OM6 as a double-bottomed pit. The name Pugdells is in the TA. Perhaps Pugdell is an original Bucgan-del, 'Bucga's quarry.' Cf. ' Bucgan Ora ' above.

10. *Of tham Delle on Beran Del:* 'From the quarry to Barley Quarry': or, reading, 'Bern-del,' 'Quarry of the Barn.' This is probably the old quarry or chalk-pit on the south edge of Barton Copse (Bere-tun) on the south boundary of Wield.

10a. (B.938). *Thonne on Mint Mere:* 'Then to the Pond where Mint grows.' It is probable that Mint Mere was at the north east corner of Medstead parish, ¼m south west of Gaston Grange. The field just west of this point is called Minchams, which is possibly a corruption of a former 'Minthammas,' 'mint enclosures'.

---

a well-known landmark at one of its corners known as Buggenore's thorn. This wood also extended to the adjacent parishes of Brown Candover and Wield for, in a conveyance of 1598, we hear of Behunger Coppice and Buggenore Coppice in Wield. In the time of John the name Buggenora is used.

16 Grundy: *V.C.H. Hants,* III, 304, 5, original perambulation in the public record office, Eccl. Comm. 136, No. 1.

17 Grundy: This word 'rod', which is very common in the charters presents great difficulty in interpretation. It can mean a 'cross' and it can also mean a 'rood' of land. But when, as is often the case, a boundary is described as passing 'along the rod' it cannot mean across; nor is it at all probable that it means a rood of land, for the reason that the Saxon surveyors never employ this mode of defining a boundary. In relation to other terms implying land areas, eg, 'aecer', they may indeed describe a boundary as running for a certain distance 'two acres broad', which means roughly 44 yards; but that is a totally different kind of statement on the face of it. Philologists are emphatic in denying that it can be a variant of Anglo-Saxon 'Rad', which is the linguistic ancestor of our word 'road'. So I must in this and other instances translate it by 'rood', though I am almost certain that it had not that meaning.

18 Grundy: This meaning of 'del' will not be found in the dictionaries; but the fact that in the Hampshire charters it is again and again used of a quarry or chalk-pit makes it quite certain that such could be its meaning. It could also mean a small stream valley; and that was probably its original meaning. Its transference to places where stone was dug was probably due to a fact which may be noticed on the boundaries of many parishes in Oxfordshire and elsewhere, namely, that stone-digging was carried on upon the narrow balks of ploughlands, and so long, narrow, trench-like excavations were made resembling small stream valleys.

11. *Thonne on Feld Dene*: 'Then on the Dean of the Open Land.'[19] The name survives in that of Velden's Copse, about 1m north of Medstead village. The wood stands in a dean. The next few points in the survey must be taken together before any attempt is made to solve the topography of this part of the boundary (B.938).

11a. *Andlang Feld Dene on thone Hagan:* 'Along Field Dean on the Game Enclosure.'[20]

12. *Andlang Dene to Wuda*: 'Along the Dean to the Wood.'

12a. (B.938). *Fha andlang Hagan to Blacan Sole:* 'Then along the Game Enclosure to the Black Slough.'

13. *Siva be Mearce to Grenmeres Stigele:* 'So by the Balk to the Stile of the Green Pond.'

14. *Thonan to Lammeres Geate*: 'Thence to Claypond Gate.'

15. *Of tharn Geate to Bocmeres Stigele:* 'From the Gate to the Stile at the Pond of the Beech-trees.'[21]

16. *Thonan to Beammeres Geate*: (? read *Beanmeres)*[22] 'Then to the Gate at the Pond where Vetches (?) grow.'

17. *Of tham Geate to Hammer dene Geate*: 'From the Gate to Hammerdean Gate.'[23]

18. *Thonne to Hremmescumbes Geate:* 'Then to Ravenscombe Gate.' This brings the boundary to a point which is clearly determinable at the present day. In the Bighton charter, this point also occurs in the form 'Brennescumbes Geat' where the 'B' is an obvious mistake for 'H'. Furthermore the name survives in that of Ranscombe Farm which is in the parish of Bishop's Sutton, ½m west of North Street in Ropley.

---

19 Grundy: 'Feld', the origin of the word 'field', does not imply enclosed land, but open, but probably fairly flat, land free from trees and brushwood.

20 Grundy: see footnote reference 'haga'.

21 Bohmers Stile is a spot on the edge of the parish on Pullinger's Farm, now called Bogmore Dell, by which the road out of the parish ran to Wield. Grundy: I have translated the 'Mere' of these names 'pond'. It is possible that the reading 'mere' is correct, for some of the charters of the high-lying lands of north west Hampshire and west Wiltshire show that artificial rain-water ponds were used on the highlands. But I strongly suspect that 'maere', 'balk of a ploughland', would be the right reading here. As regards the terms 'maere', 'gemarea', 'mearc', the last being by far the most common in Hampshire charters, it is quite evident that in the surveys they do not refer to the boundary which is being actually traced, for that would be tautology, and, to say the least of it, not very enlightening. They are the balks or strips of unploughed land which divided different ploughlands from one another and, in the case of the charters, they must be the balks which divided the ploughlands of one land-unit from those of a neighbouring one. 'Geat' and 'stigel' are frequent landmarks in the Saxon surveys. During a certain period of the year, after the crops were gathered, and before the seed for the next crop was sewn, the ploughlands were open to the common pasture of all landholders-cattle. Live hedges were hardly known, and the fences of the ploughlands were merely wattle hurdles which could be removed when the crops were off, and set up again before sowing took place. But in these fences the gates and styles were permanent structures maintained from age to age; and so they seemed to the Saxons permanent landmarks. 'Geat' may sometimes be used of a gap in a hill ridge; but it is much more commonly used of these permanent gates on the ploughlands.

22 Grundy: 'Beam' means a tree. But I have not so far come across an instance of its use in the charters saving composition with a proceeding term, eg, 'elebeam'. I think that 'beammere' is a copyist's error for 'beanmere'. But the emendation is not, perhaps, absolutely necessary.

23 Hammerdon Bottom is identified as Ropley Stoke in a Winchester College terrier of 1786 (Winchester College Archives, 21412/40). Grundy: The name might conceivably be applied to a valley with two heads; but I am inclined to think that 'hamer' is here the shortened name of one of the plants 'hamersecg', 'hammersedge', or 'hamer-wyrt', black hellebore.

'Hremmescumb' was evidently the wide hollow which runs up the south east boundary of Bighton. The 'geat' was at the northern of the two heads of the hollow, where the boundaries of Bighton, Medstead and Bishop's Sutton meet, a little more than a mile east of the north end of Bighton village. It follows that the points between this and Feld Dene were on the east and south boundaries of Medstead. Hammerdene Geat was almost certainly where the road from Soldridge running south crosses the south boundary about 150 yards north of the railway. The other intervening points are not determinable. Nor is this surprising when we consider the nature of the landmarks.[24]

19. *Thonan to Eacges Geate·*. 'Then to . . . Gate.'[25] Whatever the name may mean, it almost certainly survives in a corrupted form in Hacket, the name of three fields which lie on the east boundary of Bighton, just north of the road from Bighton to Soldridge. The 'geat' may have been on a forerunner of that road, or possibly at the head of the combe, called Stancombe in the TA., which is just north of these fields.

20. *Thonne to Dunnes Stigele*: 'Then to Dun's Stile.' This was probably at the north east corner of Bighton parish ¼m south of Heath Green.

21. *Thonan on Witleage:* 'Then on White Lea.' A variant 'Pytleage,' 'pit lea,' is found. Probably this is right. This was probably at the old gravel pits west of the south end of Bighton Wood. **21a.** (B.938). *Andlang Mearce ut aet Ricg Sceate:* 'Along the Balk out at Ridge Shot.' This is the well-marked ridge which comes down the east boundary of Alresford, about ¾m north east of Old Alresford.

22. *Thonne to there Bradan Aec:* 'Then to the Broad Oak.' Mentioned in the Bighton charter. Probably stood about a furlong north of the north east corner of Upton Park.

23. *Thonne andlang Mearce to Dreigtune on thone Ford:* 'Then along the Balk to Drayton to the Ford.' Drayton Farm stands in Bighton, 3 furlongs east of Upton Park, on a large stream which flows into Alresford Pond. The ford must have been at the south east. corner of Upton Park. It is called Tornan Ford in the Bighton charter.

24. *Of tham Forda to Wuda Forda* : 'From the Ford to Wood Ford.' This was a ford over the Alre where the boundary crosses it just ¼m above Alresford Pond. The ford has vanished; but the sixteenth-century perambulation mentions a Furdley Ditch (Ford Lea) at this point.

25. *Thonan suth andlang Mearce to the* (S) *Gares suthende* : 'Then south along the Balk to the south end of the Gore'; (B.938) *thonne andlang Mearce on thone Garanuf wearthne*: 'Then along the Balk to the Gore on its upper side.' The reference is to a gore or triangular piece of ploughland. The gore was either at or just north of the south east corner of New Alresford, about 3 furlongs east of the Alresford Union workhouse.

---

24 The tenth gate 'was undoubtedly' the point where Ropley, Bishop's Sutton and Bighton came together near Pie Corner at a spot on Stankcomb Farm, Moody (*Short History of Medstead*), p. 10. There was a half-buried, three-sided boundary stone, one face with a 'B', another with an 'M', photographed at the meeting point of Medstead, Bighton and Ropley (National Grid reference SU 636348. Photo by Martin Morris, Alton Papers, No. 13, 2009), p. 29. Ravenscombe Gate is 'clearly determined' today in Ranscombe Farm a half mile from North Street.

25 Grundy: This is called Etges Geat in B.102, and Eces or Ekes Geat in the Bighton charter. The word may be a shortened form of one of the numerous personal names beginning with ECG... Dr. Henry Bradley suggests to me a Geaces Geat, 'Cuckoo's Gate'.

25a. (B.938). *Of tham Garam north ofer tha Streat:* 'From the Gore north over the Street.' The orientation is obviously wrong; but then the extant copy of the survey attached to this charter was made by one who either did not know Saxon, or was a very careless copyist. Probably 'north' has been written for 'west.' The identity of the 'straet' is doubtful. On the whole it is possible that it is an old road which followed the line of Appledown Lane, the lane running south from a point just east of the workhouse. But the defectiveness of the survey makes it impossible to do more than hazard a guess.

26. *Thonne andlang Mearce in on Aewyllas:* 'Then along the Balk on the inside of the Springs.' The line goes along the south boundary of New Alresford to certain large springs close to the Itchen at the west corner of the parish, about ½m north of Tichborne Park.

27. *Andlang Ewyllas in on to Ticceburnan:* 'Along the Springs inside (?) the Tichborne.' In the modern map this southern tributary of the Itchen is called by the name of the main stream, Itchen. But in old times the stream now called Aire, which flows through Alresford, was regarded as the main stream and called Icene. (See note on the name Alresford).

28. *Andlang Ticceburnan on Icenan:* 'Along Ticca's Bourne to the Itchen.' This is where the modern Itchen and the modern Aire join.

29. *Andlang Icenan thaer Cendefer and Icene cumath togaedere:* 'Along Itchen to where Candover (Brook) and Itchen meet; 'where Candover Brook meets the Itchen'. The second element in the name Candefer (Candover) is the Celtic 'defr,' 'water.' The same element occurs in the name Micheldever. It is interesting to notice that the Saxons understood the meaning of this word; for they do not seem to have known the meanings of most of the Celtic river-names which they adopted. There are various other Saxon charters which refer to this land at Alresford; but only B.938, K.1189 has a survey attached to it, and that survey has been dealt with in the preceding pages, in so far as it differs from the better survey we have used.

The Alresford lands seem to have remained the same through Saxon times, consisting of the parishes of Old and New Alresford, of Medstead, and of the south west part of the parish of Wield.[26]

---

26 Grundy: Those who wish to know further the story of the ownership of the Alresford lands may find it in B.102, K.997 [A.D.701] above.

Appendix 2: Ridge villages, Domesday Survey, 1086

After Duke William of Normandy conquered England, most of the lands of the Saxon nobility were granted to his followers.[1] *The Saxon Chronicles* noted in 1085 that

> *At the midwinter was the king in Gloucester with his council .... After this had the king a large meeting, and very deep consultation with his council, about this land; how it was occupied, and by what sort of men. Then sent he his men over all England into each shire; commissioning them to find out how many hundreds of hides were in the shires, what land the king himself had, and what stock upon the land; or, what dues he ought to have by the year from the shire.*[2]

The next year, the king left England for the last time. The survey was collated at Winchester (where the bishop was the king's grandson, Henry), 'corrected, abridged, chiefly by omission of livestock and the 1066 population, and fair copied by one writer into a single volume'. The manuscript is also known by the Latin name *Liber de Wintonia*, 'Book of Winchester'. The book's purpose was that every 'man should know his right and not usurp another's'. It was called *Domesday Book*, in allusion to the Last Judgement and in specific reference to the definitive character of the record. The word 'doom' was the usual Old English term for a law or judgment; it did not carry the modern overtones of fatality or disaster. London and Winchester were not included in the survey.[3]

'Of the thousand or so individuals who held their lands directly from the king in 1086, only thirteen were English. All the rest were foreign newcomers.'[4]

Alresford (see Medstead)[5]
Land of the bishop of Winchester in Fawley Hundred (2.1)
Walkelin bishop of Winchester holds Alresford in lordship. It is and always was in the bishopric. Before 1066 it answered for 51 hides; now for 42 hides.
Land for 40 ploughs. In lordship 10 ploughs; 48 villagers and 36 smallholders with 13 ploughs.
31 slaves; 9 mills at £9 30d. Meadow, 8 acres; woodland at 10 pigs pasturage; from grazing, 50d; three churches at £4. They paid £6 a year, but they could not bear it.
Robert holds 3½ hides of the land of this manor; Walter 2 hides; Durand 4 hides in Soberton and 6 hides in Beauworth; an Englishman 1½ hides. They have in lordship 6 ploughs; 17 villagers, 6 smallholders and 19 slaves with 6 ploughs.
A mill at 20s; meadow, 6 acres.
Wulfric Chipp, Robert's predecessor, could not go whither he would, nor could Osbern, Walter's predecessor; nor Edward and Alric, Durand's predecessors.

1   Munby, 'Introduction', *The Domesday Survey*,
2   Savage, *Saxon Chronicles*, p. 213.
3   Biddle, *Winchester in the Early Middle Ages, An Edition and Discussion of The Winton Domesday*.
4   Marc Morris, *The Anglo-Saxons* (2021), p. 404.
5   Raymond Elliott ,'Alresford at Domesday', 42, 1986, Alresford Historical and Literary Society.

Value of the whole manor before 1066 £40; later £20; now, the bishop's lordship £40, Robert's £4, Walter's 40s, Durand's £11.

Bishop's Sutton (see Ropley)
Land of Count Eustace in Ashley Hundred (20.1)
Count Eustace holds (Bishops) Sutton from the King. Earl Harold held it. 25 hides there; now it answers for 10 hides, and did so before 1066, as the Hundred states.
Land for 50 ploughs. In lordship 5 ploughs; 60 villagers and 60 smallholders with 23 ploughs.
A church with 1 hide; 32 slaves; 4 mills at 35s; meadow, 6 acres; woodland at 100 pigs from pasturage.
Value before 1066 £50; later and now £60; however, it pays £80 at face value.
Land of Count Eustace in Neatham Hundred (20.2)
The count himself holds 5 hides in Headley which answered for 3 hides before 1066. Earl Godwin held it. They account it in (Bishops) Sutton.

Chawton
Land of Hugh of Port in Neatham Hundred (23.5)
Odo held it from King Edward in freehold. There were 10 hides but King Edward put it for service and tax at 4 hides and 1 virgate.
Land for 8 ploughs. In lordship 4 ploughs; 19 villagers and 8 smallholders with 5 ploughs.
6 slaves; meadow, 6 acres; woodland at 50 pigs.
Value before 1066 £10; later £10; now £12.

East Tisted
Not mentioned. West Tisted (2.22)
Ranulf holds (West) Tisted in the Ashley Hundred from the bishop. It is of the bishopric.
Before 1066 and now it paid tax for 7 hides.
Land for 8 ploughs. In lordship 3 ploughs; 15 villagers and 3 smallholders with 3 ploughs.
A church; 2 slaves
Value before 1066 and later £4; now £6.

Farringdon
Land of bishop Osbern of Exeter in Neatham Hundred (3.5)
Bishop Osbern of Exeter holds Farringdon from the King.
Godwin the priest held it from King Edward. It belongs to the church of Bosham. Then (it answered) for 10 hides; now for 5 hides.
Land for 10 ploughs. In lordship 1 plough; 11 villagers and 20 smallholders with 8 ploughs.
2 slaves; meadow, 12 acres; woodland at 30 pigs.
Value before 1066 £15; later £12: now £21.

Medstead

There is no separate mention of Medstead in the Domesday Book. If the place-names that occur in the charter of King Ine are correct, Medstead was included in a grant of forty *mansae* of land at Alresford. It consequently formed part of Alresford Liberty and the manor of Old Alresford, and is most probably included in the entry under Alresford in the Domesday Book. This is supported by a perambulation of the manor taken in the reign of Edward VI, because the tithing of Medsted sent a tithing-man to the old Alresford court-leet, and also by the report of Anthony Browne, an agent sent from London to report on the whole bailiwick of Bishop's Sutton previous to its purchase by Sir John Gate in the reign of Edward VI, which included the parish of Medsted in his survey,[6]

> *Midsted adjoyning on the sowthest side of Wild and parcell of Old Alresford manor is verie well wodded with great beches and some oks onn everie side the greate wodds thereof, which from the village roun a mile and a haulf of Alton, and onn the west side from the ferme of Alresford downe to the commen felds of Medsted and on the sowth side to London hieghwaie that leadeth from Alresford to Alton, and onn the northe side to the mannor of Wild.*

Newton Valence

Land of Thurstan Son of Rolf in Neatham Hundred (38.1)
Thurstan son of Rolf holds Newton (valence) from the King.
Brictric held it from King Edward in freehold.
Then (it answered) for 10 hides; now for 5 hides.
Land for 12 ploughs. In lordship 3 ploughs; 9 villagers and 5 smallholders with 9 ploughs.
A church; 6 slaves; 2 mills at 100d; meadow, 6 acres; woodland at 100 pigs.
Value before 1066 and later £15; now £12.

Ropley

Not mentioned. Ropley was part of the hundred of Bishop's Sutton.

---

6   *Victoria Count History of Medstead*, Vol. 3, pp. 327-9.

Appendix 3: Perambulation of the Manor of Alresford, c. 1550

Perambulation of the Manor of Alresford, c. 1550 (translation)[1]

[1] A perambulation of the manor of Alresford, beginning at New
[2] Alresford Bridge at the end of the great weir, And then turning towards
[3] the west, just as the river in that place flows, as far as the southern corner
[4] of the land named Fobdown in the tenure of Nicholas Tycheborne, opposite
[5] the Geire in the tenure of Reginald Williams, And then by the other bank
[6] leading <towards the north> on the western side of Fobdown as far as the
        corner of the lord's land, [that is] of his, the Marquess's,
[7] Manor of Abbotstone, near the fulling mill there, And
[8] then turning towards the east as far as Harmysworgate, And then[2]
[9] towards the north as far as Bugner Corner, And then on to[3]
[10] Weld Park, and thus by the aforesaid park towards the east as far as Weld
        Common,[4]
[11] And then turning thence towards Deadhob, and from Deadhob[5]
[12] as far as Weldbayle, And then as far as Feldene, and from Feldene
[13] as far as Bentworth Holt, and then to Howpen Corner, and from
[14] the said corner as far as the great beech, And then as far as a certain road
[15] near The Dell in that place, and thus turning from the said road towards the
        south
[16] by the aforesaid Dell, on a certain road between the wood of R. Lyster and
[17] the house of Bentworth within the wood, as far as the wood of the Wardens
        of
[18] New College, And then immediately towards the south, into the eastern part
        of the[6]
[19] wood of the said Wardens as far as the corner of the wood of R. L. Knight,
        just as
[20] the great ditch appears, And thus then towards the south, on the eastern side
        of the wood of
[21] R. Lyster, to another corner of the said ditch opposite Chawton Park,
[22] And thus then towards the west by the great ditch for the length of ten
        perches
[23] and more, And then the route turns to the south as far as another
[24] corner on the eastern side of R. Lyster's wood called Row Downe[7]

1 HRO, 11M59/A1/2/4, Court Rolls, pp. 117 +1. See also abstract at VCH, Vol. 3, pp. 304-6. With
    thanks to Mike Overy for the modern-day annotations
2 Armsworth / Harmsworth.
3 Bogmore Hill in Godsfield.
4 Wield.
5 Deadhob Copse in the south of Wield parish.
6 Oxford.
7 Roe Downs.

[25]   and abutting upon the road opposite the lord of this manor's Rede Busshes,[8]

[26]   And then turning towards the south, between the wood called Redbusshes on the west

[27]   and Chawton Common on the eastern side, beyond the Pase of[9]

[28]   Alton as far as the plashed beech stump being and

[29]   growing in the wood of the President of the College of Oxford, And then <towards the south> between

[30]   the said wood and the wood of the Marquess of Winchester <and the lord of this manor, and Richard Lyster,> on the west and Chawton Common

[31]   on the eastern side, as far as a certain empty place of land called

[32]   Four Marks near Bookemere, and named thus, Four Marks,

[33]   because four tithings abut there mutually, that is to say, the tithings of

[34]   Medstead, Ropley, Faryngdon and Chawton,[10]

[35]   And then the boundary turns towards the west, between the woods of Richard Lyster and the Wardens

[36]   of the College in the north, and the lord of this manor's Bookmore Launde

[37]   on the southern side, and as far as the Grene Dene, And thus

[1]   then towards the west, between the lord's woods, both of Ropley and of

[2]   Alresford, called The Holt, as far as Gullett Mere, And then[11]

[3]   between the land called Solrydge on the northern side and the land of the Wardens of the College on[12]

[4]   the south, as far as the great ditch in Ranscombe woods,[13]

[5]   And then separating [ie forking, turning off?] towards the west, just as the said ditch leads beyond Pye[14]

[6]   Way to Bickton Down, And then turning towards the north[15]

[7]   as far as the pound post, And then towards the north as far as mill

[8]   oak, and from mill oak as far as the hanging beech, and by the lane

[9]   leading to Lanham Down, And then directly turning towards[16]

[10]   the west, by Bickwood and Bickton Field as far as

[11]   Cokes Land, and thus by the said lane as far as London Way

[12]   and beyond the said road to the eastern side of the Nyther, And

[13]   then turning towards the south to Furdley Ditch Corner,

[14]   And then the route turns thence to the west, on the southern side

[15]   of the great fish pond, as far as the aforesaid bridge where this

[16]   perambulation began

---

8   Red Bushes, Boyneswood Road.
9   Pass.
10 Farringdon.
11 Gullett Wood?.
12 Soldridge.
13 Ramscomb Farm in the north of Ropley parish.
14 Pye Corner.
15 Bighton.
16 Upper and Lower Lanham Copse are in the north of the parish of Old Alresford.

Perambulation of the Manor of Alresford, c. 1550 (transcription)

P[er] Ambulac[io] Man[er]ii de Alresford

[1]   P[er]ambulac[io] Man[er]ii de Alresford incipien[s] ad pontem de Nova

[2]   Alresford ad fine[m] de Magna wara & deinde tend[ens] v[er]s[us]

[3]   occid[entem] sic[u]t Rivolu[s] ib[ide]m currit usq[ue] ad angulu[m] austral[em]

[4]   de t[er]r[a] no[m]i[n]at[a] fobdowne In ten[u]r[a] Nich[ola]i Tycheborne exopp[os]ita

[5]   le geire in ten[u]r[a] Regnold[i] Will[ia]ms & deind[e] p[er] alia[m].rip[er] iam

[6]   d[u]c[e]nt[em] <v[er]s[us] aquilone[m]> in occid[entali] p[ar]t[e] de fobdow usq[ue] angulu[m] t[er]r[e] d[omi]ni M[ar]ch[i]o[n]is

[7]   Man[er]ii s[ui] de Abbotystone p[ro]pe molendi[num] fullat[ione] ib[ide]m &

[8]   d[einde] tend[ens] v[er]s[us] orien[tem] usq[ue] harmysworgate & deinde

[9]   v[er]s[us] aquilon[em] usq[ue] bugner corner & deinde usq[ue].p[ar]c[um]

[10]   de welld & sic <p[er]> p[ar]c[um] p[re]d[ictum] v[er]s[us] orie[ntem]. usq[ue] co[mmun]ia[m] de weld

[11]   & tunc tend[ens] deinde v[er]s[us] dedhob ~~& v[er]~~ & a dedhob

[12]   usq[ue] weldbayle & deinde usq[ue] feldene & a felde[ne]

[13]   usq[ue] bentworth holt & tunc ad howpen corne[r] & a

[14]   dict[o] corn[er] usq[ue] Magn[um] fagu[m] & deinde usq[ue] qua[n]d[a]m via[m]

[15]   p[ro]pe le Dell ib[ide]m & sic a dict[a] via tend[ens] usq[ue] austru[m]

[16]   p[er] le dell p[re]d[ictum] in quad[a]m via int[er] bosc[um] R lyst[er] &

[17]   Domu[m] de bentworth infra bosc[um] usq[ue] ad bosc[um] custod[um]

[18]   novi collegii & deinde cont[inuo] v[er]s[us] austr[um] in orien[tali] p[ar]t[e]

[19]   bosc[i] d[i]c[torum] Cust[o]d[um] usq[ue] angulu[m] bosc[i] R L militis p[ro]ut p[atet]

[20]   magn[a] fossat[a] & sic deinde v[er]s[us] austr[um] in orien[tali] p[ar]t[e] bosci

[21]   R Lyst[er] ad al[iud] angulu[m] d[i]c[t]e fossat[e] exoppo[s]i[tum] p[ar] c[um] de Chawton

[22]   & sic deinde v[er]s[us] occid[entem] p[er] magn[am] fossat[am] p[er] spaciu[m] x p[ar]tic[ularum]

[23]   & Amplius & tu[n]c iter tend[ens] in austr[o] usq[ue] ad aliu[d]

[24]   angulu[m] in orie[ntali] p[ar]t[e] bosci de R lyst[er] voc[ati] Row downe

[25]   & abutt[ans] sup[er] via[m] exoppo[s]it[am] Rede busshes d[omi]ni hui[us] Man[er]ii

[26]   & deind[e] tend[ens] v[er]s[us] austr[um] int[er] bosc[um] voc[atum] Redbusshes & [in error for "in"?] occid[ente]

[27]   & co[mmun]ia[m] de chawton in orien[tali] p[ar]te ultra le pase de

[28]   Alton usq[ue] ad le stub beche plasshed existent[em] &

[29] crescen[tem] in bosco p[re]sedent[is] colleg[ii] oxo[n]is & deinde <v[er]s[us]
      austr[um]> p[er] int[er]

[30] d[i]c[tum] bosc[um] & bosc[um] de M[ar]chione Wint[onie] <ac d[omi]ni
      hui[us] Man[er]ii & Ric[hardi] Lyster> in occid[enti] & co[mmun]ia[m] de
      chawto[n]

[31] in orien[tali] p[ar]t[e] usq[ue] & ad quada[m] vacua[m] placea[m] t[er]re
      voc[atam]

[32] fowre m[ar]kes p[ro]pe bookemere & sic no[m]i[n]at[am] fowre m[ar]k[es]

[33] q[uia] iiij decenne illic adinvicem ad abutt[ant] v[idelicet] dec[enne] de

[34] Medsted dec de Ropley dec de Faryngdon & Chawton

[35] & tu[n]c bond[a] tend[it] v[er]s[us] occid[entem] int[er] bosc[os] Ri[chardi]
      lyst[er] & Custod[um]

[36] Colleg[ii] in borial[e] & bla bookmore launde d[omi]ni hu[ius]

[37] Man[er]ii in austr[ali] p[ar]te & usq[ue] le grene dene & sic

[1]   deinde v[er]s[us] occid[entem] int[er] bosc[os] d[omi]ni t[a]m de Ropley
      qu[am] de

[2]   Alresford voc[atum] le holt usq[ue] Gullett mere & deind[e]

[3]   int[er] t[er]r[am] voc[atam] solrydg in borial[i] p[ar]te & t[er]r[am] de
      Cust[o]d[um] Colleg[ii] in

[4]   Austr[o] usq[ue] magn[am] fossat[am] in Ra bosc[o] de Ranscombe

[5]   & tu[n]c sep[arans] v[er]s[us] occid[entem] p[ro]ut dict[a] fossat[a] duc[it]
      ultra Pye

[6]   wey ad byckton downe & deinde tend[ens] v[er]s[us] borea[m]

[7]   usq[ue] le pounde post & deinde v[er]s[us] borie[m] usq[ue] myll

[8]   oke & <a> myll oke usq[ue] hangyng beche & p[er] venel[lam]

[9]   duc[entem] ad layneh[a]m downe & deinde direct[e] tend[ens] v[er]s[us]

[10] Magn v occid[entem] p[er] bykwodd & byckton feld usq[ue] ad

[11] Cokes land & sic p[er] dict[am] venell[am] usq[ue] london wey

[12] & ult[ra] dict[am] via[m] ad orien[tem] p[ar]t[em] de le Nyther &

[13] deinde tend[ens] v[er]s[us] Austr[um] ad furdley dyche corn[er]

[14] & tu[n]c deinde iter tend[it] in occid[ente] in austr[ali] p[ar]t[e]

[15] magni vivar[ii] usq[ue] ip[s]o ad ponte[m] p[re]dict[um] ubi incepit

[16] p[er]ambulacio ista

Appendix 4: Chawton Courts, 1606, 1617, 1654, 1705, 1729

This particular Court was held by John Knight (now Lord of the Manor) on 11th April, 3rd of James I (1606).[1] After reciting that, according to the ancient custom of the Manor, every tenant and inhabitant had the right of feeding three sheep for every acre of land which he held in the common fields of the Manor 'at such tyme and tymes as the said fields have not been sowen,' and one 'Rother beaste' or Horse beaste' for every three of such acres; and that within these last thirty or forty years 'greate parte of the sayd fieldes' had been enclosed by divers of the said tenants and with the consent of the lord, which said tenants nevertheless still kept the same number of cattle upon the common fields as they did before, to the great prejudice of the tenants whose ground still lay in common and not enclosed, the jurors, tenants and inhabitants present proceeded to make regulations for the good government of the Manor.

First of all, they mutually consented, granted, and agreed that neither they, nor any of them, nor 'any other whatsoever, that shall hereafter inhabit dwell or have the use or occupation of any lands or Tenements within the said Manor, shall keep or have any greater number of cattle going or feeding in and upon the said waste and common fields than according unto the ancient rate and order'. They then set out at length what the ancient rate and order was, and decreed that 'evrie one that shall hereafter doe contrary to this order shall forfeyt for evrie time he shall offend, and do contrary to the same to the Lord of the said Manor for the tyme being, the sum of ten shillings, the said to be levied by waye of distress, etc'.

Next followed general regulations for the management of the Common and common fields.

All gates, hedges, and fences against and belonging to the common fields were to be repaired within six days after the first man 'hath begun to sowe in the said fields any corner or grayne and to be maynteyned according to the discretions of four men, viz., John Barnard, Laurence Alderslade, Thomas Knight, & Nicholas Moorey, upon payne of vis. viiid for everie default'. The same four men were elected 'vangers or breakers' of the Common Fields, and were directed yearly to give notice to the tenants, &c., 'when any of the said fields shall be vanged and shall from tyme to tyme present unto the Lord of this Manor all forfeitures committed and done contrary to this order within three months next after the same shall be committed upon payne of XXs. for every default.'

The next order is a self-denying one:

'We doe agree that if any of us have encroached upon any of his neighbours' lands in the Common Fields and the same shall soe appear by the vewe, judgment and discretion of any six of the Lord's Tenants then we payne everie man to lay out and amend his encroachments within ten daies after everie such vewe in such sort as the said six Tenants shall appoynte upon payne of VIs. VIIId. for everie default.'

---

1   Leigh, *Chawton Manor*, pp. 33-45.

Further orders directed that whosoever should 'drive his cattell along Broad Waie after the Corne be sowen there until the fields are all rid of the corn, shall forfeit for everie tyme IIIs. IVd'. That no person should leave behind him in the fields any of his cattle without a keeper. That no man should take any tenants, without the consent of the lord and parishioners, and that every man should from 'tyme to tyme scoure and amend his watercourses upon foure daies warning to be given by any two of the Lord's Tenants, *sub pena* VIs. VIIId. *toties quoties*'.[2]

Six years afterwards, viz. 9th October 1617, further regulations were agreed upon.

The vangers or breakers of the fields were to have power 'to order and appoynte the tyme of rynginge or pegginge of hogge and where they shall be suffered to feed and goe and whosoever shall not, upon warninge thereof given in the Church, pegge and ringe his hogge sufficientlie shall forfeyte to the lord iid. for everye hogge that shalbe not sufficientlie ringed & pegged'.

That there should be a common 'sheepe prynte made at the equal charges of the Commoners that have sheepe common within the parish of Chawton before the first daie of May next followinge'. Every one who did not pay his share of the cost of making the 'prynte' to be fined – the 'prynte' to be kept by some tenant chosen by the vangers at Easter, and to be imprinted at the expense of the owner on as many sheep as every man might lawfully keep, immediately after the sheep shearing. 'And if any Inhabitant keep more sheepe prynted than he may lawfullie doe by the Ancient rates, he shall forfeyt to the Lord of the Manor iid. for everye sheep *toties quoties*. And for everye sheepe that shalbe there taken unprynted with the same prynte shall forfeite to the Lord iiiid. for everye sheepe *toties quoties*.'

Next the vangers were authorised to order the 'layinge uppe, or freethinge of all the Common Fields as well when the same shall begin as when the same shall be layed upon publick notice thereof to be given in the Church and that every inhabitant that will not stand to their order therein shall forfeite to the Lord VIs. VIIId. *toties quoties*'.

Then, as to turning out pigs on the Common, the vangers had full power and authority to appoint to every man the rateable proportion or number of hogs he might put into the Common to mast there.

The maintenance of parish boundaries, too, was an important part of the duties of the Court. At the same Court we find them presenting that the 'Ancient bonds between the Lordships of Chawton and Alton at the end of the lane leading from Ackner were sett uppe and bounden by the Ancient men of Chawton, viz. Wm. Moorey the elder, John Alderslade, and Thomas Moorey the elder, and that the holes which were digged about the beginning of October last and filled with stones at and by the Knappe or Green Hill at the end of the said lane, and the bounds at the green hill or Knappe near Mayden Lane Gate at Robyn Hoode Butts where likewise holes are digged and filled with stones, are the utmost of the bounds by them sett and appoynted in the presence of Richard Dawes, John Barnard, Thomas Buckland, Thomas Pryor, Richard Willys, Richard Mason (clerk), and Laurence Alderslade who were then there and did see and viewed the setting forth of the said bounds'.

---

2   *Sub pena*: subpoena: A writ ordering a person to attend a court. *Toties quoties*: Repeatedly.

The 'vanngers or frethers' were to be elected yearly in the Christmas holidays by the lord's tenants, the time of meeting to be given by the outgoing vanngers in Church publicly on Christmas day. If, during their term in office, they should neglect their duties, they were to forfeit to the lord for every such careless neglect XXs.

Although there was assize of bread and ale in this Manor allowed to John de St. John in 1280, no ale-tasters were appointed at Courts, as was the case in the Manor of Alton Eastbrook; and in the matter of ale it would have been a dead letter, as no alehouse was permitted in the parish.

The Court of 9th October 1617 agreed 'that if any Inhabitant of the Parish of Chawton shall from this tyme forth keep any Ale house, victualling house taking in and selling or buying or selling forth of their house or within their house to any of the Parish of Chawton or out of the Parish of Chawton any ale or beer, he shall for everye tyme so offending forfeit to the Lord of the Manor XXVIs. VIIId. whereof we of the homage doe entreat that VIs. VIIId. of everye such payne or forfeit may be distributed amongst the poore of Chawton'.

The vangers continued to be appointed until after the Restoration; the last of such consecutive appointments having been that of Wm. Pratt and Rowland Prowting at the Court held 16th April, 14th of Charles II. From this time to the 24th October 1705 the Rolls are silent as to the stint of Common and the election of vangers, but in 1705 the usual presentments were revived and the vangers appointed. At this Court the Homage also present that the stocks and whipping ('wiping') post are out of repair. At a previous Court (6th October 1654) they had presented that 'the Lord of this Manor, upon lawful warninge or notice bee given, at his owne cost & charges ought to repayrs the Pound belonging to this Manor'.

Bees seem to have been looked upon as estrays, and in 1706 the jury present a swarm of bees found in the Manor of Chawton, 'which Bees are now in the Custody of Mr. Wm. Fisher the younger, and belong to the Lord of the Manor, having no owner appearing'. At the same Court they present Mr. William Fisher, senior, for not paying a couple of capons for his quit rent due to the lord of this Manor at Christmas.

At the Court held 24th September 1729, by Bulstrode Knight and Elizabeth his wife, the jury present that there shall be four persons chosen 'vongers' of the common fields, to be chosen in the Christmas holidays, and whoever refuses to come to the election shall forfeit to the lord 3s 4d. So by this time the ancient name of 'vangers' for the breakers up and freethers of the common fields had been corrupted into 'vongers'. Their duties came altogether to an end on the enclosure of Common and common fields in 1741.

It will interest some to know the names of those summoned to attend the Court two hundred years ago: William Fisher, Tho's Prior, John Dawes, Andrew Eyres, Rob't Boldover, Rob't Carter, John Lipscombe, Rowland Prowting, James Mumford, Tho's Eames, John Alderslade, Henry Strudwick, William Woodward, Robert Grover, Edward Harris, John Harris, Wm. French (the only name still to be found in Chawton), Thomas Oliver, Francis Pink, James Pink, John Privett, Rob't Jowning, Thomas Morley, Jethro Eames, Tho's Baker, John Nash.

The extracts from the Court Rolls which have been given above show an active life in this small village community, and a real desire to do justice between man and man. The lord was no doubt possessed of important rights and privileges, but even he had definite duties to discharge. His land was made up in great part of strips in the open field, and these would be subjected to the same course of tillage as those of his neighbours. Even in his own Court he, or rather his steward, hardly occupied the position of a judge. The tenantry, forming what answered to a jury, were virtually his assessors, and, as we have seen above, do not hesitate to call on him to carry out his obligations by repairing the stocks, whipping-post and pound; rough and ready methods, no doubt, but probably then considered necessary for ensuring the safety and good order of the community. A different set of ideas is introduced by the edicts against alehouses and indiscriminate gambling. Whether these regulations were made at the instance of the lord or tenants does not appear.

Appendix 5: Medstead's pastoral care, 1662-1869

	Bishop	Rector	Curate	Enclosure
1662	**George Morley**	George Beaument		
1663			John Carter	
1684	**Peter Mews**			
1687		William Needham		
1702			**Stephen Stephens**	
1707	**Jonathan Trelawny**			
1721	**Charles Trimnell**			
1723	Richard Willis			
1727		**Joseph Soley**		
1734	*Benjamin Hoadly*			*1735*
1737		*John Hoadly*		
1738			John Child	
1760			John Winbolt	
1761	John Thomas			
1762			John Downes	
1771			John Simpson	
1773			Alban Thomas	
1776		William Buller	John Jones	
1781	*Brownlow North*			
1789			John Docker	
1790			William Harrison	
1795			Liv Booth	
1797		*Francis North*		
1798			**Benjamine Lovell**	**1798**
1802			Michael Terry	
1811			James Digweed	
1816			George Coulthard	
1820	**George Pretyman Tomline**			
1822			W. Berry	
1823			George Coulthard	
1824			William Smith	
1827	*Charles Sumner*			
1829			August Smith	
1835			T. F. Baker	
1837			David Robinson	
1843			Nevenham Travers	
1844			Claudius Magnay	
1850		George Henry Sumner		
1851			Frederick Graeme Middleton	
1861			William Standen	
1862			John R. Gurney	
1863		M. A. Smelt		
1867		Edgar Silver		
1869	Samuel Wilberforce			

Bold: Protagonists in this book. *Italics* and underlined: Nepotism.

Appendix 6: Complaint by Robert Kerby against Charles
Heron (written Herne), c. 1707

To the Right Reverend Father in God, Jonathan, by Divine p[er]mission Lord
Bishopp of Winchester[1]

An Accounte of [those] [par]ticulers wherein Mr. Herne, your Lordshipp's Steward,
have Acted contrary to your Lordshipp's Honour and Interest, by not behaveing
himselfe According to the Dignity of his trust, humbly offered to your Lordshipp by
your Lordshipp's faithful Servant, which are as Followeth;
1. *Imprimis*[2] That the said Mr. Herne, since he has Acted as your Lordshipp's
Steward, sent to one Mr. Thomas Slatford, who is and has beene many yeares
Baker to the Colledge of Winchester, and by Character an honest Mann, and
was for many yeares past a Tennant by Lease to the Lord Bishopp Morley, and
to the late B[isho]pp Mews, and had a Lease in being att his Lordshipp's death
of some Meadow Ground belonging to your Lordshipps Pallace at Wolvesey,
wherein severall yeares were then to come and unexpired, and desired to see his
Lease, p[re]tending to renew the same; which as soone as the said Mr. Slatford
produced, notwithstanding he had before Accepted the Rent due since your
Lordshipp's Translation, Immediately tooke the said Lease and Cancelled itt,
and refused to lett the said Thomas Slatford have itt againe, and ousted the said
Thomas Slatford out of the said Meadowes, on which he had bestowed greate
Charges by way of Improvement, which was a base and dishonourable way of
proceeding, and to prove this.
2. That the said Mr. Herne hath since lett the after Grass of the said Meadows
to one Mr. Tipper, a Butcher of Winchester, by Lease, and had Five Guineas for
letting him have the bargain and makeing the Leases, and to prove this.
3. That he holds an Extraordinary Correspondence with one John Gantlett, a
Notorious lyer, and a p[er]son of Ill Fame, and a person that has said Publicly that
he wisht that my Lord Bishopp of Salisbury had beene Bishopp of Winchester, by
whome he should have gott something that he was not like to gett any thinge by
your Lordship, for he could not yett see any of your Lordshipp's Money, Butt this
p[er]son the said Mr. Herne is Introduceing in to be your Lordshipp's Housekeeper
at Wolvesey, and he is to Manage the First Cutt of the said Meadowes, and itt is
apparent that the keepeing the First cutt of those Meadows for your Lordshipp's
use, as p[re]tended, and letting the after Grass, as the same is lett, will fall short of
answereing the Rent which the said Mr. Slatford paid for the same att least tenn
pounds P[er] Annu[m], which will be soe much disadvantage to your Lordshipp,
and to prove this.

---

1   HRO, 11M59/F/BP/E/B12.
2   *Imprimis*, Latin, 'In the fist place' … in a list of items.

4. That he holds Correspondence with and Imploys severall scandalous p[er]sons, who are often his Companions and make them his Informers, and Incourages them by letters and otherwise to spread false stories to the p[re]judice of your Lordshipp's Faithfull servants and Tennants, and Especially the said Kerby, The names of which persons he Imployes are John Gantlett, Edward Hoare, John Fry, Richard Warne, Robert Rice, John Binsted, James Dagwell and several others, and to prove this.

5. That he has taken upon him to usurp the Authority of Mr. Wither your Lordshipp's steward of the Lands to your Lordshipp's B[isho]ppricke of Winchester, who is an Officer by Patent to your Lordshipp and a Gentleman by birth as well as by his Office, and of a good Family, and a person which is very honest in his office, that the said Mr. Herne has threatened him at his Perrill in Publicke, as P[ar]ticulerly att Waltham Court, because he would not submitt to doe as he would have him, and that was to doe an Act contrary to the Custome of the Mannor and to your Lordshipp's Interest to prove this.

6. That att Crawley Court the said Mr. Herne in Publicke Court told the said Mr. Wither that he would make him carry his owne Portmantle, onely because he insisted to have Oates for his Horses which were paid by the Farmer there, According to the Antient usuage and Custome of your Lordshipp's Bishoppricke, to prove this.

7. That att Bently Court he said that he would have the said Mr. Wither, your Lordshipp's Steward, tost in a Blankett if he came to your Lordshipp's Castle at Farnham, and this was said without any provocac[i]on, and to deterr him from Acquainteing your Lordshipp of his behaviour, and to p[ro]ve this. That by shewing disrespect to your Lordshipp's Steward, who in his place represents your Lordshipp, is a showing disrespect to your Lordshipp, and a lessening of your Lordshipp's honour and Interest, and an Incouragement to all Insolent P[er]sons to Affront and disrespect your Lordshipp's Steward.

8. That the said Mr. Herne att Crawley Court aforesaid said to the other Officers belonging to your Lordshipp's Court that they should carry theire owne Portmantles, which tends to a lessening of your Lordshipp's Honour for as they are your Lordshipp's Officers, they are Gentleman and above that meane Office of carrying a Portmantle, and better Men then Mr. Herne were he out of your Lordshipp's Service.

9. That the said Mr. Herne has <likewise> taken upon him <another> part of the office of your Lordshipp's Steward of the Lands of your Lordshipp's Bishoppricke, for that he has Compounded with one Mr. Spencer for a Lycence to pull downe a House in your Lordshipp's Mannor of Bishopps Waltham, and agreed itt for thirty shillinges, which was less then your Lordshipp ought to have had for the Fine, that he did itt without ever viewing the p[re]misses, or being any wayes Informed of the vallue thereof, That it is the Steward of the Lands Office to doe itt, that itt ought not to be done butt in open Court, and that for Several reasons; that the Baililffe of the Mannor is the proper Officer to value the p[re]misses, and to report itt to the Steward, and that your Lordshipp's Fine ought to be aboute one third part of the reall value of the p[re]misses taken downe as hath beene Antiently Accustomed, And that the p[re]mises were worth aboute Eight or tenn pounds to prove this.

10. That he likewise Compounded with Mr. Wavell of Winchester for another Lycence to take down a House in the Mannor of Bishopp Stoake, for a Fine of Foure

pounds on a Contract aboute buying of Wine, That the p[re]misses were worth neare Forty pounds Standing, but he Compounded the same att the rate of Foure pounds, without seeing the p[re]misses, which he did by the P[er]swasion of his Confident and Friend the said John Gantlett who is a Tennant to the said Mr. Wavell and soe made way for his said Landlord to have a good bargaine of the said Mr. Herne, whereas in reall truth your Lordshipp ought to have had Eight pounds att least for the Fine of the said Lycence, According to the Custome and useage of the said Mannor.

11. That the said Mr. Herne takes upon him to defraude your Lordshipp's officers (vizt) the Steward, Treasurer, Clerke of the Lands, Clerke of the Bailliwicke and Bailliffe of the Bailliwicke, of theire Severall Antient and Accustomed Fees b[elon]ging to theire Severall offices, and paid by your Lordshipp's Ten[nan]ts, and are grounded upon just reason and right, and have beene by them and theire p[re]decessors for time Immemorially rec[eiv]ed, that he putts them upon beareing theire owne Expenses att your Lordshipp's Courts, and pocketts the Money that should Entertaine them, and forces them to begg victualls and trespasse upon Gentleman, when they are in your Lordshipp's Business, by reason att some places noe publicke Houses are neare, that his Intent by itt must be to discourage your Lorshipp's Officers in doeing the respective dutyes of theire Severall Offices, which will be of disadvantage to your Lordshipp and B[isho]ppricke, and a lessening of the Severall Officers, and of their Offices, which are in your Lordshipp's gift as they Fall, and they are such Officers as your Lordshipp's B[isho]ppricke cannott be without, and that theire Fees are not Extravagant, Nay they are rather much to little for the Service they P[er]forme, if they doe theire duty as they ought, that it is plaine that the said Mr. Herne's intent is to breake them all, that he may be sole Officer to your Lordshipp, and then he might be att liberty to make such Accounts as he pleased, and not be detected, which liberty he cannott now have, because the Officers are a Checke one to the other, Soe that noe cann Cheate but that he may be and will be detected.

12. That the said Mr. Herne has taken upon him to Act as Bailliffe to your Lordshipp, and office below his station, and to Seize Herriotts on your Lordshipp's Tennants Deathes where none were due, as att Mr. Waights att Sutton Mannor, where he seized Five Herriotts and none due, which he did on purpose to disgrace Mr. Lacy your Lordshipps Bailliffe, and to represent him as a person not to be trusted to doe his duty, and negligent officer for not doeing his duty in due time, to prove this.

13. That the said Mr. Herne, notwithstanding he Indeavours to lessen your Lordshipp's Steward's Fees, and other your Lordshipp's Officers, yett he himself take Five pounds for a Lease granted by your Lordship as his Fee, altho' such Lease does not cost above tenn shillinges the writeing, as he has taken of severall p[er]sons.

14. That the said Mr. Herne Endeavours to make all your Lordshipp's Officers pay Eight shillinges in the Pound for taxes, for theire severall Offices, which is a greate hardshipp on them, and which they hope your Lordshipp will not Countenance him in, and that he moved the Commiss[i]on[er]s of the taxes to <th[a]t purpose, & to> prove this.

15. That the said Mr. Herne is a very haughty, Imperious Mann, and of a Rigid Temper, which renders him unfitt for doeing your Lordshipp true service, that he

uses very harsh Expressions to your Lordshipp's Tennants by Menaceing of them, That by his Pride he's above Advice of the Antient officers of your Lordshipp's B[isho]ppricke, who know the Customes thereof; and this your Lordshipp's Officers will justifie.

16. That he has used base and unmannerly Expressions to your Lordshipp's Tennants onely when they have with Civility Invited him to theire Houses, as in P[ar]ticuler he said to one William Mayhew on such an occasion, that he was not to come to such an Impudent Fellow's house as his, to prove this.

17. That he has behaved himselfe verie disrespectively to severall Clergie Men att severall Courts, and in p[ar]ticuler to Mr. Needham and Mr. Louth att Alresford Court to prove this.

18. That he has done the same to severall Gentlemen, Namely to S[i]r Harry Titchbourne and Mr Lewis &c to prove this.

19. That he breakes old Customes an[d] usuages in Minute and Small matters, which are of small value to your Lordshipp, as in perticuler he scoures servants of theire Fees att Severall places, he has denyed to Allow Five shillinges att Waltham to the Jury att the Court, and two shillinges and six at Droxford, to drinke your Lordshipp's health, a Custome that has beene used time out of Mind, that he has denyed your Lordshipp's Steward and Officers a small p[er]quisite of haveing theire Horses shood att Waltham According to an Antient usuage, which never Exceeded above six or seaven shillinges, that he denies your Lordshipps Tennants Timber for the repaire of Severall Bridges and Common Pounds where itt hath of right beene Antiently Allowed, which is a greate p[re]judice to the publicke.

20. That he refused to pay for the Game that was brought to your Lordshipp According to the rate as has beene paid for Fifty yeares last past, for which reason they that catcht them would catch noe more.

21. That he turned out James Robinson out of his business att Wolvesey without just Cause, who had served there above thirty yeares, onely to make roome for the said Mr. Gantlett his Favourite.

22. That he has att severall times Misrepresented severall thinges to your Lordshipp against your Lordshipps officers and servants, and in perticuler that he Informed your Lordshipp against Mr. Cranley and his Clerke Mr. Barton in relac[i]on to your Lordshipps Instruments on your Lordshipps Conge d'Eslire[3] to the Chapter of Winchester, that they were not readdie when he came to Winton[ia] [ie Winchester], and that the said Mr. Barton knew not how to make them readdie, when in fact there was noethinge wanting to Finish the same butt to fill a blanke with your Lordshipp's Name, That he Informed your Lordshipp that the said Robert Kerby had brought severall Acc[i]ons against severall p[er]sons for viewing your Lordshipp's Woods, which he knew to be a Falsity for that the Acc[i]ons were brought by the said Kerby against the p[er]sons for scandalizeing him, to vindicate his reputac[i]on which have <been> abused by the said Gantlett and the other Favourites of the said Mr. Herne and by his Incouragement.

---

3 Conge d'Eslire: permission from the sovereign to a dean and chapter to elect a bishop in time of vacation.

23. That the said Mr. Herne has told severall of your Lordshipp's Tennants, and in perticuler Madam Morley, that the said Kerby was the person th[a]t gave Informac[i]on of the value of theire Estates &c, which he does on purpose to Create Enemies to the said Kerby, which if the same had beene true, yet ought not to be named by him, being noe wayes Materiall to your Lordshipps Interest to Name p[er]sons, but the readdie way to discourage any body to give Informac[i]on for your Lordshipp's Interest.

24. That the said Mr. Herne has from time to time baffled your Lordshipp's Leasehold Tennants, and putt them of, with sham p[re]tences from time to time, from theire just Allowances of Wood and Timber, Altho' severall of them are justly Entituled by theire Leases to the same, which is a Dishonour to your Lordshipp, and a discouragement to them to pay theire Rents and P[er]forme theire Covennants, and a disadvantage to your Lordshipps B[isho]ppricke, by reason repaires runns on [an]d will be greate att last, That the said Mr. Herne has misrepresented the Fees and Actinges of the said Kerby your Lordshipp's Woodward to your Lordshipp, by saying that he has two parts in three of the Timber which is altogeather false, for it's not one third thereof, as your Lordshipp may be Easily satisfied, that the said Mr. Herne has taken upon him, altho' he hath noe thinge to doe with the same, to direct makeing of Hedges aboute Cheriton Wood, that the same are soe ma[de] by his direcc[i]on that the wood hath beene Extreamely Damaged.

25. That the said Mr. Herne has from time to time Harrased and perplexed many of your Lordshipp's Tennants, the Collectors of the Queenes taxes, by makeing them runn ab[ou]t after the Money, till the Expences of severall of them was as much as the tax, when the Collectors were not the persons in fault that your Lordshipp was taxt, but the Assessors, and the said Mr. Herne, has not yett taken that care to putt that matter into a proper or regular course for your Lordshipp's Interest and your Tennants ease, butt that matter stands in a Confusion throughout your Lordshipps B[isho]ppricke, which is by some threatened, if not p[re]vented, to be made a Complainte in Parliament.

26. That the said Mr. Herne is a p[er]son that sweares and Dams your Lordshipp's servants, officers and Tennants to prove this.

27. That the said Mr. Herne caused double notice to be given of your Lordshipp's Courts the last p[ro]gresse, whereby your Lordshipp's Tennants were much Dampnified by provideing for the same.

28. That the said Mr. Herne is a Frequent Sabbath breaker, and has very often taken his journeys from Winton[ia] and other places on Sundays, and has spent the Sundayes in searching Records att Wolvesey and att his Favourite's, Mr. Gantlett's, which in his Post is an Ill Example, to prove this.

29. That the said Mr. Herne is by Fame a Necessitous man and lives separate from his wife, and is very vitious, That his Actions are such as tend to your Lordshipp's dishonour, which makes people not respect him, or att least not pay him that respect which they would doe in respect to your Lordshipp, were his behaviour Accordingly, that by his unskillfull Management and Imperious way, he has occasioned some Law Suites to your Lordshipp, and is likely to be occasion of many more.

30. That the said Rob[er]t Kerby, in respect to the said Mr. Herne as he was your Lordshipp's Steward, Invited him to his House in July last was twelve Month, and att the same time shewed him all the respect he was capable of, yett the same day the said Mr. Hern declared that he would be a plague to him, for that he did not like him, And since the said Kerby Invited him att Waltham Court to Lodge at his House, which he did, Butt he then behaved himselfe soe to his Maid Servant, by using such violent temptac[i]ons to her by way of Debauchery, that she would not goe into his Chamber, and amongest the rest of his wicked Insinuac[i]ons, he told <her> that unleast that she would submitt he would tell her Master, which was a reflecc[i]on on the said Kerby, as tho' he had beene privie to his base designes, for which reasons he did not att <ye> last Court give him any Invitac[i]on, which the said Mr. Herne resents.

31. That the said Mr. Herne, Notwithstanding all his behaviour, and since your Lordshipp has had no Complaint against him, which he thought by his Menaceing of people and setting forth that your Lordshipp would not heare any body (would never have beene made) Yett he has beene soe bold as to say [*record ends*]

Appendix 7: Ropley Commons Act, 1709

Passed 27 March, p. 386; royal assent 5 April 1709.[1]

Whereas there is a tract of ground called Ropley Commons, containing by estimation five hundred acres, more or less, parcel of the manors of Bishop's Sutton and Ropley, in the county of Southampton,

- in which the tenants of the same manors have the sole right of communing, and depasturing their cattle *levant and couchant* on their respective tenements parcels of the same manors, exclusive of all others whatsoever:
- And whereas the said Ropley Commons are at present of small annual value, but capable of improvement, in case the tenants of the same manors might have the liberty of enclosing, ploughing, and sowing the same, and many poor people would be employed in making such improvements, which will tend to the public good:
- And whereas the tenants of the said manors have agreed to divide and enclose the said Ropley Commons, and to allot to every tenant of the said manors his due share and proportion, according to their respective interest and right of common therein;
- and that each and every one of them would accept and take such a proportion and share therein as shall be set forth and allotted by William Godwin, late of Ovington, in the said county of Southampton, yeoman, Richard Seward, late of Bishop's Sutton, in the said county, yeoman, and Henry Whitear, of Lanham, in the parish of Old Alresford, in the said county, yeoman, men indifferently elected and chosen by the said tenants to divide and allot the same according to the several interest and rights aforesaid;
- and that each tenant, in manner directed, should fence and hedge in the share and dividend to him so to be allotted, and keep the fences so to be made in good repair, and for ever enjoy the parts so to be respectively allotted in Severalty [owned by one person], and as part of their respective tenements, in respect or right of which such, parcels, allotments, and dividends shall be made.

And Whereas the old disparked park of Farnham, in the counties of Surrey and Southampton, part of the bishoprick of Winchester, is likewise capable of being greatly improved, in case tenants might have a certain interest therein for their encouragement to make such improvements, which would also be for the public good;

And Whereas a house, called The Lawday House, lately standing in such park, was accidentally burnt down and consumed: Wherefore, for the rebuilding of the same, and for the making of such improvements as aforesaid, and for the encouragement of the said tenants therein,

---

1   Parliamentary Archives, HL_PO_PB_1_1709_8&9An41, 8 Anne c. 16. HoC Journals, XVI, 1709.

- Jonathan, Lord Bishop of Winchester, the Warden and Fellows of Winchester College, together with the tenants of the said manors of Bishop's Sutton and Ropley, Do respectfully, and in the most humble manner beseech your Most Excellent Majesty, That it may be enacted, and be it enacted, by the Queen's Most Excellent Majesty, by and with the advice and consent of the Lords Spiritual and Temporal, and Commons in this present Parliament assembled, and by the authority of the same, that the commons called Ropley Commons, parcel of the manors of Bishop's Sutton and Ropley, in the county of Southampton, shall,

- on or before the twentieth day of December, which shall be in the year of our Lord one thousand seven hundred and ten,

- be divided and allocated by the said William Godwin, Richard Seward, and Henry Whitear, or the survivors of them, unto and amongst the said several tenants and persons according to their respective interests and right of common appertaining to their respective tenants;

- and that each tenant of the said manors shall hold and enjoy his share and part so to be allotted to and with his respective tenement, as part of the same, and to have a great and the same interest and estate in the part so to be allotted as he and they respectively now have in the respective tenements to which or in respect of whereof such allotments are to be made,

- and fence, hedge in, and enclose the same in such manner and proportion as the said William Godwin, Richard Seward, and Henry Whitear, or the survivors of them, shall at the making such allotments direct and appoint;

- and that the aforesaid allotment be in writing, and be enrolled in the courts of the said manors.

And be it further Enacted, by the authority aforesaid, That the said Lord Bishop of Winchester, and his successors for the time being, shall and may from time to time, and at all times hereafter, demise, lease, and grant all the said old disparked park to any person or persons, for any term of years not exceeding twenty-one years, from the making thereof, reserving the annual rent of seventy pounds to be paid half yearly for the same, and to continue payable during such lease or demise, to the said Lord Bishop and his successors, Bishops of Winchester;

Saving to the Queen's Most Excellent Majesty, her heirs and successors (other than the tenants of the said manors of Bishop's Sutton and Ropley, and their heirs, and the said Bishop of Winchester and his successors) all such estates, rights, and interests as they, or any, or either of them had or might have had if this Act had not been made.

Appendix 8: Ropley Commons Act: Parliament and Petitions, 1709-10

17 March 1709: Ropley Inclosure[1]

Also, the Lords have passed a Bill intituled, An Act for the inclosing of Ropley Commons, in the county of Southampton, and for the Improvement of the old disparked Park of Farnham, in the Counties of Surry [sic] and Southampton; to which the Lords desire the Concurrence of this House.

18 March 1709: Ropley Inclosure[2]

An ingrossed Bill from the Lords, intituled, An Act for the inclosing of Ropley Commons, in the county of Southampton, and for the Improvement of the old disparked Park of Farnham, in the Counties of Surry and Southampton, was read for the First time.

Resolved, That the Bill be read for a Second time.

20 March 1709: Ropley Inclosure[3]

Ordered, That the ingrossed Bill from the Lords, intitled An Act for the inclosing of Ropley Commons, in the county of Southampton, and for the Improvement of the old disparked Park of Farnham, in the Counties of Surrey and Southampton, be now read the Second time.

The Bill was accordingly read a Second time.

Resolved, That the Bill be committed to Lord *Wm. Powlett*, Mr. Chancellor of the Exchequer, Mr. *Jerveise*, Mr. *Onslow*, Mr. *Bridges*, Mr. *Austin*, Mr. *Ossley*, Lord Marquis of Winchester, Mr. *White*, Major General Rosse, Mr. *Addison*, Mr. *Dolben*, Mr. *Masters*, Sir *Rushout Cullen*, Sir *Fran. Masham*, Mr. *Bacon*, Sir *Robert Edon*, Mr. *Henley*, Mr. *Nevill*, Sir *Richard Farrington*, Major *Yate*, Sir *Walter Yonge*, Mr. *Evelyn*, Mr *Oglethorp*, Sir *Wm. Seawen*; and all, that serve for the Counties of Southampton, Surry, and Wilts: And they are to meet this Afternoon, at Five a Clock, in the Speaker's Chamber.

23 March 1709: Ropley Inclosure[4]

A Petition of *John Soper*, Esquire, *Robert Budd*, senior, *Nicholas Mayhew*, Thomas Budd, John Gilbert, *James Budd*, junior, *Robert Yalden*, and *John Mayhew*, Tenants of the Manor of Bishops Sutton and Ropeley [sic], in the County of Southampton, in behalf of themselves, and several others, Tenants of the same Manors, was presented to the House, and read; setting forth, that the Petitioners are possessed of diverse Freehold, Copyhold, and Leasehold, Estates, of the yearly value of Five hundred Pounds, and upwards, and have Right of Common in the said Ropley Commons: And praying to be heard by their Counsel against the Bill for the inclosing of Ropley Commons, in the County of Southampton, and for the Improvement of the old disparked Park of Farnham, in the Counties of Surry and Southampton.

---

1   HoC Journals, XVI, 1709, p. 374.
2   HoC Journals, XVI, 1709, p. 374.
3   HoC Journals, XVI, 1709, p. 376.
4   HoC Journals, XVI, 1709, p. 381.

Ordered, That the Consideration of the said Petition to be referred to the Committee, to whom the said Bill is committed; and that the Petitions be heard before the Committee To-morrow, who are then appointed to meet.

25 March 1709: Ropley Inclosure[5]

The Lord *William Powlet* [sic] reported from the Committee, to whom the ingrossed Bill from the Lords, intitled, An Act for the inclosing of Ropeley Commons, in the county of Southampton, and for the Improvement of the old disparked Park of *Farnham,* in the Counties of Surrey and Southampton, was committed; that they had examined the Allegations of the Bill, and heard the Petitioners upon the Petition, referred to the Committee; and that the Committee had directed him to report the Bill to the House without any Amendment: and he delivered the same in at the Clerk's Table.

About 26 March 1709

Passing of Ropley Inclosure bill.

3 February 1710: Ropley Inclosure[6]

A Petition of *John Soper,* Esquire, *John Mayhew, Nicholas Mayhew, Robert Budd,* senior, *Tho. Budd, James Budd, Robert Budd,* junior, *Richard Oliver, James Blanchard, Margaret Batell, John Oliver, Robert Yalden, John Gilbert, Jasper Smith,* and *Wm. Smith,* in behalf of themselves, and others, the Tenants of the Manor of Ropley and Bishop Sutton, was presented to the House, and read; setting forth, that an Act passed the last Session of Parliament, for inclosing Ropley Common, to be divided amongst the Tenants, having Right of Common, as Three Persons named in the … should apportion: That several of the Petitioners opposed the passing that Act, well knowing they should have no Benefit by the Inclosure; and the Three Persons have acted so partially in the Premises, that several of the Petitioners, who always had right of Common, have no Part allotted to their Estates, and to others they have not allotted half their Proportion, to their very great Oppression: And praying, that the Clause in the said Act for inclosing the said Common, may be early repealed, or that the Petitioners be otherwise relieved in the Premises, as the House shall think fit.

And a Motion being made, and the Question being put, That the said Petition be referred to the Consideration of a Committee; and that they do examine the Matter thereof, and report the same to the House;

The House divided:

The Noes go forth:

Tellers for the Yeas: Sir *Simeon Stuart,* Mr. *Cholmondley*) 129

Tellers for the Noes: Mr. *Brydges,* Mr. *Henley*) 76

So it was resolved in the Affirmative.

And it is referred to Sir *Simeon Stewart,* Mr *Sergeant Hooper,* Sir *Gilbert Dolben,* Mr. *Conyers,* Sir *Rich. Onslow,* Mr. *Moncton,* Mr. *Rodney Bridges,* Mr. *Page,* Mr. *Pocklington,* Mr. *Gore,* Mr *Lloyd,* Mr. *Hedges,* Mr. *Tilney,* Mr. *Chapman,* Mr. *Foley,* Sir *Robert Eden,*

---

5   HoC Journals, XVI, 1709, p. 385.
6   HoC Journals, XVI, 1710, p. 476.

Mr. *Goulston*, Mr. *Essington*, Mr. *Guidot*, Mr. *Onslow*, Mr. *Peyton*, Mr. *Gott*, Mr. *Pitt*, Sir *Rich. How*, Mr. *Lewis*, Sir *Robert Davers*, Mr. *Sharp*, Mr. *Campion*, Mr. *Henley*, Mr. *Morley*, Mr. *Fox*, Sir *Geo. Newland*, Lord *Powlett*, Mr. *Mew*, Mr. *Gale*, Lord *Downe*, Mr. *Jessop*, Mr. *Moor*; and all that serve for the Counties of Southampton and Surry: And they are to meet this Afternoon, at Five a Clock, in the Speaker's Chamber; and have Power to send for Persons, Papers, and Records.

A Petition of the Gentlemen, Freeholders, and others of the Counties of Southampton and Surry, and Parts adjacent, living near the Commons, called Ropley Commons, in the said County of Southampton, was presented to the House, and read; setting forth, that by inclosing the said Commons, by virtue of a late Act, and the Proceedings hitherto had thereupon, the Petitioners find, they shall be incommoded, that there will be no travelling, by themselves, their Horses, Carts, and other Carriages: And praying, that the said Act may be repealed.

Ordered, That the said Petition be referred to the Consideration of the said Committee; and that they do examine the Matter thereof, and report the same to the House.

21 February 1710: Ropley Inclosure[7]

A petition of the Reverend *John London*, Vicar of Ropley, *Robert Cranston, John Gilbert, John Bull, Tho. Warrenton, James Godwin, Robert Harwood*, on behalf of themselves, and others, the Tenants of the Manors of Bishop-Sutton [sic] and Ropley, in the county of Southampton, and other inhabitants of other parts adjacent, was presented to the House, and read; setting forth, that the Petitioners are informed, a Petition has been lately been presented to the House by a few Tenants of the said Manors, complaining, that the Persons, appointed by Act of Parliament for dividing and inclosing of Ropley Commons, have made partial and unjust Allotments: that the Petitioners hope to make it appear, that the Allotments are just; and that the Petitioners have been at great Expence fencing in the Shares allotted them; and that to repeal the said Act will be the Ruin of the Petitioners: And praying, that they may be heard before the Committee, to whom the Petition of *John Soper*, Esquire, and others, is referred.

Ordered, That the said Petition be referred to the Consideration of the said Committee; and that the Petitioners be heard by their Counsel before them, if they think fit.

After 22 February 1710

The Ropley Inclosure Petition was only referenced in the House of Commons Journal in 1710 on 3 and 21 February (see above). It was not brought back to the House after 21 February because the Committee did not *think fit*: the bill had already been given the Royal Assent and the Committee did not think it necessary to consider the bill or the petitions before the House.

---

7   HoC Journals, XVI, 1710, p. 509.

Appendix 9: The Waltham Black Act, 1723

An Act for the more effectual punishing of wicked and evil-disposed persons going armed in disguise, and doing injuries and violences to the persons and properties of his Majesty's subjects, and for the more speedy bringing the offenders to justice.[1]

I. WHEREAS several ill-designing and disorderly persons have of late associated themselves under the name of Blacks, and entered into confederacies to support and assist one another in stealing and destroying of deer, robbing of warrens and fish-ponds, cutting down plantations of trees, and other illegal practices, and have, in great numbers, armed with swords, fire-arms, and other offensive weapons, several of them with their faces blacked, or in disguised habits, unlawfully hunted in forests belonging to his Majesty, and in the parks of divers of his Majesty's subjects, and destroyed, killed and carried away the deer, robbed warrens, rivers and fish-ponds, and cut down plantations of trees; and have likewise solicited several of his Majesty's subjects, with promises of money, or other rewards, to join with them, and have sent letters in fictitious names, to several persons, demanding venison and money, and threatening some great violence, if such their unlawful demands should be refused, or if they should be interrupted in, or prosecuted for such their wicked practices, and have actually done great damage to several persons, who have either refused to comply with such demands, or have endeavoured to bring them to justice, to the great terror of his Majesty's peaceable subjects:

For the preventing which wicked and unlawful practices, be it enacted by the King's most excellent Majesty, by and with the advice and consent of the lords spiritual and temporal and commons, in parliament assembled, and by the authority of the same:

That if any person or persons, from and after the first day of June in the year of our Lord one thousand seven hundred and twenty-three, being armed with swords, fire-arms, or other offensive weapons, and having his or their faces blacked, or being otherwise disguised, shall appear in any forest, chase, park, paddock, or grounds inclosed with any wall, pale, or other fence, wherein any deer have been or shall be usually kept, or in any warren or place where hares or conies have been or shall be usually kept, or in any high road, open heath, common or down, or shall unlawfully and wilfully hunt, wound, kill, destroy, or steal any red or fallow deer, or unlawfully rob any warren or place where conies or hares are usually kept, or shall unlawfully steal or take away any fish out of any river or pond; or if any person or persons, from and after the said first day of June shall unlawfully and wilfully hunt, wound, kill, destroy or steal any red or fallow deer, fed or kept in any places in any of his Majesty's forests or chases, which are or shall be inclosed with pales, rails, or other fences, or in any park, paddock, or grounds inclosed, where deer have been or shall be usually kept; or shall unlawfully and maliciously break down the head or mound of any fish-

---

1 I Geo. c.22.

pond, whereby the fish shall be lost or destroyed; or shall unlawfully and maliciously kill, maim or wound any cattle, or cut down or otherwise destroy any trees planted in any avenue, or growing in any garden, orchard or plantation, for ornament, shelter or profit; or shall set fire to any house, barn or out-house, or to any hovel, cock, mow, or stack of corn, straw, hay or wood; or shall wilfully and maliciously shoot at any person in any dwelling-house, or other place; or shall knowingly send any letter, without any name subscribed thereto, or signed with a fictitious name, demanding money, venison, or other valuable thing; or shall forcibly rescue any person being lawfully in custody of any officer or other person, for any of the offences before mentioned; or if any person or persons shall, by gift or promise of money, or other reward, procure any of his Majesty's subjects to join him or them in any such unlawful act; every person so offending, being thereof lawfully convicted, shall be adjudged guilty of felony, and shall suffer death as in cases of felony, without benefit of clergy.

II. And whereas notwithstanding the laws now in force against the illegal practices above mentioned, and his Majesty's royal proclamation of the second day of February which was in the year of our Lord one thousand seven hundred and twenty-two, notifying the same, many wicked and evil-disposed persons have, in open defiance thereof, been guilty of several of the offences before mentioned, to the great disturbance of the publick peace, and damage of divers of his Majesty's good subjects; It is hereby enacted by the authority aforesaid, That all and every person and persons, who since the second day of February in the year of our Lord one thousand seven hundred and twenty-two, have committed or been guilty of any of the offences aforesaid, who shall not surrender him, her or themselves, before the twenty-fourth day of July in the year of our Lord one thousand seven hundred and twenty-three, to any of the justices of his Majesty's court of kings bench, or to any one of his Majesty's justices of the peace, in and for the county where he, she or they did commit such offence or offences, and voluntarily make a full confession thereof to such justice, and a true discovery upon his, her or their oath or oaths, of the persons who were his, her or their accomplices in any of the said offences, by giving a true account of their names, occupations and places of abode, and to the best of his, her or their knowledge or belief, discover where they may be found, in order to be brought to justice, being thereof lawfully convicted, shall be adjudged guilty of felony, and shall suffer death as in cases of felony, without benefit of clergy.

III. Provided nevertheless, That all and every person and persons, who have been guilty of any the offences aforesaid, and shall not be in lawful custody for such offence on the said first day of June and shall surrender him, her or themselves, on or before the said twenty-fourth day of July as aforesaid, and shall make such confession and discovery as aforesaid, shall by virtue of this act be pardoned, acquitted and discharged of and from the offences so by him, her or them, confessed as aforesaid; any thing herein contained to the contrary in any wise notwithstanding.

IV. And for the more easy and speedy bringing the offenders against this act to justice, be it further enacted by the authority aforesaid, That if any person or persons shall be charged with being guilty of any of the offences aforesaid, before any two or more of his Majesty's justices of the peace of the county where such offence or offences were or shall be committed, by information of one or more credible person or persons upon oath by him or them to be subscribed, such justices before whom such information shall be made as aforesaid, shall forthwith certify under their hands and seals, and return such information to one of the principal secretaries of state of his Majesty, his heirs or successors, who is hereby required to lay the same, as soon as conveniently may be, before his Majesty, his heirs or successors, in his or their privy council; whereupon it shall and may be lawful for his Majesty, his heirs or successors, to make his or their order in his or their said privy council, thereby requiring and commending such offender or offenders to surrender him or themselves, within the space of forty days, to any of his Majesty's justices of the court of king's bench, or to any one of his Majesty's justices of the peace, to the end that he or they may be forth coming, to answer the offence or offences wherewith he or they shall so stand charged, according to the due course of law; which order shall be printed and published in the next *London Gazette*, and shall be forthwith transmitted to the sheriff of the county where the offence shall be committed, and shall, within six days after the receipt thereof be proclaimed by him, or his officers, between the hours of ten in the morning, and two in the afternoon, in the market-places upon the respective market-days, of two market-towns in the same county, near the place where such offence shall have been committed; and a true copy of such order shall be affixed upon some publick place in such market-towns; and in case such offender or offenders shall not surrender him or themselves, pursuant to such order of his Majesty, his heirs or successors, to be made in council as aforesaid, he or they so neglecting or refusing to surrender him or themselves as aforesaid, shall from the day appointed for his or their surrender as aforesaid, be adjudged, deemed and taken to be convicted and attained of felony, and shall suffer the pains of death as in case of a person convicted and attained by verdict and judgment of felony, without benefit of clergy; and that it shall be lawful to and for the court of king's bench, or the justices of *oyer* and *terminer*, or general gaol-delivery for the county, where the offence is sworn in such information to have been committed, upon producing to them such order in council, under the seal of the said council, to award execution against such offender and offenders, in such manner, as if he or they had been convicted and attained in the said court of king's bench, or before such justices or *oyer* and *terminer*, or general gaol-delivery respectively.

V. And be it enacted by the authority aforesaid, That all and every person and persons, who shall, after the time appointed as aforesaid, for the surrender of any person or persons, so charged upon oath with any the offences aforesaid, be expired, conceal, aid, abet or succour, such person or persons, knowing him or them to have been so charged as aforesaid, and to have been required to surrender him or themselves, by such order or orders as aforesaid, being lawfully convicted thereof, shall be guilty of felony, and shall suffer death as in cases of felony, without benefit of clergy.

VI. Provided nevertheless, and it is hereby declared and enacted, That nothing herein contained shall be construed to prevent or hinder any judge, justice of the peace, magistrate, officer of minister of justice whatsoever, from taking, apprehending and securing, such offender or offenders, against whom such information shall be given, and for requiring whose surrender such order in council shall be made as aforesaid, by the ordinary course of law; and in case such offender or offenders, against whom such information, and for requiring whose surrender such order in council shall be made as aforesaid, shall be taken and secured in order to be brought to justice, before the time shall be expired, within which he or they shall be required to surrender him or themselves, by such order in council as aforesaid, that then in such case no further proceeding shall be had upon such order made in council against him or them so taken and secured as aforesaid, but he or they shall be brought to trial by due course of law; any thing herein before contained to the contrary in any wise notwithstanding.

VII. And be it enacted by the authority aforesaid, That from and after the first day of June one thousand seven hundred and twenty-three, the inhabitants of every hundred, within that part of the kingdom of Great Britain called England, shall make full satisfaction and amends to all and every the person and persons, their executors and administrators, for the damages they shall have sustained or suffered by the killing or maiming of any cattle, cutting down or destroying any trees, or setting fire to any house, barn or out-house, hovel, cock, mow or stack of corn, straw, hay or wood, which shall be committed or done by any offender or offenders against this act; and that every person and persons, who shall sustain damages by any of the offences last mentioned, shall be and are hereby enabled to sue for and recover such his or their damages, the sum to be recovered not exceeding the sum of two hundred pounds, against the inhabitants of the said hundred, who by this act shall be made liable to answer all or any part thereof; and that if such person or persons shall recover in such action, and sue execution against any of such inhabitants, all other inhabitants of the hundred, who by this act shall be made liable to all or any part of the said damage, shall be rateably and proportionably taxed, for and towards an equal contribution for the relief of such inhabitant, against whom such execution shall be had and levied; which tax shall be made, levied and raised, by such ways and means, and in such manner and form, as is prescribed and mentioned for the levying and raising damages recovered against inhabitants of hundred in case of robberies, in and by an act, intituled. *An act for the following hue and cry*, made in the twenty-seventh year in the reign of Queen Elizabeth [27 Eliz. c.13].

VIII. Provided nevertheless, That no person or persons shall be enabled to recover any damages by virtue of this act, unless he or they by themselves, or by their servants, within two days after such damage or injury done him or them by any such offender or offenders as aforesaid, shall give notice of such offence done and committed unto some of the inhabitants of some town, village, or hamlet, near unto the place where any such act shall be committed, and shall within four days after such notice, give in his, her or their examination upon oath, or the examination upon oath of his, her or their servant or servants, that had the care of his or their houses, out-houses, corn, hay, straw or wood, before any justice of the peace of the county, liberty or division, where such act shall be committed, inhabiting within the said hundred where the said act shall happen to be committed, or near unto the same, whether he or they do know the person or persons that committed such act, or any of them; and if upon such examination it be confessed, that he or they do know the person or persons that committed the said act, or any of them, that then he or they so confessing, shall be bound by recognizance to prosecute such offender or offenders by indictment, or otherwise, according to the laws of this realm.

IX. Provided also, and be it further enacted, by the authority aforesaid, That where any offence shall be committed against this act, and any one of the said offenders shall be apprehended, and lawfully convicted of such offence, within the space of six months after such offence committed, no hundred, or any inhabitants thereof, shall in any wise be subject or liable to make any satisfaction to the party injured, for the damages he shall have sustained; any thing in this act to the contrary notwithstanding.

X. Provided also, That no person, who shall sustain any damage by reason of any offence to be committed by any offender contrary to this act, shall be thereby enabled to sue, or bring any action against any inhabitants of any hundred, where such offence shall be committed, except the party or parties sustaining such damage, shall commence his or their action or suit within one year after such offence shall be committed.

XI. And for the better and more effectual discovery of the offenders above-mentioned, and bringing them to justice, be it enacted by the authority aforesaid, That it shall and may be lawful to and for any justice of the peace, to issue his warrant to any constable, headborough, or other peace-officer, thereby authorizing such constable, headborough, or other peace-officer, to enter into any house, in order to search for venison stolen or unlawfully taken, contrary to the several statutes against deer-stealers, in such manner, as by the laws of this realm such justice of the peace may issue his warrant to search for stolen goods.

XII. And be it further enacted by the authority aforesaid, That if any person or persons shall apprehend, or cause to be convicted any of the offenders above-mentioned, and shall be killed, or wounded so as to lose an eye or the use of any limb, in apprehending or securing, or endeavouring to apprehend or secure any of the offenders above-mentioned, upon proof thereof made at the general quarter-sessions of the peace for the county, liberty, division or place, where the offence was or shall be committed, or the party killed, or receive such wound, by the person or persons so apprehending, and causing the said offender to be convicted, or the person or persons so wounded, or the executors or administrators of the party killed, the justices of the said sessions shall give a certificate thereof to such person or persons so wounded or to the executors or administrators of the person or persons so killed, by which he or they shall be entitled to receive of the sheriff of the said county the sum of fifty pounds, to be allowed the said sheriff in passing his accounts in the exchequer; which sum of fifty pounds the said sheriff is hereby required to pay within thirty days from the day on which the said certificate shall be produced and shewn to him, under the penalty of forfeiting the sum of ten pounds to the said person or persons to whom such certificate is given, for which said sum of ten pounds, as well as the said sum of fifty pounds, such person may and is hereby authorized to bring an action upon the case against such sheriff, as for money had and received to his or their use.

XIII. And whereas the shortness of the time within which prosecutions for offences against the statute made in the third and fourth years of the reign of their late majesties King William and Queen Mary, intituled, *An act for the more effectual discovery and punishment of deer-stealers*, or limited to be commenced, has been a great encouragement to offenders; be it therefore enacted by the authority aforesaid, That any prosecution for any offence against the said statute, shall or may be commenced within three years from the time of the offence committed, but not after [3 & 4 W. & M. c.10].

XIV. And for the better and more impartial trial of any indictment or information, which shall be found commenced or prosecuted for any of the offences committed against this act, be it enacted by the authority aforesaid, That every offence that shall be done or committed contrary to this act, shall and may be enquired of, examined, tried and determined in any county within that part of the kingdom of Great Britain called England, in such manner and form, as if the fact had been therein committed; provided, That no attainder for any of the offences made felony by virtue of this act, shall make or work any corruption of blood, loss of dower, or forfeiture of lands or tenements, goods or chattels.

XV. And be it further enacted by the authority aforesaid, That this act shall be openly read at every quarter-sessions, and at every leet or law-day.

XVI. And be it further enacted by the authority aforesaid, That this act shall continue in force from the first day of June one thousand seven hundred and twenty-three, for the space of three years, and from thence to the end of the then next session of parliament, and no longer [Further continued by 24 Geo. 2. c.57].

XVII. And be it further enacted by the authority aforesaid, That if any venison, or skin of any deer, shall be found in the custody of any person or persons, and it shall appear that such person or persons bought such venison or skin of any one, who might be justly suspected to have unlawfully come by the same, and does not produce the party of whom he bought it, or provide upon oath the name and place of abode of such party, that then the person or persons who bought the same, shall be convicted of such offence, by any one or more justice or justices of the peace, and shall be subject to the penalties inflicted for killing a deer, in and by the statute made in the third and fourth year of the reign of their late majesties King William and Queen Mary, intituled, *An act for the more effectual discovery and punishment of deer-stealers.* [3 & 4 W. & M. c.10].

Appendix 10: Soldridge and Stankham Enclosure Act (Medstead) 1735

An Act for Dividing and Enclosing certain Commons and Waste Grounds called Stankham and Soldridge Commons, in the Parish of Old Alresford, in the County of Southampton.[1]

Whereas there are certain Commons or Tracts of Waste Grounds called Stankham and Soldridge Commons, containing by estimation five hundred Acres or thereabouts, lying and being in the Tything of Medstead, within the Parish and Manor of Old Alresford, in the county of Southampton:

And whereas the Right Reverend Father in God *Benjamin* Lord Bishop of Winchester Lord of the said Manor, and Patron of the Rectory of Old Alresford; and *John Shackleford*, Esquire, Lord of the Manor of Medstead, an inferior Manor within the said Manor of Old Alresford; and also a Proprietor of Lands within the said Tything of Medstead; and the several Proprietors of Lands, lying within the said Tything of Medstead, who have the sole Right of commoning and de-pasturing their Cattle therein, exclusive of all other Persons whatsoever, have consented and are desirous that the said Commons or Tracts of Waste Grounds shall be divided and enclosed: But although the said Division and Enclosure will tend to the Publick Good, and be a great Advantage to the several Parties concerned, yet as the same cannot be effectually settled and established to answer the Intention of the Parties interested in the said Commons or Tracts of Waste Grounds, without the Aid and Authority of Parliament:

Therefore, Your Majesty's most dutiful and loyal Subjects, the Warden and Fellows of Winchester College, the President and Fellows of Magdalen College in Oxford, *John Shackleford*, Esq; Lord of the said Manor of Medstead, *John Barnard*, [end page 1] Esq, *Joseph Soley*, Rector of Old Alresford, *Stephen Stephens*, Clerk, *John Hicks*, *John Bulbeck*, *William Budd* of *Ropley*, *William Budd* of Soldridge, *William Sawkins*, *Edward Weeks*, *John Budd* of Shaldon, *John Budd* of Tennantry, *John Budd* of Hatingly, *John Burnell*, *Richard Wake*, *John Spencer*, *John Pryor*, *Richard Bone*, *William Wake*, *John Cammish* the elder, *William Skinner*, *John Vinden*, *James Budd*, *John Beackley*, *John Harrison*, *William Pryor*, *John Hockley*, *Elizabeth Pryor*, and *Armiger Bayley*, being near all the Proprietors of Lands in the said Tything of Medstead,

Do most humbly beseech Your most Excellent MAJESTY;

That it may be **Enacted**; and be it **Enacted**, by the KING's most Excellent Majesty, by and with the Advice and Consent of the Lords Spiritual and Temporal, and Commons, in the present Parliament assembled, and by the Authority of the same, That the said Commons or Tracts of Waste Grounds called *Stankham* and *Soldridge Commons*, within the Manor of *Old Alresford* aforesaid, shall on or before the Twenty-fifth Day of *March*, which will be in the Year of our Lord One thousand seven hundred and thirty-seven, be divided, set out, and allotted by the Honourable

---

1   Private Act, 9 George II, c. 19, HL/PO/PB/1/1735/9G2n47; *HRO*, 109A05/PX/10.

Edward Stawell, Norton Pawlett, Senior, *Norton Pawlett,* Junior, *Thomas Bates, Thomas Bonham, William Yalden,* and *Thomas Hall,* Esquires; and Robert Cropp and William Yalden, of South-street in the Parish of *Ropley,* in the County aforesaid, Yeoman; Commissioners appointed by this Act, and their Successors, of the Survivors of them, or any Five of more of them, unto and amongst all such persons, Proprietors of Lands and Tenements in the said Tything, as have a Right of Common in the Commons aforesaid, in proportion and according to the annual Value of the respective Estates, by which they are respectively entitled to such Right of Common, to be holden and enjoyed in Severalty by such Persons respectively, according to their Right and Interest in their said respective Estates.

And be it further Enacted, by the Authority aforesaid, That for the better ascertaining what Share and Proportion of the said Commons and Waste Grounds each Person interested therein ought to have allotted to him, her, or them respectively, the said Commissioners, or the Survivors of them, or any Five of more of them, shall have full and free Liberty and Power, at any Time or Times whatsoever, before the said Twenty-fifth Day of *March,* One thousand seven hundred and thirty-seven, to enter into and examine into the yearly Value of each Person's Estate having Right of Common in the said Commons, and the Nature and Goodness of the Land, and to admeasure the same, and also to inspect and examine into the Land-Tax Rate and Poor's Rate in the Parish or Place where such Estates lie, and enquire and inform themselves by every other Way they shall think proper and necessary, that they may be better enabled to form a Judgement of the Value of the said respective Estates, in order to divide and said Commons or Waste Lands in a just, proportionable, and equitable manner, among the Persons interested therein, and thereupon to adjudge, ascertain, and set out the Proportion and Share of each Person in the said intended Enclosures; in the doing whereof the said Commissioners shall have a due Regard to the Goodness, Quality, and different Natures, as well as to the Quantity of the Lands so to be allotted, and shall allot and set out each Person's Share as near and convenient to his or her Tenement or Estate, in the Right of which such Allotment [end page 2] shall be made, as may be, in the most impartial Manner, without any undue Preference of one to another.

And be it further Enacted, by the Authority aforesaid, That when the said Commissioners shall have fully completed and finished the said Partitions and Allotments of the said Commons or Waste Lands, the Names of the Persons to whom such Allotments shall be made, and the Quantity of Land allotted to each Person, with the Abuttals and Boundaries thereof, shall be fairly ingrossed upon Parchment, and signed and sealed by the Commissioners making such Partition, and shall be inrolled with the Clerk of the Peace for the County of *Southampton,* to the end Recourse may be had thereto, at all Times hereafter by any Person whatsoever; and the said Clerk of the Peace is hereby required to file the same among the Records of the General Quarter Sessions of the Peace of the said County, and to let all Persons who shall desire to see the same at all Times hereafter, upon Request, have Recourse thereto, and also to make and deliver a copy thereof signed by him, to any Person who shall desire the same; and such Copies so made and signed by the Clerk of the

Peace, shall at all Times hereafter be admitted and read as Evidence in all Courts whatsoever.

And be it further Enacted, by the Authority aforesaid, That all and every Person and Persons to whom any Part of the said Commons or Waste Grounds shall be allotted in his or her own Right by Virtue of this Act, shall accept the Part or Share thereof so allotted to him, her, or them, within Six Months next after such allotment shall be made, and Notice to him, her, or them respectively given by the said Commissioners, or their Successors, of the Survivors, or any Five or more of them, for that Purpose: And in Case any Person of Persons shall upon such Notice, refuse or neglect to accept of such Part or Share of the said Commons or Waste Grounds, as shall be so allotted to him, her, or them, within the Time aforesaid, the the Person or Persons so neglecting or refusing to accept his, her, or their Part or Share of the said Commons or Waste Grounds so allotted to him, her, or their Part or Share, shall absolutely forfeit the Part or Share of the said Commons or Waste Grounds so allotted to him, her, or them, and shall be entirely excluded from all Benefit, Right of Common, Estate, or Interest in any of the Lands appointed or intended to be enclosed by Virtue of this Act; and then and in such Case, the Part or Share, and Parts and Shares which shall be so allotted and set out for the Person or Persons who shall neglect or refuse to accept the same within the Time aforesaid, shall be divided amongst the rest of the Persons, who shall accept and take the Parts and Shares of the said Commons or Waste Grounds set out for them respectively, proportionably, according to the Share so set out and accepted by them respectively.

Providing always, That the Husband, Trustee, Guardians, Attornies or Committee of any Person under Coverture,[2] Under-Age, Idiot, Lunatick, or beyond the Seas, or otherwise incapable by Law to accept such allotments as shall be made to him, her, or them, by Virtue of this Act, shall and may, and are hereby enabled and required to accept thereof, in Right of, and to and for the Use of such Person or Persons so incapacitated as aforesaid; and such Acceptance shall be and is hereby declared to be as valid and effectual, as if the Person or Persons in whose Right the same shall be respectively made, were capable of acting for themselves, and had accepted the same in their own Persons; anything herein contained to the contrary thereof in any wise notwithstanding: But the Non-acceptance of any Executor, Guardian, Husband, Trustee, Attorney or Committee, shall not exclude or prejudice the Claim or Acceptance of any Infant, *Feme Covert*,[3] or other Person intitled to any Part of the said Commons or Waste Grounds, under any Disability or Incapacity to accept the Part or Share thereof [end page 3] allotted to him, her, or them, his, her, or their Heirs, Executors, or Administrators; Provided such Persons or Persons being under such Inability or Incapacity, shall accept and take the Parts and Shares allotted to him, her, or them, within Six Months after such Inability or Incapacity shall be removed.

---

2 *Person under Coverture:* A husband and wife are one *person in* law: the very being or legal existence of the woman is suspended during the marriage.

3 *Feme couvert:* A married woman who has no rights except through her husband.

And be it further Enacted, by the Authority aforesaid, That all and every Person and Persons to whom any Share of the said Commons or Waste Grounds shall be allotted as aforesaid, shall be admitted to and shall and may from time to time, hold and enjoy his, her, or their Share and Part in Severalty, freed and discharged from all Right of Common; and shall have and enjoy the same Parts or Shares so to be allotted to him, her, or them respectively, together with and for such Estate and Interest, as he, she, or they now hath or have in the Lands or Tenements, in respect whereof such Allotments shall be made; and such Allotments shall be taken and deemed as Parcel of such Lands or Tenements, and shall from and after Setting out and Acceptance thereof, stand and be subject and liable to such Jointures, Dowers, Covenants, Settlements, Conditions, Limitations, Trusts, Charges , and Incumbrances, as at the Time of setting out the same, do or shall affect the Lands or Tenements in respect whereof such Allotments shall be made: And that such Person or Persons to whom such Allotments shall be made, shall severally well and sufficiently ditch, fence, hedge, and enclose the Land so to be allotted to him, her, or them, in such manner, as the said Commissioners or any Five or more of them shall by writing subscribed under their Hands direct and appoint: And if any Difference shall arise touching the accepting, enclosing or fencing the said respective Shares, or touching or concerning any Interest of the Proprietors, the said Commissioners, or any Five or more of them, shall have full Power and Authority, and are hereby impowered and authorized to hear and finally determine the same; And that such Order and Determination of the said Commissioners, or any Five or more of them, so far as it relates to the Right of each Proprietor in and to the Partition and Allotment of such Commons and Tracts of Land to be enclosed aforesaid, and the fencing and hedging the same, shall be binding and conclusive, and final without Appeal, and shall be obeyed and observed accordingly.

And it is hereby further Enacted, That the said Lands so to be allotted, shall not be liable to any other of greater Fines or Rents, or subject to any other Suits or Services to the Lord of the said Manor of Old Alresford for the Time being, than have been usually paid and rendered by the Tenants in respect of their several Estates which they now respectively hold of the said Manor.

Providing always, That the Right Reverend Father in God, *Benjamin* Lord Bishop of Winchester, the present Lord of the said Manor of Old Alresford, and his successors, the future Lords of the same Manor for the Time being, and also the said *John Shackleford* and his Heirs or Assigns, Lords of the said Manor of Medstead, shall, notwithstanding such Inclosure and Division of the said Common or Waste Grounds, be intitled to and have, receive, and enjoy, all Rents, Fines, Services, Suits of Court, and all Royalties belonging to the said Manors, as fully and effectually as if this Act had never been made: And the Rector of the Parish Church of Old Alresford and his successors, shall at all Times hereafter have, receive, and take, all such and the like Tythes yearly issuing and arising from or out of any of the Lands hereby Enacted to be enclosed as aforesaid, as the said Rector is now entitled to have, receive, and take from or out of any Lands within the said Parish. [end page 4]

And be it further Enacted, by the Authority aforesaid, That the said Commissioners, or any Five or more of them, shall, and they are hereby authorized and impowered, if they shall judge it necessary or expedient for the bettering or improving the Highways or Roads leading over or across the Part of the said Commons, to stop up, turn aside, or alter the Roads now respectively used, or any of them, and to ascertain, set out and appoint a competent Part of the said Commons or Wastes, for publick Roads for Horses, Cattle and Carriages through the Inclosures hereby intended to be made, in such convenient Place, other than those now used, as they shall judge most convenient and apt; and that all such Roads so to be newly made and set out, and all such roads as shall be continued in the Situation they now lie, shall from and after the Execution of the Powers by the Act given respectively, contain Sixty Feet at least in Breadth; Except where Causeways shall be made by Direction of the said Commissioners, and in such Case, not less than Thirty between Ditch and Ditch, and also convenient Foot Paths for Passengers over the said Grounds hereby intended to be inclosed; and all such Roads so to be made, enlarged or continued, shall be from Time to Time, and at all Times hereafter kept in Repair, in the same Manner as the Roads in the same Parish were to be repaired before the making of this Act: And the said Commissioners, or any Five of them, shall also set out convenient Ways and Passages for Foot Persons, Horses, Carts and other Carriages, for the respective Persons intitled to such Allotments as aforesaid, to go to and from their respective Shares and Proportions of Land to be allotted to them in Pursuance of this Act, and shall appoint and order, how, and by whom, such several Ways and Passages shall be repaired; which Order of Appointment shall be made under the Hands and Seals of the said Commissioners, or any Five or more of them, and shall be inrolled with the Clerk of the Peace for the said County; a Copy of which shall be allowed as Evidence: And that it shall not be lawful for any Person afterwards, to use any Roads or Ways, either publick or private, over the said new Inclosures, either on Foot or with Horses, Cattle or Carriages, other than such Roads, Ways and Passages, as shall be ascertained and set out as aforesaid.

And whereas Great Hurt and Damage may happen unto the planting and setting Quick Wood, or any other Wood, for the fencing in any Part or Parcel of the said new Inclosures, by Sheep or Cattle going in any of the Lanes or Roads hereby directed to be left upon enclosing the said Commons; **Be it therefore Enacted,** by the Authority aforesaid, That any proprietor or Owner of any of the new Inclosures shall have full Liberty, for and during the Term of Twelve Years from and after the said Twenty-fifth Day of March, One thousand seven hundred and thirty seven, and no longer, to erect and set up, and maintain at his, her, or their own Charge, a Gate or Gates, across any Part or Parts of the Roads or Lanes against his or their Lands, for keeping out Sheep or Cattle, to prevent their destroying any Quick Wood, or other Wood or Fence, which shall be planted for enclosing any Part or Parcel of the said Lands as aforesaid, they the said Proprietors disclaiming all Right or Property to and in the Soil of such Lane of Lanes, as are bounded by such Gates so erected and set up.

Provided also, and it is hereby declared, That is shall not be lawful for any of the Proprietors of such new Inclosures to plant any Tree or Trees so near the Hedge or Fence of any of the other Proprietors, by which the Growth of any such Hedge or Fence may be hindered or hurt. [end page 5]

And it is hereby also enacted, That all the Lanes to be made or laid out, or which now do or shall lead from any Part of the Lands intended to be enclosed to the publick Roads, shall have one Gate at each End thereof, which, with such Lanes, shall be for ever repaired in the same Manner as the publick Roads in the same Parish were to be repaired before the making of this Act.

And it is hereby further Enacted and Declared, by the Authority aforesaid, that the said Commissioners, or any Three or more of them, shall and they are hereby required to give Notice at the Door of the Parish Church of Old Alresford and Medstead, upon some Sunday Morning immediately after Divine Service, of the Time and Place of the first Meeting of the said Commissioners for the executing of the Powers herby vested in them, at least Ten Days before such Meeting, and shall and may be at every Meeting for that Purpose, adjourn from Day to Day, and appoint such Times and Places for their subsequent Meetings, as to them or any Three of more of them shall seem meet, always giving Notice of every such subsequent Meeting (except Meetings by Adjournment) at the Doors of the said Parish Church and Chapel as aforesaid, upon some Sunday Morning, at least Ten Days next proceeding such Meeting, immediately after Divine Service, in Manner before mentioned.

And, for the more effectual Execution of the Act, **Be it further Enacted,** by the Authority aforesaid, That if any of the Commissioners hereby appointed, shall die, or refuse to act, then it shall and may be lawful to and for the acting or surviving Commissioners then in being, or Five or more of them, from time to time and at all times, by Writing under their Hands and Seals, to appoint new Commissioners in the room and stead of such of the Commissioners herein before named, who shall so die, or refuse to act; and if the said Commissioners appointed by this Act shall by Death be reduced to less than Five, or all of them except four, or a less Number, shall refuse to execute the Trust hereby in them reposed, then it shall and may be lawful to and for such acting or surviving Commissioners and Three of the Persons who have Right of Common in the Commons aforesaid, to be chosen by the Majority of the rest of the Persons intitled to or having Right of Common for that Purpose, or the major Part of such surviving or acting Commissioners and Persons so chosen, by Writing under their Hands and Seals, to appoint other Commissioners in the room of such as shall die, or refuse to act, as aforesaid; and if all the Commissioners hereby nominated and appointed shall die before any other shall be appointed, or shall refuse to act, then it shall and may be lawful for the major Part in Number and Value of the Persons who have any Right of Common in the said Commons, by writing under their Hands and Seals, to appoint new Commissioners for carrying this Act into Execution, in the room of the Commissioners herein before-named; and so from time to time, and at all times hereafter, as there shall be Occasion, it shall and may be lawful for the said surviving or acting Commissioners, and the Persons having Right of Common in the said Commons, in Manner herein before directed, to supply and keep up a competent Number of Commissioners for executing all and every the Trusts and Powers by this Act vested in them; which Commissioners to be so from time to time appointed, shall have as full Authority to execute the Powers hereby given, as if they had been appointed by this Act, and particularly named herein:

But publick Notice of every Meeting for the Choice of any new Commissioner or Commissioners, in pursuance of this Act, shall be given at the Door of the Parish Church of Old Alresford and Chapel of Medstead, on a Sunday Morning, at least Ten Days before every such Meeting, immediately after Divine Service.

And be it further Enacted, by the Authority aforesaid, That as well all the Charges of passing this Act, as for surveying, allotting, dividing, and enrolling the Allotments, and all the Charges and Expenses of the said Commissioners, and all other necessary Charges in or about the same, shall be borne and paid by the Persons to whom any Part or Share of the said Commons or Wastes shall be allotted or assigned in manner hereby directed, rateably and proportionably, according to the Value of the Parts or Shares which shall be allotted to each Person to be settled, ascertained and determined by the said Commissioners, or their Successors, or the Survivors, or any Five of more of them.

Saving to the King's Most Excellent Majesty, his Heirs and Successors, and to all and every other Person and Persons, Bodies Politick and Corporate, his, her, and their Heirs and Successors, Executors and Administrators respectively, (Other than and except the said Lord Bishop of Winchester, and his Successors Bishops of Winchester, Lords of the said Manor of Old Alresford, the Lords of the said Manor of Medstead, and the Tenants of the same Manors, and all other Persons claiming any Right of Common, in and upon the Commons or Waste Grounds aforesaid, or any Part thereof, and their and each of their Heirs, Executors, Administrators and Assigns) All such Estate, Right, Title, and Interest, as they, or any, or either of them, have or hath, or might have had, in or to the said Commons or Waste Grounds, if this Act had never been made.

And be it further Enacted, by the Authority aforesaid, That this Act, and every Clause and Matter therein contained, shall by all and every Judge and Judges, and other Person and Persons, be construed and adjudged, as largely and beneficially in all Courts of Law and Equity, and all other Places, as can be, for the Ends and Purposes herein mentioned, and that a true Copy thereof, shall be deemed, taken, and allowed as Evidence, in all Courts of Law and Equity whatsoever.

Appendix 11: Soldridge and Stankham Enclosure Awards, 1736

We whose Hands and Seals are hereunto Sett, being Commissioners appointed by this Act above mentioned Have to the best of our Judgement executed the Powers and Trusts of the said Act, in manner following.[1]

First, we adjudge and Sett out to the several Proprietors entitled to Right of Common in Stankham and Soldridge Commons what to us appeareth to be their proportionate shares of Lands to be inclosed out of the said Commons.

1   To Alton and belonging to the poor of Alton forty perches little more or less:
   • The Land of John Budd of Shalden on the North and West Parts and
   • The London Road on the South and East parts thereof.

2   To John Budd of Shalden for his Copyhold of Inheritance Seventeen Acres, three Roods, and two perches with one Acre and two Roods more allow'd for Grounds Spoil'd by the Roads, lying in two pieces:
    One having:
   • The London Road on the South Side,
   • An Inclosure of his own and the Land of William Sawkins on the North,
   • A Road leading from from the said London Road towards Medstead on the west, and
   • The allotment for Alton on the East.
    The other piece:
   • The London Road on the South
   • The land of Mr. Barnard on the North,
   • A Road from South Town towards Five Ash Pond on the West, and
   • A piece of Land allotted to Mr. Shackleford on the East.

3   To William Sawkins:
    for his Lease-hold of two thousand years, (under late John Henley Esq) one Acre, one Rood, and fourteen perches:
   • The Land of John Budd of Shalden on the East,
   • The allotment for his Leasehold of one thousand years on the west
   • The land of John Budd of Shaldon on the South, and
   • A road leading into Row Downs on the North
    for his leasehold of one thousand years (under late John Henley Esq) two Roods and nine perches:
   • The Allotment for his leasehold of two thousand years on the East,
   • The land of John Budd of Shaldon on the South,
   • The Road leading into Row Downs on the North, and
   • The Land of Nicholas Wilks, Martha Stooll widow, John Doary and Joseph Smith on the west.

4   To Nicholas Wilks for his leasehold of one thousand years (under Anthony Henley Esq) fifty perches:
   • The Land of William Sawkins on the East,

---

1   HRO, 21M65/I/2/A/157.

- The Land of Martha Stooll on the South,
- The Road to Row Downs on the North, and
- A Road leading from the London Road towards Medstead on the west.

5   To John Doary for his freehold fifty perches:
- The land of the widow Stooll on the North,
- The land of William Sawkins on the East,
- The land of Joseph Smith on the South, and
- The Road leading from the London Road towards Medstead on the west.

6   To Joseph Smith for his freehold fifty perches:
- The land of John Doary on the North,
- The land of William Sawkins on the East,
- The land of John Beagley on the South, and
- The said Road leading from the London Road towards Medstead on the West.

7   To John Beagley for his leasehold of two thousand years (under late John Henley Esq) One Rood and thirty six perches:
- The land of Joseph Smith on the North,
- The land of William Sawkins on the East,
- The land of John Budd of Shalden on the South and
- The said Road leading from the London Road on the west.

8   To William Skinner for his [end page 1] freehold two acres two Roods and six perches, with two Roods more, allowing for Ground spoil'd by Roads:
- One piece of Mr. Barnard's Allotment on the west, and
- His Majesty's highway on the other parts thereof.

9   To John Shackleford Esq Lord of the Manor of Medstead, [an inferior Manor within the Manor of Old Alresford] One hundred and seven acres, one Rood and four perches with thirty perches more allow'd for a Dell, lying in four pieces:
     One piece lies on the:
- North side of the London Road
- Adjoining to the East end of a piece allotted to John Budd of Shalden,
- The Road leading from Medstead to the London Road on the North and East parts thereof.
     Two other pieces lie on the:
- Southside of the London Road,
- The Road leading from Medstead towards Farringdon on the East,
- A Lane from the London Road, between the two said pieces towards Boyn's Grounds, the Road leading from South-Town towards Lymington Grounds on the West, and
- His enclosed Lands, the Land of Richard Wake, and the Land of the Widow Prior on the South.
     One other piece:
- Lies between the Land allotted to Richard Wake and the Lymington Road,
- The Road leading from Ropley to Alton on the South, and
- The Land allotted to the Widow Prior and to James and John Budd on the North.

10 To Richard Wake for his two copyholds of Inheritance nineteen acres, two Roods and two perches:
- The Land belonging to the Parish of Ropley on the South
- The Land of John Budd of Tenantry on the west,
- The Land of Mr. Shackleford on the east, and
- A piece of Land allotted for his Copyhold under Winchester College (called high Holmes) on the North.

11 To the said Richard Wake for his copyhold under Winchester College called High Holmes, one acre three Roods and thirty two perches, having:
- The Land of John Budd of Tenantry on the west,
- The Land allotted for his Copyhold of Inheritance on the South, and
- A private Road for the House of Mr. Shackleford, the said Richard Wake and James Budd on the East, and
- The Land allotted [for] one other Copyhold under Winchester College on the North.

12 To the said Richard Wake for his Copyhold under Winchester College (called two Acres), parcel of the Land called (Lymington) one Acre one Rood, and thirty four perches:
- The Allotment of Land to the last above mentioned Copyhold on the South,
- The Land of John Budd on Tenantry on the west,
- The Land allotted to his Copyhold under Saint Mary Magdalen College in Oxford on the North & the said private Road on the East.

13 To the said Richard Wake for his Copyhold under Saint Mary Magdalen College in Oxford [the Copy says four Acres] three Roods and thirty six perches:
- Lying on the North side of the Allotment of Land last above mentioned between the Land of John Budd of Tenantry and the said private Road, and
- The allotment of Land to one other of his Copyholds under Winchester College on the North.

14 To the said Richard Wake for one other Copyhold under Winchester College [the Copy mentions six Acres] three Roods and thirty six perches:
- Between the Allotment of Land last above mentioned, and
- The allotment Land to his Leasehold of two thousand years, and
- Between the Land of John Budd of Tenantry and the said private Road.

15 To the said Richard Wake for his Leasehold of two thousand years (under late John Henley Esq) three Roods and thirty six perches:
- Between the Allotment of Land last above mentioned and the Allotment for his other Leasehold of two thousand year and between [end page 2]
- The Land of John Budd of Tenantry on the west, and
- The said private Road on the East.

16 To the said Richard Wake for his other Leasehold of two thousand years (under the late John Henley Esq) twenty Acres, three Roods and ten perches:
- The Land of John Budd of Tenantry on the west,
- The London Road on the North, and
- The said private Road on the East,

and allow'd him more to him Eight perches for a Dell in his said Lands.

17 To John Budd of Tenantry for his Copy of Lives under Winchester College (the Leasehold Lymington Close) one Acre one Rood and three perches:
   • An allotment of William Budd's of Soldridge on the west,
   • The King's Highway on the North,
   • The Garden of Thomas Cane on the East, and
   • The Land hereinafter mentioned to be allotted for his Copyhold under Magdalen College on the South.

18 To the said John Budd of Tenantry for Copyhold under Saint Mary Magdalen College in Oxford One Acre one Rood and three perches:
   • His Land for the said Copy under Winchester College last above mentioned on the North,
   • An Allotment of William Budd of Soldridge on the west,
   • The remaining part of the piece being part of his Allotment for his Copyhold of Inheritance on the South, and
   • The Soldridge Bottom Road on the East part.

19 To the said John Budd of Tenantry for his Copyhold of Inheritance of forty five Acres one Rood and five perches (and in his whole Allotment sixty eight perches more Allow'd for Dells and Ground spoil'd by Roads) lying in five pieces:
   One piece:
   • The Land of William Budd of Soldridge on the West and South-west,
   • The Road leading from Ropley to Soldridge on the East, and
   • The Land allotted to Magdalen College on the North.
   One other piece:
   • The Land of William Budd of Soldridge on the West,
   • The London Road on the North,
   • The Soldridge Bottom Road on the East and
   • The piece of Land in Soldridge Bottom, which is left waste for the use of the poor, a Cottage, Garden now of William Crockford and part of a Way leading from Allen's to Thomas Worde's on the South,
   One other piece call'd Coppice end piece:
   • The London Road on the South and East,
   • The Land and Coppice of the said John Budd on the west and North,
   One other piece:
   • The London Road on the North,
   • The Land of Richard Wake on the East,
   • The Soldridge Bottom Road and the Garden and Paddock of Thomas Budd and the widow Oakey on the west,
   • The Allotment for his other Copy of Lives under Winchester College on the South,
   One other piece:
   • The Land of John Burnel and Armiger Baily on the North,
   • Basingstoke Road on the East,
   • John Camois Way on the South, and
   • The Land of Mr. Barnard on the west.

20 To the said John Budd of Tenantry for his other Copy of Lives under Winchester
College which he purchased of John Budd of Shalden twenty eight Acres one
Rood and eight perches:
- The Land belonging to the parish of Ropley to the South,
- Soldridge Bottom Way on the West,
- An Allotment to his Copyhold of Inheritance on the North and
- The Land of Richard Wake on the East part thereof.

21 To Mary Budd of Ropley Widow for her Copyhold under Magdalen College,
two Acres two Roods and six perches with five perches more Allow'd for a Dell.
- The Land of William Budd of Soldridge on the East,
- Land belonging to Ropley on the South,
- The Land of Thomas Mould on the North, and
- A piece of her former enclosed Land on the west.

22 To James Budd for his Copyhold of Inheritance, seven Acres and four perches:
- The London Road on the North,
- The Land of his Brother John Budd on the East,
- The Land of Mr. Shackleford on the South, and
- A private Road for Mr. Shackleford, Richard Wake and the said James Budd
on the west. [end page 3]

23 To John Budd Brother of the said James Budd for his Freehold four Acres and
two Roods:
- The Land of the said James Budd on his West,
- The Land of Mr. Shackleford on the South,
- The Land of the Widow Prior, William Prior and John Finden on the East,
and
- The London Road on the North.

24 To Elizabeth Prior Widow for her Copyhold under Winchester Collage, one
acre three Roods and twenty four perches:
- The Land of Mr. Shackleford on the South,
- The Land of the above named John Budgon on the West,
- The Land of William Prior on the North, and Lymington Road on the East.

25 To the said Elizabeth Prior for her Copyhold of Inheritance, four Acres one
Rood and thirty eight perches Lying in two pieces:
One adjoins to:
- The Common field the Land of John Harrison on the South West,
- The Land of John Budd of Lower House on the Northwest, and
- Stankham Road on the South-East.
The other piece called Towzer's Bank:
- A Road leading from bottom Camois to a piece of Land belonging to John
Camois on the North,
- The land of the said John Camois on the South-East,
- A meadow plot on the West, and
- The land of Mr. Barnard, Richard Wake and John Budd of Tenantry on the
South

Through which said piece of Land call'd Towzer's Bank, there is a Road of a Rod wide for the use of the said John Camois, Mr. Barnard, Richard Wake and John Budd of Tenantry their Heirs and Assigns with Cattle Carts ploughs and Waggons at all times to pass and repass to and from their respective Lands and premises.

And Whereas there must be a good Quantity of fencing to fence off from Roads the said piece call'd Towzer's Bank, it is thought necessary and convenient that the said Elizabeth Prior her Heirs and Assigns may Erect and Sett up a Gate at the North-End of the Said Road to keep back the Cattle which are feeding in the Lanes, from feeding in the said Road and piece of Land call'd Towzer's Bank aforesaid.

26 To William Prior for his Lease of Lives which he holds under Anthony Henley Esq three Acres, three Roods, and nine perches:
  • The Land of the Widow Prior on the South,
  • The Land of the above named John Budd on the West,
  • The Land of John Finden on the North, and
  • Lymington Road on the East.

27 To John Finden for his Freehold five Acres and twelve perches:
  • The Land of William Prior on the South,
  • The Land of John Budd on the west,
  • The London Road on the North, and
  • Lymington Road on the East.

28 To William Budd of Soldridge for his Leasehold of two thousand years from James Yoolding, twelve Acres and eight perches with twenty four perches more allow'd for Dells, lying in two pieces:
    Of one piece:
  • His Majesty's Highway on the Southwest and North and
  • An Allotment of John Budd of Tenantry on the East
    the other piece:
  • The Land and Lane of Mary Budd Widow on the West,
  • The Land belonging to the Parish of Ropley on the South, and
  • An Allotment of the said John Budd's Land and the Soldridge Road on the North, North-East and East parts thereof.

29 To the Rev. Mr. Soley for this Glebe, one Acre three Roods and twenty four perches with four perches more, allow'd for part of a Dell:
  • The Land of Mr. Stephen's on the North,
  • Mr Shackleford's Wood called Hooks wood on the East,
  • A Road or way for John Camois to his land call'd great Hooks on the South, and
  Stankham Road on the Northwest.

30 To the Rev. Mr. Stephens for his Leasehold of one thousand years from Anthony Henley Esq two Roods and three perches: [end page 4]
  • The Land of John Spencer on the North,
  • Mr Shackleford's Hook's wood on the East,
  • The Land belonging to his Freehold on the South, and

- Stankham Road on the North West.

31 To the said Mr Stephens for his Freehold two Roods and thirty perches:
- Lying between the Allotments for his two Leaseholds,
- Mr. Shackleford's Hook's Wood on the East, and
- Stankham Road on the North west part thereof.

32 To the said Mr Stephens for his other Leasehold of two thousand years, which he purchased of John Camois two Roods and thirty perches, with two perches more allow'd for part of a Dell:
- Lying between his Allotment for his Freehold and the Allotment for the Glebe,
- Mr. Shackleford's Hooks wood on the East, and
- Stankham Road on the North-West.

33 To John Spencer for his Copy of Lives under Winchester College four Acres and twenty eight perches:
Lying in two pieces:
- One on the North side of Mr. Stephens' Allotment,
- Mr. Shackleford's hooks wood on the East, and Stankham Road on the North West part thereof.
  The other piece:
- The Allotment for his Copyhold under Magdalen College on the South,
- The Land of John White on the East,
- The Land of Richard Bone on the West, and
- Linsum Road on the North.

34 To the said John Spencer for his Copyhold under Saint Mary Magdalen College in Oxford one Acre one Rood and three perches of Land:
- The Garden to a Cottage in possession of William Lover on the East,
- The Land of Richard Bone on the West,
- The Road leading from William Lover's to William Moulds on the South-East,
- The Allotment for his Copy of Lives, under Winchester College on the North.

35 To John Harrison for his Copyhold of Inheritance two Acres two Roods and six perches with eight perches more allow'd for Dells:
- The Land of John Budd of Lower House on the South-West and North-West;
- The Land of Elizabeth Prior on the North-East and
- Stankham Road on the South-East part thereof.

36 To John Budd of Lower House for his Freehold seventy two Acres with eighty seven perches more allow'd for Dells and Stoney places in his Allotment:
- The Land of John Harrison on the North-East,
- Stankham Road, Silvester's Garden and Linsum Road on the South-East and South,
- The Basingstoke Road and his Allotment for his Leasehold on the West, and
- His Wood called the Grove on the North part thereof.

37 To the said John Budd of his Leasehold of one thousand years, which he purchased of John Camois two Roods and twenty one perches:

- The Land of John Burnell on the North,
- The said Basingstoke Road on the West, and
- His Allotment of Land for his Freehold on the East and South parts thereof.

38 To Thomas Hockley for his Copyhold of Inheritance, two Acres, one Rood and eleven perches:
- The Land of John White on the West,
- Linsum Road on the North,
- His Majesty's Highway on the South-East, and
- A Garden to a Cottage now in possession of the Widow Hall on the South part thereof.

39 To John White for his Copyhold of Inheritance one Acre, one Rood and three perches,
- The Land of Thomas Hockley on the East,
- The Land of John Spencer on the West,
- William Lover's Garden on the South and
- Linsum Road on the North.

40 To John Prior for his Copy of Lives under Winchester College, thirty two Acres three Roods and thirty eight perches, with fifty perches more allow'd for Dells lying in [end page 5] Three pieces:
One piece:
- Linsum Road on the North,
- The Land of Richard Bone on the East,
- William Mould's Garden and paddock on the South,
- A foot way four foot wide, of Water Way for the poor people to drive a wheel Barrow to fetch water, on the West.
One other piece:
- The Land of John Camois on the South,
- A Lane leading from the Widow Halls towards John Smith's on the North and North West, and
- His Majesty's Highway on the East.
The other piece lies:
- On the South Side of Hacket Road,
- The Basingstoke Road on the South West and
- Mr Barnard's Land on the East and South thereof.

41 To John Camois for his freehold eleven Acres, three Roods and four perches, lying in two pieces:
One contains thirty nine perches:
- The Road which leads from Medstead Street towards Soldridge on the West, and
- His buildings Barkside Garden and premises on the East.
The other piece lies:
- On the South Side of the Land of John Prior, and
- On the North side of his Allotment to his Leasehold
- Between The King's Highway on the East, and
- A Lane leading from the Widow Hall's towards Hacket Pond on the West.

42 To the said John Camois for his leasehold of two thousand years (from late John Henley Esq) Eleven Acres three Roods and four perches, with seventy five perches more for Dells and Stony Land:
  * The Hacket Road on the South,
  * The King's Highway on the East,
  * The Lane leading from John Smith's to Hacket pond on the West, and
  * His Allotment to his freehold on the North.

43 To John Burnell for his Copyholds of Inheritance thirty seven Acres one Rood and twenty eight perches, lying in three pieces (with seventy seven Rods [*taken as error for 'perches'*] more allowing for Dells):

  One piece:
  * Lies on the South of Linsum Way, and
  * On the North of John Bulbeck's Land,
  * The little four foot Water-way on the East, and
  * Basingstoke Road on the West.

  One other piece:
  * Lies between the Basingstoke Road, and the land belonging to Bighton, and
  * The Land of John Bulbeck on the South.

  The other piece:
  * Lies on the South side of Hacket Road,
  * The Land of Armiger Bayly on the East,
  * The land of John Bulbeck on the West, and
  * The Land of John Budd of Tenantry and Mr. Barnard on the South.

44 To Richard Bone for his Copyhold of Inheritance, three Acres three Roods and nine perches, with thirteen perches more allow'd for a Dell:
  * The Land of John Prior on the West,
  * The Land of John Spencer on the East
  * The Lane from the Widow Halls towards Hacket Pond on the South-East, and
  * Linsum Road on the North.

45 To John Bulbeck for his Copyright of Inheritance, Twenty eight acres and thirty one perches lying in three pieces (with forty three perches more allow'd for Dells):

  One piece hath:
  * The Land of John Burnell on the North [multi-word deletion]
  * The Land belonging to the parish of Bighton on the West,
  * The Land of John Hicks on the South and
  * Basingstoke Road on the North East.

  One other piece:
  * The land of John Burnell on the North,
  * The said John Hicks on the South,
  * Part of the Said four foot water-way, the Garden of John Smith a Cottager, and part of a Lane leading from the said John Smith's towards Hacket Pond on the East, and
  * The Basingstoke Road on the South West.

The other [end page 6] Piece:

- The Land of Mr. Barnard on the South
- The Land of John Hickson on the West,
- The Land of John Burnell on the east and
- Hacket Road on the North.

46 To John Hicks for his Copyhold of Inheritance, thirty five Acres two Roods and twenty one Perches lying in three pieces (with thirty five perches more allow'd for Dells):

One hath:

- The Land belonging to the Parish of Bighton on the West
- The Land of John Bulbeck on the North,
- Hacket Road on the South, and
- Basingstoke Road on the North East.

One other piece hath:

- The Basingstoke Road on the South West,
- The Land of John Bulbeck on the North
- Hacket Road on the South
- A Lane leading by John Smith's to Hacket pond on the East.

The other piece hath:

- The Land belonging to Bighton on the West
- The Land of John Bulbeck in the East
- Hacket Road on the North, and
- The Land of Mr Barnard on the South.

47 To Armiger Bayly for his Copy of Inheritance for twenty Sheep Commons and two Hog Commons in the Bishop of Winchester's late Wood call'd Stankham, five Acres:

- The Land of John Budd of Tenantry on the South,
- The Land of John Burnell on the West
- Basingstoke Road on the North East, and
- Hacket Road on the North

48 To John Barnard Esq for his Freehold eighty five Acres, two Roods and twenty two perches, lying in four pieces, with ninety three perches more allow'd for Dells:

One piece hath:

- Hacket Road on the North,
- A Road leading from Stankham Gate to Soldridge on the East
- London Road on the South, and
- Basingstoke Road on the South-West

One other piece:

- The Basingstoke Road on the North-East,
- The London Road on the South,
- The Land belonging to the parish of Bighton on the West,
- The Land of John Hicks, John Bulbeck, John Burnell and John Budd of Tenantry on the North

One other piece hath:

- The London Road on the North
- The Land of Edward Woolls on the East and
- Certain Lands call'd Ramscomb on the South and South-West
  His other piece:
- The Land of him the said John Barnard on the West,
- The Road leading from pace Lane towards Five Ash pond on the North
- The Land allotted to William Skinner on the East, and
- The London Road on the South.

49   To William Wake for his Leasehold of two thousand years from James Yoolding six Acres three Roods and thirty six perches, lying in two pieces with six perches more allow'd for the Picked Corner, and six perches more allow'd for a Dell:
  One piece hath:
- The London Road on the North
- The Basingstoke Road on the South-West, and
- The Lands of him the said William Wake on the South-East.
  The other piece:
- The Land of Edward Woolls on the west
- The London Road on the North,
- Basingstoke Road on the North-East, and
- Certain Lands call'd Ramscomb on the South.

50   To Edward Woolls for his Copyhold of Inheritance one Acre three Roods and twenty-four perches, with two perches more allow'd for a Dell:
- The London Road on the North
- The Land of William Wake on the East,
- Certain Lands call'd Ramscomb on the South, and
- The Land of Mr. Barnard on the West [end page 7]

Public Roads

We Sett out and Appoint the following Publick Roads on Soldridge Common:
- One Road called the London Road sixty feet wide from the East End of the said Common call'd Redhill to the West call'd Soldridge.
- One other Road thirty foot wide from pace Lane and from South-Town by five ash pond and Lymington Ground towards Ropley, and
- One Road thirty foot wide from the London Road between the Soldridge Houses in the Bottom towards Ropley.
- On Stankham Common, one Road call'd the London Road sixty foot wide from the East End of the said Common call'd Soldridge, to the West and call'd Bighton lower Way.
- One other Road thirty foot wide call'd Hacket Road, from Bighton Hacket way to Pace Lane.
- One other Road thirty foot wide call'd Linsum Road from Breath Lane By Silvesters to Stankham Road.
- One other Road, thirty foot wide from Stankham Gate, by Bottom Camois's and John Camois's to the London Road.
- One other Road thirty foot wide call'd Basingstoke Road from Gullett Lane to Heath Green.

We appoint that causeways be made in all the publick Roads which are less than sixty foot wide.

We Sett out and appoint the following private Roads.

1 To John Shackleford Esq, John Barnard Esq, Richard Wake and William Prior, their heirs, Executors and Assigns, a Lane leading from the London Road to Boynes, exclusive of all other persons, and they only to repair the same.

2 To John Barnard Esq, his heirs and Assigns, a way a Rod wide from Fielder's Corner on the North side of the Lane of John Budd of Shalden, so far Eastward as the said John Barnard's middle long Lease Gate, and the said John Budd his heirs and Assigns to keep the way in good repair; and to fence the same off if required.

3 To John Shackleford Esq, Richard Wake and James Budd, their heirs Executors and Assigns a Lane leading from the North side of the London Road into the Several lands of the said John Shackleford Richard Wake and James Budd, exclusive of all other persons, and they only to repair the same.

4 To Mary Budd of Ropley widow her heirs Executors and Assigns a Lane a Rod wide to her Land, who are to repair the Same.

5 A lane a Rod wide from the London Road at Soldridge by William Moulds and Allows for the use of the Poor and to be repaired by the Parish.

6 To John Camois his heirs Executors and Assigns the use of a Lane a Rod wide from the Stankham Road to his piece of Land call'd Great Hooks who are to repair the same.

7 To the said John Camois his heirs Executors and Assigns, a Way a Rod wide, thro' the Land of Mr. Barnard on the South Side of a piece of Land allotted to John Budd of Tenantry and into the London Road to be used with Horses Carts Waggons and Ploughs to his Lands call'd Hides keeping the said Way in good repair, and not drive any Cattle loose. [end page 8]

8 A lane a Rod and an half wide from the Widow Hall's to William Lovers, William Moulds and John Smith to Hacket Pond for the use of the poor people, and to be repair'd by the Parish.

We Sett out and appoint the Foot Ways:

1 From Silvesters thro' John Budd's Land of Lower House, to the Stile Moreys Close.

2 From Beathgreen Lane End Strait to the New Gate by Linsum Road.

3 From Moulds' and Smith's Strait to Breath Lane End.

4 From Smith's and Moulds' to Hacket Pond and then thro' the Lands of John Prior to John Camois's Draught way in Mr Barnard's Land to Pye way leading to Bighton down.

5 From the North Side of Oakleys House at Soldridge thro' the Lands of John Budd of Tenantry, Richard Wake, and Mr Shackleford to the London Road at the East End of the Widow Budd's field of Ropley.

6 From the upper end of Hacket Pond thro' Mr. Barnards New Enclosures into the Road opposite to his middle Gate in his old Enclosures call'd Soldridge.

7 From Skinners thro' the upper Side of Mr. Barnard's Close call'd little Puckerett into the London Road.

8   From Mr. Barnard's middle Long Lees Strait thro' John Budd of Shalden's Land into the London Road.

9   From the Lane end of Thomas Hanham's hedge Corner thro' the Land of William Budd of Soldridge and the Widow Budd's of Ropley to the Stile that enters into Mr. Thomas Budd of Alton's Ground.

10 From piece Lane across John Camois's Ground into the Water Lane from Smith's to Hacket Pond, and then Southwards to Hicks's Clap-Gate and so to Bighton Hacket Lane End.

We appoint that the Pond on Soldridge Common call'd five ash pond, and that on Stankham Common call'd Hacket Pond Shall remain as they were before the Enclosure, for the use of the Publick, and that no one shall enclose any part of them nor dig within their Land adjoining so as to drain the water from them.

In Witness of Dated the 22nd of March 1736.
Sign'd and Seal'd by
Edward Stawell
Norton Pawlett
Norton Pawlett Jun.
Thomas Bonham
Robert Cropp
William Yalden

Appendix 12: Chawton Commons Act and Agreement, 1740

An Act for confirming and establishing Articles of Agreement and an Award, for dividing and inclosing certain Common Fields, and a Common called Chawton Common, in the Parish of Chawton in the County of Southampton.[1]

Whereas by certain Articles of Agreement indented, bearing Date on or about the Twenty-second Day of May, in the Year of our Lord One thousand Seven hundred and Forty, under the common Seal of the Mayor, Bailiffs and Commonalty of the City of Winchester, and under the common Seal of the Feoffees of the free Grammar School of *John Eggar* of *Moungomeryes*, and under the Hands and Seals of several Persons being Commoners, and having respectively Right and Interest in, over and upon certain common Fields called *Southfield, Northfield, Ridgefield, Whitedown, Winstreetfield, Upper Eastfield, Lower Eastfield,* and a certain Common called *Chawton Common*, in the Parish of Chawton, in the County of Southampton; reciting, That the said Commoners had consented and were desirous, that the common Fields and Common should, for their mutual Benefit, be [end page 1] divided and inclosed, and to avoid Difficulties that might arise touching such Division and Inclosures) they the said Commoners did submit themselves respectively to the Award, Arbitration, Order, final Determination and Judgment of *John Barnard*, of New Alresford in the said County of Southampton, Esq; *Benjamin Reynolds*, of Fleet in the said County, Yeoman; *Bernard Burningham*, of Binsted in the said County, Yeoman; *Thomas Stevens*, of Wield in the said County, Yeoman; *Thomas Earwaker*, of Neatham in the same County, Yeoman; *John Budd*, of *Trinity* in Medstead in the said County, Yeoman; and *John Camies*, of Medstead aforesaid, Yeoman, or any Five of them, by the said Commoners by their said Articles constituted Arbitrators, as well for and concerning the respective Rights and Interest of the Parties who executed or should execute the said Articles in the said common Fields and Common, as for and concerning the apportioning, dividing and inclosing the same to and amongst the said Commoners claiming any Right in the said common Fields and Common, and allotting and laying out Highways, and Ways, Paths and Passages to and from such Apportionments and Allotments respectively, so as the same Arbitrators, or any Five of them, should and did make and publish their Award of and concerning the Premises in Writing under their Hands and Seals before the Feast-day of St. Michael the Archangel then next coming after the Date of the said Articles: And it is by the said Articles covenanted, granted condescended unto, concluded and agreed by and between the Parties, and each of them did covenant, grant, condescend unto, conclude and agree to and with every other, for themselves severally, and for their respective Heirs, Successors and Assigns, that they, and each of them, and the Heirs, Executors, Administrators, Successors and Assigns of them, and each of them, for their and each of their Parties, should and would perform and keep the Submission, and every Agreement in the said Articles mentioned: And further, in case an Award

---

1   Private Act, 14 George II, c. 12 (HL/PO/PB/1/1740/14G2n44).

should be made in pursuance thereof, that then the Parties to the said Articles, or any One or more of them, might apply to the Parliament, in order to obtain an Act for establishing and confirming such Award as should be so made of and concerning the Premises:

And whereas the said *John Barnard, Benjamin Reynolds, Bernard Burningham, Thomas Stevens, Thomas Earwaker* and *John Camies,* Six of the said Referees, afterwards (to wit, on the Twenty-seventh Day of September then next coming after the Date of the said Articles) made their Award in Writing under their Hands and Seals of that Date, (reciting that they had surveyed and viewed the said common Fields and Common, that the said common Fields had been measured, and that they had considered of the Value of each of the said common Fields by the Acre, and that each respective Commoner might have his Proportion in the said common Fields) and thereby did order, [end page 1] award and appoint to the several Commoners aforesaid the several Pieces and Allotments of Land in the said Award, and herein after particularly mentioned and expressed, as and for their several and respective Shares, Proportions and Allotments of the common Fields and Common aforesaid; [end page 2] and that they and every of them should respectively exchange and relinquish all their other Lands whatsoever in the said common Fields and Common, and their respective Rights of Common therein in lieu of the same, and should inclose and fence in such their Allotments in Manner in the said Award and herein after-mentioned; (*That is to say*) As for and concerning the said common Fields, they the said Arbitrators did award, appoint and allot:

To Thomas Knight, Esquire, Lord of the Manor of Chawton aforesaid,
1   All that Field called White Downfield, containing Thirty-three Acres Three Roods and Twenty-three Perches, abutting:
   • East to the Highway leading from Alton to Winchester,
   • South to inclosed Lands of the said Thomas Knight,
   • West to a Way leading to Ackner Coppice,
   • North to a Highway called Whitedown-Lane;
2   And also the said Thomas Knight All that Field called Lower Eastfield, containing Forty-six Acres and Thirty-one Perches, abutting:
   • East to inclosed Lands of the said Thomas Knight,
   • West to inclosed Lands of the said Thomas Knight and of the Reverend Doctor Harris and Mary Harris,
   • North to Upper Eastfield, to an Inclosure of Glebe Lands and to a Way leading to Hartley;
3   And also to the said Thomas Knight in Southfield, One Piece of Land containing Thirty-six Acres Two Roods and Thirty-three Perches, abutting:
   • East to an Allotment of Michael Harris, to an Allotment of the Glebe Land, and to inclosed Land of the said Thomas Knight,
   • South to inclosed Lands of the said Thomas Knight,
   • West to an Allotment of the said Doctor Harris and Mary Harris, and inclosed Lands of the said Thomas Knight and the said Doctor Harris,

- North to an Allotment and inclosed Lands of the said Doctor Harris and Mary Harris, and to the Way leading to Crockland and Inbook;

And that the said Thomas Knight shall make the Fences thereof against the said Way, and against the South End of the said Doctor Harris and Mary Harris Allotment in Smockveer; And that the said Thomas Knight shall have Right of the usual Way to the said Piece through the Parsonage-yard and Close, and an Allotment to the Glebe Lane;

4   And also to the said Thomas Knight in Upper Eastfield, One Piece of Land containing Sixteen Acres and Thirty-six Perches, abutting:
- East to an Allotment and an Inclosure of the said Doctor Harris and Mary Harris,
- South and West to inclosed Lands of the said Thomas Knight,
- North to an Allotment of the Corporation of Winchester, and inclosed Lands of the said Robert Eames;

and that the said Thomas Knight shall make the Fence against the said Allotment of the said Doctor Harris;

5   And also to the said Thomas Knight One other Piece of Land containing Ten Acres One Rood and Ten Perches, abutting:
- East to an Allotment of the Corporation of Winchester,
- South and West to inclosed Lands of the said Thomas Knight,
- North to the Allotment of Rowland Prowting, to the Allotment of the free Grammar-School of John Eggar, and to the Allotment of the said Robert Eames;

and that the said Thomas Knight shall make the Fence against the said Allotments of the Corporation of Winchester, and of the free Grammar School, and of the said Robert Eames.

To the Corporation of Winchester
1   All that Field called Ridgefield, containing Nineteen Acres Three Roods and Thirteen Perches, abutting
- West to the Way set out [end page 3] at the East End of Northfield,
- North to inclosed Lands of the said Corporation, and of the said Thomas Knight and Robert Eames,
- South East to inclosed Lands of the said Corporation, and of the said Robert Eames, and
- South to inclosed Lands of the said Thomas Knight;

2   And also to the said Corporation of Winchester One Piece of Land called the First or East Veer in the Northfield, containing Thirteen Acres Three Roods and Thirty-five Perches (after deducting a Way Twenty Feet wide on the East Side next to Ridgefield leading from the Shrave Road to the Paceway Road) abutting
- East to the said new Way,
- South to a Highway called the Shrave,
- West to an Allotment and Inclosure of the said Robert Eames, and
- North to the Paceway Road;

and that the said Corporation shall make the Fence next to the said new Way;

3   And also to the said Corporation One other Piece of Land in the said North
Field called the Third Veer, containing Eleven Acres, abutting
- East to an Allotment and Inclosure of the said Robert Eames,
- South to a Highway called the Shrave Road,
- West to an Allotment of the said free Grammar School, and to an Inclosure
  of the said Corporation, and
- North to the Paceway Road;
  and that the said Corporation shall make the Fence on the East Side next to
  an Allotment of the said Robert Eames;

4   And also to the said Corporation One Piece of Land in the upper East Field,
containing Twelve Acres Two Roods and Thirty-two Perches, abutting
- East to an Allotment and an Inclosure of the said Robert Eames,
- South to an Allotment of the said Thomas Knight,
- West to another Allotment of his the said Thomas Knight and of the said
  Robert Eames, and
- North to a Way leading to Hartley;
  and that the said Corporation shall make the Fences against the said Way,
  and against the said Allotment of the said Thomas Knight at the South End:

To the Reverend Master John Baker, for his Glebe Land

1   One Piece of Land in Southfield, containing Nine Acres One Rood and Fourteen
Perches, abutting
- East to two Inclosures of Glebe Lands,
- South to an Inclosure of the said Thomas Knight,
- West and North to other Allotments of his the said Thomas Knight and the
  said Michael Harris
  and that the said John Baker shall make a Fence on the West and North Side
  of the said Allotment, and shall allow a Way for the Use of the said Thomas
  Knight through the Parsonage-yard and Close, and through the said Allotment,
  to and from the Southfield:

To Doctor John Harris and Mary his Wife

1   One Piece of Land in Southfield, containing Twenty-eight Acres Two Roods
and Fourteen Perches, abutting
- East to an Inclosure of the said Doctor John Harris and Mary Harris called
  Beans-Close, and to a Way leading from Shrave Road to the Southfield,
- South to a Way leading to Crockland and Inbook and to the said Inbook
  Woods, and an Inclosure of the said Doctor Harris and Mary Harris,
- West to Chawton Common and Inbook Wood,
- North to the Shrave Road;
  and that the said Doctor Harris and Mary Harris shall make the Fence
  against the Way at the East End;

2   And also to the said Doctor John Harris and Mary Harris One other Piece of
Land in the Southfield, containing Three Acres Three Roods and Five Perches,
abutting

- East and South to an Allotment of the said Thomas Knight,
- West to an Inclosure of the said Doctor Harris and Mary Harris, and
- North to the Way leading to Crockland;

and the said Doctor Harris and [end page 4] Mary Harris shall make the Fence on the East Side and North End of the said last mentioned Allotment, and shall allow a Way where it now is, and usually has been, to and from the Inbook Woods;

3   And also to the said Doctor John Harris and Mary Harris One other Piece of Land in Upper Eastfield, called Lower Marslet-Veer, containing Five Acres Three Roods and Twenty Perches, abutting

- East and South to Lower East-field,
- West to an Allotment of the said Thomas Knight, and
- North to an Inclosure of the said Doctor Harris and Mary Harris called Summergate, and to an Inclosure of Glebe Land; which last-mentioned Allotment we judge convenient for the said Doctor Harris and Mary Harris, on account of its lying between their two Inclosures called Summergate and Holebrook-Close, there being no other Way to Holebrook:

To the Feoffees of the free Grammar-School of John Eggar

1   All that field called Winstreet-Field, containing Nine Acres and One Perch, abutting

- North-east to an Inclosure of John Goodyer,
- South-east to the Highway leading from Alton to Chawton,
- South-west to inclosed Lands of the said free Grammar-School, and of the said Thomas Knight, and Robert Eames, and
- North-west to the Highway from Alton to Chawton Common;

2   and also to the said Feoffees of the said free Grammar School, One Piece of Land in the Northfield, called the West Veer, containing Six Acres Three Roods and Five Perches, abutting

- East to an Allotment of the Corporation of Winchester,
- South to the Shrave Road,
- West to an Inclosure of the said free Grammar-School, and an Inclosure of the Corporation of Winchester, and
- North to an Inclosure of the said Corporation;

    and that the said Feoffees shall make the Fence on the East Side of the said Allotment;

3   and also the said Feoffees of the said free Grammar School, One Piece of Land in Upper Eastfield, containing Seven Acres Two Roods and Twenty-four Perches, abutting

- East to an Allotment of the said Robert Eames,
- South to an Allotment of the said Thomas Knight,
- West to an Allotment of Rowland Prowting,
- North to a Way leading to Hartley;

    and that the said Feoffees shall make the Fence on the East and North Sides of the said Allotment:

To Robert Eames

1   One Piece of Land in Northfield, called the Second Veer, from the East End, containing Six Acres One Rood and Twenty-one Perches, abutting
    • East and West to an Allotment of the said Corporation,
    • South to the Shrave Road, and
    • North to an Inclosure of the said Robert Eames;
      and that the said Robert Eames shall make a Fence on the East Side of the said Allotment:

2   And also the said Robert Eames, One other Piece of Land, in the Upper Eastfield, containing Three Acres and Two Roods, abutting
    • East to an Inclosure of the said Doctor John Harris and Mary Harris,
    • South to an Inclosure of the said Robert Eames,
    • West to an Allotment of the said Corporation of Winchester, and
    • North to a Way leading to Hartley;
      and that the said Robert Eames shall make a Fence on the West Side and North End of the said Allotment:

3   And also the said Robert Eames, One other Piece of Land in the Upper East-Field, containing Eight Acres Two Roods and Four Perches, abutting
    • East and South to an Allotment of the said Corporation of Winchester,
    • West to an Allotment of the said free Grammar-School, and
    • North to a [end page 5] Way leading to Hartley;
      and that the said Robert Eames shall make a Fence at the East-Side and the North End of the said Allotment:

To Joan Prowting, Widow, her Copyhold

1   One Piece of Land in Upper Eastfield, containing Six Acres Two Roods and Seven Perches, abutting
    • East to an Allotment of Rowland Prowting his Copyhold,
    • South to an Inclosure of the said Thomas Knight,
    • West to Inclosures of his the said Thomas Knight, and of the said Corporation of Winchester, and
    • North to the Way leading to Hartley;
      and that the said Joan Prowting shall make the Fence on the East Side and North End of the said Allotment:

To Rowland Prowting

1   his Copyhold, One Piece of Land in Upper Eastfield, containing Six Acres Two Roods and Thirty-eight Perches, abutting
    • East to an Allotment of the Feoffees of the said free Grammar School,
    • South to an Allotment and Inclosure of the said Thomas Knight,
    • West to an Allotment of the said Joan Prowting, and
    • North to the Way leading to Hartley;
      and that the said Rowland Prowting shall make the Fence on the East Side, and North End of the said Allotment:

To Michael Harris
1   his Copyhold, One Piece of Land, Part of Southfield, called Tard-Mill, containing One Rood and Nineteen Perches, abutting
    • East to Inclosures of the said Doctor John Harris and Mary Harris, and of the said Robert Eames, and of the said Michael Harris,
    • South to an Inclosure of the said Thomas Knight, and to an Allotment of the said Michael Harris,
    • West to an Inclosure of the said Doctor John Harris and Mary Harris,
    • North to an Inclosure of the said Joan Prowting:
2   And also to the said Michael Harris, his Copyhold, One other Piece of Land, in Southfield, containing Five Acres and Thirty-two Perches, abutting
    • East to an Inclosure of the said Thomas Knight, and of the said Doctor Harris and Mary Harris,
    • South to an Allotment of Glebe Land,
    • West to an Allotment of the said Thomas Knight, and
    • North to an Inclosure of the said Doctor John Harris and Mary Harris, and to the Way leading to Crockland and Inbook;
        and that the said Michael Harris shall make a Fence on the West End, and against the Way on the North Side of the said Allotment.

And the said Arbitrators did by their said Award recite, that it appeared to them, as well by the Information of Persons then living, as also by the Court-Rolls, of and by several Presentments made at several Courts held for the Manor of Chawton aforesaid, that the Right of Common upon the said Chawton Common, is by a Stint, at the Rate of Three Sheep for every Acre of the said Common Fields, and therefore in Proportion to each Person's Lands lying in the said common Fields, they the said Arbitrators did by their Award appoint and allot out of the said Common,

To the said Thomas Knight
1   One Piece of Land, containing Twenty-one Acres, abutting
    • East to Read's Coppice and Read's Close,
    • South to the lower Road upon the Common,
    • West to an Allotment of Glebe Lane, and
    • North to the upper Road upon the Common;
        and that the said Thomas Knight shall make the Fences all round the said Piece:
2   And also the said Thomas Knight, One other Piece on the South Side of the said lower Road, containing Twelve Acres and One Rood, abutting
    • East to an Allotment of the said Robert Eames,
    • South to Farringdon Common,
    • West to a Way leading to Worthimy Gate, and
    • North to the said lower Road;
        and that the said Thomas Knight, shall make the Fences against the lower Road, and against the Road leading to Worthimy [end page 6] Gate aforesaid;

3   And also the said Thomas Knight One other Piece, Part of the said Common, containing One hundred and Five Acres and Two Roods, abutting
- East to an Allotment of the Corporation of Winchester aforesaid,
- South to the said lower Road,
- West to the Road leading from Readhill to Four Mark Gate, and
- North to the upper Road;
  and that the said Thomas Knight, shall make the Fences against the said Roads on the South, West, and North Sides;

4   and also in Consideration of the Privileges and Rights upon the said Common belonging to the said Thomas Knight, as Lord of the said Manor, the said Arbitrators did in lieu thereof award and allot to him all that Piece of Land (Part of the said Common) containing Seventeen Acres Five Perches, Part of which is now planted with Wood, and abutting
- South to the said upper Road,
- West to an Inclosure of John Budd, and
- North to Chawton Park, and an Inclosure of John Budd,
  and that the said Thomas Knight shall make the Fence against the said upper Road;

5   And also, that the said Thomas Knight shall have the Herbage of all the Highways taken out of the said Common:

And the said Arbitrators, by their said Award, did appoint and allot out of the said Common;

To the Corporation of Winchester
1   one Piece of Land, containing Fifty-eight Acres Two Roods and Ten Perches, abutting
- East to an Allotment of the Glebe Lane,
- South to the lower Road,
- West to an Allotment of the said Thomas Knight, and
- North to the upper Road;
  and that the said Corporation shall make the Fences to the South, West and North Sides.

To the Reverend Master John Baker
1   his Glebe, One Piece, Part of the said Common, containing Twelve Acres Three Roods, abutting
- East to an Allotment of the said Thomas Knight,
- South to the lower Road,
- West to an Allotment of the Corporation of Winchester, and
- North to the upper Road;
  and that the said John Baker shall make the Fences on the South Side next to the lower Road, and on the West Side next to the Allotment of the Corporation of Winchester, and on the North Side next to the upper Road:

To the said Doctor John Harris and Mary Harris

1   One Piece of Land, Part of the said Common lying at the East End, containing Twenty-seven Acres, abutting
   - East to the Southfield, and Inbook Wood,
   - South to the Lands of the said Doctor John Harris and Mary Harris,
   - West to an Allotment of the Feoffees of the said free Grammar School, and
   - North to the said lower Road;
      and that the said Doctor Harris and Mary Harris shall make the Fences on the West End and North Side of the said Piece;

2   And also to the Doctor John Harris and Mary Harris, One other Piece of Land, containing Five Acres Two Roods and Seven Perches, abutting
   - East to a Coppice and inclosed Lands of the said Doctor Harris and Mary Harris,
   - South to Lands of John Finden,
   - West and North to an Allotment of the Feoffees of the said free Grammar School;
      and that the said Doctor John Harris and Mary Harris shall make the Fences on the West Side and North End next to the Allotment of the free Grammar-School of John Eggar:

To the Feoffees of the said free Grammar School [end page 7]

1   One Piece of Land, Part of the said Common, containing Twenty-four Acres and Five Perches, abutting
   - East to an Allotment and an Inclosure of the said Doctor Harris and Mary Harris,
   - South to an Allotment of the said Doctor Harris and Mary Harris, and inclosed Lands of the said John Finden, and to Farrington Common,
   - West to an Allotment of the said Rowland Prowting, and
   - North to the lower Road;
      and that the said Feoffees shall make the Fence on the West and North Sides of the said Allotment: And

To the said Rowland Prowting for

1   his Copyhold One Piece of Land in the said Common, containing Six Acres One Rood and Thirty-seven Perches, abutting on the
   - East to an Allotment of the Feoffees of the said free Grammar-School, on the
   - South to Farringdon Common aforesaid, on the
   - West to an Allotment of the said Joan Prowting, and
   - North to the said lower Road;
      and that the said Rowland Prowting shall make the Fences on the West Side and North End of the said Allotment:

To the said Joan Prowting for

1   her Copyhold One Piece of Land in the said Common, containing Seven Acres One Rood and Eight Perches, abutting on the

- East to an Allotment of the said Rowland Prowting,
- South to Farringdon Common aforesaid,
- West to an Allotment of the said Robert Eames, and
- North to the said lower Road;

and that the said Joan Prowting shall make the Fences on the West Side and North End of the said Allotment:

To the said Robert Eames

1   For One Piece of Land in the said Common, containing Seventeen Acres and Twenty-seven Perches, abutting on the
- East to an Allotment of the said Joan Prowting,
- South to Farringdon Common aforesaid,
- West to an Allotment of the said Thomas Knight, and
- North to the said lower Road;

and that the said Robert Eames shall make the Fences on the West and North Sides of the said Allotment:

To the said Michael Harris

For his Copyhold One Piece of Land containing Six Acres One Rood and Twenty-six Perches, abutting
- East to a Way leading to Worthimy-Gate aforesaid,
- South to Farringdon Common aforesaid, and
- North-west to the said lower Road;

and that the said Michael Harris shall make the Fences on the East, North and West Sides of the said Allotment;

and the said Arbitrators did by their said Award order and appoint, That the said *Thomas Knight*, as Lord of the Manor of Chawton aforesaid, shall have free Liberty at any time or times on or before the First Day of June, which shall be in the Year of our Lord One thousand Seven hundred and Forty-two, to sell, cut down, grub up, take, cart, and carry away all the Timber-Trees, Pollard-Trees, Bushes and Wood, growing and being on the respective Allotments in the said Common; and for that Purpose it shall be lawful for the Workmen and Servants of the said *Thomas Knight*, to enter into and upon the respective Allotments with or without Horses, Team, Carts, and Carriages;

and they did award and appoint, that *Edward Randall* shall set out

1   One or more Piece of Pieces of Land in the said Common, not exceeding One Acre in the whole, nor to be within any Allotment, which Piece and Pieces of Land shall remain uninclosed, and made use of by the respective Occupiers of the respective Allotments from time to time for a Pond, and digging Chalk for manuring the respective Allotments in the said Common;

and they did further order, [end page 8] award, and appoint, that so much of the said common Fields and Common as herein after-mentioned shall be left uninclosed, and take and used as common Highways, and as common Ways and Droves to and from the several Allotments before-mentioned for Carriages and driving Cattle, and for all other Intents and Purposes as common Ways and Droves are used and enjoyed; (that is to say)

1   In the *Northfield*, at the East End next to *Ridgefield*, One Way or Drove Twenty Feet wide from the *Shrave Road* to the *Pace-way* Road in *Southfield*;

2   One Way or Drove from the *Shrave* Road at the East Corner of Beans Close to the Allotments of the said Doctor *John Harris* and *Mary Harris*, of the said *Thomas Knight*, and *Michael Harris*, and to *Crockland-Gate*, and to *Inbook Woods*, where the Way now is and has usually been;

3   One Way or Drove from the Highway leading from Chawton to Farringdon, into and through the Parsonage-Yard and Close, and through One Allotment of *Glebe Land* in *Southfield* to the Allotment of the said *Thomas Knight*, in the said *Southfield*, where there now is and heretofore has been a Way;

4   That the Highway leading from Chawton to Hartley, at the North Side of the *Upper Eastfield* shall be Thirty Feet wide;

5   That the Highway at the upper Side of the Common leading from Alton to Alresford be Twelve Rods wide from the Corner of *Reads Close* to *Red Hill*;

6   that the Highway at the lower Part of the Common leading from Chawton to Four Mark Gate aforesaid, shall be not less than Forty Feet, nor exceeding Eighty Feet wide from the North-west Corner of *Southfield* so far as to the South-west Corner of *Reads Coppice*, and shall be Forty Feet wide from thence to *Bucklers Tigh*, and shall be Ten Rods wide from *Bucklers Tigh* to *Four Mark Gate* aforesaid;

7   and that the Road leading out of the said last-mentioned Road to *Worthimy-Gate* aforesaid, shall be Four Rods wide;

8   and that the Road from *Four Mark Gate* aforesaid to *Red Hill*, at the West End of the said Common, shall be Three Rods wide; and that the said *Thomas Knight* shall have Liberty of hanging Gates (not to be locked) at each End of the said last-mentioned Road;

9   and that there shall be a Road Thirty Feet wide at the West End of the first-mentioned Allotment on the Common to the said *Thomas Knight*, leading from the upper Road near the Brick-Kiln to the lower Road.

And whereas the carrying the said Award into Execution will be of great Advantage to the Parties concerned in Interest in the Premises, **But** by reason of the Disability of several of them, the same cannot be established and rendered effectual to answer their Intention, without the Aid and Authority of Parliament:

May it therefore please Your Most Excellent MAJESTY,

That it may be **Enacted; And be it Enacted**, by the KING'S Most Excellent Majesty, by and which the Advice and Consent of the Lords Spiritual and Temporal, and Commons, in this present Parliament [end page 9] assembled, and by the Authority of the same, That the said Articles of Agreement, and the said Award, and all and every the Clauses, Matters, and Things, therein respectively contained, and the Division, Distribution, Apportionments, Allotments, and Inclosures of and in the said common Fields, and Common, and the Highways, Ways and Droves, by the said Award directed, appointed, and allotted, shall be, and the same is and are hereby established, ratified, and confirmed, according to the Purport and true Meaning of the said Articles of Submission, and Award respectively; and that the several Pieces or Parcels of Land so allotted or awarded to the several Parties, shall from and after the Twenty-ninth Day of September One thousand Seven hundred and Forty-one, be, and the same is, and are hereby vested, in and to the Use of the several Persons, their Heirs, Successors, Executors, Administrators and Assigns, in Manner and Form, as in this present Act is mentioned.

Provided always, That this Act, or any thing herein contained, shall not extend, or be adjudged to revoke, vary, or annul any Settlement, Deed, Will, or any other Writing whatsoever, or to prejudice any Person or Persons having any Right or Claim of Dower, Jointure, Portion, Debt or Incumbrance of, relating to, out of, or upon, or affecting any of the Premises comprised in the said Award, and this present Act, or any Part or Parcel thereof; but that such and every Proprietor, his, her, and their Heirs, Successors, Executors, Administrators and Assigns, shall respectively stand seized and be possessed of and in the Premises under and by virtue of the aforesaid Articles, Award, and this present Act of Parliament, to such and the same Uses, and for, and subject to, such and the same Estates, Limitations, Debts, and Incumbrances, as he, she, and they respectively should and would have been seized or possessed, had the aforesaid Articles, and the said Award, and this present Act, or either of them, never been made; any thing in the said Articles, and in the said Award, and this present Act, or either of them, contained to the contrary notwithstanding.

And be it also Enacted, That the Highways in the said Award, and herein before-mentioned, shall from the said Twenty-ninth Day of September One thousand Seven hundred and Forty-one, be taken and adjudged, and they are hereby declared to be the common Highways of the said Parish of Chawton, in the said County of Southampton to all Intents and Purposes whatsoever.

And it is hereby further Enacted, by the Authority aforesaid, That the Charges and Expences of passing this Act shall be paid and borne by the Commoners aforesaid, and those having Right in, over, and upon the said common Fields, and Common, ratably in Proportion to the Number of Acres allotted to them respectively by the said Award, and by this Act established, or by such Person or Persons who at the Time of passing this Act shall for this Purpose represent him, her, or them, respectively. [end page 10]

Saving to the KING's Most Excellent Majesty, His Heirs and Successors, and to all and every other Person and Persons, Bodies Politick and Corporate, his, her, and their Heirs, Successors, Executors, and Administrators respectively, (Other than and except the several Commoners, and such as have respectively a Right and Interest to and in the said common Fields and Common aforesaid, or any or either of them, their Heirs, Successors, Executors, Administrators, and Assigns, respectively) All such Estate, Right, Title, and Interest, as they, every or any of them, had and enjoyed in, to, or out of the said common Fields and Common aforesaid, or any or either of them, before the Date of the said Articles, or making this Act, or may, might, or could have or enjoy, in case this Act had never been made. [end page 11]

2	£	s.	d.
Edward Randell's Bill for surveying & making the Common Fields and setting out the several allotments therein, being 309 acres @ 12d. per acre	15	9	0
Ditto for the Common, being 321 acres @ 8d. p. acre	10	14	0
Mr. Baker's Bill for drawing & engrossing Articles of reference, & the award, & attendance, etc.	4	12	10
Mr. Hamlyn's Bill for charge of passing the act	164	19	6
A fee to the messengers of the House of Commons	1	1	0
Edward Randell's Bill for two journeys to London and Mr. Barnard to attend the Committees of both Houses	6	9	10½
To the Referees for their trouble	9	9	0
Bills of expenses at the George at Alton at four meetings of the Referees and proprietors of the Lands	11	1	9
	£223	16	11½

---

2 Leigh, *Chawton Manor*, pp. 49-50.

Appendix 13: Chawton Commons and Common Fields, 1741

The boundary of the Common was as follows, beginning at the Lower Road or 'Shrave,' where there was a gate, called the 'Hatch Gate'. It followed the hedge of Hatchgate and Imbook to the top of the hill; then turned west to the northwest corner of Greenwood Copse, where it turned south again; outside the copse across Jays Bottom to the Faringdon boundary. Here it turned west, and continued along the parish boundary hedge to the Four Marks, where was another gate. Still keeping to the parish boundary, here against Medstead, it continued in a northerly direction as far as the bank and ditch of Red Hill Cut in Chawton Park, where it turned east, following the boundary bank of Chawton Park as far as the King Tree Gate. Here it turned south across Great Reads by the west side of Read's Copse to the Shrave, thence along the south side of Read's Copse to the Hatch Gate.[1]

The enclosure of all the common land took place in 1740-1, soon after Thomas Brodnax had succeeded to the property under the will of Mrs. Elizabeth Knight. It appears to have been carried out most carefully and systematically. Nine owners of common rights were in existence at the time, viz. Thomas Knight, Lord of the Manor, Mr. Fisher's heirs, Mr. Baker the Rector, the Corporation of Winchester (as Trustees of Peter Symonds School), Feoffees of the Free Grammar School of John Eggar of Moungomeryes, Robert Eames, Rowland Prowting, Mrs. Prowting, and Michael Harris.

The allotments were as follows:

- To Thomas Knight, as his share of the Common, on consideration of his right and privileges as lord of the Manor, Long eight acre, and Gibbetts Plantation (not then planted), and the herbage of all the highways taken out of the Common; and in consideration of his rights of common, Bineswood, Drawhole field, Gores, 12 acres by Worthimy Lane and Upper Reads, in all 156 acres; and of the common fields 143 acres.
- To Mr. Fisher's heirs, 32½ acres of the Common, viz. Great Common, Green Common, and part of Jays Bottom, and 38 acres of the common fields.
- To the Glebe, of the Common, Parsonage Common; and 9 acres of the common fields.
- To the Trustees of Peter Symonds' School, 58½ acres of the Common, viz. the block of land between Parsonage Common, Gores, and the upper and lower roads, together with 57½ acres of the common fields.
- To the Feoffees of Eggar's School, on the Common, Jays Pond Piece, Jays Hanger, and Jays Hill, and about 23 acres in the common fields.
- To Robert Eames, Merry Tree Piece and the upper part of Firtree Copse on the Common, and about 18 acres in the common fields.
- To Rowland Prowting, part of Long Common and 6½ acres in the common fields.
- To Mrs. Joan Prowting, the remainder of Long Common and 6½ acres in the common fields.
- To Michael Harris, Tanners Puddock and 5½ acres in the common fields.

---

1   Leigh, *Chawton Manor* pp. 47-9. With thanks to Mike Overy.

- Thomas Knight was to have the timber with full liberty to fell, grub up, and carry it away, before the 1st June 1742.
- A piece not exceeding an acre was to be reserved unenclosed to be used as a chalk pit for manuring the respective allotments, and a pond for watering sheep and cattle.

The highways and droveways were laid out at the same time and left unenclosed, very much as they now exist. Northfield Lane was to be from the Shrave Road to the Pace-Way Road, 20 feet wide. The lower road or Shrave, now the high road to Winchester, was to be not less than 40 feet nor more than 80 feet wide from the north-west corner of Southfield, now called Hatchgate, as far as the south-west corner of Read's Coppice, and 40 feet wide from thence to Buckler's Tigh, and 10 rods wide from Buckler's Tigh to Four Marks Gate (Buckler's Tigh must be what is now known by the less euphonious name of Lousey Dell). Worthimy Lane was to be 4 rods wide with a gate at the parish boundary; and the road from Four Marks Gate to Red Hill 3 rods, with liberty to Thomas Knight to hang gates (not to be locked) at each end.

Chawton Common Fields[2]
The acreage of the common fields was 309 acres 0 roods 32 perches and of the Common 321 acres 0 roods 5 perches.

South Field [*between The Shrave (A31) and the A32, 83/2/28*] included South Field and the plat; Lower Yew Tree Piece; the Glebe, Southfield; about 14 acres of the Glebe meadow behind the Rectory adjoining South Field; and the Strip of Land containing 28½ acres adjoining the road called the Shrave from the way to Inbrook Wood to the end of Hatchgates, except Beans Close (2/2/10).

North Field [*between Chawton Park Road, Ridge Field and the Shrave, 38/2/28*] included the four North Fields from the Shrave to the Pace way or common except the upper part of middle North Field, not including Peaseway or Paceway Close.

Ridge Field [*between Chawton Park Road, Northfield Lane and the Shrave, 19/3/13*] was much the same as the present Ridge Field now divided by the new Meon Valley Line.

White Down [*between Ackender (Bushy Leaze) Wood, The A339 and Chawton Park Road, 33/3/23*] abutted on Ackender Wood, White Down Lane and the Road from Alton to Alresford.

Winstreet [Winstreet Field, between Chawton Park Road, The Butts and Winchester Road, 9/0/1] lay between the two roads leading to the Butts or 'Robin Hood Butts', as they were then called.

Upper East Field [*between Winchester Road, Wolfs Lane and the Selborne Road, 78/0/11*] included Mingledown [Mingledown Plantation], Mounters East Field, and the other East Fields, and Great and Little Maslets. [East Field Farm is south of Wolfs Lane, the road east from Chawton to the Selborne Road]

Lower East Field [*south of the Selborne Road and east of Upper East Field, 46.0.31*] included Old Brook Vere, Style Piece and Great Field.

---

2   Leigh, *Chawton Manor*, pp. 178-9.

Appendix 14: Chawton Commons Memorandum of Agreement, 1741

That We whose Names are hereunto subscribed being Commoners and having Right of Common on Chawton Common in the County of Southampton do hereby unanimously agree that each person having an allotment or allotments Assigned have on the said Common by certain Articles of Agreement and an Award of several Arbitrators therein mentioned and by an Act of Parliament paid to confirm the same shall and may at his and their free will and pleasure Ditch in all such Allotment or Allotments so as not to to hinder any sheep from passing and repassing and Feeding thereon and on every part thereof, and also free Liberty to Denshire any part or parts of such Allotment or Allotments, Provided such person or persons do and shall immediately before he or they do begin to Denshire take and keep off from the said Common on any part thereof so many of the Sheep which he or they have thereon or doth or did usually keep thereon, as is in proportion to the Quantity of Ground which he or they do intent to Deushire as is above said.[1]

And Whereas John Budd of Shalden in the said County, Yeoman, Hath hired all those Allotments on the said Common which by the above said Agreement award and Act is assigned to Thomas Knight Esquire We do also hereby agree that the said John Budd shall immediately have the Liberty to fence in Denshire, Chalk, Break up, Plow, one piece as mentioned in the said Award and Act to contain Seventeen Acres and five Perches

And also to begin ditch and to Denshire the West end of another Allotment mentioned to contain one hundred and five Acres and two Roods but not more than [blank] Acres of the said piece and also free Liberty to Chalk all the said piece but not to hinder any Sheep from feeding at Liberty on any part of the last mentioned piece till the [blank] day of [blank] next provided Nevertheless that the said John Budd shall pay to the said Commoners so much for the said Liberty as Any three of us at Michaelmas next shall allot and appoint as Witness our hands.[2]

---

1 HRO, 39M89/E/B562.
2 Feast of Saint Michael and All Angels, 29 September.

Appendix 15: Medstead Perambulation, 1744

Perambulation & Treadings of the Bounds of the said Mannor of Medsted taken the Ninth day of October 1744 by Edward Rookes Esq, Lord of the said Mannor, Attended with Thomas Peace his Steward & Several People that are Parishioners & Inhabitants there (that is to say)[1]

Thomas Mould Aged about Seventy Two Years
John Budd of Trinity Aged about Seventy Years
Thomas Hannum Aged about Sixty Five Years
Thomas Budd Aged about Sixty Years
Richard Wake the Elder Aged about Sixty Years
William Allen the Elder Aged about Fifty Years
Nicholas Wilks Aged about Forty Five Years
John Andrews Aged about Thirty Nine Years
Richard Wake Junior, Aged about Thirty Two Years
John Wilks Aged about Twenty Years
Richard Hawkins Aged about Nineteen Years
William Allen the younger Aged about Fifteen Years

First - Beginning at Hoping Stile next New Coppice Ground where an <u>Ancient Bound Cross</u> in the Ground was Cutt afresh, & from thence to a Wood of John Budd of Tenantry up the Ditch leaving the hedge on the Left & so on in like manner to Redwood Field & from Redwood Field to Alton Lane or Hussell Lane Gate; By which Gate an <u>Ancient Bound Cross</u> Just Over the hedge was Cutt aFresh as was also <u>another Cross</u> under the hedge on the other side of the Road Way;

And from thence Over the Hedge into little & Great Park Closes (College Land) belonging to the said John Budd of Tenantry & Over the Hedge into the Four Row Down Closes & Merriots Piddles part of Mr Rookes Mannor Farme keeping *along* up the Ditch & leaving the Hedge on the left hand & so on into Mr Budd of Shalden Red Hill Close & Red Hill Coppice *in the like manner*

Then Over the hedge of Red hill Coppice by a stile or Rail next the corner of Chawton Common (now Enclosed) where another <u>ancient Bound Cross</u> was Cutt afresh, keeping along under Red Hill Coppice Hedge about Thirty Three Yards from the Hedge leaving it on the Right hand until they came into the Road leading from Alresford to Alton called Redhill Road Over the Rails into a piece of Common Ground which on the left lyes in & next Chawton Common, Hedged off & Inclosed, And all the right Hand part of it from very near the said Chawton Common Hedge lies all in Medsted where another <u>Bound Cross</u> was Cutt afresh to Shew how far from the abovesaid Hedge Medsted Bounds were;

From thence Strait along under Chawton Common Ground Hedge till they came across to an <u>Old Bound Cross</u> about Six Yards on the Right hand *Hedge* of

---

1 HRO, 107M89/22.

Boyneswood which was Cutt afresh then keeping along at the side of the Dale near Mr John Barnard's Sand Pitts where there was another <u>ancient Bound Cross</u> Cutt afresh, from thence Over the said Dale to a <u>very remarkable Ancient Bound mark</u> *this day cutt afresh <u>being an Old Bound Mark</u>* for Four Parishes (that is Medsted Rapley Chawton & Farringdon) & is about Six Yards from the hedge belonging to [erased] on Medsted Side & from theare along up the Road leading from Alton to Alresford in the Ditch Under the hedge leaving the hedge on the Right hand to a place where an <u>ancient Bound Cross</u> formerly was & where Mr Rookes has Ordered a <u>Bound Post</u> to be now Erected in Order to prevent Waggons & such like Going thereupon.

And from that Place directly across the Road Way to an <u>Ancient Bound Cross</u> Cutt afresh, near the hedge of Richard Weaks Lymington Ground, which Cross is about Nine & Twenty Yards to the left Corner Lane called Lymington Bottom Lane, & then to another <u>ancient Bound Cross</u> cutt also afresh from the other corner of the same Lane about ten Yards & from this last Cross up directly across the said Roadway to another <u>ancient Bound Cross</u> by a stile leading into Mr Rookes Feild lately Inclosed out of Medsted Common;

Then [*page 2*] Over the stile there up the Ditch of the Fields lately Inclosed out of Medsted Common leaving the Hedge which parts off Rapley Common Feilds from Medsted now Inclosed Feilds on the left Unto the Hedge next Solderidge Bottom Lane where an <u>Ancient Bound Cross</u> was Cutt a fresh then Over the Hedge into the said Lane, across the said Lane, over another Hedge into the Ground of William Budd of Solderidge, along up the Ditch leaving the Hedge & Rapley Grounds on the left

Then Over the Hedge of Mr Budd of Rapley to an <u>ancient Bound Cross</u> which was Cutt afresh & from thence directly across a Meadow into a Row of William Weaks Opposite Arnolds Coppice & from that Row to the corner of Arnold Coppice a cross a Close of William Weaks of Byton then a cross other lands to Ramscomb Gate by Gullet Lane making <u>Bound Crosses</u> at every Field Hedge to direct where they went across And by Ramscomb Gate is a <u>Very Ancient Bound Cross</u> which was Cutt afresh & from that Cross over the Hedge a cross the Roadway into Grounds of Mr John Barnards & Widow Hockley

Strait along under the left Hand Hedge against Ramscombe Ground to Pyed Corner at the lower end of John Gamises Hydes Close to an <u>Ancient Bound Cross</u> Just Over the Hedge cut a fresh;

From thence back Over the Hedge again into Hydes Close keeping under the left hand Hedge against Byton Dean Lane Unto the Bottom Lane to an <u>Old Bound Cross</u> Just by Gosberys Corner which was Cutt afresh, from this Cross over the Hedge into Mr Barnards Ground leaving the Hedge against Byton Ground all a long on the Left till they came to Byton Lane or Nacket Lane End which Lane they went a cross to a Stile & into Land of Mr Hicks's keeping up those Lands (leaving the Hedge *against* of Byton Ground Still on the left) unto Whythes Down Gate then Strait along Heath Green Lane crossing Landham Lane End which Land thro' the Chalk Dale at the Upper End at which an <u>Ancient Bound Cross</u> was Cutt a fresh & so on Up to a Close of Land of John Bulbecks called West Crofts then in at the Gate taking in about Twenty Rodd from Off the Right hand Hedge, it being a certain Noted place in Medsted Mannor where One Mesham had formerly a Cottage & Garden

And from thence into Heath Green Lane again Under the left Hand Side of the Hedge next to Bulbeck's Land (Two Bound Crosses being cutt One where they went in & the other where they came Out)

And from thence keeping up Heath Green Lane leaveing Bulbecks Hedge on the left till they came out of this Lane into the Gardens between the Hedge & the House there, leaveing the meadow Hedge on the left hand & then close by William Weaks Farm House on the right hand & then between the Stables & Wall & a cross the Farm Gate & Over the Wall & along the Ditch leaveing a little Piece of Hedge Row on the left & then across the Lane by an Old Gate Place to the Hedge on the Right Hand & then up along the Ditch leaving the Hedge on the Right & Harmsworth Heath Lane on the left then Over a Hedge by Burnt Corner Close Up the Ditch leaving Church Close Coppice on the Right to the corner in the same Close next Verneys Coppice & Going over a Hedge continuing Still up the Ditch leaving the Hedge on the Right till they came into Harmsworth Heath Lane, keeping down the Ditch leaving said Verney Coppice on the Right & the Lane left & continuing the same Ditch leaving Dead Hobb Close left

And then across Dead Hobb Lane into Down Coppice Ditch, leaving Down Coppice on the Right & William Cagers land on the left Going Over the Hedge & keeping the Ditch leaving the Hedge by the side of Balbecks Down Coppice on the Right & Stephen's Dead Hobbs Close on the left & when past the Coppice they continued Up the same Ditch leaving Burnells land on the Right & Stephens's on the left & then on up the same Ditch leaving Hocklys land on the right & Stephens's on the left then John Budds *Down* Coppice on the Right & Sir Bartley Lucys & Vickerys Lane on the left, Then Lands of John Budd of lower House on the Right & Vickerys on the left then keeping the same Ditch across [page 3] To Green lane by Wheel Bayly Gate Over into the Widow Pearcis Field leaveing College Down Coppice on the Right & vicherys Lands & Lord Lymingtons, Minchins Close on the left.

Then William *Priors* Minchin's Bottom Close & his Minchin's Coppice on the Right & Hocklys Land on the left, Then Over the Hedge into Bentworth veldon Lane to an Ancient Bound Cross which was Cutt a fresh from thence kept up the Ditch leaving said Priors Minchins Coppice Still on the Right & the said Bentworth veldon Lane on the left for a little Way,

Then over the Hedge into a Close of the said Vickerys keeping Still up the Ditch leaving the said last mentioned Coppice on the right & the said Vickerys Close on the left, Then Tenants Coppice on the Right & Vickery's veldon Close or Great Common Close on the left, Then the said veldon Lands & Burnt Coppice & Hick's Field on the Right & Mr Rookes North Readen Close on the left, Then Bulbecks Close & Lands of John Budd of Tenantry on the Right & Bentworth Lane on the left, And up the Ditch to Trinity Lane Gate & from thence turning Short on the left keeping up the Ditch to New Coppice leaving Lands of John Budd of Tenantry on the Right & Applefords New Coppice Feild on the left, Then Over the Hedge keeping still up the Ditch in New Coppice leaveing a Close of the said John Budd of Tenantry on the Right & Just out of the Coppice is an <u>Ancient Bound Cross</u> which was Cutt afresh, from thence keeping up the Ditch of New Coppice leaving Mr Rookes Six Acred Bottom Field on the Right & New Coppice on the left, And from thence *in*to Mr Rookes Hopeing Wood Close on the Right & New Coppice Seven Acres Close on the left, Still keeping the Ditch.

Then leaving Hopeing Wood on the Right & New Coppice in Hopeing Wood Close on the left, & so up to Hopeing Stile next New Coppice Ground to the <u>Bound Cross</u> (where the perambulation first begun).

Owners of Cottages built of the Waste of Medstead Mannor [17]: Joseph Smith, John Smith, Ann Mould widow, William Loveyer, Olive Hall widow, Stephen Silvester, Thomas Hannums, Thomas Mould, Elizabeth Crockford widow, William Allen, Thomas Cane, Thomas Budd, John Mould, Elizabeth Hockly, Joseph Turrell, John Dorey, John Cameis (sic).

Appendix 16: Farringdon Commons Agreement, 1749

To All Christian People to whom [] shall come Greeting

Whereas by certain articles of Agreement bearing date on or about the Twenty first day of October the [] of our Lord one thousand seven hundred and forty eight and entered into by

- Lewis Cage Esquire, Lord of the Manor of Farringdon in the County of Southampton
- William Knight
- John Finden
- William Finden
- John Tribe
- Richard Wake
- Richard Wake Junior
- Thomas Eames, Yeoman
- and Others

The Freehold and Copyhold Tenants of the said Manor whose hand and Seals are thereunto set being by much the greater part in Number and Values of those who have Right and Interest in over and upon certain waste Grounds or Common called Farringdon Common or Commons in the Parish and Manor of Farringdon aforesaid

Who were desirous that the said Common or Commons might for their mutual benefit be forthwith Surveyed Measured Divided and Allotted out in order to be inclosed and held Severally in proportion to each person's Right and Interest wherein

And in order to avoid difficulties and disputes that might arising touching such divisions and Allotments They the said Lord and Tenants Commoners aforesaid did Submit themselves to the Award Arbitration Order and determination of

- Edward Randall of Chawton in the said County Gentleman
- John Richardson of Ropley in the said County Carpenter
- John Baigen of Chawton
- John Budd of Shalden and
- John Budd of Trinity in the Parish of Medstead in the said County Yeoman

or any Three of them Arbitrators by the the said Lord and Tenants appointed as well touching and concerning the Surveying dividing and Allotting out the said Common or Commons and laying out Highways Roads and passages to and from such Allotments and portionments respectively so as the said Arbitrators or any three of them should make and [publish] such their Award of and concerning the promises in Writing under the hands and Seals on or before the first day of April then next As [] and by the said Articles of Agreements relation being thereunto had it doth may and may appear

And whereas we the said arbitrators who have hereunto set our hands and seals pursuant to the power vested in the said arbitrators having Surveyed the said common or commons and well considered the same and the said common or commons having been measured

We do hereby Order, Appoint and Allot out

- One Road or Highway leading from Bridestone Lane to Hore Thorn Lane across the said common to be 42 feet wide
- One Road or Highway leading from Vidlers Lane into the last mentioned Road and to be of 33 feet wide
- One Road or Highway leading from Headmere Lane toward Medstead into Chawton Road to be 42 feet wide
- One Road or Highway leading from Roaply Lane towards Worthimy Pond and so to Worthimy Gate to be 42 feet wide
- One Road or Highway leading from Drymere gate into the last mentioned Road to be 42 feet wide And
- One Road or Highway leading from Mr Camies's gate on Brockmore hill into Chawton Road to be of 42 feet wide

all which said Roads to be taken and devised for and as the Highways or Common Roads of the Parish of Farringdon And

- One Drove lane from Ropley lane end near Ropley Hedge to and from the allotments of William Dunce and Thomas Bridger and also
- One Drove Lane from the said Ropley lane and near Ropley Hedge Northward to and from an Inclosure of a certain Heath []

which said Drove Lane [] also devised allot and appoint to Louis Cage Esquire Lord of the said Manor

- Twenty Acres in Right of his lordship as agreed to in [] by the said Articles of Agreement And also
- Seventeen Acres and one half in Right of Cramps Farm that is to say all that piece of the said Common A butting
  - East to the Road leading from Headmere towards Medstead
  - South to the Road leading from Ropley lane to Worthimy Pond
  - North West to the Road leading from Mr Camies's gate on Brockmore Hill towards Chawton and
  - West to Inclosed land of the Parish of Ropley and to the last mentioned drove containing Thirty [1] Acres

and that the said Lewis Cage shall make all the Fences against the said Roads and Droves

Also to the said Lewis Cage

- One other piece part of the said common containing Six Acres and two Roods, abutting
  - South to the Road leading from Ropley Lane towards Worthimy Pond
  - West toward the Road leading towards Medstead
  - North to an allotment of Richard Wake and
  - East to an Allotment of Elizabeth Grossmith

and that the said Lewis Cage shall make the Fence towards the South and West against the said Roads and East against the Allotments of the said Elizabeth Grossmith

To William Knight

- One piece part of the said common called Hews Hill containing Twenty One Acres Abutting
  - East to inclosed land of the said William Knight and John Tribe []
  - South to inclosed land called Pies
  - West to inclosed lands of the said John Tribe
  - North to an Allotment of the said John Tribe and

that the said William Knight shall make the fence against the said John Tribe's, allotments

Also to the said William Knight

- One other piece of land part of the said common containing Six Acres Two Roods abutting
  - East to the Road leading from Headmere lane towards Medstead
  - South to inclosed Land of [blank]
  - West to an Allotment of Thomas Eames and
  - North to an Allotment of Robert Carrack and

that the said William Knight shall make the Fence on the East and North sides and

Also to the said William Knight

- One other piece part of the said Common containing Twenty four Acres Exclusive of a Common Chalk pit and a way to it of 30 feet wide containing One Acre Two Roods Abutting
  - East to an Allotment of John Finden and John Fry
  - South to the said Chalk pit and way and toa new Coppice
  - West to the way leading from Drymer Gate towards Worthimy pond and
  - North to an Allotment of John Tribe and to the road leading to the Worthimy pond

and that the said William Knight shall make the fence on the West and North side and also against the said Chalk pit way or having a gate on the West and thereof with a Common key for each proprietor on the said Common to have the free use of the said Chalk pit

To John Tribe for his Copyhold

- All that other part of Hews hill Part of the said common with his Forestall on the East end of Mr Cage's Coppice with
  - All that drove called Cows hill Drove except away through the said Forestall to and from the Allotment of John Finden on the North side of the said Coppice and to and from the said Coppice and also
  - Except a Freeway to and from Woodside Lane to Drymer Way on the South side of the said Mr Cage's Coppices to be 42 feet wide containing Exclusive of the said Ways Thirty four Acres

and that the said John Tribe shall make a fence from the South West Corner of New Coppice to the North East Corner of Drymer lane with a Gate not to be locked And also to the said John Tribe for his Copyhold

- One other piece of Land part of the said common containing Six Acres and One Rood abutting
  - To an allotment of John Finden towards the South
  - To the Road leading from Drymer gate towards Worthimy pond towards [torn paper]
  - Another allotment of Richard Wake toward the West and
  - Of Henry Page towards the North [torn paper] [end page 1]

And that the said John Tribe shall make the fence on the North and East sides and the northern most half of the West side against Rickard Wake and also to the said John Tribe

- One other piece in right of his freehold containing three acres one rood and sixteen perches abutting
  - To the last mentioned allotment to William Knight towards the South
  - To the last mentioned road towards the West and
  - To the allotment of William and Sarah Knight towards the North

and that the said John Tribe do make the fence on the West and North sides

To John Finden for his copyhold
One piece of the said common containing one acre and twelve perches abutting
- To inclosed land called Drymer wood towards the South
  - To an allotment to the said John Finden for his freehold towards the West and North and
  - To the way leading from Drymer gate towards the East

and that the said John Finden shall make the fence on the East, West and North sides

also to the said John Finden for his freehold
- One other piece of the said common containing eight acres abutting
  - To the last mentioned road towards the East []
  - Later mentioned allotment and lands called Drymer wood towards the South
  - To an allotment of Richard Wake towards the West and
  - To an allotment to John Tribe towards the North

and that the said John Finden shall make the Fence on the West and North sides and the southern most half against said Richard Wake to the mark [fob 5]

To the said Richard Wake second
- One piece of land part of the said common containing sixteen acres abutting
  - To inclosed lands called Drymer wood and to allotments of John Finden and of John Tribe towards the East
  - To the Road leading from Bride Stone lane to Hore Thorne to the South
  - To the road leading from Headmore towards Medstead towards the West and
  - To an allotment of Richard Wake [] and of Thomas Goff towards the North

and that the said Richard Wake shall make the Fence on the South, West and North sides and the middle half of the East side against John Finden and John Tribe

And also to the said Richard Wake
- One other piece of the said common containing seven acres abutting
  - East to a way leading from Mr Camies's gate on Breachmore hill towards Chawton
  - South West to inclosed lands of John Richardson
  - To the West of an allotment of Elizabeth Fielder and
  - North to Chawton road

and that the said Richard Wake shall make the Hedge against the said roads and also

To the said Richard Wake
- One other piece of the said common containing 17: 3: 0 abutting
  - To an allotment of Mary Windybank towards the East and
  - Of Lewis Cage Esquire and of Elizabeth Grossmith towards the South
  - To the road leading towards Medstead towards the West
  - To Chawton road towards the North

and that the said Richard Wake shall make the Fence on the South West and North and the Northern most half of the East sides

And to Richard Wake [] for his Copyhold
- One piece of the said common containing 1: 2: 34 perch abutting
  - To the road leading to Worthimy pond towards the West and
  - To an allotment of Richard Wake second towards the East and South and
  - To an allotment of Thomas Goff towards the North

and that the said Richard Wake [] do make the Fence on the West and North sides

To Robert Heath for his copyhold
- One piece of land in the said common containing 4: 1: 20 abutting
  - East to a road to Greenmere lane
  - South to inclosed lands of the said Robert Heath
  - West to the read land out of Headmere lane towards Medstead and
  - North to an allotment of Robert Rogers

and that the said Robert Heath shall make the Fence on the East, West and North sides

And to the said Robert Rogers for his freehold
- One piece of the said common containing 6: 0: 30 abutting
  - To the said way leading from Greenmere towards the East
  - To the allotment of the said Robert Heath towards the South
  - To the said road leading out of Headmere lane towards the West and
  - To a Road leading from Bride Stone lane to Hore Thorne towards the North

and that the said Robert Heath shall make the Fence on the East, West and North sides

And also to the said Robert Rodgers for his freehold
- One other piece part of the said common containing 2: 1: 10 [] abutting

- [] of Thomas Goff towards the South
- To the road leading to Headmere towards the West and
- To an allotment for his copyhold towards the North and
- To several small allotments towards the East

and that the said Robert Rodgers shall make the Fence on the West, North and East sides

Also to the said Robert Rodgers for his copyhold

- One other piece of the said common containing 4: 1: 20 abutting
  - To the last mentioned piece towards the South
  - The last mentioned road towards the West and
  - To several small allotments towards the North and East
- and the said Robert Rodgers shall make the Fence on the East, West and North sides

To the said Thomas Goff

- One piece of land of the said common for his freehold containing 8: 3: 0 abutting
  - To an allotment of Richard Wake on the South
  - To an allotment of Robert Rodgers on the North
  - To the last mentioned road on the West and
  - To small allotments on the East

and that the said Thomas Goff shall make the Fence on the East, West and North sides

To William Finden for his copyhold

- One piece part of the said common containing 15: 0: 9 abutting
  - To the road leading from Bride Stone lane to Hore Thorn towards the South
  - To the road leading from Headmere to Medstead towards the East
  - To an allotment of Thomas Fielder towards the West and
  - To an allotment of Mary Windybank towards the North

and the said William Finden shall make the Fence on the East, South and North sides

Also to the said William Finden

- One other piece containing 16: 1: 10 abutting
  - To an allotment of Elizabeth Fielder towards the East
  - To the road towards Hore Thorn towards the South and
  - To Ropely hedge towards the West and
  - To an allotment to Thomas Bridger towards the North

and that the said William Finden shall make the Fence on the East, South and North sides.

To Elizabeth Fielder for her freehold

- One piece of the said common containing 13: 2: 20 abutting
  - To the last described piece towards the West
  - To the last mentioned road South

- To an allotment of Thomas Fielder to the East and
- To an allotment of John Gunner toward the North

and that the said Elizabeth Fielder shall make the Fence on the East, South and North sides

Also to the said Elizabeth Fielder

- One piece in right of Post leasehold containing 1: 0: 30 abutting
  - To an allotment of Richard Wake on the East
  - To Ropely hedge towards the South West and
  - To Chawton road to the North and North West

and that the said Elizabeth Fielder shall make the Fence against the said Richard Wake's allotment and also against Chawton road

To Thomas Fielder for his copyhold

- One piece of land part of the said common containing 8: 0: 24 perches abutting
  - To an allotment of William Finden East
  - Elizabeth Fielder West and of
  - John Langrish towards the North and
  - The road leading from Bride Stone lane to Hore Thorn towards the South

and that the said Thomas Fielder shall make the Fence on the East, South and North sides

To Thomas Bridger for his Copyhold

- One piece of the said common containing 4: 1: 30 abutting
  - To inclosures of Ropely parish towards the West
  - To an allotment of William Finden South
  - To an allotment of John Gunner East and
  - Of William Dunce North

and that the said Thomas Bridger shall make the Fence on the East and North sides

To William Dunce for his copyhold

- One piece containing 0: 3: 7 abutting
  - To the allotment of John Gunner towards the East and North and
  - To the allotment of Thomas Bridger and a Drove lane towards the West

and that the said William Dunce shall make the Fence against the East North and West sides

To John Gunner for his copyhold

- One piece of land containing 8: 3: 20 abutting
  - East to an allotment of John Langrish
  - South to Elizabeth Fielder
  - West to Thomas Bridger and William Dunce and a Drove lane and

North to the road leading from Ropeley Lane towards Worthimy pond and that the said John Gunner shall make the Fence and on [torn paper] West and North sides and

To John Langrish for his freehold [torn paper]
- Of the said common containing 3: 3: 12 [*end of page*] Abutting
- East to his Copyhold Allotment
- South to an allotment of [blank] Fielder
- West of John Gunner and
- North to the road from Ropeley

and that the said John Langrish will make the fence on the East and North sides
Also to the said John Langrish for his Copyhold
- One other piece of the said common containing 9: 1: 10 Abutting
- East to allotments of Mary Windybank and John Battle
- South to Thomas Fielder
- West to [blank] freehold allotment and
- North that said Road

and that the said John Langrish shall make the Fence on the East and North sides

And to John Battle
- The piece part of the said common containing 5: 3: 20 Abutting
- East to the Road leading from Headmore toward Medstead
- South to an allotment of Mary Windybank
- West of John Langrish and
- North to the Road leading from Ropeley

and that the said John Battle shall make the Fence against the said Roads on the East and North

To Mary Windybank for her copyhold
- One piece containing 5: 2: 0 abutting
- East to the Road
- South to the allotment of William Finden
- West of John Langrish and
- North to that of John Battle

and that the said Mary Windybank shall make the Fence on the East and North side
And also to the said Mary Windybank
- One other piece part of the said common containing 18: 1: 0 abutting
- East to an allotment of Michael Harrison
- West to allotments of Richard Wake and Elizabeth Grossmith
- South to the Road leading from Ropely to Worthimy gate and
- North to an inclosure of the said Michael Harrison

and that the said Mary Windybank shall make the fence on the East, South and North and the Southern most half of the West side against the allotment of Richard Wake

To Michael Harrison for his Copyhold
- One piece containing 0: 1: 37 abutting
  - On the West to the allotment of Mary Windybank

To John Harrison for his Copyhold
- One piece containing 0: 1: 37 abutting
  - On the West to Michael Harrison

To Edward Harrison for Copyhold
- 1: 2 : 38 abutting
  - West to John Harrison

To James Finden for his Copyhold end of the copyhold of [grand] Garden
- One piece of the said common containing 0: 1: 18 abutting
  - West to Edward Harrison

To Edward Withers
- One piece for his Copyhold containing 0: 1: 36 abutting
  - West to James Finden

And [blank] the five last mentioned persons shall make their fences on the North East and South sides of their allotments

To Mary Vidler for her freehold
- One piece of the said common containing 2: 0: 30 abutting
  - South and West to inclosed lands of the said Mary Vidler
  - North to the Road leading from Bridestone lane to Hore Thorn East to an allotment [blank] of John Faithfull

and that the said Mary Vidler shall make the Fence on the East and North sides []

To John Faithfull for his Copyhold
- One piece of 1: 0: 15 abutting
  - West to an allotment of Mary Vidler

To William Faithfull for his Freehold
- 0: 2: 6 abutting
  - West to an allotment of John Faithfull

And to the said William Faithfull for his Copyhold
- 2: 1: 12 abutting
  - West to his allotment for said freehold and

To John Westson for his Copyhold
- One piece of the said common containing 3: 2: 8 abutting
  - West to an allotment of William Faithfull
  - East to the road leading to Vidlers lane

- North to the road leading from Bride lane to Hore Thorn and
- South to inclosed lands of [blank]

And that said John Westson, William Faithfull and John Faithfull shall each make the Fences against their respective lands on the East and North sides and

To Thomas Tayler for his Freehold
- One piece part of the said common containing 2: 0: 30 abutting
  - East to an allotment of John Neal
  - South to inclosed land of [blank]
  - West to the road leading to Vidlers and
  - North to an allotment of John Andrews
and that the said Thomas Tayler shall make the Fence on the North and West side and the Southern most half of the East side and

To John Andrews for his Copyhold
- 7: 1: 0 abutting
  - East to an allotment of John Neal
  - West to the road leading to Vidlers
  - South to an allotment of Thomas Tayler and
  - North to the Road leading to Hore Thorn
and that the said John Andrews shall make the Fence on the North and West sides and the Northern most half on the East side

To John Neal for his Copyhold
- One piece of the said common containing 7: 0: 20 abutting
  - North to the road leading to Hore Thorn
  - East to the way to a common chalk pit
  - South to [] and
  - West to the allotments of John Andrews and Thomas Tayler
and that [] fence on the North and East sides and the middle half of the West []
[end page 2]

And to William Beagley for his Copyhold
- One [piece] of [torn paper] containing 0: 0: 14 abutting
To the Road leading to Worthimy pond and that he shall [torn paper] side of the same and

To John [Kenteris] for his Copyhold
- One piece of [torn paper] containing 0: 0: 23 abutting
  - To the said Road leading to Worthimy pond
and that the said John [Kenteris] shall make the Fence against to sides of the same

And to John Gunner and John Knolton for their Copyhold
- One piece part of the said Common containing 0: 0: 38 Abutting

- To the said Road leading to Worthimy pond

and that they shall make the pond and that they shall make the Fence against two sides of the same

And to Martha Knight
- One piece for her Copyhold containing 0: 0: 12 Abutting
  - To the said road

and that the said Martha Knight shall make the Fence against two sides of the same and

To Thomas Langrish for his Copyhold
- One piece containing 0: 0: 9 abutting
  - To the said Road

and that he shall make the Fence against two sides of the same and

To George Linfield for his Copyhold
- One piece containing 0: 0: 37 abutting
  - To the said Road

and that he shall make the fence against two sides of the same and

To Francis Moreton for his Copyhold
- One piece part of the said common containing 0: 0: 36 Abutting
  - To the [torn paper]

and that the said Francis Moreton shall make the Fence against the two sides of the same and

To [torn paper] Sarah Messenger for her Copyhold
- 0: 0: 34 Abutting
  - To the said Road

and that she shall make the Fence [torn paper] two sides of the same and

To Sarah Mayhew for her Copyhold
- One piece part of the said common [torn paper] containing Five perches Abutting
  - To the said road leading to Worthimy pond

and that the said Sarah Mayhew shall make the Fence against two sides of the same and

To Elizabeth Grossmith for her Leasehold
- One piece of land part of the said common containing 6: 2: 20 Abutting
  - To an Allotment of Lewis Cage Esquire towards the West and
  - Richard Wake second towards the North and of
  - Mary Windybank towards the East and
  - To the Road leading from Roapley lane to Worthimy pond towards the South

and that the said Elizabeth Grossmith shall make the fence on the South and East sides

And also to the said John Finden for his freehold
- One other piece of land part of the said common containing 93: 2: 0 Abutting
  - East to inclosed land to the said John Finden
  - South to New Coppice
  - West to the allotments of William Knight, John Fry, Jane Fry and Robert Eames and
  - North to inclosed land of the said Robert Eames and Rowland [Prart]
and that the said John Finden [torn paper] [end page 3].

[And to Thomas Eames for] his Copyhold
- One piece part of the said common containing 6: 0: 6 abutting
  - East to an allotment of William Knight
  - South to inclosed lands of [blank] and to the common chalk pit
  - West to the common way to the said chalk pit
  - North to the Road leading to Hore Thorn
and that the said Thomas Eames shall make the fence on the East and North sides and also on the West side against the said common chalk pit way or hang up a gate not to be locked or with a common key for all the proprietors at the North side of the said way

And to the town of [Farnham poor] in right of their Copyhold belonging to Hall farm
- one piece containing 0: 1: 36 abutting
  - South and [torn paper] the allotment of Thomas Eames
  - East to Robert Carrack
  - North to the road leading from Bride Stone leading to the town of Farnham
and the said Town of Farnham shall make the Fence on the North, East and South sides

And to Robert Carrack and John Wheeler for their Copyhold
- One piece containing 2: 1: 11 abutting
  - East to the Road leading to [torn paper]
  - North to the Road leading to Bride Stone lane
  - South to an allotment of William Knight and
  - West [torn paper] to the town of Farnham
and that the said Robert Carrack shall make the fence on the East [torn paper] also

To William Tibbery for his freehold
- 1: 1: 32 abutting
  - North to an allotment of John [torn paper] an allotment to Sarah Knight
  - West to the Road to Drymer and

- [] to the road leading to [torn paper]

and that the said William Tibbery shall make the Fence on the West and North sides and

To Sarah Knight for her Leasehold
- 0: 2: 16 abutting
  - To an allotment of John Tribe South and
  - Of William Tibbery West and
  - Of William Knight East and to the road leading to Worthimy pond North

and that the said Sarah Knight shall make the Fence on the West and North sides and

To Robert Eames for his Copyhold
- One piece of Land part of the said common containing 5: 0: 30 abutting
  - To an allotment to John Finden toward the East and
  - Of Jane Fry and of James Fry South
  - To the road to Worthimy gate West and
  - To inclosures of the said Robert Eames and of Thomas Knight Esquire towards the North

and that the said Robert Eames shall make the fence on the South, North and West sides and

To Jane Fry for her Copyhold
- One piece of land part of the said common containing 9: 9: 10 abutting
  - To an allotment of John Finden East and
  - Of John Fry South and
  - To the road near Worthimy pond West and
  - To allotments of Robert Eames and James Fry North

and that the said Jane Fry shall make the Fence on the South and West sides and

To the said James Fry for his Copyhold
- One piece containing 0: 1: 2 abutting
  - East and South to an allotment to Jane Fry
  - North to an allotment to Robert Eames and
  - West to the road [torn paper] [pond]

and that the said James Fry shall make the fence on the East, West and South sides and

To John Fry his Copyhold
- One piece part of the said common containing 8: 2: 16 abutting
  - To an allotment [torn paper] Finden towards the East and
  - Of William Knight towards the South and
  - Of Jane Fry toward the North [torn paper]

said John Fry shall make the Fence on the South and West sides and

To Henry Page for his copyhold piece
- Part of the said common containing 1: 3: 30 abutting
  - To an allotment of John Tribe South [torn paper]
  - [Thomas] Goff West and
  - Of John Carter towards the North and
  - The road leading to Drymer gate towards the East [torn paper]
the said Henry Page shall make the Fence on the East and North sides and

To John Carter for his leasehold
- One piece containing 1: 2: 13 abutting
  - On the allotments to Henry Page South
  - Of Thomas Goff West
  - Of Nich [torn paper: olas Chace] North and
  - To the said road East
and that the said John Carter shall make the Fence on the North and East sides and

To Nicholas Chace for his copyhold
- One piece containing 0: 2: 20 abutting
  - To the allotments of John Carter South
  - Of Robert Rodgers West and
  - Of Henry Wells North and
  - To the said road East
and that the said Nicolas Chace shall make the Fence on the North and East sides and

To Henry Wells for his Copyhold
- One piece containing 1: 3: 38 abutting
  - East to the said road
  - South to an allotment of Nicholas Chase
  - West to Robert Rodgers
and that he shall make the Fence on the North and East sides [end page 4].

First name	Surname	Title	Identifier	Number of allotments	A	R	P	Total acres	%
Lewis	Cage	Esquire	1	2	37	2	0	37.50	8.8%
William	Knight	Yeoman	2	3	51	2	0	51.50	12.0%
John	Finden	Yeoman	3	3	42	2	12	42.58	10.0%
William	Finden	Yeoman	4	2	31	1	10	31.31	7.3%
Richard	Wake	Yeoman	5	3	40	3	0	40.75	9.5%
Richard	Wake	Junior	6	1	1	2	34	1.71	0.4%
John	Tribe	Yeoman	7	3	43	2	16	43.60	10.2%
Mary	Windybank		8	2	23	3	0	23.75	5.6%
Elizabeth	Fielder		9	2	14	3	10	14.81	3.5%
Thomas	Fielder		10	1	8	0	24	8.15	1.9%
John	Langrish		11	2	13	0	22	13.14	3.1%
Thomas	Goff	Mr	12	1	8	3	0	8.75	2.0%
John	Gunner		13	1	8	3	20	8.88	2.1%
Robert	Rodgers		14	3	12	3	30	12.94	3.0%
John	Andrews		15	1	7	1	0	7.25	1.7%
John	Neal		16	1	7	0	20	7.13	1.7%
Thomas	Eames		17	1	6	0	0	6.00	1.4%
Elizabeth	Grossmith		18	1	6	2	20	6.63	1.6%
Robert	Heath		19	1	4	1	20	4.38	1.0%
Robert	Eames		20	1	5	0	30	5.19	1.2%
John	Fry		21	1	8	2	16	8.60	2.0%
Jane	Fry		22	1	3	3	10	3.81	0.9%
James	Fry		23	1	0	1	2	0.26	0.1%
John	Battle		24	1	5	3	20	5.88	1.4%
Thomas	Bridger		25	1	4	1	30	4.44	1.0%
William	Dunce		26	1	0	3	7	0.79	0.2%
Mary	Vidler		27	1	2	0	30	2.19	0.5%
John	Faithfull		28	1	1	0	15	1.09	0.3%
William	Faithfull		29	2	2	3	18	2.86	0.7%
John	Westson	Gent.	30	1	3	2	8	3.55	0.8%
Thomas	Tayler		31	1	2	0	30	2.19	0.5%
Robert	Carrack & Wheeler		32	2	2	1	11	2.32	0.5%
Poor of Farnham			33	1	0	1	36	0.48	0.1%
Henry	Page		34	1	1	3	30	1.94	0.5%
Henry	Wells		35	1	1	3	38	1.99	0.5%

John	Carter		36	1	1	2	13	1.58	0.4%
Nicholas	Chace		37	1	0	2	20	0.63	0.1%
William	Tibbery		38	1	1	1	32	1.45	0.3%
Sarah	Knight		39	1	0	2	16	0.60	0.1%
Michael	Harrison		40	1	0	1	37	0.48	0.1%
John	Harrison		41	1	0	1	37	0.48	0.1%
Edward	Harrison		42	1	1	2	38	1.74	0.4%
James	Finden		43	2	0	1	18	0.36	0.1%
Edward	Withers		44	1	0	1	36	0.48	0.1%
William	Beagley		a	1	0	0	14	0.09	0.0%
John	Kenteris?		b	1	0	0	23	0.14	0.0%
John	Gunner & Knolton		c	1	0	0	38	0.24	0.1%
Martha	Knight		d	1	0	0	12	0.08	0.0%
Thomas	Langrish		e	1	0	0	9	0.06	0.0%
George	Linfield		f	1	0	0	37	0.23	0.1%
Francis	Moreton		g	1	0	0	36	0.23	0.1%
Sarah	Messenger		h	1	0	0	34	0.21	0.0%
Sarah	Mayhew		i	1	0	0	5	0.03	0.0%
								427.40	100.0%

Appendix 17: Chawton Manor Lands, 1768-1852

Chawton Manor map references[1]

Names of fields, etc.		Acres	Roods	Perches
1	Farm House, yard, outbuildings & garden	2	21	
2	Small piece of coppice behind the house	4		
3	Upper Barn Field	6	1	17
4	Row	3	0	11
5	Lower Barn Field including row & road (0.0.35)	7	2	20
6	Row	2	25	
7	Row	1	0	6
8	Green Common including row & dell (0.2.13)	11	1	11
9	Great Common	17	0	30
10	Upper Greenwood, including row (0.1.35)	10	2	..6
11	Lower Greenwood, including row (0.1.29)	7	1	..6
12	Greenwood Coppice	12	0	38
13	Jays Bottom, including dell (0.0.15)	..5	3	9
14	Old Gardens, including row (0.0.20	15	3	36
15	Row	1	0	27
16	The Six Acres	6	0	19
17	Row	1	0	30
18	The Seven Acres, including row (0.032)	8	0	16
19	Long Close	11	2	20
20	Row	2	2	12
21	Crocklands Coppice	7	0	0
22	Little Crocklands, including row (0.1.16)	3	3	37
23	Row	1	5	
24	Crooked Crocklands, including row & road (0.3.33)	8	0	3
25	Row	1	23	
26	Hatch Gates, including row (0.0.12)	7	1	19
27	Upper South Field, including bank & dell (0.1.24)	8	2	30
28	Lower South Field, including road (0.0.23)	10	1	..0
29	Yew Tree Piece, including row, road & dell (0.1.36)	15	0	36
30	Row	1	16	
31	Great Bean Field, including row & road (0.1.13)	6	3	35
32	Little Bean Field, including row (0.0.20)	1	2	15
	Total	**200**	**2**	**20**

---

1   HRO, 18M61/MP3. With thanks to Mike Overy.

Appendix 18: Medstead, Old Alresford terrier, 1776

To my successor - Old Alresford – Guilford – Terrier of the Rectory - 1776[1]
The Admeasurement of the Tything of Medsted: As far as the Plough and Scythe go

A Summary of all the Lands in the Tything of Medsted		a	r	p
Lands occupied	By Charles Hobbs	446	0	6
	By Robert Tollfree	368	0	13
	By Richard Wake	94	3	34
	By William Budd of Tenantry	278	1	10
	By William Budd of Soldridge	37	1	0
	By William Bone	126	3	9
	By William Shawyer	42	3	13
	By William White	1	0	22
	By Mrs Tollfree	316	1	9
	By Richard Bone	12	1	9
	By William Dory	13	2	25
	By John Newland	99	1	12
	By William Andrews	106	1	4
	By William Crosswell	42	2	32
	By Phillip Vidler	19	3	30
	By John Lindon	5	2	39
	By John Wilks	19	2	23
	By John Wilks … Glebe	5	2	22
	By William Budd of Ropley	8	3	0
	By John Beagley		3	13
	By John Camies, arable	83	1	31
	By John Camies, Hop Ground	3	0	23
	By John Hunt	112	2	32
		2,245	**3**	**11**
Little Common Down		12	0	7
	Total	**2,257**	**3**	**18**

1 HRO, 43M74/PB1.

Church Field

	Occupiers	Proprietors	a	r	p
Middle Child acre on head land	Charles Hobbs	William Jolliffe Esq	1	0	14
Piece south of the last	William Budd of Tenantry	William Budd of Tenantry	2	1	2
Moory piece	Charles Hobbs	William Jolliffe Esq	3	1	6
Moory Bottom piece	Richard Wake	William Andrews	1	0	10
Cuckoo Bush piece	Robert Tollfree	William Wake		1	2
Cuckoo Bush piece	Richard Wake	Richard Wake		1	11
		Total	**8**	**1**	**5**

Little Millway Furlong begins South, and heads great Millway furlong

1	Richard Wake	William Andrews		1	7
2	William Budd of Tenantry	William Budd of Tenantry		2	13
3	Charles Hobbs	William Jolliffe Esq		1	21
		Total	**1**	**1**	**1**

Great Millway Furlong begins East

1	William Budd of Tenantry	William Budd of Tenantry		1	17
2	Glebe John Wilks	The Reverend Mr Butler		1	5
3	Robert Tollfree	Elizabeth Hurst			34
4	Richard Wake	Richard Wake		3	17
5	William Budd of Tenantry	William Budd of Tenantry		3	9
6	Glebe John Wilks	The Reverend Mr Butler		2	18
7	William Budd of Tenantry	William Budd of Tenantry		1	20
8	Charles Hobbs	William Jolliffe Esq		1	23
9	William Budd of Tenantry	William Budd of Tenantry		3	33
10	Charles Hobbs	William Jolliffe Esq	1	2	19
11	William Budd of Tenantry	William Budd of Tenantry	1	1	17
12	Charles Hobbs	William Jolliffe Esq	1	3	20
13	Richard Wake	William Andrews		3	20
14	Richard Wake	Richard Wake	1	3	17
15	William Budd of Tenantry	William Budd of Tenantry		3	6
16	Charles Hobbs	William Jolliffe Esq		3	24
17	William Budd of Tenantry	William Budd of Tenantry	1	0	30
		Total	**15**	**1**	**9**
	A piece abutting on the south end of the last furlong Ric. Wake				24

Hattenly Furlong begins East, and abuts on Great Millway Furlong

1	Mrs Tollfree	Mr Richard Woolls	1	3	5
	John Newland	Richard Wake		1	14
2	John Hunt	Andrew Woodley		2	7
3	William Bone	William Bone	1	0	15

4	Mrs Tollfree	Mr Richard Woolls	1	1	5
5	John Hunt	Andrew Woodley	1	0	17
6	John Newland	Richard Wake		2	35
	Richard Bone, the South End	Richard Bone		3	25
7	Mrs Tollfree	Mr Richard Woolls	1	0	9
8	John Hunt	Andrew Woodley			23
		Total	**8**	**3**	**35**

A summary of Church Field

Several pieces of different names in page (1)	8	1	5
Little Millway furlong	1	1	1
Great Millway furlong	15	1	33
Hattenly furlong	8	3	35
Total	**33**	**3**	**34**

Middle Field

Head piece by hoar Dell, Charles Hobbs	William Jolliffe Esq		2	39

Elder Furlong begins East

1	Robert Tollfree	William Wake		1	29
2	Charles Hobbs	William Jolliffe Esquire		1	36
3	William Andrews	William Andrews	2	0	38
4	William Budd of Tenantry	William Budd of Tenantry		3	38
5	Charles Hobbs	William Jolliffe Esq		3	38
6	William Budd of Tenantry	William Budd of Tenantry		3	34
7	Charles Hobbs	William Jolliffe Esq	2	0	3
8	William Andrews	William Andrews		2	6
9	Robert Tollfree	William Wake		2	18
10	Robert Tollfree	Richard Wells		3	28
11	William Andrews	William Andrews		2	15
12	Robert Tollfree	William Wake	1	0	9
13	Willam Budd of Tenantry	William Budd of Tenantry	1	0	9
	Charles Hobbs (South End)	William Jolliffe Esq			39
14	Robert Tollfree	Richard Woolls	1	1	0
15	Charles Hobbs	William Jolliffe Esq			25
16	Glebe, John Wilks the north End	The Reverend Mr Butler		2	9
	Charles Hobbs, the south End	William Jolliffe Esquire	2	2	3
17	William Andrews	William Andrews		3	17
18	Charles Hobbs	William Jolliffe Esq	2	0	9
		Total	**20**	**2**	**3**

Hooks Corner Furlong begins south

1	Robert Tollfree	Richard Woolls	1	2	30
2	Robert Tollfree	William Wake		1	9
3	Charles Hobbs, on head piece	William Jolliffe Esq		2	6
		Total	**2**	**2**	**5**

Gore Furlong begins north

1	William Andrews	William Andrews		1	33
2	Charles Hobbs	William Jolliffe Esq		1	15
3	Robert Tollfree	Elizabeth Hunt		1	30
4	John Camies	John Camies	2	2	22
5	Charles Hobbs William Andrews (the west end)	William Jolliffe Esq William Andrews		1	7 11
6	John Wilks	John Wilks		2	1
7	Richard Wake	Richard Wake	1	3	12
8	William Budd of Tenantry	William Budd of Tenantry		1	32
9	Robert Tollfree	Richard Woolls		1	38
10	Charles Hobbs	William Jolliffe Esq	1	0	28
11	William Budd of Tenantry	William Budd of Tenantry			10
12	Robert Tollfree	Richard Woolls			9
		Total	**8**	**3**	**8**

A Furlong at the West end of the Field, begins north

1	John Camies	John Camies	1	0	31
2	Robert Tollfree	Richard Woolls		3	18
3	William Andrews	William Andrews		2	13
4	Robert Tollfree	Elizabeth Hunt		1	21
5	John Camies	John Camies		1	23
6	Robert Tollfree	Richard Woolls		1	29
		Total	**3**	**3**	**15**

Another Furlong at the West End of the Field, south of Last, and abuts and heads last

1	Charles Hobbs	William Jolliffe Esq	1	2	37
2	Robert Tollfree	William Proyer		1	33
3	Charles Hobbs	William Jolliffe Esq	3	1	32
		Total	**5**	**2**	**22**
	Gore Piece ...... Charles Hobbs	William Jolliffe Esq	4	1	21

Lonong Oak Stile Furlong begins Weft

1	Robert Tollfree	Elizabeth Hunt	1	1	9
2	John Camies	John Camies	1	0	24
3	Richard Wake	Richard Wake		2	7
4	Robert Tollfree	Richard Woolls	1	3	9
		Total	**4**	**3**	**9**

Furlong abutting on Long Oak Stile Furlong, begins north

1	Robert Tollfree	William Wake		2	8
2	William Andrews	William Andrews		1	26
3	Robert Tollfree	William Proyer		1	29
4	Charles Hobbs	William Jolliffe Esq		1	24
5	Robert Tollfree	Richard Woolls	1	0	19

6	William Budd of Tenantry	William Budd of Tenantry	1	0	6
7	Robert Tollfree	Elizabeth Hunt		1	3
8	Robert Tollfree	Richard Woolls	2	0	5
		Total	**6**	**1**	**0**
	Head piece, Charles Hobbs	William Jolliffe Esq		3	11

Square Close Furlong, begins south

1	Charles Hobbs	William Jolliffe Esq		1	7
2	William Budd of Tenantry	William Budd of Tenantry		3	35
3	Robert Tollfree	Richard Woolls		3	16
4	Robert Tollfree	William Wake		1	12
5	Charles Hobbs	Williamm Jolliffe Esq		2	0
6	William Andrews	William Andrews		1	4
7	Robert Tollfree	Richard Woolls	6	0	4
		Total	**9**	**0**	**38**

Crook Lane Furlong, begins north

1	Charles Hobbs	William Jolliffe Esq	1	2	20
2	Robert Tollfree	Elizabeth Hunt		1	25
3	Robert Tollfree	Richard Woolls	1	3	31
4	Charles Hobbs	William Jolliffe Esq		3	12
5	Robert Tollfree	Richard Woolls	1	0	23
		Total	**5**	**3**	**31**
	A piece heading Bathstile Furlong – Charles Hobbs	William Jolliffe Esq	1	1	36
	A piece under Banaker Hedge – William Budd of Tenantry	William Budd of Tenantry	1	2	13

Yellow Land Furlong, begins south

1	William Budd of Tenantry	William Budd of Tenantry	2	2	37
2	Charles Hobbs	William Jolliffe Esq		1	27
3	William Budd of Tenantry	William Budd of Tenantry	5	0	35
4	Charles Hobbs	William Jolliffe Esq	4	3	29
5	Robert Tollfree	William Wake		1	35
6	William Budd of Tenantry	William Budd of Tenantry		1	36
		Total	**14**	**0**	**39**

Bath Stile Furlong, begins north

1	Robert Tollfree	Richard Woolls		1	15
2	William Andrews	William Andrews		1	19
3	William Budd of Tenantry *	The Poor of Alton		2	35
4	Charles Hobbs	William Jolliffe Esq		1	20
5	Robert Tollfree	William Wake		1	14
6	William Budd of Tenantry	William Budd of Tenantry		1	22
7	Charles Hobbs	William Jolliffe Esq	1	2	21
8	Robert Tollfree	Elizabeth Hunt		3	4

9	William Budd of Tenantry	William Budd of Tenantry	1	2	12
		Total	6	2	2

* This piece of land was given by two maiden ladies at a time when the plague was so bad in Alton, that the streets were green with grass

A Summary of Middle Field

Head piece by hoare dell		2	39
Elder Furlong	20	2	3
Hooks Corner Furlong	2	2	5
Gore Furlong	8	3	8
A Furlong at the West End of the Field	3	3	15
Another Furlong at the West End of the Field	5	2	22
Gore piece	4	1	21
Long Oak Stile furlong	4	3	9
A Furlong abutting on long Oak Stile furlong	6	1	0
A Head piece		3	11
Square Close furlong	9	0	38
Crook Lane furlong	5	3	31
Yellow Land furlong	14	0	39
Bathstile furlong	6	2	2
A piece heading the Last furlong	1	1	36
A piece under Banaker Hedge	1	2	13
Total	97	1	12

North Pace Field

Beech Land Furlong, begins East

1	William Budd of Tenantry	William Budd of Tenantry	1	0	36
2	Robert Tollfree	Richard Woolls		2	32
3	John Camies	John Camies			28
		Total	2	0	11

Hacket Furlong, begins north

1	William Budd of Tenantry	William Budd of Tenantry	2	2	37
2	Charles Hobbs	William Jolliffe Esq		1	27
3	William Budd of Tenantry	William Budd of Tenantry	5	0	35
4	Charles Hobbs	William Jolliffe Esq	4	3	29
5	Robert Tollfree	William Wake		1	35
6	William Budd of Tenantry	William Budd of Tenantry		1	36
		Total	14	0	39
	White peace at the Lower End of the Field C Hobbs	William Jolliffe Esq	1	0	22
	Piece by pace Lane William Budd of Tenantry	William Budd of Tenantry		1	15
		Total	1	1	37

Longhill Furlong, begins West

1	Richard Wake	Richard Wake	2	1	31
2	Robert Tollfree	William Proyer		3	9
3	William Andrews	William Andrews		3	6
4	Charles Hobbs	William Jolliffe Esq	1	2	24
		Total	**5**	**2**	**30**

Gore Furlong, begins north

1	William Andrews	William Andrews		2	5
2	Charles Hobbs	William Jolliffe Esq	1	3	2
3	Robert Tollfree	Elizabeth Hunt		3	19
4	Robert Tollfree	Richard Woolls		3	34
5	William Budd of Tenantry	William Budd of Tenantry		2	8
6	Robert Tollfree	Richard Woolls	1	3	30
7	William Budd of Tenantry	William Budd of Tenantry		2	10
8	Charles Hobbs	William Jolliffe Esq		1	4
9	Robert Tollfree	William Wake		1	15
10	Robert Tollfree	Richard Woolls		1	4
		Total	**8**	**3**	**13**
	A piece heading the East End of the last field – Robert Tollfree	Richard Woolls	1	0	39

Fan Furlong, begins south

1	Robert Tollfree	William Wake		2	17
2	Robert Tollfree	Richard Woolls		2	0
3	Robert Tollfree	Elizabeth Hunt			38
4	William Budd of Tenantry	William Budd of Tenantry		2	24
5	Robert Tollfree	William Woolls		3	35
6	Robert Tollfree	Elizabeth Hurst		2	27
7	Robert Tollfree	Richard Woolls		3	3
8	William Andrews	William Andrews		2	15
9	Robert Tollfree	Richard Woolls		2	28
10	John Camies	John Camies		2	27
11	Robert Tollfree	Richard Woolls		2	25
	Charles Hobbs	William Jolliffe Esq		2	36
12	Robert Tollfree	William Wake		2	6
13	Glebe, John Wilks	The Reverend Mr Butler		1	15
		Total	**8**	**2**	**16**

Ash Furlong, begins west

1	Robert Tollfree	Elizabeth Hunt		2	2
2	Robert Tollfree	Richard Woolls		2	2
3	John Wilks	John Wilks		2	4
4	Glebe John Wilks	The Reverend Mr Butler		3	25
		Total	**2**	**1**	**33**

A Summary of North Pace Field

Beech Land furlong	2	0	11
Hacket Furlong	5	2	5
Whitepiece and a piece by pace Lane	1	1	37
Longhill furlong	5	2	30
Gore furlong	8	3	13
A Headpiece	1	0	39
Fan furlong	8	2	16
Ash furlong	2	1	33
Total	**35**	**3**	**24**

South Pace Field

Picked Furlong, begins north

1	Robert Tollfree	Robert Woolls	2	0	0
2	William Budd of Tenantry	William Budd of Tenantry		3	27
3	Charles Hobbs	William Jolliff Esq		1	14
4	Robert Tollfree	William Wake			27
		Total	**3**	**1**	**28**

Soldridge Acre Furlong, begins south

1	Robert Tollfree	William Wake		3	2
2	Robert Tollfree	Richard Woolls		3	37
3	Charles Hobbs	William Jolliffe Esq	1	3	28
		Total	**3**	**2**	**27**
	A piece heading pudding furlong on the north – Robert Tollfree	William Proyer		1	32
	A piece at the south end of pudding furlong – R Tollfree	Elizabeth Hunt	1	0	2
	Havershot headpiece – Robert Tollfree	Richard Woolls	2	0	34
		Total	**3**	**2**	**28**

Pudding Furlong, begins west

1	William Andrews	William Andrews		2	19
2	Robert Tollfree	Richard Woolls		2	33
3	Charles Hobbs	William Jolliffe Esq	1	1	8
4	Robert Tollfree	Elizabeth Hunt		2	7
5	William Budd of Tenantry	William Budd of Tenantry		2	14
6	Charles Hobbs	William Jolliffe Esq	1	1	39
7	William Budd of Tenantry	William Budd of Tenantry			34
8	Robert Tollfree	William Wake		1	15
9	William Budd of Tenantry	William Budd of Tenantry		2	9
10	John Wilks	John Wilks		1	14
11	Charles Hobbs	William Jolliffe Esq		3	3
12	Robert Tollfree	William Woolls		3	10

13	Robert Tollfree	William Wake	1	0	11
	Robert Tollfree	William Andrews			22
14	Robert Tollfree			1	31
15	Robert Tollfree		1	0	32
16	Robert Tollfree	William Wake		3	11
17	William Budd of Tenantry	William Budd of Tenantry		3	1
18	Charles Hobbs	William Jolliffe Esq		2	2
19	Richard Wake	Richard Wake		2	15
20	Charles Hobbs	William Jolliffe Esq	1	0	10
21	Robert Tollfree	Elizabeth Hunt		3	9
22	Charles Hobbs	William Jolliffe Esq		1	16
23	Robert Tollfree	Richard Woolls		1	21
24	Charles Hobbs	William Jolliffe Esq	2	3	32
25	William Andrews	William Andrews		2	7
26	Charles Hobbs	William Jolliffe Esq		1	35
		Total	**20**	**1**	**20**

A Summary of South Pace Field

Picked Furlong	3	1	28
Soldridge Acre furlong	3	2	27
Pudding furlong	20	1	20
3 Head pieces	3	2	28
Total	**31**	**0**	**23**
Little Common Down	12	0	7

Appendix 19: Ropley Manor terrier, 1786-8

Terrier, Lifehold Lands, Ropley Manor: Began and finished in the Years 1786, 1787 and 1788 by Morley Copeland

Premises & tenant	Arable			Out to Out			Annual value		
	a	r	p	a	r	p	£	s	d
1 John Mayhew, Ropley									
A Purrock of Land having the Farm Lands on the East & North parts the said John Mayhew Garden Dry Mead and Backside on the West part and William Budd's Land on the South part thereof	1	3	38	2	0	0	2	0	0
2 Barned Woods / Later William Grant, Bighton									
A Messuage Backside & Barton									
Water Mead in Drayton		3	12		3	18			
Pasture in Drayton		1	23		1	26			
Pasture by the tenement		2	7		2	11			
Fulflood Close	2	0	11	2	0	28			
Backside Close	1	1	27	1	2	24			
East Upper Hagdel Close	2	0	4	2	3	8			
East Lower Hagdel Close	1	3	21	2	1	5			
West Upper Hagdel Close	1	3	7	2	1	39			
West Lower Hagdel Close	2	1	35	9	3	23			
East Swelling Close	3	2	28	3	2	36			
West Swelling Close	3	1	19	3	2	24			
A Wood in Bishop's Sutton				13	0	36	21	18	6
	19	3	36	36	0	1			
3 Thomas Oliver now William Budd, Ropley									
A Cottage and Garden									
A close by Wm Newland's House	2	1	3	2	1	23			
The Hanger piece	2	2	21	2	3	13			
Home Close	1	1	19	1	1	39			
Upper Cleve	2	0	30	2	1	27	6	0	0
	8	1	32	9	0	22			

Aug 18 1802: It seems that the Premises of this copy are only the Close behind Newlands house called Hamerton Bottom containing two Acres & half and 3 perches; and also the piece called Half here received in exchange for the two pieces called Cockshott. Aug 18 1802: It appears from the rent which William Budd gives for Nos. 21, 46, 15, 29 that the Hangar Piece, Home Close, Cottage & Garden belong to those numbers: for Copeland's Valuation will not bring those numbers to £15 per annum which is the annual rent paid for them. This copy was held by lease under Bishop of Winchester which lease was renewed in 1852 under consent of the College to H J Mulcock.

4 John Andrews, Ropley

Great Mancroft	4	3	18	5	1	8			
Little Mancroft	2	3	21	3	0	13	5	0	0
	7	**2**	**39**	**8**	**1**	**21**			

5 Richard Woolls, Medsted

Lower Church Close	3	0	39	3	1	27			
Middle Church Close	5	1	34	6	0	2			
Upper Church Close	8	1	22	8	2	6			
Great Minchins	10	2	19	11	0	18			
Bottom Minchins	3	3	33	4	2	3			
Little Minchins	1	2	15	2	1	17			
Hether Minchins	3	3	20	4	1	3			
North Field	2	1	34	2	2	10			
North Field purrock	0	3	4	0	3	16			
Swanmore piece	2	1	26	2	2	15			
Stankham Common or Close by Camies's	5	1	5	5	2	4			
Stankham Hill Close	11	1	6	12	0	20			
Frog Acre by Crooked Close	0	3	29	1	0	4			
Crooked Close	2	3	19	3	0	10			
Long Acre in Church Filed	1	1	18	1	1	29			
Willmead piece in Church Field	1	2	30	1	2	36			
Square acre in Church Field	1	0	6	1	0	9			
Cockshot Close	4	2	15	4	3	34			
Church Close Coppice				7	2	30			
Minchins Coppice				3	3	2	37	17	0
	88	**2**	**23**						

6 Richard Wake, James Knight 1828, Medsted

Cuckoo Bush piece in Church Field		1	10		1	11			
Old Mead	1	0	39	1	1	16			
Withey piece	1	3	20	2	0	7			
A piece in pudding Furlong in South paice Field		2	13		2	15			
Bramble halve by Oak Stile in Middle Field		2	6		2	10			
The Common piece which is thrown to the Common piece No 11	1	0	0	1	0	7	2	8	0
	5	**2**	**8**	**5**	**3**	**26**			

7 John Wilks, Medsted

This Copy is the same as No. 8 which see

8 John Spencer since John Wilks. James Usher 1832. James Jeffery, Medsted

Home purrock		1	5		1	14			
The Dry Meadow adjoining to the last		3	22		3	35			
A purrock at the Lower End of the last		3	28	1	0	3			

Picked Hook - Common Ground	1	1	33	1	2	10			
Piece of Common Ground near Lavers House	2	0	37	2	1	16			
A Messuage and Garden							5	0	0
	4	**3**	**5**	**6**	**0**	**38**			

9   Late Thomas Hall Esq now John Bernard Esq. William Budd, Ropley

Hayling Hills or Hazledon Piece	3	3	5	4	0	1			
The Read Piece	1	3	33	2	0	1			
Compton's or Coopers Croft abutting on the North side of Gilberts Street	3	3	27	4	0	27			
Further Piece on Swelling Hill	3	3	33	4	1	3			
Middle Piece on Swelling Hill	5	3	21	6	1	31			
A piece by the Messuage on Swelling Hill	4	0	26	4	2	4			
A piece of Common Ground	2	1	14	2	2	12			
A Messuage & Garden on Swelling Hill							15	10	0
	25	**3**	**29**	**27**	**3**	**39**			

10   Rechab Thorne. 1828 Alex. Barrington, Itchen Stoke

Upper Field

A piece in the lower Shot by the Down				2	0	34	
A piece in the upper Shot					3	21	
A piece by Serles Bushes				2	1	15	
Chalk Dell piece					2	13	
A piece near the last					3	1	
A piece in the Shot by Road Hedge					2	23	
Another piece					2	11	
Tidbut piece					2	19	
A Head Acre					1	28	
A piece by Serles Bush Shot				1	0	14	
Another piece in Serles Bush Shot					2	26	
A piece East of the Road					2	6	
				11	**1**	**11**	

Home Field

A piece heading the lower Shott					1	14	
A piece in the lower Shott				1	0	38	
Another piece in the same Shott				1	3	16	
Another piece heading the lower Shott				2	2	38	
A piece abutting on the last piece				2	2	5	
A piece in the Slade Shott				1	0	34	
A piece heading Slade Shott					2	1	
Another piece in Slade Shott				1	0	19	
Chalk Dell piece abutting on Upper Field Hedge					2	24	
				12	**0**	**29**	

Water Meadow

Wigmore Mead: The Lower half Acre					1	10		
Wigmore Mead: The square half Acre					2	32		
Wigmore Mead: Another half Acre					1	8		
Wigmore Mead: A piece by the parish Acre					2	37		
Bullingham Mead				2	3	32		
				4	**3**	**39**		

Pasture Land

A purrock by the Dwelling House			2	19	

Lower Field

A piece in piddle Shott				1	1	10		
A piece in lower Shott					2	7		
Another piece in the same Shott					2	12		
Another piece in the same Shott				1	1	0		
Great head Acre piece					3	34		
Headpiece by Thursdays Bush				1	1	12		
Tinepiece				1	0	30		
A piece in little Shott					1	32		
Another piece in the same Shott					1	32		
A piece in the upper Shott by new Broak Land					3	20		
A piece in the Lower Shott by new Broak Land				1	2	8		
Thursdays piece					2	10		
Two Acre piece by Thursdays Bush				1	1	15		
A piece in the Shott heading the lower Shott					2	20		
A piece at Shiphouse Bank				1	3	26		
Another piece by the same					2	10		
A Messuage Backside & Barton							21	0	0
	15	**1**	**38**	**44**	**2**	**16**		

11   Richard Wake. 1828: James Knight, Medsted

South Upper Lymington Close	3	0	37	3	1	29			
South Lower Lymington	3	2	34	3	3	27			
North Upper Lymington	3	2	34	3	3	27			
North Lower Lymington	3	1	21	3	2	38			
The common piece, which piece is thrown to his common piece No. 6	1	3	31	2	0	13	5	0	0
	15	**3**	**37**	**17**	**0**	**15**			

12   John Luff. Arnold. Ropley

Further Close	1	2	21	2	0	33			
Hether Close	1	3	26	2	0	35			
A piece of Common Land	1	2	13	1	2	30			
A Messuage Garden & Yard							5	12	0
	5	**0**	**20**	**6**	**0**	**18**			

13   Henry Budd of Alton. Worthington. Ropley

A Grove of Wood called Cuninger	1	0	0					
Land called Cuninger	1	0	26					
	2	**0**	**26**					

14   John Egby, Ropley

This copy appears to be the same as No. 57 which see

15   Thomas Oliver. William Budd. Ropley

A Close of Land adjoining to a Close called Rowlands lying on the south part of Hammerdon Bottom [Saxon], or Ropley Soke, and on the East part of a Close of Land late Thomas Andrews now the said Thomas Oliver's being Copy No. 21	2	1	19	2	1	32	1	5	0

16   Samuel Smither. 1825: William Smith. Ropley

A piece of Land called Mancroft		3	9		3	24			
A piece by the Cottage		2	20		2	32			
A piece of the inclosed Common allotted to the same having the King's Highway leading from Medsted to East Tisted on the North West, John Andrews Land on the west and the South parts and John Budd's Land on the East part thereof	4	2	5	4	2	7			
A Messuage & Garden							4	16	0
	5	**3**	**34**	**6**	**0**	**23**			

17   Charles Daniels late Robert Smith. John Passingham, Ropley

A Cottage Orchard and Garden									
A purrock of Land adjoining to the Cottage		1	34		2	8	2	0	0

18   John Duthy Esq (part Bp. of Winton), Roppley

Kitwood Lands									
A purrock by Horethorne	1	0	26	1	2	6			
A piece by the road leading to Tisted	2	3	20	3	1	17			
Blanchards Close north of the last	8	2	10	8	3	8			
Middle piece or Dell piece	15	2	20	16	1	7			
A piece adjoining to the East part of Kitwood	5	2	30	6	0	2			
The long Slip south of the Wood		3	23	1	0	25			
A slip on the West side of the Wood	2	1	25	2	1	32			
The Great piece west of the last	15	2	18	16	1	13			
Home Field	11	3	13	12	1	30			
Kitwood Wood				11	2	28			
A Messuage Backside and Barton							33	16	0
	68	**1**	**20**	**79**	**3**	**28**			

19 Nicholas Mayhew. Michael ?Ribits, Bishop's Sutton

Bakers purrock by Water Lane	3	2	10	3	2	29			
North Street Close	3	0	16	3	1	15			
Hasledon Bottom piece	2	3	37	3	0	32			
A Close east of Hasledon Bottom	4	3	3	5	2	19			
East Honey Linch	3	2	33	4	0	20			
West Honey Linch	6	0	30	6	2	38			
Greenaway Close	10	0	36	11	0	0			
A Cottage Garden and Orchard							20	10	0
	37	**3**	**8**	**41**	**0**	**33**			

20 Richard Andrews. 1827: James Knight, Medsted

Lower Lymington Close	6	0	7	6	2	33			
Upper Lymington Close	6	3	35	7	1	11			
A piece in Medsted Common. Aug 18 1802: This is let for £5 per annum	1	13	6	1	3	39	4	16	0
	14	**3**	**18**	**16**	**0**	**3**			

21 Thomas Oliver. William Budd. Ropley

A Close of Land abutting on the Cottage and Garden belonging to the same	2	0	27	2	1	37	2	5	0

22 Executors of J Duthy Esq. M Duthie, Ropley

Great Broom Fields heretofore called Out Croft	13	2	15	14	1	16			
Little Broom Field, a piece of inclosed Common Ground	1	2	30	1	3	24			
Two Acre Close by Old Down being inclosed Common Land	1	3	20	2	0	12			
Brickiln piece ?? Land. 1795: NB: A mistake was made in assigning Brickiln to the College. That belongs to Mr Duthy. The College has seven acres in a large field lying behind Brickiln, which seven acres constitute the quantity of Land mentioned after the first Item in the above description.	4	0	0	4	0	35	13	4	0
	21	**0**	**25**	**22**	**2**	**7**			

23 John Long, Ropley

Great Meerlands	5	0	25	5	1	29			
Little Meerlands	3	3	4	4	0	6			
Stadeham or Sladenham	5	3	2	6	0	39			
A piece of Common to the above	6	0	16	6	1	6	13	4	0
	20	**3**	**7**	**22**	**0**	**0**			

24 Sarah Andrews, Ropley

House Lower Close		2	13		3	32

Middle Lower Close	1	2	36	1	3	27			
Further Lower Close	1	1	22	1	2	31			
Further Upper Close	1	0	28	1	1	6			
Middle Upper Close	2	1	8	2	2	17			
Hether Upper Close	2	0	17	2	2	10			
A Cottage Garden Barn& Backside							4	16	0
	9	**0**	**38**	**11**	**0**	**3**			

25   Stephen Hockley. 1827: Rev G Coulthard, Wield

A piece near Michens Coppices	3	2	11	3	3	2			
A piece by Dirty Lane Gate Piece	5	1	30	5	3	31			
Long Close	4	2	17	4	3	24			
A piece East of the Last	8	1	11	8	3	19	8	0	0
	21	**3**	**29**	**23**	**1**	**26**			

26   Hannah Budd. Chris Pickering. Bighton

Messuage and Garden						10	2	0	0

27   John Long, Ropley

Soly or Silly House Close by the Grove	5	1	6	5	2	8			
Moonburn Piece adjacent to Sladeham	4	3	32	5	0	21			
Long Buckingham	2	1	19	2	1	34			
Square Buckingham	3	2	25	4	0	34			
Short Buckingham	2	0	5	2	0	25			
A Close called Chacys abutting on the south side of Gilbert Street	1	3	14	1	3	38			
A piece of the Common inclosed	8	2	5	8	3	23			
Soly or Silly House Coppice				1	2	35			
A Barn in Chacys Close but no Messuage							13	5	0
	28	**2**	**26**	**32**	**0**	**18**			

28   Thomas Bartlett Esq late Thomas Stevens. 1829: John Lavender. Ropley

A Close called Coppers abutting on the North side of South Street. A Malthouse Granary.	2	2	29	2	3	10	4	16	0

29   Thomas Oliver. William Budd. Ropley

A Cottage and Garden called Squirrels. A purrock adjoining to the same		3	3		3	15	2	0	0

30   John Eames Waight. Also Waight's copy 29 May 1809 on facing page - not transcribed. Bishop's Sutton

Gullet Close	8	0	28	9	0	37			
East piece in Broaks	2	1	3	2	3	12			
West piece in Broaks	2	0	29	2	2	12			
Dell piece at Broaks	3	2	4	4	1	6			

Long piece at Broaks	2	3	19	3	1	19		
Upper Shott in Ropley Mark	2	1	27	2	1	29		
Lower Shott in Ropley Mark	3	3	18	3	3	21		
One Acre piece in Ropley Mark	1	0	11	1	0	14		
Greenaway Close	3	3	14	4	0	35		
Medsted Acre		2	17		2	30		
North Street Close	3	3	20	4	0	1		
Bottom piece in Bradly Field	4	3	18	4	3	18		
Long piece in Bradly Field	3	3	31	3	3	33		
A piece in Salden Field by Bradly Field Gate		3	2		3	5		
Roundabout Acre by Whiteway		3	39	1	0	38		
Bush piece between the Linches	1	2	35	1	2	38		
Harber Close	6	0	17	7	0	24		
Upper Potters	3	2	15	3	3	17		
Lower Potters	2	1	20	2	2	13		
A piece in Colden Bottom		2	38		3	2		
Honey Linch	11	1	14	12	2	36		
	71	**0**	**10**	**78**	**1**	**10**		
The Water Meadow	4	1	7	4	1	19		
Coppice Ground								
Upper Gullet coppice				5	1	35		
Lower Gullet coppice				4	3	4		
Broak Coppice				4	3	4	49	7	6
				97	**2**	**32**		

31 William Budd Senior: Ropley Manor (two copies), Medsted

Wilsons lower Soldridge Common piece	13	2	25	13	3	11
Wilsons upper Soldridge Common piece	14	1	6	14	2	11
Havershop paice Field Close	5	1	4	5	2	5
Barr Acre in Great paice Field		2	14		2	18
Whitehill piece			34			36
Picked Acre in South paice Field		3	20		3	28
A piece by the Lane in Little paice Field		1	16		1	21
Head piece ascending the Hill	1	1	14	1	1	16
Beechling hill piece			36			36
White piece upon the Hill		1	2		1	4
Waterdell piece in Middle Field	1	0	0	1	0	37
Staple Acre	1	0	8	1	0	11
Waterdell piece in Long Oak stile furlong	1	0	0	1	0	2
A piece in Yellow Lanes by Square Close		1	28		1	31
A piece just within Middle Field Gate	1	2	19	1	2	28
Crooked Lane piece		2	6		2	9
The Great piece in Yellow Lands	5	0	14	5	0	17
A piece by Summerlease Hedge		1	37		2	0

Willsons Lower Close	6	1	6	6	2	25			
Willsons Home Close	3	2	21	3	3	10			
Willsons Dry Mead	2	2	18	2	3	11			
Great Park Close and little Park Close both in one	16	3	18	17	1	8			
Willsons Down piece by the Coppice	4	3	17	5	0	20			
Willsons Down piece by the last piece	4	2	5	4	2	39			
Ryfield	8	2	4	8	3	4			
Bonts Close	4	0	29	4	1	16			
Shepards Close		1	28		1	37			
Summerlease	1	2	35	1	3	10			
Crab-Corner Close	3	1	17	3	1	20			
Great Hursles, pond Hursles and a piece called Redwood, now all one Close	12	1	23	12	3	7			
Church Field									
The Bottom piece		3	9		3	9			
?Cuffle Acre		3	5		3	7			
A piece abutting on Birds purrock		2	30		2	33			
A piece south of the Glebe Land		1	15		1	16			
A piece in Millway Furlong		2	11		2	13			
	120	3	5	124	3	6			
Wood Ground									
Down Coppice				6	0	18			
Great Coppice				14	1	11			
Little Coppice at the south end of the Last				2	0	34	61	0	0
				147	1	29			

32 Richard Andrews late Eldridges, Ropley

Lower Purrock		3	1		3	22			
Middle Purrock	1	0	14	1	0	28			
Upper Purrock	1	2	19	1	2	39	1	10	0
The above pieces lye on the South side of the Road leading from Ropley to Newton									
	3	1	14	3	3	9			

33 Benjamin Nevill, Bighton

Old Alresford Close	2	0	8	2	1	10
Ash Garden Piece	3	0	5	3	1	12
Ferney Close	13	1	11	13	2	16
Dobbs Stile Close	2	1	22	2	2	7
Backside Close	8	1	23	8	3	6
The Drove			18			19
Maple Close	4	3	10	5	1	27
Fullers Horn Close	10	1	3	10	2	16
Eight Acre Piece	8	0	24	8	1	32

Kite's Hill piece	10	2	27	10	3	12			
Nythe Piece	12	1	1	12	2	30			
	75	**1**	**32**	**78**	**2**	**27**			
Upper Water Mead	1	3	7	1	3	15			
Lower Water Mead		2	15		2	25			
	77	**3**	**14**	**81**	**0**	**27**			
A Messuage Backside & Barton to the above							45	0	0

34 Thomas Moon, Bighton

A Cottage and Garden · 11 1 0

35 Edward Goffe, Bighton

Barton Piece	2	1	17	2	2	27			
Backside Close	2	2	15	2	3	10			
A Close abutting on Mitchels Garden		2	25		2	25			
A Messuage Garden and Barn							4	0	0
	5	**2**	**7**	**6**	**0**	**30**			

36 John Andrews, Ropley

See No. 17 being the same premises

37 Charles Ward. William Budd, Ropley

A piece of the Common inclosed abutting on the Road leading from Medstead to Tisted and adjoins to the Kitwood Road	9	0	11	9	1	12
A piece of the Common inclosed at Bogmere	3	0	15	3	0	38
A piece of the Common inclosed abutting on the north side of the Turnpike Road near Ropley Soke	3	3	21	4	0	29
Long Purrock adjoining to the North Side of the Turnpike Road	0	3	6	1	0	17
Hook Field	1	1	34	1	2	37
A piece near Drumer Budd's Cottage	2	3	16	3	0	17
Home Close adjoining to the Messuage	7	3	36	8	2	10
South Hasle Close	5	1	21	5	3	14
North hasle Close	5	3	33	6	0	16
	40	**1**	**33**	**43**	**0**	**30**

Great Grove or Wood	5	0	4
Little Grove		3	0
	48	**3**	**34**

A Messuage Backside & Barton · 25 2 8

[The file contains a sheet of 1882 headed Copies
31, 38 & 41 which lists later arrangements]

38 **William Budd Senior. Jane Morey 1836. Medsted**

Lymington Bottom Close	4	1	33	5	0	21		
A piece of Common Ground in Camies's piece	1	1	0	1	1	3	2	0	0
	5	2	33	6	1	24		

39 **William Budd of Ropley. Ropley**

A Coppice called West Grove adjoining to Bowers Grove				4	3	9	2	17	0

40 **William Budd of Ropley. Ropley**

Bowyer's Grove East of West Grove (+ full page map)				13	3	23		
A piece of Common inclosed adjoining to the north side of the road by Farringdon Common	4	0	4	4	0	29	9	13	0
	4	0	4	18	0	12		

1797: Much dispute having arisen between the College and Mr William Budd respecting the value of his Copies Estate at Ropley of Mr William Budd held under the Warden and Fellows of Winton College Containing a Messuage Garden Barns and Farm Yard with the following pieces of Arable Land: No. 39, 40, 48, 51, 52, 53.

It was at length agreed by the parties that Mr Tredgold [1799 Medstead enclosure commissioner] should survey and value them and that his valuation should regulate the fine. The Lands at Ropley differ greatly in value: those of the North side are by no means as good as those on the South. Mr Budd's Lands lie chiefly on the North side.

Mr Tredgold however has set them very low indeed and perhaps before another renewal takes place it may be advisable for the College to have the Lands again valued. But Mr Tredgold's Survey has at least been attended with one advantage. From Mr Budd's having thrown together Copyhold, Bishop's holding, and Freehold Land, it was difficult to ascertain the College property. The different fields were made out by Mr Tredgold and are now referred to their respective numbers.

[There is a separate sheet headed] Value of an Estate at Ropley of Mr William Budd held under the Warden and Fellows of Winton College Containing a Messuage Garden Barns and Farm Yard with the following pieces of Arable Land. [Tredgold's signed list dated 23 May 1797 of 19 pieces follows amounting to 148 acres/2/18 valued at £49/3/9¾ plus a wood called Collins at £1/16/6¼, total £51/0/4].

41 **John Luff late Crockford. John Arnold. Ropley**

A purrock of Land having ?Wards Hook Close on the North and the said John Luffs Garden and part of his other Land on the South		2	22		3	6		9	0

42 **Samuel Smithers, Ropley**

A Close called Hook or Hook Close having Swelling Lane or the Kings highway on the North the said Samuel Smithers Land, held under the Bishop of Winton, on the West part, a Lane leading out of Swelling Lane to John Budd's Land called Heldens on the East part and John Andrews Land on the South part thereof	2	3	1	3	1	32	2	0	0

43 William Faithfull. Thomas Moore. Ropley

A Cottage, Barn, Yard and Garden									
A piece South of the Road by the Cottage	4	2	13	5	0	4			
Middle Close	3	1	6	3	2	36			
Further Close adjoining to the Road leading from Ropley to Newton Common	2	0	5	2	1	19			
Further piece adjoining to Newton Common	2	1	12	2	2	31			
Hether piece adjoining to the last	1	0	28	1	1	28			
A Close by the Messuage & Garden	2	0	30	2	2	36			
A Close North of the last Close	2	0	20	2	2	30			
A Cottage & Garden to the above							7	7	0
	17	**2**	**43**	**20**	**2**	**24**			

44 John Andrews. 1836: William Smither. Ropley

A Close near Fry Wood. (1882: Tithe 440, 1a/3/17)	1	1	24	1	2	22	1	0	0

45 John Andrews. 1836: William Smither. Ropley

A Close called Amerkin	1	0	10	1	0	34	1	5	0

46 Thomas Oliver. William Budd. Ropley

A Close adjoining to Olivers Garden	1	0	21	1	1	16			
A piece North of the Last Close	2	0	2	2	0	18			
A Close East and adjoining to the two Last Closes	3	1	36	3	2	22			
The above three pieces are called Rowlands							3	0	0
	6	**2**	**19**	**7**	**0**	**16**			

47 William Budd Junior. 1836 Jane Morey. Medsted

South upper Lymington Close	3	1	22	3	2	34			
North upper Lymington Close	3	1	18	3	2	13			
Little Lymington Close at the bottom of the Last	1	0	27	1	1	9			
A piece of inclosed Common Ground	1	3	21	1	3	30	3	3	0
	9	**3**	**8**	**10**	**2**	**6**			

48 William Budd of Alton, Ropley

Starve Acre Close	4	3	31	5	0	6			
Wansors Close West of the Last	7	0	6	7	1	14			
Cowpens Close North of the Last	2	3	37	3	2	26			
Seven Acre Close	6	0	21	6	2	3			
Eight Acre Close	6	3	33	7	0	27			
The Hanger Piece being inclosed Common Ground and adjoins to Collins Wood	9	0	25	9	2	3			
A piece adjoining to the Turnpike Road and Arnolds or Luffs House	0	3	3	0	3	7			
	37	**3**	**36**	**39**	**3**	**36**			

Collins's Wood				7	1	19			
				47	**0**	**15**			
A Messuage Garden Barn and Backside belonging to the same							19	16	0

49 Stephen Smith. 1832: George Hetherington. Ropley

A Tenement and Garden on the South side of the Soke						2	1	10	0

50 Frances Newton, Winnall

Four Acre Close	4	0	3	4	1	13			
Ten Acre Close	8	1	12	10	3	24			
Three Acre Close	4	0	0	4	0	20			
A Close by the Cottage		1	22		1	27			
A Close abutting on the Turnpike (This Close is sold to Mr Deverell)	1	0	22	1	0	34			
	17	3	19	20	3	38			
A Cottage & Garden to the above							16	0	0

51 William Budd of Alton, Ropley

A piece of Land called Rowlands having the Lands of Thomas Oliver on the South and East parts thereof and is thrown to the said William Budds Land Copy No. 52	5	2	26	6	0	23	2	14	0

52 William Budd of Alton, Ropley

A piece called Bruslands	3	2	31	5	1	35			
Rowlands Wood piece	6	0	26	6	1	30			
Pinks Close	13	0	26	13	1	35			
The upper Hangar	8	2	24	9	0	1			
Magpye piece on holts hill	7	1	7	7	2	8			
A piece East of and adjoining to Gullet Lane	3	3	12	4	1	8			
Purrock by the House late Drumer Budd		2	21		2	21			
A Close called Squirrels	3	2	19	4	1	11			
Berry piece, late Mayhews	2	3	14	3	0	1			
Long Acre on the South side of Gaston Lane	1	1	1	1	2	8			
West Gaston piece		2	26		2	30			
East Gaston piece		3	2		3	10			
Bogmere piece	5	3	6	6	0	1			
	58	**1**	**15**	**63**	**0**	**19**			
A Tenement & Garden							22	4	0

53 William Budd of Alton, Ropley

Wares Wood				3	2	6			
A Close adjoining to Wares Wood	8	1	2	8	1	2			
	8	**1**	**2**	**12**	**0**	**9**			

								£	s	d
A Barn & Yard belonging								5	6	0
54 Robert Gibbs, Ropley										
A Cottage and Garden							20	2	0	0
55 Richard Woolls. 1834: George Newberry, Medsted										
A piece in Stankham Common near Stankham Barn	15	3	17	16	1	8		6	8	0
56 Hannah Budd. 1832 Richard Bone. Medsted										
Breach Close	3	0	10	3	1	1				
Summerleaze	2	0	34	2	2	7				
New Close	5	0	1	5	1	2				
Well Mead	1	1	8	1	1	19				
Upper Mead	1	3	16	2	0	9				
Chalkdell Piece		2	9		2	18				
Little Mead		2	9		2	22				
	14	**2**	**7**	**15**	**2**	**38**				
A Messuage Garden & Barn								7	10	0
57 John Egby, Ropley										
A Cottage and Garden No. 61										
A Close adjoining to the same No 57	1	2	32	1	3	5		2	11	0
A Close adjoining to the same No. 57	1	2	32	1	3	5		2	11	0
58 John Lockett. 1825: William Budd. Ropley										
A Cottage & Garden							4	1	0	0
59 Moses Portsmouth, Ropley										
?Bue Kingham Common	3	0	7	3	1	9				
Upper Grove Purrock		2	2		2	9				
Lower Grove Purrock		3	25	1	0	5				
Little ?Ruttly	2	0	0	2	0	2		4	4	0
	6	**1**	**34**	**6**	**3**	**35**				
Total				1074	2	39		613	5	3

Appendix 20: Medstead and Bentworth Enclosure Act, 1798

An Act for Dividing, Allotting and Inclosing, the Open and Common Fields in the Parishes of Medstead and Bentworth, in the County of Southampton.[1]

Whereas there are within the several Parishes of Medstead, otherwise Meidstead, and Bentworth, in the County of Southampton, certain Open and Common Fields, containing together, by Estimation, Four Hundred Acres, or thereabouts:

And whereas

- Charles Drummond, Esquire, and
- George Wheatley, Gentlemen, (as Devisees in Trust of the last will and Testament of Henry Drummond, Esquire, deceased)
- Ann Woolls, Widow
- Edward Wools, Esquire
- Francis North, Clerk, as Rector of Old Alresford, with the Chapelries of New Alresford and Medstead, otherwise Meidstead, annexed
- John Hicks
- William Budd
- Richard [end page 1] Wake
- John Camies
- John Andrews
- William Andrews

and divers other Persons, and Owners of the said Open and Common Fields lying within the said Parish of Medstead, otherwise Meidstead

And Thomas Coulthard, Esquire, Thomas Hall, Esquire, John Calland, Clerk, as Rector of the said Parish of Bentworth, Stephen Dicker, Joseph Page, John Andrews the Younger, Thomas Vickery, William Winter, John Paddick, and divers other Persons, are Owners of the said Open and Common Fields lying with the said Parish of *Bentworth*

And whereas the Lands of the several Proprietors in all the said Open and Common Fields lie intermixed and dispersed in small Parcels, and in their present State are incapable of any considerable Improvement, and it would be advantageous to the said Proprietors if all the same Open and Common Fields were divided and inclosed, and specific Parts thereof allotted to them in Lieu of, and in Proportion to their Estates and Properties therein respectively: But such Division and Inclosure cannot be effected without the Authority of Parliament.

MAY IT THEREFORE PLEASE YOUR MAJESTY

That it may be enacted, and be it enacted by the King's Most Excellent Majesty, by and with the Advice and Consent of the Lords, Spiritual and Temporal, and Commons, in this present Parliament assembled, and by the Authority of the same, That Thomas Hasker of Chineham, in the County of Southampton, Esquire, John Tredgold, of the City of Winchester, in the same County, and Thomas Fleet, of the

---

1   Parliamentary Archives: Private Act, 38 George III, c. 35, HL/PO/PB/1/1798/38G3n99.

Parish of Preston Candover, in the same County, Yeoman, shall be, and they are hereby appointed, Commissioners for setting out, dividing, and allotting, all the said Open and Common Fields within the said several Parishes of Medstead, otherwise Meidstead, and Bentworth.

And be it further enacted, That if any one or more of the said Commissioners hereby appointed, or any Commissioner or Commissioners to be nominated and appointed in Manner hereinafter mentioned, shall die or refuse to act, then, and from Time to Time, as often as Occasion shall require, it shall be lawful for the major Part in Value of the several Owners, for the Time being, of the lands hereby directed to be inclosed, their Agents or Attornies, attending at a Meeting to be appointed for that Purpose, by Writing under their Hands, [end page 2] to nominate and appoint One other proper Person, not interested in the said intended Inclosure, in the Room of every such Commissioner to be nominated and appointed, shall, from thenceforth, have the same Powers and Authorities to put this Act in Execution, as if he had been hereby nominated and appointed such commissioner.

Provided, That Eight Days previous Notice of the Time and Place of holding every such Meeting under the Hands of Three or more of the said Proprietors be affixed on the principal Doors of the Parish Churches of Medstead, otherwise Meidstead, and Bentworth aforesaid.

Provided always, That it shall be lawful for any Two or more of the said Commissioners for the Time being, and they are hereby fully authorised and impowered to execute, do and perform, every any every Act, Matter and Thing whatsoever, by this Act authorised to be executed, done and performed by the said Commissioners; and every such Act, Matter, or Thing, which shall be executed, done, and performed by any Two of the said Commissioners for the Time being, shall be as valid and effectual, to all Intents and Purposes, as if all the said Commissioners, hereinbefore named and appointed, had been present, and had executed, done, and performed the same.

Provided always, and be it further enacted, That no Person shall be capable of acting in the execution of this Act, as a Commissioner (except in appointing the First Meeting of the Commissioners, and administering the following Oath) or as a Surveyor, until he shall have taken and subscribed the Oath following (that is to say):

> *I A. B. do swear, that I will faithfully, impartially and honestly, to the best of my Judgement, do and execute all Things appertaining to the Office and Duty of a Commissioner [or Surveyor, as the Case may be] by virtue of an Act, passed in the Thirty-eight Year of the Reign of his Majesty King George the Third, intituled [here set forth the Title of the Act]; and that* [end page 3] *without Favour of Affection, Prejudice or Malice, to any Person or Persons whomsoever. So help me God.*

Which Oath shall be lawful for any One of the said Commissioners to administer; and the said Oath, so taken and subscribed by each Commissioner, shall be inrolled with any Award of the said Commissioners hereinafter directed to be made.

And be it further enacted, That Notice shall be affixed on the principal Doors of the Parish Churches of Medstead, otherwise Meidstead, and Bentworth, respectively, of the Time and Place of the First, and every subsequent Meeting of the said Commissioners, for putting this Act in Execution, at least Eight Days before every such Meeting (Meetings by Adjournment only excepted); and that all such Meetings shall be held in the Villages of Medstead and Bentworth, or one of them, or within the Distance of Ten Miles therefrom.

Providing always, That if, at any Meeting appointed to be holden as aforesaid, only one Commissioner shall attend, he may adjourn such meeting, to such Time and Place as he shall think most convenient, giving Notice thereof to the absent Commissioners.

And, For the more just and regular Division of the said Open and Common Fields, and other Commonable Grounds, **Be it further Enacted,** That the Commissioners shall, as soon as conveniently may be, view, examine, and value all the said Lands and Grounds hereby intended to be inclosed, and all or such Parts of the Old Inclosures within the said Parishes, or either of them, as the said Commissioners shall think fit; and shall cause true and perfect Surveys, Admeasurements, and Plans to be made thereof, by such Person or Persons as they shall appoint; and such Surveys, Admeasurements, and Plans, shall be reduced into Writing, and all the Contents of the whole Lands to be inclosed, and the several Parcels of Land, and Numbers of Acres, Roods, and Perches shall, when completed, be laid before the said Commissioners, to be used by them for the Purposes of this Act; and the Person or [end page 4] Persons who shall make such Survey, Admeasurement, and Plan, shall verify the same, upon Oath, at some Meeting of the said Commissioners, before the Allotments hereinafter mentioned are made, which Oath the said Commissioners are hereby impowered to administer.

Provided always, That if any Survey, Admeasurement, or Plan, made within the Period of Five Years last past, or any of the Lands hereby directed to be surveyed, shall be produce to, and approved by the said Commissioners; then the said Commissioners may, if they shall think proper, make use of the same, for the Purposes aforesaid, instead of having the same Lands re-surveyed.

And be it further enacted, That it shall be lawful for the said Commissioners, and every of them, and all Persons appointed to make such Surveys, Admeasurements, Plans, and Valuations, together with their Assistants and Servants, from Time to Time, as often as it shall be necessary, to enter into and upon the Lands hereby directed to be surveyed and valued as aforesaid, and every or any Part or Parts thereof, for the Purposes of this Act, without any hindrance or molestation whatsoever.

And be it further enacted, That all Persons claiming any Lands, Right of Common, or Right of Soil, or other Property in or upon the said Lands or Grounds hereby directed to be inclosed, shall lay their respective Claims, in Writing, before the said Commissioners, at some meeting to be held for that Purpose, of which, at least, Fourteen Days previous Notice shall be given by Advertisements, in the *Salisbury and Winchester Journal* and *Hampshire Chronicle* (if such papers then be circulated), and by affixing such Notice, in Writing, on the principal Doors of the Parish Churches of Medstead, otherwise Meidstead, and Bentworth, aforesaid, on a Sunday, immediately before Divine Service, in which Notice the said Commissioners shall require all Persons claiming and Right, Property, or Interest, in or upon the said

Lands and Grounds hereby directed to be inclosed, or any Part thereof, to lay such Claims before them in Writing, at or within the time to be limited for that Purpose; and that it shall be lawful for the said Commissioners to reject any [end page 5] Claim or Claims which shall not be delivered at such Meeting.

And be it further enacted, That if any Dispute or Difference shall arise between the Parties interested in the said intended Division, touching the respective Rights, Shares, Interests, and Proportions, which they or any of them shall Claim to have of, and in the said Lands and Grounds hereby directed to be inclosed, it shall be lawful for the said Commissioners, by the Examination of Witnesses upon Oath (which Oath any One of the said Commissioners is hereby empowered to administer) and upon other proper and sufficient Enquiry, Evidence, and Examination, to hear and determine all such Disputes and Differences, and to make such order therein as they shall think fit, which Determination shall be binding and conclusive to all Parties; and if the said Commissioners shall, upon any such Dispute or Difference, think it expedient to have the Assistance of Counsel, learned in the Law; or if either of the Parties at variance shall, by Writing under their Hands, request the said Commissioners to nominate one or more such Counsel for that Purpose, who shall, jointly with the said Commissioners, hear and determine such Dispute or Difference, and shall have the like Power and Authority in that behalf, as is hereinbefore given to the said Commissioners.

Provided always, That nothing herein contained shall authorize the said Commissioners to determine any Difference or Dispute which shall arise, touching the Title of any Person or Persons to any Estate, Right, or Interest, in or to any of the Lands of Grounds hereby directed to be inclosed; but the said Commissioners shall distinguish the Land which shall be allotted in Lieu of such disputed Property, which shall be taken by the Person or Persons who shall establish his Title thereto, by Law.

And be it further enacted, That the said Commissioners shall set out and appoint such Public and Private Roads and Ways, and also such ditches, Mounds, Fences, Drains, Watercourses, Bridges, Banks, Gates and Stiles, in, over, through, and upon the Lands and Grounds hereby directed to be inclosed, as they, in their direction, shall think requisite; all which public Carriage-Roads [end page 6] shall be well and sufficiently fenced out on both sides, from the Lands adjoining, by such of the Owners of the said Lands and Grounds, and within such Time as the said Commissioners shall appoint; and that it shall not be lawful for any Person to erect any Gate across any of the said public Carriage-Roads, or to plant any Trees on the Sides thereof, nearer each other than Fifty Yards; and the said Commissioners are hereby impowered and required to appoint One or more Surveyor or Surveyors, for first forming and putting into good and sufficient Repair all such public Carriage-Roads, who shall be allowed such Salary or Salaries as the said Commissioners shall direct; which Salary or Salaries and also the Expences of first forming and putting into good and sufficient Repair the same Roads (over and above the Statute Duty) shall be raised and paid in the same manner as the Costs and Charges of obtaining and executing this Act are hereinafter directed to be raised and paid; and that no Person, other than the Owners of the said Lands and Grounds hereby directed to be inclosed, shall be charged towards the first forming, making, and repairing the same Roads, other than the Statute Duty, until the same shall be certified, in Writing, by such Surveyor or Surveyors, to be delivered to the Justices at some Quarter Sessions of the Peace for the County of *Southampton*, to be completely formed, and until such Certificate shall have been allowed and confirmed by them, which said Certificate the said Surveyor or Surveyors shall deliver to the said Justices at their Quarter Sessions, to be holden next after the same Roads shall be formed and put into good and sufficient Repair as aforesaid, and within Two Years after the execution of the Award of the said Commissioners, unless sufficient Reason be given, to the satisfaction of the said Justices, that further Time is necessary for that Purpose, in which Case they may allow a further Time for delivering in the said Certificate, not exceeding One Year: And, in Case the said Surveyor or Surveyors shall neglect, or refuse, to deliver in such Certificate within the Time before limited, or shall certify contrary to the Truth of the Case, each such Surveyor shall forfeit and pay the Sum of Ten Pounds, to be levied and recovered by such Ways and Means, and applied in like Manner, as hereinafter is directed or provided, with respect to the Money to be raised for defraying the Expences of obtaining and executing this Act; and that, from and after such Certificate or Certificates shall have been delivered, and allowed and confirmed as aforesaid, [end page 7] the same Roads shall be amended and kept in Repair, in the same Manner as other Public Highways are, by Law, to be amended and kept in Repair, and the Grass and Herbage growing thereon, shall belong to the Person or Persons to whom the said Commissioners shall allot the same; and that after such Public and Private Roads and Ways shall be set out and made, it shall not be lawful for any Person or Persons to use any other Roads or Ways either Public or Private, in, over, through, and upon the Lands and Grounds hereby directed to be inclosed, either on Foot, or with Horses, Cattle, or Carriages; and that all other Roads and Ways through the same Lands and Grounds, which shall not be set out or continued in pursuance of this Act, shall be deemed Parts of the Lands and Grounds to be divided by this Act, and shall be divided and allotted accordingly: And all such Public Bridle Roads and Footways, and also such Private Roads and Ways, and also all such Hedges, Ditches, Fences, Banks, Drains, Bridges, Gates, and Watercourses, which shall be set out and appointed in pursuance of this Act, shall be made, and afterwards cleansed, maintained, and kept in repair by such Person or Persons, and in such Manner, as the said Commissioners, by any Award or other Writing, under their Hands, shall appoint.

And be it further enacted, That in Case it shall appear to the said Commissioners, from the Certificate of the major Part in Value of the Owners of Lands in the several Parishes of Medstead otherwise Meidstead, and Bentworth, or either of them, that there are any Bridle Roads, or Footways, in, through, over, or on the sides of any of the inclosed Lands within the said Parishes, or either of them which may be diverted and turned without inconvenience to the Public into any other Public Highways, Bridle Roads, or Footways, or be diverted and turned, through or over any such inclosed Lands, so as to make the same more convenient to the Public, and the said Commissioners shall approve thereof, that then, and in such Case, it shall be lawful for the said Commissioners, by their Award, to order and direct such Public

Highways, Bridle Roads, and Footways, to be altered and turned, in such Manner as the said Commissioners shall (agreeably to the Intent and Meaning of such Certificate) think proper. [end page 8]

Provided, That it shall not be lawful for the said Commissioners, by Virtue of this Act, to turn or alter any Turnpike Road or Roads.

And be it further enacted, That the said Commissioners shall set out, divide, assign, allot, and award, all the Residue of the said Open and Common Fields hereby directed to be inclosed, after deducting the public Carriage Roads set out therein, unto and amongst the several Owners and Proprietors thereof, and Persons having Rights of Common thereon, Rights of Soil, or other Property therein, in Proportion to their respective Rights and Properties, due regard being had to the Quality, Situation, and Convenience, as well as the Quantity of the Lands to be allotted as aforesaid, which said Allotments shall be laid as near to and convenient for Occupation, with the other Estates of the several Persons entitled to the same as may be; and such Allotments are hereby declared to be a full Satisfaction and Compensation for all such former Rights and Properties in the said Open and Common Fields, and shall accordingly be accepted and taken by the Person or Persons to whom the same are allotted immediately after the Execution of the Award of the said Commissioners.

And be it further enacted, That the several Allotments which shall be set out in pursuance of this Act, shall be Ring Fenced by the Owners thereof, either with or without Quicksets or sufficient Stake Hedges, within such Time and in such Manner as the said Commissioners shall, by their Award, or other Writing under their Hands, direct and appoint, and if any Person shall neglect or refuse to make such Fences according to the Directions of the said Commissioners, then it shall be lawful for any Person interested in the Lands next adjoining to such unfenced Lands to exhibit a Complaint in Writing against the Persons who ought to have fenced the same before Two or more Justices of the Peace for the said County of Southampton, who shall inquire into the Nature of the Complaint, and examine Witnesses upon Oath (which Oath such Justices are hereby empowered to administer) and shall and may, if they shall see Cause, order the Person exhibiting such Complaint to make such Fences; and when the same shall be so made, such Justices shall ascertain the Expences thereof, and by Warrant under their Hands and Seals, directed to any Person whomsoever, cause the said Expences to be levied by Distress and Sale of [*end of page 9*] the Goods and Chattels of the Persons so neglecting or refusing as aforesaid, rendering the Overplus (if any) to the Owner of such Goods and Chattels after deducting the Costs and Charges of such Distress and Sale. **Provided always,** that the Allotments to be made to the said Rectors shall be fenced round with Quickset Hedges, or such other proper Mounds and Fences as the said Commissioners shall direct, at the Expence of the other Proprietors of Lands and Grounds hereby directed to be inclosed, or such of them as the Commissioners shall appoint.

Provided always, That it shall be lawful for any of the said Owners after their Allotments shall have been staked out, and before the signing of any Award, with the consent of the said Commissioners in Writing, to Ring Fence their Allotments or any Part thereof, in such Manner as the said Commissioners shall think proper.

And be it further enacted, That in the mean Time and until such Divisions and Allotments shall be made as aforesaid, all the Tillage and other Lands, hereby directed to be inclosed, shall be cropped and sown with such sort of Corn, Grain, Turnips, or Grass Seeds, in such Proportions, and shall be kept, ordered, and continued in such Course of Husbandry as the said Commissioners shall, by any Writing or Writings, under their Hands, in that behalf, order and appoint any Usage or Custom to the contrary thereof notwithstanding.

Be it further enacted, That it shall be lawful for all or any of the Owners and Proprietors of any Manors, Messuages, Lands, Tenements or Hereditaments, New Allotments or Old Inclosures, within the said respective Parishes, being Tenants in Tail, or for Life, or by Copy of Court Roll, or for a Term of Years at a small Rent; and also for the Husbands, Guardians, Trustees, Committees, or Attornies, acting on behalf of any such Owners or Proprietors respectively, who are under Coverture, Minors, Lunatics, or beyond the Seas, or under any other legal Disability to exchange all or any of their said Manors, Messuages, Buildings, Lands, Tenements or Hereditaments, New Allotments or Old Inclosures, situate in the said respective Parishes of *Medstead* and *Bentworth*, for any other Manors, Messuages, Buildings, Lands, Tenements or Hereditaments, New Allotments or Old Inclosures, within the same respective [end page 10] Parishes, or within any adjoining Parish, Township, or Place, so as all such Exchanges be made with the Consent of the said Commissioners, and be specified and declared by the Award of the said Commissioners, or by any other Deed executed by them within the Space of Twelve Calendar Months after the Execution of such Award: and all such Exchanges shall be good, valid, and effectual in Law to all Intents and Purposes, notwithstanding the Interests of the Persons exchanging in the Properties exchanged may be of a Nature different from each other; and notwithstanding the Want of sufficient Title in the exchanging Parties, provided that no such Exchange shall be made by the said Rectors, or either of them, without the Consent, in Writing, of the Lord Bishop of Winchester, and of the Patrons for the Time being.

And be it further enacted, That all and singular the Lands and Hereditaments which shall be so respectively allotted or exchanged by Virtue of this Act, shall immediately after the making such Allotments and Exchanges be, remain, and enure, and the several Persons to whom the same shall be allotted, or given in Exchange, as aforesaid, shall, from thenceforth stand, and be seized thereof and interested therein, to, for, and upon, such and the same Estates, Uses, Trusts, and Purposes, and under, and subject to, the same Wills, Settlements, Leases, Limitations, Powers, Remainders, Charges, and Incumbrances, and shall be of such and the same Tenures, and held by such and the same Rents, Fines, Heriots, and other Duties and Services, as the several and respective Lands and Hereditaments, in lieu, or in respect whereof such Allotments and Exchanges shall be respectively made as aforesaid, now are, or might, would, or ought to have been, held subject or liable to, or charged with, or affected by, in Case this Act had not been made: subject, nevertheless, to such Mortgages, Charges, and Incumbrances, and such additional Rents as shall be made in pursuance of this Act.

And be it further enacted, That in Case any Lands or Grounds whereon any Trees, Thorns, Hedges, Bushes, or Shrubs, shall, at the Time of making such Allotments, be standing, growing, or being, shall be allotted to any Person or Persons, other than such as was or were the Proprietor or Proprietors, Owner or Owners thereof, at and immediately before such Allotments were made, then it shall be lawful for such former Owners and Proprietors [end page 11] respectively at any reasonable Time or Times, to be appointed by the said Commissioners, after such Allotments shall be made, to enter upon the Lands and Grounds, upon which such Trees, Thorns, Hedges, Bushes, or Shrubs shall be standing, and to cut down and carry away the same; Provided nevertheless; That no Bushes, Hedges, or Trees, shall be cut down, unless the Owners thereof shall first have Licence under the Hands of the said Commissioners respectively so to do; and in Case the said Commissioners shall think it proper, that any such Trees, Thorns, Hedges, Bushes, or Shrubs shall be left standing and remaining on any such Allotment or Allotments, that then they shall order and direct the same accordingly; and that the Person or Persons to whom such Allotments shall be made on which such Trees, Thorns, Hedges, Bushes, or Shrubs, shall be left standing and being, shall pay for the same as the said Commissioners shall direct; and in Default of such Payment, the same shall be levied and recovered in like Manner as the Costs and Expences of obtaining and executing this Act are herein after authorized to be recovered.

And be it further enacted, That it shall be lawful for the said Commissioners, by Writing under their Hands, to order and direct any Lessees or Tenants at Rack Rents of any Allotment or Allotments to be made, in Pursuance of this Act, to pay such additional Rent or Rents to the Lessors or Owners of such Allotment or Allotments, and for, and on Account of, the Improvements to be made by such Lessors or Owners, in the annual Value of such Leasehold Tenements, as the said Commissioners in their Judgment shall think fair and reasonable; which additional Rent and Rents shall be payable at such Times as the said Commissioners shall appoint, during the remainder of such Lessees or Tenants, Term or Interest therein, and shall be recoverable in the same Manner as any other Rents are by Law recoverable.

And be it further enacted, That as soon as conveniently may be after the Divisions and Allotments of the said Lands and Grounds shall be finished pursuant to the Purport and Directions of this Act, the said Commissioners shall form and draw up, or cause to be formed and drawn up, two several Awards, one relating separately and exclusively to the Lands, Estates, and Hereditaments in the Parish of Medstead, otherwise Meidstead, aforesaid; and the other relating, separately and exclusively to the Lands, Estates and [end of page 12] Hereditaments in the Parish of Bentworth aforesaid; which said respective Awards shall express the Quantity of Acres, Roods, and Perches, in Statute Measure, contained in the said Open and Common Fields, and the Quantity of each and every Part and Parcel thereof assigned, or allotted, or given in Exchange, to and for each of the Proprietors, and the Situation, Buttals, and Boundaries, of the same respectively; and where any Person or Persons shall be seised of, or entitled to, any Lands or other Hereditaments in the said Open and Common Fields, by different Tenures, or for different Estates, the said Commissioners shall distinguish what Parcels or Allotments are by them awarded, in lieu of Freehold, Copyhold, and Leasehold Lands or Hereditaments, and are in future to be deemed Freehold, Copyhold, and Leasehold, respectively; and the said respective Awards shall also contain proper Orders and Directions for fencing and mounding the said several Allotments, and for keeping the said Mounds and Fences in repair, and also a Description of the Roads, Ways, and Footpaths, to be set out and appointed by the said Commissioners, in, over, and through, the said Premises, and shall likewise express and contain such other Orders, Regulations, and Determinations, as the said Commissioners shall think proper and necessary to be inserted therein, respectively, conformable to the Tenet and Purport of this Act, and which said several Awards shall be fairly engrossed or written on Parchment, and signed and sealed by the said Commissioners and shall within Twelve Calendar Months next after the same shall be so signed and sealed as aforesaid, be enrolled in one of His Majesty's Courts of Record at *Westminster*, or with the Clerk of the Peace of the County of Southampton, to the end Recourse may be had to the same respectively, by any Person or Persons interested therein, for the inspecting and perusing whereof the Sum of One Shilling shall be paid, and no more; and a true Copy thereof, or of any Part thereof, signed by the proper Officer, purporting the same to be a true Copy, shall, from Time to Time, be made and delivered by such Officer to any Person requesting the same, for which no more shall be paid than Fourpence for every Sheet of Seventy-two Words; and the said several Awards or a true examined Copy thereof, or of the Enrolment thereof, or of any part thereof respectively, shall be admitted and allowed as legal Evidence; and that the said several original Awards after the same shall have been respectively enrolled as aforesaid, shall be deposited in such secure Place in each of the said [end page 13] Parishes as the said Commissioners shall order and direct, for the Perusal, Use, and Benefit, of all Parties interested therein; and the said several Awards, and the Allotments, Partitions, Regulations, Agreements, Exchanges, Orders, Directions, Determinations, and all other Matters and Things therein mentioned and contained, shall, to all Intents and Purposes, be binding and conclusive, unto and upon the said Proprietors and all other Persons concerned or interested therein; or in any of the Lands, Grounds, or Premises aforesaid, to all Intents and Purposes whatsoever.

And be it further enacted, That one Moiety of the Expences incident to the obtaining and passing of this Act, shall be paid and defrayed by the several Proprietors to whom Allotments shall be made, or whose Property shall be exchanged in the said Parish of Medstead, otherwise Meidstead, in such Proportions, at such Times, and to such Persons, as the said Commissioners shall appoint; and that the other Moiety thereof shall be paid and defrayed by the several Proprietors to whom Allotments shall be made, or whose Property shall be exchanged in the said Parish of Bentworth, in such Proportions, at such Times, and to such Persons, as the said Commissioners shall appoint: And that all Charges and Expences of carrying the said Act into Execution, as to the Lands and Hereditaments in the Parish of Medstead, otherwise Meidstead, aforesaid, shall be paid and defrayed by the Proprietors of Lands in the same Parish to whom Allotments shall be made, or whose Property shall be exchanged by Virtue of this Act, in such Proportions, at such Times, and to such Persons, as the said Commissioners shall, by Writing under the Hands, order and direct, and as to the Lands and Hereditaments in the Parish of Bentworth aforesaid, shall be paid and defrayed by the Proprietors of Lands in the same Parish, to whom Allotments shall be made, or whose Property shall be exchanged by Virtue of this Act, in such

Proportions, at such Times, and to such Persons, as the said Commissioners shall, in like Manner, direct:

And in Case any Person shall refuse or neglect to pay his or her Proportion of such Charges and Expences, according to such Directions of the said Commissioners, then the said Commissioners are hereby authorized, by Warrant under their Hands and Seals, directed to any Person or Persons, to cause the same to be levied by Distress and Sale of the Goods and Chattels of the Person neglecting or refusing to pay as aforesaid, rendering the Overplus (if any) to the Owners of such Goods and [end page 14] Chattels, after deducting the Costs and Charges of making such Distress and Sale; and in Case no sufficient Distress can be had, it shall be lawful for the said Commissioners, by Writing under their Hands, to authorize any Person to enter into and upon the Lands and Hereditaments to be allotted to the Person refusing to pay as aforesaid, and to have and receive the Rents and Profits thereof until thereby his or her Proportion of the said Costs and Charges, and also the Costs and Charges attending such entry upon, and Receipt of the said Rents and Profits, shall be fully paid: **Provided always,** That the Rectors of Medstead, otherwise Meidstead, and Bentworth, aforesaid, shall not be charged with or contribute to the Charges and Expences aforesaid, or any Part thereof.

And be it further enacted, That if any of the Owners and Proprietors of the Lands hereby directed to be inclosed as aforesaid, or any other Person shall advance any Sum or Sums of Money for the Purpose of defraying the Expences of obtaining and passing this Act, and of putting the same into Execution every such Owner and Proprietor or other Person shall be repaid the same, with Interest, at the Rate of Five Pounds *per Centum per Annum*, out of the first Money that shall be raised for defraying such Expences by Virtue of this Act.

And be it further enacted, That it shall be lawful for the several Owners and Proprietors of the Lands and Grounds to be allotted and divided as aforesaid, and for the Husbands, Guardians, Trustees, Committees, Executors in Trust, or Attornies of any of the Owners and Proprietors of the said Allotments, being *Femes Covert* or Lunatics, or under any other Disabilities, and Attornies lawfully constituted for and on the Behalf of Persons beyond the Seas, and for any of the said Owners and Proprietors being Tenants in Tail, or for Life or Lives only, or for any Term or Terms of Years, at small Rents, or upon any Contingency, to whom any Allotments shall be made in Pursuance of this Act, and to and for every of them, for the Time being, other than and except the said respective Rectors and their Successors, to charge the said Allotments, with such Sum and Sums of Money as the said Commissioners respectively shall, by any Writing under their Hands, adjudge necessary to pay and defray their respective Shares and Proportions of the Charges and Expences incident to obtaining this Act, [end page 15] and carrying the same into Execution, and of making interior or subdivision Ditches, Mounds, and Fences, within the said Allotments, so that such Money do not exceed Three Pounds an Acre, the same to be paid to such Person or Persons, and applied in such Manner as the said Commissioners shall direct: And for securing the Repayment of such Money, with Interest, to grant, mortgage, or demise the Lands so to be charged unto any Person or Persons, who shall advance such Money, his or her Executors, Administrators, or Assigns, so as in every such Grant, Mortgage, or Demise, to be made by any Person being Tenant in Tail, or for Life or Lives only, or for any Term or Terms of Years, at small Rents, or upon Contingency as aforesaid, there be contained a Covenant to pay and keep down the Interest of the Money to be thereby secured during his or her Life, or other Estate in the Premises; and that no Person afterwards becoming intitled to the Premises shall be liable to pay any larger Arrear of Interest than for One Year preceding the Time that the Title to such Possession shall accrue; and every Charge, Grant, Mortgage, and Demise, to be made as aforesaid, shall be valid and effectual in Law, notwithstanding any want of Title or any Settlement, Will, Trust, Limitation, or Incumbrance, affecting such Lands, or any Part thereof, then in being, or capable of taking effect to the contrary; and that no Mortgagee or Mortgagees advancing or lending Monies upon such Security or Securities, shall be liable to fee to the Application, or answerable for the Misapplication of the Money so advanced and lent.

And be it further enacted, That the said Commissioners shall, and they are hereby required, to enter into a Book or Books an Account of all Money which shall be assessed upon the said Owners and Proprietors, and which shall come to their Hands, and of all Charges, Expences, and Disbursements, which shall accrue, be made, and paid, or charged by them, by Virtue of this Act; and such Book or Books shall be signed by the said Commissioners, and shall be produced by them to the said Owners or Proprietors, at a Meeting to be appointed for the Execution of the said Award, with the Bills and Vouchers concerning the same.

And be it further enacted, That each of the said Commissioners who shall act in the Execution of the Trusts and Powers hereby vested in them, shall be allowed and paid the Sum of [end page 16] Two Guineas for each Day he shall act or travel for the Purpose of acting, or in returning Home from acting therein, in full Satisfaction for his Trouble and Expences in the Execution of this Act.

Provided always, and be it further enacted, That if any Person or Persons shall think him, her, or themselves aggrieved by any Thing done in pursuance of this Act, then, and in every such Case (except in such Cases where the Orders and Determinations of the said Commissioners are directed to be final and conclusive) he, she, or they, may appeal to any General Quarter Sessions of the Peace, which shall be held in and for the said County of Southampton, within Four Calendar Months next after the signing and sealing of the said Awards respectively, such Appellant or Appellants first giving Fourteen Days Notice at least, in Writing, of his, her, or their Intention to bring such Appeal, and of the Matter thereof, to the Commissioners, or some One of them; and the Justices in the said General Quarter Sessions are hereby required to hear the Matter of every such Appeal, and to make such Order therein, and Award such Costs as to them, in their Discretion, shall seem reasonable; and by their Order or Warrant to levy the Costs so awarded by Distress and Sale of the Goods and Chattels of the Party or Parties, Person or Persons, liable to pay the same, rendering the Overplus (if any) to the Owner or Owners of such Goods and Chattels, after deducting the reasonable Charges of such Distress and Sale, which Determination or Order of the said Justices, shall be final and conclusive to all Parties or Persons therein concerned.

Provided always, and be it further enacted, That nothing in this Act contained shall prejudice, lessen, or defeat, the Right, Title, or Interest of the Lords of the Manors of Medstead, otherwise Meidstead, and Bentworth, or either of them, or of any other Manor or Manors.

Saving always, To the King's Most Excellent Majesty, His Heirs, and Successors, and to all and every other Person and Persons, Bodies Politic and Corporate, his, her, and their respective Heirs, Successors, Executors, and Administrators, all such Estate, Right, Title, and Interest (other than, and except such, as are meant and [end page 17] intended to be barred and destroyed by this Act) as they, any, or every of them had and enjoyed of, in, to, out, or in respect of the said Lands, Grounds, and Premises hereby intended to be divided and allotted before the passing of this Act, or could, might, or ought to have had and enjoyed, in case the same had not been made. [end page 18]

Appendix 21: Medstead Enclosure Award & Exchanges, 1799

To all whom these Presents shall come[1]

- Thomas Hasker of Chineham in the county of Southampton, Esquire
- John Tredgold, late of the City of Winchester and now of Chilbolton in the same County, Gentleman
- Thomas Fleet of Preston Candover in the said County, Yeoman
- Charles Drummond of Spring Garden in the parish of Saint Martin-in-the-Fields within the Liberty of Westminster in the County of Middlesex, Esquire, Surviving Trustee named and appointed in and by the last Will and Testament of Henry Drummond, late of St James's Square in the parish of St James within the Liberty of Westminster, Esquire, deceased
- Ann Woolls of New Alresford in the said County of Southampton, Widow
- Edward Woolls of Farringdon in the same County, Esquire
- The Reverend Francis North, Rector of Old Alresford with the Chapelries of New Alresford and Medstead, otherwise Meidstead, annexed
- John Hicks of West Meon in the said County, Gentleman
- William Budd
- Richard Wake
- John Camies
- William Andrews
- Richard Andrews and
- Richard Bone, all of Medstead in the said County, Yeomen
- Robert Pullinger of Itchinswell[2] in the same County, Yeoman
- John Andrews of Farringdon in the same County, Yeoman; and
- John Hoar of Froxfield in the same County, Yeoman

Send Greeting Whereas in and by an Act of Parliament made and passed in the thirty eighth year of the reign of his present Majesty King George the third entitled 'An Act for dividing allotting and inclosing the open and Common fields in the parishes of Medstead and Bentworth in the County of Southampton'

After Reciting that there were in the Several Parishes of Medstead, otherwise Meidstead, and Bentworth in the County of Southampton certain Open and Common fields containing together by estimation Four Hundred Acres or thereabouts,

And that the said Charles Drummond, Ann Woolls, Edward Woolls, Francis North, John Hicks, William Budd, Richard Wake, John Camies, William Andrews, Richard

---

1   HRO, Q23/2/82. Also Winchester College Archives, 3538. [ ] signifies unreadable or unsure content and, on occasion, suggestions. There were at least three copyists: capitalisation and spelling varied between them and within their own parts. There was almost no punctuation or breaks in flow so what punctuation you see is mostly introduced by me to aid understanding. There was duplication (deleted) and several obvious errors (corrected). I have also standardised a minimum of spellings, mostly major place names and, for example, variations of 'allotment'. I have used 'inclosure' throughout rather than the modern 'enclosure'. I have not used 'sic' to identify unusual or old spellings, etc, as there are so many of them, so words like 'Expence' are left as written. Thus, the document contains fields called 'Summerleys', 'Summer leys' and 'Summerlands'; likewise 'Southtown' and 'South Town'. Spreadsheets are available upon enquiry.

2   Probably Ecchinswell in Kingsclere.

Andrews, and divers other persons were Owners of the said Open and Common fields lying within the said parish of Medstead, otherwise Meidstead

And further Reciting that the Land of the several Proprietors in all the said Open and Common fields lay intermixed and dispersed in Small Parcels and in their present state were incapable of any Considerable Improvement and that it would be advantageous to the said proprietors if all the same Open and Common fields were divided and inclosed and specific parts thereof allotted to them in lieu of and in proportion of their Estates and properties therein respectively

It was and is by the said Act of Parliament Enacted that the said Thomas Hasker, John Tredgold and Thomas Fleet should be and they were thereby appointed commissioners for setting and dividing and allotting all the said Open and Common fields lying within the said several parishes of Medstead, otherwise Meidstead, and Bentworth

And that it should be lawful for any two or more of the said Commissioners for the time being and they were thereby fully authorized and impowered to execute, do, and perform every and any Act, Matter or thing whatsoever by the said Act authorized to be executed, done, and performed by the said Commissioners and for every such Act, Matter or thing which should be executed done or performed by any two of the said Commissioners for the time being should be as valid and effectual to all Intents and purposes as if all the said Commissioners had been present and had executed, done and performed the same

And that no person should be capable of acting in the Execution of the said Act as a Commissioner, Except in appointing the first Meeting of the Commissioners and administering the Oath thereinafter mentioned or a Surveyor until he should have taken and subscribed the Oath therein mentioned Which Oath it should be lawful for any one of the said Commissioners to administer and the said Oath so taken and subscribed by each Commissioner should be inrolled with any award of the said Commissioners thereinafter directed to be made

And that Notice should be affixed on the principal Doors of the parish Churches of Medstead, otherwise Meidstead, and Bentworth, respectively, of the time and place of the first and every Subsequent Meeting of the said Commissioners for putting the said Act into execution at least Eight days before every such Meeting (Meetings by adjournment only Excepted)

And that all such Meetings should be held in the villages of Medstead and Bentworth, or one of them, or within the distance of Ten Miles therefrom

And that if any meeting appointed to be holden as aforesaid only one Commissioner should attend he might adjourn such Meeting to such time and place as he should think most convenient giving Notice thereof to the absent Commissioners And for the more just and regular division of the said Open and Common fields and other Commonable Grounds

It was further enacted that the Commissioners should as soon as conveniently might be view examine and value all the said Lands and Grounds thereby intended to be inclosed and all or such parts of the Old Inclosures within the said parishes or either of them as the said Commissioners should think fit and should cause true and perfect Surveys Admeasurements and plans to be made thereof by such person or persons as they should appoint and such Surveys Admeasurements and plans should be reduced into writing and the Contents of the whole Lands to be inclosed and the several parcels of land and number of Acres Roods and Perches belonging to each Proprietor respectively should be therein set forth ascertained and described and the said surveys and plans should when Completed be laid before the said Commissioners to be used by them for the purposes of the said Act and the person or persons who should make such Survey Admeasurements and plan should verify the same upon Oath at some Meeting of the said Commissioners before the Allotment thereinafter mentioned were made which Oath the said Commissioners and thereby impowered and required to administer

And it was further Enacted that all persons claiming any Land right of Common or right of Soil or other property in or upon the said Lands or Grounds thereby directed to be inclosed should lay their respective Claims in Writing before the Said Commissioners at some Meeting to be held for that purpose of which at least Fourteen Days previous Notice should be given by advertisements in the Salisbury and Winchester Journal and Hampshire Chronicle[3] if such papers were then circulating and by fixing such Notice in Writing on the principal Doors of the parish Churches of Medstead otherwise Meidstead and Bentworth aforesaid on a Sunday immediately before Divine Service in which Notice the said Commissioners should require all persons claiming any right property or Interest in or upon the said Lands or Grounds thereby directed to be inclosed of any part thereof to lay such Claims before them in Writing at or within the time to be limited for that purpose and that it should be lawful of the said Commissioners to reject any Claim or Claims which should not be delivered to them at such Meeting

And it was further Enacted that the said Commissioners should set out and appoint such public and private Roads and Ways, and also such Ditches, Mounds, Fences, Drains, Watercourses, Bridges, Banks, Gates and Stiles, in, over, through, and upon the Lands and Grounds thereby directed to be inclosed, as they, in their direction, shall think requisite and that after such public and private Roads and Ways should be set out and made it should not be lawful for any person or persons to use any other Roads or Ways either public or private in through over and upon the Lands and Grounds thereby directed to be inclosed either on foot or with Horses, Cattle and Carriages and that all other Roads and Ways through the same Lands and Grounds which should not be set out or continued in pursuance of the said Act should be deemed parts of the Lands and Ground to be divided by the said Act and should be divided and allotted accordingly

And all such public bridle Roads and footways and also such private Roads and Ways and all such Hedges, Ditches, Fences, Banks, Drains, Bridges, Gates and Watercourses which should be set out and appointed in pursuance of the said Act should be made and afterwards cleansed, maintained and kept in repair by such person and persons and in such Manner as the said Commissioners by any Award or other Writing under their Hands should appoint

And it was further Enacted that in Case it should appear to the said Commissioners, from the Certificate of the Major part in Value of the owners of Lands in the several parishes of Medstead otherwise Meidstead, and Bentworth, or either of them, that there were any Bridle Roads, or Footways, in, through, over, or on the Sides of any of the inclosed Lands within the said parishes, or either of them which might be diverted and turned without Inconvenience to the public into any other public Highways, Bridle Roads, or Footways, or be directed and turned, through or over any such inclosed Lands, so as to make the same more Convenient to the public, and the said Commissioners should approve thereof, that then, and in such Case, it should be lawful for the said Commissioners, by their Award, to order and direct such public highways, Bridle Roads,

---

3 *Hampshire Chronicle*, 14/8/1798.

and footways, to be altered and turned, in such Manner as the said Commissioners shall (agreeably to the intent and Meaning of such certificate) think proper

And it was further Enacted that the said Commissioners should set out, direct [end page 1], assign, allot, and award, all the residue of the said Open and Common fields thereby directed to be inclosed, after deducting the public Carriage Roads set out therein, unto and amongst the several Owners and proprietors thereof, and persons having rights of Common thereon, rights of soil, or other property therein, in proportion to their respective rights and properties, due regard being had to the Quality, situation, and Convenience, as well as the Quantity of the Lands to be allotted as aforesaid, which said Allotments should be laid as near to and Convenient for Occupation, with the other Estates of the several persons entitled to the same as might be; and such Allotments are thereby declared to be in full satisfaction and compensation for all such former rights and properties in the said Open and Common fields, and should accordingly be accepted and taken by these person or persons to whom the same should be allotted immediately after the Execution of the Award of the said Commissioners

And be it further Enacted that the several Allotments which should be set out in pursuance of the said Act, should be ring fenced by the owners thereof, either with or without quicksets or sufficient stake Hedges, within such time and in such Manner as the said Commissioners should, by their Award, or other writing under their Hands, direct and appoint, and if any person should neglect or refuse to make such fences according to the directions of the said Commissioners, then it should be lawful for any person interested in the Lands next adjoining to such unfenced Lands to exhibit a Complaint in Writing against the persons who ought to have fenced the same before two or more Justices of the Peace for the said County of Southampton, who should inquire into the Nature of the Complaint, and Administer such relief as in the said Act is mentioned

And it is thereby Provided that the Allotments to be made to the said Rectors should be fenced around with Quickset Hedges or such other proper Mounds and fences as the said Commissioners should direct at the Expence of the other proprietors of Lands and Grounds thereby directed to be inclosed or such of them as the Commissioners should appoint

And it was further Enacted that it should be lawful for all or any of the Owners and proprietors of any Manors, Messuages, Lands, Tenements or Hereditaments, New Allotments or Old Inclosures, within the said respective Parishes, being Tenants in Tail, or for life, or by Copy of Court Roll, or for a Term of Years at a Small Rent; and also for the Husbands, Guardians, Trustees, Committees, or Attornies, acting on behalf of any such owners or proprietors respectively, who are under Coverture, Minors, Lunatics, or beyond the Seas, or under any other legal disability to exchange all or any of their said Manors, Messuages, buildings, Lands, Tenements or Hereditaments, New Allotments or Old Inclosures, situate in the said respective parishes of Medstead and Bentworth, for any other Manors, Messuages, Buildings, Lands, Tenements or Hereditaments, New Allotments or Old Inclosures, within the same respective parishes, or within any adjoining parish, Township, or Place, so as all such Exchanges be made with the Consent of the said Commissioners, and were specified and declared by the Award of the said Commissioners, or by any other Deed executed by them within the space of twelve Calendar Months after the execution of such Award: and all such Exchanges should be good, valid, and effectual in the Law to all Intents and purposes, notwithstanding the Interests of the persons exchanging in the properties Exchanged might be of a

Nature different from each other; and notwithstanding the want of Sufficient Title in the exchanging parties, provided that no such Exchange should be made by the said Rectors, or either of them, without the Consent, in Writing, of the Lord Bishop of Winchester, and of the Patrons for the Time being

And it was further Enacted that all and singular the Lands and Hereditaments which should be so respectively allotted or exchanged by virtue of the said Act, should immediately after the making such Allotments and exchanges be, remain, and enure, and the several persons to whom the same should be allotted, or given in Exchange, as aforesaid, should, from thereforth stand, and be seized thereof and interested therein, to, for, and upon, such and the same Estates, Uses, Trusts, and Purveyors, and under, and Subject to, the same Wills, Settlements, Leases, Limitations, Powers, Remainders, Charges, and Incumbrances, and should be of such and the same Tenures, and held by such and the same Rents, Fines, Heriots, and other Duties and Services, as the several and respective Lands and Hereditaments, in lieu, or in respect whereof such Allotments and Exchanges should be respectively made as aforesaid, then were, or might, would, or ought to have been, held subject or liable to, or exchanged with, or affected by, in Case the said Act had not been made: subject, nevertheless, to such Mortgages, Charges, and Incumbrances, and such additional Rents as should be made in pursuance of the said Act

And it was further Enacted that it should be lawful for the said Commissioners, by writing under their Hands, to order and direct any Lessees or Tenants at Rack Rents of any allotment or Allotments to be made, in pursuance of this Act, to pay such additional Rent or Rents to the Lessors or Owners of such allotment or Allotments, and for, and on Account of, the improvements to be made by such Lessors or Owners, in the annual value of such Leasehold Tenements, as the said Commissioners in their Judgment should think fair and reasonable; which additional Rent and Rents shall be payable at such Times as the said Commissioners should appoint, during the remainder of such Lessees or Tenants, Term or Interest therein, and should be recoverable in the same Manner as any other Rents are by law recoverable

And it was further Enacted that as soon as conveniently might be after the divisions and Allotments of the said Lands and Grounds should be finished pursuant to the purport and directions of this Act, the said Commissioners shall form and draw up, or caused to be formed and drawn up, two Several Awards, one relating separately and exclusively to the Lands, Estates, and Hereditaments in the Parish of Medstead, otherwise Meidstead, aforesaid; and the other relating, separately and exclusively to the Lands, Estates and Hereditaments in the Parish of Bentworth aforesaid; which said respective Awards should express the quantity of Acres, Roods, and Perches, in Statute Measure, contained in the said Open and Common fields, and the quantity of each and every part and parcel thereof assigned, or allotted, or given in Exchange, to and for each of the proprietors, with the Situation, Buttals, and Boundaries, of the same respectively; and where any person or persons should be seised of, or entitled to, any Lands or other Hereditaments in the said Open and Common Fields, by different Tenures, or for different Estates, the said Commissioners should distinguish what parcels or Allotments are by them awarded, in lieu of Freehold, Copyhold, and Leasehold Lands or Hereditaments, and were in future to be deemed freehold, Copyhold, and Leasehold, respectively; and the said respective Awards shall also contain proper Orders and Directions for fencing and mounding the said several Allotments, or for keeping the said Mounds and Fences in repair, and also a Description of the Roads, Ways, and Footpaths, to be set out and appointed by the said

Commissioners, in, over, and through, the said premises, and should likewise express and Contain such other Orders, Regulations, and Determinations, as the said Commissioners shall think proper and necessary to be inserted therein, respectively, Conformable to the Tenor and Purport of the said Act, and which several Awards should be fairly engrossed or written on parchment, and Signed and Sealed by the said Commissioners and should within twelve Calendar Months next after the same should be so signed and sealed as aforesaid, be enrolled in one of his Majesty's Courts of Record at Westminster, or with the Clerk of the Peace of the County of Southampton, to the end recourse might be had to the same respectively, by any person or persons interested therein, for the inspecting and perusing whereof the sum of One Shilling should be paid, and no more; and a true copy thereof, or of any Part thereof, signed by the proper Officer, purporting the same to be a true Copy, should, from time to time, be made and delivered by such Officer to any person requesting the same, for which no more should be paid than fourpence for every sheet of seventy-two Words; and the said several Awards or a true examined Copy thereof, or of the enrolments thereof, or of any part thereof respectively, should be admitted and allowed as legal evidence; and that the said several original Awards after the same should have been respectively enrolled as aforesaid, should be deposited in such secure place in each of the said parishes as the said Commissioners shall Order and direct, for the Perusal, Use, and Benefit [end page 2] of all Parties interested therein; and the said several Awards, and the Allotments, Partitions, Regulations, Agreements, Exchanges, orders, directions, determinations, and all other Matters and things therein mentioned and contained, should, to all Intents and purposes, be binding and Conclusive, unto and upon the said proprietors and all other persons concerned or interested therein; or in any of the Lands, Grounds, or premises aforesaid, to all Intents and purposes whatsoever

And it was further Enacted that one Moiety of the Expences incident to the obtaining and passing of said Act, should be paid and defrayed by the several proprietors to whom Allotments shall be made, or whose Property should be exchanged in the said parish of Medstead, otherwise Meidstead, in such proportions, at such times, and such persons, as the said Commissioners should appoint; and that the other Moiety thereof should be paid and defrayed by the several proprietors to whom Allotments should be made, or whose Property should be exchanged in the said parish of Bentworth, in such proportions, at such times, and to such persons, as the said Commissioners should appoint: And that all Charges and Expences for carrying the said Act into Execution, as to the Lands and Hereditaments in the arish of Medstead, otherwise Meidstead, aforesaid, should be paid and defrayed by the proprietors of Lands in the same parish to whom Allotments should be made, or whose Property should be exchanged by Virtue of the said Act, in such proportions, at such times, and to such persons, as the said Commissioners should, by Writing under the Hands, order and direct, and as to the Lands and Hereditaments in the parish of Bentworth aforesaid, should be paid and defrayed by the Proprietors of Lands in the same parish, to whom Allotments should be made, or whose Property should be exchanged by Virtue of the said Act, in such Proportions, at such times, and to such persons, as the said Commissioners should, in like Manner, direct: with such Ways Means for the Recovery of such expenses upon refusal or neglect of payments as in the said Act are mentioned

And in Case any Person shall refuse or neglect to pay his or her Proportion of such Charges and Expences, according to such Directions of the said Commissioners, then the said Commissioners are hereby authorized, by Warrant under their Hands and Seals, directed to any Person or Persons, to cause the same to be levied by Distress and Sale of the Goods and Chattels of the Person neglecting or refusing to pay as aforesaid, rendering the Overplus (if any) to the Owners of such Goods and Chattels, after deducting the Costs and Charges of making such Distress and Sale; and in Case no sufficient Distress can be had, it shall be lawful for the said Commissioners, by Writing under their Hands, to authorize any Person to enter into and upon the Lands and Hereditaments to be allotted to the Person refusing to pay as aforesaid, and to have and receive the Rents and Profits thereof until thereby his or her Proportion of the said Costs and Charges, and also the Costs and Charges attending such entry upon, and Receipt of the said Rents and Profits, shall be fully paid

Provided always That the Rectors of Medstead, otherwise Meidstead, and Bentworth, aforesaid, shall not be charged with or contribute to the Charges and Expences aforesaid, or any Part thereof

And it was further Enacted that the said Commissioners should, and they are thereby required, to enter into a Book or Books an Account of all Money which should be assessed upon the said Owners and Proprietors, and which should come to their Hands, and all Charges, Expences, and Disbursements, which should accrue, be made, and paid, or charged by them, by Virtue of the said Act; and such Book or Books should be signed by the said Commissioners, and should be produced by them to the said Owners and Proprietors, at a Meeting to be appointed for the Execution of the said Award, with the Bills and Vouchers concerning the same

As in and by the said Act of Parliament reference being thereunto had will more fully appear and whereas soon after passing the said Act of Parliament the said Commissioners named therein did appoint their first Meeting for executing the powers vested in them by the said Act to be holden on Monday, the twenty first day of May which was in the Year of our Lord One Thousand Seven Hundred and Ninety eight at the Swan Inn in the Town of New Alresford in the said County And in pursuance of the directions given them by the said Act did Cause public notice to be given and affixed on the principal Doors of the said parish Church of Medstead on Sunday the thirteenth day of May in Same Year of the time and place of their first Meeting for executing the powers vested in them by the said Act more than eight Days before such Meeting And the said Commissioners did also give or Cause eight days previous Notice to be given of every their subsequent Meetings for the like purpose Meetings by adjournment only excepted

And Whereas the said Thomas Hasker John Tredgold and Thomas Fleet did meet at the Swan Inn in New Alresford aforesaid on the said twenty first day of May pursuant to the said first Notice and before they began to act in the Execution of the Powers given by the said Act saving that of administering the Oath prescribed by the said Act for each Commissioner to take and of giving or causing Notice to be given of the said first Meeting Did severally take and subscribe the Oath directed by the said Act which Oath so taken and subscribed is hereunto annexed to the Intent that the same may be enrolled therewith and the said Commissioners immediately after they had taken the said Oath duly appointed Thomas Richardson of Chelsea in the county of Middlesex, Gentleman, to be Surveyor of the said Land so intended to be inclosed and ordered Notice to be given pursuant to the said Act for a Meeting to be held on Monday the third day of September then next at the House of Mr William Budd at Medstead aforesaid that all persons claiming any right, property or Interest in or upon the Land or Grounds in the said parish of Medstead intended by the said Act to be diverted, allotted and inclosed should lay their respective claims in Writing before the said Commissioners at such Meeting

And Whereas the said Commissioners did meet at the House of the said William Budd at Medstead aforesaid on Monday the said third day of September pursuant to Notice by Advertisements in the Salisbury and Winchester Journal and Hampshire Chronicle on Sundays the nineteenth and twenty sixth days of August and Sunday the second day of September last and affixed on the principal Doors of the parish Church of Medstead, otherwise Meidstead, aforesaid immediately before Divine Service on each of those days and in pursuance of the powers vested in and the directions given to them by the said Act did receive the different Claims of the respective proprietors and hear and determine all Disputes and differences which arose between the parties who before making their Award were interested in the said division and inclosure directed by the said Act touching and Concerning the respective Shares Rights and Interests which they, or any, of them claimed in the said Lands and Grounds by the said Act directed to be divided, allotted and inclosed as aforesaid

And whereas the said Commissioners in execution of the powers vested in them by the said Act have caused true and perfect surveys Admeasurements and plans to be made taken and Completed of all the said open and Common fields in the said parish of Medstead by the said Thomas Richardson which Surveys Admeasurements and plans have been reduced into writing and numbers of Acres Roods and perches belonging to each proprietor are there set forth and described and such Surveys Admeasurement and plans have been verified on Oath by the said Thomas Richardson and laid before the said Commissioners at their several Meetings held in pursuance of the said Act

And whereas the said Commissioners have carefully viewed all the said open and Common fields in the said parish of Medstead by the said Act directed to be divided allotted and enclosed and also such Lands in the said parish as have been exchanged pursuant to the powers in the said Act and have carefully considered and made distinct valuation thereof respectively

And as soon as the said Surveys Admeasurements and plans were made and laid before them and before they proceeded to make the General Allotments by the said Act directed have set out and appointed such public and private footroads and ways in through and over the said Open and Common fields as are hereinafter mentioned

And the said Commissioners have also completed the division and Allotment of the said Open and Common fields in the said parish of Medstead in Manner hereinafter expressed and have done all things incumbent on them for Carrying the said Act into complete execution according to the true Intent and Meaning thereof previous to making this their Award

Now know ye that the said Commissioners have awarded ascertain set out and appointed And by these presents do Award ascertain set out and appoint the several private Carriage Roads and public footpaths in through and over the Lands and Grounds hereinafter divided and allotted in such directions and Situations as are hereinafter made that is to say

- **One Private Road** of the breadth of twelve feet leading from and out of the village of Hattingley commencing at the usual Entrance in North field crossing the South East and of the first Allotment hereinafter awarded to the said John Hicks and following the hedge on the South West side through the several allotments of John Hicks, Richard Bone and Robert [*Richard deleted*] Pullinger to the entrance of certain old Inclosures belonging to the Hicks and Robert Pullinger which said Road shall be deemed taken and enjoyed as a private Carriage Road or Driftway for the use and Convenience of the said John Hicks, John [*Robert deleted*] Pullinger and Richard Bone respectively and the owners and occupiers of the said Allotment in the said fields and Old Inclosures to where said Roads lead for the time being for ever

- **And the other Private Road** of the breadth of twenty feet leading from and out of the said Village of Hattingley commencing at its usual Entrance into Lower Church field crossing the North West side of the Second Allotment hereinafter awarded to the said John Hicks which said Road shall be taken deemed and enjoyed as a private [*end of page 3*] carriage road and or driftway for the use and Convenience of the said Richard Wake and the future owners and occupiers of the said Allotment for the time being, for ever
- **One public Footway** of the breadth of six feet leading from Medstead Street to Hattingley on the North side of lower Church field commencing at the Gate leading into the said field and passing in its usual direction to the Lane which leads into the same field from Hattingley
- **One other Public footway** of the same breadth commencing at the Style on the South side of a certain field called Whore Dell belonging to Richard Wake crossing Middle field to a little inclosed Meadow and then Crossing upper pace field to pace Lane [*Bars*] from thence across the said Lane and lower pace field to a field called Camies's Close leading to Soldridge
- **One other public Footway**, of the same breadth, commencing at Bar Stile on the North side of Middle field crossing Middle field to the [*East*] of crooked Lane along the side of the Lane to Southtown Gate
- **One other Public Footway**, of the same breadth, commencing at a Stile on the East Side of Whore Dell belonging to the said Richard Wake leading from thence on the North side of Middle field to the Gate leading into Little Down
- **And one other Footway**, of the same breadth, commencing at the Gate leading into Upper Church field and crossing the same field to a Stile on the North East side of a field belonging to John Camies

Which said several public footways shall be taken, deemed, used and enjoyed as public footways by all persons whomsoever

And furthermore know Ye that the said Commissioners in further pursuance of the directions of the said Act Have and by this their Award Do after having set out and appointed the said private Carriage Roads and public footways as herein before described and having had due regard as well to the Quality, Convenience and Situation as to the Quantity of the Lands contained in the Allotments hereinafter described and as to make the same as convenient as possible to the respective Messuages, Barns, and inclosed properties of the several proprietors divide, set out and allot the remainder of the said Open and Common fields in the said parish of Medstead by the said Act directed to be divided allotted and inclosed as applicable and award and confirm the same as follows, that is to say,

Unto and for the Reverend Francis North and his successors as rector of the parish of Old Alresford with Chapelries of New Alresford and Medstead annexed for and in regard of his Glebe Land in the common fields of the said parish of Medstead

- The Plot or parcel of Land in Lower Church field containing three acres two Roods and thirty four perches bounded
  - On the North and West by a certain field called Barrow Close belonging to the Trustees of Henry Drummond Esquire
  - On the South West by the first allotment hereinafter awarded to the said Richard Andrews and William Andrews and given in Exchange by them to William Budd and by him to Richard Wake as hereinafter mentioned and
  - On the South East by the public Highway leading from Medstead to Alresford

The Fences for inclosing the said Allotment to the said Francis North against the said Highway to be made and planted by the said Francis North with Quickset who is hereby directed to fence the same with sufficient posts and rails in [*it*] such Quickset plants shall be of sufficient age to make an effectual fence against the said Road in Consideration of the sum of Ten pounds and Ten Shilling which the said Commissioners have ordered to be paid to him for that purpose [] of the levy hereinafter directed to [*be*] made

Unto and for the said Charles Drummond as Trustee as aforesaid the three following Allotments, that is to say,

- One plot or parcel of Land situate in Lower pace field containing fourteen Acres and thirty perches bounded
  - On the North by a certain Lane called pace lane
  - On the South by the second Allotment hereinafter mentioned to the said Richard Wake
  - The fifth allotment hereinafter awarded to the said Ann Woolls and by her given in Exchange to the said William Budd as hereinafter mentioned and
  - Certain old Inclosures belonging to the said William Budd
  - On the East by an Inclosure belonging to Richard Wake and
  - On the West by the seventh allotment hereinafter awarded to the said Ann Woolls which said allotment is hereinafter Given in exchange to the said [Ann Woolls]

- One other plot or parcel of Land situate in Upper pace field containing eleven acres two Roods and thirteen perches bounded
  - On the north by the third Allotment hereinafter awarded to the said Charles Drummond
  - On the South by pace lane
  - On the East by the Copyhold and third freehold Allotments herewith awarded to the said John Camies and by him given in Exchange to the said John Andrews as hereinafter mentioned and
  - On the West by the second allotment hereinafter awarded to the said Ann Woolls and by her exchanged to the said John Camies as hereinafter mentioned

- And one other Plot or Parcel of Land situate in Middle field containing forty one Acres three Roods and four perches bounded

- On the North by an old Inclosure called Mayple Acre belonging to the said William Budd and an Old Inclosure called Whore Dell belonging to the said Richard Wake Which two old Inclosures are given in Exchange by the said William Budd and Richard Wake to the said Charles Drummond as hereinafter mentioned and one other old Inclosure called Lower Hooks belonging to the said Charles Drummond
- On part of the South by the fourth allotment hereinafter awarded to the said Anne Woolls and by her given in Exchange to the said John Andrews as hereinafter mentioned
- On other part of the South by an old Inclosure belonging to the said John Andrews
- On further part of the South by the first allotment hereinafter awarded to the said John Andrews and
- On the remaining part of the South by the second allotment hereinafter awarded to the said Charles Drummond
- On part of the East by the Allotments hereinafter awarded to the said William Budd as Copyhold Tenant of the Manor of Old Alresford and given in Exchange by him to the said Charles Drummond and
- On other part of the East by the allotment hereinafter awarded to Richard Wake as Copyhold Tenant for [] of the Manor of Ropley and by him given in Exchange to the said Charles Drummond and
- On the remaining part of the East by a Little Meadow belonging to the said John Andrews
- On part of the West and North West by certain old Inclosures belonging to the said John Camies
- On other part of the West by an old Inclosure called Millberrys belonging to the said John Andrews and given in Exchange by him to the said John Camies and
- On the remaining part of the West by the third allotment hereinafter awarded to the said Ann Woolls and given in Exchange by her to the said John Camies

The Fences for inclosing the first described allotment against pace Lane and against the second freehold allotment of the said Richard Wake for inclosing the second described allotment against the allotment to the said John Camies as Copyhold Tenant of the Manor of Old Alresford and the third freehold allotment of the said John Camies against pace Lane and against the second allotment of the said Ann Woolls to be made and for ever thereafter kept in repair by and at the Expence of the said Charles Drummond and the future owners and Occupiers of the said several Allotments for the time being

Unto and for the said Ann Woolls the seven following freehold Allotments, that is to say,
- One Plot or Parcel of Land situate in Upper pace field containing thirteen Acres three Roods and seventeen perches bounded
  - On part of the North by an old inclosure belonging to the said John Camies and
  - On the remaining part of the North by the third allotment hereinafter awarded to the said Ann Woolls and given in Exchange by her to the said John Camies
  - On the South by pace Lane
  - On the East by the second allotment hereinafter awarded to the said Ann Woolls and given in Exchange by her to the said John Camies and

- On the West by old Inclosures belonging to the said John Camies

which said allotment is hereinafter to given in exchange to the said John Camies

- One other plot or parcel of Land situate in Upper Pace field containing seven Acres one Rood and nine perches bounded
  - On the North by the third allotment hereinafter awarded to the said Ann Woolls and given in Exchange by her to the said John Camies
  - On the South by pace Lane
  - On the East by the second allotment hereinbefore awarded to the said Charles Drummond and
  - On the West by the first allotment hereinbefore awarded [end page 4] to the said Ann Woolls

which said allotment is also hereinafter given in exchange to the said John Camies

- One other plot or parcel of Land situate in Middle field containing twenty Acres one Rood and thirteen perches bounded
  - On the North by the first Allotment hereinafter awarded to the said John Camies and several old Inclosures belonging to the said John Camies and Richard Wake
  - On the South by old Inclosures belonging to the said John Camies and the first and second Allotments hereinbefore awarded to the said Ann Woolls and given in Exchange to the said John Camies as aforesaid
  - On the East by the third Allotment hereinbefore awarded to the said Charles Drummond and
  - On the West by old Inclosures belonging to the said John Camies

which said Allotment is hereinbefore given in exchange to the said John Camies

- One other plot or parcel of Land situate in Middle field containing one Acre Two Roods and one perch bounded
  - On the North by the third Allotment hereinbefore awarded to the said Charles Drummond and
  - On the South East and West by old Inclosures belonging to the said John Andrews which said Allotment is hereinafter given in Exchange to the said John Andrews
- One other plot or parcel of Land situate in Lower pace field containing three Roods and eight perches bounded
  - On the North by the first Allotment hereinbefore awarded to the said Charles Drummond
  - On the South by the public Highway leading from five Ash Pond to Soldridge
  - On the East by the second freehold Allotment hereinafter awarded to the said Richard Wake
  - On the West by an old Inclosure of the said William Budd and the third allotment hereinafter awarded to the said William Budd and the third freehold Allotment hereinafter awarded to William Budd

which said Allotment is hereinafter give in Exchange to the said William Budd

- One other plot or parcel of Land situate in Middle field containing one Acre two Roods and twenty seven perches bounded
  - On part of the North by the Allotment to the said William Budd, tenant of the Manor of Ropley
  - On other part of the North by the first freehold Allotment of the said William Budd and

- The remaining part of the North by the Allotment of the said William Budd as copyhold tenant of the Manor of Old Alresford as hereinafter severally awarded

which three last mentioned Allotments are hereinafter given in Exchange by him to the said Charles Drummond bounded
  - On the South and West by the first freehold Allotments hereinafter awarded to the said Richard Wake and exchanged by him with the said Charles Drummond as hereinafter mentioned and
  - On the East by the public highway leading from Medstead to Southtown

which said Allotment is hereinafter given in Exchange to the said Richard Wake and by him to the said Charles Drummond
  - And one other plot or parcel of land situate in Lower pace field containing sixteen Acres two Roods and seventeen perches bounded
    - On the North by old Inclosures belonging to the said Ann Woolls and
    - By pace Lane on the South, by old Inclosures belonging to the said Ann Woolls, the Allotments hereinafter awarded to the Executors of the late William Budd and other old Inclosures belonging to the said William Budd
    - On the East by the first Allotment hereinbefore awarded to the said Charles Drummond and Exchanged with the said Ann Woolls as aforesaid
    - On the North West by an old Inclosure called Hackett field belonging to the said John Andrews and Exchanged with the said Ann Woolls as hereinafter mentioned and
    - On the South West by a public highway leading from Medstead to Stankham Farm

The Fences for inclosing the first and second described Allotments against pace Lane bounding the Same, for inclosing the third described Allotment against the third Allotment of the said Charles Drummond bounding the Same, for inclosing the fourth described Allotment against the third Allotment of the said Charles Drummond, for inclosing the fifth Allotment against the said second freehold Allotment of the said Richard Wake and against the first Allotment of the said Charles Drummond, and for inclosing the seventh Allotment against pace Lane and against the North side of the Allotment to the East of the said William Budd to be made and for ever thereafter maintained and kept in repair and at the expence of the said Ann Woolls and the future owners and Occupiers of the said Allotment respectively for the time being

Unto the said William Budd the three following freehold Allotments, that is to say,
  - One plot or parcel of Land situate in Middle field containing one Acre three Roods and two perches bounded
    - On the North by an old Inclosure of the said Richard Wake called Summerland hereinafter given in Exchange to the said Charles Drummond
    - On the South by the sixth Allotment awarded to the said Ann Woolls as aforesaid
    - On the East by the Allotment to the said William Budd as copyhold Tenant of the Manor of Ropley as aforesaid And
    - On the West by the Allotment to the said William Budd as Copyhold Tenant of the Manor of Old Alresford as aforesaid which said Allotment is hereinafter given in Exchange to the said Charles Drummond

- One other field or parcel of Land situate in Lower Church field containing three Acres and twenty two perches bounded
  - On the North West and North East by old inclosures belonging to William Budd
  - On other part of the North East by the second Allotment of the said William Andrews as copyhold Tenant of the Manor of Old Alresford
  - On the South East by the Allotment hereinafter awarded to the said William Budd as copyhold Tenant of the Manor of Selborne
  - On the South West by the second Allotment hereinafter awarded to the said Edward Woolls as Copyhold Tenant of the Manor of Ropley which said Allotment is hereinafter given in Exchange to the said Richard Wake
- One other Plot or parcel of Land situate in Broom Corner in lower pace field containing one Rood and twenty three perches bounded
  - On the North West by an Inclosure of the said William Budd
  - On the North East by the fifth Allotment hereinbefore awarded to the said Ann Woolls
  - On the South East by the public Highway leading from five ash Pond to Soldridge and
  - On the South West by an old Inclosure belonging to William Budd and
  - On the other part of the South West by an old Inclosure belonging to the said John Hoar hereinafter given in Exchange to the said William Budd

Unto and for the said William Budd as Copyhold Tenant of the Manor of Old Alresford
- One Plot or parcel of Land situate in Middle field containing nine Acres and fourteen perches bounded
  - On the North West by an Allotment of Richard Wake called Summerlays hereinafter give in Exchange to the said Charles Drummond
  - On the North East by the said William Budd's first freehold Allotment
  - On the South East by the sixth Allotment hereinbefore awarded to the said Ann Woolls
  - On other part of the South East by the freehold Allotment hereinafter awarded to the said Richard Wake and the said Richard Wake's Allotment as Copyhold Tenant of the Manor of Ropley
  - On the South West by an old Inclosure of the said Richard Wake hereinafter given in Exchange to the said Charles Drummond And
  - On other part of the South West by the third Allotment hereinbefore awarded to the said Charles Drummond

which said described Allotment is hereinafter given in exchange to the said Charles Drummond

Unto and for the said William Budd as Copyhold Tenant of the Manor of Ropley the following Allotment, that is to say,
- One plot or parcel of Land situate in the Middle field containing thirteen acres two Roods and thirty perches bounded
  - On the North West by an old Inclosure of the said Richard Wake called Summerleys hereinafter given in Exchange to the said Charles Drummond

- On other part of the North by an old Inclosure of the said Charles Drummond hereinafter given in Exchange to the said William Budd and
- On other part of the North by an inclosed Meadow of the said William and Richard Andrews
- On the East by a little inclosed Meadow of the said Charles Drummond
- On the South East by the public Highway leading from Medstead to Southtown
- On other part of the South East by two cottages and gardens belonging to the said Richard Wake and John Andrews
- And on the other part of the South East by the sixth Allotment hereinbefore awarded to the said Ann Woolls and
- On the South West by the first freehold Allotment hereinbefore awarded to the said William Budd

which said described Allotment is hereinafter given in Exchange to the said Charles Drummond

Unto and for the said William Budd as copyhold Tenant of the Manor of Selborne the following Allotment, that is to say,

- One plot or parcel of Land situate in lower Church field containing four Acres one Rood and thirty nine perches bounded
- On the North East by the second Allotment hereinafter awarded to the said Richard and William Andrews
- On the South East by the public Highway leading from Medstead to Alresford
- On the South West by the first Allotment hereinafter awarded to the said Robert Pullinger and by him given in Exchange to the said [end page 5] Richard Wake
- On other part of the South West by the second Allotment hereinafter awarded to the said Edward Woolls and by him given in Exchange to the said Richard Wake And
- On the North West by the second freehold Allotment hereinbefore awarded to the said William Budd and by him given in Exchange to the said Richard Wake

Unto and for the said Richard Wake the four several Allotments [] Leasehold for one thousand Years following, that is to say,

- One plot or parcel of Land situate in Middle field containing ten Acres one Rood and fifteen Perches bounded
- On the North West by the sixth Allotment hereinbefore awarded to the said Ann Woolls and by her given in Exchange to the said Richard Wake and by him to the said Charles Drummond
- On the other part of the North West by the Allotment of the said William Budd as copyhold Tenant of the Manor of Old Alresford
- On the East by the public Highway leading from Medstead to Southtown
- On the South by old inclosures belonging to the said John Andrews
- On other part of the South by the third Allotment hereinbefore awarded to the said Charles Drummond And
- On the West by the Allotment of the said Richard Wake hereinafter awarded to him as Copyhold Tenant of the Manor of Ropley and by him given in Exchange to the said Charles Drummond, Which said described Allotment is hereinafter given in Exchange to the said Charles Drummond [*repetition*]

- One other plot or parcel of Land situate in Broom Corner in Lower pace field containing four Acres two Roods and one perch bounded
  - On the North West by the first Allotment hereinbefore awarded to the said Charles Drummond and by him hereinafter given in Exchange to the said Ann Woolls
  - On other part of the North West by Old Inclosures of the said Richard Wake
  - On other part of the North East by an old Inclosure of the said Charles Drummond hereinafter given in Exchange by him to the said Richard Wake
  - On the South East by the public Highway leading from five ash pond to Soldridge And
  - On the South West by the fifth Allotment hereinbefore awarded to the said Ann Woolls and by her given in Exchange to the said William Budd

- One other Plot or parcel of Land comprizing the whole of Upper Church field containing two Acres and fifteen perches bounded
  - On the North West by an old Inclosure of the said Charles Drummond and by him hereinafter given in Exchange to the said Richard Wake
  - On the North East by an Old Inclosure of the said Richard Wake
  - On the South East by another old Inclosure of the said Richard Wake hereinafter given in Exchange by him to the said Charles Drummond and
  - On the South West by an old Inclosure of the said John Camies
- And one other Plot or parcel of Land situate in lower Church field containing two Roods bounded
  - On the North West by the public highway leading from Medstead to Alresford
  - On the North East by an old Inclosure of the said Richard Wake
  - On the South by an old Inclosure of the said Charles Drummond hereinafter given in Exchange to the said Richard Wake and
  - On the South West by the first Allotment hereinafter awarded to the said Richard Wake as Copyhold Tenant of the Manor of Old Alresford

The Fence for inclosing the last described Allotments against the public Highway aforesaid to be made and for ever thereafter maintained and kept in repair by the said Richard Wake and the future owners and occupiers of the said Allotments for the time being

Unto and for the said Richard Wake as Copyhold Tenant of the Manor of Old Alresford the two following Allotments, that is to say,
- One plot or parcel of Land situate in Lower Church field containing two Acres three Roods and eleven perches bounded
  - On the North West by the public Highway leading from Medstead to Alresford
  - On the North East by a Leasehold Allotment hereinbefore awarded to the said Richard Wake
  - On other part of the North East by an Inclosure of the said Charles Drummond hereinafter given in Exchange to the said Richard Wake
  - On the South East by old Inclosures of the said John Camies and
  - On the South West by the second freehold Allotment of the said John Camies hereinafter given in Exchange to the said William Budd and by him to the said Richard Wake

- And one other plot or parcel of Land situate in Lower Church field containing two Acres and twenty three perches bounded
  - On the North West by an old Inclosure of the said Edward Woolls
  - On the North East by the second Allotment hereinafter awarded to the said Edward Woolls and by him given in Exchange to the said Richard Wake
  - On the South East by the first Allotment hereinafter awarded to the said Robert Pullinger and by him given in Exchange with the said Richard Wake and
  - On the South West by the said Allotment hereinafter awarded to the said Edward Woolls

Unto and for the said Richard Wake as Copyhold Tenant of the Manor of Ropley, the following Allotment, that is to say,
- One plot or parcel of Land situate in Middle Field containing One Acre and twenty six perches bounded
  - One the North, South and West by the third Allotment hereinbefore awarded to the said Charles Drummond And
  - On the East by the first Leasehold Allotment awarded to the said Richard Wake and by him to be given in Exchange as aforesaid which said described Allotment is hereinafter given in Exchange to the said Charles Drummond

Unto and for the said Edward Woolls as Copyhold Tenant of the Manor of Ropley the two following Allotments that is to say
- One plot of parcel of Land situate in lower church field containing two Roods and thirty three perches bounded
  - On the North West and South West by old Inclosures of the said Edward Woolls and the second Allotment hereinbefore awarded to the []
  - On the North East by the second Allotment hereinbefore awarded to the said Richard Wake as Copyhold Tenant of the Manor of Old Alresford And
- One other plot or Parcel of Land situate in lower Church field containing seven Acres two Roods and twenty three perches bounded
  - On the North East by the second freehold Allotment of the said William Budd and his Allotment as Copyhold Tenant of the Manor of Selborne
  - On the North West and South West by old Inclosures of William Budd
  - On other part of the South West by the Allotment hereinafter awarded to the said John Hicks
  - On other part of the South West by the Allotment hereinafter awarded to the said John Hoare
  - On other part of the South West by an old Inclosure to the said Edward Woolls And
  - On other part of the South West by the Allotment hereinbefore awarded to the said Richard Wake as Copyhold Tenant of the Manor of Old Alresford and
  - On the South the first Allotment hereinafter awarded to the said Robert Pullinger which said last described is hereinafter given in Exchange to the said Richard Wake

The fences for inclosing the first described Allotment against the second Allotment hereinbefore awarded to the said Richard Wake as Copyhold Tenant of the Manor of

Old Alresford be made and for ever after maintained and kept in repair by and at the Expence of the said Edward Woolls and the future owners and Occupiers of the said first described Allotment for the time being

Unto and for the said Robert Pullinger as Copyhold Tenant of the Manor of Old Alresford the two following Allotments, that is to say,
- One Plot or parcel of Land situate in Lower Church field containing two Acres thirty perches bounded
  - On the North West by the second Allotment hereinbefore awarded to the said Richard Wake as Copyhold Tenant of the Manor of Old Alresford and
  - On other part of the North West by the second Allotment hereinbefore awarded to the said Edward Woolls
  - On the North East by the Allotment hereinbefore awarded to the said William Budd as Copyhold Tenant of the Manor of Selborne
  - On the South East by the public Highway leading from Medstead to Alresford
  - On the South West by an old Inclosure of the said John Hicks

which said described Allotment is hereinafter given in Exchange to the said Richard Wake And

- One other plot or parcel of Land situate in North field containing One Acre and twenty two perches bounded
  - On the North by a private carriage way
  - On the North West and South East by the Inclosures of the said Robert Pullinger
  - On other part of the South East by the Allotments hereinafter awarded to the said Richard Bone
  - On the South West by old Inclosures of the said John Hicks and Richard Wake

The Fences for inclosing the first described Allotment against the public Highway and for inclosing the second described Allotment against the Allotment of the said Richard Bone to be made and for ever thereafter maintained and kept in repair by and at the Expence of the said Robert Pullinger and the future owners and Occupiers of the Allotments for the time being

Unto and for the said John Hicks as Copyhold Tenant of the Manor of Old Alresford [end page six] the two following Allotments, that is to say,
- One Plot or parcel of Land situate in North field containing One Acre two Roods and eight perches bounded
  - On the North East and South East by the old Inclosures of the said John Hicks and
  - On the other part of the South East by old Inclosures of the said William Budd and Richard Bone
  - On the South West by an old Inclosure of the said Robert Pullinger and
  - On the North West by another old Inclosure of the said Robert Pullinger and the Allotment hereinafter awarded to the said Richard Bone and

- One other Plot of parcel of Land situate in Lower church field containing three Roods and nine perches bounded

- On the North West by an old Inclosure of the said William Budd
- On the North East and part of the South East by the second Allotment hereinbefore awarded to the said Edward Woolls
- On the other part of the South East by the Allotment hereinafter awarded to the said John Hoare and
- On the South West by an old Inclosure of the said Richard Wake

The Fences for inclosing the second described Allotment against the same Allotment hereinbefore awarded to the said Edward Woolls and against the Allotment hereinafter awarded to the said John Hoare to be made and for ever thereafter maintained and kept in repair by and at the Expence of the said John Hicks and the future owners and Occupiers of the second described Allotment for the time being

Unto and for the said Richard Andrews and William Andrews as Copyhold Tenants of the Manor of Old Alresford the two following Allotments according to their respective Estates rights and Interests therein, that is to say,

- One Plot or parcel of Land situate in Lower Church field containing three Acres and twenty seven perches bounded
  - On the North West by an old Inclosure of the said Charles Drummond and by him hereinafter given in Exchange to the said Richard Wake
  - On the North East by the Allotment hereinbefore awarded to the said Francis North
  - On the South East by the public Highway leading from Medstead to Alresford and
  - On the South West by the second Allotment hereinafter awarded to the said Richard and William Andrews which said described Allotment is hereinafter given in Exchange to the said William Budd and by him to the said Richard Wake

- And one other Plot or parcel of Land situate in Lower Church field containing eight Acres One Rood and five perches bounded
  - On the North by an old Inclosure of the said William Budd and
  - On other part of the North by an Inclosure of the said Charles Drummond hereinafter exchanged with the said Richard Wake
  - On the North East by the last described Allotment
  - On the South East by the public Highway leading from Medstead to Alresford and
  - On the South West by the freehold Allotment and the Copyhold Allotment of the Manor of Selborne hereinbefore awarded to the said William Budd

which said described Allotment is hereinafter given in Exchange to the said Richard Wake

The Fences for inclosing the first described Allotment against the Allotment to the said Francis North and against the said public Highway and for inclosing the said second described Allotment against the said public Highway to be made and for ever thereafter maintained and kept in repair by and at the expence of the said Richard Andrews and William Andrews and the future owners and Occupiers of the said Allotments for the time being

Unto and for John Hoar and Ann his Wife as Copyhold Tenants of the Manor of Old Alresford the following Allotment, that is to say,

- One Plot or parcel of Land situate in Lower Church field containing One Acre One Rood and thirteen perches bounded
  - On the North West and South West by old Inclosures of the said Richard Wake
  - On the North East by the second Allotment hereinbefore awarded to the said Edward Woolls and
  - On the South East by the old Inclosure of the said Richard Wake

Unto and for the said Richard Wake as acting Trustee under the Will of the late William Budd late of Soldridge Yeoman deceased as Copyhold Tenant of the Manor of Old Alresford the following Allotment, that is to say

- One plot or parcel of Land situate in Lower pace field containing One Acre three Roods and thirty nine perches bounded
  - On the North East and West by the seventh Allotment hereinbefore awarded to the said Ann Woolls and
  - On the South by old inclosures of the late William Budd

The Fence for inclosing this Allotment in the East and West ends there against the seventh Allotment hereinbefore awarded to the said Ann Woolls to be made and for ever thereafter maintained and kept in repair by and at the Expence of the said Trustee of the said William Budd and the future owners and Occupiers of the said Allotment for the time being

Unto and for the said John Andrews the two following freehold Allotments, that is to say

- One Plot or parcel of Land situate in Middle field containing One Rood and fifteen perches bounded
  - On the North by the third Allotment hereinbefore awarded to the said Charles Drummond
  - On the East by old Inclosures of the said John Andrews and
  - On the South by the second Allotment hereinafter awarded to the said John Andrews and the third freehold Allotment hereinafter awarded to the said John Camies

- One other Plot or parcel of Land situate in Upper pace field containing three Acres three Roods and seventeen perches bounded
  - On the North by the first Allotment hereinbefore awarded to the said John Andrews
  - On the remainder part of the North and on the East by old Inclosures of the said John Andrews
  - On the South by pace Lane and
  - On the West by the Allotment hereinafter awarded to the said John Camies as Copyhold Tenant of the Manor of Selborne and also the third freehold Allotment hereinafter awarded to the said John Camies

The Fences for inclosing the first described Allotment against the third Allotment hereinbefore awarded to the said Charles Drummond for inclosing the said second described described Allotment against Pace Lane to be made and for ever thereafter maintained and kept in repair by and at the expence of the said John Andrews and the future owners and occupiers of the said two Allotments for the time being

Unto and for the said John Camies the three following freehold Allotments, that is to say
- One plot or parcel of land situate in Middle field containing one Acre and thirty seven perches bounded
  - On the North and West by two old Inclosures of the said John Camies
  - On the East and on the South by the third Allotment hereinbefore awarded to the said Ann Woolls and hereinafter given in Exchange to the said John Camies

- One other Plot or parcel of Land situate in Lower Church field containing three Roods and thirty perches bounded
  - On the North West by the Highway leading from Medstead to Alresford
  - On the North East by the first Allotment hereinbefore awarded to the said Richard Wake as Copyhold Tenant of the Manor of Old Alresford
  - On the South East and South West by old Inclosures of the said John Camies which said described Allotment is hereinafter given in Exchange to the said William Budd and by him to the said Richard Wake

- One other Plot of parcel of Land situate in Upper pace field containing one Acre and fifteen perches bounded
  - On the North and East by the first and second Allotments hereinbefore awarded to the said John Andrews
  - On the South by the Allotment hereinafter awarded to the said John Camies as Copyhold Tenant of the Manor of Selborne and
  - On the West by the second Allotment hereinbefore awarded to the said Charles Drummond which said described Allotment is hereinafter given in Exchange to the said John Andrews

The Fence for inclosing the second described Allotment against the public Highway leading from Medstead to Alresford to be made and for ever thereafter maintained and kept in repair by and at the expense of the said John Camies and the future owners and Occupiers of the said Allotment

Unto and for the said John Camies as Copyhold Tenant of the Manor of Selborne, that is to say
- One Plot or parcel of land situate in Upper pace field containing two Acres two Roods and seven perches bounded
  - On the North by the third freehold Allotment hereinbefore awarded to the said John Camies
  - On the East by the second Allotment hereinbefore awarded to the said John Andrews
  - On the South by pace Lane and
  - On the West by the second Allotment hereinbefore awarded to the said Charles Drummond which said described Allotment is herein[] given in Exchange to the said John Andrews

The Fence for inclosing the inclosing the second described Allotment against the public Highway leading from Medstead to Alresford to be made and for ever thereafter maintained and kept in repair by and at the expence of the said John Camies and the future owners and Occupiers of the said Allotment for the time being

Unto and for the said Richard Bone as Copyhold Tenant of the Manor of Old Alresford, the following Allotment that is to say
- One Plot or parcel of Land situate in North Field containing One Acre and four perches bounded
  - On the North West by the second Allotment hereinbefore awarded to the said Robert Pullinger
  - On the North East by an old Inclosure of the said Robert Pullinger
  - On the remaining part of the North East and South East by the first Allotment hereinbefore awarded to the said John Hicks and
  - On the South West by old Inclosures of the said Richard Wake, John Hicks and Edward Woolls

The Fence for inclosing this Allotment against the first Allotment hereinbefore awarded to the said John Hicks to be made and for ever thereafter maintained [end page 7] and kept in repair by and at the Expence of the said Richard Bone and the future owners and Occupiers of the said Allotment for the time being

All which said Allotments hereinbefore set out and awarded to the said several and respective proprietors are situate in the several Open and Common fields in the said parish of Medstead and contain together Two Hundred and twenty nine Acres One Rood and twenty eight perches which with the said private Carriage Roads and footways hereinbefore described and set out within the said Parish containing two Acres and thirty eight perches make up and amount to Two Hundred and thirty one Acres Two Roods and twenty six perches being the whole Measure and Contents of the said open and Common fields by the said Act directed to be divided allotted and inclosed
And the said Commissioners Do hereby award order and direct that the said hereinbefore described Allotments are and shall be taken deemed and accepted by the several and respective proprietors to whom the said Allotments are respectively awarded as aforesaid in full [care] of and in full satisfaction and compensation for their several and respective pieces or parcels of Land and Ground which were heretofore and before the passing the said Act lying dispersed in the said open and Common fields
And also in full [] satisfaction and compensation for their several and respective rights of Common and all other rights and properties whatsoever in over and upon the whole of the said open and Common fields in the said parish of Medstead or any part thereof
And the said Commissioners Do hereby further direct appoint that the fences hereinbefore allotted and awarded shall be well and sufficiently made by the Owners or Occupiers by whom the same are hereinbefore ordered and directed to be respectively made as aforesaid on or before the first day of December next
And that the several proprietors making such fences shall in such places where any foot Roads shall cross the same erect and set up good and sufficient stiles with planks over the Ditches for the Convenience of persons passing along such Roads

And the said Commissioners do hereby declare that by a certain Notice in Writing affixed on the principal Door of the parish Church of Medstead aforesaid on the Nineteenth day of December last they have extinguished all rights of Common in over and upon the Lands and Grounds divided and inclosed as aforesaid and no rights of Common shall hereinafter be claimed or enjoyed over all or any part of the said Lands or Grounds or any part thereof

And for the more convenient situation and disposition of the several farms Lands and Estates within the said parish of Medstead the following several Exchanges of Lands and Tenements have been made by the several proprietors thereof respectively and whose consent thereto is testified by their being parties to and sealing and executing these presents and by and with the Consent and approbation of the said Commissioners and by virtue of the powers and authority granted in the said Act for that purpose, that is to say

The said Charles Drummond as Trustee as aforesaid Hath given and granted And by these presents Doth give and grant unto the said Ann Woolls
- All that his first Allotment hereinbefore described situate in Lower pace field containing fourteen Acres and thirty perches In exchange for
- All that piece or parcel of Coppice Land part of North Ridding Coppice containing One Acre and Eleven perches bounded
  - On the North West by other part of the said Coppice belonging to the said Charles Drummond
  - On the South East by other part of the said Coppice belonging to the said William Budd and hereinafter given in Exchange to the said Charles Drummond and
  - On the North East by Lands of the Manor Farm of the parish of Bentworth
- And also one piece of inclosed Land called Great down containing Eleven Acres one Rood and seventeen perches bounded
  - On the North West by old Inclosures of the said Charles Drummond
  - On the North East by two Coppices belonging to the said John Andrews and Ann Woolls
  - On the South East by the Barns and Yard of the said Charles Drummond and
  - On the South West by the public Highway leading from Redhill to Medstead

And the said Ann Woolls have given and granted and by these presents Doth give and grant to the said Charles Drummond
- All that piece or parcel of Coppice Land in North Ridding Coppice containing one Acre and eleven perches in Exchange for
- All that first Allotment hereinbefore awarded to the said Charles Drummond containing fourteen Acres and thirty perches And

The said Charles Drummond hath given and granted and these presents Doth give and grant unto the said William Budd the several freehold Inclosures after mentioned, that is to say,
- All that old Inclosure called Puckritt containing four Acres three Roods and thirty one perches bounded
  - On the North and East by old Inclosures belonging to the said Ann Woolls
  - On the South by the public Highway leading from five ash Pond to Soldridge and

- On the West by the second freehold Allotment hereinbefore awarded to the said Richard Wake and an old Inclosure of the said Richard Wake and also

- All that old Inclosure called Spruce field containing ten Acres two Roods and twenty perches bounded
  - On the North West by an Old Inclosure of the said William Budd
  - On the North East by Beech Wood belonging to the said Richard Wake
  - On the East by a Coppice belonging to the said Charles Drummond
  - On the South East by a Lane called Foul Lane and
  - On the South by the Common called Little Down
- And also all that old Inclosure called Rye field containing two Roods and thirty two perches bounded
  - On the South East by an old Inclosure belonging to the said Ann Woolls and
  - On every other part thereof by an old Inclosure belonging to the said William Budd
- Also all that old Inclosure called Green Style containing four Acres and four perches bounded
  - On the North East by the public Highway leading from Southtown to Medstead
  - On the North West by a Lane leading into Upper Church field
  - On the South West by an old Inclosure of the said Richard Wake and
  - On the South East by an old Inclosure of the said Richard and William Andrews and William Budd also
- All that old Inclosure called Barstyle containing four Acres and twenty one perches bounded
  - On the North West and North East by old Inclosures belonging to the said Richard and William Andrews
  - On the South west by Upper church field and
  - On the South East by the Allotment hereinbefore awarded to the said William Budd as Copyhold Tenant of the Manor of Ropley and also

- All that old Inclosure called Redwood Close containing five Acres two Roods and twenty five perches bounded
  - On the North West by a Beechwood of the said William Budd
  - On the South West by an old Inclosure of the said John Andrews
  - On the North East by an old Inclosure of [] Austin Esquire and
  - On the South East by the public Highway leading from Medstead to Alton

In Exchange for
- The first freehold Allotment hereinbefore awarded to the said William Budd containing One Acre three Roods and two perches
- Also the Allotment hereinbefore awarded to the said William Budd as Copyhold Tenant of the Manor of Old Alresford containing Nine Acres and fourteen perches
- Also the Allotment hereinbefore awarded to the said William Budd as Copyhold Tenant of the Manor of Ropley containing Thirteen Acres two Roods and thirty perches

- Also all that freehold piece of Coppice Ground part of North Ridding Coppice containing one Rood and twenty two perches bounded
  - On the North West by the Lands of Bentworth Manor Farm and
  - On every other part thereof by Inclosures of the said Charles Drummond and
- Also all that old Inclosure being Copyhold of the Manor of Ropley called Mayple Close containing One Acre two Roods and twenty one perches bounded
  - On the North West by old Inclosures belonging to the said Charles Drummond
  - On the North East by the old Inclosure of the said Richard Wake hereinafter given in Exchange to the said Charles Drummond and
  - On every other part thereof by the third Allotment hereinafter awarded to the said Charles Drummond

And the said William Budd Hath given and granted And by these presents Doth give and grant unto the said Charles Drummond

- All that his first freehold Allotment containing One Acre three Roods and two perches and Also
- The Copyhold Allotment of the Manor of Old Alresford containing Nine Acres and twelve perches [*fourteen perches earlier*] and also
- His Copyhold Allotment of the Manor of Ropley containing Thirteen Acres two Roods and thirty perches and also
- His freehold piece of Coppice Land part of North Ridding Coppice containing one Rood and twenty two perches and Also
- His old Inclosure called Mayple Acre being Copyhold of the Manor of Ropley

In Exchange for

- The said old Inclosures as the same have hereinbefore described called Puckritt containing four Acres three Roods and thirty two perches [*thirty one perches earlier*]
- Spruce field containing Ten Acres two Roods and Ten Perches [*twenty perches earlier*]
- Rye field containing two Roods and thirty two perches
- Green Style containing four Acres and four perches
- Bar Style containing four Acres and twenty one perches and
- Redwood Close containing five Acres two Roods and five perches [*twenty five perches earlier*] and

The said Charles Drummond Hath given and granted and by these presents Doth give and grant unto the said Richard Wake the several freehold Inclosures after mentioned, that is to say

- All that old Inclosure called [Lethen] Gate Meadow containing four Acres and thirty six perches bounded
  - On the North East by the Highway leading from Medstead to Alresford
  - On the South East by a Lane leading into upper Church field and
  - On every other part thereof by old Inclosures of the said Richard Wake Also
- All that old inclosure called Church field [end page 8] containing two Acres one Rood and twenty three perches bounded
  - On the South East by Upper Church field

- On the South West by a Old Inclosure belonging to the said John Camies
- On the North West by Lower Church field and
- On the North East by old Inclosures of the said Richard Wake Also
- All that piece of Land part of Bridle Close containing three Acres two Roods and twenty one perches bounded
  - On the North West by the public Highway leading from Medstead to Alresford
  - On the North East by an old Inclosure of the said John Camies
  - On the South East by an old Inclosure of the said William Budd and
  - On the South West by the remaining part of the said piece called Bridle Close

The Fence for inclosing the part of Bridle Close is hereby given in Exchange to the said Richard Wake against the remaining part of the said Close to be made and for ever thereafter kept in repair by and at the Expence of the said Charles Drummond and the future Owners and Occupiers of the remaining part of the said Close for the time being Also all

- That piece of Land part of Upper Hooks containing one Acre two Roods and two perches bounded
  - On the North West and North East by an old Inclosure of the said William Budd
  - On the South East by an old Inclosure of the said Richard Wake and
  - On the South West by the remaining part of the said fields called upper Hooks

The Fence for inclosing the part of upper Hooks hereby given in Exchange to the said Richard Wake against the remaining part of the said field to be made and for ever thereafter maintained and kept in repair by and at the Expence of the said Charles Drummond and the future Owners and Occupiers of the remaining part of the said field for the time being And also

- All that old Inclosure called Barrow Close containing seven Acres and twelve perches bounded
  - On the North by the public Highway leading from Medstead to Hattingley
  - On the South East by the public Highway leading from Medstead to Alresford
  - On the West by old Inclosures of the said Robert Pullinger and [blank] Budd and
  - On the South by Lower Church field

In Exchange for
- The first Leasehold Allotment hereinbefore awarded to the said Richard Wake containing Ten Acres one Rood and fifteen perches
- Also the Allotment hereinbefore awarded to the said Richard Wake as Copyhold Tenant of the Manor of Ropley containing One Acre and twenty six perches
- Also the sixth Allotment hereinbefore awarded to the said Ann Woolls and by her hereinafter given in Exchange to the said Richard Wake containing One Acre two Roods and twenty seven perches
- Also all that old Inclosure called Whore dell held by Lease for One Thousand Years containing five Acres and twenty nine perches bounded
  - On the North West by old Inclosures of the said Charles Drummond, William Budd and John Camies
  - On the North East by an old Inclosure of the said Richard Wake and Middle field

- On the South West by an old Inclosure of the said William Budd and
- On the South East by Middle field Also
- All that piece of Coppice Land part of North Ridding Coppice containing three Roods and two perches held also by Lease for One Thousand years bounded
  - On the North East by the Lands of Bentworth Manor Farm and
  - On every other part thereof by Coppice Lane of the said Charles Drummond Also
- All that old Inclosure being also Leasehold for one thousand years called Little Summer leys containing one Acre one Rood and twenty perches bounded
  - On the North West by an old Inclosure of the said John Camies and upper Church field
  - On the South West and North East by old Inclosures of the said Richard Wake and
  - On the South East by Middle field.

The Fence for inclosing the South End of Great Summerleys to be made and for ever thereafter maintained and kept in repair by and at the Expence of the said Charles Drummond And also

- And also all that piece of Land part of Great Summerleys containing two Roods and thirty seven perches held also by Lease for one Thousand years bounded
  - On the North West by the remaining part of the said piece and an old Inclosure of the said Charles Drummond
  - On the South West by Little Summerleys Exchanged as aforesaid and
  - On the South East by Middle Field

The Fence for inclosing the part of Great Summerleys hereby given in Exchange against the remaining part thereof to be made and for ever thereafter maintained and kept in repair by and at the Expence of the said Charles Drummond and his future owners and Occupiers of the remaining part of the said piece for the time being Also all

- That old Inclosure called Shoulder of Mutton containing six Acres and thirty four perches bounded
  - On the North West by the public Highway leading from Medstead to Alresford
  - On the North East by a small old Inclosure of the said William Budd and
  - On every other part thereof by old Inclosures of the said Charles Drummond And also
- All that old Inclosure called Shoulder of Mutton hereinafter given in Exchange by the said William Budd to the said Richard Wake containing three Roods and sixteen perches bounded
  - On the North West by the public Highway leading from Medstead to Alresford
  - On the South West by the said Inclosure of the said Richard Wake called Shoulder of Mutton and
  - On the North East and South East by an inclosure of the said Charles Drummond called Bridle Close

And the said Richard Wake Hath given and Granted and by these presents Doth give and grant unto the said Charles Drummond

- All that his first freehold Allotment containing Ten Acres One Rood and fifteen perches

- Also his Allotment as Copyhold Tenant of the Manor of Ropley containing one Acre and twenty six perches
- Also the sixth Allotment of the said Ann Woolls containing one Acre two Roods and twenty seven perches
- Also the several old Inclosures called Whore Dell containing five Acres and twenty nine perches
- Part of North Ridding Coppice containing three Roods and two perches
- Little Summerleys containing One Acre one Rood and twenty perches
- Part of Great Summerleys containing two Roods and thirty seven perches
- Shoulder of Mutton containing six Acres and thirty four perches and
- The old Inclosure of the said William Budd called Shoulder of Mutton containing three Roods and sixteen perches

In Exchange for
- The several old Inclosures of the said Charles Drummond hereinbefore described called Silten Gate Meadow containing four Acres and thirty six perches
- Church field containing two Acres one Rood and twenty three perches
- Bridle Road Close containing three Acres two Roods and twenty one perches
- Part of Upper Hooks containing One Acre two Roods and two perches and
- Barrow Close containing seven Acres and twelve perches

And the said Ann Woolls Hath given and granted and by these presents Doth give and grant unto the said William Budd
- All that her fifth Allotment hereinbefore described containing three Roods and twenty eight perches and also
- All that old Inclosure called Long Down containing five Acres and three perches bounded
  - On the South West by the public Highway leading from Redhill to Medstead
  - On the North East and South East by inclosures of the said Charles Drummond and
  - On the North West by inclosures of the said William Budd

In Exchange for
- The piece or parcel of Land hereinbefore given in Exchange to the said William Budd by the said Charles Drummond called Puckritt containing four Acres three Roods and thirty one perches

And the said William Budd Hath given and granted and by these presents Doth give and Grant unto the said Ann Woolls
- The said piece of Land called Puckritt containing four Acres three Roods and thirty one perches

In Exchange for
- The said fifth Allotment of the said Ann Woolls containing three Roods and twenty eight perches and
- The said old Inclosure called Long Down containing five Acres and three perches

And the said Ann Woolls Hath given and granted and by these presents Doth give and grant unto the said Richard Wake

- All that her sixth Allotment hereinbefore described containing one Acre two Roods and twenty seven perches and also
- All that old Inclosure called Morecroft containing one Acre two Roods and sixteen perches bounded
  - On the North West and South West by an old Inclosure of the said John Andrews and
  - On the North East and South by the public Highway leading from Southtown to Alresford

In Exchange for

- All that old Inclosure called Puckritt held by Copy of Court Roll of the Manor of Old Alresford containing one Acre two Roods and five perches bounded
  - On the South East by the public Highway leading from five ash pond to Stankham farm and
  - On every other part thereof by a certain old Inclosure called Puckritt hereinbefore given in Exchange to the said William Budd and by him to the said Ann Woolls
- Also all that old Inclosure called Rye field of the same Tenure containing One Acre and eighteen perches bounded
  - On the West by the public Highway leading from Southtown to Medstead
  - On the North East by an Inclosure of the said William Budd and
  - On every other part thereof by inclosures of the said Ann Woolls And
- Also all that piece of Land part of an old Inclosure called Withy piece of the same Tenure containing one Rood and thirty eight perches bounded
  - On the West by other part of the said piece
  - On the North by an old Inclosure of the said Edward Woolls and
  - On the East and South by the said Inclosure called Puckritt

The Fence for inclosing the said last mentioned piece called Withy piece against the remaining part thereof to be made and for ever thereafter maintained and kept in repair by and at the Expence of the said Ann Woolls and the future owners and Occupiers of the remaining part of the said piece for the time being

And the said Richard Wake [end page 9] Hath given and granted And by these presents Doth give and grant unto the said Ann Woolls

- The several old Inclosures hereinbefore described called Puckeritt containing one Acre two Roods and five perches
- Rye field containing one Acre and Eighteen perches and
- Part of Witting piece containing one Rood and thirty eight perches

In Exchange for

- The sixth Allotment hereinbefore awarded to the said Ann Woolls containing one Acre two Roods and twenty seven perches and
- The said old Inclosure called Morecroft containing one Acre two Roods and sixteen perches

And the said Ann Woolls Hath given and granted and by these presents doth give and grant unto the said John Andrews

- All that her fourth freehold Allotment hereinbefore described containing one Acre two Roods and one perch

In Exchange for

- All that old freehold Inclosure called Hackett field containing two Acres One Rood and thirty one perches bounded
  - On the North West by pace Lane and an old Inclosure of the said Richard and William Andrews
  - On the South West by the public Highway leading from Medstead to Stankham Farm and
  - On the South East by an old Inclosure of the said Ann Woolls and the seventh Allotment hereinbefore awarded to the said Ann Woolls

And the said John Andrews Hath given and granted and by these presents Doth give and grant unto the said Ann Woolls

- All that old Inclosure hereinbefore described called Hackett field containing two Acres one Rood and thirty one perches

In Exchange for

- The said fourth freehold Allotment of the said Ann Woolls containing one Acre two Roods and one perch

And the said Ann Woolls Hath given and granted And by these presents Doth give and grant unto the said John Camies

- All that her second freehold Allotment hereinbefore described containing seven Acres one Rood and nine perches and also
- All that her third freehold Allotment hereinbefore described containing twenty Acres one Rood and thirteen perches

In Exchange for

- All that old freehold Inclosure called Rye field containing three Acres three Roods and thirty eight perches bounded
  - On the West by a private road
  - On the East by an old Inclosure of the said Charles Drummond and
  - On every other part thereof by Inclosures of the said Ann Woolls And also
- All that Meadow called Southtown Mead containing two Acres and twenty four perches bounded
  - On the North West by the public Highway leading from Southtown to Alresford
  - On the North East by the public Highway leading from Southtown to Five Ash pond And
  - On every other part thereof by an old Inclosure of the said Ann Woolls and also
- All that old Inclosure called Stankham piece containing three Acres and three Roods surrounded
  - On the North West by an Inclosure belonging to the said Robert Pullinger
  - On the North East by a public Highway there and

- On every other part thereof by Inclosures of the said Ann Woolls

And the said John Camies Hath given and granted and by the presents Doth give and grant to the said Ann Woolls
- All those his said three old Inclosures called Rye field containing three Acres three Roods and thirty eight perches
- Southtown Mead containing two Acres and twenty four perches and
- Stankham farm containing Three acres and three Roods

In exchange for
- The second and third freehold Allotments of the said Ann Woolls hereinbefore described And

The said Ann Woolls Hath further given and granted and by these presents Doth give and grant unto the said John Camies
- All that her first freehold Allotment hereinbefore described containing Thirteen Acres Three Roods and seventeen perches

In Exchange for
- All that old Inclosure called Hydes being Copyhold of Inheritance of the Manor of Old Alresford containing seven Acres one Rood and twenty four perches bounded
  - On the North by the public Highway leading from Stankham farm to Alresford
  - On the West by a way leading to Sutton Wood
  - On the South by Inclosures of William Budd Gentleman and
  - On the East by an inclosure of the said Ann Woolls

And the said John Camies Hath further given and granted and by these presents Doth further give and grant unto the said Ann Woolls
- All that his said Copyhold Inclosure hereinbefore described called Hydes containing seven Acres one Rood and twenty four perches

In Exchange for
- The first freehold Allotment of the said Ann Woolls hereinbefore described containing thirteen Acres three Roods and seventeen perches

And the said Ann Woolls Hath given and granted and by these presents Doth give and grant unto the said Richard Wake as acting Trustee of the late William Budd
- All that piece or parcel of Land part of [Pye] Corner containing one Acre three Roods and thirty nine perches bounded
  - On the North by the public Highway leading from Alton to Alresford by Stankham farm
  - On the East by an old Inclosure of the said Trustees of the late William Budd
  - On the South by an old inclosure of William Budd of Ropley, Gentleman, and
  - On the West by the remaining part of the said Inclosure

In Exchange for

- The Allotment hereinbefore awarded to the said Richard Wake as Trustee as aforesaid containing one Acre three Roods and thirty nine perches and

The said Richard Wake as Trustee as aforesaid Hath given and granted and by these presents Doth give and grant unto the said Ann Woolls

- The said Allotment hereinbefore described containing one Acre three Roods and thirty nine perches

In Exchange for
- The said piece of Land parcel of [Pye] Corner containing one Acre three Roods and thirty nine perches

The Fence for inclosing the remaining part of [Pye] Corner shall be made and for ever thereafter maintained and kept in repair by and at the Expence of the said Ann Woolls her Heirs and Assigns for ever

And the said William Budd Hath given and granted And by these presents Doth give and grant unto the said Richard Wake
- All that his second freehold Allotment hereinbefore described containing three Acres and twenty two perches Also
- All that his Allotment hereinafter described as Copyhold Tenant of the Manor of Selborne containing four Acres one Rood and thirty nine perches Also
- The first Copyhold Allotment hereinbefore awarded to the said Richard and William Andrews and by them hereinafter given in Exchange to the said William Budd containing three Acres and twenty seven perches Also
- The second freehold Allotment hereinbefore awarded to the said John Camies and by him hereinafter given in Exchange to the said William Budd Also
- All that old inclosure called Crab Close held by Copy[hold] of the Manor of Ropley containing three Acres and thirty eight perches bounded
  - On the North East by an inclosure of the said John Camies and
  - On every other part thereof by inclosures of the said Charles Drummond And Also
- All that old Inclosure being Copyhold of the Manor of Old Alresford called Shoulder of Mutton containing three Roods and sixteen perches bounded
  - On the North West by the public Highway leading from Medstead to Alresford
  - On the South West by an old Inclosure of the said Charles Drummond And Also
- All that old Inclosure called Summerleys situate near the Dwelling House of the said Richard Wake and held by copy[hold] of the Manor of Ropley containing one Acre three Roods and ten perches and
- All that old Inclosure called Shepherds Meadow containing One Rood and thirty six perches of the same Tenure bounded
  - On the North and East by old Inclosures of the said Richard Bone
  - On the South by the public highway leading from Medstead to Alresford and
  - On the West by an old Inclosure of the said Richard Wake

In Exchange for

- All that old Inclosure called Old Acres held by Copy of Court Roll of the Manor of Old Alresford containing three Acres three Roods and sixteen perches bounded
  - On the North by the Common called Little Down
  - On the West by the public Highway leading from Medstead to Southtown
  - On the East by the public Highway leading from Redhill to Medstead and
  - On the South West by an old Inclosure of the said William Budd Also
- All that old Inclosure called Long Down held by Copy of the Manor of Old Alresford containing five Acres two Roods and twenty seven perches And
- All that old Inclosure called Down Close held by Lease for One thousand Years containing two Acres three Roods and fourteen perches severally bounded
  - On the North West by the said Common called Little Down and a Lane called Fowl Lane
  - On the West by the public Highway leading from Redhill to Medstead and
  - On every other part thereof by old Inclosures of the said William Budd
- Also all that old Inclosure called Redwood Close held by Lease for One thousand Years containing three Acres bounded
  - On the South West and North West by the old Inclosures of the said William Budd
  - On the South East by the public Highway leading from Medstead to Alton and
  - On the North East by Redwood Close hereinbefore given in Exchange by the said Charles Drummond to the said William Budd And

- Also all that Old Inclosure called Redwood Close containing two Acres three Roods and thirty one perches being bounded [end page 10]
  - On the North by a Wood belonging to the said William Budd called Redwood and
  - On the East by the said old Inclosure called Redwood Close hereinbefore given in exchange by the said Richard Wake to the said William Budd
  - On the South by public highway leading from Medstead to Alton and
  - On the West by an old Inclosure called Hurtle piece belonging to the said William Budd

- **And also** the right of Cutting Taking and carrying away two loads of Underwood or Rice from a certain Coppice called Wilsons Grove held of the Manor of Ropley belonging to the said William Budd

And the said Richard Wake given and granted and by these presents doth give and grant unto the said William Budd the said old Inclosures hereinbefore described called
- Old Acres containing three Acres three Roods and sixteen perches
- Long Down, containing five Acres two Roods and twenty seven perches
- Down Close, containing two Acres three Roods and fourteen perches
- Redwood Close containing three Acres; and
- One other close called also Redwood Close, containing two Acres three Roods and thirty one perches and
- The said right or privilege of cutting taking and carrying away the said two loads of underwood or rice from the said coppice called Wilsons Grove which right the said Richard Wake doth hereby forever give up and relinquish

In exchange for
- The second freehold allotment of the said William Budd hereinafter described containing three acres and twenty two perches
- The allotment before awarded to the said William Budd as tenant of the Manor of Selborne containing four Acres one Rood and thirty nine perches
- The first allotment hereinbefore awarded to the said Richard and William Andrews
- The second freehold allotment hereinbefore awarded to the said John Camies and
- The said Old Inclosures hereinbefore described severally called
  - Crab Close containing three Acres and thirty eight perches and
  - Shoulder of Mutton containing three roods and sixteen perches

And the said Edward Woolls hath given and granted and by these presents doth give and grant unto the said Richard Wake
- All that his second copyhold allotment hereinbefore described containing seven Acres two Roods and twenty three perches

In Exchange for
- All that old inclosures called Horsleys held by copy of the Manor of Old Alresford containing three Acres three Roods and one perch bounded
  - On the North East by North field
  - On the North West by an old inclosure of the said Robert Pullinger
  - On the South East by an old inclosure of the said John Hicks and
  - On the South West by an old Inclosure of the said Edward Woolls and also
- All that old Inclosure called Hirdle Gate of the same tenure containing two acres two roods and thirty one perches bounded
  - On the East by a Lane and
  - On every other part thereof by Inclosures of the said Edward Woolls

And the said Richard Wake hath given and granted and by these presents doth give and grant unto the said Edward Woolls all those two Inclosures hereinbefore described called
- Horseleys containing three acres three roods and one perch and
- Hirdle Gate containing two acres two roods and thirty one perches

In exchange for the second allotment hereinbefore awarded to the said Edward Woolls containing seven acres two roods and twenty three perches

And the said Edward Woolls hath given and granted and by these present doth give and grant until the said Robert Pullinger
- All that old Inclosure called Horseleys containing three acres three roods and one perch hereinbefore given in Exchange to him by the said Richard Wake also
- All that old Inclosure called north field Purrock containing three roods and eighteen perches bounded
  - On the North East by North field
  - On the North West by an inclosure of the said John Hicks and
  - On the South West by a field called Horsleys belong to the said Edward Woolls and also

- All that piece of parcel of land part of Horsleys containing three acres and sixteen perches bounded
  - On the East by an Inclosure and the Rick Yard of the said Robert Pullinger
  - On the North East by the said slip of land above described and inclosures of John Hicks and Richard Wake
  - On the South by the public highway leading from Hattingley to Medstead and
  - On the West by a meadow of the said Edward Woolls and by other part the said field called Horseleys belonging to the said Edward Woolls

The fence for inclosing the said piece or parcel of land last described as part of Horseleys to be made in equal moieties and
- One half thereof to be made by the said Edward Woolls and
- The other half to be made by the said Robert Pullinger
- and for ever thereafter to be kept in repair in such moieties by and at the expence of the said Edward Woolls and Robert Pullinger and the future owners and occupiers of the said piece or parcel of land and of the said piece of land called Horseleys for the time being

In exchange for
- An old Inclosure called Common End containing one Acre two Roods and twenty one perches bounded
  - On the North West by a public highway leading from Hattingley to Lasham and
  - On every other part thereof by old Inclosures of the said Edward Woolls also
- All that old Inclosure called West Field containing four Acres three Roods and twenty four perches and Also
- All that Old Inclosure called also West Field containing two Acres three Roods and twelve perches bounded
  - On every part thereof by old inclosures of the said Edward Woolls

And the said Robert Pullinger hath given and granted and by these presents doth give and grant unto the said Edward Woolls the said old Inclosures hereinbefore described called
- Common End containing One acre two Roods and twenty one perches
- Westfield containing four Acres three Roods and twenty four perches and
- Also Westfield containing two Acres three Roods and twelve perches

In exchange for the several old inclosures of the said Edward Woolls hereinbefore described called Horseleys received in **exchange** with the said Richard Wake
- containing three Acres three Roods and one perch
- North field Purrock containing three Roods and eighteen perches and
- Part of Horseleys containing three Acres and sixteen perches

And the said Richard Wake hath given and granted [repeated - and granted] And by these presents doth give and grant unto the said Robert Pullinger
- All that old inclosure called Carpenters Paddock held by copy of the Manor of Old Alresford containing one Acre one Rood and twenty five perches bounded

- On the North by the public Highway leading from Hattingley to Alresford
- On the North West and South West by Inclosures belonging to the said John Hicks and
- On the South East by an Inclosure of the said Robert Pullinger

In exchange for
- All that the first allotment hereinbefore awarded to the said Robert Pullinger containing two Acres and thirty perches

And the said Robert Pullinger hath given and granted and by these presents doth give and grant unto the said Richard Wake
- All that allotment hereinbefore awarded to him containing two Acres and thirty perches

In exchange for
- All that old Inclosure above described called Carpenters Paddock containing one Acre one Rood and twenty five perches

And the said William Budd hath given and granted and by these present doth give and grant unto the said Richard Andrews and William Andrews
- All that old freehold Inclosure called five Ash Close containing five Acres and sixteen perches bounded
  - On the North West by a public highway leading from five Ash pond to Soldridge and
  - On the North East by the public highway leading from Southtown to the Ropley Turnpike Road

In exchange for the first allotment hereinbefore awarded to the said Richard and William Andrews containing three acres and twenty seven perches and the said Richard Andrews and William Andrews hath given and granted and by these presents doth give and grant unto the said William Budd
- All that their first allotment hereinbefore awarded containing three Acres and twenty seven perches

In exchange for
- All that old Inclosure above described called Five Ash Close containing five Acres and sixteen perches

And the said William Budd hath further given and granted and by these presents doth give and grant unto the said Richard Andrews and William Andrews
- All those three old Inclosures in the said parish of Medstead called respectively
  - South upper Lymington Close, containing three Acres two Roods and thirty four perches
  - North upper Lymington Close containing three Acres two Roods and thirteen perches and
  - Little Lymington Close containing one Acre one Rood and nine perches
which said three Inclosures are held by copy of the Manor of Ropley aforesaid

In exchange for an old Inclosure of the said Richard Andrews and William Andrews called
- Shoemaker Close with the garden and orchard adjoining containing together six Acres and one Rood held by copy of the Manor of Old Alresford

And the said Richard Andrews and William Andrews have further given and granted and [end page 11] by these presents Do further give and grant unto the said William Budd
- All that said old Inclosure called Shoemaker Close with the Garden and Orchard adjoining containing six acres and one rood

In Exchange for the said three old Inclosures called
- South Upper Lymington Close containing three Acres two roods and thirty four perches
- North Upper Lymington containing three Acres two roods and thirteen perches and
- Little Lymington Close containing one Acre one rood and nine perches and

The said Richard Wake hath Given and Granted and by these presents doth Give and Grant unto the said Richard Andrews and William Andrews
- All that old Inclosure called Boynes held by copy of the Manor of Old Alresford containing eight acres and eight perches bounded
  - On the North West by an old Inclosure of the said Richard and William Andrews and
  - On the North East by a Wood belonging to Richard Westbrook and
  - On the South West by a Public highway and a Wood of Edward Woolls Esquire

In Exchange for
- All that second Allotment hereinbefore awarded to the said Richard Andrews and William Andrews containing eight Acres one rood and five perches and

The said Richard Andrews and William Andrews Have Given and Granted and by these presents Do give and grant unto the said Richard Wake
- All that their second allotment hereinbefore awarded containing eight acres one rood and five perches

In Exchange for
- All that old Inclosure above described called Boynes containing eight Acres and eight perches and

The said Richard Wake hath Given and Granted and by these presents Doth give and grant unto the said John Hoar and Ann his wife
- All that old Inclosure held by copy of Court Roll of the Manor of Ropley called Dell Lymington containing three Acres more or less

In Exchange for

- All that old Inclosure of the same tenure called Medstead Common containing two acres more or less and
- All that Allotment hereinbefore awarded to the said John Hoar and Ann his wife containing one Acre one Rood and thirteen perches

And the said John Hoar and Ann his wife Have Given and Granted and by these presents Do Give and Grant unto the said Richard Wake

- All that old Inclosure above described called Medstead Common containing two acres and
- The allotment hereinbefore awarded to them containing one acre one rood and thirteen perches

In Exchange for

- All that old Inclosure above described called Lymington containing three acres and

The said William Budd hath Given and Granted and by these presents doth Give and Grant unto the said John Camies

- All that old Inclosure held by Copy of Court Roll of the Manor of Old Alresford called Milberry Close containing one acre one rood and twenty six perches

In Exchange for

- All that second freehold Allotment hereinbefore awarded to the said John Camies containing three roods and thirty perches

And the said John Camies hath given and granted and by these presents doth give and grant unto the said William Budd

- All that his second freehold allotment hereinbefore described containing three roods and thirty perches

In Exchange for

- All that old Inclosure called Milberry Close containing one acre one rood and twenty six perches and

The said William Budd hath given and granted and by these presents doth give and grant unto the said John Hoar and Ann his wife

- All that old Inclosure called Lymington held by copy of Court Roll of the Manor of Ropley containing five Acres more or less

In Exchange for

- All that old Inclosure called Pace field held by copy of Court Roll of the Manor of Selbourne containing four Acres more or less

And the said John Hoar and Ann his wife have given and granted and by these presents do give and grant unto the said William Budd all that the said old Inclosure called Pace field containing four Acres

In Exchange for
- All that old Inclosure called Lymington containing five Acres

And the said John Andrews hath given and granted and by these presents doth give and grant unto the said John Camies
- All that old freehold Inclosure called Stankham or Milberry Close containing three acres and one rood

In Exchange for
- The third freehold allotment hereinbefore awarded to the said John Camies containing one acre and fifteen perches and
- The allotment hereinbefore awarded to the said John Camies as Copyhold Tenant of the Manor of Selborne containing two Acres two Roods and seven perches

And the said John Camies hath given and granted and by these presents doth give and grant Unto the said John Andrews
- All that his third freehold allotment hereinbefore awarded containing one Acre and fifteen perches and
- The said allotment hereinbefore awarded to him as Copyhold Tenant of the Manor of Selborne containing two acres two roods and seven perches

In Exchange for the
- Said freehold Inclosure called Stankham containing three acres and one rood

And the said William Budd hath given and granted and by these presents doth give and grant Unto the said John Andrews
- All those two freehold Inclosures called Giblets containing one Acre three Roods and eight perches and Southtown Meadow containing two roods and ten perches and
- All that piece of land in Middle Common field containing one acre held by copy of Court Roll of the Manor of Old Alresford which said piece or parcel of land hath been taken up In the Name of the said John Andrews and hereinbefore awarded to him and also
- All that old Inclosure called Priors situate near Five Ash pond held by copy of a Court Roll of the Manor of Ropley containing one acre three roods and Ten perches

In Exchange for nine small pieces of land lying dispersedly in the said Common Fields of Medstead containing together four Acres and two roods which said several pieces of land have been taken up in the Name of the said William Budd and hereinbefore awarded to him

And the said John Andrews Hath Given and Granted and by these presents Doth Give and Grant unto the said William Budd
- All those Nine several pieces of land above mentioned containing together four Acres two roods

In exchange for
- The said two pieces of freehold Land called Giblets containing two Roods and ten perches
- Southtown Meadow containing one Acre
- Piece of Land in Middle field containing one acre and
- An old Inclosure called Priors containing one Acre three Roods and ten perches and

The said Robert Pullinger Hath Given and Granted and by these presents doth Give and Grant unto the said Richard Bone
- All that old Inclosure called Carpenters Paddock containing one Acre one Rood and twenty five perches hereinbefore given in Exchange of the said Richard Wake and
- All that old Inclosure also called Carpenters Paddock containing one Acre one Rood and thirteen perches bounded
  - On the North by the public Highway leading from Harmsworth to Medstead
  - On the West by the aforesaid carpenters paddock
  - On the South by old Inclosures of the said John Hicks and Edward Woolls and
  - On the East by an old Inclosure of the said Richard Bone And also
- All that piece or parcel of Land part of Home Close containing two Roods and eighteen perches bounded
  - On the North East by North field
  - On the North West by the remaining part of the said piece called Home Close and
  - On every other part thereof by old Inclosures of the said Richard Bone

In Exchange for
- The Allotment hereinbefore awarded to him containing one Acre and four perches And
- All that old Inclosure called Church Close containing two Acres one Rood and thirty five perches bounded
  - On the North East by an Inclosure of the said John Hicks
  - On the South East by an old Inclosure of the said Robert Pullinger and
  - On the North West and South West by old Inclosures of the said Edward Woolls

And the said Richard Bone hath Given and Granted and by these presents Doth Give and Grant unto the said Robert Pullinger
- All that said Allotment hereinbefore awarded to him containing one Acre and four perches
- And all that said old Inclosure called Church Close containing two Acres one Rood and thirty five perches

In Exchange for
- The said old Inclosure called Carpenters Paddock received **In Exchange** of the said Richard Wake and [end page 12] containing One Acre One Rood and twenty five perches Also
- The other the other old Inclosure called [] Also

- Carpenters Paddock containing One Acre one Rood and thirteen perches And
- Part of Home Close containing two Roods and Eighteen perches

And the said Robert Pullinger Hath Given and Granted and by these presents Doth Give and Grant unto the said John Hicks
- All that old Inclosure called Church Close containing two Acres and one Rood and thirty five perches hereinbefore received in Exchange of the said Richard Bone And
- All old Inclosure called Coles Paddock containing One Acre and twelve perches bounded
  - On the North East by a Lane called Green Lane
  - On the South East by an old Inclosure of [blank] Budd of Bighton
  - On the North West and South West by old inclosures of the said John Hicks

In Exchange for
- The first Allotment hereinbefore awarded to him the said John Hicks containing one Acre two Roods and eight perches And
- All that old Inclosure called Home Acre containing one Acre one Rood and thirteen perches bounded
  - On the North East by North field
  - On the North West by an old Inclosure of the said Richard Wake hereinbefore given in Exchange to the said Robert Pullinger and
  - On the South East and South West by old Inclosures of the said Edward Woolls hereinbefore given in Exchange to the said Robert Pullinger

And the said John Hicks Hath given and granted And by these presents Doth Give and Grant unto the said Robert Pullinger
- All that his first Allotment hereinbefore described containing one Acre two Roods and and eight perches and
- All that old Inclosure called Home Acre containing one Acre one Rood and thirteen perches

In Exchange for
- Church Close hereinbefore given in Exchange to the said Richard Bone containing two Acres one Rood and thirty five perches And
- All that old Inclosure called Coles Paddock containing one Acre and twelve perches

And the said John Hicks Hath given and granted and by these presents Doth Give and Grant unto the said Richard Wake
- All that the second Allotment hereinbefore awarded to him the said John Hicks containing three Roods and Nine perches And
- All that old Inclosure called Little Stankham piece containing one Acre and Nineteen perches bounded
  - On the North by Lower Church field
  - On the East by the public Highway leading from Medstead to Alresford and
  - On the South and West by old Inclosures of the said Edward Woolls

In Exchange for
- All that old Inclosure called Little Sheep Croft containing one Acre one Rood and seventeen perches bounded
  - On the North East by the said Lane called Green Lane
  - On part of the South East by an old Inclosure of the said Robert Pullinger hereinbefore given in Exchange to the said John Hicks called Coles Paddock and
  - On the remaining part of the South East and on every other part thereof by old Inclosures of the said John Hicks

And the said Richard Wake Hath Given and Granted and by these presents Doth Give and Grant unto the said John Hicks
- All that old Inclosure called Little Sheeps Croft hereinbefore described containing one Acre one Rood and seventeen perches

In Exchange for
- All that second Allotment hereinbefore described containing three Roods and three perches and
- All that old Inclosure called Little Stankham piece hereinbefore described containing one Acre and nineteen perches

All which Exchanges hereinbefore ascertained set forth are hereby declared to be made by and with the Consent and Approbation of the said Commissioners

And further Know Ye that the said Edward Woolls in order to lay his Lands in the said parish of Medstead which are held of the said Manor of Ropley more contiguous to each other and to render the same of greater value Hath Exchanged And by these presents Doth Exchange All those his two freehold Inclosures hereinafter described, that is to say,
- All that piece or parcel of Land called the Down containing thirteen Acres two Roods and twelve perches bounded
  - On the North by the Inclosures belonging to the right Honorable George Lord Rodney
  - On the East by the said Lane called Green Lane
  - On the South by old Inclosures of the said Robert Pullinger and Richard Wake and
  - On the West by a Coppice called Down Coppice belonging to the said Edward Woolls And also
- All that piece of parcel of Land part of Lower Creach field containing seven Acres two Roods and thirty four perches bounded
  - On the West by the public Highway leading from Medstead to Wield
  - On the South West by the remaining part of the said piece called Lower Creach and
  - On every other part thereof by old Inclosures of the said Edward Woolls

In Lieu of and in Exchange for the several Allotments and old Inclosures hereinafter mentioned which are held by him as Copyhold Tenant of the Manor of Ropley, that is to say,

- The first Allotment hereinbefore awarded to him the said Edward Woolls containing two Roods and thirty three perches
- The second Allotment hereinbefore awarded to him containing seven Acres two Roods and twenty three perches which said second Allotment is hereinbefore given in Exchange to the said Richard Wake And
- All that old Inclosure called Swanmore piece containing two Acres and three Roods bounded
  - On the North by the public Highway leading from Medstead to Harmsworth
  - On the West by an old Inclosure of the said Richard Bone and
  - On every other part thereof by old Inclosures of the said Edward Woolls And
- All those old Inclosures called Crooked Close and [Prey] Acre now laid together containing four Acres and thirty two perches bounded
  - On parts of the North and East by an old Inclosure of the said John Hicks
  - On the other parts of the North and West by old Inclosures of the said Robert Pullinger hereinbefore given in Exchange to the said Edward Woolls and
  - On every other part thereof by old Inclosures of the said Edward Woolls and
- All that old Inclosure called Cockshot Close containing four Acres two Roods and eight perches bounded
  - On the North by an old Inclosure of the said Robert Pullinger hereinbefore given in Exchange by the said Edward Woolls
  - On the South by a Coppice called the close belonging to the said Edwards Woolls
  - On every other part thereof by old Inclosures belonging to the said Edward Woolls

And Also
- All that old Inclosure called North field Purrock containing three Roods and Eighteen perches hereinbefore given in Exchange to the said Robert Pullinger

Which said two several freehold Inclosures as hereinbefore first described shall be from the date of this Award be held deemed taken and enjoyed by the said Edward Woolls as part of his Copyhold Estate held of the Manor of Ropley aforesaid in lieu of the several allotments and old Inclosures hereinbefore last described

And further Know Ye the said William Budd in order to ascertain the situation of the Lands held by him of the Manor of Ropley to lay the same as contiguous and convenient to each other as possible and to render them of greater value Hath Exchanged and by these presents Doth Exchange the several old Inclosures hereinafter described Which are held by him the said William Budd as Copyhold Tenant of the Manor of Old Alresford, that is to say,
- All that old Inclosure called Long Down containing five Acres two Roods and twenty seven perches received in Exchange of the said Richard Wake and
- All that old Inclosure called Down close containing three Acres three Roods and fourteen perches hereinbefore received in Exchange of the said Richard Wake
- Old inclosure called Redwood Close containing three Acres hereinbefore received in Exchange of the said Richard Wake And
- All that old Inclosure called Long Down containing four Acres and three Roods bounded
  - On the North East by a Lane called Dirty Lane

- On the South East by a Coppice called Wilsons Down Close belonging to the said William Budd
- On the North West by a small beech wood of the said Richard Wake and
- On every other part thereof by the aforesaid old Inclosures called Long Down and Down Close and

- All that old Inclosure called Great Down containing Eight Acres two Roods and two perches bounded
  - On the North West and North East by a beech wood of the said Richard Wake
  - On the South West by the said Lane called Dirty Lane
  - And on the South East by an old Inclosure called Park Close belonging to the said William Budd And
- All that old Inclosure called Redwood Close containing five Acres two Roods and twenty five perches hereinbefore received in Exchange of the said Charles Drummond and Also
- All that old Inclosure called Lower Ground bounded
  - On the North East by a Public Highway leading from Medstead to Bentworth
  - On the North [end page 13] West by an Inclosure of the said Richard Wake
  - On the South West by a Coppice called Wilsons Grove belonging to the said William Budd and
  - On the South East by a coppice called Trinity Coppice

In Lieu of and in Exchange for All that the Allotment and the several old Inclosures hereinafter described belonging to him the said William Budd as Copyhold Tenant of the Manor of Ropley, that is to say,
- All that Allotment hereinbefore awarded to him containing thirteen Acres two Roods and thirty perches and
- All that old Inclosure called Rye field containing Eight Acres two Roods and one perch situate on the South West side of Down Lane And
- All that old Inclosure called Mayple Acre containing one Acre two Roods and Twenty one perches hereinbefore given in Exchange to the said Charles Drummond And
- All that old Inclosure called Crab piece containing three Acres and thirty eight perches hereinbefore given in Exchange to the said Richard Wake And
- All that old Inclosure called Bonts Close containing four Acres one Rood and sixteen perches and situate on the South side of the public Highway leading from Medstead to Alton and
- All that old inclosure called Havershop pace field Close containing five Acres two Roods and five perches situate on the South side of Lower pace field And
- All that old Inclosure called Lymington Bottom containing five Acres and twenty one perches hereinbefore given in Exchange to the said John Hoar and Ann his wife, And also
- All that old Inclosure called Priors Lymington Common containing one Acre three Roods and thirty perches hereinbefore given in Exchange to the said John Andrews

Which said several old Inclosures hereinbefore first described as part of the Copyhold Estate of the said William Budd held of the Manor of Old Alresford shall from the date of this Award be held deemed taken and enjoyed by the said William Budd as part of his Copyhold Estate of the said Manor of Ropley

And further Know Ye that the said William Budd in order to ascertain the situation of the Lands held by him of the Manor of Selborne Hath Exchanged and by these presents Doth Exchange

- All that old inclosure called Bar Stile containing four Acres and twenty one perches hereinafter received in Exchange of the said Charles Drummond

In Lieu of and in Exchange for

- All that the Allotment hereinbefore awarded to him the said William Budd as Copyhold Tenant of the Manor of Selborne containing four Acres one Rood and thirty nine perches and hereinbefore given in Exchange to the said Richard Wake which said old Inclosure called Bar Stile shall for ever hereafter be deemed taken and enjoyed by the said William Budd as for and in Lieu of his Allotment as Copyhold Tenant of the said Manor of Selborne

And further more Know Ye that the said William Budd in order to ascertain the future situation of his freehold Lands in the parish of Medstead which said heretofore laid intermixed with Lands of different Tenures as of those Lands which have been given and received in Exchange by him in this Award and to lay the same as Contiguous and Convenient to each other as possible Hath Exchanged and by these presents Doth Exchange

- All that old Inclosure called Green Stile containing four Acres and four perches hereinbefore received in Exchange of the said Charles Drummond and
- All that old Inclosure called Banniker containing three Acres and five perches adjoining the said piece called Green Stile and which said two Closes are now in one

In Lieu of and in Exchange for the several freehold Allotments hereinbefore awarded to him and the old Inclosure following, that is to say,

- The first Allotment containing one Acre three Roods and two perches hereinbefore given in Exchange to the said Charles Drummond and
- The second Allotment containing three Acres and twenty two perches hereinbefore given in Exchange to the said Richard Wake and
- The said third Allotment containing one Rood and twenty three perches And
- All that old inclosure called Five Ash Close containing five Acres and sixteen perches hereinbefore given in Exchange to the said Richard Andrews And Also
- All that piece of Coppice Ground part of North Ridding Coppice containing one Rood and twenty two perches hereinbefore given in Exchange to the said Charles Drummond which said old Inclosures first described shall for ever hereafter be held and enjoyed by the said William Budd as his freehold Estate in Lieu of the said Allotments and old Inclosures last described

And Further Know Ye the said Richard Wake in order to lay his Lands in the said parish of Medstead which are held of the said Manor of Ropley more contiguous to each other and to render them of greater value Hath Exchanged and by these presents Doth Exchange the several old Inclosures following which are held by him as Copyhold Tenant of the Manor of Old Alresford, that is to say

- All that old Inclosure called Medstead Common containing ten Acres and twenty eight perches and
- All that old Inclosure also called Medstead Common containing four Acres three Roods and thirteen perches and also
- All that old Inclosure called also Medstead Common containing four Acres three Roods and thirty perches which said several old Inclosures are bounded
  - On the North by an old Inclosure of the said John Hoar hereinbefore given in Exchange to the said Richard Wake
  - On the East by Inclosures of the said Charles Drummond
  - On the South by old Inclosures in the parish of Ropley belonging to Rubin Hunt and William Budd and
  - On the West by old Inclosures of the said William Budd

In Lieu of and in Exchange for the following old Inclosures held by   him   as Copyhold Tenant of the Manor of Ropley, that is to say,

- All that old Inclosed Meadow called Shepherds Mead containing one Rood and thirty six perches hereinbefore received in Exchange of the said William Budd and
- All that old Inclosure called Towngate Meadow containing one Acre one Rood and twenty seven perches situate near the Farm House of the said Richard Wake And
- All that old Inclosure called Dell Lymington containing three Acres hereinbefore received in Exchange of the said John Hoar And
- All that old Inclosure called Withy piece containing two Acres and thirteen perches and also
- All that old Inclosure called Little Medstead Common containing three Acres

Which said old Inclosures hereinbefore first described and mentioned to be held of the Manor of Old Alresford shall from the date of this Award and for ever thereafter be held deemed taken and enjoyed by the said Richard Wake as part of the Copyhold Estate held of the Manor of Ropley in Lieu of the several old Inclosures hereinbefore last mentioned to be held of that Manor All which Exchanges are made and are hereby declared to be made by and with the Consent and Approbation of the said Commissioners and are hereby ratified and Confirmed by them accordingly

And Further Know Ye that the said Commissioners in further pursuance and by virtue of the powers and directions Given them by the said Act and pursuant to the Certificate of the Major part in value of the owners of Lands in the said Parish of Medstead have ordered and directed and by this their Award Do order and direct that the several Bridle Roads and footways in the said parish of Medstead hereinafter mentioned shall be diverted and turned agreeable to the intent and Meaning of the said Certificate in Manner hereinafter expressed, that is to say, That

- A certain footway in the said Parish commencing at the West side of the Great Meadow on the Manor Farm and leading in the front of the House to Hustle Lane shall be diverted and turned into the Footway behind the Manor House from the Corner of the Rick Yard in a straight Lane into Hustle Lane at the end of Adams's Garden and that
- The footway commencing at the Corner of the said Rick Yard and leading through William Budd's field called Hustle shall also be diverted and turned into the Footway above mentioned and that
- One other footway Commencing at the end of Little Down near Foul Lane end and leading across Richard Wake's Round wood shall be diverted and turned into the said Lane called Foul Lane and that
- One other footway commencing at Pace field Bars leading to Southtown through Mrs Woolls's Farm Yard across the Highway to Bulters Lane and from thence across Down Lane to Chawton Parish shall be diverted and turned into the footway leading from Southtown to Redhill And that
- One other footway commencing at Skinners Nap leading through Southtown Mead across Middle field through Church field to Hattingley shall be diverted and turned into the footpath leading from the [broom] [end page 14] Priors to Medstead Church and
- That one other Footway commencing at the end of Crooked Lane near Little Down and leading through Granary piece across Rutters Lane to five ash Lane and from thence through Lower Wood to the Turnpike Road shall be diverted and turned into the Road leading from South town to Red Hill And
- That one other Footway commencing at Skinners Nap and leading through Terrells Common shall be diverted and turned into the footpath leading to Soldridge And
- That one other footway commencing at Dell piece Soldridge leading through [Great] Common into the Turnpike Road shall be diverted and turned into the Highway leading from five ash pond to Lymington Bottom And
- That one other Footway commencing at the upper End of South Pace field near John [P] [h]ouse and leading through Broom Corner into the Highway leading from Soldridge shall be diverted and turned [into] the Footway leading from Medstead Church to Soldridge And
- That one Public Highway or Bridle Road leading from Redhill through [] field called Upper Boynes belonging to Medstead Manor Farm through a piece of land called Windmill piece belonging to Richard Wake And also
- One other Public Highway or public Bridle Road leading also from Redhill through Upper and Lower Boynes Wood into the Turnpike Road shall be diverted and turned into the public Highway leading from Red hill to the said Turnpike as the Lane leading immediately into Boynes Wood from Red hill is agreed to be given up to the said Charles Drummond the right of the said Ann Woolls of carrying the Wood when she cuts Boynes Wood through the fields called Little Boynes and Dell piece is hereby reserved to her And
- That one other Bridle Road or footway commencing at the Clap Gate adjoining the Lane near the Grove Barn leading to the late William Budd's Cottages shall be diverted and turned into the Public Highway by Oakley's Cottage into the Lane leading from Bighton to South town And

- That one other Footway commencing at the Gate near Hackett Pond leading across the Cottage field late Priors into the Basingstoke Road shall be diverted and turned into the public Highway leading from the aforesaid Budd's Cottage to Gullett Lane And
- That one other Footway commencing at the said Budd's Cottages and leading to Pullinger's Barn shall be diverted and turned into the public Highway leading from South town to Bighton And
- That one other Footway commencing at the Clap Gate near Grove Barn and leading to Lanham Chalk Pit shall be diverted and turned into the public Highway leading from the aforesaid Clap Gate to Pullinger Barn And
- That one other Footway leading from Hattingley House through Puddicks to the aforesaid Chalk Pit shall be diverted and turned into the public Highway leading from Hattingley to Heath Green And
- That one other public Highway commencing at Bulberks Meadow running through Hattingley Farm Yard to Swanmore piece And
- Also one other footway leading from the aforesaid Bulberks Meadow to the Style opposite Pullinger's Carthouse And also
- One other Footway leading from the aforesaid stile to Hattingley House And also
- One private carriage Road leading from Green Lane into Richard Wake's Middle Reeds on the South East side of the said Robert Pullinger's Upper Reeds shall be diverted and turned into the said Richard Wake's Inclosure called Upper Reeds shall be severally diverted and turned into the Footway leading through Bulberks piece to Heath Green And
- That one other Footway commencing at the East end of Bulberks Meadow leading through Bulberks Farm yard into Hattingley Street shall be diverted and turned into Hockleys Lane And
- That one other Footway commencing at the Chalk Dell in Hattingley field leading through [Dor/ys]Farm Yard shall be diverted and turned into the aforesaid Lane called Hockleys Lane And
- That one other Footway commencing at Pullinger's Farm Yard and leading through Richard Bone's Meadow and Hockleys and from thence into North field shall be diverted and turned into the footpath leading through the Upper part of Home Close to North field And
- That one other Footway commencing at the South End of North field and leading through Crofts Acre into Green Lane shall be diverted and turned into the Footpath leading from the aforesaid North field by John Bone's Cottage into Green Lane And
- That one other Bridle Road leading from Foul Lane through Richard Wake's Redwood and Hustle Lane shall be diverted and turned into a Highway leading from the Middle of Little Down to Hustle Lane
- One other Footway commencing at Farmer Bone's Gorey Close and through Coles Purrock into Green Lane shall be diverted and turned into the said Footway leading from the aforesaid North Field by John Bone's Cottage into Green Lane And
- That one other Footway Commencing opposite the Church Rails and preceding through Church field into Hattingley field And Also

- One other Footway leading through Little Summerleys shall be diverted and turned into the public Highway leading by Farmer Wake's House from Hattingley to Lower Common And
- That one other Footway commencing at Hattingley Cowpasture and leading across the further Breach into Ferney Lane shall be diverted and turned into the public Highway leading from Hattingley to Heath Green

All which said Bridle Roads and Footways are hereby directed to be diverted and turned accordingly and that it shall not be lawful for any persons or persons whomsoever to use or pass the said Bridle Roads and Footpaths or any of them after the Execution of this Award on any account or pretence whatsoever

And the said Commissioners Do further award order direct and appoint that where any Trees Thorns Hedges Bushes or Shrubs shall be Standing or Growing on the Allotment or Allotments Exchange or Exchanges of any Proprietor or Proprietors other than such as was or were the former proprietor or proprietors Owner or Owners of such Trees Thorns Hedges Bushes or Shrubs that it shall and may be lawful to and for such owners or proprietors their Servants or Workmen respectively at any seasonable time or times on or before the twenty first day of December next ensuing the date of this Award or Instrument to enter upon such Lands and Grounds upon which such Trees Thorns Hedges Bushes or Shrubs are standing and to cut down grub up and with Horses and Carriages to carry away the same doing as Little Damage as possible and levelling the Ground [re] the same shall be broken up

Provided nevertheless that no Trees Thorns Hedges Bushes or Shrubs shall be cut down unless the owner thereof shall first have Licence in Writing under the Hands of the said Commissioners and that no Trees Thorns Hedges Bushes or Shrubs shall be cut down grubbed up or carried away that have been valued and appraised by the said Commissioners or such persons as they shall appoint and paid for according to such valuation

And Moreover Know Ye that the said Commissioners in further pursuance and exercise of the Power and Authorities vested in them by the said Act after having taken into their Consideration the improvements in value of the Farm and Lands in the Occupation of John Wyeth in the said parish of Medstead as Tenant to the said Charles Drummond in Consequence of the inclosure of the Common fields which heretofore belonged to the said Farm and of the General improvements of the said Farm by such Inclosure Do hereby award order and direct that the said John Wyeth his Executors Administrators or Assigns shall pay the sum of Ten pounds and fifteen Shillings being five per cent upon the Expenses which the said Charles Drummond has sustained in such Inclosure as an increased Rent for the said farm and for the improvements made thereon which additional Rent shall commence and take effect from the Tenth day of October now next ensuing and be payable Half yearly and recoverable in the same Manner as the former Rent for the said Term is now by Law recoverable

And Lastly concerning the charges and expenses incident to and attend the obtaining and passing the said Act and all the Expenses of the Division and Allotment of the Lands and Grounds by the said act directed to be divided inclosed or exchanged and for preparing and inrolling this Award and for paying the Commissioners their reasonable Charges Troubles and Expenses in an about the Execution of the Trusts and powers vested in them by the said Act and all other Necessary Expenses in and about the Execution of the said Act incurred as well before as after passing the said Act The Commissioners have ascertained the same and find that they amount in the whole to the Sum of Five Hundred Pounds And for raising such Sum of Five Hundred Pounds the said Commissioners have made a Levy on all to whom Allotments are awarded or exchanged made and which Levy is hereunder written entitled "A Schedule or Levy for raising the Expenses of this Inclosure"

And the said Commissioners do order award and direct that the several Persons named and mentioned in the said Schedule or Levy who have not already paid the Sums set against their respective Names shall within Ten Days after the execution of these presents pay into the Hands of Edward Hopkins of New Alresford Clerk to the said Commissioners the several and respective Sums set and affixed against their several and respective Names And the said Edward Hopkins after receiving the whole amount of such Levy is hereby directed and impowered to lay out and dispose of the same in discharging and paying such Costs and expenses according to an account thereof made out and inserted in a certain Book signed by the said Commissioners [end page 15] and intended to be deposited with these presents in the parish Chest of the Church of Medstead aforesaid

In Witness whereof the said Commissioners parties hereto have to this Award or Instrument of Allotments in writing and Deed of Exchange and Confirmation written on Twenty two skins of parchment Annexed to each Skin thereof severally subscribed their Names and to the last skin thereof severally set Hands and Seals and all and every the said several other persons named after the said Commissioners and made exchanging parties hereto have hereunto severally subscribed and set their hands and seals at a Meeting held for that purpose at the Swan Inn in the town of New Alresford in the said County of Southampton this twenty first day of May in the thirty ninth year of the Reign of our Sovereign Lord George the third by the Grace of God of Great Britain France and Ireland King defender of the faith and so forth and in the year of our Lord one Thousand seven Hundred and ninety nine

A Schedule or Levy for Raising the Expences of this Inclosure

	£	s	d	%
The Trustees of the late Henry Drummond Esquire	135	2	2	27.0
Mrs Ann Woolls	64	1	1	12.8
Mr William Budd	99	2	6	19.8
Robert Pullinger	18	8	5	3.7
John Hicks	5	17	3	1.2
Edward Woolls Esquire	19	12	3	3.9
Richard Wake	104	5	2	20.9
John Camies	31	13	7	6.3
Richard Bone	4	18	11	1.0
John Andrews	10	3	3	2.0
Richard and William Andrews	3	16	9	0.8
John Hoare	1	13	5	0.3
Late William Budd	1	5	3	0.3
Amount of the Rate	500	0	0	

Thomas Hasker	(LL)
John Tredgold	(LS)
HW Fleet	(LS)
Wm Budd	(LS)
Richd Wake	(LS)
John Andrews	(LP)

Signed Sealed and delivered being first duly stamped in the presence of us
Edward Hopkins New Alresford
David Weddell his clerk

9th May 1800 Examined with the original by me
Peter Kerby Deputy Clerk of the peace

Appendix 22: The Second Annual Enclosure Act (Newton Valence), 1848

An Act to authorize the Inclosure of certain Lands in pursuance of a Special report of the Inclosure Commissioners for England Wales.[1]

Whereas the Inclosure Commissioners for England and Wales have, in pursuance of an Act passed in the Ninth Year of the Reign of Her present Majesty,[2] intituled An Act to facilitate the Inclosure and Improvement of Commons and Lands held in Common, the Exchange of Lands, and the Division of intermixed Lands; to provide Remedies for defective or incomplete Executions, and for the Nonexecution of the Powers of general and local Inclosure Acts; and to provide for the Revival of such Powers in certain Cases, since the Date of their Third Annual General Report, issued their Provisional Orders for and concerning the proposed Inclosures mentioned in the Schedule to this Act, and the requisite Consents thereto have been given;

And whereas the said Commissioners have, by a Special Report, certified their Opinion that such proposed Inclosures would be expedient; but the same cannot be proceeded with without the previous Authority of Parliament: Be it enacted by the Queen's most Excellent Majesty, by and with the Advice and Consent of the Lords Spiritual and Temporal, and Commons, in this present Parliament assembled, and by the Authority of the same, That the said several proposed Inclosures mentioned in the Schedule to this Act be proceeded with.

II. And be it enacted, That in citing this Act in other Acts of Parliament, and in legal Instruments, it shall be sufficient to use the Expression 'The Second Annual Inclosure Act, 1848'.

III. And whereas since the Presentation by the Inclosure Commissioners of the said Special Report the necessary consents to the Provisional Order have been given in the Matter of the Warley Inclosure in the County of York: And whereas the several Parties consenting thereto are desirous that certain Agreements already entered into between the Lord of the Manor of Wakefield, of which the Township of Warley is Parcel, and Commoners thereof, who have consented to such Provisional Order, should be carried out with respect to certain Matters which unless provided for it would not be advisable that such Inclosure should proceed: Be it therefore enacted, That it shall be lawful for the said Commissioners, if they shall think fit, and they are hereby authorized, by Order under their Seal, to direct that the said Inclosure be proceeded with upon the Terms and Conditions of such Provisional Order and of the said Agreements, or such of them as the said Commissioners shall think just and reasonable; and thereupon such Inclosure shall be proceeded with, and the Award to be made in pursuance of such Order shall be binding and conclusive, in the same Manner as if the said Warley Inclosure had been mentioned in the Schedule to this Act, and as if the Terms and Conditions of the said Agreements, or such of them as the Commissioners shall think just and reasonable as aforesaid, had been included in and incorporated with the Provisional Order in the Matter of such Inclosure, and had been authorized by the said recited Act.

---

1 Parliamentary Archives, HL_PO_PU_1_1848_11&12V_Inclosure Act, 11 & 12 Victoria, c. 109, 4/9/1848.

2 8 & 9 Victoria, c. 118.

Schedule to which this Act refers.

Inclosure	County	Date of Provisional Order
Ash Moor	Devon	2 February 1848
Cottisford	Oxford	2 February 1848
Kildwick	York	5 April 1848
Winterbourn Dantsey	Wilts	2 December 1847
Littleton	Middlesex	15 June 1848
Newton Valence	Southampton	24 May 1848
Discoyed Hill	Radnor	24 May 1848
Greatham	Southampton	10 December 1847
Newbiggin Moor	Westmorland	18 May 1848
Harras Moor	Cumberland	15 June 1848
Drinkstone	Suffolk	15 July 1848
South Common	Somerset	15 July 1848
Standlake, Brighthampton, and Hardwicke	Oxford	19 July 1848
Hebden Moor	York	18 May 1848
Hodnet Heath	Salop	5 July 1848
Thatcham	Berks	31 July 1848
Germans Week Common	Devon	19 July 1848

Appendix 23: Newton Valence enclosure agreement, 1850

To all to whom these Presents shall come[1]
I Richard Wakefield Attree of the Parish of Bishearne Liss in the County of
Southampton Land Surveyor send greeting.

Whereas by a Provisional Order under the Seal of the Inclosure Commissioners
for England and Wales dated the Twenty fourth day of May one thousand eight
hundred and forty eight by the necessary consents given to such Order and by *The
Second Annual Inclosure Act 1848* the Inclosure of Newton Valence Commons situate
in the parish of Newton Valence in the County of Southampton has been duly
authorised under the provisions of the Act passed in the Eighth and Ninth years of
the reign of Her present Majesty, Chapter 118.

And Whereas I the said Richard Wakeford Attree have been appointed the Valuer
in the matter of the said Inclosure and having made the declaration required by the
said last mentioned Act have duly held all necessary meetings and drawn up and sent
to the said Inclosure Commissioners my Report in writing in the matter of the said
Inclosure with Maps marked **A** and **B** thereunto annexed and in all other respects
complied with the provisions of the said last mentioned Act.[2]

And Whereas all such objections as have been made to my said Report having
been heard and all such enquiries having been made in relation thereto, as the said
Inclosure Commissioners have thought fit, for the said Inclosure Commissioners
have authorised and directed me to cause to be drawn up and engrossed on Parchment
my Award in the matter of such Inclosure.

Now Know Ye that in pursuance of the provisions of the said Acts and by virtue
of the powers and authorities in me vested I the said Richard Wakeford Attree the
Valuer as aforesaid do make and declare this to being Award in the matter of the
said Inclosure, and to this my Award I have annexed the Maps referred to in my said
Report.

And first I declare that I have discontinued and stopped up A certain public Carriage
Road or Highway in the said Parish of Newton Valence commencing at a point
marked **A** passing through the north end of Rotherfield Park to a point marked **C**
on Lower Common as shown by the said Map **B** hereunto annexed

And I do hereby declare that I have set out and appointed, and do hereby set out and
appoint the following Public Carriage Roads of Highways, that is to say:

- One public Carriage Road or Highway of the width of twenty six feet and a
half to be called the Common Road and commencing at a point marked **D** on
the said Map A and extending across the Lower Common to a point marked
E. And from thence Westward to a point marked **F** on Upper Common
where it joins the existing Road leading to Ropley.

---

1   HRO, Q23/2/94.
2   TNA MAF 1/543. Maps redrawn in Chapter 10.

- One other Public Carriage Road on Highway of the width of twenty six feet and a half to be called the new Road commencing at a point marked **G** on the said Map **A** and extending thence westwards and southward to a point marked **H** passing thence over the old existing road on Lane to a point marked **J** in Upper Common and extending thence to a point marked **F** on the said map where the same joins the other Road leading to Ropley

- And one other public Carriage Road on highway of the width of twenty six feet and a half to be called the Stoney Road commencing at a point marked **K** on the said Map **A** and extending thence to a point marked **L** on the same map.

- And I declare that I have set out and do hereby set out all of allot and award unto the Churchwardens and Overseers of the Poor of the said parish of Newton Valence. All that piece or parcel of Land numbered **12** on the said Map **A** containing two acres to be held by them and their successors in Trust as a place of exercise and recreation for the Inhabitants of the said Parish and neighbourhood. And I direct that the fences on the north and south west sides of such allotment shall from time to time be repaired and maintained by and at the expense the Churchwardens and Overseers of the Poor of the said Parish for the time being.

- And I declare that I have set out and appointed and do hereby set out and appoint the following Public Pond or Watering Place; that is to say: one public Pond situate on the Upper Common and marked **M** on the said Map **A**.

- And I declare that the said Pond shall be from time to time properly cleansed and repaired by the owner for the time being of the allotment numbered **4** on the said Map **A**.

- And I have also according to the directions of the Provisional Order of the said Commissioners set out and do hereby set out; allot and award unto Henry Chawner Esquire the Lord of the Manor of Newton Valance all that piece or parcel of Land numbered **9a** on the said Map **A** and containing six acres and twenty four perches, and also that other piece or parcel of Land numbered **9b**. On the same map containing three acres two Roods and two perches, which two pieces of parcels of Land I adjudge and declare to be equal in value to one sixteenth part of the residue of the said Commons and to be in lieu and in full compensation for the right and interest of the said Henry Chawner on the Soil of the said Commons inclusively of his right and interest in all mines, minerals, stone and other substrata under the Land to be inclosed.

- And I direct the Fence on the South West side of the said allotment numbered **9a** against the Common Road and the fence on the North East side of the said allotment numbered **9b** against the same road shall be made and repaired and maintained by and at the expense of the owner of the said allotment respectively for the time being.

- And I further declare that have set all the remainder of the said Newton Valence Commons among the several persons hereinafter named, being all the persons interested therein in the shares of allotments following set opposite to their respective names which allotments which I have adjudged and determined to be proportionate to the value of the respective rights and interests of such seral persons which have been claimed and allowed under the provisions of the said last mentioned Act, that is to say

I do set out allot and award unto:

	map	a	r	p	total	%
William Carter	7	0	3	11	0.82	0.5
Henry Chawner Esq	8b	6	1	0	6.25	
Henry Chawner Esq	8c	15	1	16	15.35	
Henry Chawner Esq	4	21	1	15	21.28	27.7
Robert & Henry Knight	10	22	2	19	22.62	
Robert & Henry Knight	6	3	0	32	3.20	
Robert & Henry Knight	5	7	2	23	7.52	21.6
Capt. George Ouvry Sampriere	3	15	3	33	15.96	10.3
John & Edward Hunt	11	1	3	5	1.97	1.3
James Winter Scott Esq	13	17	2	26	17.66	11.4
The Rev. Thomas Snow	1	13	0	31	13.19	8.5
Eli Turvill	14	21	3	4	21.46	13.9
William Warner	2	0	3	8	0.93	0.6
Roads and Pond	M (pond)	6	1	29	6.43	4.2
					154.64	
plus Overseers of the Poor	12	2	0	0	**156.64**	

And I the said Richard Wakeford Attree do hereby order direct and appoint that the several hedges, Banks, Fences and ditches for inclosing the several Allotments hereinbefore described not already set up and made shall be raised set up and made respectively within the space of one year from the confirmation by the said Inclosure Commissioners of this my Award by the several persons owners for the time being of the said several Allotments on the sides hereinbefore in that behalf prescribed on which sides a star is marked or drawn thus **T** on the said Map **A**.

In Testimony whereof I the said Richard Wakeford Attree have to this my award which I have under the directions of the said Inclosure Commissioners for England and Wales caused to be drawn up and engrossed on Parchment set my hand this 30th day of May in the year of our Lord one thousand eight hundred and fifty.
[*Signature*] R Wakeford Attree

In Witness and Confirmation whereof We the Undersigned Inclosure Commissioners for England and Wales have hereunto subscribed our respective names and caused our Official Seal to be affixed this Twentieth day of June in the year of our Lord one thousand eight hundred and fifty.

[*Signature*] Wm Blamire

Appendix 24: Owners of over 4,000 acres in Hampshire and owners of ridge land, 1873

Owners of over 4,000 Hampshire acres[1]

Name		Address	Acres
Bolton	Lord (Harry Powlett)	Hackwood Park, Winslade	18,808
Portsmouth	Earl of	Hurstbourne Park, Whitchurch	16,401
Wellington	Duke of	Stratfield Saye House	15,847
Ashburton	Lord (Alexander Baring)	The Grange, Alresford	15,330
Heathcote	Sir William, Bart	Hursley House, Hursley	14,189
Portal	Melville	Laverstoke House, Micheldever	10,566
Carnarvon	Earl of	Highclere Castle, Newbury	9,294
Normanton	Earl of (James Agar)	Somerley House, Ringwood	9,286
Northbrook	Lord	Lowndes Square, London	9,236
Scott	Lord Henry	Beaulieu	8,922
Fleming	John B W, execs	Hambledon	8,843
Simeon	Sir J B	Swainstone	8,724
Woods	Henry	Warnford Park	8,649
McCreagh	Lady	Deal	8,600
Chamberlayne	Thomas	Cranbury Park, Otterbourne	8,535
Thistlewayte	Thomas	Southwick Park	8,084
Baring	Thomas	Norman Court, Stockbridge	8,058
Jervoise	Sir J C	Idsworth	7,877
College	of Winchester	Winchester	7,629
Tichborne	Sir A H	Tichborne	7,270
Mildmay	Sir Henry B P St John	Dogmersfield Park	6,762
Delme	H P	Fareham	6,258
Jervoise	F J E	Herriard Park	6,183
Best	Rev. Thomas	Upper Clatford	6,134
Beach	W W B	Oakley Hall Park	6,099
Dean & Chapter	of Winchester	Winchester	5,837
Cowper-Temple	W F	Romsey	5,780
Carter	John Bonham	Petersfield	5,621

---

1   *The Return of Owners of Land*, 1873, uncorrected returns. Many of these landowners have significant additional holdings outside of the county. See Cahill, *Who Owns Britain*, p. 239.

Morant	John	Brockenhurst House, Lymington	5,596
Kingsmill	Wm. H.	Newbury	5,361
Heytesbury	Lord	Heytesbury	5,195
Drummond	Edgar A	Fawley	5,155
Stanmore	William H S	Eling	5,150
Iremonger	William H	Brighton	5,103
Knight	Edward	Chawton House	5,044
Mill	Lady Jane	Romsey	5,040
Shelley	Edward	Avington	4,996
Winchester	Marquis of	Amport House	4,785
Hulse	Sir Edward	Breamore	4,518
War Department		Pall Mall, London	4,467
Dutton	Hon. John	Alresford	4,293
Gervis	Sir G	Christchurch	4,286
Malmesbury	Earl of	Christchurch	4,155
Mills	John	Bisterne, Ringwood	4,144
Seely	Sir Charles	Brooke House, IoW	4,086
Miller	Sir Charles J H H	Froyle Place	4,008

Chawton

Owner surname	Owner first name	Residential address	Acres in Hampshire
Clement	Rev B	Chawton	16
Knight	Edward	Chawton House	5,044
Knight	Rev E B	Chawton	70
Spencer	Wm, execs	Chawton	70
London S-W Railway[2]	In parish	Waterloo	42
Stevens	George	Chawton	3
			5,245
	Parish	1908 acreage	**4,684**
	Minimum	external owned	**0**

---

2 The figures for the London and South-Western Railway are for that parish. That railway owned 1,450 acres in Hampshire in 1873. With thanks to Roger Burt and Dr. Keith Brown.

East Tisted

Allam	John	East Tisted	18
Howlett	Rev	East Tisted	8
			26
	Parish	1908 acreage	**2,649**
	Minimum	external owned	**2,623**

Farringdon

Andrews	W P	Farringdon	1
Banks	Caroline	Farringdon	6
Ben	General P	Farringdon	15
Bennett	John	Farringdon	7
Carter	William	Farringdon	38
Clinker	William	Farringdon	5
Copland	Thomas	Farringdon	24
Fielder	John	Farringdon	1
Grover	Sarah	Farringdon	1
Harding	Albert J	Farringdon	3
Harding	Cornelius	Farringdon	3
Harding	E B	Farringdon	5
Keat	William	Farringdon	1
Leadbiter	Mrs	Farringdon	2
Leach	Mrs	Farringdon	8
Massey	Rev T H	Farringdon	7
Penton	Mrs	Farringdon	8
Stoner	James	Farringdon	2
Streeter	George	Farringdon	6
Trimmer	George	Farringdon	88
			231
	Parish	1908 acreage	**2,358**
	Minimum	external owned	**2,127**

Medstead

Andrews	William	Medstead	84
Bone	Nancy	Medstead	30
Bone	William	Medstead	3

Cannons	Charles	Medstead	1
Curtis	W C	Medstead	430
Holliday	Fras.	Medstead	32
Knight	George	Medstead	2
Knight	John	Medstead	32
Lambert	Mrs	Medstead	78
Lambourne	James	Medstead	1
London S-W Railway	In parish	Waterloo	26
Potter	William	Medstead	2
Silver	Rev E	Medstead	8
Stevens	Louisa	Medstead	3
Wake	George	Medstead	96
Wake	Lucy	Medstead	13
Westbrook	William	Medstead	2
Wyeth	Robert	Medstead	8
Wyeth	William	Medstead	6

				853
		Parish	1908 acreage	**2,484**
	Minimum		external owned	**914**

Newton Valance

Chawner	Capt. Edward	Newton Valence	643
Haines	Harriet	Newton Valence	60
Howe	Frances	Newton Valence	3
Lempriere	A. T.	Newton Valence	460
Lempriere	Mrs	Newton Valence	112
Maclaclan	Rev A C N	Newton Valence	94
Munday	James	Newton Valence	14
Turvill	Eli	Newton Valence	184
Warner	Hy.	Newton Valence	25
Warner	William	Newton Valence	108

			1,703
	Parish	1908 acreage	2,258
	Minimum	external owned	555

Ropley

Bennett	William	Ropley	72
Charrett	Jane	Ropley	6
Deacon	Hy.	Ropley	18
Fisher	John	Ropley	6
Hagen	Mrs	Ropley	507
Hale	William	Ropley	20
Hall	Thomas	Ropley	1
Mulcock	H J	Ropley	2,572
Lailey	George	Ropley	175
Lillywhite	John	Ropley	80
London & S-W Railway	In parish	Waterloo	38
Long	David	Ropley	1
Mayhews	Mrs	Ropley	92
Stevens	Wm, execs	Ropley	10
Turner	H	Ropley	1
Woodhouse	Rev Thos.	Ropley	31
Young	Arthur	Ropley	6
Young	George	Ropley	172
			3,808
	Parish	1908 acreage	**4,684**
	Minimum	external owned	**914**

Appendix 25: Colonel Lorents Rathbone, A Chronicle of Medstead: Extract 1966

If even one person delves deeper than I into the old records, then this small booklet will have been justified.[1]

Customs of the Manor[2]

There is a document in the British Museum of about 1250 which, because of its great interest, is worth dealing with in detail and at some length. It begins:

> These are the customs and services of the manor of Alresford by the enquiry on oath of Roger Faber, William de Wodeford, Andrew of the Hill, Robert of Upton. Daniel of Estune, Nicholas of Kullane, Eli Albus, John de la Ware, Hugh de Solrigge, Senior and Richard Uudeman Jurors.

It gives the names of the Bishop's (the lord's) tenants and, after each name, is given the size or nature of his holding, the rent he, or she, paid in money and/or services, the nature of those services and the official positions he might be called upon to fill and 'benefits' attached thereto.

The crops mentioned are corn, barley and oats and there were meadows and feeding grounds for pigs. The main livestock consisted of sheep and pigs. Horses and oxen were kept for ploughing and carting. It would appear that about half of the land of the manor was let off and that the remainder was the lord's demesne (home farm), common land and woodland. Before filling in the details of the picture we must visualize the general system of farming in those days. Usually a manor was divided into two or three large fields of which one would lie fallow each year. From later evidence, (which will be considered in the next chapter) it is probable that *Medestede* was an exception with six or seven fields. Each arable field was usually divided into strips of half or a quarter of an acre. Each farmer, including the lord, owned strips all over the field thus ownership might be:-

Strip 1.   Daniel de Hattingele.
Strip 2.   Stephen de Solrigge.
Strip 3.   The lord.
Strip 4.   Joanna Blanchard.
Strip 5.   Stephen de Solrigge, and so on.

There were various grazing rights on the common land, the fallow and the lord's land. From later evidence it seems probable that Alresford, Harmesworth and Medestede each had their own field systems.

One interesting feature of the document is that people's names appear in a sort of 'class' order, the most important coming at the top of the list and the least important at the bottom. This order will be adhered to in the following paragraphs.

---

1   Lorents Rathbone.
2   *HRO, 32M 94/1/71.*

- The Mother Church held 2 virgates 'freely', i.e. with no money rent and no obligations. The Parson had the following privileges – he could gather wood for fencing and fire-wood in the lord's wood; he could graze 2 horses and 8 oxen on the lord's pasture, 100 sheep and 1 ram could graze with those of the lord and he did not have to pay pannage for up to 100 pigs.
- William de Houtot held a knight's fee in the vill of Medested and he had two parts of the same vill and the lord the third part. He paid no money rent but he owed military service or payment in lieu. He had to fence, with his own men, part of the park of the lord's palace at Waltham. If any one of his tenants had a plough then he had to plough, for the lord, 1 acre in the winter and 1 during Lent; he was paid 2d. for each acre.
- William de Hattyngele held 1 hide (4 Virgates) and paid no money rent. But he had to do riding service, if the lord pleased within the County of Southampton. Presumably he had to provide other horse-men as well as himself. An early example of a postal service?
- Daniel de Hattyngele held 2 virgates for 5s free of all services except fencing the park at Waltham.
- Hugo de Solrigge, junior, held 1 virgate for 6s for all services except that if he put his pigs in the lord's feeding grounds he must pay 2d for each yearling pig, 1½d for each of 9 months old, 1d for each of 6 months old and 1d per piglet up to six months.
- John Yunge had 2 virgates for 10s. He had to fence at Waltham and mow the meadow at the lord's palace at Wolvesey; he must plough 1 acre in winter and 1 in Lent receiving 4d for it. He paid pannage for his pigs if on the lord's ground. If the lord required he had to be Forester and Warden of the lord's woods; in which case 'he must give 400 eggs to the lord at Christmas. For this he shall have 5 cartloads of branches and he shall have branches which fall for sale if worth less than 4d.' And 'when he dies there is due to the lord the best beast by way of Heriot and if he is so rich that he has a horse it shall be sent to the court with harness'. A precursor of modern Estate Duty!

All the above owed suit of court at the hundred court of Alresford twice in the year 'and whenever thieves are to be tried there'. They also had to do suit at the court of the hundred of Falele (Fawley) to which hundred Alresford belonged.

The vill of Alresford had land called Prenete for 100s free of all services.

There is then a group of people (24) holding from 2 virgates for 13s 4d to 1 linch for 1d and some paid for 'certain waters'. These rents were for all services. Fishing rights? Water-cress beds?

Then come the holders of four mills whose money rents varied from 30s to 13s 8d. Each had, if needed, to provide a carpenter for the lord's hall; to do carting anywhere in the manor; to take nets or fish to Farnham, Waltham, Marwell or Bitterne. They could be called on to do additional work. They were released of these works if they paid the lord annually 1½ silver marks. Those with a wife had to give the lord 4 hens, if no wife then 2 hens. Using the lord's barley they had to bake, and take to the harvesters in the field, 100 loaves.

There was a fulling mill whose owner paid 33s and another miller who paid 66s, both for all services.

The next group of fifty people were 'virgaters', each one farming 1 virgate or ½ virgate at money rents varying from 4s to 10s per virgate. Of these people six were women (widows) who had security of tenure. The services required of them seem hard when we remember that, in order to live, they had to cultivate their own land. These services were:-

- If owning a plough they had to plough 1 acre in winter and 1 in Lent being paid 4d. If they had a horse they had to harrow 1 acre in winter and another in Lent when they had to harrow every day until the lord's oats were sown.
- They had to do 3 boonworks in autumn with 2 of their men.
- They must fence at Waltham and mow at Wolvesey. (Each some fifteen miles from Medested.)
- If needed they must make malt with the lord's barley and attend the Scot-Ale.
- They had to pay pannage for their pigs and they must cart as follows:

    1 cartload of barley to Wolvesey at Easter and Christmas. 1 quarter of hard corn or 2 quarters of oats to the four neighbouring markets 'at whatever occasion'. If the lord wanted to build a barn, they must cart the material, as well as any corn to the Grange throughout the autumn.

    'He shall not give his son nor his daughter in marriage nor sell his horse or his ox or young stock without licence.' This applied to them all as indeed did all the services specified above.

    These virgaters were liable to be appointed to the following official positions at 'the lord's will'.

Reeve This was the most important job within the manor, in fact equivalent to the modern farm manager. His benefits were: he was quit of all services except fines for the marriage of his offspring and paying pannage and he was quit of 5s of his rent. He had 1 acre of corn, barley or compost at his choice and had his lamb, piglet and cheese 'according to custom'. He could put 2 animals with the lord's stock and received a portion of wine. At Christmas and Easter he had to provide 400 eggs.

Granger Responsible for the storage of grain. He was quit of 3s rent and half his services excepting pannage and paying a fine for the marriage of this children.

Hayward Looked after fences and hedges. He was responsible for all damage done to the lord's corn. He had to provide iron for 2½ ploughs and their wheels and 150 eggs at Christmas and 250 at Easter. He was quit of 4s 6d rent and services except fines for the marriage of his children. He 'shall have 3 outlying portions of land which he shall sow with his own seed if he wishes'. He had 1½ acres of corn or barley of the lord's for his own use; he had 1 piglet and 1 lamb 'according to custom', and grazed 1 horse and 2 stock animals anywhere. At every boonwork he had two loaves for his food and 'peas porrage' to the value of ½d.

Shepherd to the Wethers. Was quit of 3s rent and half his services except the fine for the marriage of his children. He got one cloak and could run 2 animals with the lord's and 60 sheep and 1 ram with the lord's wethers.

The next group was made up of 22 cottagers owning a cottage and cotland for 3s. These appear to have had even more onerous services than the others.

- If they did not pay their rent they had to do day work, presumably in addition to the works to be described.
- From 29th September to 1st August they had to do three days' work in any one week without pay, except the Christmas, Easter and Whitsun weeks, and in the period 1st August to 29th September day work on any day, and, if ordered, had to do an extra day's work until 'tierce' (9 am when 'Tierce' the canonical office was said) 'getting nothing for it'.
- If threshing corn they did as many day's works as made up three bushels and if barley six and if oats twelve bushels.
- If felling for fencing they felled for one day work until tierce, likewise for fencing and collecting 'twigs' for wattle fencing (hurdles).
- They each had to weed 7½ acres between 1st August and 29th September.
- If they had a cow or an ox they paid 7d a year for summer pasture for them and if the animals were two years old they paid 2d and for bullocks 1d, but they had to be gelded in the lord's pasture.
- If they had a wife they provided 4 hens, if not, 2.
- If they reaped they had to reap ½ an acre of corn or ½ an acre of barley each day and received 1 sheaf, and if oats then 1 acre, receiving 2 sheafs.
- If they did not reap they had to bind 1½ acres for the day's work and received 1 sheaf, when they gathered stubble they got 1 sheaf for one day's work and when twigs or branches in the autumn, 1 armful. If they threshed they got 1 measure of the corn; they had to thresh as many measures in the day as made up 1 bushel at 7 measures to the bushel.
  - A Ploughman was quit of services and rent in autumn and any other time. If he had a plough he had to plough 8 acres.
  - If Ploughman and Ox-herd he had to plough 8 acres.
  - If Ox Drover and not Ox-herd he ploughed 7 acres.
  - A Shepherd for Ewes had the same benefits as those of a virgater acting as shepherd.
  - A Shepherd of Hoggets was quit of rent and services and could pasture 25 sheep with the lord's hoggets.
  - A Cowman was quit of rent and services, could keep 1 cow with the lord's and had 1 strip of land to sow.
  - A Swineherd was quit as above and could pasture 2 cows with the lord's and if he was in the lord's feeding ground for swine he got one quarter of barley and if he was looking after the pigs outside the hundred he had one quarter of barley. If with suckling pigs he had the 'escheat' complete, that is to say he was quit of his customary duties.
  - Whoever owed day work could, in no circumstances, be quit of pannage or of church-scot nor the marriage of a son or daughter without payment of a fine nor of the sale of a horse, ox or young stock without a licence.
  - If a tenant was a ploughman and there was boonwork to be done he had to find one man for the plough and another for the boonwork.

- The Smith held 1 virgate of land for 5s and owed the same services as the other virgaters for this. He also had a cotland and provided, for it, fore-iron for 3 ploughs and had 3 trees for his charcoal and had up to 4 animals with the lord's for the same services. He also had a croft of 3 acres for which he shod the cart horses at his own expense. If a horse died he had the leather.

There are only two mentions of land being held 'freely', in both cases as part of a holding for the rest of which the occupier owed services.

There are five other people mentioned who, in addition to the normal services, had to wash and shear the lord's sheep.

It is apparent from the context that many of the Bishop's tenants sublet their land and it is likely that substantial holders of land such as the Church, William de Houtot and William de Hactyngele had their own smiths, especially the latter two who had the need of horses to carry out their services.

From a scrutiny of the names it seems as if the bulk of the population lived near Alresford and that Harmesworth and Medested were comparatively sparsely peopled; this would be logical owing to Alresford having a river with, presumably, the lusher meadows, a market and a fair.

The obligation some of them had, i.e. to mow the Bishop's lawns at Wolvesey (by hand with a sickle) and to fence his park at Waltham – each a day's walk away – must have been quite a burden.

A Court Roll of 1750 shows that copyhold tenants of the Bishop were obliged to repair parts of the road running across the weir at Alresford; each district having a section for which is was responsible.

The villeins (virgaters, cottagers and millers) owed onerous services which appear to have given them little time to look after their own land, but land they had and, by custom of the manor, security of tenure; this meant that, except in times of prolonged and universal crop failures which affected rich and poor alike, they could not starve. Whilst they were bound to their land it was in the interest of the lord to protect them from all except himself.

This document shows, by its mixture of money rents and services, that, slowly, the villein was gaining his freedom and at the same time losing the security that his land had given him. The lord's managers were finding that the men who did obligatory work for no reward were, if possible, more trouble than those who came to work for money.

Farm Sale

In 1392 Roger Gerways (or Gerveys), probably a descendant of William Gerways, who is known to have owned land in Medested and other places before 1272, released 340 acres of land, 2 acres of meadow, 30 acres of pasture and 60 of woodland for £10 rent and 11lb. of cumin (a form of parsley with an aromatic seed used to flavour liqueurs) to the then Bishop of Winchester – William of Wykeham, who made over the land to Winchester College, which he had founded. This land was located in six villages, including Medested, but, owing to the strip system, lay scattered around each parish. The interest of this is that the land was handed over 'lock stock and barrel', consequently there exists what appears to be a complete inventory of the live and dead stock carried on those lands. I am giving this inventory, virtually in full, in the text as I think that it makes a good supplement to the custumal of one hundred and forty years earlier which was given in the preceding paragraphs. Customs and farming methods changed very slowly in those days.

The stock comprised:

1 iron fastened cart, 6 collars, 5 pairs of traces, 1 cart saddle, 2 cart ropes, 1 new cart ladder, 1 dung cart, 6 headstalls (3 of leather), 3 threshing sledges, 1 shovel, 1 dung 'pylce', 5 ploughs, 2 plough shares, 2 iron coulters, 1 winnowing fan, 1 sieve, 3 screens, 1 prong, 1 oak table top with 2 trestles, 1 fixed table, 1 four gallon brass pot, 1 old brass 'posncet', 2 vats made of hog's heads, 3 hogs' heads of cider and 60 gallons more, 3 cheese vats, 3 pails, 5 cheese boards, 1 new salting trough, 1 iron hooped bucket, 1 well rope, 1 moulding board, 8 harrows, 4 hay racks, 8 sheep racks, 6 gallons tar to dress sheep, 5 quarters of lime, 3 'col' hurdles, 1 12-gallon tub.

There are many points of interest in this inventory, especially if studied in conjunction with the thirteenth century custumal. There are several things to be borne in mind at this point; the stock listed would have belonged to the various sub tenants of Gerways who were being transferred to a different lord. The Black Plague, which killed between one third and one half of the population of all England within a year, had happened forty years before (1348/9). The old feudal system whereby men held land by reason of services to the lord was, as we saw in the custumal, being commuted to money rents either fully or in part.

Boundaries

A perambulation, of about 1556, made of the manor of old Alresford, shows that the boundaries were still virtually the same as they were in the seventh century and are today. Minchins Copse is still on the north-east of the parish boundary, in 650 A.D. Mint Mere (Minthammas) marked this same spot on the same boundary. A little south of this point was, in Saxon times, Feldene, in 1556 it was spelt Feldens, by 1845 it was spelt, as it is today, Veldens.

Fields

Another document of the same date shows Medested as having seven fields – they were called North Feld, West Feld, South Feld, Myddel Feld, Ry Feld, Grete Pace Feld and Little Pace Feld. Each field was divided into a number of furlongs, each of which was further divided into a number of strips whose sizes varied from one rod to six acres, the majority being of half an acre. By now the strip system was beginning to break down, and a number of people were owning contiguous pieces of land. The manor of Medested was bought by Sir Richard Lyster in 1530 and sold by his grandson in 1556. It would seem, from a survey made at that time, that the Lysters did what they could to get their holdings together, since the majority of them were of two or more acres. Altogether twenty two owners of land are listed. Nine hundred acres of the parish are accounted for, some blocks of pasture and wood of up to twenty acres as shown.

Amongst the names are three Budds and two Wakes.

In July 1561 Robert Wacke (Wake) died worth some £12. He had lived in a cottage having a hall, a chamber and a kitchen. The hall contained a table and a form, an old chest, a painted cloth and other things worth altogether 3s. The chamber contained two bedsteads and one flock bed. There was one pair of blankets, one coverlet, one pair of sheets and a chest, these were worth 28s altogether. Among the few items in the kitchen were the only candlestick, three pans, three platters, four porringers and a chafing dish; the total value of everything in the kitchen was £1 10s 2d His only tools were a bill and an axe. He left an acre of wheat (16s), an acre of barley (8s) and one bushel of old wheat (1s 6d). His livestock consisted of one horse (10s), one cow (26s 8d), one steer and two heifers (26s 8d), fourteen ewes, four lambs and twenty-two wethers together with one sow and five 'pyggys'. He bequeathed one sheep for the repairing of the Church at Medstyd and to the poore folke of Medstyd one bushel of wheat.

Nine years later John Bud of Medstead, who must have been quite a substantial farmer, died. He had lived in a house having, downstairs, a hall, a chamber, a back chamber, a servant's chamber, a buttery and a kitchen. Upstairs there were two lofts and a cheese loft, the latter containing thirteen cheeses worth 8s. There were two feather and two flock beds together with six bedsteads. He had also owned fifteen pairs of sheets, eight table cloths, six table napkins and three towels. The outbuildings comprised a malt house with a loft, a wheat barn containing two stacks of wheat worth £5 and a barley barn with forty quarters of barley worth £4 10s. Amongst the tools was a dung pick. The livestock comprised six horses, one gelding, one complete with harness – £13 6s 8d. One bull, one steer, six cows and six heifers – £8, eleven score and three wethers, ewes and teggs – £22. Two iron bound carts were worth £1. He left 4s to the "Trinity of Winchester," one bushel of wheat to the poore people of Medsteid and two sheep towards maintaining of the Church of Medsteid.

Forty-five years later, in 1625, William Budd, yeoman, of Hattyngley died. His house had five rooms including the kitchen. Amongst his effects were one Bible and other small books priced at 15s. All his clothes were valued £3 5s, and he had a £1 in his purse. His linen, including sheets, etc., was worth £15. There were a mill house and a malt house. His barns held, threshed and unthreshed, wheat (£8), barley (£17s 5s), and oats (£3 10s). The corn and all other grains sown on the land were worth £24. Five horses with harness were valued at £20 and all the carts, ploughs, harrows, etc., at £6 6s 8d. He had kept cattle, sheep and pigs worth some £33, also 10s 6d worth of geese and poultry 'about the house.' He had timber worth 10s lying at Heth Green. His probate value was £203 1s 4d. He left 12s to Winchester Cathedral, 11s 8d for repairing the Parish Church and left £1 5d. for the poor people of Medsted.

In 1613, widow Joane Budd left one ewe sheep to her servant boy, 10s to the poore of Medsted, and to the Trinity of Winchester 4s. She grew wheat, vetches, barley, oats and peas and had four bushels of malt. Her estate was valued at £35 4d.

The following opening lines of one will is typical of them all:

In the name of God Amen. The XXIXth day of June anno domini 1561 I, Robert Wacke of the parish of Medstyd within the diocese of Winchester, being of good and perfecte remembrance, thanks be unto God, do make and ordeyne my

last wyll and testament in manner and forme following, that is to say First I
bequeath my Soull to Almighty God, my maker and Saviour, and my body to be
buried wythin the Church of Medstyd aforesaid. I bequeath ...

Then comes the detailed disposal of the testator's property. Great care was taken to ensure that the widow, if there was one, was fully provided for. The majority of bequests were in kind although some money gifts were made. There was not so much money about in those days.

Poor Laws

It is in the late seventeenth century that we get positive local evidence of the coming of enclosures and the dispossession of many people of their land. It is then that the burial records of the Church show men who were styled 'yeoman' – substantial farmers who had bought their neighbour's strips who, in their turn, became labourers, depending for their entire living on wages and not on ownership of land, whether free or copyhold. The import of this gradual change of status and other factors are shown in the next paragraphs.

By 1600, poverty had become a vast problem, desperate men, without land and unable to get any work, went round the land robbing in order to live. The causes were the change in the system of agriculture, noted above, numbers of ex-solders and feudal retainers returning from the French wars (as always, not wanted when the fighting was done), and the Dissolution of the Monasteries which had been great charities administering to the needy.

In 1597, the first proper Poor Law was enacted and this was confirmed in 1601. These laws placed the onus of responsibility fairly and squarely on the parish, that is to say onto the church wardens and the recently created overseers of the poor. They were made responsible (under the Vestry) for all poor people in the parish whether they were sick, old, unemployed or just lawless. In 1662 an Act of Settlement was passed which forced people to remain in their own parish unless they had substantial means of support.

A few entries from the burial section of the parish registers give point to the above.

- 10 January 1670. Griffen wife of Thomas 'a wandering woman.'
- 26 November 1680. Abigail Livington, single woman, who had been for many years kept by the parish.
- 18 May 1684, Nicholas Harris, a poor man, kept by the alms of the parish.
- June 1695. William Moule a poor labourer hanged himself on the thirtieth day of June 'not having the fear of God before his eyes'.

There were many such entries at this period.

Farming

By 1845, the lay out of fields was much as it is today except that many roadside fields of that date have since been encroached on by bungalows and their gardens. Land was owned and farmed in large blocks in a 'ring fence'; the 'strip' system of agriculture had finally disappeared.

The tithe apportionment map of 1845 shows that there were eight holdings of more than a hundred acres; John Wyeth and George Wake farmed, as tenants, 544 and 188 acres respectively. John Wake owned and let 188 acres. Henry Budd had 8 acres in hand and William Budd let 5 acres. The eight biggest farms occupied more than 2,200 acres. In 1966, five men own and farm holdings of comparable size totalling about 1,200 acres.

In 1851, James Yalden lived at Hattingley and farmed 230 acres employing eleven labourers; today Mr. Robin Swan farms 450 acres (325 in this parish) with three men and he has a large milking herd of cows.

The same map shows a hop garden which lay immediately south of the junction of Common Hill, Goatacre Road and Homestead Road. One must presume that at one time hops were grown there and wonder how successful they were.

GLOSSARY

Acre An area of land equal to 4,047 square metres or 4,840 square yards.

Admeasurement The act of measuring and apportioning fair shares in land.

Advowson The right of a patron to present to a diocesan bishop a nominee for appointment to a vacant church living.

Allotment A piece of land which is allotted or given.

Assart Wood converted into arable by grubbing up the trees and brushwood.

Bailiff The officer responsible for executing the decisions of a Norman court; a Saxon reeve.

Bailiwick Area of jurisdiction of a bailiff.

Balk, baulk A strip of ground left unploughed as a boundary between two ploughed portions.

Beadle A parish constable of the Anglican Church.

Boonwork Work due to the lord as part of the rent.

Botes Small wood for fencing, building repair and fuel.

Bovate An oxgang, or as much land as one ox could plough in a year (between ten and eighteen acres).

Butt A ridge when cut short of its full length by the irregular shape of a field.

Catchpole A man who paid a lump sum to collect taxes and was able to keep whatever was extracted after using almost any method. Later, a legal debt collector, working for the bailiff.

Ceorl An Anglo-Saxon freeman of the lowest class, ranking directly below a thane.

Church-Scot Customary obligations paid to the parish priest; from which duties the religious sometimes purchased an exemption for themselves and their tenants.

Close A permanently enclosed pasture.

Copyhold An entry in the manorial roll of the services a tenant was to render to the lord and the rights he received in return. The tenant was given a copy, hence 'copyhold'. These transactions might include rent, days of work, access to wood and pasture, numbers of animals allowed on the common, and heriots.

Copyhold of Inheritance Where one tenant pays rent and undertakes duties to the lord. When the tenant died, the holding passed to his heir depending on the custom of the manor. This type of copyhold could be sold through the lord.

Copyhold for Lives Several, usually three, named persons hold the premises for the duration of their lives. The first-named paid rents and heriots. The other two formed a queue. When the first died, the second named inherited and nominated a new third life for the end of the queue.

Cot, Cotland The land belonging to a cottager or cotter, usually about five acres.

Court-baron The assembly of the freehold tenants of a manor under the presidency of the lord or his steward.

Court-leet A court of record held periodically in a hundred, lordship or manor before the lord or his steward and attended by the residents. It held jurisdiction over petty offences and performed administrative functions.

Coverture A husband and wife were one *person in* law: the very being or legal existence of the woman was suspended during marriage.

Croft A piece of inclosed land used for tillage or pasturage, in most cases adjacent to a home.

Customary Court The assembly of the copyhold tenants of a manor under the presidency of the lord or his steward.

Denshire To improve land by burning heaps of earth, turf, and stubble and then spreading the ashes over the ground as a compost.

Demesne All the land retained and managed by a lord of the manor for his own use, occupation or support.

Dower A provision, settled on a bride by agreement, to provide for her support if she became widowed.

Ealdorman In the tenth century, the most prestigious royal appointments. Local representatives of the West Saxon king. They would lead in battle, preside over courts and levy taxation.

Essoin An excuse for non-appearance in court at the appointed time.

Estover Small wood for fencing, building repair and fuel.

Estray A stray animal.

Fallow Ground that is well ploughed and harrowed, but left uncropped for a year or more.

Feme Covert A married woman who has no rights except through her husband.

Feoffee A trustee who holds a fief (or 'fee'), a piece of land, for the benefit of an owner, sometimes a charity and often used to evade taxes or death duties.

Forestall A physical obstruction to stop someone accessing or doing something to a piece of land.

Forestaller A person who buys goods before they can be sold on the open market in anticipation of rising prices.

Freehold A property or piece of land which is owned outright. The freeholder is responsible for all maintenance.

Furlong Originally the length of the furrow in the common field which was theoretically regarded as a square containing ten acres.

Furrow A long, narrow trench made in the ground by a plough, especially for planting seeds or irrigation.

Gate A right to run or a pasturage for an animal on a common field, representing a share of the joint ownership; a barrier to privatised land.

Glebe An area of land within an ecclesiastical parish used to support a parish priest. The land may be owned by the church or its profits may be reserved to the church.

Gore A wedge-shaped strip of land on the side of an irregular field.

Harrow An implement consisting of a heavy frame set with teeth or tines which is dragged over ploughed land to break up clods, remove weeds and cover seed.

Headland A strip of land in a ploughed field left for convenience in turning the plough at the end of the furrows, or a boundary.

Hectare 10,000 square metres (a square with 100 metre sides), equivalent to just under 2½ acres.

Heriot A tribute paid to the lord of the manner out of the belongings of a tenant who died, often a live animal.

Hereditament Rented land or building that can be inherited.

Hey Hedge or hedged field.

Hide A unit which represented the amount of land sufficient to support a household, traditionally 120 acres (49 hectares). It was also a variable measure of value and tax assessment. A hide was divided into four yardlands or virgates.

Hogget A sheep between one or two years or a sheep not yet shorn.

Hundred In the south of England, a hundred was the division of a shire for military and judicial purposes under the common law, which could vary one to another depending on feudal and ecclesiastical rights of ownership. Hundred boundaries were independent of both parish and county boundaries, although often aligned, meaning that a hundred could be split between counties, or a parish could be split between hundreds. The importance of the hundred courts declined from the seventeenth century and most of their powers were extinguished with the establishment of county courts in 1867.

Inclosure The old spelling of enclosure.

Kersey Coarse, ribbed cloth with a short nap, woven from short-stapled wool.

Leasehold A contract granting use of a property for a specified time (like a hundred or a thousand years) in exchange for rent or another form of payment; a leaseholder.

Levant and couchant Rising up and lying down; mostly used of trespassing cattle which have been long enough on land to lie down and rise up to feed, a day and night at the least, and being required as grounds for legal distraint.

Linch, lynchet A ridge or ledge formed by ploughing along the downhill side of a plot.

Mansae 100 hides of land.

Manor A mansion or the district over which a lord exercises rights and privileges.

Marling In local lands, the use of chalk from pits to neutralise acid soil and to lighten surface clay. Chalk pits also provided flint for building.

Mast Beechnuts, acorns, chestnuts, etc., especially as food for hogs.

Mere A small lake, pond or marsh.

Merestone A boundary, or an object indicating a boundary, or a landmark.

Moiety A part or share of something, especially when it is divided into two parts, often equal.

Offal Waste wood.

Out-ranger A sinecure with the duty to preserve any deer which escaped the bounds of a royal forest.

Owlers Wool smugglers.

Pannage Pasturage for pigs, especially in a wood, or the right to pasture pigs, or the payment for pasturage, or the acorns or beech mast on which pigs feed.

Pasture Land covered with grass and other low plants suitable for grazing animals, especially cattle or sheep.

Parish In the Church of England, an area with its own church cared for by one priest; in government in England, the smallest local unit.

Partageur (or partageux) One who shares, especially willingly.

Perambulation Walking around the boundaries of a manor or parish and, usually, checking and re-establishing boundary markers.

Perch A rod, pole or perch is a measure of land equal to 1/160th of an acre.

Pindar An impounder of strayed cattle.

Pinfold A place for confining stray or distrained beasts.

Piscary The right to fish in nominated waters.

Prebendary Most prebends disappeared in 1547 as part of the Reformation. The office of prebendary was retained by some Church of England dioceses as an honorary title for senior parish priests, usually awarded for long and dedicated service to the diocese. They may have a role in cathedral administration.

Purpresture Wrongful appropriation of land subject to the rights of others, for instance, an encroachment upon common land.

Purrock (or parrock) A small field or enclosure; a pen.

Pylce Anglo- Saxon container made of skin.

Quatern loaf A loaf of bread weighing four pounds.

Quillet A small plot or narrow strip of land.

Rack rent The full economic value of the land to a tenant.

Reeve Saxon term for the person who ran *manors in England and saw to feudal obligations on behalf of the landlord; later, a Norman bailiff.*

Regrater A middleman who travels the country buying farm produce to sell at market.

Rice Cross stakes used for fences or for clay or dung walls.

Rod A rod, pole or perch is a measure of land equal to 1/160th of an acre.

Rood A measure of land equal to a quarter of an acre.

Rother A horned bovine, especially ox or cattle.

Sainfoin A perennial legume, known as 'holy hay', that thrives on thin chalk, limestone or stony soils typical of the South Downs. It produces large spikes of pink flowers in early summer that are a magnet to insects.

Severalty Sole, separate and exclusive ownership.

Scot-Ale A compulsory feast at which subscriptions are taken for the upkeep of the nave of the church.

Shack The period after the harvest when there is a common right to graze.

Shot A division of land.

Snapwood Wood easily snapped off a tree, or pulled down with a pole, or the lops and tops of trees, or dry and fallen wood, but not the timber.

Socage Tenure of land by agricultural service fixed in amount and kind or by payment of money rent only.

Stack wood Wood which is stacked with enough space in between logs to allow air drying.

Stint The limited number of cattle allotted to each portion of divided pasture or common land, or to each person entitled to the right of common pasturage, or the right of pasturage according to a fixed rate.

Terrier A register of landed property, including lists of vassals and tenants, with particulars of their holdings, services or rents.

Toft A whole homestead with its holding and outbuildings; toft and croft.

Tithe The right to receive tithes, a tenth of annual income or produce, was granted to the English churches by King Ethelwulf in 855. The dissolution of the monasteries led to the transfer of many rights to tithe to secular landowners and to the Crown. The system for produce was abolished in 1836. An act in 1936 began the process of ending tithe payments by, at least, 1996.

Tithing (or 'tything') A legal, administrative or territorial unit, originally ten hides (and hence, one tenth of a hundred). Tithings later became subdivisions of a manor or civil parish.

Turbary Turves and peat for fuel.

Vanger A person who captures and holds people or animals.

Virgate About 32 acres.

Waste Common land not in cultivation or used as pasture.

Woodward Occupational name for a forester employed to look after the trees and game in a forest.

Woad A yellow-flowered plant of the cabbage family that was once widely grown as a source of blue dye which was extracted from the leaves.

Wong A piece of meadow land; a portion of uninclosed land under the open-field system.

READING LIST

Adair, *Cheriton 1644, The Campaign and the Battle* (Roundwood Press, Warwick 1973)

Adeane, Charlies, and Savill, Edwin, *The Land Retort, A Study of the Land Question with an Answer to the Report of the Secret Enquiry Committee* (Murray, London 1914)

Addington, Stephen, *An inquiry into the reasons for and against inclosing open-fields* (1772; Gale 2021)

Andrews, Thomas, *An Enquiry into the Causes of the Encrease and Miseries of the Poor of England* (1738; Sagwan Press 2021)

Anon, *The History of the Blacks of Waltham in Hampshire; and those under the like Denomination in Berkshire* (London, 1723)

Anon, *The Countrey mans chat wherein you shall finde how each man doth talke to please his owne minde* (London 1632).

Appleby, Andrew B., *Famine in Tudor and Stuart England* (Liverpool University Press 1978)

Bailey, Brian J., *The Luddite Rebellion* (NYU Press 1998)

Bainbridge, John, *The Compleat Trespasser, Journeys into Forbidden Britain* (Author, revised 2020)

Balen, Malcolm, *A Very English Deceit, The Secret History of the South Sea Bubble and the First Great Financial Scandal* (Fourth Estate, London 2003)

Biddle, Martin, edited, *Winchester in the Early Middle Ages, An Edition and Discussion of The Winton Domesday*, Winchester Studies 1 (Oxford University Press 1976)

Bate, Jonathan, *John Clare, A Biography* (Picador, London 2004)

Beckett, Arthur, *The Spirit of the Downs* (1909; Bramble Hill Press, Cork 2021)

Beggs, Thomas, 'Freehold Land Societies', *Journal of the Statistical Society of London*, 1853, Vol. 16, No. 4, pp. 338-346

Beloff, Max, *Public Order and Popular Disturbances, 1660-1714* (Frank Cass, London 1963)

Beresford, Maurice, and Hurst, John G., edited, *Deserted Medieval Villages* (Sutton, Stroud 1989)

Biddell, Barbara, 'Jacobitism in Bishop's Waltham and East Hampshire', *Proceedings of the Hampshire Field Club and Archaeological Society*, Vol. 60, 2005, pp. 229-241

Black, Jeremy, *Walpole in Power* (Sutton Publishing, Stroud 2001)

Blackstone, Sir William, *Commentaries on the Laws of England*, Vol. IV (Clarendon Press, Oxford 1778)

Blomley, Nicholas, 'Making Private Property: Enclosure, Common Right and the Work of Hedges', *Rural History*, Vol. 18/1, 2007, pp. 166-186

Bovill , E. W., *English Country Life 1780-1830* (Country Book Club, London 1964)

Box, E. G., 'Hampshire in Early Maps and Early Road-Books', *Hampshire Field Club*, Papers and Proceedings, Part 1, 1934, pp. 221-235; Part 2, 1937, pp. 61-68

Bramwell, George, *An Analytical Table of The Private Statutes passed between the 1st Geo II AD 1727 and 52nd Geo III 1812* (Bramwell, London 1813)

Britnell, Richard, *The Winchester Pipe Rolls and Medieval English Society* (Boydell, Woodbridge 2003)

Broad, John, 'Whigs and Deer Stealers in Other Guises: A Return to the Origins of the Black Act', *Past and Present*, 119, May 1988, pp. 56-72

Bromley, Nick, 'Enclosure, Common Right and the Property of the Poor', *Social and Legal Studies*, 17, 2008

Bruce, Susan, *Three Early Modern Utopias: Utopia, New Atlantis and The Isle of Pines* (Oxford University Press 2008)

Cahill, Kevin, *Who Owns Britain, The Secret Facts Behind Landownership in Britain and Ireland* (London, Canongate, 2001)

Capes, W. W., *Scenes of Rural Life in Hampshire among the Manors of Bramshott* (Macmillan, London 1901)

Cassan, Stephen Hyde, *The Lives of the Bishops of Winchester from Birinus, the first bishop of the West Saxons, to the Present Time*, Vol. 2 (Rivington, London 1827)

Chambers, J. D., 'Enclosure and Labour Supply in the Industrial Revolution', *The Economic History Review*, New Series, Vol. 5, No. 3, 1953, pp. 319-343

Chambers, J. D., and Mingay, G. E., *The Agricultural Revolution 1750-1880* (Batsford, London 1966)

Chapman, John, and Seeliger, Sylvia, 'Formal Agreements and the Enclosure Process: The Evidence from Hampshire', *Agricultural History Review*, Vol. 43/1, 1995, pp. 35-46; *A Guide to Enclosure in Hampshire, 1700-1900*, Hampshire Record Series, 15, 1997; 'Formal and Informal Enclosures in Hampshire, 1700–1900', *Hampshire Papers*, 12, 1997; 'Charities, Rents, and Enclosure: A Comment on Clark', *The Journal of Economic History*, Vol. 59/2, June, 1999

Chase, Malcolm, 'Out of Radicalism: the Mid-Victorian Freehold Land Movement', *English Historical Review*, 1991, pp. 319-345; *Early Trade Unionism, Fraternity, skill and the politics of labour* (Aldershot, Ashgate 2000)

Chibnall, Marjorie, *The Normans* (Blackwell, Oxford 2000)

Christophers, Brett, *The New Enclosure, The Appropriation of Public Land in Neoliberal Britain* (Verso, London 2019)

Clare, John, *Major Works* (Oxford University Press 2004)

Clanchy, M. T., edited, 'Highway Robbery and trial by battle in the Hampshire eyre of 1249', in Hunnisett, R. F., and Post, J. B., *Medieval Legal Records, edited in the memory of C. A. F. Meekings* (HMSO, London 1978); *From Memory to Written Record, England 1066-1307*, third edition (Wiley-Blackwell, Chichester 2013)

Clay, Christopher, '"The Greed of Whig Bishops"?: Church Landlords and their Lessees 1660–1760', *Past & Present*, Vol. 87/1, May 1980, pp. 128–157

Cobbett, William, *Cottage Economy* (1822; Oxford University Press 1979); *Rural Rides* (1830; Penguin, London 1967); *Legacy to Parsons* (1835; Watts, London 1947)

Colgate, E. J., *The Power and The Poverty* (George Mann, Winchester 2008)

Collins, E. J. T., edited, *The Agrarian History of England and Wales*, Vol. VII, 1850–1914 (Cambridge University Press 2000)

Cornick, David, *Early Memories of Four Marks* (no publisher, undated)

Coventry, Thomas, *Observations on The Title to Lands Derived Through Inclosure Acts* (Butterworth, London 1827)

Cruickshanks, E., and Erskine-Hill, H., 'The Waltham Black Act and Jacobitism', *Journal of British Studies*, Vol. xxiv, 1985, pp. 358-65

Curtler, W. H. R., *The Enclosure and Redistribution of Our Land* (Oxford University Press 1920)

Curtis, William, *A Short History and Description of the Town of Alton* (1896; Noverre Press, Binsted 2012)

Darvall, Frank Ongley, *Popular Disturbances and Public Order in Regency England, being an account of the Luddite and other disorders in England during the years 1811-1817 and of the attitude and activity of the authorities* (Oxford University Press 1934)

Davey, C. R., edited, *The Hampshire Lay Subsidy Rolls, 1586* (Hampshire Record Series, Vol. IV, Hampshire County Council 1981)

Defoe, Daniel, *A Tour Thro' the Whole Island of Great Britain* (1724-27; Harmondsworth, 1971)

Duthy, John, 'Observations on the present high price of provisions', *Letter to the Lord Lieutenant and inhabitants of Hampshire* (1800; Gale Ecco reprint, 2020); *Sketches of Hampshire; embracing the architectural antiquities, topography, etc* (Jacob and Johnson, Winchester 1839; British Library 2018)

Dyer, Christopher, and Jones, Richard, edited, *Deserted Villages Revisited* (University of Hertfordshire Press, Explorations in Local and Regional History, Vol. 3 1988)

East Hampshire District Council, *Four Marks Village Design Statement* (2001)

Erskine-Hill, Howard, *The Social Milieu of Alexander Pope: Lives, Example and the Poetic Response* (Yale University Press, London 1975)

Everitt, Alan, *The Pattern of Rural Dissent: the Nineteenth Century* (Leicester University Press 1972)

Fairlie, Simon, 'A Short History of Enclosure in Britain', *The Land*, Summer 2009

Fletcher, Holly, *Four Marks Population Study* (Private, Four Marks 2020)

Fritz, Paul S., *The English Ministers and Jacobitism between the Rebellions of 1715 and 1745* (University of Toronto Press 2017)

Gash, Norman, *Aristocracy and People, 1815-1865* (Harvard University Press 1981)

Edwin F, 'Inclosures in England in the Sixteenth Century', *The Quarterly Journal of Economics*, Vol. 17/4, August 1903, pp. 566-597

Gibson, Elizabeth, 'The Rodney Family and Wield', *About Alresford*, No. 80, Issue 18, 1993

Gibson, William, *Enlightenment Prelate: Benjamin Hoadly, 1676-1761* (James Clark, Cambridge 2004)

Gilbey, Sir Walter, and Cuming, E. D., *George Morland, His Life and Works* (Adam and Charles Black, London 1907)

Gillespie, Frances Elma, *Labor and Politics in England: 1850-1867* (1927; Frank Cass, London 1966)

Godwin, George Nelson, *The Civil War in Hampshire, 1642-45* (1882, Kindle 2020)

Gonner, E. C. K., *Common Land and Inclosure* (Macmillan, London 1912)

Gray, Howard Levi, *English Field Systems* (1915; Harvard University Press 1959)

Groves, Reg, *Sharpen The Sickle!, The History of the Farm Workers' Union* (Porcupine Press, London 1949)

Grundy, George Beardoe, 'The Saxon Land Charters of Hampshire with Notes on Place and Field Names', *The Archaeological Journal*, No. 1, Vol. 83, 1921, pp. 55-173

Hagen, Marianna S., *Annals of Old Ropley* (Private, 1929)

Hamer, D. A., *The Politics of Electoral Pressure, A Study in the history of Victorian Reform Agitations* (Harvester Press, Hassocks 1977)

Hammond, J. L. and Barbara, *The Village Labourer, 1760–1832: A Study of the Government of England before the Reform Bill* (1911; Longmans, Green, London, 1995)

Harwood, Winfred A., 'The Household of Winchester College in the later Middle Ages 1400-1560', *Proceedings of the Hampshire Field Club Archaeological Society*, 59, 2004, pp. 163-179

Hawker, Colonel Peter, *The Diary, 1802-53*, Vol. II (1893; Greenhill, London 1968)

Hawkes, C. F. C., 'Old Roads in Central Hants', *Hampshire Field Club*, Vol. 9, Part 3, 1925, pp. 324-333

Hayes, Nick, *The Book of Trespass, Crossing the lines that divide us* (Bloomsbury, London 2020)

Heal, Chris, *Felt-Hatting in Bristol & South Gloucestershire: the Rise and the Fall* (Avon LH&A 2013); *Disappearing* (Chattaway & Spottiswood, Somerset 2019); *The Four Marks Murders* (Chattaway & Spottiswood, Somerset 2020)

Healey, Jonathan, 'The political culture of the English Commons, c. 1550-1650', *The Agricultural History Review*, Vol. 60/2, 2012, pp. 266-287

Hill, Christopher P., *British Economic and Social History, 1700–1982*, 5th edition (London, Hodder Arnold 1985)

Hilton, Boyd, *A Mad, Bad, and Dangerous People? England 1783-1846* (Oxford, Clarendon Press 2006)

Hindle, Steve, 'A sense of place? Becoming and belonging in the rural parish, 1550-1650', in Shepard, Alexandra, and Withington, Phil, edited, *Communities in early modern England, Networks, place, rhetoric* (Manchester University Press 2000)

Hobsbawm, E. J., 'The Machine Breakers', *Past & Present*. Vol. 1/1, pp. 57-70; *Industry and Empire from 1750 to the Present Day* (Penguin, Harmondsworth 1972)

Homer, Henry Sacheverell, *An essay on the nature and method of ascertaining the specifick shares of proprietors upon the inclosure of common fields; with observations on the inconveniences of open fields, and upon the objections to this inclosure, particularly as far as they relate to the public and the poor* (Parker, Oxford, 1766; 2021 reprint)

Horn, Pamela, *Joseph Arch, The Farm Workers' Leader, 1826-1919* (Roundwood Press, Kineton 1971)

Howlett, John, *Examination of Dr. Price's Essay on the Population of England & Wales, and the Doctrine of an Increased Population in this Kingdom, established by Facts* (1781; Augustus M., New York 1968)

Hubbard, John, and Griffin, Henry, *Neolithic Dew-Ponds and Cattle-Ways* (1905; Sagwan Press 2021)

Hunt, E. H., and Pam, S. J., 'Responding to Agricultural Depression, 1873–1896: Managerial Success, Entrepreneurial Failure?', *The Agricultural History Review*, Vol. 50/2, 2002

Hunter, Robert, 'The Movements of the Inclosure and Preservation of Open Lands', *Journal of the Royal Statistical Society*, Vol. 60/2, June 1897

Hurst, Jane, 'Baigens, Chawton', *Hampshire Field Club and Archaeology Society Newsletter*, 44, Autumn 2005

Hutchinson, John, *Men of Kent and Kentishmen, A Manual of Kentish Biography* (1892; Forgotten Books 2021)

Johnson, Arthur H., *The Disappearance of the Small Landowner* (1909, Oxford; reprint London, Merlin Press 1979)

Jones, J. D., 'The Hampshire Beacon Plot of 1586', *Proceedings of the Hampshire Field Club and Archaeological Society*, Vol. 7/1, 1968, pp. 105-118

Jones, Richard, and Dyer, Christopher, edited, *Farmers, Consumers, Innovators, The World of Joan Thirsk* (University of Hertfordshire, 2016)

Kain, Roger J. P., Chapman, John, and Oliver, Richard R., *The Enclosure Maps of England and Wales 1595-1918* (Cambridge University Press 2004)

Kehoe, Timothy J., and Prescott, Edward C., *Great Depressions of the Twentieth Century* (Federal Reserve Bank of Minneapolis 2007)

Kent, David, *Popular Radicalisation and the Swing Riots in Central Hampshire* (HCC, Hampshire Papers, No. 11, 1997)

Kerridge, Eric, *The Agricultural Revolution* (Allen & Unwin, London 1967); Agrarian Problems in the Sixteenth Century and After (Allen & Unwin, London 1969)

Kirby, T. F., *The Charters of the Manor of Ropley, Hants* (The Society of Antiquaries, London 1902)

Land Enquiry Committee, report, *The Land*, Vol. 1, Rural (Hodder and Stoughton, London 1913)

Langlands, Alastair, edited, *Hampshire through writers' eyes* (Eland, London 2017)

Laurence, Edward, *The Duty of a Steward to his Lord* (1727; Gregg, Farnborough 1971)

Leigh, William Austen, and Knight, Montagu George, *Chawton Manor and its Owners, A Family History* (Smith, Elder, London 1911)

Lenman, Bruce, *The Jacobite Risings in Britain 1689-1746* (Scottish Cultural Press, Aberdeen 1995)

Linebaugh, Peter, *Stop, Thief! The Commons, Enclosures, and Resistance* (Spectre, Oakland, California 2014)

Mabey, Richard, *Plants with a Purpose, A guide to the everyday use of wild plants* (Collins, London 1977)

Mackay, James, A., *Sub Office Rubber Date Stamps of England and Wales* (Self-published, Dumfries 1986)

Mandeville, Bernard, *The Fable of the Bees* (1705; Penguin, London 1989)

Manning, R. B., *Village Revolts, Social Protest and Popular Disturbances in England 1509-1640* (Oxford University Press 1988)

Mason, Frederick, edited, *Ropley Past and Present, A Brief History of a Hampshire Village* (Scriptmate Editions, London 1889)

Moore Adam, *Bread for the Poor and advancement of the English Nation promised by Enclosure of the Wastes and Common Grounds of England* (Nicholas Bourn, London 1653)

Mathew, W. M., 'Marling in British Agriculture: A Case of Partial Identity', *Agricultural History Review*, 41/II, pp. 97-110

Martin, J. M., 'The Small Landowner and Parliamentary Enclosure in Warwickshire', *Economic History Review*, Vol. 32, 1979, pp. 328-43

Martin, Edward Alfred, 'Dew-Ponds' (Reprint, BiblioLife 2021; *Knowledge*, May/June 1907)

Martin, Robert Bernard, *Enter Rumour: Four Early Victorian Scandals* (Faber and Faber, London 1962)

Mayhew, Susan, *Dictionary of Geography* (Oxford University Press 1997)

McCloskey, D., 'The Enclosure of Open Fields: Preface to a Study of Its Impact on the Efficiency of English Agriculture in the Eighteenth Century', *Journal of Economic History*, 32, 1972, pp. 15-35

Mills, Betty, *Four Marks its Life and Origins* (Repton Publishing, Four Marks 1995)

Mingay, G. E., *Enclosure and the Small Farmer in the Age of the Industrial Revolution* (Economic History Society, London 1971); *The Gentry, The Rise and Fall of a Ruling Class* (Longman, New York 1976)

Monod, Paul Kléber, *Jacobitism and the English people, 1688-1788* (Cambridge University Press 1989); 'Dangerous Merchandise: Smuggling, Jacobitism, and Commercial Culture in Southeast England, 1690–1760', *Journal of British Studies*, Vol. 30/2, April 1991, pp. 150-182

Montgomery, Roy, *The Villages of Medstead and the parishes of St Andrew* (01); *Farringdon, All Saints* (15); *Ropley, St Peter* (20); *Bighton, All Saints* (27); *Chawton, St Nicholas* (47); *Itchen Stoke, St Mary the Virgin* (64); *Bishops Sutton, St Nicholas* (68); *Hartley Mauditt & West Worldham, St Leonard and St Nicholas* (80); *East Tisted, St James* (98); *Old Alresford, St Mary the Virgin* (100); *Wield, St James* (103) (Hampshire Genealogical Society)

Moody, Nellie, *A Short History of Medstead* (The Women's Institute, Medstead 1932)

Munby, Julian, edited, Domesday Book, 4, Hampshire (1086; Phillimore, Chichester 1982)

Munden, Alan, *Thomas Snow and the Western Schism* (private, undated)

Munsche, P. B., *Gentlemen and Poachers, The English Game Laws 1671-1831* (Cambridge University Press 1981)

Neeson, J. M., *Commoners: Common Right, Enclosure and Social Change in England, 1700–1820* (Cambridge University Press 1996)

Newby, Howard, 'The Deferential Dialectic, *Comparative Studies in Society and History*, Vol. 17, No. 2, April 1975, pp. 139-164

Nourse, Timothy, *Campania Foelix* (1700; Garland, New York 1982)

Office for National Statistics, *National Censuses* (1811-2011); *Official Labour Market Statistics, Four Marks Parish* (2011)

Orth, John V., *Combination and Conspiracy, A Legal History of Trade Unionism 1721-1906* (Oxford at the Clarendon Press 1991)

Orwin, C.S and C.S., *The Open Fields* (Oxford at the Clarendon Press 1967)

Outhwaite, R. B., *Dearth, public policy and social disturbance in England, 1550-1800* (Economic History Society, Cambridge 1991)

Page, William, edited, *The Victoria History of Hampshire*, Vol. 3 (Archibald Constable, London 1908)

Palmer, Stanley H., *Police and Protest in England and Ireland, 1780-1850* (Cambridge University Press 1988)

Pelteret, David A. E., *Slavery in Early Medieval England from the Reign of Alfred until the Twelfth Century* (Boydell Press, Woodbridge 1995)

Pennington, W., *Reflections on the various Advantages resulting from the Draining, Inclosing and Allotting of Large Commons and Common Fields* (White, London 1769)

Perry, P.J., edited, *British Agriculture 1875–1914* (London, Methuen 1973)

Poole, Steve, *The Politics of Regicide in England, 1760–1850* (Manchester University Press 2002)

Prest, John, *Politics in the Age of Cobden* (Macmillan, Basingstoke 1977)

Pryor, Francis, *Britain AD* (Harper, London 2005)

Pugh, Reverend Dr. R. K., 'Bishop Hoadly: A Plea in Mitigation', *Proceedings of the Hampshire Field Club and Archaeological Society,* Vol. 41, 1985, pp. 243-252

Pugsley, Alfred J., *Dewponds in Fable and Fact* (Country Life, London 1939)

Radzinowicz, L., 'The Waltham Black Act, A Study of the Legislative Attitude Towards Crime in the Eighteenth Century', *The Cambridge Law Journal,* Vol. 9/1, March 1945, pp. 56-81

Reed, M., 'Enclosure in North Buckinghamshire, 1500-1750', *Agricultural History Review,* Vol. xxxii, 1984, pp. 133-44

Ritchie, J. Ewing, *Freehold Land Societies: Their history, present position, and claims* (William Tweedie, London 1853)

Roberts, Edward, 'The Bishop of Winchester's Deer Parks in Hampshire, 1200-1400', *Hampshire Field Club,* Vol. 44, 1968, pp. 67-86

Rodney, Sir George Brydges, 'An Account of Alresford', c. 1768-1782, *Hampshire Field Club,* Vol. 9/3, 1925, pp. 334-341

Rogers, Pat, 'The Waltham Blacks and the Black Act', *The Historical Journal,* Sep. 1974, Vol. 17/3, pp. 465-486

Rose, R. B., 'Eighteenth Century Price Riots and Public Policy in England', *International Review of Social History,* Vol. 6, Issue 2, August 1961, pp. 277-292

Rowntree, B., Seebohm, F., and Kendall, May, *How the Labourer Lives, A Study of the Rural Labour Problem* (Nelson, London 1913)

Rudé, George, *The Crowd in History, A Study of Popular Disturbances in France and England, 1730-1748* (John Wiley, New York 1964)

Rutherford, Susan, 'Benjamin Hoadly: Sacramental Tests and Eucharistic thought in early eighteenth-century England', *Anglican and Episcopal History,* Dec. 2002, Vol. 71/4, pp. 473-497

Savage, Anne, translated and collated, *The Anglo-Saxon Chronicles* (Macmillan, London 1982)

Scriven, John, *A Treatise on Copyholds, Customary Freeholds, Ancient Demesne, and the Jurisdiction of Courts* (Butterworth, London 1821)

Scrutton, Thomas Edward, *Commons and the Common Fields; Or, the History and Policy of the Laws Relating to Commons and Enclosures in England* (1886, Cambridge University Press)

Seebohm, Frederic, *The English Village Community examined in its relations to the manorial and tribal systems and to the common or open field system of husbandry* (1905, fourth edition; Longmans, Green, London 1915)

Sharp, Buchanan, *In Contempt of All Authority: Rural Artisans and Riot in the West of England, 1586-1660* (1980; Breviary Stuff Publications, London 2010)

Shaw-Taylor, Leigh, 'Labourers, Cows, Common Rights and Parliamentary Enclosure: The Evidence of Contemporary Comment c. 1760-1810', *Past and Present*, Vol. 171/1, May 2001, pp. 95-126

Shore, T. W., *A History of Hampshire* (Elliot Stock, London, 1892); 'Springs and Streams of Hampshire', *Hampshire Field Club*, Vol. 2, 1890, pp. 33-57; 'Hampshire Valleys and Waterways', *Hampshire Field Club*, Vol. 3, Part 2, 1894, pp. 29-51

Shrubsole, Guy, *Who Owns England?, How We Lost Our Land and How to Take It Back* (William Collins, London 2019)

Slater, Gilbert, *The English Peasantry and the Enclosure of Common Fields* (Constable, London 1907)

Smith, M. G., *'Fighting Joshua', A Study of the Career of Sir Jonathan Trelawny, bart, 1650-1721, Bishop of Bristol, Exeter and Winchester* (Dyllansow Truran, Redruth 1985)

Snell, K. D. M., Annals of the Labour Poor: Social Change and Agrarian England 1660-1900 (Cambridge University Press 1985)

Strickland, Agnes, *The Lives of the Seven Bishops Committed to the Tower in 1688* (Bell and Daldy, London 1866)

Tate, W. E., 'The Commons' Journals as Sources of Information Concerning the Eighteenth-Century Enclosure Movement', *The Economic Journal*, Vol. 54, No. 213, 1944, pp. 75-95; 'A New Domesday of (Georgian) Enclosures, Hampshire Section', Vol. 15/3, 1943; 'Field Systems and Enclosures In Hampshire', *Proceedings of the Hampshire Field Club and Archaeological Society*, Vol. 16/3, 1947; *The English Village Community and The Enclosure Movements* (London, Gollancz 1967)

Tawney, R. H., *The Agrarian Problem in the Sixteenth Century* (Burt Franklin, New York 1912)

Thirsk, Joan, 'The Common Fields', *Past & Present*, Vol. 29/1, December 1964; *Economic Policy and Projects, The Development of a Consumer Society in Early Modern England* (Oxford University Press 1978); *The Rural Economy of England* (Hambledon Press, London 1984)

Thompson, E. P., *The Making of the English Working Class* (1963; London, Penguin 1980); 'The Moral Economy of the English Crowd in the Eighteenth Century', *Past & Present*, No. 50, February 1971, pp. 76-136; *Whigs and Hunters, The Origin of the Black Act* (Allen Lane, London 1975); *Albion's Fatal Tree, Crime and Society in Eighteenth Century England*, with Hay, Douglas; Linebaugh, Peter; Winslow, Cal; Rule, John G. (Allen Lane, London 1975); *Customs in Common* (Penguin, London 1991)

Thomson, Andrew, 'Estate Management in the Winchester Diocese before and after the Interregnum: A Missed Opportunity', *Proceedings of the Hampshire Field Club and Archaeological Society*, Vol. 61, 2006, pp. 182-199

Trollope, Anthony, *The Warden* (1855; Wordsworth Editions, Ware 1995)

Tusser, Thomas, *Five Hundred Points of Good Husbandry: As Well for the Champion or Open Country, as for the Woodland or Several; Together with a Book of Huswifery. Being a Calendar of Rural and Domestic Economy, for Every Month in the Year* (2021; Mavor, 1812; Tottel, London 1557)

Vancouver, Charles, *General View of the Agriculture of Hampshire* (The Board of Agriculture, London 1810)

Wallis, Rose, 'We do not come here … to inquire into grievances; we come here to decide law', *Southern History*, Vol. 32, 2010, pp. 159-175

Ward, Colin, *Cotters and Squatters, Housing's Hidden History* (Five Leaves, Nottingham 2009)

Ward, W. R., edited, *Parson and Parish in Eighteenth Century Hampshire: Replies to Bishop's Visitations* (Hampshire County Council 1995)

Webb, Sidney and Beatrice, *The History of Trade Unionism* (1894; revised edition extended to 1920, London, Longmans, Green 1926); *English Local Government: The Parish and the County* (1906; Frank Cass, London 1963)

White, Gilbert, *Natural History of Selborne* (1860; Gresham, Old Woking 1979)

White H. T., 'A Hampshire Plot', *Proceedings of the Hampshire Field Club and Archaeological Society*, Vol. 12, 1934, pp. 54-60

Wood, Andy, *Riot, Rebellion and Popular Politics in Early Modern England* (Palgrave, Basingstoke 2002)

Wordie, J. R., 'The Chronology of English Enclosure, 1500-1914', *The Economic History Review*, November 1983, Vol. 36/4, pp. 483-505

Wrightson, Keith, *Earthly Necessities: Economic Lives in Early Modern Britain, 1470-1750* (Yale University Press, 2000)

Wrigley, E. A., and Schofield, R. S., *The Population History of England 1541-1871: A Reconstruction* (Cambridge University Press 1989)

Wyeth, Gerald, *Four Marks School Boy's Memories* (No publisher, undated)

Yelling, J. A., *Common Field and Enclosure in England, 1450-1850* (MacMillan, London 1977)

Young, Arthur, *General Report on Enclosures* (Board of Agriculture, London 1808)

INDEX

This index covers only the main text; it does not include footnotes or appendices. Explanations of unusual words and phrases are included in the Glossary.

Other books by Chris Heal
www.candspublishing.org.uk and online bookstores

The Four Marks Murders
Twenty grisly tales from a sleepy corner of Hampshire between the years 400 and 2020
'I couldn't put it down. So exciting and so much to learn about my home village.'
978-1-9161944-2-7 • Paperback • 331 pages • 234 x 155 mm
55 B&W illustrations • 18 maps • 2 charts • 1 table
Published by Chattaway & Spottiswood • October 2020 • reprint January 2021

Sound of Hunger
One German family's chronicle of the chivalry, politics, lies, murder and aftermath of war
'A distinctive and valuable contribution to the history of the First World War.'
978-1-911604-41-9 • Hardback • 768 pages • 240 x 165 mm
100 B&W illustrations • 12 colour maps
Published by Uniform • Unicorn Publishing Group • June 2018

Disappearing (also available from stock at £8 plus £3 p&p)
The part-autobiographical story of a modern nomad and the people he upset.
'This is a subversive book that should not receive the breath of publicity.'
978-1-9161944-0-3. Paperback • Ebook • 324 pages • 234 x 155 mm
55 B&W illustrations • 4 maps
Published by Chattaway & Spottiswood • June 2019

Reappearing
The nomad keeps on running. China takes the world to the very edge
'An intelligent detective story wrapped up in a global travel adventure.'
978-1-9161944-1-0 • Paperback • 306 pages • 234 x 155 mm
40 B&W illustrations • 8 maps
Published by Chattaway & Spottiswood • July 2020

Felt-Hatting in Bristol & South Gloucestershire (£5 each plus p&p)
The complete story of a leading craft industry from 1530-1909
'Immensely impressive scholarship, well written and thoroughly researched.'
Pamphlets • Both parts 42 pages • 147 x 210 mm
Part 1: the Rise (ALHA 13) • 10 illustrations • 3 maps • 1 figure 978-1-9115921-3-6
Part 2: the Fall (ALHA 14) • 3 illustrations • 6 maps • 6 figures 978-1-9115921-4-3
Published by ALHA • June 2013, reprints 2015, 2018, 2020

Lightning Source UK Ltd.
Milton Keynes UK
UKHW020639201221
395957UK00003B/232

Ferreting Around

A contemporary sampler quilt

Happy Quilting

Ferret

by Ferret

Thank you

I've had a lot of help and support in producing this book and I would like to thank you all for your part in bringing this project to fruition. Special thanks go to Husqvarna Viking for their support. The Sapphire is great machine for quilters.

Jenny and Doug Stafford at Patchwork Corner in Hemel Hempstead tried to talk me out of this absurd career choice, and when it became clear I wasn't going to take any notice, they supported me wholeheartedly. Without Jenny pushing me to teach, I know this book wouldn't have happened, and without their ongoing advice I know I would have found things a lot harder.

Cy has done a fine job of showing me how you should produce and launch a book, and Nic is an endless source of marketing advice. Who would have thought there was so much in common between comics and quilting?

My students have been stars. They are not all keen on standing in front of a camera, but they did it for me. They put up with my poor pictures and error filled instructions to test this book for you. They have even allowed me to use their quilts on the covers of my book. But the best thing they give me are classes I can really enjoy working with.

Finally, my greatest thanks have to go to Tet. My long suffering partner has not only had to put up with me working on this book but he has also got involved. He has done the editing, diagrams, proof reading and typesetting for this book. He even went so far as to make the quilt. For this and all the other daft things I rope him into, I thank him.

Ferreting Around

Published by
Ferret Fabrications
11 Grosvenor Avenue
Harrow
HA2 7AR
United Kingdom

+44 (20) 8861-6410

http://www.ferfab.co.uk

©2009 Ferret

First printing August 2009

A catalogue record for this book is available from the British Library.

ISBN 978-1-907193-01-9

Foreword

Every now and again, a new talent emerges in the quilt world that transcends the ordinary and is instantly unforgettable. I witnessed this first hand at the Festival of Quilts in Birmingham in August of 2008 when an emerging artist's name was announced again and again as a winner. Not only were her quilts fresh and exciting, but so was the artist who stepped on stage to receive the awards. It was a thrill to see a young talent making her mark in the quilting kingdom. It is obvious to quilters worldwide that the general quilting demographic is of a 'certain' age. It is therefore exceptional to me when someone from a younger generation latches on to this timeless art/craft and puts a fresh spin on it. To this I say, "Hear, hear!"

However, I have discovered that Ferret enjoys creating her work using a variety of quilting techniques, many of which are rooted in tradition. She does not fly in the face of traditional quilting, but rather she embraces it and includes it into her extraordinary 'quilting toolbox'. Ferret is young and talented. But being young and talented are not the qualities that I most have come to admire in Ferret. It is her enthusiasm and heartfelt desire to share her passion with others.

Many artists have a selfish side—or at least they hoard a few secrets to themselves in fear that someone else might rise above them. Not so with Ferret. She has not chosen to write a book about shocking and unorthodox techniques. Instead she polled individuals to find out what they most wanted to learn. In turn she has authored her first book with you in mind. The techniques included here range from simple to complex, but in every aspect it is written with easy-to-understand language and presented with excellent illustrations.

I am honored that Ferret asked me to write a foreword for her first book (thank you, Ferret). I hope she will pursue quilting and fiber arts as a lifelong career. If she does, you are no doubt holding in your hand a collector's item for it will always and forever be—Ferret's first book!

Ricky Tims
La Veta, CO, USA
July 2009

Introduction

It's all my students' fault. I'd had a plan to write a book. I'd designed a very contemporary sampler quilt. So contemporary that I didn't think most people would even recognise it as a sampler. Then things changed.

I am lucky enough to teach several regular classes of wonderful ladies. Each class has its own character, which keeps teaching really interesting. My Thursday night class are especially characterful, and they have a Christmas Party every year. At the first of the parties after I started teaching the class, it seemed like a good time to find out what they liked about the classes and what I needed to change. So we got to the question of what they wanted to do in the next term. The replies were:

- We should all work on the same quilt

- But we have to all be able to take it home

- We have to be able to use our own fabric

- We will be broke after Christmas so we can't buy any fabric for a while

- It's got to be a lap quilt

- It's got to be a single bed quilt

- It's got to be a king size quilt

- It has to be quilt as you go

Hmmm. Well it was clear enough what was wanted, but was it possible? I certainly hadn't seen anything that would fit the bill. I was thinking about this when they started coming up with techniques they wanted to learn:

- Celtic knots

- Half square triangles

- Flying geese

- Foundation piecing

Just to round it off, it had to work for a lady who was going to join us the next term to start learning quilting

6

and yet still teach something to those who have been quilting longer than I have. So, no pressure, then...

I have to admit it was a daunting specification. But I do like a challenge, and during the course of the party, I started sketching some ideas. Over the Christmas holiday, I designed the quilt and wrote the first chapter. The following term the class worked steadily on their quilts. We made it as a round robin project with ten people involved. Everyone made the center piece and then put all their fabrics with it in a box. At the end of each section, the box with the quilt in progress was passed the next person. Every so often, people added more fabric to their boxes. The quilt is intended to be made as a scrap project, but as you will see it can be made from as little as three different fabrics.

My job for the next two terms was to write the next section before the class needed it, and complete my section of the group quilt. My students had to just keep going, without any real idea what they were making. They all worked very hard, and working on somone else's quilt is stressful, but it does bring out the best in most people, and the finished quilts do reflect this. I was so flattered that they would take such a huge chance on my idea, and I'm very proud of what they produced.

After this group started the quilt, word started to get around, as I write this, over a year after the first ones were started, students from my other classes now want to make their own versions of this quilt. I love teaching it, and my students seem to enjoy making it. I think the main feature of this quilt is it will teach you a good range of techniques, and then help you produce a truly unique quilt. The center piece is very structured. But once you've completed the block border (chapter 14) it's up to you where you go from there. You could stop there and have a useful lap quilt, or a large wallhanging. Maybe you could add borders on two sides to make the quilt rectangular and build up to a single bed quilt or you can expand all the way arround to make a bed topper, a double, or even a king size. As it is quilt as you go, you can make a really big quilt on a small domestic machine. Imagine what you can make.

You will notice that I haven't given overall fabric requirements. There are two reasons for this. Firstly, as I have said above this was intended to be a scrap quilt, so people could add more fabric as required and were often using odd pieces which are very hard to quantify. Secondly, evey quilt has ended up a different design and in a range of sizes, and so has needed different amounts of fabric. I would suggest for your first one of these quilts, you choose a palette and buy fabric as required that fits with your colours. This also allows the quilt to talk to you and grow with you, which can be very rewarding.

I am well known with my students for being quite relaxed about many quilting rules. Often I will say something needs to be about or approximately a given size, and that is exactly what I mean. You don't need to stress over those pieces. Close enough is good enough. However on the few ocassions where I do say something needs to be accurate or pinned, that is also exactly what I mean. I try very hard to eliminate rules for the sake of rules, so if I've put one in it's probably required. Please trust me, and relax where you can.

If you've got this far you might be wondering about the book I said I had planned originally. Well, as you might have gathered, this isn't it. When I finished this book, the same students came up with another clever set of

requirements for a quilt. So not wanting to disappoint, I came up with another design for them, and yes that will also be available in book form. Once we've all had a break, that first design will get written up and I hope my students will be up for trying it out for me.

I hope you will enjoy this book as much as my students have. Please do play with the design, see what you can change and what you can do with it. I would love to hear from you and see how your quilts come out. My current contact details are always available on my web site at http://ferfab.co.uk.

Now, go sew....

CHAPTER ONE

Celtic Knot

Fabric Requirements

A 13" square of background fabric (if you are using a fabric with a directional pattern, you may need closer to a 15" square instead)

A 14" square of backing fabric

A 14" square of wadding

1 fat quarter of fabric to make bias, or a roll of pre-made bias tape

You should use a cotton or cotton blend wadding. In particular, do not use a polyester wadding.

Helpful Tools

Applique pins

These pins are shorter than normal pins and when working in tight spaces they do make things a lot easier. These are sometimes called sequin pins.

Bias tape maker

If you are making your own bias tape you will need one of these clever little tools. I recommend the 6mm or 8mm tape makers from Clover.

Spray baste

This is an aerosol adhesive which you can use to temporarily hold fabrics together. It is very useful for holding the layers of small quilts together while you quilt them.

Mini iron

If you are using the pre-made fusible bias this is the easiest way to fuse it into place. It isn't necessary, but it does make life easier.

Blue washout marker pen

If you have a light background fabric this is a great way to put your design onto the fabric. However heat will set the ink so if you are using fusible tape you must completely cover the marks or remove them before fusing.

Dressmakers transfer paper

For dark coloured fabrics you will probably find dressmakers carbon paper will be easier to see.

Light box

Using a light box can help you trace the design onto your background fabric, with a good light box you might even be able to trace onto a dark fabric. If you don't have a proper light box you can tape your design to a sunny window instead.

Instructions

1. Two knotwork designs are provided in Appendix A. Select the one you wish to use for the centre of your quilt and photocopy it. You need to ensure that the copier doesn't change the size of the design.

> **Tip:** Alternatively, you can download the PDF designs from my web site and print them out yourself:
> http://ferfab.co.uk/ferreting_around/

2. The knot is split over two pages, and the two halves will need to be joined together again along the dotted line. I recommend using Scotch Magic Tape for this.

3. Cut and press the background and backing fabrics.

> **Tip:** If you're using a background fabric with a directional pattern, you may need to cut the square on the bias in order to ensure that the pattern is oriented correctly

4. We now need to transfer the design onto the fabric. If you are using a light coloured fabric, you will probably be able to trace the design directly onto the centre of the fabric, by laying the fabric over the paper pattern and drawing on it with a washout pen. If you do have access to a light box, you can try tracing directly onto a darker fabric, although you may need to use a chalk pencil rather than the washout pen.

5. If you are using a dark background fabric without a light box, lie the fabric face up on a hard surface, then the dressmakers carbon waxy side down on the fabric. I line up one corner of the paper with a corner of the fabric. Then place the pattern centred on the fabric and trace the lines with either a pen or a dressmaker's tracing wheel. If you've aligned the corners as I suggested above,

the centre of the design should then be 6½" from each of the edges. In the illustration 1, I have used the dressmaker's wheel and just one line as I couldn't remove my marks.

6. In both cases, pin the fabric to the paper to prevent it from moving around while you are tracing the design.

7. Test your chosen marking tool on an off-cut of your background fabric. Make sure you can remove the marks. If the marks are stubborn, don't despair. You can still use them but you have to be certain you will cover the marks with the tape, so rather than drawing a double line (as on the pattern) draw a single line down the middle of each section.

Illustration 1: Marking the knot

8. If you are using pre-made bias tape skip to step 13.

9. Press the fabric you are going to use for the bias tape and fold it

in half diagonally. The sides will not line up as a fat quarter is not a perfect square, don't worry about this.

10. Fold the fabric in half again, bringing the point down to the centre of the first fold. Press gently.

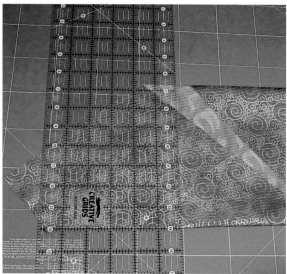

Illustration 2: Preparing to cut the strips

11. We are now going to cut strips from this fabric. Because of the way we have folded it, the strips will be on the bias and very stretchy, so handle them very gently. To make the first cut, line up the markings on your ruler with the longer folded edge, and position it at the start of the shorter fold. Illustration 2 shows the position of the ruler for a right handed quilter. If you are left handed, you can simply start from the other end of the fabric, and yours will be the mirror image of this. Make the first cut with the rotary cutter, and move the small triangular piece out of the way.

12. For the 6mm tape maker I cut ½" strips and for the 8mm I use ¾". Illustration 2 shows ½" strips. Align the marks for the width of strip with the cut edge, and check that the markings going the other direction still line up with the long fold. This should ensure you get straight strips.

Illustration 3: Half inch strips

13. Start by cutting seven strips. You may need a couple more but it is easy to cut these later and it saves having some left over. You now need to use the bias tape maker to fold the strip into a neat tape. Start by threading the tape right side facing towards the pin slot in the tape maker, as shown in illustration 3, and use a pin to pull the strip through the maker until there is about ½" protruding.

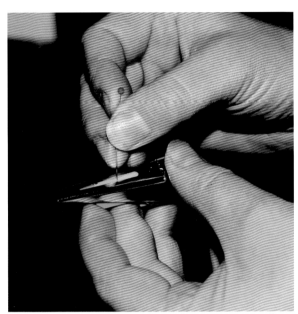

Illustration 4: Threading the strips into the tape maker

14. For the next step I have found it easier to use the tool upside down. You might like to try it both ways and see which gives you the best result. Pull the bias maker gently along the strip, following it closely with the iron. I use steam when setting these folds, but if you are going to do this you need to be very careful to pull the tape maker in a straight line. Bias tape is very easy to distort, a feature that will be very useful when we start making the applique.

Tip: If you're using steam to set the folds in your tape, remember to move each completed tape off the ironing board before pressing the folds on subsequent strips. If you don't, the steam is likely to open up the folds that you just pressed into place.

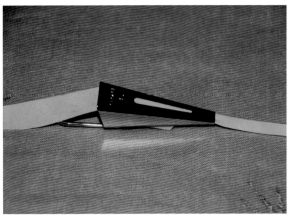

Illustration 5: Making the bias tape

15. Repeat for all the strips you have cut. They will be different lengths, but this will not be a problem. There are a lot of places in these designs where we can hide the ends of the tape.

16. Lay your background fabric on a table and choose a crossing place to start laying down the tape. Decide which part of the design will be underneath, and this is where you will start. If you are using purchased tape, cut yourself a half metre length to start working with.

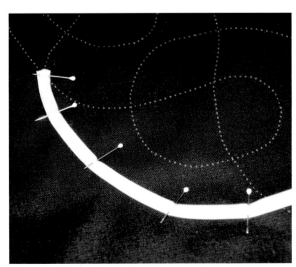

Illustration 6: Pinning the tape

17. Trim the end of the tape, and pin it to be in the middle of the junction where you are starting.

18. Slowly work your way around the design stretching the tape to make curves as needed. Pin at regular intervals. On straighter sections every couple of inches will be plenty but in tighter corners you may find you need more pins. Do not pin at junctions, as you may need to pass the tape under this one as you complete the knot.

19. If you are using fusible tape, you can iron it in place, rather than pinning it. The easiest method is to use a miniature iron and work your way around the design, fusing it as you go. When you have fused it all, turn it over and press again from the back.

20. If you have been able to mark two lines it is easy to see how the knot crosses, but if you have only one line it is a bit trickier. If you can't see which way it should be it is very easy to work out. The junctions alternate, so where the tape started it is under another, the next junction it will be over, then under again. If you're using fusible tape, add a small piece of the backing tape at junctions to prevent it from fusing there.

21. When you are about to run out of tape you need to work out the last junction where the tape will be crossed by another and cut the tape to the right length to hide the end in the junction. Then simply carry on with a new piece.

Illustration 7: Passing the tape under itself

22. At some point you will need to pass the tape under a piece you have already laid down. This is a lot easier if you use a pair of tweezers to help. Slide the tweezers under from the far side and pull the end of the tape through underneath itself, as shown in illustration 7.

Tip: Although you should alternate the junctions to be over and under at successive crossings, it's not strictly necessary. If you're not feeling confident about threading the tape under itself, you can just keep the tape on top at each junction, and it won't be a problem.

23. The stitching that holds the applique in place is also going to be the quilting for the centre of our quilt, so we now need to make up the quilt sandwich.

Spread the backing fabric on the table face down. If you are using spray baste, give the backing fabric a light spray.

24. Lay the wadding on top of the backing fabric, smooth out any wrinkles. Spray the wadding with basting spray (if you're using it). Centre the applique top on the wadding and backing fabric and smooth out any wrinkles.

25. If you have chosen not to use spray baste, you will need to use another method to hold the sandwich together while you stitch. Options include pins, safety pins or hand sewing large tacking stitches.

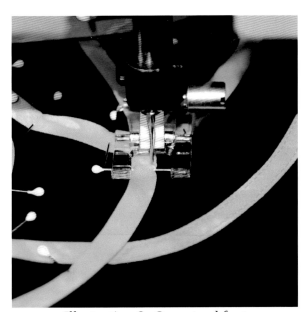

Illustration 8: Open toed foot

26. To make sewing the tape as easy as possible, put a foot on your machine that has good visibility. I used the plastic open toed foot shown in illustration 8, but any open foot will work well. If your

walking foot is an open design, that would be perfect for this process.

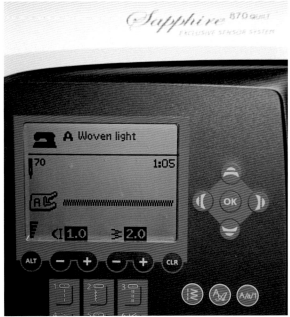

Illustration 9: Selecting a zigzag stitch

27. There are several options for securing the tape. The easiest is probably a zigzag stitch, although any decorative stitch would also work. Alternatively you could use a blind hem, or blanket stitch, with the long part of the pattern running next to the tape and the across part of the stitch catching the applique. This method can give the look of hand applique. Finally, and my preferred option, is to put a line of straight stitching close to the edge of the tape. Whichever stitch you choose you will need to run your machine slowly and move the fabric steadily to follow the lines.

CHAPTER TWO

Sawtooth Border

Fabric Requirements

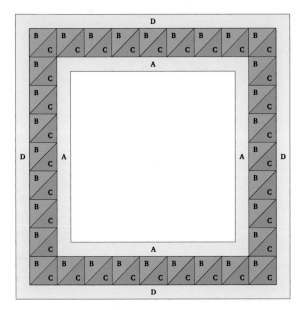

Inner border (A)

About half a fat quarter of a fabric that contrasts well with the centre square and the fabrics you will use for the half square triangles

Half square (B)

Approximately 13" square of light fabric

Half square (C)

Approximately 13" square of dark fabric

Outer border (D)

About half a fat quarter of a fabric that contrasts well the centre square and the fabrics you will use for the half square triangles. It needs to be at least 21½" along one side, unless you want to piece the longer strips. You could use the same fabric as for A or you could try something different.

You will need similar amounts of backing and wadding.

Helpful Tools

Large square ruler

A large square ruler is very useful for squaring up quilt blocks but they are quite expensive and tricky to store. It might be a good tool to buy with a group of friends and share.

Shape Cut Ruler

This is another specialist ruler. I love it for cutting strips as it is quick and accurate. It has many slots that allows you to line the ruler up once then cut several strips. I used it for cutting the narrow border strips.

Instructions

1. Trim your centre square to be 12½" square. Try to keep the design centred as you trim. We will now add the narrow border of contrasting fabric.

2. Cut two 12½" x 2" strips from each of the three layers, the top (A), the wadding and the backing. Press the top and backing fabrics.

Illustration 1: Cutting strips using the Shape Cut Ruler

3. Take the strip cut from the top fabric and lie it along one side of the centre square, right sides together. Start by pinning the ends into place then add a few more pins to secure the middle of the strip.

Illustration 2: Pin the border to the centre square

4. Using a scant ¼" seam, sew the strip to one side of the centre square.

Tip: A scant ¼" seam should be very slightly smaller than a full quarter inch, ideally by two or three threads on the fabric you're sewing.

5. Check your seam has caught all the layers of the centre square.

6. Place the square face down on the table and lie the strip of backing face down along the side to which you have just attached the top strip.

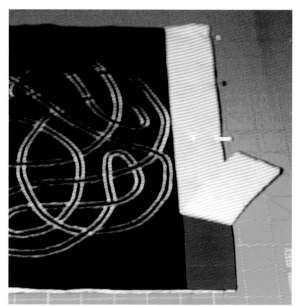

Illustration 3: Adding the backing fabric and wadding

7. On top of the strip of backing, place the strip of wadding. Pin all the layers together.

8. Flip the square over so you can see the seam you just stitched.

9. Resew the seam through all the layers taking a slightly deeper seam so your previous stitching will be hidden within it.

10. Flip the layers open and press aggressively. This is why I said

to avoid using polyester wadding, as it melts during pressing. Make sure both the backing and the top fabrics are spread out from the seam. Repeat steps 3 to 10 on the opposite side of the square.

11. Cut two 16" x 2" strips from each of the three layers.

12. Apply these strips in the same way as the shorter ones to other two sides, creating a border for the centre square. The ends will probably overlap a bit at this point. Don't worry, that's not a problem.

13. We have made this border slightly oversize. This was to allow for shifting when learning these techniques. It is quite tricky to get the perfect ¼" seam on the first attempt with this many layers. So we now need to trim up again. The quilt needs to be trimmed down so that the combined centre piece and the inner borders measures 14½" square. This can be done easily with a straight ruler. When trimming, take care to ensure that the borders are the same width on either side of the centre square.

14. Take the lighter fabric (B) that you selected for the half square triangles, press it and lie it face down on the table.

15. With a pencil, mark a 3" grid on the fabric. Make the grid four squares by four squares, for a total of sixteen.

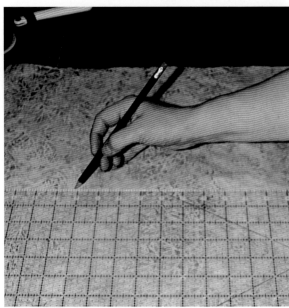

Illustration 4: Marking the grid

16. Mark in diagonal lines as shown in figure 5. Note each square has just one line through it.

Illustration 5: Diagonal lines

17. Lay the darker of your half square fabrics (C) face up on the table and place the lighter fabric face down on top of it. A couple of pins might help you keep the two layers together as you start stitching.

18. Stitch slightly less than ¼" away from each side of the diagonal lines. You will find that you can sew from one line to the next rather than cutting the thread and restarting each time.

Illustration 6: Sew each side of the diagonal lines

19. When you have sewn on both sides of each diagonal line, press your work and double check you haven't missed a line of stitching. Using a ruler and your rotary cutter, cut along all the drawn lines. Remember to cut along both the grid and the diagonals.

20. Open each triangle out to form a square, and press the seams towards the darker side.

Tip: You may find the tips of the triangles are stitched together, which is preventing you from opening them. If so, simply remove the offending thread before opening. There should be no more than a small handful of stitches, and they should be quite easy to remove.

Illustration 7: Seam pressed to the dark side of square

21. You will have thirty two squares made of two half square triangles. They will probably look a little off square but that's fine. They are slightly oversize so we can trim them up to be more accurate. This method also avoided having to cut on the bias then sew a seam, which is very prone to stretching out of shape.

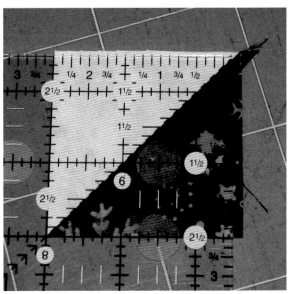

Illustration 8: Trim to 2½" square

22. Use a small square ruler to trim up the squares. Try to position the seam exactly on the diagonal as shown in illustration 8, and trim up two sides at a time. Then rotate the block and trim the other two sides to make a 2½" square.

23. Lay the squares out around the centre square to create a pattern you like. Decide on a pattern to use. The fabric requirements diagram shows one option, but you may be able to come up with something you like better. There are an almost infinite number of ways the squares can be joined together. Which one you choose is up to you.

24. A few ideas are shown in illustrations 11 and 12 at the end of the chapter.

25. Sew the squares together using a scant ¼" into two rows of 9 squares and two rows of 7 squares, taking care to maintain your chosen pattern.

26. Press the seams towards the darker side.

> **Tip:** After joining the first three squares together, press them open and measure the inner of the three squares. It should be exactly 2" wide, which will let you know if you've got your seam allowance right before you go too much further.

27. When you have completed your four rows, measure the distance between the outermost seams. For the longer rows, this should be 14". For the shorter rows, it should be 10". If your rows are too long, redo some of the seams, taking a little bit more seam allowance. If your rows are too short, you can stretch the fabric a little during pressing to make up the shortfall.

28. Cut two 2½" x 14½" strips of wadding and backing fabric.

29. Apply the seven square strips and and the wadding and backing as you did for the inner border in steps 3 to 10. When you sew the initial seam holding the squares to the quilt, fold it open and check that you haven't caught the points of the triangles in the seam. As you will be resewing the seam, you need there to be a little space. If there is a problem it is easy to undo and try again. This is why we sew the top layer on its own first.

30. Illustration 9 shows what we are trying to achieve after sewing the seam the second time. Once attached and pressed open, the points of the half square triangles should just be touching the inner border.

Illustration 9: Half square border attached, with the points just touching the inner border

31. Cut two 2½" x 18½" strips of wadding and backing fabric.

32. Sew the longer strips of nine squares into place as you did above for the shorter strips.

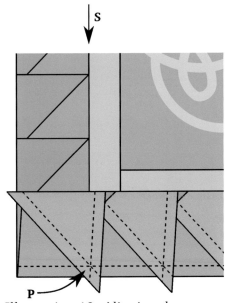

Illustration 10: Aligning the seams

33. When pinning the squares on, make sure the seam between the last two squares at each end match the seams where the other squares were sewn onto the centre section. In illustration 10, point P should align with seam S, to ensure that your borders look right at the corners.

34. The outer narrow border is made in exactly the same way as the inner one was. This time the smaller strips are cut 2" x 18½" and the longer ones 2" x 21½". If your fabric isn't long enough to cut the 21½" strips you can join two 11" strips with a ¼" seam to make each one. Follow steps 3-9 to complete this section of your quilt.

Tip: When adding the outer borders, fold the top fabric back before you add the second line of stitching to secure the backing and wadding. This will show you how close the points on your triangles are to the first seam, which will give you some guidance on how close to the first seam you should make your second seam.

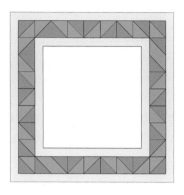

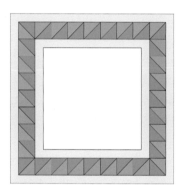

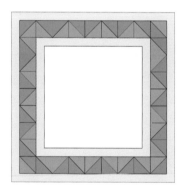

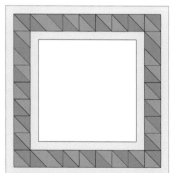

*Illustration 11: Alternate
layouts*

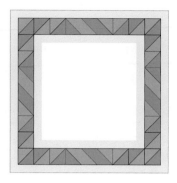

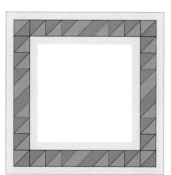

*Illustration 12: Alternate
layouts*

CHAPTER THREE

Mariners' Compass

Fabric Requirements

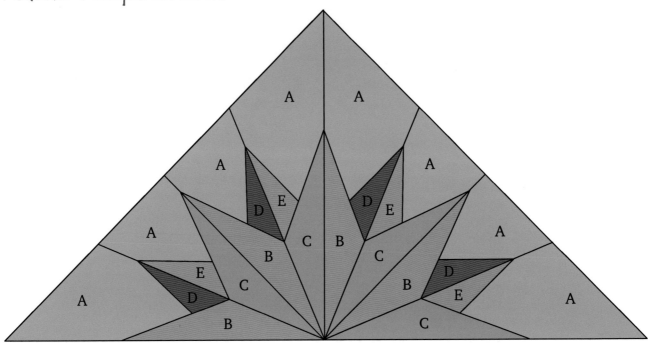

A (Compass background)   1m
B (Half the large points)   ½m
C (Half the large points)   ½m

D (Half the small points)   ¼m
E (Half the small points)   ¼m
Backing: two squares, each 16" × 16"
Wadding: two squares, each 16" × 16"

Helpful Tools

Add-a-quarter Ruler

This small ruler has a lip on one side which makes it excellent for trimming up the seam allowance as you foundation piece.

Portable Ironing Pad

As you need to press each seam as you sew it, it is really handy to have your iron right next to your sewing machine. A little ironing pad is a real asset for this technique.

Instructions

1.   Foundation piecing is a very accurate method of producing spiky designs. The fabric is laid on one side of the paper foundation and sewn from the other, so sometimes you will make a mistake. Be nice to yourself and try to stay calm. If this is your first time trying this method you might want to make an extra copy of one of the pattern pages and practice with some scraps. The letters on the pieces relate to the fabric needed for each section, the numbers tell you the order you will be adding the pieces. You will notice that a seam allowance has been added around the

foundation piece. This is not accurate and is merely there to remind you to leave the extra fabric while you are piecing.

2. Photocopy the foundation pieces in Appendix B. If you have a choice, use the cheapest, thinnest paper you can, and make eight copies of each of the two pages. Alternatively, as with the celtic knotwork in chapter 1, you can download and print the designs from my web site.

3. Using the plan in the fabric requirements above, select your fabrics. You might find it easier to keep track of your fabrics if you either make a note of which is which, or pin a label to each fabric.

4. I strongly suggest you work on the pieces one page number at a time. It makes it easier to keep the pieces in order. Start with the eight copies of page one.

5. Roughly separate the two pattern pieces, there is no need to cut them out carefully.

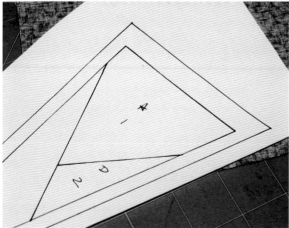

Illustration 1: Foundation paper in place on the background fabric

6. Place the background (fabric A) face down on the table and position the foundation pattern face up on top of it, as shown in illustration 1. Make sure that the whole of the 1A area, and the surrounding seam allowances are over the fabric. Put a pin in to stop the layers moving.

7. With the aid of a piece of cardboard (I use a postcard), fold back the paper along the line between areas 1 and 2. Using either the Add-a-quarter ruler or any small ruler to trim the fabric ¼" away from the paper, this will become the seam allowance.

Illustration 2: Using a postcard, trim ¼" from the fold between areas 1 and 2

8. Repeat for the line between areas 1 and 3. Unfold the paper and turn the piece over so the fabric is face up with the paper below it.

9. Take a piece of the fabric you are going to use for area 2, and place it face down on the first piece of fabric aligning a straight edge with the cut edge.

10. Pin along the seam line from the printed side of the paper. This

allows us to check the positioning before sewing.

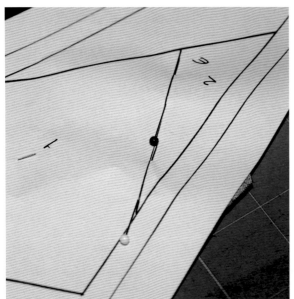

Illustration 3: Pin what will become the seam between areas 1 and 2

11. Imagine those pins are a sewn seam. Fold the second piece of fabric out to cover area 2. Hold the paper up to the light to check area 2 is fully covered. If not, unpin and reposition.

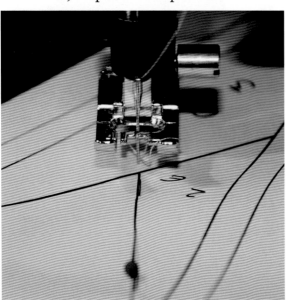

Illustration 4: Sew along the pinned line

12. Once you have the fabric in the right place, you can sew the seam. This is done from the printed side of the foundation. Set your sewing machine for a smaller than usual stitch, I use a 1.5mm stitch length, and use a foot that gives you good visibility. I like the one shown in illustration 4 because I find it easy to line up the red mark on the foot with the line I need to stitch on. Start your stitching a little before the line starts and continue right through the outer seam allowance. Remove the pins as you come to them.

13. Fold the paper back along the line you have just stitched, and using an Add-a-quarter ruler if you have one, or a small ruler if you don't, trim the seam allowance to ¼".

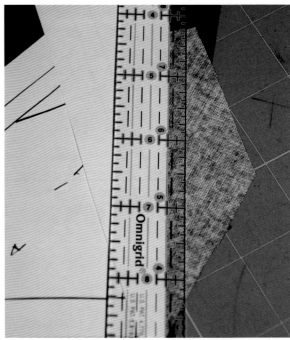

Illustration 5: Trim seam allowance to ¼"

14. From the fabric side, press the second fabric into position.

15. Repeat steps 9-14 for the third piece of fabric.

16. This process is repeated for each of the foundations.

17. Each page is a quarter of one star, and a good place to start is getting these together. Before joining the pieces, trim the long sides of the wedges to leave a ¼" seam allowance, but don't trim the short edge for now. When trimming, use your ruler to measure the allowance. You will probably find that you are trimming just inside the drawn line.

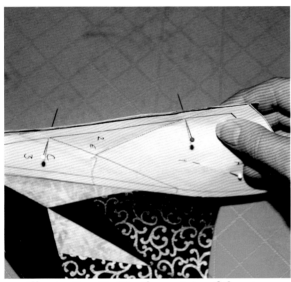

Illustration 6: Pin the points of the star

18. When joining the wedges, the most important parts to have lined up are the points of the star. To do this, poke a pin through the exact point where your stitching crosses the outer seam line from the printed side of the paper. Push the point of the pin through the matching point on the next piece. Leave this pin as it is and do the same with any other points that need to match on the seam line. Don't worry too much about the outer edge aligning.

19. Next to each of the pins that you've poked straight through

the piece, put in a pin normally to hold the layers in place.

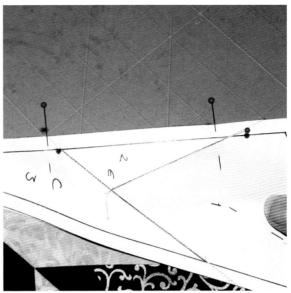

Illustration 7: Pin next to the pins you just added

20. Remove the first set of pins, and stitch along the printed seam line.

21. Before pressing the seam, I suggest that you remove the paper from the seam allowances, and any piece that has been sewn on all sides (the small points) This will make pressing the seam a lot easier.

22. Continue working through the pages of foundations until you have four sets of four pairs.

Illustration 8: Four pairs of wedges

23. Then proceed to join those together to get the four compass triangles. Remove the foundation paper from the parts of the triangle that will attach to the quilt centre.

Illustration 9: Completed compass triangle

24. Trim your quilt centre so that it is 20½" square.
25. Cut two 16" squares of backing then cut each in half diagonally so you have four large triangles.
26. Cut two 16" squares of wadding then cut each in half diagonally so you have four large triangles.
27. Fold the quilt centre in half to find the mid-point of one edge, and use a pin to mark this point. This is where we want the middle of the compass to fall, so with right sides together, pin a compass corner onto the quilt, matching the centres. The ends will overhang the quilt. Sew this into place with a very scant ¼" seam. Check to see that the centre point is not caught in the seam. If the centre is too far from the seam you can take a bigger seam when you sew on the backing and wadding.
28. Pin the backing (right sides together) to the back of the quilt on the same edge. Add the wadding and then resew the seam.
29. Press the pieces into position, making sure there are no folds left at the seam. Pin the outer edge of the triangles to hold the layers together.

Illustration 10: Compass attached to quilt

30. As these triangles are quite large, they need a little more quilting than the other borders have. The simplest way to do this is to "stitch in the ditch". That means to run a line of quilting along the seam lines of the compass. If you are not confident of your ability to sew a perfectly straight line of quilting, you might want to consider a decorative machine stitch. Curvy lines or feather stitches are especially good with this style of block. Start at the seam with the quilt and stitch out along the large points towards the outer edge of the triangle.
31. Repeat steps 27 to 30 for the opposite triangle.
32. Finally, put on the remaining two corners. Once you have quilted the triangles you can remove the pins from around the outer edge.

CHAPTER FOUR

Flying Geese

Fabric Requirements

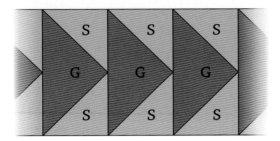

Sky (S)   ½m

Geese (G)   ½m

There is no need for the fabric to be two large pieces, it is quite possible to use up scraps for this border. When selecting your fabrics, make sure that there is good contrast between the geese and the sky. The minimum size scrap you can use for the sky is 2½" square, and for the geese a 4½" x 2½ rectangle.

Instructions

1.   From your sky fabric, cut one hundred and twenty 2½" squares.

Tip: If you are cutting your squares from larger sections of fabric, first cut 2½" strips, then cross cut them to make squares. This is a lot quicker and more accurate than trying to cut each square individually.

2.   From your geese fabrics, cut sixty rectangles measuring 4½" x 2½ .

3.   Lay one sky fabric face up on the table.

4.   Take one goose, and fold it in half so it is almost square, do not press.

Illustration 1: Folded goose

5.   Place goose on square with the fold towards the top of the square as seen in the picture. Align the raw edges. The fold of the goose should be ¼" down from the top of the square, as seen in illustration 1.

Illustration 2: Aligning the edges

6. Place a second sky square face down over the first square. Match all edges, with the aligned edges at the bottom, as shown in illustration 2.Place two or three pins along the right hand edge to hold all the layers together as shown in illustration 3.

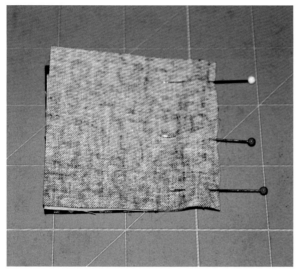

Illustration 3: PIn the right hand edge

7. Stitch the pieces together along this edges with a ¼" seam.

8. Repeat for the other fifty nine geese.

Illustration 4: Open out the sky

9. When you have all your geese, press them open. Start by lifting

one sky square and press the seam, as show in illustration 4. Try to avoid pressing the fold of the goose.

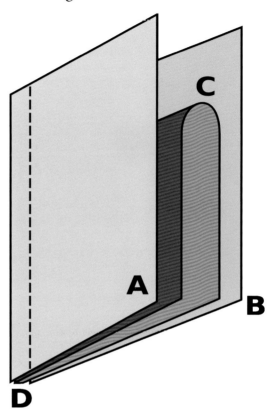

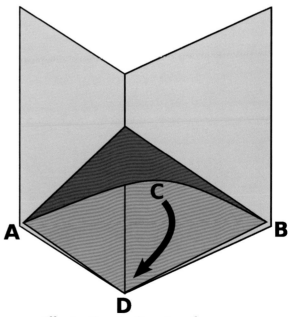

Illustration 6: Opening the goose

10. Then open out the goose. Pull its lower corners towards the lower corners of the sky, as shown in illustration 5, then press gently.

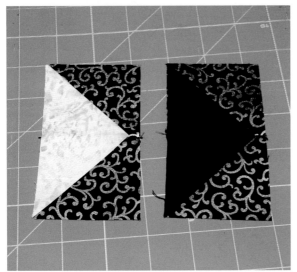

Illustration 7: Laying out the geese

11. Lay out your geese in a pattern you like. You will have 15 geese for each side of the quilt.

12. Flip the geese over, and press the seam allowance on alternate geese in opposite directions. This will make it easier to sew the geese together.

Illustration 8: Interlock the seams

13. Sew your sets of geese together with a ¼" seam. When you place two together, if you have pressed your seams in opposite directions they will interlock at the center of the seam, as shown in illustration 7. Snug them together and pin. Add more pins to hold the ends of the seam in place. Take care to pin the outer corners of the geese into place when you pin the seam.

14. Once your individual geese are joined into four rows of fifteen geese each, gently press the seams between geese towards the points. Your geese are now complete. If you are making this as a round robin quilt, you will swap before joining these borders to the quilt.

CHAPTER FIVE

Pinwheel Corners

Fabric Requirements

Although this chapter is called Pinwheel Corners, we're actually going to be making not only the corners, but also the narrow borders that separate the geese in the previous chapter from the rest of the quilt.

Pinwheel

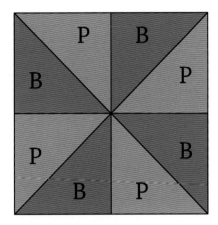

Background (B)   sixteen 2½" squares

Pinwheels (P)   sixteen 2½" squares

Backing fabric - two pieces 4½" x 30½" and two pieces 4½" x 38½"

Wadding - two pieces 4½" x 30½" and two pieces 4½" x 38½"

There is no need for the fabric to be two large pieces. It is quite possible to use up scraps for this border. When selecting your fabrics, make sure that there is good contrast between the pinwheel and background.

Inner border

Front fabric - two pieces 3" x 30½" and two pieces 3 x 28½"

Backing fabric - four pieces 3" x 30½"

Wadding - four pieces 3" x 30½"

Note that the precise lengths of the inner border fabrics are calculated in steps 15 to 18.

Outer border

Front Fabric - two pieces 2½" x 38½" and two pieces 2½" x 42½"

Backing fabric - two pieces 2½" x 38½" and two pieces 2½" x 42½"

Wadding - two pieces 2½" x 38½" and two pieces 2½" x 42½"

Instructions

1.   From your background fabric cut sixteen 2½" squares.

> **Tip:** For cutting your sixteen background and pinwheel squares, you can cut a single 2½ strip across the width of the fabric, and then cross cut it to give you your sixteen squares.

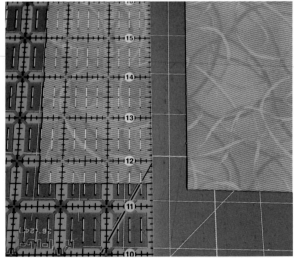

Illustration 1: Cut 2½" strips

2.   From your pinwheel fabrics, cut sixteen 2½" squares. As above,

consider cutting strips and then cross cutting to get squares.

3. Take a pinwheel square and fold it in half diagonally with wrong sides together.

Illustration 2: Folded pinwheel

4. Place a background square right side up on your table, then align the now triangular piece of pinwheel so the raw edges align with two sides of the background square.

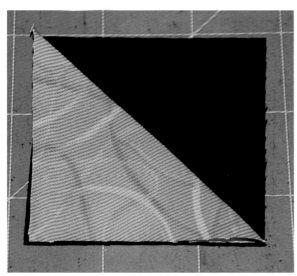

Illustration 3: Aligned edges

5. Stitch the triangle into place less than ¼" from the raw edge.

6. Repeat for the other fifteen of each square, making sixteen folded half squares.

7. Join pairs of the squares exactly as shown in illustration 4. Use a ¼" seam.

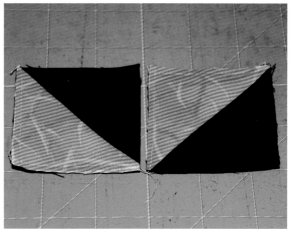

Illustration 4: Pair of squares

8. Press the seam so that it lies behind the background fabric.

9. Sew two of these pairs together to make a pinwheel block. You should find that the seams and folds nestle into each other to correctly align the points at the center of the block.

10. Repeat to make four pinwheel squares. Press the centre seam open.

11. Take out the rows of flying geese you made in the last chapter and work out where you want to place them. Take two of those rows and attach a finished pinwheel to each end of them.

12. Press seams towards the geese.

13. Put the borders to one side and prepare the quilt center. The first step is to trim it up. You want to end up with a perfect square, with more than ¼" beyond all the points, including the point where the triangles met in the middle of each side. If you have a square ruler larger than 15" square, you can use that.

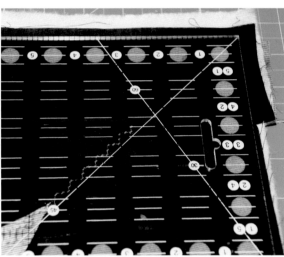

Illustration 5: Misaligned diagonal

14. Align the square so it is at least ¼" past the points, and with the same measurement showing at that point on each side of the ruler. Ideally the diagonal line on the ruler will match with the mid-point of the compass triangle. However, it won't always align. This isn't a problem, and the two can be out of line as shown in illustration 5 without causing problems. I strongly suggest you make the cutting line in chalk first rather than just cutting it. This will allow you to change the cutting line if need be.

15. Work around the quilt marking each corner in the same way. If you do not have a large square you can use your long ruler to trim up instead.

16. After trimming, measure your quilt. It should measure around 28¼" square. However, it doesn't always go according to plan, and I've seen quilts that have ended up anywhere between 26" square and 31" square. We need to get the centre piece to be a 30.5" square. If you can trim it to that size directly, then do so and skip to step 21. If the quilt is too large, you may have to accept that you'll need to trim the tips of some of the points. If your quilt is smaller than 30.5" square, we will insert a border to make it up to that size.

17. From the inner border fabric, cut two strips 3" wide and the same length as your square. Cut the same size pieces from the wadding and backing.

Tip: Your quilt is now at the size where you may not have a large enough piece of wadding to hand. If necessary, you can create a larger piece of wadding by joining two smaller pieces. Trim them so that they both have a suitably straight edge, and butt the two edges together. Then join the two with a wide zigzag stitch.

18. Apply these strips to opposite sides of the quilt as described in

Chapter 2.

19. Again from the inner border fabric, cut two strips 3" wide and the length as long as your square plus 5". Cut the same size pieces from the wadding and backing.

20. Apply these pieces to your quilt, and trim the quilt to 30½" square.

21. Cut two pieces of wadding 4½" x 30½", and the same from backing fabric.

Illustration 6: Stitched edge

22. Apply the two short strips of flying geese borders (those without the pinwheels attached) to opposite sides of the quilt, in the same way as the narrow border. Take care to keep your finished seam allowance to ¼", as we don't want to lose the

points of the geese.

23. Stitch a line of straight stitching, less than ¼" from the outside edge of the borders you have just attached to keep the three layers together.

24. Cut two pieces of wadding 4½" x 38½", and the same from backing fabric.

25. Apply the geese and pinwheel borders to the other two sides of the quilt.

26. Again, stitch a line of straight stitching, less than ¼" from the outside edge of the borders you have just attached to keep the three layers together.

Illustration 7: Pinned curves

27. We are now ready to make our geese and pinwheels curve. If you gently fold back the folded edge of the geese it will make a curve. I suggest you start with the pinwheels, as they only have

one side to turn down. Push the fold back until you have a curve you like the look of, then pin in place.

28. Test some decorative stitches on a scrap of fabric, when you have one you like use it to sew the folded piece into place. If you don't have a decorative stitch you like, a simple straight stitch can look very elegant.

29. With the geese it is entirely up to you how many you make curved. You could do all of them, every alternate one, or any other number and pattern that you think looks good.

30. Finally, add the outer border, using the same method that you used for the inner one.

Illustration 8: Sewn curves

CHAPTER SIX

Friendship Stars

The last set border is made up of eight different 6" blocks. Each block in the border is intended to show you another technique. The blocks have also been designed to help use up the smaller pieces of fabric you have left from the other chapters.

The first of these blocks is known as a friendship star. This block shows you another method of making half square triangles, one that is good for smaller pieces of fabric. It also shows how pressing can make putting a block together a lot easier and more accurate.

Fabric Requirements

These are the requirements for one block. You will need to make four blocks in total.

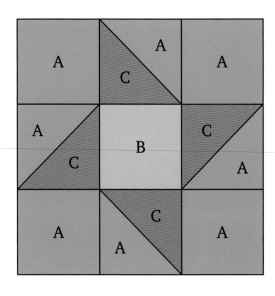

A   four 2½" and two 3" squares

B   one 2½" square

C   two 3" squares

Instructions

1.   Cut the fabrics as listed in the requirements. Remember that you need to make four of these blocks, although they do not need to all use the same fabrics. For the sample, I have used the same fabric for B and C.

2.   Place a 3" square of A right sides together with a 3" square of C.

3.   Mark a line from one corner to the one diagonally opposite. Use any marking tool that will show up well, as this line will end up in the seam allowance.

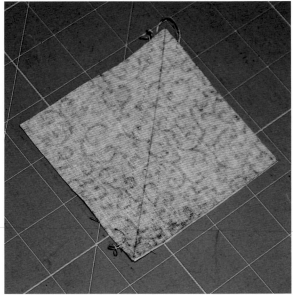

Illustration 1: Sew ¼" each side of the diagonal line

4.   Stitch the squares together a ¼" from each side of this line.

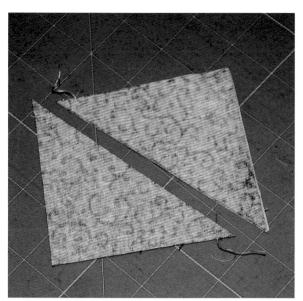

Illustration 2: Cut along the diagonal line

5. Cut the squares apart along the marked line, then open up the half square triangle blocks. Press the seam towards the darker fabric.

6. Trim the square to 2½" square. Repeat with the other pair of 3" squares.

7. Layout the block taking care to get the triangles correctly positioned.

Illustration 3: Layout the block

8. Join the pieces to make 3 rows, using a scant ¼" seam so that the finished squares will be 2".

Illustration 4: Press seams away from the triangles

9. Press all the seams away from the half square triangles. This will mean the seams on the top and bottom rows will be pressed outward and those on the middle row will be pressed inward. This allows the seams to interlock and makes the points very accurate.

10. Sew the rows together carefully aligning the seams between the blocks.

11. Pin the junctions if you find it helpful.

12. Make three more of these blocks.

CHAPTER SEVEN

Partial Ring

OK, you've caught me. The ring is whole. It's the seams that are partial. This is a really useful technique for putting together all kinds of designs.

Fabric Requirements

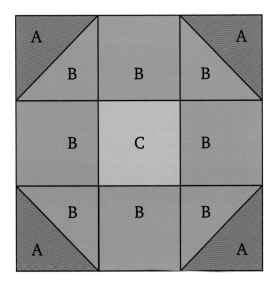

You will need to make four blocks. Each block requires:

A   four 2½" squares

B   four 2½" x 4½" rectangles

C   one 2½" square

Instructions

1. Cut the pieces as listed in the requirements. Remember you need to make four copies of this block, but they need not use the same fabrics.

2. Place an A square right sides together on top of a B rectangle. Align it to one end of the rectangle as shown in illustration 1. Mark the diagonal line exactly as in the picture.

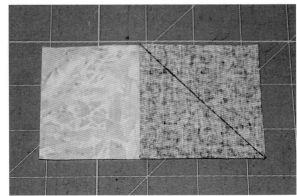

Illustration 1: Align the pieces and mark the diagonal

3. Stitch along this line. You might find this easier to do with the sewing machine needle in it's centre position and a foot with a centre mark. Alternatively, an open toed foot can give good visibility for when you need to follow a line.

Illustration 2: Sew the diagonal

4. Trim off the corner ¼" beyond the sewn line, open and press the seam towards the darker fabric. Make three more of these AB units to complete one block.

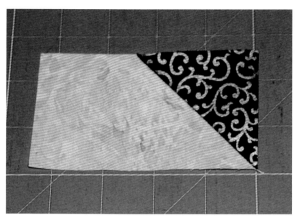

Illustration 3: Open and press the seam

5.   Lay out the block so you can see where the pieces need to fit.

Illustration 4: Layout the AB units

6.   Take the top AB unit (as seen in illustration 4) and the centre square. Using a ¼" seam allowance, start sewing the seam between them. Stop sewing two thirds of the way along the square, as shown in illustration 5.

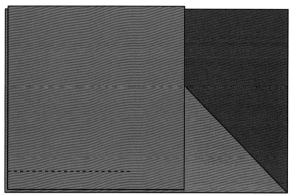

Illustration 5: Sew 2/3rds of the seam

7.   Press the part of the seam you have sewn away from the center square.

8.   If you put the part stitched pieces back into the block layout, you can see that it is now possible to sew the left hand AB unit into place.

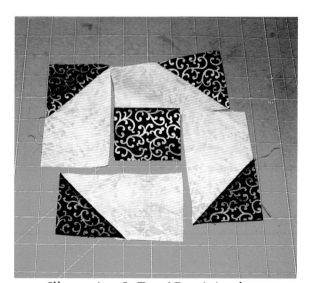

Illustration 6: Top AB unit in place

9.   Press the seam away from the center square.

Illustration 7: The lower AB unit attached

10. Once you have the left piece in place, the bottom AB unit can be attached.

11. Again, press the seam away from the center square.

12. Now the right hand side piece can be put on, pressing seam away from the center square.

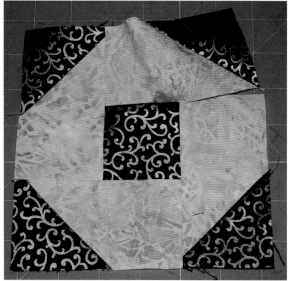

Illustration 9: Three complete seams and one partial seam

13. Now the only seam left is the one you started first. You can now complete this one. Restart sewing where you stopped and press the seam away from the center square when you have finished.

Illustration 10: The completed block

14. Make three more of these blocks.

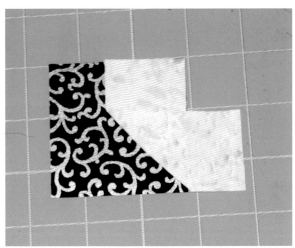

Illustration 2: Fold the rectangle

4. Firmly press the fold with your finger, to make a hard crease, and unfold the strip. If you finish stitching exactly on this crease, it will be exactly your seam allowance from the corner.

Illustration 3: Sew to the crease

5. Sew the second strip to the bottom side of the so it will overhang the same corner as the first strip. Again, stop sewing ¼" from the corner. This will be exactly the spot where you stopped sewing on the last strip.

6. Fold the square in half, wrong sides together, along the diagonal through the corner where the strips overhang. Pin the strips so they are perfectly aligned.

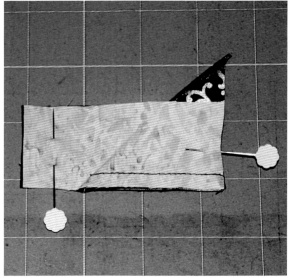

Illustration 4: Pinned strips

7. Line a ruler up with the fold of the square, and its point with the end of the stitching lines, as shown in illustration 5.

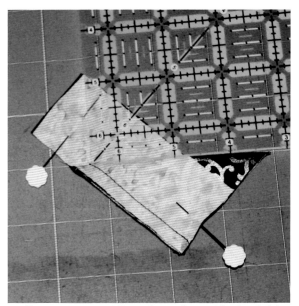

Illustration 5: Align the ruler with the fold and the end of the stitching

8. Draw a line from the end of the sewing along the side of the ruler, so it is at 90° to the fold. You should find the line goes to the corner of the strip.

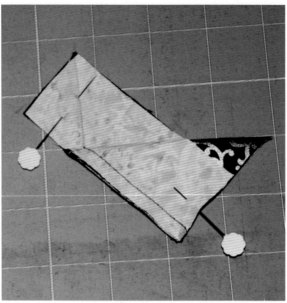

Illustration 6: Mark a line from the end of the stitching at right angles to the fold

9. Stitch along the drawn line. Start exactly where the stitching finished and sew to the edge of the fabric.

10. Open out the block and check your mitered corner. If there is a little tuck, you will need to find the stitch that is causing it and snip it.

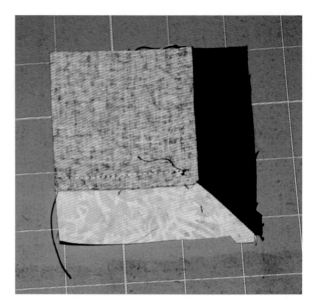

11. Trim off the excess fabric in the seam allowance. Press the seams towards the strips, and press the mitre seam open. This will give the flattest finish to the corner.

12. Make three more of these attic windows to complete one block, and then make three more blocks. As mentioned at the start of the chapter, the windows can be joined in several ways to make the finished block. A couple of possibilities are shown in illustrations 7 and 8.

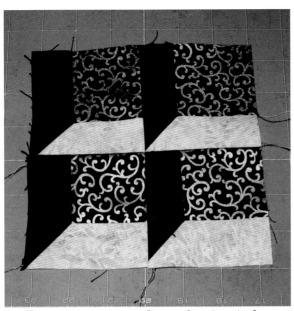

Illustration 7: A traditional attic window block

Illustration 8: An alternative layout, using the same attic window pieces

CHAPTER NINE

Chequerboard

This very simple block is a very versatile one. It is often forgotten, which I think it a great shame. If you need a quick quilt or a zingy border, this block could be just what you are looking for.

Fabric Requirements

A	B	A
B	A	B
A	B	A

A   Three 2½" x 18" strip

B   Three 2½" x 18" strip

That will make all four blocks. In this case it is a lot easier and quicker to make the four blocks together.

Instructions

1.   Sew the strips together to make these strip sets using a scant ¼ seam. You will have two sets, one with the light fabric in the centre, and one with the darker fabric in the centre.

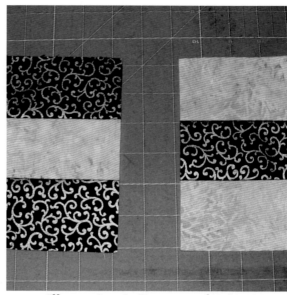

Illustration 1: Two sets of strips

Tip: To help keep the strips as straight as possible, stitch the seams in opposite directions. On such short strips you are unlikely to see much distortion anyway, but on longer strips this will make a big difference.

2.   Press the seams towards the darker fabric. Take care while pressing not to stretch or curve the strips.

3.   From each set, cut six slices 2 ½ wide. Line up the horizontal lines on the ruler with the seams in the strip and use this to judge when the cut will be straight.

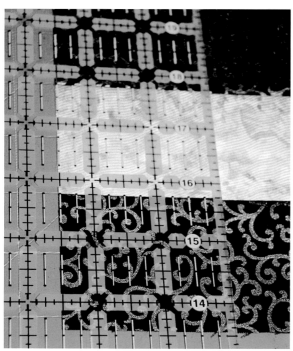

Illustration 2: Cut the strips

4. Join these slices of three 'squares' into blocks. You will have two of each of two blocks, one being the inverse of the other, as shown in illustrations 3 and 4. You should find the seams will nicely lock together and help you match the points.

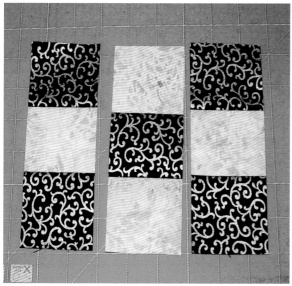

Illustration 3: Chequerboard layout

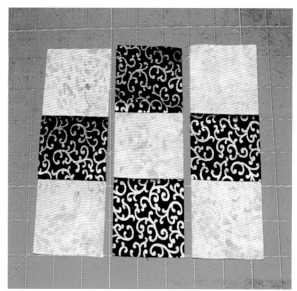

Illustration 4: Inverse chequerboard layout

5. You should have enough slices to make two blocks in each colour way.

CHAPTER TEN

Delectable Mountains

This traditional block is very striking yet very easy. It is not the most efficient use of fabric, but sometimes the impact of the design makes it worth while.

Fabric Requirements

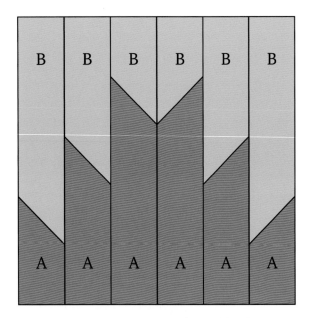

You will need to make four blocks. Each block requires:

A   one 7½" square

B   one 7½" square

Instructions

1.   Cut the pieces as listed in the requirements. Remember you need to make four copies of this block, but they need not use the same fabrics.

2.   Place the squares right sides together, and lay them on your table with the lighter fabric uppermost.

3.   Mark a diagonal line on the lighter fabric.

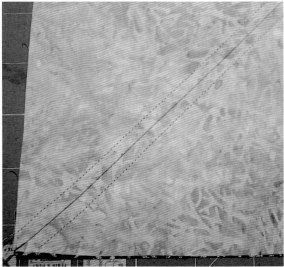

Illustration 1: Sew either side of the diagonal

4.   Sew a seam a ¼ to each side of this line, and press flat.

5.   Cut apart on the drawn line then open the square and press the seam towards the darker colour.

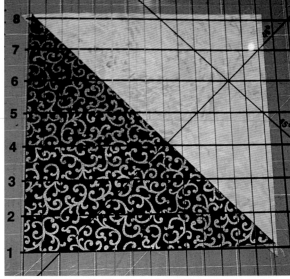

Illustration 2: Square 1 cutting orientation

6.   You now need to cut your squares into strips. Make sure you cut them with the blocks positioned exactly as shown in the diagrams. It is very easy to

cut them both the same and only be able to make one side of the block. If you have one, this job is a lot easier with a strip cutter. It can of course be done perfectly well with a long ruler.

8. Now cut a series of three strips each 1½" wide.

9. Keep these three pieces safe and discard the first and last strips.

Illustration 5: Rearrange the strips

Illustration 3: Strips from square 1

7. Cut the first strip 1" from the left hand edge of the block. There is no need to square up the block before cutting, as this strip and the last one will be discarded.

10. Rearrange the strips as shown in illustration 5, and sew them together with a scant ¼" seam.

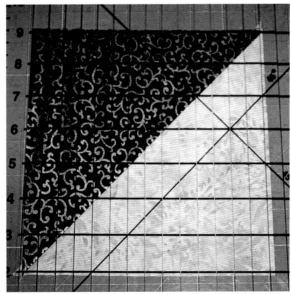

Illustration 6: Square 2 cutting orientation

Illustration 4: Discard the outer strips

11. Cut the second square into the same strips, but with the square placed as in illustration 6.

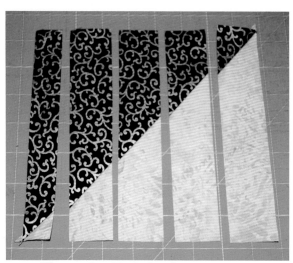

Illustration 7: Strips from square 2

Tip: When trimming it is a good idea to align the lines on the ruler with the seams in the block before cutting. This will make your block look more square.

12. Join the two halves together to make the finished block. The only point that needs matching is the point on the centre seam between the two halves where the light and dark fabrics meet.

13. Press the block. It should be 6½" wide and somewhat taller. Trim the block down to 6½" square.

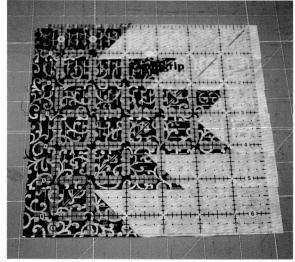

Illustration 8: Trim the block to 6½" square

14. Make the other three blocks.

CHAPTER ELEVEN

Windmills

This block can also be assembled as the pattern called Rail Fence. This strip piecing technique is very useful for making really quick quilts.

Fabric Requirements

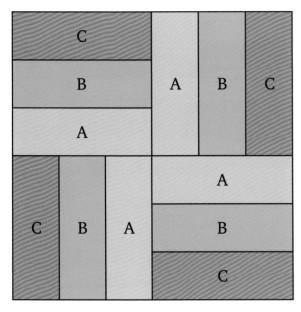

Again, you need to make four blocks. Each one requires:

A - 1½" x 15" strip

B - 1½" x 15" strip

C - 1½" x 15" strip

If you are using up scraps, you could use pieces as small as 1½" x 3 ½", but this will lose you the advantage of strip piecing.

If you are making the blocks all the same you could use longer strips. You will need a minimum of 42" of usable fabric to make all four, but you will probably need slightly more to allow for distortion of the set while you sew and press.

Instructions

1. Cut the pieces as listed in the requirements. Remember you need to make four copies of this block, but they need not use the same fabrics.

2. Sew strips together to make a set of three using a scant ¼" seam. Depending on how long the strips are, you may have one set or several. You need to be able to cut four 3½" slices from each set, as that will make one block. You don't need to make every block from the same colours.

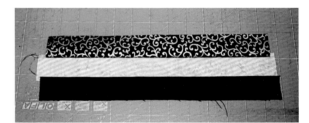

Illustration 1: Set of three strips

3. Press the seams towards the darker colour. Take care to keep the strips straight as you press. It is quite easy on long strips to allow them to curve.

4. Cut four 3½" slices from the set. As you cut, check you are cutting perpendicular to the seams. This means lining up the horizontal markings on your ruler with the seams before cutting. You may find you have to square up the strip more than once as you cut it. This will ensure your block is as accurate as possible.

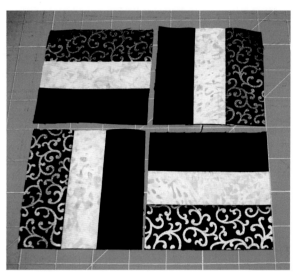

Illustration 2: Laying out the pieces

5.   Lay out the block as shown in illustration 2. Sew the top pair of squares together with a scant ¼" seam and press the seam to the side without seams.

Illustration 3: Join the top and bottom pairs

6.   Join the lower pair in the same manner.

7.   The seams you have just sewn should now interlock to make aligning the pairs easy. Join the pairs to complete the block, and press the seam.

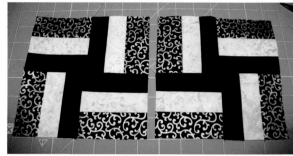

Illustration 5: Windmills rotating in opposite directions to each other

8.   Make three more of these blocks. You can choose to make them all the same. Alternatively, you can make some that rotate in the opposite direction, as shown in illustration 5.

CHAPTER TWELVE

Square In A Square
(In A Square In A Square)

Fabric Requirements

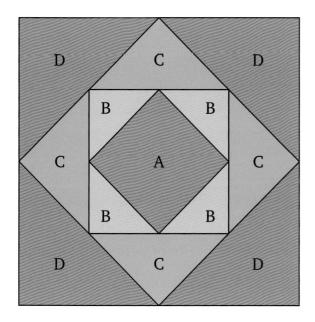

For one block you need,

Centre square

2 ¾ x 2 ¾

Second square

two squares, 2½" x 2½"

Third square

two squares 3" x 3"

Outermost square

two squares 4" x 4"

You need to make four blocks in total, but they need not use the same fabrics.

Instructions

1. Cut the pieces as listed in the requirements. Remember you need to make four copies of this block, and it is quicker to piece them all at the same time.

2. Cut the squares for the second square in half diagonally, so you have four triangles for each block.

Illustration 1: Diagonal cut

3. For this block, use a full ¼" seam rather than a scant one.

4. This slightly larger seam allowance allows us to cut more convenient size squares than a scant seam would.

5. Stitch the long side of one of these triangles to the side of the centre square. The triangle will be slightly longer than the side of the square, so make sure it overhangs the same amount at

each end. One way to do this is to fold both the square and the triangle in half and align the centre points.

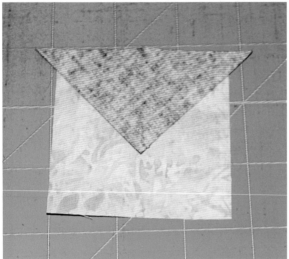

Illustration 2: Triangle overhanging the square

6. Repeat with another triangle on the opposite side of the square. Press the seams towards the triangles.

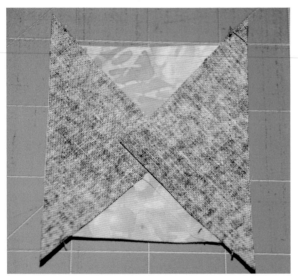

Illustration 3: Both triangles attached

7. Stitch the remaining two triangles to the other two sides

of the square.

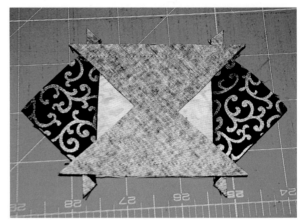

Illustration 4: Add the remaining triangles

8. Press the seams towards the triangles.

Illustration 5: Press seams outwards

9. Cut the two squares for the third square in half diagonally, to give four triangles for each block.

70

Illustration 6: The completed 3rd square

10. Repeat steps 5, 6 and 7. When you are sewing the triangles onto the square, stitch with the pieced square uppermost so you can make sure your seam goes just to the seam side of the point of the innermost square.

Illustration 7: Align the seam with the point of the inner square

11. Repeat for the outermost square. Your block should now look like illustration 7. Make four of these blocks.

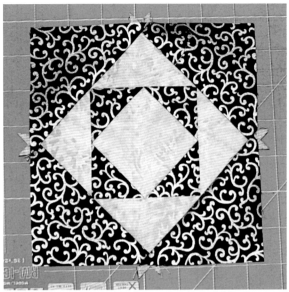

Illustration 8: The completed block

71

CHAPTER THIRTEEN

Star On A Star

Fabric Requirements

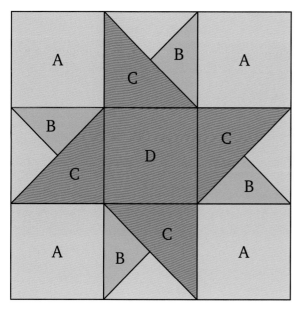

These blocks are made two at a time, so these requirements will make two of the four blocks you'll need.

Background (A)   Eight 2½ x 2½ squares and two 4" x 4" squares

Lower star (B)   Two 4" x 4" squares

Upper star (C)   Four 3½" x 3½"

Centre (D)   One 2½" x 2½" square

Instructions

1. Cut the pieces as listed in the requirements.

2. Place a 4" square of A and a 4" square of B right sides together.

3. On the lighter fabric, mark a line diagonally across the square.

4. Stitch ¼" to each side of this line as shown in illustration 1.

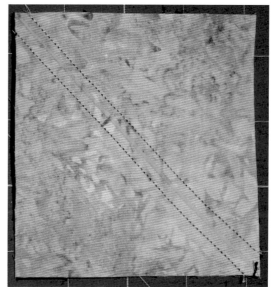

Illustration 1: Diagonal line

5. Cut apart along the drawn line. Press the seam towards the darker fabric.

6. Repeat with other pair of squares to make four half square triangle blocks.

Illustration 2: The opposite diagonal

7. Place a 3½" square of fabric C right sides together on top of one of these half square triangle blocks. Mark the opposite diagonal line, i.e. the one that is

perpendicular to the seam in the half square triangle.

8. Stitch ¼" to each side of this line. Lift the top fabric and check you have the seam in the right place to get blocks like those shown in illustration 3. The two sides will be different, one for each of the two finished blocks.

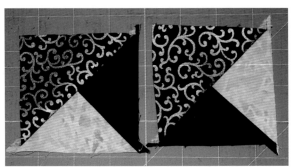

Illustration 3: Background with both upper and lower stars

9. Cut apart along the drawn line. Press the seam towards the larger triangle (fabric C).

10. Repeat with the other three half square triangles, making a total of eight blocks, each made up of three triangles.

11. Trim up the three triangle blocks to 2½" squares. Start by lining up the diagonal line on a square ruler with the last seam you stitched, and place the 1¼" mark on the seam between the smaller two triangles. This will mean both the diagonal lines will run exactly through corners of the square.

12. Separate the blocks into their two types. Layout your star blocks.

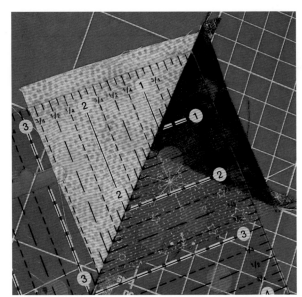

Illustration 4: Trim to 2½" squares

13. Join the pieces in rows. Press the seams towards solid squares.

14. Join the rows to complete the blocks. You will end up with two blocks, with the stars rotating in opposite directions.

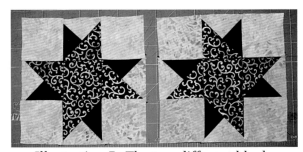

Illustration 5: The two different blocks

15. Make another pair of blocks to get to the required four.

CHAPTER FOURTEEN

Block Border

You should now have thirty two 6½" blocks, four each of the designs from the last eight chapters. In this chapter, we will put the blocks together as a border to be added to the quilt centre.

Fabric Requirements

Wadding

One piece 42½" x 6½"

One piece 54½" x 6½"

Backing fabric

One piece 42½" x 6½"

One piece 54½" x 6½"

Instructions

1. Layout your quilt centre and the blocks in a way that suits you. It will look as thought the block border will be too long as there are a lot of seams to be sewn.

2. Once you have a layout you like, you need to join the blocks to each other to make border strips. Leave the corner blocks for the moment and just join the other blocks together with a scant ¼" seam allowance.

3. To attach the border to the quilt, place one border right sides together along one edge of the quilt. Pin in place then stitch with a very narrow seam.

4. Place a short strip of backing right sides together with the back of the quilt along the same edge, with the wadding on top of it. Pin in place and then resew the seam with a ¼" seam allowance, catching all the layers.

5. Unfold the border into place and press well. Pin the raw edges to hold the layers aligned.

6. Stitch in the ditch between the blocks. This means run a line of quilting along the seam lines between the blocks. You can use a decorative stitch to make this easier and more interesting. The faux herringbone stitch and the wavy stitches look particularly good.

7. Repeat steps 4 to 7 on the opposite side of the quilt.

8. Attach the corner blocks to the ends of the remaining strips of blocks. Then attach these to the other two sides of the quilt. Try to align the seams of the corner blocks with the seams that attached the first two sides. If they don't match perfectly you can use the quilting to hide this.

9. You can add more quilting if you want. If you find one fabric is standing out too much quilting it in a contrasting thread can tone it down. Conversely if there isn't enough contrast in a block you can use your quilting to make the pattern clearer.

CHAPTER FIFTEEN

Outer Border

Congratulations! You have now completed all the techniques. I hope you've learned some things that you will find useful in your future quilt making. You now need to decide how you will finish your quilt.

As you can see from the photographs of finished quilts, there are many ways to complete this quilt depending largely on what you wish to use it for. The simplest option would be to bind the quilt at this point. This will give you a quilt approximately 54" square.

This size would be ideal as a lap quilt or a wall hanging. However if this is roughly the finished size you want I would strongly suggest adding a final narrow border of 2" or 3" all the way around the quilt. The reason for this is that binding is often slightly over ¼" on the front of the quilt and would remove the points on the pieced blocks. A narrow outer border stops this happening, and it gives the finished quilt a frame which is often more pleasing to the eye.

To make this quilt into a bed quilt you will need to add some more borders. Exactly how many will depend on how large you want the finished quilt to be. Although the measurements can vary, as a rough guideline, you should be looking at the following sizes:

- Single/twin - 70"x90"

- Double - 85"x100"

- King - 110"x110"

The best option is to measure the bed for which the quilt is intended, allowing the tape measure to drape over the sides as required. Alternatively, measure an existing quilt that is about the size you want. It doesn't matter if your quilt is a completely different size to those listed above, so long as it is right for you. This is your quilt and you can make is however you like. For example, although I have a king size bed, I find 110" far too long, but not quite wide enough so I like to have quilts that are wider than they are long. The following diagrams (which aren't to scale) give some ideas for layout that will result in quilts of various sizes.

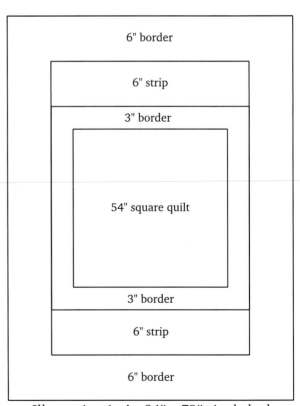

Illustration 1: An 84" x 72" single bed

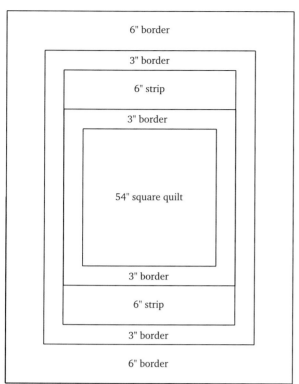

Illustration 2: A 90" x 78" queen size

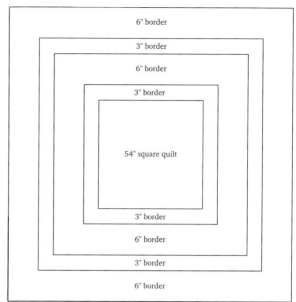

Illustration 4: A 90" x 90" double bed

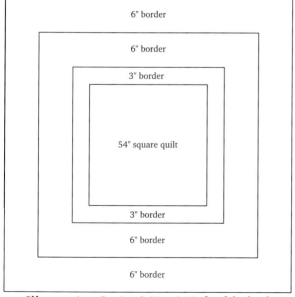

Illustration 3: An 84" x 84" double bed

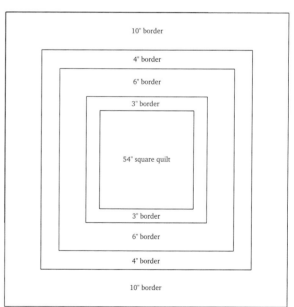

Illustration 5: A 100" x 100" king size

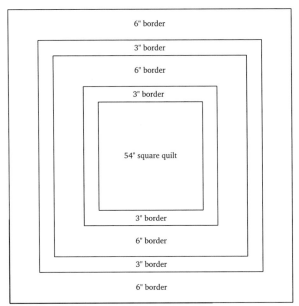

Illustration 6: A 108" x 108" king size

Once you know what size you are aiming for, you can start designing your borders. When planning your borders, you need to bear in mind than the blocks you have just been making are all 6" square and to fit nicely into a border it needs to be a multiple of 6". In the layouts given the narrow borders are all 3" wide finished (so cut pieces 3½" wide, which includes a seam allowance). When they are added to two opposite sides of the quilt they will add 6", one complete block. If you stick to adding combinations of narrow 3" borders and pieced 6" borders, the maths will all take care of itself. The exception to this rule is the outermost border. This can be any width you like, which allows you to fine tune the measurements of your quilt.

If you are designing your own layout (and I really hope you will), I suggest drawing out the design on paper like the layouts here. Mark the dimensions on each of the borders (remember these are finished dimensions) and it will make it easy to add them up to see if you are close to the size you want.

Once you have your layout selected you can think about the blocks you want to use in your borders. Most people find there are some blocks they enjoyed making more than the others, and I suggest those would be a good choice for additional borders. You don't want to be making lots of copies of a block you don't enjoy. Maybe some of the example quilts will give you some ideas as to how the different blocks can be used.

To work out how many you will need you need to work out the size of each of the borders that will be filled with blocks and then divide the number by 6 (yes you can use a calculator - in fact I would recommend it). If you want to make it really simple, put together the quilt to the point where you want to add the border then measure the quilt across the centre parallel to where the border will go, remember this number will include an extra ½" of seam allowance.

All of the borders except the last one are put on in exactly the same way as you have been doing throughout the book.

If you would like to put celtic knots on the last border there is a corner design and an edge design included in

Appendix C, although you may have others you would rather use which is a great way to personalize your quilt. The designs given are sized to fit a 6" border, so you may need to scale them up or down for wider or smaller borders.

If you are adding celtic knots I have a few tricks to make this a bit easier:

1. Start by cutting the pieces for your shorter two borders. Cut them to the correct length for your quilt by measuring your quilt from edge to edge through the center of the quilt.

2. Next, mark your patterns and apply the tape as described in chapter 1.

3. Cut the wadding to roughly match the border piece (slightly bigger is just fine).

4. Tack the wadding to the back of the border fabric by whatever means you prefer, I like to use 505 spray baste glue for this.

5. Now stitch down the tape through just these two layers. I find that it is a lot easier to manoeuvre under the sewing machine if I roll it up like a scroll. I put a couple of pins into each roll just to hold in in place. Doing the stitching this way means you can machine the tape in place and use the wadding as stabilizer. It also helps quilt the wadding

(although not the backing). You should find that even very long borders are pretty easy to handle in this way.

6. Once you have completed the stitching on the bias tape, you can apply the border to the quilt. Pin the pre-quilted front right sides together with the front of your quilt. The best way I have found to do this is to align the pieces at each end and pin them in place. Then fold both quilt and border in half and pin the mid points. Fold each half in half again and pin the mid point of that section. Repeat until the pins are no more than about 6" apart. This will spread any fullness along the whole length of the seam. Stitch the border on with the very narrow seam as described in previous chapters.

7. Then pin the backing right sides together on the back of the quilt and resew the seam with the back of the quilt.

If your outer border is more than about 4" wide it really needs some quilting in it. The simplest option it do sew plain straight lines parallel to the seams. If you want something more fancy try a decorative stitch perhaps in a variegated thread. You can also try following a wavy line rather than a straight one, or even do free hand quilting in the border. Remember you will only ever be working on the outer most few inches of your quilt and you can quilt each border as you attach it.

All that is left to do is to bind your quilt. If you have a preferred technique for this then go ahead and use it. If this is your first quilt, I would suggest the following method. It is quick and simple. Your binding will be what is called a double fold binding, which means that there are two layers of fabric over the edge of the quilt. This is much harder wearing than just one layer. The step involved are:

1. Cut fabric strips 2½" wide and long enough to go all the way around your quilt with about 12" spare. You can piece it out of your leftovers if you like, which can make quite a funky binding.

2. Once you have a long length of binding press it in half length-wise. As you do so, make sure any seams with in the binding are pressed open to reduce the bulk in any one place.

3. Aligning the raw edges of the binding with the raw edges of the front of the quilt, stitch the binding to one side of the quilt down it's complete length with a ¼" seam.

4. Cut the binding off flush with the edge of the quilt.

5. Now wrap the folded edge of the binding around the edge of the quilt and hand sew it to the back of the quilt so the fold in

the binding covers the line of stitching holding the binding in place. Repeat this process on the opposite edge of the quilt.

6. Putting the binding on the remaining two sides is almost the same as for the first two but you need to leave about 1" of binding beyond each side of the quilt. This spare fabric can then be wrapped around the corner of the quilt to avoid leaving raw edges showing

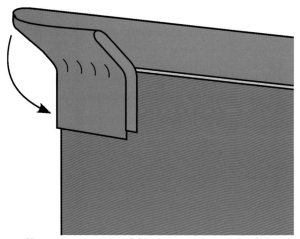

Illustration 7: Folding over the end of the binding

And that's that. I hope you will get years of enjoyment from your quilt, and that you will be inspired to take the blocks and techniques to make many more.

I would love to see what you have made from this book, so please do get in touch. My contact details can always be found on my web site at `http://ferfab.co.uk`

The quilters

Lesley

I have been going to Patchwork Corner on a Thursday evening for the past 5 years. I really enjoy patchwork and quilting, especially choosing the fabrics, mixing and matching colours and designs. Like most patchworkers, I have a fairly large selection of fat quarters. I also have a large selection of other materials, threads, paints, card, stamps and a variety of tools as I enjoy all types of craft from free style embroidery to painting and card making. I find that what I learn in one medium is always useful in another and I love to combine techniques to see what will happen. Our Thursday night class is great fun because, not only do we make lovely quilts, but we forge great friendships and share all the ups and downs in life over the sewing machines, always ending up laughing. Ferret is a great teacher because she always looking for new ways to encourage us to try something different and to stretch our abilities so we never get bored and we never stop learning. If you haven t tried patchwork yet, do you will soon get hooked!!

Barbara

From the moment I entered my local patchwork group on a dark, cold January evening 18 months ago, I have made genuine friends, shared many hours of fun and support and enjoyed completing a round robin quilt. My love of quilting has grown and grown, and I shall carry on the skills learned in my new life in Ibiza. A big thank you especially to Ferret, our brilliant tutor, and to everyone for allowing my many opportunities to have my mad and boisterous moments.

Eileen

Eileen is new to patchwork and quilting. On joining one of my regular classes, she dove straight into this quilt. Despite being initially concerned by the apparent complexity of the centre block, she completed it in her first class, impressing her family. This is her first ever quilt, and she even felt confident enough to enter it into a show.

Margaret

 I never knew that inside this predictable pillar of the teaching establishment who is me, lurked another more exciting and dynamic persona. I liken it to sherbet; innocuous on the outside but when triggered explodes through the body stimulating all the senses. Ferret has triggered that sherbet and this first quilt of mine releases so much of my inner colour, chaos and unrestrained enthusiasm that I am left reeling. So who am I? Well, I don t quite know any more but over the next few years I m looking forward to finding out!! Thank you Ferret.

Margaret was horrified when I told her that I planned to use her quilt for the front cover of the book, and insisted that I point out it wasn't all her own work, and that other members of the class had contributed to this round robin quilt.

Mary

Mary is one of the most experienced of the quilters that have made this quilt, and was already a member of the class when I started teaching it. She is always keen to take on a challenge. She progressed through this quilt rapidly, often getting slightly ahead of me. Near the end of the quilt, she ran short of the backing fabric, but everyone rallied around and raided their stashes to help find enough fabric to finish the quilt.

Angela

Angela does a lot of sewing. Outside of the quilting world, she is an accomplished dressmaker. When I told her this was a scrap quilt, she raided her stash and found large amounts of purple. She had also just dyed a bed sheet lime green, and decided to combine the two. The resulting quilt is loud, but not as garish as might be expected given the fabrics involved. This is a good example of how different the back can be to the quilt top. In Angela's case, her back is very subdued in comparison. She does confess that she doesn't know what she will do with the quilt, as it doesn't go with the decor of any of her rooms. Fortunately for her, the quilt is on tour with me for when I talk to quilting groups, so she doesn't need to make that decision just yet.

Claire

I came, with my friend Angela, to a course as a patchwork novice. We became completely hooked and haven't been able to leave!! So much to learn and so little time! Ferret has filled me with confidence and self belief. Her work is inspirational and with her enthusiasm, encouragement and straightforward instructions, she makes you believe you can tackle any project or attempt any technique. I can thoroughly recommend making this sampler quilt - lots of new and old blocks and lots of new ideas and methods. An absolute delight being able to assemble and quilt it as you go. Have a stab at this quilt - you won't be disappointed.

Tethys

This wasn't planned. I'd studiously avoided getting into quilting, despite it having taken over Ferret's life and much of our house in the last few years. But I'd agreed to proofread the book on Ferret's behalf, and I decided that I couldn't adequately do that by just reading it. I needed to follow the instructions and see if they made sense. So that's how I ended up making this, my first quilt. One of the things I noticed from looking at her students' quilts was that the backs always seemed a little dull when compared to the quilt tops, so I tried to make my back a little more interesting.

Happy quilting
Tet

Ferret

As the author, I suppose I should include my own quilt in here! I'd told my students that the quilt could be made with only three colours, and then decided that I really should make the quilt to see if it was true. I used a black, a black and silver and a mottled blue. This was the quilt that was used for many of the illustrations in the book. It was only afterward that I noticed the blue fabric really didn't photograph well, and ended up looking dirty in some of the photographs. But by then it was too late to change it. For the back, I decided to use black and a selection of reds.

87

Joan

Joan was initially less than enthralled by my pattern. I think the word hideous was used. However, as she saw the other students' quilts grow, she became inspired to have a go herself. From this unpromising start, she really got into the spirit of taking this pattern and designing her own quilt, with impressive results. You might notice that she has eschewed the varied block border, and gone for a border made solely from friendship stars instead.

Everyone

I didn't think it was fair to ask the experienced quilters to trust the newcomers in the class with their work. So I started this quilt to add an extra member to the round robin group so that the less experienced students could add to my centre piece and build their confidence, and also to show the more experienced quilters what they were capable of. I handed over a box full of a large amount of black plus several of my own hand dyed fabrics, the quilt made its way around the entire class, and this was what came back. I was expecting the quilt to come back much darker, but the black was barely touched and it came back much more vibrant than I anticipated.

Foundation Piece Patterns

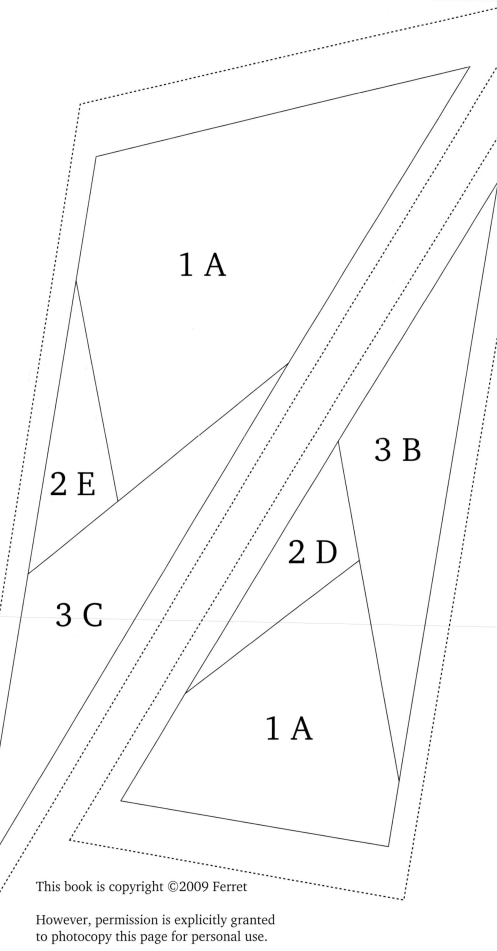

1 A

2 E

3 B

2 D

3 C

1 A

Foundation Piece Patterns

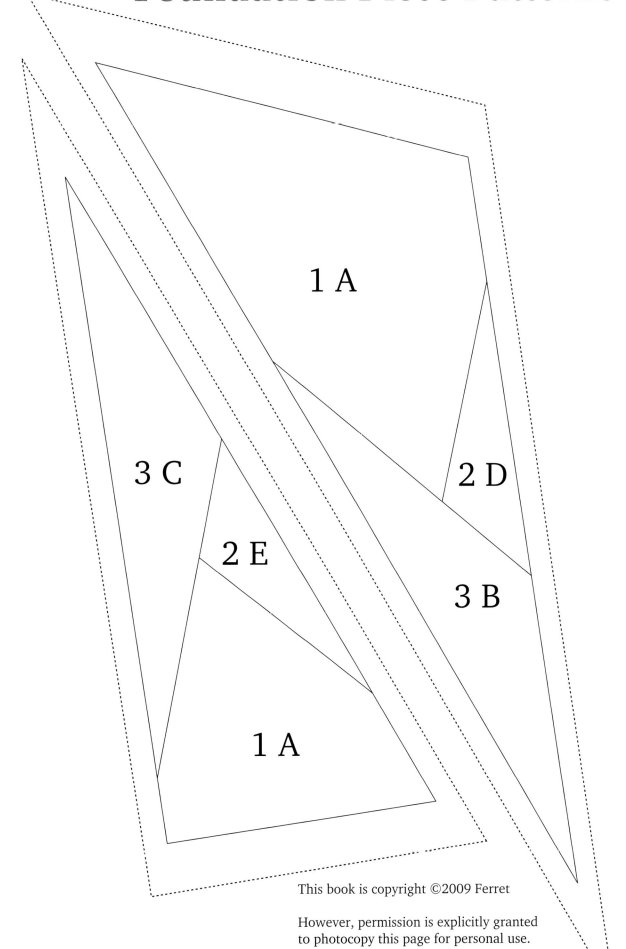

1 A

3 C

2 D

2 E

3 B

1 A

Celtic Knots

Celtic Knots

Appendix C

Celtic Knots

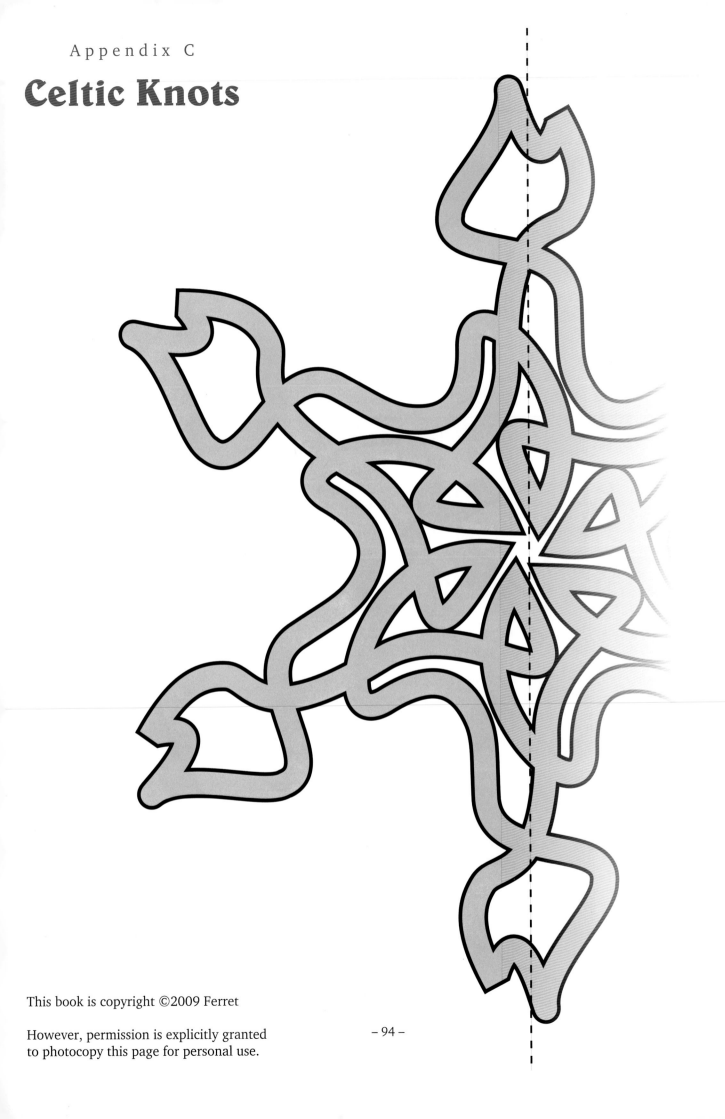

Celtic Knots

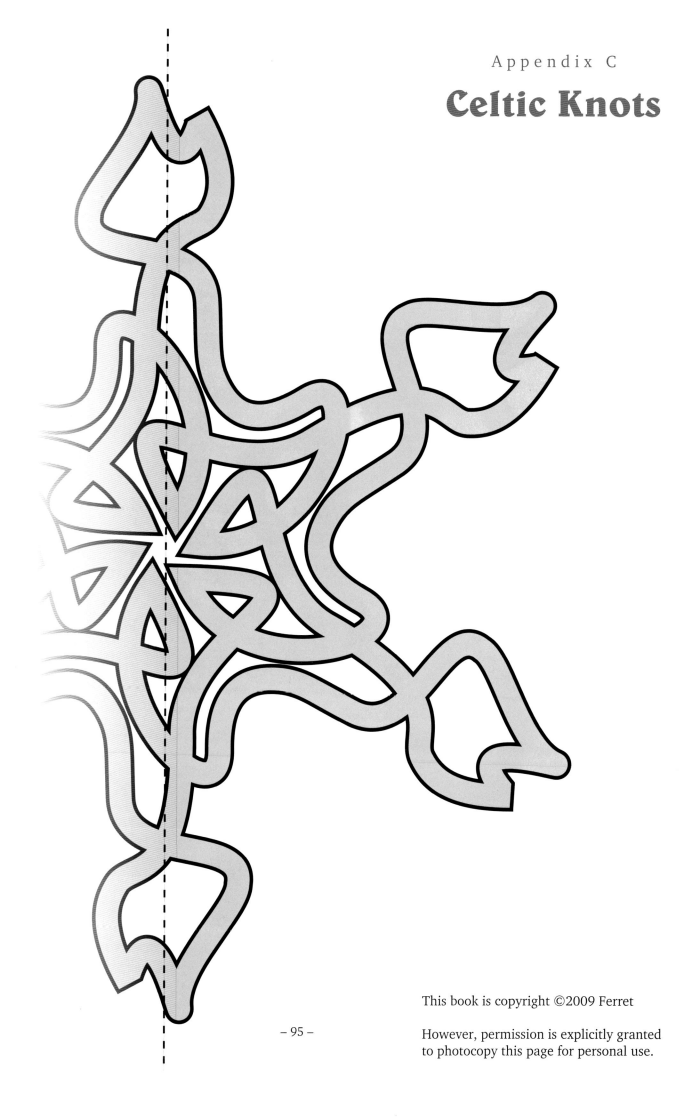

Appendix C

Celtic Knots